African Language Grammars and Dictionaries

Chief Editor: Adams Bodomo
Editors: Ken Hiraiwa, Firmin Ahoua

In this series:

1. Schrock, Terrill B. The Ik language: Dictionary and grammar sketch.

2. Brindle, Jonathan. A dictionary and grammatical outline of Chakali.

The Ik language

Dictionary and grammar sketch

Terrill B. Schrock

Terrill B. Schrock. 2017. *The Ik language: Dictionary and grammar sketch*
(African Language Grammars and Dictionaries 1). Berlin: Language Science
Press.

This title can be downloaded at:
http://langsci-press.org/catalog/book/98
© 2017, Terrill B. Schrock
Published under the Creative Commons Attribution 4.0 Licence (CC BY 4.0):
http://creativecommons.org/licenses/by/4.0/
ISBN: 978-3-944675-95-4 (Digital)
    978-3-944675-96-1 (Hardcover)
    978-3-944675-68-8 (Softcover)
    978-1-544669-06-9 (Softcover US)
DOI:10.5281/zenodo.344792

Cover and concept of design: Ulrike Harbort
Typesetting: Sebastian Nordhoff, Terrill B. Schrock
Illustration: Monika Feinen
Proofreading: Ahmet Bilal Özdemir, Andreas Hölzl, Bev Erasmus, Christian Döhler, Claudia Marzi, Don Killian, Eitan Grossman, Esther Yap, Greg Cooper, Kilu von Prince, Mykel Brinkerhoff, Rosey Billington, Steve Pepper, Tom Gardner
Fonts: Linux Libertine, Arimo, DejaVu Sans Mono
Typesetting software: X∃LATEX

Language Science Press
Unter den Linden 6
10099 Berlin, Germany
langsci-press.org
Storage and cataloguing done by FU Berlin

Language Science Press has no responsibility for the persistence or accuracy of URLs for external or third-party Internet websites referred to in this publication, and does not guarantee that any content on such websites is, or will remain, accurate or appropriate.

For Amber Dawn

Contents

Preface ix

Acknowledgements xi

Abbreviations xiii

I **Introduction** 1
   1   The Ik language 3
   2   The dictionary 3
   3   Using the dictionary 7
        3.1   Writing system 7
        3.2   Structure of entries 7
        3.3   Tips for finding words 9

II **Ik-English dictionary** 11
   a 13
   b 18
   ɓ 27
   c 32
   d 35
   ɗ 41
   dz 48
   e/ɛ 50
   f 54
   g 57
   h 63
   ɦy 66
   i/ɨ 68
   j 121
   ɟ 122

Contents

```
k  . . . . . . . . . . . . . . . . . . . . . . . . . . . . . . .  125
ɓ  . . . . . . . . . . . . . . . . . . . . . . . . . . . . . . .  143
l  . . . . . . . . . . . . . . . . . . . . . . . . . . . . . . .  148
m  . . . . . . . . . . . . . . . . . . . . . . . . . . . . . . .  161
n  . . . . . . . . . . . . . . . . . . . . . . . . . . . . . . .  170
ɲ  . . . . . . . . . . . . . . . . . . . . . . . . . . . . . . .  179
ŋ  . . . . . . . . . . . . . . . . . . . . . . . . . . . . . . .  205
o/ɔ . . . . . . . . . . . . . . . . . . . . . . . . . . . . . . .  215
p  . . . . . . . . . . . . . . . . . . . . . . . . . . . . . . .  219
r  . . . . . . . . . . . . . . . . . . . . . . . . . . . . . . .  223
s  . . . . . . . . . . . . . . . . . . . . . . . . . . . . . . .  229
t  . . . . . . . . . . . . . . . . . . . . . . . . . . . . . . .  236
ts . . . . . . . . . . . . . . . . . . . . . . . . . . . . . . .  259
ts' . . . . . . . . . . . . . . . . . . . . . . . . . . . . . . .  264
u/ʉ . . . . . . . . . . . . . . . . . . . . . . . . . . . . . . .  267
w  . . . . . . . . . . . . . . . . . . . . . . . . . . . . . . .  268
x  . . . . . . . . . . . . . . . . . . . . . . . . . . . . . . .  272
y  . . . . . . . . . . . . . . . . . . . . . . . . . . . . . . .  275
z  . . . . . . . . . . . . . . . . . . . . . . . . . . . . . . .  276
```

III English-Ik reversal index   279

IV Grammar sketch   475

   1   Introduction 477
   2   Phonology 477
         2.1   Consonants and vowels 477
         2.2   Consonant devoicing 478
         2.3   Vowel devoicing 478
         2.4   Morphophonology 478
         2.5   Vowel harmony 485
         2.6   Tone 488
   3   Morphology 490
         3.1   Overview 490
         3.2   Nouns 491
         3.3   Pronouns 491
         3.4   Demonstratives 491

		3.5	Quantifiers	492
		3.6	Numerals	493
		3.7	Prepositions	493
		3.8	Verbs	495
		3.9	Adverbs	495
		3.10	Ideophones	496
		3.11	Interjections	497
		3.12	Nursery words	497
		3.13	Complementizers	497
		3.14	Connectives	498
4	Nouns			501
		4.1	Overview	501
		4.2	Number	502
		4.3	Compounds	508
5	Pronouns			512
		5.1	Overview	512
		5.2	Personal pronouns	512
		5.3	Impersonal possessum pronoun (PSSM)	514
		5.4	Indefinite pronouns	514
		5.5	Interrogative pronouns	515
		5.6	Demonstrative pronouns	516
		5.7	Relative pronouns (REL)	517
		5.8	Reflexive pronoun	518
6	Demonstratives			519
		6.1	Overview	519
		6.2	Spatial demonstratives (DEM)	520
		6.3	Temporal demonstratives (DEM.PST)	520
		6.4	Anaphoric demonstratives (ANAPH)	521
		6.5	Adverbial demonstratives	522
7	Case			524
		7.1	Overview	524
		7.2	Nominative (NOM)	526
		7.3	Accusative case (ACC)	528
		7.4	Dative (DAT)	529
		7.5	Genitive (GEN)	530
		7.6	Ablative (ABL)	531
		7.7	Instrumental (INS)	532
		7.8	Copulative (COP)	533

Contents

		7.9	Oblique (OBL)	534
8	Verbs			534
		8.1	Overview	534
		8.2	Infinitives (INF)	535
		8.3	Deverbalizers	539
		8.4	Directionals	542
		8.5	Aspectuals	544
		8.6	Voice and valence	545
		8.7	Subject-agreement	549
		8.8	Dummy pronoun (DP)	551
		8.9	Mood	552
		8.10	Verb paradigms	553
		8.11	Adjectival verbs	558
9	Adverbs			561
		9.1	Overview	561
		9.2	Manner adverbs	561
		9.3	Temporal adverbs	562
		9.4	Epistemic adverbs	565
10	Basic syntax			567
		10.1	Noun phrases	567
		10.2	Clause structure	569
		10.3	Subordinate clauses	575
		10.4	Questions	578
		10.5	Quotations	580
		10.6	Complements	581
		10.7	Comparatives	582
		10.8	Clause combining	583

Appendix A: Ik affixes 589

References 593

Subject index 595

Preface

When I first heard about the Ik back in September 2005, I was thoroughly intrigued. Here was a people just emerging from the mists of time, from that now dark and shrouded realm of African prehistory. Judging by appearances, their journey had not been easy. Their story spoke of great suffering in the form of sickness, suppression, starvation, and slaughter. And yet, somehow, there they were, limping into the 21st century as survivors of conditions most of us cannot imagine. Having grown up in a safe and serene community in the American South, I thought the Ik seemed stranger than fiction. People like this actually exist out there? I found myself wanting to know more about them, wanting to know who they are. Subconsciously I sensed that anyone who could endure what they had endured could perhaps teach me something about being truly human.

My quest to know the Ik has led me down a winding path to the present. Over the years I have been frustrated by my inability to enter fully into their world, to see reality through their eyes. More than once I wished I were an anthropologist, so I could get a better grasp of their essence as a people. But time and time again, life steered me right back to the language – to *Icétôd*. I gradually learned to accept that their language is a doorway to their spirit, and that as a linguist, I could only open the door for others, and point the way to the Promised Land while I remain at the threshold. This book can act as a key to that door, a key that has been carefully shaped and smoothened by hands tired yet trembling with purpose.

Living in Ikland has taught me a lot about being human, but not in the way I expected. It was not by becoming 'one with the people' that I learned what it is like to survive subhuman conditions. And it was not physical starvation, or sickness, or slaughter that I was forced to endure. No, I was spared those things. Yet all the same, in Ikland I became acquainted with spiritual starvation, social sickness, and the wholesale slaughter of my cultural, religious, and intellectual idols. And just as the Ik have learned that life does not consist in 'bread alone', nor in health, nor in security – but can carry on living with dignity and humanity – I have learned that at the rock bottom of my soul, where my self ends and the world begins, there is where Life resides. That realization is my 'pearl of great price' for which I have sold everything else and would do it all over again.

Acknowledgements

Compiling a dictionary such as this one is a massive undertaking, far more so than I ever imagined it would be. Although I myself spent many hours, days, and months working alone on this project, a whole host of people put me in a position to do so. And it is here that I wish to acknowledge and thank them all.

First, I want to express a heartfelt *Ɨlákásʉkɔtíàà zùkᵘ* to all the Ik people of the Timu Forest area for welcoming us into their community and patiently putting up with the long process of a foreigner trying to learn their language. To the following Ik men and women, I give thanks for their participation in a word-collecting workshop that took place in October 2009, during which roughly 7,000 Ik words were amassed: Ariko Hillary, Kunume Cecilia, Lochul Jacob, Lokure Jacob, Longoli Philip, Losike Peter, Lotuk Vincent, Nakiru Rose, Nangoli Esther, †Ngiriko Fideli, Ngoya Joseph, Ochen Simon Peter, Sire Hillary, and Teko Gabriel.

A second group of Ik men are sincerely thanked for giving me a clearer view of the Ik sound system and for helping me edit several hundred words during an orthography workshop in April 2014: Amida Zachary, Dakae Sipriano, Lokauwa Simon, Lokwameri Sylvester, Lomeri John Mark, Longoli Philip, Longoli Simon, Lopeyok Simon, †Lopuwa Paul, and Lotuk Paul. One of those men, Longoli Philip, deserves special thanks for the years he spent as my main guide into the grammar and lexicon of his mother tongue. The number and quality of entries in this book are owed in large part to his skillful labors. Four other men – Lojere Philip, †Lochiyo Gabriel, Lokwang Hillary, and †Lopuwa Paul – also deserve my thanks for teaching me bits of the language at various points along the journey.

But it is another group of Ik men that I wish to give special honor. These are the ones who for an entire year went with me through every word in this dictionary to refine their spellings and define their meanings. They include the respectable elders Iuɗa Lokauwa, Locham Gabriel, and Lemu Simon, as well as our translators Kali Clement, Lotengan Emmanuel, and Lopeyok Simon. The three elders not only shared their intimate knowledge of the language with me but also befriended me with a grace and humility that can only come with age. Every moment I spent with them was a blessing I will never forget. As they said, if I ever come back, I should ask if those old men are still around. I pray they are.

Acknowledgements

Although teaching foreigners Ik-speak has usually been the domain of men, I wish to bring special attention to two Ik women who, through their resilient friendship and lively conversation, greatly enhanced my grasp of the language. These are the highly esteemed Nachem Esther and Nakiru 'Akóóro' Rose.

Next, I want to gratefully mention those in the long line of linguists who worked on the Ik language and – in person or publication – passed their knowledge down to me: Fr. J. P. Crazzolara who wrote the first recorded grammatical description of the language; A. N. Tucker whose series of articles on Ik expanded my knowledge considerably; Fritz Serzisko who penned several insightful articles and books on Ik and Kuliak; Bernd Heine who wrote numerous works on Ik and Kuliak and authored a grammar sketch and dictionary of the language (1999); Richard Hoffman who studied the grammar and lexicon, devised a practical orthography, and tirelessly supported language development efforts on behalf of the Ik; Christa König who wrote several articles and an entire book on the Ik case system; Ron Moe who helped me lead a word-collection workshop; Keith Snider who trained me in tone analysis; Kate Schell who collected dozens of hours of recorded Ik texts; and Dusty Hill who supervised me throughout the process.

Another group I wish to thank are our friends and family members whose generous and faithful donations have made it possible for us to live and work in Uganda since 2008. It has been a privilege to be financially supported in doing long-term work on the Ik language, and I do not take that for granted.

For all their hard work pushing this project through to completion, I gratefully acknowledge the series editors: Adams Bodomo, Ken Hiraiwa, and Firmin Ahoua. My sincere thanks also go the reviewers and proofreaders who helped me improve this manuscript, to Monika Feinen for drawing up a lovely map of Ikland (Figure 1), and lastly to Sebastian Nordhoff, whose patient help and technical expertise in manuscript preparation I could never have done without.

I also want to thank my dear family: my two adopted Ik daughters, Kaloyang Mercy and Lemu Immaculate, and my wife Amber Dawn. Their loving presence enabled me to carry out this long work in an otherwise isolated and often very lonely environment. The existence of this book is owed in large measure to Amber's innumerable sacrifices big and small. It came into being at great cost to her. For that and many other reasons, I thank her from the bottom of my heart.

Above all else, I want to praise the God whose Word became flesh – ὁ λόγος σὰρξ ἐγένετο – making a linguistic cosmos where my mind and the Ik language could collide and radiate bright rays of new knowledge out into the world.

Abbreviations

A	transitive subject	GEN	genitive
ABST	abstractive	H	high tone
ACC	accusative	HYPO	hypothetical
ADJ.PL	adjectival plural	ideo.	ideophone
adv.	adverb	IMP	imperative
AND	andative	INC	inclusive
ANAPH	anaphoric	INCH	inchoative
ANTICIP	anticipative	INF	infinitive
ATR	advanced tongue root	INFR	inferential
AUX	auxiliary	INS	instrumental
BHVR	behaviorative	INT	intentional
C	consonant	interj.	interjection
CAUS	causative	IPFV	imperfective
CC	copula complement	IPS	impersonal passive
COMP	completive	IRR	irrealis
compl.	complementizer	L	low tone
COND	conditional	lit.	literal
CONF	confirmational	M	mid tone
coordconn.	coordinating connective	MED	medial
		MID	middle
COP	copulative	n.	noun
CS	copula subject	NF	non-final form
DAT	dative	NOM	nominative
dem.	demonstrative	num.	numeral
DIST	distal	nurs.	nursery word
DISTR	distributive	O	object
DP	dummy pronoun	OBL	oblique
DUR	durative	OPT	optative
E	extended object	PASS	passive
EXC	exclusive	PAT	patientive
FF	final form (pre-pause)	PHYS	physical property adverb

Abbreviations

pl.	plural	STAT	stative
PLUR	pluractional	SUBJ	subjunctive
prep.	preposition	subordconn.	subordinating connective
PRF	present perfect		
pro.	pronoun	v.	verb
PROX	proximal	VEN	venitive
PSSM	impersonal possessum	1	first person
PST1	recent past tense	2	second person
PST2	removed past tense	3	third person
PST3	remote past tense	Ø	zero realization
PST4	remotest past tense	-	morpheme boundary
quant.	quantifier		
REAL	realis	=	clitic boundary
RECENT	recentive	[…]	phonetic form
RECIP	reciprocal	/…/	phonemic form
REFL	reflexive	…	morphemic form
rel.	relativizer	[́]	high tone
S	intransitive subject	[̀]	low tone
SEQ	sequential	[̂]	high-falling tone
sg.	singular	†	deceased
SIM	simultaneous	§	section

Part I

Introduction

1 The Ik language

Ik is the native language of the Ik people who live on a narrow swath of land in the northeastern corner of Uganda, East Africa. The people call their language *Icétôd*, which means 'Ik-speech' or 'Ik-talk' and is pronounced *ee-CHAY-TOad* or in phonetic symbols, [ītʃétôḑ]. Ik belongs to a small cluster of languages called 'Kuliak', which also includes Nyang'ía of Lobalangit and Soo/Tepeth of Mounts Moroto, Napak, and Kadam – all in Uganda's magnificent Karamoja Region.

At the outset, let me state definitively that Ik is *not* a dialect of Karimojong, nor is it even Nilotic or 'Hamitic'. And it is certainly not Bantu (as some have asked me). Scholars disagree as to whether it is related to Karimojong at all, but if it is, it would be a distant relationship within the great Nilo-Saharan language family, much as English is related to Russian or Hindi within Indo-European.

One reason people assume Ik is a dialect of Karimojong is that the Ik have long been surrounded and dominated by the pastoralist Dodoth, Toposa, Turkana, and Jie. These groups, as well as the Karimojong proper, all speak mutually intelligible forms of a speech variety called 'Ateker', 'Teso-Turkana', or 'Tunga'. Another reason Ik seems similar to Karimojong is that it has borrowed many hundreds of words from Teso-Turkana speech varieties over the centuries. In addition to lexical borrowing, the close contact between the Ik and Teso-Turkana peoples has caused Ik grammar to become more like Teso-Turkana in various ways.

But despite the many superficial similarities one may see between Ik and Teso-Turkana, their grammatical systems are actually quite different. For instance, while their vowel inventories are similar, Ik has many more consonants than Teso-Turkana, including the ejectives /k̓/ and /ts'/, which are found in no other Ugandan language. Ik also has an elaborate case system with eight cases all marked with suffixes, whereas Teso-Turkana languages mark only four cases, some using only tone to do so. And although both Ik and Teso-Turkana order their words as Verb-Subject-Object in main clauses, in subordinate clauses, Ik changes the order to Subject-Verb-Object. These are but a few examples among others that show the significant differences between Ik and Teso-Turkana.

2 The dictionary

This book contains a bilingual Ik-English dictionary and an English-Ik reversal index. The dictionary section lists all the Ik words I have recorded up to now and offers English definitions for them. Including proper names, there are approximately 8,700 entries in the dictionary. While I have done all I could to collect as many words as possible within the limits of time and resources, no doubt many hundreds of other words still lurk out there in the recesses of Ikian minds. It will not be until more texts are written in Ik that these missing words might be gently coaxed out onto the page and into more books like the present one.

Although the presumed purpose of a dictionary is to propound the current meanings of the words of a language, I fear that purpose is only partly achieved in this volume. The true meanings of words are lived meanings, intended by living beings in a living world. To capture them on a page is to encase them in black rock and white ice. A native speaker of Ik may recognize in my English definitions familiar traces of true meaning but never all of it. As a foreign, non-native speaker of the language, my grasp of the living meanings of Ik words is severely limited. For the only way to learn living linguistic meanings is to experience life linguistically, *through* a language, through its words and phrases and tropes. Still, I have been fortunate enough to have had a few real-life experiences in Ik, for instance, when I learned the living meaning of the verb *isɛɛs* 'to miss' by actually missing a bushpig boar as I tried to spear it when it charged toward me out of a thicket. The young Ik hunters never let me forget that miss, and as they retold the story with glee, they always used that particular verb. So when I hear it, I not only know what it means in terms of 'missing', but I also *feel* the living overtones that include shame, regret, loss of opportunity, diminution of manhood, and so on. *That* is how one learns the meanings of words.

Due to the exceptional nature of such experiences, most of the Ik words in this volume I have had to define extrinsically, from the outside. Unfortunately, as a foreign lexicographer, *I do not inhabit the words*. All I could really do was try to understand the words as best I could and render them in perspicacious English, marking out a felicitous meeting place between two very different modes of linguistic being-in-the-world. To the degree that I succeeded in this endeavor, this is what I hope to be a worthwhile first full-scale Ik-English lexicon.

The English definitions the reader will find are of various types. Some Ik words lend themselves easily to one-word, entirely accurate glosses, for example, *gɨbérá-* as 'leopard'. Others require a short phrase in English, for instance, *kóré-* as the 'back of the knee'. Still others, the ones that are conceptually more distant from English, call for longer descriptions, as when *makúlí-* is defined as a 'round grass beehive cover that goes over the end of a hollow beehive'.

As well as being a record of modern Ik to be used for modern purposes, this dictionary also provides much data for historical research. Because the Ik have left little in the way of archaeology over the ages, and because oral histories tend to be vague, inconsistent, and undated, language is one of the few lenses through which to investigate prehistory. Already the Ik lexicon gives some tantalizing hints as to the ancient northern East African origins of the Ik, for example in the link between words like sɔkɔ́- 'hoof' and Arabic *saaq* 'foot' and Gumuz *tʃagw* 'foot', or between *kídz-* 'bite' and Maltese Arabic *gidem* 'bite' and Uduk *k'ūcūr* 'suck'. Every Ik word is a cultural relic, a linguistic artifact sticking out of the red clays of time and memory. Each one has been molded by a million mouthings, much as grains of sand are ground down by wind and water. Each has its own history, an origin and a tortuous path of descent to its present form, the same path, we can assume, that its many speakers have taken. This is where the fields of etymology and historical linguistics (or 'paleolinguistics') can provide some evidence on which to build a grounded sense of identity and cultural history.

A deeply rooted sense of history and identity is important because it could help give the Ik a more sure footing as they transition into a nationally-minded Ugandan society and a globally-minded international society. If I imagine the future fate of the Ik language, I can see two possible developmental paths it could take. The first is that it could be lost by being totally assimilated by Karimojong, much like Nyang'ía already has and Soo/Tepeth is in danger of doing, or by succumbing to the dazzling promise of upward mobility that English seems to offer. If either of these forms of language death should take place, at least this book would remain as a monument to a once noble language-mediated world-view.

The second path the Ik language could take into the future is the one I have often daydreamed of. It is the one that would fulfill my scholarly strivings and confirm my greatest hopes for the Ik. In this path, Ik would go on to become the language of a highly literate populace who would use it skillfully to promote their own well-being. With explicit knowledge of their grammar and lexicon, educated Ik people would harness the expressive power of their native-born tongue and make it a vehicle of music, poetry, fiction, philosophy, theology, medicine, education, policy – the full gamut of human expression. This scrappy language that has barely scraped by countless threats to its existence yet somehow managed to pull through, this language that contains the linguistic genes of so many other languages from unrelated stocks, this small language of a small people in small place, could go on to become an enduring symbol of the Ikian spirit.

As portrayed in Figure 1, the Ik language area can be viewed imaginatively from an 'Ik-centric' perspective as a 'heart' of East Africa. There it lies, near the arterial convergence of four East African nations: Uganda, South Sudan, Ethiopia, and Kenya. Over the centuries the Ik have migrated through and throughout each of these four countries. While doing so, their language absorbed words and grammatical traits from the many languages spoken there. So, in a real sense, Ik

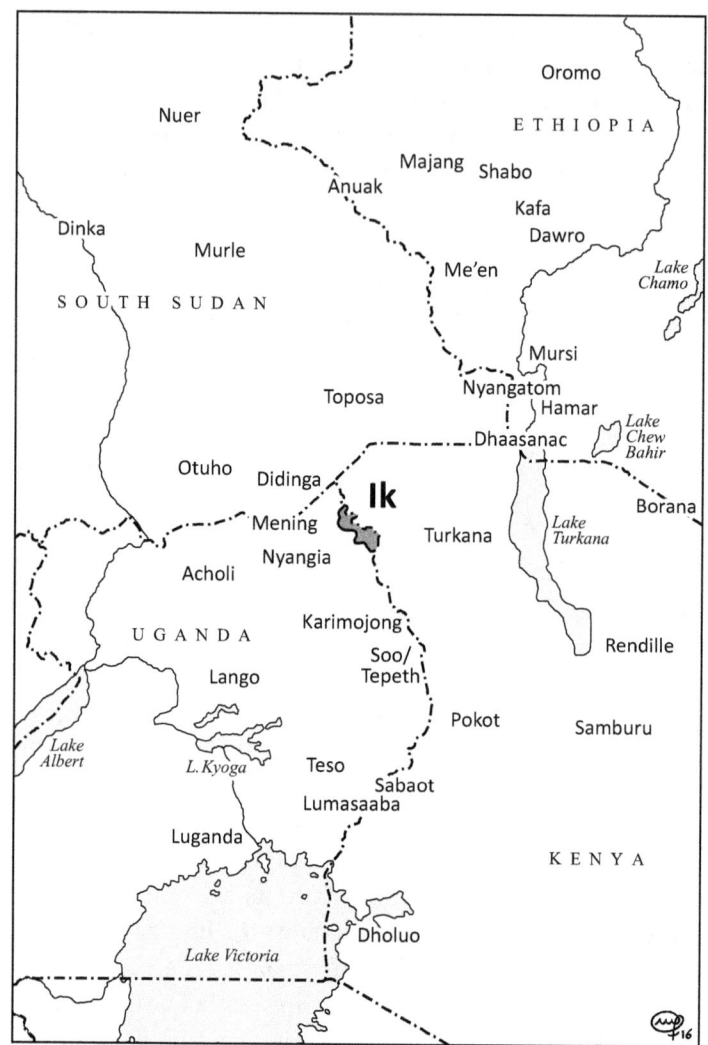

Figure 1: Ik language area in an 'Ik-centric' perspective (CC-BY Monika Feinen)

embodies the linguistic heritage of northern East Africa. Thus, could it be that Ik is providentially situated to blossom into a language that can serve the full range of communicative needs of a modernized Ik society, and then extend its fruited boughs over the escarpment in four directions to become a blessing to the neighboring nations? In the end, only time will tell, and yet it is toward the fulfillment of that dream that this work on Ik has been lovingly consecrated.

3 Using the dictionary

3.1 Writing system

The Ik script used in this dictionary and grammar sketch is based on what is called the Linguistic Orthography (LingO) as described in Schrock (2015). The LingO is a compromise between the simpler Popular Orthography (PopO) and a more scientific writing system. The main reason for choosing the LingO over the PopO is that the LingO encodes three very important features of the Ik sound system: voiceless vowels, vowel harmony, and tone. Although these three features are difficult to remember and write, they are indispensable for the correct pronunciation of Ik. Therefore it was decided that for this book to be an accurate and reliable record of the language, the proper pronunciations would have to be reflected in the spellings. LingO writing can easily be converted to PopO, but the reverse is not true, since it requires greater linguistic awareness.

The alphabetical order of Ik letters is given below. Note that the vowel pairs E/Ɛ, I/Ɨ, O/Ɔ, and U/Ʉ – whose two members differ only in terms of a linguistic feature called Advanced Tongue Root [ATR] – are alphabetized as if they were the same letter. This is done to assist non-native speakers of Ik in finding words beginning with vowels they might not be able to distinguish at first. Also note that the letter (Ʒ) is in parentheses because even though it belongs to the alphabet, no recorded Ik word begins with it. For the pronunciation of these letters, the reader is referred ahead to §2.1 of the grammar sketch section.

- Ik alphabetical order: A B Ɓ C D Ɗ Dz E/Ɛ F G H Hy I/Ɨ J J' K K L M N Ɲ Ŋ O/Ɔ P R S T Ts Ts' U/Ʉ W X Y Z (Ʒ)

3.2 Structure of entries

The Ik-English dictionary section contains entries of the following kinds of Ik words: nouns, pronouns, demonstratives, quantifiers, numerals, prepositions, verbs, adverbs, ideophones, interjections, nursery words, complementizers, and connectives (or conjunctions). For a brief description of each word class, the reader is referred to §3 of the grammar sketch at the back of the book. The goal of the present section is to explain to the user the structure of lexicographical entries. To do this, an example of a noun entry and a verb entry are discussed.

A typical noun entry has several components. To identify them, match the numbered components in this explanatory paragraph with the superscript number in the model entry below. 1) The lexical headword is in bold typeface. It is the citation form of the noun, that is, the form of the noun spoken in isolation. In Ik, the citation form takes the nominative case (see §7.2). 2) The root or lexical form is in parentheses. It is hyphenated to show that it still needs a case ending, and it is the form on which to base all other case forms of this noun. This particular noun is also hyphenated in the middle to signify that it is a compound noun made of two parts (see §4.3 of the grammar). 3) This is an abbreviation for 'plural', indicating that the next item is the plural form of the headword. 4) This is the plural form of the singular headword *bàdìàm*. 5) This number (1) indicates that what follows is the first and primary sense or meaning of the headword. 6) This is an abbreviation of the grammatical category of the word, in this case *n.* for 'noun'. 7) After the primary sense, one or more other numbered senses of the word may be added. 8) After the senses, one or more notes may mention further information about the entry, for example cultural details or suggestions for synonyms or near-synonyms.

> [1]**bàdìàm** [2](bàdì-àmà-) [3]*pl.* [4]badiik[a] [5]1) [6]*n.* sorcerer, wizard [7]2) anything spooky, weird, or uncanny | [8]The concept of *bàdìàm* includes nocturnal animals like bats, hyenas, and owls that have strange characteristics... tobacco is also called *bàdìàm* because its strong physiological effects are not attributable to human agency.

A typical verb entry has similar components but also some different ones: 1) Just as with nouns, the verbal headword is shown in bold typeface. This is the citation form of the verb, which in Ik appears in the infinitive form and nominative case (see §8.2 in the grammar). As an infinitive, the verb is acting as a noun at this point, much like 'to go' or 'going' in English. To use an Ik infinitive as a verb, simply remove the infinitive suffix (either *-ònì-* or *-ésí-*) and use the appropriate suffixes (see §8.7). 2) Then, the form in the parentheses is the lexical form of the infinitival headword, the one that is the base for all other case-inflected forms of the verb. 3) This number (1) indicates that what follows is the first and primary sense or meaning of the headword. 4) This is an abbreviation of the grammatical category of the headword, in this case *v.* for 'verb'. 5) After the

3 Using the dictionary

primary sense, one or more other senses of the headword may be added. 6) This short note directs the user to a synonym or near-synonym of the headword.

¹**betsínón** ²(betsínónì-) ³1) ⁴*v.* to be awkward, gauche, inept ⁵2) to be left-handed, sinistral | ⁶See also *ɨɓaŋɨɓáŋɔn*.

Over a hundred Ik verb roots end in /a/, /e/, or /ɛ/, meaning that when an infinitive suffix is added to the root, these root-final vowels are assimilated (see §2.4.4). For example, though the root for 'miss' is *ɨsá-*, the infinitive form is *ɨsɛɛs*, which obscures the root-final vowel. Lest the dictionary user hear a form of the root *ɨsá-* in speech and then fail to deduce that its infinitive is *ɨsɛɛs*, both root and infinitive have been listed in the dictionary. The entry for *ɨsá-* includes the notation (<*ɨsɛɛs*) which indicates that *ɨsɛɛs* is the entry the user should go to for the definition. Conversely, the entry for *ɨsɛɛs* 'to miss' includes both the lexical form of the infinitive and the bare root, as in: **ɨsɛɛs** (ɨsɛɛsɨ́-/ɨsá-).

3.3 Tips for finding words

Finally, because a good number of Ik words have more than one form, and because many of them can be reasonably spelled in multiple ways, let me offer the user the following tips for locating polymorphous words in the dictionary:

- If you are looking up a verb beginning with /i/ or /ɨ/ and cannot find it, remove the /i/ or /ɨ/ and try again. Conversely, if you are looking up a verb and cannot find it, try adding an /i/ or /ɨ/ to see if that takes you to a word.

- If you are looking up a word beginning with /w/ and cannot find it, try replacing the /w/ with /ɔ/, /o/, /ʉ/, or /u/ and vice versa.

- If you are looking up a word beginning with /y/ and cannot find it, try placing the /y/ with /i/ or /ɨ/ and vice versa.

- If you are looking up a noun beginning with /ɲa/ and cannot find it, try replacing it with /ɲe/ and vice versa.

- If you are looking up a noun beginning with /ɲe/ and cannot find it, try replacing it with /ɲo/ and vice versa.

- If you are looking up a word beginning with /ts/ and cannot find it, try replacing it with /ts'/ and vice versa.

- If you are looking up a word beginning with /dz/ and cannot find it, try replacing it with /ts/ or /ts'/ and vice versa.

- If you are looking up a word beginning with /d/ and cannot find it, try replacing it with /ɗ/ or /t/ and vice versa.

- If you are looking up a word beginning with /g/ and cannot find it, try replacing it with /ƙ/ or /ŋ/ and vice versa.

- If you are looking up a word containing the vowels /e, i, o, u/ and cannot find it, try replacing the vowel with /ɛ, ɨ, ɔ, ʉ/.

Part II

Ik-English dictionary

a

aaii (aaii) *interj.* ouch! ow! (an expression of pain).

abáŋ (abáŋɨ̀-) *pl.* **abáŋín.** *1 n.* my father. *2 n.* my uncle (father's brother). *3 n.* pope of the Catholic church.

ábaŋ (ábaŋ) *interj.* oh! wow! (an expression of amazement). *Lit.* 'my father'.

abáŋɨ́dzàƙᵃ (abáŋɨ́-dzàƙà-) *n.* son of my father (brother or male cousin on father's side).

abáŋɨ̀ɲòtᵃ (abáŋɨ̀-ɲòtà-) *n.* my father-in-law (sibling's spouse's father).

abér (abérí-) *pl.* **áberaikw**ᵃ. *n.* termite colony actively flying and mound-building.

àbètᵃ (àbètà-) *n.* lesser kudu. *Tragelaphus imberbis*.

abûbᵃ (abúbà-) *pl.* **abúbìk**ᵃ. *1 n.* spider. *2 n.* cobweb, spiderweb, web.

ábʉbʉƙɛ́s (ábʉbʉƙɛ́sɨ́-) *v.* to dip out (liquid with a vessel).

ábùbùƙɔ̀n (ábùbùƙɔ̀nɨ̀-) *1 v.* to bubble, burble, gurgle. *2 v.* to bellow, roar (like a charging animal or angry person). See also *béúrèton*.

abʉtɛtɛ́s (abʉtɛtɛ́sɨ́-) *v.* to sip, take a sip. See also *tsʉɓɛtɛ́s*.

abutiam (abutiamá-) *n.* sippable food like beer or porridge.

abutiés (abutiesí-) *v.* to sip or slurp continually. See also *tsʉɓɛ́s*.

aɓɨ́ɓɨ́lánón (aɓɨ́ɓɨ́lánónì-) *v.* to roll around.

aɓúlúkánón (aɓúlúkánónì-) *v.* to flip, flip over, somersault.

Acókᵃ (Acókò-) *n.* a personal name.

Acúkwa (Acúkwaá-) *n.* a personal name.

àdàbì (àdàbìà-) *n.* vine species found growing on rocky outcroppings and whose leaves are crushed, soaked in water, and applied to the skin to treat acne and rashes.

àdɛ̀nɛ̀s (àdɛ̀nɛ̀sà-) *n.* bird species.

áduduƙɛ́s (áduduƙɛ́sɨ́-) *v.* to pour from a small opening.

aɗáɗá (aɗáɗáà-) *n.* ringworm: an itchy, circular skin fungus.

àɗᵉ (àɗè) *num.* three.

àɗèɲèlìò (àɗèɲèlìò-) *n.* large hardwood tree that grows in the ravines and riverbeds of Rift Valley escarpments; Heine (1999) reports that its fruits may be eaten raw. *Allophylus sp.*

àɗᵒ *num.* three times, thrice.

àɗòn (àɗònì-) *v.* to be three.

aɗoniɛn (aɗoni-ɛnɨ́-) *n.* third time.

àɗònìkᵉ *n.* for the third time.

aɗúŋkú (aɗúŋkúù-) *pl.* **aɗúŋkúik**ᵃ. *n.* guitar-like stringed instrument found in many East African cultures (and whose body was traditionally made from a tortoise shell).

Àɗùpà (Àɗùpàà-) *n.* a personal name.

aeam (aeamá-) *n.* any food that is ripe or otherwise ready to be eaten.

aeásá bùbùì *n.* gluttony. *Lit.* 'ripeness of the belly'.

aeétón (aeétónì-) *1 v.* to ripen up, start ripening. *2 v.* to light up. *3 v.* to catch fire. *4 v.* to switch or turn on (of electricity).

aeitetés (aeitetésí-) *1 v.* to light (a fire or lamp). *2 v.* to switch or turn on (an electronic device or electric switch).

aeitetésíàwᵃ (aeitetésí-àwà-) *pl.* **aeitetésíawíkᵃ**. *n.* ignition, switch.

Aemun (Aemuní-) *n.* a personal name.

àèòn (àèònì-) *1 v.* to be ripe, ready to eat. *2 v.* to be lit.

aeonƙotᵃ (aeonƙotí-) *v.* to become ready to eat, ripen.

aeonƙota kíjáᵉ *n.* readying for harvest (of people's gardens).

ágɨrɨkácà (ágɨrɨkácàà-) *1 n.* agricultural training course. *2 n.* tall variety of maize.

àgɨtᵃ (àgɨtà-) *pl.* **ágɨtɨkᵃ**. *n.* metal ringlet sown on women's traditional aprons.

águjés (águjésí-) *v.* to gulp, guzzle. Also pronounced as *ígujés*.

áí (áí) *interj.* ouch! ow! (an expression of pain).

àjᵃ (àjɨ-) *pl.* **ájɨtín**. *n.* pestle. See also *iwótsídàkwᵃ* and *kuɲukᵃ*.

akᵃ (aká-) *pl.* **akɨtín.** *1 n.* mouth, oral cavity. *2 n.* entrance, opening. *3 n.* burrow, den, hole, lair.

aka gwaáᵉ *n.* beak.

akáám (aká-ámà-) *pl.* **akáíkᵃ**. *n.* one skilled at talking deceptively or persuasively. *Lit.* 'mouth-person'.

Akaɗéérótᵃ (Akaɗéérótò-) *n.* a personal name.

akákwáywᵃ (aká-kwáyò-) *pl.* **akákwáítín**. *n.* lip. *Lit.* 'mouth-tooth'.

akáƙúm (aká-ƙúmù-) *pl.* **akáƙúmítín**. *n.* cheekbone, malar, zygomatic bone.

akánɨ́ (akánɨ́) *prep.* until, up to (an event or place). A noun following this word takes the oblique case.

akarér (akaréri-) *pl.* **akarérikᵃ**. *n.* hole dug to trap edible termites.

akatɛ́tᵃ (akatɛ́tí-) *pl.* **akatɛ́tíkᵃ**. *n.* gourd plug (made from a gourd tip cut off and inverted).

akáts'ɛa na pakós *n.* cleft palate. *Lit.* 'mouth skin that is split'.

akɛdᵃ (akɛdɛ-) *1 n.* mouth, opening. *2 n.* muzzle of a weapon.

akɨ́lɨkᵃ (akɨ́lɨkà-) *1 n.* intelligence, mind. *2 n.* skill, talent.

àkɨ̀lɔ (àkɨ̀lɔ) *prep.* instead (of). A noun following this word takes the oblique case.

akɨn (akɨ́nɔ́-) *n.* greater kudu. *Tragelaphus strepsiceros*.

Akɔl (Akɔlɨ́-) *n.* a personal name.

akɔ́ŋikɔŋ (akɔ́ŋikɔŋɨ́-) *n.* cliff chat. *Myrmecocichla cinnamomeiventris*.

Akóóro (Akóóroó-) *n.* a personal name.

Akúɗúkori (Akúɗúkorií-) *n.* a personal name.

akúkúròn (akúkúrònì-) *v.* to crawl. See also *tolíón*.

akwétékwétánón (akwétékwétánónì-) *v.* to wriggle or writhe around.

áƙáfòn (áƙáfònì-) *v.* to yawn.

aƙár (aƙáró-) *pl.* **aƙáríkwᵃ**. *n.* palate, roof of the mouth.

aƙatᵃ (aƙatí-) *pl.* **áƙátɨkᵃ**. *1 n.* nose. *2 n.* nostril.

aƙatiékwᵃ (aƙatí-ékù-) *pl.* **aƙatiékwitín**. *n.* nostril. *Lit.* 'nose-eye'.

áƙátɨkìn (áƙátɨkìnì-) *n.* points, topics. *Lit.* 'its nostrils'.

aƙatiɔ́kᵃ (aƙatí-ɔ́kà-) *pl.* **aƙatiɔ́kɨ́tín**. *n.* nasal bone, nosebone.

aƙóláánón (aƙóláánónì-) *v.* to swing.

aƙúƙúrɔ̀n (aƙúƙúrɔ̀nì-) *v.* to creep.

akwᵃ (akɔ́-) *pl.* **akwitín.** *n.* inside, interior.

ák̂wêdᵃ (ák̂wédè-) *n.* inner part, inside, interior.

alálá (alálàà-) *n.* augur buzzard. *Buteo augur.*

alámááránón (alámáárànónì-) *v.* to disperse, dissipate (like ants or a crowd of people). See also *ɨlámááránón.*

alárá (aláràà-) *n.* shrub species whose red or yellow berries are eaten raw and whose stems are made into arrows, spears, and walking sticks and are used to build houses and granaries. *Grewia tenax.* See also *ɔgɔn.*

álìf (álìfù-) *pl.* **álìfìkᵃ.** *n.* thousand.

alólóánitetés (alólóánitetésí-) *v.* to dangle, suspend in the air.

alólóánón (alólóánónì-) *v.* to dangle, hang freely.

alólóés (alólóésí-) *v.* to dangle, hold up, suspend in the air.

alólóŋòn (alólóŋònì-) *v.* to be anxious, fret, worry.

ám (ámá-) *pl.* **ròɓᵃ.** *n.* person.

ámá na biyáᵉ *n.* foreigner, outsider. See also *ɦyɔ̀ɔ̀m* and *ɲeɓúkúitᵃ.*

ámá nà mìɲ *n.* deaf person.

ámá nà ŋwàx *n.* disabled person.

ámácèkᵃ (ámá-cèkì-) *pl.* **roɓacikám.** *n.* someone's wife.

ámáìdwᵃ (ámá-ìdò-) *n.* breast milk. *Lit.* 'person-milk'.

ámáìm (ámá-ìmà-) *pl.* **roɓawikᵃ.** *n.* someone's child.

ámákɔrɔ́ɓâdᵃ (ámá-kɔrɔ́ɓádì-) *pl.* **ámákurúɓâdᵃ.** *n.* personal item, personal property.

ámánànès (ámánànèsì-) *n.* humanness, personhood.

ámáze (ámá-zeá-) *pl.* **roɓazeíkᵃ.** *1 n.* big man, boss, chief, head honcho. *2 n.* mister, sir. *3 n.* lord, master. *4 n.* adult, big person, grown-up.

ámázeám (ámá-ze-ámà-) *pl.* **roɓazeíkᵃ.** *1 n.* big man, boss, chief, head honcho. *2 n.* mister, sir. *3 n.* lord, master.

ámázeáma awáᵉ *1 n.* chief village elder. *2 n.* village chairperson.

ámázeáma na kɔ́nɔ̀nɨ *n.* councilor in the Local Council I (LCI), a unit in the Ugandan government at the village level.

ámázeáma ɲápukanɨ *n.* government official.

ámázeáma ɲépárìxì *n.* parish chief.

ámázeáma ɲésukúluⁱ *n.* headmaster, head teacher, principal.

ámázeáma teréɡì *1 n.* boss, employer. *2 n.* crew chief, foreman.

ámêdᵃ (ámédè-) *pl.* **ámín.** *n.* one responsible, owner, proprietor.

ámédà kíjáᵉ *1 n.* landowner. *2 n.* indigenous person, local, native. *3 n.* God.

Amérìkà (Amérìkàà-) *n.* America.

Amérìkààm (Amérìkà-àmà-) *pl.* **Amérikaikᵃ.** *n.* American.

amózà (amózàà-) *n.* small black flying ant species that often appears after a rain as a sign of the coming emergence of edible termites.

amɨ́tsᵃ (amɨ́tsá-) *pl.* **amɨ́tsɨ́kᵃ.** *n.* debt, obligation (like having drunk someone's beer without having paid for it by doing work in their garden).

amɨ́tsáàm (amɨ́tsá-àmà-) *pl.* **amɨ́tsɨkaikᵃ.** *n.* debitor, debtor.

amʉtsanés (amʉtsanésí-) *v.* to collect on a debt.

anás (anásɨ-) *n.* male greater kudu. *Tragelaphus strepsiceros.*

ànɛ̀ (ànɛ̀ɛ̀-) *n.* vine species whose tuberous roots are peeled and eaten raw or roasted and whose beanlike seeds are cooked and eaten. *Vigna frutescens.* Possibly the same vine as *málákʉ́r.*

anɛsʉ́ƙɔt[a] (anɛsʉ́ƙɔtɨ́-) *v.* to recall, remember (often with regret).

anɛtés (anɛtésɨ́-) *v.* to recall, recollect, remember. See also *tamɛtés.*

aniesʉ́ƙot[a] (aniesʉ́ƙotí-) *v.* to recall repeatedly (often with regret).

aŋaras (aŋarasá-) *n.* gravel.

aŋarasááƙw[a] (aŋarasá-áƙɔ-) *n.* gravelly area.

Aŋatár (Aŋatárɨ-) *n.* name of a hill or mountain.

aŋaw[a] (aŋaú-) *n.* yellowish tobacco leaves.

aŋirɛs (aŋirɛsɨ́-) *1 v.* to turn, twist. *2 v.* to steer (a vehicle).

aŋiriesón (aŋiriesónì-) *v.* to swerve or veer repeatedly.

Aŋolekók[a] (Aŋolekókò-) *n.* name of a hill or mountain.

Apáálokiɓúk[a] (Apáálokiɓúkù-) *n.* personal ox-name of a colonial British District Commissioner.

Apáálokúk[a] (Apáálokúkú-) *n.* name of an Italian priest (Father Daniel) who founded the Kaabong Catholic mission and was killed by the Turkana.

Apáálomúƙ[a] (Apáálomúƙú-) *n.* a personal name.

Apáálòŋìrò (Apáálòŋìròò-) *n.* a personal name.

Apáásiá (Apáásiáà-) *n.* a personal name.

apápánà (<apápánɔ̀ɔ̀n) *v.*

apápánɛ̀ɛ̀tɔ̀n (apápánɛ̀ɛ̀tɔ̀nì-) *v.* to make peace, reconcile (often for self-centered purposes).

apápánɔ̀ɔ̀n (apápánɔ̀ɔ̀nɨ-/apápána-) *v.* to make peace, reconcile (often for self-centered purposes).

apéléle (apéléleí-) *pl.* **apélélèik**[a]. *n.* cestode, tapeworm.

Apérít[a] (Apérítì-) *n.* a personal name.

apɛ́tɛ́pɛ́tánón (apɛ́tɛ́pɛ́tánónì-) *1 v.* to be scattered around, strewn about. *2 v.* to wave limbs wildly during a seizure or when dying. See also *idɛrídɛ́rɔ́s.*

apíìròn (apíìrònì-) *1 v.* to jump down, jump off. *2 v.* to jump to it, leap into action. See also *ipíìròn.*

Apʉs (Apʉsɨ́-) *n.* a personal name.

arágwan (arágwanɨ́-) *pl.* **arágwànɨk**[a]. *1 n.* moon. *2 n.* month.

arágwànà kɔ̀n *n.* maize variety. *Lit.* 'one month'. Also called *katʉmán.*

arágwanɨ́ɛ́bitɨ́n (arágwanɨ́-ɛ́bitɨ́nɨ́-) *n.* new moon. *Lit.* 'moon-horns'.

arágwanɨ́ɛ́kw[a] (arágwanɨ́-ɛ́kù-) *n.* full moon. *Lit.* 'moon-eye'.

Aramasán (Aramasánɨ-) *n.* personal name of a Bokora man who settled in Ikland and married an Ik.

Árápííjí (Árápííjìì-) *n.* place named after rocket-propelled grenades (RPG).

arasí (arasîi-) *n.* councillor in the Local Council I (LCI), an administrative unit in the Ugandan government at the village level.

arétón (arétónì-) *v.* to cross (this direction, to this side).

arɨ́ (arɨ́ɛ́-) *pl.* **arɨ́ɨ́k**[a]. *n.* section of the small intestine.

Aríkó (Aríkóò-) *n.* a personal name.

àrɨŋàs (àrɨŋàsɨ) *adv.* all the time, always.

arír (arírá-) *pl.* **arírík**[a]. *n.* flame mixed with smoke.

àrònìàw[a] (àrònì-àwà-) *pl.* **aroniawík**[a]. *n.* crossing, bridge, ford.

aronuƙot[a] (aronuƙotí-) *v.* to cross (to that side).

arúrúbɔ̀n (arúrúbɔ̀nɨ-) *v.* to stalk.

arútón (arútónì-) *1 v.* to make noise, resound, sound. *2 v.* to be famous, well-known (when one's name resounds).

arútónuƙot[a] (arútónuƙotí-) *v.* to make a noise, sound out.

Áryánkòrì (Áryánkorií-) *n.* a personal name.

as (asɨ-) *pl.* **ásík**[a]. *pro.* self, -self.

àsàk[a] (àsàkà-) *pl.* **asákík**[a]. *1 n.* door, doorway. *2 n.* patriclan: clan based on the father's lineage. *3 n.* verse.

àsàkànèb[a] (àsàkà-nèbù-) *n.* main body of a door.

asínítòn (asínítònì-) *v.* to dream, envision (at night or prophetically).

asínítònìàm (asínítònì-àmà-) *pl.* **asínítoniik**[a]. *n.* dreamer, fortuneteller, prophet.

asínón (asínónì-) *v.* to delay. See also *itɨón*.

Asiróy[a] (Asiróì-) *n.* a personal name.

asʉnán (asʉnánɨ-) *pl.* **asʉnáník**[a]. *n.* African pencil cedar, a tall evergreen tree whose fragrant poles are used for building and whose bark is pounded and soaked as a decoction against stomach ailments. *Cupressus lusitanica*.

át[a] (átí-) *n.* um: a filler word that can replace a forgotten word of any grammatical category.

átà (átà) *subordconn.* even if.

atɔŋ (atɔŋɔ́-) *n.* spotted hyena. *Crocuta crocuta*. See also *natɨŋá*.

àtsòn (àtsònì-) *v.* to come.

áts'[a] (áts'á-) *pl.* **áts'ítín**. *n.* Sycamore fig: huge branching tree in which beehives are placed, whose fruits are eaten raw, and whose wood is used to carve bowls and troughs. *Ficus sycomorus*.

ats'am (ats'amá-) *n.* gnawable food (like maize or meat).

áts'ɛ́s (áts'ɛ́sɨ-) *1 v.* to chew, gnaw. *2 v.* to bite, sting (of insects). *3 v.* to ache, cause pain, hurt. See also *kɨ́dzɛ̀s*.

áts'ɛ́sà bùbùì *n.* bellyache, stomach ache.

áts'ɛ́sa gʉ́ró[e] *1 n.* acid reflux, heartburn. *2 n.* heartache.

áts'ɛ́sɨ̀àmà ròɓà[e] *n.* cannibal.

áts'ɛ́suƙot[a] (áts'ɛ́sʉƙotɨ́-) *1 v.* to eat all, eat up (by chewing or gnawing). *2 v.* to bite or sting thoroughly.

áts'ietés (áts'ietésí-) *v.* to hurt intermittently.

ats'ímétòn (ats'ímétònì-) *v.* to wear out (of clothes, shoes, etc.).

aúgòn (aúgònì-) *v.* to emerge and feed at night (of termites).

aukes (aukesí-) *v.* to fill (one's mouth) with drink before/without swallowing.

aw[a] (awá-) *pl.* **àwìk**[a]. *1 n.* abode, home, homestead, manyatta, village. *2 n.* place.

awa ná zè *1 n.* big home or village. *2 n.* capital city. *3 n.* Heaven.

awa Ɲákují *n.* Heaven.

awáákw[a] (awá-áƙɔ̀-) *1 n.* compound, grounds, yard. *2 n.* home life.

awáám (awá-ámà-) *pl.* **awáík**[a]. *n.* homebody, stay-at-home person.

ay[a] (aí-) *pl.* **aitín**. *1 n.* side. *2 n.* area, location.

b

bàbà (bàbàà-) *pl.* **bábàɩkᵃ**. *n.* armpit, underarm.

babatᵃ (babatí-) *pl.* **babátíkwᵃ**. *1 n.* his/her/its father. *2 n.* his/her uncle (father's brother).

babatíím (babatí-ímà-) *pl.* **babatíwíkᵃ**. *n.* his/her cousin (father's brother's child).

babatínánès (babatínánèsì-) *n.* fatherhood, fatherliness.

babatíɲótᵃ (babatí-ɲótà-) *n.* his/her father-in-law (sibling's spouse's father).

bábò (báboò-) *pl.* **báboín**. *1 n.* your father. *2 n.* your uncle (father's brother).

bábòìm (bábò-ìmà-) *pl.* **bábowikᵃ**. *n.* your cousin (father's brother's child).

báboɲótᵃ (bábo-ɲótá-) *n.* your father-in-law (sibling's spouse's father).

bácɩ́kᵃ (bácɩ́kà-) *pl.* **bácɩ́kɩ̀kᵃ**. *1 n.* area, place, spot. *2 n.* corridor, walkway. *3 n.* part, section.

bàdᵃ (bàdì-) *n.* giant, goliath: any huge person or thing.

bàdìàm (bàdì-àmà-) *pl.* **badiikᵃ**. *1 n.* sorcerer, wizard. *2 n.* anything spooky, weird, uncanny.

bàdìàm (bàdì-àmà-) *n.* canine tooth, cuspid.

badirétᵃ (badirétí-) *n.* devilry, sorcery, wizardry.

badirétínànès (badirétínànèsì-) *n.* sorcery, wizardry. See also *kʉtsʼánánès*.

badítésukotᵃ (badítésukotí-) *1 v.* to make die. *2 v.* to make break.

bàdòn (bàdònì-) *1 v.* to die. *2 v.* to be in a coma, unconscious. *3 v.* to be broken.

badona arágwanɨ *n.* lunar eclipse. *Lit.* 'death of the moon'.

badona fetí *n.* solar eclipse. *Lit.* 'death of the sun'.

badona ná jèjèⁱ *n.* natural death. *Lit.* 'death on a sleeping mat'.

bàdònìàm (bàdònì-àmà-) *pl.* **badoniikᵃ**. *n.* dead person, deceased.

bàdònìsìm (bàdònì-sìmà-) *pl.* **badonisimitín**. *n.* sisal species whose flat white leaves are cut into strips and used to bind bodies for burial.

badonukotᵃ (badonukotí-) *1 v.* to die. *2 v.* to collapse, go unconscious. *3 v.* to break.

bàɗᵃ (bàɗà-) *n.* muscle twitching.

baɗɨbaɗas (baɗɨbaɗasɨ́-) *pl.* **báɗɨ́bàɗàsɨ̀kᵃ**. *n.* fontanelle, soft spot. See also *bɔdɨbɔdɔs*.

bakutsᵃ (bakutsí-) *pl.* **bákútsɩ̀kᵃ**. *n.* breast, chest, pectus, thorax.

bakútsêdᵃ (bakútsédè-) *1 n.* middle, central part. *2 n.* belly (of a pot). *Lit.* 'its chest'.

bakutsísíts'ᵃ (bakutsí-síts'à-) *n.* chest hair.

bakáíkᵃ (bakáíkà-) *n.* exhaustion brought on by exertion, hunger, or thirst.

bakúlúmòn (bakúlúmònì-) *v.* to be thickly round (of long objects like rope, string, trees, etc.).

bálábálatés (bálábalatésí-) *v.* to disregard, ignore, tune out.

balés (balésɨ́-) *v.* to disregard, ignore, neglect.

balésá asɨ́ *v.* to neglect oneself (e.g. in hygiene or work).

balɛtés (balɛtésɨ́-) *v.* to disregard, ignore, neglect.

banés (banésɨ́-) *v.* to sharpen, whet.

bàr (bàrɔ̀-) *pl.* **bárɨ́tɨ́n**. *1 n.* flock, herd. *2 n.* riches, wealth.

barájónuƙot[a] (barájónuƙotí-) *v.* to sleep (of more than one person).

barat[a] (baratɨ́-) *pl.* **bárátɨ̀k**[a]. *n.* sisal species with flat leaves whose fibers are used to make string, rope, hunting nets, and termite traps; pieces of the plant may be tied to the limbs of the dead before they are burried. *Sansevieria sp.*

barat[a] (baratɨ́-) *pl.* **bárátɨ̀k**[a]. *n.* large fig tree species whose fruits are eaten and whose sap is chewed as gum; beehives are placed in its branches. *Ficus platyphylla*.

baratɨ́dɛ̀ (baratɨ́-dɛ̀a-) *n.* base or foot of a fig tree (*Ficus platyphylla*), often a sacred place or the site of significant cultural activities like dances and prayers.

baratɨ́gwà (baratɨ́-gwàà-) *n.* yellow white-eye. *Lit.* 'fig tree bird'. *Zosterops senegalensis.*

baratɨ́sím (baratɨ́-símà-) *pl.* **baratɨ́símɨ́tín**. *n.* rope made of the fibers of a *Sanseviera* sisal plant.

barats[a] (baratsó-) *pl.* **barátsíkw**[a]. *1 n.* morning. *2 n.* morrow.

barats[o] *n.* in the morning.

báretɔ̀n (bárétɔ̀nɨ̀-) *v.* to start getting rich or wealthy.

barís (barísá-) *pl.* **barísík**[a]. *n.* rock hyrax. *Procavia johnstoni.*

barɨ́tésuƙot[a] (barɨ́tésuƙotí-) *v.* to enrich, make rich (originally in terms of livestock).

bàrɔ̀am (bàrɔ̀-àmà-) *pl.* **baroik**[a]. *n.* rich or wealthy person (originally in terms of livestock). See also *bàrɔ̀nɨ̀am*.

bàròìm (bàrò-ìmà-) *pl.* **bárɨ́tɨ́níwik**[a]. *n.* small flock or herd.

bàrɔ̀n (bàrɔ̀nɨ̀-) *v.* to be rich, wealthy, well-off (originally in terms of livestock).

bàrɔ̀nɨ̀am (bàrɔ̀nɨ̀-àmà-) *pl.* **barɔniik**[a]. *n.* rich or wealthy person (originally in terms of livestock). See also *bàrɔ̀am*.

barɔnuƙot[a] (barɔnuƙotí-) *v.* to get rich or wealthy.

bás (básá-) *pl.* **básín**. *n.* beam, ray, or shaft of light. See also *súw*[a].

basaúr (basaúré-) *n.* eland. *Tragelaphus (Taurotragus) oryx.*

basaúréèkw[a] (basaúré-èkù-) *n.* medium-sized tree species found growing down the Rift Valley escarpment; it has red flowers and extremely hard wood used for roof rafters. *Lit.* 'eland-eye'.

Basaúréik[a] (Basaúré-icé-) *n.* traditional men's age-group with the eland as its totem (# 6 in historical line). *Lit.* 'Eland-Folk'. Also called *Nɨ́wápɛtoik*[a].

bàsɔ̀n (bàsɔ̀nɨ̀-) *v.* to dot, fleck, spot (e.g. insect droppings).

batánón (batánónì-) *1 v.* to be easy, simple. *2 v.* to be 'easy', easily seduced. *3 v.* to be gentle, kind. *4 v.* to be humble. *5 v.* to be cheap.

bàts[e] (=bèè/bɛ̀ɛ̀) *adv.* last, yester-: yester-hour, yesterday, yesteryear.

bátsés (bátsésɨ̀-) *v.* to scrape off (e.g. bark, peelings, skin). See also *sɛkés* and *tukurɛs*.

báts'ᵃ (báts'á-) *n.* pus, suppuration.

baúcùè (baú-cùè-) *n.* amniotic fluid.

bébam (bébamá-) *1 n.* fat slug (describing termites with fatty bodies). *2 n.* fat-ass, fatso.

béberés (béberésí-) *1 v.* to pull, tow. *2 v.* to draw out, extract (e.g. blood or information).

béberésúƙotᵃ (béberésúƙotí-) *v.* to drag away/off, pull away.

béberésuƙota así *1 v.* to scoot, skid. *2 v.* to refuse treatment for oneself.

béberetés (béberetésí-) *1 v.* to pull in, pull this way. *2 v.* to imbibe, ingest, take (drink or medicine).

béberiés (béberiesí-) *v.* to drag or pull along.

bèɗᵋ (bèɗè) *1 ideo.* thinly. *2 ideo.* lightly in color.

bɛɗɛ́ɗɔ̀n (bɛɗɛ́ɗɔ̀nɨ̀-) *1 v.* to be delicately thin, gossamer. *2 v.* to be light in color.

béɗés (béɗésɨ-) *1 v.* to need, want. *2 v.* to look or search for, seek. *3 v.* to intend (to do). *4 v.* to almost do (by accident).

béɗésa fiyekesí *v.* to try to earn a living. *Lit.* 'to look for life'.

béɗésa wasɔ́ᵋ *v.* to stand (for nomination).

bɛɗɛtés (bɛɗɛtésɨ́-) *v.* to look or search for, seek. See also *iƙujɛs*.

béɗíbeɗú (béɗíbeɗúù-) *pl.* **béɗíbeɗúikᵃ**. *1 n.* butterfly. *2 n.* letter, missive. See also *bóɗíboɗú*.

beemón (beemónì-) *v.* to crack slightly without coming apart.

bɛf (bɛfá-) *pl.* **bɛfitín**. *n.* puff adder or viper in general. *Bitis arietans*.

bèf (bèfù) *ideo.* bulkily, heftily.

bɛfa na gógòròjìkàᵉ *n.* Gaboon viper. *Lit.* 'adder with ridges'. *Bitis gabonica*.

bɛfácɛ́mɛ́r (bɛfá-cɛ́mɛ́rɨ́-) *n.* small reed-like plant species with thorns and whose roots are pounded, ground, and applied to snake-bites; legend is that puff adders themselves taught people about this treatment. *Lit.* 'puff adder herb'. *Cissus rhodesiae*.

bɛfúdɔ̀n (bɛfúdɔ̀nɨ̀-) *v.* to be bulky, hefty. See also *bɛfúƙúmɔ̀n*.

bɛfúƙúmɔ̀n (bɛfúƙúmɔ̀nɨ̀-) *v.* to be bulky, hefty. See also *bɛfúdɔ̀n*.

bèkwᵃ (bèkù-) *pl.* **bekwitín**. *n.* warthog boar. *Phacochoerus aethiopicus*.

bɛná (<bɛnɔ́ɔ́n) *v.*

beniitesa kíjáᵉ *n.* transformation of the land (e.g. due to development or weather patterns).

benión (beniónì-) *1 v.* to not be (someone or something). *2 v.* to be unique. See also *bɛnɔ́ɔ́n*.

beniónuƙotᵃ (beniónuƙotí-) *v.* to change, transform.

bɛnɔ́ɔ́n (bɛnɔ́ɔ́nɨ̀-/bɛná-) *1 v.* to not be (someone or something). *2 v.* to be unique. See also *benión*.

bɛrés (bɛrésɨ́-) *1 v.* to build, construct, mould, make. *2 v.* to develop, raise up (e.g. a community or country). *3 v.* to braid, plait, weave. *4 v.* to bombard with spears, spear (many animals at once).

bɛrésá mɛnáᵋ *v.* to go over matters, process issues. *Lit.* 'to build matters'.

bɛrésɨ́am (bɛrésɨ́-àmà-) *pl.* **bɛrésíikᵃ**. *n.* builder.

bɛrésíama dómítíní *n.* potter.

bɛrɛtés (bɛrɛtésɨ́-) *v.* to craft, form, shape, sculpt.

bɛrɛtésá mɛná⁽ᵉ⁾ v. to come to a consensus.

bèrrr (bèrrr) ideo. baa! (bleating sound of goats and sheep).

betsínákwètᵃ (betsíná-kwètà-) pl. betsínákwɛtɨ́kᵃ . n. left hand.

betsínáŋabér (betsíná-ŋabérí-) pl. betsínáŋabérɨ́kᵃ. n. lefthand rib.

betsínón (betsínónì-) 1 v. to be awkward, gauche, inept (e.g.in one's limbs or speech). 2 n. to be left-handed, sinistral. See also ɨɓaɲɨ́ɓáŋɔ̀n.

bèʉ̀r (bèʉ̀rà-) n. fork-tailed drongo. Dicrurus adsimilis. See also mɛ̀ʉ̀r.

béúrètòn (béúrètònì-) v. to bellow, roar. See also áɓʉ̀ɓʉ̀kɔ̀n.

bezekanitetésá tódàᵉ v. to exchange words.

bezekánón (bezekánónì-) v. to fail to cross paths or meet.

bézèkètìkìn (bézèkètìkìnì-) n. crossroad, junction.

bì (bì-) pl. bìtᵃ. pro. you/your (singular).

bîbᵃ (bíbà-) n. dove, pigeon.

bibɨjᵃ (bibɨjɨ́-) pl. bɨ́bɨjɨ̀kᵃ. n. chicken breastbone.

bicékᵃ (bi-cékì-) n. your wife.

bɨɗᵃ (bɨɗà-) pl. bɨɗitɨ́n. 1 n. bile, gall. 2 n. gallbladder.

bɨɗàhò (bɨɗà-hòò-) pl. bɨɗahoíkᵃ. n. gallbladder.

biéákwᵃ (bi-eákwá-) n. your husband.

biemetá (bi-emetáà-) pl. biemetátikwᵃ. n. your parent-in-law (of men).

biɛ́n (bi-ɛ́nɨ́-) pro. yours (singular).

biím (bi-imá-) pl. biwíkᵃ. 1 n. your child. 2 n. your niece or nephew (brother's child).

bɨlamúsɨ̀àm (bɨlamúsɨ́-àmà-) pl. bɨlamúsíikᵃ. n. village elder who adjudicates community matters.

bɨ́lɨ́kɛrɛtɛ́ (bɨ́lɨ́kɛrɛtɛ́ɛ̀-) n. crested francolin. Francolinus sephaena.

bilóbà (bi-lóbàà-) n. your grandchild.

bɨ́lɔɔrɔ́ (bɨ́lɔɔrɔ́ɔ̀-) n. fiscal, shrike. Lanius sp.

binamúí (bi-namúíì-) pl. binamúátikwᵃ. 1 n. your sibling-in-law (husband's sibling). 2 n. your sister-in-law (brother's wife).

binamúíìm (bi-namúí-ìmà-) pl. binamúíwikᵃ. n. your niece or nephew (husband's sibling's child).

binêbᵃ (bi-nébù-) n. yourself (singular). Lit. 'your body'.

bɨɲ (bɨɲɨ̀-) n. tiny red waterworm that swims vertically.

bɨɲɛ́s (bɨɲɛ́sɨ́-) v. to push nearer to.

bɨɲótᵃ (bi-ɲótá-) 1 n. your foreign friend. 2 n. your sibling-in-law (child's spouse's parent).

bɨɲótáìm (bi-ɲótá-ìmà-) pl. bɨɲótáwikᵃ. n. your niece or nephew-in-law (child's spouse's sibling).

bɨrá (<bɨrɔ́ɔ́n) v.

bɨráútɔ̀n (bɨráútɔ̀nì-) v. to be decreased, less.

bɨ́rɛ́s (bɨ́rɛ́sɨ̀-) v. to avail, give, help.

bíro (bíroó-) n. bird species.

bɨrɔ́ɔ́n (bɨrɔ́ɔ́nɨ̀-/bɨrá-) v. to be lacking, not there, unavailable.

bɨrɔ́ɔ́nɨ̀mɛ̀n (bɨrɔ́ɔ́nɨ̀-mɛ̀nà-) n. lack (as in 'due to the lack of ...').

bisákᵃ (bisáká-) n. appetite for meat, meat hunger.

bìtᵃ (bìtì-) pro. you/your (plural).

bitáŋá (bi-táŋáɨ̀-) *n.* your co-: cohort, colleague, comrade, etc.

bítés (bítésì-) *v.* to spray.

bitétɔ́n (bitétɔ́nɨ̀-) *v.* to increase, multiply.

bitiɛn (biti-ɛnɨ́-) *pro.* yours (plural).

bitinebitín (biti-nebitíní-) *n.* yourselves (plural). *Lit.* 'your bodies'.

bititam (bititamá-) *n.* increase, profit.

bititɛtés (bititɛtésɨ́-) *v.* to increase, multiply.

bitsétón (bitsétónì-) *1 v.* to expire, pass away, perish. *2 v.* to be exhausted, used up (energy, wealth).

biy[a] (biyá-) *n.* outside.

biyáxán (biyá-xánà-) *n.* outside.

bízès (bízèsì-) *v.* to press, push, squeeze.

bízetés (bízetésí-) *v.* to press out, squeeze out.

bízibizatés (bízibizatésí-) *v.* to press or squeeze all over.

bɔ (bɔɔ̀-) *pl.* bɔitín. *n.* section of the large intestine.

bɔbá (bɔbáà-) *pl.* bɔbáɨn. *1 n.* my grandfather. *2 n.* my father-in-law (of women).

bɔbat[a] (bɔbatí-) *pl.* bɔbatíkw[a]. *1 n.* his/her grandfather. *2 n.* her father-in-law.

bɔ́bɔ (bɔ́bɔɔ̀-) *pl.* bɔ́bɔɨn. *1 n.* your grandfather. *2 n.* your father-in-law (of women).

bɔɗibɔɗɔs (bɔɗibɔɗɔsí-) *pl.* bɔ́ɗibɔɗɔsɨk[a]. *n.* fontanelle, soft spot. See also *baɗibaɗas*.

bóɗíboɗú (bóɗíboɗúù-) *pl.* bóɗiboɗúik[a]. *1 n.* butterfly. *2 n.* letter, missive. See also *bédíbeɗú*.

bɔɗɔ́k[a] (bɔɗɔ́kú-) *pl.* bɔɗɔ́kɨk[a]. *1 n.* bark, husk, rind. *2 n.* gun safety mechanism.

bɔ̀f (bɔ̀fɔ̀) *ideo.* puffily.

bofétón (bofétónì-) *v.* to shout, yell.

bɔfɔ́dɔ̀n (bɔfɔ́dɔ̀nɨ̀-) *v.* to be puffy, tumid, turgid.

bɔfɔkɔr (bɔfɔkɔ́rɛ́-) *pl.* bɔfɔkɔ́rɨk[a]. *n.* ram: uncastrated male goat.

bófón (bófónì-) *v.* to shout, yell.

bógès (bógèsì-) *v.* to catch off guard, storm, surprise, take by surprise. See also *itúúmés*.

bɔibɔ́ɔ́n (bɔibɔ́ɔ́nɨ̀-) *v.* to be reddish-brown.

bɔ̀k[a] (bɔ̀kà-) *pl.* bɔ́kɨtɨ́n. *n.* crotch or fork in a plant or tree.

bɔ̀kɛ̀d[a] (bɔ̀kɛ̀dɛ̀-) *pl.* bɔ̀kɨn. *n.* crotch or fork in a plant or tree.

bòkìbòk[a] (bòkìbòkì-) *pl.* bokíbókik[a]. *n.* jowl.

bokímón (bokímónì-) *v.* to get caught or stuck in/on.

bɔkɔ́k[a] (bɔkɔ́kɔ́-) *pl.* bɔkɔ́kɨk[a]. *n.* old black honeycomb.

bɔkɔs (bɔkɔ́sɨ́-) *pl.* bɔkɔ́sɨ́k[a]. *n.* neckbone, upper cervical vertibrae.

bɔkátín (bɔkátɨ́nɨ́-) *pl.* bòkèt[a]. *1 n.* bride. *2 n.* daughter-in-law.

bɔkátɨ́nɨ̀èàkw[a] (bɔkátɨ́nɨ́-èàkwà-) *n.* bridegroom, groom.

bɔlɛ́sɨ́kɔt[a] (bɔlɛ́sɨ́kɔtɨ́-) *v.* to forego, give up, relinquish.

bɔlitɛ́sɨ́kɔt[a] (bɔlitɛ́sɨ́kɔtɨ́-) *v.* to make someone stop doing.

bɔlɔl (bɔlɔlɔ́-) *pl.* bolólíkw[a]. *n.* backyard: spot outside a home where ashes/rubbish are dumped and where people go for their toilet.

bɔlɔnukɔt[a] (bɔlɔnukɔtɨ́-) *v.* to cease, desist, stop doing.

bòmòn (bòmònì-) *1 v.* to be dense, thick (of undergrowth). *2 v.* to be fertile, prolific (of people and animals).

bɔn (bɔnɛ́-) *n.* caretaking, provision (for dependent persons).

bɔnán (bɔnánɨ́-) *pl.* **bɔnánáikw**[a]. *n.* dependent, orphan.

bɔnánɛ́s (bɔnánɛ́sì-) *n.* dependence, orphanhood.

bɔnɛ́ám (bɔnɛ́-ámà-) *pl.* **bɔnɛ́ík**[a]. *n.* caretaker, provider.

bɔnɛ́s (bɔnɛ́sɨ́-) *1 v.* to care or provide for (esp. with food). *2 v.* to feed, give food relief. *3 v.* to domesticate, tame (by feeding).

bònìt[a] (bònìtà-) *pl.* **bonítík**[a]. *1 n.* kind, species, type, variety. *2 n.* clan. See also *ɲákabɨ́lá*.

bɔɲ (bɔɲɔ́) *ideo.* brittlely.

bɔɲɔ́dɔ̀n (bɔɲɔ́dɔ̀nì-) *v.* to be brittle.

bɔ́ŋɔ́n (bɔ́ŋɔ́nɨ̀-) *1 v.* to be nearly ripe (showing some color). *2 v.* to be fruit-laden.

boŋórén (boŋórénì-) *pl.* **boŋórénik**[a]. *n.* red dirt or soil (naturally occuring or from being burnt).

bòrèn (bòrènì-) *pl.* **bórénìk**[a]. *1 n.* fatty chicken tail. *2 n.* small bottle-like gourd used as a butter or oil flask.

bɔrɛ́tɔ́n (bɔrɛ́tɔ́nɨ̀-) *1 v.* to become tired, tire. *2 v.* to become bored, lose interest.

bɔrɔ́ɗɔ́mɔ̀n (bɔrɔ́ɗɔ́mɔ̀nɨ̀-) *v.* to be shriveled, shrunken (like a deflated ball or one's eyes).

bòròk[a] (bòròkù-) *n.* bushpig. *Potamochoerus porcus.*

borokucúrúk[a] (boroku-cúrúkù-) *n.* bushpig boar.

bòròkùìm (bòròkù-ìmà-) *pl.* **borokuwik**[a]. *n.* bushpig piglet.

borokuŋwa (boroku-ŋwaá-) *n.* bushpig sow.

bɔrɔkɔk[a] (bɔrɔkɔkɔ́-) *pl.* **bɔrɔ́kɔ́kɨ̀k**[a]. *n.* tobacco cone.

bɔ́rɔ́n (bɔ́rɔ́nɨ̀-) *1 v.* to be tired. *2 v.* to be bored, uninterested.

bɔrɔ́ɔ́n (bɔrɔ́ɔ́nɨ̀-) *1 v.* to be ajar, open. *2 v.* to be loud (of a voice). See also *ŋawɨ́ɔ́n*.

bɔ́rɔ́rɔ̀n (bɔ́rɔ́rɔ̀nɨ̀-) *v.* to cry out (in alarm, fear, or pain). See also *werétsón*.

bɔ̀rɔ̀ts[a] (bɔ̀rɔ̀tsà-) *n.* erosion, landslide, mudslide. See also *dìdìàk*[a].

Bɔ̀rɔ̀tsààk[a] (Bɔ̀rɔ̀tsà-àkà-) *n.* name of a place. *Lit.* 'erosion-mouth'.

borotsiɛ́s (borotsiɛsí-) *v.* to blow gently on.

bɔrɔ́tsɔ́mɔ̀n (bɔrɔ́tsɔ́mɔ̀nɨ̀-) *v.* to be goopy, sludgy (of any viscous liquid). See also *bɔrɔ́tɔ́mɔ̀n*.

bòs (bòsì-) *pl.* **bositín**. *n.* ear.

bósánòn (bósánònì-) *v.* to be blue-gray. See also *kábusubusánón*.

bɔsɛtɛ́s (bɔsɛtɛ́sɨ́-) *1 v.* to collect, gather (e.g. contributions, donations). *2 v.* to summarize, sum up. See also *itsʉnɛtɛ́s*.

bòsìèkw[a] (bòsì-èkù-) *pl.* **bosiekwitín**. *n.* ear hole.

bòsìɔ̀k[a] (bòsì-ɔ̀kà-) *pl.* **bosiɔkitín**. *1 n.* temporal (outer ear) bone, os temporale. *2 n.* inner ear bone.

bòsìsìts'[a] (bòsì-sìts'à-) *n.* ear hair.

bɔsitɛtɛ́s (bɔsitɛtɛ́sɨ́-) *v.* to extract contributions from.

bositíniàm (bositíní-àmà-) *pl.* **bositíniik**[a]. *1 n.* deaf person. *2 n.* nickname for a hare or rabbit.

botᵃ (botá-) *pl.* **botitín.** *1 n.* burden, cargo, load. *2 n.* migration, movement, wave.

botáám (botá-ámà-) *pl.* **botaíkᵃ**. *n.* immigrant, migrant.

botedᵒ *n.* all, as a whole, entirely.

bɔ́tɛ́s (bɔ́tɛ́sɨ-) *v.* to shape (with a blade), shave.

bɔtɛtam (bɔtɛtamá-) *n.* wood shaving.

botétón (botétónì-) *v.* to migrate or move this way.

botibotos (botibotosí-) *v.* to be migratory, nomadic.

botibotosíám (botibotosí-ámà-) *pl.* **botibotosiíkᵃ**. *n.* drifter, migrant, nomad.

botitín (botitíní-) *n.* baggage, cargo, luggage.

bòtòn (bòtònì-) *v.* to migrate, move.

botonukotᵃ (botonukotí-) *v.* to migrate or move away.

bótsón (bótsónì-) *1 v.* to be clear, open, vacant. *2 v.* to be empty, hollow.

bótsóna ikáᵉ *v.* to be clear, sober (of one's mind).

bóx (bóxá-) *1 n.* nightjar. *2 n.* idiot, moron, stupid person.

boxokorétᵃ (boxokorétí-) *pl.* **boxokorétíkᵃ**. *n.* tall softwood tree species whose bland, red berries are eaten by children and whose wood is carved into bowls and cups. *Cussonia arborea*.

bú (búá-) *n.* airborn dust, dust cloud.

buanítésukotᵃ (buanítésukotí-) *v.* to lose, hide, make disappear, misplace.

buanón (buanónì-) *v.* to be lost, disappeared, misplaced.

buanónukotᵃ (buanónukotí-) *v.* to disappear, fade, evaporate, get lost.

bubú (bubú) *nurs.* nighty-night! (a nursery word for sleeping).

bùbù (bùbùà-) *pl.* **búbùìkᵃ**. *n.* abdomen, belly, gut.

bùbùàkwᵃ (bùbù-àkɔ̀-) *1 n.* abdominal cavity, bowel, gut. *2 n.* bolt carrier.

búbùedᵃ (búbùèdè-) *n.* underbelly, underside. *Lit.* 'its belly'.

búbuiem (búbui-emé-) *n.* back part or underpart of an animal's leg, from the ankle to the thigh, which is the women's special cut of meat.

bubʉn (bʉbʉná-) *pl.* **búbʉnɨkᵃ**. *1 n.* cinder, coal, ember. *2 n.* bullet, slug.

bʉbʉnɔ́ɔ́jᵃ (bʉbʉnɔ́-ɔ́jà-) *pl.* **bʉbʉnɔ́ɔ́jɨtín**. *n.* bullet or gunshot wound.

bùbùɔj ᵃ (bùbù-ɔ̀jà-) *pl.* **bubuɔjitín**. *n.* stomach ulcer.

bubuxánón (bubuxánónì-) *1 v.* to be soft (like ripe figs). *2 v.* to blistered, vesicated.

bubuxánónukotᵃ (bubuxánónukotí-) *1 v.* to become soft, soften (like ripe figs). *2 v.* to blister, vesicate. See also *ileɓíléɓòn*.

budés (budésí-) *v.* to conceal or hide oneself.

búdès (búdèsì-) *1 v.* to bury, inhume, inter, lay to rest. *2 v.* to conceal, hide. See also *mudés* and *tʉnʉkɛs*.

budésón (budésónì-) *v.* to be concealed, hidden.

budésónukotᵃ (budésónukotí-) *v.* to become hidden.

búdesukotᵃ (búdesukotí-) *1 v.* to bury. *2 v.* to conceal, hide.

búdòs (búdòsì-) *v.* to be concealed, covert, hidden, private, secret.

bùɗàm (bùɗàmà-) *n.* darkness.

buɗamaakón (buɗamaakónì-) *1 v.* to be dark (of many). *2 v.* to be black (of many). *3 v.* to be dirty (of many). *4 v.* to be dim (of many).

buɗamés (buɗamésí-) *v.* to move after dark.

buɗámón (buɗámónì-) *1 v.* to be dark. *2 v.* to be black. *3 v.* to be dirty. *4 v.* to be dim (of eyesight). *5 v.* to be dim or dull in intellect. *6 v.* to be meaningless, pointless.

buɗámónìàm (buɗámónì-àmà-) *pl.* **buɗámóniik**[a]. *1 n.* black person. *2 n.* African. *3 n.* human being.

Buɗámóniicékíj[a] (Buɗámóni-icé-kíjà-) *n.* Africa.

bùɗ[u] (bùɗù) *ideo.* softly.

buɗúditésúkot[a] (buɗúditésúkotí-) *v.* to make soft, soften up.

buɗúdòn (buɗúdònì-) *v.* to be soft.

bùf (bùfù) *ideo.* spongily.

bufúdòn (bufúdònì-) *v.* to be spongy.

bugwám (b-ugwámá-) *pl.* **bugwámátikw**[a]. *1 n.* your sibling-in-law (wife's sibling). *2 n.* your sibling-in-law (brother's wife's sibling). *3 n.* your brother-in-law (sister's husband). *4 n.* your sibling-in-law (sister's husband's sibling).

bukites (bukitesí-) *v.* to lay prostrate.

bùkòn (bùkònì-) *v.* to be or lie prostrate.

bukonukot[a] (bukonukotí-) *v.* to lie down prostrate. See also *eponukot*[a] and *itsólóŋòn*.

bukukánón (bukukánónì-) *v.* to be or lie prostrate (e.g. while deep in thought).

bukures (bukuresí-) *v.* to overturn, turn over, upset. See also *iɓéléés and iɓélúkéés*.

bukúresukot[a] (bukúresukotí-) *1 v.* to overturn, turn over, upset. *2 v.* to cover up.

bukúresukota así *v.* to dump over, overturn, spill.

buƙ[a] (buƙú-) *n.* brideprice (and all associated ceremonies).

buƙés (buƙésí-) *v.* to pay for a bride by giving gifts and doing work for her family on a continual basis.

buƙésúƙot[a] (buƙésúƙotí-) *v.* to pay out for a bride by giving gifts and doing work for her family on a continual basis.

buƙetés (buƙetésí-) *v.* to start paying for a bride by giving gifts and working for her family on a continual basis.

buƙitetés (buƙitetésí-) *v.* to extract brideprice.

buƙós (buƙósí-) *v.* to be married (of a woman) by virtue of having been paid for with brideprice.

buƙotam (buƙotamá-) *n.* anything payable as part of the brideprice.

buƙúám (buƙú-ámà-) *pl.* **buƙúík**[a]. *n.* brideprice payer: the groom and any of his relatives.

buƙusítésuƙot[a] (buƙusítésuƙotí-) *v.* to overturn, turn over, upset.

bʉlájámòn (bʉlájámònì-) *v.* to be debile, sapless, weak (from fatigue or sickness). See also *dakwádòn*.

bùlòn (bùlònì-) *1 v.* to be empty, void. *2 v.* to be unoccupied, vacant. *3 v.* to be free, unburdened. *4 v.* to be destitute, impoverished, poor.

bulonukot[a] (bulonukotí-) *1 v.* to empty out. *2 v.* to become unoccupied or vacant. *3 v.* to die off/out, go extinct.

bulubulátᵃ (bulubulátɨ-) *pl.* **bulubulátɨk**ᵃ. *n.* fire lily: plant species whose bulb is used to store tobacco (promoting fermentation) and is made into a thread to patch beehives or gourds; its large red or pink flowers are worn on the head by children during its brief blooming season. *Drimia altissima.*

bulubuláta na sábàìkàᵉ *n.* plant species whose leaves are made into children's bracelets. *Lit.* 'lily of the rivers'. *Typha sp.*

bulubulɔs (bulubulɔsɨ-) *1 v.* to be froofy, poofy, puffy (of animal tails and hairstyles). *2 v.* to be bristling, bristly (of hedgehogs, porcupines, and women with lots of jewelry).

bulukétᵃ (bulukétí-) *pl.* **bulukétík**ᵃ. *n.* small gourd used as an enema to rectally self-administer concoctions against intestinal illness.

bùlùƙᵘ (bùlùƙù) *ideo.* splash! (sound made by something landing in water).

bulúƙúmòn (bulúƙúmònì-) *v.* to be bulbous, bulging (like a gourd or a head). See also *lɔrɔ́dɔ̀n*.

bulútésuƙotᵃ (bulútésuƙotí-) *1 v.* to empty out. *2 v.* to clear out, vacate. *3 v.* to eradicate, wipe out.

bunétón (bunétònì-) *v.* to come across, happen upon.

bùnòn (bùnònì-) *v.* to come across, happen upon.

bùɲ (bùɲà) *ideo.* crumbly.

buɲádòn (buɲádònì-) *v.* to be crumbly.

búɲèn (búɲènì-) *pl.* **buɲéník**ᵃ. *n.* crumbly substance (like rock or soil that crumbles to powder when you pinch it between your fingers).

bur (buré-) *n.* dust.

bùr (bùrà) *ideo.* mushily.

burádòn (burádònì-) *v.* to be mushy, soft (like boiled pumpkin, damp soil, or egg yolk). See also *dabúdòn*.

bùràtsᵃ (bùràtsɨ-) *pl.* **burátsɨk**ᵃ. *n.* bat-eared fox. *Otocyon megalotis.*

burétɔ́n (burétɔ́nɨ-) *1 v.* to fly, take flight, take off flying. *2 v.* to wake suddenly.

bùrɔ̀n (bùrɔ̀nɨ-) *v.* to fly.

burɔnuƙotᵃ (burɔnuƙotɨ-) *v.* to fly off/away, take off flying.

Burukáyᵃ (Burukáí-) *n.* Turkanaland, northwest Kenya.

bùrùkùtsᵃ (bùrùkùtsɨ-) *pl.* **burúkútsɨk**ᵃ. *n.* kneecap, patella.

bùsùbùs (bùsùbùsɨ-) *pl.* **búsùbùsɨk**ᵃ. *n.* papyrus-like water plant species whose stalks are used as drinking straws and whose white pith is used to kill owls, hyenas, and other wizardly creatures. *Cyperus alternifolius.*

bútés (bútésɨ-) *v.* to drink like a cow in long slow drags.

bùtsᵃ (bùtsà-) *pl.* **butsitín**. *n.* patch of ground where birds dust-bathe.

búúbuanón (búúbuanónì-) *v.* to be infrequent, rare, scarce.

buúù (buúù) *ideo.* moo! (sound of cows lowing).

ɓ

ɓa (ɓa) *ideo.* unliftably.

ɓá (ɓá) *nurs.* yum-yum! (a nursery word for food or eating). See also *mamá*.

ɓaaɓánón (ɓaaɓánónì-) *v.* to be cracked.

ɓaɓaránón (ɓaɓaránónì-) *v.* to linger, loiter (sitting or standing).

ɓàj[a] (ɓàjì-) *pl.* **ɓajitín**. *n.* large tree species whose bark is decocted and drunk for heartburn and whose parasitic plant is applied to swollen body parts; its bark may also be chewed and applied to one's head and attached to one's bracelet as a charm to make one attractive to friends and invisible to enemies. *Boscia angustifolia*.

ɓakɨɓákɔ́n (ɓakɨɓákɔ́nɨ-) *v.* to be slightly bitter.

ɓaláŋ (ɓaláŋɨ-) *pl.* **ɓaláŋɨk**[a]. *n.* toothbrush tree: species whose stems are used to clean teeth, whose root decoction is drunk for chest or stomach pain (esp. women after delivery), and whose fruits are eaten raw. *Salvadora persica*.

ɓalídɔ̀n (ɓalídɔ̀nɨ-) *v.* to be gleaming, glistening. See also *pirídòn*.

ɓaŋás (ɓaŋásɨ-) *1 n.* looseness, slackness. *2 n.* plainness, simplicity.

ɓàŋɔ̀n (ɓàŋɔ̀nɨ-) *1 v.* to be free, loose, slack. *2 v.* to be plain, simple, uncomplicated.

ɓaram (ɓaramá-) *n.* sour porridge used as mash to make beer.

ɓarán (ɓaránɨ-) *pl.* **ɓaránɨk**[a]. *n.* inner chamber of an anthill or termite mound.

ɓariɓarítésukɔt[a] (ɓariɓarítésukɔtí-) *v.* to enlarge slightly, make a bit bigger (from small to medium).

ɓariɓárón (ɓariɓárónì-) *v.* to be piquant, sharp in taste, tart. See also *ɓárikíkón*.

ɓariɓárɔ̀n (ɓariɓárɔ̀nɨ-) *v.* to be medium-sized. See also *jɔ̀kɔ̀n* and *lerúkúmòn*.

ɓariɓárɔ́nukɔt[a] (ɓariɓárɔ́nukɔtí-) *v.* to become a bit bigger, enlarge slightly (from small to medium).

ɓárikíkón (ɓárikíkónì-) *v.* to be piquant, sharp in taste, tart. See also *ɓariɓárón*.

ɓarites (ɓaritesí-) *1 v.* to make sour. *2 v.* to make feel bad, upset.

ɓarítésukɔt[a] (ɓarítésukɔtí-) *1 v.* to make sour. *2 v.* to make feel bad, upset.

ɓáritson (ɓáritsoní-) *n.* small black ant species that causes pain if it gets in an eye. Also called *siŋíl*.

ɓàròn (ɓàrònì-) *v.* to be sour, tart.

ɓaronukɔt[a] (ɓaronukɔtí-) *v.* to ferment, sour.

ɓatísimú (ɓatísimúù-) *n.* baptism.

ɓatísimúêd[a] (ɓatísimú-édì-) *pl.* **ɓatísimúéditín**. *n.* baptismal name, Christian name.

ɓatísimúkabáɗ[a] (ɓatísimú-kabáɗá-) *pl.* **ɓatísimúkabáɗík**[a]. *n.* baptismal certificate.

ɓátsés (ɓátsésɨ-) *v.* to spread around (e.g. food in order to cool it). See also *iwies*.

ɓátsésa asɨ *v.* to spread oneself open (that is, one's legs while sitting, often immodestly).

ɓatsilárón (ɓatsilárónì-) *v.* to be acerbic, acrid.

ɓa[u] (ɓau) *ideo.* seriously, steadily.

ɓàz (ɓàzì) *1 interj.* so then, then. *2 interj.* so there, you see?

ɓéɓélés (ɓéɓélésí-) *v.* to split open/apart.

ɓéɓélɔ́s (ɓéɓélɔ́sɨ́-) v. to be split open/apart.

ɓɛiɓéɔ́n (ɓɛiɓéɔ́nɨ̀-) v. to burn or sting (of pain).

ɓɛjékwᵃ (ɓɛjékù-) n. late-flying edible termites that are less nutritious and tasty than their forerunners.

ɓɛkam (ɓɛkamá-) n. incitement, provocation.

ɓɛkánón (ɓɛkánónì-) v. to be incitive, inflammatory, provoking, rankling.

ɓɛkᵋ (ɓɛkɛ) ideo. snap! (sound of something thin snapping).

ɓɛkés (ɓɛkésɨ́-) v. to perforate, puncture.

ɓɛkɛtés (ɓɛkɛtésɨ́-) 1 v. to perforate, puncture. 2 v. to incite, provoke, rankle.

ɓɛkétɔ́n (ɓɛkétɔ́nɨ̀-) v. to hatch (of chicks). See also iɓéɓéètɔ̀n.

ɓɛkiɓékɔ́n (ɓɛkiɓékɔ́nì-) v. to rustle.

ɓɛkés (ɓɛkésɨ́-) 1 v. to walk. 2 v. to travel. 3 v. to move.

ɓɛkésá buɗámíkᵉ v. to move blindly.

ɓɛkésá kútúŋikᵒ v. to walk on the knees.

ɓɛkésá kwètɨkᵓ v. to walk on the hands.

ɓɛkésá turúùkᵉ v. to stumble ahead.

ɓɛkésá wɛwɛɛs v. to walk leisurely.

ɓɛkésá ziál v. to walk laboriously (like an obese or pregnant person).

ɓɛkésɨ́àm (ɓɛkésɨ́-àmà-) pl. ɓɛkésíikᵃ. 1 n. pedestrian, walker. 2 n. traveler, wayfarer.

ɓɛkésɨ́ama mukú n. one who walks at night (like a lover or wizard or merely someone who has not reached their destination by dark).

ɓɛkésɨ́kabáɗᵃ (ɓɛkésɨ́-kabáɗá-) pl. ɓɛkésɨ́kabáɗíkᵃ. n. identity card, passport.

ɓɛkɛ́sɨ́nɔ́s (ɓɛkɛ́sɨ́nɔ́sɨ́-) 1 v. to walk together. 2 v. to travel together.

ɓɛkɛsɔs (ɓɛkɛsɔsɨ́-) v. to be ambulatory, mobile, on the move.

ɓɛkɛsɔsɨ́ám (ɓɛkɛsɔsɨ́-ámà-) pl. ɓɛkɛsɔsíikᵃ. n. roamer, rover, wanderer.

ɓɛléɓélánón (ɓɛléɓélánónì-) v. to be chapped, cracked, split open.

Bèlèkwᵃ (Bèlèkù-) n. name of a flat area in Turkanaland, Kenya.

ɓɛlɛlɛtsᵋ (ɓɛlɛlɛtsɛ) ideo. flatly, pronely.

ɓelémón (ɓelémónì-) 1 v. to crack or split open (like burnt skin). 2 v. to break (of day), dawn.

ɓɛlérémɔ̀n (ɓɛlérémɔ̀nɨ̀-) v. to be bug-eyed.

ɓɛlés (ɓɛlésɨ́-) v. to crack, split.

ɓɛlɛtés (ɓɛlɛtésɨ́-) v. to crack, split.

ɓeletiés (ɓeletiesí-) v. to split apart multiply.

ɓɛlɔ́s (ɓɛlɔ́sɨ́-) v. to be cracked, split.

ɓerɲiés (ɓerɲiesí-) v. to pry open/apart (like grass so one can look through, or one's eyelids when fighting sleep).

ɓɛtélémɔ̀n (ɓɛtélémɔ̀nɨ̀-) v. to be flatly or shallowly concave. See also fɛtélémɔ̀n.

ɓets'aakón (ɓets'aakónì-) 1 v. to be white (of many). 2 v. to be light in color (of many). 3 v. to be clear, transparent (of many).

ɓets'akáwᵃ (ɓets'a-káú-) n. shrub species with ash-white bark, found growing down the escarpment; a decoction of its bark can be applied as a salve for skin abrasions. Lit. 'white-ash'. Olinia rochetiana.

ɓèts'ìɓèts'òn (ɓèts'ìɓèts'ònì-) 1 v. to be slightly white, whitish. 2 v. to be slightly light (of daytime).

ɓɛts'idɔ́dɔ́n (ɓɛts'idɔ́dɔ́nɨ̀-) *v.* to be whitish.

ɓets'itetés (ɓets'itetésí-) *1 v.* to make white, whiten. *2 v.* to embarrass, humiliate, shame.

Ɓèts'òn (Ɓèts'ònì-) *n.* February: month of white dryness. See also *Lokwaŋ*.

ɓèts'òn (ɓèts'ònì-) *1 v.* to be white. *2 v.* to be light in color. *3 v.* to be clear, transparent. *4 v.* to be clean, pure. *5 v.* to be holy.

ɓèts'ònìàm (ɓèts'ònì-àmà-) *pl.* ɓets'oniik[a]. *n.* white person: American, European, or any Caucasian. See also *ɲémúsukit[a]*.

Ɓets'oniicékíj[a] (Ɓets'oni-icé-kíjà-) *n.* America (North), Europe. *Lit.* 'white people land'.

Ɓets'oniicétôd[a] (Ɓets'oni-icé-tódà-) *n.* English or any European language. *Lit.* 'white people talk'. See also *Ɲímusukúitòd[a]*.

ɓìɓ[a] (ɓìɓà-) *n.* egg, ovum.

ɓiɓáhò (ɓiɓá-hòò-) *pl.* ɓiɓáhoík[a]. *n.* egg-sack, ovary.

ɓíɓités (ɓíɓítésí-) *v.* to drink with a straw.

ɓíkìrà (ɓíkìràà-) *pl.* ɓíkirain. *n.* nun, Catholic sister.

ɓilés (ɓilésí-) *v.* to cut out, excise, resect (something soft like an organ).

ɓilésúƙot[a] (ɓilésúƙotí-) *v.* to disembowel, eviscerate, gut.

ɓilíɓílés (ɓilíɓílésí-) *v.* to break into pieces, shatter.

ɓilímón (ɓilímónì-) *v.* to burst, deflate, erupt, explode.

ɓir (ɓirì) *ideo.* squashily, squishily.

ɓirés (ɓirésí-) *v.* to squash, squish. See also *reɗés*.

ɓirídòn (ɓirídònì-) *v.* to be squashy, squishy (like boiled greens or wet ground). See also *rɔjɔ́dɔ̀n*.

ɓirímón (ɓirímónì-) *v.* to get squashed or squished.

ɓirítésuƙot[a] (ɓirítésuƙotí-) *v.* to squash, squish.

ɓis (ɓisá-) *pl.* ɓísítín. *1 n.* spear. *2 n.* baby boy.

ɓisáák[a] (ɓisá-ákà-) *pl.* ɓisáákítín. *n.* spearhead. *Lit.* 'spear-mouth'.

ɓisáɓóló (ɓisá-ɓólòò-) *pl.* ɓisáɓólóíkw[a]. *n.* neck of a spearhead. *Lit.* 'spear-gourd'.

ɓisáím (ɓisá-ímà-) *pl.* ɓísítíníwik[a]. *n.* dart.

ɓo (ɓoó-) *pl.* ɓoitín. *n.* escarpment.

ɓóák[a] (ɓó-ákà-) *n.* top edge of an escarpment. *Lit.* 'escarpment-mouth'.

ɓòɓòn (ɓòɓònì-) *1 v.* to be deep. *2 v.* to be high-pitched, shrill. *3 v.* to be sexually insatiable (of a woman).

ɓoɓonuƙot[a] (ɓoɓonuƙotí-) *v.* to become deeper, deepen.

ɓɔɗ[a] (ɓɔɗá-) *pl.* ɓɔɗitín. *n.* clearing or glade where crops are dried and threshed. See also *dípɔ̀*.

ɓɔɗájúm (ɓɔɗá-júmù-) *n.* dirt mixed with threshed grain that is then sifted.

ɓóéɗ[a] (ɓó-éɗì-) *n.* shrub species whose round roots are peeled, boiled, and eaten during times of famine; they are said to cause severe itching in the throat and are thus swallowed quickly without chewing. *Lit.* 'escarpment-grain'. *Arisaema ruwenzoricum*.

ɓokóánètòn (ɓokóánètònì-) *v.* to be tri-colored.

ɓɔ́kɔ̀ɲ (ɓɔ́kɔ̀ɲɨ̀-) *pl.* ɓokóɲíkw[a]. *n.* bank, embankment, slope.

ɓɔ́l (ɓɔ́lá-) *pl.* ɓɔ́lɨ́tɨ́n. *n.* shin.

ɓòlìɓòl (ɓòlìɓòlì-) *pl.* ɓolíɓólìᵃ. *1 n.* dewlap: fold of loose skin on a animal's throat. *2 n.* hood (of a snake). *3 n.* goiter.

ɓólìs (ɓólìsò-) *pl.* ɓolísíkᵃ. *n.* tree species whose leaves are burnt green, together with the *ɲɛɛkɨmá* tree to smoke insect pests out of a garden. *Croton dichogamus.*

ɓoló (ɓolóò-) *pl.* ɓólóikwᵃ. *n.* big round gourd.

ɓólóèdᵃ (ɓólóèdè-) *n.* place where an arrowhead and shaft meet.

ɓòlòkòtsᵃ (ɓòlòkòtsì-) *pl.* ɓolókótsìkᵃ. *n.* scoop made from a small bisected gourd which often has a beaded handle sewn into it.

ɓolóɲómòn (ɓolóɲómònì-) *v.* to be widemouthed (of any opening like an anus, gourd, hole, or circumcized penis).

ɓɔlɔrɔtsᵃ (ɓɔlɔrɔtsɔ́-) *pl.* ɓɔlɔ́rɔ́tsɨ̀kᵃ. *n.* milkweed locust. *Phymateus sp.*

ɓòŋ (ɓòŋì-) *pl.* ɓoŋitín. *n.* tree species whose bitter yellow fruits are boiled multiple times, exposing the seeds which are eaten only during famines. *Balanites pedicellaris.*

ɓór (ɓóré-) *pl.* ɓórítín. *n.* boma, corral, kraal, livestock pen.

ɓórítɔ̀n (ɓórítɔ̀nì-) *v.* to discharge, emit, secrete (like pus or snot).

ɓɔrɔ́tɔ́mɔ̀n (ɓɔrɔ́tɔ́mɔ̀nì-) *v.* to be goopy, gunky (like millet beer, coagulating blood, drying eye drainage, snot, or saliva). See also *bɔrɔ́tsɔ́mɔ̀n.*

ɓotɨ́ (ɓɔtɨ́ɨ-) *n.* bland, watery meal mush (posho) eaten without accompanying sauce in times of famine.

ɓotólómòn (ɓotólómònì-) *v.* to be pooched out, protruding.

ɓòtòŋ (ɓòtòŋù-) *pl.* ɓótóŋɨ̀kᵃ. *n.* bunch, clump, cluster (like a swarm of bees, a regime of bananas, a cluster of figs).

ɓotsetés (ɓotsetésí-) *v.* to pluck or pull off.

ɓòtsᵒ (ɓòtsò) *ideo.* rigidly, stiffly.

ɓotsódòn (ɓotsódònì-) *1 v.* to be inflexible, rigid, stiff. *2 v.* to be absent-minded, inattentive. See also *kɛtérémɔ̀n.*

ɓɔtsɔ́tᵃ (ɓɔtsɔ́tɨ́-) *pl.* ɓɔtsɔ́tɨ́kᵃ. *n.* awl.

ɓotsotiés (ɓotsotiesí-) *v.* to pluck or pull off continually (as when harvesting).

ɓúɓús (ɓúɓúsà-) *pl.* ɓúɓúsɨ̀kᵃ. *n.* natural perfume made from the dried heart of the *tsʉ́ʉr* tree.

ɓʉɓʉsánón (ɓʉɓʉsánónì-) *1 v.* to be rotten at the core, have the heart-rot disease (of trees). *2 v.* to be indolent, slothful.

ɓukúlá (ɓukúláɨ-) *pl.* ɓukúláìkᵃ. *n.* Gerrard's acacia: hardwood tree whose wood is used for building and fencing, whose bark fiber makes a rope for tying, and whose bark decoction is drunk to cleanse the gut. *Acacia gerrardii.*

ɓukés (ɓukésí-) *v.* to elevate, lift, raise (as onto someone's head). See also *ikɛɛtés.*

ɓukésá botáᵉ *v.* to load a load.

ɓuketés (ɓuketésí-) *v.* to lift off, lower, unload (as from someone's head).

ɓuketésá botáᵉ *v.* to offload or unload a load.

ɓuketésá mɛnáᵋ *v.* to cause problems. *Lit.* 'to unload issues'.

ɓukétón (ɓukétónì-) *v.* to enter, go in.

ɓukítésukotᵃ (ɓukítésukotí-) *1 v.* to make enter, put in, take in. *2 v.* to enter, include. *3 v.* to employ, hire.

ɓukítésukotíám (ɓukítésukotí-ámà-) *pl.* **ɓukítésukotíík**ᵃ. *n.* employer, hirer.

ɓùkòn (ɓùkònì-) *v.* to enter, go in. Not to be confused with *ɓúkón*.

ɓúkón (ɓúkónì-) *v.* to commit adultery. Not to be confused with *ɓùkòn*.

ɓúkóniàm (ɓúkónì-àmà-) *pl.* **ɓúkóniik**ᵃ. *n.* adulterer, adulteress.

ɓukonuƙotᵃ (ɓukonuƙotí-) *1 v.* to enter, go in. *2 v.* to join in, participate. *3 v.* to pass through (specifically the legs of an old person during a ceremony of blessing the next generation). *4 v.* to go under, sink.

ɓulɛs (ɓulɛsɛ) *ideo.* in large numbers.

ɓuluɓul (ɓuluɓulu) *ideo.* sound of quaking or shaking (like an earthquake).

ɓulúrúmòn (ɓulúrúmònì-) *v.* to be callous, scarred.

ɓúnés (ɓúnésɨ-) *v.* to cut through a tubular object (like a pipe or log).

ɓunɛtam (ɓunɛtamá-) *n.* something cuttable cylindrically, tubularly (like a beehive).

ɓunɛtés (ɓunɛtésɨ-) *v.* to cut through a tubular object (like a pipe or log).

ɓùnɔn (ɓùnɔnɨ-) *v.* to move past, pass by.

ɓunɔnuƙotᵃ (ɓunɔnuƙɔtí-) *v.* to go past, pass by going.

ɓunúmɔn (ɓunúmɔnɨ-) *v.* to disperse, scatter. See also *iwéélánón*.

ɓunúmɔnà sèàᵉ *1 v.* to blush, flush, run hot (of one's blood out of excitement or embarrassment). *2 v.* to run cold (of one's blood out of terror). *Lit.* 'dispersal of blood'.

ɓunutés (ɓunutésɨ-) *v.* to disperse, scatter.

ɓunutiés (ɓunutiesí-) *v.* to scarify: make small cuts for cosmetic or medical reasons.

ɓúrukúkón (ɓúrukúkónì-) *v.* to germinate, sprout.

ɓútánés (ɓútánésí-) *v.* to have sex repeatedly and often.

ɓutᵘ (ɓutu) *ideo.* all, entirely.

ɓutúrúmòn (ɓutúrúmònì-) *v.* to be bulky, hulky.

ɓuumón (ɓuumónì-) *v.* to get dislocated, out-of-joint.

C

caál (caalɨ́-) *pl.* **caalɨ́k**[a]. *1 n.* cooking stone, hearthstone. *2 n.* supporting stone.

Caalíím (Caalí-ímà-) *n.* name of a place. *Lit.* 'hearthstone-child'.

càc[i] (càcɨ̀) *adv.* carelessly, heedlessly.

Cakalatɔ́m (Cakalatɔ́mɛ́-) *n.* name of a river near *Lòsòlìà* and *Píré*. Also called *Oŋorisabá*.

calúɓ[u] (calúɓú) *ideo.* splish-splash! (sound of walking in water).

cɛbɛn (cɛbɛnɨ́-) *pl.* **cébènɨ̀k**[a]. *1 n.* white concave container used for scooping. *2 n.* wooden spatula. *3 n.* gearshift. See also *ɲémiikó*.

cébès (cébèsɨ̀-) *v.* to roughen (esp. the surface of a grinding stone).

cɛɓés (cɛɓésɨ́-) *v.* to scoop up (with a ladle or spoon). See also *tɛ́bès*.

cédicedí (cédicedîi-) *n.* hopscotch.

cɛés (cɛɛsɨ́-) *1 v.* to kill, murder, slay (singly). *2 v.* to break. Compare with *sáɓés*.

cɛɛsá rié sàbàk[e] *v.* to immerse a sacrificial goat in the river, then roast it, and then dance around it as a prayer for rain. *Lit.* 'to kill a goat at the river'.

cɛɛsɨ́ám (cɛɛsɨ́-ámà-) *n.* killer, murderer (of one living thing).

cɛɛsúƙɔt[a] (cɛɛsúƙɔtɨ́-) *1 v.* to kill, murder (singly). *2 v.* to break.

cɛɛtés (cɛɛtésɨ́-) *v.* to harvest bountifully, produce a lot of.

Cegem (Cegemú-) *n.* a personal name.

ceím (ceímá-) *1 n.* lubricant, oil, oily substance (cooking oil, cream, lotion, motor oil). *2 n.* adipose tissue, blubber, fat. *3 n.* fuel: diesel, paraffin (kerosene), petrol (gas).

cek[a] (cekí-) *pl.* **cɨkám**. *1 n.* woman. *2 n.* wife.

cekínánès (cekínánèsì-) *n.* femininity, womanhood, womanliness.

cɛma kíjíkà[e] *n.* war. *Lit.* 'fighting of countries'.

cɛmáám (cɛmá-ámà-) *pl.* **cɛmáík**[a]. *n.* combatant, fighter.

cɛmɛkánón (cɛmɛkánónì-) *v.* to be a fighter.

cèmèr (cèmèrì-) *pl.* **cɛmɛrík**[a]. *1 n.* medicinal herb. *2 n.* drug, medicine, treatment. *3 n.* chemical. *4 n.* poison.

cèmèrɨ̀èkw[a] (cèmèrɨ̀-èkù-) *pl.* **cɛmɛriekwitín**. *n.* pill, tablet. *Lit.* 'drug-eye'.

cɛmérɨ́kààm (cɛmérɨ́kà-àmà-) *pl.* **cɛmérɨ́kaik**[a]. *n.* herbalist, traditional healer. See also *wetitésíàm*.

cɛmicɛmɔs (cɛmicɛmɔsɨ́-) *v.* to be bellicose, combative.

cèmɔ̀n (cèmɔ̀nɨ̀-) *1 v.* to fight, struggle against/with. *2 v.* to be doing something.

céŋ (céŋá-) *n.* humor, joke, joking.

cɛŋ (cɛŋá-) *n.* woodpecker.

céŋáám (céŋá-àmà-) *pl.* **céŋáik**[a]. *n.* joker, jokester, teaser.

ceŋánón (ceŋánónì-) *v.* to joke around, tease.

ceŋetíám (ceŋetí-ámà-) *pl.* **ceŋetíík**[a]. *n.* in-law.

ceŋetínánès (ceŋetínánèsì-) *n.* being in-laws.

cèrɔ̀n (cèrɔ̀nɨ̀-) *v.* to have breastmilk, let down milk (of mammals and humans).

Cerûb[a] (Cerúbè-) *n.* name of a river.

cicianón (cicianónì-) *v.* to reform, repent.

cicídè (cicídèà-) *n.* bird species.

ciitésuƙɔt[a] (ciitésuƙɔtí-) *1 v.* to fill, sate, satiate, satisfy. *2 v.* to charge (electrically).

cikám (cikámá-) *1 n.* women. *2 n.* wives.

cíkóróìkànànès (cíkóróìkànànèsì-) *n.* boundedness, having boundaries.

cíkóroy[a] (cíkóroí-) *pl.* **cíkóróìk**[a]. *n.* border, boundary, limit.

cikw[a] (cikó-) *pl.* **cikóík**[a]. *n.* male animal.

cìɔ̀n (cìɔ̀nì-) *v.* to be full, sated, satiated, satisfied.

ciɔnuƙɔt[a] (ciɔnuƙɔtí-) *v.* to become full, sated, satiated.

Cɔ́ƙɔ́tɔ̀m (Cɔ́ƙɔ́tɔ̀mè-) *n.* Dodoth people.

Cɔ́ƙɔ́tɔ̀mèàm (Cɔ́ƙɔ́tɔ̀mè-àmà-) *n.* Dodoth person.

còòkààm (còòkà-àmà-) *pl.* **cookaik**[a]. *1 n.* cowherd, shepherd. *2 n.* guard, watchman. *3 n.* defender, guardian, protector.

cookaama zíkésiicé *n.* prison guard.

cookaika ínó[e] *n.* wildlife authorities. *Lit.* 'guardians of animals'.

cookés (cookésí-) *1 v.* to shepherd, tend (livestock). *2 v.* to defend, guard, protect.

cookotós (cookotósí-) *v.* to be guarded, protected, tended.

coór (coorí-) *pl.* **coorík**[a]. *n.* leg rattle tied below the knee.

coorígwà (coorí-gwàà-) *n.* bee-eater. *Lit.* 'rattle-bird'. *Merops sp.* See also *kesenígwà*.

cuáák[a] (cuá-ákà-) *n.* permanent water source (like a spring or well). *Lit.* 'water-mouth'.

cuanón (cuanónì-) *v.* to be fluid, liquid.

cuanónuƙot[a] (cuanónuƙotí-) *v.* to become liquid, liquify, melt.

cuc[u] (cucu) *ideo.* very black.

cucue (cucué-) *n.* damp chill.

cucuéétòn (cucuéétònì-) *1 v.* to cool down/off (of pain or weather). *2 v.* to feel mercy, sympathize.

Cùcuèìk[a] (Cùcuè-ìkà-) *n.* name of a hill or mountain.

cucuéítésuƙot[a] (cucuéítésuƙotí-) *v.* to chill, cool down.

cucuéítésuƙota gúró[e] *v.* to calm or cool down one's heart.

cucuéón (cucuéónì-) *1 v.* to be chilly, cool. *2 v.* to be weak. *3 v.* to be bland, stale.

cucuéónuƙot[a] (cucuéónuƙotí-) *v.* to cool down/off (of pain or weather).

cue (cué-) *1 n.* liquid, water. *2 n.* baby girl. *3 n.* taboo of failing to give water to the elders first.

cúédòm (cúé-dòmà-) *pl.* **cúédomitín**. *n.* water pot used to keep clean water inside the hut.

cueina mésè *n.* beer leftover from a ceremony or group work-day. *Lit.* 'waters of beer'.

cúémúcè (cúé-múcèè-) *pl.* **cúémúcèìk**[a]. *n.* ditch, watercourse, waterway.

cúénêb[a] (cúé-nébù-) *pl.* **cúénébitín**. *n.* body of water.

cúkúɗùm (cúkúɗùmù-) *n.* male mountain reedbuck. *Redunca fulvorufula*.

Curuk[a] (Curukú-) *n.* name of a hill or mountain. *Lit.* 'bull'.

cúrúk[a] (cúrúkù-) *pl.* **cúrúkaikw**[a]. *1 n.* bull. *2 n.* male, sire, stud.

cúrúkà mèsè *n.* barm or yeast used in brewing beer. *Lit.* 'sire of beer'.

Curukúdè (Curukú-dèà-) *n.* base of *Curuk* mountain. *Lit.* 'bull-foot'.

cwɛtᵃ (cwɛtá-) *pl.* **cwɛ̀tɨkᵃ**. *n.* upper arm. An older form of the word *kwɛtᵃ* 'arm, hand' that may have taken on a narrower meaning for some Ik speakers.

cwɛtéém (cwɛté-émè-) *n.* bicep and/or tricep. *Lit.* 'upper arm flesh'.

d

dà (<dòòn) *v.*

daás (daasɨ́-) *1 n.* beauty, handsomeness, loveliness, prettiness. *2 n.* generosity, magnanimity, philanthropy. *3 n.* agreeableness, niceness, pleasantness. *4 n.* glory, radiance, splendor. *5 n.* holiness, sanctity.

dàbɨ̀j[a] (dàbɨ̀jà-) *n.* bird species.

dàb[u] (dàbù) *ideo.* mushily, softly, tenderly.

dabúdòn (dabúdònì-) *1 v.* to be mushy, soft (like a ripe avocado). *2 v.* to be soft and tender (like a baby). See also *burádòn*.

dadáŋ (dadáŋɨ̀-) *pl.* **dadáŋín**. *1 n.* my grandmother. *2 n.* my mother-in-law (of women).

dádàt[a] (dádàtì-) *pl.* **dadatíkw**[a]. *1 n.* his/her grandmother. *2 n.* her mother-in-law.

dádata dáŋá[e] *n.* queen of an edible-termite colony.

dádò (dádòò-) *pl.* **dádoín**. *1 n.* your grandmother. *2 n.* your mother-in-law (of women).

daiƙot[a] (<doonuƙot[a]) *v.*

daites (daitesí-) *v.* to adorn, beautify, embellish, make lovely or nice.

daitetésá asɨ́ *v.* to beautify oneself, make oneself look good.

dàj[a] (dàjà-) *pl.* **dajitín**. *n.* beer residue, draff, dregs. See also *dʉká*.

Dakáy[a] (Dakáɨ̀-) *n.* a personal name.

dakúáƙw[a] (dakú-áƙɔ̀-) *n.* forest, woodland. See also *ríjáàƙw*[a].

dakúɓɔ́l (dakú-ɓɔ́lè-) *pl.* **dakwitíníɓɔlitín**. *n.* tree trunk. Lit. 'tree-shin'.

dakúdè (dakú-dèà-) *pl.* **dakwitínídɛík**[a]. *n.* base/foot of a tree. Lit. 'tree-foot'.

dakúkwɛ́t[a] (dakú-kwɛ́tà-) *pl.* **dakúkwɛ́tɨ́k**[a]. *n.* bough, branch, limb. Lit. 'tree-arm'.

dakúsɔ́k[a] (dakú-sɔ́kɔ̀-) *pl.* **dakúsɔ́kɨ́tín**. *n.* root. Lit. 'tree-hoof'.

dakw[a] (dakú-) *pl.* **dakwitín**. *1 n.* plant, shrub, tree. *2 n.* wood. *3 n.* piece of wood, pole, stick. *4 n.* firewood.

dakwa kɔn *n.* one million. Lit. 'one tree'.

dàƙw[a] (dàƙwà) *ideo.* weakly.

daƙwádòn (daƙwádònì-) *v.* to be debile, sapless, weak. See also *bʉlájámɔ̀n*.

dàlìs (dàlìsà-) *1 n.* small plant species whose roots are peeled, crushed, and used as soap, especially as laundry detergent. *Dolichos oliveri*. *2 n.* soap.

dàn (dànɨ̀) *adv.* exactly, precisely.

Dáŋ (Dáŋá-) *n.* March: month of edible termites. See also *Lɔdʉ́ŋɛ*.

dáŋ (dáŋá-) *n.* termite species whose winged alates are traditionally caught and consumed as a major source of nutrition.

dáŋáàk[a] (dáŋá-àkà-) *pl.* **dáŋáakitín**. *n.* opening in an edible-termite mound. Lit. 'termite-mouth'.

dáŋádadát[a] (dáŋá-dadátí-) *pl.* **dáŋádadátíkw**[a]. *n.* queen of an edible-termite colony. Lit. 'termite-grandmother'.

dáŋádè (dáŋá-dèà-) *pl.* **dáŋádɛík**[a]. *n.* base of an edible-termite mound. Lit. 'termite-foot'.

dáŋádidí (dáŋá-didíì-) *n.* annual rain which stimulates the mass flight of edible termites.

dáŋáhò (dáŋá-hòò-) *pl.* **dáŋáhoík**[a]. *n.* housing of grass and soil made to trap edible termites as they emerge from the ground to fly.

dáŋájùm (dáŋá-jùmù-) *n.* dirt mixed with edible termites inside a trapping hole.

dáŋákìts[a] (dáŋá-kìtsà-) *pl.* **dáŋákitsitín**. *n.* abandoned edible-termite mound.

dáŋámorók[a] (dáŋá-morókú-) *pl.* **dáŋámorókík**[a]. *n.* hollow clay column built up by edible termites. *Lit.* 'termite-throat'.

dáŋátsóy[a] (dáŋá-tsóí-) *n.* season for harvesting edible termites (usually around March).

dáŋéèkw[a] (dáŋé-èkù-) *pl.* **dáŋéekwitín**. *n.* outlet in the ground from which edible termites emerge to fly. *Lit.* 'termite-eye'.

dayaakón (dayaakónì-) *v.* to be good, nice, proper (of many).

dɛ (dɛá-) *pl.* **dɛìk**[a]. *1 n.* foot, leg. *2 n.* footprint. *3 n.* base, foot (of non-animal things). *4 n.* tire, tire track, wheel. *5 n.* taboo of neglecting to share the hind-quarters of bushmeat with the elders.

dɛáákw[a] (dɛá-ák̓ɔ-) *n.* sole of the foot.

dɛáám (dɛá-ámà-) *pl.* **dɛikaik**[a]. *1 n.* courier, footman, messenger. *2 n.* disciple, follower.

dɛágwarí (dɛá-gwarîi-) *n.* top of the foot.

dɛákɔrɔk[a] (dɛá-kɔrɔkú-) *pl.* **dɛákɔrɔkík**[a]. *n.* toe. *Lit.* 'foot-finger'.

dɛámórók[a] (dɛá-mórókú-) *pl.* **dɛikamorókík**[a]. *n.* ankle. *Lit.* 'foot-throat'. See also *kɔpɨkɔp*[a].

dèdès (dèdèsà-) *n.* willow warbler. *Phylloscopus trochilus*.

déé (=déé) *dem.* that (one already known or mentioned).

dɛɛd[a] (dɛɛdɛ-) *pl.* **dèìkìn**. *1 n.* foot, leg (of a particular person or thing). *2 n.* base, foot (of a particular non-animal thing). *3 n.* handle. *4 n.* butt of a gun.

dèèdà hò[e] *n.* footer, foundation, groundwork. *Lit.* 'foot of a house'.

dégèmɔn (dégèmɔnɨ-) *v.* to crouch, duck down. See also *rábùxɔn*.

dèìkà àd[e] *n.* traditional three-legged stool. *Lit.* 'three legs'.

dèìkà[ɔ] *1 n.* on the feet or legs. *2 n.* underfoot.

dɛikatsirím (dɛika-tsɨrímú-) *pl.* **dɛikatsirímík**[a]. *n.* metal anklet.

dèìk[ɔ] *n.* by foot, on foot.

dèj[ɛ] (dèjè) *ideo.* chubbily, plumply.

dɛjédɔn (dɛjédɔnɨ-) *v.* to be chubby, plump.

dek[a] (deké-) *pl.* **dekitín**. *n.* long decorated goat-leather hind-apron worn by women and swished like a tail during dances.

dekitíníàm (dekitíní-àmà-) *pl.* **dekitíníik**[a]. *n.* an unmarried woman who may be promiscuous and who may have had a child out of wedlock; hussy.

dèk̓w[a] (dèk̓ù-) *n.* argument, dispute, quarrel.

dék̓widek̓os (dék̓widek̓osí-) *v.* to be argumentative, contentious, quarrelsome.

dék̓widek̓osíám (dék̓widek̓osí-ámà-) *pl.* **dék̓widek̓osíík**[a]. *n.* quarreler, quarrelsome person.

dék̓wítetés (dék̓wítetésí-) *v.* to argue with, contradict, fight, start a quarrel with.

dèmìywᵃ (dèmìyò-) *pl.* demííkwᵃ. *n.* wild olive: tree whose termite-proof wood is used in building and for firewood and whose black berries are eaten and used as a dye, whose bark is crushed, soaked, and drunk for malaria, and whose roots are pounded and used for stomach ailments. *Olea europaea (africana)*.

dèŋ (dèŋè) *ideo.* a long time (esp. waiting in vain).

dɛŋɛlɛs (dɛŋɛlɛsɨ́-) *1 v.* to raise (the leg) to kick. *2 v.* to spread (legs) apart while standing.

dɛŋɛlɛsá dɛáᵋ *1 v.* to stride. *2 v.* to straddle.

dɛŋúɲúnɔ́s (dɛŋúɲúnɔ́sɨ́-) *v.* to hate each other.

dèr (dèrè) *ideo.* anemically, feebly, frailly.

dèrèdèr (dèrèdèrè) *ideo.* sound of a metal saucepan rolling.

dɛrɛ́dɔ̀n (dɛrɛ́dɔ̀nɨ̀-) *v.* to be anemic, feeble, frail.

dɛrɛ́ƙᵃ (dɛrɛ́ƙɨ̀-) *pl.* dɛrɛ́ƙɨ́kᵃ. *1 n.* hornet, vespid, wasp. *2 n.* desert rose: flowering plant species with a big base, long thin branches, and pink flowers that attract bees and wasps; its oblong root is dug and rolled by children who pretend it is prey in their spearing practice. *Adenium obesum*.

detés (detésí-) *v.* to bring.

dèwòn (dèwònì-) *v.* to be extremely hard (of wood).

dɨ́ (dɨ́) *nurs.* poo-poo! (a nursery word for defecating or feces).

dìdì (dìdìì-) *1 n.* weather (especially rain). *2 n.* precipitation, rain. *3 n.* small blackish shrub species whose root decoction is drunk as a remedy for rainy weather ailments like body aches and pains. *4 n.* soldiers.

Dìdìàkᵃ (Dìdì-àkà-) *n.* name of a river. Lit. 'rain-mouth'.

dìdìàkᵃ (dìdì-àkà-) *pl.* didiakitín. *n.* erosion, landslide, mudslide. Lit. 'rain-mouth'. See also *bɔ̀ròtsᵃ*.

didigwarí (didi-gwaríì-) *1 n.* atmosphere, sky, outer space. *2 n.* afterlife, heaven. *3 n.* God. *4 n.* salt. Lit. 'weather-top'.

dìdìkᵉ *n.* up, upward.

didiɲeɗeké (didi-ɲeɗekéè-) *n.* sickness associated with rainy weather or drinking cold water (thus being perhaps flu or pneumonia).

dìdìɔ̀kᵃ (dìdì-ɔ̀kà-) *n.* clear sky. Lit. 'rain-bone'.

didis (didisá-) *pl.* dídìsìkᵃ. *n.* female genitalia, pubic area, pudendum.

didisíɔ́kᵃ (didisí-ɔ́kà-) *n.* pubic bone, pubis.

didisísíts'ᵃ (didisí-síts'à-) *n.* pubic hair. Lit. 'pubis-hair'. See also *ɔ́zàsìtsᵃ*.

diditsóyᵃ (didi-tsóí-) *n.* rainy season. See also *ɔtáyᵃ*.

díí (=díí) *dem.* those (already known or mentioned).

dikwᵃ (dikwá-) *pl.* dikwitín. *1 n.* dance, song. *2 n.* ring-tone.

dikwa na tsokóbè *n.* zigzagging men's dance modeled on the flight of Abdim's stork.

dikwáhò (dikwá-hòò-) *pl.* dikwáhoíkᵃ. *n.* dance hall, disco.

dikwétón (dikwétònì-) *v.* to dance.

dikwétóna ŋabɔ́bɔ̀ɔ̀ *v.* to dance at the danceground (where it is forbidden to dance before the chief elder sings his ox-song).

dikwidikos (dikwidikosí-) *v.* to always be dancing, like to dance.

dìkwòn (dìkwònì-) *v.* to beat, palpitate, pulsate, throb, thump. See also *kádikádòn*.

diƙwam (diƙwamá-) *pl.* **diƙwámíkᵃ**. *n.* headrest, pillow (traditionally a stone or stool).

diƙwés (diƙwésɨ-) *v.* to prop or rest (the head on a stone or stool).

dililits'ᵃ (dililits'á-) *n.* dipteran, gnat.

Dɨmán (Dɨmánɨ-) *n.* name of a large area to the south of *Lopokókᵃ*.

Dɨmánɨakᵃ (Dɨmánɨ-àkà-) *n.* name of a mountain and associated river. *Lit.* '*Dɨmán*'s mouth'.

dimés (dimésí-) *v.* to deny, refuse, reject.

dimésá bubue ŋɔɛsɨ *n.* dyspepsia, indigestion. *Lit.* 'refusal of the stomach to grind'.

dimités (dimitésí-) *v.* to forbid, prohibit, proscribe. See also *itáléés*.

dimitetés (dimitetésí-) *v.* to forbid, prohibit, proscribe.

dìr (dìrì) *ideo.* compactedly.

diriɓá (<diriɓóón) *v.*

diriɓóón (diriɓóónì-/diriɓá-) *v.* to be immovable, stabile, stationary.

diridírón (diridíróni-) *v.* to be sugary, sweet.

dirídòn (dirídòni-) *1 v.* to be compacted, hard (of a full container like a bag of cement or sack of grain). *2 v.* to be insolent, insubordinate.

dirijijᵃ (dirijijí-) *pl.* **diríjíjìkᵃ**. *n.* gingiva, gum.

diriɲíɲón (diriɲíɲóni-) *v.* to be tough: hard to chew or crush.

dìyòàm (dìyò-àmà-) *pl.* **diyoikᵃ**. *n.* elder who sits at the lookout.

diyoama ná zè *n.* chief local elder.

dìywᵃ (dìyò-) *pl.* **diitín**. *1 n.* lookout or observatory that serves as a local meeting place for men. *2 n.* ethnic group, people, tribe.

dɔ́bàtòdᵃ (dɔ́bà-tòdà-) *n.* muddled talk, nonsense. *Lit.* 'mud-talk'.

dódètòn (dódètòni-) *v.* to begin aching or hurting.

dodíkᵃ (dodíkí-) *n.* plant species whose big brown fruits are edible and sweet and whose branching stems are used to make mingling sticks. *Canthium sp.*

dodimórón (dodimóróni-) *v.* to be frozen or paralyzed (out of fear).

Dɔ́dɔ̀f (Dɔ́dɔ̀fà-) *n.* name of a river.

dódòkᵃ (dódòkù-) *pl.* **dódokaikwᵃ**. *n.* malnourished child (as when births are not spaced adequately, leading to a lack of breastmilk).

dódòn (dódòni-) *v.* to ache, be painful, hurt.

dɔ́dɔ̀rɔ̀n (dɔ́dɔ̀rɔ̀ni-) *v.* to move on one's buttocks.

dɔ́dɔrɔnuƙɔtᵃ (dɔ́dɔrɔnuƙɔtí-) *v.* to move away on one's buttocks.

dòɗᵃ (dòɗì-) *pl.* **doɗitín**. *n.* vagina.

dòɗidòɗigwà (dòɗidòɗi-gwàà-) *n.* bird species. *Lit.* 'vagina-vagina bird'.

dòɗièkwᵃ (dòɗì-èkù-) *n.* uterine cervix. *Lit.* 'vagina-eye'.

dɔ́gɔ̀lɔ̀mɔ̀n (dɔ́gɔ̀lɔ̀mɔ̀ni-) *v.* to be bent, bowed (like a bow or bowlegged person).

dojánónuƙotᵃ (dojánónuƙotí-) *v.* to freak out, go crazy, panic, go into pandemonium.

dòkìr (dòkìrà-) *pl.* **dokíraikw**ᵃ. *n.* old honeycomb filled with crystallized honey.

doƙofiés (doƙofiesí-) *v.* to bark at, speak harshly to.

dòl (dòlò) *ideo.* loosely or unfastenedly.

dolés (dolésí-) *v.* to pull back, retract (e.g. the foreskin). See also *rʉjés*.

doletés (doletésí-) *v.* to pull back, retract (esp. the foreskin).

doletésá kwaní *v.* to pull back or retract the foreskin.

doletésá ɔ́zàᵋ *v.* to project an anorectal appendage (to catch prey).

dolódòn (dolódònì-) *v.* to be loose, unaffixed, unfastened (like a hoe on its handle). See also *roiróón*.

dololoƙᵃ (dololoƙí-) *pl.* **dolólóƙìk**ᵃ. *n.* grain kernels hollowed out by weevils. See also *dololots*ᵗᵃ.

dololotsᵗᵃ (dololots'í-) *pl.* **dolólóts'ìk**ᵃ. *n.* grain kernels hollowed out by weevils. See also *dololoƙ*ᵃ.

dóm (dómá-) *pl.* **dómítín**. *n.* cooking pan or pot.

dómá na buɗám *n.* clay pot blackened from soot.

dómáìm (dómá-ìmà-) *pl.* **dómítíníwik**ᵃ. *n.* small cooking pan or pot.

dómóɔz (dómó-ɔ̀zà-) *pl.* **dómítíníɔzitín**. *n.* bottom of a cooking pot or pan.

dómóɔ̀zà mèsè *n.* beer dregs left at the bottom of a pot.

dónés (dónésì-) *v.* to donate, give out, present.

dónésìàm (dónésì-àmà-) *pl.* **dónésiik**ᵃ. *n.* donor, philanthropist.

dónésuƙotᵃ (dónésuƙotí-) *v.* to donate, give out, present.

donitiésuƙotᵃ (donitiesúƙotí-) *v.* to donate or give out sporadically.

dòòn (dòònì-/da-) *1 v.* to be attractive, beautiful, fair, fine, good-looking, handsome, lovely, pretty. *2 v.* to be agreeable, nice, pleasant. *3 v.* to be generous, magnanimous, philanthropic. *4 v.* to be glorious, radiant, resplendent, splendid. *5 v.* holy, saintly.

dòònìàm (dòònì-àmà-) *pl.* **dooniik**ᵃ. *n.* generous, magnanimous person.

doonuƙotᵃ (doonuƙotí-/daiƙot-) *v.* to become better, improve (in any of the characteristics expressed by *dòòn*). See also *xɔ́dɔnʉƙɔt*ᵃ.

dosés (dosésí-) *v.* to thatch.

dɔ̀x (dɔ̀xà-) *pl.* **dɔxitín**. *n.* dried rheum, mucopurulent discharge: thin mucus secreted from the eyes, nose, or mouth.

dɔxés (dɔxésí-) *v.* to berate, chide, rebuke, reprimand, scold.

dɔxésúƙotᵃ (dɔxésúƙotí-) *v.* to berate, chide, rebuke, reprimand, scold.

dɔ́bᵃ (dɔ́bà-) *pl.* **dɔ́bitín**. *n.* mire, muck, mud.

dʉbam (dʉbamá-) *n.* dough. *Lit.* 'kneadable'.

dʉbés (dʉbésí-) *1 v.* to knead, work (mixing a solid with a liquid). *2 v.* to ruffle, tousle. *3 v.* to call for rain by putting leaves in water in a calabash and then sprinkling water into the air.

dúbès (dúbèsì-) *v.* to capture, catch (with the hands).

dúduránón (dúduránónì-) *v.* to be puffy, swollen (of skin, as from a bee-sting, poisonous plant, or rash). See also *leɓúdòn*.

39

dʉɗέr (dʉɗέrὲ-) *pl.* **dʉɗέrɨ́k**ᵃ. *n.* biting water beetle (reported to draw blood if swallowed).

dúgʉ̀mὲtɔ̀n (dúgʉ̀mὲtɔ̀nɨ-) *v.* to bend or hunch over.

dúgʉ̀mɔ̀n (dúgʉ̀mɔ̀nɨ-) *v.* to be bent or hunched over.

duƙésúƙotᵃ (duƙésúƙotí-) *v.* to take (somewhere).

duƙésúƙota mòràᵉ *v.* to flee, run away. *Lit.* 'to take the fear'.

dùl (dùlù) *ideo.* mushily, squishily.

duláts'ámòn (duláts'ámònì-) *v.* to be juicy (of oily foods like meat).

Dúlél (Dúlélí-) *n.* name of a certain stream with a rock beehive.

dulúdòn (dulúdònì-) *v.* to be mushy, squishy (like feces, mud, or rotten fruit). See also *duxúdòn*.

dúlúƙuƙú (dúlúƙuƙúù-) *pl.* **dúlúƙuƙúik**ᵃ. *n.* small round or oval gourd used as cup or container.

dulúmón (dulúmónì-) *1 v.* to become suddenly diarrheal, loose. *2 v.* to erupt, flare up, ignite.

dʉmέɗέmɔ̀n (dʉmέɗέmɔ̀nɨ-) *v.* to be distractible, have a short attention span.

dʉmún (dʉmúná-) *pl.* **dʉmúnáikw**ᵃ. *n.* dung beetle.

dʉmʉ́ná mòrɩ̀ɗòᵉ *n.* bruchid beetle. *Lit.* 'beetle of beans'. *Bruchidae.*

dunaakón (dunaakónì-) *v.* to be elderly, old (of many).

dunaakóniikᵃ (dunaakóni-icé-) *n.* the elderly, old people.

dúnéìm (dúné-ìmà-) *pl.* **dúnéikw**ᵃ. *n.* old woman.

Dúnémorókᵃ (Dúné-morókú-) *n.* name of a hill or mountain. *Lit.* 'old-voice'.

dúnésìàm (dúnésì-àmà-) *pl.* **dúnésiik**ᵃ. *n.* elderly or old person.

dúnésòn (dúnésònì-) *1 v.* to be elderly, old. *2 v.* to be doddery, senile.

dunétón (dunétónì-) *v.* to age, grow old.

dununúòn (dununúònì-) *v.* to be miniscule, tiny.

duŋúlúmòn (duŋúlúmònì-) *1 v.* to be blunt, dull. *2 v.* to be born without a hand. See also *líídòn* and *tufádòn*.

dùràtsᵃ (dùràtsɨ-) *pl.* **dúrátsɨk**ᵃ. *n.* brown jewel beetle. *Buprestidae.*

dʉrʉdʉr (dʉrʉdʉrá-) *pl.* **dʉrúdʉ̀rɨ̀k**ᵃ. *1 n.* carpenter bee. *Xylocopa sp.* *2 n.* radio. *3 n.* mobile phone.

dʉrʉdʉra na tímoí *n.* hand-held HF radio, walkie-talkie. *Lit.* 'carpenter bee with a tail'.

dús (dúsé-) *pl.* **dúsítín**. *n.* grassland, plain, savannah.

dùù (dùù) *ideo.* deeply.

dʉʉdʉ́ (dʉʉdʉ́) *nurs.* sitty-sit! (a nursery word for sitting down).

dùx (dùxù) *ideo.* mushily, squishily.

duxúdòn (duxúdònì-) *v.* to be mushy, squishy (like feces, mud, or rotten fruit). See also *dulúdòn*.

ɗ

ɗa (ɗi-) *pro.* these ones.

ɗa (ɗi-) *pro.* this one.

ɗa áɗònì *pro.* the third (one).

ɗa jɨ́rɨ̀ *pro.* the last (one).

ɗa kɔ́nɔ̀nɨ̀ *pro.* the first (one).

ɗa leɓétsónì *pro.* the second (one).

ɗa na *pro.* this one.

ɗa ne *pro.* that one.

ɗa ni *pro.* these ones.

ɗa ts'agúsónì *pro.* the fourth (one).

ɗa túdònì *pro.* the fifth (one).

ɗa wáxɨ̀ *pro.* the first (one).

ɗaɗ^a (ɗàɗà-) *pl.* ɗaɗitín. *n.* honey.

ɗàɗàgwà (ɗàɗà-gwàà-) *n.* dragonfly. Lit. 'honey-bird'.

ɗàɗàhò (ɗàɗà-hòò-) *pl.* ɗaɗahoík^a. *n.* honeycomb. Lit. 'honey-house'. See also ts'ɨkáhò.

ɗaɗátésukot^a (ɗaɗátésukotí-) *1 v.* to drop or spill. *2 v.* to hold or push down (e.g. a person in a fight).

ɗàɗèèw^a (ɗàɗè-èò-) *pl.* ɗaɗeewitín. *n.* leather honey bag.

ɗáɗítés (ɗáɗítésí-) *v.* to consume, devour, inhale (food or drink).

ɗáɗítésa ríjá^e *v.* to crash through brush. Lit. 'to devour forest'.

ɗak^a (ɗàkà) *ideo.* dryly as a bone.

ɗakitár (ɗakɨtárɨ-) *pl.* ɗakɨtárɨk^a. *n.* clinic, health center, hospital, infirmary.

ɗakɨtárɨ̀àm (ɗakɨtárɨ̀-àmà-) *pl.* ɗakɨtáriik^a. *1 n.* doctor, physician. *2 n.* nurse.

ɗakɨtáriama ínó^e *n.* animal doctor, veterinarian, vet.

ɗakón (ɗakónì-) *v.* to slur, speak indistinctly. See also iɲájápánón.

ɗalés (ɗalésí-) *v.* to scoop out (water slowly seeping out of river sand). See also ɨlaɓetés and téɓetés.

ɗálútés (ɗálútésí-) *v.* to hit, strike.

ɗam (ɗamú-) *pl.* ɗamitín. *n.* brain.

ɗamatés (ɗamatésí-) *1 v.* to set fire to. *2 v.* to fire or open fire on.

ɗamɨɗámón (ɗamɨɗámónɨ-) *v.* to jump up and down excitedly.

ɗàmùs (ɗàmùsù) *1 adv.* fast, quickly. *2 subordconn.* before. *3 subordconn.* unless. *4 subordconn.* until. See also dɛ̀mùs.

ɗàɲɨɗàŋ (ɗàŋɨɗàŋɨ̀) *quant.* all, entire, whole.

ɗapálámɔ̀n (ɗapálámɔ̀nì-) *v.* to be flat (of objects rather than land).

ɗaráɗáránón (ɗaráɗáránónì-) *v.* to be losing, molting, or shedding.

ɗarámɔ́n (ɗarámɔ́nɨ-) *v.* to slide or slough off (like boiled feathers or dead tissue).

Dàsòk^a (Dàsòkò-) *n.* Dodoth County, area around Kàlàpàtà.

ɗàsòn (ɗàsònì-) *v.* to be even, flat, level (of an area).

ɗataɗatánón (ɗataɗatánónì-) *v.* to be decayed, decomposed, rotted.

ɗataɲámòn (ɗataɲámònì-) *v.* to be barrel-shaped, cylindrical.

ɗatólóɲòn (ɗatólóɲònì-) *v.* to be unstable, unsturdy. See also ɨkáɓóɓánón.

ɗàw^a (ɗàò-) *pl.* ɗáwítín. *1 n.* blade, knife. *2 n.* propeller blade.

ɗɛɗɛanón (ɗɛɗɛanónì-) v. to crack, crackle, pop (like roasting maize, tree on fire, thunder, gunfire, or people talking angrily). See also rɛɗɛɗánón.

ɗɛ́f (ɗɛ́fɛ́-) pl. ɗɛ́fɨ́tín. n. small well-worn leather mat (often used as a sleeping mat for children).

ɗɛ̀kᵃ (ɗɛ̀kà-) pl. ɗɛ́kɨ́tín. n. small gourd used to churn butter.

ɗɛ̀kwɔ̀n (ɗɛ̀kwɔ̀nɨ̀-) 1 v. to be bland, flavorless, tasteless, vapid. 2 v. to not make any sense. See also jɔ̀lɔ̀n.

ɗɛlɛ́mɔ́n (ɗɛlɛ́mɔ́nɨ̀-) 1 v. to cling, stick (e.g. parasites). 2 v. to stick to, stick with (as in to continue on, remain with).

ɗɛm (ɗɛ̀mɛ̀) ideo. chattily, talkatively.

ɗɛmɛ́dɔ̀n (ɗɛmɛ́dɔ̀nɨ̀-) v. to be chatty, talkative. See also ɗɛmɨɗɛ́mɔ́n and ikútúkánón.

ɗɛmɨɗɛ́mɔ́n (ɗɛmɨɗɛ́mɔ́nɨ̀-) v. to be chatty, talkative. See also ɗɛmɛ́dɔ̀n and ikútúkánón.

ɗɛ̀mùs (ɗɛ̀mùsù) 1 adv. fast, quickly. 2 subordconn. before. 3 subordconn. unless. 4 subordconn. until. See also ɗàmùs.

ɗɛ̀ɲ (ɗɛ̀ɲɛ̀) ideo. flatly.

ɗɛɲiɗɛɲɔs (ɗɛɲiɗɛɲɔsɨ́-) v. to be restless, uncomfortable.

ɗɛ̀pᵋ (ɗɛ̀pɛ̀) ideo. thinly.

ɗɛpɛ́dɔ̀n (ɗɛpɛ́dɔ̀nɨ̀-) v. to be undesirably thin (like a thin sleeping mat). Compare with bɛɗɛ́dɔ̀n.

ɗɛr (ɗɛ́rɔ́-) n. mouse, rat.

ɗɛ́rá na áwìkàᵉ n. house rat.

ɗɛrɛ́tᵃ (ɗɛrɛ́tú-) pl. ɗɛrɛ́tíkwᵃ. n. Sudan gum arabic or gum acacia: tree species with hooked thorns that rip skin and clothing; hunters often remove clothing before trying to penetrate its brush; found down in the Turkana plains, it is used for fencing and is eaten by livestock. *Acacia senegal*. See also lofílitsí.

ɗɛ̀rɛ̀tsᵃ (ɗɛ̀rɛ̀tsà-) n. small pieces or sticks of kindling or tinder.

ɗɛ́rɔ́cɛmɛ́r (ɗɛ́rɔ́-cɛmɛ́rɨ́-) n. rat poison (modern or traditional).

ɗɛ́rɔ́dɛɨ́kᵃ (ɗɛ́rɔ́-dɛɨ́ká-) n. pitter-pattering rain. Lit. 'mouse-feet'.

ɗɛsɛ́ɗɛ́sánón (ɗɛsɛ́ɗɛ́sánónɨ̀-) v. to break or come apart (like an old rope).

ɗɛsɛ́mɔ́n (ɗɛsɛ́mɔ́nɨ̀-) 1 v. to break, cut (like a rope or wire). 2 v. to connect, join, rejoin.

ɗɛtɛ́ɗɛ́tánón (ɗɛtɛ́ɗɛ́tánónɨ̀-) 1 v. to be strewn about (like bones or feces). 2 v. to laugh uproariously ('fall over laughing').

ɗɛ́tɛ́s (ɗɛ́tɛ́sɨ̀) v. to blow (a projectile).

ɗɛ̀tsᵋ (ɗɛ̀tsɛ̀) ideo. fetidly, foully.

ɗɛtsɨɗɛ́tsɔ́n (ɗɛtsɨɗɛ́tsɔ́nɨ̀-) v. to be fetid, foul, rank.

ɗɛuɗɛ́wɔ́n (ɗɛuɗɛ́wɔ́nɨ̀-) v. to ring hollow, sound empty.

ɗewen (ɗewení-) pl. ɗewéníkwᵃ. n. large tree species with small edible yellow fruits and whose bark is decocted and drunk for abdominal ailments associated with the appendix, pancreas, liver, pancreas, etc. *Berchemia discolor*.

ɗêgᵃ (ɗégɛ̀-) n. tamarind seeds.

ɗɨ (ɗɨ̀) 1 ideo. switch! (sound made by a small stick hitting skin). 2 ideo. snap! (sound of small sticks breaking).

ɗiakᵃ (ɗiaká-) pl. ɗiakáikwᵃ. n. baby, infant, suckling.

ɗîdᵃ (ɗîdɛ̀-) n. ass, donkey.

Dìɗèàwᵃ (Dìɗè-àwà-) *n.* name of a place in Timu Forest. *Lit.* 'donkey-place'.

ɗiɗecúrúkᵃ (ɗiɗe-cúrúkù-) *n.* jack: male donkey.

ɗiɗèìm (ɗìɗè-ìmà-) *pl.* **ɗiɗewik**ᵃ. *n.* foal: young donkey.

ɗiɗèkwàtsᵃ (ɗìɗè-kwàtsì-) *n.* stale, watery beer (often with a reddish color). *Lit.* 'donkey-piss'.

ɗiɗèŋàm (ɗìɗè-ŋàmà-) *n.* sorghum variety with brownish-gray seeds. *Lit.* 'donkey-sorghum'.

ɗiɗeŋwa (ɗiɗe-ŋwaá-) *n.* jenny: female donkey.

ɗiɗèsɔkᵃ (ɗìɗè-sɔ̀kɔ̀-) *n.* stool with two legs and circular foot and head. *Lit.* 'donkey-hoof'.

ɗiɗèwàz (ɗìɗè-wàzò-) *n.* female foal: young female donkey.

ɗiɗítésukotᵃ (ɗiɗítésukotí-) *v.* to pick-pocket, sneak, snitch.

ɗiɗítɛtés (ɗiɗítɛtésí-) *v.* to pick-pocket, sneak, snitch.

ɗiɗítɔ̀n (ɗiɗítɔ̀nì-) *v.* to breathe fitfully (like a crying child or someone dying).

ɗiisí (ɗiisîì-) *n.* District Commissioner.

ɗiitᵃ (ɗiití-) *n.* bird species.

ɗilatᵃ (ɗilatí-) *pl.* **ɗilátikw**ᵃ. *n.* vine species whose root decoction is highly medicinal.

ɗinés (ɗinésí-) *v.* to block, obstruct, stop up.

ɗinɔ́s (ɗinɔ́sí-) *1 v.* to be blocked, obstructed, stopped up. *2 v.* to be congested (e.g. from nasal allergies). *3 v.* to be stone-deaf.

ɗipímón (ɗipímónì-) *1 v.* to calm, cool, die, or settle down. *2 v.* to descend, go down low (e.g. into a deep valley). *3 v.* to screw around on an errand.

ɗípɔ̀ (ɗípɔ̀ɔ̀-) *pl.* **ɗipɔ́ík**ᵃ. *1 n.* clearing or glade where crops are dried and/or threshed. *2 n.* animal bed. *3 n.* open air market. See also *ɓɔd*ᵘ.

ɗír (ɗírì) *adv.* right or straight away.

ɗír (ɗírá-/ɗíró-) *1 n.* semen, sperm. *2 n.* nocturnal emission.

ɗis (ɗisá-) *n.* belowground, underground.

ɗítá (ɗítá) *prep.* as, like. A noun following this word takes the genitive case.

ɗítés (ɗítésì-) *v.* to remove or take gingerly (as when uprooting seedlings for transplating).

ɗítésukotᵃ (ɗítésukotí-) *v.* to remove or take away gingerly.

ɗiwaakón (ɗiwaakónì-) *v.* to be red (of many).

Ɗiwamúce (Ɗiwa-múceé-) *n.* August: month of worn trails. *Lit.* 'the trail is worn'. See also *Idátáŋér* and *Lósúbán*.

ɗiwiɗíwón (ɗiwiɗíwónì-) *v.* to be pinkish-red.

ɗiwítésukotᵃ (ɗiwítésukotí-) *v.* to make red, redden.

ɗiwòn (ɗiwònì-) *1 v.* to be red. *2 v.* to be brown-skinned. *3 v.* to be well worn (of footpaths or roads).

ɗiwònìàm (ɗìwònì-àmà-) *pl.* **ɗiwoniik**ᵃ. *n.* brown-skinned person.

ɗiwonukotᵃ (ɗiwonukotí-) *v.* to become red, redden.

Ɗɔan (Ɗɔaní-) *n.* a personal name.

ɗɔan (ɗɔaní-) *1 n.* weed(s). *2 n.* weeding.

ɗɔanés (ɗɔanésí-) *v.* to weed.

ɗoɗékwᵃ (ɗoɗékú-) *n.* corner of the eye, peripheral vision.

ɗóɗés (ɗóɗésì-) *1 v.* to indicate, point at/to/out. *2 v.* to show.

ɗóɗésa muceé *v.* to get going, set out, take off. *Lit.* 'to show the way'.

ɗoɗésúƙotᵃ (ɗoɗésúƙotí-) *1 v.* to indicate, point at/out/to. *2 v.* to demonstrate, illustrate, show. *3 v.* to expose, reveal. *4 v.* to introduce. *5 v.* to announce, report.

ɗoɗésúƙota ɲásáatí *v.* to tell the time. *Lit.* 'to point to the hour'.

ɗóɗiés (ɗóɗiesí-) *1 v.* to pinpoint. *2 v.* to bewitch by pointing, point to secretly so as to curse.

ɗóɗiesá tsòònì *v.* to point at the sunset as a curse: "Go down with the sun at sunset!".

ɗóɗítetés (ɗóɗítetésí-) *v.* to reveal, show. See also *enitésúƙotᵃ*.

ɗóɗítetésá asɨ *v.* to let oneself be known, show oneself.

Ɗóɗò (Ɗóɗòò-) *n.* name of a river. *Lit.* 'sheep'.

ɗóɗò (ɗóɗòò-) *pl.* ɗóɗòikwᵃ. *n.* sheep.

ɗoɗóbᵃ (ɗoɗóbà-) *pl.* ɗoɗóbikᵃ. *n.* baby carrier or sling.

ɗóɗòbàr (ɗóɗò-bàrɔ̀-) *pl.* ɗóɗobaritín. *n.* flock of sheep.

ɗóɗocurúkᵃ (ɗóɗo-curúkú-) *n.* ram: male sheep.

ɗóɗòèm (ɗóɗò-èmè-) *n.* mutton: sheep meat.

ɗóɗòìm (ɗóɗò-ìmà-) *pl.* ɗóɗowikᵃ. *n.* lamb: young sheep.

ɗóɗòƙwàz (ɗóɗò-ƙwàzà-) *1 n.* sheep-leather clothing (with wool removed). *2 n.* short sheep-leather skirt worn by young girls.

ɗóɗoŋwa (ɗóɗo-ŋwaá-) *n.* ewe: female sheep.

ɗóɗòsìts'ᵃ (ɗóɗò-sìts'à-) *n.* fleece, wool.

ɗóɗotimóyᵃ (ɗóɗo-timóí-) *pl.* ɗóɗotimóíkᵃ. *n.* tail of fat-tailed sheep, highly prized for its oil content.

ɗɔ́f (ɗɔ́fá-) *n.* shrew.

ɗɔ́giɗɔ̀gᵃ (ɗɔ́giɗɔ́gɔ̀-) *pl.* ɗɔ́giɗɔ́gìkᵃ. *n.* yellow sugar-ant species often found eating honey.

ɗɔ̀kᵓ (ɗɔ̀kɔ̀) *ideo.* scrumptiously, yummily.

ɗɔkɔ́dɔ̀n (ɗɔkɔ́dɔ̀nɨ̀-) *v.* to be scrumptious, yummy.

ɗɔkɔ́lɔ́mɔ̀n (ɗɔkɔ́lɔ́mɔ̀nɨ̀-) *v.* to stammer, stutter. See also *ɗákón* and *ikʉjʉ́kʉ́jɔ̀n*.

ɗókótsᵃ (ɗókótsì-) *n.* sorghum variety with yellow seeds and sweet canes.

ɗòkᵘ (ɗòkù) *adv.* sole, solitary.

ɗɔƙítésʉƙotᵃ (ɗɔƙítésʉƙotɨ́-) *v.* to dampen, make wet, moisten.

ɗɔ̀ƙɔ̀n (ɗɔ̀ƙɔ̀nɨ̀-) *1 v.* to be damp, moist, wet. *2 n.* mucus, phlegm, snot, sputum.

ɗɔƙɔnʉƙotᵃ (ɗɔƙɔnʉƙotɨ́-) *v.* to become damp, moist, or wet.

ɗòl (ɗòlì-) *pl.* ɗólítín. *1 n.* tattered animal carcass with only the skin remaining. *2 n.* shell of an abandoned beehive.

ɗɔ̀l (ɗɔ̀lè-) *pl.* ɗɔ́lɨ́tín. *1 n.* small unripe pumpkin. *2 n.* ulcer. See also *ɲíkalʉtʉ́rɔ*.

ɗòlà kòn *n.* one billion. *Lit.* 'one beehive shell'.

ɗɔ̀m (ɗɔ̀mɔ̀) *ideo.* gluily, gooily.

ɗɔmɔ́dɔ̀n (ɗɔmɔ́dɔ̀nɨ̀-) *v.* to be gluey, gooey.

Ɗómòkᵃ (Ɗómòkò-) n. name of a place in Timu and its associated human habitations.

ɗooɲómòn (ɗooɲómònì-) 1 v. to be deformed or missing (of an eye). 2 v. to have a bad eye, monocular vision.

ɗɔ̀r (ɗɔ̀rɔ̀) ideo. slickly, slipperily.

ɗoriɗóron (ɗoriɗórónì-) v. to happen quickly (like a person appearing near after being seen from afar, or foods that are cooked quickly, like rice).

ɗɔrɔ́dɔ̀n (ɗɔrɔ́dɔ̀nɨ̀-) v. to be slick, slippery.

ɗorôgᵃ (ɗorógè-) pl. ɗorógìkᵃ. n. roan antelope. *Hippotragus equinus*.

ɗòs (ɗòsì-) n. gum, mucilage.

ɗɔ̀s (ɗɔ̀sɔ̀) ideo. gummily.

ɗɔsɔ́ (ɗɔsɔ́ɔ̀-) n. vine species whose seeds are eaten raw or cooked and whose roots are eaten raw, cooked, or roasted. *Vigna sp.*

ɗɔsɔ́dɔ̀n (ɗɔsɔ́dɔ̀nɨ̀-) v. to gummy.

ɗotíɗótòn (ɗotíɗótònì-) v. to go restlessly from place to place.

ɗɔtɔ́ (ɗɔtɔ́ɔ̀-) 1 n. rubbery gum (like that of baratᵃ). 2 n. rubber. 3 n. chewing gum.

ɗɔtsánón (ɗɔtsánónì-) 1 v. to be joined together. 2 v. to cooperate. 3 v. to be compacted. See also *kumutsánón*.

ɗɔtsánónuƙotᵃ (ɗɔtsánónuƙotí-) 1 v. to join or meet together. 2 v. to cooperate.

ɗɔtsɛ́s (ɗɔtsɛ́sɨ́-) 1 v. to add. 2 v. to add or mix in. 3 v. to add together, combine, join.

ɗɔtsɛ́sá ɦyekesí v. to contribute resources. Lit. 'to add life'.

ɗɔtsɛ́súƙɔtᵃ (ɗɔtsɛ́súƙɔtɨ́-) 1 v. to add. 2 v. to add or mix in. 3 v. to add together, combine, join.

ɗɔtsɛ́súƙɔta mɛnáᵉ v. to summarize, sum up.

ɗɔtsɛtés (ɗɔtsɛtésɨ́-) 1 v. to add up, combine. 2 v. to attach, join. 3 v. to list.

ɗɔtsɛtésá asɨ́ v. to gather oneselves.

ɗɔtsɛtésá tódàᵉ v. to negotiate, reach a consensus. Lit. 'to add up speech'.

ɗɔtsɔ́s (ɗɔtsɔ́sɨ́-) 1 v. to be added. 2 v. to be attached, joined. 3 v. to be compacted.

ɗòwòn (ɗòwònì-) 1 v. to be pristine, unspoiled, untouched, virginal (like a forest). 2 v. to be left alone, unused (like a path or old village).

ɗòx (ɗòxò) ideo. fitly, healthily.

ɗɔ̀x (ɗɔ̀xɔ̀) ideo. unsteadily.

ɗóxɛátᵃ (ɗóxɛatí-) pl. ɗóxɛatíkᵃ. n. star.

Ɗóxɛatá na baratsóᵉ n. morning star.

ɗóxɛatá na ɓeƙés n. satellite. Lit. 'star that moves'.

ɗóxɛatá na tsúwà n. meteor, shooting star. Lit. 'start that runs'.

Ɗóxɛatá tsòònì n. morning star.

Ɗóxɛatá xìŋàtàᵉ n. evening star.

ɗoxódòn (ɗoxódònì-) v. to be fit, healthy, in shape.

ɗɔxɔ́dɔ̀n (ɗɔxɔ́dɔ̀nɨ̀-) v. to be rickety, wobbly (of people, while walking).

ɗɔ̀xɔ̀ƙᵃ (ɗɔ̀xɔ̀ƙɔ̀-) pl. ɗɔxɔ́ƙɨ́kᵃ. n. gourd flesh, pulp.

ɗuɗuanón (ɗuɗuanónì-) v. to growl, grumble, gurgle (of digestion).

ɗùɗùŋ (ɗùɗùŋù) ideo. to the end. See also *tùtùr*.

ɗués (ɗuesí-) v. to deracinate, extirpate, pull up, uproot. See also *rués*.

ɗuetés (ɗuetésí-) v. to deracinate, extirpate, pull up, uproot.

ɗuká (ɗukáí-) pl. ɗukáíkᵃ. n. beer residue, draff, dregs. See also dàjᵃ.

ɗukán (ɗukánɨ-) pl. ɗukánɨkᵃ. n. kiosk, shop, store. See also pádukán.

ɗukes (ɗukesí-) 1 n. pollen. 2 n. egg yolk. 3 n. yellow color.

ɗukés (ɗukésí-) v. to strain (muscles, causing burning pain, especially when climbing a steep hill or mountain).

ɗùkᵘ (ɗùkù) ideo. circularly, roundly.

ɗùkᵘ (ɗùkù) ideo. very smelly or stinky.

ɗukúditésúƙotᵃ (ɗukúditésúƙotí-) v. to make round, round.

ɗukúdòn (ɗukúdònì-) 1 v. to be circular, round. 2 v. to be in large denominations, undivided (of cash).

ɗukuɗúkón (ɗukuɗúkónì-) v. to boom, rumble, thunder.

ɗukúmétòn (ɗukúmétònì-) v. to crumble, disintegrate, fall apart.

ɗukúmón (ɗukúmónì-) v. to crumble, disintegrate, fall apart.

ɗukúkón (ɗukúkónì-) v. to suffer internally or quietly (from hunger or sickness).

ɗùl (ɗùlù) ideo. thud! (sound of a person landing on the ground).

ɗúlúnós (ɗúlúnósí-) v. to be at odds, uncooperative with each other.

ɗúlútés (ɗúlútésí-) v. to pound, pummel (with a fist or stick).

ɗùm (ɗùmù) ideo. very well-cooked.

Ɗumánámérìx (Ɗumáná-mérìxì-) n. name of a hill or mountain.

ɗumés (ɗumésí-) v. to pick up. See also iɗɛpɛs.

ɗumɛtés (ɗumɛtésí-) 1 v. to pick up. 2 v. to choose, pick, select. See also iɗɛpɛtés.

ɗumúdòn (ɗumúdònì-) v. to be cooked well-done.

ɗúó pro. because (of), due to (the fact that). This word is followed either by a noun in the genitive case or a subordinate clause with the dummy pronoun on its verb.

ɗúr (ɗúrá-) pl. ɗúrítín. n. fetus.

ɗúrés (ɗúrésɨ-) v. to pull on, tug, yank. See also ɗutés.

ɗurɛtés (ɗurɛtésí-) v. to pull out, yank out. See also ɗutɛtés.

ɗùrù (ɗùrùù-) n. mild vulgarity: a damn thing, shit, squat.

ɗúruɗɔ́ɔ (ɗúruɗɔ́ɔ) interj. fool! idiot! (an insult to someone who made a mistake).

ɗusés (ɗusésí-) 1 v. to break, pull apart, separate, sever, tear. 2 v. to harvest (honey by pulling out honeycombs).

ɗusésúƙotᵃ (ɗusésúƙotí-) v. to break off, pull apart, separate, sever, tear off.

ɗusúmón (ɗusúmónì-) v. to break, come apart, cut, snap, tear (of rope-like objects).

ɗusutes (ɗusutesí-) v. to break, cut, pull apart, sever, tear (rope-like objects).

ɗusutesíáwᵃ (ɗusutesí-áwà-) pl. ɗusutesíáwíkᵃ. n. breakage point.

ɗùtᵃ (ɗùtà-) pl. ɗútítín. n. huge wide-bottom gourd.

ɗutés (ɗutésí-) v. to pull on, tug, yank. See also ɗúrés.

ɗutɛtés (ɗutɛtésí-) v. to pull out, yank out. See also ɗurɛtés.

ɗùtᵘ (ɗùtù) ideo. very decayed or rotten.

ɗutúdòn (ɗutúdònì-) *v.* to be decayed, decomposed, rotten.

ɗutúɗútánón (ɗutúɗútánónì-) *v.* to be decaying, decomposing, rotting.

ɗutúɗútánónukot[a] (ɗutúɗútánónukotí-) *v.* to decay, decompose, rot. See also *masánétòn* and *mʉsánétòn*.

dz

dzàbùl (dzàbùlà-) *pl.* **dzábùlìk**[a]. *n.* female eland. *Tragelaphus (Taurotragus) oryx.*

dzàƙ[a] (dzàƙà-) *pl.* **dzáƙaikw**[a]. *n.* son.

dzàƙèd[a] (dzàƙèdè-) *n.* his/her son.

dzálón (dzálónì-) *v.* to cry easily (usually for no good reason). See also *ɲééмɔ̀n.*

dzàr (dzàrà-) *n.* red-billed oxpecker, tickbird. *Buphagus erythrorhynchus.*

dzɛ́rɛ́dzɛránón (dzɛ́rɛ́dzɛránónì-) *v.* to be in shreds, shredded.

dzɛrɛ́s (dzɛrɛ́sí-) *1 v.* to rend, rip, shred, tear. *2 v.* to strike (a match). *3 v.* to gash, slash.

dzeretiés (dzeretiesí-) *1 v.* to shred, strip, tear off. *2 v.* to make facial incisions. *3 v.* to stripe.

dzeretiésuƙot[a] (dzeretiesúƙotí-) *v.* to shred, strip, tear off.

dzèrɔ̀n (dzèrɔ̀nɨ-) *v.* to dash, tear off.

dzɛrɔ́sɔ́n (dzɛrɔ́sɔ́nɨ-) *v.* to be rent, ripped, shredded, torn.

dzibér (dzibérí-) *pl.* **dzíbèrìk**[a]. *n.* axe, hatchet.

dzíbèrìkàmès (dzíbèrìkà-mèsè-) *n.* annual agricultural ceremony during which beer is drunk as a reward for clearing new gardens and beer dregs are poured all over the axes used for clearing. *Lit.* 'axes-beer'.

dzígw[a] (dzígwà-) *1 n.* business, commerce, trade. *2 n.* price.

dzígwààm (dzígwà-àmà-) *pl.* **dzígwaik**[a]. *n.* buyer, customer.

dzígwààw[a] (dzígwà-àwà-) *pl.* **dzígwaawík**[a]. *n.* market. See also *ɲámákèt*[a].

dzígwam (dzígwamá-) *n.* commodity, merchandise, product, or ware (bought or sold).

dzígwès (dzígwèsì-) *v.* to do commerce, trade (sell or buy).

dzígwèsèd[a] (dzígwèsèdè-) *n.* price.

dzígwèsìàm (dzígwèsì-àmà-) *pl.* **dzígwesiik**[a]. *n.* buyer, customer.

dzígwesuƙot[a] (dzígwesuƙotí-) *v.* to sell.

dzígwesuƙotíám (dzígwesuƙotí-ámà-) *pl.* **dzígwesuƙotíík**[a]. *n.* seller.

dzígwetam (dzígwetamá-) *n.* commodity, merchandise, product, or ware (to be bought). *Lit.* 'buyable'.

dzígwetés (dzígwetésí-) *v.* to buy.

dzííƙotam (dzííƙotamá-) *n.* commodity, merchandize, product, or ware (to be sold). *Lit.* 'sellable'.

dziŋ (dziŋá-) *pl.* **dziŋitín**. *n.* base, foot, floor (of a house or hill).

dziŋánànès (dziŋánànèsì-) *n.* lowland living.

dzɔɗát[a] (dzɔɗátɨ-) *pl.* **dzɔɗátɨk**[a]. *n.* rectum.

dzɔɗátɨnànès (dzɔɗátɨnànèsì-) *n.* grabbiness, greediness. *Lit.* 'acting like a rectum'.

dzôg[a] (dzógà-) *pl.* **dzógitín**. *n.* large tree species whose small red berries are loved by children and baboons alike; the seeds, when dried and ground, yield a sooty black, smelly paste that women put into their hair and onto their skin for cosmetic purposes; this paste is also used to tan hides; the tree's twigs make toothbrushes, and its wood is used for building and fencing. *Pappea capensis.*

dzolugánón (dzolugánónì-) *v.* to have hidden motives.

dzòn (dzònì-) *pl.* **dzóníkw**[a]. *n.* hand-dug well.

dzònìàm (dzònì-àmà-) *pl.* **dzoniik**[a]. *n.* Toposa person. *Lit.* 'well-person'.

dzú (dzúú-) *n.* burglary, larceny, theft, thievery.

dzúám (dzú-ámà-) *pl.* **dzúík**[a]. *n.* burgler, stealer, thief.

dzuesés (dzuesésí-) *v.* to burgle, steal, thieve.

dzuesésúƙota asɨ *v.* to sneak off/away.

dzuesetés (dzuesetésí-) *v.* to burgle, steal, thieve (and bring this way).

dzuƙés (dzuƙésí-) *1 v.* to displace, move, relocate. *2 v.* to pass, waste (time).

dzuƙésúƙot[a] (dzuƙésúƙotí-) *v.* to displace, move, or relocate away.

dzuƙetés (dzuƙetésí-) *v.* to displace, move, or relocate this way.

dzúƙudzuƙiés (dzúƙudzuƙiesí-) *v.* to postpone or put off repeatedly.

dzúnánès (dzúnánèsì-) *n.* thievery, thieving.

e/ɛ

eakwᵃ (eakwá-) *pl.* **ɲɔtᵃ**. *1 n.* man. *2 n.* husband.

eakwánánès (eakwánánèsì-) *n.* manhood, manliness, masculinity.

ɛán (ɛánɨ-) *pl.* **ɛáníkwᵃ**. *1 n.* co-wife: one of multiple wives of one man. *2 n.* sister-in-law (wife of one's husband's brother).

eaŋanes (eaŋanesí-) *v.* to be happy, joyful.

eas (easí-) *1 n.* truth, verity. *2 n.* honesty, integrity, transparency.

easíám (easí-ámà-) *pl.* **easíikᵃ**. *n.* honest person, truthful person.

easíkᵉ *n.* really, truly.

ɛ́bàdè (ɛ́bà-dèa-) *pl.* **ɛ́badɛíkᵃ**. *n.* gunstock, stock. *Lit.* 'gun-foot'.

ɛbam (ɛbamá-) *pl.* **ɛ́baikwᵃ**. *n.* fellow, in-group friend (an Ik or an incorporated foreigner only). Compare with *ɲòtᵃ*.

ɛbamánánès (ɛbamánánèsì-) *n.* friendliness, friendship (with Ik or in-group members).

ébetiés (ébetiesí-) *v.* to blaspheme, curse, cuss out.

ɛ́ɓútòn (ɛ́ɓútònì-) *v.* to groan, moan. See also *émɨ́tɔ̀n* and *émúròn*.

èeòn (èeònì-) *v.* to get out of the way, move aside. Also pronounced as *èkòn*.

êdᵃ (édì-) *pl.* **éditín**. *n.* name.

éda na moranâdᵉ *n.* name of honor, title. *Lit.* 'name that is feared'.

ɛdɛ́ (ɛdɛ́è-) *pl.* **ɛdɛ́ɨn**. *1 n.* my brother. *2 n.* my cousin (father's brother's son).

ɛdɛ́cèkᵃ (ɛdɛ́-cèkì-) *n.* wife of my brother or of a paternal male cousin.

ɛdéìm (ɛdé-ìmà-) *pl.* **ɛdéwikᵃ**. *n.* my niece or nephew (brother's child).

édès (édèsì-) *v.* to carry on the back.

éditínikabáɗᵃ (éditíni-kabáɗá-) *n.* list of names, record of attendance.

eɗᵃ (eɗí-) *1 n.* cereal, grain. *2 n.* tip, top.

ɛɗá (ɛɗá) *adv.* alone, only, solely.

eɗa ni erútsᵃ *n.* harvest of new grain.

eɗeɗᵃ (eɗede-) *pl.* **eɗin**. *1 n.* kernel, seed. *2 n.* embryo. *3 n.* bullet. *4 n.* glans penis. See also *ekʷeɗᵃ*.

eɗímɛ́s (eɗí-mɛ́sè-) *n.* grain beer.

eɗin (eɗini-) *n.* fruit(s).

ee *interj.* yeah, yes. The tone on this word may vary in pronunciation.

éétòn (éétònì-) *v.* to become full, fill.

ɛfás (ɛfásɨ-) *pl.* **ɛfásíkᵃ**. *n.* adipose tissue, fat (esp. when eaten).

ɛfitɛs (ɛfitɛsí-) *1 v.* to flavor, season, spice (especially with oil). *2 v.* to sweeten (a deal or offer). *3 v.* to spice up: make it fun or funny.

ɛ̀fɔ̀n (ɛ̀fɔ̀nɨ-) *1 v.* to be flavorful, tasty, well-seasoned. *2 v.* to be funny, interesting. *3 v.* to be entertaining, fun.

ɛfɔnʉkɔtᵃ (ɛfɔnʉkɔtɨ́-) *1 v.* to be become flavorful or tasty. *2 v.* to become fun or funny. *3 v.* to become ecstatic, orgasmic, or rapturous.

egés (egésí-) *v.* to place, put.

egésá ekwí *v.* to go to seed, produce seeds, seed. *Lit.* 'to put an eye'.

egésá hòòkᵉ *v.* to imprison, jail, lock up. *Lit.* 'to put in the house'.

egésá itsikɛsí *v.* to pass a law. *Lit.* 'to put a law'.

egésá kwɛtáᵋ v. to sign. *Lit.* 'to put the hand'.

egésá ɲájálaákᵉ v. to jail, put in jail.

egésá zɨ́kɛsɨkᵋ v. to imprison, jail, lock up. *Lit.* 'to put in tying'.

egetés (egetésí-) v. to place, put.

éítɛsuƙotᵃ (éítésuƙotí-) v. to fill up.

éítetés (éítetésí-) v. to fill up. *See also* **ilíliés**.

ejá (ejá) *adv.* not: do not, let not.

ɛkɛwᵃ (ɛkɛú-) *pl.* **ɛkéwɨ́kᵃ**. *n.* iliolumber ligament that joins the backbone to the pelvis.

Ékɨtɛ̀là (Ékɨtɛlaá) *n.* a personal name.

ekoɗitᵃ (ekoɗití-) *n.* tree species whose young roots are eaten raw and whose fruit is liked by children and birds; its bark is chewed as medicine for coughing, and its wood is used to carve stools and wooden containers. *Lannea schimperi. See also* **meleke**.

èkòn (èkònì-) v. to get out of the way, move aside. *Also pronounced as* **ècòn**.

ekúám (ekú-ámà-) *pl.* **ekúíkᵃ**. *n.* one with the 'evil eye': the magical power to cause harm by staring too long or too intensely at something admirable. *Lit.* 'eye-person'.

ekúcé (ekú-céè-) *n.* tears. *Lit.* 'eye-water'.

ekúcúédidí (ekú-cúé-didíi-) *n.* teardrop rain: light drizzle after a death or during a funeral.

ekúkɔ́ɔ́kwarósíts'ᵃ (ekú-kɔ́ɔ́-kwarósíts'à-) *n.* eyebrow. *Lit.* 'north-of-eye hair'.

ekúnánès (ekúnánèsì-) *n.* having the 'evil eye': the magical power to cause harm by staring too long at something admirable.

ekúɔ́kᵃ (ekú-ɔ́kà-) *pl.* **ekwitíníɔkɨtín**. *n.* brow bone, supraorbital bone.

ekúsíts'ᵃ (ekú-síts'à-) *1 n.* eyelash. *2 n.* eyebrow.

ekwᵃ (ekú-) *pl.* **ekwitín**. *1 n.* eye. *2 n.* seed. *3 n.* center, center point, point.

ekwedᵃ (ekwede-) *pl.* **ekwin**. *1 n.* kernel, seed. *2 n.* core, essence, point. *See also* **eɗedᵃ**.

ɛkwétɔ́n (ɛkwétɔ́nɨ-) v. to start early or first.

ekwin (ekwini-) *1 n.* seeds. *2 n.* points.

ɛkwitɛs (ɛkwitɛsí-) v. to put ahead or in front.

ɛkwɨ́tɛ́suƙotᵃ (ɛkwɨ́tɛ́suƙotí-) v. to put ahead or in front.

ɛ̀kwɔ̀n (ɛ̀kwɔ̀nɨ-) *1 v.* to be early or first. *2 v.* to be ahead or in front.

elánétòn (elánétònì-) v. to accompany here, come after/with.

elánónuƙotᵃ (elánónuƙotí-) v. to accompany away, follow or go after.

eletiesá mɛnáᵋ v. to blunder, blurt out news or secrets.

eletiésuƙotᵃ (eletiesúƙotí-) v. to blow, squander, waste. *See also* **iɲékésuƙotᵃ**.

em (emé-) *1 n.* flesh, meat. *2 n.* muscle.

emetá (emetáa-) *pl.* **emetátikwᵃ**. *n.* parent in-law (of men).

eminés (eminésí-) v. to draw, pull.

eminésúƙotᵃ (eminésúƙotí-) v. to draw or pull away/off.

eminetés (eminetésí-) v. to draw or pull out/up.

eminiés (eminiesí-) v. to draw apart, pull apart, stretch.

emitaakón (emitaakónì-) v. to swell (of many).

emites (emitesí-) *v.* to make swell, tumefy.

ɛmítɔ̀n (ɛmítɔ̀nɨ̀-) *1 v.* to groan, moan. *2 v.* to wheeze. See also *ébútòn* and *émúròn*.

èmòn (èmònì-) *v.* to swell, tumefy.

émúròn (émúrònì-) *v.* to groan, moan. See also *ɛmítɔ̀n* and *ébútòn*.

èmùsìà (èmùsìà-) *n.* tree species used for fencing and whose black seeds are eaten raw and whose bitter roots are eaten by children, turning their tongues yellow; also, the root rinds are crushed and added to water or porridge to cleanse the digestive system. *Euclea schimperi.*

emut[a] (emutí-) *pl.* **emútík**[a]. *1 n.* narrative, story, tale. *2 n.* news. *3 n.* information.

emuta ínó[e] *n.* animal fable.

emútík[a] (emútíkà-) *1 n.* storytelling. *2 n.* news. *3 n.* information.

emutíká nùù kɔ̀w[a] *n.* history. *Lit.* 'stories of old'.

emútíkààm (emútíkà-àmà-) *pl.* **emútíkaik**[a]. *n.* narrator, storyteller. See also *isíséésíàm*.

enés (enésí-) *1 v.* to see. *2 v.* to feel, perceive. *3 v.* to know, underestand. *4 v.* to discover. *5 v.* to achieve, attain.

enésá mɛná[ɛ] *v.* to confirm the case, find proof. *Lit.* 'to see matters'.

enésúkot[a] (enésúkotí-) *v.* to catch sight of, see.

ɛ́nɛ́sʉ̀kɔt[a] (ɛ́nɛ́sʉ̀kɔtɨ́-) *v.* to seize, take by force.

enésúkotíám (enésúkotí-ámà-) *pl.* **enésúkotíík**[a]. *n.* spectator, witness.

énímós (énímósí-) *v.* to visit. *Lit.* 'to see each other'.

enitésúkot[a] (enitésúkotí-) *v.* to reveal, show. See also *dódítetés*.

Enitetés (Enitetésí-) *n.* Revelation: last book in the New Testament.

enitetés (enitetésí-) *1 v.* to clarify, explain. *2 v.* to reveal, show.

eŋún (eŋúnú-) *pl.* **eŋúnáikw**[a]. *n.* last-born. See also *jɨrɨàm*.

eŋúnúnànès (eŋúnúnànèsì-) *n.* being the last born in a family.

eódòn (eódònì-) *v.* to be full.

ɛ̀ɔ̀m (ɛ̀ɔ̀mɔ̀) *ideo.* breakably, brittlely.

ɛɔmɔ́dɔ̀n (ɛɔmɔ́dɔ̀nì-) *v.* to be breakable, brittle. See also *wɛts'édɔ̀n* and *pokódòn*.

ep[a] (epú-) *1 n.* sleep, slumber. *2 n.* sex, sexual relations or intercourse.

epítésukot[a] (epítésukotí-) *1 v.* to lay down. *2 v.* to put to sleep. *3 v.* to settle down.

epítésúkòtà ɗèɲ *v.* to flatten, lay flat.

epítésúkota tódà[e] *v.* to resolve an issue, settle a dispute.

èpòn (èpònì-) *1 v.* to be lying down. *2 v.* to be sleeping, sleep, slumber. *3 v.* to have sex, make love.

epona ŋabér[o] *v.* to lie on the side. *Lit.* 'to lie on the rib'.

eponukot[a] (eponukotí-) *1 v.* to lie down, recline. *2 v.* to go to sleep. See also *bukonukot*[a] and *itsólóŋòn*.

epopos (epoposí-) *1 v.* to sleep a lot. *2 v.* to sleep around, be sexually promiscuous.

epúám (epú-ámà-) *pl.* **epúík**[a]. *1 n.* lover of sleep, sleeper. *2 n.* lover.

epúáw[a] (epú-áwà-) *pl.* **epúáwík**[a]. *1 n.* sleeping place. *2 n.* hostel, hotel, lodge, motel, inn. *3 n.* uterus, womb. See also *ɲapéryét*[a].

erégam (erégamá-) *n.* useable, useful.

eréges (erégesí-) *1 v.* to employ, make use of, use. *2 v.* to deploy, send.

erégesíám (erégesí-ámà-) *pl.* **erégesíík**[a]. *n.* emissary, envoy, errand-runner.

érítòn (érítònì-) *v.* to flitter, flutter (of termite alates underground just before emerging and taking flight).

eruméń (eruméní-) *pl.* **eruméník**[a]. *n.* short spear shaft (with *pɛlɨrát*[a] as its spearhead).

erúń (erúná-) *pl.* **erúník**[a]. *n.* edible termite alate that takes flight during the night just before the day when the rest of the colony does the same.

Erupe (Erupeé-) *n.* a personal name.

erutánón (erutánónì-) *1 v.* to low, moo. *2 v.* to roar (e.g. lions).

erútsón (erútsónì-) *1 v.* to be new. *2 v.* to be fresh. *3 v.* to be recent.

eruxam (eruxamá-) *n.* loose feces or stool.

erúxón (erúxónì-) *v.* to have loose feces or stool.

ɛs (ɛsá-) *n.* termite(s).

ɛ́s (ɛ́sá-) *n.* alcoholism, drunkenness, inebriation.

ɛ́sáàm (ɛ́sá-àmà-) *pl.* **ɛ́sáik**[a]. *n.* alcoholic, drunkard, drunk.

ɛsánón (ɛsánónì-) *v.* to be drunk, inebriated, intoxicated.

ɛ́sátòd[a] (ɛ́sá-tòdà-) *n.* drunken talk.

eséánètòn (eséánètònì-) *v.* to be tricolored (brown, ruddy, yellow).

esetés (esetésí-) *1 v.* to ask, inquire. *2 v.* to assess, test. *3 n.* inquiry, question.

esetésúƙot[a] (esetésúƙotí-) *v.* to ask, inquire.

esetetés (esetetésí-) *v.* to ask, inquire.

esetiés (esetiesí-) *v.* to question, interrogate, investigate.

ets'[a] (ets'í-) *n.* droppings, dung, excrement, feces, poop, scat, stool.

ets'íhò (ets'í-hòò-) *pl.* **ets'íhoík**[a]. *n.* latrine, outhouse, toilet. See also *pótsorón*.

ets'íƙwâz (ets'í-ƙwázà-) *pl.* **ets'íƙwázík**[a]. *n.* diaper, nappy.

eûz (eúzè-) *pl.* **eúzìk**[a]. *n.* buffalo bull. *Syncerus caffer.*

eúzòn (eúzònì-) *v.* to be predawn, in the small or 'wee' hours of the morning (3:00-4:00 am, when buffalos come to waterholes to drink).

èw[a] (èò-) *pl.* **ewitín**. *n.* leather bag used for carrying honey and other wild foods.

ewanes (ewanesí-) *1 v.* to notice, take note off. *2 v.* to attend to, show hospitality to, welcome warmly.

ewanetés (ewanetésí-) *1 v.* to notice, take note of. *2 v.* to attend to, show hospitality to, welcome warmly.

ewêd[a] (ewédì-) *n.* wild potato-like vine species whose tubers are peeled and cooked multiple times to remove toxins and are then eaten. *Dioscorea sp.*

ey[a] (eí-) *n.* chyme: stomach contents. See also *ŋkújít*[a].

êb[a] (ɛ́bà-) *pl.* **ɛ́bitín**. *1 n.* antler, horn. *2 n.* insect antenna. *3 n.* musical horn traditionally made from an animal horn (often oryx). *4 n.* firearm, gun, weapon.

f

fá (<féés) v.

fáɗᵃ (fáɗò-) pl. **fáɗikwᵃ**. n. scale, shell.

faɗás (faɗásɨ́-) n. divination, prophecy.

faɗetés (faɗetésí-) v. to extract, pull out (like jiggers or a thorn).

faɗétón (faɗétónì-) v. to be casual, cavalier, nonchalant about life.

fàɗìgùr (fàɗì-gùrò-) n. grass species with a pungent odor and taste, used for thatching houses; the Didinga are said to use a decoction of its roots to treat children's diarrhea. Lit. 'bitter-heart'. *Fadigura sp.*

faɗites (faɗitesí-) 1 v. to make bitter in taste. 2 v. to discourage, embitter.

fàɗòn (fàɗònì-) 1 v. to be bitter. 2 v. to divine, prophesy.

fàɗònìàm (fàɗònì-àmà-) pl. **faɗoniikᵃ**. n. diviner, prophet.

fáídomés (fáídomésí-) v. to brew beer and/or cook food for a housewarming party. Lit. 'to pot-boil'.

fàìdwᵃ (fàìdò-) pl. **faidíkwᵃ**. n. hardwood tree species with a black heart that is used for making beautiful black-brown walking sticks.

fàkᵃ (fàkà) ideo. broad-bladedly.

fakádòn (fakádònì-) v. to be broad-bladed (like a leaf or spearhead).

fàlòn (fàlònì-) v. to fail to get, miss, miss out on.

fàr (fàrà) adv. in the future. Also pronounced as *fàrò*.

fátár (fátárà-) pl. **fátárikwᵃ**. n. ridge running vertically. See also ɲɔɗɔ́kɛ́tᵃ.

fátáràakᵃ (fátárà-àkà-) pl. **fátárikóákɨ́tín**. n. top of a vertically running ridge. Lit. 'ridge-mouth'.

fátáràakànànès (fátáràakànànèsì-) n. having the habit of going to the escarpment's vertical-running ridges and valleys to look for food as a way to escape domestic problems like conflict or hunger.

fatsámánòn (fatsámánònì-) v. to be laid flat.

fatsifatsos (fatsifatsosí-) v. to lie around or sleep flat on one's back.

fátsón (fátsónì-) v. to like on the back, lie face-up.

féés (féèsì-/fá-) v. to cook by boiling.

féésa íditíní v. to cook for one's unmarried friends (of a newly married man, as a celebration of getting access to 'breasts', i.e. his new wife). Lit. 'to cook breasts'.

féiàwᵃ (féí-àwà-) pl. **féiawíkᵃ**. n. bath, bathroom, shower.

féítetés (féítetésí-) v. to bathe.

fekifekos (fekifekosí-) v. to be giggly, laugh a lot.

fekitetés (fekitetésí-) v. to amuse, entertain, make laugh.

fèkòn (fèkònì-) v. to laugh.

fen (fení-) pl. **fenitín**. n. digging stick with a wide flat end.

fèn (fènì-) n. fart, flatulence, gas.

fɛ̀n (fɛ̀nɛ̀) ideo. flatulently, gassily.

fɛnɛ́dɔ̀n (fɛnɛ́dɔ̀nì-) v. to be flatulent, gassy.

fenétón (fenétónì-) v. to break wind, fart, pass gas.

féón (féónì-) *v.* to bathe, shower.

fet[a] (fetí-) *1 n.* sun. *2 n.* thirst. *3 n.* clock, watch.

fɛtélémɔ̀n (fɛtélémɔ̀nɨ̀-) *v.* to be flatly or shallowly concave. See also *ɓɛtélémɔ̀n*.

Fetíám (Fetí-ámà-) *pl.* **Fetíík**[a]. *n.* Jie person. *Lit.* 'sun-person'.

fetíbàs (fetí-bàsà-) *pl.* **fetíbàsìn**. *n.* sunbeam, sunray.

fetíékùàm (fetí-ékù-àmà-) *pl.* **fetíékuik**[a]. *n.* easterner. *Lit.* 'sun-eye person'.

fetíékuxan (fetí-éku-xaná-) *dem.* easterly direction.

fetíékw[a] (fetí-ékù-) *n.* east. *Lit.* 'sun-eye'.

fètìfèt[a] (fètìfètì-) *pl.* **fetífétìk**[a]. *n.* nape of the neck, scruff.

fetígwà (fetí-gwàà-) *n.* bird species. *Lit.* 'sun bird'.

fetíhò (fetí-hòò-) *pl.* **fetíhoík**[a]. *n.* range on both horizons in which the sun rises and sets relatively constantly during dry and rainy seasons. *Lit.* 'sun-hut'.

Fetíícétôd[a] (Fetí-ícé-tódà-) *n.* Jie dialect of the Ateker (Teso-Turkana) speech varieties. *Lit.* 'sun-people speech'.

féy[a] (féí-) *n.* bathing, showering.

fifòn (fifònì-) *v.* to be annoying, bothersome, irritating. See also *itsánánòn*.

fiifión (fiifiónì-) *v.* to be felt on the skin (like a breeze or scratching an itch).

fɨr (fɨrɨ̀) *ideo.* fully.

firifíránón (firifíránónì-) *v.* to be avoidant, circumventing, evasive, steering clear. See also *wirifíránón*.

firimón (firimónì-) *v.* to be clogged or constipated from overeating.

fírits'ár (fírits'árì-) *n.* bird species.

fírits'és (fírits'ésí-) *v.* to trample to pieces.

fités (fitésì-) *v.* to clean, wash.

fitésa kíjá[e] *v.* to create peace. *Lit.* 'to wash the land'.

fitésuƙot[a] (fitésuƙotí-) *v.* to wash up/away.

fitésuƙota gúró[e] *v.* to repent, self-cleanse. *Lit.* 'to wash the heart'.

fitésuƙota kwétɨkà[ɛ] *v.* to wash hands (for health or peace).

fitetés (fitetésí-) *v.* to wash up.

fitídòn (fitídònì-) *v.* to be dull (of blades).

fit[i] (fitì) *ideo.* dully (of blades).

fiuu (fiuu) *ideo.* zing! (sound of a bullet passing close by). The vowels in this word are pronounced silently.

fɔɗ[a] (fɔɗɛ́-) *pl.* **fɔɗɨtín**. *1 n.* long goat-leather loincloth worn by women (wider at the waist and at the knees, narrower in between). *2 n.* tiny garden plot. *3 n.* mudflap.

fɔɗɨtíníàm (fɔɗɨtíní-àmà-) *pl.* **fɔɗɨtíníik**[a]. *n.* old woman. *Lit.* 'loincloths-person'. See also *dúnéim*.

fɔfɔj[a] (fɔfɔjá-) *pl.* **fɔfɔjɨk**[a]. *n.* dried fruit of the *ts'ɔkɔm* tree.

fɔfɔtés (fɔfɔtésí-) *v.* to drag, grate, scrape (along the ground). See also *ifɔɛs*.

fójón (fójónì-) *v.* to whistle.

fɔk[ɔ] (fɔkɔ̀) *ideo.* lightweightly.

fɔkɔ́dòn (fɔkɔ́dònì-) *v.* to be lightweight. See also *ɔfɔ́dòn* and *olódòn*.

folólómòn (folólómònì-) *v.* to be wide open (like an open road).

fòlòn (fòlònì-) *v.* to exuviate, molt, shed (scales or skin).

fɔrɔ́sɨtà (fɔrɔ́sɨtàà-) *n.* forest.

fɔrɔ́ts'ɔ́mɔ̀n (fɔrɔ́ts'ɔ́mɔ̀nɨ̀-) *v.* to be deflated, flat (like a ball or tire).

fɔ́tés (fɔ́tésɨ̀-) *v.* to winnow by tossing up and down in an open container (using one's breath or the wind to remove chaff).

fotólón (fotólónì-) *v.* to be clear, open, unobstructed (like a line-of-sight).

fòts[a] (fòtsà-) *pl.* **fotsitín**. *n.* gorge, ravine. See also *ɲɔ́kɔ́pɛ*.

fòtsàɨk[a] (fòtsà-ɨkà-) *pl.* **fotsitíníikitín**. *n.* top end of a steep gorge. *Lit.* 'gorgehead'.

fɔts'ɔ (fɔ̀ts'ɔ̀) *ideo.* boggily, marshily, swampily.

fɔts'ɔ́dɔ̀n (fɔts'ɔ́dɔ̀nɨ̀-) *v.* to be boggy, marshy, soggy, swampy.

fúfút[a] (fúfútà-) *pl.* **fúfútɨk**[a]. *n.* fresh footpath or trail (of animals or people, e.g. through grass).

fujúlúmòn (fujúlúmònì-) *v.* to be clifflike, cliffy.

fúluƙurú (fúluƙurúù-) *n.* turaco (Ross's and white-crested species). Also pronounced as *kúlufurú*.

fùr (fùrù) *ideo.* streaming out, going separate ways.

furés (furésí-) *1 v.* to scavenge, scrounge for. *2 v.* to be sexually promiscuous.

furésíàm (furésí-àmà-) *pl.* **fúrésiik**[a]. *n.* scavenger.

furúdòn (furúdònì-) *v.* to pour out or stream out (and part ways).

fútés (fútésì-) *v.* to blow.

fútésuƙot[a] (fútésuƙotí-) *v.* to blow off/away.

fútón (fútónì-) *1 v.* to blow. *2 v.* to make noise (vehicle).

fùts'àts'[a] (fùts'àtsà) *ideo.* carelessly, heedlessly.

futs'áts'ésuƙot[a] (futs'áts'ésuƙotí-) *v.* to throw down carelessly.

fúts'iés (fúts'iesí-) *1 v.* to resuscitate, revive (especially with steam). *2 v.* to rekindle (with one's breath).

fùt[u] (fùtù) *ideo.* cut off completely.

fùù (fùù) *ideo.* sound of an empty gourd.

fúútòn (fúútònì-) *1 v.* to breathe heavily. *2 v.* to hiss (of snakes).

fùùt[u] (fùùtù) *ideo.* whoosh! (sound of flowing).

g

gaanaakón (gaanaakónì-) *v.* to be bad, evil, wicked (of many).

gaánàs (gaánàsɨ̀-) *1 n.* badness, evil, wickedness. *2 n.* anger, annoyance, fury, rage. *3 n.* danger, peril, risk.

gàànìkᵉ *v.* badly, poorly.

gaanítésuƙotᵃ (gaanítésuƙotí-) *1 v.* to make bad, worsen. *2 v.* to anger, annoy, upset.

gaanón (gaanónì-) *1 v.* to be bad, evil, wicked. *2 v.* to be angry, annoyed, upset. *3 v.* to be dangerous, perilous, risky. *4 v.* to really like, be 'into' (e.g. playing football).

gaanónuƙotᵃ (gaanónuƙotí-) *1 v.* to become worse, worsen. *2 v.* to become angry, annoyed, upset.

gaɗᵃ (gaɗɛ́-) *n.* destruction and violence directed treacherously towards one's own family, property, clan, neighbor, etc. See also *gaɗɛ́s*.

gaɗár (gaɗárá-) *pl.* **gaɗáríƙ**ᵃ. *1 n.* goo, goop, slime. *2 n.* chyme. *3 n.* cervical mucus.

gaɗɛ́ám (gaɗɛ́-ámà-) *pl.* **gaɗɛ́íƙ**ᵃ. *n.* person who destroys property and assaults people from within his own home, garden, or community.

gaɗɛ́s (gaɗɛ́sɨ́-) *v.* to violently destroy one's own property, leading to the cessation of rain and a poor harvest for the whole community.

gaɗikam (gaɗikamá-) *n.* foraging.

gaɗikamáám (gaɗikamá-ámà-) *pl.* **gaɗikamáíƙ**ᵃ. *n.* forager. See also *wààm*.

gàɗɔ̀n (gàɗɔ̀nɨ̀-) *v.* to be insufficient, lacking, not be enough.

Gaɗukúɲ (Gaɗukúɲù-) *n.* Gaɗukuɲ: one of the Ik's twelve clans.

Gaɗukúɲùàm (Gaɗukúɲù-àmà-) *pl.* **Gaɗukúɲuik**ᵃ. *n.* Gaɗukuɲ clan member.

gafarɛs (gafarɛsí-) *v.* to jab, stab. Also pronounced as *gɛfɛrɛs*.

gafariés (gafariesí-) *1 v.* to jab or stab repeatedly. *2 v.* to scoop up and eat with fingers.

gàfigàf (gàfigàfù-) *pl.* **gafígáfik**ᵃ. *1 n.* lung. *2 n.* radiator.

gafígáfikaɲeɗeké (gafígáfika-ɲeɗekèè-) *n.* pulmonary tuberculosis in animals. *Lit.* 'lung-disease'.

gagaanón (gagaanónì-) *v.* to chuckle, giggle.

gáí (gáí) *quant.* both.

gàjᵃ (gàjà) *ideo.* stammeringly, stutteringly.

gajádòn (gajádònì-) *v.* to be stammering, stuttering. See also *iƙʉjúkʉ́jɔn*.

gajádònìtòdᵃ (gajádònì-tòdà-) *n.* stammering or stuttering speech.

gakímón (gakímónì-) *v.* to lurch, reel, stagger (due to drunkenness, sickness, or old age).

gáƙón (gáƙónì-) *v.* to leave early (before dawn). See also *isókón*.

gaƙúrúmòn (gaƙúrúmònì-) *v.* to be grouchy, grumpy. See also *ɲízɨmɔ́ɔ̀n*.

Gàlàtsᵃ (Gàlàtsɨ̀-) *n.* name of a hill or mountain.

gamam (gamamá-) *n.* firewood, kindling, tinder. *Lit.* 'kindlable'.

gamés (gamésí-) *v.* to kindle, light or start (a fire).

gamésá ts'aɗí v. to kindle, light, or start a fire.

gàràjᵃ (gàràjɨ-) pl. **gárájɨkᵃ**. n. tree species with slick, reddish bark and branches which are ideal for placing beehives; its seed-pods split open exposing little black seeds with red tips and itchy hairs; these are fried, ground, and cooked, yielding a nice edible seed-butter. *Sterculia stenocarpa*.

Gàràjɨàwᵃ (Gàràjɨ-àwà-) n. name of a place and village near *Lopokókᵃ*. Lit. '*gàràj*-place'.

gárés (gárésì-) v. to dish out/up, serve (food).

gáruɓúɓón (gáruɓúɓónì-) v. to flourish, thrive (of plants). Also pronounced as *karuɓúɓón*.

gàsàr (gàsàrà-) n. Cape buffalo. *Syncerus caffer*.

Gasaraikᵃ (Gasara-icé-) n. traditional men's age-group with the cape buffalo as its totem (#10 in historical line). Lit. 'Buffalo-Folk'.

gàsàràìm (gàsàrà-ìmà-) pl. **gasarawikᵃ**. n. buffalo calf.

gàsàràkwàtsᵃ (gàsàrà-kwàtsì-) n. small plant species that resembles a potato and smells like buffalo urine; its leaves are rubbed curatively into foot sores. Lit. 'buffalo-urine'. *Plecthranthus sp*.

gasaraŋwa (gasara-ŋwaá-) n. buffalo cow.

gaso (gasoó-) 1 n. warthog. *Phacochoerus aethiopicus*. 2 n. military tank.

gasoa na ilɨr n. armored military vehicle with machine-gun turret. Lit. 'warthog that rotates'.

gasóím (gasó-ímà-) pl. **gasówíkᵃ**. n. warthog piglet.

gasoŋwa (gaso-ŋwaá-) n. warthog sow.

gàtsᵃ (gàtsà) ideo. rockily, stonily.

gatsádòn (gatsádònì-) v. to be rocky, stony.

gaúsúmòn (gaúsúmònì-) v. to be shaggy, unruly (of hair).

gáʒàdᵃ (gáʒàdɨ-) pl. **gáʒàdɨkᵃ**. n. red-pod terminalia: large shady tree species whose branches can support beehives and whose trunks are carved into beehives; the heart is ground and mixed with oil to make a perfume called *ɓúɓús*; and a bark decoction is drunk with *rukûdzᵃ* and *tikorotótᵃ*. *Terminalia brownii*.

gáʒadɨŋwa (gáʒadɨ-ŋwaá-) n. blabbermouth, gossiper.

gɛbɛjᵃ (gɛbɛjɨ-) pl. **gɛbéjɨkᵃ**. n. shrub species found down in the Kenyan plains where the Turkana eat its fruits. *Boscia coriacea*.

gɛf (gɛfá-) n. deadly abdominal disease (possibly cancer).

gɛfɛrɛs (gɛfɛrɛsɨ-) v. to jab, stab. Also pronounced as *gafarɛs*.

gégès (gégèsì-) v. to chug, gulp, guzzle. See also *iɟɨɾésʉkɔtᵃ*.

gɛrésà (gɛrésàà-) n. British colonial government in East Africa.

gerúsúmòn (gerúsúmònì-) v. to be flabby, pudgy, tubby. See also *rexúkúmòn*.

gìdᵃ (gìdà-) pl. **gíditín**. n. cloud.

gida ná buɗám n. dark raincloud.

gìdà nà ɓèts'ᵃ n. rainless cloud.

gìdòɔ̀kᵃ (gìdò-ɔ̀kà-) 1 n. clear, cloudless sky. 2 n. Heaven. Lit. 'cloud-bone'. See also *dìdiɔ̀kᵃ*.

gìgᵃ (gìgà-) pl. **gígitín**. n. elephant trunk, proboscis.

gígìr (gígìrò-) *n.* downward place, lowland.

gígìròk[e] *n.* down, downward.

gígiroxan (gígiro-xaná-) *dem.* southerly direction.

gíjɛ́s (gíjɛ́sɨ̀-) *v.* to shave (hair).

gìjɛtɛ́s (gìjɛtɛ́sɨ́-) *1 v.* to shave off (hair). *2 v.* to massacre, raze.

gìjìt[a] (gìjìtà-) *pl.* **gíjítìk**[a]. *n.* handmade razor.

girɛ́s (girɛ́sɨ́-) *1 v.* to keep, save, store. *2 v.* to have, possess.

girɛ́sá asɨ́ *v.* to keep one's business to oneself.

girɛ́sá ɨ̀tsɨ̀kà[ɛ] *v.* to keep the law.

girɛ́sá mɛná[ɛ] *v.* to keep one's thoughts secret.

girɛ́síàw[a] (girɛ́sí-àwà-) *pl.* **girɛ́síawík**[a]. *n.* storage place, store (cupboard, cabinet, cave, etc.).

girú (girúù-) *n.* locust.

gɨzá (gɨzáɨ̀-) *pl.* **gɨzáɨk**[a]. *n.* large flat boulder or table rock (where many people can grind their grains together at one time).

gobétón (gobétónì-) *v.* to become overcast, cloud up.

gɔɓ[a] (gɔɓà-) *pl.* **gɔ́ɓítín**. *n.* knot in wood.

gɔɓ[ɔ] (gɔɓɔ) *ideo.* hardly.

gɔɓɔ́dɔ̀n (gɔɓɔ́dɔ̀nɨ̀-) *v.* to be impenetrably hard (like a tree knot or the seeds of the *tɨ́laŋ* tree).

godiyw[a] (godiyó-) *pl.* **godiík**[a]. *n.* large shady tree species whose wood is used to make digging sticks and in whose branches beehives can be placed. *Diospyros scabra*.

gɔɗɨrɨ́mɔ̀n (gɔɗɨrɨ́mɔ̀nɨ̀-) *v.* to be puny, tiny, weeny.

gɔɗɔ́ɛ̀ (gɔɗɔ́ɛ̀-) *pl.* **gɔɗɔ́ɨk**[a]. *n.* brownish-black worm that eats bee larvae and honeycomb.

góges (gógèsì-) *v.* to nail, peg, perforate with a tool.

gɔgɔm (gɔgɔmɔ́-) *pl.* **gɔ́gɔ̀mɨ̀k**[a]. *n.* breastbone, sternum. See also *toroɓ*[a].

gògɔ̀r (gògɔ̀rɔ) *ideo.* decrepitly.

gògòròj[a] (gògòròjì-) *pl.* **gógòròjìk**[a]. *1 n.* spine. *2 n.* midrib. *3 n.* straight middle part. *4 n.* ridge.

gògòròjòòk[a] (gògòròjò-ɔ̀kà-) *n.* backbone, spine, vertebrae.

gógòrɔ̀mɔ̀n (gógòrɔ̀mɔ̀nɨ̀-) *v.* to be bony, decrepit, rickety, scraggy.

gòk[a] (gòkà-) *n.* insomnia, sleeplessness, wakefulness.

gɔ̀k[a] (gɔ̀kà-) *pl.* **gɔ́kɨ́tɨ́n**. *1 n.* larynx, voicebox. *2 n.* eyeball.

gokirós (gokirósí-) *v.* to be unsettled.

gɔ̀k[ɔ] (gɔ̀kɔ) *ideo.* stiffly.

gɔkɔ́dɔ̀n (gɔkɔ́dɔ̀nɨ̀-) *v.* to be stiff : impliable or unsupple.

gòkòn (gòkònì-) *1 v.* to be sleepless, have insomnia. *2 v.* to be awake for sex. Not to be confused with *gókón*.

góƙ[a] (góƙá-) *n.* sitting as a group.

gokaakétòn (gokaakétònì-) *v.* to sit down (of many).

góƙáàw[a] (góƙá-àwà-) *pl.* **góƙáawík**[a]. *n.* place where groups of people sit together.

góƙón (góƙónì-) *v.* to be seated, sitting (of many). Not to be confused with *gòkòn*.

gólɨ̀d[a] (gólɨ̀dɨ̀-) *n.* gold.

gólɔ́gɔlánón (gólɔ́gɔlánónì-) *v.* to be crooked, twisted (like a river or stick).

gomóí (gomóíá-) *n.* small shrub species whose bitter yellow berries are cooked and eaten; the plant is beaten on paths to thwart enemies, and it also serves as a treatment for stomach ailments. *Maerua pseudopetalosa.*

Gomóíàw[a] (Gomóí-àwà-) *n.* name of a hill. *Lit.* 'gomóí-place'.

gòmòjòj[a] (gòmòjòjì-) *n.* small plant species whose round roots are worn around the neck and whose smell is believed to frighten snakes away; the roots (or seeds, Heine 1999) are chewed and the bitter juice swallowed for colds and coughs. *Cyperus distans.*

gɔmɔr (gɔmɔrú-) *pl.* **gɔmɔ́rɨ́k**[a]. *n.* Nubian acacia: thorn tree species whose bark is pounded and added to porridge or the juice is mixed with sheep blood and fat and taken as a treatment for the *loɓáí* disease; the bark is also made into children's necklaces and charms for spiritual protection. *Acacia nubica.*

gɔn (gɔnɛ́-) *pl.* **gɔ́nɨ́tɨ́n**. *n.* stump.

gònè (gònè) *prep.* all the way to, until, up to. A noun following this word takes the oblique case.

gonés (gonésí-) *1 v.* to check out, inspect, look at, view. *2 v.* to be alert, awake.

gonésá kom° *v.* to be wide-eyed (when alert to danger or embarassed). *Lit.* 'to see much'.

gonésétòn (gonésétònì-) *v.* to awaken, wake up.

gonésúƙot[a] (gonésúƙotí-) *v.* to check out, inspect, look at, view (over there).

gonetés (gonetésí-) *v.* to check out, inspect, look at, view (here).

gónímós (gónímósí-) *v.* to look at each other.

góózés (góózésí-) *1 v.* to cast, throw, toss. *2 v.* to abandon, desert, forsake. *3 v.* to vote for.

góózésíàm (góózésí-àmà-) *pl.* **góózésiik**[a]. *1 n.* one who throws meat at people sitting in age-groups. *2 n.* voter.

góózésíàw[a] (góózésí-àwà-) *pl.* **góózésiawík**[a]. *n.* polling station.

góózesuƙot[a] (góózesuƙotí-) *1 v.* to cast, throw, or toss away. *2 v.* to abandon, desert, forsake. *3 v.* to lose, misplace.

góózetés (góózetésí-) *v.* to cast, throw, or toss this away.

góózinósúƙot[a] (góózinósúƙotí-) *v.* to forsake each other.

góózosuƙot[a] (góózosuƙotí-) *1 v.* to be abandoned, deserted, forsaken. *2 v.* to be lost, misplaced.

górés (górésì-) *1 v.* to cross over, go across, pass over. *2 v.* to pass (an examination or test). Also pronounced as *ígorés.*

góriés (góriesí-) *v.* to cross over, go across, or pass over repeatedly. Also pronounced as *ígoriés.*

góriesá ɓisá[ɛ] *v.* to cross or pass over a spear.

gòrìgòr (gòrìgòrì-) *pl.* **górígòrìk**[a]. *1 n.* hoof. *2 n.* bare foot.

górígòrìk[ɔ] *n.* barefoot. *Lit.* 'on hooves'.

Gɔris (Gɔrisí-) *n.* name of a river near *Kàlàpàtà* where the Dodoth and Turkana fought each other.

gɔrɔ́x (gɔrɔ́xɨ-) *pl.* **gɔrɔ́xɨ́k**[a]. *n.* eyelid, palpebra (upper and lower).

góʒòw[a] (góʒòù-) *pl.* **góʒòwìk**[a]. *n.* fog, mist.

Góʒòwìk[a] (Góʒòwìkà-) *n.* name of a hill or mountain. *Lit.* 'mists'.

gubes (gubesí-) *pl.* **gúbèsìk**[a]. *n.* thigh.

gubés (gubésí-) *v.* to blanket, cover.

gubesíɔk[a] (gubesí-ɔ́kà-) *pl.* **gúbesikɔɔkɨtɨ́n**. *n.* femur, thighbone.

gubésúƙot[a] (gubésúƙotí-) *v.* to blanket over, cover or wrap up.

gʉɓɛ́r (gʉɓɛ́rá-) *n.* leopard. *Panthera pardus.*

gúɗúsam (gúɗúsamá-) *n.* fragment, shard.

guf (gufá-) *pl.* **gúfɨtɨ́n**. *n.* foam, froth.

guféém (gufé-émè-) *n.* armpit muscle, teres major. *Lit.* 'froth-muscle'.

gúgùrɔ̀n (gúgùrɔ̀nɨ̀-) *v.* to be severely hunched or stooped over.

gùj[a] (gùjè-) *n.* small plant species whose flat leaves tortoises like to eat and people may boil as an edible vegetable. *Commelina sp.*

gùlùj[u] (gùlùjù) *ideo.* gulp! (sound of swallowing something big).

gúr (gúró-) *pl.* **gúrítín**. *1 n.* inner chest containing the 'heart' (emotional and physical). *2 n.* heart, soul, psyche. *3 n.* battery. *4 n.* engine, motor. See *gúróeɗ* for the physical heart.

gùr (gùrà-) *pl.* **gúrítín**. *n.* sickle bush: small, fast-growing hardwood tree species with strong thorns and which is used in blacksmithing and building and whose bark juice can act as a mouthwash. *Dichrostachys cinerea.* Not to be confused with *gúr*.

gúránòn (gúránònì-) *v.* to be hotheaded, hot-tempered, irascible.

gúránós (gúránósí-) *v.* to be hotheaded, hot-tempered, irascible.

gúréda dakwí *n.* duramen, heartwood.

gúróàm (gúró-àmà-) *pl.* **gúróik**[a]. *1 n.* hothead, hot-tempered person. *2 n.* calm, even-keeled person.

gúróeɗ[a] (gúró-èɗì-) *n.* physical heart. *Lit.* 'heart-kernel'. See *gúr* for the emotional heart.

gúróɛn[ɔ] *n.* from the heart, sincerely.

Gutí (Gutîi-) *n.* a personal name.

gʉts'ʉrɛs (gʉts'ʉrɛsí-) *v.* to do away with, get rid of, rid oneself of.

gʉts'ʉriés (gʉts'ʉriesí-) *v.* to do away with, get rid of.

gʉts'ʉriesá tódà[e] *v.* to speak harshly, meanly. *Lit.* 'to get rid of speech'.

gʉts'ʉ́rínɔ́s (gʉts'ʉ́rínɔ́sí-) *v.* to repulse each other out of mutual hatred.

gwa (gwaá-) *1 n.* bird, fowl. *2 n.* air, sky. Not to be confused with *gwà*.

gwà (gwàà-) *pl.* **gwaitín**. *1 n.* stomach. *2 n.* craw, crop. Not to be confused with *gwa*.

gwaa na awá[e] *n.* domestic bird.

gwáák[a] (gwá-ákà-) *pl.* **gwáákɨtɨ́n**. *n.* beak, bill. *Lit.* 'bird-mouth'.

gwábàr (gwá-bàrɔ̀-) *pl.* **gwábaritín**. *n.* flock of birds.

gwácúrúk[a] (gwá-cúrúkú-) *n.* male bird: cock, rooster, tercel, etc.

gwadam (gwadamá-) *1 n.* congealed animal fat. *2 n.* delicacy, treat.

Gwágwààm (Gwágwà-àmà-) *pl.* **Gwágwaik**[a]. *n.* Dodoth person.

Gwágwaicétôd[a] (Gwágwaicé-tódà-) *n.* Dodoth dialect of the Ateker (Teso-Turkana) speech varieties.

gwáho (gwá-hoó-) *pl.* **gwáhoík**[a]. *n.* birdhouse, nest.

gwáím (gwá-ímà-) *pl.* **gwáwík**[a]. *n.* chick.

gwaítón (gwaítónì-) *v.* to leave in a huff, storm off. See also *ígwɨ̀jìrɔ̀n*.

gwaɨ́ts'[a] (gwaɨ́ts'ɨ́-) *1 n.* giraffe. *Giraffa camelopardalis*. *2 n.* camel.

gwaɨ́ts'ɨ́cikw[a] (gwaɨ́ts'ɨ́-cikó-) *n.* giraffe bull.

Gwaɨ́ts'íik[a] (Gwaɨ́ts'í-icé-) *n.* traditional men's age-group with the giraffe as its totem (#8 in the historical line). *Lit.* 'Giraffe-Folk'.

gwaɨ́ts'íìm (gwaɨ́ts'í-ìmà-) *pl.* **gwaɨ́ts'ɨ́-wik**[a]. *n.* giraffe calf.

gwaɨ́ts'ɨ́lɔ̀d[a] (gwaɨ́ts'ɨ́-lɔ̀dà-) *pl.* **gwaɨ́ts'ɨ́lɔ́ditín**. *n.* tassel made from the bushy end of a giraffe's tail.

gwaɨ́ts'ɨ́ŋwa (gwaɨ́ts'ɨ́-ŋwaá-) *n.* giraffe cow.

gwàj[a] (gwàjà) *ideo.* wham! (sound of hitting the ground heavily).

gwàj[a] (gwàjì-) *pl.* **gwajitín**. *n.* belly, paunch, pot-belly.

gwalát[a] (gwalátɨ́-) *pl.* **gwalátík**[a]. *n.* labret, lip plug.

gwamétón (gwamétónì-) *v.* to stand up (of more than one person).

gwámón (gwámónì-) *v.* to stand (of more than one person).

gwan (gwanɨ́-) *1 n.* bushbaby, lesser galago. *Galago senegalensis*. *2 n.* pair of trousers.

gwaŋwa (gwa-ŋwaá-) *n.* female bird, biddy, hen.

gwarés (gwarésí-) *v.* to throw multiple things in a downward motion.

gwarí (gwarîi-) *1 n.* top. *2 n.* location, presence.

gwarîêd[a] (gwaríédè-) *n.* top part.

gwaríedek[e] *n.* on, on top.

gwárixan (gwári-xaná-) *dem.* northerly direction.

gwas (gwasá-) *pl.* **gwàsɨ̀k**[a]. *1 n.* pebble, small rock, stone. *2 n.* grinding stone. *3 n.* nugget. *4 n.* battery. *5 n.* medal.

gwasa na féí *n.* bathing stone (for rubbing one's heels).

gwàsɨ̀kàkɨ̀ts[a] (gwàsɨ̀kà-kɨ̀tsà-) *n.* grave marked by a pile of stones. *Lit.* 'stones-pile'.

gwɛɛ́ts'ɛ́mɔ̀n (gwɛɛ́ts'ɛ́mɔ̀nɨ̀-) *v.* to stop seasonal swarming (of termites).

gwegweritiés (gwegweritiesí-) *v.* to scratch, scribble, scrawl.

gwegweritiós (gwegweritiosí-) *1 v.* to be scratched, scribbled, scrawled. *2 v.* to be striped.

gwèj[e] (gwèjè) *ideo.* roughly.

gwèlèj[e] (gwèlèjè) *1 ideo.* unsteadily, wobbly. *2 ideo.* empty-handedly.

gwelítésuƙot[a] (gwelítésuƙotí-) *v.* to distract, make forget.

gwèlòn (gwèlònì-) *v.* to be forgotten. See also *iɓílérɔ̀n*.

gwɛɲémɔ́n (gwɛɲémɔ́nɨ̀-) *1 v.* to be bright, brilliant (of the sun at daybreak). *2 v.* to be wide awake, wide open (of one's eyes).

gwɛrɛ́jɛ́jɔ̀n (gwɛrɛ́jɛ́jɔ̀nɨ̀-) *v.* to be coarse, gritty, mealy (like poorly ground flour or boiled maize with loose shells).

gwéts'ón (gwéts'ónì-) *v.* to be sweet, tasty, yummy.

gwi (gwié-) *pl.* **gwiitín**. *n.* grove, stand. May also be spelled as *guy*[a].

gwidídòn (gwidídònì-) *v.* to be limber, lithe.

gwìd[i] (gwìdì) *ideo.* limberly, lithely.

gwɨ̀rɔ̀n (gwɨ̀rɔ̀nɨ̀-) *v.* to squirm away, wriggle out.

h

hà (hà) *interj.* whatever! (an expression of scornful disbelief).

hàbᵃ (hàbù-) *pl.* **hábikw**ᵃ. *n.* natural beehive in a hollow tree trunk.

hábàs (hábàsɨ-) *n.* selfishness, stinginess. *Lit.* 'hotness'.

hábatsésúkotᵃ (hábatsésúkotí-) *v.* to cast away, discard, ditch, toss aside. Also pronounced as *ábadzésúkot*ᵃ.

hábatsetés (hábatsetésí-) *v.* to cast down, discard, toss aside. Also pronounced as *ábadzetés*.

hábètòn (hábètònì-) *v.* to become hot, heat up.

hábitésúkotᵃ (hábitésúkotí-) *1 v.* to heat up, make hot. *2 v.* to charge (electrically).

hábòn (hábònì-) *1 v.* to be hot. *2 v.* to be selfish, stingy.

hábona kíjáᵉ *n.* hot weather. *Lit.* 'heat of the land'.

hábona nébwì *n.* fever, high temperature. *Lit.* 'heat of the body'.

hábonukotᵃ (hábonukotí-) *v.* to become hot, heat up.

hádaadánón (hádaadánóní-) *v.* to be inept, maladroit, uncoordinated.

hádoletés (hádoletésí-) *v.* to open wide, set agape.

hádòlòmòn (hádòlòmòní-) *v.* to be gaping, yawning (of any opening).

hàjᵃ (hàjà) *ideo.* loosely.

hajádòn (hajádòní-) *v.* to be loosely tied, unsecured. See also *lajádòn* and *yaŋádòn*.

hakaikés (hakaikésí-) *v.* to forget, neglect, overlook.

hakaikitetés (hakaikitetésí-) *v.* to distract, make forget.

hakaikós (hakaikósí-) *v.* to be forgotten, neglected, overlooked.

hákátòn (hákátòní-) *v.* to clear the throat, harrumph, hawk. See also *xakarés*.

hákátònìàm (hákátòní-àmà-) *pl.* **hákátoniik**ᵃ. *n.* one who speaks harshly or meanly.

hakítésukotᵃ (hakítésukotí-) *v.* to lead astray, mislead. See also *itwáŋítésúkot*ᵃ.

hakonukotᵃ (hakonukotí-) *1 v.* to drift off, get lost, go astray, lose the way, stray off. *2 v.* to err, make a mistake. *3 v.* to digress, go off topic. *4 v.* to be forgotten, leave one's memory.

hakwés (hakwésí-) *v.* to harvest (wild foods like honey and edible termites).

hakwésá dáŋáᵉ *v.* to harvest edible termites.

hamomos (hamomosí-) *v.* to sample or try out in large numbers.

hamʉjés (hamʉjésí-) *1 v.* to finish grinding well (grain that had been poorly ground). *2 v.* to botch, bungle, do wrongly, mess or screw up.

hár (hárɨ-) *pl.* **hárítɨn**. *n.* diarrhea.

hárá na gwɛrɛjɛjᵃ *n.* chunky diarrhea.

hárá na tɨliwᵃ *n.* liquid diarrhea.

hárá ná zè *n.* severe diarrhea.

hárɨgad́ár (hárɨ-gad́árá-) *n.* diarrheal mucus.

harítɔ́n (harítɔ̀nɨ-) *v.* to diarrhate, have diarrhea.

harítɔ́na pìɔ *v.* to have liquidy diarrhea. The sound represented by *pìɔ* is whispered.

hataikánón (hataikánónì-) *1 v.* to ripen quickly. *2 v.* to cook quickly.

haú (haúù-) *n.* hyena.

haúdòn (haúdònì-) *1 v.* to be be tough when cooked. *2 v.* to be munchy (hungry between meals).

hàᵘ (hàù) *ideo.* cooked very tough.

hèɓᵘ (hèɓù) *ideo.* softly, squeezably.

heɓúdòn (heɓúdònì-) *v.* to be soft, squeezable, squeezy (like a ball, belly, or breast).

heɓúlúmòn (heɓúlúmònì-) *v.* to be paunchy, potbellied (like beer-drinkers or pregnant women).

héɗɔ́nʉkɔtᵃ (héɗɔ́nʉkɔtí-) *v.* to shrink or shrivel up. See also *kiɗɔnʉkɔt*ᵃ.

héé' (héé') *interj.* yeah right! (an expression of disbelief or doubt). The apostrophe at the end marks a glottal stop, which makes an abrupt end to the word's voicing.

hègᵃ (hègà-) *pl.* **hégitín**. *n.* bone marrow.

hejú (hejúù-) *pl.* **hejúik**ᵃ. *n.* suprapubic area: space above the pubis but below the abdomen.

hèz (hèz) *interj.* hey! (an expression of strong disapproval).

hɨɨjᵃ (hɨɨjá) *1 adv.* slowly. *2 adv.* carefully.

hɨɨjᵓ (hɨɨjɔ́) *1 adv.* slowly. *2 adv.* carefully.

hɨ́kɔ́ (hɨ́kɔ́ɔ̀-) *pl.* **hɨ́kɔ́ɨk**ᵃ. *n.* chameleon.

hò (hòò-) *pl.* **hóík**ᵃ. *1 n.* house, hut. *2 n.* casing, housing. *3 n.* class, grade, level (in school).

hoákwᵃ (ho-akɔ́-) *n.* inside of a house or hut.

hɔɓɔ́mɔ́n (hɔɓɔ́mɔ́nì-) *v.* to be hungry quickly, have a high metabolism.

hodzíŋ (ho-dzíŋá-) *n.* porch, veranda.

hoɗés (hoɗésí-) *1 v.* to free, liberate, release, set free. *2 v.* to divorce. See also *talakes*.

hoɗésúkotᵃ (hoɗésúkotí-) *1 v.* to free, liberate, release, set free. *2 v.* to remove, take off, undress. *3 v.* to fire, sack, terminate (from employment).

hoɗetés (hoɗetésí-) *1 v.* to free, liberate, release, set free. *2 v.* to remove, take off, undress. *3 v.* to save spiritually.

hoɗetésá asɨ *1 v.* to free oneself. *2 v.* to be born again, get saved (in the Christian sense).

hoɗetésá takáɨkàᵋ *v.* to remove or take off shoes.

hoɗetésíàm (hoɗetésí-àmà-) *pl.* **hoɗetésíik**ᵃ. *1 n.* freer, releaser (e.g. of prisoners or trapped animals). *2 n.* redeemer, savior.

hoɗómón (hoɗómónì-) *v.* to come free/off/undone, loosen.

hoés (hoesí-) *1 v.* to cut, slice. *2 v.* to butcher, slaughter. *3 v.* to skin. *4 v.* to operate on, perform a surgery on. See also *tɔŋɔlɛs*.

hoesíàm (hoesí-àmà-) *pl.* **hoesíik**ᵃ. *1 n.* butcher. *2 n.* surgeon.

hoesího (hoesí-hoó-) *pl.* **hoesíhoík**ᵃ. *1 n.* abattoir, butchery, slaughterhouse. *2 n.* operating room (OR), surgery, theater.

hoetés (hoetésí-) *1 v.* to cut into/out/up. *2 v.* to do surgery on, operate on. *3 v.* to figure out, solve. *4 v.* to divide or divvy up.

hoetésá ɲásáatí *v.* to plan a time. *Lit.* 'to cut out an hour'.

hogwarí (ho-gwarîi-) *n.* roof.

hóítá kwí *interj.* oh my goodness/God/word! (an expression of strong emotions like fear or astonishment). Borrowed from Ateker (Teso-Turkana).

hoƙuts'ᵃ (ho-ƙʉts'á-) *n.* type of biting worm that lives in dirt floors.

hómò (hómòò-) *n.* laundry detergent or soap. From the detergent brand called OMO; see also *ɲéómò*.

hɔnɛ́s (hɔnɛ́sɨ́-) *1 v.* to drive (a vehicle). *2 v.* to ride (a bicycle or motorcycle). Not to be confused with *hónɛ́s*.

hónɛ́s (hónɛ́sɨ-) *v.* to drive (animals). Not to be confused with *hɔnɛ́s*.

hɔnɛ́súƙɔtᵃ (hɔnɛ́súƙɔtɨ́-) *1 v.* to drive off/away. *2 v.* to exorcize.

hɔnɛtɛ́s (hɔnɛtɛ́sɨ́-) *v.* to drive out (in this direction).

hɔnɛtɛ́sá ínóᵉ *v.* to drive out animals (as from a thicket).

hɔ́tɔ̀ (hɔ́tɔ̀ɔ̀-) *n.* bustard.

hòwɛ̀l (hò-wɛ̀là-) *pl.* **howélíkwᵃ**. *n.* house window.

húbutɛ́s (húbutɛ́sɨ́-) *v.* to perforate, punch (e.g. a hole in a gourd or a skull). See also *pulɛ́s*.

hyeaa (hyeaa) *ideo.* sound of a tree falling.

ɦy

ɦyakwés (ɦyakwésí-) *v.* to hush, shush.

ɦyàƙàtàk[a] (ɦyàƙàtàkà-) *n.* a bit far, far-away, some distance away.

ɦyàtàk[a] (ɦyàtàkà-) *n.* close by, nearby, in the vicinity.

ɦyeés (ɦyeesí-) *v.* to know. Another form of the root of this word is *íye-*.

ɦyeésúƙot[a] (ɦyeésúƙotí-) *v.* to come to know, learn, learn how.

ɦyeímós (ɦyeímósí-) *v.* to be kin, related. *Lit.* 'to know each other'. Also pronounced as *ɦyeínós*.

ɦyeínós (ɦyeínósí-) *v.* to be kin, related. *Lit.* 'to know each other'. Also pronounced as *ɦyeímós*.

ɦyeínósá ƙwaaté[o] *v.* to be related by birth.

ɦyeínósá na ƙɔ́ɓà[ɛ] *v.* kinship or relation by birth. *Lit.* 'relation of the umbilical cord'.

ɦyeínósá na séà[e] *v.* to be related by blood. *Lit.* 'relation of blood'.

ɦyeínósá sits'ésú *v.* to be related by marriage.

ɦyeités (ɦyeitésí-) *1 v.* to check out, familiarize oneself with, get to know. *2 v.* to discern, recognize, tell apart. *3 v.* to prospect, survey.

ɦyeitésá arííkà[ɛ] *v.* to haruspicate: to divine the future by inspecting patterns in animal entrails.

ɦyeítésihò (ɦyeítési-hòò-) *pl.* **ɦyeítésihoík**[a]. *n.* examination room.

ɦyeitésúƙot[a] (ɦyeitésúƙotí-) *v.* to inform, let know, tell.

ɦyeitetés (ɦyeitetésí-) *v.* to inform, let know, tell.

ɦyekes (ɦyekesí-) *1 v.* to be alive, live. *2 n.* being, existence, life. *3 n.* livelihood, living, survival.

ɦyekesíám (ɦyekesí-ámà-) *pl.* **ɦyekesíík**[a]. *n.* dependant, long-term guest (who may be asked to help work without payment).

ɦyekétón (ɦyekétónì-) *v.* to come back to life, resurrect, revive.

ɦyekitetés (ɦyekitetésí-) *v.* to reanimate, resurrect, revive.

ɦyɛnɛ́tɔn (ɦyɛnɛ́tɔnɨ-) *v.* to barf, hurl, puke, regurgitate, vomit, upchuck.

ɦyɛnɛ́tɔna pɨɔ *v.* to vomit pure liquid. The sound represented by *pɨɔ* is whispered.

ɦyɛ̀nɔ̀n (ɦyɛ̀nɔ̀nɨ-) *v.* to barf, hurl, puke, regurgitate, vomit, upchuck.

ɦyɛtás (ɦyɛtásí-) *n.* ferocity, fierceness, meanness, savagery.

ɦyɛtiɦyɛtɔs (ɦyɛtiɦyɛtɔsí-) *v.* to be ferocious, fierce, mean, savage.

ɦyɛ̀tɔ̀n (ɦyɛ̀tɔ̀nɨ-) *v.* to be ferocious, fierce, mean, savage.

ɦyɔ (ɦyɔɔ-) *n.* cattle, cow(s). Can refer to one or more cattle/cows.

ɦyɔ̀àm (ɦyɔ̀-àmà-) *pl.* **ɦyoik**[a]. *n.* foreigner: non-Ik, especially a member of a pastoralist tribe. *Lit.* 'cattle-person'.

ɦyɔ̀bàr (ɦyɔ̀-bàrò-) *pl.* **ɦyɔbarítín**. *n.* herd of cattle.

ɦyɔcèk[a] (ɦyɔ̀-cèkì-) *pl.* **ɦyɔcikám**. *n.* foreign woman: non-Ik, especially a member of a pastoralist tribe. *Lit.* 'cattle-woman'.

ɦyɔɛn (ɦyɔ-ɛnɨ-) *n.* foreign language: any but especially that of a pastoralist tribe. *Lit.* 'cattle's (language)'.

ɦyɔ̀ets'ᵃ (ɦyɔ̀-èts'ì-) *n.* cowdung, manure. See also *ŋɔtᵃ*.

ɦyòìdwᵃ (ɦyò-ìdò-) *pl.* ɦyoiditín. *1 n.* cow udder. *2 n.* cow milk.

ɦyòìm (ɦyò-ìmà-) *pl.* ɦyowikᵃ. *n.* foreign child: non-Ik, especially of any pastoralist tribe. *Lit.* 'cattle-child'.

ɦyɔjejé (ɦyɔ-jejéì-) *n.* cowhide, cow leather, cowskin.

ɦyɔ̀jàn (ɦyɔ̀-jànɨ-) *n.* short grass species loved by cattle and used to make brooms. *Eragrostis braunii.*

ɦyɔ̀m (ɦyòmò) *ideo.* crack! (sound of a stick breaking easily).

ɦyɔŋwa (ɦyɔ-ŋwaá-) *n.* cow. This is the term for a female cow; see *ɦyɔ̀* for 'cow' in general.

ɦyoós (ɦyoosí-) *v.* to be famous, known, reputed, well-known.

ɦyɔtaƙáyᵃ (ɦyɔ-taƙáɨ-) *pl.* ɦyɔtaƙáɨkᵃ. *n.* cow-leather shoe.

ɦyɔ̀tòdᵃ (ɦyɔ̀-tòdà-) *pl.* ɦyɔtodaicíkᵃ. *n.* foreign language: any but especially that of a pastoralist tribe like the Dodoth, Toposa, and Turkana. *Lit.* 'cattle-talk'.

ɦyɔtógètɔ̀n (ɦyɔtógètɔ̀nɨ-) *1 v.* to approach, come close, draw near. *2 v.* to be approximate.

ɦyɔtógimɔ́s (ɦyɔtógimɔ́sɨ-) *v.* to be close/near to each another.

ɦyɔtógɔ̀n (ɦyɔtógɔ̀nɨ-) *1 v.* to be close, near. *2 v.* to be approximate. *3 v.* to be almost.

ɦyɔtógɔ̀nɨ̀àm (ɦyɔtógɔ̀nɨ̀-àmà-) *pl.* ɦyɔtógɔniikᵃ. *n.* friend or neighbor whom you want to stay close to.

ɦyɔtógɔnʉƙɔtᵃ (ɦyɔtógɔnʉƙɔtɨ́-) *v.* to approach (going), go near.

ɦyʉƙum (ɦyʉƙumú-) *pl.* ɦyúƙumɨkᵃ. *n.* neck.

ɦyʉƙuma ƙwázàᵉ *n.* collar, neckband. *Lit.* 'neck of clothing'.

ɦyʉƙumúɔ́kᵃ (ɦyʉƙumú-ɔ́kà-) *n.* cervical vertebrae, neckbone.

ɦyʉƙumútsɨrím (ɦyʉƙumú-tsɨrímú-) *pl.* ɦyʉƙumútsɨrímɨkᵃ. *n.* metal neckring worn as jewelry.

ɦyʉƙún (ɦyʉƙúná-) *pl.* ɦyʉƙúnɨkᵃ. *n.* back interior wall of a house/hut (opposite the front door).

i/ɨ

iáɨ́á (<iáɨ́ɛ́ɛ́s) *v.*

iákɛsʉƙotᵃ (iákɛsʉƙotí-) *v.* to take away. See also *duƙésúƙotᵃ*.

iakɛtés (iakɛtésɨ́-) *v.* to bring. See also *detés*.

iatɛs (iatɛsɨ́-) *v.* to add, increase.

iatiés (iatiesí-) *v.* to add repeatedly, keep adding.

iatiésuƙotᵃ (iatiesúƙotí-) *v.* to add repeatedly, keep adding.

iatímétòn (iatímétònì-) *v.* to be added, grow, increase.

iatɔs (iatɔsɨ́-) *1 v.* to added, increased. *2 v.* to be expanded, widened.

ɨàwɨ̀àwᵃ (ɨ̀àwɨ̀àʉ̀-) *pl.* **iáɨwɨ́áwɨkᵃ**. *n.* creek, small stream.

ɨbaɗés (ɨbaɗésɨ́-) *v.* to bang into, bump, hit, knock, run into.

ɨbaɗiés (ɨbaɗiesí-) *v.* to bang into, bump, hit, knock, run into repeatedly.

íbànètòn (íbànètònì-) *v.* to come in the late afternoon or evening. See also *irípétòn*.

íbànòn (íbànònì-) *v.* to go in the late afternoon or evening. See also *iripón*.

ɨbatalés (ɨbatalésɨ́-) *v.* to put in a sling, sling.

ɨbatés (ɨbatésɨ́-) *v.* to knock down/over, topple, tumble.

ɨbatɛsa asɨ́ *v.* to tumble down.

ɨbatɛtés (ɨbatɛtésɨ́-) *v.* to knock down/over, topple, tumble.

ɨbatiés (ɨbatiesí-) *v.* to knock down/over, topple, or tumble repeatedly.

ɨ̀bèɗɨ̀bèɗɔ̀n (ɨ̀bèɗɨ̀bèɗɔ̀nì-) *1 v.* to blink, nictate, wink. *2 v.* to creep or sneak up. See also *irwapírwápòn*.

ibétᵃ (ibétí-) *pl.* **ibètìkᵃ**. *n.* thorn-tree species whose wood is used for building, fencing, and carving tool handles; its twigs are used as toothbrushes, and its red seeds are worn as beads by the Turkana. *Commiphora africana*.

íbìrìbìròn (íbìrìbìrònì-) *v.* to babble, blather.

ɨbités (ɨbitésɨ́-) *v.* to plant, sow.

ɨbɔbɔtsɛ́s (ɨbɔbɔtsɛ́sɨ́-) *v.* to agitate, churn, shake vigorously.

iboboyᵃ (iboboí-) *n.* African paradise flycatcher (both rufous and white). *Terpsiphone viridis*.

íboɗolés (íboɗolésí-) *v.* to lean or tip over (e.g. a beer gourd in order to drink from it).

íbòfòn (íbòfònì-) *v.* to make an alarm call (of animals, like a baboon's bark an oribi's whistle).

íbokés (íbokésí-) *1 v.* to put up: elevate for safe storage. *2 v.* to postpone, put off.

ibɔtᵃ (ibɔtá-) *pl.* **ɨbɔ̀tɨkᵃ**. *1 n.* ring of dried out pumpkin. *2 n.* wrist knife. See also *ɲáɓaarátᵃ*.

íbotitésúƙotᵃ (íbotitésúƙotí-) *v.* to bounce, jounce, make jump.

íbotitetés (íbotitetésí-) *v.* to bounce, jounce, make jump.

Íbotokokᵃ (Íbotokokó-) *n.* name of a river.

íbòtòn (íbòtònì-) *1 v.* to jump, leap, spring. *2 v.* to bounce, rebound.

ɨbɔtsam (ɨbɔtsamá-) *n.* butter. Lit. 'churnable'.

ɨbɔtsɛ́s (ɨbɔtsɛ́sɨ́-) *v.* to agitate, churn, shake vigorously.

íbɔtsésá así *v.* to be agitated, churn, roil.

íbubuŋés (íbubuŋésí-) *1 v.* to inclose, insert, slip or tuck into (e.g. when one is secretly passing an item into a friend's pocket). *2 v.* to butt in, disrupt, interfere.

íbubuŋésúkɔt[a] (íbubuŋésúkɔtí-) *1 v.* to inclose, insert, slip or tuck into (e.g. when one is secretly passing an item into a friend's pocket). *2 v.* to butt in, disrupt, interfere.

íbudés (íbudésí-) *v.* to trample, tromp.

íbudésá cué *v.* to slosh through water. *Lit.* 'to trample water'.

íbunutsés (íbunutsésí-) *v.* to brace, splint.

íburubúrés (íburubúrésí-) *v.* to mingle or stir in (e.g. flour into water to make meal mush).

íbutsés (íbutsésí-) *v.* to beat down, beat out (e.g. to put out fire by beating it with leafy branches; to clear away brush before cutting larger trees; to beat dust out of clothing).

íbutsurés (íbutsurésí-) *v.* to flavor, season. See also *iwéwérés* and *iwówórés*.

iɓááŋàs (iɓááŋàsɨ-) *1 n.* innocence, naivete. *2 n.* folly, foolishness. *3 n.* idiocy, stupidity. *4 n.* illiteracy.

iɓááŋàsìam (iɓááŋàsɨ-àmà-) *pl.* **iɓááŋasiik**[a]. *n.* idiot, imbecile, moron, stupid person.

iɓááŋàsìtòd[a] (iɓááŋàsɨ-tòdà-) *n.* bunk, hogwash, nonsense.

iɓááŋɔ̀n (iɓááŋɔ̀nɨ-) *1 v.* to be innocent, naive, unknowing. *2 v.* to be foolish, unwise. *3 v.* to be dumb, idiotic, stupid, unintelligent. *4 v.* to be illiterate, uneducated.

iɓáɓá (<iɓáɓɛ́ɛ́s) *v.*

iɓáɓɛ́ɛ́s (iɓáɓɛ́ɛ́sɨ-/iɓáɓá-) *v.* to handle carefully, treat gently.

iɓákɨ́nɔ́s (iɓákɨ́nɔ́sɨ-) *v.* to be next to each other.

iɓákɔ́n (iɓákɔ́nɨ-) *v.* to be adjacent, beside, next to.

iɓákɔ́nukɔt[a] (iɓákɔ́nukɔtí-) *v.* to move adjacent, beside, or next to.

iɓálétɔ̀n (iɓálétɔ̀nɨ-) *v.* to appall, astonish, horrify, shock. The one who experiences this sensation takes the dative case in a sentence.

iɓalíɓálés (iɓalíɓálésɨ-) *v.* to consume, misuse, waste.

iɓálɔ́n (iɓálɔ́nɨ-) *v.* to be appalling, astonishing, horrifying, shocking. See also *toɓúlón*.

iɓámɔ́n (iɓámɔ́nɨ-) *1 v.* to be free, unoccupied. *2 v.* to be extra, spare, unused. *3 v.* to be loose, unfixed. *4 v.* to be free of charge. *5 v.* to be plain, simple, unadorned.

iɓámɔ́nìàm (iɓámɔ́nɨ-àmà-) *pl.* **iɓámɔ́niik**[a]. *n.* care-free person.

iɓámɔ́nìtòd[a] (iɓámɔ́nɨ-tòdà-) *n.* pointless talk.

iɓaɲɛs (iɓaɲɛsí-) *v.* to bump, jab (e.g with the elbow).

iɓaŋíɓáŋɔ̀n (iɓaŋíɓáŋɔ̀nɨ-) *v.* to be awkward, clumsy, uncoordinated (in movement or speech). See also *betsínón*.

iɓatɛs (iɓatɛsí-) *1 v.* to block, deflect, knock back, parry. *2 v.* to hamper, handicap, hinder, impede, stymie. See also *ikiɛs*.

iɓátésukɔta mɛná[ɛ] *v.* to digress, sidetrack a discussion.

iɓatíɓátés (iɓatíɓátésɨ-) *1 v.* to block, deflect, knock back, or parry repeatedly. *2 v.* to hamper, handicap, hinder, impede, or stymie repeatedly.

iɓatíɓátɔ̀n (iɓatíɓátɔ̀nɨ̀-) *v.* to be hampered, handicapped, hindered.

iɓátísa (<iɓátíseés) *v.*

iɓátíseés (iɓátíseesí-/iɓátísa-) *v.* to dunk, baptize.

iɓɛ́ɓɛ́ (<iɓɛ́ɓɔ́ɔ̀n) *v.*

iɓɛ́ɓɛɛsuƙɔt[a] (iɓɛ́ɓɛɛsuƙɔtí-) *v.* to lay (eggs).

iɓɛ́ɓɛ́ètɔ̀n (iɓɛ́ɓɛ́ètɔ̀nɨ̀-) *v.* to hatch out (of chicks). See also *ɓeƙétón*.

iɓɛ́ɓɛ́lés (iɓɛ́ɓɛ́lésɨ́-) *v.* to split into pieces.

iɓɛ́ɓɔ́ɔ̀n (iɓɛ́ɓɔ́ɔ̀nɨ̀-/iɓɛ́ɓɛ́-) *v.* to hatch (of chicks).

iɓɛkíɓékés (iɓɛkíɓékésɨ́-) *v.* to break or snap off (e.g. dry sticks).

iɓέlέ (<iɓέlɔ́ɔ̀n) *v.*

iɓέléánón (iɓέléánónì-) *v.* to be impetuous, impulsive.

iɓéléés (iɓéléésí-) *1 v.* to overturn, roll or turn over. *2 v.* to alter, change, transform. See also *bukures* and *iɓélúƙéés*.

iɓéléésuƙota asɨ́ *v.* to change one's direction, turn oneself around.

iɓéléetés (iɓéléetésí-) *v.* to overturn, roll or turn over.

iɓéléìmètòn (iɓéléìmètònì-) *1 v.* to overturn, roll or turn over (on its own). *2 v.* to change, transform. See also *iɓékúkáìmètòn*.

iɓeliɓélésa tódà[e] *v.* to change statements or the story.

iɓélɔ́ɔ̀n (iɓélɔ́ɔ̀nɨ̀-/iɓέlέ-) *v.* to be impetuous, impulsive.

iɓélúƙá (<iɓélúƙéés) *v.*

iɓélúƙáìmètòn (iɓélúƙáìmètònì-) *v.* to overturn, turn over (on its own). See also *iɓéléìmètòn*.

iɓélúƙéés (iɓélúƙéésí-/iɓélúƙá-) *v.* to overturn, turn over, upset. See also *bukures* and *iɓéléés*.

iɓɛ́rɔ́ánón (iɓɛ́rɔ́ánónì-) *v.* to be energetic, hard-working, industrious.

iɓɛsíɓésés (iɓɛsíɓésésɨ́-) *v.* to break up into small pieces (like sticks for kindling).

iɓíléròn (iɓíléròní-) *1 v.* to be forgotten, misplaced. *2 v.* to be baffled, confused, perplexed. See also *gwèlòn*.

iɓíléronuƙot[a] (iɓíléronuƙotí-) *v.* to become forgotten or misplaced.

iɓilíɓílésá asɨ́ *v.* to keep turning oneself over (e.g. in bed at night).

iɓɨ́ɔ́n (iɓɨ́ɔ́nì-) *v.* to shart: defecate unintentionally while passing gas.

iɓitsíɓítsés (iɓitsíɓítsésɨ́-) *v.* to struggle or wriggle into (an opening).

iɓóɓólés (iɓóɓólésí-) *v.* to chip or pull (bark) off in pieces (rather than strips).

iɓóɓóŋètòn (iɓóɓóŋètònì-) *v.* to come back, return, turn around this way. See also *itétón*.

iɓóɓóŋòn (iɓóɓóŋòní-) *v.* to go back, return, turn around.

iɓóɓórés (iɓóɓórésí-) *v.* to core or hollow out.

iɓóɓórós (iɓóɓórósí-) *v.* to be cored or hollowed out.

iɓokes (iɓokesí-) *v.* to jiggle, shake.

iɓókésuƙot[a] (iɓókésuƙotí-) *v.* to shake or throw off.

iɓoletés (iɓoletésí-) *v.* to covenant, promise.

iɓolíɓólés (iɓolíɓólésí-) *v.* to plunder, ransack, rifle through.

iɓolíɓólésuƙot[a] (iɓolíɓólésuƙotí-) *v.* to plunder, ransack, rifle through.

iɓólínós (iɓólínósí-) *v.* to enter a covenant with each other, promise each other.

iɓólínósa na séà[e] *v.* blood covenant.

iɓólóɲés (iɓólóɲésí-) *v.* to hole, make a hole in.

iɓɔ́lɔ́tsɛ́s (iɓɔ́lɔ́tsɛ́sí-) *v.* to strip off (e.g. strips of sisal or tree bark). See also *iɓɔtɛs*.

iɓɔníɓɔ́nés (iɓɔníɓɔ́nésí-) *v.* to caress, stroke afffectionately.

iɓoníɓóniés (iɓoníɓóniesí-) *v.* to caress, stroke affectionately.

iɓóŋón (iɓóŋóní-) *v.* to do again, repeat.

iɓóótánón (iɓóótánóní-) *v.* to be hermitic: living in solitude.

iɓɔtɛs (iɓɔtɛsí-) *v.* to strip off (e.g. strips of sisal or tree bark). See also *iɓɔ́lɔ́tsɛ́s*.

iɓótóŋés (iɓótóŋésí-) *v.* to lock, shut up.

iɓótóŋésá aká[e] *v.* to keep one's mouth shut, shut up (e.g. in anger).

Iɓùɓù (Iɓùɓùù-) *n.* December: month of clearing. See also *Raraan*.

iɓúɓués (iɓúɓuésí-) *v.* to clear off/out (uncut brush for a garden).

iɓues (iɓuesí-) *v.* to sear (e.g. fresh animal hides).

iɓúlíánón (iɓúlíánóní-) *v.* to be destitute, dirt-poor.

iɓúlíánóníàm (iɓúlíánóní-àmà-) *pl.* **iɓúlíánoniik**[a]. *n.* destitute, dirt-poor person (who does not work).

iɓúŋá (<iɓúŋéés) *v.*

iɓúŋéés (iɓúŋéésí-/iɓúŋá-) *v.* to flog, lash, scourge.

iɓúŋón (iɓúŋóní-) *v.* to be in a hurry, hurry, rush.

iɓures (iɓuresí-) *v.* to replant (a garden a second time in a single year).

iɓurɛtésíàm (iɓurɛtésí-àmà-) *pl.* **iɓurɛtésíik**[a]. *n.* attractive or vivacious person. *Lit.* 'warm-person'.

iɓúrétɔ̀n (iɓúrétɔ̀nì-) *1 v.* to warm up. *2 v.* to arouse, incite desire.

iɓurímétòn (iɓurímétònì-) *1 v.* to warm up. *2 v.* to be aroused, turned on, worked up (sexually).

iɓúrítésuƙot[a] (iɓúrítésuƙotí-) *v.* to make warm, warm up.

iɓúrón (iɓúróní-) *v.* to be warm.

iɓurúɓúrɔ̀n (iɓurúɓúrɔ̀nì-) *v.* to do quickly, hasten, hurry.

iɓutes (iɓutesí-) *v.* to atone for, expiate.

iɓutsɛs (iɓutsɛsí-) *v.* to elude, evade, get away from.

iɓutsɛtésá así *v.* to evade, elude, get away from.

iɓutsúmétòn (iɓutsúmétònì-) *v.* to escape, evade, get away.

iɓutúɓútés (iɓutúɓútésí-) *v.* to dump or shake out (of a container).

iɓutúɓútòn (iɓutúɓútònì-) *1 v.* to defecate frequently (of children). *2 v.* to be obese, overweight.

iɓútúŋɔ̀n (iɓútúŋɔ̀nì-) *v.* to pout, sulk. See also *imutúmútòn*.

iɓuyákòn (iɓuyákònì-) *v.* to enter puberty, mature sexually (of boys).

iɓwates (iɓwatesí-) *v.* to jerk, pull, yank. See also *ipoles*.

iɓwátésuƙot[a] (iɓwátésuƙotí-) *v.* to shove away.

iɓwatetés (iɓwatetésí-) *v.* to pull forcefully, yank over (this way).

Icéám (Icé-ámà-) *pl.* **Ik**[a]. *n.* Ik person.

Icédìkw[a] (Icé-dìkwà-) *pl.* **Icédikwitín**. *n.* Ik dance.

Icédìyw[a] (Icé-dìyò-) *n.* Ik tribe.

Icéén (Icé-ɛnɨ-) *n.* Ik culture and/or language.

Icého (Icé-hòò-) *pl.* **Icéhoík**ᵃ. *n.* traditional beehive-shaped grass hut once the primary dwelling of the Ik people. *Lit.* 'Ik-hut'.

Icékíjᵃ (Icé-kíjà-) *n.* Ikland, Ik country or county.

Icémóríɗᵃ (Icé-móríɗó-) *n.* cowpeas. *Lit.* 'Ik-beans'.

Icémóríɗókàkᵃ (Icé-móríɗó-kàkà-) *n.* cowpea leaves (which the Ik eat as a vegetable). *Lit.* 'Ik-bean leaves'.

Icénáƙáf (Icé-náƙáfʉ-) *n.* Ik language, the Ik tongue. *Lit.* 'Ik-tongue'. See also *Icétôd*ᵃ.

Icénánès (Icénánèsì-) *n.* Iklikeness, Ikness.

icéɲjeés (icéɲjeesí-) *v.* to change.

icéɲjèimètòn (icéɲjèimètònì-) *v.* to change.

Icéódòwᵃ (Icé-ódòʉ-) *n.* Ik day: a general Ik gathering held every January in Kamion to celebrate Ik identity and discuss challenges.

Icétôdᵃ (Icé-tódà-) *n.* Ik language. *Lit.* 'Ik-speech/talk'. See also *Icénáƙáf*.

icɔ́ɲáimetona ikáᵉ *v.* to be baffled, confused, perplexed.

ɨdadamɛ́s (ɨdadamɛ́sɨ-) *v.* to fondle, grab, grope. See also *tárábes*.

ɨdadamɔ́s (ɨdadamɔ́sɨ-) *v.* to be groping (e.g. walking in darkness or on a slope).

ídèm (ídèmè-) *pl.* **ídèmìk**ᵃ. *1 n.* serpent, snake. *2 n.* intestinal worm.

ídemecɛmɛ́r (ídeme-cɛmɛ́rɨ-) *n.* small plant species with yellow flowers; its roots, when roasted and ground, are used to treat snakebites. *Lit.* 'snake-herb'. Also called *ídèmèdàkw*ᵃ.

ídèmèdàkwᵃ (ídèmè-dàkʉ-) *n.* small plant species with yellow flowers; its roots, when roasted and ground, are used to treat snakebites. *Lit.* 'snake-plant'. Also called *ídemecɛmɛ́r*.

ídèmèìm (ídèmè-ìmà-) *pl.* **ídemewik**ᵃ. *n.* earthworm. *Lit.* 'snake-child'.

ídèmèkwàywᵃ (ídèmè-kwàyò-) *pl.* **ídemekwaitín**. *n.* snake fang.

ídemeƙidzɛ́s (ídeme-ƙidzɛ́sɨ-) *n.* snakebite.

ídèmètàtᵃ (ídèmè-tàtì-) *n.* snake venom. *Lit.* 'snake-spit'.

ídirés (ídirésí-) *v.* to smack.

ídocɛmɛ́r (ído-cɛmɛ́rɨ-) *n.* herb that is soaked in water with hot quartz and applied as a treatment to women's swollen breasts. *Lit.* 'breast-herb'. *Evolvus alsinoides*.

ídoeɗᵃ (ído-eɗí-) *pl.* **ídoeɗitín**. *n.* breast areola. *Lit.* 'breast-kernel'.

ídoho (ído-hoó-) *pl.* **ídohoík**ᵃ. *n.* udder. *Lit.* 'milk-housing'.

ídòkàkᵃ (ídò-kàkà-) *n.* milk-leaf: a shrub species whose bark fibers are used for tying and whose large leaves are used to wrap meat, honeycomb, or mira (khat); livestock also eat this plant. *Abutilon sp.*

ídòkàtsᵃ (ídò-kàtsì-) *pl.* **ídokatsín**. *n.* nipple. *Lit.* 'breast-tip'.

ídòkwàywᵃ (ídò-kwàyò-) *pl.* **ídokwaitín**. *n.* milk tooth.

ídoɲeɗeké (ído-ɲeɗekéè-) *n.* mastitis. *Lit.* 'breast-disease'.

ídulés (ídulésí-) *v.* to commingle, commix, mix in (e.g. contaminating a liquid or refreshing beer by adding more porridge).

ɨdulɨdulɛ́s (ɨdulɨdulɛ́sɨ-) *1 v.* to pour out noisily (from a small opening). *2 v.* to rub vigorously (e.g. when one is hit on the body, or to soften up a fruit).

íduliduĺesa tódàᵉ *v.* to murmur, mutter.

íduludulés (íduludulesí-) *v.* to commingle, commix, mix in (e.g. by kneading or mashing).

ídulumona cué *v.* to flow in waves (of water).

ídurés (ídurésí-) *v.* to bombard, pelt, shower, spray (with projectiles).

ídurésá tódàᵉ *v.* to barrage or bombard with words.

îdwᵃ (ídò-) *pl.* íditín. *1 n.* breast. *2 n.* teat. *3 n.* milk. *4 n.* young maize kernels filled with a milky white liquid. *5 n.* sebum: whitish oily substance exuded from skin pores.

ídwà nì ɓàr *n.* sour milk.

ídzànànès (ídzànànèsì-) *n.* affluence, prosperity, success.

ídzès (ídzèsì-) *1 v.* to discharge, emit, expel. *2 v.* to fire, shoot.

ídzesa así *v.* to shoot across/over, whiz by (e.g. a shooting star or a person dashing somewhere).

ídzesuƙotᵃ (ídzesuƙotí-) *1 v.* to discharge, emit, expel. *2 v.* to fire, shoot, take a shot at.

ídziidziés (ídziidziesí-) *1 v.* to discharge, emit, or expel continuously. *2 v.* to fire or shoot repeatedly.

ídzòn (ídzònì-) *v.* to discharge, drain, emit, run out.

iɗá (<iɗɛɛs) *v.*

iɗaarés (iɗaarésí-) *v.* to ambush, lie in wait for, waylay. See also *taɗapes.*

iɗafes (iɗafɛsí-) *1 v.* to slap. *2 v.* to clap.

iɗafesa kwétìkàᵋ *v.* to clap the hands.

iɗafesa sáwátìkàᵋ *v.* to slap the shoulders.

iɗáfɛsuƙotᵃ (iɗáfɛsuƙotí-) *1 v.* to slap. *2 v.* to beat back/down, repel, subdue, suppress.

iɗáfɛsuƙota así *v.* to be beat back, repelled, subdued, suppressed.

iɗafiés (iɗafiesí-) *v.* to slap around.

iɗáíƙotᵃ (<iɗɛ́ɛsuƙotᵃ) *v.*

iɗáínɔs (iɗáínɔsí-) *v.* to murder each other.

iɗaiyes (iɗaiyesí-) *1 v.* to hide repeatedly, keep hiding. *2 v.* to keep murdering, murder repeatedly.

iɗakᵃ (iɗakí-) *pl.* iɗákíkᵃ. *n.* small plant species whose salty-tasting leaves are boiled as a vegetable or mixed in with meal mush or edible termites. *Portulaca quadrifida.*

iɗakés (iɗakɛsí-) *v.* to lack, miss.

iɗákɔ́n (iɗákɔ́nì-) *v.* to be deficient, insufficient, lacking.

iɗalɛs (iɗalɛsí-) *v.* to spring, trigger, trip (a trap).

iɗáĺesuƙota así *v.* to spring, trip (of a trap).

iɗámɔ́n (iɗámɔ́nì-) *v.* to go for a walk.

iɗaɲɛtés (iɗaɲɛtésí-) *v.* to accumulate, amass. See also *torítéetés.*

iɗaŋíɗáŋés (iɗaŋíɗáŋésí-) *v.* to knead, press repeatedly.

iɗaŋíɗáŋòn (iɗaŋíɗáŋònì-) *v.* to persist, persevere, press on.

iɗásón (iɗásónì-) *v.* to be sneaky, stealthy.

Iɗátáŋér (Iɗátá-ŋérá-) *n.* August: the month when mingling sticks are heard banging on cooking pots (due to the presence of food from freshly harvested gardens). *Lit.* 'mingling sticks are banging'. See also *Diwamúce* and *Lósúbán*.

iɗates (iɗatesí-) v. to bang on, pound (e.g. a hammer on metal).

iɗébetés (iɗébetésí-) v. to amass or accumulate one-by-one.

iɗéɗέ (<iɗéɗɔ́ɔn) v.

iɗéɗéŋés (iɗéɗéŋésí-) v. to necrotize: eat away body tissue.

iɗéɗɔ́ɔn (iɗéɗɔ́ɔnì-/iɗéɗέ-) v. to lie on one's back, recline, repose.

iɗeɛs (iɗeɛsí-/iɗá-) 1 v. to conceal, hide. 2 v. to bump off, get rid of, murder, off.

iɗéέsukɔt[a] (iɗéέsukɔtí-/iɗáíkɔt-) 1 v. to conceal, hide away. 2 v. to bump off, get rid of, kill off.

iɗéέtɔn (iɗéέtɔnì-) v. to jump out or up, launch, spring (e.g. a grasshopper or snake, or popcorn or pumpkin seeds when heated up).

iɗeiɗéés (iɗeiɗéέsí-) 1 v. to rap or tap repeatedly. 2 v. to burn around the edge of, make a firebreak on. See also *iɫɛrílérés*.

iɗéke (iɗékèè-) pl. iɗékèìk[a]. n. aircraft, airplane, plane (with propellers).

iɗɛmɛs (iɗɛmɛsí-) v. to bewitch by staring at with the 'evil eye'.

iɗenes (iɗenesí-) v. to borrow, credit, take on credit.

iɗenetés (iɗenetésí-) v. to borrow, credit, take on credit. See also *wáánɛtés*.

iɗeŋɛs (iɗeŋɛsí-) 1 v. to pack down, tamp (e.g. cement or dirt). 2 v. to cover, scour, or search (an area).

iɗeŋiɗéŋés (iɗeŋiɗéŋésí-) v. to pack down or tamp repeatedly (e.g. cement or dirt floor).

iɗéŋímètòn (iɗéŋímètònì-) 1 v. to become packed or tamped down. 2

v. to be covered, scoured, searched over thoroughly.

iɗέɔ́n (iɗέɔ́nì-) v. to be jumping out/up, springing, striking (e.g. a grasshopper or snake, or pumpkin seeds in a pan).

iɗɛpɛs (iɗɛpɛsí-) v. to pick up. See also *dumés*.

iɗɛpɛtés (iɗɛpɛtésí-) v. to pick up. See also *dumɛtés*.

iɗɛpíɗépés (iɗɛpíɗépésí-) v. to pick up (many things).

iɗɛpíɗépɛtés (iɗɛpíɗépɛtésí-) v. to pick up (many things).

iɗɛrɛs (iɗɛrɛsí-) 1 v. to scatter, strew (e.g. seeds). 2 v. to bead, decorate with beads (e.g. gourds or hides).

iɗɛríɗérés (iɗɛríɗérésí-) v. to scatter around, strew about.

iɗɛríɗérɔ́s (iɗɛríɗérɔ́sí-) v. to be scattered around, strewn about. See also *apétépétánón*.

iɗɛrɔs (iɗɛrɔsí-) 1 v. to be scattered, strewn. 2 v. to be beaded, decorated with beads. See also *kazaanón*.

iɗɛtɛs (iɗɛtɛsí-) v. to cut, mow, or slash (vegetation).

iɗiɗɛs (iɗiɗɛsí-) v. to cut into strips.

iɗíɗíwés (iɗíɗíwésí-) v. to clear a narrow furrow or path in.

iɗíiɗés (iɗíiɗésí-) v. to swish, swoosh.

iɗíkétòn (iɗíkétònì-) 1 v. to clot, coagulate, congeal, solidify, thicken. 2 v. to escalate, intensify.

iɗíkílɔ̀n (iɗíkílɔ̀nì-) v. to be obstinate, stubborn.

iɗikitetés (iɗikitetésí-) 1 v. to clot, coagulate, congeal, solidify, thicken. 2 v. to esclate, intensify.

idíkón (idíkónì-) *1 v.* to be clotted, coagulated, congealed, solidifed, thickened. *2 v.* to be intense.

idiles (idilesí-) *1 v.* to gain ground or make headway on. *2 v.* to work on/over: slang for clobbering somebody.

idiles (idilesí-) *v.* to bundle, jam, pack.

idílón (idílónì-) *v.* to get a headstart (e.g. on the day by leaving early).

idimés (idimésí-) *1 v.* to fix, make, repair. *2 v.* to organize, prepare, ready.

idimésá así *v.* to sit decently (by arranging your legs and clothes modestly).

idimésá buƙú[i] *v.* to arrange a marriage.

idimésá ìùmà[ɛ] *v.* to arrange a marital engagement.

idimésíàm (idimésí-àmà-) *pl.* **idimésíik**[a]. *1 n.* fixer, mechanic. *2 n.* artist, creator, inventor.

idimésón (idimésónì-) *v.* to be prepared, ready.

idimésúƙot[a] (idimésúƙotí-) *1 v.* to fix, make, repair. *2 v.* to organize, prepare, ready.

idimɛtés (idimɛtésí-) *1 v.* to create, make. *2 v.* to fix, repair. See also *iroketes* and *tɔsubɛs*.

idimɛtésíàm (idimɛtésí-àmà-) *pl.* **idimɛtésíik**[a]. *n.* creator, maker.

idimiés (idimiesí-) *v.* to organize, plan, prepare, ready.

idimiesá así *v.* to prepare or ready oneself.

idimiesíàm (idimiesí-àmà-) *pl.* **idimiesíik**[a]. *1 n.* organizer. *2 n.* usher.

idimiesúƙot[a] (idimiesúƙotí-) *v.* to organize, plan, prepare, ready.

idímón (idímónì-) *v.* to speak a foreign language, talk foreignly.

idimós (idimósí-) *1 v.* to be fixed, made, repaired. *2 v.* to be organized, prepared, tidy.

idimɔtós (idimɔtósí-) *1 v.* to be created, made. *2 n.* creature.

idimɔtósá kwètìk[ɔ] *v.* to be hand-crafted, handmade.

idimɔtósá ròɓ[o] *v.* to be artificial, man-made.

idíɲón (idíɲónì-) *v.* to grunt, strain.

idíŋón (idíŋónì-) *1 v.* to be narrow. *2 v.* to be tight (of a space, e.g. inside a vehicle).

idíón (idíónì-) *v.* to drop down (of seeds from a dried out plant pod).

idíóna iká[e] *v.* migraine headache.

idipes (idipesí-) *v.* to dip into (e.g. a container, fire, etc.).

idírírɔ̀n (idírírɔ̀nì-) *v.* to move straight ahead.

idírítésuƙot[a] (idírítésuƙotí-) *v.* to straighten, unbend.

idírón (idírónì-) *1 v.* to be or move in a straight line. *2 v.* to aim, take aim.

iditsɛs (iditsɛsí-) *v.* to cane, lash, whip.

idóbès (idóbèsí-) *v.* to arrange, order. See also *inábès* and *itíbès*.

idóbetés (idóbetésí-) *v.* to arrange, order.

idóɗóés (idóɗóésí-) *v.* to cook up, rustle up (a light meal or snack).

idóɗókánón (idóɗókánónì-) *v.* to be heaped, piled or stacked up.

idóɗókés (idóɗókésí-) *v.* to heap, pile, or stack on top of.

idoes (idoesí-) *v.* to drop into (e.g. food in the mouth).

idokes (idokesí-) *v.* to add on top.

idókóliés (idókóliesí-) *v.* to choose, pick, select (e.g. fruit that is ripe).

iɗolíɗólés (iɗolíɗólésí-) *v.* to dot, speckle, stipple.

iɗolíɗólòn (iɗolíɗólònì-) *1 v.* to be dotted, speckled, spotted. *2 v.* to get rusty.

iɗomes (iɗomesí-) *v.* to do in intervals, intersperse.

iɗómíòn (iɗómíònì-) *v.* to be alternated, in intervals, interspersed.

iɗómóés (iɗómóésí-) *v.* to toss in the mouth one by one.

iɗɔ́nɔ́n (iɗɔ́nɔ́nɨ̀-) *v.* to dribble, drip continously. See also *ts'òlòn*.

iɗoŋes (iɗoŋesí-) *v.* to punish (often by beating or caning).

iɗɔŋíɗɔ́ŋés (iɗɔŋíɗɔ́ŋésɨ́-) *v.* to knock or rap on (esp. wood, e.g. a beehive). See also *ikoŋíkóŋés*.

iɗɔ̀r (iɗɔ̀rɔ̀-) *n.* cultivation done early in the farming season.

iɗɔ́rɛ́ʉkɔt[a] (iɗɔ́rɛ́ʉkɔtɨ́-) *v.* to cultivate early in the farming season.

iɗoses (iɗosesí-) *v.* to crush, pound (often between stones, e.g. the spermatic cords of an animal during castration).

iɗotíɗótòn (iɗotíɗótònì-) *1 v.* to hop along. *2 v.* to appear randomly at different places.

iɗótón (iɗótónì-) *1 v.* to bound, hop, jump, leap, spring. *2 v.* to bounce or glance off, rebound, ricochet.

iɗɔtsɛs (iɗɔtsɛsɨ́-) *v.* to belabor, press, push.

iɗɔ́tsɔ́n (iɗɔ́tsɔ́nɨ̀-) *v.* to jam, stick (e.g. of a gun).

iɗúkóós (iɗúkóósí-) *v.* to stay put, stick around one place.

iɗupes (iɗupesí-) *v.* to follow, stick to, trace (specifically landscape features like rivers, ridges, or roads).

iɗúzòn (iɗúzònì-) *v.* to flee, fly, or run away (as a group).

iɗyates (iɗyatesí-) *v.* to blend, combine, mix. See also *iɲales*.

iɛ́bɛ̀s (iɛ́bɛ̀sɨ̀-) *1 v.* to bump, glance, sideswipe. *2 v.* to go by, pass via, swing by. *3 v.* to give a lift or ride to, pick up and take. See also *toyeres*.

iɛ́bɛsʉkɔt[a] (iɛ́bɛsʉkɔtɨ́-) *1 v.* to bump, glance, swipe. *2 v.* to go by, pass via, swing by. *3 v.* to give a lift or ride to, pick up and take.

iɛ́bɛtés (iɛ́bɛtésí-) *1 v.* to bump, glance, swipe. *2 v.* to come by, pass here via, swing by. *3 v.* to give a ride to, pick up and bring. See also *tɔmɛɛtés*.

iɛ́ɓɛ́tɔ̀n (iɛ́ɓɛ́tɔ̀nì-) *1 v.* to become cold. *2 v.* to become ashamed or embarrassed.

iɛ́ɓítésʉkɔt[a] (iɛ́ɓítésʉkɔtɨ́-) *v.* to make cold.

iɛ́ɓítésʉkɔta gúró[e] *v.* to calm or cool down emotionally.

iɛ́ɓítɛtés (iɛ́ɓítɛtésí-) *v.* to douse, soak, souse (e.g. flour in a pot).

iɛ́ɓɔ́n (iɛ́ɓɔ́nɨ̀-) *1 v.* to be cold. *2 v.* to be weak. *3 v.* to be meek, mild. *4 v.* to be frigid: sexually unresponsive.

iɛ́ɓɔ́na kíjá[e] *v.* cold weather.

iɛ́ɓɔ́nʉkɔt[a] (iɛ́ɓɔ́nʉkɔtɨ́-) *1 v.* to become cold. *2 v.* to clear up (of sickness).

iɛƙás (iɛƙásɨ́-) *n.* distance, farness.

iɛƙiɛƙ[a] (iɛƙiɛƙɨ́-) *n.* vine species whose hollow yellow seedpods children like to use as rattles or blow as whistles (with the seeds inside). *Crotalaria lachnocarpoides*.

iɛƙíɛ́ƙɔ̀n (iɛƙíɛ́ƙɔ̀nì-) *v.* to be slightly distant or far.

iɛ́ƙímɔ́s (iɛ́ƙímɔ́sɨ́-) *v.* to be far from each other.

iɛkítésʉkɔtᵃ (iɛkítésʉkɔtɨ́-) *v.* to distance, take far away.

i̱ɛkɔ̀n (i̱ɛkɔ̀nɨ̀-) *v.* to be distant, far.

iɛmɛs (iɛmɛsɨ́-) *v.* to lead slowly and gently.

iɛmɛtés (iɛmɛtésɨ́-) *v.* to bring slowly and gently.

iɛmɨ́ɛmɛ́s (iɛmɨ́ɛmɛ́sɨ́-) *v.* to mangle, mutilate.

iɛmɔ́n (iɛmɔ́nɨ̀-) *v.* to walk slowly (e.g. when sick). See also *isɔ́wɔ́ɔ̀n*.

iɛ́nétɔ̀n (iɛ́nétɔ̀nɨ̀-) *v.* to discuss, have a talk, talk.

iɛnítɛtés (iɛnítɛtésɨ́-) *v.* to draw out, elicit speech, get to talk. See also *tóítetés*.

iɛnɔ́n (iɛnɔ́nɨ̀-) *v.* to converse, discuss, speak, talk. See also *tódòn*.

i̱ɛŋààwᵃ (i̱ɛŋà-àwà-) *pl.* iɛŋaawíkᵃ. *n.* resting place.

iɛŋɔ́n (iɛŋɔ́nɨ̀-) *1 v.* to breathe, respire. *2 v.* to rest. See also *sʉ̀pɔ̀n*.

iɛŋɔ́nʉkɔtᵃ (iɛŋɔ́nʉkɔtɨ́-) *1 v.* to catch one's breath. *2 v.* to rest up, take a break.

iɛpɛs (iɛpɛsɨ́-) *v.* to ease: place slowly and carefully.

iɛpɛsa asɨ́ *v.* to ease over: move slowly and carefully.

iɛpɛsa asɨ́ɛ ámákᵉ *v.* to ease up on someone.

iɛpésʉkɔtᵃ (iɛpésʉkɔtɨ́-) *v.* to ease off with: move away with slowly and carefully.

iɛpésʉkɔta asɨ́ *v.* to ease off: move away slowly and carefully.

iɛpɛtés (iɛpɛtésɨ́-) *1 v.* to ease down: put down slowly and carefully. *2 v.* to abduct, kidnap, smuggle.

iɛpɔ́nʉkɔtᵃ (iɛpɔ́nʉkɔtɨ́-) *v.* to ease off: move away slowly and carefully.

iɛ́s (iɛ́sɨ̀-) *v.* to clear or hoe (grass, leaving only soil). See also *irɛɲes*.

iɛtés (iɛtésɨ́-) *v.* to defend, rescue, save. See also *hodés*.

iɛtésá asɨ́ *v.* to save oneself.

iɛtésá isɨ́ítésʉ́ *v.* to acquit, clear, exonerate. *Lit.* 'to save from accusation'.

iɛtésíàm (iɛtésɨ́-àmà-) *pl.* iɛtésíikᵃ. *n.* defender, rescuer, savior.

ifáfáɲés (ifáfáɲésɨ́-) *v.* to scramble, stir around (e.g. coals to put out fire, or grain spread out to dry).

ifáfúkés (ifáfúkésɨ́-) *v.* to gobble down or wolf down. See also *ŋɔfés*.

ifáfúkós (ifáfúkósɨ́-) *v.* to be comatose, unconscious.

ifalífálés (ifalífálésɨ́-) *v.* to chase, drive, impel (e.g. animals, wild or domestic).

ifátésʉkɔtᵃ (ifátésʉkɔtɨ́-) *v.* to check on/out, keep an eye on, monitor.

ifédélés (ifédélésɨ́-) *v.* to scramble, scurry, or shinny up.

ifɛlɛsa asɨ́ *1 v.* to glide, slide, slip (like an adze off of wood). *2 v.* to slip or sneak away/off.

ifélónʉkɔtᵃ (ifélónʉkɔtɨ́-) *v.* to glide, skid, slide (e.g. on one's buttocks).

ifitífités (ifitífitésɨ́-) *v.* to cut bluntly, saw away at.

ifɔɛs (ifɔɛsɨ́-) *v.* to drag, grate, scrape (along the ground). See also *fɔ́fɔ́tés*.

ifɔɛsa asɨ́ *v.* to drag oneself.

ifófóés (ifófóésɨ́-) *n.* taboo of eating the year's new crops prematurely, before the culturally appointed time.

ifúkúfukés (ifúkúfukésɨ́-) *v.* to snort or snuffle at loudly.

ifúlón (ifúlónɨ̀-) *v.* to go at dawn.

ifulúfúlòn (ifulúfúlònì-) *1 v.* to be violent. *2 v.* to have explosive diarrhea. See also *irépíánón*.

ɨgaɗɛ́s (ɨgaɗɛ́sɨ́-) *v.* to displease, dissatisfy.

ɨgatsɨgatsɛ́s (ɨgatsɨgatsɛ́sɨ́-) *v.* to chink or clink against (e.g. rocks in soil).

ígòmòn (ígòmònì-) *1 v.* to bark, woof. *2 v.* to bluster, boast, brag.

ɨgɔɲɛ́s (ɨgɔɲɛ́sɨ́-) *v.* to cater or provide for, supply (e.g. people working your garden whom you had already paid in beer earlier).

ígorɛ́s (ígorɛ́sɨ́-) *v.* to cross over, go across, pass over. Also pronounced as *górɛ́s*.

ígorɛ́súƙot[a] (ígorɛ́súƙotɨ́-) *1 v.* to cross over, go across, pass over. *2 v.* to give across/over the top (e.g. of a fence).

ígoriɛ́s (ígoriɛ́sɨ́-) *1 v.* to cross over, go across, or pass over repeatedly. *2 v.* to leapfrog: jump over repeatedly. Also pronounced as *góriɛ́s*.

ígoriɛsá simá[e] *v.* to jump or skip rope.

ɨgɔ̀rɔ̀bɔ̀n (ɨgɔ̀rɔ̀bɔ̀nɨ̀-) *v.* to bound, leap, spring.

ɨgʉjɛ́s (ɨgʉjɛ́sɨ́-) *v.* to guzzle. Also pronounced as *ágʉjɛ́s*.

ɨgʉjʉgʉjɛ́s (ɨgʉjʉgʉjɛ́sɨ́-) *v.* to rinse, swish (the mouth). See also *ɨmʉ́mʉ́jɛ́s*.

ígujugujɛ́s (ígujugujɛ́sɨ́-) *v.* to fiddle with, twiddle.

ígujugujɛ́sa tódà[e] *v.* to repeat a point of discussion endlessly. *Lit.* 'to twiddle (one's) talk'.

ígùjùgùjòn (ígùjùgùjònì-) *v.* to be busy, preoccupied (e.g. in the house or in the garden).

ígulajitetɛ́s (ígulajitetɛ́sɨ́-) *v.* to boil, make bubble.

ígùlàjòn (ígùlàjònì-) *1 v.* to boil, bubble. *2 v.* to churn, roil. See also *wádòn*.

ígùm (ígùmà-) *pl.* **ígùmɨ̀k**[a]. *n.* unripe maize (with small milky kernels). See also *kárubú* and *paɲárʉ́tɛ̀*.

ɨgwɨgwɨjɛ́s (ɨgwɨgwɨjɛ́sɨ́-) *v.* to beautify, embellish.

ɨgwɨ̀jɨ̀rɔ̀n (ɨgwɨ̀jɨ̀rɔ̀nɨ̀-) *v.* to leave in a huff, storm off. See also *gwaitón*.

iíɗón (iíɗónì-) *v.* to clench one's buttocks.

ɨɨ́ɗɔ́n (ɨɨ́ɗɔ́nɨ̀-) *v.* to disappear, vanish. See also *wɨdɨ́mɔ́nʉƙot*[a].

iikííkɛ́s (iikííkɛ́sɨ́-) *v.* to rock back and forth (like a tree loose in its hole, a rock rooted in the soil, or one's body in dancing). May also be spelled as *iyikíyíkɛ́s*. See also *iukúúkɛ́s*.

ijákáánón (ijákáánónì-) *v.* to be rich, wealthy, well-off.

ijaƙɨjáƙɛ́s (ijaƙɨjáƙɛ́sɨ́-) *v.* to lap up.

ijárɔ́n (ijárɔ́nì-) *v.* to be dazed, in shock, stunned (e.g. over bad news). See also *jarámétòn*.

Íjéekw[a] (Íjéekú-) *n.* a personal name.

ijɛ́ɛ́lɔ̀n (ijɛ́ɛ́lɔ̀nɨ̀-) *v.* to grow underground (of roots).

ijɛ́mɨ́tɛ́sʉƙot[a] (ijɛ́mɨ́tɛ́sʉƙotɨ́-) *v.* to hush, quiet down, shut up, silence.

ijɛ́mɔ́n (ijɛ́mɔ́nɨ̀-) *v.* to be hushed, quiet, silent, still.

ijɛ́mɔ́nʉƙot[a] (ijɛ́mɔ́nʉƙotɨ́-) *v.* to become still, calm down, hush up, quiet down, shut up.

ijɨ́ɨ́lɔ̀n (ijɨ́ɨ́lɔ̀nɨ̀-) *v.* to move in single file.

ijɨ́ɨ́rɛ́s (ijɨ́ɨ́rɛ́sɨ́-) *v.* to pour to the last drop.

ijɨ́ɨ́rɛ́sʉƙot[a] (ijɨ́ɨ́rɛ́sʉƙotɨ́-) *1 v.* to pour out to the last drop. *2 v.* to chug, down, drink to the last drop. See also *gégès*.

ijilɛtés (ijilɛtésɨ-) *v.* to cream or skim off (e.g. cream from liquid milk).

ijíŋáánón (ijíŋáánónì-) *v.* to be dull, sluggish, torpid.

ijiwɛs (ijiwɛsɨ-) *v.* to filter, strain. See also *itiwɛs*.

ijokes (ijokesɨ-) *v.* to give, leave to, pass off/on, transfer, transmit.

ijokesa mɛnáᵋ *v.* to pass on problems, transmit trouble.

ijókésuƙotᵃ (ijókésuƙotɨ-) *v.* to give, leave to, pass off/on, transfer, transmit.

ijókón (ijókónì-) *v.* to drivel, drool, slaver, slobber.

ijɔƙɨjɔ́ƙɛ́s (ijɔƙɨjɔ́ƙɛ́sɨ-) *v.* to stick in and out repeatedly (e.g. the penis during sexual intercourse or one's finger in and out of mud).

ijɔƙɨjɔ́ƙɛ́sá kwaní *v.* to masturbate (of males).

ijʉkes (ijʉkɛsɨ-) *v.* to push.

ijʉkɛsííka búbùìkàᵉ *n.* obese elders (of long ago). *Lit.* 'pushers of bellies'.

ijúkésʉƙɔtᵃ (ijúkésʉƙɔtɨ-) *v.* to push away.

ijʉketés (ijʉkɛtésɨ-) *1 v.* to pull. *2 v.* to bring.

ijúkítɛtɛs (ijúkítɛtésɨ-) *v.* to make pull.

ijʉkújúkɛ́s (ijʉkújúkɛ́sɨ-) *v.* to goad, push along, spur (e.g. an animal).

ijúkúmiés (ijúkúmiesɨ-) *v.* to push aside brusquely and repeatedly.

ijʉƙújúƙɛ́s (ijʉƙújúƙɛ́sɨ-) *v.* to break apart/up, dismantle, take apart.

ijʉlɛs (ijʉlɛsɨ-) *v.* to flip, switch, turn.

ijʉlɛsa tódàᵉ *v.* to change the subject.

ijʉlɛtés (ijʉlɛtésɨ-) *1 v.* to flip, switch, or turn around/over. *2 v.* to give birth to (a child legs first).

ijʉlɔs (ijʉlɔsɨ-) *v.* to be flipped, switched, turned.

ijúrújúròn (ijúrújúrònì-) *v.* to be downcast, downward (of eyes).

ijúrúròn (ijúrúrònì-) *v.* to be downcast, downward (of eyes or head, e.g. in prayer, deep thought, or timidity).

Ikᵃ (Icé-) *n.* Ik people.

ikᵃ (iká-) *pl.* **ikitín.** *n.* head.

ikáábɛs (ikáábɛsɨ-) *v.* to pick or skim off (e.g. the top of hot food to cool it, or the top layer of termites in a trapping hole). See also *ikákápés*.

ikáburés (ikáburésɨ-) *v.* to enshroud, enwrap, wrap (the body in clothing).

ikáɓóɓánón (ikáɓóɓánónì-) *v.* to be unstable, unsteady: not having good contact with a surface. See also *ɗatólóɲòn*.

ikáɗóés (ikáɗóésɨ-) *v.* to blend, combine, or mix (different kinds of grain). See also *itsɔɓítsóɓés* and *itsulútsúlés*.

ikágwarí (iká-gwarîi-) *n.* crown, pate, top of head, vertex.

ikágwarîikᵉ *n.* midday, noon. *Lit.* 'at the top of the head'.

ikaiká (<ikaiƙéés) *v.*

ikaiƙéés (ikaiƙéésɨ-/ikaiká-) *v.* to flit (from one person or thing to another).

ikáká (<ikákéés) *v.*

ikákáiƙotᵃ (<ikákéésʉƙɔt**ᵃ**) *v.*

ikákápés (ikákápésɨ-) *v.* to pick or skim off (e.g. the top of hot food to cool it, or the top layer of termites in a trapping hole). See also *ikáábɛs*.

ikákéés (ikákéésɨ-/ikáká-) *v.* to separate by shaking (e.g. unground grains from ground ones, or seeds from dirt).

ikákɛ́ɛ́sʉkɔtᵃ (ikákɛ́ɛ́sʉkɔtɨ́-/ ikákáɨkɔt-) *v.* to separate out by shaking (e.g. unground grains from ground ones, or seeds from dirt).

ikálájaránón (ikálájaránónɨ̀-) *v.* to be feckless, inept, irresponsible.

ikálámɛ́s (ikálámɛ́sɨ́-) *v.* to gap, leave gaps in (e.g. when taking big steps, or when sewing in wide passes).

ikámárɛ́s (ikámárɛ́sɨ́-) *v.* to stretch across.

ikamɛs (ikamɛsɨ́-) *v.* to grip, handle, hold. See also *tokopɛs*.

ikamɛ́sʉ́kɔtᵃ (ikamɛ́sʉ́kɔtɨ́-) *1 v.* to catch, grab, grip, take hold of. *2 v.* to capture, seize. See also *ikamɛs*.

ikamɛtɛ́s (ikamɛtɛ́sɨ́-) *1 v.* to catch, grab, grip, take hold of. *2 v.* to build on the ground (e.g. a granary or roof).

ikamɨ́kámɛ́s (ikamɨ́kámɛ́sɨ́-) *v.* to grab or grip repeatedly, hold onto (e.g. a tree when climbing it).

ikámʉ́nɔ́sʉ́kɔtᵃ (ikámʉ́nɔ́sʉ́kɔtɨ́-) *v.* to take hold of each other.

ikanɛ́s (ikanɛ́sɨ́-) *v.* to appease, placate (e.g. the bride's parents by negotiating favorably for a reasonable brideprice).

ikanɨ́kánɛ́s (ikanɨ́kánɛ́sɨ́-) *v.* to appease, pacify, placate (e.g. an infant by rocking it back and forth).

ikáɲón (ikáɲónɨ̀-) *v.* to abstain, fast.

ikaɲɨ́káŋɛ́s (ikaɲɨ́káŋɛ́sɨ́-) *1 v.* to grind coarsely. *2 v.* to chew roughly (e.g. uncooked maize). See also *iŋaɨŋɛ́ɛ́s*.

ikarɛtɛ́s (ikarɛtɛ́sɨ́-) *v.* to discourage, frustrate.

ikarímétòn (ikarímétònɨ̀-) *v.* to be depleted, exhausted, wiped out.

ikárímétòn (ikárímétònɨ̀-) *v.* to become fruitless, futile, or vain.

ikárɔ́n (ikárɔ́nɨ̀-) *v.* to be gaunt, haggard, ragged, thin. See also *kɔrɔ́ɗɔ́mɔ̀n*.

ikásíɛ́s (ikásíɛ́sɨ́-) *v.* to work. See also *tereganɛ́s*.

ikásíetam (ikásíetamá-) *v.* doable, feasible, viable, workable.

ikásîìmètòn (ikásîìmètònɨ̀-) *v.* to happen, occur, take place, transpire. See also *itíyáìmètòn*.

ikásíitetɛ́s (ikásíitetɛ́sɨ́-) *v.* to employ, hire, put to work, work. See also *teréganitetɛ́s*.

ikásíts'ᵃ (iká-síts'à-) *n.* head hair.

ikatɛs (ikatɛsɨ́-) *v.* to assay, attempt, try.

ikatɨ́kátɛ́s (ikatɨ́kátɛ́sɨ́-) *v.* to attempt or try repeatedly.

ikátɨ́nɔ́s (ikátɨ́nɔ́sɨ́-) *v.* to compete with each other. See also *ilɔ́ɨnɔ́s*.

ikatsɛs (ikatsɛsɨ́-) *v.* to care, mind. See also *imisɛs*.

ikáʉ́tɛ́s (ikáʉ́tɛ́sɨ́-) *v.* to cool down (e.g. food by pouring or stirring).

ikáwɨ́lɔ̀n (ikáwɨ́lɔ̀nɨ̀-) *v.* to burn poorly (of firewood, when it burns quickly and does not hold fire).

ikáyá (<ikáyɛ́ɛ́s) *v.*

ikáyɛ́ɛ́s (ikáyɛ́ɛ́sɨ́-/ikáyá-) *v.* to canvass, cover, or spread over (an area). See also *iɗɛŋɛs*.

ikázànà (<ikázànòòn) *v.*

ikázànòòn (ikázànòònɨ̀-/ɨ́kazana-) *v.* to be ambituous, determined, tenacious.

ikedᵃ (ikede-) *1 n.* head, top part, upper end. *2 n.* heading, title.

ikeda ƙwázàᵉ *1 n.* collar. *2 n.* waist, waistline (of clothing). *Lit.* 'head of the cloth'.

ikeda mɛ́sɛ̀ *n.* beer head: the foamy, frothy top layer of beer.

ikɛɗɛs (ikɛɗɛsɨ́-) *v.* to curse with a difficult labor and delivery.

ikɛɗíkɛɗɛ́s (ikɛɗíkɛɗɛ́sɨ́-) *v.* to stimulate digitally, titillate, touch lightly. See also *ikwatíkwátés*.

ikɛɗɔs (ikɛɗɔsɨ́-) *v.* to be cursed by relatives with a difficult birth.

ikéé kɔ̀n *n.* at once, in concert, simultaneously, together. *Lit.* 'at one head'.

ikéésukɔt[a] (ikéésukɔtɨ́-) *v.* to elevate, lift or raise up.

ikɛɛtés (ikɛɛtésɨ́-) *v.* to elevate, lift or raise up. See also *ɓukés*.

ikeimétòn (ikeimétònì-) *1 v.* to be lifted, raised up. *2 v.* to be developed.

ikéítetés (ikéítetésɨ́-) *1 v.* to make elevate, lift, or raise. *2 v.* to benefit, profit.

ikékémɔ̀n (ikékémɔ̀nɨ̀-) *v.* to cackle.

ikékéɲòn (ikékéɲònì-) *1 v.* to be stable, steady, sturdy. *2 v.* to be dependable, reliable (in work).

ikeɲíkéɲés (ikeɲíkéɲésɨ́-) *v.* to kill serially.

ikeɲíkéɲésíàm (ikeɲíkéɲésɨ́-àmà-) *pl.* **ikɛɲíkéɲésíik**[a]. *n.* serial killer.

ikéɲéɗés (ikéɲéɗésɨ́-) *v.* to break, cut, pull apart, sever, tear (rope-like objects). See also *ɗusutes* and *tɔɲeɗɛs*.

iketɛs (ikɛtɛsɨ́-) *1 v.* to choke. *2 v.* to hang (by the neck to kill).

ikɛtesa asɨ́ *v.* to hang oneself.

iketiés (iketiesɨ́-) *v.* to choke, strangle, throttle.

ikíɗítsés (ikíɗítsésɨ́-) *v.* to stick out of sight, tuck away.

ikíkóanón (ikíkóanónì-) *v.* to convene, meet (for a discussion).

ikílɔ́n (ikílɔ́nì-) *1 v.* to rumble, thunder. *2 v.* bellow, holler, shout, yell. *3 v.* to trumpet.

ikiríkírɔ̀n (ikiríkírɔ̀nì-) *v.* to get a move on, hurry, rush.

ikit[a] (ikitɨ́-) *pl.* **ikítík**[a]. *n.* head-pad: twisted clothing, grass, or leaves used to cushion the weight of a load on the head.

ikitínícɛmér (ikitíní-cɛmérɨ́-) *n.* shrub species whose roots are crushed, soaked in water, and drunk as a remedy for headaches. *Lit.* 'heads-herb'. *Withania somnifera*. See also *ɲónomokére*.

ikɔɓɛs (ikɔɓɛsɨ́-) *1 v.* to hand, pass, transfer. *2 v.* to render, translate.

ikɔ́ɓésukɔt[a] (ikɔ́ɓésukɔtɨ́-) *v.* to hand over, pass along/on, transfer there.

ikɔɓetés (ikɔɓetésɨ́-) *1 v.* to hand over, pass along/on, transfer (this way). *2 v.* to translate.

ikɔ́ɓínɔ́s (ikɔ́ɓínɔ́sɨ́-) *1 v.* to pass around to each other. *2 v.* to translate back and forth.

ikɔɗíkɔ́ɗɔ̀n (ikɔɗíkɔ́ɗɔ̀nì-) *v.* to meander, weave, zigzag. See also *ikulúkúlòn* and *lúkúɗukuɗánón*.

ikokes (ikokesɨ́-) *v.* to crack open (bones to extract the marrow).

ikókíánón (ikókíánónì-) *v.* to be orphaned.

ikókórés (ikókórésɨ́-) *v.* to crawl up, scale.

ikókóretés (ikókóretésɨ́-) *v.* to crawl up or scale this way.

ikókótés (ikókótésɨ́-) *v.* to shadow, tail, trail.

ikɔ́kɔ́yà (ikɔ́kɔ́yàà-) *n.* armoured ground cricket. *Bradyporidae*.

ikólípánón (ikólípánónì-) *v.* to be barren, childless, infertile, sterile. See also *osorosánón*.

ikómá (<ikómóòn) *v.*

ikómáikotᵃ (<ikómóonukotᵃ) *v.*

ikómééton (ikómééètònì-) *v.* to come quickly, hasten here, hurry this way.

ikómóòn (ikómóònì-/ikómá-) *v.* to hasten, hurry, move quickly.

ikómóonukotᵃ (ikómóonukotí-/ikómáikot-) *v.* to go quickly, hasten there, hurry over there.

ɨkɔ̀ŋ (ɨkɔ̀ŋà-) *pl.* **ikɔ́ŋíkᵃ**. *n.* malt: soaked flour that is fried and dried for brewing beer.

ikoŋetés (ikoŋetésí-) *v.* to corral, round up. See also *kalíkálés*.

ikoŋíkóŋés (ikoŋíkóŋésí-) *v.* to knock or rap on (e.g. a door). See also *idɔŋídɔ́ŋés*.

ikoŋíkóŋòn (ikoŋíkóŋònì-) *v.* to live long.

ikóŋítetés (ikóŋítetésí-) *v.* to make swear.

ikóŋón (ikóŋónì-) *v.* to avow, swear, take an oath.

ikóóbés (ikóóbésí-) *1 v.* to close, fold up or in half (e.g. a book or leather mat). *2 v.* to collect, gather (e.g. yard rubbish).

ikóóbetés (ikóóbetésí-) *1 v.* to close, fold up or in half (e.g. a book or leather mat). *2 v.* to collect, gather up (e.g. rubbish).

ikóóbetésá asɨ *v.* to come together, congregate.

ikóɔ́kᵃ (ikó-ɔ́kà-) *pl.* **ikitíníɔkitín**. *n.* cranium, skull. *Lit.* 'head-bone'.

ikɔɔtɔ́s (ikɔɔtɔ́sɨ-) *v.* to be elevated, lifted or raised up.

ikópíòn (ikópíònì-) *v.* to condense (of water vapor). See also *tsɨpitsɨpɔ́n*.

ikórímés (ikórímésí-) *v.* to peek or peep at (by bobbing the head up-and-down like small animals do). See also *ilóíkés*.

ikóteré (ikóteré) *1 prep.* because of, due to. *2 subordconn.* because, due to the fact that, for the reason that. *3 subordconn.* in order that, so that. A noun following this word takes the oblique case. See also *kóteré*.

ikuɗúkúɗés (ikuɗúkúɗésí-) *v.* to dig or pick out with a finger (e.g. from an ear or a nostril).

ikues (ikuesí-) *v.* to warm up (e.g. porridge or water).

ikuetés (ikuetésí-) *v.* to warm up (e.g. porridge or water).

ikujɛs (ikujɛsí-) *v.* to look or search for, seek. See also *bɛdɛtés*.

ikújíánón (ikújíánónì-) *1 v.* to perform a miracle. *2 v.* to prophesy.

ikúkúrés (ikúkúrésí-) *v.* to claw or dig up by scratching.

ikulɛs (ikulɛsí-) *1 v.* to clean, clear (a surface). *2 v.* to even, plane, shave (e.g. tool handles or poles). See also *ikwalɛs*.

ikúlésukotᵃ (ikúlésukotí-) *1 v.* to clean or clear off (a surface). *2 v.* to plane off, shave off (e.g. tool handles or poles).

ikulɛtés (ikulɛtésí-) *1 v.* to clean or clear up (a surface). *2 v.* to even out, plane, shave (e.g. tool handles or poles).

ikúrúfánón (ikúrúfánónì-) *1 v.* to be destitute, poor, poverty-stricken. *2 v.* to be undeveloped.

ikúrúfánóníàm (ikúrúfánóní-àmà-) *pl.* **ikúrúfánóníikᵃ**. *n.* destitute, poor, poverty-stricken person.

ikutses (ikutsesí-) *v.* to chase off/away, run off (e.g. a beggar or a dog).

ikútsésukotᵃ (ikútsésukotí-) *v.* to chase off/away, run off (e.g. a beggar or a dog).

ikútúkánón (ikútúkánónì-) *v.* to be chatty, talkative. See also *dɛmédɔn*.

ikutúkútés (ikutúkútésí-) *v.* to back up, reverse.

ikutúkútòn (ikutúkútònì-) *v.* to back up, reverse.

ikwá (<ikwóón) *v.*

íkwà (íkwà) *adv.* apparently, seemingly, it seems. See also *ókò*.

ikwáánitetés (ikwáánitetésí-) *1 v.* to equalize, equate, treat equally. *2 v.* to model, simulate. See also *iriánitetés*.

ikwáánòn (ikwáánònì-) *1 v.* to be the same. *2 v.* to resemble, be similar. *3 v.* to be symmetrical.

ikwákwárés (ikwákwárésí-) *v.* to spread around.

ikwalɛs (ikwalɛsí-) *1 v.* to clean, clear (a surface). *2 v.* to even, plane, shave (e.g. tool handles or wooden poles). See also *ikulɛs*.

ikwárétòn (ikwárétònì-) *v.* to resuscitate, revive.

ikwaríkwárɛs (ikwaríkwárɛ́sí-) *1 v.* to spread around. *2 v.* to spend wildly.

ikwaríkwarɔs (ikwaríkwárɔ́sí-) *v.* to be spread around.

ikwatíkwátés (ikwatíkwátésí-) *v.* to stimulate digitally, titillate, touch lightly. See also *ikɛdíkédɛs*.

ikwɛ́rɛ́ɗɔ̀n (ikwɛ́rɛ́ɗɔ̀nì-) *v.* to wrestle out, wriggle free (of a hold).

ikwɛtíkwétés (ikwɛtíkwétésí-) *v.* to corral, round up (e.g. animals, by lightly hitting them).

ikwilíkwílés (ikwilíkwílésí-) *v.* to tickle.

ikwílílòn (ikwílílònì-) *v.* to scream, shriek.

ikwiɲíkwíɲɔ́n (ikwiɲíkwíɲɔ́nì-) *v.* to be active, energetic. See also *kwiɲídɔ̀n*.

ikwóón (ikwóónì-/ikwá-) *v.* to crow.

iƙáálɛs (iƙáálɛ́sí-) *v.* to skim off. See also *iripetɛ́s*.

iƙaíƙá (<iƙaíƙéés) *v.*

iƙaíƙéés (iƙaíƙéésí-/iƙaíƙá-) *v.* to fight, oppose, resist.

iƙáƙá (<iƙáƙéés) *v.*

iƙáƙéés (iƙáƙéésí-/iƙáƙá-) *v.* to fight, oppose, resist.

iƙáƙɛɛtɛ́s (iƙáƙɛɛtɛ́sí-) *v.* to fight, oppose, resist.

iƙalíƙálɛs (iƙalíƙálɛ́sí-) *v.* to confine, hold back/in, restrain (e.g. animals in a pen or someone in a fight).

iƙaŋɛs (iƙaŋɛsí-) *v.* to hold or prop up, support.

iƙárárɔ̀n (iƙárárɔ̀nì-) *v.* to sit on a stool.

iƙɛɓíƙɛ́ɓésa ts'aɗí *v.* to slash a firebreak.

iƙéƙéés (iƙéƙéésí-) *1 v.* to crack open (e.g. the seeds of gourds or pumpkins). *2 v.* to pick out, select.

iƙélémés (iƙélémésí-) *v.* to castrate (by crushing the spermatic cords).

iƙɛlɛs (iƙɛlɛsí-) *v.* to choose, pick out, select.

iƙɛlɛtɛ́s (iƙɛlɛtɛ́sí-) *v.* to choose, pick out, select.

iƙémíƙémés (iƙémíƙémésí-) *v.* to cut or slice away, fillet (i.e. meat or skin).

iƙenes (iƙenesí-) *1 v.* to beseech, entreat, plead with. *2 v.* to forgive, have mercy on, pardon.

iƙɛníƙɛ́nés (iƙɛníƙɛ́nésí-) *v.* to cluck at (e.g. animals or a honeyguide).

iƙerɛs (iƙerɛsí-) *v.* to draw, mark, trace (non-linguistically).

iƙiɛs (iƙiɛsí-) *v.* to block, deflect, shield. See also *iɓatɛs*.

iƙilíƙílòn (iƙilíƙílònì-) *v.* to drip. See also *ilímón*.

iƙirɛs (iƙirɛsí-) *v.* to draw, mark, write (linguistically).

iƙirɔs (iƙirɔsɨ́-) *1 v.* to be recorded, written. *2 v.* to be striped.

iƙofes (iƙofesí-) *v.* to cut off, interrupt.

iƙóƙós (iƙóƙósí-) *v.* to be doubtful, dubious.

iƙólésuƙot[a] (iƙólésuƙotí-) *v.* to score (a goal).

iƙòlòt[a] (ìƙòlòtà-) *pl.* **iƙólótaikw**[a]. *n.* dried out gourd.

iƙɔmɛs (iƙɔmɛsɨ́-) *v.* to annihilate, obliterate, wipe out.

iƙɔ́nɔ́nɔ̀ɔ̀n (iƙɔ́nɔ́nɔ̀ɔ̀nɨ̀-) *v.* to droop, sag (e.g. an overloaded fruit tree, or someone hunched over in hunger).

iƙɔŋɛs (iƙɔŋɛsɨ́-) *1 v.* to lean, prop, or rest on/against. *2 v.* to depend or rely on. See also *tonokes*.

iƙɔ́ɲítés (iƙɔ́ɲítésɨ́-) *v.* to lean, prop, or rest on/against.

iƙɔ́ɲítésuƙɔt[a] (iƙɔ́ɲítésuƙɔtɨ́-) *v.* to lean, prop, or rest on/against.

iƙɔ́ɲítɔ́s (iƙɔ́ɲítɔ́sɨ́-) *v.* to be leaned, propped, or rested on/against.

iƙɔ́ɔ́résá asɨ́ *v.* to strut, swagger. See also *kɔrɔn*.

iƙoríƙórés (iƙoríƙórésí-) *v.* to work with a long tool (e.g. stir gourd innards or shave the interior of a hive or mortar when making it).

iƙórú (iƙórúù-) *pl.* **iƙórúìk**[a]. *1 n.* millipede. *2 n.* trailer.

iƙúétòn (iƙúétònì-) *1 v.* to howl, wail. *2 v.* to holler, shout, yell.

iƙujúƙújɔ̀n (iƙujúƙújɔ̀nɨ̀-) *v.* to stammer, stutter (when cold). See also *dákón* and *gajádòn*.

iƙúƙúrés (iƙúƙúrésí-) *v.* to enlarge, erode (a hole in the ground).

iƙulúƙúlòn (iƙulúƙúlònì-) *v.* to meander, weave, wind around. See also *iƙɔdíƙɔ́dɔ̀n* and *lúƙúdukudánón*.

iƙulúƙúlɔ̀n (iƙulúƙúlɔ̀nɨ̀-) *v.* to come back around, retrace one's steps.

iƙumes (iƙumesí-) *v.* to jab, poke, prod (physically or verbally).

iƙúmúnós (iƙúmúnósí-) *v.* to bicker, clash, fight, skirmish, squabble. *Lit.* 'to jab each other'.

iƙúón (iƙúónì-) *1 v.* to howl, wail. *2 v.* to holler, shout, yell.

iƙúónuƙot[a] (iƙúónuƙotí-) *1 v.* to howl, wail. *2 v.* to holler, shout, yell.

iƙures (iƙuresí-) *1 v.* to stir. *2 v.* to paddle, row. *3 v.* to confound, confuse.

iƙurúƙúròn (iƙurúƙúrònì-) *v.* to be corrupt, crooked.

iƙúrúmétona iƙá[e] *v.* to be confounded, confused.

iƙúrúmós (iƙúrúmósí-) *v.* to be agitated, incited, roused, stirred up (as a group).

iƙúúlɛ́s (iƙúúlɛ́sɨ́-) *v.* to swipe or wipe clean (e.g. a bowl, with one's finger). See also *itsídɛs*.

iƙwáƙwárés (iƙwáƙwárésí-) *v.* to prune, trim.

iƙwɛ́ƙwɛ́rɛ́s (iƙwɛ́ƙwɛ́rɛ́sɨ́-) *v.* to shave off (e.g. thorns from a tree's trunk or branches).

iƙwéón (iƙwéónì-) *v.* to yelp, yip.

iƙwɛrɛs (iƙwɛrɛsɨ́-) *1 v.* to brush, comb. *2 v.* to rake. See also *ɲírés*.

iƙwɛ́rɛ́suƙɔt[a] (iƙwɛ́rɛ́suƙɔtɨ́-) *v.* to brush or comb out.

iƙwɛrɔs (iƙwɛrɔsɨ́-) *1 v.* to be brushed, combed. *2 v.* to be down-striped.

ilá (<ɨlɔ́ɔ́n) *v.*

ilaɓɛtés (ilaɓɛtésí-) *v.* to scoop or skim off (e.g. water from sand). See also *d'alés* and *tébɛtés*.

iláɓúés (iláɓúésí-) *v.* to smoothen (with water).

iláfúkòn (iláfúkònì-) *v.* to hurt in the chest (e.g. from acid reflux or heart-attack).

iláíkɔt[a] (<ilɔ́ɔ́nukɔt[a]) *v.*

ilailá (<ilailɛ́ɛ́s) *v.*

ilailɛ́ɛ́s (ilailɛ́ɛ́sí-/ilailá-) *v.* to rinse. See also *ilɔ́lɔ́tsés*.

iláítésukɔt[a] (iláítésukɔtí-) *v.* to take for a walk, walk.

ilaɟíláɟés (ilaɟíláɟésí-) *1 v.* to loosen. *2 v.* to fail, neglect, overlook.

ilákásítésukɔt[a] (ilákásítésukɔtí-) *1 v.* to delight, make happy, please. *2 v.* to appreciate, thank. See also *imúmúitɛtés*.

ilákásòn (ilákásònì-) *v.* to be glad, happy.

ilákásónukɔt[a] (ilákásónukɔtí-) *1 v.* to become glad or happy. *2 v.* to be appreciative, thankful.

ilakɛs (ilakɛsí-) *v.* to pan, shake in a pan (e.g. looking for gold).

ilakílákés (ilakílákésí-) *v.* to pan, shake in a pan (e.g. looking for gold).

ilákízòn (ilákízònì-) *v.* to feel ill, nauseated, queasy.

ilálákés (ilálákésí-) *v.* to pan, shake in a pan (e.g. looking for gold).

iláláŋés (iláláŋésí-) *v.* to eat gingerly (hot food).

ilálátés (ilálátésí-) *v.* to add water to (e.g. cement, grist, or flour).

ìlàm (ìlàmà-) *n.* curse, imprecation, malediction.

ilámááránón (ilámááránónì-) *v.* to disperse, dissipate (like ants or a crowd of people). See also *alámáárón*.

ilamɛs (ilamɛsí-) *v.* to curse, damn, imprecate.

ilámɔ́n (ilámɔ́nì-) *v.* to go through, pass, succeed, win.

ilamɔs (ilamɔsí-) *v.* to be cursed, damned, doomed.

iláŋ (iláɲí-) *pl.* iláɲík[a]. *n.* Indian jujube: a tree whose round yellow fruits are eaten by people and goats and whose roots are decocted as a cure for stomach and chest ailments; its forked poles are used for building houses and platforms. *Ziziphus mauritiana*.

ilaŋés (ilaŋésí-) *v.* to leave behind, overtake, pass.

iláɲígwì (iláɲí-gwìè-) *pl.* iláɲígwiitín. *n.* grove of Indian jujube trees.

ilápétòn (ilápétònì-) *v.* to overflow, spill over.

ilarɛs (ilarɛsí-) *v.* to abuse, misuse, utilize inappropriately. See also *ilwarɛs*.

ilárímétòn (ilárímétònì-) *v.* to become distressed or stressed out. See also *ilwárímétòn*.

ilaritɛtés (ilaritɛtésí) *v.* to keep waiting, make wait, waste the time of. See also *ilwaritɛtés*.

ilárɔ́n (ilárɔ́nì-) *v.* to be inactive, idle, unused, unutilized. See also *ilwárɔ́n*.

ilatɛs (ilatɛsí-) *v.* to add water to (e.g. cement, grist, or flour).

ílebéd'[a] (ílebéd'é-) *n.* small green snake (possibly a boomslang).

ilébìlèbètòn (ilébìlèbètònì-) *v.* to be saturated, water-logged (e.g. cement or sand).

ileɓílébòn (ileɓíléɓònì-) *v.* to blister, vesicate. See also *bubuxánónuƙotᵃ*.

ileɗɛs (ilɛɗɛsí-) *v.* to crush, smash, squash. See also *itsakɛs*.

ilééránitetés (ilééránitetésí-) *v.* to disclose, expose, reveal, show.

ilééránón (ilééránónì-) *v.* to be clearly seen, exposed, visible.

ilɛ́ɛ́tòn (ilɛ́ɛ́tònì-) *v.* to come for a visit, travel here.

ílegûgᵃ (ílegúgù-) *1 n.* black ant species that transports grain.

iléjíánón (iléjíánónì-) *v.* to be undependable, unreliable.

ilɛjɨ́lɛ́jɛ́s (ilɛjɨ́lɛ́jɛ́sí-) *v.* to do odd jobs, work temporarily.

ilɛjɨ́lɛ́jitɛtɛ́s (ilɛjɨ́lɛ́jitɛtɛ́sí-) *v.* to hire temporarily.

ilɛkɨ́lékɛ́s (ilɛkɨ́lékɛ́sí-) *v.* to waste. See also *iɲekíɲékés*.

íleƙó (íleƙóò-) *pl.* **íleƙóiƙ**ᵃ. *n.* edible yellow seeds of the *jàw*ᵃ shrub.

ilɛ́ƙwérɛs (ilɛ́ƙwérɛsí-) *v.* to make stumble, trip.

ilɛ́ƙwérɛtɛs (ilɛ́ƙwérɛtɛsí-) *v.* to make stumble, trip up.

ilɛ́ƙwéries (ilɛ́ƙwériesí-) *1 v.* to thread, weave around (e.g. reeds to build a granary). *2 v.* to whip all over.

ilélébés (ilélébésí-) *1 v.* to lift and carry together (as when a killed animal or a prisoner is being hauled by more than one person). *2 v.* to winnow.

ilélébètòn (ilélébètònì-) *v.* to buoy, float.

ilélébonuƙotᵃ (ilélébonuƙotí-) *v.* to drift or float away.

ilélɛ́ɛs (ilélɛ́ɛsí-) *v.* to despise, detest, disdain.

ilélɛ́imɔ́s (ilélɛ́imɔ́sí-) *v.* to despise each other.

ilélɛ́itɛtɛ́s (ilélɛ́itɛtɛ́sí-) *v.* to disgust, repulse, revolt.

ilélémùòn (ilélémùònì-) *v.* to be loud, noisy, make a racket.

ilemílémòn (ilemílémònì-) *v.* to blabber, jabber, prattle.

Iléŋ (Iléŋí-) *n.* Iléŋ: one of the Ik's twelve clans.

ileŋes (ileŋesí-) *v.* to be higher than, surpass in height.

Iléŋíàm (Iléŋí-àmà-) *pl.* **Iléŋíik**ᵃ. *n.* Iléŋ clan member.

ilɛ́ɔ́n (ilɛ́ɔ́nì-) *v.* to rage, rampage.

ilépésuƙotᵃ (ilépésuƙotí-) *v.* to clamber or scramble up.

ilépón (ilépónì-) *v.* to meet a member of the opposite gender in the middle of a dance circle during a group dance.

ilépɔ́n (ilépɔ́nì-) *v.* to clamber, scramble (e.g. like monkeys).

ilɛrɨ́lérɛ́s (ilɛrɨ́lérɛ́sí-) *v.* to rap on repeatedly (e.g. a gourd or head). See also *iɗɛiɗéés*.

ilérón (ilérónì-) *v.* to be bare, naked, nude.

ilérúmùòn (ilérúmùònì-) *v.* to argue, dispute, quarrel (as a large group).

ilététà (<ilététòòn) *v.*

ilététaitetés (ilététaitetésí-) *v.* to expose, leave out in the open.

ilététòòn (ilététòònì-/ilététa-) *v.* to be exposed, left out in the open, unprotected.

ilɛtɨ́létòn (ilɛtɨ́létònì-) *v.* to be insensitive, unresponsive. See also *ilétúránón*.

ilétúránón (ilétúránónì-) *v.* to be insensitive, unresponsive. See also *ilɛtɨ́létòn*.

iléúrés (iléúrésí-) *1 v.* to light up (e.g. with fire or a torch). *2 v.* to view (e.g. through binoculars or a microscope). See also *inwakes*.

ilíánòn (ilíánònì-) *v.* to reek, stink (e.g. the stench of blood).

iliɓaakón (iliɓaakónì-) *v.* to be green (of many).

iliɓaakónuƙot[a] (iliɓaakónuƙotí-) *v.* to turn green (of more than one).

ilíɓɔ́n (ilɨ́ɓɔ́nɨ̀-) *1 v.* to be green. *2 v.* to be new (of foliage).

ilɨ́ɓɔ́nuƙɔt[a] (ilɨ́ɓɔ́nuƙɔtɨ́-) *v.* to turn green.

iliɗés (iliɗésí-) *v.* to tie off (e.g. one's stomach when very hungry, or one's gold flecks in a small pouch, or a penis in a practical joke boys play on each other).

iliɗɛtés (iliɗɛtésí-) *v.* to tie off (e.g. one's stomach when very hungry, gold flecks in a small pouch, or a penis in a practical joke boys play on each other).

iliɗɔ́s (iliɗɔ́sí-) *v.* to be tied off.

ilies (iliesí-) *v.* to paste, seal.

iliíliés (iliíliésí-) *v.* to paste, seal.

iliílíós (iliílíósí-) *v.* to be pasted, sealed, seamless.

ilíítés (ilíítésí-) *v.* to snitch, tattle, or tell on.

ilikílíkés (ilikílíkésí-) *v.* to jerk, jiggle, tug back and forth (e.g. a dog with cat in its mouth, or jerking a kid's ears).

ilílíés (ilílíésí-) *v.* to fill up. See also *éítetés*.

ilíliés (ilíliésí-) *v.* to dry over fire (e.g. meat or tobacco).

ilɨ́lɨinɔ́s (ilɨ́lɨinɔ́sí-) *v.* to be angry at each other.

ilɨ́liŋés (ilɨ́liŋésí-) *v.* to shake back and forth or side to side (like one's head saying 'no' or like a dog with something in its mouth).

ilɨ́liɔ̀n (ilɨ́liɔ̀nɨ̀-) *v.* to be angry, annoyed, heated, pissed. See also *gaanón*.

ilɨ́liɔnuƙɔt[a] (ilɨ́liɔnuƙɔtɨ́-) *v.* to become angry, annoyed, heated, or pissed off.

ilílítsés (ilílítsésí-) *v.* to shake off/out (e.g. how a bird or dog shakes off dust or water).

ilimɛs (ilimɛsí-) *v.* to pare, trim (e.g. a tanned skin or a piece of wood). See also *ipɛlɛs*.

ilimɛsa asɨ́ *v.* to drip.

ilimɛtés (ilimɛtésí-) *v.* to pare down, trim back.

ilimílímɔ̀n (ilimílímɔ̀nɨ̀-) *1 v.* to drizzle. *2 v.* to be flecked, spotted.

ilímítés (ilímítésí-) *v.* to bring up, mention.

ilɨ́mɔ́n (ilɨ́mɔ́nɨ̀-) *v.* to drip. See also *ikilíkɨ́lɔ́n*.

ilíɲánètòn (ilíɲánètònì-) *v.* to be streaked, striped.

Ilíɲééts'[a] (Ilíɲé-èts'ì-) *v.* July: month when feces have streaks in them due to a change in diet resulting from seasonal foods. *Lit.* 'the feces are streaked'. See also *Lomoɗokogéc*.

iliɲɛs (iliɲɛsí-) *v.* to do partially, streakily (e.g. cut only a portion of one's hair, or bathe only a portion of one's body).

iliɲɨ́liŋés (iliɲɨ́liŋésí-) *v.* to shake back and forth or side to side (like one's head saying 'no' or like a dog with something in its mouth). See also *ilitsílítsés*.

ilíɲírés (ilíɲírésí-) *1 v.* to cut around, cut a ring in, ring. *2 v.* to circumcise. Also pronounced as *iléŋérés*. See also *ilirɛs*.

iliŋírésîawᵃ (iliŋírésí-àwà-) *pl.* **iliŋírésíawík**ᵃ. *n.* place on an arrow where grooved rings have been made for holding while nocking the arrow.

iliŋɔ́n (iliŋɔ́nɨ̀-) *v.* to be streaked, striped.

ilios (iliosí-) *1 v.* to be pasted, sealed. *2 v.* to be deaf, hard-of-hearing.

ilírá (<ilíróòn) *v.*

ilíráitetés (ilíráitetésí-) *v.* to coordinate, synchronize.

ilɨram (ilɨramá-) *n.* meal mush stirred solid. *Lit.* 'rotatable'. See also *tɔbɔŋ* and *tɨdɨtam*.

ilíréètòn (ilíréètònì-) *v.* to act in sync or in unison (e.g. vehicles in a convoy, birds in an echelon, or people mourning a death).

ilɨrɛs (ilɨrɛsí-) *1 v.* to circumvolve, move around, rotate (e.g. when stirring food). *2 v.* to circumcise, cut around, ring (e.g. when removing the anus of a wild animal). See also *ilíŋírés*.

ilɨrílírés (ilɨrílírésí-) *v.* to circumvolve, move around, or rotate repeatedly (e.g. when trying to balance something).

ilíróòn (ilíróònì-/ilírá-) *v.* to be coordinated, synchronized, in unison.

ilitsílítsés (ilitsílítsésí-) *v.* to shake back and forth or side to side (like one's head saying 'no' or like a dog with something in its mouth). See also *iliŋílɨŋés*.

ilɨwɛs (ilɨwɛsí-) *v.* to clean, clear (e.g. smooth surfaces). See also *ikɨlɛs*.

ilɨwɨ́lɨwɛtés (ilɨwɨ́lɨwɛtésí-) *v.* to clean or clear off (e.g. smooth surfaces).

ilɨwɨ́lɨwɔ́s (ilɨwɨ́lɨwɔ́sí-) *v.* to be cleaned or cleared off (e.g. smooth surfaces).

ilɔɓílɔ́ɓés (ilɔɓílɔ́ɓésí-) *v.* to plaster.

ilɔ́ɓɔtɛtés (ilɔ́ɓɔtɛtésí-) *v.* to hurl, spew, upchuck, vomit.

ilɔ́ɗétɔ̀n (ilɔ́ɗétɔ̀nì-) *v.* to come around.

ilɔɗílɔ́ɗɔn (ilɔɗílɔ́ɗɔ̀nì-) *v.* to go round and round.

ilɔ́ɗíŋánón (ilɔ́ɗíŋánónì-) *v.* to be discriminatory, marginalizing, segregative.

ilɔ́ɗíŋés (ilɔ́ɗíŋésí-) *v.* to discriminate, isolate, marginalize, segregate.

ilɔ́ɗɔnɨkɔtᵃ (ilɔ́ɗɔnɨkɔtí-) *v.* to go around.

ilɔɛs (ilɔɛsí-) *1 v.* to beat, defeat, exceed, outdo, surpass. *2 v.* to be more or less than (in terms of an attribute). See also *kurés*.

ilɔɛtés (ilɔɛtésí-) *v.* to beat, defeat, outdo, surpass.

ilɔ́étɔ̀n (ilɔ́étɔ̀nì-) *v.* to be beat, bored, tired out, worn out.

ilɔ́gɔtsés (ilɔ́gɔtsésí-) *v.* to drape, lay over.

ilóíkés (ilóíkésí-) *v.* to peek or peep at (by bobbing the head up-and-down like small animals do). See also *ikórímés*.

iloílóés (iloílóésí-) *v.* to dislodge, loosen by moving back and forth.

iloimétòn (iloimétònì-) *v.* to be defeated or overcome, lose.

ilɔ́ímɔ́s (ilɔ́ímɔ́sí-) *v.* to compete, contend.

ilɔ́ínɔ́s (ilɔ́ínɔ́sí-) *v.* to compete, contend. See also *ikátínɔ́s*.

ilɔ́ítésɨkɔtᵃ (ilɔ́ítésɨkɔtí-) *v.* to beat down, discourage, frustrate, wear down.

ilójésɨkɔtᵃ (ilójésɨkɔtí-) *v.* to displace, relocate, transfer.

ilɔkɨ́lɔ́kés (ilɔkɨ́lɔ́késí-) *v.* to wind or wrap around.

ilɔkílɔ́kɛtés (ilɔkílɔ́kɛtésɨ́-) *v.* to wind or wrap around.

ilókótsés (ilókótsésɨ́-) *v.* to exchange, swap, trade. See also *ixɔtsɛs* and *xɔ́tsés*.

ilókótsésa mɛná[ε] *v.* to exchange words.

ilɔ́ƙɛ́rés (ilɔ́ƙɛ́résɨ́-) *v.* to interlace, interlock, interweave, mesh.

ilɔƙɛs (ilɔƙɛsɨ́-) *v.* to dissolve, emulsify.

ilɔ́lɨ́és (ilɔ́lɨ́ésɨ́-) *v.* to displace, expel, force out, oust.

ilɔ́lɨ́ésá asɨ *v.* to drift, wander.

ilɔ́lɨ́ɛtés (ilɔ́lɨ́ɛtésɨ́-) *v.* to threaten to displace (by encircling several times).

ilɔ́lɔ́kés (ilɔ́lɔ́késɨ́-) *v.* to space, thin out (e.g. seedlings).

ilɔ́lɔ́mɔ̀n (ilɔ́lɔ́mɔ̀nɨ̀-) *v.* to be roomy, spacious. See also *lalújón*.

ilɔ́lɔ́ŋés (ilɔ́lɔ́ŋésɨ́-) *v.* to agitate, stir.

ilɔ́lɔ́rés (ilɔ́lɔ́résɨ́-) *v.* to smear, smudge (e.g. food on a child's face to trick its parents into believing it has eaten).

ilɔ́lɔ́tsés (ilɔ́lɔ́tsésɨ́-) *v.* to rinse. See also *ilailéés*.

ilólúés (ilólúésɨ́-) *v.* to bombinate, buzz around.

ilɔmɨ́lɔ́mɔ̀n (ilɔmɨ́lɔ́mɔ̀nɨ̀-) *v.* to circulate, move around (e.g. a snake or a thief in a house).

ilɔŋɛs (ilɔŋɛsɨ́-) *v.* to chase, go after, pursue. See also *irukes*.

ilɔ́ŋésukɔt[a] (ilɔ́ŋésukɔtɨ́-) *v.* to chase, go, or pursue after.

ilɔ́ɔ́n (ilɔ́ɔ́nɨ̀-/ilá-) *v.* to go for a visit, take a trip, travel. See also *ipásóòn*.

ilɔ́ɔ́nukɔt[a] (ilɔ́ɔ́nukɔtɨ́-/iláíkɔt-) *v.* to go for a visit or on a trip, travel away.

ilɔpɛs (ilɔpɛsɨ́-) *v.* to move, reassign, transfer.

ilɔpɨ́lɔ́pés (ilɔpɨ́lɔ́pésɨ́-) *v.* to move around in (e.g. a crowd or village).

ilores (iloresɨ́-) *v.* to intersperse, space.

ilɔ́tésuƙɔt[a] (ilɔ́tésuƙɔtɨ́-) *v.* to wash.

ilɔ́tésuƙɔta kíjá[e] *v.* to create peace. *Lit.* 'to wash the land'.

ilotses (ilotsesɨ́-) *1 v.* to change, transform. *2 v.* to relay, translate. *3 v.* to confuse, mistake for, mix up.

ilotsesa mɛná[ε] *v.* to change decisions, override, veto.

ilotsesa zɛƙɔ́[ε] *v.* to migrate, move, relocate one's home.

ilotsímétòn (ilotsímétònɨ̀-) *v.* to change, transform. See also *iβéléìmètòn*.

ilɔ́yɔ́n (ilɔ́yɔ́nɨ̀-) *v.* to be beat, bored, tired, weary.

ilujúlújés (ilujúlújésɨ́-) *v.* to fill up to the brim.

ilúkánètòn (ilúkánètònɨ̀-) *v.* to point downward (of horns).

ilukɛs (ilukɛsɨ́-) *v.* to carry under (e.g. tucked under one's arm).

Ilúkɔ́l (Ilúkɔ́lɨ̀-) *n.* a personal name.

ilúkúɗon (ilúkúɗonɨ̀-) *v.* to arc, curve.

ilúkútsés (ilúkútsésɨ́-) *v.* to inject, interject, interpose (objects or comments, e.g. in a conversation without knowing the topic).

ilúkúretés (ilúkúretésɨ́-) *v.* to coil, curl, spiral, wind.

ilúkúrètòn (ilúkúrètònɨ̀-) *v.* to coil or curl up (as in the fetal position).

ilúkúròn (ilúkúrònɨ̀-) *v.* to be coiled or curled up (as in the fetal position).

ilúlúés (ilúlúésɨ́-) *v.* to badger, bug, pester.

ilúlúmùòn (ilúlúmùònɨ̀-) *v.* to swim.

iluluŋam (iluluŋamá-) *1 n.* fist. *2 n.* fistful, handful. See also *mukutam*.

ilúlúŋɛ́s (ilúlúŋɛ́sɨ́-) v. to make ball-shaped, round, or spherical.

ilúlúŋɔ́s (ilúlúŋɔ́sɨ́-) v. to be made ball-shaped, round, or spherical.

ilumɛs (ilumɛsɨ́-) v. to dip (into liquid), immerse, submerge.

ilúmésuƙotª (ilúmésuƙotɨ́-) v. to dip (into liquid), immerse, submerge.

ilumɛtésá asɨ́ v. to enter, immerse onself.

ilúmúlúmɛ́s (ilúmúlúmɛ́sɨ́-) v. to munch happily.

ilúɲón (ilúɲónì-) v. to go by, pass, pass by (e.g. a person or time).

ilúɲónuƙotª (ilúɲónuƙotɨ́-) v. to go by, pass, pass by (e.g. a person or time).

iluŋúlúŋɛ́s (iluŋúlúŋɛ́sɨ́-) 1 v. to bribe, corrupt, buy or pay off. 2 v. to pay to have killed.

ilúrón (ilúrónì-) v. to mourn.

Ilúúkori (Ilúúkoríí-) n. name of a place.

ilúzɛ̀tòn (ilúzɛ̀tònì-) v. to doze or nod off.

ilúzɔ̀n (ilúzɔ̀nì-) v. to feel drowsy or sleepy.

ilwarɛs (ilwarɛsɨ́-) v. to abuse, misuse, utilize inappropriately. See also ilarɛs.

ilwárímétòn (ilwárímétònì-) v. to become distressed or stressed out. See also ilárímétòn.

ilwaritɛtés (ilwaritɛtésɨ́-) v. to keep waiting, make wait, waste the time of. See also ilaritɛtés.

ilwárɔ́n (ilwárɔ́nì-) v. to be inactive, idle, unused, unutilized. See also ilárɔ́n.

ilwárɔ́na tɛrégù v. to be jobless, out of work, unemployed.

im (imá-) pl. wikª. n. baby, child, kid, youngster.

imá (<imɛɛs) v.

ima na interj. this kid, I tell you! (an expression of any positive or negative opinion about a single object or person). Lit. 'this child'.

imaarɛ́s (imaarɛ́sɨ́-) v. to count, enumerate, number.

imaarɛ́sá dèɨ̀kàᵋ v. to pace or step off. Lit. 'to count feet'.

imaarɔ́s (imaarɔ́sɨ́-) v. to be few, numbered.

imácékª (imá-cékì-) pl. wicécíkám. n. daughter-in-law. Lit. 'child's-wife'.

imadɛs (imadɛsɨ́-) v. to apply heat to, heat.

imadɛsa ɔ́jáᵋ v. to treat a wound.

imádɛ́suƙotª (imádɛ́suƙotɨ́-) v. to apply heat to, heat up.

imadɨ́mádɔ̀n (imadɨ́mádɔ̀nì-) v. to to treacherous, tricky (e.g. enemies that come in peace and then turn violent, or a sickness that sets in slowly but then worsens rapidly).

imádɨ́ŋánón (imádɨ́ŋánónì-) v. to be forgetful, undependable, unreliable (e.g. when given a message to deliver to someone).

imakɛs (imakɛsɨ́-) v. to bandage, bind.

imakɨ́mákɛ́s (imakɨ́mákɛ́sɨ́-) v. to wind up. See also ilɔkɨ́lɔ́kɛ́s.

imákóitɛtés (imákóitɛtésɨ́-) 1 v. to contort, distort, twist up. 2 v. to get to misbehave, make difficult.

imákóòn (imákóònì-) 1 v. to be contorted, distorted, twisted up. 2 v. to be in a long and difficult labor. 3 v. to be difficult, misbehaving, unmanageable.

imákwéètòn (imákwéètònì-) 1 v. to become contorted, distorted, or twisted up. 2 v. to become unmanageble, grow difficult, misbehave.

imákɔ́fɔ́ (imá-kɔ́fɔ́ɔ̀-) *pl.* **imákófóikw**ᵃ. *n.* child's small gourd bowl.

imáláánón (ɨmáláánònì-) *v.* to be sexually loose or promiscuous.

imalímálɛs (imalímálɛsɨ́-) *v.* to spread around in a circular motion (e.g. lotion on skin or peanuts in a frying pan).

imámáɗós (imámáɗósɨ́-) *v.* to deviate, go off track, wander off (as if innocently, e.g. to look for food or escape captivity).

imámɛɛs (imámɛɛsɨ́-) *v.* to cajole, coax, sweet-talk, wheedle.

imámɛɛtɛs (imámɛɛtɛ́sɨ́-) *v.* to call sweetly, coax into coming.

imánán (imánáni-) *pl.* **imánànɨ̀k**ᵃ. *n.* castor-oil plant: large shrub species whose hollow stems are used to make pipes and straws (for drinking from rock wells) and whose seeds are friend, ground, and made into a body lotion for women. *Ricinus communis*.

imánànɛs (imánánèsì-) *n.* childhood, childlikeness, childishness. *Lit.* 'being a child'.

imanɛs (imanɛsɨ́-) *v.* to plot against, vow to harm.

imánétòn (imánétònì-) *v.* to connect, encounter, meet, run into.

imanímánɛs (imanímánɛ́sɨ́-) *v.* to curl or wind around (e.g. a vine on a tree).

imánónuƙotᵃ (imánónuƙotɨ́-) *v.* to connect, encounter, join up, meet up, run into.

imáráɗàɗà (<imáráɗàɗòòn) *v.*

imáráɗàɗòòn (imáráɗàɗòònì-/imáráɗàɗa-) *v.* to be fancy, flashy, gaudy.

imasɛs (imasɛsɨ́-) *v.* to hurl, throw, toss.

imásɛ́suƙotᵃ (imásɛ́suƙotɨ́-) *v.* to hurl, throw, or toss away.

imasɛtɛs (imasɛtɛ́sɨ́-) *v.* to hurl, throw, or toss this way.

imásíts'ᵃ (imá-síts'à-) *n.* baby hair.

imátáŋɛs (imátáŋɛ́sɨ́-) *v.* to chew, masticate (esp. tobacco). Also pronounced as *mataŋɛs*.

imátôdᵃ (imá-tódà-) *n.* babble, baby talk.

imátsárɛs (imátsárɛ́sɨ́-) *v.* to brand, label, mark.

imaúròn (imaúrònì-) *v.* to feel dizzy, lightheaded, woozy.

imáxánɛs (imáxánɛ́sɨ́-) *1 v.* to wave. *2 v.* to greet, say hello to.

imáxánínɔs (imáxánínɔ́sɨ́-) *v.* to great each other.

imeda gwasáᵉ *n.* grinding stone held in the hand. *Lit.* 'child of the stone'.

iméɗélɛs (iméɗélɛ́sɨ́-) *v.* to rebuff, reject, snub, spurn, turn down.

iméɗétɔn (iméɗétɔ̀nì-) *v.* to flare up, flash.

iméɗétɔna ekwí *v.* to see stars (when concussed). *Lit.* 'flashing of the eye'.

imɛdímɛ́ɗɔn (imɛdímɛ́ɗɔ̀nì-) *v.* to flicker, glitter.

iméɗɔn (iméɗɔ̀nì-) *1 v.* to flare, flash. *2 v.* to be bright, brilliant.

iméɗɔ̀nà dìdìi *n.* lightning. *Lit.* 'flashing of rain'.

iméérɛs (iméérɛ́sɨ́-) *v.* to shift, transfer (from one like thing to another, i.e. container, place, etc.).

imɛɛs (imɛɛsɨ́-/imá-) *v.* to warm (by fire or sunlight).

imɛlɛs (imɛlɛsɨ́-) *v.* to flicker, flitter (e.g. the tongue).

iméníkánón (iméníkánònì-) *v.* to be untrue to one's word, untrustworthy.

Ìmèr (Ìmèrà-) *n.* name of a hill or mountain.

imetsés (imetsésí-) *1 v.* to fill in for, replace, substitute for, take over for. *2 v.* to inherit.

imetsités (imetsitesí-) *v.* to fill or put in, replace, substitute.

imidímídés (imidímídésí-) *v.* to dilate, enlarge (a small hole).

imidímídésa mɛná[ɛ] *1 v.* to elaborate or expand on the issues. *2 v.* to exaggerate or hyperbolize.

imídítsés (imídítsésí-) *v.* to fill, plug, stop up (a hole).

imídítsésa así *v.* to commit, devote, or plug oneself in.

imíjílés (imíjílésí-) *v.* to wink.

imilɛtés (imilɛtésí-) *v.* to dribble, drip, drop.

imilímílɔ̀n (imilímílɔ̀nì-) *v.* to pool, puddle (in small amounts).

imímíjés (imímíjésí-) *1 v.* to convulse, twitch (the face for fun). *2 v.* to shrug.

imínímínés (imínímínésí-) *1 v.* to feel, finger, play with. *2 v.* to conserve, economize, ration. See also *minímínatés*.

imíŋá (<imíŋóòn) *v.*

imíŋóòn (imíŋóònì-/imíŋá-) *v.* to come uninvitedly, show up unwelcomely.

imisɛs (imisɛsí-) *v.* to care, mind. See also *ikatsɛs*.

imítíŋa (<imítíŋɛɛs) *v.*

imítíŋɛɛs (imítíŋɛɛsí-/imítíŋa-) *v.* to pursue, seek (e.g. a wife).

imítíròn (imítírònì-) *v.* to be hazy, indistinct, vague.

imɔdɛs (imɔdɛsí-) *1 v.* to deceive, trick. *2 v.* to cheat, con, rip off, swindle.

imɔ́dɛ́sukɔt[a] (imɔ́dɛ́sukɔtí-) *v.* to cheat, heist, rip off.

imɔdɛtés (imɔdɛtésí-) *v.* to allure, bait, entice, lure.

imɔdímɔ́dés (imɔdímɔ́désí-) *v.* to slather, smear, spread.

imɔ́dɔ́rɔ̀n (imɔ́dɔ́rɔ̀nì-) *v.* to be sooty.

imɔ́jírés (imɔ́jírésí-) *v.* to intertwine, twine, twist.

imɔlɛs (imɔlɛsí-) *v.* to administer, allot, apportion, deal or dish out.

imɔlɛsiám (imɔlɛsí-ámà-) *pl.* **imɔlɛsíík**[a]. *n.* administrator.

imɔ́lɔ́ŋetés (imɔ́lɔ́ŋetésí-) *v.* to heat or warm up (e.g. water for bathing).

imɔ́métɔ̀n (imɔ́métɔ̀nì-) *v.* to hesitate, pause, stop, take a break. See also *mɔ́métɔ̀n*.

imɔ́mɔ́dés (imɔ́mɔ́désí-) *v.* to slather, smear, spread.

imɔ́ɲíka (<imɔ́ɲíkees) *v.*

imɔ́ɲíkees (imɔ́ɲíkeesí-/imɔ́ɲíka-) *1 v.* to dishevel, rumple, tangle. *2 v.* to mess up, ruin, spoil.

imɔ́ɲíkeetés (imɔ́ɲíkeetésí-) *1 v.* to dishevel, rumple up, tangle up. *2 v.* to mess up, ruin, spoil.

imɔrímɔ́rés (imɔrímɔ́résí-) *v.* to jumble, mix, or scramble up.

imɔrímɔ́rɔ́s (imɔrímɔ́rɔ́sí-) *v.* to be jumbled, mixed, or scrambled up.

imudúmúdɔ̀n (imudúmúdɔ̀nì-) *v.* to squint. See also *wízilɛ́s*.

imúítɛtés (imúítɛtésí-) *v.* to bear twins.

imujúmújɔ̀n (imujúmújɔ̀nì-) *v.* to draw or gather saliva.

imúká (<imúkɔ́ɔ̀n) *v.*

imúkáánón (imúkáánónì-) *v.* to be determined, driven.

imúkáitetés (imúkáitetésí-) *v.* to encourage, spur on, urge.

imúkɔ́ɔ̀n (imúkɔ́ɔ̀nì-/imúká-) *v.* to endure, persevere, press on.

imúmúitɛtés (imúmúitɛtésí-) *v.* to delight, make smile, please. See also *ilákásítésʉkɔtᵃ*.

imúmújés (imúmújésí-) *v.* to rinse, swish (the mouth). See also *igʉjʉgʉjés*.

imúmúɔ̀n (imúmúɔ̀nì-) *v.* to grin, smile. May also be spelled as *imúmwɔ́ɔ̀n*.

imúmúrés (imúmúrésí-) *v.* to do faster than others (e.g. eating at a feast).

imúmúrɔ̀n (imúmúrɔ̀nì-) *v.* to be faster than others (in doing, eating, etc.).

imúmwárés (imúmwárésí-) *v.* to amuse, entertain, regale, treat (with singing and dancing, e.g. visitors or one's in-laws during marriage ceremonies).

imúnúkukúón (imúnúkukúónì-) *1 v.* to ball up, clench (e.g. fists or clouds). *2 v.* to cramp up (of limbs).

imúnúkùkùɔ̀n (imúnúkùkùɔ̀nì-) *v.* to be numb (of body parts).

imúɲésʉkɔtᵃ (imúɲésʉkɔtí-) *v.* to finish off, wipe out (e.g. food, enemies, work). See also *iɲódésʉkɔtᵃ*.

imuɲɛtés (imuɲɛtésí-) *v.* to finish off, wipe out (e.g. food, enemies, work).

imúɲúmétòn (imúɲúmétònì-) *v.* to be finished off.

imúɔ́n (imúɔ́nì-) *v.* to be a twin.

imúránón (imúránónì-) *v.* to be undercooked. See also *kìtsòn*.

imúsá (<imúsɔ́ɔ̀n) *v.*

imúsɛ́ɛ̀tòn (imúsɛ́ɛ̀tònì-) *v.* to become foul, rank, smelly, or stinky.

imúsɔ́ɔ̀n (imúsɔ́ɔ̀nì-/imúsá-) *v.* to be foul, rank, smelly, stinky. See also *wízilílón*.

imutúmútòn (imutúmútònì-) *v.* to pout, sulk (often expressed in refusing food). See also *iɓútúŋɔ̀n*.

imutúmútɔ́s (imʉtúmútɔ́sí-) *v.* to be pouty, sulky.

imwaímwá (<imwaímwɛ́ɛ́s) *v.*

imwaímwɛ́ɛ́s (imwaímwɛ́ɛ́sí-/imwaímwá-) *1 v.* to spit on. *2 v.* to bless. See also *tatiés*.

imwáŋón (imwáŋónì-) *v.* to look around cautiously (e.g. so as to avoid enemies or one's mother-in-law).

ín (ínà) *1 adv.* what exactly ...? (an expression of uncertainty). *2 adv.* wow! (an expression of surprise).

inábɛs (inábɛsí-) *v.* to arrange, order, stack. See also *idɔ́bɛ̀s* and *itíbɛs*.

inábèsìàwᵃ (inábèsì-àwà-) *pl.* **inábɛsiawíkᵃ**. *n.* parking place.

inábèsùkɔtᵃ (inábèsùkɔ̀tí-) *v.* to arrange, put in order, stack up.

inábɛtés (inábɛtésí-) *v.* to arrange, order, set up, stack up.

inakᵃ (inakí-) *n.* nit(s): lice egg(s).

ináƙúés (ináƙúésí-) *v.* to destroy, ruin, wreck. May also be spelled as *ináƙwíés*.

ináƙúetés (ináƙúetésí-) *v.* to destroy, ruin, wreck. May also be spelled as *ináƙwietés*.

ináƙúós (ináƙúósí-) *v.* to be destroyed, ruined, wrecked. May also be spelled as *ináƙwóós*.

ináƙúotós (ináƙúotósí-) *v.* to be destroyed, ruined, wrecked. May also be spelled as *ináƙwíotós*.

inapɛs (inapɛsí-) *v.* to put alongside or beside.

inápésʉkɔtᵃ (inápésʉkɔtí-) *v.* to leave or put aside (e.g. in someone's care).

ɨnapɛtés (ɨnapɛtésɨ́-) v. to bring alongside or beside.

ɨnapɛtésá asɨ́ v. to come.

ɨnatsɨ́nátsés (ɨnatsɨ́nátsɛ́sɨ́-) v. to pat down (e.g. dough, hair, or mud).

inénéés (inénéésí-) v. to hang or tie up.

inénéésukotᵃ (inénéésukotí-) v. to hang or tie up.

ɨnɛpɨ́nɛ́pɔ̀n (ɨnɛpɨ́nɛ́pɔ̀nɨ̀-) v. to lick (of flames).

ínés (ínésì-) v. to inhabit, live or stay in.

ínésá (<inésóòn) v.

inésóòn (inésóònì-/inésá-) v. to parade about, show off.

ínésukotᵃ (ínésukotí-) v. to colonize, inhabit, move in, populate, settle.

iníámésukotᵃ (iníámésukotí-) v. to accompany, escort.

inietés (inietésí-) v. to pull down (e.g. a tree branch).

ɨnɨkwɨ́nɨ́kwés (ɨnɨkwɨ́nɨ́kwésɨ́-) v. to wiggle, wriggle, or work in (e.g. a stick to support something).

ɨnɨnés (ɨnɨnésɨ́-) v. to interrogate, press for details, probe.

inínós (inínósí-) v. to coinhabit, live or stay together.

iniŋes (iniŋesí-) 1 v. to assess, evaluate, test. 2 v. to try in court.

iniŋíníŋés (iniŋíníŋésí-) v. to make flinch, startle (e.g. by pretending to hit).

inipes (inipesí-) v. to bash, wallop, whack.

inípónítésúkotᵃ (inípónítésúkotí-) v. to delay, retard, slow down.

inípónòn (inípónònì-) v. to be slow, move slowly.

ɨnɔɛs (ɨnɔɛsɨ́-) v. to coil, loop, wind (e.g. a snake, or beads around the neck).

ɨnɔɛtés (ɨnɔɛtésɨ́-) v. to coil, loop around, or wind around.

ɨnɔɨnɔés (ɨnɔɨnɔésɨ́-) v. to loosen by pulling back and forth.

ínóƙwàz (ínó-ƙwàzà-) pl. ínóƙwazíkᵃ. n. leather clothing. Lit. 'animal-cloth'.

ɨnɔmɛs (ɨnɔmɛsɨ́-) v. to beat, cane, whip.

ɨnɔmɛtés (ɨnɔmɛtésɨ́-) v. to 'hit': exploit, harvest, take advantage of.

ínónànès (ínónànèsì-) n. animal-likeness, animateness.

ínósìts'ᵃ (ínó-sìts'à-) n. fur, pelt.

ɨnɔtsɛs (ɨnɔtsɛsɨ́-) v. to adhere, cling, or stick to.

ɨnʉɛs (ɨnʉɛsɨ́-) 1 v. to burden, encumber, weigh down. 2 v. to make ill.

ɨnʉ́ítésʉ́ƙotᵃ (ɨnʉ́ítésʉ́ƙotɨ́-) v. to make heavy.

ɨnʉkúnúkés (ɨnʉkúnúkésɨ́-) v. to mound: heap or pile up in a mound.

ɨnʉƙúnúƙwés (ɨnʉƙúnúƙwésɨ́-) v. to dissolve, melt (in the mouth, e.g. soft foods).

ɨnʉmúnúmés (ɨnʉmúnúmésɨ́-) v. to celebrate, observe.

ɨnʉ́númés (ɨnʉ́númésɨ́-) v. to celebrate, observe.

inunúmétòn (inunúmétònì-) v. to approach death or near death, be dying.

inunúmónukotᵃ (inunúmónukotí-) v. to be almost dead or dying.

ínwᵃ (ínó-) n. animal(s), beast(s), brute(s).

inwᵃ (inɔ́-) pl. initín. 1 n. arboreal vine species with square stems and milky sap. 2 n. milk bush: a euphorbia species with narrow round stems containing milky sap toxic to the eyes; it is used widely as a protective hedge around homes. *Euphorbia tirucalli*.

ínwá na awáᵉ *n.* domestic animal.

ínwá na rijáákɔ̀ᵉ *n.* wild animal.

iɲakes (iɲakesí-) *1 v.* to light up (e.g. with fire or a torch). *2 v.* to view (e.g. through binoculars or microscope). See also *iléúrés*.

iɲáɗútés (iɲáɗútésí-) *v.* to chew, masticate, ruminate.

iɲakes (iɲakesí-) *v.* to do again, redo, repeat. Also pronounced as *iɲokes*.

iɲales (iɲalesí-) *v.* to blend, combine, fuse, mix. See also *idyates*.

iɲatɛs (iɲatɛsí-) *v.* to knock, thump, whack (e.g. with a gunstock or stick).

iɲatiés (iɲatiesí-) *v.* to knock, thump, or whack repeatedly.

iɲatiesá kíjáᵉ *v.* to stumble or trip repeatedly.

iɲɛ́ɓɛ́rɛ́s (iɲɛ́ɓɛ́rɛ́sí-) *v.* to grimace: contort the face to show emotion.

iɲɛ́ɛ́mɔ̀n (iɲɛ́ɛ́mɔ̀nì-) *1 v.* to cry easily when threatened. *2 v.* to snarl, snap. *3 v.* to be fierce, savage, vicious. See also *dzálón*.

iɲɛɛs (iɲɛɛsí-) *1 v.* to enlarge, expand. *2 v.* to elaborate or expound on. See also *taɲɛɛs*.

iɲekes (iɲekesí-) *1 v.* to blow, squander, waste. *2 v.* to lose (something valuable).

iɲékésuƙotᵃ (iɲékésuƙotí-) *1 v.* to blow, squander, waste. *2 v.* to lose (something valuable). See also *eletiésuƙot*ᵃ.

iɲekíɲékés (iɲekíɲékésí-) *v.* to blow, squander, waste.

iɲéráánón (iɲéráánònì-) *v.* to be girl-crazy, obsessed with girls.

iɲés (iɲésì-) *1 v.* to pound (with a pestle, e.g. termites or tobacco). *2 v.* to pump (e.g. water from a borehole).

iɲétsé (<iɲétsóón) *v.*

iɲétséetés (iɲétséetésí-) *v.* to abort, miscarry, terminate. See also *iyétséetés*.

iɲétsóòn (iɲétsóònì-/iɲétsé-) *1 v.* to act, feign, pretend. *2 v.* to abort, fail (e.g. of weather, being drier than normal). See also *iyétsóòn*.

iɲibɛs (iɲibɛsí-) *v.* to nibble. See also *tɔjipɛs*.

iɲiiɲɔ̀n (iɲiiɲɔ̀nì-) *v.* to mewl, whimper. See also *iɲíɲɔ̀n*.

iɲíkáiƙotᵃ (<iɲíkéésuƙot**ᵃ) *v.*

iɲíkéésuƙotᵃ (iɲíkéésuƙotí-/ iɲíkáiƙot-) *v.* to flatten, stamp down, trample.

iɲíkétòn (iɲíkétònì-) *1 v.* to change, fluctuate. *2 v.* to begin frowning or scowling.

iɲikiétòn (iɲikiétònì-) *v.* to fluctuate, vacillate.

iɲikíɲíkòn (iɲikíɲíkònì-) *v.* to fluctuate, vacillate.

iɲíkón (iɲíkónì-) *1 v.* to be in flux, fluctuate. *2 v.* to frown, scowl.

iɲiliɲílánón (iɲiliɲílánònì-) *v.* to be disintegrating, falling apart.

iɲíɲiés (iɲíɲiésí-) *v.* to erase, rub off.

iɲíɲínés (iɲíɲínésí-) *v.* to dole, mete, or parcel out (e.g. food or money).

iɲíɲɔ̀n (iɲíɲɔ̀nì-) *v.* to mewl, whimper. See also *iɲiiɲɔ̀n*.

iɲipes (iɲipesí-) *v.* to snip, tip.

iɲipíɲípòn (iɲipíɲípònì-) *v.* to smolder.

iɲóɗésuƙotᵃ (iɲóɗésuƙotí-) *v.* to finish off. See also *imúɲésuƙot*ᵃ.

iɲokes (iɲokesí-) *v.* to do again, redo, repeat. Also pronounced as *iɲakes*.

iɲókésuƙotᵃ (iɲókésuƙotí-) *v.* to do again, redo, repeat.

iɲóɲóés (iɲóɲóésí-) *v.* to anoint, besmear.

íɲós (íɲósɨ-) *v.* to be pounded (with a pestle).

iɲɔ́táánón (iɲɔ́táánónì-) *v.* to be men-crazy, obsessed with men.

iɲúɲúánón (iɲúɲúánónì-) *1 v.* to be faint, obscure, vague (e.g. in a fog). *2 v.* to be jinxed: bring bad luck in food-gathering activities like hunting and gathering.

iɲúɲúrɔ̀n (iɲúɲúrɔ̀nɨ-) *v.* to bicker, quibble, squabble. See also *ɲúzʉmánón*.

iŋaalés (iŋaalésɨ-) *1 v.* to poison. *2 v.* to blackmail, threaten.

iŋaalésɨ̀am (iŋaalésɨ-àmà-) *pl.* **iŋaalésíik**ᵃ. *n.* poisoner.

iŋáámɛs (iŋáámɛsɨ-) *v.* to grind coarsely (into large particles).

iŋaarés (iŋaarésɨ-) *v.* to aid, assist, help.

iŋaarésɨ̀am (iŋaarésɨ-àmà-) *pl.* **iŋaarésíik**ᵃ. *n.* assistant, helper.

iŋaarímétòn (iŋaarímétònì-) *v.* to be aided, assisted, helped.

iŋááɨ́nɔ́s (iŋááɨ́nɔ́sɨ-) *v.* to help each other.

iŋaaɨ́nɔ́sá ƙwaatéᵒ *v.* to help give birth.

iŋábólés (iŋábólésí-) *v.* to leave open.

iŋábúkés (iŋábúkésí-) *v.* to grind a second time, regrind (e.g. after first pounding the grain).

iŋáɗá (<iŋáɗɛ́ɛs) *v.*

iŋáɗáiƙɔtᵃ (<iŋáɗɛ́ɛsuƙotᵃ) *v.*

iŋáɗɛ́ɛs (iŋáɗɛ́ɛsɨ-/iŋáɗá-) *v.* to put or set aside.

iŋáɗɛ́ɛsuƙotᵃ (iŋáɗɛ́ɛsuƙotí-/iŋáɗáiƙɔt-) *v.* to put or set aside.

iŋaíŋá (<iŋaíŋɛ́ɛs) *v.*

iŋaíŋɛ́ɛs (iŋaíŋɛ́ɛsɨ-/iŋaíŋá-) *1 v.* to grind coarsely. *2 v.* to chew roughly (e.g. uncooked maize). See also *ikaɲíkáɲés* and *iŋáɲɛ́ɛs*.

iŋaíŋɛ́ɛsa tódaᵉ *v.* to speak vaguely. *Lit.* 'to grind speech coarsely'.

iŋájápánón (iŋájápánónì-) *v.* to slur, speak indistinctly. See also *ɗákón*.

iŋáléètòn (iŋáléètònì-) *v.* to ease up, get better, get well, heal up, improve.

iŋáléòn (iŋáléònì-) *v.* to be healthy, in good condition, well.

iŋáɲá (<iŋáɲɛ́ɛs) *v.*

iŋáɲárɛtés (iŋáɲárɛtésɨ-) *1 v.* to collaborate or cooperate on. *2 v.* to gang up on (e.g. in a fight).

iŋáɲɛ́ɛs (iŋáɲɛ́ɛsɨ-/iŋáɲá-) *1 v.* to grind coarsely. *2 v.* to chew roughly (e.g. uncooked maize). See also *ikaɲíkáɲés* and *iŋaíŋɛ́ɛs*.

iŋárúrètòn (iŋárúrètònì-) *1 v.* to form seeds, seed (esp. grains). *2 v.* to break out, flare up (e.g. skin bumps or rashes).

iŋárúròn (iŋárúrònì-) *1 v.* to be seeded, have seeds (esp. grains). *2 v.* to be broken out, flared up (of skin bumps due to feeling cold, shaving the head, or getting a rash).

iŋátsátsá (<iŋátsátsóòn) *v.*

iŋátsátsóòn (iŋátsátsóònì- /iŋátsátsá-) *v.* to sit with one's legs apread apart.

iŋáúánón (iŋáúánónì-) *v.* to sit indecently (e.g. a woman with an open skirt).

iŋáyá (<iŋáyéés) *v.*

iŋáyéés (iŋáyéésí-/iŋáyá-) v. to doubt, question.

iŋilíŋílánón (iŋilíŋílánónì-) v. to be cut up in pieces.

iŋilíŋílés (iŋilíŋílésí-) v. to cut up into pieces.

iŋiníŋínɔ̀n (iŋiníŋínɔ̀nì-) v. to coo (of infants).

iŋísímɔ̀n (iŋísímɔ̀nì-) v. to be bucktoothed, toothy.

iŋitɛs (iŋitɛsí-) v. to reenact, retell.

iŋitiés (iŋitiesí-) v. to copy, emulate, imitate.

iŋɔ́ɓélés (iŋɔ́ɓélésí-) v. to glance sidelong at.

iŋóɗyàimètòn (iŋóɗyàimètònì-) v. to become chaotic, descend into chaos.

iŋókíánón (iŋókíánónì-) v. to be as poor or wretched as a dog.

iŋolíŋólés (iŋolíŋólésí-) v. to oscillate, swing side to side.

iŋolíŋólésa tódàᵉ v. to garble one's speech.

iŋolíŋólós (iŋolíŋólósí-) v. to be wary: looking this way and that.

iŋɔ́lɔ́ɓɔ́ɲés (iŋɔ́lɔ́ɓɔ́ɲésí-) v. to roll around (in one's mouth).

iŋomes (iŋomesí-) v. to chomp.

iŋɔ́písà (<iŋɔ́písɔ̀ɔ̀n) v.

iŋɔ́písɔ̀ɔ̀n (iŋɔ́písɔ̀ɔ̀nì-/iŋɔ́písa-) v. to bounce along, walk with springy steps.

iŋóyáánón (iŋóyáánónì-) v. to be angry, annoyed, upset.

iŋulúŋúlés (iŋulúŋúlésí-) 1 v. to cut with a dull knife. 2 v. to spear with a blunt tip. 3 v. to gum, mumble: chew without teeth.

iŋúŋúnɔ̀n (iŋúŋúnɔ̀nì-) v. to whine.

iŋʉrúŋúrɔ̀n (iŋʉrúŋúrɔ̀nì-) v. to complain, grumble, murmur.

iɔ́ɓɔ́rɛ́s (iɔ́ɓɔ́rɛ́sí-) 1 v. to lightly roast, toast. 2 v. to intimidate.

iɔkᵃ (iɔkɔ́-) n. nectar, pollen.

iɔ́kɔ̀n (iɔ́kɔ̀nì-) 1 v. to bloom, blossom, flower. 2 v. to be fertile, flourish.

iɔ́lɔ́lɔ̀n (iɔ́lɔ́lɔ̀nì-) v. to be steep.

iòn (iònì-) 1 v. to be (somewhere). May also be spelled as iyòn.

iona arágwaníkᵉ v. to flow, menstruate. Lit. 'to be in the month'.

iònà ɗòkᵘ v. to be alone, solitary, the only/sole.

iona ɛɗá v. to be alone, solitary.

iona muceékᵉ v. to be en route, on the way.

iona ńdà v. to be with, have.

iona ńda sea ni itsúr v. to be active, energetic. Lit. 'to have blood that boils'.

iona ɲítsaníkᵉ v. to be in trouble, have problems.

iɔ́ɔ́rɛ́s (iɔ́ɔ́rɛ́sí-) v. to glide, send soaring, sail.

iɔ́ɔ́rɔ̀n (iɔ́ɔ́rɔ̀nì-) v. to glide, sail, soar.

iɔ́s (iɔ́sì-) v. to be cleared, hoed up (e.g. patch of ground).

ipáɗáɲɔ̀n (ipáɗáɲɔ̀nì-) v. to be flat, level.

ipájɔ́n (ipájɔ́nì-) v. to sit on the ground.

ipakɛs (ipakɛsí-) v. to swipe: make a sweeping motion with one's hand.

ipakɛsa cué v. to fling water.

ipákɛsʉkɔtᵃ (ipákɛsʉkɔtí-) v. to fling, swipe away/off.

ipálákɔ̀n (ipálákɔ̀nì-) 1 v. to be feeble, frail, weak. 2 v. to be fickle at work, reliable only when the boss is around. See also juódòn.

ipalípálés (ipalípálésí-) *v.* to brush or sweep aside (e.g. the layer of slime on top of stagnant water so one can drink).

ipáŋka (<ipáŋkeés) *v.*

ipáŋkeés (ipáŋkeesí-/ipáŋka-) *1 v.* to hire, lease, rent. *2 v.* to organize, make plans, plan.

ipáŋwá (<ipáŋweés) *v.*

ipáŋweés (ipáŋweésí-/ipáŋwá-) *v.* to conceal, hide, hold in (e.g. food or emotions).

ipápá (<ipápɛɛ́s) *v.*

ipápɛɛ́s (ipápɛɛ́sí-/ipápá-) *v.* to moisten.

ipáríés (ipáríésí-) *v.* to demolish, destroy, wreck (e.g. a house during a robbery or vandalism). See also *itɔ́tɔ́és*.

ipáríŋánón (ipáríŋánóní-) *v.* to be perilous, precarious.

ìpàs (ìpàsɔ̀-) *n.* dance involving walking and the stomping of feet.

ipásɛ́tɔ̀n (ipásɛ́tɔ̀nì-) *v.* to dance by singing, stomping, and walking.

ipásóòn (ipásóònì-) *1 v.* to be unoccupied, have free time, kill time. *2 v.* to go for a visit. See also *ilɔ́ɔ́n*.

ipátsésuƙot[a] (ipátsésuƙɔtí-) *v.* to isolate, seclude, sequester (often in anger).

ipátsésuƙɔta así *v.* to isolate, seclude, or sequester oneself (often in anger).

ìpèɗààm (ìpèɗà-àmà-) *pl.* **ipeɗaik**[a]. *n.* bewitcher, hexer, jinxer.

ipeɗes (ipeɗesí-) *v.* to bewitch, hex, jinx. See also *suɓés*.

ipɛ́ɛ́pɛ́sá así *v.* to amble, saunter (esp. with flat, thin buttocks).

ipɛ́ɛ́rɔ̀n (ipɛ́ɛ́rɔ̀nì-) *v.* to get away, retreat, withdraw (e.g. from home).

ipɛipɛ́ɛ́s (ipɛipɛ́ɛ́sí-) *v.* to do aimlessly.

ipɛipɛ́ɛ́sá kíjá[e] *v.* to wander aimlessly.

ipɛipɛ́ɛ́sá tódà[e] *v.* to speak pointlessly.

ipɛlɛs (ipɛlɛsí-) *v.* to pare, peel, shave. See also *ilimɛs*.

ipɛlɛtam (ipɛlɛtamá-) *n.* peeling, shaving.

ipɛlípɛ́lɔ̀n (ipɛlípɛ́lɔ̀nì-) *v.* to be sleek, slick. See also *piɗíɗɔn*.

ipépétánón (ipépétánóní-) *v.* to sprawl.

ipépétánónuƙot[a] (ipépétánónuƙotí-) *v.* to sprawl out.

ipépétɛ́s (ipépétɛ́sí-) *v.* to lay out, spread about.

iperípérɔ̀n (iperípérɔ̀nì-) *v.* to flit around, flitter (e.g. in fighting, speaking).

ipés (ipésí-) *1 v.* to thresh. *2 v.* to thrash, trounce. *3 v.* to cast, toss (for divination).

ipésá gwàsìkà[e] *v.* to cast or toss stones (to divine the future).

ipésá taƙaíkà[ɛ] *v.* to cast or toss sandals (to divine the future).

ipétá (<ipétɛ́ɛ́s) *v.*

ipétɛ́ɛ́s (ipétɛ́ɛ́sí-/ipétá-) *v.* to make a platform or scaffolding.

ipéyeés (ipéyeésí-) *v.* to kill (an animal) and serve (to one's friends or relatives as a part of initiation to an age-group). See also *topues*.

ipéyéitésúƙot[a] (ipéyéitésúƙotí-) *v.* to make (an initiate) kill and serve (a ritual animal).

ipiipíòn (ipiipíònì-) *v.* to blow (of a chilly breeze).

ipiipíyeés (ipiipíyeesí-) *v.* to smoothen.

ipííríánón (ipííríánóní-) *v.* to have a great memory, remember clearly.

ipíìròn (ipíírònì-) *1 v.* jump down/off. *2 v.* to jump to it, leap into action. See also *apííròn*.

ipíjikɛ́s (ipíjikɛ́sí-) *v.* to inspect, investigate, scrutinize (e.g. someone on trial, or an animal's footprints).

ipíjikimɔ́s (ipíjikimɔ́sí-) *v.* to suspect each other.

ipíká (<ipíkéés) *v.*

ipíkéés (ipíkéésí-/ipíká-) *v.* to paddle, spank.

ipimɛs (ipimɛsí-) *1 v.* to measure, weigh. *2 v.* to diagnose, test. *3 v.* to aim for, target.

ipinípínòn (ipinípínònì-) *v.* to dribble, leak. See also *tɔléléòn*.

ipírintiŋeetés (ipírintiŋeetésí-) *v.* to print.

ipirípírés (ipirípírésí-) *v.* to bore, drill. See also *pulutiés*.

ipirípírètòn (ipirípírètònì-) *v.* to dawn red (before the orb of the sun is visible).

ipírisɛtés (ipírisɛtésí-) *v.* to pop or squeeze out (e.g. pus from a wound).

ipitɛs (ipitɛsí-) *v.* to tighten hard (e.g. a cap or rope).

ipitɔs (ipitɔsí-) *v.* to be tight, tightened hard.

ipíyáiƙot[a] (<ipíyéésuƙot[a]) *v.*

ipíyéésuƙot[a] (ipíyéésuƙotí- /ipíyáiƙot-) *v.* to defeat, outdo, overcome.

ipɔkɛs (ipɔkɛsí-) *v.* to slosh, splosh (a liquid in a container).

ipɔ́kɔ́n (ipɔ́kɔ́nì-) *v.* to be stuck (e.g. from sloshing back and forth).

ipoles (ipolesí-) *v.* to jerk, pull, yank. See also *iɓwates*.

ipoletés (ipoletésí-) *v.* to jerk, pull, or yank out/up.

ipɔ́pírés (ipɔ́pírésí-) *v.* to roll or twist up (e.g. cigarette or mat).

ipúká (<ipúkéés) *v.*

ipúkákòn (ipúkákònì-) *v.* to congeal when cooled (of hot foods). See also *tɔsɔ́dɔ́kɔn*.

ipúkéés (ipúkéésí-/ipúká-) *v.* to govern, reign over, rule.

ipúkéésíàm (ipúkéésí-àmà-) *pl.* **ipúkéésíik**[a]. *n.* governor, ruler, sovereign. See also *tòtwàrààm*.

ipukes (ipukesí-) *1 v.* to fan. *2 v.* to wave (e.g. objects for wishes and blessings).

ipukúpúkés (ipukúpúkésí-) *1 v.* to flap, flutter. *2 v.* to batter, clobber.

ipúkútsésuƙot[a] (ipúkútsésuƙotí-) *v.* to jam, push, or ram into.

ipúmɛ́tòn (ipúmɛ́tònì-) *v.* to dart or dash out.

ipúmɔ́nuƙot[a] (ipúmɔ́nuƙotí-) *v.* to dart or dash away/off.

ipunɛs (ipunɛsí-) *1 v.* to push (e.g. someone on a swing). *2 v.* to grind quickly (by pushing one stone against another).

ipúɲá (<ipúɲéés) *v.*

ipúɲéés (ipúɲéésí-/ipúɲá-) *v.* to make a funeral goat sacrifice to prevent the deceased's ghost from disturbing the relatives (by stunting their growth and the yield of their crops). See also *séés*.

ipuŋes (ipuŋesí-) *1 v.* to tilt. *2 v.* to tuck (into one's clothing).

ipuŋetés (ipuŋetésí-) *v.* to tilt over.

ipúpúŋés (ipúpúŋésí-) *v.* to enclose, wrap (e.g. in clothing or leaves).

ipúpúŋetés (ipúpúŋetésí-) *v.* to enclose, wrap up (e.g. in clothing or leaves).

ipúrá (<ipúréés) *v.*

ipúrá (<ipúróòn) *v.*

ipúréés (ipúréésí-/ipúrá-) *1 v.* to fumigate, smoke out. *2 v.* to ritually cover in smoke (by sacrificing a chicken). See also *iwaɲíwáŋés* and *ts'udités*.

ipúréètòn (ipúréètònì-) *v.* to begin to smoke, billow up, evaporate.

ipúróòn (ipúróònì-/ipúrá-) *v.* to billow, fume, smoke, waft.

ipʉtɛs (ipʉtɛsí-) *v.* to beat or knock down/off (e.g. dew from grass).

ipútésʉkɔta así *v.* to rush or take off.

ipútésʉkɔta muceé *v.* to blaze a trail.

ipʉtsɛs (ipʉtsɛsí-) *v.* to plaster.

ipwáákés (ipwáákésí-) *v.* to accuse or act falsely.

irá (<irɛɛs) *v.*

irábɛs (irábɛsí-) *v.* to harvest finger millet.

Iraf (Irafá-) *n.* name of a river that flows down from Kamion.

iraɨrá (<iraɨróòn) *v.*

iraɨróòn (iraɨróònì-/iraɨrá-) *v.* to glare, shine brightly.

irákáánás (irákáánàsì-) *n.* envy, jealousy.

irákáánón (irákáánònì-) *v.* to be envious, jealous.

irakɛs (irakɛsí-) *v.* to daze, stun (e.g. by slapping very hard).

irakɛsa así *v.* to make oneself envious or jealous.

irákésʉkɔt[a] (irákésʉkɔtí-) *v.* to daze, stun.

irákésʉkɔta así *1 v.* to get oneself high (on drugs). *2 v.* to be in ecstasy, have an orgasm.

irakiesúkota así *v.* to have seizures, seize.

irákímétòn (irákímétònì-) *1 v.* to have a seizure, seize. *2 v.* to feel sexual afterglow. *Lit.* 'to be stunned'.

iram (iramá-) *pl.* **irámík**[a]. *n.* thinly-sliced dehydrated food (e.g. meat and pumpkin). *Lit.* 'sliceable'.

iramɨrámés (iramɨrámɛsí-) *v.* to hit repeatedly.

iraɲ (iraɲí-) *n.* small corncobs and pieces of cobs left over after the larger cobs have been tied together by the husks.

iraŋɛs (iraŋɛsí-) *v.* to ruin, spoil.

iraŋɛtés (iraŋɛtésí-) *v.* to ruin, spoil.

iraɲímétòn (iraɲímétònì-) *1 v.* to become ruined or spoiled. *2 v.* to become upset.

iraŋɔs (iraŋɔsí-) *v.* to be ruined, spoiled.

iráɲúnánón (iráɲúnánònì-) *1 v.* to be ruined, spoiled. *2 v.* to be corrupt, depraved. *3 v.* to be dirty, soiled.

irapɛs (irapɛsí-) *v.* to reclaim, recover.

irápésʉkɔt[a] (irápésʉkɔtí-) *v.* to reclaim, recover.

irapɛtés (irapɛtésí-) *v.* to reclaim, recover.

irárákés (irárákésí-) *v.* to crack into pieces .

irárátés (irárátésí-) *v.* to gather, glean, harvest, reap (from the ground).

irarɛs (irarɛsí-) *v.* to gather, glean, harvest, reap (from the ground). See also *irárátés* and *tararɛs*.

iratɨrátés (iratɨrátésí-) *v.* to spatter, splatter (e.g. heavy rain on the ground). See also *irwatɛs* and *irwaɨrwéés*.

irɛɓɛs (irɛɓɛsí-) *v.* to clip, snip.

irébésuk̢otᵃ (irébésuk̢otí-) v. to clip or snip off.

irɛɓírɛ́ɓés (irɛɓírɛ́ɓésí-) v. to cause sharp pain in.

irɛɗɛs (irɛɗɛsí-) v. to grab, seize, snatch.

irɛɛs (irɛɛsí-/irá-) v. to beat, trounce, vanquish (in a game).

irɛɛsa dikwáᵉ v. to keep the beat (of a dance by clapping).

irɛjes (irɛjesí-) v. to cut, mow, slash (vegetation).

irékóɗiŋa (<irékóɗiŋeés) v.

irékóɗiŋeés (irékóɗiŋeesí- /irékóɗiŋa-) v. to record (music, voice, etc.).

irɛmɛs (irɛmɛsí-) v. to frighten or scare off/away.

irémóòn (irémóònì-) v. to cause conflict, create insecurity.

ireɲes (ireɲesí-) v. to clear, hoe up (grass, leaving only soil). See also iés.

iréɲésuk̢otᵃ (iréɲésuk̢otí-) v. to clear away (grass, leaving only soil).

iréɲíánón (iréɲíánónì-) v. to be violent. See also ifulúfúlòn.

irés (irésí-) v. to medicate, treat.

írés (irésì-) 1 v. to cut in slices, slice. 2 n. to conduct a ceremony, do a ritual. See also irikírikés.

irésíàm (irésí-àmà-) pl. irésiikᵃ. n. traditional healer. See also ŋkwa.

írésiŋk̢ák̢ᵃ (írési-ŋk̢ák̢á-) n. banquet, ceremonial meal, feast.

iretes (iretesí-) v. to do like, make like.

irɛtɛs (irɛtɛsí-) v. to prevent, resist (e.g. diseases).

irex (irexí-) pl. iréxíkᵃ. n. shell of a small white water-snail.

iríá (<iríóòn) v.

iríáik̢otᵃ (<iríóonuk̢otᵃ) v.

iriánitetés (iriánitetésí-) 1 v. to equalize, make equal (amounts, portions). 2 v. to compare, equate. 3 v. to balance (figures, the books). See also ikwáánitetés.

iriánòn (iriánònì-) v. to be equal, the same.

iriánònà dèìkàᵋ v. to march. Lit. 'the being equal of legs'.

iriánonuk̢otᵃ (iriánonuk̢otí-) v. to become equal, equate.

iríɓá (<iríɓéés) v.

iríɓéés (iríɓéésí-/iríɓá-) v. to assault, attack, conduct an operation against, mount an offensive against.

iríɗòn (iríɗònì-) v. to gravitate, move to a point.

iriɗɛs (iriɗɛsí-) 1 v. to bind, constrict, squeeze. 2 v. to confine, limit, restrict.

iriɗɛsá bùbùàᵉ v. to bind the stomach (to relieve hunger pangs).

iriɗɛtés (iriɗɛtésí-) 1 v. to bind, compress, constrict, squeeze. 2 v. to confine, limit, restrict.

iriɗétòn (iriɗétònì-) v. to decease, expire, perish.

iriɗɔ́n (iriɗɔ́nì-) v. to hurt, suffer.

iriɗɔs (iriɗɔsí-) 1 v. to be bound, compressed, constricted, narrow, tight. 2 v. to be constrained, limited, restricted.

iriétòn (iriétònì-) v. to come of age, grow, mature.

iriìtánón (iriìtánónì-) v. to be gluey, sticky (e.g. gum, honey, okra).

iriítés (iriítésí-) v. to ferry, transfer, transport.

irijɛs (irijɛsí-) v. to tie tightly.

irijɔs (irijɔsí-) v. to be tied tightly.

Irikakokor (Irika-kokoró-) *n.* name of a ridge where there used to be several Ik villages. *Lit.* 'surround-the-ridge'.

irikɛs (irikɛsí-) *v.* to encircle, surround.

iríkɛsukɔtᵃ (iríkɛsukɔtí-) *1 v.* to encircle, surround. *2 v.* to finish, fulfill (e.g. a work contract). *3 v.* to finish off.

irikɛtés (irikɛtésí-) *v.* to encircle, surround.

irikíríkés (irikíríkésí-) *v.* to cut in slices, slice up. See also *írés*.

irikíríkòn (irikíríkònì-) *1 v.* to twitch, vellicate (e.g. an eyelid or muscle). *2 v.* to quake, tremor. See also *kwalíkwálòn*.

iríƙá (<iríƙéés) *v.*

iríƙéés (iríƙéésí-/iríƙá-) *v.* to polish, rub (e.g. wax in a beehive, mud on a sculpture, or sand to clean pots).

iríƙímánón (iríƙímánónì-) *v.* to lounge, sit around (as a group, e.g. while taking a break from work).

irikíríkés (irikíríkésí-) *v.* to saw.

irímá (<iríméés) *v.*

iríméés (iríméésí-/irímá-) *v.* to treat respectfully.

irimes (irimesí-) *v.* to circulate, go around, or rotate around in.

irimesíám (irimesí-ámà-) *pl.* **irimesíík**ᵃ. *1 n.* scout, spy. *2 n.* roamer, rover.

irimétòn (irimétònì-) *v.* to circulate, come around, rotate.

irimírímés (irimírímésí-) *v.* to recce, reconnoiter, scout out.

irimítetés (irimítetésí-) *v.* to circulate, rotate, spin.

irímón (irímónì-) *v.* to circulate, move around, rotate, spin.

irinɛs (irinɛsí-) *v.* to peer over the side at (e.g. of a cliff or container).

iríŋétòn (iríŋétònì-) *v.* to turn this way.

iríŋítés (iríŋítésí-) *v.* to spin, turn.

iríŋítésukɔtᵃ (iríŋítésukɔtí-) *v.* to turn around/away.

iríŋón (iríŋónì-) *1 v.* to spin, turn. *2 v.* to orbit, revolve.

iríŋónukɔtᵃ (iríŋónukɔtí-) *v.* to turn around/away (that way).

iríóòn (iríóònì-/iríá-) *v.* to spend or take time (during the day).

iríóonukɔtᵃ (iríóonukɔtí-/iríáiƙot-) *v.* to spend the day, spend time.

iripetés (iripetésí-) *v.* to skim off (the top layer, e.g. cream from milk or leaves from the surface of water. See also *iƙáálés*.

irípétòn (irípétònì-) *v.* to come late in the afternoon or evening. See also *íbànètòn*.

irípón (irípónì-) *v.* to go late in the afternoon or evening. See also *íbànòn*.

irírá (<iríréés) *v.*

irírá (<iríréés) *v.*

iríráiƙɔtᵃ (<iríréésuƙɔt**ᵃ**) *v.*

iríréés (iríréésí-/irírá-) *v.* to feed or fuel (fire).

iríréés (iríréésí-/irírá-) *v.* to collect, gather. See also *itsunɛtés*.

iríréésuƙɔtᵃ (iríréésuƙɔtí-/iríráiƙɔt-) *v.* to assemble, collect, gather up.

iríréetés (iríréetésí-) *1 v.* to feed or fuel (fire). *2 v.* to mobilize, muster, rally, summon.

iríréɛtésá así *v.* to assemble, congregate, gather oneselves.

iríríjés (iríríjésí-) *v.* to spread around (coals in a fire, to reduce heat).

iríríkòn (iríríkònì-) *v.* to be ready to fight, in a fighting posture.

iritsésí (iritsésí-) *1 v.* to guard, hang on to, keep. *2 v.* to care for, take care of. *3 v.* to manage, oversee, supervise. *4 v.* to contain.

iritsésá así *1 v.* to care for oneself. *2 v.* to be self-controlled.

iritsésá ɲeɗekéicíká° *v.* to keep healthy (from illnesses).

iritsésíàm (iritsésí-àmà-) *pl.* **iritsésíik**[a]. *1 n.* caretaker, keeper, manager. *2 n.* heir, inheritor. *3 n.* deacon.

iriwes (iriwesí-) *v.* to fence (the outer fence).

irɔɗíróɗés (irɔɗíróɗésí-) *v.* to burn a little in a controlled manner (e.g. some grass around the village, still a bit green).

irójíés (irójíésí-) *v.* to search for in vain.

irɔjírójés (irɔjírójésí-) *v.* to clack, crack, crunch (to evoke such sounds, e.g. cracking knuckles or a plastic bottle, or cocking a gun).

irɔjírójésá kɔrókíkà[ɛ] *v.* to crack the knuckles.

iroketés (iroketésí-) *1 v.* to create, devise, invent, make up. *2 v.* to compose (music). See also *iɗimɛtés* and *tɔsʉɓɛs*.

iróƙóòn (iróƙóònì-) *v.* to be bony, cadaverous, emaciated, skeletal. See also *itóƙóƙòòn* and *kwéɗekwedánón*.

irɔmɛs (irɔmɛsí-) *v.* to cycle, recycle.

ìròn (ìrònì-) *v.* to be (somehow).

ironuƙot[a] (ironuƙotí-) *v.* to become (somehow).

iróríkés (iróríkésí-) *n.* to ceremonially finish off (the crops by harvesting last seedheads and cutting and chewing the stalks).

iróróbes (iróróbesí-) *v.* to burn off (land).

irórókánón (irórókánónì-) *v.* to have an appetite, craving, hankering.

iróróƙés (iróróƙésí-) *v.* to hollow out.

iróróòn (iróróònì-) *v.* to corrode, rust. See also *simírón*.

iroroy[a] (iroroí-) *n.* tree species used for fencing and whose root decoction is mixed with the contents of the third stomach and stomach fat of goats or sheep and drunk as a cure for headaches and a head disease called *lokóú*. *Maerua triphylla*.

irotes (irotesí-) *1 v.* to shift, ship, transfer, transport. *2 v.* to transplant. *3 v.* to delegate.

irotírótés (irotírótésí-) *1 v.* to shift, ship, or transfer repeatedly. *2 v.* to postpone or put off repeatedly.

iruɓes (iruɓesí-) *v.* to crunch, munch.

ìrùk[a] (ìrùkà-) *n.* singing, song, vocals.

ìrùkààm (ìrùkà-àmà-) *pl.* **irukaik**[a]. *n.* singer, vocalist. See also *irukósíàm*.

ìrùkàhò (ìrùkà-hòò-) *pl.* **irukahoík**[a]. *n.* singing hall.

irukes (irukesí-) *v.* to chase or run after. See also *ilɔɲɛs*.

irúkésuƙot[a] (irúkésuƙotí-) *v.* to chase or run after.

iruketés (iruketésí-) *v.* to heap or pile up. See also *kitsetés*.

irúkón (irúkónì-) *v.* to sing.

irukósíàm (irukósí-àmà-) *pl.* **irukósíik**[a]. *n.* singer, vocalist. See also *ìrùkààm*.

irʉmɛs (irʉmɛsí-) *v.* to cling to, embrace, hug.

irúmúnós (irúmúnósí-) *v.* to embrace or hug each another.

irúpá (<irúpóòn) *v.*

irúpèètòn (irúpèètònì-) *v.* to be the final one to come, last to show up (e.g. a person to a meeting or the last rain of the season).

irúpóòn (irúpóònì-/irúpá-) *v.* to be the final one to arrive, last to show up (e.g. a person to a meeting or the last rain of the season).

irúrúɓɛ́s (irúrúɓɛ́sɨ́-) *n.* to brace, stabilize (e.g. a beehive's grass cover by inserting several small sticks to hold it in place).

irúrúƙɛ́s (irúrúƙɛ́sɨ́-) *v.* to push in and out (back and forth, like a stick in a fire).

irúrúmà (<irúrúmòòn) *v.*

irúrúmòòn (irúrúmòònì-/irúrúma-) *v.* to howl, roar, thunder (e.g. a woman in labor, a swarm of bees, or a jet plane taking off).

irᵾtsɛs (irᵾtsɛsɨ́-) *v.* to fling, hurl, project (e.g. food in the mouth, or bullets).

irᵾtsɛsa asɨ *v.* to dart, race, speed.

irutumén (irutuméní-) *n.* half of a butchered hyrax, including the front leg, ribs, and the back leg on one side.

irúútés (irúútésí-) *v.* to ream out: clear out with a back and forth motion.

irwaírwá (<irwaírwéés) *v.*

irwaírwéés (irwaírwéésí-/irwaírwá-) *v.* to spatter, sprinkle. See also *iratɨ́rátɛ́s* and *irwates*.

irwanes (irwanesí-) *v.* to cache, hoard, stash.

irwapírwápòn (irwapírwápònì-) *v.* to blink, nictate, wink. See also *ɨɓèdɨ̀ɓèdɔ̀n*.

irwápón (irwápóní-) *v.* to droop, sag (of eyelids).

Irwátà (Irwátàà-) *n.* a personal name.

irwates (irwatesí-) *v.* to spatter, sprinkle. See also *iratɨ́rátɛ́s* and *irwaírwéés*.

irwatesa kíxᵒ *v.* to whip lightly. *Lit.* 'to spatter with a switch'.

iryámétòn (iryámétònì-) *v.* to acquire, get, meet with. The object acquired takes the dative case.

iryámétona ŋiléétsìkᵉ *v.* to become ashamed, disgraced, or embarrassed.

iryámíryámètòn (iryámíryámètònì-) *v.* to assemble, congregate, meet together.

iryámítetésá ŋiléétsìkᵉ *v.* to disgrace, embarrass, shame.

Iryɔ́kɔ́ (Iryɔ́kɔ́ɔ̀-) *n.* name of a river and ravine near *Lopokókᵃ*.

ɨs (ìsì-) *pro.* what?

isá (<isóón) *v.*

isá (<isɛɛs) *v.*

isáánɨŋa (<isáánɨŋeés) *v.*

isáánɨŋeés (isáánɨŋeesí-/isáánɨŋa-) *v.* to sign.

isáɓɨ́sɨŋa (<isáɓɨ́sɨŋɛɛs) *v.*

isáɓɨ́sɨŋɛɛs (isáɓɨ́sɨŋɛɛsɨ́-/isáɓɨ́sɨŋa-) *v.* to maintain, service (a vehicle).

isaɨsáyá (<isaɨsáyées) *v.*

isaɨsáyées (isaɨsáyéesí-/isaɨsáyá-) *v.* to miss repeatedly.

isalɛs (isalɛsɨ́-) *1 v.* to sieve, sift, sort. *2 v.* to disprove, refute. See also *rɔrɛ́s*.

isalɛtɛ́s (isalɛtɛ́sí-) *1 v.* to sieve, sift, sort. *2 v.* to disprove, refute.

isálílètòn (isálílètònì-) *v.* to go asleep, go into paresthesia (of limbs).

isálílòn (isálílònì-) *1 v.* to ache, hurt (of teeth, e.g. when exposed to sourness). *2 v.* to be asleep or in paresthesia (of limbs).

isálímétòn (isálímétònì-) *v.* to be disproven, refuted.

isalités (isalitésí-) *1 v.* to make sieve, sift, or sort. *2 v.* to disprove, refute, show to be wrong.

ísánòn (ísánònì-) *v.* to be apprehensive, concerned, worried.

ísánonuƙot[a] (ísánonuƙotí-) *v.* to become apprehensive, concerned or worried.

Ísɛ (Ísɛ́ɛ̀-) *n.* name of a river.

isɛbɛs (isɛbɛsí-) *1 v.* to notch, mark, score. *2 v.* to scarify: make cosmetic cuts or marks on the skin.

isɛbísébɛ́s (isɛbísébɛ́sí-) *v.* to scarify: make cosmetic cuts or marks on the skin.

isɛbɔs (isɛbɔsí-) *1 v.* to be notched, marked, scored. *2 v.* to be scarified: have cosmetic cuts or mark on the skin.

isɛɛs (isɛɛsí-/isá-) *1 v.* to miss (a shot). *2 v.* to survive (a mishap).

isɛɛsa mɛná[ɛ] *v.* to miss the point.

iséétòn (iséétònì-) *v.* to begin, commence, start. See also *itsyákétòn*.

iséísɛ́ɔn (iséísɛ́ɔnì-) *v.* to drizzle.

isɛkísékés (isɛkísékésí-) *v.* to sample from (e.g. different grains during a famine, so as to not eat all of one kind, leaving some for planting).

isɛ́ƙɔ́ánón (isɛ́ƙɔ́ánónì-) *v.* to be disobedient, insubordinate.

isélétésuƙota así *v.* to glide, slide, or slip through (e.g. the air).

iséméés (iséméésí-) *v.* to admire, check out, eye, inspect, look over.

isémeétés (iséméetésí-) *v.* to admire, check out, eye, inspect, look over.

isémúra (<isémúreés) *v.*

isémúreés (isémúreesí-/isémúra-) *v.* to fall for, fall in love with.

isépón (isépónì-) *v.* to course, flow.

isɛ́pɔ́n (isɛ́pɔ́nì-) *v.* to gimp, hobble. See also *itɔ́kɔ́ɔ̀n* and *itsúkúkòn*.

isépónuƙot[a] (isépónuƙotí-) *v.* to flow away.

isér (iserá-) *n.* jackal (black-backed and/or side-striped). *Canis sp.*

isérérèòn (isérérèònì-) *1 v.* to be horizontally straight. *2 v.* to go straight ahead.

iséréròn (iséréròni-) *v.* to be vertically straight, upright.

isésékés (isésékésí-) *v.* to sample from (e.g. different grains during a famine, so as to not eat all of one kind, leaving some for planting).

isésélés (isésélésí-) *v.* to crop, lop, prune, trim back.

isíɗá (<isíɗóòn) *v.*

isíɗéètòn (isíɗéètònì-) *v.* to fall back/behind, lag. See also *maɗámón*.

isíɗóòn (isíɗóònì-/isíɗá-) *v.* to hang back, lag, stay behind.

isiɛnɨk[ɛ] *n.* for what? why?

isíílés (isíílésí-) *v.* to assort, categorize, classify.

isíílɛtés (isíílɛtésí-) *v.* to pick or select according to categories.

isíítés (isíítésí-) *v.* to accuse, charge.

isíítésìàm (isíítésɨ̀-àmà-) *pl.* **isíítésiik**[a]. *n.* accuser, prosecutor.

isɨk[a] (isɨkà-) *n.* bullrush, cat's-tail, nail-rod, reedmace.

isikares (isikaresí-) *v.* to press, pressure, pressurize.

isikɛs (isikɛsí-) *1 v.* to cram, pack, stuff. *2 v.* to inflate, pump up (e.g. a ball). See also *rʉtsés*.

isíƙá (<isíƙéés) *v.*

isíƙá (<isíƙóòn) *v.*

isíƙéés (isíƙéésí-/isíƙá-) *v.* to hold back, prevent, restrain (some intended action).

isíƙóòn (isíƙóònì-/isíƙá-) *v.* to hesitate, pause, waver.

isɨ́lɨ́ánitɛtés (isɨ́lɨ́ánitɛtésɨ́-) *v.* to devastate, lay waste to, ravage (e.g. what bushpigs do to a garden, or sexual violence against women).

isɨ́lɨ́ánón (isɨ́lɨ́ánónì-) *v.* to be brutal, feral, savage, vicious.

isɨ́lɨ́tésuƙotᵃ (isɨ́lɨ́tésuƙotɨ́-) *v.* to conciliate, harmonize, make peace, reconcile.

isɨ́lɔ́n (isɨ́lɔ́nì-) *v.* to be harmonious, peaceful.

isɨ́lɔ́nìàm (isɨ́lɔ́nì-àmà-) *pl.* **isɨ́lɔ́niik**ᵃ. *n.* peaceful person.

isɨ́lɔ́nuƙotᵃ (isɨ́lɔ́nuƙotɨ́-) *v.* to become peaceful, stabilize.

isimam (isimamá-) *n.* food peelable with the teeth (e.g. the sweet canes of maize and sorghum).

isimɛs (isimɛsɨ́-) *v.* to peel with the teeth (e.g. the sweet canes of maize and sorghum).

isɨ́nákòn (isɨ́nákònì-) *v.* to sprout (of maize cobs).

isipísipòn (isipísipònì-) *v.* to jog, lope, trot. See also *isɔƙɨ́sɔ́ƙɔ̀n* and *isumúsúmɔ̀n*.

isires (isiresí-) *v.* to decorate, embellish, embroider.

isiresa aƙáᵉ *v.* to speak eloquently, wax eloquent. *Lit.* 'to embellish the mouth'.

isirísɨ́rɔ́n (isirísɨ́rɔ́nì-) *v.* to have a squeaky voice.

isiros (isirosí-) *v.* to be decorated, embellished, embroidered.

isísá (<isíséés) *v.*

isíséés (isíséésí-/isísá-) *v.* to narrate, recount, tell.

isíséésìàm (isíséésí-àmà-) *pl.* **isíséésiik**ᵃ. *n.* narrator, storyteller. See also *emútíkààm*.

isites (isitesí-) *v.* to burden, encumber, make heavy, weigh down.

isítíya (<isítíyeés) *v.*

isítíyeés (isítíyeesí-/isítíya-) *v.* to expend, use, utilize.

isɔ́ɓɔ́lés (isɔ́ɓɔ́lésɨ́-) *v.* to maintain poorly, neglect (e.g. home or garden).

isɔɛs (isɔɛsɨ́-) *v.* to slide, slip (e.g. when swallowing food without chewing).

isɔɛtés (isɔɛtésɨ́-) *1 v.* to slide, slip (e.g. when swallowing without chewing). *2 v.* to give birth to prematurely.

isɔɛtésá así *v.* to slide or slip oneself through.

isókétòn (isókétònì-) *v.* to get up and come early.

isókítésuƙotᵃ (isókítésuƙotí-) *v.* to get up and send away early.

Isókóìàƙwᵃ (Isókóì-àƙɔ-) *n.* name of a place. *Lit.* 'among euphorbias'.

isókón (isókónì-) *v.* to get up and go early.

isɔ́kɔ́ta (<isɔ́kɔ́teés) *v.*

isɔ́kɔ́teés (isɔ́kɔ́teesí-/isɔ́kɔ́ta-) *v.* to smoke (a cigarette).

isókóyᵃ (isókóì-) *pl.* **isókóik**ᵃ. *n.* tall euphorbia tree species from which bees makes bitter honey. *Euphorbia bussei.*

isɔƙɨ́sɔ́ƙɔ̀n (isɔƙɨ́sɔ́ƙɔ̀nì-) *v.* to jog, lope, trot. See also *isipísipòn* and *isumúsúmɔ̀n*.

isólólòètòn (isólólòètònì-) *v.* to clear off/up visually (eyes, skies).

isólólòòn (isólólòònì-) *v.* to be visually clear (eyes, sky).

isómá (<isómééś) *v.*

isómáìmètòn (isómáìmètònì-) *v.* to be legible, readable.

isómáitetés (isómáitetésí-) *v.* to educate, teach to read.

isómééś (isómééśí-/isómá-) *1 v.* to read. *2 v.* to study.

isómééśíàm (isómééśí-àmà-) *pl.* **isómééśíik**[a]. *1 n.* reader. *2 n.* pupil, student.

isɔmɛs (isɔmɛsí-) *v.* to toss out of sight (e.g. into tall grass or brush).

ìsòn (ìsònì-) *v.* to be burdensome, heavy, weighty.

isɔ́nɛ́sɔ̀n (isɔ́nɛ́sɔ̀nì-) *v.* to be dejected, depressed, downcast.

isóón (isóónì-/isá-) *1 v.* to begin, commence, start. *2 n.* taboo of eating before the elders eat.

Isópìà (Isópìà-) *n.* Abyssinia, Ethiopia. See also *Sópìà*.

isɔrɔɓam (isɔrɔɓamá-) *n.* slurpable food (e.g. thick porridge).

isɔ́rɔ́ɓɛ́s (isɔ́rɔ́ɓɛ́sí-) *v.* to slurp. See also *xáɓútés*.

isɔ́rɔ́kánón (isɔ́rɔ́kánónì-) *v.* to be a youth.

isósóŋós (isósóŋósí-) *v.* to shift, stir (while sitting or sleeping).

isɔ́wá (<isɔ́wɔ́ɔ̀n) *v.*

isɔ́wɔ́ɔ̀n (isɔ́wɔ́ɔ̀nì-/isɔ́wá-) *v.* to walk feebly (e.g. from sickness or thirst). See also *iɛmón*.

isuɗam (isuɗamá-) *pl.* **isúɗámìk**[a]. *n.* false information, lie.

isuɗes (isuɗesí-) *v.* to distort, falsify, make up, perjure.

isuɗesa mɛná[ɛ] *v.* to be 'full of it', lie, prevaricate. *Lit.* 'to distort matters'.

isuɗetés (isuɗetésí-) *v.* to distort, falsify, make up, perjure.

isukɛs (isukɛsí-) *1 v.* to bypass, go around, overtake. *2 v.* to exceed, surpass, top . *3 v.* to win. See also *súkɛ́s*.

isúmétòn (isúmétònì-) *v.* to sneak up: come without informing anyone.

isúmón (isúmónì-) *v.* to sneak: come or go without informing anyone.

isúmónukɔt[a] (isúmónukɔtí-) *v.* to sneak off: go without informing anyone.

isumúsúmòn (isumúsúmònì-) *v.* to jog, lope, trot. See also *isipísípòn* and *isɔkísókɔ̀n*.

isuɲɛs (isuɲɛsí-) *v.* to take all of.

isúɲésukɔt[a] (isúɲésukɔtí-) *v.* to give or take away all of.

isuɲetés (isuɲetésí-) *v.* to bring all of.

isúŋúrés (isúŋúrésí-) *v.* to entice, get to come, lure (e.g. by pinching, poking, or winking, esp. to do something like eat or have sex).

isúrúmòn (isúrúmònì-) *v.* to back out, draw back, withdraw (e.g. an animal from a trap).

isúsúés (isúsúésí-) *v.* to egg on, incite, provoke, urge on. See also *itsótsóés*.

isutɛs (isutɛsí-) *v.* to move (an object).

isútésukɔt[a] (isútésukɔtí-) *v.* to move (an object) away/off.

isutɛtés (isutɛtésí-) *v.* to move (an obect) this way.

isútɔ́n (isútɔ̀nì-) *v.* to change position, move, shift.

isúwá (<isúwɔ́ɔ̀n) *v.*

isúwɔ́ɔ̀n (isúwɔ́ɔ̀nì-/isúwá-) *1 v.* to be sterile, unproductive (e.g. of grains which are overcrowded, thereby no producing heads). *2 v.* to be overfull to the bursting point of the container (e.g. a granary or a sack).

íswᵃ (ísó-) *n.* flood, torrent.

isyá (<isyees) *v.*

isyees (isyeesí-/isyá-) *v.* to harass, harry.

isyones (isyonesí-) *v.* to have mercy or take pity on.

isyónón (isyónónì-) *v.* to be merciful, have pity.

isyónónkotᵃ (isyónónkotí-) *v.* to become merciful, soften (emotionally).

itá (<itɔ́ɔ́n) *v.*

itáɓóòn (itáɓóònì-) *v.* to drip, drizzle.

itaités (itaitésí-) *v.* to get there, make reach.

itaitetés (itaitɛtésí-) *v.* to get here, make reach here.

itakɛs (itakɛsí-) *v.* to strip, unstick (e.g. an adhesive bandage).

itákɛsukotᵃ (itákɛsukotí-) *v.* to strip off, unstick (e.g. a bandage).

itákálés (itákálésí-) *1 v.* to mislay, misplace. *2 v.* to do/make poorly.

itákálésá así *v.* to hibernate, hole up.

itákúòn (itákúònì-) *v.* to go on, follow, proceed.

itáléánón (itáléánónì-) *v.* to be forbidden, off limits, prohibited, taboo.

itáléés (itáléésí-) *1 v.* to forbid, prohibit, make taboo. *2 v.* to menstruate. See also *dimités*.

italɛs (italɛsí-) *v.* to accustom, habituate, make used to.

itálóós (itálóósí-) *v.* to be forbidden, off limits, prohibited, taboo.

italɔs (italɔsí-) *v.* to be accustomed, habituated, used to.

itam (itamá-) *n.* carrion. *Lit.* 'findable'.

itámáánón (itámáánónì-) *v.* to be necessary: must, ought, should. Must be followed by another verb.

ítánésukotᵃ (ítánésukotí-) *v.* to hope, long, or yearn for.

ítánòn (ítánònì-) *v.* to hope, long, yearn.

itáɲátɔ̀n (itáɲátɔ̀nì-) *v.* to like or tend (to do). Must be followed by another verb in the infinitive.

itaósés (itaósésí-) *v.* to slight, snub (by giving a lesser portion to).

itapítápɔ̀n (itapítápɔ̀nì-) *v.* to feel or fumble around (e.g. on the ground like a small child or elderly person).

itárákáɲés (itárákáɲésí-) *v.* to hide where easily found.

itásónòn (itásónònì-) *v.* to be sad, sorrowful. See also *tasónón*.

itátá (<itátéés) *v.*

itátámés (itátámésí-) *1 v.* to instruct, teach, train. *2 v.* to evangelize, preach. See also *nɔɔsanitetés*.

itátámésìam (itátámésí-àmà-) *pl.* **itátámésiikᵃ**. *1 n.* instructor, teacher, trainer. *2 n.* evangelist, preacher. See also *ɲímaalímùàm*.

itátéés (itátéésí-/itátá-) *1 v.* to take for a walk, walk. *2 v.* to balance (e.g. on one's head).

itátsámánón (itátsámánónì-) *v.* to be lazy, negligent, slack. See also *wéésánón*.

itɛɓɛs (itɛɓɛsí-) *1 v.* to nick (e.g. the branch stubs off of the reeds used for building granaries and houses). *2 v.* to notch (the ears of oxen for decoration).

itéɓúkòn (itéɓúkònì-) *1 v.* to swell, be swollen (body part or whole body). *2 v.* to be gorged, stuffed (from eating).

iteɗes (iteɗesí-) *v.* to cut or lop off (e.g. branches from a trunk).

itéélòn (itéélònɨ-) *v.* to lie or sit with legs straight.

itééritɛtés (itééritɛtésɨ́-) *v.* to face in one direction.

itééròn (itéérònɨ-) *v.* to face in one direction.

itɛítéés (itɛítéésɨ́-) *v.* to break up into pieces (e.g. when making aggregate).

itéƙélés (itéƙélésí-) *v.* to dam up (i.e. using logs or rocks).

itéƙítéƙés (itéƙítéƙésí-) *v.* to nod, shake up and down (as when saying 'yes').

iteles (itelesí-) *v.* to watch.

itelesa bàrìrrr *v.* to gaze or stare at emptily (e.g. when angry, pregnant, or in pain).

itelesa ceŋetíámà[e] *n.* taboo of watching one's mother-in-law.

itelesa fetí *1 v.* to watch the sun (to predict the seasons). *2 v.* to tell the time.

itelesíám (itelesí-ámà-) *pl.* **itelesíík**[a]. *1 n.* sentry, watchman. *2 n.* caretaker. *3 n.* witness. See also *ŋítsaɗénìàm*.

itelesíáma fetí *n.* sun watcher: an elder who is an expert in observing the seasonal cycle of the sunrise and sunset.

itelesíáma kíjá[e] *pl.* **itelesííka kíjá**[e]. *n.* sentry, watchman.

itelesíáwa fetí *n.* point from which an elder observes solar cycles.

itélésuƙot[a] (itélésuƙotí-) *v.* to watch (there).

iteletés (iteletésí-) *v.* to watch (here).

itélínós (itélínósí-) *v.* to watch each other.

itɛmá (<itɛmɔ́ɔ̀n) *v.*

itemes (itemesí-) *v.* to continue, keep on.

itemetés (itemetésí-) *v.* to continue, keep on.

itemités (itemitésí-) *1 v.* to make ready, prepare, ready. *2 v.* to resolve, solve.

itémítuƙotam (itémítuƙotamá-) *n.* solvable problem.

itémón (itémónì-) *v.* to be appropriate, enough, fitting, proper, suitable.

itɛmɔ́ɔ̀n (itɛmɔ́ɔ̀nɨ-/itɛmá-) *1 v.* to be at leisure, hang out, pass time. *2 v.* to stroll, walk leisurely.

itɛ́nitɛtés (itɛ́nitɛtésɨ́-) *v.* to set straight, straighten.

itɛ́nitɛtésá tódà[e] *v.* to set the record straight, talk straight to the issue. *Lit.* 'to straighten speech out'.

itɛ́nɔ́n (itɛ́nɔ́nɨ-) *v.* to be straight.

itéón (itéónì-) *v.* to go back, return there.

itɛpɛs (itɛpɛsɨ́-) *1 v.* to inseminate (of animals). *2 v.* to fuck.

itɛrítɛ́ròn (itɛrítɛ́rònɨ-) *v.* to reel, stagger.

ítés (itésì-) *1 v.* to find missing. *2 v.* to find the remains of (left by thieves or predators).

itétémés (itétémésí-) *1 v.* to demonstrate, illustrate, show. *2 v.* to exercise, practice.

itétón (itétónì-) *v.* to come back, return here. See also *iɓóɓóŋètòn*.

itétɔ́n (itétɔ́nɨ-) *1 v.* to arrive (here). *2 v.* to get, find.

itíbès (itíbèsì-) *v.* to arrange, order, put in order. See also *idɔ́bès* and *inábès*.

itíbesúƙot[a] (itíbesúƙotí-) *v.* to arrange, order, put in order.

itiɓes (itiɓesí-) *v.* to section, segment (e.g. a felled tree).

itiɓítíɓés (itiɓítíɓésí-) *v.* to section, segment (e.g. a felled tree).

itiɓítíɓɔ̀n (itiɓítíɓɔ̀nì-) *v.* to contract, cramp (during childbirth or defecation).

itídídés (itídídésí-) *v.* to filch, lift, pilfer, sneak.

itídídésá así *v.* to slink, sneak, tiptoe.

itíílés (itíílésí-) *v.* to repel, repulse, turn away.

itíírà (<itííròòn) *v.*

itííròòn (itííròònì-/itííra-) *v.* to hold fast, stand firm.

itikes (itikesí-) *1 v.* to hold down, overpower, subdue, suppress. *2 v.* to chase down (food or drink by eating or drinking something else).

itiketésá gúróe kíják[e] *v.* to calm down. *Lit.* 'to suppress the heart'.

itikiesúƙot[a] (itikiesúƙotí-) *v.* to rape, assault or violate (sexually). *Lit.* 'to suppress repeatedly'.

itikítíkòn (itikítíkònì-) *v.* to feel queasy, sick, woozy (as when oil or sugar enters one's bloodstream). The experiencer of this feeling is marked with the dative case.

itíƙírà (<itíƙíròòn) *v.*

itíƙíròòn (itíƙíròònì-/itíƙíra-) *v.* to rumble or thunder off (e.g. a vehicle taking off quickly or a herd of animals stampeding). Also pronounced as *itíríkòòn*.

itílésuƙot[a] (itílésuƙotí-) *v.* to push over.

itilɛtés (itilɛtésí-) *v.* to pull over.

itílétɔ̀n (itílétɔ̀nì-) *v.* to come in a convoy or procession.

itilítílɔ̀n (itilítílɔ̀nì-) *v.* to ache (of joints).

itílɔ́nuƙot[a] (itílɔ́nuƙotí-) *v.* to go in convoy or procession.

itinítínés (itinítínésí-) *v.* to move rhythmically (e.g. a body part while dancing).

itinítínésá así *v.* to move oneself rhythmically (as in dancing).

ítínós (ítínósí-) *v.* to find each other missing.

itíŋá (<itíŋéés) *v.*

itíŋéés (itíŋéésí-/itíŋá-) *v.* to compel, force. See also *itiŋɛs*.

itiŋés (itiŋésí-) *v.* to cook, prepare (food). Compare with *kɔŋés*.

itiŋɛs (itiŋɛsí-) *v.* to compel, force. See also *itíŋéés*.

itiŋɛsa así *v.* to force oneself.

itiŋésíàw[a] (itiŋésí-àwà-) *pl.* **itiŋésíawík**[a]. *n.* cooking place, kitchen.

itión (itiónì-) *v.* to go back, return there. See also *iteón*.

itíɔn (itíɔnì-) *v.* to delay. See also *asínón*.

itiónàs (itiónàsì-) *n.* miracles, wonders.

itiónòn (itiónònì-) *1 v.* to be difficult, hard. *2 v.* to do miracles, wonders. *3 v.* to be important, significant. *4 v.* to be expensive, exorbitant, high.

itípá (<itípéés) *v.*

itípéés (itípéésí-/itípá-) *v.* to deviate, divert (e.g. enemies by making a preventative sacrifice or by talking them down from their plan).

Itírá (Itíráà-) *n.* a personal name.

itírákés (itírákésí-) *v.* to recoil from, shrink back from (i.e. something dangerous or embarrassing).

itíríkà (<itíríkòòn) *v.*

itíríkòòn (itíríkòònì-/itíríka-) *v.* to rumble or thunder off (e.g. a vehicle taking off quickly or a herd of animals stampeding). Also pronounced as *itíkíròòn*.

itirítírés (itirítírésí-) *v.* to stamp, stomp, tamp.

itírónòn (itírónònì-) *v.* to be fast, quick, speedy. See also *wéénɔn*.

itítí (itítíi-) *pl.* **itítíik**[a]. *n.* flame tree: emblematic East African tree species with brilliant red flowers; its seeds are used as necklace beads; its wood is used to make door planks, bowls, and containers, and a decoction of its bark or flowers is used as a treatment for chicken and dog diseases. *Erythrina abyssinica*.

itítíkés (itítíkésí-) *v.* to hold back, restrain, retain.

itítíketés (itítíketésí-) *v.* to hold back, restrain, retain.

itítíŋòn (itítíŋònì-) *v.* to be brave, courageous, dauntless, fearless, intrepid.

itítírés (itítírésí-) *v.* to hinder, obstruct, prevent.

itiwɛs (itiwɛsí-) *v.* to filter, strain. See also *ijɨwɛs*.

itíyá (<itíyéés) *v.*

itíyáìmètòn (itíyáìmètònì-) *v.* to be done, happen, occur, take place, transpire. See also *ikásîimètòn*.

itíyéés (itíyéésí-/itíyá-) *v.* to do.

itíyéetam (itíyéetamá-) *n.* actionable, doable, feasible, possible.

itíyéetés (itíyéetésí-) *v.* to do, get done.

itoɓes (itoɓesí-) *1 v.* to hole, make a hole in. *2 v.* to cut in, interrupt.

itoɓítóɓés (itoɓítóɓésí-) *v.* to hole or make holes in repeatedly.

itoɓítóɓésa tódà[e] *v.* to cut in or interrupt a conversation or discussion. *Lit.* 'to make holes in speech'.

itoɗítóɗés (itoɗítóɗésí-) *v.* to peck, pick at.

itɔɗɔn (itɔɗɔnì-) *v.* to wilt, wither.

itojiés (itojiesí-) *v.* to pick a fight with, start a fight with.

itɔkɔánòn (itɔkɔánònì-) *v.* to be grabby, grasping (e.g. of food from others).

itɔkɔɗɛs (itɔkɔɗɛsí-) *v.* to clench, grip (e.g. one's side while running).

itókókòòn (itókókòònì-) *v.* to be bony, cadaverous, emaciated, skeletal. See also *irókòòn* and *kwédekwedánón*.

itɔkɔɔn (itɔkɔɔnì-) *v.* to gimp, hobble. See also *isépón* and *itsúkúkòn*.

itɔlɛs (itɔlɛsí-) *v.* to barbeque, grill.

itɔlɔs (itɔlɔsí-) *v.* to be barbequed, grilled.

itɔmɔn (itɔmɔnì-) *v.* to be near, next to.

itɔmɔnìàm (itɔmɔnì-àmà-) *pl.* **itɔmɔniik**[a]. *n.* neighbor.

itɔmúnɔs (itɔmúnɔsí-) *v.* to be neighbors, next to each other.

ítón (ítónì-) *v.* to be (some size or amount).

ítónà dìdìk[e] *v.* to become big or many. *Lit.* 'to reach high'.

ítóna kíjée ts'ɛɛ *v.* to dawn, get light.

ítónuƙot[a] (ítónuƙotí-) *v.* to become (some size or amount).

itoŋes (itoŋesí-) *v.* to twine, twist.

itoŋetésá tódà[e] *v.* to lie, prevaricate, twist the truth. *Lit.* 'to twist up speech'.

itóŋílés (itóŋílésí-) *v.* to hurt (of teeth, from coldness or sourness).

itɔŋítɔ́ŋɛ́s (itɔŋítɔ́ŋɛ́sɨ́-) *v.* to tap out (e.g. salt or tobacco from a container).

itɔ́ŋɔ́ɛ́s (itɔ́ŋɔ́ɛ́sɨ́-) *v.* to get a rise out of, incite or provoke verbally.

itóŋóiesá mɛnáᵋ *v.* to doubt matters, question things.

itóŋóòn (itóŋóònì-) *v.* to doubt, hesitate, waver.

itɔ́ɔ́n (itɔ́ɔ́nì-/itá-) *1 v.* to reach (a destination). *2 v.* to find, get.

itópénòn (itópénònì-) *1 v.* to be hideous, ugly, unattractive. *2 v.* to be boring, dull, monotonous, uninteresting. See also *làlòn*.

itóróɲɛ́s (itóróɲésɨ́-) *v.* to make ridges in, ridge (e.g. for planting potatoes).

itórópés (itórópésɨ́-) *v.* to cut out the meat and organs of the respiratory and upper digestive systems (i.e. the tongue, throat, lungs, and heart).

itɔ́tɔ́ɛ́s (itɔ́tɔ́ɛ́sɨ́-) *v.* to demolish, destroy (sth. hard). See also *ipáríés*.

itotoles (itotolesí-) *v.* to crack or split apart (e.g. hard roots or seeds).

itɔ́tɔ́ŋɛ́s (itɔ́tɔ́ŋɛ́sɨ́-) *v.* to peck, rap or tap on (e.g. wood, like a woodpecker).

itɔ́tɔ́rɔ̀n (itɔ́tɔ́rɔ̀nì-) *v.* to wipe after defecating.

itówá (<itówéés) *v.*

itówá (<itówóòn) *v.*

itówéés (itówéésɨ́-/itówá-) *n.* to kick off, inaugurate, launch, or usher in (the new year of agriculture by conducting a ceremony).

itówóòn (itówóònì-/itówá-) *v.* to be enhaloed, ringed (e.g. the moon, sun, or a saint).

itóyá (<itóyéés) *v.*

itóyéés (itóyéésɨ́-/itóyá-) *v.* to assemble, bring or put together.

itóyéésa asɨ́ *v.* to assemble, congregate, converge, meet.

itsáɗénés (itsáɗénésɨ́-) *v.* to attest, bear witness, or testify to.

itsakɛs (itsakɛsɨ́-) *v.* to crush, smash (e.g. melon, pumpkin, squash). See also *ilɛɗɛs*.

itsakítsákɛ́s (itsakítsákɛ́sɨ́-) *v.* to crush or smash up (e.g. bark or roots as medicine).

itsánánòn (itsánánònì-) *v.* to be annoying, bothersome, irritating. See also *fifòn*.

itsanɛs (itsanɛsɨ́-) *v.* to annoy, disturb, irritate.

itsánitɛtɛ́s (itsánitɛtɛ́sɨ́-) *v.* to cause problems or make trouble for.

itsanítsánɛ́s (itsanítsánɛ́sɨ́-) *v.* to anguish, torment, torture.

itsanítsánitɛtɛ́s (itsanítsánitɛtɛ́sɨ́-) *v.* to cause anguish or torment for.

itsárɨ́ánón (itsárɨ́ánónì-) *1 v.* to be fake, hypocritical, insincere, phony. *2 v.* to be unwanted, useless.

itsɛɗítsɛ́ɗɛ́s (itsɛɗítsɛ́ɗɛ́sɨ́-) *v.* to dig randomly (e.g. holes for seeds).

itsɛɗítsɛ́ɗòn (itsɛɗítsɛ́ɗònì-) *1 v.* to tiptoe, walk on tippytoes. *2 v.* to get a running jump, take off hopping (like a vulture).

itsɛ́ɛ́rà (<itsɛ́ɛ́rɔ̀ɔ̀n) *v.*

itsɛ́ɛ́rɔ̀ɔ̀n (itsɛ́ɛ́rɔ̀ɔ̀nì-/itsɛ́ɛ́rɛ-) *v.* to cloud up but only rain elsewhere.

itsékʼé (<itsékʼóòn) *v.*

itsékʼéés (itsékʼéésɨ́-) *v.* to climb with gear (e.g. a honey-tree or mountain).

itsékʼóòn (itsékʼóònì-/itsékʼé-) *1 v.* to climb with gear (e.g. a honey-tree or mountain). *2 v.* to walk with a cane.

itséléèòn (itséléèònì-) *v.* to perch, roost.

itsemes (itsemesí-) *1 v.* to poke, prod. *2 v.* to provoke, push buttons.

itsemítsémés (itsemítsémésí-) *v.* to poke around in/on (e.g. a patch of ground being prospected for minerals or tapped on with a cane).

itsenes (itsenesí-) *1 v.* to beg. *2 v.* to curse.

itseniés (itseniesí-) *1 v.* to beg relentlessly. *2 v.* to lament, wail for.

itsenietés (itsenietésí-) *v.* to begin begging relentlessly.

itsétséés (itsétséésí-) *1 v.* to clamber or scamper up (e.g. a mountain or tree). *2 v.* to spear from a distance.

itsiɗɛs (itsiɗɛsí-) *v.* to wipe clean (e.g. with a finger). See also *ikúúlés*.

itsikɛs (itsikɛsí-) *1 v.* to charge, instruct, order. *2 n.* law, rule.

itsikɛsa Ɲákují *v.* divine commandment, law of God.

itsikɛsíám (itsikɛsí-ámá-) *pl.* **itsikɛsíík**[a]. *n.* commander.

itsikɛsíícíká kíjá[e] *v.* laws of the land, local laws.

itsipítsipés (itsipítsipésí-) *1 v.* to tattoo: mark skin with a piece of grass used in a twirling motion to leave pock-marks that scar. *2 v.* to immunize, vaccinate (by injection).

itsírítetés (itsírítetésí-) *1 v.* to erect, put or set upright. *2 v.* to aim, direct, guide. *3 v.* to correct, make right, rectify. See also *tɔɓɛitɛtés* and *tsírítɛtés*.

itsírón (itsírónì-) *1 v.* to be erect, upright. *2 v.* to go directly, hit the target. *3 v.* to be correct, right, true. See also *tɔɓéón* and *tsírón*.

itsírɔna tódàk[e] *v.* to tell the truth. *Lit.* 'to go directly to truth'.

itsɔɓítsɔ́ɓés (itsɔɓítsɔ́ɓésí-) *1 v.* to blend, commingle, conflate, mix. *2 v.* to dapple, mottle, spot. See also *iɲales* and *itsulútsúlés*.

itsɔɓítsɔ́ɓòn (itsɔɓítsɔ́ɓònì-) *1 v.* to be blended, commingled; conflated, mixed. *2 v.* to be dappled, mottled, spotty.

itsɔɓítsɔ́ɓós (itsɔɓítsɔ́ɓósí-) *1 v.* to be blended, commingled, conflated, mixed. *2 v.* to be dappled, mottled, spotted.

itsoɗiétòn (itsoɗiétònì-) *v.* to come edging or inching one's way (e.g. to get food where one is not invited).

itsóɗókòn (itsóɗókònì-) *v.* to hop on one leg.

itsóɗón (itsóɗónì-) *1 v.* to edge, inch. *2 v.* to limp. *3 v.* to hedge, skirt, surround.

itsóɗóniàw[a] (itsóɗónì-àwà-) *pl.* **itsóɗóniawík**[a]. *n.* hunting ground: where hunters split up, edge forward, and hedge animals in between two phalanxes.

itsɔ́ítésuƙɔt[a] (itsɔ́ítésuƙɔtí-) *v.* to satisfy (someone's) hunger for meat.

itsók[a] (itsókó-) *n.* sunbird.

itsɔƙítsɔ́ƙés (itsɔƙítsɔ́ƙésí-) *v.* to whip back and forth.

itsól (itsólá-) *n.* bird species.

itsólóŋòn (itsólóŋònì-) *1 v.* to lie down, recline. *2 v.* to go down, set (of sun). See also *eponuƙot*[a].

itsomes (itsomesí-) *v.* to crush into powder, pulverize.

itsomítsómés (itsomítsómésí-) *v.* to pound repeatedly (e.g. grain, edible termites).

itsɔŋɛtés (itsɔŋɛtésɨ-) *v.* to chance, come across, happen upon. See also *ŋawilɛs*.

itsɔ́ɔ́n (itsɔ́ɔ́nɨ-) *v.* to satisfy hunger for meat.

itsɔ́ɔ́nukɔt[a] (itsɔ́ɔ́nukɔtɨ-) *v.* to satisfy hunger for meat.

itsópé (<itsópóòn) *v.*

itsópóòn (itsópóònɨ-/itsópé-) *v.* to be alert, attentive, watchful.

itsɔ́rɛ́sukɔt[a] (itsɔ́rɛ́sukɔtɨ-) *v.* to heave or shove away.

itsɔrɛtés (itsɔrɛtésɨ-) *v.* to pull or yank this way.

itsɔrɛtésá así *v.* to clamber down.

itsɔ́rónukɔt[a] (itsɔ́rónukɔtɨ-) *v.* to clamber down (e.g. a steep slope).

itsótsóés (itsótsóésɨ-) *v.* to egg on, incite, provoke, urge on. See also *isúsúés*.

itsúbùɗɔn (itsúbùɗɔnɨ-) *v.* to be herniate, invert, prolapse.

itsúbùɗùmɔ̀n (itsúbùɗùmɔ̀nɨ-) *v.* to be herniated, inverted, prolapsed.

itsuɗútsúɗés (itsuɗútsúɗésɨ-) *v.* to crowd, space too closely (e.g. hair when braiding, grass when thatching, or seeds when planting). See also *ituɗútúɗés*.

itsues (itsuesɨ-) *1 v.* to emit, give off, let out (e.g. a gas). *2 v.* to let or set loose, release (e.g. an animal). *3 v.* to cauterize.

itsuetés (itsuetésɨ-) *1 v.* to emit, give off, let out (e.g. a gas). *2 v.* to let or set loose, release (e.g. an animal).

itsúkúkòn (itsúkúkònɨ-) *v.* to gimp, hobble. See also *isɛpón* and *itɔ́kɔ́ɔ́n*.

itsúkúk[u] (itsúkúkù) *ideo.* gimpily, hobblingly.

itsulɛs (itsulɛsɨ-) *v.* to pay a fine for (impregnating a girl out of wedlock).

itsúlítɛtés (itsúlítɛtésɨ-) *v.* to fine for unlawful impregnation.

itsulútsúlés (itsulútsúlésɨ-) *v.* to blend, commingle, conflate, mix. See also *iɲales* and *itsɔbítsɔ́bɛ́s*.

itsumés (itsumésɨ-) *v.* to pierce, puncture.

itsunɛs (itsunɛsɨ-) *v.* to collect, gather.

itsunɛtés (itsunɛtésɨ-) *1 v.* to collect, gather. *2 v.* to summarize. See also *bɔsɛtés* and *irírɛ́ɛ́s*.

itsunɛtésá así *v.* to gather socially, get together, meet.

itsúnétòn (itsúnétònɨ-) *v.* to assemble, congregate, gather, meet.

itsuŋɛs (itsuŋɛsɨ-) *1 v.* to burn. *2 v.* to fire. *3 v.* to brand. *4 v.* to mend with fire.

itsúŋɛ́sukɔt[a] (itsúŋɛ́sukɔtɨ-) *v.* to burn up.

itsúrítetés (itsúrítetésɨ-) *v.* to boil, bring to a boil.

itsúrón (itsúrónɨ-) *v.* to boil.

itsúrúés (itsúrúésɨ-) *v.* to do away with, get rid of, rid oneself of.

itsúrútsa (<itsúrútseés) *v.*

itsúrútseés (itsúrútseesɨ-itsúrútsa-) *v.* to do business, make money.

itsúrútsúrés (itsúrútsúrésɨ-) *v.* to spill all over.

itsúrútsúrésúkɔt[a] (itsúrútsúrésúkɔtɨ-) *v.* to spill all over.

itsutɛs (itsutɛsɨ-) *v.* to finish off, wipe out (e.g. food, people, etc.).

itsútésukɔt[a] (itsútésukɔtɨ-) *v.* to do in, finish off, wipe out.

itsútúmétòn (itsútúmétònɨ-) *v.* to be finished off (of what had remained from earlier).

itswɛtítswétɔ̀n (itswɛtítswétɔ̀nì-) *v.* to click or cluck with disapproval.

itsyákétòn (itsyákétònì-) *1 v.* to begin, commence, start. *2 v.* to take office. See also *iséétòn*.

itsyákétòniàw[a] (itsyákétònì-àwà-) *pl.* **itsyákétoniawík**[a]. *n.* beginning point, origin, source.

itsyátón (itsyátónì-) *1 v.* to be impervious, resilient, resistant, tough. *2 v.* to be 'in shape', physically fit.

its'íɗèètòn (its'íɗèètònì-) *v.* to be the very last (in class, in line, etc.).

its'ɔ́kón (its'ɔ́kónì-) *v.* to be nearly ripe (of grains).

itúɓ[a] (itúɓá-) *pl.* **itúɓík**[a]. *1 n.* manger, trough. *2 n.* bathtub, tub. *3 n.* boat, vessel, watercraft.

ituɗútúɗés (ituɗútúɗésí-) *v.* to crowd, space too closely (e.g. hair when braiding, grass when thatching, or seeds when planting). See also *itsuɗútsúɗés*.

itues (ituesí-) *v.* to form, make, shape.

ituetés (ituetésí-) *v.* to form, make, shape.

ituetésá así *v.* to form, take form, take shape (like a raincloud).

ituetésá tódà[e] *v.* to discuss all points in detail, from all angles. *Lit.* 'to form speech'.

itukanetésá mɛná[e] *v.* to discuss matters (as a group).

itukanitetés (itukanitetésí-) *v.* to orchestrate, organize (a meeting).

itukánón (itukánónì-) *v.* to congregate, convene, gather, meet.

itukes (itukesí-) *v.* to gather, heap, pile.

ituketés (ituketésí-) *v.* to gather, heap, or pile up.

itúkúɗetòn (itúkúɗetònì-) *v.* to bend, crook, flex.

itúkúɗon (itúkúɗònì-) *v.* to bend, crook, flex.

itúlákáɲés (itúlákáɲésí-) *v.* to down, gulp, quaff. See also *lakatiés*.

itúlɛɛtés (itúlɛɛtésí-) *v.* to attract, catch the attention of.

itúléròn (itúlérònì-) *v.* to be doddery, senile.

itúléronuƙot[a] (itúléronuƙotí-) *v.* to become doddery or senile.

itúlésuƙota así *v.* to die suddenly (of unknown reasons).

itúlúmà (<itúlúmòòn) *v.*

itúlúmòòn (itúlúmòònì-/itúlúma-) *v.* to hurdle, vault.

itúmésuƙot[a] (itúmésuƙotí-) *v.* to delay, detain, hold up, keep back.

itumetésíàm (itumetésí-àmà-) *pl.* **itumetésiik**[a]. *n.* companion, company. *Lit.* 'detainer'.

itúmétòn (itúmétònì-) *v.* to company, hang out, keep company.

itúmúránitésúƙot[a] (itúmúránitésúƙotí-) *v.* to absorb, distract, preoccupy.

itúmúránón (itúmúránónì-) *v.* to be absorbed, distracted, preoccupied.

iturɛs (iturɛsí-) *1 v.* to pour into. *2 v.* to give rectally. See also *otés*.

itúrón (itúrónì-) *v.* to be arrogant, conceited, proud, vain.

itúrónìtòd[a] (itúrónì-tòdà-) *n.* boasting, bragging. *Lit.* 'pride-speech'.

itúrúmés (itúrúmésí-) *v.* to defame, denigrate, slander, smear.

itúrútés (itúrútésí-) *1 v.* to exalt, extol, praise. *2 v.* to revere, worship.

itúrútésá así *v.* to praise oneself.

itúrútésìàm (itúrútésì-àmà-) *pl.* **itúrútésiik**[a]. *n.* worshipper.

itúrútésiho (itúrútési-hoó-) *pl.* **itúrútésihoík**[a]. *n.* house of worship.

iturútúrés (iturútúrésí-) *v.* to pat (e.g. a baby to burp or a mat to remove dust).

itusɛtés (itusɛtésí-) *1 v.* to scrunch up. *2 v.* to hog-tie.

itútsón (itútsónì-) *v.* to be cruddy, filthy, nasty (e.g. one who never bathes or a smelly billy goat). See also *ts'ágòn*.

itútúés (itútúésí-) *v.* to brush or dust off (e.g. charcoal from roasted meat, crumbs from clothing, dirt from roots, etc.).

itútúésuƙot[a] (itútúésuƙotí-) *v.* to brush or dust off (e.g. charcoal from roasted meat, crumbs from clothing, dirt from roots, etc.).

itútúrés (itútúrésí-) *v.* to twist round (like cloth into a head-pad).

itútúrɔs (itútúrɔsí-) *v.* to be twisted round (e.g. a head-pad).

itúúmés (itúúmésí-) *v.* to catch off guard, storm, surprise, take by surprise. See also *bógès*.

itúwá (<itúwéés) *v.*

itúwéés (itúwéésí-/itúwá-) *v.* to break into.

itwáŋítésúƙot[a] (itwáŋítésúƙotí-) *v.* to lead astray, mislead, trick. See also *hakítésuƙot*[a].

itwáŋón (itwáŋónì-) *1 v.* to get lost, go astray, lose the way. *2 v.* to go grazy, lose one's mind.

itwares (itwaresí-) *v.* to dispel, disperse, scatter (e.g. birds or children).

itwelítwélés (itwelítwélésí-) *v.* to mark, pock, speckle.

itwelítwélós (itwelítwélósí-) *v.* to be marked, pocked, speckled.

itweɲítwéɲòn (itweɲítwéɲònì-) *1 v.* to flicker, twinkle (e.g. fire or the stars). *2 v.* to flash (e.g. headlights or a gunshot at night).

ìtyàkààm (ìtyàkà-àmà-) *pl.* **ityakaik**[a]. *n.* blacksmith, forger, metalworker.

ityakes (ityakesí-) *v.* to forge, hammer.

ityakesígwàs (ityakesí-gwàsà-) *pl.* **ityakesígwasík**[a]. *n.* forging stone, stone anvil.

Ìɨɗà (Ìɨɗàà-) *n.* a personal name.

ɨɨɗààm (ɨɨɗà-àmà-) *pl.* **iɨɗaik**[a]. *n.* mobilizer, organizer.

iɨɗɛs (iɨɗɛsí-) *v.* to assemble, collect, gather.

iɨɗɛtés (iɨɗɛtésí-) *v.* to assemble, collect, gather.

iújietés (iújietésí-) *v.* to make into porridge.

iukúúkés (iukúúkésí-) *v.* to rock back and forth (like a tree loose in its hole, a rock rooted in the soil, or one's body in dancing). See also *iikííkés*.

ɨɨƙɔ́n (ɨɨƙɔ́nì-) *1 v.* to be heavy-laden, loaded or weighed down. *2 v.* to be uncertain, unsure.

ɨɨm (ɨɨmà-) *n.* marital engagement.

iɨmɛs (iɨmɛsí-) *v.* to marry (by taking a girl away from her parents' home, sometimes forcibly).

ɨɨmésuƙot[a] (ɨɨmésuƙɔtí-) *v.* to marry by taking away (a girl from her home, sometimes forcibly).

iɨmɨɨɨmés (iɨmɨɨɨmésí-) *v.* to crunch, scrunch (e.g. broken glass or dry leaves).

iúpétòn (iúpétònì-) *v.* to dip or duck down.

iúpón (iúpóni-) *v.* to dip, duck. May also be spelled as *iwúpón*.

iúpónuƙotᵃ (iúpónuƙotí-) *v.* to dip or duck away.

iupúúpòn (iupúúpònì-) *v.* to bob, duck up and down.

iúrá (<iúréés) *v.*

iúréés (iúréésí-/iúrá-) *v.* to pick clean, scavenge.

iwá (<iwees) *v.*

Íwá (Íwáà-) *n.* name of an original Ik settlement.

iwáákós (iwáákósí-) *1 v.* to be sounding an alarm. *2 v.* to be wailing.

iwáíƙotᵃ (<ɨwɔ́ɔ́nʉƙɔtᵃ) *v.*

iwákón (iwákónì-) *1 v.* to sound an alarm (e.g. when enemies are coming or when a hunted animal is headed in a certain direction). *2 v.* to wail. *3 v.* to ring (of ears).

iwakúwákòn (iwakúwákònì-) *v.* to flap (e.g. wings or one's arms while dancing).

iwales (iwalesí-) *v.* to put on, wear (non-clothing accessories).

iwalesa túkàᵉ *v.* to put on a feather (often from an ostrich).

iwalɛtés (ɨwalɛtésɨ́-) *v.* to peel or scrape off (e.g. meat from a bone, pumpkin from its peel).

iwálílòn (iwálílònì-) *v.* to escape, get away, fly (e.g. an animal with a spear or a hawk with a chick).

Iwam (Iwamá-) *n.* name of a river.

iwanetés (iwanetésí-) *v.* to enlarge, expand, make bigger. See also *zeites*.

iwánétòn (iwánétònì-) *v.* to become bigger, enlarge, expand. See also *zoonuƙot*ᵃ.

iwàŋ (ìwàŋà-) *n.* warming by radiated heat (i.e. fire or sunshine).

iwaŋíwáŋés (iwaŋíwáŋésí-) *v.* to fumigate, smoke. See also *ipúréés* and *ts'udités*.

iwáŋón (iwáŋónì-) *v.* to warm up by radiated heat (i.e. fire or sunshine).

Iwar (Iwarɨ-) *n.* name of a hill or mountain.

iwarɛs (ɨwarɛsɨ́-) *v.* to daub, plaster (with a swirling motion).

iwarɨ́wárɛs (ɨwarɨ́wárɛ́sɨ́-) *v.* to move around, swirl (e.g. one's hand as when plastering).

ɨwarɔs (ɨwarɔsɨ́-) *v.* to be daubed, plastered.

ɨwasɛs (ɨwasɛsɨ́-) *v.* to moisturize (e.g. skin by applying lotion).

iwásíòn (iwásíònì-) *v.* to stand apart (e.g. being the first or last in a line).

iwatíwátés (iwatíwátésí-) *v.* to shake off (e.g. water from hands or one's hand when burnt by fire).

ɨwáwá (<ɨwáwɛ́ɛ́s) *v.*

ɨwáwáɗés (ɨwáwáɗésɨ́-) *v.* to bisect, cut in two (meat only). See also *pakés*.

ɨwáwɛ́ɛ́s (ɨwáwɛ́ɛ́sɨ́-/ɨwáwá-) *v.* to caress, fondle, stroke.

ɨwɛ́ɛ́lánón (ɨwɛ́ɛ́lánónì-) *1 v.* to disperse, dissipate, scatter, spread out. *2 v.* to spatter, splatter. See also *ɓʉnʉ́mɔ́n*.

ɨwɛ́ɛ́lés (ɨwɛ́ɛ́lésɨ́-) *v.* to break up, disperse, scatter, spread. See also *toɓwaŋes*.

ɨwɛ́ɛ́lésá jʉmwɨ *v.* to spread soil (as part of cursing or making threats).

ɨwɛ́ɛ́lésʉƙotᵃ (ɨwɛ́ɛ́lésʉƙɔtí-) *v.* to disperse, dissipate, scatter, spread out.

ɨwɛ́ɛ́lɛtés (ɨwɛ́ɛ́lɛtésɨ́-) *v.* to disperse, dissipate, scatter, spread out.

iwéélɔ́s (ɨwéélɔ́sɨ́-) *v.* to be dispersed, dissipated, scattered, spread out.

iwees (iweesí-/iwá-) *v.* to kick off, initiate, or start off (a group dance).

iwɛlɛ́wɛ́lánón (ɨwɛlɛ́wɛ́lánónì-) *v.* to be brittle, crumbly.

iwés (iwésí-) *1 v.* to hit, strike. *2 v.* to ring (a bell).

iwésá dakwí *v.* to thump a tree (to call a honey-guide bird).

iwésá ɲéɓulókìkàᵉ *v.* to make blocks or bricks.

iwésá ɲémusaláɓàᵉ *v.* to make the sign of the cross.

iwésúƙotᵃ (iwésúƙotí-) *1 v.* to hit, strike. *2 v.* to call on the phone, phone out (in that direction).

iwetés (iwetésí-) *1 v.* to depict, draw. *2 v.* to photograph, snap a photo of, take a picture of. *3 v.* to mark, sign. *4 v.* to call on the phone, phone in. *5 v.* to fasten, lock.

iwɛtɛs (ɨwɛtɛsɨ́-) *v.* to drink slowly, sip (e.g. hot drinks).

iwetésá ɲáɓúkwì *v.* to print or publish a book.

iwetésá ɲépítsaáᵉ *v.* to snap a photo, take a picture.

ɨwɛts'ɨ́wɛ́ts'ɛ́s (ɨwɛts'ɨ́wɛ́ts'ɛ́sɨ́-) *v.* to break, chip, or knap off pieces repeatedly. See also *wɛts'ɛ́s*.

iwéwérés (iwéwérésí-) *1 v.* to summon by whistling, whistle for. *2 v.* to flavor, season. See also *íbutsurés* and *iwówórés*.

iwɨɗɛs (ɨwɨɗɛsɨ́-) *v.* to grind finely.

iwɨɗíwɨ́ɗés (ɨwɨɗíwɨ́ɗésɨ́-) *v.* to wag, waggle (tail only).

iwɨɗɔs (ɨwɨɗɔsɨ́-) *v.* to be finely ground, powdery.

iwies (iwiesí-) *v.* to spread around (e.g. food in order to cool it). See also *ɓátsés*.

iwííɲés (iwííɲésí-) *v.* to singe.

iwɨ́rétɔ̀n (ɨwɨ́rétɔ̀nɨ̀-) *v.* to begin shining.

iwɨ́rɔ́n (ɨwɨ́rɔ́nɨ̀-) *v.* to shine.

iwítésuƙotᵃ (iwítésuƙotí-) *v.* to hide away, make disappear.

iwitités (iwititésí-) *v.* to deviate, divert.

iwitíwítòn (iwitíwítònì-) *1 v.* to swerve or veer repeatedly. *2 v.* to avoid, dodge, or evade repeatedly.

iwítón (iwítónì-) *v.* to swerve, veer.

iwitses (iwitsesí-) *v.* to miss narrowly (e.g. a bullet or a flame).

iwítsíwítsés (iwítsíwítsésí-) *v.* to wag, waggle, wave around.

iwitsíwítsésá ekwitíní *v.* to wave around in front of the eyes.

iwɨ́tsɔ́n (ɨwɨ́tsɔ́nɨ̀-) *v.* to be pointed, tipped (e.g. a needle or thorn).

iwɨ́wɨ́nés (ɨwɨ́wɨ́nésɨ́-) *v.* to aggravate, exasperate.

iwoɗíwóɗés (iwoɗíwóɗésí-) *v.* to insert, work into (e.g. a finger into a hole).

iwɔkɛs (ɨwɔkɛsɨ́-) *v.* to empty by shaking (e.g. a gourd with pulp inside).

iwɔ́ƙɔ́n (ɨwɔ́ƙɔ́nɨ̀-) *v.* to be arrogant, cocky, self-important.

iwɔ́ƙɔ́nɨ̀àm (ɨwɔ́ƙɔ́nɨ̀-àmà-) *pl.* **iwɔ́ƙɔ́niik**ᵃ. *n.* arrogant or cocky person.

iwoles (iwolesí-) *v.* to fold, turn (e.g. a page).

iwoletés (iwoletésí-) *v.* to fold or turn over (e.g. a page).

iwolíwólòn (iwolíwólònì-) *v.* to flitter, flutter (e.g. in the wind).

Íwɔlɔ́ (Íwɔlɔ́ɔ̀-) *n.* name of a dance-ground at the foot of a fig tree.

iwóŋón (iwóŋónì-) *v.* to exult, shout triumphantly (e.g. having won a contest or killed a wild animal).

ɨwɔ́ŋɔ́n (ɨwɔ́ŋɔ́nɨ̀-) *v.* to intend or mean (to do), premeditate. Must be followed by an infinitive in the dative case.

ɨwɔ́ɔ́n (ɨwɔ́ɔ́nɨ̀-) *v.* to be flagging, slacking, slowing.

ɨwɔ́ɔ́nʉkɔt[a] (ɨwɔ́ɔ́nʉkɔtɨ́-/ɨwáɨ́kɔt-) *v.* to ease up, flag, slack off, slow down.

iwórón (iwórónì-) *v.* to roam, stray, wander.

iwóróniàm (iwóróni-àmà-) *pl.* **iwóróniik**[a]. *n.* roamer, stray, wanderer.

iworós (iworósí-) *v.* to be crazy, deranged.

iwósétòn (iwósétònì-) *v.* to be dangerously steep, preciptious.

iwóts[a] (iwótsí-) *pl.* **iwótsík**[a]. *1 n.* mortar. *2 n.* drum.

iwotses (iwotsesí-) *v.* to pound (with mortar and pestle).

iwótsíàk[a] (iwótsí-àkà-) *n.* mouth of a mortar.

iwótsídàkw[a] (iwótsí-dàkù-) *pl.* **iwótsídakwitín**. *n.* pestle. *Lit.* 'mortar-stick'. See also **àj**[a] and **kuɲuk**[a].

iwótsígwà (iwótsí-gwàà-) *n.* chin-spot batis. *Lit.* 'mortar-bird'. *Batis molitor*. See also **nàŋʉ̀ràmbɔ̀**.

iwótsíɔ̀z (iwótsí-ɔ̀zà-) *1 n.* bottom of mortar. *2 n.* pounded edible termites at the bottom of a mortar.

iwótsóòn (iwótsóònì-) *v.* to binge, glut, overeat, pig out.

iwówá (<iwówéés) *v.*

iwówéés (iwówéésí-/iwówá-) *v.* to swarm over, teem around.

iwówórés (iwówórésí-) *v.* to summon by whistling, whistle for. See also **iwéwérés**.

ɨwɔxɨ́wɔ́xɛ́s (ɨwɔxɨ́wɔ́xɛ́sɨ́-) *v.* to cut noisily (making a *shw-shw* sound).

iwúlákés (iwúlákésí-) *v.* to aerate, loosen or turn over (soil).

ɨwʉ́lɔ́n (ɨwʉ́lɔ́nɨ̀-) *v.* to boast, brag.

iwulúwúlés (iwulúwúlésí-) *v.* to rub around (e.g. on the ground to make dirty).

ɨxáxá (<ɨxaxɛɛs) *v.*

ɨxaxɛɛs (ɨxaxɛɛsɨ́-/ɨxáxá-) *v.* to shake out noisily (making a *sha-sha* sound).

ɨxɔtsɛs (ɨxɔtsɛsɨ́-) *v.* to exchange, swap, trade. See also **ilókótsés** and **xɔ́tsés**.

ixóxókés (ixóxókésí-) *v.* to dump or shake out (e.g. honey from a container or seeds from a gourd). See also **ixúxúkés**.

ixukúxúkés (ixukúxúkésí-) *v.* to dump or shake out (e.g. honey from a container or seeds from a gourd).

ixúxúkés (ixúxúkésí-) *v.* to dump or shake out (e.g. honey from a container or seeds from a gourd). See also **ixóxókés**.

iyalíyálòn (iyalíyálònì-) *v.* to be drowsy, sleepy.

iyaŋes (iyaŋesí-) *v.* to abuse verbally, insult.

iyaɲíyáɲés (iyaɲíyáɲésí-) *v.* to shuffle (like peanuts in a frying pan).

iyaɲíyáɲòn (iyaɲíyáɲònì-) *v.* to feel flushed or flustered.

ɨyáyá (<ɨyáyɛ́ɛ́s) *v.*

ɨyáyɛ́ɛ́s (ɨyáyɛ́ɛ́sɨ́-/ɨyáyá-) *v.* to shout or yell 'ya ya!' at (e.g. to drive animals or control a crowd).

íyeés (íyeesí-) *v.* to know. A form of the word 'know' used by younger generations of Ik speakers; see words beginning with *ɦye-* for the older and more standard form.

iyééseetés (iyééseetésí-) *v.* to pour down/out.

iyééseetésá asɨ *v.* to lower oneself.

iyérón (iyéróniì-) *1 v.* to be coiled, spiraled, whorled (e.g. a horn or a tree). *2 v.* to be rifled.

iyérólƙot[a] (iyéróƙotí-) *v.* to spiral, whorl.

iyétsé (<iyétsóòn) *v.*

iyétséetés (iyétséetésí-) *v.* to abort, miscarry, terminate. See also *iɲétséetés*.

iyétséyeés (iyétséyeesí-) *v.* to abort or miscarry repeatedly.

iyétsóòn (iyétsóòniì-/iyétsé-) *1 v.* to act, feign, pretend. *2 v.* to abort, fail (e.g. the weather, being drier than normal). See also *iɲétsóòn*.

iyikes (iyikesí-) *v.* to sprinkle, spritz.

iyíyá (<iyíyéés) *v.*

iyíyéés (iyíyéésí-/iyíyá-) *1 v.* to screech, shriek (of raptors). *2 v.* to ululate.

iyoes (iyoesí-) *v.* to aim, direct, train.

iyoesa asɨ *v.* to aim for, go directly.

iyolíyólés (iyolíyólésí-) *v.* to let down, lower (e.g. by rope or vine).

iyomam (iyomamá-) *pl.* **iyómík**[a]. *n.* masterpiece, work of art.

iyomes (iyomesí-) *v.* to do properly, make excellently.

iyɔŋɨyɔ́ŋɛ́s (iyɔŋɨyɔ́ŋɛ́sɨ-) *v.* to jiggle.

iyóómètòn (iyóómètòniì-) *v.* to celebrate, enjoy, have fun, party.

iyóón (iyóóniì-) *v.* to be correct, right.

iyopíyópòn (iyopíyópòniì-) *v.* to move up and down alternately, seesaw (e.g. the way women jump alternately during group dances).

iyópón (iyópóniì-) *v.* to vary in height.

iyótsóós (iyótsóósí-) *v.* to be deliberate, intentional.

ɨzaɓizaɓés (ɨzaɓizaɓésɨ-) *v.* to switch or whip lightly. See also *zaɓatiés*.

ɨzidesa tóda[e] *v.* to measure or weigh one's words (e.g. when talking during a sad or serious time).

ɨzìɗòn (ɨzìɗòniì-) *v.* to speak slowly, intermittently, or thoughtfully (e.g. an elder giving his last advice to his family before death).

ízokomés (ízokomésí-) *v.* to strap across or wear across (e.g. the chest or shoulder).

ízotam (ízotamá-) *n.* food with a consistency between thick porridge and watery mush.

ízuzués (ízuzuesí-) *v.* to dust, sprinkle (e.g. flour on water, salt on food). See also *xεés*.

j

jèjè (jèjèì-) *pl.* **jéjèìk**[a]. *1 n.* leather. *2 n.* leather mat, sleeping skin.

jíjè (jíjèì-) *pl.* **jíjèìk**[a]. *n.* opposite side of a ravine, river, or valley.

j

já (=já) *adv.* just, then.

jâbᵒ (jábò) *adv.* after all (an expression of counter-expectation).

jáɓúgwà (jáɓú-gwàà-) *n.* helmeted guineafowl. *Numida meleagris*.

jàgwᵃ (jàgò-) *pl.* **jágwitín**. *n.* daughter.

jágwèdᵃ (jágwèdè-) *n.* his/her daughter.

jákᵃ (jáká-) *n.* elders, old men.

jàkàlùkà (jàkàlùkàà-) *n.* ecstatic spiritual dance during which drums are beated, songs are sung, and a mentally/spiritually disturbed person goes into a trance and dances in order for the spirit to leave him/her.

jákám (jákámà-) *pl.* **jákᵃ**. *n.* elder, old man.

jákámànànès (jákámànànèsì-) *n.* elderliness, eldership (of men).

jaƙátós (jaƙátósí-) *v.* to gag, heave, retch. See also *xáƙátòn*.

jàƙwᵃ (jàƙwà) *ideo.* cowardly, fearfully.

jaƙwádòn (jaƙwádònì-) *v.* to be cowardly, faint-hearted, fearful.

jalájálánón (jalájálánónì-) *v.* to be different, diverse, several, various.

jalanites (jalanitesí-) *v.* to differentiate, distinguish.

jalánón (jalánónì-) *1 v.* to be different, dissimilar. *2 v.* to be alien, foreign, unrelated.

jalánónuƙotᵃ (jalánónuƙotí-) *v.* to become different, differ.

jálátsᵃ (jálátsɨ-) *pl.* **jálátsɨkᵃ**. *n.* plant species found on the Turkana plains and whose large tubers are dug up, roasted, and eaten.

jàm (jàmù) *ideo.* silkily, smoothly.

jamúdòn (jamúdònì-) *v.* to be silky-smooth, velvety.

jan (janɨ-) *pl.* **janitɨn**. *1 n.* broomgrass: grass species used to make brooms and to cover beehives and granaries. *Andropogon chinensis*. *2 n.* broom. See also *jɛn*.

J'àòàwᵃ (J'àò-àwà-) *n.* name of a deserted village in the east where *jàwᵃ* shrubs used to grow.

jaoboɗókᵃ (jao-boɗóká-) *n.* bark of the *jàwᵃ* shrub used as soap.

jarámétòn (jarámétònì-) *v.* to be dazed, in shock, stunned. See also *ijárón*.

jaulímòn (jaulímònì-) *v.* to be soft, supple (like Caucasian hair).

jàwᵃ (jàò-) *pl.* **jáwítín**. *n.* shrub species whose yellow fruits are eaten raw, whose interior bark is used as soap and treatment against head-lice, and whose wood and stem are used for flutes, switches, sticks, tool handles, and roof rafters. *Grewia bicolor*.

jayᵃ (jaɨ-) *pl.* **jaitín**. *n.* grass species used for thatching huts and for holding a woman's placenta when it is collected and thrown out. *Gramineae sp*.

jɛjétón (jɛjétònì-) *1 v.* to remain, stay on. *2 v.* to be extra, leftover.

jèjòn (jèjònɨ-) *1 v.* to remain, stay. *2 v.* to live on, survive.

jɛn (jɛnɨ-) *pl.* **jɛnitɨn**. *1 n.* broomgrass: grass species used to make brooms and to cover beehives and granaries. *Andropogon chinensis*. *2 n.* broom. See also *jan*.

jíikⁱ (jíikì) *adv.* all the time, always.

jijîdᵃ (jijɨ́dɔ̀-) *pl.* **jijídikw**ᵃ. *n.* plant species whose whitish reeds are used to make granaries, houses, and termite traps. *Acalypha fruticosa.*

jɨkᵋ (=jɨ̀ɨ̀) *adv.* also, as well, in addition, too.

jikijíkón (jikijíkónì-) *v.* to sway gently.

jɨlífifɨ (jɨlífifɨ̀-) *n.* bird species (possibly a red-winged starling).

jilíwᵃ (jilɨ́ú-) *n.* yellow-rumped seedeater. *Serinus reichenowi.*

jɨr (jɨ̀rɨ̀-) *n.* back, behind, rear.

jɨr (jɨ̀rɨ̀) *ideo.* hushedly, quietly, silently.

jɨrêdᵃ (jɨ́rédɛ̀-) *pl.* **jɨrín**. *1 n.* leftover, remainder. *2 n.* back part, rear end.

jɨ̀rɨ̀àm (jɨ̀rɨ̀-àmà-) *pl.* **jɨriik**ᵃ. *1 n.* last/latest person. *2 n.* lastborn. See also *eŋún. 3 n.* last wife who follows one around, attending to every need. See also *kárátsɨ̀kààm*.

jɨríjɨrɛ̀tɔ̀n (jɨríjɨrɛ̀tɔ̀nɨ̀-) *v.* to fill, swell, or well up (e.g. tears, tide, water).

jɨríjɨrɔ̀n (jɨríjɨrɔ̀nɨ̀-) *v.* to fill, swell, or well up (e.g. tears, tide, water).

jɨ̀rɨ̀kᵋ *n.* back, backward, behind, to the rear.

jɨrín (jɨ́rɨ́nɨ̀-) *n.* leftovers, remainders.

jɨ̀rɔ̀kᵃ (jɨ̀rɔ̀kù-) *pl.* **jɨrókɨk**ᵃ. *n.* sharpened stick-spear used in spear-throwing practice.

jɨrù *1 n.* after, later. *2 n.* behind, in the back/rear.

jikɨ (jɨ́kɨ̀) *1 adv.* completely, totally, very. *2 adv.* forever. *3 adv.* never. See also *mùkà*.

jɔɓétón (jɔɓétónɨ̀-) *v.* to grow back, regrow, resprout.

jɔ́ɓɔ̀n (jɔ́ɓɔ̀nɨ̀-) *v.* to be regrowing, resprouting.

jɔ́kɔ̀n (jɔ́kɔ̀nɨ̀-) *v.* to be medium-sized. See also *ɓarɨɓárɔ́n* and *lerúkúmòn*.

jolíl (jolílé-) *n.* black kite. *Milvus migrans.*

jɔ́lɔ̀n (jɔ́lɔ̀nɨ̀-) *1 v.* to be bland, flavorless, tasteless, vapid. *2 v.* to be boring, dull, lackluster, uninteresting. See also *dɛ̀kwɔ̀n*.

joojo (joojoó-) *n.* vine species whose potato-like roots are edible.

jòrìjòr (jòrìjòrì-) *pl.* **joríjórìk**ᵃ. *n.* cricket.

jɔrɔr (jɔrɔrɔ́-) *pl.* **jɔrɔ́rɨ́k**ᵃ. *1 n.* singing ants: large black ants that can be heard as they march to and from raids on termite mounds. *Pachycondyla spp. 2 n.* soldiers.

jɔrɔrɔ́ám (jɔrɔrɔ́-ámà-) *pl.* **jɔrɔr**. *n.* soldier. *Lit.* 'singing-ant person'. See also *kéààm*.

jɔtᵃ (jɔté-) *n.* desert rose: flowering plant species with a big base, long thin branches, and pink flowers that attract bees and wasps; its oblong root is dug and rolled by children who pretend it is prey in their spearing practice. *Adenium obesum.* Not to be confused with *jɔ́d*ᵃ. See also *dɛrɛ́k*ᵃ.

jɔ́dᵃ (jɔ́dɛ̀-) *n.* sisal plant whose fibers are used to make hunting nets. *Sansevieria sp.* Not to be confused with *jɔt*ᵃ.

jʉɛ́s (jʉɛsɨ́-) *1 v.* to roast. *2 v.* to bake.

júétɔ̀n (júétɔ̀nɨ̀-) *v.* to come out, shine forth (of heavenly bodies).

jùjù (jùjùù-) *n.* small plant species with edible cucumber-like roots.

julam (julamá-) *pl.* **julámík**ᵃ. *n.* chunk, piece, segment.

julamáím (julamá-ímà-) *pl.* **julámíkawik**ᵃ. *n.* small chunk, piece, or segment.

julés (julésí-) *v.* to section, segment, cut in chunks.

jʉm (jʉmú-) *1 n.* dirt, earth, soil. *2 n.* ground.

jʉma na zîz *n.* fertile soil. *Lit.* 'soil that is plump'.

jʉmáákw[a] (jʉmá-ákɔ̀-) *n.* underground.

jʉmúcúé (jʉmú-cúè-) *n.* groundwater, water table.

jʉmʉjʉmás (jʉmʉjʉmásí-) *n.* sand.

jʉmúkábaɖ[a] (jʉmú-kábaɖá-) *pl.* **jʉmúkábàɖik**[a]. *n.* land deed or title.

jù[o] (jùò) *ideo.* feebly, frailly, weakly.

juódòn (juódònì-) *v.* to be feeble, frail, weak. See also *ɨpálákɔ̀n*.

jùɔ̀n (jùɔ̀nɨ̀-) *v.* to be out: visible and shining (of heavenly bodies).

jʉɔ́s (jʉɔsí-) *1 v.* to be roasted. *2 v.* to be baked.

júránànès (júránànèsì-) *n.* provocativeness.

júránòn (júránònì-) *v.* to be provoking, pushing.

júrés (júrésɨ-) *1 v.* to massage, press on, rub, work. *2 v.* to sniff, snuff (tobacco through the nose).

júrésɨ̀àm (júrésɨ-àmà-) *pl.* **júrésiik**[a]. *1 n.* midwife (who massages the womb). *2 n.* massager, masseuse, physical therapist.

júrésʉkɔt[a] (júrésʉkɔtí-) *1 v.* to massage out, press out, rub down/out. *2 v.* to snuff (tobacco).

jʉrɛtés (jʉrɛtésí-) *v.* to massage out, press out, rub down/out.

jʉrʉm (jʉrʉmú-) *pl.* **jʉrúmík**[a]. *n.* crook, rod, staff, stick.

júrút[u] (júrútù) *ideo.* schlip! (sound of slipping). See also *sèlèt*[ɛ].

jʉrútúmɔ̀n (jʉrútúmɔ̀nì-) *v.* to be slick, slippery. See also *jʉrʉtútɔ́n*.

jʉrʉtútɔ́n (jʉrʉtútɔ́nì-) *v.* to be slick, slippery. See also *jʉrútúmɔ̀n*.

jútés (jútésɨ-) *1 v.* to squeeze, wring (e.g. chyme from intestines). *2 v.* to milk. See also *jútés*.

jútésʉkɔt[a] (jútésʉkɔtí-) *v.* to squeeze or wring out (e.g. chyme from intestines).

k

Kaaɓɔ́ŋ (Kaaɓɔ́ŋɨ̀-) *n.* Kaabong town.

Kaaɓɔ́ŋimucé (Kaaɓɔ́ŋɨ-mucéè-) *n.* Kaabong Road.

Kaacikóy[a] (Kaacikóì-) *n.* name of a hill or mountain.

Kaakámár (Kaakámárɨ̀-) *n.* name of a rocky hill near Kaabong.

Káákuma (Káákumaá-) *n.* Kaakuma town.

Kaaláɓè (Kaaláɓèè-) *n.* name of a place.

Kaatíríám (Kaatíríámù-) *n.* name of a hill or mountain.

kàbàɗ[a] (kàbàɗà-) *pl.* **kábàɗìk**[a]. *1 n.* rag, shred. *2 n.* document, paper, sheet of paper. *3 n.* ballot.

kabaɗa na ɓɛkɛ́sɨ́ *n.* passport. *Lit.* 'paper for traveling'.

kabaɗa na hɔnɛ́sɨ́ɛ kàèè *n.* driver's license, driving permit. *Lit.* 'paper for driving of a vehicle'.

kabaɗa na terégì *n.* work contract. *Lit.* 'paper for work'.

kabas (kabasá-) *pl.* **kábàsìk**[a]. *1 n.* flour, grist. *2 n.* dust, powder.

kábàsìn (kábàsìnì-) *n.* dust, powder. *Lit.* 'its powders'.

kábìlànètòn (kábìlànètònì-) *1 v.* to be black with white patches. *2 v.* to be flecked or mixed with fat.

kábùn (kábùnù-) *pl.* **kábùnìk**[a]. *n.* clique, coterie, social group.

kábusubusánón (kábusubusánónì-) *v.* to be blue-gray (e.g. haze over the land, or the color of tobacco mixed with soda ash). See also *bósánòn*.

kàɓ[a] (kàɓà-) *pl.* **káɓítín**. *n.* diaphragm, midriff.

kàɓàɲ (kàɓàɲà-) *pl.* **káɓáɲìk**[a]. *n.* big bowl made from half a gourd.

kaɓéléɓelánón (kaɓéléɓelánónì-) *v.* to bank, roll (e.g. when flying or sleeping).

kaɓúrútsánón (kaɓúrútsánónì-) *v.* to be dirty, murky, turbid.

Kaɓútákurí (Kaɓútákurîi-) *n.* name of a hill or mountain.

kadɨx (kadɨxá-) *pl.* **kádɨxɨk**[a]. *n.* sorghum flowers.

Kádzàn (Kádzànɨ̀-) *n.* name of a mountain.

káɗìò (káɗìò) *subordconn.* while (not yet).

kaɗokóy[a] (kaɗokóì-) *n.* vervet monkey. *Ceropithecus aethiops.*

kaɗóts[o] (kaɗótsó) *ideo.* slenderly, slimly.

kaɗótsómòn (kaɗótsómònì-) *v.* to be slender, slim. See also *sɨ́dɔ̀rɔ̀mɔ̀n* and *tɔ̀kɔ̀n*.

kàè (kàèè-) *1 n.* tortoise. *Kinixys belliana.* *2 n.* small truck, vehicle.

Kaehɨ́ƙɔ́ (Kae-hɨ́ƙɔ́ɔ̀-) *n.* name of a place. *Lit.* 'tortoise-chameleon'.

kàèìm (kàè-ìmà-) *pl.* **kaewik**[a]. *1 n.* tortoise hatchling, young tortoise. *2 n.* car, small vehicle.

kàèƙwàz (kàè-ƙwàzà-) *pl.* **kaeƙwazík**[a]. *n.* tortoise shell. *Lit.* 'tortoise-clothing'.

kaetaƙáy[a] (kae-taƙáɨ́-) *pl.* **kaetaƙáɨ́k**[a]. *n.* tire shoe. *Lit.* 'car (tortoise)-shoe'.

kàf (kàfù-) *n.* sticker, thorn.

kaiɗeíáƙát[a] (kaiɗeí-áƙátí-) *n.* pumpkin stem base. *Lit.* 'pumpkin-nose'.

kaiɗeíbɔrɔkɔ́kᵃ (kaiɗeí-bɔrɔkɔ́kɔ́-) *pl.* **kaiɗeíbɔrɔkɔ́kɨ́kᵃ.** *n.* piece of a cut up pumpkin. *Lit.* 'pumpkin-cone'.

kaiɗeícúé (kaiɗeí-cúè-) *n.* pumpkin juice. *Lit.* 'pumpkin-water'.

kaiɗeiékwᵃ (kaiɗeí-ékù-) *pl.* **kaiɗeiékwítín.** *n.* pumpkin seed.

kaiɗeyᵃ (kaiɗeí-) *n.* pumpkin.

kaiká (<kaikóón) *v.*

Kaikɛm (Kaikɛmɛ́-) *n.* name of a campground near *Lowákuj* which was used during the era of British road construction in Karamoja.

Kaikɔ́ɓà (Kaikɔ́ɓàà-) *n.* name of a place in *Tímù* and associated human habitations.

kaikóón (kaikóónì-/kaiká-) *v.* to dim, darken.

kain (kainí-) *pl.* **kainíkᵃ.** *n.* year.

kainíka ńda kainíkᵃ *n.* forever and ever. *Lit.* 'years and years'.

kainíkò nùkᵒ *n.* long ago, years ago. *Lit.* 'in those years'.

kainɔ na *n.* this year. See also *nakaina*.

kainɔ na far *n.* three years from now.

kainɔ na táà *n.* a year from now, next year.

kainɔ na tso *n.* two years from now, year after next.

kainɔ nɔkᵓ *n.* three years ago.

kainɔ nɔɔ kɛ *n.* four years ago.

kainɔ nótso *n.* two years ago, year before last. See also *nɔkɛina*.

kainɔ sin *n.* a year ago, last year, yesteryear.

kaites (kaitesí-) *1 v.* to taste. *2 v.* to sample, test, try.

kakᵃ (kaká-) *n.* leaf, leaves.

kakáánón (kakáánónì-) *v.* to be antsy, fidgety, moving restlessly.

Kakaɗᵃ (Kakaɗɨ-) *n.* name of a hill or mountain.

kakɨrɛ́s (kakɨrɛ́sɨ́-) *v.* to roll or twist up (e.g. grass for a head-pad, or clothing at the waist).

Kàkùtà (Kàkùtàà-) *n.* name of a mountain.

Kàkòlò (Kàkòlòò-) *n.* name of a river.

kál (kálé-) *pl.* **kálítín.** *n.* credit, debt, loan.

kalápátánitetés (kalápátánitetésí-) *v.* to flatten or level out.

kalápátánón (kalápátánónì-) *v.* to be flat, level (of landscapes).

kalápátánónukotᵃ (kalápátánónukotí-) *v.* to flatten or level out.

Kàlèànàŋìrò (Kàlèànàŋìròò-) *n.* name of a hill or mountain.

kalɛ́ɛ́tsɛránón (kalɛ́ɛ́tsɛránónì-) *1 v.* to be scrawny, scrubby (e.g. crops or trees). *2 v.* to be wimpy, wussy. See also *sikwárámòn*.

Kàlèwèr (Kàlèwèrì-) *n.* name of a flat hilltop where some Ik lived in the mid-1900s.

Kali (Kalií-) *n.* a personal name.

Kalɨmapús (Kalɨmapúsɨ-) *n.* a personal name.

Kalɔbɛɲɛ́ɲ (Kalɔbɛɲɛ́ɲɨ-) *n.* name of a hill or mountain.

Kàlɔ̀jɔ̀kèès (Kàlɔ̀jɔ̀kèèsè-) *n.* name of a river.

Kaloŋoléárɛ́ŋan (Kaloŋoléárɛ́ŋaní-) *n.* name of a hill or mountain.

Kalɔtúkɔ́ (Kalɔtúkɔ́ɔ̀-) *n.* name of a river.

Kaloturum (Kaloturumú-) *n.* name of a river.

Kalouwan (Kalouwaná-) *n.* name of a river.

Kalɔyáŋ (Kalɔyáŋɨ-) *n.* a personal name.

kámáránón (kámáránónì-) *1 v.* to be horizontal, cross, go across. *2 v.* to point backward (of horns). *3 v.* to be cross-eyed, strabismic.

kámáránónuƙotᵃ (kámáránónuƙotí-) *v.* to cross, go across, go horizontally.

kámáriés (kámáriesí-) *1 v.* to horizontalize: to make or mark horizontally. *2 v.* to weave the weft or woof.

kámáriésúƙotᵃ (kámáriesúƙotí-) *v.* to horizontalize: to make or mark horizontally.

kámáriós (kámáriosí-) *1 v.* to be horizontalized: made or marked horizontally. *2 v.* to be side-striped.

Kámíón (Kámíónò-) *n.* Kamion: the administrative center of Ikland and its associated human habitations.

Kámíónòàkᵃ (Kámíónò-àkà-) *n.* name of a spring and stream near Kamion. *Lit.* '*Kámíon*-mouth'.

Kámíónomucé (Kámíóno-mucéè-) *n.* Kamion Road.

Kamɔ́rɔ́mɔrátᵃ (Kamɔ́rɔ́mɔrátɨ́-) *n.* name of a hill or mountain.

kamudurudádòn (kamudurudádònì-) *v.* to be doddering, senile.

kan (kaná-) *pl.* **kanɨtín**. *n.* upper back.

Kanaɗápᵃ (Kanaɗápʉ̀-) *n.* name of a river.

Kanákɛrɛtᵃ (Kanákɛrɛté-) *n.* name of a river.

Kanamúto (Kanamútóò-) *n.* name of a hill or mountain.

Kanarɔ́ (Kanarɔ́ɔ̀-) *n.* name of a place in *Tímù* and its associated human habitations.

Kanatárúkᵃ (Kanatárúkù-) *n.* name of a small hill in Kenya that often has vultures perched on it. The Ik name is *Kɔ̀pàkwàr*.

kànàxà (kànàxàà-) *pl.* **kanáxáɨk**ᵃ. *n.* beehive (traditional or modern).

kànàxàdɛ̀ (kànàxà-dɛ̀à-) *pl.* **kanáxáɨkadɛɨk**ᵃ. *n.* base of a tree containing a beehive. *Lit.* 'beehive-foot'.

kanɛdᵃ (kanɛdɛ-) *1 n.* back, behind, rear. *2 n.* outer part.

kànèdèkᵋ *1 n.* behind. *2 n.* outside. *Lit.* 'in its back'.

kánɛs (kánɛ́sɨ-) *1 v.* to lick. *2 v.* to wipe off/up. *3 v.* to annihilate, exterminate, wipe out.

kánɨ (kánɨ) *subordconn.* in order that, so that.

kánɨ mookóo *subordconn.* in order that ... not, so that ... not.

kánɨ náa táa *subordconn.* in order that, so that.

kanímétòn (kanímétònì-) *v.* to go extinct, be annihilated, wiped out.

kanɨtínú *n.* behind. *Lit.* 'at/from their backs'.

kánɔ́n (kánɔ́nɨ-) *v.* to be clear, cloudless, unclouded.

Kaɲɨ́kààl (Kaɲɨ́kààlɨ-) *n.* name of a river.

kaɲʉm (kaɲʉmʉ́-) *n.* sesame, simsim. *Sesamum indicum*.

kàŋ (kàŋa) *ideo.* chewily.

kaŋádòn (kaŋádònì-) *1 v.* to be chewy, tough to chew. *2 v.* to be stammering, stuttering. See also *kwaídòn*.

kàŋèr (kàŋèrà-) *pl.* **kaŋɛ́rɨ́k**ᵃ. *n.* calabash, gourd.

kàŋèrèèkwᵃ (kàŋèrè-èkù-) *pl.* **kaŋɛreekwitín**. *n.* gourd seed.

Kapalú (Kapalúù-) *n.* name of a place in *Tímù* between *Lokinéne* and *Tulútúl*.

Kàpètà (Kàpètàà-) *n.* name of a mountain pass between *Lɔɓáláŋɨt* and *Ɔrɔ́m*.

Kapɛtapús (Kapɛtapúsɨ-) *n.* name of a hill or mountain.

Kapísima (Kapísimaá-) *n.* name of a place in Kenya.

kapʉrat[a] (kapʉratá-) *n.* vine species whose leaves cause skin itchiness. *Ipomoea wightii*.

karám (karámʉ́-) *pl.* **karámɨ́k**[a]. *n.* male eland. *Tragelaphus (Taurotragus) oryx*.

karámá (<karámóòn) *v.*

karámóòn (karámóònɨ-/karámá-) *v.* to be irresponsible, lax, lazy.

karan (karanɨ́-) *pl.* **karánɨ́k**[a]. *n.* assistant, secretary.

kàràts[a] (kàràtsɨ-) *pl.* **kárátsɨ̀k**[a]. *1 n.* headrest, neckrest that doubles as a stool. *2 n.* chair, seat, stool.

kárátsɨ̀k[a] (kárátsɨ̀kà-) *n.* court fee: fine a defendent must pay. *Lit.* 'seats'.

kárátsɨ̀kààm (kárátsɨ̀kà-àmà-) *pl.* **kárátsɨkaik**[a]. *1 n.* stool carver. *2 n.* jury member. *3 n.* last wife who attends to every need. *Lit.* 'chairs-person'.

karatsʉ́na (karatsʉ́naá-) *n.* young men. See also *ɲɨ́mɔ́kɔ́ka*.

karatsʉ́náám (karatsʉ́na-ámà-) *pl.* **karatsʉ́na**. *n.* young man.

kàrè (kàrèè-) *pl.* **karɛ́ɨ́k**[a]. *n.* tree species whose wood is used to carve stools. *Canthium sp.*

Karéɲaŋ (Karéɲaŋá-) *n.* name of a mountain spring with yellow soil.

Kàrèŋà (Kàrèŋàà-) *n.* name of a river with reddish soil.

Kàrèŋààm (Kàrèŋà-àmà-) *pl.* **Karɛŋaik**[a]. *n.* Napore person.

kárɨká (kárɨká) *1 adv.* most likely, probably. *2 adv.* actually, certainly, really.

karimésém (kariméséma-) *n.* small, reddish weed that grows on overturned soil and chokes out young crops.

kàròƙ[a] (kàròƙò-) *pl.* **karóƙɨ́k**[a]. *n.* burnt ground, scorched earth.

karɔŋ (karɔŋɔ́-) *pl.* **karɔ́ŋɨ́k**[a]. *n.* harvest, harvest time. See also *watsóy*[a].

káruɓú (káruɓúù-) *pl.* **káruɓúìk**[a]. *n.* unripe maize. See also *ígùm* and *ɲaɲárʉ́tè*.

karuɓúɓón (karuɓúɓónɨ-) *v.* to flourish, thrive (of plants). See also *gáruɓúɓón*.

Karʉmɛmɛ́ (Karʉmɛmɛ́ɛ̀-) *n.* name of a hill or mountain.

kárʉ̀ts'[a] (kárʉ̀ts'ʉ̀-) *pl.* **karúts'ɨ́k**[a]. *n.* carrot.

karúts'ʉ́mɔ̀n (karúts'ʉ́mɔ̀nɨ-) *v.* to be crunchy (like a carrot).

Kàsìlè (Kàsìlèè-) *n.* Kathile town and surrounding area.

kasɨ́r (kasɨ́rá-) *n.* cane, stalk (esp. the ones with sweet pith, like maize, sorghum, and sugarcane).

kásɨ́t[a] (kásɨ́tà-) *pl.* **kásɨ́tɨ̀k**[a]. *n.* hookthorn acacia: tree species with white flowers and whose branches are used in fencing and whose twigs are used to make the lower (female) firesticks. *Acacia mellifera*.

kasurúɓé (kasurúɓéè-) *n.* fine for sexual misconduct: adultery or illegitimate impregnation.

kàsw[a] (kàsò-) *pl.* **kásítín**. *n.* stick bent over as the spring mechanism for a snare.

katálámòn (katálámònɨ-) *v.* to be large and leaflike (e.g. elephant ears or figtree leaves).

Kátárʉkɔ́t[a] (Kátárʉkɔ́tɔ́-) *n.* name of a hill or mountain.

Katólìkà (Katólìkàà-) *1 n.* Catholic church. *2 n.* Catholicism.

katólìkà (katólìkàà-) *n.* maize variety with multicolored kernels.

Katólìkààm (Katólìkà-àmà-) *pl.* **Katólikaik**[a]. *n.* Catholic person.

Katoposiɲaŋ (Katoposiɲaŋá-) *n.* name of a river in Turkanaland.

Kátɔ́rɔ̀sà (Kátɔ́rɔ̀sàà-) *n.* name of a river.

kàts[a] (kàtsɨ̀-) *pl.* **kátsɨ́n.** *n.* tip, top.

Katsakól (Katsakólí-) *n.* name of a hill and an associated river.

Kátsápeto (Kátsápetoó-) *n.* name of a river.

katsés (katsésí-) *v.* to gaze or squint at while shielding the eyes.

kátsêd[a] (kátsɛ́dɛ̀-) *n.* tip, top.

Katsolé (Katsoléè-) *n.* name of a hill or mountain.

katʉmán (katʉmánɨ́-) *n.* maize variety with white kernels that matures quickly and has short stems and short cobs.

katúrúturánón (katúrúturánónì-) *v.* to be broken out, bumpy, rashy (of skin).

kaûdz[a] (kaúdzò-) *1 n.* money tree: tree species whose flat, round, brown, and sweet oily fruits are boiled many times and eaten, and whose wood is used for building houses and fencing. *Craibia laurentii.* *2 n.* money. For some speakers, the root has the form of *kaúdzè-* See also *ŋárɔpɨyá.*

kaúdzà nì ɓèts[a] *n.* cash, hard currency. *Lit.* 'money that is white'.

kaúdzèèkw[a] (kaúdzè-èkù-) *pl.* **kaúdzeekwitín.** *1 n.* coin. *2 n.* shilling. *Lit.* 'money-tree eye'.

kaúdzokabáɗ[a] (kaúdzo-kabáɗá-) *pl.* **kaúdzokabáɗík**[a]. *1 n.* bill, note (of money). *2 n.* bank check, check. *Lit.* 'money-tree paper'.

kaúdzòmèn (kaúdzò-mènà-) *n.* finance, financial matters.

káw[a] (káú-) *pl.* **káwítín.** *n.* ash(es).

Kawalakɔ́l (Kawalakɔ́lɨ̀-) *n.* name of a place.

Kàwàlèès (Kàwàlɛ̀ɛ̀sɛ̀-) *n.* name of a river near *Lódwàr.*

kawam (kawamá-) *n.* area clearable by cutting (e.g. to make a new garden).

Kawes (Kawesí-) *n.* a personal name.

Kawés (Kawésí-) *n.* November: month of clearing woodland. See also *Loipo.*

kawés (kawésí-) *v.* to cut with a bladed tool (e.g. an axe or machete).

Kàxɨ̀èrà (Kàxɨ̀èràà-) *n.* name of a hill or mountain.

kaxit[a] (kaxɨtɨ́-) *n.* grass species whose fruits are a staple food.

kazaanón (kazaanónì-) *v.* to be scattered, strewn. See also *idɛrɔs.*

kazit[a] (kazɨtɨ́-) *pl.* **kázɨtɨk**[a]. *n.* anus.

kâʒw[a] (káʒò-) *pl.* **káʒitín.** *1 n.* torch made of a bundle of small sticks. *2 n.* maize tassel.

ke (=ke) *dem.* that (over there).

kéà (kéàà-) *n.* army, military, soldiers. From the British King's African Rifles (KAR).

kéààm (kéà-àmà-) *pl.* **kéà.** *n.* soldier. See also *jɔrɔrɔ́ám.*

kéám (kéámà-) *n.* every person.

kébàdà (kébàdì-) *n.* colossus, giant, monster of a, whale of a. Referring to an entity some distance away.

kêd[a] (kédì-) *n.* degree, measure.

kéda ke *dem.* over there, there (far).

kéda zikîb[a] *n.* a long time or while.

kedíánètòn (kedíánètònì-) *v.* to be black with a white rump.

kédìè kòn *n.* at one time, together. *Lit.* 'in one measure'.

kédie kwáts[a] *n.* slowly.

kédìim (kédì-ìmà-) *1 n.* a bit. *2 n.* a time, a while.

kédiima kwáts[a] *1 n.* a little bit. *2 n.* a little while, a short time.

kédò kòn *n.* at one time, together. *Lit.* 'by one measure'.

kɛɗa (kɛ-ɗɨ-) *pro.* that one (over there).

kɛɗá (kɛ-ɗɨ́-) *pro.* that one (just there).

kèɗ[a] (kèɗà-) *pl.* **kéɗɨ́tɨ́n.** *n.* reed.

kèɗè (kèɗè) *1 coordconn.* or. *2 adv.* incorrectly, mistakenly.

Kéékoŋa (Kéékoŋaɨ́-) *n.* name of a river east of *Lopokók*[a].

Keepák[a] (Keepákà-) *n.* name of a rocky hill with two peaks near Kaabong.

keîdz[a] (keídzò-) *n.* wild potato: plant species with edible tubers.

kɛɨnats[a] *n.* next year, the coming year. A contraction of *kaɨna na ats*[a] 'the year that is coming'.

kéíta ke *dem.* over there, there (far).

kɛkɛrɛs (kɛkɛrɛsɨ́-) *v.* to tie or wind around.

kɛ́láy[a] (kɛ́láɨ-) *pl.* **kɛ́láɨk**[a]. *n.* small fruited teclea: hardwood tree species growing near rivers and whose wood is used for building. *Teclea nobilis*. See also *ɲɛmaɨlɔŋ*.

kèlèrw[a] (kèlèrò-) *pl.* **kelérík**[a]. *n.* thorny plant species whose root decoction is drunk hot as a remedy for stomach acidity. *Harrisonia abyssinica*.

kémús (kémúsì-) *pl.* **kémúsìk**[a]. *1 n.* old, dry, matted grass. *2 n.* long, matted hair.

kémúsánón (kémúsánónì-) *v.* to be felted, matted.

kèɲ (kèɲè) *ideo.* killing one-by-one.

Kéɲà (Kéɲàà-) *n.* Kenya.

kéɲán (kéɲánà-) *n.* each one.

kerêb[a] (kerébè-) *pl.* **kerébìk**[a]. *n.* layer of a grass-thatched roof.

kèrèmìdz[a] (kèrèmìdzà-) *n.* an inedibly bitter thing (e.g. some kinds of gourd).

kɛrɛ́s (kɛrɛ́sɨ-) *v.* to falsely accuse.

kerets'[a] (kerets'ú-) *pl.* **keréts'ík**[a]. *n.* termite soil: soil dampened by fresh termite dung and saliva.

kɛrɨ́nɔ́s (kɛrɨ́nɔ́sɨ́-) *v.* to falsely accuse each other.

kɛrɨ́nɔ́sɨ̀am (kɛrɨ́nɔ́sɨ́-àmà-) *pl.* **kɛrɨ́nɔ́síik**[a]. *n.* false accuser or witness. See also *lóliit*[a].

Kerûb[a] (Kerúbè-) *n.* name of a river.

kɛs (kɛsà-) *pl.* **késɨ́tɨ́n.** *n.* cataract.

kesen (kesení-) *pl.* **késénìk**[a]. *n.* shield.

kesenígwà (kesení-gwàà-) *n.* bee eater. *Lit.* 'shield-bird'. *Merops sp*. See also *coorígwà*.

Kétél (Kétélà-) *n.* name of a hill or mountain.

kɛtélitɛtɛ́s (kɛtélitɛtɛ́sɨ́-) *v.* to make seen or visible.

kɛtélɔ́n (kɛtélɔ́nɨ̀-) *v.* to be clearly seen, visible, stand out.

kɛtɛ́rɛ́mɔ̀n (kɛtɛ́rɛ́mɔ̀nɨ̀-) *v.* to be inflexible, rigid, stiff, unbending. See also *ɓotsódòn*.

kétsóibaráts[a] (kétsói-barátsó-) *n.* day after tomorrow, tomorrow next.

kétsóita ke *n.* three days from now.

kéxána kɛ *dem.* that direction/way.

kéxés (kéxésɨ̀-) *1 v.* to fry (with or without oil). *2 v.* to dry by cooking (when no oil is used).

kéxésìàm (kéxésì-àmà-) *pl.* **kéxésiik**ᵃ. *1 n.* fryer: one who fries food. *2 n.* Didinga man.

ki (=ki) *dem.* those (over there).

kíbàdà (kíbàdì-) *n.* overabundance, plentitude (over there).

kìɓèɓè (kìɓèɓèì-) *pl.* **kiɓéɓéik**ᵃ. *n.* prolapsed uterus. See also *kɨtʉ̀lɛ̀*.

kìɓèɓèàm (kìɓèɓè-àmà-) *pl.* **kiɓeɓeik**ᵃ. *n.* greedy, selfish person. *Lit.* 'one like a prolapsed uterus'.

kíɓɛzam (kíɓɛzamá-) *n.* chip, flake (of wood).

kɨɓɨɓɨtᵃ (kɨɓɨɓɨtà-) *n.* dwarf gecko. *Lygodactylus sp.*

Kiɓícᵃ (Kiɓícì-) *n.* name of a place in Kenya. Also pronounced as *Gìbíj*ᵃ.

kɨɓɔ̀ɔz (kɨɓɔ̀ɔzà-) *1 n.* heartburn, pyrosis. *2 n.* phlegm in the mouth of a newborn baby.

kídzìmètòn (kídzìmètònì-) *v.* to climb down this way, come down, descend this way. Also pronounced as *tsígìmètòn*.

kídzìmòn (kídzìmònì-) *v.* to descend, move down.

kídzimonuƙotᵃ (kídzimonuƙotí-) *v.* to climb down, descend, or go down that way.

kiɗa (ki-ɗi-) *pro.* those ones (over there).

kiɗá (ki-ɗí-) *pro.* those ones (just there).

kɨɗapánɛ́tòn (kɨɗapánɛ́tònɨ-) *v.* to be black with white cheeks.

kiɗíása (ki-ɗíá-saí-) *pro.* other(s), the others.

kiɗíwítsánón (kiɗíwítsánónì-) *v.* to be slender, slim, slight (like a needle or a thin person).

kɨɗɔ̀ (kɨɗɔ̀ɔ-) *n.* tchagra (black-and brown-crowned). *Tchagra australis/senegala.*

kiɗoɗotsᵃ (kiɗoɗotsí-) *pl.* **kiɗóɗótsìk**ᵃ. *n.* atom, molecule, particle, speck.

kɨɗɔlɛ́ (kɨɗɔlɛ́ɛ̀-) *pl.* **kɨɗɔlɛ́ɨk**ᵃ. *n.* baby primate, primate infant.

kiɗonuƙɔtᵃ (kiɗonuƙɔtí-) *1 v.* to shrink, shrivel (e.g. one's stomach when inhaling). *2 v.* to dodge, sidestep. See also *hɛ́ɗɔ́nuƙɔt*ᵃ.

Kiɗorinamótᵃ (Kiɗorinamótí-) *n.* name of a river.

kíjᵃ (kíjá-) *pl.* **kíjík**ᵃ. *1 n.* earth, globe, world. *2 n.* cosmos, universe. *3 n.* environment, nature. *4 n.* land, property, real estate. *5 n.* location, place. *6 n.* country, nation, state. *7 n.* floor.

kíjá na iɗimotós *n.* creation.

kíjáìm (kíjá-ìmà-) *pl.* **kíjáwik**ᵃ. *n.* fairy, imp, sprite: small humanoid that inhabits the wild places, has magical powers, and interacts with humans in mischievous and mysterious ways. *Lit.* 'earth-child'.

kíjákᵉ *n.* down.

kíjámèn (kíjá-mènà-) *n.* current issues, recent news. *Lit.* 'land-matters'.

kíjíkààm (kíjíkà-àmà-) *pl.* **kíjíkaik**ᵃ. *n.* alien, foreigner, outsider.

kikímón (kikímónì-) *v.* to be stocky, thickset.

kileleɓú (kileleɓúù-) *pl.* **kileleɓúik**ᵃ. *n.* intercostal muscle: meat between two ribs.

kɨlɨkilɨká (kɨlɨkilɨkáà-) *n.* long-crested eagle. *Lophaetus occipitalis.*

kɨlɨɲɨtᵃ (kɨlɨɲɨtà-) *n.* bull (male) elephant. *Loxodonta africana.*

kiɨíwítánón (kiɨíwítánónì-) *v.* to be clean, clear (e.g. area, sky, water).

kìlòlòɓ[a] (kìlòlòɓà-) *n.* bird species.

kílootór (kílootóró-) *n.* kingfisher (African pygmy or malachite). *Alcedo cristata/Ispidina picta*.

kìlɔ́rít[a] (kìlɔ́rítà-) *n.* Egyptian thorn or scented-pod acacia: tree species whose inner bark is chewed as cough remedy and whose seed-juice is used as a disinfectant. *Acacia nilotica*.

Kilóróŋ (Kilóróŋò-) *n.* name of a mountain pass.

kímáts[a] (kímátsa) *ideo.* thump thump (sound of feet stepping).

kímáts[a] (kímátsɨ-) *pl.* **kímátsɨk**[a]. *n.* footfall, footstep, step.

kimír (kimírá-) *n.* red-billed quelea. *Quelea quelea*.

kìmɔ̀ɗɔ̀rɔ̀ts[a] (kìmɔ̀ɗɔ̀rɔ̀tsà-) *n.* flowering plant species whose sap, when heated up, is used as glue to fix metal implements or to mend gourds. *Kleinia sp.*

kímúr (kímúrà-) *n.* mosquito.

kíná (kíná) *coordconn.* so then, then.

Kinám (Kinámá-) *n.* May: month of mushrooms. See also *Titímá*.

kɨnám (kɨnámá-) *pl.* **kɨnámík**[a]. *n.* mushroom.

kɨnata (kɨnataá-) *pl.* **kɨnátáɨk**[a]. *n.* handheld grinding stone.

kíníám (kíní-ámá-) *n.* strangers, unrecognized people (e.g. those seen from afar without being recognized). Plural form of *kɔ́nɔ́m*.

kíníén (kíní-ɛ́nɨ́-) *pro.* a few, some (plural).

Kinimé (Kiniméè-) *n.* a personal name. Also pronounced as *Kunumé*.

kínɨ́ŋàn (kínɨ́ŋànɨ̀-) *pl.* **kínɨ́ŋanín**. *n.* each one.

kínítòd[a] (kíní-tòdà-) *n.* incomprehensible speech, strange talk.

kìnòròt[a] (kìnòròtì-) *pl.* **kinórótìk**[a]. *n.* peg, stake (e.g. used to tack down animal skins).

kiɲom (kiɲomú-) *pl.* **kiɲómík**[a]. *n.* seed(s).

kìŋ (kìŋì) *ideo.* for good, permanently.

kíón (kíónì-) *v.* to be less-than-full, not full.

kɨpúránètòn (kɨpúránètònì-) *v.* to be maroon: dark-brownish to purplish-red.

kɨrarap[a] (kɨrarapá-) *1 n.* green scum or slime found on top of stagnant water. *2 n.* skin on boiled milk. *3 n.* soft outer layer of stomach.

kírérebú (kírérebúù-) *n.* millet left in the field to sprout the next year.

kirot[a] (kirotí-) *n.* perspiration, sweat.

kirotánón (kirotánónì-) *v.* to perspire, sweat.

kís (kísá-) *n.* dispersion, distribution.

kísáàm (kísá-àmà-) *pl.* **kísáik**[a]. *n.* distributor.

kisanes (kisanesí-) *v.* to dispense, disperse, distribute, divide out/up. See also *tɔkɔrɛs*.

kisanesíám (kisanesí-ámà-) *pl.* **kisanesíík**[a]. *n.* distributor.

kísés (kísésì-) *v.* to dispense, disperse, distribute, divide out/up. See also *tɔkɔrɛs*.

kitétón (kitétónì-) *v.* to begin quivering, shaking, shivering, or trembling.

kitítésukotᵃ (kitítésukotí-) *1 v.* to make quiver, shake, shiver, or tremble. *2 v.* to frighten, intimidate, scare, threaten. See also *xɛɓitésúkotᵃ*.

kìtòn (kìtònì-) *1 v.* to shake, quiver, shiver, tremble. *2 v.* to be aflutter, jittery, nervous.

kɨtɔ́ɔ́sɔ̀n (kɨtɔ́ɔ́sɔ̀nɨ̀-) *v.* to be what color? what shape? what texture?

kìtsᵃ (kìtsà-) *pl.* **kítsín**. *1 n.* heap, mound, pile. *2 n.* tall anthill. See also *ɲatúkítᵃ*.

kɨ̀tsàɗɔ̀s (kɨ̀tsàɗɔ̀sɨ̀-) *n.* vine species whose roots are eaten raw or roasted. *Vigna oblongifolia*.

kitsetés (kitsetésí-) *v.* to heap or pile up. See also *iruketés*.

kìtsòn (kìtsònì-) *1 v.* to be undercooked. *2 v.* to be unclear, vague (of information). See also *ɨmɨ́ránón*.

kitsonukotᵃ (kitsonukotí-) *1 v.* to undercook (due to waning fire). *2 v.* to lose interest. *3 v.* to fade (of color). See also *sɛkɔnʉkotᵃ*.

kɨ̀tʉ̀lɛ̀ (kɨ̀tʉ̀lɛ̀ɨ̀-) *pl.* **kitúlɛ́ɨkᵃ**. *n.* prolapsed uterus. See also *kìɓèɓè*.

kiwíl (kiwílá-) *pl.* **kiwílíkᵃ**. *n.* area newly cleared and burnt off for cultivation.

kíxána ke *n.* over there, that way.

kíxwᵃ (kíxó-) *pl.* **kíxítín**. *n.* freshly cut switch.

kiyá ki *dem.* those areas or places.

kiyér (kiyérí-) *n.* bird species.

kɨ́yɔɔrɔ́ (kɨ́yɔɔrɔ́ɔ́-) *n.* white-crested helmet shrike. *Prionops plumatus*.

kó (kó) *nurs.* wa-wa! (a nursery word for drinking or water).

kɔ́ɓɔ̀n (kɔ́ɓɔ̀nɨ̀-) *v.* to be ripening (e.g. maize when its kernels are still hard).

Kocí (Kocîi-) *n.* a personal name.

Kɔ́cɔ́kɨɔ (Kɔ́cɔ́kɨɔ́-) *n.* name of a mountain slope, associated river, and associated human habitation.

Kocom (Kocomó-) *n.* name of a mountainous area with a huge cavern that used to be frequented by baboons.

kodowᵃ (kodoú-) *pl.* **kódòwìkᵃ**. *1 n.* gazelle (possibly Grant's). *Gazella granti*. *2 n.* yellowish color (like that of a gazelle).

Kodowííkᵃ (Kodowí-ícé-) *n.* traditional men's age-group with a gazelle as its totem (11th and final Ik age-group). *Lit.* 'Gazelle-Folk'.

kɔ̀dzᵃ (kɔ̀dzà-) *n.* yellow-necked spurfowl. *Francolinus leucoscepus*.

koɗó (koɗóò-) *n.* pestilence, plague (partially manifested in skin boils).

koɗósón (koɗósónì-) *v.* to be bent forward (of horns).

Kɔés (Kɔésɨ́-) *n.* a personal name. May also be spelled as Kwɛés.

kɔés (kɔɛsɨ́-) *1 v.* to await, expect, wait (for/on). *2 v.* to attend to, tend (e.g. a garden, keeping watch for animal and human crop thieves).

kɔ́ɛ́s (kɔ́ɛ́sɨ̀-) *v.* to bleed for healing, leech, phlebotomize.

kɔɛsɨ́àm (kɔɛsɨ́-àmà-) *pl.* **kɔɛsíikᵃ**. *n.* bird-scarer, garden attendant.

kɔɛtés (kɔɛtésɨ́-) *v.* to await, expect, wait (for/on).

koferemáásìò (koferemáásìò-) *n.* Confirmation: Catholic sacrament allowing a baptized person to fully participate in the church.

Kòfòè (Kòfòèò-) *n.* name of a hill or mountain.

kɔín (kɔíná-) *pl.* **kɔíníkᵃ**. *n.* scent, whiff.

koisiés (koisiesí-) *v.* to wait in vain.

kój[a] (kójà) *adv.* may ..., please.

kɔk[a] (kɔ̀kà-) *n.* small reeds woven together to make granaries.

kɔkés (kɔkɛ́sɨ́-) *1 v.* to close, shut. *2 v.* to cover. See also *muts'utɛs*.

kɔkésá asɨ́ *1 v.* to shut oneself in. *2 v.* to cover oneself (e.g. in clothing).

kɔkésá mɛná[ɛ] *v.* to conceal matters, cover up issues.

kɔkésúƙɔt[a] (kɔkɛ́súƙɔtí-) *v.* to shut out.

kɔkɛtés (kɔkɛtésɨ́-) *1 v.* to close, shut. *2 v.* to cover. *3 v.* to shut down, turn off.

kɔkɛtésá mɛná[ɛ] *v.* to bring to a close, conclude, wrap up (matters).

kokímétòn (kokímétònì-) *v.* to close, shut.

kɔkɨ́rɨ́kɔk[a] (kɔkɨ́rɨ́kɔkɔ́-) *n.* bush barbet, tinkerbird (red-fronted). *Pogoniulus sp./Tricholaema sp.*

kɔkitɛtés (kɔkitɛtésɨ́-) *v.* to make to close/shut.

Kɔkɔ́ (Kɔkɔ́ɔ̀-) *n.* a personal name.

kɔkɔ́ (kɔkɔ́) *nurs.* no-no! (a nursery word for 'Don't touch!').

kokoes (kokoesí-) *v.* to entrap, trap (termites by digging a hole and lining it with sisal leaves).

kokór (kokóró-) *pl.* **kokóríkw**[a]. *n.* ridge.

kòkòròts[a] (kòkòròtsì-) *n.* small plant species with nasty hooked thorns and which is burned in fields to kill pests or to stop rain. *Asparagus flagellaris.*

kɔkɔsánón (kɔkɔsánónì-) *v.* to be mature (of plants or people).

Kókósowa (Kókósowaá-) *n.* name of a hill or mountain.

Kokóy[a] (kokóí-) *n.* a personal name.

kɔl (kɔlá-) *pl.* **kólíkw**[a]. *n.* young goat ram (uncastrated).

kɔlánétòn (kɔlánétònì-) *1 v.* to have a stripe down the spine. *2 v.* to be clear (of a path).

kɔlérà (kɔléràà-) *n.* cholera.

kɔlil (kɔlilɨ́-) *n.* cucumber.

kɔlilɨ́cúé (kɔlilɨ́-cúè-) *n.* cucumber juice.

kɔlilɨ́ékw[a] (kɔlilɨ́-ékù-) *pl.* **kɔlilɨ́ékwítín**. *n.* cucumber seed.

kɔlilɨ́kú (kɔlilɨ́-kúà-) *n.* cucumber grass: short grass species used for picking up slippery things (like cucumber seeds) and wiping the rear ends of infants. *Gramineae sp.*

koliméw[a] (koliméù-) *n.* patas monkey. *Erythrocebus patas.*

kɔlɔlánón (kɔlɔlánónì-) *1 v.* to be derelict, dilapidated, ramshackle, run-down. *2 v.* to be dried up, wasted away (crops or cadavers).

kólór (kólórò-) *n.* bird species.

kɔ́lɔ́ts[a] (kɔ́lɔ́tsɨ̀-) *pl.* **kɔ́lɔ́tsɨ̀k**[a]. *n.* men's coverall, overall, or smock made of animal skin.

kom (komá-) *n.* lots, many, multitude.

kòm (kòmà) *quant.* many.

komás (komásɨ́-) *n.* manyness, multiplicity, plurality.

kombót[a] (kombótì-) *n.* liquor, strong drink. See also *tule*.

kóméts'àɗ[a] (kómé-ts'àɗì-) *n.* conflagration, inferno, wildfire.

komikómón (komikómónì-) *v.* to be slightly numerous, not few-not many.

komitésá asɨ́ *v.* to multiply oneselves.

komítésuƙot[a] (komítésuƙotí-) *v.* to increase, multiply.

Kòmòkùà (Kòmòkùàà-) *n.* Komokua (I & II): two of the Ik's twelve clans.

Kòmòkùààm (Kòmòkùà-àmà-) *pl.* **Komokuaik**ᵃ. *n.* Komokua clan member.

komolánón (komolánónì-) *v.* to be patched, spotted (in color). See also *koríánètòn* and *tábàsànètòn*.

kómoló (kómolóò-) *pl.* **kómolóik**ᵃ. *n.* tree species whose large fruits are sucked like an orange and from whose wood branched mingling sticks are made and whose strong wood is used for building. *Canthium lactescens*.

kɔmɔ́m (kɔmɔ́má-) *pl.* **kɔmɔ́mɨ́k**ᵃ. *1 n.* scale, scurf. *2 n.* cracked skin on the foot. *3 n.* small plant species with painful, paper-thin thorns that stick in the feet of baboons and humans.

kòmòn (kòmònì-) *v.* to be many, multitudinous, plural.

komos (komosí-) *pl.* **kómósìk**ᵃ. *n.* butt cheek, buttock.

kómósikaa ɓets'aakátìkᵉ *n.* young children. *Lit.* 'buttocks being white'. So-called from their scooting around in the dust.

komótsᵃ (komótsá-) *pl.* **komótsík**ᵃ. *1 n.* elephant trunk. *2 n.* plant species whose hollow bamboo-like stems are used to blow spirits out of any bodily orifice and whose root decoction is fed to dogs to make them fierce.

komótsɛ́ɛ̀bᵃ (komótsɛ́-ɛ̀bà-) *pl.* **komótsɛ́ɛbitín**. *n.* artillery gun, cannon. *Lit.* 'elephant-trunk gun'.

kon (koní-) *pl.* **konitín**. *n.* ligament, sinew, tendon.

kɔn (kɔnɨ́-) *pro.* another, some other.

kɔ̀n (kɔ̀nà) *num.* one.

kónáxàn (kóná-xànà-) *n.* unusual way.

kɔ́náyᵃ (kɔ́n-áí-) *pro.* somewhere else.

kɔ́nɛ́ɛ́ná ámáᵉ *n.* somebody, someone.

kɔ́nɛ́ɛ́ná kɔ́rɔ́ɓádì *n.* something.

kɔníám (kɔnɨ́-ámà-) *pro.* someone.

kóníátìkᵉ *v.* one at a time, one-by-one.

kɔ́nɨ́ɛ́n (kɔ́nɨ́-ɛ́nɨ́-) *pro.* a/an, some (singular).

kónión (kóníónì-) *v.* to be one at a time, one-by-one.

kónionúkotᵃ (kónionúkotí-) *v.* to go off one-by-one.

kɔ́nɨ́s (kɔ́nɨ́sɨ̀-) *n.* inbreeding, incest.

kɔ́nɨ́sɨ̀àm (kɔ́nɨ́sɨ̀-àmà-) *pl.* **kɔ́nɨ́siik**ᵃ. *n.* inbreeder, incestuous person.

kɔnɨ́tésukɔtᵃ (kɔnɨ́tésukɔtɨ́-) *v.* to make into one, unite.

kɔnitɛtés (kɔnitɛtésɨ́-) *1 v.* to take nearly everything (e.g. food or things). *2 v.* to hit from behind.

kɔ́nɨ́tiákᵉ *1 pro.* once and for all. *2 pro.* completely, totally.

kónító ódòwì *n.* another day, one day, once upon a time. Often shortened to *kóntódòwì*.

kɔnɔ *num.* once, one time. *Lit.* 'by one'.

kɔ́nɔ́m (kɔ́nɔ́mà-) *pl.* **kíníám**. *n.* stranger.

kɔ̀nɔ̀n (kɔ̀nɔ̀nɨ̀-) *1 v.* to be one. *2 v.* to be alone.

kɔnɔna áɗònù *v.* to be a third (fraction).

kɔnɔna leɓétsónù *v.* to be a half.

kɔnɔna toomínú *v.* to be a tenth (fraction).

kɔnɔna ts'agúsónù *v.* to be a fourth (fraction).

kɔnɔna túdònù *v.* to be a fifth (fraction).

kɔŋés (kɔŋésɨ́-) *v.* to cook (by heating water and stirring). Compare with *itiŋés*.

kɔŋɛ́sɨ̀àm (kɔŋɛ́sɨ́-àmà-) *pl.* **kɔŋɛ́síik**[a]. *n.* chef, cook.

kɔŋɛ́sɨ́dàkw[a] (kɔŋɛ́sɨ́-dàkù-) *pl.* **kɔŋɛ́sɨ́dakwitín**. *n.* cooking stick (for stirring food).

Kóŋgò (Kóŋgòò-) *n.* Congo, Democratic Republic of Congo (DRC).

kɔ́ɔ́ (kɔ́ɔ́) *dem.* there. A noun following this word takes the genitive case.

kɔ́ɔ́ kɛ *dem.* in that direction, over there, there.

kɔ́ɔ́ kíj[o] *1 n.* down, downward. *2 n.* below. *3 n.* south, southward. *Lit.* 'there by the land'.

kɔ́ɔ́ kwar[ɔ] *1 n.* up, upward. *2 n.* north, northward. *Lit.* 'there by the mountain'.

kɔ́ɔ́kíjóàm (kɔ́ɔ́kíjó-àmà-) *pl.* **kɔ́ɔ́kíjóik**[a]. *n.* southerner.

kɔ́ɔ́kwarɔ́ám (kɔ́ɔ́kwarɔ́-ámà-) *pl.* **kɔ́ɔ́kwaróík**[a]. *n.* northerner.

kɔ̀p[a] (kɔ̀pà-) *1 n.* vulture. *2 n.* funerary goat killed to appease the spirit of the deceased. See also *ɲépúɲa*.

Kɔ̀pàkwàr (Kɔ̀pà-kwàrà-) *n.* name of a small hill in Kenya that often has vultures perched on it. *Lit.* 'vulture-mountain'. Also called *Kanatárúk*[a].

kɔpɨkɔp[a] (kɔpɨkɔpɨ́-) *pl.* **kɔpɨ́kɔ́pɨ̀k**[a]. *n.* ankle. See also *dɛámórók*[a].

kɔr (kɔrɛ́-) *n.* charred meat, muchomo.

kɔrɛtɛ́s (kɔrɛtɛsɨ́-) *v.* to blacken, char, scorch.

kɔrɛ́tón (kɔrɛ́tònɨ̀-) *v.* to get blackened, charred, scorched.

kòrì (kòrì) *coordconn.* or.

koríánètòn (koríánètònì-) *v.* to be patched, spotted (like a giraffe). See also *komolánón* and *tábàsànètòn*.

kóríètòn (kóríètònì-) *v.* to contend, struggle, wrestle.

koríón (koríónì-) *v.* to be in labor, parturiency.

kɔrɨtɛtɛ́s (kɔrɨtɛtɛ́sɨ́-) *1 v.* to blacken, char, scorch. *2 v.* to beat, crush, or destroy (slang for defeating someone).

Koríye (Koríyeé-) *n.* a personal name.

kɔrɔanón (kɔrɔanónì-) *v.* to struggle, wrestle. See also *koríón*.

kɔ́rɔ́ɓâd[a] (kɔ́rɔ́ɓádì-) *pl.* **kúrúɓâd**[a]. *n.* entity, item, object, thing.

kɔ́rɔ́ɓáìdàkw[a] (kɔ́rɔ́ɓáì-dàkù-) *n.* unidentified or unknown plant or tree.

Koroɓé (Koroɓéè-) *n.* a personal name.

kɔrɔ́ɗɔ́mɔ̀n (kɔrɔ́ɗɔ́mɔ̀nɨ̀-) *v.* to be gaunt, haggard, ragged, thin. See also *ɨkárɔ́n*.

kɔrɔ́k[a] (kɔrɔ́kú-) *pl.* **kɔrɔ́kɨ́k**[a]. *n.* digit, finger, toe.

kɔrɔ́ká ná zè *1 n.* thumb. *2 n.* big toe. *Lit.* 'digit that is big'.

kɔrɔ́kɨ́kààm (kɔrɔ́kɨ́kà-àmà-) *pl.* **kɔrɔ́kɨ́kaik**[a]. *n.* kleptomaniac. *Lit.* 'fingers-person'.

kɔrɔ́kɨ́kànànès (kɔrɔ́kɨ́kànànèsì-) *n.* kleptomania.

kɔrɔ́kɔ́ɔ̀k[a] (kɔrɔ́kɔ́-ɔ̀kà-) *pl.* **kɔrɔ́kɨ́kɔɔkitín**. *n.* finger bone, toe bone.

Kɔrɔmɔt[a] (Kɔrɔmɔtá-) *n.* Toposa.

Kɔrɔmɔtáhó (Kɔrɔmɔtá-hóò-) *pl.* **kɔrɔmɔtáhóík**[a]. *n.* conical hut made in the style of the Toposa people.

Kɔrɔmɔtáŋám (Kɔrɔmɔtá-ŋámà-) *n.* sorghum variety associated with the Toposa tribe, with white stalks, stems, and seeds.

Kɔrɔmɔtátôd[a] (Kɔrɔmɔtá-tódà-) *n.* Toposa dialect of the Ateker (Teso-Turkana) speech varieties.

Koror (Kororí-) *n.* name of a place.

kɔrɔ́bᵃ (kɔrɔ́bè-) *pl.* **kɔrɔ́baikwᵃ**. *n.* calf.

kòrrr (kòrrr) *ideo.* swish swish (sound of someone moving by).

Koryaŋ (Koryaɲí-) *n.* a personal name.

Kɔsɔŋ (Kɔsɔŋɔ́-) *n.* personal name of an Ik man who was shot by the Turkana for beating up a warrior who was stealing from his garden.

kòsòwᵃ (kòsòù-) *n.* dried out figs (of any of the various fig tree species).

kóteré (kóteré) *1 prep.* because of, due to. *2 subordconn.* because, due to the fact that, for the reason that. *3 subordconn.* in order that, so that. A noun following this word takes the oblique case. See also *ikóteré*.

kɔ́tɛ́s (kɔ́tɛ́sɨ-) *1 v.* to curse, cuss out. *2 v.* to exorcize (e.g. evil spirits).

kɔ́tésa súgùrìkàᵉ *v.* to exorcize spirits.

kɔ́tésɨàm (kɔ́tésɨ-àmà-) *pl.* **kɔ́tésiikᵃ**. *n.* exorcist.

kotím (kotímá-) *pl.* **kotímíkᵃ**. *n.* hole or hollow in a tree.

kotímácùè (kotímá-cùè-) *1 n.* water found in a tree hollow. *2 n.* black tea.

kòtᵒ (kòtò) *1 coordconn.* so, then, therefore, thus. *2 coordconn.* but.

kòtòbᵃ (kòtòbà-) *pl.* **kotóbaikwᵃ**. *n.* female greater kudu. *Tragelaphus strepsiceros.*

kɔtɔl (kɔtɔlí-) *n.* African white-backed vulture. *Gyps africanus.*

kɔtɔ́r (kɔtɔ́rá-) *n.* oribi. *Ourebia ourebi.*

Kotorúbé (Kotorúbéè-) *n.* name of a hill or mountain.

kɔ́tsᵃ (kɔ́tsá-) *n.* scabies.

kotsés (kotsésí-) *v.* to fetch, get (water).

kotsetés (kotsetésí-) *v.* to fetch, get (water).

kotsítésuƙotᵃ (kotsítésuƙotí-) *v.* to ensnare, entrap, snare, trap. See also *ságwès*.

kòtsòn (kòtsònì-) *v.* to be ensnared, entrapped, snared, trapped. See also *ságoanón*.

kotsonuƙotᵃ (kotsonuƙotí-) *v.* to become ensnared, entrapped, snared, or trapped.

kɔ̀wɛ̀ nòkᵒ *v.* long ago.

kɔ̀wɔ̀n (kɔ̀wɔ̀nɨ̀-) *1 v.* to be ancient, old. *2 v.* to be chronic. *3 v.* to be old-fashioned, outmoded. *4 v.* to have been around already a while.

koxésúƙotᵃ (koxésúƙotí-) *v.* to scratch vigorously to the point of bleeding.

kù (kùà-) *n.* grass.

kua mínésiɛ kwaitíní *n.* grass toothpick. *Lit.* 'grass of the picking of teeth'.

kua ni ɲeryaɲí *n.* iron sheets used for roofing houses. *Lit.* 'grasses of modernity'.

kûbᵃ (kúbà-) *pl.* **kúbitín**. *n.* unseen hillside.

kúbam (kúbamá-) *n.* more. *Lit.* 'unseeable'.

kúbèl (kúbèlà-) *pl.* **kúbèlìkᵃ**. *n.* push hoe.

kúbèlèmɔ̀n (kúbèlèmɔ̀nɨ̀-) *v.* to be precipitous, steep (on two sides).

kúbòn (kúbònì-) *v.* to be invisible, out of sight, unobserved, unseen.

kúbonuƙotᵃ (kúbonuƙotí-) *v.* to disappear, go out of sight, vanish.

kúbùr (kúbùrà-) *pl.* **kúburaikwᵃ**. *n.* big container (e.g. gourd, jerrycan, tank).

kùɓᵃ (kùɓà-) *pl.* **kúɓítín**. *n.* hill.

kʉɓá (kʉɓáà-) *pl.* **kʉɓáátikw**ᵃ. *n.* husband of my wife's sister.

kùɓààƙwᵃ (kùɓà-àƙɔ̀-) *n.* flat hilltop.

Kùɓààwᵃ (Kùɓa-àwà-) *n.* name of a hill. *Lit.* 'hill-place'.

kuɓagwarí (kuɓa-gwaríì-) *n.* hilltop.

kúcᵃ (kúcé-) *pl.* **kúcítín.** *n.* outcropping, rocky outcrop. May also be spelled as *kwíc*ᵃ.

kúɗaakón (kúɗaakónì-) *v.* to be low, short (of many).

kuɗás (kuɗásɨ́-) *n.* lowness, shortness.

kuɗítésuƙotᵃ (kuɗítésuƙotí-) *v.* to make short, shorten.

kúɗón (kúɗónì-) *v.* to be low, short.

kúf (kúfá-) *pl.* **kúfítín.** *n.* light rain, sprinkle (just enough to moisten surfaces).

kukátᵃ (kukátɨ́-) *pl.* **kukátɨ́k**ᵃ. *n.* half-grown primate.

kukú (kukú) *nurs.* up-up! (a nursery word for riding on mother's back).

kùkᵘ (kùkù) *ideo.* on an empty stomach, without eating.

kùkᵘ (kùkù) *ideo.* thump thump (sound of someone running).

kukuanón (kukuanónì-) *v.* to scramble down.

kukuɗetsᵃ (kukuɗetsí-) *n.* slate-colored boubou. *Laniarius funebris*.

kùkùsèn (kùkùsènì-) *pl.* **kukúsénìk**ᵃ. *1 n.* subterranean hive built by ground bees. *2 n.* underground hole used for storage.

kʉkúúkᵘ (kʉkúúkù) *ideo.* cockle-doodle-doo! (sound of a rooster crowing).

kʉláɓᵃ (kʉlaɓá-) *n.* bushbuck. *Tragelaphus scriptus*.

kʉláɓákàkᵃ (kʉláɓá-kàkà-) *n.* bushbuck leaf: shrub species that bushbucks like to eat and whose leaves yield a red dye. *Fuerstia africana*.

kùm (kùmù) *ideo.* flop! wham! (sound of hitting the ground hard).

Kumetᵃ (Kumetí-) *n.* name of a river.

kumutsánón (kumutsánónì-) *v.* to be joined together. See also *ɗɔtsánón*.

kunétᵃ (kunétá-) *n.* tree species whose yellow fruits are eaten raw, whose oily seeds are fried, mashed, and used as smearing oil or soap, and whose wood is used for fencing. *Ximenia americana*.

kuɲukᵃ (kuɲukú-) *pl.* **kúɲúkìk**ᵃ. *n.* pestle. See also *àfᵃ* and *iwótsídàkwᵃ*.

kuɲukúdzibér (kuɲukú-dzibérí-) *pl.* **kuɲukúdzibérík**ᵃ. *n.* traditional axe or hatchet.

kùpᵃ (kùpà-) *n.* cloud cover, cloudiness.

kùpààƙwᵃ (kùpà-àƙɔ̀-) *n.* cloudiness, overcast weather.

kʉpés (kʉpésɨ́-) *1 v.* to burn, scald. *2 v.* to affect, move emotionally.

kʉpésúƙɔtᵃ (kʉpésúƙɔtɨ́-) *v.* to burn, scald.

kupétón (kupétónì-) *v.* to cloud over/up, get cloudy.

Kùpòn (Kùpònì-) *n.* January: month of cloudiness. See also *Lomukᵃ*.

kùpòn (kùpònì-) *v.* to be cloudy, gray (of weather), overcast.

kupukúpón (kupukúpónì-) *v.* to cloud over/up, get cloudy.

kur (kurí-) *pl.* **kuritín.** *1 n.* shade. *2 n.* shelter. *3 n.* assembly, gathering, meeting (i.e. people sitting in the shade).

kùr (kùrì-) *pl.* **kúrítín.** *n.* tree species whose bark, leaves, or roots are pounded and soaked in water yielding a decoction that is drunk for chest problems; the residue can also be applied to alleviate back and chest pain. *Vepris glomerata.*

kùr (kùrù) *ideo.* klop klop (sound of trotting footsteps).

kúrà (kúràɨ-) *pl.* kurá‍ɨkᵃ. *n.* wait-a-bit acacia: small tree species whose wood is used for building and fencing, whose sticks are used to thresh grain, and whose roots are crushed, soaked, and drunk to ward off evil spirits. *Acacia brevispica.*

Kʉráhò (Kʉrá-hòò-) *n.* name of a hill or mountain. *Lit.* 'wait-a-bit acacia hut'.

Kúràɨakwᵃ (Kúràɨ-àkɔ̀-) *n.* name of a place. *Lit.* 'among wait-a-bit acacias'.

kúràkᵃ (kúràkɨ-) *1 n.* fan-tailed raven. *Corvus rhipidurus.* *2 n.* pied crow. *Corvus albus.*

kurés (kurésí-) *v.* to beat, defeat, overwhelm. See also *ilɔɛs*.

kurésúƙotᵃ (kurésúƙotí-) *v.* to beat, defeat, overwhelm.

kurétón (kurétóni-) *v.* to jar, jolt. The object of this verb takes the dative case.

kuritésúƙota asɨ *v.* to forfeit, give in/up, quit.

kurósúƙotᵃ (kurósúƙotí-) *v.* to become difficult, overwhelming.

kúrúɓáa ni cɛmáᵋ *n.* arms, weapons.

kúrúɓáa ni epwí *n.* beddings.

kúrúɓáà nùù kɔ̀wᵃ *n.* artifacts. *Lit.* 'things that are old'.

kúrúɓâdᵃ (kúrúɓádì-) *1 n.* entities, items, objects, things. *2 n.* goods, belongings.

kúrúɓáicíkᵃ (kúrúɓá-icíká-) *n.* belongings, commodities, goods, stuff. *Lit.* 'various things'.

kúrúɓáìnòìn (kúrúɓáì-nòìnì-) *n.* new discovered things.

kurukur (kurukurí-) *n.* black wingless insect that devours clothing.

kùrùkùr (kùrùkùrù) *ideo.* sound of a gourd rolling.

kúrúkúr (kúrúkúrí-) *pl.* kúrúkúríkᵃ. *1 n.* shadow. *2 n.* apparition, ghost, shade, specter, wraith. *3 n.* reflection. *4 n.* photo(graph), picture, snapshot. *5 n.* idol.

kurukúrétòn (kurukúrétònì-) *v.* to darken with shade or shadows.

kúrúkúríka ni ɓɛƙɛ́s *n.* film, movie, television, video. *Lit.* 'shadows that move'. See also *ɲévídyo*.

kurukúrón (kurukúrónì-) *v.* to avert the eyes, avoid eye contact.

kʉrúkúrɔ́s (kʉrúkúrɔ́sɨ-) *v.* to be active, energetic. See also *kwiɲɨ́dɔ̀n*.

Kúrúlè (Kúrúlèè-) *n.* personal name of a former Ik chief elder.

Kùrùmò (Kùrùmòò-) *n.* name of a place on Mount Morúŋole.

Kʉsɛ́m (Kʉsɛ́mʉ̀-) *n.* a personal name. Also pronounced as *Kʉsám*.

kùtɔ̀n (kùtɔ̀nɨ̀-) *1 v.* to say. *2 v.* to name. *3 v.* to go___: make a sound or perform an action that is expressed with one of the language's many ideophones. *4 v.* to intend to do. *5 v.* to arrive in.

kʉtɔnʉƙotᵃ (kʉtɔnʉƙotɨ́-) *1 v.* to pronounce, say, utter. *2 v.* to 'do' or 'go': make a sound or perform an action that is expressed with one of the language's many ideophones.

kʉtsáƙáàwᵃ (kʉtsáƙá-àwà-) *pl.* kʉtsáƙáawíkᵃ. *n.* urinating spot.

kʉtsáƙón (kʉtsáƙóni-) *v.* to pee, urinate.

kutsúbàè (kutsúbàè-) *n.* vine species which is peeled and whose pith is roasted and eaten; a root decoction is drunk for body pain.

kútúkᵃ (kútúkù-) *n.* first portion of edible termites to be eaten. See also *wàxɨ̀dòm*.

kútúŋ (kútúŋù-) *pl.* **kútúŋìk**ᵃ. *n.* knee.

kutúŋétòn (kutúŋétònì-) *v.* to genuflect, kneel.

kutúŋón (kutúŋónì-) *v.* to be kneeling.

kútúŋùdàdᵃ (kútúŋù-dàdà-) *n.* small red flying ant species that appears at evening time.

kutútᵃ (kutútá-) *pl.* **kutútík**ᵃ. *n.* anthill, termite mound.

Kʉwám (Kʉwámù-) *n.* a personal name.

kùx (kùxù) *ideo.* greasy, oily.

kwàà (kwàà) *nurs.* pee-pee: a nursery word for urine or urinating.

kwààkᵉ *n.* ago, before, since. May also be spelled as *kɔ̀wà kè*.

kwaake nákᵃ *n.* since earlier today. May also be spelled as *kɔwa ke nák*ᵃ.

kwààkè nòkᵒ *n.* long since, since long ago. May also be spelled as *kɔ̀wà kè nòk*ᵒ.

kwààkè sɨ̀n *n.* since yesterday. May also be spelled as *kɔ̀wà kè sɨ̀n*.

kwaár (kwaárá-) *pl.* **kwaárík**ᵃ. *n.* troop of baboons.

kwaídòn (kwaídònì-) *v.* to be chewy, tough to chew. See also *kaɲádòn*.

kwàin (kwàinì-) *1 n.* edges, sides. *2 n.* vulval (genital) labia.

kwalíkwálɔ̀n (kwalíkwálɔ̀nì-) *v.* to quake, quiver, shake, shiver, tremble. See also *irikírikòn*.

kwan (kwanɨ́-) *pl.* **kwanɨtɨ́n**. *1 n.* penis, phallus. *2 n.* stinger.

kwanɛdᵃ (kwanɛdɛ-) *n.* tiny stick used as a trigger in a bird snare. *Lit.* 'its penis'.

kwanɨ́ɗᵃ (kwanɨ́-éɗì-) *n.* glans penis. *Lit.* 'penis-kernel'.

kwanɨ́ékwᵃ (kwanɨ́-ékù-) *n.* penis hole, urethral meatus. *Lit.* 'penis-eye'.

kwanɨ́ts'ɛ́ (kwanɨ́-ts'ɛ́à-) *n.* foreskin. *Lit.* 'penis-skin'.

kwaɲɛ́s (kwaɲɛ́sɨ́-) *v.* to foil, thwart.

kwaɲɛ́súƙɔtᵃ (kwaɲɛ́súƙɔtɨ́-) *v.* to foil, thwart.

kwar (kwará-) *pl.* **kwàrɨ̀k**ᵃ. *n.* mountain.

kwarádɛ̀ (kwará-dɛ̀à-) *pl.* **kwarɨkadɛɨ́k**ᵃ. *n.* base or foot of a mountain.

kwarágwarí (kwará-gwarîi-) *n.* mountaintop, peak, summit.

kwaréékwᵃ (kwaré-ékù-) *n.* mountain saddle. *Lit.* 'mountain-eye'.

kwàrɨkààm (kwàrɨkà-àmà-) *pl.* **kwarɨkaik**ᵃ. *n.* mountain dweller.

Kwarɨkabubúíkᵃ (Kwarɨka-bubúíkà-) *n.* name of a place. *Lit.* 'mountain-bellies'.

kwatsᵃ (kwatsí-) *1 n.* pee, urine. *2 n.* offspring, progeny.

kwatsíém (kwatsí-émè-) *n.* soft flesh below the buttock. *Lit.* 'urine-meat'.

kwátsíkaakón (kwátsíkaakónì-) *1 v.* to be little, small (of many). *2 v.* to be young (of many).

kwatsítésuƙotᵃ (kwatsítésuƙotí-) *v.* to decrease size, make smaller, shrink down.

kwatsitésúƙota así *v.* to humble oneself.

kwátsón (kwátsónì-) *1 v.* to be little, small. *2 v.* to be young.

kwátsónuƙotᵃ (kwátsónuƙotí-) *v.* to become little or small, decrease in size, shrink down.

kwayɔ́ɔ́kᵃ (kwayɔ́-ɔ́kà-) *pl.* **kwaitíníɔkitín**. *n.* root of a tooth. *Lit.* 'toothbone'.

kwaywᵃ (kwayó-) *pl.* **kwaitín**. *1 n.* tooth. *2 n.* edge, fringe, side.

kwàⁱ (kwàì) *ideo.* chewily.

kwédekwedánón (kwédekwedánónì-) *v.* to be bony, cadaverous, skeletal.

kwédɔ̀n (kwédɔ̀nì-) *1 v.* to bend sideways. *2 v.* to go off course, veer. *3 v.* to split open (of bean pods).

kweedᵃ (kweede-) *n.* edge, fringe, side. *Lit.* 'its tooth'.

kweeda ƙwázàᵉ *n.* hem.

kweelémòn (kweelémònì-) *1 v.* to protrude, stick out (of ears). *2 v.* to be ashamed, embarrassed, humiliated.

kwɛlɛ́ɗᵃ (kwɛlɛ́ɗá-) *n.* blackish-brown edible flying ant species.

kwɛ́rɛɗɛ́ɗɔ́n (kwɛ́rɛɗɛ́ɗɔ́nì-) *v.* to balk, refuse to comply, resist.

kwɛ̀rɛ̀tᵉ (kwɛ̀rɛ̀tɛ̀) *ideo.* totally finished.

kwɛrɛ́xɔ́n (kwɛrɛ́xɔ́nì-) *v.* to be gray-haired, grizzly, hoary.

kwɛtᵃ (kwɛtá-) *pl.* **kwɛ̀tìkᵃ**. *1 n.* arm. *2 n.* hand. *3 n.* arm-like appendage or extremity. *4 n.* branch. *5 n.* sleeve.

kwɛtááƙwᵃ (kwɛtá-áƙɔ̀-) *n.* palm of the hand. *Lit.* 'inner hand'.

kwɛtákán (kwɛtá-kánà-) *n.* back of the hand. *Lit.* 'hand-back'.

kwɛtákɔ́rɔ́ɓádᵃ (kwɛtá-kɔ́rɔ́ɓádì-) *pl.* **kwɛtákúrúɓádᵃ**. *n.* handmade object. *Lit.* 'hand-thing'.

kwɛtámórókᵃ (kwɛtá-mórókú-) *n.* wrist. *Lit.* 'hand-throat'.

kwɛtɨ́kɨ́nᵓ *n.* empty-handed, unrewarded. *Lit.* 'with hands (only)'.

kwɛts'ɛ́mɔ́n (kwɛts'ɛ́mɔ́nì-) *1 v.* to get damaged or shattered (esp. a gourd). *2 v.* to be divulged, let out, revealed (a secret).

kwɛts'ɛ́s (kwɛts'ɛ́sɨ́-) *1 v.* to damage, shatter. *2 v.* to divulge, let out, reveal (a secret).

kwɛ̀x (kwɛ̀xɛ̀) *ideo.* thinly.

kwɛxɛ́dɔ̀n (kwɛxɛ́dɔ̀nì-) *v.* to be thin (of flat surfaces, like cloth or leather).

kwídètòn (kwídètònì-) *v.* to have a penile erection.

kwídikwidós (kwídikwidósí-) *v.* to be aroused, horny, turned on (sexually).

kwídòn (kwídònì-) *v.* to have a penile erection.

kwɨ́lilɨ́ (kwɨ́lilɨ́-) *1 n.* ripe desert dates. *2 n.* local Ik tobacco variety (possibly indigenous?).

kwɨniƙᵃ (kwɨniƙɨ́-) *n.* dassie, hyrax.

kwɨniƙɨ́kú (kwɨniƙɨ́-kúà-) *n.* hyrax grass: tall grass species eaten by hyraxes and used to store tobacco in and to make beehive plugs. GRAMINEAE *sp.*

kwɨɲ (kwɨɲì) *ideo.* actively, energetically.

kwɨɲídɔ̀n (kwɨɲídɔ̀nì-) *v.* to be active, energetic. See also *kʉrʉ́kʉ́rɔ́s*.

kwɨ́ɲɨ́kà (<kwɨ́ɲɨ́kɔ̀ɔ̀n) *v.*

kwɨ́ɲɨ́kɔ̀ɔ̀n (kwɨ́ɲɨ́kɔ̀ɔ̀nì-/kwɨ́ɲɨ́ka-) *v.* to bare the teeth.

kwìr (kwìrì) *ideo.* slickly, slipperily.

kwɨ́rɛ́s (kwɨ́rɛ́sɨ̀-) *v.* to anoint, embrocate, inunct (the victorious, e.g. with soot, marrow, tobacco, or crushed termites). See also *tsáŋés*.

kwirídòn (kwirídònì-) *v.* to be slick, slippery, slippy (like a raw tendon).

kwɨ́tsɨ́ladidí (kwɨ́tsɨ́ladidîi-) *n.* Jackson's francolin. *Francolinus jacksoni.*

kwits'ídòn (kwits'ídònì-) *v.* to be juicy.

kwits'íkwíts'ánón (kwits'íkwíts'ánónì-) *v.* to be moody, tempermental.

kwìts'ⁱ (kwìts'ì) *ideo.* juicily.

ƙ

ƙà (<ƙòòn) v.

ƙádès (ƙádèsì-) v. to shoot.

ƙádesuƙotᵃ (ƙádesuƙotí-) v. to shoot.

ƙádetésá kadixáᵋ v. to flower, go to flower (of sorghum). Lit. 'to emit flowers'.

ƙádiƙádès (ƙádiƙádèsì-) v. to thud, thump (e.g. a beehive to check its contents).

ƙádiƙadiés (ƙádiƙadiesí-) v. to shoot repeatedly.

ƙádiƙádòn (ƙádiƙádònì-) v. to beat, pulsate, pulse (of blood in veins). See also dìkwòn.

ƙádòn (ƙádònì-) v. to ripen (of tree fruit).

ƙáidetés (ƙáidetésí-) v. to go bring, go get.

ƙàƙᵃ (ƙàƙà-) n. hunt, hunting.

ƙaka ŋúnítínᵒ n. hunting with rope neck-snares.

ƙàƙààm (ƙàƙà-àmà-) pl. kaƙaikᵃ. n. hunter.

ƙakates (ƙaƙatesí-) n. to brace or stabilize (a trap, e.g. with several sticks).

ƙaƙés (ƙaƙésí-) v. to hunt.

ƙaƙótsómòn (ƙaƙótsómònì-) v. to be wide-legged (in stance and stride).

ƙaƙúŋ (ƙaƙúŋù-) pl. ƙaƙúŋìkᵃ. n. back corner of the lower jawbone, mandibular angle.

ƙalíƙálés (ƙalíƙálésí-) v. to corral, round up. See also ikoŋetés.

ƙálíts'ᵃ (ƙálíts'ì-) pl. ƙálíts'ìkᵃ. n. jaw, mandible.

ƙálíts'ìɔkᵃ (ƙálíts'ì-ɔkà-) pl. ƙálíts'ikɔɔkitín. n. jawbone, mandibular bone.

ƙámá kiɗíé v. maybe, perhaps. Lit. 'it's like those (words)'.

ƙámétòn (ƙámétònì-) v. to become like.

ƙámítetés (ƙámítetésí-) v. to compare, liken.

ƙámón (ƙámónì-) v. to be like, resemble.

ƙámónà ts'èèn v. to be like this.

ƙámónuƙotᵃ (ƙámónuƙotí-) v. to become like.

ƙánàkᵃ (ƙánàà) adv. would have ... (earlier today).

ƙanés (ƙanésí-) v. to take in hand.

ƙanésúƙotᵃ (ƙanésúƙotí-) 1 v. to remove, take away. 2 v. to subtract.

ƙanésúƙota gwaáᵉ v. to solve a bird problem in the garden by burying a bird alive as a sacrifice. Lit. 'to take away the bird'. See also muɗésá gwaáᵉ.

ƙanetés (ƙanetésí-) 1 v. to get, take hold of. 2 v. to remove, take out. 3 v. to desire, wish for (of one's heart). 4 v. to apprehend, sense.

ƙanitetés (ƙanitetésí-) v. to cause to get.

ƙánòkᵒ (ƙánòò) adv. would have ... (long ago).

ƙanotós (ƙanotósí-) v. to be chosen, elect, special.

ƙáraƙár (ƙáraƙárà-) n. green woodhoopoe. Phoeniculus purpureus.

ƙásàm (ƙásàmù) adv. would have ... (yesterday).

ƙédaikén (ƙédaikén) dem. there.

ƙeɗétón (ƙeɗétónì-) v. to be newly pregnant (showing no sign).

143

ƙèƙᵋ (ƙèƙɛ̀) *ideo.* crunch crunch (sound of feet on hard ground).

ƙɛƙɛanón (ƙɛƙɛanónì-) *v.* to walk making a crunching sound.

ƙɛƙɛ́r (ƙɛƙɛ́rá-) *n.* grasshopper.

ƙɛƙɛram (ƙɛƙɛramá-) *n.* traditional Ik food made of honey mixed with edible termites.

ƙɛ́ƙɛ́rɛ́s (ƙɛ́ƙɛ́résɨ́-) *v.* to mix (specifically honey and edible termites).

ƙeƙérón (ƙeƙeróni-) *v.* to detour, steer clear, take a wide detour (so as to avoid something dangerous or unpleasant). See also *wédɔn*.

ƙɛ́lɛ́s (ƙɛ́lɛ́sɨ-) *v.* to pick out, select (one's portion or property from others, e.g. goats from a herd).

ƙɛ́lɛ́sukɔta asɨ *v.* to set oneself apart.

ƙɛlɛtɛ́sá asɨ *v.* to pull oneself away.

ƙélietés (ƙélietesí-) *v.* to select iteratively.

ƙérikérɔ́n (ƙérikérɔ́nɨ-) *v.* to be astringent. See also *tererɛ́ɔ́n*.

ƙídiƙídɔ̀n (ƙídiƙídɔ̀nɨ-) *v.* to pour, stream, teem (e.g. ants, water, enemies, vehicles in a convoy, etc.).

ƙídzatiés (ƙídzatiesí-) *1 v.* to bite repeatedly. *2 v.* to interlace, interlock, mesh.

ƙídzès (ƙídzèsɨ-) *1 v.* to bite, chomp. *2 v.* to sting. *3 v.* to overcrowd, overrun. See also *átsʼɛ́s*.

ƙídzesa dáŋáᵉ *v.* to 'bite' or eat whole termites alive.

ƙídzèsɨkwàywᵃ (ƙídzèsɨ-kwàyò-) *pl.* ƙídzɛsɨkwaitín. *n.* fang, incisor. *Lit.* 'biting-tooth'.

ƙídzɨkà (<ƙídzɨkɔ̀ɔ̀n) *v.*

ƙídzɨkɔ̀ɔ̀n (ƙídzɨkɔ̀ɔ̀nɨ-/ƙídzɨka-) *v.* to clench the teeth (visibly). See also *wɨdɨdánón*.

ƙídzinɔ́s (ƙídzinɔ́sɨ́-) *1 v.* to bite each other. *2 v.* to move in single file.

ƙídzitɛtɛ́s (ƙídzitɛtɛ́sɨ́-) *v.* to join end-to-end. *Lit.* 'to make bite'.

ƙídzɔn (ƙídzɔ̀nɨ-) *1 v.* to adhere, cling, stick. *2 v.* to emerge and begin to fly away (of edible termites).

ƙíɛƙíɛƙíɛ (ƙíɛƙíɛƙíɛ) *ideo.* cheep cheep! chirp chirp! (sound made by young birds).

ƙíítínɨsɔ̀kᵃ (ƙíítínɨ́-sɔ̀kà-) *pl.* ƙíítínɨsɔkitín. *n.* leather tassel. *Lit.* 'strap-root'.

ƙìrɔ̀n (ƙìrɔ̀nì-) *v.* to thunder.

ƙironuƙotᵃ (ƙironuƙotí-) *1 v.* to thunder. *2 v.* to thunder off (like an elephant).

ƙìrɔ̀tᵃ (ƙìrɔ̀tì-) *pl.* ƙirɔ́tíkᵃ. *n.* opposite riverbank.

ƙitɛ́s (ƙitɛ́sɨ́-) *v.* to pinch off (e.g. tobacco leaves).

ƙíwᵃ (ƙíɔ́-) *pl.* ƙíítín. *n.* strap made of leather or any other material.

ƙó (<ƙòòn) *v.*

ƙɔ́ɓᵃ (ƙɔ́ɓà-) *pl.* ƙɔ́ɓítín. *1 n.* belly button, navel. *2 n.* pistol grip.

ƙɔɓa na zikîɓᵃ *n.* umbilical hernia. *Lit.* 'navel that is long'.

ƙɔɓasim (ƙɔɓa-simá-) *pl.* ƙɔ́ɓítínɨsimitín. *n.* umbilical cord.

ƙɔ́ɓàsìtsʼᵃ (ƙɔ́ɓà-sìtsʼà-) *n.* navel hair.

ƙɔ́ɓuƙɔ́ɓᵃ (ƙɔ́ɓuƙɔ́ɓù-) *n.* large tree species (possibly fig) with edible yellow fruits.

ƙɔ́dɔ̀l (ƙɔ́dɔ̀lɛ̀-) *pl.* ƙɔ́dɔ̀lɨkᵃ. *1 n.* forearm. *2 n.* section of stalk above a maize cob. See also *ɲepɨkɨ́sɨtᵃ*.

ƙɔ́dɔxɔ́ (ƙɔ́dɔxɔ́ɔ̀-) *pl.* ƙɔ́dɔxɔ́ɨkᵃ. *n.* centipede.

ƙɔditɛs (ƙɔditɛsɨ́-) *v.* to make cry.

ƙɔdɔ̀n (ƙɔdɔ̀nɨ-) *1 v.* to cry, wail, weep. *2 v.* to call (of animals and birds). *3 v.* to bemoan, complain, lament. See also *topódón*.

ƙɔɗɔ̀t^a (ƙɔɗɔ̀tà-) *pl.* ƙɔɗɔ́tɨ́k^a. *n.* climbing crook: hooked stick used for climbing trees.

ƙɔés (ƙɔɛsɨ́-) *v.* to straighten, stretch. See also *kɔkatés*.

ƙɔfɔ́ (ƙɔfɔ́ɔ̀-) *pl.* ƙofóikw^a. 1 *n.* round gourd traditionally cut in half to make two bowls. 2 *n.* bowl made from half of a round gourd.

ƙɔfɔ́èɗ^a (ƙɔfɔ́-èɗì-) *n.* first harvest of grain. *Lit.* 'gourd-bowl grain'.

ƙɔfóìm (ƙɔfó-ìmà-) *pl.* ƙofóikówík^a. *n.* small round gourd.

ƙɔkatés (ƙɔkatésí-) 1 *v.* to straighten, stretch. 2 *v.* to exercise (the body). See also *ƙɔés*.

ƙokó (ƙokóò-) *pl.* ƙokóikw^a. *n.* big wide-mouthed gourd.

ƙɔkɔanón (ƙɔkɔanónì-) 1 *v.* to stretch. 2 *v.* to advertise, flaunt (one's physical attributes).

ƙokórómòn (ƙokórómònì-) *v.* to be gruff, hoarse, husky. See also *rókɔ́rɔkánón*.

ƙɔ̀ƙɔ̀t^a (ƙɔ̀ƙɔ̀tà-) *n.* red-billed hornbill. *Tockus erythrorhynchus*.

ƙolom (ƙolomú-) *pl.* ƙólómìk^a. *n.* wooden spoon.

Kolomúsábá (Kolomú-sábáà-) *n.* name of a river and associated human habitations in Kenya; now called *Oropoi*. *Lit.* 'spoon-river'.

ƙòlòn (ƙòlònì-) *v.* to bleed from the nose, have a nosebleed.

ƙɔɔlɔ́mɔ̀nà dèɨ̀kà^ɛ *v.* to be clubfooted, have talipes.

ƙòòn (ƙòònì-/ƙa-) *v.* to go, leave.

ƙooná dìdìk^e *v.* to go up.

ƙooná gìdààkɔ̀k^ɛ *v.* to go behind the clouds.

ƙoona gígìròk^e *v.* to go down.

ƙòònà jɨ̀r *v.* to go away forever.

ƙoona jɨ́rɨ̀k^ɛ *v.* to go back or behind.

ƙoona rutet^o *v.* to go along the side.

ƙoona wáxɨ̀k^ɛ *v.* to go ahead or in front.

ƙòònìàm (ƙòònì-àmà-) *pl.* ƙooniik^a. *n.* goer, traveler.

ƙór (ƙóré-) *pl.* ƙórítín. *n.* back of knee, posterior knee. Not to be confused with *ƙɔ́r*.

ƙɔ́r (ƙɔ́ré-) *pl.* ƙóríkw^a. *n.* dipper, ladle (made from cutting a small gourd in two). Not to be confused with *ƙór*.

ƙóróèm (ƙóró-èmè-) *n.* plantaris muscle: behind the knee.

ƙɔ́rɔmɔmɔ́n (ƙɔ́rɔmɔmɔ́nɨ̀-) *v.* to be shriveled, withered (like dry leaves or an old corpse).

ƙɔ̀rɔ̀n (ƙɔ̀rɔ̀nɨ̀-) *v.* to strut, swagger. See also *iƙɔ́ɔ́résá asɨ́*.

ƙórór (ƙórórò-) *n.* African scops-owl. *Otus senegalensis*.

ƙɔxés (ƙɔxésɨ́-) *v.* to manually maneuver, or manipulate into the right position (e.g. a midwife guiding a preborn infant).

ƙúdès (ƙúdèsì-) 1 *v.* to dump, pour, spill. 2 *v.* to pay (poll-tax).

ƙúdesa ɗíróe asɨ́ *v.* to be emitted nocturnally (of semen).

ƙúdesa káue mucéíkàk^e *v.* to sprinkle ashes along paths.

ƙúdèsìàm (ƙúdèsì-àmà-) *pl.* ƙúdesiik^a. *n.* dump truck, tipper.

ƙúdesuƙot^a (ƙúdesuƙotí-) *v.* to dump or pour out, spill.

ƙúdetés (ƙúdetésí-) 1 *v.* to dump out, pour out, spill. 2 *v.* to miscarry.

ƙúdetésá ɗíróᵉ *v.* to come, ejaculate. *Lit.* 'to spill semen'.

ƙúduƙûdᵃ (ƙúduƙúdù-) *n.* safari ant. *Dorylus spp.*

ƙuɗɛ́s (ƙuɗɛ́sɨ́-) *v.* to suck, suck on. See also *ts'ʉ́tés*.

ƙuɗɛtɛ́s (ƙuɗɛtɛ́sɨ́-) *v.* to suck out (e.g. bone marrow).

ƙúɗúnɔ́s (ƙúɗúnɔ́sɨ́-) *v.* to suck on each other (e.g. during foreplay).

ƙujʉ́dɔ̀n (ƙujʉ́dɔ̀nɨ̀-) *v.* to garble.

ƙúƙᵃ (ƙúƙá-) *pl.* ƙúƙítín. *n.* runt.

ƙúƙín (ƙúƙínɨ̀-) *n.* brood, litter, pack of runts. Also used disparagingly of human children.

ƙuƙumanés (ƙuƙumanésɨ́-) *v.* to turn one's back to (e.g. one's mother-in-law).

ƙuƙumánítésuƙotᵃ (ƙuƙumánítésuƙotí-) *v.* to turn back to back.

ƙuƙumánón (ƙuƙumánónì-) *v.* to face back to back.

ƙuƙumánónuƙotᵃ (ƙuƙumánónuƙotí-) *v.* to turn back to back.

ƙúl (ƙúló-) *pl.* ƙúlítín. *n.* log.

ƙulɛ́ (ƙulɛ́ɛ̀-) *pl.* ƙulɛ́ɨ̀kᵃ. *n.* elbow.

ƙulɛ́èm (ƙulɛ́-èmè-) *n.* lower tricep. *Lit.* 'elbow-flesh'.

ƙumúƙúmánón (kumúƙúmánónì-) *1 v.* to be bumpy, pot-holed, rough. *2 v.* to be hilly, rough, uneven.

ƙutsʼᵃ (ƙutsʼá) *1 n.* grub, worm. *2 n.* bug, insect. *3 n.* germ, microbe, parasite.

ƙutsʼáám (ƙutsʼá-ámà-) *pl.* ƙutsʼaíkᵃ. *n.* creep, freak, weirdo (e.g. the members of tribes who practice sorcery). *Lit.* 'worm-person'.

ƙutsʼácémɛ́r (ƙutsʼá-cémɛ́rɨ́-) *n.* insecticide (modern or traditional). *Lit.* 'bug-medicine'.

ƙutsʼánánès (ƙutsʼánánèsì-) *1 n.* harmfulness, ruinousness. *2 n.* sorcery, wizardry. *Lit.* 'being wormlike'. See also *badirétínànès*.

ƙùtsʼàtsʼᵃ (ƙùtsʼàtsʼì-) *pl.* ƙutsʼátsʼíkᵃ. *n.* gland, lymph node, secretor.

ƙutsʼátsʼíka ni tatí *n.* salivary glands.

ƙútᵘ (ƙútú) *ideo.* cluck! (the sound a hen makes).

ƙúzùmòn (ƙúzùmònì-) *v.* to be bent over.

ƙwáaƙwá (ƙwáaƙwáà-) *n.* white-bellied go-away bird. *Corythaixoides leucogaster.*

ƙwaátᵃ (ƙwaatá-) *n.* frog, toad.

ƙwaátᵃ (ƙwaaté-) *n.* birth, birthing, giving birth.

ƙwaata ɓíɓàᵉ *n.* laying of eggs.

ƙwaatá na áwìkàᵉ *n.* toad. *Lit.* 'frog of homes'.

ƙwaata ná gààn *n.* birthing complications, difficult labor (breach, miscarriage, etc.). *Lit.* 'birth that is bad'.

ƙwaatetés (ƙwaatetésí-) *v.* to bear, deliver, give birth to.

ƙwaatetésíàm (ƙwaatetésí-àmà-) *pl.* ƙwaatetésiikᵃ. *n.* parent (by birth).

ƙwaatítetés (ƙwaatítetésí-) *1 v.* to help give birth, midwife. *2 v.* to produce.

ƙwaatítetésíàm (ƙwaatítetésí-àmà-) *pl.* ƙwaatítetésiikᵃ. *n.* midwife.

ƙwaatón (ƙwaatónì-) *v.* to give birth.

ƙwàɗᵉ (ƙwàɗè) *quant.* few.

ƙwaɗíƙwáɗón (ƙwaɗíƙwáɗónì-) *v.* to be fewer.

ƙwàɗòn (ƙwàɗònì-) *v.* to be few, little.

ƙwaɗonuƙotᵃ (ƙwaɗonuƙotí-) *v.* to become fewer, decrease in number.

ƙwár (ƙwárá-) *pl.* ƙwárítín. *1 n.* cicatrix, scar. *2 n.* bruise, contusion.

ƙwàz (ƙwàzà-) *pl.* ƙwázìkᵃ. *n.* cloth, clothes, clothing, garment.

ƙwàzàìm (ƙwàzà-ìmà-) *pl.* ƙwázikawikᵃ. *n.* small cloth.

ƙwèjᵋ (ƙwèjɛ̀) *ideo.* bllgh bllgh (sound of water boiling in a pot).

ƙwɛjɛ́dɔ̀n (ƙwɛjɛ́dɔ̀nɨ̀-) *v.* to be boiling, boil (with a rattling sound).

ƙwɛjɨ́ƙwɛ́jɔ̀n (ƙwɛjɨ́ƙwɛ́jɔ̀nɨ̀-) *v.* to be boiling (with a rattling sound).

ƙwɛsɛ́ (ƙwɛsɛ́ɛ̀-) *pl.* ƙwéséikwᵃ. *1 n.* broken gourd. *2 n.* piece of junk, scrap.

ƙwɨjɛ́s (ƙwɨjɛ́sɨ́-) *v.* to dislocate (a joint), luxate.

ƙwɨjɨ́mɔ́n (ƙwɨjɨ́mɔ́nɨ̀-) *v.* to get dislocated, luxated.

ƙwɨ́l (ƙwɨ́lɨ́) *ideo.* clink! (sound of metal on metal).

ƙwɨx (ƙwɨ̀xɨ̀) *ideo.* greenly.

ƙwɨxɨ́dɔ̀n (ƙwɨxɨ́dɔ̀nɨ̀-) *v.* to be verdant, very green. See also *xɨ́dɔ̀n*.

l

Laatso (Laatsoó-) *n.* name of a hill or mountain.

laɓᵃ (laɓá-) *pl.* **láɓíkw**ᵃ. *n.* cache, stash (whose location may be forgotten).

laɓáɲámòn (laɓáɲámònì-) *v.* to be gaping, wide-mouthed, yawning. See also *lafárámòn*.

làf (làfù-) *pl.* **láfítín**. *n.* breast (of meat), pec, pectoral muscle.

lafárámòn (lafárámònì-) *v.* to be gaping, wide-mouthed, yawning. See also *laɓáɲámòn*.

lágalagetés (lágalagetésí-) *v.* to check or spy on/out.

làjᵃ (làjà) *ideo.* loosely.

lajádòn (lajádònì-) *v.* to be loosely tied down, unsecured. See also *hajádòn* and *yaŋádòn*.

lajámétòn (lajámétònì-) *1 v.* to collapse, crumple, fall down. *2 v.* to wilt, wither. *3 v.* to dissolve, melt (of fat). See also *ɲalámétòn*.

lajetés (lajetésí-) *1 v.* to lay down/over loosely (e.g. the last layer of grass on a thatched roof). *2 v.* to take off (e.g. beads from one's neck).

lakámétòn (lakámétònì-) *v.* to descend, go down (out of sight).

lakámón (lakámónì-) *v.* to descend, go down (out of sight).

lakates (lakatesí-) *v.* to push into/over the side.

lakatiés (lakatiesí-) *1 v.* to push into/over the side repeatedly. *2 v.* to down, gulp down, inhale (food). See also *itúlákaɲés*.

láládziránón (láládziránónì-) *v.* to be ripped, shredded, in shreds.

lalatíɓón (lalatíɓónì-) *pl.* **lalatíɓónìk**ᵃ. *n.* flat stone, stone slab (used to grind tobacco, carry rubbish, cover granaries, or cover a rock well to protect it from the befouling of baboons).

làlòn (làlònì-) *v.* to be hideous, ugly. See also *itópénòn*.

lalújón (lalújónì-) *v.* to be roomy, spacious. See also *ilɔ́lɔ́mɔ̀n*.

láŋ (láŋá-) *pl.* **láŋítín**. *n.* bogus, counterfeit, fake, phoney, pseudo-.

laŋádòn (laŋádònì-) *v.* to be stifling, sultry, unpleasantly warm.

laŋírímòn (laŋírímònì-) *v.* to be broad, stout (e.g. bodies, buildings).

laŋírón (laŋírónì-) *v.* to be broad, stout (e.g. bodies, buildings).

làr (làrà-) *pl.* **láríkw**ᵃ. *n.* tobacco pipe.

laradakwᵃ (lara-dakú-) *pl.* **lárákódakwitín**. *n.* pipe-stem (often made from Carissa stems).

látsó (látsóò-) *pl.* **látsóìk**ᵃ. *n.* drop-off, edge of a cliff or rock, precipice.

látsóìkᵃ (látsóìkà-) *n.* falls, waterfall. *Lit.* 'cliff edges'.

leatᵃ (leatí-) *pl.* **leatíkw**ᵃ. *1 n.* his/her/its brother. *2 n.* his/her cousin (father's brother's son).

leatíím (leatí-ìmà-) *pl.* **leatíwík**ᵃ. *n.* his/her niece or nephew (brother's child).

leatínánès (leatínánèsì-) *n.* brotherhood, brotherliness.

lèɓᵃ (lèɓà-) *n.* liquid honey.

lɛɓéɲémɔ̀n (lɛɓéɲémɔ̀nɨ̀-) *v.* to be open-topped, unlidded.

lèɓèts[e] (lèɓètsè) *num.* two.

lɛɓetsíòn (lɛɓetsíónì-) *v.* to be in twos, two-by-two.

lɛɓetsítésuƙot[a] (lɛɓetsítésuƙotí-) *v.* to make two, put in twos or two-by-two.

lèɓèts[o] *num.* twice, two times.

lɛɓétsón (lɛɓétsónì-) *v.* to be two.

lèɓ[u] (lèɓù) *ideo.* pudgily, puffily.

lɛɓúdòn (lɛɓúdònì-) *v.* to be pudgy, puffy (like a plump person or swollen body part). See also *dúdúránón*.

lèdèr (lèdèrè) *ideo.* running naked.

léɗ[a] (léɗá-) *n.* gecko species?

lɛɛmétɔ̀n (lɛɛmétɔ̀nɨ̀-) *v.* to stick out/up (like a snake from the grass).

legé (legéè-) *1 n.* craziness, insanity, madness, mental illness. *2 n.* demon possession. See also *lejé*.

lejé (lejéè-) *1 n.* craziness, insanity, madness, mental illness. *2 n.* demon possession. Also pronounced as *legé*.

lejéàm (lejé-àmà-) *pl.* **lejéik**[a]. *n.* mad person, demon-possessed person. Also pronounced as *legéàm*.

lejéèd[a] (lejéèdè-) *1 n.* craziness, insanity, madness, mental illness. *2 n.* demon possession.

lejénánès (lejénánèsì-) *1 n.* craziness, insanity, mental illness. *2 n.* demonic possession.

lejétòd[a] (lejé-tòdà-) *n.* insane talk.

léj[ɛ] (léjɛ́) *ideo.* flash!: sound of bursting in flames.

léjétón (léjétónɨ̀-) *v.* to catch fire, erupt in flames, ignite.

lɛkés (lɛkésɨ́-) *v.* to retrieve from storage (e.g. grain from a granary).

lɛkésɨ̀àm (lɛkésɨ́-àmà-) *pl.* **lɛkésíik**[a]. *n.* food retriever (esp. stored food in granaries).

lɛlɛmánétòn (lɛlɛmánétònì-) *v.* to appear, come into view, emerge.

lɛlɛmánón (lɛlɛmánónì-) *v.* to be appearing, coming into view, emerging (e.g. a snake from a hole, or a vehicle over a hill).

lɛlétɔ́n (lɛlétɔ́nɨ̀-) *v.* to appear, come into view, emerge. See also *pɛlémétɔ̀n*.

lɛ́lɔ́n (lɛ́lɔ́nì-) *v.* to be fully seen, completely visible.

Lemú (Lemúù-) *n.* a personal name.

lemúánètòn (lemúánètònì-) *1 v.* to be hornless. *2 v.* to be bare, naked, nude.

lɛŋ (lɛŋá-) *n.* honey badger, ratel. *Mellivora capensis*.

lɛŋérémɔ̀n (lɛŋérémɔ̀nɨ̀-) *v.* to be circumcised.

lɛŋés (lɛŋésɨ́-) *1 v.* to hunt (for honey). *2 v.* to bum, cadge, freeload, mooch, sponge.

lɛŋésɨ̀àm (lɛŋésɨ́-àmà-) *pl.* **lɛŋésíik**[a]. *1 n.* honey hunter. *2 n.* bum, cadger, freeloader, moocher, sponge.

lɛŋúrúmòn (lɛŋúrúmònì-) *v.* to be bare, naked, nude.

léó (léóò-) *pl.* **léóín**. *1 n.* your brother. *2 n.* your cousin (father's brother's son).

léóím (léó-ímá-) *pl.* **léówík**[a]. *n.* your niece or nephew (brother's child).

lèr (lèrà-) *pl.* **lérɨ́tɨ́n**. *n.* fever tree, or Naivasha thorn: tall acacia with powdery green-white bark, whose wood is used to carve stools. *Acacia xanthophloea*.

lèr (lèrè) *ideo.* hardly, unbreakably.

Lèràà̀kw[a] (Lèrà-àkɔ̀-) *n.* name of a place. *Lit.* 'among fever trees'.

lɛrédɔ̀n (lɛrédɔ̀nɨ̀-) *1 v.* to be hard, unbreakable (e.g. bone, hardwood, rock). *2 v.* to be frozen still, still, stock-still, stone-still (e.g. an eagle's unblinking eyes). *3 v.* to be blockheaded, boneheaded.

lɛrékɛ́mɔ̀n (lɛrékɛ́mɔ̀nɨ̀-) *v.* to be gnarled, knobby (like bones or bulging, dried out eyes).

lerúkúmòn (lerúkúmònì-) *v.* to be medium-sized. See also *ɓarɨɓárɔ́n* and *jɔ́kɔ̀n*.

lèt[a] (lètà-) *pl.* **létítín.** *n.* girl's loincloth made of beaded strings.

léts[a] (létsá-) *n.* tiny termite species.

lɛtsékɛ́ɛd[a] (lɛtsékɛ́ɛdɛ-) *n.* purity of food (e.g. white-ants with no wings or dirt, honey with no rubbish, or grain with no chaff).

lèts'[ɛ] (lèts'è) *ideo.* bendily, whippily.

lɛts'édɔ̀n (lɛts'édɔ̀nɨ̀-) *v.* to be bendy, whippy (like a limber body, or long hair whipping back and forth).

leûz (leúzò-) *n.* charcoal.

leúzìn (leúzìnì-) *n.* gunpowder. *Lit.* 'its charcoal'.

lèwèɲ (lèwèɲì-) *n.* common ostrich. *Struthio camelus.*

lèwèɲìdè (lèwèɲì-dèà-) *pl.* **leweɲidɛ́ík**[a]. *n.* tripod. *Lit.* 'ostrich-foot'.

Leweɲiik[a] (Leweɲi-icé-) *n.* traditional men's age-group with the ostrich as its totem (#9 in the historical line). *Lit.* 'Ostrich-Folk'.

lêz (lézà-) *pl.* **lézɨtín.** *n.* mistletoe, parasitic plant (sometimes used for medicine and witchcraft).

lì (lìì) *1 ideo.* bluntly, dully. *2 ideo.* quietly, silently.

lìà (lìà) *ideo.* bright white, milky white, pure white.

líídòn (líídònì-) *1 v.* to be blunt, dull. *2 v.* to be quiet, silent. See also *duŋúlúmòn* and *tufádòn*.

likiɗes (likiɗesí-) *v.* to reach and pull down.

likɨ́ɗɨ́mɔ̀n (likɨ́ɗɨ́mɔ̀nɨ̀-) *v.* to be cuneal, wedge-shaped (e.g. container, upper body).

likɛ́s (likɛ́sí-) *v.* to lean, tilt (e.g. one's head backward).

lilétón (lilétònì-) *v.* to appall, astonish, shock, horrify. The experiencer of this feeling is marked with the dative case.

lìr (lìrì) *ideo.* heavily.

lɨtɔ̀n (lɨtɔ̀nɨ̀-) *v.* to be new (of plant growth).

líùù (líùù) *ideo.* zing! (sound of a bullet passing close by). The vowels of this word are pronounced silently.

lɨ̀w (lɨ̀wɨ̀) *ideo.* smoothly.

lɨwɨ́dɔ̀n (lɨwɨ́dɔ̀nɨ̀-) *v.* to be smooth (e.g. a book, skin, or wood).

lobá (lobáà-) *pl.* **lóbaatikw**[a]. *n.* grandchild.

Lɔbɛɛ́l (Lɔbɛɛ́lɛ̀-) *n.* name of a rocky hill far south of Ikland where Jie warriors used to ambush vehicles.

lóburuj[a] (lóburují-) *n.* mildew, mold. See also *ɲóróiroy*[a].

lɔɓaɓal (lɔɓaɓalɨ́-) *n.* drying rack (on which grass is put below and above the grain being dried).

Lɔɓalɛl (Lɔɓalɛlɛ́-) *n.* month of weeding.

loɓáy[a] (loɓáí-) *n.* unknown kind of sickness that causes emaciation (said to originate in Turkanaland).

lɔɓɛlɛɲ (lɔɓɛlɛɲɨ́-) *n.* plant disease that shrivels grain seed-heads and destroys the seeds.

lóɓíliwás (lóɓíliwásɨ̀-) *n.* white-tailed mongoose. *Ichneumia albicauda.*

lóɓɨ́rɨɓɨ́r (lóɓɨ́rɨɓɨ́rá-) *pl.* lóɓɨ́rɨɓɨ́rɨ́k[a]. *n.* medulla spinalis, spinal cord.

lɔɓîz (lɔɓízɨ̀-) *pl.* lɔɓízìk[a]. *n.* inner rooftop, upper ceiling (where roof sticks are jammed into a point).

lɔ́ɓᵓ (lɔ́ɓɔ́) *ideo.* thickly.

lɔɓódɪtɛtɛ́s (lɔɓódɪtɛtɛ́sɨ́-) *v.* to thicken up optimally (e.g. beer, cement, porridge).

lɔɓɔ́dɔ̀n (lɔɓɔ́dɔ̀nɨ̀-) *v.* to be optimally thick (e.g. beer, cement, porridge).

lòɓòlìà (lòɓòlìà-) *n.* morning glory: flowery vine whose leaves are cooked and eaten as a vegetable. *Basella alba.*

loɓóɲiɓóŋ (loɓóɲiɓóŋì-) *n.* small flowering plant species whose bark and/or stems are crushed, cooked, and taken for stomach ailments. *Kleinia sp.*

Lɔɓɔsɔɔŋɔ́r (Lɔɓɔsɔɔŋɔ́rɨ̀-) *n.* name of a river and ravine running northeast from *Loodói.*

loɓôz (loɓózò-) *pl.* loɓózìk[a]. *n.* neb, snout.

Loɓúɓúwo (Loɓúɓúwoó-) *n.* a personal name.

lɔɓúkɛjɛ́n (lɔɓúkɛjɛ́nɨ̀-) *n.* stunted growth.

lóɓúlukúɲ (lóɓúlukúɲù-) *1 n.* rhinocerus beetle grub. *Oryctes sp. 2 n.* HIV-AIDS. See also *sílím.*

Lɔɓʉrák[a] (Lɔɓʉráká-) *n.* name of a small hill where Ik lived in the mid-1900s.

loɓúrútùt[a] (loɓúrútùtù-) *n.* bishop bird (red or yellow). *Euplectes sp.*

Lɔcám (Lɔcámù-) *n.* a personal name.

Lɔcáp[a] (Lɔcápù-) *n.* a personal name.

Lɔcárák̫wat[a] (Lɔcárák̫watɨ́-) *n.* name of a hill or mountain and surrounding area.

lɔcègèr (lɔcègèrè-) *pl.* lɔcégérìk[a]. *n.* three-legged stool with a round seat.

lócén (lócénì-) *n.* shrub species that, at the order of a witchdoctor, may be put on one's threshold to counteract the curse of dead person; it may also be put in one's bathwater to ward off trouble or sprayed on a trap for success. *Asclepiadaceae sp.*

Locíyo (Locíyoó-) *n.* a personal name.

Locom (Locomó-) *n.* name of a hill or mountain.

Locóm (Locómò-) *n.* a personal name.

Locómín (Locómínì-) *n.* a personal name.

Lɔcɔ́rɨ́àlɔ̀sɨ̀à (Lɔcɔ́rɨ́àlɔ̀sɨ̀à-) *n.* name of a hill or mountain and associated river.

lòcòrò (lòcòròò-) *n.* water scorpion. *Nepidae.*

Locóto (Locótoó-) *n.* name of a place.

lɔ́d[a] (lɔ̀dà-) *pl.* lɔ́dɪtɪ́n. *1 n.* animal-tail tassel worn by men as an accessory. *2 n.* silky hair at the end of animal tails.

loɗeɗ[a] (loɗeɗé-) *n.* vine species with cucumber-like fruits and leaves that are rubbed on the inner thighs of a birthing mother and tied to the waist of the newborn to prevent diarrhea. *Cucumis figarei.*

lóɗíkór (lóɗíkóró-) *n.* scorpion.

lóɗíkórócɛmɛ́r (lóɗíkóró-cɛmɛ́rɨ́-) *n.* scorpion herb: succulent plant species whose latex is applied to scorpion stings and whose reddish stems may be worn by girls as a kind of wig. *Euphorbia prostrata.*

lódíwé (lódíwéí-) *n.* tree species whose bitter leaves are eaten as a vegetable. *Maerua angolensis.*

Lɔ́ɗɔ́wɔ̀n (Lɔ́ɗɔ́wɔ̀nɔ̀-) *n.* name of a hill or mountain.

lɔ́ɗúmɛ́l (lɔ́ɗúmɛ́lá-) *n.* firefly (that glows green).

Lɔɗúŋɛ (Lɔɗúŋɛɛ́-) *n.* March: month of edible termites. See also *Dáŋ.*

Lɔɗúr (Lɔɗúrù-) *n.* name of a hill or mountain and associated river.

loɗúrú (loɗúrúù-) *pl.* **loɗúrúìk**[a]. *n.* granary, storehouse.

loɗúrúdè (loɗúrú-dèà-) *pl.* **loɗúrúdɛìk**[a]. *n.* base of a granary.

loɗúrúkɔ̀k[a] (loɗúrú-kɔ̀kà-) *n.* granary reed: shrub whose stems are used to make granaries and whose reddish parasitic plant is worn as a charm or ground and blown into the air to ward off enemies.

loɗúwa (loɗúwaá-) *n.* jet, jet plane.

Lóɗwàr (Lóɗwàrɨ̀-) *1 n.* Lodwar town in Turkanaland, Kenya. *2 n.* name of a cave with a lot of edible termites.

lofílitsí (lofílitsîi-) *n.* Sudan gum arabic or gum acacia: tree species with nasty hooked thorns that rip skin and clothing; hunters often remove clothing before trying to penetrate its brush; this tree, found down in the Turkana plains is used for fencing and is eaten by livestock. *Acacia senegal.* See also *ɗerét*[a].

lófúk[a] (lófúkù-) *n.* Verreaux's eagle-owl. *Bubo lacteus.*

lɔgém (lɔgémù-) *n.* game warden, game ranger, wildlife authorities. From English 'game' park.

logeréɲo (logeréɲoó-) *n.* green stink bug. *Pentatomidae.*

Lɔgyél (Lɔgyélɨ̀-) *n.* a personal name.

loiɓóròk[a] (loiɓóròkù-) *n.* tall grass species found in the forest which is used to rain-proof granaries.

Loíkí (Loíkîi-) *n.* a personal name.

Loipo (Loipoó-) *n.* November: month of clearing woodland. See also *Kawés.*

Lɔisɨ́ká (Lɔisɨ́káà-) *n.* name of a river.

Lòìtà (Lòìtàà-) *n.* name of a place in *Tímù* and its associated human habitations.

Lɔitánit[a] (Lɔitánitɨ́-) *n.* name of a river and surrounding area in *Lɔkitɔ́ɨ* where the Ik used to initiate age-groups.

lɔjála (lɔjálaá-) *n.* jail. See also *ɲájála.*

lojeméy[a] (lojeméí-) *n.* shrub whose milky white sap is put in sores.

Lójérè (Lójérèè-) *n.* a personal name. Also pronounced as *Lójórè.*

lójɔjɔ́ (lójɔjɔ́ɔ̀-) *n.* regrown grain (i.e. when millet or sorghum grow back and produce again).

lɔjɔkɔtáw[a] (lɔjɔkɔtáù-) *n.* philanthopist: donor, humanitarian, missionary, non-governmental organization (NGO). From the Ateker (Teso-Turkana) word meaning 'good-hearted'.

lɔ̀jùrùtà (lɔ̀jùrùtàà-) *n.* slipknot.

lojúulú (lojúulúù-) *n.* sorghum variety with drooping seed-heads, red seeds; it is very bitter and used to make leaven.

Lɔkaaƙilit[a] (Lɔkaaƙilitɨ́-) *n.* name of a hill or mountain.

Lòkààpèlòt[a] (Lòkààpèlòtò-) *n.* name of the river draining *Nàkòrìtààw*[a].

lɔkaapɨ́n (lɔkaapɨ́nɨ́-) *pl.* **lɔkaapɨ́nɨ́k**[a]. *n.* shoelace, shoe-strap.

lɔkabúás (lɔkabúásɨ̀-) *n.* crumbly rock.

lɔkájʉ́ (lɔkájʉ́ʉ̀-) n. water running down a flat surface (e.g. over a rock, into a cave, over a tin roof).

lokaliliŋ (lokaliliɲí-) n. lineolate blind snake. *Typhlops lineolatus*.

Lokapel (Lokapelí-) n. a personal name.

lɔkapɛtᵃ (lɔkapɛtá-) pl. lɔkápɛ́tɨ̀kᵃ. 1 n. appendix. 2 n. appendicitis.

lɔkapʉ́r (lɔkapʉ́rá-) n. steam, vapor.

Lɔkasaŋatɛ́ (Lɔkasaŋatɛ́ɛ̀-) n. name of a river near *Lowákuɟᵃ*.

lɔ̀kàtàtᵃ (lɔ̀kàtàtà-) pl. lɔ̀kátátɨ̀kᵃ. n. African wild date palm. *Phoenix reclinata*.

lɔkátɔ́rɔ̀tᵃ (lɔkátɔ́rɔ̀tɔ̀-) n. breakfast beer drunk early in the morning to warm up the body, e.g. before going to the garden to work.

Lɔ̀kàtsᵃ (Lɔ̀kàtsɨ̀-) n. a personal name.

lɔkaʉɗᵃ (lɔkaʉɗɛ́-) n. maize weevil. *Sitophilus spp*.

Lokauwa (Lokauwaá-) n. a personal name.

lokemú (lokemúʉ̀-) pl. lokemúɨ̀kᵃ. n. mbira, sanza, thumb piano.

Lokéɲéribɔ (Lokéɲéribɔɔ́-) n. a personal name.

lɔ́kérʉ́ (lɔ́kérʉ́ʉ̀-) n. tree species with a distinctive pungent odor and whose berries are eaten by children; its leaves are pounded, soaked, and the juice is poured into infected ears. *Cassia singueana*.

loki (lokií-) n. brown parrot. *Poicephalus meyeri*.

lókíbobó (lókíboɓóò-) n. gecko.

Lokicókio (Lokicókió-) n. Lokichokio town in northwest Kenya.

Lɔkɨjʉká (Lɔkɨjʉkáà-) n. name of rebel group who resisted colonial British rule in northeast Uganda and northwest Kenya.

Lòkìlè (Lòkìlèè-) n. name of a hill or mountain and associated river.

lokilókón (lokilókònì-) v. to be loose, wiggly (e.g. a tooth or stump).

lókílóróŋ (lókílóróŋó-) n. queen bee. Also called *okílóɲór*.

Lokinéne (Lokinéneé-) n. name of a ridge in Timu and its associated human habitations.

Lɔkɨ́ŋɔ́l (Lɔkɨ́ŋɔ́lɨ̀-) n. an older name for Oropoi, Kenya.

Lokipáka (Lokipákaá-) n. name of a hill or mountain and associated river.

lɔkɨram (lɔkɨramá-) n. garden edge (not the same as the boundary between gardens).

lɔkɨ́rídɨdɨ́ (lɔkɨ́rídɨdɨ̀ɨ̀-) n. maize variety with small cobs and mixed black and white kernels.

Lókírù (Lókírùù-) n. a personal name.

lɔkɨsɨ́ná (lɔkɨsɨ́náà-) n. a condition that involves a twitching under the skin of the left breast/pec, which is believed to be a disease.

Lɔkɨtɛlɛ́ɛ́lɔɓᵃ (Lɔkɨtɛlɛ́ɛ́lɔɓá-) n. name of a place in the east near *Tulútúl*.

lokítoɲí (lokítoɲîî-) n. smooth, black, and very hard kind of stone (used as a blacksmith's hammer). Also called *sàbàgwàs*.

lòkìtòŋ (lòkìtòŋò-) pl. lokítóŋɨkᵃ. n. doorstep, threshold. See also *lòrìòŋòn*.

Lɔkitɔ́yᵃ (Lɔkitɔ́ɨ̀-) n. name of a river and associated human habitations.

Lɔkitɔ́yᵃ (Lɔkitɔ́ɨ̀-) n. name of a hill, the surrounding area, and associated human habitations.

lɔkitúr (lɔkitúrá-) *n.* pinworms.

lokiyo (lokiyoó-) *n.* eye disease that closes the eyes and causes tears.

lòkᵒ (lòkò) *ideo.* jiggily, loosely.

lokoɓél (lokoɓélè-) *pl.* lokoɓélín. *n.* grain thief.

lokódòn (lokódònì-) *v.* to be jiggly, loose (e.g. a car part or tool-head).

lɔkɔ́ɗᵃ (lɔkɔ́ɗá-) *pl.* lɔkɔ́ɗɨ́kᵃ. *n.* hooked stick.

lókóɗém (lókóɗémá-) *n.* thorny vine species used in house-building. *Toddalia asiatica.*

lɔkɔɗɛtɛ́s (lɔkɔɗɛtɛ́sɨ́-) *v.* to pull down (with a hooked stick).

lɔkɔɗɨ́kɔ́ɗɔ́n (lɔkɔɗɨ́kɔ́ɗɔ́nɨ̀-) *v.* to have a crooked neck.

lɔkɔ́ɗɔ́n (lɔkɔ́ɗɔ́nɨ̀-) *v.* to be hooked, hook-shaped. See also *sokóɗómòn*.

lòkòɗòŋìrò (lòkòɗòŋìròò-) *n.* gluttony, gobbling (food to the deprivation of others).

lòkòɗòŋìròàm (lòkòɗòŋìrò-àmà-) *pl.* lokiɗoŋiroikᵃ. *n.* glutton, gobbler, gourmand. See also *lokekes*.

lokoɗoŋironánés (lokoɗoŋironánésí-) *n.* gluttonousness, rapaciousness.

lokoitᵃ (lokoití-) *pl.* lokóítìkᵃ. *n.* big white waist bead.

lókókᵃ (lókókò-) *n.* solider ant or termite.

Lɔkɔl (Lɔkɔlɨ́-) *n.* a personal name.

Lɔ́kɔ̀l (Lɔ́kɔ̀lɨ̀-) *n.* name of a place.

lokóoɗo (lokóoɗoó-) *pl.* lokóòɗòìkᵃ. *n.* large leather sack.

lɔkɔ́r (lɔkɔ́rɨ́-) *pl.* lɔkɔ́rɨ́kᵃ. *n.* crotch, groin.

Lòkòrìkìpì (Lòkòrìkìpìì-) *n.* name of a place near *Loyóro*.

lòkòsòs (lòkòsòsì-) *pl.* lokósósìkᵃ. *n.* anthill or termite mound with large holes.

Lòkùɗà (Lòkùɗàà-) *n.* personal name of a Dodoth man from Loyoro who administered the Ik during the reign of the Baganda king Mutesa I.

lɔkúɗᵃ (lɔkúɗá-) *pl.* lɔkúɗɨ́kᵃ. *n.* small garden barn or granary with a door on the side.

lókúɗukuɗétᵃ (lókúɗukuɗétí-) *n.* vine species that is highly poisonous and whose fruits are ground, mixed with food, and used as rat poison. *Capparis tomentosa.*

Lɔkulitᵃ (Lɔkulitɨ́-) *n.* Year of *Lɔkulit*, a good year following *Lotíira*.

lokum (lokumú-) *pl.* lokúmíkᵃ. *n.* large, tall tree species whose yellow fruits are eaten raw and which vultures like to nest in. *Mimusops kummel.*

Lɔkúma (Lɔkúmaɨ́-) *n.* name of a river.

Lókúrúkᵃ (Lókúrúkú-) *n.* name of a place where ravens used to come to bathe in a rock pool.

lɔkutúr (lɔkutúrá-) *pl.* lɔkutúrɨ́kᵃ. *n.* gourd with a funnel-like stem.

Lɔkuwám (Lɔkuwámù-) *n.* a personal name.

Lɔkwakaramɔ́yᵃ (Lɔkwakaramɔ́ɨ̀-) *n.* name of a mountainside, the surrounding area, and associated human habitations.

Lokwaŋ (Lokwaŋá-) *n.* February: month of planting. See also *Bèts'òn*.

Lokwaŋ (Lokwaŋá-) *n.* a personal name.

lokekes (lokekesí-) *pl.* lokékésìkᵃ. *n.* glutton, gobbler, gourmand. See also *lòkòɗòŋìròàm*.

lokírotᵃ (lokírotí-) *n.* robin-chat (white-browed and others?). *Cossypha sp.*

lokól (lokólé-) *n.* eagle.

lókólíl (lókólílá-) *pl.* **lókólílíkᵃ**. *n.* swing.

lɔ́kɔ́ŋ (lɔ́kɔ́ŋù-) *pl.* **lɔ́kɔ́ŋɨkᵃ**. *n.* sacred tree where ceremonies like *itówéés* are held. Also called *ɲɔ́kɔ́ŋ*.

lɔ́kɔ́ŋùdɛ̀ (lɔ́kɔ́ŋù-dɛ̀à-) *pl.* **lɔ́kɔ́ŋɨkadɛ́ɨkᵃ**. *n.* base of the sacred tree.

lokózòmòn (lokózòmònì-) *v.* to be long-necked (of gourd or women who wear neck-beads).

lokú (lokúù-) *pl.* **lokúaikwᵃ**. *n.* medium-sized, small-mouthed gourd (used for storing water, beer, or grain).

Lokúm (Lokúmú-) *n.* name of a savannah area south of *Tímù*.

lolataɓᵃ (lolataɓá-) *n.* large, flat floor-like boulder.

lɔlɛɛú (lɔlɛɛúù-) *n.* cattle disease that causes meat to become bitter.

Lɔlɛ́lɨ́à (Lɔlɛ́lɨ́à-) *n.* name of a place.

Lolém (Lolémù-) *n.* a personal name.

lolemukán (lolemukánɨ́-) *pl.* **lolemukánɨ́kᵃ**. *n.* tool or weapon without a handle.

lóliitᵃ (lóliití-) *n.* false accuser or witness. See also *kérɨ́nɔ́sɨ́àm*.

lolítsᵃ (lolítsí-) *n.* dense forest, jungle.

Lolítsíàkwᵃ (Lolítsí-àkɔ̀-) *n.* name of a densely forested place. *Lit.* 'in the jungle'.

lɔlɔanón (lɔlɔanónì-) *v.* to be discontent, dissatisfied.

Lɔlɔɓáyᵃ (Lɔlɔɓáɨ́-) *n.* October. See also *Terés*.

lolómónukotᵃ (lolómónukotí-) *1 v.* to shrivel up (e.g. seeds in the ground). *2 v.* to decay, dry out (e.g. bones, hair).

lòlòtᵃ (lòlòtà-) *n.* giant Gambian rat. *Cricetomys gambianus*.

lolotánón (lolotánónì-) *v.* to be crowded or jammed together.

lɔ́lɔwɨ́ (lɔ́lɔwɨ́ɨ̀-) *n.* tall tree species whose sap is rubbed into wounds as a disinfectant, whose wood is used for carving wooden containers, and whose trunk is used to support the sacred tree (*lɔ́kɔ́ŋ*). *Commiphora campestris*.

Lóloyᵃ (Lóloí-) *n.* name of a river.

Lɔmaanɨ́kɔ (Lɔmaanɨ́kɔɔ́-) *n.* name of a river.

Lɔmacarɨwárɛtᵃ (Lɔmacarɨwárɛtɛ́-) *n.* name of a river.

Lɔmálɛ́r (Llɔmálɛ́rɨ̀-) *n.* name of a place.

Lomarukᵃ (Lomarukú-) *n.* April: month of mushrooms. See also *Lɔmɔ́y*ᵃ.

Lomataŋaáwᵃ (Lomataŋá-áwà-) *n.* name of a place where some Ik used to live.

Lɔmɛ́jᵃ (lɔmɛ́jà-) *n.* name of a mountain sloping westward off *Morúŋole*.

lɔmɛ́jékɛlé (lɔmɛ́jékɛlɛ́ɛ̀-) *n.* cockroach, roach.

lóméléwᵃ (lóméléwá-) *pl.* **lóméléwáikw**ᵃ. *n.* widow(er). See also *ɲepúrósit*ᵃ.

loménio (loménió-) *n.* swallow, swift.

Lɔmɛ́r (Lɔmɛ́rà-) *n.* a personal name.

Lomérídokᵃ (Lomérídokó-) *n.* name of a hill or mountain.

lomerúkᵃ (lomerúká-) *n.* sweet-smelling plant species growing underground, invisible until guinea-fowl uncover it; a decoction from its red roots is drunk as a medicine.

Lɔmɨ́jᵃ (Lɔmɨ́jí-) *n.* name of a mountain and surrounding area that was home to a fairy who told on wrongdoers.

Lómìl (Lómìlà-) *n.* name of a river.

Lómil (Llómilí-) *n.* name of a hill or mountain.

lòmìl (lòmìlà-) *n.* new honeycomb deposits.

lɔ́milí (lɔ́milíì-) *n.* scincid, skink. *Mabuya margaritifer.*

lɔ́mílimíl (lɔ́mílimílá-) *n.* glandular swelling.

lɔ́mɔ́ɗaát[a] (lɔ́mɔ́ɗaátí-) *n.* short grass species with small hooks that catch clothing and itch and which is tied to sorghum stalks to discourage birds from landing. *Triumfetta annua.*

Lomoɗokogéc (Lomoɗokogecí-) *n.* July: month of gourd harvest. See also *Ikíŋéèts*[a].

Lomoɗóɲ (Lomoɗóɲó-) *n.* name of a mountain and associated human habitations.

lómoloró (lómoloróò-) *n.* sharp stick forming the pinnacle of a traditional hut.

Lomoŋin (Lomoŋiní-) *n.* a personal name.

lomóŋin (lomóŋiní-) *pl.* **lomóŋiník**[a]. *n.* large gunny sack. See also *ɲáwaawá.*

Lɔmɔ́y[a] (Lɔmɔ́í-) *n.* a personal name.

Lɔmɔ́y[a] (Lɔmɔ́í-) *n.* April: month of mushrooms. See also *Lomaruk*[a].

lɔmɔ́y[a] (lɔmɔ́ì-) *n.* plant whose parts are rubbed on the open wounds of cattle to ward off flies and biting insects. *Datura stramonium.*

lɔmɔ́y[a] (lɔmɔ́í-) *n.* poisonous mushroom species with a conical top.

lomucir (lomucirí-) *pl.* **lomúcírik**[a]. *n.* type of bolt-action rifle.

Lomuk[a] (Lomukú-) *n.* January: month of grass burning. See also *Kùpòn.*

lomuƙe (lomuƙeí-) *n.* courgette, edible gourd, squash, zucchini. *Lagenaria sp.*

Lɔmúɲén (Lɔmúɲénì-) *n.* a personal name.

Lómúrìà (Lómúrìà-) *n.* a personal name.

Lomutsú (Lomutsúù-) *n.* a personal name.

Loɲá (Loɲàà-) *n.* a personal name.

Loɲákw[a] (Loɲákú-) *n.* name of a mountain pass.

Loɲáŋálem (Loɲáŋálemú-) *n.* a personal name.

Lòɲàŋàsùwà (Lòɲàŋàsùwàà-) *n.* a personal name.

Lɔŋása (Lɔŋásaí-) *n.* name of a river.

loŋazut[a] (loŋazutú-) *n.* mixture of seeds from the bride and bridegroom's families that is ceremonially planted as a symbol of the admixed fertility of bodies and lands.

lòŋìr (lòŋìrò-) *n.* short tree species found growing in thick groves and whose sweet black fruits are eaten. *Meyna tetraphylla.*

lɔŋizɛt[a] (lɔŋizɛté-) *n.* black cleg, biting fly (associated with warthogs).

lóŋízìŋíz (lóŋízìŋízá-) *1 n.* burrowing ground beetle (that can ring trees). *2 n.* cut that develops spontaneously under the toes, which the Ik treat with earwax.

lɔŋɔanón (lɔŋɔanónì-) *v.* to be confused, disorderly, jumbled, topsy-turvy.

lɔŋɔanónuƙot[a] (lɔŋɔanónuƙotí-) *1 v.* to become confused, disorderly, or jumbled up. *2 v.* to go into pandemonium, panic.

Loŋóle (Loŋóleé-) *n.* a personal name.

Lòŋòlè (Lòŋòlèè-) *n.* a personal name.

loŋóléhò (loŋólé-hòò-) *pl.* **loŋóléhoík**[a]. *n.* hip joint socket.

Loŋólépalɔ́r (Loŋólépalɔ́rɔ́-) *n.* a personal name.

Loŋólì (Loŋólìì-) *n.* a personal name.

loŋórómòn (loŋórómònì-) *v.* to be domical, hemispherical (like a round hut).

lɔŋɔ́t[a] (lɔŋɔ́tá-) *n.* enemies, foes.

lɔŋɔ́tánànès (lɔŋɔ́tánànèsì-) *n.* enmity, hostility.

lɔŋɔ́tásìts'[a] (lɔŋɔ́tá-sìts'à-) *n.* sacrifice for warding off enemies.

lɔŋɔ́tɔ́m (lɔŋɔ́tɔ́mà-) *pl.* **lɔŋɔ́t**[a]. *n.* enemy, foe.

Lɔ́ŋúsul (Lɔ́ŋúsʉlʉ́-) *n.* name of a hill or mountain.

Loocíkwa (Loocíkwaá-) *n.* name of a hill.

Lɔɔɗíŋ (Lɔɔɗíŋì-) *n.* name of a mountain in Didingaland, South Sudan. Also called *Lotukéì*.

Lòòɗòs (Lòòɗòsì-) *n.* name of a hill or mountain.

Looɗóy[a] (Looɗóì-) *n.* name of a hill in Timu, the surrounding area, and associated human habitations.

lɔɔmúyá (lɔɔmúyáà-) *n.* blue-eared starling (greater or lesser). *Lamprotornis.*

lɔɔrán (lɔɔránɨ́-) *n.* glow of a fire at night.

lóórì (lóórìì-) *pl.* **lóórìik**[a]. *n.* lorry, truck. See also *ɲolórì*.

lɔɔrúk[a] (lɔɔrúkú-) *n.* whydah (Eastern paradise or pin-tailed). *Vidua sp.*

Lɔɔsɔ́m (Lɔɔsɔ́mɔ̀-) *n.* name of a river.

lɔ́péɗepéɗ[a] (lɔ́péɗepéɗé-) *n.* bat.

Lopéɗó (Lopéɗòò-) *n.* name of a mountainous area south of Ikland.

Lopeleméri (Lopelemérií-) *n.* a personal name.

Lɔpɛlipɛl (Lɔpɛlipɛlɨ́-) *n.* name of a place far southwest of Ikland.

lopem (lopemú-) *pl.* **lopémík**[a]. *1 n.* flat area. *2 n.* plateau, tableland. *3 n.* level, storey.

lopemúím (lopemú-ímà-) *pl.* **lopémíkawik**[a]. *n.* stair, step.

lopéren (lopérení-) *n.* ghost, ghoul, phantom, wraith (associated with rivers).

Lɔpét[a] (Lɔpétɨ́-) *n.* name of a hill or mountain.

lópey[a] (lópeí-) *pl.* **lópèik**[a]. *n.* pancreas.

Lopéyók[a] (Lopéyóko-) *n.* a personal name.

Lopíar (Lopíarɨ́-) *n.* Year of *Lopíar* (1980), a year that brought disease and famine on the Ik, leading to the death and displacement of many.

Lopíè (Lopíè-) *n.* a personal name.

lɔ́pɨ́ripɨ́r (lɔ́pɨ́ripɨ́rá-) *n.* wood-boring insect (identified by the piles of sawdust it leaves below).

lɔpitá (lɔpitáɨ́-) *pl.* **lɔpitáɨ́k**[a]. *1 n.* drying rack. *2 n.* platform, podium. *3 n.* altar.

lɔpitáá na ƙófóikó[e] *n.* dish-drying rack.

Lopokók[a] (Lopokókò-) *n.* name of a mountain to the east of Timu. Also called *Sokogwáás*.

Loporukɔlɔ́ŋ (Loporukɔlɔ́ŋɨ̀-) *n.* name of a place.

lɔpɔ́ts[a] (lɔpɔ́tsá-) *n.* clear fluid found in an elephant's stomach.

lɔ́púl (lɔ́púlɨ̀-) *pl.* **lɔ́púlɨ̀k**[a]. *n.* small oblong edible gourd. *Lagenaria sp.*

Lopúsór (Lopúsórì-) *n.* a personal name.

Lopúwà (Lopúwàà-) *n.* name of a mountain where there is a large well.

Lópúwà (Lópúwàà) *n.* a personal name.

lɔ̌r (lɔ̀rɔ̀) *ideo.* bulbously, bulgingly.

Lɔrɛŋ (Lɔrɛŋé-) *n.* name of a flat place in Turkanaland, Kenya.

Loriɓóɓó (Loriɓóɓóò-) *n.* name of an area at bottom of a ridge along the Ik escarpment.

lɔrɨ́ɗ[a] (lɔrɨ́ɗá-) *n.* urinary tract infection (possibly sexually transmitted, manifested in painful urination).

lɔ̀rɨ̀kɨ̀là (lɔ̀rɨ̀kɨ̀làà-) *n.* genet. *Genetta tigrina*.

loriónómor (loriónómorí-) *n.* long-leaf tobacco (now found growing in the wild). See also *péléɗèk*[a].

lòrìòŋòn (lòrìòŋònì-) *n.* doorstep, threshold. See also *lòkìtòŋ*.

lorít[a] (lorítá-) *n.* shrub species growing at the base of boulders; its small black roots are dug up and crushed during termite harvest to ensure a good harvest; roots may also be ground, dried, and applied to sores as a disinfectant, or drunk as a remedy for underarm and back pain.

lɔrɔ́dɔn (lɔrɔ́dɔ̀nɨ̀-) *v.* to be bulbous, bulging. See also *bulúkúmòn*.

lorokon (lorokoní-) *pl.* **lorókónìk**[a]. *n.* adze.

Lorokonídàkw[a] (Lorokoní-dàkù-) *n.* constellation of seven-stars resembling an adze handle. *Lit.* 'adze-wood'.

lorokonígwà (lorokoní-gwàà-) *n.* bird species. *Lit.* 'adze-bird'.

Lorukuɗe (Lorukuɗeé-) *n.* personal name of a Jie shopkeeper.

lorwaneta (lorwanetaá-) *pl.* **lorwánétàìk**[a]. *n.* Maasai blanket.

lɔsalát[a] (lɔsalátɨ́-) *n.* plant species whose root decoction is blown into the anus with a pipe to treat diarrhea. *Gomphocarpus fruticosus*.

Lɔ̀sèrà (Lɔ̀sèràà-) *n.* name of a hill.

Losíke (Losíkeé-) *n.* a personal name.

Lósíl (Lósílì-) *n.* name of a hill or mountain.

lósínák[a] (lósínáká-) *n.* smut fungus (on maize or sorghum).

Losíroíáw[a] (Losíroí-áwà-) *n.* name of an Ik home that was burned down long ago by a boy named *Losíroi*. *Lit.* '*Losíroi*'s place'.

Losíroy[a] (Losíroí-) *n.* a personal name.

Lòsòlìà (Lòsòlìà-) *n.* name of a mountain northwest of Ikland that the Ik used to hunt and gather on. Also called *Mt. Zulia*.

Losor (Losoró-) *n.* name of a place.

lósùaɲ (lósùàɲà-) *pl.* **losúáɲìk**[a]. *n.* sharpening stone, whetstone.

Lósúɓán (Lósúɓáná-) *n.* August. See also *Diwamúce* and *Iɗátáŋér*.

losúk[a] (losúkù-) *n.* candidiasis, moniliasis: fungal infection of the mouth and throat.

lòtàbùsèn (lòtàbùsènì-) *pl.* **lotábùsènìk**[a]. *n.* dust devil, whirlwind.

lotáɗá (lotáɗáà-) *n.* bandit, robber.

lotáɗánànès (lotáɗánànèsì-) *n.* banditry, robbery.

lɔ̀tàfàr (lɔ̀tàfàrà-) *n.* grass species whose seeds are ground and eaten; children also use it in play-fighting. *Gramineae sp.*

Loteteleít[a] (Loteteleítì-) *n.* name of a river near *Ròŋòt*[a]. Also called *Sógɛsabá*.

Lotííra (Lotííraá-) *n.* Year of *Lotííra* that brought famine to the Ik.

lɔtɨ́litɨ́l (lɔ́tɨ́litɨ́lɨ̀-) *n.* grass species whose long, sharp seeds stick to clothing and prick the skin; Ik children pretend they are spears.

Lotim (Lotimá-) *n.* name of a small mountain, the surrounding area, and associated human habitations.

lotímálèmòn (lotímálèmònì-) *v.* to be emaciated, gaunt, skeletal.

Lotíɲam (Lotíɲamá-) *n.* name of a place between *Kámíón* and *Lɔkwakaramɔ́ɨ* and its villages.

Lotirém (Lotirémò-) *n.* name of a verticle ridge running up to *Gàlàts*[a], where the Ik used to live in the mid-1900s.

lotiwúót[a] (lotiwúótò-) *n.* bird species (possibly an oriole).

Lotíyá (Lotíyáà-) *n.* name of a hill or mountain.

lɔ́tɔ́ɓa[a] (lɔ́tɔ́ɓà-) *n.* tobacco.

lɔ́tɔ́ɓa ná zè *n.* cannabis, marijuana. *Lit.* 'tobacco that is big'.

lɔ́tɔ́ɓààm (lɔ́tɔ́ɓà-àmà-) *pl.* lɔ́tɔ́ɓaik[a]. 1 *n.* tobacco user. 2 *n.* Didinga person.

lɔ́tɔ́ɓabɔrɔkɔ́k[a] (lɔ́tɔ́ɓa-bɔrɔkɔ́kɔ̀-) *pl.* lɔ́tɔ́ɓabɔrɔkɔ́kík[a]. *n.* tobacco cone.

lɔ́tɔ́ɓàgwàs (lɔ́tɔ́ɓà-gwàsà-) *pl.* lɔ́tɔ́ɓagwasík[a]. 1 *n.* tobacco grinding stone. 2 *n.* young monkeys.

lɔ́tɔ́ɓàɲèk[a] (lɔ́tɔ́ɓà-ɲèkè-) *n.* hunger for tobacco, urge for nicotine.

lɔ́tɔ́ɓàsèd[a] (lɔ́tɔ́ɓà-sèdà-) *pl.* lɔ́tɔ́ɓasedík[a]. *n.* tobacco garden.

lɔtɔ́k[a] (lɔtɔ́kɔ́-) *pl.* lɔtɔ́kík[a]. *n.* garden rain shelter.

Lɔtɔ́kɨ́kààw[a] (Lɔtɔ́kɨ́kà-àwà-) *n.* name of a place. *Lit.* 'garden shelters place'.

Lɔtɔlér (Lɔtɔlérè-) *n.* name of a place and associated human habitations.

lótórobét[a] (lótórobétí-) *n.* vine with long edible seed-pods. *Zehneria scabra.*

Lotséto (Lotsétoó-) *n.* month of bad honey.

lɔtsɔ́gɔ̀m (lɔtsɔ́gɔ̀mà-) *n.* millet-like grass that is an inedible weed.

lòtsòr (lòtsòrò-) *n.* firefinch (red-billed and others?). *Lagonosticta senegala.*

Lòtsòròɓò (Lòtsòrò-ɓòò-) *n.* name of a hill or mountain and associated river. *Lit.* 'firefinch-escarpment'.

lótsóts[a] (lótsótsò-) *n.* biting fly, cowfly.

Lotsul (Lotsulú-) *n.* a personal name.

lótsúm (lótsúmù-) *pl.* lótsúmìk[a]. *n.* thatched storehouse.

lots'ilots'[a] (lots'ilots'í-) *pl.* lots'ílóts'ìk[a]. *n.* animal-hoof rattle.

Lɔ̀tùɗɔ̀ (Lɔ̀tùɗɔ̀ɔ̀-) *n.* a personal name.

lotúɗuzé (lotúɗuzèè-) *n.* nickname for a hyrax.

Lotuk[a] (Lotukú-) *n.* a personal name.

Lotukéy[a] (Lotukéì-) *n.* a personal name.

lótúrum (lótúrumú-) *n.* olive pigeon. *Columba arquatrix.*

Lotyak[a] (Lotyakí-) *n.* September. See also *Nakariɓ*[a].

Lotyaŋ (Lotyaɲí-) *n.* a personal name.

loúk[a] (loukú-) 1 *n.* carnivore, predator. 2 *n.* greedyguts.

Loukómor (Loukómorú-) *n.* name of a mountain in Turkanaland, Kenya.

loukúets'[a] (loukú-éts'ì-) *n.* cadaver, corpse. *Lit.* 'predator-shit'.

Loúnoy[a] (Loúnoí-) *n.* World Vision: NGO that administered relief food distributions to the Ik in the 2010s.

loúpal (loúpalɨ́-) *n.* cobra. *Naja sp.*

lóúpè (loúpèè-) *n.* shrub species whose bitter roots are chewed or pounded, soaked in water, and drunk for stomachaches. *Pachycarpus schweinfurthii*.

Lourien (Louriení-) *n.* a personal name.

Loúsúnà (Loúsúnàà-) *n.* name of a place.

lɔutsúr (lɔutsúrá-) *n.* freshly pounded tobacco, still green.

Lowákuj[a] (Lowákují-) *n.* name of a mountain southwest of Ikland.

lɔwíɗ[a] (lɔwɨ̞ɗɨ́-) *pl.* **lɔwíɗík**[a]. *n.* small-animal trap (e.g. for hyraxes and squirrels).

lɔwiɲ (lɔwiɲɨ́-) *n.* stingless bee, sweat bee. *Hypotrigona sp.*

lɔ́wíriwír (lɔ́wíriwírɨ́-) *n.* optical illusion of having seen something distant moving quickly.

Loyaŋorok[a] (Loyaŋorokó-) *n.* a personal name.

loyeté (loyetéè-) *n.* ground barbet (d'Arnaud's or red-and-yellow). *Trachyphonus sp.*

Loyóro (Loyóroó-) *n.* name of a place far southeast of Ikland.

lozikinet[a] (lozikinetí-) *n.* rope stretched horizontally to support neck snares. See also *lozikit*[a].

lozikit[a] (lozikití-) *n.* rope stretched horizontally to support neck snares. See also *lozikinet*[a].

luɗés (luɗésí-) *v.* to dent, depress, indent. See also *rábaɗamitésúƙot*[a].

luɗúmón (luɗúmónì-) *v.* to be dented, depressed, indented.

lúgùm (lúgùmà-) *1 n.* solidified meal mush (posho). *2 n.* tough maize kernels (past maturation).

lùj[u] (lùjù) *ideo.* flabbily, flaccidly.

lujúdòn (lujúdònì-) *v.* to be flabby, flaccid.

lujulújɛ́s (lujulújɛ́sɨ́-) *v.* to fill completely.

lujulújón (lujulújónì-) *v.* to be completely full.

Lúkà (Lúkàà-) *1 n.* Luke. *2 n.* Luke: book in the New Testament.

luk[a] (luká-) *n.* tree squirrel.

lúkúɗukuɗánón (lúkúɗukuɗánónì-) *1 v.* to slither. *2 v.* to meander, weave, wind, zigzag. See also *ikɔɗɨ́kɔ́ɗɔ̀n* and *ikulúkúlòn*.

lukutiés (lukutiesí-) *v.* to down, gulp down, inhale (food). See also *lakatiés*.

luƙáámitésúƙot[a] (luƙáámitésúƙotí-) *v.* to make inadequate, insufficient, or lacking.

luƙáámòn (luƙáámònì-) *v.* to be inadequate, insufficient, lacking.

luƙés (luƙésí-) *v.* to down, swallow.

lúl (lúlà-) *n.* heavens, firmament, sky.

lùm (lùmù) *ideo.* malleably, pliably, softly.

lumúdòn (lumúdònì-) *v.* to be malleable, pliable, soft.

lúulú (lúulúù-) *1 n.* kindling, tinder, touchwood. *2 n.* lizard species that lives in Kenya.

lwàŋ (lwàŋà) *ideo.* out of sight.

lyàm (lyàmà) *ideo.* powderily.

lyamádòn (lyamádònì-) *v.* to be powdery. See also *ɲapíɗímòn*.

m

mà (<mòòn) *v.*

mà (<meés) *v.*

máa (máa) *adv.* not: do not, did not, has/have not.

Maarʉkᵃ (Maarʉkú-) *n.* a personal name.

maɗámón (maɗámóni-) *v.* to fall back, remain behind. See also *isíɗéètòn*.

máɗíŋ (máɗíŋi-) *pl.* **máɗíŋik**ᵃ. *1 n.* spleen. *2 n.* organ, organization.

maimoos (maimoosí-) *v.* to be chronically ill.

maimoosíám (maimoosí-ámà) *pl.* **maimoosíík**ᵃ. *n.* chronically ill person.

maímós (maímósí-) *1 v.* to give each other. *2 v.* to face each other.

máɨ̀rɔ (máɨ̀rɔɔ̀-) *pl.* **máɨ̀rɔ̀ɨk**ᵃ. *n.* mile.

máɨ̀rɔ̀ɛdᵃ (máɨ̀rɔ̀ɛdɛ̀-) *n.* distance, mileage.

maitetés (maitetésí-) *v.* to care for, nurse (the sick).

makúl (makúlí-) *pl.* **makúlík**ᵃ. *n.* round grass beehive cover (that goes over the two ends of a beehive).

maƙésúƙotᵃ (maƙésúƙotí-) *v.* to give away/out.

maƙésúƙota así *v.* to give oneself away.

málákʉr (málákʉrá-) *n.* vine species with edible seed-pods. *Vigna sp.* Possibly the same vine as *ànè*.

màlòr (màlòrì-) *1 n.* sisal species with sharp tips and fibers that are used for tying; the Turkana thatch with it. *Sansevieria robusta.* *2 n.* sisal rope. *3 n.* corn, maize.

màlòrìɛdᵃ (màlòrì-ɛdì-) *n.* corn, maize . *Lit.* 'sisal-grain'.

mamá (mamá) *nurs.* yum-yum! (a nursery word for food or eating). See also *ɓá*.

Mamʉkíria (Mamʉkíriá-) *n.* personal name of a woman from Kamion.

màŋ (màŋà) *ideo.* thickly.

maŋádòn (maŋádòni-) *v.* to be undesirably thick (e.g. an axe, shoes, etc.). Compare with *maŋídòn*.

maŋídòn (maŋídòni-) *v.* to be thick (of flat objects like honeycomb).

Máóikᵃ (Máó-icé-) *n.* traditional men's age-group with the lion as its totem (second oldest, #2, in the historical line). *Lit.* 'Lion-Folk'.

maráŋ *interj.* fine! good! okay! *Lit.* 'It's good!'.

maráŋaakón (maráŋaakóni-) *v.* to be good (of many).

maráŋás (maráŋásɨ-) *n.* goodness.

màràŋgwà (màràŋgwàà-) *n.* red bean variety (called K20). From the Swahili word *maharagwe* 'beans'.

maráŋíkᵉ *v.* nicely, well.

maraŋités (maraŋitesí-) *v.* to ameliorate, enhance, improve, make good.

maraŋitésuƙotᵃ (maraŋitésuƙotí-) *1 v.* to ameliorate, enhance, improve, make good. *2 v.* to cure, heal.

maráŋón (maráŋóni-) *1 v.* to be good. *2 v.* to be kind.

maráŋóniàm (maráŋóni-àmà-) *pl.* **maráŋóniik**ᵃ. *n.* good, kind person.

maráŋónuƙotᵃ (maráŋónuƙotí-) *1 v.* to become good, improve. *2 v.* to get better, heal.

Máríkò (Máríkòò-) *1 n.* Mark. *2 n.* Mark: New Testament book.

mariŋ (mariɲí-) *n.* wooden fence (inner or outer).

mariŋídɛ̀ (mariɲí-dèà-) *n.* base or foot of a fence. *Lit.* 'fence-foot'.

mariŋímóríɗ[a] (mariɲí-móríɗó-) *n.* variety of red, white, or pink beans planted near the wooden fences built around homesteads.

marúkúcɛmér (marúkú-cɛmérí-) *n.* shrub species that grows down the escarpment and whose root decoction is drunk for body pain.

másálúk[a] (másálúká-) *n.* paste made of ground, undried edible termites.

masánétòn (masánétònì-) *v.* to decay, go off, rot, spoil. See also *ɗutúɗútánónukot*[a] and *mʉsánéton*.

masánón (masánónì-) *v.* to be off, rotten, spoiled.

matáŋ (matáɲí-) *pl.* **matáŋìk**[a]. *n.* temple (zygomatic) area.

mataŋɛs (mataŋɛsí-) *v.* to chew, masticate (esp. tobacco). Also pronounced as *ɨmátáŋɛs*.

matáŋɨ́gwarí (matáɲɨ́-gwaríi-) *n.* upper frontal bone, upper temple (zygomatic) area.

matáŋɨ̀ɔk[a] (matáɲɨ́-ɔ̀kà-) *n.* temple (sphenoid) bone.

matáŋitɛtés (matáŋitɛtésí-) *v.* to give (chewing tobacco). *Lit.* 'to make chew'.

Matéò (Matéòò-) 1 *n.* Matthew. 2 *n.* Matthew: New Testament book.

Matsú (Matsúù-) *n.* a personal name.

máw[a] (máó-) *n.* lion. *Panthera leo*.

máxìŋ (máxìɲì-) *n.* epicardium, epicardial (heart) fat.

máyá (máyáà-) *n.* kob. *Kobus kob (thomasi)*.

mayaakón (mayaakónì-) *v.* to be ill or sick (of many people).

mayaakóniicéhò (mayaakóni-icé-hòò-) *pl.* **mayaakóniicéhoík**[a]. *n.* hospital ward.

mayaakóniik[a] (mayaakóni-icé-) *n.* patients.

máyákù (máyá-kùà-) *n.* kob grass: species of grass the reddish color of a Ugandan kob, used widely by the Ik for thatching. *GRAMINEAE sp.*

màyw[a] (màyò-) *pl.* **mayoicík**[a]. *n.* disease, illness, malady, sickness.

mázɨmázɔ̀n (mázɨmázɔ̀nɨ̀-) *v.* to be tangy, tart (like liquid at the onset of fermentation or some tree bark concoctions).

mbáyà (mbáyà) *adv.* a lot, very much. A slang expression based on the Swahili word *mbaya* 'bad'.

médemedánón (médemedánónì-) *v.* to be cracked, fissured (floor, soil, walls, etc.). See also *takátákánón*.

mɛ́ɛ̀ɛ̀ (mɛ́ɛ̀ɛ̀) *ideo.* baa! (bleating sound of goats and sheep).

meés (meesí-/ma-) *v.* to give.

meesíám (meesí-ámà-) *pl.* **meesíík**[a]. *n.* giver.

meetam (meetamá-) *n.* gift.

meetés (meetésí-) *v.* to give.

meetésiicík[a] (meetésí-icíká-) *n.* gifts, offerings, tribute.

meetón (meetónì-) *v.* to fall sick, get sick.

mɛkɛlɔ́n (mɛkɛlɔ́nɨ̀-) *v.* to be unbreakable, unchewable (e.g. bone or metal).

mɛkɛmɛkán (mɛkɛmɛkánɨ́-) *n.* Temminck's ground pangolin. *Manis temmincki*.

meleke (melekeí-) *n.* tree species whose young roots are eaten raw and whose fruit is liked by children and birds; its bark is chewed as medicine for coughing, and its wood is used to carve stools and wooden containers. *Lannea schimperi*. See also *ekoɗitᵃ*.

mèlètᵃ (mèlètì-) *n.* grass species resembling millet, and whose seeds are dried, ground, and used to make meal mush.

Meletisabá (Meleti-sabáà-) *n.* name of a river. *Lit.* '*mèlèt*-river'.

mɛn (mɛná-) *1 n.* issues, matters. *2 n.* problems, troubles.

mɛnáám (mɛná-ámà-) *pl.* **mɛnaíkᵃ**. *n.* outlaw, rebel, troublemaker.

mɛnaícíkᵃ (mɛná-ícíká-) *n.* stuff, things.

mɛnééкwᵃ (mɛné-ékù-) *pl.* **mɛn**. *n.* point, topic, word. *Lit.* 'matters-eye'. See also *tódèèkwᵃ*.

mɛnétɔ́n (mɛnétɔ̀nì-) *v.* to send in a message (e.g. by phoning or shouting).

mɛnɔnʉkɔtᵃ (mɛnɔnʉkɔtɨ́-) *v.* to send out a message (by phoning or shouting).

méréɗeɗé (méréɗeɗéɛ̀-) *n.* short plant species whose roots are decocted and applied to hurting or diseased eyes. *Vernonia cinerascens*.

mɛrimɛ́ránètòn (mɛrimɛ́ránètònì-) *v.* to have multiple varied patterns.

mérímeritsíò (mérímeritsíò) *interj.* ready, set, go! (an expression issuing a challenge or initiating a competition of some sort).

merixánón (merixánónì-) *v.* to be dotted or spotted (like a leopard).

mès (mèsè-) *n.* beer, brewski.

mɛsa édì *n.* beer drunk at a newborn's naming ceremony.

mɛsa ƙwaaté *n.* beer drunk as part of the traditional Ik birth ceremony.

mɛsɛcue (mɛsɛ-cué-) *n.* watery beer leftover from a ceremony or work-day. *Lit.* 'beer-water'.

mèsèdòm (mèsè-dòmà-) *pl.* **mɛsɛdomitín**. *n.* beer pot.

mèsèɲèƙᵃ (mèsè-ɲèƙè-) *n.* craving for alcohol, hunger for beer.

métᵃ (métá-) *n.* shrub species used for firewood and eaten by livestock; it often provides shade for tobacco gardens; elders use its branches to ceremonially whip hunters before their departure on a hunt. *Cadaba farinosa*. See also *súr*.

mɛtsés (mɛtsésɨ́-) *v.* to fence with poles and sticks.

mèùr (mèùrà-) *n.* fork-tailed drongo. *Dicrurus adsimilis*. See also *bèùr*.

méyᵃ (méyá-) *pl.* **méítín**. *n.* bundle, package, packet (of mira or tobacco wrapped in grass or leaves).

mɨdɨƙᵃ (mɨdɨƙɨ́-) *n.* parrot-billed sparrow. *Passer gongonensis*.

mídzatés (mídzatésí-) *1 v.* to smell, sniff. *2 v.* to smell in order to kill.

mídzatetés (mídzatetésí-) *v.* to catch scent of, smell.

mídzitésúƙotᵃ (mídzitésúƙotɨ́-) *v.* to make smelly.

mídzòn (mídzònì-) *v.* to smell (good or bad), stink.

mídzona ɗɛtsɨɗétsɨ́kᵋ *v.* to reek, smell fetid, stink.

mídzònà ɗùkᵘ *v.* to reek, smell rotten, stink.

mígirigíránón (mígirigíránónì-) *v.* to be dusky, twilit (at dawn or dusk).

míjés (míjésì-) *v.* to decline, reject, scorn, turn down.

mijílímɔ̀n (mijílímɔ̀nɨ̀-) *v.* to be slitted (like squinted eyes).

miƙídòn (miƙídònɨ̀-) *v.* to be legion, very numerous (e.g. trees or people).

mìƙⁱ (mìƙì) *ideo.* numerously.

mɨ̀l (mɨ̀lɨ̀) *ideo.* glitterily, sparkely.

mɨ̀l (mɨ̀lɔ̀) *ideo.* sleekly.

milékwᵃ (milékú-) *pl.* **milékwíkᵃ**. *n.* shrub species whose brown fruits are eaten raw. *Canthium sp.*

milɨ́ár (milɨ́árɨ̀-) *n.* grass species which is used to tie up a piece of broken pot to calm strong winds or is put at the threshold of a sick person's door, and when crossed, leads to healing. *Gramineae sp.*

milɨ́dòn (milɨ́dònɨ̀-) *v.* to be glittery, sparkly.

milílón (milílónɨ̀-) *v.* to be gelatinous, jelly-like (egg yolk, okra).

milɔ́dɔ̀n (milɔ́dɔ̀nɨ̀-) *v.* to be sleek, streamlined (like a snake).

mínés (mínésɨ̀-) *1 v.* to affix, fix on (a tool on a handle). *2 v.* to pick (the teeth).

mínés (mínésɨ̀-) *1 v.* to adore, cherish, love. *2 v.* to cure, heal.

mínésìàm (mínésɨ̀-àmà-) *pl.* **mínésiikᵃ**. *n.* admirer, devotee, lover.

mínésìàwᵃ (mínésɨ̀-àwà-) *pl.* **mínésiawíkᵃ**. *n.* fixture of a metal tool to its handle.

mínésìèdᵃ (mínésɨ̀-èdì-) *pl.* **mínésieditín**. *n.* term of endearment. *Lit.* 'love-name'.

miníƙímɔ̀n (miníƙímɔ̀nɨ̀-) *1 v.* to be gummy, sticky. *2 v.* to be stingy.

minímínatés (minímínatésí-) *v.* to feel, finger, play with. See also *imínímínés*.

mínínɔ́s (mínínɔ́sɨ̀-) *v.* to love each other.

mínínɔ́sá na áwìkàᵉ *v.* love between community members, neighbors. *Lit.* 'love of villages'.

mínínɔ́sá na iɓám *v.* feigned love.

mínínɔ́sìàm (mínínɔ́sí-àmà-) *pl.* **mínínɔ́siikᵃ**. *n.* lover.

minítᵃ (minítá-) *n.* African civet. *Civettictis civetta.*

mìɲɔ̀n (mìɲɔ̀nɨ̀-) *v.* to be deaf, mute.

miɲɔna íkèdè *v.* to be dumb, slow or 'thick' mentally. *Lit.* 'deafness of the head'.

míɔ̀kᵃ (míɔ̀kɔ̀-) *n.* mamba (black or green).

miríɗímɔ̀n (miríɗímɔ̀nɨ̀-) *v.* to be tiny (of an opening, like a pin hole).

mirimírón (mirimírónɨ̀-) *v.* to trickle.

misá (misáɨ́-) *n.* shrub species whose berries are eaten raw or crushed to flavor porridge; berries are also chewed as a treatment for tongue blisters; wood is used for fencing, and the leaves are used to filter dirty water. *Rhus natalensis.*

misáɨ́cùè (misáɨ́-cùè-) *n.* wine made from the fermenting juice of the *misá* shrub, obtained by soaking seeds, squeezing out the juice, and letting it sit in the sun.

misáɨ̀ètsˈᵃ (misáɨ́-ètsˈì-) *n.* feces containing *misá* seeds that cause the fecal matter to disperse loosely.

mísɨ̀ (mísɨ̀) *subordconn.* if, whether.

mísi ... mísi ... *coordconn.* either ... or ....

misíás (misíásɨ̀-) *n.* shrub species. *Gnidia subcordata.*

misimísón (misimísónɨ̀-) *v.* to be seen dimly or faintly (e.g. because of a great distance, like the Turkana plains below Ikland).

mitimítɔ́n (mitimítɔ́nì-) v. to be sweet-and-sour. See also taasámòn.

mitɨrímɔ̀n (mitɨrímɔ̀nɨ̀-) v. to be shriveled, withered.

mititɛs (mititɛsɨ́-) v. to make be (someone or something).

mìtɔ̀n (mìtɔ̀nɨ̀-) v. to be (someone or something).

mitɔna ɗɨ́ɛ áɗònì v. to be the third.

mitɔna ɗɨ́ɛ jɨ̀rɨ̀ v. to be the last.

mitɔna ɗɨ́ɛ lɛɓétsónì v. to be the second.

mitɔna ɗɨ́ɛ tûbᵃ v. to be the next.

mitɔna ɗɨ́ɛ wàxɨ̀ v. to be the first.

mitɔna eas v. to be the truth.

mitɔna síriàs v. to be serious.

mitɔnukɔtᵃ (mitɔnukɔtɨ́-) v. to become (someone or something).

míts'ᵃ (míts'á-) pl. míts'ítín. n. testicle, testis.

mízɨ̀ʒ (mízɨ̀ʒɔ̀-) pl. mízɨ̀ʒɨ̀kᵃ. n. vine species used as for building granaries, strapping beehives to trees, and lowering men or honey from high places; its seeds are ground, soaked, and then the infusion acts as a treatment for headlice. *Hippocratea africana*.

mɔ́ɗᵃ (mɔ́ɗɛ́-) n. ground bee.

Moɗiŋ (Moɗiŋí-) n. a personal name.

Moɗó (Moɗóò-) n. a personal name.

mɔɗɔ́ɗᵃ (mɔɗɔ́ɗɔ́-) 1 n. bagworm. Psychididae. 2 n. cocoon. 3 n. sleep, slumber.

mɔɗɔ́ɗɔ́ekwᵃ (mɔɗɔ́ɗɔ́-èkù-) 1 n. cocoon opening. 2 n. threshold consciousness: state of being half-asleep or half-awake. Lit. 'cocoon-eye'.

môgᵃ (mógà-) n. dense thicket, thick brush (often found in riverbeds where it avoids being burned).

mogánétòn (mogánétònì-) v. to become dense or thick (of brush).

mogánón (mogánónì-) v. to be dense, thick (of brush).

mɔkɛ́s (mɔkɛ́sɨ́-) v. to cover, enclose (a termite hole with a dome of sticks, grass, and soil, leaving one opening out which the ants can be collected).

mókol (mókoló-) pl. mókòlìkᵃ. n. hardwood tree species whose wood is used in building and fencing and whose bark decoction is drunk as a treatment for abdominal pains; pipes and beehives are carved from its branches and trunk. *Ozoroa insignis (reticulata)*.

mɔkimɔ́kɔ́n (mɔkimɔ́kɔ́nɨ̀-) v. to cloud up, form rainclouds.

mɔkɔr (mɔkɔrɔ́-) pl. mokóríkwᵃ. n. well deeply embedded in a large rock. Compare with sátᵃ.

Mɔkɔ́ríkᵃ (Mɔkɔ́ríkà-) n. name of a river. Lit. 'rock wells'.

mɔkɔrɔ́ám (mɔkɔrɔ́-ámà-) pl. mɔkɔróíkᵃ. n. Bokora person. Lit. 'rock-pool person'.

mɔkɔrɔ́cúé (mɔkɔrɔ́-cúè-) n. water from a well deep inside a rock.

Mɔkɔrɔ́gwàs (Mɔkɔrɔ́-gwàsà-) n. name of a hill or mountain. Lit. 'well-rock'.

mɔ́métòn (mɔ́métònì-) v. to hesitate, pause, stop, take a break. See also mɔ́métòn.

momó (momóò-) pl. momóín. 1 n. uncle (mother's brother). 2 n. nephew (sister's son).

momócèkᵃ (momó-cèkì-) n. aunt (mother's brother's wife).

momóìm (momó-ìmà-) pl. momówikᵃ. n. cousin (mother's brother's child).

momotᵃ (momotí-) pl. momotíkwᵃ. n. his/her uncle (mother's brother).

momotícékᵃ (momotí-cékì-) *n.* his/her aunt (mother's brother's wife).

momotíím (momotí-ímà-) *pl.* **momotíwík**ᵃ. *n.* his/her cousin (mother's brother's child).

mɔ́ɲɛ́s (mɔ́ɲɛ́sɨ̀-) *v.* to gossip about, talk about.

mɔɲimɔɲɔs (mɔɲimɔɲɔsɨ́-) *v.* to be gabby, gossipy.

mòò (mòò) *adv.* not: and then ... do(es) not.

mòòn (mòònì-/ma-) *v.* to be ill, sick.

moona gúróᵉ *v.* to be heartsick (from anger, guilt, sadness, etc.).

moós (moosí-) *v.* to be given.

morétón (morétónì-) *1 v.* to germinate, grow, sprout. *2 v.* to come in (of teeth). *3 v.* to break out (of skin problems).

Morícoro (Morícoroó-) *n.* name of an area where the road from *Kàlàpàtà* slopes upward at the border of Ikland.

mòriɗᵃ (mòrìɗò-) *n.* bean(s).

mórímós (mórímósí-) *v.* to respect each other.

Móróɗᵃ (Móróɗò-) *n.* name of a deserted village.

morókᵃ (morókú-) *pl.* **morókík**ᵃ. *1 n.* throat. *2 n.* voice. *3 n.* shaft. *4 n.* stalk.

moróká na kwátsᵃ *1 n.* esophagus, gullet. *2 n.* soft voice. *Lit.* 'throat that is small'.

moróká ná zè *1 n.* trachea, windpipe. *2 n.* loud voice. *Lit.* 'throat that is big'.

morókêdᵃ (morókédè-) *n.* gun barrel. *Lit.* 'its throat'.

mòròn (mòrònì-) *1 v.* to fear. *2 v.* to respect, revere, venerate.

moronuƙotᵃ (moronuƙotí-) *v.* to flee, run away.

Morúaɲáo (Morúaɲáoó-) *n.* name of a hill or mountain.

Moruaɲákiné (Moruaɲákinéì-) *n.* name of a hillside and associated human habitations.

Morúaɲápiɔn (Morúaɲápiɔnɔ́-) *n.* name of a hill or mountain.

Moruaɲípi (Moruaɲípií-) *n.* name of a mountain in Toposaland, South Sudan.

Morúaɲítà (Morúaɲítàà-) *n.* name of a hill or mountain.

Morúápólón (Morúápólóní-) *n.* name of a mountain in Turkanaland, Kenya.

Morúárɛ́ɲán (Morúárɛ́ɲánɨ̀-) *n.* name of a hill or mountain.

Morúatapᵃ (Morúatapá-) *n.* name of a hilltop in Kamion where the British used to come for picnics and on which the Ik now live.

Morúédikayᵃ (Morúédikaí-) *n.* name of a hill or mountain.

Morúéris (Morúérisá-) *n.* name of a hill or mountain.

Morukoyan (Morukoyanɨ-) *n.* name of a hill.

Morúlem (Morúlemú-) *n.* name of a hill or mountain.

Morúɲaŋ (Morúɲaŋá-) *n.* name of a hill with yellowish grass.

Morúŋole (Morúŋoleé-) *n.* name of a tall mountain in the west of Ikland.

mɔsɨ́mɔ́sɔ̀n (mɔsɨ́mɔ́sɔ̀nɨ̀-) *v.* to be lightly parched, partially dry.

mɔ̀sɔ̀n (mɔ̀sɔ̀nɨ̀-) *v.* to be dried out, parched, withered.

mɔsɔnuƙotᵃ (mɔsɔnuƙotɨ́-) *v.* to dry out, parch, wither up.

moxés (moxésí-) *v.* to peel or pick off (e.g. a scab).

mɔz (mɔzà-) *n.* shrub species whose reddish-brown fruits are eaten and whose branches are made into weapons. *Grewia villosa*.

mozokoɗᵃ (mozokoɗí-) *n.* softwood tree species whose wood is used for fencing and whose branches are used as fighting sticks. *Ormocarpum trichocarpum*.

muce (muceé-) *pl.* **mucéík**ᵃ. *1 n.* path, road, trail, way. *2 n.* method, way (of doing). *3 n.* fortune, lot, luck.

mucea na ɓáriɓár *n.* average luck, decent fortune.

mucea na ináƙúós *n.* awful luck, terrible fortune.

mucea ná jɔl *n.* bad luck, ill fortune. *Lit.* 'way that is bland'.

mucea na títìan *n.* good fortune or luck. *Lit.* 'way that is hot'.

mucéákᵃ (mucé-ákà-) *pl.* **mucéíkaakitín**. *n.* middle of a path. *Lit.* 'path-mouth'. See also *mucéékw*ᵃ.

mucédè (mucé-dèà-) *pl.* **mucéíkadɛík**ᵃ. *n.* trailhead. *Lit.* 'path-foot'.

mucéékwᵃ (mucé-ékù-) *pl.* **mucéíkeekwitín**. *n.* middle of a path. *Lit.* 'path-eye'. See also *mucéák*ᵃ.

mʉɗáŋámɔ̀n (mʉɗáŋámɔ̀nì-) *v.* to be unpierced (of ears, lips).

múɗèr (múɗèrì-) *1 n.* dwarf mongoose. *Helogale parvula*. *2 ideo.* very black.

muɗés (muɗésí-) *v.* to bury, inhume, inter, lay to rest. See also *búdès* and *tʉnʉkɛs*.

muɗésá cɛméríkàᵉ *v.* to bury medicine (a metaphor for items like a butter flask, chicken, or shard of broken pottery, buried as a way to prevent enemies or sickness).

muɗésá gwaáᵉ *v.* to bury a bird alive (as a sacrifice in order to prevent them from consuming the crops). See also *ƙanésúkota gwaá*ᵉ.

muɗésá ɦiyekesíé wicé *v.* to bury the life of one's children (a metaphor for making a pronouncement over one's children, for example when a father is nearing his death).

muɗésá logeréɲoé *v.* to bury a stink-bug (as a sacrfice to prevent them from eating up all the grain in one's garden).

muɗésíàm (muɗésí-àmà-) *pl.* **muɗésíik**ᵃ. *n.* gravedigger. See also *tʉnʉkɛsíám*.

múɗuɗú (múɗuɗúù-) *n.* white-browed coucal (possibly Senegal as well). *Centropus superciliosus*.

Múɗùgùrìtòdᵃ (Múɗùgùrì-tòdà-) *n.* Arabic language.

múɗúkánón (múɗúkánónì-) *1 v.* to be blind, unsighted. *2 v.* to have poor eyesight. *3 v.* to close the eyes.

múɗúkánónìtòdᵃ (múɗúkánónì-tòdà-) *n.* careless speech, reckless talk. *Lit.* 'blindness-talk'.

mujálámòn (mujálámònì-) *1 v.* to be bland, flavorless, tasteless, vapid. *2 v.* to be lukewarm, tepid.

mʉ̀kà (mʉ̀kà) *1 adv.* really, totally. *2 adv.* forever. *3 adv.* never. See also *jîkⁱ*.

mukétᵃ (mukétí-) *pl.* **mukétík**ᵃ. *n.* mylohyoid muscle: thin muscle that connects to the inner front of the jawbone and pulls it down.

múkò *n.* en route, on the way.

mukú (mukúà-) *pl.* **mukúaicík**ᵃ. *n.* night, nighttime.

mukú *n.* at night, by night, during the night.

mukúádàŋ (mukúá-dàŋà-) *n.* noctural edible termite species.

mukúágwà (mukúá-gwàà-) *n.* nocturnal bird (in general).

mukúásɨ́sɨ́k[a] (mukúá-sɨ́sɨ́ká-) *n.* midnight.

Mukulit[a] (Mukulití-) *n.* name of a river.

mʉkʉtam (mʉkʉtamá-) *n.* fist. *Lit.* 'clenchable'. See also *ilʉlʉŋam*.

mʉkʉtɛs (mʉkʉtɛsɨ́-) *v.* to clasp, clench.

mʉkʉtɛtés (mʉkʉtɛtésɨ́-) *v.* to clasp, clench up.

múƙás (múƙásɨ̀-) *n.* small honeybee species that nests in trees.

Mùƙè (Mùƙèì-) *n.* name of a hill or mountain.

muƙíánètòn (muƙíánètònì-) *v.* to be brown.

mʉƙúrʉ́mɔ̀n (mʉƙúrʉ́mɔ̀nɨ̀-) *v.* to be hunched, stooped. See also *rʉ́gʉ̀dʉ̀mɔn*.

múlʉƙúƙɔ́n (múlʉƙúƙɔ́nɨ̀-) *v.* to salivate (when gagging or vomiting).

mulúráŋòn (mulúráŋònì-) *v.* to lurch, sink (of one's heart when hearing or suspecting bad news).

mumúánón (mumúánónì-) *v.* to be myopic, shortsighted.

múmùt[a] (múmùtà-) *n.* evergreen mosslike plant species used as livestock fodder and whose bark is pounded, soaked and drunk as stomach medicine. *Selaginella phillipsiana*.

múmútètòn (múmútètònɨ̀-) *v.* to putrefy.

múmútòn (múmútònɨ̀-) *v.* to be putrid, rank (e.g. body odor, rotting meat).

mùɲ (mùɲù) *1 quant.* all, entire, whole. *2 quant.* any, whatsoever.

mùɲùmùɲ (mùɲùmùɲù) *quant.* all, entire, whole.

mʉránón (mʉránónì-) *v.* to be sour (of malt grains).

mʉrɛ́s (mʉrɛ́sɨ́-) *v.* to mash, soak (i.e. grist for beer-brewing).

mʉrɔn (mʉrɔnɨ́-) *1 n.* grass species that grows like a vine and whose leaves are chewed and applied to wounds to stop pain; it is prescribed as a charm to ward of diseases and spirits; tobacco is often planted where it grows. *Cynodon dactylon*. *2 n.* grassy tobacco garden.

múrotsíò (múrotsíò-) *n.* shrub species used for making house poles. *Maytenus undata*.

murut[a] (murutá-) *n.* watershed: ridge separating adjacent river systems.

murutéékw[a] (muruté-ékù-) *n.* centerpoint of a watershed.

mʉs (mʉ̀sà-) *pl.* **músɨ́tín**. *n.* candelabra tree: cactus-like tree whose sap is used as a glue to fix tools and whose ashes are used as fertilizer for pumpkin and tobacco fields. *Euphorbia candelabrum*.

mʉsánétòn (mʉsánétònì-) *v.* to decay, decompose, go off, rot. See also *dutúdútánónukot*[a] and *masánétòn*.

mususánón (mususánónì-) *v.* to be groggy, hungover.

mútèts[a] (mútètsì-) *n.* Egyptian mongoose. *Herpestes ichneumon*. Also called 'gray mongoose' or 'ichneumon'.

mʉts'ʉtɛs (mʉts'ʉtɛsɨ́-) *v.* to close, shut. See also *kɔkɛ́s*.

mʉts'ʉ́tésʉkɔt[a] (mʉts'ʉ́tésʉkɔtɨ́-) *v.* to close or shut up. See also *kɔkɛ́sʉ́kɔt*[a].

muts'utiesúkot[a] (muts'utiesúkotí-) *v.* to keep closing or shutting up (e.g. termite holes where one doesn't want them exiting).

mutu (mutuú-) *pl.* **mutuík**[a]. *1 n.* thick needle/pin with a wooden handle (used for mending gourds and leather skins). *2 n.* firing pin.

Mutúnan (Mutúnaní-) *n.* name of a river.

n

na (na=) *subordconn.* if, when (hypothetically). The main verb in the clause that follows this particle takes the sequential aspect. Note also that for some Ik speakers, this particle has a 'floating' high tone after it, making the first syllable of the next word have a high tone.

na (=na) *1 dem.* this. *2 rel.* that/which (singular).

nà (<nɛɛ́s) *v.*

na tsóíta kɔnɨ́ *n.* one day.

náà (náà) *subordconn.* when ...(earlier today). The main verb in the clause that follows this word takes the dummy pronoun.

náà (náà) *subordconn.* when. The main verb that follows this word takes the simultaneous aspect.

náa táà *1 subordconn.* when. *2 subordconn.* lest, otherwise.

náabús (náabúsɨ-) *n.* four-toed hedgehog. *Erinaceus albiventris.*

nááƙwa (nááƙɔ-) *n.* even, including.

Náápoŋo (Náápoŋoó-) *n.* name of a hillside, the surrounding area, and associated human habitations.

naarákiɫɛ (naarákiɫɛɛ́-) *n.* large tree species whose reddish berries are eaten but whose bark is poisonous; wood is used for house-building or making tool-handles.

naaseɲaŋ (naaseɲaŋá-) *n.* worker bee.

náàtì (náàtì) *coordconn.* and then.

nábàdà (nábàdì-) *n.* colossus, giant, monster of a, whale of a. This word refers to an entity close by.

nábàts[e] (nábèè) *adv.* must have ... (earlier today).

nábèè (nábèè) *subordconn.* if ... had (yesterday). The main verb in the clause that follows this word takes the sequential aspect.

nabêz (nabézà-) *n.* allergic skin reaction, skin allergy.

nabidit[a] (nabiditɨ́-) *pl.* **nábiditik**[a]. *n.* adjoining area, quarter, section.

nábɔnʉkɔt[a] (nábɔnʉkɔtɨ́-) *1 v.* to be done, completed, finished. *2 v.* to be enough, plenty, sufficient. See also *ŋábɔnʉkɔt*[a].

naɓálámorú (naɓálámorúù-) *n.* mouse species.

naɓó (naɓó) *1 adv.* again. *2 coordconn.* furthermore, moreover.

Nacákʉ́nèt[a] (Nacákʉ́nètɨ-) *n.* name of a place southwest of Ikland where a girl threw herself to her death to avoid marrying a man she did not want.

Nacapíò (Nacapíò-) *n.* a personal name.

nàdèkwèl (nàdèkwèlà-) *n.* edible melon (desert vine) species whose soft leaves are also eaten; its seeds are dried, fried, ground, and mixed with vegetables to be eaten. *Citrullus sp.*

nádzàƙ[a] (nádzàƙà-) *n.* my friend.

naɗa na *pro.* this one.

naɗɛ́p[a] (naɗɛ́pɛ̀-) *pl.* **naɗɛ́pik**[a]. *n.* flea(s). *Siphonaptera.* See also *ŋíkaɗɛpíɗɛ́p*[a].

nàɗɨ̀ak[a] (nàɗɨ̀akà-) *pl.* **naɗɨ́akɨk**[a]. *1 n.* patch of styled, colored hair on the back of men's heads. *2 n.* men's nylon skullcap in which feathers are stuck.

Naɗóóɲ (Naɗóóɲò-) *n.* a nickname for a one-eyed person.

Nàɗù (Nàɗùù-) *n.* a personal name.

náganâgᵃ (náganágà-) *n.* Nile monitor lizard. *Varanus niloticus.*

Nagomocóm (Nagomocómò-) *n.* name of a hill or mountain.

naídòn (naídònì-) *v.* to be viscous (like honey or oil).

Naiɗíɗᵃ (Naiɗíɗì-) *n.* name of a hill in Timu.

naíké *dem.* here.

naíkɔtᵃ (<nɛɛsúkɔtᵃ) *v.*

náìlòn (náìlònì-) *n.* nylon.

naínɛɛtés (naínɛɛtésí-) *v.* to accustom, acquaint, familiarize, habituate.

náínɛnɛ́ (náínɛnɛ́ɛ-) *n.* large fig tree species whose dark fruits are eaten raw. *Ficus sp.*

naínɔ́s (naínɔ́sɨ́-) *v.* to be mutually acquainted, used to each other.

Náìtà (Náìtàà-) *n.* name of a rocky hill.

naítá (naítá) *1 subordconn.* how, like, the way (something is or is done). *2 subordconn.* seeing as how, since.

náíta na *dem.* here.

naitakípúratᵃ (naitakípúratá-) *n.* caracal. *Caracal caracal.*

Náìtáyᵃ (Náìtáɨ-) *n.* name of a hill or mountain.

naítésʉkɔtᵃ (naítésʉkɔtɨ́-) *v.* to accustom, acquaint, familiarize, habituate.

nákᵃ (=náà) *1 dem.* that (earlier today). *2 rel.* that/which (earlier today). *3 adv.* earlier today.

Nakaɓinín (Nakaɓiníní-) *n.* month of honey.

Nakaɗapaláítᵃ (Nakaɗapaláítɨ-) *n.* name of a hill or mountain.

nakaɨn *n.* this year. See also *kaɨnɔ na.*

nakaɨna far *n.* in three years, three years from now.

nakaɨna tso *n.* in two years, two years from now, year after next.

Nakalalé (Nakalaléè-) *n.* name of a hill or mountain.

Nakalelé (Nakaleléè-) *n.* name of a place.

Nakamemeotᵃ (Nakamemeotó-) *n.* name of a natural well.

Nakariɓᵃ (Nakariɓá-) *n.* September: month of chaff. See also *Lotyakᵃ.*

nakariɓᵃ (nakariɓá-) *n.* chaffs, husks (from millet, rice, sorghum).

nakatʉmán (nakatʉmání-) *n.* maize variety with white kernels that matures quickly and has short stems and short cobs. See also *katʉmán.*

Nakɨ́ŋa (Nakɨ́ŋaá-) *n.* a personal name.

Nakɨríkètᵃ (Nakɨríkètè-) *n.* name of a hill or mountain.

nakɨríkètᵃ (nakɨríkètɨ-) *pl.* **nakɨríkɛtík**ᵃ. *n.* barbeque spot, roasting ground (where men cook and eat some of the meat taken during a successful hunt).

nakɨrɔ́r (nakɨrɔ́rɨ́-) *pl.* **nakɨrɔ́rík**ᵃ. *n.* sheath. See also *ɲaɓúrétᵃ.*

Nákírù (Nákírùù-) *n.* a personal name.

nakítsòɗᵃ (nakítsòɗì-) *n.* hedging in or surrounding of animals during a hunt.

Nakoɗíle (Nakoɗíleé-) *n.* name of a river.

nakɔlitákᵃ (nakɔlitákà-) *n.* sand snake. *Psammophis sp.*

Nakɔŋ (Nakɔŋʉ́-) *n.* a personal name.

Nàkòrìtààwᵃ (Nàkòrìtà-àwà-) *n.* name of a hill and surrounding area in Timu.

Nakɔrɔɗɔ́ (Nakɔrɔɗɔ́ɔ̀-) *n.* name of a mountain pass in Toposaland, South Sudan.

nakús (nakúsó-) *pl.* **nakúsík**ᵃ. *n.* animal bed. See also *ɗípɔ̀.*

nakút[a] (nakútá-) *pl.* **nakútík**[a]. *n.* wooden spade used for planting and weeding.

Nàkwàŋà (Nàkwàŋàà-) *n.* name of a river.

Nakyéɲ (Nakyéɲì-) *n.* a personal name.

naƙaf (naƙafú-) *pl.* **náƙáfɨk**[a]. *1 n.* tongue. *2 n.* language. *3 n.* arrowhead.

náƙáfɛd[a] (náƙáfɛdɛ̀-) *n.* point. *Lit.* 'its tongue-tip'.

naƙánàk[a] (naƙánàà) *1 subordconn.* if ... would . *2 subordconn.* if ... would have (earlier today). The main verb in the clause the follows this conjunction takes the sequential aspect.

naƙánòk[o] (naƙánòò) *subordconn.* if ... would have (a while ago). The main verb in the clause the follows this conjunction takes the sequential aspect.

naƙásàm (naƙásàmù) *subordconn.* if ... would have (yesterday). The main verb in the clause following this word takes the sequential aspect.

naƙɨlɨƙɨl (naƙɨlɨƙɨlɨ̀-) *pl.* **naƙɨlɨƙɨlɨk**[a]. *n.* chopper, helicopter, whirlybird.

náƙɨ́rà (náƙɨ́ràà-) *n.* aardwolf. *Proteles cristatus*.

naƙólít[a] (naƙólítì-) *pl.* **naƙólítìk**[a]. *n.* log or wooden bar used to block a gate or trap entrance.

naƙúlé (naƙúléɛ̀-) *pl.* **naƙúléɨk**[a]. *n.* division, partition, room, section.

nàƙw[a] (nàƙwà) *ideo.* bendily, flexibly.

naƙwádòn (naƙwádònì-) *v.* to be bendy, flexible. See also *naúdòn* and *nɔkɔ́dɔ̀n*.

naƙwés (naƙwésɨ-) *v.* to breastfeed, suckle.

naƙwésúƙɔt[a] (naƙwésúƙɔtɨ-) *v.* to breastfeed, suckle.

nàƙw[i] (nàƙwɨ̀) *ideo.* looking very good, very dressed up.

naƙwɨ́dɛtɛ́s (naƙwɨ́dɛtɛ́sɨ-) *v.* to adorn, beautify, decorate, dress up.

naƙwɨ́dɔ̀n (naƙwɨ́dɔ̀nɨ̀-) *v.* to be decked out, dressed up, looking great.

naƙwɨ́n (naƙwɨ́nɨ-) *pl.* **naƙwɨ́nɨ́k**[a]. *n.* forked stick used to hold up hunting nets.

naƙwɨtɛs (naƙwɨtɛsɨ-) *v.* to breastfeed, give suck to, suckle.

nàlèmùdzòɗà (nàlèmùdzòɗàà-) *n.* common rock-thrush. *Monticola saxatilis*.

nalɨ́ɨlɨ́ (nalɨ́ɨlɨ́ɨ̀-) *n.* sorghum variety with round seed-heads, whitish-yellowish seeds, and curved stalks.

nalójón (nalójónì-) *v.* to ill-fitting, loose.

nalɔŋizat[a] (nalɔŋizatá-) *n.* desert.

Nàmàƙàr (Nàmàƙàrà-) *n.* June. See also *Yɛlɨ́yél*.

nàmɛ̀ɗɔ̀ (nàmɛ̀ɗɔ̀ɔ̀-) *pl.* **namɛ́ɗɔ́ɨk**[a]. *n.* occipital bone (back of skull).

namɛ́ɗɔ́ɛ̀d[a] (namɛ́ɗɔ́ɛ̀dɛ̀-) *n.* back side (e.g. of an axehead or human head). *Lit.* 'its occipital bone'.

Namerí (Namerîi-) *n.* name of a river flanked with spotted rocks.

Namétúròn (Namétúrònì-) *n.* name of a river in Turkanaland, Kenya.

Namórú (Namórúù-) *n.* name of a river. Also called *Gwasikasabá*.

Namɔ́y[a] (Namɔ́ɨ̀-) *n.* a personal name.

namúɗit[a] (namúɗitɨ-) *n.* large fig tree species whose small yellow berries are eaten raw. *Ficus ingens*.

námúí (námúíì-) *pl.* **námúatikw**[a]. *1 n.* sibling-in-law (husband's sibling). *2 n.* sister-in-law (brother's wife).

nanáà (nanáà) *subordconn.* when ... had (earlier today). The main verb in the clause that follows this word takes the dummy pronoun.

nanáá (nanáá) *subordconn.* if ... had (earlier today). The main verb in the clause that follows this word takes the sequential aspect.

naniŋiniŋ (naniŋiniŋí-) *pl.* **naníŋiniŋìk**[a]. *n.* modern axe or axehead (with a hole for the handle). See also *naɲiniŋin*.

nánòk[o] (nánòò) *adv.* must have ... (long ago).

nànòò (nànòò) *1 subordconn.* when ... had (a while ago). *2 subordconn.* if ... had (a while ago).

Naŋetéɓ[a] (Naŋetéɓè-) *n.* a personal name.

naɲiniŋin (naɲiniŋiní-) *pl.* **naɲíníŋìnìk**[a]. *n.* modern axe or axehead (with a hole for the handle). See also *naniŋiniŋ*.

Naŋóléɓok[a] (Naŋóléɓokó-) *n.* name of a boulder and associated river.

Náŋòlì (Náŋólìì-) *n.* a personal name.

nàŋùràmɓɔ (nàŋùràmɓɔɔ̀-) *n.* chin-spot batis. *Batis molitor.* See also *iwótsígwà*.

Naɔyakíŋɔ́l (Naɔyakíŋɔ́lì-) *n.* name of a place.

nápáka na *adv.* now, presently. A phrase borrowed from Ateker (Teso-Turkana) languages.

nàpèì (nàpèì) *1 prep.* from. *2 subordconn.* from the time when, since. A noun following this word takes the ablative case. See also *ɲàpèì*.

napérít[a] (napériti-) *pl.* **napérítik**[a]. *n.* bivouac, bushcamp, camp.

naperorwá (naperorwáà-) *pl.* **naperorwáìk**[a]. *n.* oblong purple or yellow pumpkin variety.

napɛtés (napɛtésɨ-) *v.* to bring alongside or beside. See also *inapɛtés*.

Napitiro (Napitiroó-) *n.* name of a hill or mountain and associated river.

Nápíyò (Nápíyòò-) *n.* a personal name.

napóɗè (napóɗèè-) *n.* bird species.

Napoliso (Napolisoó-) *n.* a personal name.

nápɔ́n (nápɔ́nɨ-) *v.* to come alongside or beside.

Nàpɔ̀rèàm (Nàpɔ̀rèà-àmà-) *pl.* **Napɔrɛaik**[a]. *n.* Napore person.

Napóroto (Napórotoó-) *n.* name of a hill or mountain.

narɛ́w[a] (narɛ́ù-) *n.* dwarf adder species that lives in northwest Kenya. *Bitis sp.*

Narót[a] (Narótò-) *n.* a personal name.

narúét[a] (narúétì-) *pl.* **narúétík**[a]. *n.* community, neighborhood.

narúétiàm (narúétì-àmà-) *pl.* **narúétiik**[a]. *n.* neighbor.

narúétinós (narúétinósí-) *v.* to be neighbors, neighbor each other.

Narúkyeŋ (Narúkyeŋí-) *n.* name of a hill or mountain and surrounding area.

narwá (narúà-) *pl.* **narúáik**[a]. *n.* long spear shaft (with *ɲéɓíli* as its head).

nàsàm (násàmù̀) *adv.* must have ... (yesterday).

nàsàmù (nàsàmù) *subordconn.* when ... had (yesterday). The main verb that follows this word takes the dummy pronoun.

nasɛmɛ́ (nasɛmɛ́ɛ̀-) *pl.* **nasémɛ́ɨk**[a]. *n.* oblong gourd with a handle sown onto it.

nasoroɲ (nasoroɲí-) *pl.* **nasóróɲìk**ᵃ. *n.* intestine.

Nasurukéɲ (Nasurukéɲì-) *n.* name of a hill or mountain.

natɛ́ɓᵃ (natɛ́ɓà-) *n.* sorghum variety with yellow seeds.

nateɓú (nateɓúù-) *pl.* **nateɓúìk**ᵃ. *n.* worker termite that cares for the queen.

natélétsìò (natélétsìò-) *n.* earwig. *Dermaptera.*

natélewá (natélewáà-) *n.* rat species.

natiɓᵃ (natiɓá-) *pl.* **natíɓɨ́k**ᵃ. *n.* braided twine (used in snaring).

natiŋá (natiŋáà-) *n.* spotted hyena. *Crocuta crocuta.* See also *atɔŋ.*

Natípem (Natípemú-) *n.* name of a hill or mountain and surrounding area.

Natɔkɔ́ɔ́ŋɔr (Natɔkɔ́ɔ́ŋɔrɨ́-) *n.* name of a river.

nàtɔ̀lɔ̀kà (nàtɔ̀lɔ̀kàà-) *pl.* **natɔ́lɔ́kɨ̀k**ᵃ. *n.* rainbow.

Nátɔmɛ́ (Nátɔmɛ́ɨ-) *n.* a personal name.

Natɔ́rɔ́kɔkɨ́tɔ́ (Natɔ́rɔ́kɔkɨ́tɔ́ɔ̀-) *n.* name of a place.

Natsapúó (Natsapúó-) *n.* a personal name.

nàtsèr (nàtsèrà-) *n.* striped ground rat.

natsés (natsésɨ́-) *v.* to cook out (bitterness or poison by boiling, pouring the water, and reboiling one or more times).

Natsíámu (Natsíámù-) *n.* a personal name. Also pronounced as *Nacém.*

Natsíátà (Natsíátàà-) *n.* name of a hill or mountain.

natsɨ́ɓɨlɨ́ (natsɨ́ɓɨlɨ̀ɨ̀-) *n.* female bushbuck. *Tragelaphus scriptus.*

nàtsìkwᵃ (nàtsìkò-) *pl.* **natsíkwík**ᵃ. *n.* ring or wreath of twisted reeds.

Natsuƙúl (Natsuƙúlù-) *n.* name of a seasonal stream west of *Lokinéne.*

natúɗusé (natúɗuséè-) *n.* woodland crombec (northern or red-faced). *Sylvietta sp.*

natúkᵃ (natúkù-) *n.* group discussion.

Naturukan (Naturukanɨ́-) *n.* name of a river.

naturutur (naturuturú-) *pl.* **natúrútùrɨ̀k**ᵃ. *n.* cracked gourd.

nàᵘ (nàù) *ideo.* bendily, flexibly.

naúdòn (naúdònì-) *v.* to be bendy, flexible.

náʉ́mɔ (náʉ́mɔɔ́-) *n.* lappet-faced vulture. *Torgos tracheliotus.*

Naʉratᵃ (Naʉratá-) *n.* name of a mountain connected to *Morúŋole.*

Nàwà (Nàwàà-) *n.* a personal name.

Nawáɗowᵃ (Nawáɗoú-) *n.* name of a hill and associated human habitations.

Nawólójam (Nawólójamú-) *n.* Year of *Nawólójam,* when many cattle died of rinderpest.

náxána na *dem.* this direction, this way.

nayá (naí-) *n.* here.

Nayaón (Nayaóní-) *n.* a personal name.

Nayapan (Nayapanɨ́-) *n.* name of a place in Dodoth country where the British cleared land to reduce the problem of tsetse flies in mid-1900s.

nayé *dem.* here.

nayé kɔ̀nà *dem.* right here.

nayé na *dem.* here.

nayé ne *dem.* just there, there.

názèkwà (názèkwà) *1 n.* while. *2 n.* now, soon. When used in the sense of 'while', this word is followed by a verb with the dummy pronoun attached to it.

nà[i] (nàì) *ideo.* viscously.

ńdà (ńdà) *1 coordconn.* and. *2 prep.* with. In a series of nouns linked by this word, every noun after the first takes the oblique case.

ńda nébèè kɔ̀n *n.* eleven.

ndaicé (ndaicé-) *n.* um, uh, whatca-ma-callit.

ndaík[e] *pro.* where?

nday[o] *n.* by what path? which way?

ndayúk[o] *n.* it is where?

ndéé *1 n.* from where? *2 interj.* whatever! (an expression of disagreement).

ǹdò *pl.* **ndoín**. *pro.* who?

ndóó *1 prep.* what about ...? *2 subordconn.* what about (when) ...? When acting as a preposition, this word is followed by a noun in the nominative case.

ndóó fiyè *n.* maybe, perhaps, who knows?

ndóó mìtìè *v.* what if (it is ...).

ne (=ne) *dem.* that (just there).

ne (ne) *interj.* here! here you go! (an expression of giving).

nêb[a] (nébù-) *pl.* **nébitín**. *1 n.* body. *2 n.* self.

nébàdà (nébàdì-) *n.* colossus, giant, monster of a, whale of a. Referring to an entity a slight distance away.

nébèd[a] (nébèdè-) *pl.* **nébìn**. *n.* himself, herself, itself: the very person/thing.

nébùnànès (nébùnànèsì-) *n.* bodiliness, embodiment.

nébùsìts'[a] (nébù-sìts'à-) *n.* body hair.

nédà (nédì-) *dem.* there (near).

néda ne *dem.* just there, there.

nɛ́ɛ́ (nɛ́ɛ́) *subordconn.* when. The main verb that follows this word takes the simultaneous aspect.

nɛ́ɛ́ (nɛ́ɛ́) *1 prep.* from. *2 prep.* through. A noun following this word takes the genitive case.

nɛɛ́s (nɛɛsí-/na-) *v.* to abide, bear, deal with, endure, tolerate.

nɛɛsúkɔt[a] (nɛɛsúkɔtí-/naikɔt-) *v.* to abide, bear, deal with, endure, tolerate.

néita ne *dem.* just there, there.

nɛpɛ́káàm (nɛpɛ́ká-àmà-) *pl.* **nɛpɛ́káik**[a]. *1 n.* arguer, argumentative person. *2 n.* atheist, unbeliever.

nɛpɛkanitetés (nɛpɛkanitetésí-) *v.* to challenge, contradict.

nɛpɛkánón (nɛpɛkánónì-) *v.* to argue, debate, disagree, protest.

nɛ̀rɛ̀ (nɛ̀rɛ̀) *ideo.* teeteringly.

nɛrédɔ̀n (nɛrédɔ̀nì-) *v.* to be teetering, tottering.

nérìnérɔ́n (nérìnérɔ́nì-) *1 v.* to quiver, shudder. *2 v.* to lurch, stagger.

nés (nésé) *adv.* oh, I see; oh, you mean.

nɛsɛkánón (nɛsɛkánónì-) *v.* to be healthy, hygienic.

nesés (nesésí-) *v.* to hear. See also *nesíbès*.

nesíbes (nesíbesí-) *1 v.* to hear. *2 v.* to listen. *3 v.* to comprehend, understand. *4 v.* to heed, obey. See also *nesés*.

nesíbesíám (nesíbesí-ámà-) *pl.* **nesíbesíík**[a]. *n.* listener.

nesíbiés (nesíbiesí-) *v.* to obey habitually.

nesíbos (nesíbosí-) *v.* to be understood.

nesíbunós (nesíbunósí-) *1 v.* to understand each other. *2 v.* to be understood.

ni (=ni) *1 dem.* these. *2 rel.* that/which (plural).

nɩ́ám (nɩ́ámà-) *n.* every person.

níbàdà (níbàdɨ̀-) *n.* overabundance, plentitude (here).

niɗa ni *pro.* these ones.

nɩ̀kwⁱ (nɩ̀kwɨ̀) *ideo.* resistantly, toughly.

nɩ̀kwɩ́dɔ̀n (nɩ̀kwɩ́dɔ̀nɨ̀-) *v.* to be resistant, tough, unyielding.

níkⁱ (=níì) *1 dem.* those (earlier). *2 rel.* that/which (earlier; plural).

nɩ̀kwⁱ (nɩ̀kwɨ̀) *ideo.* sweetly.

nɩ̀kwɩ́dɔ̀n (nɩ̀kwɩ́dɔ̀nɨ̀-) *v.* to be slightly sweet (like porridge with a little sugar).

nɩ̀kwɩ́nɩ́kɔ̀n (nɩ̀kwɩ́nɩ́kɔ̀nɨ̀-) *v.* to whip back and forth.

ninɛtés (ninɛtésɨ́-) *v.* to confirm, corroborate.

nɩ̀r (nɩ̀rɨ̀) *ideo.* doughily, gooily.

nirídɔ̀n (nirídɔ̀nɨ̀-) *v.* to be doughy, gooey.

nɩ̀tsɩ̀nɩ̀tsᵃ (nɩ̀tsɩ̀nɩ̀tsɨ̀-) *pl.* **nitsínítsɩ̀k**ᵃ. *n.* fatty nape of neck, fat scruff.

niyá ni *dem.* these areas or places.

Nòf (Nòfò-) *n.* name of a river and large ravine separating Kamion from Timu to the south.

nòìn (nòìnì-) *n.* discovery, find.

nɔkɛin *n.* two years ago, year before last. See also *kainɔ nótso*.

nɔkɛina ke *n.* three years ago.

nɔkɛina kenóó ke *n.* four years ago.

nòkᵒ (=nòò/nɔ̀ɔ́) *1 dem.* that (long ago). *2 rel.* that/which (long ago). *3 adv.* long ago.

nɔkɩnɔ́kɔ́n (nɔkɩnɔ́kɔ́nɨ̀-) *v.* to bend, flex.

nɔ̀kᵓ (nɔ̀kɔ̀) *ideo.* bendily, flexibly.

nɔkɔ́dɔ̀n (nɔkɔ́dɔ̀nɨ̀-) *v.* to be bendy, flexible. See also *lɛts'édɔ̀n* and *nakwádòn*.

nòò (nòò) *subordconn.* when ... (long ago). The main verb in the clause that follows this word takes the dummy pronoun.

nɔ́ɔ́ (nɔ́ɔ́) *dem.* here, in this direction. If this word is followed by a noun, the noun takes the genitive case.

nɔ́ɔ́ kíjᵒ *1 n.* below, down. *2 n.* south.

nɔ́ɔ́ kwarᵓ *1 n.* above, up. *2 n.* north.

nɔ́ɔ́ na *dem.* in this direction, over here.

nóódwáá (nóódoú-) *n.* today.

nɔɔ́s (nɔɔsá-) *1 n.* cleverness, intelligence, knowledge, shrewdness, wisdom. *2 n.* craftiness, cunning, guile. *3 n.* erudition, literacy.

nɔɔsáám (nɔɔsá-àmà-) *pl.* **nɔɔsáik**ᵃ. *n.* clever, intelligent, or wise person.

nɔɔsánétòn (nɔɔsánétònɨ̀-) *v.* to gain experience, grow wiser, learn.

nɔɔsanitetés (nɔɔsanitetésɨ́-) *v.* to instruct, teach, train. See also *itátámés*.

nɔɔsánón (nɔɔsánónɨ̀-) *1 v.* to be clever, intelligent, knowledgeable, shrewd, wise. *2 v.* to be crafty, cunning, guileful, sly. *3 v.* to be erudite, literate.

nɔ̀s (nɔ̀sà-) *n.* noise, racket, shouting.

nɔ̀sáàm (nɔ̀sà-àmà-) *pl.* **nɔsaik**ᵃ. *n.* loud person, shouter, yeller.

nɔsátón (nɔsátónɨ̀-) *v.* to make a racket, shout, yell.

nótsò (=nótsòò/nɔ́tsɔ̀ɔ́) *1 dem.* that (a while ago). *2 rel.* that/which (a while ago). *3 adv.* a while ago.

nótsò (nótsò) *subordconn.* when (a while ago). The main verb in the clause that follows this word takes the dummy pronoun.

nòtsᵓ (nòtsɔ̀) *ideo.* adhesively, stickily.

nótso kaɨnɔ sɨn *n.* last year.

nɔtsɔ́dɔ̀n (nɔtsɔ́dɔ̀nɨ̀-) *v.* to be adhesive, sticky.

nɔtsɔ́mɔ́n (nɔtsɔ́mɔ́nɨ̀-) *v.* to adhere, bond, stick.

nótsóò nòkᵒ *n.* day before yesterday.

ńtᵃ (ńtí-) *pro.* they/them/their. 'Their' and 'them' are formed by adding the appropriate case ending to this pronoun.

ńtá (ńtá) *adv.* not: do(es) not, will not. Used to negate statements in the present or future tense.

ńtá (ńtá) *pro.* where?

ńtɛ́ɛ́n (ńtɛ́-ɛ́nɨ́-) *pro.* which (one)?

ńtí (ńtía) 1 *adv.* how? 2 *adv.* like this!. 3 *interj.* like that! yeah! (an expression of approval).

ńtía jà *adv.* like that! (an expression of approval).

ńtía jɨ̀kⁱ *adv.* like that! (an expression of approval).

ńtíèn (ńtí-ènɨ̀-) *pro.* theirs.

ńtíén (ńtí-ɛ́nɨ́-) *pro.* which (ones)?

ńtínebitín (ńtí-nebitíní-) *n.* themselves. *Lit.* 'their bodies'.

ńtóodó (ńtóodó) *interj.* nah, no. See also *ńtóondó*.

ńtóódò *n.* when?

ńtóondó (ńtóondó) *interj.* nah, no. See also *ńtóodó*.

ntsᵃ (ntsí-) *pl.* ńtᵃ. *pro.* she/her, he/him/his, it/its. 'Him', 'his', and 'her' are formed by adding on the appropriate case ending.

ntsɛ́n (nts-ɛ́nɨ́-) *pro.* his, hers, its.

ntsícékᵃ (ntsí-cékì-) *pl.* ntsícɨ́kám. *n.* his wife.

ntsíéákwᵃ (ntsí-éákwà-) *n.* her husband.

ntsíémetá (ntsí-émetáà-) *pl.* ntsíémetátikwᵃ. *n.* his parent-in-law.

ntsíím (ntsí-ímà-) *pl.* ntsíwíkᵃ. 1 *n.* his/her/its child. 2 *n.* his niece or nephew (brother's child).

ntsílóbà (ntsí-lóbàà-) *n.* his/her grandchild.

ntsínámúí (ntsí-námúíì-) *pl.* ntsínámúatikwᵃ. 1 *n.* her sibling-in-law (brother's sibling). 2 *n.* his sister-in-law (brother's wife).

ntsínámúíìm (ntsí-námúí-ìmà-) *pl.* ntsínámúíwikᵃ. *n.* her niece or nephew (husband's sibling's child).

ntsínêbᵃ (ntsí-nébù-) *n.* himself, herself, itself. *Lit.* 'his/her/its body'.

ntsíɲótᵃ (ntsí-ɲótà-) 1 *n.* his/her foreign friend. 2 *n.* his/her sibling-in-law (child's spouse's parent).

ntsíɲótàìm (ntsí-ɲótà-ìmà-) *pl.* ntsíɲótawikᵃ. *n.* his/her niece or nephew-in-law (child's spouse's sibling).

ntsúgwám (nts-úgwámà-) *pl.* ntsúgwámatikwᵃ. 1 *n.* his sibling-in-law (wife's sibling). 2 *n.* his sibling-in-law (brother's wife's sibling). 3 *n.* his/her brother-in-law (sister's husband). 4 *n.* his/her sibling-in-law (sister's husband's sibling).

ntsúó ts'ɔɔ *pro.* it's likely, probably.

nts'áƙáàwᵃ (nts'áƙá-àwà-) *pl.* nts'áƙaawíkᵃ. *n.* defecation spot, place to defecate.

nts'áƙón (nts'áƙónì-) *v.* to crap, defecate, poop, take a shit.

nts'áƙóna sèrèikᵉ *v.* to leave a big mess behind, muck things up, spoil everything. *Lit.* 'to crap in the basin'.

nuélì (nuélìì-) *n.* Christmas service.

nùkᵘ (=nùkù) *1 dem.* those (from a while ago). *2 rel.* that/which a long time ago (plural).

nɨ́nɨ́tɔ̀n (nɨ́nɨ́tɔ̀nɨ̵-) *v.* to slink away/off (in a crouched posture).

nʉs (nʉsá-) *n.* male leopard. *Panthera pardus.*

nʉ̀s (nʉ̀sʉ̀) *ideo.* sleeping deeply.

Nʉsííkᵃ (Nʉsí-ícé-) *n.* traditional men's age-group with the leopard as its totem (#7 in the historical line). *Lit.* 'Leopard-Folk'.

nʉsɨ́dɔ̀n (nʉsɨ́dɔ̀nɨ̵-) *v.* to be deep asleep, sleeping deeply.

nutsés (nutsésí-) *v.* to mend with mud.

nútsù (=nútsùù) *1 dem.* those (a while ago). *2 rel.* that/which (a while ago, plural).

nʉʉnɨ́ (nʉʉnɨ́) *nurs.* yum-yum! (a nursery word for breastfeeding!.

ɲ

ɲáaɲún (ɲáaɲúnì-) *n.* dormouse. *Graphiurus sp.*

ɲábaŋgí (ɲábaŋgîi-) *n.* bhang, hemp.

ɲábʉlán (ɲábʉlánì-) *pl.* **ɲábʉlánɨkᵃ**. *n.* vest. Also pronounced as *ɲébʉlán*.

ɲáɓá (ɲáɓáà-) *pl.* **ɲáɓáɨkᵃ**. *n.* bar, saloon.

ɲáɓaarátᵃ (ɲáɓaarátɨ-) *pl.* **ɲáɓaarátɨkᵃ**. *n.* wrist knife. See also *iɓɔtᵃ*.

ɲáɓaasá (ɲáɓaasáà-) *pl.* **ɲáɓaasáɨkᵃ**. *n.* envelope.

ɲaɓáátᵃ (ɲaɓáátɨ-) *pl.* **ɲaɓáátɨkᵃ**. *n.* fortune, lot, luck.

ɲaɓaɓa (ɲaɓaɓaá-) *n.* crack skin on the feet (especially the heels).

ɲáɓáɓú (ɲáɓáɓúù-) *n.* small plant species with reddish stems and edible leaves.

ɲáɓáf (ɲáɓáfù-) *pl.* **ɲáɓáfɨkᵃ**. *n.* basin.

Ɲáɓáɨɓɔl (Ɲáɓáɨɓɔlɔ̀-) *pl.* **ɲáɓáɨɓɔlɨkᵃ**. *n.* Bible, Christian scripture.

ɲaɓáɨtᵃ (ɲaɓáɨtɨ̀-) *n.* predawn.

ɲaɓáɨtᵒ *n.* at dawn, before dawn.

ɲáɓákɛtᵃ (ɲáɓákɛtɛ̀-) *pl.* **ɲáɓákɛtɨkᵃ**. *n.* bucket, pail.

ɲaɓáláŋitᵃ (ɲaɓáláŋitɨ́-) *n.* soda ash, sodium carbonate. See also *ɲámakadí*.

ɲáɓáŋkᵃ (ɲáɓáŋkì-) *pl.* **ɲáɓáŋkíkᵃ**. *n.* bank.

ɲáɓáo (ɲáɓáoó-) *pl.* **ɲáɓáòìkᵃ**. 1 *n.* board, plank. 2 *n.* blackboard, chalkboard. 3 *n.* cage trap.

ɲáɓáòìkààm (ɲáɓáòìkà-àmà-) *pl.* **ɲáɓáoikaikᵃ**. *n.* carpenter, woodworker.

ɲáɓaraɓín (ɲáɓaraɓínì-) *pl.* **ɲáɓaraɓínɨkᵃ**. *n.* binoculars, field glasses.

ɲáɓárákɨs (ɲáɓárákɨsɨ̀-) *pl.* **ɲáɓárakɨsíkᵃ**. *n.* army barrack.

Ɲáɓarásà (Ɲáɓarásàà-) *pl.* **ɲáɓarásàɨkᵃ**. *n.* Monday. See also *Nákásíá kɔ̀nɨkᵋ*.

ɲáɓarasán (ɲáɓarasánɨ̀-) *pl.* **ɲáɓarasánɨkᵃ**. *n.* first and thickest layer of thatched grass.

ɲáɓarútᵃ (ɲáɓarútù-) *pl.* **ɲáɓarútɨkᵃ**. *n.* dynamite.

ɲáɓáruwa (ɲáɓáruwaá-) *pl.* **ɲáɓárùwàɨkᵃ**. *n.* epistle, letter, missive.

ɲáɓás (ɲáɓásɨ̀-) *pl.* **ɲáɓásɨkᵃ**. 1 *n.* bus. 2 *n.* campaign advertisements.

ɲáɓata (ɲáɓataá-) 1 *n.* duck, goose. 2 *n.* tree whose roots are dug up, crushed, and decocted for stomach ailments and eye problems; its roots are also stuck in paths thwart enemies; if left there, it prevents rain and causes problems.

Ɲáɓatsᵃ (Ɲáɓátsɨ̀-) *n.* personal name of a rebel leader who wanted to take power from the colonial British in northeastern Uganda.

ɲáɓol (ɲáɓolí-) *pl.* **ɲáɓòlikᵃ**. *n.* decorative garment consisting of circular plates of patterned beads covering the chest and upper back, connect by straps going over the shoulders; worn by girls and women only.

Ɲáɓoligúr (Ɲáɓoligúró-) *n.* a personal name.

ɲaɓolya (ɲaɓolyaá-) 1 *n.* game, play, sport. 2 *n.* dancing. See also *wáákᵃ*.

ɲáɓúkᵃ (ɲáɓúkù-) *pl.* **ɲáɓúkɨkᵃ**. *n.* book.

ɲáɓúka wáánᵋ *n.* prayer book.

ɲaɓʉra (ɲaɓʉraí-) *n.* corn, maize.

ɲaɓʉraídàkwᵃ (ɲaɓʉraí-dàkù-) *pl.* **ɲaɓʉraídakwitín**. *n.* corncob, maize cob.

ɲábúrás (ɲábúrásɨ̀-) *pl.* **ɲábúrásɨ̀k**ᵃ. *n.* toothbrush. See also *súkútésídàkw*ᵃ and *tsɨtsín*.

ɲabúrétᵃ (ɲabúrétɨ̀-) *pl.* **ɲabúrétɨ́k**ᵃ. *n.* sheath. See also *nakɨrɔ́r*.

ɲábús (ɲábúsì-) *pl.* **ɲábúsɨ̀k**ᵃ. *1 n.* parasitic plant species with red berries and that is used to treat aching knees. *2 n.* large boil.

ɲáɓwa (ɲáɓwaá-) *n.* scrubland.

ɲácáɗa (ɲácáɗaá-) *pl.* **ɲácáɗáɨ̀k**ᵃ. *n.* men's white leather anklet/bracelet made from the pelts of rabbits, reedbuck bellies, etc.

ɲácakwarátᵃ (ɲácakwarátɨ́-) *pl.* **ɲácakwarátɨ́k**ᵃ. *n.* fork. See also *ɲɔ́fɔ́k*ᵃ.

ɲaɗaɗés (ɲaɗaɗésí-) *v.* to collect rubbish (like uprooted weeds).

ɲáɗasɨtá (ɲáɗasɨtáá-) *pl.* **ɲáɗasɨtáɨ̀k**ᵃ. *n.* chalkboard eraser, duster.

ɲaɗés (ɲaɗésí-) *v.* to flatten, level.

ɲaɗésá ŋkákáᵉ *v.* to overeat, pig out. *Lit.* 'to flatten food'.

ɲaɗésúkotᵃ (ɲaɗésúkotí-) *v.* to flatten out, level out, raze.

ɲaɗiés (ɲaɗiesí-) *v.* to flatten or level repeatedly.

ɲáɗís (ɲáɗísì-) *pl.* **ɲáɗísɨ̀k**ᵃ. *n.* cloud.

ɲáɗís (ɲáɗísì-) *pl.* **ɲáɗísɨ̀k**ᵃ. *n.* account, narrative, story.

ɲáɗukán (ɲáɗukánɨ̀-) *pl.* **ɲáɗukánɨ̀k**ᵃ. *n.* kiosk, shop, store. See also *ɗukán*.

ɲáɗúle (ɲáɗúleé-) *pl.* **ɲáɗúlèɨ̀k**ᵃ. *n.* type of gun.

ɲáɗúyᵃ (ɲáɗúì-) *pl.* **ɲáɗúɨ̀k**ᵃ. *n.* vertical cave or cavern, volcano, volcanic vent.

ɲáfaɨ́n (ɲáfaɨ́nɨ̀-) *pl.* **ɲáfaɨ́nɨ̀k**ᵃ. *n.* fine, penalty.

ɲágaaɗi (ɲágaaɗií-) *pl.* **ɲágaaɗìk**ᵃ. *n.* balefire, bonfire.

ɲágaɗigáɗᵃ (ɲágaɗigáɗì-) *pl.* **ɲágaɗigáɗɨ̀k**ᵃ. *n.* wheelbarrow. See also *ɲakaari*.

ɲágám (ɲágámù-) *n.* glue, gum.

ɲágás (ɲágásɨ̀-) *n.* propane gas.

ɲájarán (ɲájaránɨ̀-) *pl.* **ɲájaránɨ̀k**ᵃ. *n.* sewing machine.

ɲájaará (ɲájaaráá-) *pl.* **ɲájaaráɨ̀k**ᵃ. *n.* button.

ɲájála (ɲájálaá-) *pl.* **ɲájálàɨ̀k**ᵃ. *n.* jail. See also *lɔjála*.

ɲájore (ɲájoreé-) *pl.* **ɲájòrèɨ̀k**ᵃ. *n.* crew, gang, group (organized for dancing, fighting, or hunting).

ɲákᵃ (ɲáà) *1 adv.* just. *2 adv.* why ... of course!. *3 adv.* in the hell, in the world.

ɲákááɗoŋotᵃ (ɲákááɗoŋotí-) *pl.* **ɲákááɗoŋotɨ́k**ᵃ. *n.* cowbell.

ɲákáal (ɲákáalɛ́-) *pl.* **ɲákáalɨ́k**ᵃ. *n.* camel.

ɲákaasó (ɲákaasóò-) *pl.* **ɲákaasóɨ̀k**ᵃ. *n.* robe.

ɲákábàtᵃ (ɲákábàtɨ̀-) *pl.* **ɲákábatɨ́k**ᵃ. *n.* cabinet, cupboard.

ɲakáɓétᵃ (ɲakáɓétɨ̀-) *pl.* **ɲakáɓétɨ̀k**ᵃ. *n.* spade.

ɲákáɓìc (ɲákáɓìcì-) *n.* cabbage.

ɲákaɓɨlá (ɲákaɓɨláá-) *pl.* **ɲákaɓɨláɨ̀k**ᵃ. *1 n.* ethnic group, people, tribe. *2 n.* kind, species, type, variety. See also *dìyw*ᵃ.

ɲákaɓír (ɲákaɓírì-) *n.* sorghum variety with red or white seeds and coarse hairs on the seed-heads like those of bullrush.

ɲákaɓɔɓwáátᵃ (ɲákaɓɔɓwáátá-) *pl.* **ɲákaɓɔɓwáátɨ́k**ᵃ. *n.* finger ring.

ɲákaɓurúr (ɲákaɓurúrù-) *pl.* ɲákaɓurúrùìk[a]. *1 n.* large tree species in whose branches beehives are put. *2 n.* large tin can.

ɲákáɗ[a] (ɲákáɗɨ-) *pl.* ɲákáɗɨk[a]. *1 n.* identity card. *2 n.* playing card.

ɲákáɗeŋo (ɲákáɗeŋoó-) *pl.* ɲákáɗèŋòìk[a]. *n.* women's loincloth decorated with metal ringlets all around the edges.

ɲákáɗɨk[a] (ɲákáɗɨkà-) *n.* playing cards.

ɲakaɨta (ɲakaɨtaá-) *n.* sweet potato.

ɲakaɨtákák[a] (ɲakaɨtá-kákà-) *n.* edible sweet potato leaves.

ɲákakar (ɲákakará-) *pl.* ɲákàkàrɨk[a]. *n.* chapeau, wide-brim hat.

ɲákakurá (ɲákakuráà-) *pl.* ɲákakuráìk[a]. *n.* hoe. Also called *ɲémɛlɛkɨ́*.

ɲákaláát[a] (ɲákaláátà-) *pl.* ɲákaláátɨk[a]. *n.* pan (for cooking, mining, etc.).

ɲákalám (ɲákalámù-) *pl.* ɲákalámɨk[a]. *n.* pen.

Nakalees (Nakaleesí-) *n.* a personal name.

ɲákaléńɗà (ɲákaléńɗàà-) *pl.* ɲákaléńɗàìk[a]. *n.* calendar.

ɲákálɨrikɨt[a] (ɲákálɨrikɨtɨ́-) *pl.* ɲákálɨrɨkɨtɨk[a]. *n.* stick with a metal nut affixed on the end.

ɲakalo (ɲakaloó-) *pl.* ɲakalóik[a]. *n.* alarm, alert.

ɲákamariɗúk[a] (ɲákamariɗúkù-) *pl.* ɲákamariɗúkùìk[a]. *n.* heavy cotton blanket worn as clothing.

ɲákamarɨkán (ɲákamarɨkánɨ̀-) *pl.* ɲákamarɨkánɨk[a]. *n.* women's lightweight cotton shawl.

ɲákamɓí (ɲákamɓíì-) *pl.* ɲákamɓíik[a]. *n.* bivouac, camp, encampment.

ɲákamɔ́ŋɔ (ɲákamɔ́ŋɔɔ́-) *n.* pumpkin-like vine species with white milk-sap and that grows in ravines and riverbeds down the escarpment and whose fruits and leaves are eaten raw. *Cynachium sp.*

Nákamʉ (Nákamʉʉ́-) *n.* personal name of the Ik Catholic priest of the *Sikètìà* clan who first brought Christianity to the Ik.

ɲákamúka (ɲákamúkaá-) *n.* vine whose yellow roots are decocted and drunk or given rectally as a treatment for stomach ailments.

ɲákamʉlára (ɲákamʉláraá-) *pl.* ɲákamʉláràìk[a]. *n.* red pepper.

ɲákámus (ɲákámusí-) *n.* pitch darkness (i.e. no moon, thick clouds).

ɲákáńsɔ̀là (ɲákáńsɔ̀làà-) *pl.* ɲákáńsɔ̀làìk[a]. *n.* councillor.

ɲákáparat[a] (ɲákáparatá-) *pl.* ɲákáparatɨk[a]. *n.* metal nose-ring and mouth cover.

ɲákápɨrit[a] (ɲákápɨrɨtɨ́-) *pl.* ɲákápɨritɨk[a]. *n.* modern metallic whistle.

ɲákarám (ɲákarámù-) *n.* holiday, time off, vacation.

ɲakárámit[a] (ɲakárámitɨ́-) *pl.* ŋikárám. *n.* do-nothing, idler, lazy bum, loafer, slacker.

ɲákárat[a] (ɲákáratɨ́-) *n.* fig tree whose fruits are eaten raw and whose wood is carved into stools and other items; also a favorite place to put beehives. *Ficus sp.*

ɲákaratás (ɲákaratásɨ̀-) *pl.* ɲákaratásɨk[a]. *1 n.* paper. *2 n.* document.

ɲákási (ɲákásií-) *pl.* ɲákásiicík[a]. *n.* employment, job, task, work.

Nákásiá àɗɨk[e] *n.* Wednesday. *Lit.* 'work(day) being three'.

Ɲákásíá kɔ̀nɨ̀kᵋ *n.* Monday. *Lit.* 'work(day) being one'. See also *Nábarásà*.

Ɲákásíá lèɓètsìkᵉ *n.* Tuesday. *Lit.* 'work(day) being two'.

Ɲákásíá ts'agúsíkᵉ *n.* Thursday. *Lit.* 'work(day) being four'.

Ɲákásíá tùdìkᵉ *n.* Friday. *Lit.* 'work(day) being five'.

ɲákásìàm (ɲákásì-àmà-) *pl.* **ɲákásiikᵃ**. *n.* employee, worker.

ɲákásìèdᵃ (ɲákásìèdè-) *n.* function, purpose, use.

ɲákatékísìmù (ɲákatékísìmùù-) *n.* catechism.

ɲákátɨrɨ́ɓa (ɲákátɨrɨ́ɓaá-) *n.* tree species whose sweet fruits are eaten raw and whose wood is used to make planks for doors.

ɲákáúńtì (ɲákáúńtìì-) *pl.* **ɲákáúńtìikᵃ**. *n.* county: governmental administrative unit below district and above subcounty. The Ik were granted their own county in 2015, which meant they also received their first Member of Parliament. Lokwang Hillary was elected the first Ik MP in February 2016. This was a major step toward counteracting political marginalization.

ɲakawᵃ (ɲakaʉ́-) *1 n.* bow (weapon). *2 n.* fiddle, violin.

ɲákáwa (ɲákáwaá-) *n.* coffee.

Ɲákáyᵃ (Ɲákáɨ-) *n.* a personal name.

ɲákɨláƙᵃ (ɲákɨláƙà-) *pl.* **ɲákɨláƙɨkᵃ**. *1 n.* bra, brassiere. *2 n.* traditional leather brassiere worn for dancing.

ɲákitamɓára (ɲákitamɓáraá-) *pl.* **ɲákitamɓáràikᵃ**. *n.* handkerchief.

ɲákol (ɲákolí-) *pl.* **ɲákòlìkᵃ**. *1 n.* twisted nylon string. *2 n.* nylon neck snare.

ɲákopiyá (ɲákopiyáà-) *pl.* **ɲákopiyáìkᵃ**. *n.* cap, hat.

Ɲakujᵃ (Ɲakují-) *pl.* **ɲakujíkᵃ**. *1 n.* god, God. The Christian word for 'God'; see *didigwarí* for the traditional name of the Creator. *2 interj.* oh my God! (an expression of strong emotion).

ɲakújá (ɲakújáà-) *pl.* **ɲakújáìkᵃ**. *n.* spring where water seeps out of sand (e.g. in a riverbed).

ɲakujíám (ɲakují-ámà-) *pl.* **ɲakujííkᵃ**. *n.* devout, godly person.

ɲakujíhò (ɲakují-hòò-) *pl.* **ɲakujíhoikᵃ**. *n.* church, house of worship. *Lit.* 'God-house'.

ɲakujíícíkᵃ (ɲakují-ícíká-) *1 n.* gods. *2 n.* animism.

ɲakujíícíkáàm (ɲakují-ícíká-àmà-) *pl.* **ɲakujíícíkáikᵃ**. *1 n.* animist. *2 n.* oracle, prophet, seer.

ɲakujímɛ́n (ɲakují-mɛ́nà-) *n.* religious matters, theology.

ɲakujínánès (ɲakujínánèsì-) *n.* divinity, godhood.

Ɲakujíwáán (Ɲakují-wáánà-) *n.* Lord's Prayer: Matthew 6:9-13.

ɲakwaanja (ɲakwaanjaá-) *pl.* **ɲakwáánjàikᵃ**. *1 n.* ball field, field, soccer pitch. *2 n.* airfield, airport, airstrip.

ɲákwác (ɲákwácɨ-) *pl.* **ɲákwácɨkᵃ**. *n.* safety pin.

Ɲakwácᵃ (Ɲakwácì-) *n.* name of a rock hill.

ɲákwálikwal (ɲákwálɨkwalɨ́-) *pl.* **ɲákwálɨkwàlɨkᵃ**. *n.* abdominal muscle, ab.

ɲákwáya (ɲákwáyaá-) *pl.* **ɲákwáyàikᵃ**. *n.* choir, chorus.

ɲaƙaari (ɲaƙaarií-) *pl.* **ɲaƙáárìikᵃ**. *n.* wheelbarrow. See also *ɲágadɨgádᵃ*.

ɲaƙóƙóŋ (ɲaƙóƙóŋù-) *n.* strength.

ɲakwárétᵃ (ɲakwárétɛ̀-) pl. ɲakwárétíkᵃ. n. rake.

ɲàl (ɲàlì) ideo. squashily, squishily.

ɲálaajáítᵃ (ɲálaajáítɨ̀-) n. tall grass species used for thatching houses. Gramineae sp.

ɲáláɗa (ɲáláɗaá-) pl. ɲáláɗàìkᵃ. n. ladder.

ɲálaín (ɲálaínì-) pl. ɲálaínìkᵃ. 1 n. line. 2 n. town, trading center. See also táùn.

ɲáláínìkààm (ɲáláínìkà-àmà-) pl. ɲáláínikaikᵃ. n. town-dweller, urbanite.

ɲalakas (ɲalakasɨ́-) n. happiness.

ɲalakas (ɲalakasɨ́-) n. vine species that is wrapped around other tree species in the sacred tree monument of agricultural ceremonies. Securinega virosa.

ɲalakutsᵃ (ɲalakutsɨ́-) n. ceremonial beer prepared by a newly married woman for the elders of her husband's clan.

ɲálaƙamááìtìɔ̀kᵃ (ɲálaƙamááìtì-ɔ̀kà-) pl. ɲálaƙamááitiɔkitín. n. clavicle, collarbone.

ɲálaƙamáítᵃ (ɲálaƙamáítì-) pl. ɲálaƙamáítíkᵃ. n. cowl muscle, trapezius.

ɲalamatsar (ɲalamatsarɨ́-) pl. ɲalámátsàrɨkᵃ. n. perineal muscle: between the anus and genitalia. See also ɲekiɗoɲitᵃ.

ɲalamétòn (ɲalamétònì-) v. to collapse, crumble, fall down (e.g. plaster from a wall). See also lajámétòn and taɲálóòn.

ɲalamónuƙotᵃ (ɲalamónuƙotí-) v. to collapse, crumble, fall down (e.g. plaster from a wall).

ɲálamorú (ɲálamorúù-) pl. ɲálamorúìkᵃ. 1 n. plant species. 2 n. flute. 3 n. drinking straw.

Nálámʉɲɛna (Nálámʉɲɛnaá-) n. name of a place with colored soil.

ɲálámʉɲɛna (ɲálámʉɲɛnaá-) n. colored soil (black, red, yellow, etc.).

ɲálán (ɲálánɨ̀-) pl. ɲálánɨ̀kᵃ. n. right hindleg: portion of meat reserved for elders consisting of the whole right leg including the gluteus medius.

Nálem (Nálemú-) n. a personal name.

ɲálem (ɲálemú-) pl. ɲálèmìkᵃ. n. crest, crown (e.g. of a rooster).

ɲaléso (ɲálésoó-) pl. ɲálésòikᵃ. n. light cloak or shawl.

ɲalídòn (ɲalídònì-) v. to be squashy, squishy (easily compressible).

ɲalɨ́ɲalɨ́ (ɲalɨ́ɲalɨ̀-) n. assortment, melange, mixture, variety.

ɲalúkétᵃ (ɲalúkétɛ̀-) pl. ɲalúkétíkᵃ. n. round coppice or thicket.

ɲálukutúju (ɲálukutújuú-) n. serval. Felis serval.

ɲámá (ɲámáà-) n. grass species used for thatching. Gramineae sp.

ɲámaamɓátᵃ (ɲámaamɓátɨ̀-) pl. ɲámaamɓátɨ̀kᵃ. n. metal roofing sheet.

ɲamaɗaŋ (ɲamaɗaɲɨ́-) n. tick.

ɲamaɗaŋɨ́kú (ɲamaɗaɲɨ́-kúa-) n. tick grass: grass species used to cover termite traps. Eragrostis superba.

ɲámakaɗá (ɲámakaɗáà-) pl. ɲámakaɗáikᵃ. n. AK-47 assault rifle.

ɲámakaɗí (ɲámakaɗìì-) n. soda ash, sodium carbonate. See also ɲaɓáláɲitᵃ.

ɲamakaje (ɲamakajeé-) n. sexually-transmitted disease (possibly gonorrhea or syphills).

ɲámakás (ɲámakásɨ̀-) pl. ɲámakásɨ̀kᵃ. n. scissors.

ɲámakáyᵃ (ɲámakáɨ̀-) n. charcoal.

ɲámákɛ̀tᵃ (ɲámákɛ̀tɛ̀-) pl. ɲámákɛtɨ́kᵃ. n. market. See dzígwààwᵃ.

ɲámakukᵃ (ɲámakukú-) pl. ɲámàkùkɨ̀kᵃ. n. two-legged stool.

ɲámáƙᵃ (ɲámáƙɨ-) pl. ɲámáƙɨkᵃ. n. mug, mugful.

ɲámal (ɲámalɨ́-) pl. ɲámàlɨ̀kᵃ. 1 n. arrow or bullet. 2 n. boy.

ɲamáláitᵃ (ɲamáláitɨ́-) pl. ŋimálá. n. prostitute.

ɲámáli (ɲámálií-) n. possessions, property, wealth.

ɲámalɨákᵃ (ɲámalɨ́-ákà-) pl. ɲámalikaakitɨ́n. n. arrow hole, bullet hole.

ɲámalɨ́dàkwᵃ (ɲámalɨ́-dàkù-) pl. ɲámalikadakwitín. n. arrow shaft.

ɲamalil (ɲamalilí-) n. small riverside tree with blackish bark and leaves and whose stems are used to build granaries. Saba comorensis.

ɲámanikór (ɲámanikóɾì-) pl. ɲámanikórìkᵃ. n. farmland, large field including many gardens.

ɲámápᵃ (ɲámápɨ̀-) pl. ɲámápɨ̀kᵃ. n. map.

ɲámára (ɲámáraá-) n. arithmetic, math, mathematics.

ɲámaritóítᵃ (ɲámaritóítì-) pl. ɲámaritóítìkᵃ. 1 n. gold anklet or bracelet. 2 n. golden earring.

ɲámasín (ɲámasínì-) pl. ɲámasínìkᵃ. 1 n. machine. 2 n. grinding mill.

ɲámátᵃ (ɲámátɨ-) pl. ɲámátɨkᵃ. n. mat.

ɲamatiɗa (ɲamatiɗaá-) pl. ɲamátíɗàikᵃ. n. homemade gun.

ɲámátsar (ɲámátsarɨ́-) pl. ɲámátsarɨ́kᵃ. n. brand, mark, sign (e.g. cattle brands or clan emblems).

ɲamiili (ɲamiilií-) pl. ɲamíílìkᵃ. n. bicycle, bike.

ɲamiilia ŋwáxɔ̀nɨ̀àmà̀ᵉ n. wheelchair. Lit. 'bicycle of a lame person'.

ɲámiliɔŋɔ́r (ɲámiliɔŋɔ́rɨ-) n. gecko species?

ɲámisípᵃ (ɲámisípù-) pl. ɲámisípɨkᵃ. n. belt.

ɲámoɗᵃ (ɲámoɗó-) pl. ɲámòɗikᵃ. n. thigh meat.

ɲámucúŋƙà (ɲámucúŋƙàà-) pl. ɲámucúŋƙàikᵃ. n. citrus fruit: lemon or orange.

ɲanákɛ́tᵃ (ɲanákɛ́tɨ-) pl. ɲanákɛ́tɨkᵃ. n. age-group, age-set: traditional grouping of men according to generation and initiation.

ɲánam (ɲánamú-) pl. ɲánàmɨ̀kᵃ. n. lake, ocean, sea.

ɲánambá (ɲánambáà-) pl. ɲánambáikᵃ. n. digit, number.

ɲánɨbàkᵃ (ɲánɨbàkɨ-) pl. ɲánɨbakɨ́kᵃ. n. handbag, purse.

ɲánɨnɔ́ (ɲánɨnɔ́ɔ̀-) pl. ɲánɨnɔ́ɨkᵃ. n. leather whip. Traditionally made from twisted buffalo or rhino hide.

ɲanúpítᵃ (ɲanúpítɨ-) n. belief, faith.

ɲaɲɛnijɛ́n (ɲaɲɛni-jɛ́nɨ-) n. grass species with little round seed-pods that is picked from rocky outcroppings and used to make brooms.

ɲaŋáánètòn (ɲaŋáánètònì-) 1 v. to be yellow. 2 v. to be jaundice.

ɲaŋálómòn (ɲaŋálómònì-) v. to be gappy (in teeth), have a tooth gap.

ɲaŋalúr (ɲaŋalúrá-) pl. ɲaŋalúrɨ́kᵃ. n. kidney.

ɲaŋárútɛ̀ (ɲaŋárútɛ̀ɛ̀-) pl. ɲaŋárútɛ̀ɨkᵃ. n. unripe maize (with small kernels). See also ígùm and káruɓú.

Ɲaŋasir (Ɲaŋasirí-) n. a personal name.

ɲaŋés (ɲaŋésí-) v. to avenge, get payback, retaliate, revenge.

ɲaŋésúkotᵃ (ɲaŋésúkotí-) v. to avenge, get payback, retaliate, revenge.

ɲaŋólé (ɲaŋóléè-) pl. ɲaŋóléìkᵃ. n. horse.

Naŋorokᵃ (Naŋorokú-) n. a personal name.

ɲaŋu (ɲaŋuú-) pl. ɲaŋúíkᵃ. n. monster, mythical beast.

ɲápaalí (ɲápaalíi-) pl. ɲápaalíikᵃ. n. small plastic bag or sack.

ɲapaaru (ɲapaaruú-) pl. ɲapáárùikᵃ. n. catapult, sling, slingshot (made of a leather patch with string attached to each side).

ɲápaɗɛr (ɲápaɗɛrɨ́-) pl. ɲápàɗɛ̀rɨ̀kᵃ. n. big, round, inedible gourd used as a basin or bottle.

ɲápaín (ɲápaínì-) pl. ɲápaínìkᵃ. n. fine for an illegal marriage.

ɲápaɨpáyᵃ (ɲápaɨpáɨ-) pl. ɲápaɨpáɨ̀kᵃ. n. papaya, pawpaw. Carica papaya.

ɲapala (ɲapalaá-) n. bright red soil.

ɲápalís (ɲápalísì-) pl. ɲápalísìkᵃ. 1 n. cushion, mattress. 2 n. cushion.

ɲápáma (ɲápámaá-) n. cotton.

ɲápaŋká (ɲápaŋkáà-) pl. ɲápaŋkáìkᵃ. n. machete, panga.

ɲápaŋkaláɨ́tᵃ (ɲápaŋkaláɨ́tɨ̀-) pl. ɲápaŋkaláítɨ̀kᵃ. n. type of short bolt-action rifle.

ɲápár (ɲápárɨ-) pl. ɲápárɨ̀kᵃ. n. flat cover or lid (made from metal, reeds, or anything).

ɲápárìx (ɲápárìxì-) pl. ɲápárixíkᵃ. n. parish: governmental administrative unit below the subcounty and above the ward.

ɲápatᵃ (ɲápatɨ́-) n. plant species with no known uses. Thunbergia alata.

ɲápáti (ɲápátií-) pl. ɲápátììkᵃ. n. celebration, party, shindig.

ɲapatsole (ɲapatsoleé-) pl. ɲapátsóleìkᵃ. n. bare patch or spot (e.g. where no grass or hair is growing).

ɲapáyál (ɲapáyálɨ-) pl. ɲapáyálɨkᵃ. n. hard, bare patch of ground where no grass grows.

ɲapéɗór (ɲapéɗórì-) n. ability, capability, power.

ɲàpèì (ɲàpèì) 1 prep. from. 2 subordconn. from the time when, since. A noun following this word takes the ablative case. See also nàpèì.

ɲapéryɛ́tᵃ (ɲapéryɛ́tɨ-) pl. ɲapéryɛ́tɨ́kᵃ. n. uterus, womb. See also epúáwᵃ.

ɲapíɗímòm (ɲapíɗímònì-) v. to be powdery soft. See also lyamádòn.

ɲápís (ɲápísì-) pl. ɲápísìkᵃ. n. office.

ɲápukán (ɲápukánɨ́-) pl. ɲápukánɨ́kᵃ. n. administration, government, regime.

ɲápukánɨ̀ám (ɲápukánɨ́-àmà-) pl. ɲápukáníikᵃ. n. government employee.

ɲapʉɔ́tᵃ (ɲapʉɔ́tí-) pl. ɲapʉɔ́tíkᵃ. n. offering of a slaughtered animal.

ɲáráɓa (ɲáráɓaá-) pl. ɲáráɓaìkᵃ. n. eraser, rubber.

ɲárakɔ́ákwᵃ (ɲárakɔ́-ákɔ̀-) n. wild, wilderness.

ɲárakwᵃ (ɲárakɔ́-) n. wild, wilderness. See also ɲékítɛla.

ɲàràm (ɲàràmà-) pl. ɲèr. 1 n. daughter, girl, maiden, young woman (unmarried). 2 n. girlfriend.

ɲarama na ɓéts'ᵃ n. virgin. Lit. 'girl who is white'.

ɲarama na tɨ́liwᵃ n. virgin. Lit. 'girl who is pure'.

ɲàràmàìm (ɲàràmà-ìmà-) *pl.* ɲerawik[a]. *n.* little girl.

Nárámìram (Nárámìramʉ́-) *n.* Saturday.

ɲáraŋgí (ɲáraŋgîì-) *n.* paint, pigment.

ɲárará (ɲáraráà-) *pl.* ɲáraráìk[a]. *n.* cheetah. *Acinonyx jubatus.*

ɲárásɨ́ám (ɲárásɨ́-ámà-) *pl.* ɲárásîik[a]. *n.* miscreant, pervert, reprobate.

ɲarátát[a] (ɲarátátà-) *pl.* ɲarátátɨ́k[a]. *n.* wall of a building.

ɲárém (ɲárémò-) *n.* danger, insecurity, unrest.

ɲaréréŋ (ɲaréréŋì-) *n.* good fortune or luck.

ɲarúkʉ́m (ɲarúkʉ́mʉ̀-) *1 n.* mucus, phlegm, snot; sputum. *2 n.* cold, flu. See also *dɔ́kɔ́n.*

ɲárʉ́má (ɲárʉ́máà-) *pl.* ɲárʉ́máɨ̀k[a]. *n.* injury.

ɲárʉpɛpɛ́ (ɲárʉpɛpɛ́ɛ̀-) *pl.* ɲárʉpɛpɛ́ɨ̀k[a]. *n.* wooden voice-amplifying horn (3-4 ft. long, open on each end, mouthpiece in the middle, crack between two halves sealed by a leather wrap).

ɲásaaj[a] (ɲásaajɨ́-) *pl.* ɲásààjɨ̀k[a]. *n.* donkey saddle.

ɲásaaní (ɲásaanîì-) *pl.* ɲásaanîik[a]. *n.* plate, saucer.

ɲásáat[a] (ɲásáatɨ́-) *pl.* ɲásáàtɨ̀k[a]. *1 n.* hour. *2 n.* time. *3 n.* wristwatch.

ɲásáatɨ́á kɔ̀nɨ̀k[e] *n.* seven o'clock (7:00). *Lit.* 'the hour being one'.

ɲásáatikaa aɗátìk[e] *n.* nine o'clock (9:00). *Lit.* 'the hours being three'.

ɲásáatikaa lɛɓetsátìk[e] *n.* eight o'clock (8:00). *Lit.* 'the hours being two'.

ɲásáatikaa mɨtátie toomín *n.* four o'clock (4:00). *Lit.* 'the hours being ten'.

ɲásáatikaa mɨtátie toomíní ńdà kèɗɨ̀ kɔ̀n *n.* five o'clock (5:00). *Lit.* 'the hours being ten and one'.

ɲásáatikaa mɨtátie toomíní ńda kiɗi lɛ́ɓèts[e] *n.* six o'clock (6:00). *Lit.* 'the hours being ten and two'.

ɲásáatikaa ts'agúsátìk[e] *n.* ten o'clock (10:00). *Lit.* 'the hours being four'.

ɲásáatikaa tudátie ńdà kèɗɨ̀ kɔ̀n *n.* twelve o'clock (12:00). *Lit.* 'the hours being five and one'.

ɲásáatikaa tudátie ńdà kìɗì àɗ[e] *n.* two o'clock (2:00). *Lit.* 'the hours being five and three'.

ɲásáatikaa tudátie ńda kiɗi lɛ́ɓèts[e] *n.* one o'clock (1:00). *Lit.* 'the hours being five and two'.

ɲásáatikaa tudátie ńda kiɗi ts'agús *n.* three o'clock (3:00). *Lit.* 'the hours being five and four'.

ɲásáatikaa tudátìk[e] *n.* eleven o'clock (11:00). *Lit.* 'the hours being five'.

ɲásáàtɔ̀ kɔ̀n *n.* at once, at the same time. *Lit.* 'by one time'.

Násaɓét[a] (Násaɓétì-) *n.* Sunday.

ɲásaɓét[a] (ɲásaɓétì-) *pl.* ɲásaɓétik[a]. *n.* week.

ɲásáɓúkáúntì (ɲásáɓúkáúntìì-) *pl.* ɲásáɓúkáúntìɨ̀k[a]. *n.* subcounty: governmental administrative unit below county and above parish.

ɲásaɓuní (ɲásaɓunîì-) *n.* detergent, soap.

ɲásáɓúpárìx (ɲásáɓúpárìxì-) *pl.* ɲásáɓúparixík[a]. *n.* subparish: governmental administrative unit below the parish and above the ward.

ɲásaɗukú (ɲásaɗukúì-) *pl.* ɲásaɗukúìk[a]. *n.* box, storage chest.

ɲásakaraméntù (ɲásakaraméntùù-) *n.* Catholic sacrament.

ɲasal (ɲasalɨ́-) *n.* small plant species with bluish leaves which when ground and mixed with oil are applied to heads to counteract lice. *Cassia hildebrandtii.*

ɲásalátà (ɲásalátàà-) *n.* spinach.

ɲásánɗɔl (ɲásánɗɔ̀lɔ̀-) *pl.* ɲásánɗɔlɨ́kᵃ. *n.* rubber sandal.

ɲásáníɟìn (ɲásáníɟìnì-) *n.* Sunny Gin: a Ugandan brand of cheap gin.

ɲásaŋáɲo (ɲásaŋáɲoó-) *n.* bee species that builds nests in flat ground.

ɲásápari (ɲásáparií-) *pl.* ɲásápàrììkᵃ. *1 n.* round, time. *2 n.* expedition, journey, trip.

ɲásáti (ɲásátií-) *pl.* ɲásátììkᵃ. *n.* shirt.

ɲasécón (ɲasécónì-) *pl.* ɲasécónikᵃ. *n.* error, mistake, sin. See also *ɲɔ́mɔkɔsá*.

ɲásím (ɲásímù-) *pl.* ɲásímìkᵃ. *n.* mobile phone.

ɲásipiryá (ɲásipiryáà-) *pl.* ɲásipiryáìkᵃ. *n.* metal cooking pan or pot, saucepan. See also *ɲésipiryá*.

ɲásírìàm (ɲásírì-àmà-) *pl.* ɲásíriikᵃ. *n.* fine dresser, fashionista.

ɲátaayá (ɲátaayáà-) *pl.* ɲátaayáìkᵃ. *n.* kerosene lantern.

ɲatal (ɲatalɨ́-) *pl.* ɲatálɨ́kᵃ. *1 n.* custom, tradition. *2 n.* taboo, prohibition.

ɲátám (ɲátámù-) *pl.* ɲátámìkᵃ. *n.* school term, semester.

ɲátamɨtám (ɲátamɨtámù-) *pl.* ɲátamɨtámìkᵃ. *n.* candy, sweet.

ɲátamóómìtà (ɲátamóómìtàà-) *pl.* ɲátamóómìtàìkᵃ. *n.* thermometer.

ɲátatsᵃ (ɲátatsɨ́-) *pl.* ɲátátsɨ̀kᵃ. *n.* spike trap.

ɲátauló (ɲátaulóò-) *pl.* ɲátaulóìkᵃ. *n.* towel.

ɲátáyᵃ (ɲátáì-) *pl.* ɲátáìkᵃ. *n.* necktie, tie.

ɲátóè (ɲátóè-) *pl.* ɲátóìkᵃ. *n.* beaded belt worn by females.

ɲatsʉʉma (ɲatsʉʉmaá-) *pl.* ɲatsʉ́ʉ́màìkᵃ. *n.* borehole.

ɲatsʉʉmááɾɨ (ɲatsʉʉmá-áɾɨ́ɛ́-) *pl.* ɲatsʉʉmááɾɨ́ɨ́kᵃ. *n.* borehole pipe. Lit. 'borehole-intestine'.

ɲatsʉʉmácúé (ɲatsʉʉmá-cúè-) *n.* borehole water.

ɲatsʉʉmádɛ̀ (ɲatsʉʉmá-dɛ̀à-) *n.* borehole footing. Lit. 'borehole-foot'.

ɲatsʉʉmáhò (ɲatsʉʉmá-hòò-) *pl.* ɲatsʉ́ʉ́maɨkahoíkᵃ. *n.* borehole housing or shaft.

ɲatsʉʉmákwɛ́tᵃ (ɲatsʉʉmá-kwɛ́tà-) *pl.* ɲatsʉ́ʉ́maɨkakwɛtɨ́kᵃ. *n.* borehole handle. Lit. 'borehole-arm'.

ɲatsʉʉmánêb^a (ɲatsʉʉmá-nébù-) *pl.* ɲatsʉ́ʉ́maɨkanébitín. *n.* borehole casing. Lit. 'borehole-body'.

ɲátúɗu (ɲátúɗuú-) *pl.* ɲátúɗuìkᵃ. *n.* big oblong gourd used as a general container.

ɲatúkítᵃ (ɲatúkítì-) *pl.* ɲatúkítíkᵃ. *n.* heap, mound, pile. See also *kìtsᵃ*.

ɲatúkɔ́tᵃ (ɲatúkɔ́tɔ̀-) *pl.* ɲatúkɔ́tíkᵃ. *n.* assembly, congregation, gathering.

ɲátúm (ɲátúmù-) *pl.* ɲátúmìkᵃ. *n.* spear with long, flat head (18-24 inches long).

ɲáturugéyᵃ (ɲáturugéì-) *pl.* ɲáturugéìkᵃ. *n.* type of large-bore, five-round elephant gun.

ɲàʉ (ɲàʉ̀) *ideo.* crystallizedly.

ɲaʉ́dɔn (ɲaʉ́dɔ̀nì-) *v.* to be crystallized, effloresced.

ɲaʉ́dɔnʉkɔtᵃ (ɲaʉ́dɔnʉkɔtɨ́-) *v.* to crystallize, effloresce.

ɲáwaawá (ɲáwaawáà-) *pl.* ɲáwaawáìkᵃ. *n.* large gunny sack. See also *lomóŋin*.

ɲáwáɗᵃ (ɲáwáɗɨ-) *pl.* ɲáwáɗɨkᵃ. *n.* ward: governmental administrative unit above the village and below the subparish.

ɲáwáro (ɲáwároó-) *pl.* ɲáwáròìkᵃ. *n.* cloak, shawl. Called a 'sheet' in Karamojan English.

ɲáwáróófúr (ɲáwáró-ófúrí-) *n.* bag made from the fabric of a cloak.

ɲáwáya (ɲáwáyaá-) *pl.* ɲáwáyàɨkᵃ. *1 n.* wire. *2 n.* wire neck snare.

ɲ̀cìcèkᵃ (ɲ̀cì-cèkì-) *n.* my wife.

ɲ̀cìèàkwᵃ (ɲ̀cì-èàkwà-) *n.* my husband.

ɲ̀ciemetá (ɲ̀ci-emetáà-) *pl.* ɲ̀ciemetátíkwᵃ. *n.* my parent-in-law (of men).

ɲ̀cìim (ɲ̀cì-ìmà-) *pl.* ɲ̀ciwikᵃ. *1 n.* my child. *2 n.* my niece of nephew (brother's child).

ɲ̀cilobá (ɲ̀ci-lobáà-) *n.* my grandchild.

ɲ̀cinamúí (ɲ̀ci-namúíì-) *pl.* ɲ̀cinamúátikwᵃ. *1 n.* my sibling-in-law (husband's sibling). *2 n.* my sister-in-law (brother's wife).

ɲ̀cinamúíìm (ɲ̀ci-namúí-ìmà-) *pl.* ɲ̀cinamúíwikᵃ. *n.* my niece or nephew (husband's sibling's child).

ɲ̀cinèbᵃ (ɲ̀cì-nèbù-) *n.* myself. *Lit.* 'my body'.

ɲ̀ciɲòtᵃ (ɲ̀cì-ɲòtà-) *pl.* ɲ̀ciɲotikwᵃ. *1 n.* my foreign friend. *2 n.* my in-law (my child's spouse's parent).

ɲ̀cìɲòtàìm (ɲ̀cì-ɲòtà-ìmà-) *pl.* ɲ̀ciɲotawikᵃ. *n.* my niece or nephew-in-law (child's spouse's sibling).

ɲ̀citaŋá (ɲ̀ci-taŋáɨ-) *pl.* ɲ̀citaŋáɨkɨn. *n.* my co-: cohort, colleague, etc.

ɲ̀cugwám (ɲ̀c-ugwámá-) *pl.* ɲ̀cugwámátikwᵃ. *1 n.* my sibling-in-law (my wife's sibling, my brother's wife's sibling, my sister's husband). *2 n.* my sister's husband's sibling).

ɲébenɗéra (ɲébenɗéraá-) *pl.* ɲébenɗéràìkᵃ. *n.* flag.

ɲébeŋgí (ɲébeŋgíì-) *pl.* ɲébeŋgíìkᵃ. *n.* safe, safe-box.

ɲébʉlán (ɲébʉláni-) *pl.* ɲébʉlánɨkᵃ. *n.* vest. Also pronounced as *ɲábʉlán*.

ɲébákètᵃ (ɲébákètè-) *pl.* ɲébákɛtɨkᵃ. *n.* bucket, pail. See also *ɲábákètᵃ*.

ɲébatál (ɲébatálì-) *pl.* ɲébatálìkᵃ. *n.* battalion.

ɲébéбutᵃ (ɲébéбutí-) *n.* Defassa's waterbuck. *Kobus ellipsiprymnus defassa*.

ɲɛ́бɛ́kᵃ (ɲɛ́бɛ́kɨ-) *pl.* ɲɛ́бɛ́kɨkᵃ. *n.* bag.

ɲɛ́бɛ́ɲc (ɲɛ́бɛ́ɲcɨ-) *pl.* ɲɛ́бɛɲcɨ́kᵃ. *n.* bench.

ɲɛбɛ́s (ɲɛбɛ́sɨ-) *1 v.* to chew on, ruminate. *2 v.* to contemplate, mull over, ponder, think on.

ɲɛбɛ́sá tódàᵉ *v.* to grumble to oneself. *Lit.* 'to chew on speech'.

ɲébésèn (ɲébésènì-) *pl.* ɲébésenìkᵃ. *n.* basin.

ɲébeterí (ɲébeteríì-) *pl.* ɲébètèrìkᵃ. *n.* battery.

ɲébéyᵃ (ɲébéì-) *pl.* ɲébéìkᵃ. *n.* cost, expense, price.

ɲébía (ɲébíaá-) *pl.* ɲébíaìkᵃ. *n.* bottled beer.

ɲɛбɨás (ɲɛбɨásɨ-) *n.* Irish or white potato(es), spud.

ɲébíliòn (ɲébíliònì-) *pl.* ɲébílioníkᵃ. *n.* billion.

ɲébiró (ɲébiróò-) *pl.* ɲébiróìkᵃ. *n.* stick with a round head. Well-known as a 'rungu' in Swahili.

ɲébɨsár (ɲébɨsárɨ-) *n.* flavoring, seasoning (e.g. local Royco brand).

ɲéɓisikótᵃ (ɲéɓisikótì-) *pl.* ɲéɓisikótìkᵃ. *n.* cookie, cracker, sweet biscuit.

ɲéɓíti (ɲéɓítií-) *pl.* ɲéɓítììkᵃ. *n.* short-necked, oval spearhead.

ɲɛɓɔŋ (ɲɛɓɔɲí-) *n.* egret.

ɲéɓúku (ɲéɓúkuú-) *pl.* ɲéɓúkùìkᵃ. *n.* crowd, mob, throng.

ɲéɓukuɓúkᵃ (ɲéɓukuɓúkù-) *pl.* ɲéɓukuɓúkìkᵃ. *n.* jerrycan cut in half to be an open container.

ɲeɓúkúitᵃ (ɲeɓúkúití-) *pl.* ŋíɓúkúyᵃ. *n.* foreigner, outsider. See also *ɦyɔ̀àm*.

ɲéɓulókᵃ (ɲéɓulókì-) *pl.* ɲéɓulókìkᵃ. *n.* block, brick.

ɲeɓune (ɲeɓuneé-) *pl.* ɲeɓúnéìkᵃ. *n.* drinking straw (esp. for beer).

ɲéɓur (ɲéɓurí-) *pl.* ɲéɓùrìkᵃ. *1 n.* butter flask made of leather and wood. *2 n.* drum.

ɲéɓurankítᵃ (ɲéɓurankítì-) *pl.* ɲéɓurankítìkᵃ. *n.* blanket.

ɲeɓuri (ɲeɓurií-) *n.* Bohor reedbuck. *Redunca redunca.*

ɲéɓurocó (ɲéɓurocóò-) *pl.* ɲéɓurocóìkᵃ. *n.* cartridge, shell, shell casing.

ɲéɓúruɓur (ɲéɓúruɓurí-) *pl.* ɲéɓúrùɓùrìkᵃ. *n.* floodplain, wide flat valley.

ɲeɓuryaŋ (ɲeɓuryaɲí-) *pl.* ɲeɓúryáŋìkᵃ. *n.* snuff container, tobacco horn.

ɲéɓusitá (ɲéɓusitáà-) *pl.* ɲéɓusitáìkᵃ. *n.* booster or relay tower for cellular networks or radio.

ɲéɓwál (ɲéɓwálì-) *pl.* ɲéɓwálìkᵃ. *n.* riverbed pool of standing water (found in large rivers).

ɲecaako (ɲecaakoó-) *pl.* ɲecáákòìkᵃ. *n.* scrub brush, washing brush.

ɲécaal (ɲécaalá-) *n.* tree species whose wood is carved into spoons and stools.

ɲécaal (ɲécaalí-) *n.* tree species whose fruits are eaten raw and whose wood is used to carve stools. *Cyphostemma junceum.*

ɲɛcáátᵃ (ɲɛcáátì-) *pl.* ɲɛcáátìkᵃ. *n.* men's colored handband.

ɲɛcaɓoyᵃ (ɲɛcaɓoí-) *n.* small plant species whose leaves are boiled as greens and whose small fruits are ground and applied to skin cuts.

ɲécapatí (ɲécapatíí-) *pl.* ɲécapatîìkᵃ. *n.* chapati, fried flatbread (of Indian origin).

ɲécápɔl (ɲécápɔlɔ̀-) *pl.* ɲécápɔlíkᵃ. *n.* chapel.

ɲécáyᵃ (ɲécáì-) *n.* tea.

ɲécipitá (ɲécipitáà-) *pl.* ɲécipitáìkᵃ. *n.* arrow.

ɲécɔ́ka (ɲécɔ́kaá-) *pl.* ɲécɔ́kàìkᵃ. *n.* chalk.

ɲécuma (ɲécumaá-) *n.* black-and-white colobus monkey. *Colobus guereza polykomos.*

ɲèɗᵋ (ɲèɗɛ̀) *ideo.* chafedly, frayedly.

ɲɛɗédɔn (ɲɛɗédɔ̀nì-) *v.* to be chafed, frayed (e.g. a rope or vine).

ɲeɗeke (ɲeɗekeé-) *pl.* ɲeɗekéícíkᵃ. *n.* disease, illness, sickness.

ɲeɗekea bákútsìkàᵉ *n.* chest disease (e.g. pneumonia, tuberculosis, etc.).

ɲeɗekea na itɛnítúkɔta ámákᵃ *n.* lockjaw, tetanus. *Lit.* 'disease that straightens a person'.

ɲeɗekea sakámáᵉ *n.* liver disease.

ɲeɗekéím (ɲeɗeké-ímà-) *pl.* ɲeɗekéwíkᵃ. *1 n.* spirit that causes sickness. *2 n.* mild disease, illness, or sickness. *Lit.* 'sickness-child'.

ɲédépe (ɲédépeé-) *pl.* ɲédépèikᵃ. *n.* large can: unit of measurement of 20 liters.

ɲédɛpiɗépᵃ (ɲédɛpiɗépè-) *pl.* ɲédɛpiɗépɨkᵃ. *n.* gunny sack.

ɲɛdésêdᵃ (ɲɛdésédè-) *n.* trigger. See also *ɲétíka*.

ɲédɨitᵃ (ɲédɨití-) 1 *n.* tsetse fly. Glossinidae. 2 *n.* talking drum.

ɲédíkixònàrì (ɲédíkixònàrìɨ-) *n.* dictionary, lexicon.

ɲédíni (ɲédínií-) *pl.* ɲédíniìkᵃ. 1 *n.* faith, religion. 2 *n.* religious denomination.

ɲédiŋ (ɲédiŋí-) *pl.* ɲédiŋikᵃ. *n.* long digging stick.

ɲédíol (ɲédíolí-) 1 *n.* tallow: fat of cattle, goats, or sheep. 2 *n.* cheese.

ɲédípor (ɲédíporí-) 1 *n.* tobacco soot (found in pipes). 2 *n.* earwax.

ɲédísítùrìkᵃ (ɲédísítùrìkì-) *pl.* ɲédísítùrìkìkᵃ. *n.* district: governmental administrative unit above the county and below the region.

ɲédɨtác (ɲédɨtácɨ-) *pl.* ɲédɨtácɨkᵃ. *n.* military detachment.

ɲédivíxìòn (ɲédivíxìònì-) *pl.* ɲédivíxìònìkᵃ. *n.* military division.

ɲédɔ́nɨɗɔn (ɲédɔ́nɨɗɔnɨ-) *n.* polydactyly: extra fingers or toes.

ɲɛduar (ɲɛduarɨ-) *n.* grass species which is tied with *mɨʒɨʒ* fibers to block wind and to ward off evil spirits from one's home. Aristida adoensis.

ɲɛdúkór (ɲɛdúkórì-) *pl.* ɲɛdúkórikᵃ. *n.* claimed spot, owned plot (e.g. a home or place of harvesting termites).

ɲɛdupɛ (ɲɛdupɛɛ́-) *n.* procession, succession.

ɲédurápᵃ (ɲédurápù-) *n.* checkers.

ɲédurípᵃ (ɲédurípɨ-) *n.* intravenous drip.

ɲéduruɗur (ɲéduruɗurí-) *n.* food that is burnt or stuck on the bottom of a pot.

ɲéɛkimá (ɲéɛkimáà-) *n.* small plant species whose leaves are crushed, mixed with oil, and applied as a perfumed lotion for men and women; its leaves are also mixed with those of the *ɓólɨs* tree and burnt green to fumigate gardens for insect pests.

ɲéɛkiɛ́kᵃ (ɲéɛkiɛ́kɨ-) *pl.* ɲéɛkiɛ́kɨkᵃ. *n.* small gourd rattle (with small stones inside).

ɲéema (ɲéemaá-) *pl.* ɲéèmàikᵃ. 1 *n.* tent. 2 *n.* tarp, tarpaulin.

ɲéɛ́s (ɲéɛ́sè-) *n.* bozo, dude, guy.

ɲéɛ́sɛ (ɲéɛ́sɛɛ́-) *pl.* ɲéɛ́sèikᵃ. *n.* crag: tall cliff or rock with unscalable sides.

ɲéfɨl (ɲéfɨlɨ-) *n.* market in Kenya held during British colonial rule.

ɲéfɨrɛ́m (ɲéfɨrɛ́mù-) *pl.* ɲéfɨrɛ́mɨkᵃ. *n.* door-frame.

ɲégelesíà (ɲégelesíàà-) *pl.* ɲégelesíàikᵃ. *n.* church.

ɲégetsᵃ (ɲégetsí-) *pl.* ɲégètsìkᵃ. 1 *n.* spur. 2 *n.* stiff leg hair (of insects). 3 *n.* stiff tail-tip of a python.

ɲégilás (ɲégilásɨ-) *pl.* ɲégilásìkᵃ. *n.* mirror. See also *ɲérúétᵃ*.

ɲégirasíà (ɲégirasíàà-) *n.* divine grace in Catholicism.

ɲégiróyᵃ (ɲégiróì-) *n.* mountain bamboo. Arundinaria alpinia.

ɲégitá (ɲégitáà-) *pl.* ɲégitáikᵃ. *n.* guitar.

ɲéguniyá (ɲéguniyáà-) *pl.* ɲéguniyáikᵃ. *n.* burlap bag, gunny sack.

ɲégurúf (ɲégurúfù-) *pl.* ɲégurúfikᵃ. *n.* club, co-op, group, organization.

ɲéguruwé (ɲéguruwéè-) *pl.* ŋ́guruwóy[a]. *n.* hog, pig, swine.

ɲégutá (ɲégutáà-) *pl.* ɲégutáɨ̀k[a]. *n.* alphabetical letter. See also *ɲéɲugutá*.

ɲɛitánit[a] (ɲɛitánɨtɨ́-) *pl.* ɲɛitánɨ̀tɨ́k[a]. *n.* fountain, spring.

ɲéjá (ɲéjáà-) *pl.* ɲéjáɨ̀k[a]. *n.* jug.

ɲɛjákáɨt[a] (ɲɛjákáɨtɨ́-) *pl.* ŋɨ́jákáɛ̀. *n.* sub-county chief.

ɲéjákɛ̀t[a] (ɲéjákɛ̀tɛ̀-) *pl.* ɲéjákɛtɨ́k[a]. *n.* jacket.

ɲéjem (ɲéjemú-) *n.* marsh, swamp.

ɲéjigón (ɲéjigónì-) *pl.* ɲéjigónɨ̀k[a]. *n.* cooking hut, kitchen.

ɲéjɨ́p[a] (ɲéjɨ́pɨ̀-) *pl.* ɲéjɨ́pɨ̀k[a]. *n.* zipper.

ɲéjirikán (ɲéjɨrɨkánɨ̀-) *pl.* ɲéjɨrɨkánɨ̀k[a]. *n.* jerrycan.

ɲéjúùs (ɲéjúùsì-) *n.* juice.

ɲékakúŋ́gù (ɲékakúŋ́gùù-) *pl.* ɲékakúŋ́gùɨ̀k[a]. *n.* small plastic barrel or drum.

ɲékeikéy[a] (ɲékeikéɨ̀-) *pl.* ɲékeikéɨ̀k[a]. *n.* sieve, strainer.

ɲékel (ɲékelí-) *pl.* ɲékèlìk[a]. *1 n.* articulation, joint. *2 n.* plant section or segment (e.g. of grass or sugarcane).

ɲékɛ́n (ɲékɛ́nɨ̀-) *pl.* ɲékɛ́nɨ̀k[a]. *n.* 4-liter metal can (based on USAID vegetable oil cans).

ɲeker (ɲekerí-) *pl.* ɲekérík[a]. *n.* custom, tradition.

ɲékerum (ɲékerumú-) *n.* fig tree species whose fruits are eaten raw. *Ficus sp.*

ɲékés (ɲékésì-) *pl.* ɲékésìk[a]. *n.* case, suit, trial.

ɲɛkɛ́sɛ́t[a] (ɲɛkɛ́sɛ́tɛ̀-) *pl.* ɲɛkɛ́sɛ́tɨ́k[a]. *n.* comb.

ɲɛkɛsʉpan (ɲɛkɛsʉpanɨ́-) *n.* rebel, subverter, underminer.

ɲékiɓirít[a] (ɲékiɓirítì-) *pl.* ɲékiɓirítìk[a]. *n.* match, matchstick.

ɲékiɗɛkiɗɛ́ (ɲékiɗɛkiɗɛ́ɛ̀-) *n.* sunflower (plant and seeds). *Helianthus sp.* See also *ɲétɔɔkɨ́ɗɛ́*.

ɲekiɗoŋit[a] (ɲekiɗoŋití-) *pl.* ɲekíɗóŋìtìk[a]. *n.* perineal muscle: between the anus and genitalia. See also *ɲalamatsar*.

ɲékifúl (ɲékifúlù-) *pl.* ɲékifúlìk[a]. *n.* lock, padlock.

ɲékíɨ̀kò (ɲékíɨ̀kòò-) *pl.* ɲékíɨ̀kòɨ̀k[a]. *n.* assembly, meeting.

ɲékijikó (ɲékijikóò-) *pl.* ɲékijikóɨ̀k[a]. *n.* metal spoon.

ɲékɨ́lama (ɲékɨ́lamaá-) *pl.* ɲékɨ́làmàɨ̀k[a]. *n.* sacrificial goat or ox killed by a groom for his new bride. See also *ɲɛkʉma*.

ɲékɨlás (ɲékɨlásì-) *pl.* ɲékɨlásìk[a]. *n.* class, classroom.

ɲékilelés (ɲékilelésì-) *n.* mancala: game with many names in different countries that involves counting and moving objects from hole to hole.

ɲekiliriŋ (ɲekiliriŋí-) *n.* golden jackal. *Canis aureus.*

ɲékilitón (ɲékilitónì-) *n.* plant species with edible leaves.

ɲékɨ́lɔɗa (ɲékɨ́lɔɗaá-) *pl.* ɲékɨ́lɔ̀ɗàɨ̀k[a]. *n.* coiled metal anklet or bracelet.

ɲɛkɨmar (ɲɛkɨmarɨ́-) *n.* census, population.

ɲékimyét[a] (ɲékimyétí-) *n.* sorghum variety grown by the Turkana.

ɲekiner (ɲekinerí-) *pl.* ɲekínérik[a]. *n.* body part, meat or portion.

ɲékiɲés (ɲékiɲésí-) *n.* hairstyle in which sides are short and the top is longer.

ɲɛkipanɗɛ (ɲɛkipanɗɛɛ́-) *pl.* ɲɛkípánɗèɪ̀kᵃ. *n.* Kenyan identification card.

ɲékipɛtétᵃ (ɲékipɛtétɪ̀-) *pl.* ɲékipɛtétɪ̀kᵃ. *n.* lower back.

ɲékipeyés (ɲékipeyésɪ̀-) *1 n.* initiation into a higher age-group (done by killing a goat for the next age-group). *2 n.* religious confirmation.

ɲɛkípɔ́r (ɲɛkípɔ́rɔ̀-) *pl.* ɲɛkípɔ́rɪ́kᵃ. *n.* seasonal marsh or swamp. See also *ɲotóbòr*.

ɲɛkípyɛ́ (ɲɛkípyɛ́ɛ̀-) *pl.* ɲɛkípyɛ́ɪ̀kᵃ/ɲípyɛn. *n.* demon, earth spirit, evil spirit. See also *ɲípyɛn*.

ɲékiráɓᵃ (ɲékiráɓù-) *pl.* ɲékiráɓɪ̀kᵃ. *n.* beer brewed for sale.

ɲékisakátᵃ (ɲékisakáté-) *pl.* ɲékisakátɪ̀kᵃ. *n.* grass shelter (used as a shower or toilet).

ɲékisɛsɛ́ (ɲékisɛsɛ́ɛ̀-) *pl.* ɲékisɛsɛ́ɪ̀kᵃ. *n.* nylon sack used for wringing beer from beer mash.

ɲékisɪ́ (ɲékisɪ̀ɪ-) *n.* large hardwood tree species in which beehives are placed and whose wood is used to carve stools.

ɲekísíɓitᵃ (ɲekísíɓitɪ̀-) *pl.* ɲekísíɓitɪ̀kᵃ. *n.* evidence, exhibit.

ɲɛkisil (ɲɛkisilɪ́-) *n.* lawful order, peace, security, stability. See also *ɲíkísila*.

ɲékisirán (ɲékisiránɪ̀-) *n.* maliciousness, spitefulness.

ɲékisiránɪ̀àm (ɲékisiránɪ̀-àmà-) *pl.* ɲékisiráníikᵃ. *n.* malicious or spiteful person.

ɲekísóritᵃ (ɲekísórìtɪ̀-) *n.* poison, toxin, venom.

ɲékɪ́taɗa (ɲékɪ́taɗaá-) *pl.* ɲékɪ́tàɗàɪ̀kᵃ. *n.* bed, cot.

ɲékiteitéyᵃ (ɲékiteitéɪ̀-) *pl.* ɲékiteitéɪ̀kᵃ. *n.* dress, gown.

ɲékɪ́tɛla (ɲékɪ́tɛlaá-) *pl.* ɲékɪ́tɛ̀làɪ̀kᵃ. *n.* wilderness. See also *ɲárakwᵃ*.

ɲékitiyó (ɲékitiyóò-) *pl.* ɲékitiyóɪ̀kᵃ. *n.* shovel, spade.

ɲékɪ́tɔ́wɔ́ (ɲékɪ́tɔ́wɔ̀ɔ̀-) *n.* exhaustion, extreme fatigue.

ɲɛkitsul (ɲɛkitsulɪ́-) *pl.* ɲɛkɪ́tsúlɪ̀kᵃ. *n.* fine for unlawful impregnation (incestuous or out of wedlock).

ɲɛkɪ́wɔ́rɪ̀tᵃ (ɲɛkɪ́wɔ́rɪ̀tɪ̀-) *pl.* ɲɛkɪ́wɔ́rɪ̀tɪ́kᵃ. *n.* holy ground, sacred place.

ɲékiyóɪ̀kᵃ (ɲékiyóɪ̀kà-) *n.* eyeglasses, glasses, spectacles.

ɲékiyóika ni fetí *n.* shades, sunglasses.

ɲékɔ́kɔ́tɛ́ (ɲékɔ́kɔ́tɛ́ɛ̀-) *n.* aggregate rock.

ɲékuduŋkúru (ɲékuduŋkúruú-) *pl.* ɲékuduŋkúrùɪ̀kᵃ. *n.* onion.

Nékuɗuɗᵃ (Nékuɗuɗú-) *n.* nickname of the late Luka of *Looɗói*.

ɲékúkuse (ɲékúkuseé-) *n.* soft rock.

ɲékukwá (ɲékukwáà-) *n.* conversation, discussion.

ɲékulukúl (ɲékulukúlù-) *n.* turkey.

ɲɛkʉlʉmɛ (ɲɛkʉlʉmɛɛ́-) *pl.* ɲɛkúlʉ́mɛ̀ɪ̀kᵃ. *n.* wooden jug or pitcher.

ɲɛkʉma (ɲɛkʉmaá-) *pl.* ɲɛkʉ́máɪ̀kᵃ. *n.* sacrificial goat or ox killed by a groom for his new bride. See also *ɲékílama*.

ɲékúŋutᵃ (ɲékúŋutú-) *pl.* ŋikúŋúí. *n.* parish chief.

ɲékúrara (ɲékúraraá-) *n.* mange.

ɲekúrúm (ɲekúrúmù-) *pl.* ɲekúrúmíkᵃ. *1 n.* gourd used as a milk flask by the Turkana. *2 n.* pair of panties, underclothes, underwear.

ɲékútàm (ɲékútàmà-) *pl.* **ɲékútàmìk**ᵃ. *n.* small gourd used as a flask to hold butter or oil.

ɲékwaŋa (ɲékwaŋaá-) *n.* large shrub or tree species with whitish bark and whose wood is used to carve stools. *Pittosporum viridiflorum.*

ɲɛkwɨ (ɲɛkwɨɛ́-) *n.* huge scrotal swelling (probably filiariasis). May also be spelled as *ɲɛkʉyᵃ*.

ɲɛ́kwiɲcá (ɲɛ́kwiɲcáà-) *n.* orange-flavored drink.

ɲɛ̀ƙᵃ (ɲɛ̀ƙɛ̀-) *n.* hunger, hungriness.

ɲɛƙánón (ɲɛƙánónì-) *v.* to be famished, starving.

ɲɛƙil (ɲɛƙilɨ́-) *pl.* **ɲéƙílìk**ᵃ. *n.* necktie with a pouch for keeping money.

ɲéƙínᵒ *n.* with hunger, while hungry.

ɲéƙiriƙír (ɲéƙiriƙírì-) *pl.* **ɲéƙiriƙírìk**ᵃ. *n.* handsaw, saw.

ɲeƙulu (ɲeƙuluú-) *pl.* **ɲeƙúlúìk**ᵃ. *n.* small clay pot (for side dishes).

ɲéƙúruƙur (ɲéƙúruƙurú-) *1 n.* corruption, subversion. *2 n.* conflict, discord, strife.

ɲéƙúrumotᵃ (ɲéƙúrumotí-) *pl.* **ɲéƙúrùmòtìk**ᵃ. *n.* gully or trench formed by running water. See also *urúr.*

ɲéleɓuléɓu (ɲéleɓuléɓuú-) *1 n.* tree species whose berries are eaten raw and whose wood is used as poles for building; a decoction of its bark is drunk to induce vomiting. *Ochna sp.* *2 n.* blistered burn.

ɲéléjilɛjᵃ (ɲéléjilɛjɨ́-) *n.* odd jobs, temporary work.

ɲéleƙeré (ɲéleƙeréì-) *pl.* **ɲéleƙeréìk**ᵃ. *n.* horizontal ring of reeds in a series that supports thatching.

ɲélɛl (ɲélɛlɨ́-) *pl.* **ɲélɛ̀lìk**ᵃ. *n.* cadaver, corpse.

Ɲéléle (Ɲéléleé-) *n.* a personal name.

ɲɛlélyá (ɲɛlélyáà-) *pl.* **ɲɛlélyáɨk**ᵃ. *n.* natural well, spring.

ɲélɛmá (ɲélɛmáà-) *n.* style of dance in which two or three dancers (male or female) stand together with arms around each other's waists.

ɲelépítᵃ (ɲelépítì-) *pl.* **ɲelépítík**ᵃ. *n.* milking gourd.

ɲelerum (ɲelerumú-) *n.* argument, disputation, quarreling.

Ɲɛlɛtsa (Ɲɛlɛtsaá-) *n.* a personal name.

ɲɛlil (ɲɛlilɨ́-) *n.* anger, annoyance, fury, rage. See also *gaánàs.*

ɲélímilim (ɲélímilimɨ́-) *n.* drizzle, drizzling rain.

ɲélimirá (ɲélimiráà-) *pl.* **ɲélimiráɨk**ᵃ. *n.* gun sight.

ɲelirátᵃ (ɲelirátɨ́-) *pl.* **ɲélirátíkw**ᵃ. *n.* long-necked spearhead.

ɲéliwolíwo (ɲéliwolíwoó-) *n.* transgender, transvestite (male or female).

ɲélɔ́kilɔkᵃ (ɲélɔ́kilɔkɨ́-) *n.* creeper, vine.

ɲélúɗo (ɲélúɗoó-) *n.* Ludo game.

ɲélúru (ɲélúruú-) *n.* quail.

ɲɛmailɔŋ (ɲɛmailɔŋɔ́-) *n.* small fruited teclea: hardwood tree growing near rivers and whose wood is used for building houses. *Teclea nobilis.* See also *kéláyᵃ.*

ɲémékweɲ (ɲémékweɲí-) *pl.* **ɲémékwèɲìk**ᵃ. *n.* omasum: third stomach of ruminants.

ɲémele (ɲémeleé-) *pl.* **ɲémélèìk**ᵃ. *n.* metal jewelry woven into women's hair.

ɲémɛlɛkú (ɲémɛlɛkúù-) pl. ɲémɛlɛkúìkᵃ. n. hoe.

ɲémɛlɛkúà nà ɦyɔ̀ɔ̀ᵋ n. ox plow.

ɲémɛlɛkúdàkwᵃ (ɲémɛlɛkú-dàkù-) pl. ɲémɛlɛkúìkadakwitín. n. hoe handle.

ɲɛmɛrayᵃ (ɲɛmɛraí-) n. sorghum variety with tall, red seed-heads and sweet canes.

ɲémɛza (ɲémɛzaá-) pl. ɲémɛzàìkᵃ. n. table.

ɲémɛza na íkìrà̀ᵋ n. desk, writing desk.

ɲémɛzagwarí (ɲémɛza-gwaríì-) n. table-top.

ɲémíɗimíɗᵃ (ɲémíɗimíɗí-) n. ear infection.

ɲémíémɓè (ɲémíémɓèè-) pl. ɲémíémɓèìkᵃ. n. mango (tree and fruit). Mangifera indica.

ɲémiikó (ɲémiikóò-) pl. ɲémiikóikᵃ. n. wooden spatula. Also called cɛɓɛn.

ɲémíli (ɲémílií-) n. salt.

ɲémílìòn (ɲémílìònì-) pl. ɲémílioníkᵃ. n. million.

ɲémirínɗà (ɲémirínɗàà-) pl. ɲémirínɗàìkᵃ. n. skirt.

ɲémisípᵃ (ɲémisípù-) pl. ɲémisípìkᵃ. n. belt.

ɲémíso (ɲémísoó-) pl. ɲémísòìkᵃ. n. conclusion, end, ending.

ɲémíta (ɲémítaá-) pl. ɲémítàìkᵃ. n. meter. See also ɔkɔ́tsᵃ.

ɲémítìŋ (ɲémítìŋì-) pl. ɲémítìŋíkᵃ. n. assembly, meeting.

ɲémíxòn (ɲémíxònì-) pl. ɲémíxoníkᵃ. n. mission, station.

ɲémúɗetsᵃ (ɲémúɗetsí-) n. carbon black, crock, soot. See also ɲémúɗuɗu.

ɲémúɗuɗu (ɲémúɗuɗuú-) n. carbon black, crock, soot. See also ɲémúɗetsᵃ.

ɲémúkùɲ (ɲémúkùɲì-) n. small biting black ant species.

Ɲémuƙᵃ (Ɲémuƙé-) n. a personal name.

ɲémúƙetᵃ (ɲémúƙetí-) n. topi. Damaliscus lunatus (tiang?).

ɲɛmᵾna (ɲɛmᵾnaá-) pl. ɲɛmᵾnáìkᵃ. n. delicacy, specialty, treat.

ɲémᵾnᵾkú (ɲémᵾnᵾkúù-) n. body numbness.

ɲémurúŋgù (ɲémurúŋgùù-) n. khat, mira. Catha edulis.

ɲémurúŋgùàm (ɲémurúŋgù-àmà-) pl. ɲémurúŋguikᵃ. 1 n. khat-chewer. 2 n. Didinga person.

Ɲémusaláɓà (Ɲémusaláɓàà-) n. Southern Cross constellation.

ɲémusaláɓà (ɲémusaláɓàà-) pl. ɲémusaláɓàìkᵃ. n. cross.

ɲémúsukitᵃ (ɲémúsukití-) pl. ɲímúsúkwí. n. white person: American, European, or any Caucasian. See also ɓèts'ònìàm.

ɲémᵾsᵾmén (ɲémᵾsᵾménì-) pl. ɲémᵾsᵾméníkᵃ. n. hacksaw.

ɲénéne (ɲénéneé-) pl. ɲénéneikᵃ. 1 n. bundle or sheaf of harvested crops. 2 n. bunch of bees (e.g. a swarm clumped up in a tree).

ɲénétìwàkᵃ (ɲénétìwàkà-) pl. ɲénétìwakíkᵃ. n. cellular network.

ɲénis (ɲénisí-) n. fine attire, regalia.

ɲénᵾkᵾnúkᵾ (ɲénᵾkᵾnúkᵾú-) n. mole.

ɲénús (ɲénúsì-) pl. ɲénúsìkᵃ. n. half.

ɲéɲaaɲá (ɲéɲaaɲáà-) pl. ɲéɲaaɲáìkᵃ. n. tomato (plant and fruit). Lycopersicon esculentum.

ɲéɲam (ɲéɲamá-) n. cancellous bone, spongy bone. Lit. 'nibblable'.

ɲeɲerɛs (ɲeɲerɛsɨ́-) *v.* to heave, heft, shove (e.g. a heavy object along the ground). See also *toremes*.

ɲéɲɛ́s (ɲéɲɛ́sɨ̀-) *v.* to nibble, pick (e.g. meat from a bone).

ɲéɲɛwán (ɲéɲɛwánɨ̀-) *n.* succulent plant species with sweet, yellow, edible fruits.

ɲéɲíɲí (ɲéɲíɲíɨ̀-) *n.* gold dust.

ɲéɲɔndʼɔ́ (ɲéɲɔndʼɔ́ɔ̀-) *pl.* **ɲéɲɔndʼɔ́ɨ̀k**ᵃ. *n.* hammer.

ɲéɲugutá (ɲéɲugutáà-) *pl.* **ɲéɲugutáɨ̀k**ᵃ. *n.* alphabetical letter. See also *ɲéguta*.

ɲéŋedʼo (ɲéŋedʼoó-) *n.* vine species whose root decoction is drunk as a treatment for coughing, especially coughing up blood.

ɲéŋɛ́s (ɲéŋɛ́sɨ̀-) *v.* to spear all the way through.

ɲéŋéso (ɲéŋésoó-) *n.* tree whose root decoction is drunk by women to stop postnatal bleeding and whose seeds are used as beads in girls' necklaces; its roots and leaves are crushed, mixed, and flung on crops to make them better than the neighbors'. *Rhynchosia hirta*.

ɲéómò (ɲéómòò-) *n.* laundry detergent or soap. From the detergent brand called OMO; see also *hómò*.

ɲéótèl (ɲéótèlì-) *pl.* **ɲéótelík**ᵃ. *n.* café, eatery, restaurant.

ɲépáɨl (ɲépáɨ̀lɨ̀-) *n.* file paper, thin cardboard.

ɲépalatún (ɲépalatúnì-) *pl.* **ɲépalatúnɨ̀k**ᵃ. *n.* platoon.

ɲépédʼe (ɲépédʼeé-) *pl.* **ɲépédʼeɨ̀k**ᵃ. *n.* small aluminum disc worn with beads over women's chests.

ɲépeelí (ɲépeelíì-) *n.* metal bucket or pail.

ɲepɛlɛrɛŋ (ɲepɛlɛrɛŋɨ́-) *pl.* **ɲepɛ́lɛ́rɛ̀ŋɨ̀k**ᵃ. *n.* piece of scrap metal used as a frying pan.

ɲépélu (ɲépéluú-) *pl.* **ɲépélùɨ̀k**ᵃ. *n.* furrow, line.

ɲépɛn (ɲépɛnɨ́-) *pl.* **ɲépɛ̀nɨ̀k**ᵃ. *n.* long-barreled gun with a vented muzzle.

ɲépénɛkᵃ (ɲépénɛké-) *pl.* **ɲépénɛkík**ᵃ. *n.* beard, goatee. See also *tèmùr*.

ɲéperétᵃ (ɲéperétì-) *pl.* **ɲéperétik**ᵃ. *n.* march, parade.

ɲépɛtá (ɲépɛtáà-) *pl.* **ɲépɛtáɨ̀k**ᵃ. *n.* hinge.

ɲépetorón (ɲépetorónì-) *n.* gasoline, petrol.

ɲépɨ́dʼipɨ́dʼᵃ (ɲépɨ́dʼipɨ́dʼɨ̄-) *n.* conflict, discord, strife.

ɲépɨɨrá (ɲépɨɨráà-) *pl.* **ɲépɨɨráɨ̀k**ᵃ. 1 *n.* ball, football, soccer. 2 *n.* rubber Y-handled slingshot.

ɲépilipíli (ɲépilipílií-) *n.* pepper.

ɲépɨ́nɨ́sɨ̀l (ɲépɨ́nɨ́sɨ̀lɨ̀-) *pl.* **ɲépɨ́nɨ́silík**ᵃ. *n.* pencil.

ɲépípa (ɲépípaá-) *pl.* **ɲépípàɨ̀k**ᵃ. *n.* large barrel or drum.

ɲépípa (ɲépípaá-) 1 *n.* tree species whose roots are tied as charms on gates/doors to make any enemies forget their evil intentions. 2 *n.* diversionary tactic (e.g. against enemies, in the form of persuasion or a sacrifice).

ɲépírìà (ɲépírìàà-) *n.* hippo, hippopotamus, river horse. *Hippopotamus amphibius*.

ɲepísíkitᵃ (ɲepísíkití-) *pl.* **ɲepísíkìtìk**ᵃ. 1 *n.* forearm. 2 *n.* foreleg. See also *kɔ́dɔl*.

ɲépísikitíém (ɲépísikití-èmè-) *n.* muscle (meat) of the forearm or foreleg.

ɲépɨ́sɨ́tɔl (ɲépɨ́sɨ́tɔ̀lɔ̀-) *pl.* **ɲépɨ́sɨ́tɔlík**ᵃ. *n.* handgun, pistol, sidearm.

ɲépiskóópì (ɲépiskóópìì-) *pl.* **ɲépiskóópììk**ᵃ. *n.* bishop.

ɲɛpitɛ (ɲɛpitɛɛ́-) *pl.* **ɲɛpiteicík**ᵃ. *1 n.* behavior, habit, manner. *2 n.* method, procedure, way.

ɲɛpitɛa ámáᵉ *n.* personal attribute, personality trait.

ɲépítsa (ɲépítsaá-) *pl.* **ɲépítsàɨk**ᵃ. *n.* photo(graph), picture, snapshot.

ɲépɔrésɨ̀tà (ɲépɔrésɨ̀tàà-) *1 n.* eucalyptus tree species. *Eucalyptus sp.* *2 n.* planted forest (typically of eucalyptus).

ɲépóros (ɲépórosí-) *pl.* **ɲépóròsɨ̀k**ᵃ. *n.* big scar, keloid scar.

ɲépɔ́sɨ̀tᵃ (ɲépɔ́sɨ̀tɨ̀-) *pl.* **ɲépɔ́sitík**ᵃ. *n.* police post.

ɲéprójèkɨ̀tᵃ (ɲéprójèkɨ̀tɨ̀-) *pl.* **ɲéprójekitík**ᵃ. *n.* work project (especially of NGOs).

ɲépulé (ɲépuléè-) *n.* groundnut(s), peanut(s). See also *tarádá*.

Nɛpulɔ (Nɛpulɔɔ́-) *n.* a personal name.

ɲépunɨkᵃ (ɲépunɨkú-) *pl.* **ɲépùnùkɨ̀k**ᵃ. *n.* rumen: first stomach of ruminants.

ɲépúɲa (ɲépúɲaá-) *pl.* **ɲépúɲàɨk**ᵃ. *n.* funerary goat killed to appease the spirit of the dead. See also *kɔ̀p*ᵃ.

ɲépúɲáám (ɲépúɲá-ámà-) *pl.* **ɲépúɲaík**ᵃ. *n.* one who acquires and kills a funerary goat.

ɲepúrósitᵃ (ɲepúrósití-) *pl.* **ɲepúrósitík**ᵃ. *n.* widow(er). See also *lómélew*ᵃ.

ɲèr (ɲèrà-) *n.* daughters, girls, maidens, young unmarried women.

ɲèràaƙwᵃ (ɲèrà-aƙɔ̀-) *n.* company of girls. *Lit.* 'among girls'.

Nèràdzògᵃ (Nèrà-dzògà-) *n.* name of a hillside where girls used to pick *dzôg* berries for dying their hair. *Lit.* 'girls-dzôg'.

ɲèràkù (ɲèrà-kùà-) *n.* girls' grass: grass species which resembles sorghum during rainy season and which girls wear on their heads as decoration; said to be harmful to the eyes. *Gramineae sp.*

Nerasabá (Nera-sabáà-) *n.* name of a river. *Lit.* 'girls-river'.

Nèràtàɓᵃ (Nèrà-tàɓà-) *n.* name of a mountainside where a huge boulder once broke apart and crushed some Ik girls. *Lit.* 'girls-rock'.

ɲératíl (ɲératílì-) *pl.* **ɲératílìk**ᵃ. *n.* scale for weighing.

Nerawikᵃ (Nera-wicé-) *n.* constellation of five stars resembling a group of little girls.

ɲerawikᵃ (ɲera-wicé-) *n.* little girls.

ɲéréɗi (ɲéréɗìì-) *pl.* **ɲéréɗììk**ᵃ. *n.* radio, tuner.

ɲɛrétᵃ (ɲɛrétí-) *pl.* **ɲerétíkw**ᵃ. *n.* drainage area, river basin, watershed.

ɲériɓá (ɲériɓáà-) *pl.* **ɲériɓáìk**ᵃ. *n.* cordonsearch military operation.

ɲéríɓiriɓᵃ (ɲéríɓiriɓí-) *pl.* **ɲéríɓiriɓík**ᵃ. *n.* mirage.

ɲéríkirikᵃ (ɲéríkirikí-) *pl.* **ɲéríkirikík**ᵃ. *n.* earthquake, quake, seism.

ɲérikiríkᵃ (ɲérikirɨ́kɨ̀-) *n.* shrub whose red berries are eaten by people and snakes. *Hoslundia opposita*.

ɲérímama (ɲérímamaá-) *n.* rubbish or trash carried by a flashflood.

ɲeriŋƙís (ɲériŋƙísì-) *pl.* **ɲériŋƙísìk**ᵃ. *n.* line.

ɲeríósitᵃ (ɲéríósití-) *pl.* **ɲéríósitík**ᵃ. *n.* chief, king.

ɲéripipí (ɲéripipíì-) *pl.* **ɲéripipíìk**ᵃ. *n.* brick furnace, kiln.

ɲerípírìpᵃ (ɲerípírìpì-) pl. ɲerípíripíkᵃ. n. crowd, multitude, throng.

ɲéripótᵃ (ɲéripótì-) pl. ɲéripótìkᵃ. n. message, news, report.

ɲéritá (ɲéritáà-) pl. ɲéritáìkᵃ. n. house trap used to catch larger animals.

ɲéríwi (ɲéríwií-) pl. ɲéríwìikᵃ. n. outer barrier or fence made of branches and thorns.

ɲérɔɓirɔ́ɓᵃ (ɲérɔɓirɔ́ɓù-) pl. ɲérɔɓirɔ́ɓìkᵃ. n. plastic bottle.

ɲérúétᵃ (ɲérúétè-) pl. ɲérúétìkᵃ. n. mirror. See also ɲégílás.

ɲerukuɗe (ɲerukuɗeé-) pl. ɲerúkúɗèikᵃ. n. highway, road.

ɲérúmatsᵃ (ɲérúmatsí-) pl. ɲérúmàtsìkᵃ. n. rear speartip.

ɲerupe (ɲerupeé-) pl. ɲerúpéikᵃ. n. lingering, intermittent rains between wet and dry seasons.

ɲérupɛpɛ́ (ɲérupɛpɛ́é-) pl. ɲérupɛpɛ́ikᵃ. 1 n. musical horn traditionally made from an animal horn (often oryx). 2 n. trumpet.

ɲérwám (ɲérwámù-) pl. ɲérwámìkᵃ. n. traditional style grass hut. Similar to the Icéhò.

ɲeryaŋ (ɲeryaɲí-) 1 n. administration, government, regime. 2 n. modernity, modern society.

ɲeryaŋíɓór (ɲeryaɲí-ɓórè-) pl. ɲeryaŋíɓórítín. n. army barrack. Lit. 'government-corral'.

ɲeryaŋíhò (ɲeryaɲí-hòò-) pl. ɲeryaŋíhoíkᵃ. n. modern building.

ɲeryaŋínánès (ɲeryaɲínánèsì-) n. working for the government.

ɲeryaŋíŋókᵃ (ɲeryaɲí-ŋókì-) n. alsatian, German shepherd. Lit. 'modernity-dog'.

ɲéséànìs (ɲéséànìsì-) n. science.

ɲésɛɛɓɔ́ (ɲésɛɛɓɔ́ɔ̀-) pl. ɲésɛɛɓɔ́ìkᵃ. 1 n. crook, hooked staff. 2 n. penile shaft. 3 n. gearshift, gearstick.

ɲésékíxìòn (ɲésékíxìònì-) pl. ɲésékíxionίkᵃ. n. military section.

ɲésɛ́kɔ (ɲésɛ́kɔɔ́-) n. disobedience, insubordination.

ɲésɛ́kɔ́ám (ɲésɛ́kɔ́-ámà-) pl. ɲésɛ́kóíkᵃ. n. disobedient person.

ɲéséminà (ɲéséminàà-) pl. ɲéséminàikᵃ. n. colloquium, seminar.

ɲɛsɛpɛɗɛ (ɲɛsɛpɛɗɛɛ́-) pl. ɲɛsɛpɛ́ɗɛ̀ikᵃ. n. cartridge, shell, shell casing.

ɲésiɓalitútu (ɲésiɓalitútuú-) n. fool's gold, pyrite: small, smooth, gold-colored stones. *Iron disulfide*.

ɲésíitᵃ (ɲésíití-) n. ground bee species that builds nests in anthills.

ɲésiláx (ɲésiláxì-) pl. ɲésiláxìkᵃ. n. slasher. Also called ɲásiláx.

ɲésiliɓá (ɲésiliɓáà-) pl. ɲésiliɓáikᵃ. n. aluminum knitting needle.

ɲésílisil (ɲésílisilí-) n. rhomboid muscle.

ɲésímìtᵃ (ɲésímìtì-) n. cement.

ɲésimón (ɲésimónì-) pl. ɲésimónìkᵃ. n. coin.

ɲésinɗán (ɲésinɗánì-) pl. ɲésinɗánìkᵃ. n. needle.

ɲɛsiŋkiri (ɲɛsiŋkirií-) pl. ɲɛsiŋkíriìkᵃ. n. cooker, stove.

ɲésipíɗᵃ (ɲésipíɗì-) n. speed, velocity.

ɲésipiriyá (ɲésipiriyáà-) pl. ɲésipiríyáikᵃ. n. metal cooking pan or pot, saucepan. See also ɲásipiryá.

ɲésiriwáli (ɲésiriwálií-) pl. ɲésiriwáliìkᵃ. n. pair of short pants, shorts, or trunks.

ɲésitó (ɲésitóò-) pl. ɲésitóìkᵃ. n. outbuilding, shed, storeroom, store.

ɲésóto (ɲésótoó-) *pl.* **ɲésótòìkᵃ**. *n.* pointed granary cover. Also called *ɲósóto*.

ɲésukukú (ɲésukukúù-) *pl.* **ɲésukukúìkᵃ**. *n.* national holiday.

ɲésukúl (ɲésukúlù-) *pl.* **ɲésukúlùìkᵃ**. *n.* college, institute, school.

ɲesuƙuru (ɲesuƙuruú-) *n.* small plant species with painful thorns that grows along the ground and is said to be eaten by all types of livestock. *Tribulus cistoides*.

ɲɛsupᵃ (ɲɛsupá-) *n.* influence, sway.

ɲésurúr (ɲésurúrù-) *pl.* **ɲésurúrìkᵃ**. *n.* pick, pickaxe.

ɲésútɛ̀ (ɲésútɛ̀ɛ̀-) *n.* leafy plant species whose roots are eaten raw or roasted. *Hypoxis obtusa*.

Ɲétayoŋ (Ɲétayoŋó-) *n.* a personal name.

ɲeteeɗe (ɲeteeɗeé-) *pl.* **ɲetéɛ́ɗèìkᵃ**. *1 n.* spring for holding decorative feathers on the head. *2 n.* front sight of a weapon.

ɲétɛɛr (ɲétɛɛrí-) *pl.* **ɲétèèrìkᵃ**. *n.* area, locality, region, zone.

ɲétéƙe (ɲétéƙeé-) *pl.* **ɲétéƙèìkᵃ**. *n.* metal leg trap.

ɲétélitɛl (ɲétélitɛlí-) *1 n.* lappet, wattle. *2 n.* earlobe scar.

ɲétɛmá (ɲétɛmáà-) *n.* leisure, leisure time, leisurely walk.

ɲétémetsᵃ (ɲétémetsí-) *pl.* **ɲétémètsìkᵃ**. *n.* vertical granary reed.

ɲétenɗé (ɲétenɗèè-) *n.* palm tree species.

ɲétenús (ɲétenúsí-) *pl.* **ɲeténúsìkᵃ**. *n.* large intestine.

ɲétépes (ɲétépesí-) *pl.* **ɲétépèsìkᵃ**. *n.* combination of a lip plug and a chin cover made of woven wires.

ɲétɛrɛƙéƙɛ (ɲétɛrɛƙéƙɛɛ́-) *n.* meningitis. See also *tɛ́rɛƙéƙɛ*.

ɲétɛrɛƙita (ɲétɛrɛƙitaá-) *pl.* **ɲétɛ̀rɛ̀ƙìtàìkᵃ**. *n.* tractor.

ɲétɛrɛƙitaa na kwɛtáᵋ *n.* digger, excavator, power shovel. *Lit.* 'tractor of an arm'.

ɲétɛrɛƙitaa na kwétìkàᵋ *n.* hand tiller, hand tractor. *Lit.* 'tractor of arms'.

ɲétésɨ̀tᵃ (ɲétésɨ̀tɨ̀-) *pl.* **ɲétésɨ̀tɨ̀kᵃ**. *n.* exam, examination, test.

ɲétíƙa (ɲétíƙaá-) *pl.* **ɲétíƙàìkᵃ**. *n.* trigger. See also *ɲeɗésêdᵃ*.

ɲétíli (ɲétílií-) *n.* antelope whose horns whistle in the wind (possibly the Ugandan or South Sudan kob).

ɲétílitil (ɲétílitilí-) *pl.* **ɲétílìtìlìkᵃ**. *n.* earring.

ɲétím (ɲétímù-) *pl.* **ɲétímìkᵃ**. *n.* team.

ɲétíɲáŋ (ɲétíɲáŋà-) *n.* Nile crocodile. *Crocodylus niloticus*.

ɲétípa (ɲétípaá-) *pl.* **ɲétípàìkᵃ**. *n.* dump truck, tipper.

ɲétiriƙá (ɲétiriƙáà-) *pl.* **ɲétiriƙáìkᵃ**. *n.* woven doorway curtain for traditional grass huts. Made from *mɨ́ʒɨ̀ʒ*.

ɲetitsᵃ (ɲetitsí-) *n.* duty, job, task, work.

ɲétɔɔkɨɗɛ (ɲétɔɔkɨɗɛ̀ɛ̀-) *n.* sunflower (plant and seeds). *Helianthus sp*. See also *ɲékɨɗɛkɨɗɛ́*.

ɲétorós (ɲétorósì-) *pl.* **ɲétorósìkᵃ**. *n.* pair of pants or trousers. Also called *ɲótorós*.

ɲɛtsir (ɲɛtsirí-) *n.* sacral muscle: muscle attached to the sacrum.

ɲɛtsirɨ́ɔkᵃ (ɲɛtsirɨ́-ɔ́kà-) *n.* sacrum: triangular bone above the tailbone.

ɲétsúpa (ɲétsúpaá-) *pl.* ɲétsúpàìkᵃ. *n.* glass bottle.

ɲétsúur (ɲétsúurí-) *pl.* ɲétsúùrìkᵃ. *n.* hole in a riverbed hollowed out by churning water.

ɲétúle (ɲétúleé-) *pl.* ɲétúlèìkᵃ. *n.* traditional wooden whistle.

ɲétúlerú (ɲétúlerúu-) *n.* plant species whose nectar children like to suck out. *Leonotis sp.*

ɲɛtʉnɛ (ɲɛtʉnɛɛ́-) *n.* chickenpox, varicella. See also *puurú*.

ɲétʉráwèl (ɲétʉráwèlɨ-) *pl.* ɲétʉráwèlɨkᵃ. *n.* trowel.

ɲɛtʉréélà (ɲɛtʉréélàà-) *pl.* ɲɛtʉréélàìkᵃ. *n.* trailer.

ɲéturukúku (ɲéturukúkuú-) *pl.* ɲéturukúkùìkᵃ. *n.* chicken backbone.

ɲetutu (ɲetutuú-) *n.* striped hyena. *Hyaena hyaena.*

ɲéúɗe (ɲéúɗeé-) *n.* plant whose carrot-like roots are eaten raw.

ɲéuɗuúɗu (ɲéuɗuúɗuú-) *n.* grass species similar to bullrush.

ɲéúji (ɲéújií-) *n.* gruel, porridge. See also *ɲáítɔ*.

ɲéúlam (ɲéúlamá-) *n.* plant species with no reported uses. *Helichrysum odoratissimum.*

ɲéʉrɛrɛ́ (ɲéʉrɛrɛ́ɛ̀-) *n.* sweet-smelling, yellow-flowered weed species whose leaves resemble marijuana.

ɲèùrìà (ɲèùrìà-) *n.* duel or sparring held for friendly competition or to settle disputes in the community.

ɲeuríétòn (ɲeuríétònì-) *v.* to duel, spar.

ɲɛʉrʉlatsᵃ (ɲɛʉrʉlatsɨ́-) *n.* small plant species whose leaves are ground up and used as a perfume and whose roots are ground, cooked, and drunk for stomachache. *Indigofera arrecta.*

ɲéʉrʉmɛmɛ́ (ɲéʉrʉmɛmɛ́ɛ̀-) *n.* plant species whose roots are pounded or chewed to treat stomach ailments. *Conyza sp.*

ɲéúsi (ɲéúsií-) *pl.* ɲéúsììkᵃ. *n.* thread.

ɲéutsúr (ɲéutsúrù-) *pl.* ɲéutsúrìkᵃ. *n.* levy, tax.

ɲéútsuríám (ɲéútsurí-ámà-) *pl.* ɲéútsurííkᵃ. *n.* tax collector.

ɲévíɗyo (ɲévíɗyoó-) *pl.* ɲévíɗyòìkᵃ. *n.* film, movie, television, video.

ɲévíɗyòhò (ɲévíɗyò-hòò-) *pl.* ɲévíɗyohoíkᵃ. *n.* cinema, movie theater.

ɲéviiní (ɲéviiníì-) *1 n.* wine. *2 n.* grapes.

ɲéviinísèdᵃ (ɲéviiní-sèdà-) *pl.* ɲéviinísedíkᵃ. *n.* vinery, vineyard.

ɲɛ́wakɔ́l (ɲɛ́wakɔ́lɨ-) *pl.* ɲɛ́wakɔ́lɨkᵃ. *n.* headband heavily beaded with small beads in decorative colored patterns.

ɲewale (ɲewaleé-) *pl.* ɲewáléìkᵃ. *n.* adornment, decoration (e.g. putting on an ostrich feather).

ɲewatajá (ɲewatajáà-) *pl.* ɲewatajáìkᵃ. *n.* pitcher, pitcherful.

ɲéwiinó (ɲéwiinóò-) *n.* ink.

ɲéwíɲiwiɲ (ɲéwíɲiwiɲí-) *n.* sweet fermenting wort (mixture of malt and yeast).

ɲewuruŋorokᵃ (ɲewuruŋorokó-) *n.* striped polecat, zorilla. *Ictonyx striatus.*

ɲéyoroeté (ɲéyoroetée-) *n.* medium-sized tree species found in Timu Forest whose branches are used to make wooden flutes and hunting horns. *Crataeva adansonii.*

ɲéyúnìfòm (ɲéyúnìfòmò-) *pl.* ɲéyúnifomíkᵃ. *n.* outfit, uniform.

ɲezeí (ɲezeíì-) *pl.* **ɲézeíìkᵃ**. *n.* inkpad, stamp pad.

ɲícwéɲé (ɲícwéɲéè-) *n.* sugar bush: hardwoood tree species whose wood is used for building but which nails cannot pierce. *Protea gaguedi.*

ɲíkwaamwíyá (ɲíkwaamwíyáà-) *n.* bird species.

ɲimánétòn (ɲimánétònì-) *v.* to encounter, meet, run into. Also pronounced as *ɲimánétòn.*

ɲimanites (ɲimanitesí-) *v.* to join, mend, repair.

ɲimanitésíàwᵃ (ɲimanitésí-àwà-) *pl.* **ɲimanitésíawíkᵃ**. *n.* edge, joint.

ɲimánón (ɲimánónì-) *v.* to encounter, meet.

ɲimíɲímàtòn (ɲimíɲímàtònì-) *v.* to cause sharp abdominal pain. The experiencer of the pain is marked grammatically with the dative case.

ɲimirés (ɲimirésí-) *v.* to wipe off with a hand or finger (e.g. food from a plate, sweat from one's forehead).

ɲipídòn (ɲipídònì-) *v.* to be soft (e.g. fur, grass, mattress).

ɲìpⁱ (ɲìpì) *ideo.* softly.

ɲjén (ɲj-éní-) *pro.* mine.

ɲjín (ɲjíní-) *pro.* we/our/us (inclusive of addressee). This pronoun includes the addressee. Contrast with *ŋgwᵃ.*

ɲjíníèn (ɲjíní-ènì-) *pro.* ours (including the addressee).

ɲjínínebitín (ɲjíní-nebitíní-) *n.* ourselves (including the addressee). *Lit.* 'our bodies'.

ɲɔɓɔ́ka (ɲɔ́ɓɔ́kaá-) *n.* broth, gravy.

ɲóɓókotᵃ (ɲóɓókotó-) *pl.* **ɲóɓókòtìkᵃ**. *n.* bowl-shaped cap made of human hair.

ɲɔ́ɓɔɔ́ (ɲɔ́ɓɔɔ́ɔ̀-) *n.* lentils.

ɲóɓóotᵃ (ɲóɓóotí-) *pl.* **ɲóɓóòtìkᵃ**. *1 n.* garden camp where people stay during harvest. *2 n.* abandoned homestead.

ɲoɗôdᵃ (ɲoɗódè-) *n.* aardvark, antbear, anteater. *Orycteropus afer.*

ɲɔɗɔ́kétᵃ (ɲɔɗɔ́kétè-) *pl.* **ɲɔɗɔ́kétɨkᵃ**. *n.* ridge running vertically. See also *fátár.*

ɲoɗokole (ɲoɗokoleé-) *pl.* **ɲoɗókólèìkᵃ**. *1 n.* uvula. *2 n.* plant species.

ɲɔɗɔ́la (ɲɔɗɔ́laá-) *pl.* **ɲɔɗɔ́làìkᵃ**. *n.* buck, dollar.

ɲóɗomé (ɲóɗoméè-) *n.* tree species whose gummy yellow fruits are eaten raw and found mostly in Turkana country; its leaves are used for polishing stools, and its wood is used for house poles and carving sticks and hoe handles. *Cordia sinensis.*

ɲóɗòmòŋòlè (ɲóɗòmòŋòlèè-) *n.* sweet yellow maize variety that matures quickly.

ɲɔɗɔrɔcá (ɲɔɗɔrɔcáà-) *pl.* **ɲɔɗɔrɔcáɨkᵃ**. *n.* bridge.

ɲóɗós (ɲóɗósì-) *n.* colostrum, foremilk.

ɲɔ́fɔ́kᵃ (ɲɔ́fɔ́kɔ̀-) *pl.* **ɲɔ́fɔ́kɨkᵃ**. *n.* fork. See also *ɲácakwarátᵃ.*

ɲófóm (ɲófómù-) *pl.* **ɲófómìkᵃ**. *n.* bench. See also *ɲéɓéɲc.*

ɲófuŋƙúwo (ɲófuŋƙúwoó-) *pl.* **ɲófuŋƙúwòìkᵃ**. *n.* key.

ɲógóva (ɲógóvaá-) *n.* guava (tree and fruit). *Psidium guajava.*

ɲɔkɔ́ɗɛ́tᵃ (ɲɔkɔ́ɗɛ́tɨ̀-) *pl.* **ɲɔkɔ́ɗɛ́tɨkᵃ**. *n.* handle, handgrip.

ɲɔ́kɔɗɔɔŋɔ́r (ɲɔ́kɔɗɔɔŋɔ́rɨ̀-) *n.* bird species.

ɲokoɗopeyᵃ (ɲokoɗopeí-) *n.* grass species that grows as a weed and has many roots. *Gramineae sp.*

Nókoɗós (Nókoɗósí-) *n.* a personal name.

ɲókóìn (ɲókóìnì-) *pl.* **ɲókóìnìk**ᵃ. *n.* coin.

ɲókokor (ɲókokorí-) *pl.* **ɲókòkòrìk**ᵃ. *1 n.* stick ring rolled as a target for spearing practice. *2 n.* steering wheel. See also *ɲɔkɔlɔɓɛr*.

ɲókɔkɔr (ɲókɔkɔrɔ́-) *n.* chicken, poultry. *Gallus gallus.*

ɲɔ́kɔkɔrɔ́hò (ɲɔ́kɔkɔrɔ́-hòò-) *pl.* **ɲɔ́kɔkɔrɔ́hoík**ᵃ. *n.* chicken coop, henhouse.

ɲɔ́kɔkɔróím (ɲɔ́kɔkɔró-ímà-) *pl.* **ɲɔ́kɔkɔrɔ́wík**ᵃ. *n.* biddy, chick.

ɲókólíƙètᵃ (ɲókólíƙèti-) *n.* dentifrice, toothpaste.

ɲokólípᵃ (ɲokólípì-) *n.* barren, childless, infertile, or sterile animal or person. See also *òsòròs*.

ɲɔkɔlɔɓɛr (ɲɔkɔlɔɓɛrɛ́-) *pl.* **ɲɔ́kɔ́lɔ́ɓɛ̀rìk**ᵃ. *n.* stick ring rolled as a target for spearing practice. See also *ɲókokor*.

ɲókompyútà (ɲókompyútàà-) *pl.* **ɲókompyútàìk**ᵃ. *n.* computer.

ɲɔkɔ́ɲɛ́tᵃ (ɲɔkɔ́ɲɛ́tì-) *pl.* **ɲɔkɔ́ɲɛ́tìk**ᵃ. *n.* pair of forceps, pliers, or tongs.

ɲɔkɔɔna (ɲɔkɔɔnaá-) *pl.* **ɲɔkɔ́ɔ́nàìk**ᵃ. *n.* corner.

ɲɔ́kɔ́pè (ɲɔ́kɔ́pɛɛ́-) *pl.* **ɲɔ́kɔ́pèìk**ᵃ. *n.* gorge, ravine. See also *fòts*ᵃ.

ɲókópo (ɲókópoó-) *1 n.* cup. *2 n.* clip, magazine (of a gun).

ɲókorimítᵃ (ɲókorimítì-) *pl.* **ɲókorimítìk**ᵃ. *n.* garden boundary (often made of grass and other rubbish piled into rows).

ɲókorotᵃ (ɲókorotó-) *n.* dance involving clapping and singing.

ɲókós (ɲókósì-) *pl.* **ɲókósìk**ᵃ. *n.* class, course, training, workshop.

ɲókótᵃ (ɲókótì-) *pl.* **ɲókótìk**ᵃ. *n.* court, courthouse, tribunal.

ɲókóti (ɲókótií-) *pl.* **ɲókótìik**ᵃ. *n.* coat.

ɲókotitᵃ (ɲókotití-) *n.* tree species whose fruits are eaten by children and whose wood is carved into stools and wooden containers. *Pseudocedrela sp.*

ɲɔ́kuɗɔmútù (ɲɔ́kuɗɔmútùù-) *n.* skunk-like animal that catches its prey with an anorectal protrusion.

ɲóƙoloƙolétᵃ (ɲóƙoloƙolétí-) *n.* tree whose large yellow fruits are eaten raw and from whose wood three-legged stools are carved.

ɲɔ́ƙɔ́ŋ (ɲɔ́ƙɔ́ŋù-) *pl.* **ɲɔ́ƙɔ́ŋìk**ᵃ. *n.* sacred tree where ceremonies like *itówéés* are held. Also called *lɔ́ƙɔ́ŋ*.

ɲól (ɲólí-) *n.* Gunther's dik-dik. *Madoqua guentheri.*

ɲólídɛrɛ́ƙᵃ (ɲólí-dɛrɛ́ƙì-) *n.* small black and yellow wasp. *Lit.* 'dik-dik wasp'.

ɲólíkàf (ɲólí-kàfù-) *n.* dik-dik thornbush: nettle-like plant species whose thorns cause itching and which is eaten by livestock. *Barleria acanthoides.*

ɲólíkinám (ɲólí-kinámá-) *n.* cone-shaped 'dik-dik' mushroom.

ɲoloɗiŋ (ɲoloɗiɲí-) *n.* discrimination, marginalization, segregation.

ɲolóɗo (ɲolóɗoó-) *pl.* **ɲolóɗòìk**ᵃ. *n.* horizontal ring-beam of flexible sticks that support a hut roof.

ɲólóitᵃ (ɲólóití-) *pl.* **ɲólóitìk**ᵃ. *n.* anchor, ground (like a log or rock).

ɲólójᵃ (ɲólójì-) *pl.* **ɲólójik**ᵃ. *n.* hostel, hotel, inn, lodge, motel.

ɲolókér (ɲolókérè-) *pl.* **ɲolókérìk**ᵃ. *n.* level, line.

ɲɔlɔlɔtᵃ (ɲɔlɔlɔtɨ́-) n. okra (plant and fruit). *Hibiscus esculentus*.

ɲolórì (ɲolórìi-) pl. ɲolórììkᵃ. n. lorry, truck. See also *lóórì*.

ɲomokojo (ɲomokojoó-) n. leftovers, remainder. See also *ógoɗesam*.

ɲɔ́mɔkɔsá (ɲɔ́mɔkɔsáà-) n. error, fault, mistake. See also *ɲasécón*.

ɲɔ́mɔkɔsáàm (ɲɔ́mɔkɔsá-àmà-) pl. ɲɔ́mɔkɔsáikᵃ. n. criminal, offender, wrongdoer.

ɲómoŋgó (ɲómoŋgóò-) n. cassava, manioc (plant and roots). *Manihot sp.*

ɲɔmɔránón (ɲɔmɔránónì-) v. to be impudent, insolent.

ɲomórótòtᵃ (ɲomórótòtò-) n. African rock python. *Python sebae*.

ɲómóta (ɲómótaá-) pl. ɲómótàìkᵃ. n. howitzer, mortar.

ɲómotoká (ɲómotokáà-) pl. ɲómotokáìkᵃ. n. automobile, car, vehicle.

ɲómotokátáƙáyᵃ (ɲómotoká-táƙáɨ-) pl. ɲómotokátáƙáɨkᵃ. n. shoe made of tire rubber.

ɲómotokéèkwᵃ (ɲómotoké-èkù-) pl. ɲómotokéekwitín. n. headlight. Lit. 'vehicle-eye'.

ɲómototó (ɲómototóò-) n. banana, plantain (plant and fruit). *Musa sp.*

ɲónomokére (ɲónomokéreé-) n. shrub species whose roots are crushed, soaked in water, and drunk as a remedy for headaches. *Withania somnifera*. See also *ikitínicɛmɛ́r*.

ɲónótᵃ (ɲónótì-) pl. ɲónótìkᵃ. n. monetary bill or note.

Noŋoleɓókᵃ (Noŋoleɓókó-) n. a personal name.

ɲɔ́ŋɔmɓɛ́ (ɲɔ́ŋɔmɓɛ́è-) pl. ɲɔ́ŋɔmɓɛ́ìkᵃ. n. razorblade.

ɲɔŋɔ́rɔ́mɔ̀n (ɲɔŋɔ́rɔ́mɔ̀nì-) v. to be dirty, soiled, unclean (from dirt or food). See also *ŋɔrɔ́ɲɔ́mɔ̀n*.

ɲɔ́ŋɔtsán (ɲɔ́ŋɔtsánɨ́-) n. bedlam, pandemonium, panic.

ɲɔ́pɔ́c (ɲɔ́pɔ́cɨ̀-) pl. ɲɔ́pɔ́cɨ̀kᵃ. n. billfold, wallet.

ɲɔpɔɗɛ (ɲɔpɔɗɛɛ́-) n. flesh left on a freshly skinned hide. Compare with *xáƙwᵃ*.

ɲɔ́pɔɗɔkɨ́ (ɲɔ́pɔɗɔkɨ́ɨ̀-) n. biting fly, cleg. *Haematopota sp.*

ɲɔ́pɔkɔca (ɲɔ́pɔkɔcaá-) n. false testimony, perjury.

ɲopol (ɲopolɨ́-) n. best and/or first portion of beer or meat.

ɲɔpɔl (ɲɔpɔlɨ́-) n. external oblique: muscle from the upper thigh to the lower ribs.

ɲɔpɔ́táyᵃ (ɲɔpɔ́táɨ̀-) pl. ɲipɔ́táyᵃ. n. slave. See also *ɲipɔ́táɨ̀àm*.

ɲópoté (ɲópotéè-) n. grain regrown the second time.

Nɔrɔbatᵃ (Nɔrɔbatɨ́-) n. name of a river.

Nɔrɔbatᵃ (Nɔrɔbatɨ́-) n. Norobat: one of the Ik's twelve clans.

Nɔrɔbatɨ́ám (Nɔrɔbatɨ́-ámà-) pl. Nɔrɔbatíikᵃ. n. Norobat clan member.

Nɔ́rɔ́cɔm (Nɔ́rɔ́cɔmɔ́-) n. a personal name.

ɲóróiroyᵃ (ɲóróiroí-) n. mildew, mold. See also *lóburuɟᵃ*.

ɲɔrɔkɔ (ɲɔrɔkɔɔ́-) pl. ɲɔrɔ́kɔ̀ɨkᵃ. n. famine, starvation.

ɲɔrɔn (ɲɔrɔnɨ́-) n. drought.

ɲorópúò (ɲorópúò-) n. ritual organs from the tongue downward (designated for the elders; not including the liver, stomach, or intestines).

ɲorótónitᵃ (ɲorótónití-) *pl.* ɲorótónìtìkᵃ. *n.* upper arm.

ɲorótónitíém (ɲorótónití-émè-) *n.* bicep and/or tricep.

ɲorótónitíɔ́kᵃ (ɲorótónití-ɔ́kà-) *pl.* ɲorótónitikɔɔkɨtín. *n.* humerus: bone of the upper arm.

ɲɔ́sɔ́ɗa (ɲɔ́sɔ́ɗaá-) *pl.* ɲɔ́sɔ́ɗàɨkᵃ. *n.* carbonated drink, pop, soda.

ɲɔsɔkatá (ɲɔsɔkatáà-) *pl.* ɲɔsɔkatáɨkᵃ. *n.* cigarette.

ɲósóƙis (ɲósóƙisí-) *pl.* ɲósóƙisíkᵃ. *n.* sock.

ɲosoƙoloké (ɲosoƙolokéè-) *pl.* ɲosoƙolokéìkᵃ. *n.* shorts, pair of trunks.

ɲɔ́sɔ́la (ɲɔ́sɔ́laá-) *pl.* ɲɔ́sɔ́làɨkᵃ. *n.* solar panel.

ɲósomá (ɲósomáà-) *n.* education, schooling, studies.

ɲósomáám (ɲósomá-ámà-) *pl.* ɲósomáíkᵃ. *n.* pupil, student.

ɲósomáicíkᵃ (ɲósomá-icíká-) *n.* readings.

ɲɔ́sɔ́ɔ́ƙatᵃ (ɲɔ́sɔ́ɔ́ƙatá-) *pl.* ɲɔ́sɔ́ɔ́ƙàtìkᵃ. *n.* large pitfall trap for big game.

ɲósóto (ɲósótoó-) *pl.* ɲósótòikᵃ. *n.* pointed granary cover. Also called ɲésóto.

ɲósukarí (ɲósukaríí-) *n.* sugar.

ɲɔ́sʉmár (ɲɔ́sʉmárɨ-) *pl.* ɲɔ́sʉmárɨkᵃ. *n.* nail.

ɲòtᵃ (ɲòtà-) *pl.* ɲótíkwᵃ. *1 n.* foreign friend (out-group). *2 n.* in-law (distant or removed).

ɲɔtᵃ (ɲɔtɔ́-) *1 n.* men. *2 n.* husbands.

ɲotánánès (ɲotánánèsì-) *1 n.* friendliness, friendship (with non-Ik). *2 n.* to be related indirectly by marriage (e.g. to the parents of a child's or sibling's spouse).

ɲotánónuƙotᵃ (ɲotánónuƙotí-) *v.* to make friends (with non-Ik).

ɲótíkónánès (ɲótíkónánèsì-) *n.* friendliness, friendship (with non-Ik foreigners).

ɲɔto ni *interj.* these guys, I tell you! (an expression of any positive or negative opinion about men or multiple objects). *Lit.* 'these men'.

ɲotóbòr (ɲotóbòrì-) *pl.* ɲotóbòrìkᵃ. *n.* seasonal marsh or swamp. See also ɲɛkɨpɔ́r.

ɲɔ́tɔɗɔpá (ɲɔ́tɔɗɔpáà-) *pl.* ɲɔ́tɔɗɔpáɨkᵃ. *n.* small oil lamp.

ɲotókósitᵃ (ɲotókósití-) *pl.* ɲotókósìtìkᵃ. *n.* tall column of hair colored with red clay.

ɲotolim (ɲotolimí-) *pl.* ɲotólímìkᵃ. *n.* large metal crowbar or pry bar (used to break and move rocks).

ɲótooɗó (ɲótooɗóò-) *pl.* ɲótooɗóikᵃ. *n.* crook, curve-necked cane (preferred by Turkana women).

ɲótorós (ɲótorósì-) *pl.* ɲótorósìkᵃ. *n.* pair of pants or trousers. Also called ɲétorós.

ɲótótsᵃ (ɲótótsì-) *pl.* ɲótótsìkᵃ. *1 n.* flashlight, torch. *2 n.* lip herpes.

ɲɔ́tsɔ́ɓɛ (ɲɔ́tsɔ́ɓɛɛ́-) *pl.* ɲɔ́tsɔ́ɓèɨkᵃ. *n.* cap made of giraffe-tail hairs.

ɲɔ́tsɔ́ɓitsɔɓᵃ (ɲɔ́tsɔ́ɓitsɔɓɨ́-) *n.* hodgepodge, melange, mishmash.

ɲótsorón (ɲótsorónì-) *pl.* ɲótsorónìkᵃ. *n.* latrine, outhouse, toilet. See also ets'-íhò.

ɲóvakáɗò (ɲóvakáɗòò-) *n.* avocado (tree and fruit). *Persea americana*.

ɲówoɗí (ɲówoɗíì-) *n.* seed butter, tahini (miture of peanut and sesame pastes).

ɲʉmés (ɲʉmésɨ-) *v.* to want, wish for.

ɲumɛtés (ɲumɛtésɨ-) *v.* to choose, decide on, settle on. See also *tɔsɛɛtés* and *xɔ́bɛtés*.

ɲúɲɛ́s (ɲúɲɛ́sɨ-) *v.* to gather and move (e.g. grain, rubbish, soil).

ɲúɲɛ́sukɔt[a] (ɲúɲɛ́sukɔtɨ-) *v.* to gather up and remove (e.g. grain, rubbish, soil).

ɲuɲɛtés (ɲuɲɛtésɨ-) *v.* to gather up and move (e.g. grain, rubbish, soil).

ŋ

ŋabér (ŋabérí-) *pl.* **ŋábèrìk**ᵃ. *n.* rib.

ŋabérá ƙwàzàᵋ *n.* side part of clothing. *Lit.* 'rib of clothing'.

ŋábèrèdᵃ (ŋábèrèdè-) *pl.* **ŋabérík ìn**. *n.* flank, side part. *Lit.* 'its rib'.

ŋábèrìkàdè (ŋábèrìkà-dèà-) *pl.* **ŋáberikadɛík**ᵃ. *n.* costovertebral joint: where ribs join the backbone.

ŋábèrìkèèm (ŋábèrìkè-èmè-) *n.* rib meat.

ŋabérɔ̀kᵃ (ŋabérí-ɔ̀kà-) *pl.* **ŋáberikɔɔkìtín**. *n.* costal bone, rib bone.

ŋabérᵒ *n.* beside, obliquely, sideways. *Lit.* 'by rib'.

ŋábès (ŋábèsì-) *v.* to dress, put on, wear.

ŋábɛsʉkɔtᵃ (ŋábɛsʉkɔtí-) *v.* to complete, finish.

ŋabitᵃ (ŋabití-) *n.* beads, beadwork.

ŋábitetés (ŋábitetésí-) *v.* to dress up, get dressed.

ŋabɔ́bɔ̀ (ŋabɔ́bɔ̀ɔ̀-) *n.* danceground.

ŋabɔ́bòìm (ŋabɔ́bò-ìmà-) *pl.* **ŋabɔ́bowik**ᵃ. *n.* bastard, illegitimate child, love child. *Lit.* 'danceground-child'.

ŋábɔnʉkɔtᵃ (ŋábɔnʉkɔtí-) *1 v.* to be completed, done, finished. *2 v.* to be enough, plenty, sufficient. See also *nábɔnʉkɔt*ᵃ.

ŋaɓiŋáɓón (ŋaɓiŋáɓónì-) *v.* to burn (of the eyes when something foreign enters them).

ŋàɓòn (ŋàɓònì-) *v.* to burn (of eyes when something foreign enters them).

ŋáɓɔ́ɔla (ŋáɓɔ́ɔlaá-) *pl.* **ŋáɓɔ́ɔ̀làìk**ᵃ. *n.* cent, penny.

ŋáɓutús (ŋáɓutúsù-) *pl.* **ŋáɓutúsìk**ᵃ. *n.* boot.

ŋáɓʉʉrá (ŋáɓʉʉráà-) *pl.* **ŋáɓʉʉráìk**ᵃ. *n.* modern leather shoe.

ŋadétá (ŋadétáì-) *pl.* **ŋadétáìk**ᵃ. *n.* sandal, slipper.

ŋáítɔ̀ (ŋáítɔ̀ɔ̀-) *n.* gruel, porridge. See also *ɲéúji*.

ŋakiɓʉkᵃ (ŋakiɓʉkú-) *n.* yogurt.

Ŋákiswahílìtòdᵃ (Ŋákiswahílì-tòdà-) *n.* Swahili language.

ŋáƙiran (ŋáƙiraní-) *n.* designs, emblems, etchings (e.g. on gourds according to Ik clan).

ŋálàkᵃ (ŋálàkà) *ideo.* for nothing, in vain.

ŋalɛ́pán (ŋalɛ́pánà-) *n.* fresh milk.

ŋalólómòn (ŋalólómònì-) *v.* to be toothless.

ŋálómóyá (ŋálómóyáà-) *n.* small plant whose roots are eaten (baboons also like them) and whose leaves are sour like tamarind. *Oenanthe palustris*.

ŋalúɓᵃ (ŋalúɓá-) *1 n.* soft fruit of the *ts'ɔkɔm* tree. *2 n.* toothless gums.

ŋàm (ŋàmà) *ideo.* abruptly, suddenly.

ɲám (ŋámá-) *n.* sorghum.

ŋámá na buɗám *n.* sorghum variety with black seeds.

ŋámá nà ɓèts'ᵃ *n.* sorghum variety with white seeds.

ŋámá nà ɗìwᵃ *n.* sorghum variety with red seeds.

ŋamarʉwáyᵃ (ŋamarʉwáì-) *n.* millet beer. See also *rébèmɛs*.

ŋamíá (ŋamíáì-) *n.* hundred (100). No plural form.

ŋamiɲámɔ́n (ŋamiɲámɔ́nì-) *v.* to rush into things (eating, talking, etc.).

ŋámɨ́rɔ̀ (ŋámɨ́rɔ̀ɔ̀-) *n.* beer grist: moist fermented flour used to make beer.

ŋamɔ́lɔ́l (ŋamɔ́lɔ́lɔ̀-) *n.* leather strips worn by a killer from the animal he slew as an atoning sacrifice for taking the life of a human being.

ŋamur (ŋamurí-) *n.* common duiker. *Cephalophus grimmia.*

ŋàn (ŋànà-) *pro.* each one.

ŋáɲámòn (ŋáɲámònì-) *v.* to open.

ŋáɲɛ́s (ŋáɲɛ́sɨ-) *v.* to open.

ŋáɲɛ́sɨ̀àw[a] (ŋáɲɛ́sɨ̀-àwà-) *pl.* ŋáɲɛ́siawík[a]. *n.* gun safety lever.

ŋáɲɛ́sʉkɔt[a] (ŋáɲɛ́sʉkɔtɨ́-) *1 v.* to open up. *2 v.* to uncover.

ŋaɲɛtɛ́s (ŋaɲɛtɛ́sɨ́-) *v.* to open up.

ŋáɲɔ́s (ŋáɲɔ́sɨ-) *1 v.* to be open. *2 v.* to be public.

ŋapokóy[a] (ŋapokóɪ-) *n.* white leather leggings (from knee to ankle).

ŋápʉp[a] (ŋápʉpú-) *n.* beer grist: dry fermented flour used to make beer.

ŋàr (ŋàrù) *ideo.* gravelly, rockily.

ŋaráɓámòn (ŋaráɓámònì-) *v.* to be rough (e.g. landscape, sandpaper, or any surface).

ŋaríám (ŋaríámù-) *n.* ironstone.

ŋárɔpɨyá (ŋárɔpɨyáɨ-) *n.* money. See also *kaûdz[a]*.

ŋárɔpɨyéékw[a] (ŋárɔpɨyé-ékù-) *n.* coin. *Lit.* 'money-eye'.

ŋarúdɔ̀n (ŋarúdɔ̀nɨ-) *v.* to be gravelly, rocky. See also *rakákámòn*.

ŋarúxánòn (ŋarúxánònì-) *v.* to be coiled loosely (like feces or a snake).

ŋásɛntáɨ̀èkw[a] (ŋásɛntáɨ̀-èkù-) *n.* cent, shilling. *Lit.* 'shillings-eye'.

ŋásɛntáy[a] (ŋásɛntáɨ-) *n.* cents, shillings.

Ŋasɛp[a] (Ŋasɛpɛ́-) *n.* name of a hill or mountain.

ŋasɨ́ƙáárɨ̀àm (ŋasɨ́ƙáárɨ̀-àmà-) *pl.* ŋasɨ́ƙáár. *n.* guard.

ŋásír (ŋásírì-) *n.* decoration.

ŋátámɛta (ŋátámɛtaá-) *n.* mind, thoughts.

ŋatɛ́tɔ́n (ŋatɛ́tɔ́nɨ̀-) *v.* to run this way.

ŋatíón (ŋatíónì-) *v.* to run multiply.

ŋátíónis (ŋátíónisí-) *n.* difficulty.

ŋatɨ́tɛ́sʉkɔt[a] (ŋatɨ́tɛ́sʉkɔtɨ́-) *v.* to send off running.

ŋàtɔ̀n (ŋàtɔ̀nɨ̀-) *v.* to run (a certain direction).

ŋatɔnʉkɔt[a] (ŋatɔnʉkɔtɨ́-) *v.* to run off/away, take off running.

ŋátɔɔsa (ŋátɔɔsaá-) *n.* biltong, dried meat, jerky.

ŋátuɓe (ŋátuɓeé-) *n.* edible gourd leaves.

ŋátur (ŋáturú-) *n.* blossom, flower.

ŋawɨ́l (ŋawɨ́lá-) *n.* chaff dust.

ŋawɨlɛs (ŋawɨlɛsɨ́-) *v.* to chance, come across, happen upon. See also *itsɔŋɛtɛ́s*.

ŋawɨ́ɔ́n (ŋawɨ́ɔ́nɨ̀-) *v.* to be ajar, open (e.g. a door, jerrycan, or window). See also *bɔrɔ́ɔ́n*.

ŋaxɛ́tɔ́n (ŋaxɛ́tɔ́nɨ̀-) *1 v.* to be frightened, startled. *2 v.* to cringe, flinch.

ŋaxɨtɛtɛ́s (ŋaxɨtɛtɛ́sɨ́-) *v.* to frighten, startle.

ŋaxɔ̀b[a] (ŋaxɔ́bù-) *pl.* ŋaxɔ́bɨ̀k[a]. *n.* placenta.

ŋazul (ŋazulú-) *n.* grume: coagulated blood.

ŋɛlɛ́mɛ́tɔ̀n (ŋɛlɛ́mɛ́tɔ̀nɨ̀-) *v.* to chip off (e.g. the edge of a pot).

ŋɛlɛ́s (ŋɛlɛ́sɨ́-) *v.* to chip. See also *tɛŋɛlɛs*.

ŋér (ŋérá-) *pl.* ŋeríkwᵃ. *n.* five-pronged mingling stick. Often made from the *rukûdz* tree.

ŋgóɛ́n (ŋgó-ɛ́nɨ́-) *pro.* ours (excluding the addresse).

ŋgóím (ŋgó-ímà-) *pl.* ŋgóímín. *1 n.* sibling. *2 n.* my cousin (father's brother's child).

ŋgónébitín (ŋgó-nébitíní-) *n.* ourselves (excluding the addressee). *Lit.* 'our bodies'.

ŋgúf (ŋgúfù-) *n.* power, strength. See also *ŋixás*.

ŋgwᵃ (ŋgó-) *pro.* we/our/us (exclusive of addressee). This pronoun excludes the addressee. Contrast with *ɲjín*.

ŋɓalɛl (ŋɨ́ɓalɛlɛ́-) *n.* brown edible mushroom species.

ŋɨ́ɓarɛn (ŋɨ́ɓarɛnɨ́-) *n.* flocks, herds, livestock.

Ŋɨ́ɓɔ́kɔráám (Ŋɨ́ɓɔ́kɔrá-ámà-) *pl.* Ŋɨ́ɓɔ́kɔra. *n.* Bokora person.

Ŋɨ́ɓɔ́ŋɔrɔna (Ŋɨ́ɓɔ́ŋɔrɔnaá-) *n.* Ŋiɓoŋorona: one of the Ik's twelve clans.

Ŋɨ́ɓɔ́ŋɔrɔnááм (Ŋɨ́ɓɔ́ŋɔrɔná-ámà-) *pl.* Ŋɨ́ɓɔ́ŋɔrɔnáíkᵃ. *n.* Ŋiɓoŋorona clan member.

ŋɨɓóóìam (ŋɨɓóóì-àmà-) *pl.* ŋɨɓóóiikᵃ. *n.* loader.

ŋɨ́ɓúkúìam (ŋɨ́ɓúkúì-àmà-) *pl.* ŋɨ́ɓúkúyᵃ. *n.* foreigner, outsider.

ŋɨ́ɗɛrɛpáɨ̀am (ŋɨ́ɗɛrɛpáɨ̀-àmà-) *pl.* ŋɨ́ɗɛrɛpáɨ̀. *n.* driver, operator.

Ŋɨ́ɗóŋiro (Ŋɨ́ɗóŋiroó-) *n.* Dhaasanac people.

Ŋɨ́ɗɔ́tsa (Ŋɨ́ɗɔ́tsaá-) *n.* Ŋiɗotsa: one of the Ik's twelve clans.

Ŋɨ́ɗɔ́tsááм (Ŋɨ́ɗɔ́tsá-ámà-) *pl.* Ŋɨ́ɗɔ́tsáíkᵃ. *n.* Ŋiɗotsa clan member.

ŋɨɗukan (ŋɨɗukaná-) *n.* African fan palm or Borassus palm: palm species with a deep taproot and whose fruits are eaten; its branches are used as sleeping mats and for house building.

Ŋɨ́eɓuráiikᵃ (Ŋɨeɓurái-icé-) *n.* Hebrews: book in the New Testament.

Ŋɨ́epesóíkᵃ (Ŋɨepesó-ícé-) *n.* Ephesians: book in the New Testament.

ŋɨ́funɗíàm (ŋɨ́funɗí-àmà-) *pl.* ŋɨ́funɗíikᵃ. *n.* builder, mechanic, handyman of any kind.

Ŋɨ́galatíaikᵃ (Ŋɨ́galatía-icé-) *n.* Galatians: book in the New Testament.

Ŋɨ́gɨríkɨ̀am (Ŋɨ́gɨríkɨ̀-àmà-) *pl.* Ŋɨ́gɨríkᵃ. *n.* Greek person.

Ŋɨ́gɨríkɨtôdᵃ (Ŋɨ́gɨríkɨ̀-tòdà-) *n.* Greek language.

ŋɨɨɗɛ́s (ŋɨɨɗɛ́sɨ́-) *v.* to clean, rub, wipe.

ŋɨɨɗɛ́sɨ̀kwàz (ŋɨɨɗɛ́sɨ̀-ƙwàzà-) *pl.* ŋɨɨɗɛ́sɨkwazíkᵃ. *n.* baby wipe, wipe (cloth for cleaning a soiled baby).

ŋɨɨɗɛ́súƙɔtᵃ (ŋɨɨɗɛ́súƙɔtɨ́-) *1 v.* to clean, rub, or wipe off. *2 v.* to call off, cancel.

ŋɨɨɗetɛ́s (ŋɨɨɗetɛ́sɨ́-) *v.* to clean up, wipe up.

Ŋɨɨɗɨŋáám (Ŋɨɨɗɨŋá-ámà-) *pl.* Ŋɨɨɗɨŋa. *n.* Didinga person.

Ŋɨɨɗɨŋátôdᵃ (Ŋɨɨɗɨŋá-tódà-) *n.* Didinga language.

ŋɨɨɗɨ́tɛ́súƙɔtᵃ (ŋɨɨɗɨ́tɛ́súƙɔtɨ́-) *v.* to cancel.

ŋiites (ŋiitesí-) *v.* to grease, lubricate (with lotion or oil).

ŋiitésúƙotᵃ (ŋiitésúƙotí-) *v.* to grease up, lubricate (with lotion or oil).

ŋɨ́jokopí (ŋɨ́jokopíà-) *n.* topophagnosia: navigational disorientation.

ŋɨ́kaɗɛpɨ́ɗɛ́pᵃ (ŋɨ́kaɗɛpɨ́ɗɛ́pù-) *n.* fleas. See also *naɗɛ́pᵃ*.

ŋíkaɗiiɗí (ŋíkaɗiiɗíì-) *n.* red-cheeked cordon-bleu. *Uraeginthus bengalus.*

ŋíkafɨ̀rɨ̀àm (ŋíkafɨ̀rɨ̀-àmà-) *pl.* **ŋíkafɨ́r.** *n.* heathen, pagan.

ŋíkalʉtʉ́rɔ (ŋíkalʉtʉ́rɔɔ́-) *n.* small unripe pumpkin. See also *ɗɔ́l.*

Ŋíkátapʉ́ám (Ŋíkátapʉ́-ámà-) *pl.* **Ŋíkátap**[a]. *n.* Napore person. See also *Tɔbɔŋɔ́ám.*

ŋíkatikisítààm (ŋíkatikisítà-àmà-) *pl.* **ŋíkatikisítà.** *n.* catechist.

Ŋíkátsolíám (Ŋíkátsolí-ámà-) *pl.* **Ŋíkátsol.** *n.* Acholi person.

Ŋíkátsolítôd[a] (Ŋíkátsolí-tódà-) *n.* Acholi language.

Ŋíkiristóìàm (Ŋíkiristóì-àmà-) *pl.* **Ŋíkiristóì.** *n.* Christian.

ŋíkiristóìnànès (ŋíkiristóìnànèsì-) *n.* Christianity, Christlikeness.

ŋíkísila (ŋíkísilaá-) *n.* lawful order, peace, security, stability. See also *ɲekisil.*

Ŋíkolosáik[a] (Ŋíkolosá-icé-) *n.* Colossians: book in the New Testament.

Ŋíkoríntoik[a] (Ŋíkorínto-icé-) *n.* Corinthians: books in the New Testament.

Ŋíkósowa (Ŋíkósowaá-) *n.* Ateker name for the traditional Ik men's age-group with the buffalo as its totem (#10 in the historical line).

ŋìl (ŋìlà-) *pl.* **ŋílítín.** *n.* gastric mill, gizzard, ventriculus.

ŋiléɓùiàm (ŋiléɓùi-àmà-) *pl.* **ŋiléɓúy**[a]. *n.* servant indentured to pay off a tax debt.

ŋiléɓúinànès (ŋiléɓúinànèsì-) *1 n.* indentureship (to pay off tax debt). *2 n.* enslavement, slavery. See also *ŋipɔ́tá̀inànès.*

ŋilééts[a] (ŋiléétsì-) *n.* disgrace, shame.

ŋiléétsiàm (ŋiléétsì-àmà-) *pl.* **ŋiléétsiik**[a]. *n.* disgraceful, shameful person.

ŋiléétsìnànès (ŋiléétsìnànèsì-) *n.* disgracefulness, shamefulness.

ŋilíŋílánón (ŋilíŋílánónì-) *1 v.* to break into pieces. *2 v.* to break off in groups.

ŋimaalímùàm (ŋimaalímù-àmà-) *pl.* **ŋimaalím.** *n.* instructor, teacher, trainer. See also *itátámésíàm.*

ŋɨ́máarɔy[a] (ŋɨ́máarɔɨ́-) *n.* small plant whose roots are dug up and eaten raw. *Stathmostelma peduncalatum.*

ŋɨ́maláɨ̀kàn (ŋɨ́maláɨ̀kànɨ̀-) *n.* angel.

ŋɨ́mamɓúsɨ̀àm (ŋɨ́mamɓúsɨ̀-àmà-) *pl.* **ŋɨ́mamɓús.** *n.* prisoner.

ŋimánétòn (ŋimánétònì-) *v.* to encounter, meet. Also pronounced as *ɲimánétòn.*

Ŋímaraɓúiàm (Ŋímaraɓúi-àmà-) *pl.* **Ŋímaraɓúy**[a]. *n.* Arab.

Ŋɨ́mariɔkɔ́t[a] (Ŋɨ́mariɔkɔ́tɔ̀-) *n.* Ateker name for the traditional Ik men's age-group known for struggling for blood (the oldest, #1). The Ik name is *Ŋuesííka Sèà*[e].

Ŋímeniŋíám (Ŋímeniŋí-ámà-) *pl.* **Ŋímeniŋ.** *n.* Mening person.

Ŋímeniŋítôd[a] (Ŋímeniŋí-tódà-) *n.* Mening language.

Ŋímérimoŋ (Ŋímérimoŋá-) *n.* Ateker name for the traditional Ik men's age-group with the ostrich as its totem (#9 in the historical line).

Ŋímiiɗiàm (Ŋímiiɗí-àmà-) *pl.* **Ŋímiiɗí.** *n.* Indian.

ŋɨ́mɔ́kɔka (ŋɨ́mɔ́kɔkaá-) *n.* young men. See also *karatsɨ́na.*

ŋɨ́mɔ́kɔkáám (ŋɨ́mɔ́kɔkáámà-) *n.* male youth, young man.

Ŋímorokóléìàm (Ŋímorokóléì-àmà-) *pl.* Ŋímorokólé. *n.* Charismatic or Pentecostal Christian. Based on a Luganda word meaning 'Are you born again?'

Ŋímúgandáéàm (Ŋímúgandáé-àmà-) *pl.* Ŋímúgandáᵉ. *n.* Muganda.

Ŋímúgandáétòdᵃ (Ŋímúgandáé-tòdà-) *n.* Luganda.

ŋímúí (ŋímúíì-) *n.* twins.

Ŋímusukúìtòdᵃ (Ŋímusukúì-tòdà-) *n.* English or any European language. See also *Bets'oniicétôdᵃ*.

ŋímutsurúsìàm (ŋímutsurúsì-àmà-) *pl.* ŋímutsurús. *n.* hawker, peddler, trader.

ŋímutsurúsìnànès (ŋímutsurúsìnànèsì-) *n.* being a hawker, peddler, or trader.

ŋíɲampáràyàm (ŋíɲampáràyà-àmà-) *pl.* ŋíɲampáray ᵃ. *n.* guard of the local council official who used to assist in the collection of taxes.

Ŋíɲaɲíyààm (Ŋíɲaɲíyá-àmà-) *pl.* Ŋíɲaɲíyᵃ. *n.* Nyang'ia person.

Ŋíɲaɲíyátòdᵃ (Ŋíɲaɲíyá-tòdà-) *n.* Nyang'ia language.

Ŋíɲaŋkóléfiyɔ́ (Ŋíɲaŋkólé-fiyɔ́ɔ̀-) *n.* Ankole cow.

Ŋíɲéɲéyᵃ (Ŋíɲéɲéɨ̀-) *n.* Sudanese rebels that used to live on mountains Lomil and Zulia in the late 20th century.

Ŋíɲátuɲo (Ŋíɲátuɲoó-) *n.* Ateker name for the traditional Ik men's age-group with the lion as its totem (#2 in the historical line). The Ik name is *Máóikᵃ*.

Ŋíɲóleɲaŋ (Ŋíɲóleɲaŋá-) *n.* Ateker name for the traditional Ik men's age-group with the gazelle as its totem (#11 in the historical line).

ŋìòn (ŋìònì-) *v.* to be slick (e.g of skin, from oil or sweat).

Ŋíóyatom (Ŋŋíóyatomé-) *n.* Nyangatom people.

ŋípákásíàm (ŋípákásí-àmà-) *pl.* ŋípákásí. *n.* servant, slave.

ŋipɔ́táɨ̀àm (ŋipɔ́táɨ̀-àmà-) *pl.* ŋipɔ́táyᵃ. *n.* slave. See also *ɲopɔ́táyᵃ*.

ŋipɔ́táɨ̀nànès (ŋipɔ́táɨ̀nànèsì-) *n.* enslavement, slavery. See also *ŋilébúìnànès*.

ŋípyà (ŋípyà) *n.* new thing, novelty.

ŋípyɛn (ŋípyɛnɨ́-) *n.* demon, earth spirit, evil spirit. See also *ɲekípyé*.

ŋírés (ŋírésì-) *v.* to rake. See also *ikwɛrɛs*.

ŋirɨ́ɓɨ́mɔ̀n (ŋirɨ́ɓɨ́mɔ̀nɨ̀-) *1 v.* to be stubby (e.g. of maize kernels or teeth). *2 v.* to be stubby-toothed, have stubby teeth.

Ŋiriko (Ŋirikoó-) *n.* a personal name.

Ŋɨ́rɔmánɔ́niikᵃ (Ŋɨ́rɔmánɔ́ni-icé-) *n.* Romans: New Testament book.

ŋirotsánón (ŋirotsánónì-) *v.* to be tan, tawny.

ŋirúkóìnànès (ŋirúkóìnànèsì-) *n.* banditry, brigandry.

Ŋísaakɔ́lɨ̀àm (Ŋísaakɔ́lɨ̀-àmà-) *pl.* Ŋísaakɔ́l. *n.* Nyangatom person. Also called *Ŋísɔɔkɔ́lɨ̀àm*.

ŋísil (ŋísilɨ̀-) *1 n.* fiber, silk (of hair or any other substance). *2 n.* nerve.

Ŋɨ́silám (Ŋɨ́silámʉ-) *n.* Islam.

Ŋisíráyᵃ (Ŋisíráɨ̀-) *n.* Ateker name for the traditional Ik men's age-group with the leopard as its totem (#7 in the historical line). The Ik name is *Nʉsííkᵃ*.

ŋɨ́sɔrɔkᵃ (ŋɨ́sɔrɔkɔ́-) *n.* teenage boys, young men. See also *pànèès*.

ŋɨ́sɔrɔkɔ́ám (ŋɨ́sɔrɔkɔ́-àmà-) *pl.* ŋɨ́sɔrɔkᵃ. *n.* teenage boy, young men.

Ŋɨ́sʉmálɨ̀àm (Ŋɨ́sʉmálɨ̀-àmà-) *pl.* Ŋɨ́sʉmál. *n.* Somali person.

Ŋísumáłitòdᵃ (Ŋɨ́sʉmáłɨ-tòdà-) *n.* Somali language.

Ŋítéɓuríám (Ŋítéɓurí-ámà-) *pl.* **Ŋítéɓur**. *n.* Labworian, Thur person.

Ŋítéɓurítôdᵃ (Ŋítéɓurí-tódà-) *n.* Ethur language (of Abim).

Ŋítépes (Ŋítépesí-) *n.* Soo/Tepeth people.

Ŋítépesítôdᵃ (Ŋítépesí-tódà-) *n.* Soo/Tepeth language.

Ŋítesalóníkaikᵃ (Ŋítesalóníka-icé-) *n.* Thessalonians: books in the New Testament.

Ŋítésóàm (Ŋítésó-àmà-) *pl.* **Ŋítésó**. *n.* Teso person.

Ŋítésótôdᵃ (Ŋítésó-tódà-) *n.* Ateso language.

ŋítésurɔ (ŋítésurɔɔ́-) *n.* plant species that resembles a banana but is inedible; its small black seeds are used as beads.

Ŋítɨ́ira (Ŋítɨ́iraá-) *n.* Ateker name for the traditional Ik men's age-group with the Umbrella Thorn tree as its totem (#3 in the historical line).

Ŋitɔ́mé (Ŋitɔ́mɛ́ɨ-) *n.* Ateker name for the traditional Ik men's age-group with the elephant as its totem (#5 in the historical line). The Ik name is *Oŋoriikᵃ*.

ŋítsaɗéníàm (ŋítsaɗéníàmà-) *pl.* **ŋítsaɗéniik**ᵃ. *n.* witness. See also *itelesíám*.

ŋítsan (ŋítsaní-) *n.* hardship, problems, troubles.

ŋítsen (ŋítsení-) *n.* curses.

ŋits'e (ŋits'eí-) *n.* small white mushroom that is dried and then boiled in soup where it tastes like meat.

Ŋítúkoyᵃ (Ŋítúkoí-) *n.* Ateker name for the traditional Ik men's age-group with the zebra as its totem (#4 in the historical line). The Ik name is *Zɨnáíkᵃ*.

ŋítúmɨkᵃ (ŋítúmɨkà-) *n.* bedbugs, chinces.

ŋítúrumúám (ŋítúrumú-ámà-) *pl.* **ŋítúrum**. *n.* betrayer, slanderer, sower of dissension.

Ŋɨ́wápɛtɔ (Ŋɨ́wápɛtɔɔ́-) *n.* Ateker name for the traditional Ik men's age-group with the eland as its totem (#6 in the historical line).

ŋixás (ŋixásɨ́-) *n.* power, strength. See also *ŋgúf*.

ŋixɨ́tésukɔtᵃ (ŋixɨ́tésukɔtɨ́-) *1 v.* to harden, make hard. *2 v.* to fortify, strengthen, toughen.

ŋìxɔ̀n (ŋɨ̀xɔ̀nɨ̀-) *1 v.* to be hard. *2 v.* to be powerful, strong. *3 v.* to be expensive.

ŋixɔna ikáᵉ *v.* hardheadedness.

ŋixɔnukɔtᵃ (ŋixɔnukɔtɨ́-) *1 v.* to become harder, harden. *2 v.* to become stronger, strengthen.

Ŋíyuɗáíàm (Ŋíyuɗáí-àmà-) *pl.* **Ŋíyuɗáy**ᵃ. *n.* Hebrew, Jew.

Ŋíyuɗáítôdᵃ (Ŋíyuɗáí-tòdà-) *n.* Hebrew language.

ŋɨ́zɛ̀s (ŋɨ́zɛ̀sɨ̀-) *v.* to alert, signal (e.g. by coughing or clearing one's throat).

ŋɨ́zɨ̀mà (<ŋɨ́zɨ̀mɔ̀ɔ̀n) *v.*

ŋɨ́zɨ̀mɔ̀ɔ̀n (ŋɨ́zɨ̀mɔ̀ɔ̀nɨ̀-/ŋɨ́zima-) *v.* to be grouchy, grumpy. See also *gakúrúmòn*.

ŋká (<ŋkóón) *v.*

ŋkaɗɛɛɗéyᵃ (ŋkaɗɛɛɗɛ́ɨ-) *1 n.* sparks. *2 n.* gold flecks.

ŋkaión (ŋkaiónì-) *v.* to get up (several times or of several people).

ŋkáítetés (ŋkáítetésí-) *v.* to get up, raise, stand up.

ŋkéétòn (ŋkéétònì-) *v.* to get up, rise, stand up.

ŋkérépᵃ (ŋkérépè-) *1 n.* craziness, madness, mental illness. *2 n.* demon possession. See also *lejé*.

ŋkɔ́lɨ̀à (ŋkɔ́lɨ̀à-) *n.* fish.

ŋkóón (ŋkóónì-/ŋká-) *v.* to get up, rise, stand up.

Ŋkóryó (Ŋkóryóo-) *n.* Ateker name for the traditional Ik men's age-group with the giraffe as its totem (#8 in the historical line). The Ik name is *Gwaɨts'íikᵃ*.

ŋkújɨ́tᵃ (ŋkújɨ́tɨ̀-) *n.* chyme: stomach contents. See also *eyᵃ*.

Ŋkúlákᵃ (Ŋkúlákà-) *n.* Kuliak: a name given the Ik, Nyang'i, and So/Tepeth peoples as a group.

ŋkwáŋáyᵃ (ŋkwáŋáɨ̀-) *1 n.* aluminum. *2 n.* aluminum lip plug.

ŋƙáƙᵃ (ŋƙáƙá-) *1 n.* food, grub. *2 n.* eating, feeding.

Ŋƙáƙá Komúnióᵉ *n.* Holy Communion: a Catholic ritual.

ŋƙáƙá na baratsóᵉ *n.* breakfast.

ŋƙáƙá na wídzòᵉ *n.* dinner, supper.

ŋƙáƙáàyᵃ (ŋƙáƙá-àì-) *pl.* ŋƙáƙáaitín. *n.* dining area, eating place.

ŋƙáƙáhò (ŋƙáƙá-hòò-) *pl.* ŋƙáƙáhoíkᵃ. *1 n.* camp kitchen. *2 n.* cafe, restaurant.

ŋƙáƙákwètᵃ (ŋƙáƙá-kwètà-) *n.* right hand. *Lit.* 'eating-hand'.

ŋƙáƙáŋabér (ŋƙáƙá-ŋabérí-) *n.* right-hand rib. *Lit.* 'eating-rib'.

ŋƙáƙés (ŋƙáƙésí-) *v.* to consume, eat. See also *ŋƙés*.

ŋƙáƙésuƙotᵃ (ŋƙáƙésuƙotí-) *v.* to devour, eat up.

ŋƙáƙínósìàm (ŋƙáƙínósí-àmà-) *pl.* ŋƙáƙínósiikᵃ. *n.* neighbor (with whom one eats).

ŋƙáƙítetés (ŋƙáƙítetésí-) *v.* to feed, give food to. See also *bɔnés* and *ŋƙitɛtés*.

ŋƙam (ŋƙamá-) *n.* eatable, edible, victual.

ŋƙés (ŋƙɛ́sɨ́-) *v.* to consume, eat. See also *ŋƙáƙés*.

ŋƙitɛtés (ŋƙitɛtésɨ́-) *1 v.* to feed, give food to. *2 v.* to charge (electrically). See also *bɔnés* and *ŋƙáƙítetés*.

ŋƙwa (ŋƙwaá-) *pl.* ŋƙwáatikwᵃ. *1 n.* traditional healer, witchdoctor. *2 n.* maize deformity in which the cob grows protrusions. See also *irésîám*.

ŋɔ́ (ŋɔ́ɔ̀-) *pl.* ŋɔ́ɨ́n. *1 n.* your mother. *2 n.* your aunt (father's brother's wife).

ŋɔam (ŋɔamá-) *n.* grindable.

ŋɔ̀ɓɔ̀ (ŋɔ̀ɓɔ̀) *ideo.* wide-eyedly.

ŋɔɓódɔ̀n (ŋɔɓódɔ̀nɨ̀-) *v.* to be wide-eyed from fear or guilt.

ŋɔ̀ɓɔ̀n (ŋɔ̀ɓɔ̀nɨ̀-) *v.* to be wide-eyed from fear or guilt.

ŋɔɗólómòn (ŋɔɗólómònì-) *v.* to be gimpy, hobbling.

ŋɔ́és (ŋɔ́ésɨ̀-) *1 v.* to grind, mill. *2 v.* to digest.

ŋɔɛsɨ́gwàs (ŋɔɛsɨ́-gwàsà-) *pl.* ŋɔɛsɨ́gwasíkᵃ. *1 n.* grinding stone. *2 n.* grinding mill.

ŋɔfɛ́s (ŋɔfɛ́sɨ́-) *v.* to gobble down or wolf down (food). See also *ifáfúƙés*.

ŋɔɨtésuƙɔtᵃ (ŋɔɨtésuƙɔtɨ́-) *v.* to make grind.

ŋókᵃ (ŋókí-) *pl.* ŋókítín. *1 n.* dog. *2 n.* poor person. *3 n.* you dog! (term of disrespect).

ŋókícikwᵃ (ŋókí-cikó-) *pl.* ŋókícikwitín. *n.* male dog, sire.

ŋókièts'ᵃ (ŋókí-ètsì-) *1 n.* doggy-doo, dog poop. *2 n.* earwax.

ŋókíìm (ŋókí-ìmà-) *pl.* ŋókíwik^a. *n.* puppy, whelp.

ŋókínànès (ŋókínànèsì-) *n.* impoverishment, poverty.

ŋókíŋwa (ŋókí-ŋwaá-) *n.* bitch: female dog.

ŋókítsùts^a (ŋókí-tsùtsà-) *n.* dogfly: species of fly associated with dogs.

ŋoléánètòn (ŋoléánètònì-) *1 v.* to be white-faced. *2 v.* to be bald. *3 v.* to be treeless.

ŋɔ́ɲót^a (ŋɔ́-ɲótá-) *n.* your mother-in-law (sibling's spouse's mother).

ŋɔ́ɔ́s (ŋɔ́ɔ́sɨ-) *1 v.* to be ground, milled. *2 v.* to be digested.

ŋɔr (ŋɔrɛ́-) *pl.* ŋɔritín. *1 n.* colored clay, ocher. *2 n.* color.

ŋɔra na buɗám *n.* black clay.

ŋɔra na ɗíw^a *n.* red clay.

ŋɔrɛ́ám (ŋɔrɛ́-ámà-) *pl.* ŋɔréík^a. *n.* Turkana person (who wears a colored clay headdress).

ŋɔritɛtɛ́s (ŋɔritɛtɛ́sɨ-) *1 v.* to smear with clay (to mitigate impending misforture). *2 v.* to paint.

ŋɔrɔɓɔɓ^a (ŋɔrɔɓɔɓɔ́-) *pl.* ŋɔrɔ́ɓɔ́ɓɨk^a. *n.* cartilage, gristle.

ŋorokánón (ŋorokánónì-) *v.* to be spotted black-and-white.

ŋorókón (ŋorókónì-) *v.* to be spotted black-and-white.

ŋɔ́rɔn (ŋɔ́rɔnɨ-) *v.* to have done already, earlier.

ŋɔrɔ́ɲɔ́mɔn (ŋɔrɔ́ɲɔ́mɔnɨ-) *v.* to be dirty, soiled, unclean (from dirt or food). See also ɲɔŋɔ́rɔ́mɔn.

ŋɔ́rɔ́rɔn (ŋɔ́rɔ́rɔnɨ-) *1 v.* to saw logs, snore. *2 v.* to growl. *3 v.* to purr.

ŋorótsánón (ŋorótsánónì-) *v.* to be filthy, nasty, putrid (e.g. of water or wounds).

ŋɔt^a (ŋɔtá-) *1 n.* cowdung, manure. See also ɦyɔ̀èts^a. *2 n.* millet heads when they turn brown and curl.

ŋɔtsɛ́s (ŋɔtsɛ́sɨ-) *v.* to cling to, grasp, hold onto.

ŋɔ̀tsɔ̀n (ŋɔ̀tsɔ̀nɨ-) *v.* to be fastened or tied very tightly.

Ŋoya (Ŋoyaá) *n.* a personal name.

ŋɔ́zɛ̀s (ŋɔ́zɛ̀sɨ-) *v.* to glare at, glower at, stare at (using the 'evil eye').

ŋɔ́zɛ̀sɨ̀àm (ŋɔ́zɛ̀sɨ̀-àmà-) *pl.* ŋɔ́zɛsiik^a. *n.* glarer, starer (who bewitches with the 'evil eye').

ŋɔ́ziés (ŋɔ́ziesí-) *v.* to glare or stare at repeatedly (thereby using the 'evil eye').

ŋɔ́zɨnɔ́s (ŋɔ́zɨnɔ́sɨ-) *v.* to glare or stare at each other (thereby giving each other the 'evil eye').

ŋùɓ^u (ŋùɓù) *ideo.* breakably, brittlely.

ŋuɓúɗɔ̀n (ŋuɓúɗɔ̀nì-) *v.* to be breakable, brittle (like a dry stick).

ŋúɗúŋúɗ^a (ŋúɗúŋúɗú-) *n.* pollywog, tadpole.

ŋuɗuŋúɗɔ́n (ŋuɗuŋúɗɔ́nɨ-) *v.* to squiggle, wriggle (like lizard, snake, or tadpole).

ŋuɗúsúmɔ̀n (ŋuɗúsúmɔ̀nì-) *1 v.* to be low, short. *2 v.* to be limbless.

ŋués (ŋuesí-) *v.* to struggle for/over.

ŋuésíàm (ŋuésí-àmà-) *pl.* ŋuésíik^a. *n.* robber.

Ŋuésíìkà sèà^e *n.* traditional men's age-group known as the ones who struggled for blood (oldest, #1).

ŋumúŋúmánón (ŋumúŋúmánónì-) *v.* to be chunky, crumby.

ŋún (ŋúnó-) *pl.* ŋúnítín. *n.* rope. See also *ún*.

ŋʉr (ŋʉrá-) *n.* cane rat. *Thryonomys swinderianus*.

Ŋʉrak[a] (Ŋʉraká-) *n.* name of a huge boulder near *Mukulit[a]*.

ŋʉrés (ŋʉrésɨ́-) *1 v.* to cut. *2 v.* to break (e.g. a rule or law). *3 v.* to cross. *4 v.* to adjudicate, judge.

ŋʉrésá ɨ̀tsɨ̀kà[ɛ] *v.* to break the law.

ŋʉrésɨ́àm (ŋʉrésɨ́-àmà-) *pl.* ŋʉrésíik[a]. *n.* breaker (e.g. of the law).

ŋʉrésúkɔt[a] (ŋʉrésúkɔtɨ́-) *v.* to cut away/off.

ŋʉrɛtés (ŋʉrɛtésɨ́-) *1 v.* to cut up. *2 v.* to analyze, interpret, judge.

ŋʉrɛtɛsɨ́àm (ŋʉrɛtɛsɨ́-àmà-) *pl.* ŋʉrɛtɛsíik[a]. *n.* judge.

ŋʉrɔ́s (ŋʉrɔ́sɨ́-) *v.* to be broken, cut.

ŋurúmétòn (ŋurúmétònì-) *1 v.* to be cut off. *2 v.* to cut short, end.

ŋʉrúmɔ́n (ŋʉrúmɔ́nɨ̀-) *1 v.* to break, get broken. *2 v.* to go broke.

ŋʉrúmɔ́na kwaaté[o] *v.* cessation of childbirth, menopause. *Lit.* 'breaking off of childbirth'.

ŋurúɲúɲètòn (ŋurúɲúɲètònì-) *v.* to sprout up (of many shoots).

ŋʉrúŋúránón (ŋʉrúŋúránónì-) *v.* to be all broken or cut up.

ŋʉrʉrúɲɔ́n (ŋʉrʉrúɲɔ́nɨ̀-) *1 v.* to sprout up (of many things, like grass). *2 v.* to regrow (of hair).

ŋʉrúsá (ŋʉrúsáɨ̀-) *pl.* ŋʉrúsáɨ̀k[a]. *n.* hardwood tree species with dark wood that burns well. *Haplocoelum foliolosum*.

ŋurutiés (ŋurutiesí-) *1 v.* to chop or cut up into pieces, dice. *2 v.* to adjudicate, judge, solve.

ŋurutiesá tódà[o] *pl.* ŋurutiesíícíká tódà[o]. *n.* consonant. *Lit.* 'chopping up of speech'.

ŋurutiesíàm (ŋurutiesí-àmà-) *pl.* ŋurutiesíik[a]. *n.* judge.

ŋurutiesíama mɛná[ɛ] *n.* councillor, official.

ŋurutiesíama tódà[e] *n.* elder, officer (in the church or community).

ŋurutiesúkɔt[a] (ŋurutiesúkɔtí-) *1 v.* to chop or cut up in pieces, dice up. *2 v.* to adjudicate, judge, solve.

ŋurutiós (ŋurutiosí-) *1 v.* to be chopped, cut, diced, or divided in pieces. *2 v.* to be adjudicated, judged, solved. *3 v.* to be half-striped.

ŋusés (ŋusésí-) *v.* to grab, snatch, take hold of, wrest. See also *taŋates* and *tokopes*.

ŋusésúkɔt[a] (ŋusésúkɔtí-) *v.* to grab, snatch, take hold of.

ŋusetésá asɨ́ *v.* to hurry this way.

ŋusúlúmɔ̀n (ŋusúlúmɔ̀nɨ̀-) *v.* to be low, short. See also *ŋuɗúsʉ́mɔ̀n*.

Ŋusuman (Ŋusumaná-) *n.* name of a mountain with a sharp peak.

Ŋúupéám (Ŋúupé-ámá-) *pl.* ŋúupéík[a]. *n.* Pokot or Suk person.

ŋúzʉmánón (ŋúzʉmánónì-) *v.* to bicker, squabble. See also *iɲúɲúrɔ̀n*.

ŋwa (ŋwaá-) *pl.* ŋwáátíkw[a]. *n.* female (animal).

ŋwáát[a] (ŋwáátì-) *pl.* ŋwáátìn. *1 n.* his/her/its mother. *2 n.* his/her aunt (father's brother's wife).

ŋwááta dáŋá[e] *n.* queen of an edible termite colony.

ŋwááteda gwasá[e] *n.* lower grinding stone (on which the thing being ground is lain). *Lit.* 'mother of the stone'.

ŋwáátìnànès (ŋwáátìnànèsì-) *n.* motherhood, motherliness.

ŋwáátìɲòtᵃ (ŋwáátì-ɲòtà-) *n.* his/her mother-in-law (sibling's spouse's mother).

ŋwan (ŋwaná-) *pl.* **ŋwáníkw**ᵃ. *n.* garden cultivated for more than one year.

ŋwanɨ́ŋwánìtɛ́s (ŋwanɨ́ŋwánìtɛ́sɨ́-) *v.* to better or improve slightly.

ŋwanɨŋwánɔ́n (ŋwanɨŋwánɔ́nɨ̀-) *v.* to be average, mediocre, so-so.

ŋwaxás (ŋwaxásɨ́-) *n.* disability, handicap, lameness.

ŋwàxɔ̀n (ŋwàxɔ̀nɨ̀-) *v.* to be crippled, disabled, handicapped, lame.

ŋwaxɔna ekwitíní *v.* to have poor eyesight.

ŋwàxɔ̀nɨ̀àm (ŋwàxɔ̀nɨ̀-àmà-) *pl.* **ŋwaxɔniik**ᵃ. *n.* cripple, disabled, handicapped, or lame person.

ŋ́kᵃ (ɲcì-) *pro.* I/me/my.

Ŋ́kaleesó (Ɨ́)kaleesóò-) *n.* Ateker name for the traditional Ik men's age-group with the ostrich as its totem (#9 in the historical line). The Ik name is *Leweɲiik*ᵃ.

ŋ́kaŋókᵃ (ŋ́kaŋókì-) *n.* acne, pimples.

ŋ́karakocóyᵃ (ŋ́karakocóì-) *n.* bottlecap game.

o/ɔ

ɔ́bᵃ (ɔ́bà-) *pl.* **ɔ́bɨtín**. *n.* cheek (inner and outer).

ɔ́bèr (ɔ́bèrà-) *n.* plant whose edible leaves are cooked and whose seeds are eaten raw, fried, or mixed with honey. *Hibiscus cannbinus.*

ɔ́bèràkàkᵃ (ɔ́bèrà-kàkà-) *n.* edible leaves of the *ɔ́bèr* plant.

ɔ́bès (ɔ́bèsɨ-) *1 v.* to dominate, occupy (e.g. an area or conversation). *2 v.* to boom, rise (of voices).

óbìjᵃ (óbìjò-) *n.* black rhinoceros. *Diceros bicornis.* Also called *óbùjᵃ*.

óbijoets'ᵃ (óbijo-ets'í-) *n.* vine species thought to grow where rhinos dropped their dung; its bulbous fruits are made into gourds. *Lit.* 'rhino-droppings'. *Lagenaria sphaerica.*

óbìjòkwàtsᵃ (óbìjò-kwàtsì-) *n.* inedible gourd that is extremely bitter and without use. *Lit.* 'rhino-urine'.

óbìjòɔz (óbìjò-ɔ̀zà-) *n.* tree species whose leaves rhinos like to eat and whose bitter bark infusion is drunk as an anthelmintic (anti-worm) drug. *Lit.* 'rhino-bottom'. *Albizia anthelmintica.*

obólén (obóléni-) *pl.* **óbòlènìk**ᵃ. *1 n.* hip. *2 n.* eastern rains.

obóléniɔ̀kᵃ (obóléni-ɔ̀kà-) *pl.* **óbolenikɔɔkitín**. *n.* greater trochanter: lower hipbone.

òɓà (òɓà) *interj.* folks! people! (a term for addressing a group). Contracted form of *ròɓᵃ* 'folks'.

Océn (Océní-) *n.* a personal name.

ôdᵃ (ódà-) *pl.* **ódikw**ᵃ. *n.* ford, river crossing.

ódàtù *n.* all day, the whole day.

ódeedóó *n.* on that day.

ódèèkwᵃ (ódè-èkù-) *pl.* **ódeekwík**ᵃ. *n.* ford, river crossing.

òdìòs (òdìòsì-) *n.* crowd, multitude.

ɔ́dɔ̀kᵃ (ɔ́dɔ̀kà-) *pl.* **ɔ́dɔkík**ᵃ. *1 n.* gate, gateway. *2 n.* patriclan: clan based on the father's lineage. *3 n.* chapter.

ódòᵒ *n.* at daytime, during the day.

ódoo bɨrɨr *n.* midday, noon.

ódòwᵃ (ódòù-) *pl.* **ódoicík**ᵃ. *n.* day.

ódowa ná zè *n.* big day, national holiday.

ódowicíká kì nùù kì *n.* back then, long ago. *Lit.* 'those days then'.

ódowicíká nì kòm *n.* a long time or while. *Lit.* 'days that are many'.

ódowicíká nì ƙwàɗᵉ *n.* a short time or while. *Lit.* 'days that are few'.

ódowicíkó nì *n.* nowadays, these days.

ódowicíkó nì kɔ̀nà *n.* nowadays, these very days.

ódowicíkó nùkᵘ *n.* back then, long ago, those days.

ôdzᵃ (ódzà-) *pl.* **ódzitín**. *n.* dry season.

ódzadidí (ódza-didíi-) *n.* light rain at the beginning of dry season.

ódzàkàkᵃ (ódzà-kàkà-) *n.* dry, crackly leaves of dry season.

ódzatsóyᵃ (ódza-tsóí-) *n.* dry season.

òɗòmòr (òɗòmòrì-) *n.* male bushbuck. *Tragelaphus scriptus.*

óés (óésì-) *1 v.* to call, summon. *2 v.* to invite. *3 v.* to call (a name), name. May also be spelled as *wéés*.

óésa édie imáᵉ *v.* to name a newborn child.

óésés (óésésì-) *v.* to call repeatedly.

oetés (oetésí-) *v.* to call here.

ɔf (ɔ̀fà-) *n.* cough.

ɔfàgwà (ɔ̀fà-gwàà-) *n.* bird species. *Lit.* 'coughing-bird'.

ɔfɔ́dɔ̀n (ɔfɔ́dɔ̀nɨ̀-) *1 v.* to be lightweight. *2 v.* to be easy, manageable. See also *fɔkɔ́dɔ̀n* and *olódòn*.

ɔfɔ̀n (ɔ̀fɔ̀nɨ̀-) *v.* to cough.

ɔfɔrɔkᵃ (ɔfɔrɔkɔ́-) *pl.* **ɔfɔ́rɔ́kɨ̀k**ᵃ. *1 n.* dry honeycomb. *2 n.* eggshell.

ofur (ofurí-) *pl.* **ofúrík**ᵃ. *1 n.* bag, pouch (often made of leather). *2 n.* pocket. Also called *ofir*.

ofura na jɨ́rɨ̀ *n.* back pocket.

ofura na wáxɨ̀ *n.* front pocket.

ɔ̀gɛr (ɔ̀gɛrà-) *pl.* **ɔ́gɛraikw**ᵃ. *n.* male monkey or primate of any kind.

ɔgɛraŋwa (ɔgɛra-ŋwaá-) *n.* female monkey or primate of any kind.

ógoɗés (ógoɗésí-) *v.* to keep aside, put aside/away, store.

ógoɗesam (ógoɗesamá-) *n.* leftover, remainder. *Lit.* 'keepable'. See also *jɨ̀rêd* and *ɲomokojo*.

ógoɗésúkotᵃ (ógoɗésúkotí-) *v.* to keep aside, put or store away (for later). See also *okésúkot*ᵃ.

ógoés (ógoesí-) *1 v.* to leave, let. *2 v.* to excuse, exempt. *3 v.* to concede, renounce claim over. *4 v.* to forgive, pardon. May also be spelled as *ógweés*.

ógoesíám (ógoesí-ámà-) *pl.* **ógoesíík**ᵃ. *n.* judge who pardons.

ɔgɔn (ɔgɔnɔ́-) *n.* shrub species whose red or yellow berries are eaten raw and whose stems are made into arrows, spears, and walking sticks and are used to build houses and granaries. *Grewia tenax.* See also *alárá*.

ógoós (ógoosí-) *1 v.* to be left, let. *2 v.* to be excused, exempt.

òìdìkwòn (òì-dìkwònì-) *v.* to dance and sing simultaneously.

óímós (óímósí-) *v.* to call each other.

óisiés (óísiesí-) *v.* to call continuously, keep on calling.

ɔ́jᵃ (ɔ́já-) *pl.* **ɔ́jɨ́tín**. *1 n.* sore, wound. *2 n.* knot in wood.

ɔ́jáìm (ɔ́já-ìmà-) *pl.* **ɔ́jɨ́tínɨ́wík**ᵃ. *n.* bleb, blister, small sore.

ɔ́játàs (ɔ́já-tàsà-) *n.* scar.

ɔ́jɨ́tínɨ́cɛmɛ́r (ɔ́jɨ́tíní-cɛmɛ́rɨ́-) *n.* small plant species with milky sap that is applied to wounds in order to dry them out. *Lit.* 'wounds-herb'. *Becium sp.*

ɔkᵃ (ɔká-) *pl.* **ɔkitín**. *n.* bone, osseous tissue.

ɔka ikáᵉ *n.* cranium, skull. *Lit.* 'bone of the head'.

okílóŋór (okílóŋóró-) *n.* queen bee. Also called *lókílóróŋ*.

ókísèn (ókísènì-) *pl.* **ókísènìk**ᵃ. *n.* auction, vendue.

ɔkitín (ɔkitíní-) *n.* skeleton. *Lit.* 'bones'.

ókò (ókò) *adv.* apparently, seemingly, it seems. See also *ɨ́kwà*.

ɔkɔ́tsᵃ (ɔkɔ́tsɨ́-) *pl.* **ɔkɔ́tsɨ́k**ᵃ. *1 n.* step, stride. *2 n.* meter, yard.

okésúkotᵃ (okésúkotí-) *v.* to keep aside, put or store away (for later). See also *ógoɗésúkot*ᵃ.

ókírotᵃ (ókírotí-) *n.* bird species.

ɔlɨ́ (ɔlɨ́ɨ̀-) *n.* grass whose millet-like seeds are ground into flour.

olíɓó (olíɓóò-) *n.* freeloading, mooching, sponging.

òlìotᵃ (òlìòtà-) n. alpha male baboon. See also *timùòz*.

ɔlír (ɔlírì-) pl. ɔlíraikwᵃ. n. bush hyrax. *Heterohyrax brucei*.

olódòn (olódònì-) 1 v. to be lightweight. 2 v. to be eager, enthusiastic. 3 v. to be easy to manage, manageable. See also *fɔkɔ́dɔ̀n* and *olódòn*.

omén (oméní-) pl. oméníkᵃ. n. barb, spike (used in a spike trap).

ɔmɔ́x (ɔmɔ́xá-) pl. ɔmɔ́xɨ́kᵃ. 1 n. peel, skin. 2 n. crust, scab.

on (oní-) pl. onitín. n. abandoned homestead or village, ghost town.

ɔn (ɔná-) n. odor, smell, stench.

ɔnɛdᵃ (ɔnɛdɛ-) n. odor, smell, stench (of a particular person or thing).

oníáwᵃ (oní-áwà-) pl. oníáwíkᵃ. n. abandoned homestead or village.

oɲaŋ (oɲaŋá-) n. sorghum variety with big, yellowish seeds. Also called *aɲaŋ*.

oŋerepᵃ (oŋerepé-) n. rufous beaked snake. *Rhamphiophis oxyrhynchus*.

òŋòr (òŋòrì-) n. elephant, tusker. *Loxodonta africana*.

Ɔŋɔr (Ɔŋɔrɨ́-) n. a personal name.

ɔŋɔ́ránètòn (ɔŋɔ́ránètònì-) v. to be brown, gray, gray-brown.

Òŋòrìàwᵃ (Òŋòrì-àwà-) n. name of a place where many elephants were killed. *Lit*. 'elephant-place'.

oŋoridɛrɛ́kᵃ (oŋori-dɛrɛ́kɨ̀-) n. elephant wasp: large black wasp.

Oŋoriikᵃ (Oŋori-icé-) n. traditional men's age-group with the elephant as its totem (#5 in the historical line). *Lit*. 'Elephant-Folk'.

oŋorikɨnám (oŋori-kɨnámá-) n. elephant mushroom: species with a broad, flat top.

òŋòrìkù (òŋòrì-kùà-) n. elephant grass: tall grass species used for thatching. *Panicum maximum*.

òŋòrìkwàtsᵃ (òŋòrì-kwàtsì-) n. elephant urine: a plant species with no known uses. *Satureja sp*.

òŋòrìkwàywᵃ (òŋòrì-kwàyò-) pl. oŋorikwaitín. n. elephant tusk, ivory.

òŋòrìkwɛ̀tᵃ (òŋòrì-kwɛ̀tà-) 1 n. elephant trunk. 2 n. digger, excavator.

oŋoriŋwa (oŋori-ŋwaá-) n. cow elephant (female).

Òŋòrìpàkwᵃ (Òŋòrì-pàkò-) n. name of a cave at the base of Ŋurakᵃ. *Lit*. 'elephant-cave'.

Oŋorisabá (Oŋori-sabáà-) n. name of a river near *Lòsòlìà* and *Píré*. *Lit*. 'elephant-river'. Also called *Cakalatɔ́m*.

oŋoritakáyᵃ (oŋori-takáɨ́-) pl. oŋoritakáɨ́kᵃ. n. elephant-leather shoe.

Oŋórîz (Oŋórízà-) n. name of a river and ravine.

òrègèm (òrègèmè-) n. lone male baboon.

Oríáé (Oríáé-) n. Arab or Somali.

Oríáénítòdᵃ (Oríáéní-tòdà-) n. language of Arab or Somali Muslims.

Óríɓò (Órí-ɓòò-) n. name of a river and ravine in the east of Ikland, as well as the surrounding area and its human habitations.

Óríɓosabá (Órí-ɓo-sabáà-) n. name of a river. *Lit*. 'Ori's escarpment-river'.

òrìkìrìkᵃ (òrìkìrìkì-) n. large object (esp. a house, rock, or tree).

ɔrɨ́yɔ́ (ɔrɨ́yɔ̀-) n. bird species.

Ɔrɔ́m (Ɔrɔ́mù-) n. name of a mountain on the border of Karamoja and Acholiland.

oromén (oroméní-) *n.* bateleur. *Terathopius ecaudatus.*

orómó (orómóò-) *n.* green-pigeon (Bruce's and maybe African). *Treron sp.*

ɔrɔr (ɔrɔrɔ́-) *pl.* **orórίkw**ᵃ. *n.* large stream, small river (and associated ravine).

òsòròs (òsòròsì-) *pl.* **osórósaikw**ᵃ. *n.* barren, childless, infertile, or sterile person. See also *ɲokólíp*ᵃ.

osorosánón (osorosánónì-) *v.* to be barren, childless, infertile, sterile. See also *ikólípánón.*

ɔtáyᵃ (ɔtáί-) *pl.* **ɔtáíkw**ᵃ. *n.* rainy season. See also *diditsóy*ᵃ.

otés (otésí-) *1 v.* to pour into. *2 v.* to infix, insert, put in (e.g. poles for a fence or house). *3 v.* to brew. *4 v.* to miscarry. *5 v.* to put on, wear (many beads like Turkana women). *6 v.* to thank someone for helping in the garden by pouring into their containers a portion of the grain. See also *itʉrɛs.*

otésúƙotᵃ (otésúƙotí-) *v.* to pour into.

otetés (otetésí-) *1 v.* to pour out into. *2 v.* to miscarry.

otí (otí) *interj.* whoa! (an expression of awe or mystery).

otsés (otsésí-) *v.* to board, climb, get on, mount, ride.

otsésíama haúù¹ *n.* hyena rider, hyena-riding wizard.

otsésúƙotᵃ (otsésúƙotí-) *v.* to climb on/up, get on, mount up.

òtsìɓìl (òtsìɓìlà-) *n.* common bulbul. *Pycnonotus barbatus.* Also called *tsìɓìl.*

òwà (òwàà-) *n.* yellow desert date(s).

oyóŋ (oyóŋò-) *n.* hyena species.

ɔ́zàakᵃ (ɔ́zà-àkà-) *n.* anus.

ɔ́zàhò (ɔ́zà-hòò-) *pl.* **ɔ́zitɨ́nɨ́hoík**ᵃ. *n.* anal sphincter.

ɔ́zàsìts'ᵃ (ɔ́zà-sìts'à-) *n.* pubic hair. See also *didisísíts'*ᵃ.

ɔ́zɛ̀dᵃ (ɔ́zɛ̀dɛ̀-) *1 n.* back, backside, bottom, rear, rear end. *2 n.* cap, primer (that ignites gunpowder).

ɔ́zɛ̀dà mɛ̀sɛ̀ *n.* bottom layer of beer.

Ɔ́pʉs (Ɔ́pʉsí-) *n.* name of a huge rocky cliff.

ɔ́z (ɔ́zà-) *pl.* **ɔ́zitɨ́n.** *n.* ass, backside, bottom, butt, rear.

p

pààɗòk⁰ (pààɗòkò) *ideo.* bang! kaboom! (sound of a gunshot).

pààì (pààì) *ideo.* very slowly.

Paalakán (Paalakánɨ̀-) *n.* name of a mountainside and its human habitation on *Morúŋole*.

páɗɛ̀r (páɗɛ̀rɛ̀-) *pl.* **páɗɛrín.** *n.* Roman Catholic priest.

Páɗɛ̀rɛ̀hò (Páɗɛrɛ-hoó-) *n.* name of a hill where the Italian priest *Apáálolúk* used to stop for the night. *Lit.* 'priest-hut'.

paɗókómòn (paɗókómònì-) *v.* to be caved in, collapsed (e.g. one's stomach).

pàɗwᵃ (pàɗò-) *pl.* **páɗíkwᵃ.** *n.* small cave (often used for secret storage).

pákà (pákà) *1 prep.* all the way to, until, up to (followed by a noun). *2 subordconn.* until (followed by a dependent clause). *3 adv.* forever, indefinitely. As a preposition, this word is followed by a noun in the oblique case.

pakámón (pakámónì-) *v.* to split in two.

pakatiés (pakatiesí-) *v.* to cut or split multiply (e.g. a tree into planks).

pakés (pakésí-) *v.* to bisect, dissect, divide, split in two. See also *ɨwáwáɗɛ́s*.

pakóáƙwᵃ (pakó-áƙɔ̀-) *n.* cave interior.

Pakóám (Pakwá-ámà-) *pl.* **Pakóíkᵃ.** *n.* Turkana person. *Lit.* 'cave-person'.

pakóásákᵃ (pakó-ásáká-) *n.* cave entrance.

Pakóícéɲám (Pakó-ícé-ɲàmà-) *n.* Turkana sorghum: variety grown by the Turkana that has with white stalks, stems, and seeds.

Pakóícétôdᵃ (Pakó-ícé-tódà-) *n.* Turkana language.

Pakósábà (Pakó-sábàà-) *n.* name of a river. *Lit.* 'cave-river'.

pakwᵃ (pakó-) *pl.* **pakwitín.** *n.* cave (often used for shelter or storage).

pàkⁱ (pàkì) *ideo.* bright white, milkily white, pure white.

palórómòn (palórómònì-) *v.* to be bald on top.

Palú (Palúù-) *n.* name of a river and ravine in Timu.

Palúùkùɓᵃ (Palúù-kùɓà-) *n.* name of a hill in Timu. *Lit.* 'Palu-hill'.

pànɛ̀ɛ̀s (pànɛ̀ɛ̀sɨ̀-) *n.* teenage boys, young men. See also *ɲɨsɔ́rɔkᵃ*.

pápà (pápàà-) *n.* pope: head of the Roman Catholic church.

papaɗós (papaɗósí-) *n.* small stash hidden from others (e.g. food).

paripárɔ́n (paripárɔ́nɨ̀-) *v.* to gleam, glisten. See also *piripírón*.

pás (pásì-) *n.* lousy, pathetic, or useless person or thing. See also *tsar*.

pásìnànès (pásìnànèsɨ̀-) *n.* patheticness, lousiness, uselessness. See also *tsarínánès*.

pásìtà (pásìtàà-) *pl.* **pásìtàìkᵃ.** *n.* minister, pastor, rector.

patsólómòn (patsólómònì-) *v.* to be bare (of a patch or spot).

páupáwᵃ (páupáù-) *n.* scout bee that scouts out sources of food and water.

paupáwón (paupáwónì-) *1 v.* to be parched, thirsty (e.g. after eating honey and then walking in the sun). *2 v.* to be afraid, dread, have qualms (e.g. over a bad premonition).

pɛɗɛ́pɛ́ɗánón (pɛɗɛ́pɛ́ɗánónì-) *v.* to be flapping, fluttering.

pɛdɛpédɔ́n (pɛdɛpédɔ́nì-) *v.* to flutter (of hearts, wings).

pɛɛɲémòn (pɛɛɲémònì-) *v.* to walk in a small-buttocked way.

pèl (pèlè) *ideo.* slickly, slipperily.

pɛlédòn (pɛlédònì-) *v.* to be precariously slick or slippery.

pɛ́lɛ́dɛ̀k[a] (pɛ́lɛ́dɛ̀kɛ̀-) *n.* long-leaf tobacco. See also *loríónómor*.

pɛlémétɔ̀n (pɛlémétɔ̀nì-) *v.* to appear, come into view, emerge. See also *lɛlétɔ́n*.

pɛlémɔna fetí *v.* dawn, daybreak, sunrise. Lit. 'appearance of the sun'.

Pelén (Peléní-) *n.* a personal name.

pelérémòn (pelérémònì-) *v.* to be squinted, squinty.

penitésìyà (penitésìyàà-) *n.* Catholic sacrament of penance.

pɛntɛkɔ́stɛ̀ (pɛntɛkɔ́stɛ̀ɛ̀-) *n.* Pentecost: seventh Sunday after Easter.

pèsɛ (pèsɛ̀) *ideo.* boom! (sound or effect of something explosive).

pɛsɛlam (pɛsɛlamá-) *n.* chip, small piece.

pɛ́sɛ́lamed[a] (pɛ́sɛ́lamede-) *n.* chip, small piece (of sth. in particular).

pɛsɛlɛs (pɛsɛlɛsí-) *v.* to break a piece off, chip, knap.

pɛsɛmétɔ̀n (pɛsɛmétɔ̀nì-) *v.* to break, chip, or crumble off in small pieces.

pɛsɛpɛ́sánón (pɛsɛpɛ́sánónì-) *v.* to be brittle, crumbly (e.g. biscuits).

Pétèrò (Pétèròò-) *1 n.* Peter. *2 n.* Peter: short New Testament letters.

pɨ̀c (pɨ̀cɨ̀) *ideo.* very full.

pidés (pidésí-) *v.* to cut across, go through, traverse. See also *tɔkɛ́ɛ́rɛ́s*.

pɨd[i] (pɨdɨ) *ideo.* sleekly, slickly.

pidɨ́dɔ̀n (pidɨ́dɔ̀nɨ̀-) *v.* to be sleek, slick. See also *ipɛlɨ́pélɔ̀n*.

Píipí (Píipíì-) *n.* a personal name.

pikódòn (pikódònì-) *v.* to be worn smooth (of ground, stones, etc.).

pɨ̀l (pɨ̀lɔ̀) *ideo.* smoothly.

pílè (pílè) *ideo.* all, completely, totally.

Pilɛmɔ́nɛ̀ (Pilɛmɔ́nɛ̀ɛ̀-) *n.* Philemon: book in the New Testament.

Pɨ́líkɨ̀ts[a] (Pɨ́líkɨ̀tsɨ̀-) *n.* name of a mountain near *Káákʉma* in Turkanaland, Kenya.

Pilípoik[a] (Pilípo-icé-) *n.* Philippians: book in the New Testament.

pilírímɔ̀n (pilírímɔ̀nì-) *v.* to have strabismal amblyopia: a lazy eye that looks in different directions.

pilís (pilísì-) *n.* game of tag.

pilɔ́ditɛ́súkɔt[a] (pilɔ́ditɛ́súkɔtí-) *v.* to make smooth, smoothen out.

pilɔ́dòn (pilɔ́dònì-) *v.* to be smooth.

pɨ̀ɔ̀ (pɨ̀ɔ̀) *ideo.* splat! spoot! (sound of diarrhea or vomit). The vowels in this word are pronounced silently.

pír (pírí) *ideo.* glittering white.

Píré (Piréè-) *n.* name of a slope on the north of *Morúŋole* where some Ik used to be congregated.

pirídòn (pirídònì-) *v.* to be gleaming, shiny (like a bald head). See also *barídòn*.

piripírón (piripírónì-) *v.* to gleam, glisten. See also *paripárɔ́n*.

pɨris (pɨrisɨ) *ideo.* pop! (sound of coming or popping out, as in pus from a wound or an animal from a thicket).

pìrrr (pìrrr) *ideo.* very hot (of the weather).

pìr[i] (pìrì) *ideo.* appearing suddenly, out of nowhere.

pìs (pìsɨ̀) *ideo.* quish! (sound of flesh being punctured). See also *tùs*.

pít¹ (pítí) *ideo.* all.

pìùù (pìùù) *ideo.* zing! (sound of a bullet passing over). The vowels of this word are pronounced silently.

pɔ́ɗɛ̀ (pɔ́ɗɛ̀ɛ̀-) *n.* small Japanese car.

poɗés (poɗésí-) *v.* to husk, shuck.

poɗetés (poɗetésí-) *v.* to husk, shuck.

pɔ̀ɗᵒ (pɔ̀ɗɔ̀) *ideo.* agilely, nimbly, spryly.

pɔɗɔ́dɔ̀n (pɔɗɔ́dɔ̀nɨ̀-) *v.* to be agile, nimble, spry.

pokés (pokésí-) *1 v.* to break off. *2 v.* to stick, wedge (e.g. what mud does to a vehicle). See also *wakés*.

poketés (poketésí-) *v.* to break off.

pókietésá asɨ́ɛ kédìè kɔ̀n *v.* to break off in groups.

pòkᵒ (pòkò) *ideo.* breakably, brittlely.

pokódòn (pokódònì-) *v.* to be breakable, brittle. See also *ɛɔmɔ́dɔ̀n* and *wɛts'édɔ̀n*.

pokómón (pokómónì-) *v.* to break off.

pólìs (pólìsì-) *n.* police.

poŋórómòn (poŋórómònì-) *v.* to be stumpy, tubby.

Popá (Popáà-) *n.* name of a hand-dug well and its run-off on Lotim.

pɔ̀pɔ̀s (pɔ̀pɔ̀sà-) *n.* lizard.

pórón (pórónì-) *v.* to go on, keep going, proceed.

porór (porórí-) *n.* nearly ripe crops (e.g. maize, millet, sorghum).

pòròtᵃ (pòròtì-) *pl.* pórótìkᵃ. *n.* hooked stick used to remove flesh from inside a gourd.

pɔsɔ́kɔ́mɔ̀n (pɔsɔ́kɔ́mɔ̀nɨ̀-) *v.* to be awkward, clumsy, clunky, cumbersome (due to size).

pɔ̀tᵓ (pɔ̀tɔ̀) *ideo.* slickly, slipperily.

pɔtɔ́dɔ̀n (pɔtɔ́dɔ̀nɨ̀-) *v.* to be slick, slippery (e.g. a slimy wet rock).

pòx (pòxò) *ideo.* chattily, talkatively.

poxés (poxésí-) *v.* to peel, skin.

poxésúƙotᵃ (poxésúƙotí-) *v.* to peel or skin off.

poxódòn (poxódònì-) *v.* to be chatty, talkative.

pùà (pùà) *ideo.* chop! (sound of cutting a tree).

pùɗᵃ (pùɗà) *ideo.* dryly as dust.

puɗádòn (puɗádònì-) *v.* to be dry and dusty.

Puɗápúɗᵃ (Puɗápúɗà-) *n.* name of a river.

pukés (pukésí-) *v.* to overturn, turn out (solid substances).

pukésúƙotᵃ (pukésúƙotí-) *v.* to overturn away, turn out away (solid substances).

puketés (puketésí-) *v.* to overturn, turn out (solid substances).

pùkᵘ (pùkù) *1 ideo.* zlop! (sound of something solid being dumped). *2 ideo.* whack! (sound of hitting).

pulés (pulésí-) *v.* to make a hole in, perforate, pierce, punch, puncture.

Pʉlʉkól (Pʉlʉkólɨ̀-) *n.* a personal name.

pulúmétòn (pulúmétònì-) *v.* to come out, egress, emerge.

pulúmítésúƙotᵃ (pulúmítésúƙotí-) *v.* to take out.

pulúmón (pulúmónì-) *v.* to exit, go out.

pulutetés (pulutetésí-) *v.* to bring out, issue, produce (e.g. newborn twins out of the hut).

pulutiés (pulutiesí-) *1 v.* to perforate, pierce, or puncture repeatedly. *2 v.* to bore, drill. See also *ipɨrɨ́pɨ́rés*.

pulutiesíàm (pulutiesí-àmà-) *pl.* pulutiesíik[a]. *1 n.* piercer (e.g. of ears). *2 n.* driller (e.g. of wood).

pún (púnú) *ideo.* a lot, really.

pùnùk[ʉ] (pùnùkù) *ideo.* flat to the ground.

pʉŋúrʉ́mòn (pʉŋúrʉ́mònɨ-) *v.* to be rotund (e.g. a gourd or fat pig).

pʉrákámòn (pʉrákámònì-) *v.* to be chalky dry, moisture or water-resistant (e.g. dry meat, powders, soil). See also *pʉráŋámòn* and *pʉsélémɔ̀n*.

pʉráŋámòn (pʉráŋámònì-) *v.* to be chalky dry, moisture or water-resistant (e.g. dry meat, powders, soil). See also *pʉrákámòn* and *pʉsélémɔ̀n*.

pùròn (pùrònɨ-) *v.* to live through, survive.

púrurú (púrurúù-) *n.* measles, rubeola.

pùrùs (pùrùsù) *ideo.* schunk! (sound of deep stabbing into flesh).

purutél (purutélè-) *n.* friar, mendicant.

pùs (pùsù) *ideo.* plop! (sound of food falling on the ground).

pʉsélémɔ̀n (pʉsélémɔ̀nɨ-) *v.* to be chalky dry, moisture or water-resistant (e.g. dry meat, powders, soil). See also *pʉrákámòn* and *pʉráŋámòn*.

Pútá (Pútáà-) *n.* name of a hill or mountain.

pʉtʉ́mɔ́n (pʉtʉ́mɔ́nɨ-) *v.* to go or pass through to the other side.

puurú (puurúù-) *n.* chickenpox, varicella. See also *ɲetʉnɛ*.

púùs (púùsì-) *n.* cat, housecat. *Felis libyca*.

puusúmòn (puusúmònì-) *v.* to be bantam, dwarfish, midget (with poochy belly and rear end).

pùùt[ʉ] (pùùtù) *ideo.* phoot! (sound made when a spear pierces an animal's body and comes out the other side). See also *rès*.

r

ràaràarà (ràaràarà) *ideo.* clap clap! (sound of applause).

rábaɗamitésuƙot[a] (rábaɗamitésúƙotí-) *v.* to dent, ding, put a dent/ding in. See also *luɗés*.

rábàɗàmòn (rábàɗàmònì-) *v.* to be dented, dinged.

rábaɗamonuƙot[a] (rábaɗamonuƙotí-) *v.* to get dented or dinged.

rábùxòn (rábùxònì-) *v.* to crouch, hunker (often in order to hide). See also *dégèmɔ̀n*.

rágàn (rágànì-) *n.* wild yam-like plant whose tubers are boiled many times, crushed, soaked, dried, and ground into edible flour.

rágòdìkw[a] (rágò-dìkwà-) *pl.* **rágodikwitín**. *n.* ox song: composed and sung in honor of a man's totemic ox.

rágòèd[a] (rágò-èdì-) *pl.* **rágoeditín**. *n.* ox name: taken in honor of a man's totemic ox.

râgw[a] (rágò-) *pl.* **ráíkw**[a]. *n.* ox.

rajámón (rajámónì-) *v.* to go down, recede, reduce.

rajánón (rajánónì-) *1 v.* to back up, move back, retreat. *2 v.* to regress, revert. *3 v.* to go down, recede, reduce (e.g. swelling or tumors).

rajés (rajésí-) *1 v.* to return. *2 v.* to answer, reply, respond. *3 v.* to hold back/off, resist. *4 v.* to set (i.e. a dislocated joint).

rajésúƙot[a] (rajésúƙotí-) *v.* to return: give, put, send, or take back.

rajetés (rajetésí-) *1 v.* to return: bring, give, or put back. *2 v.* to answer, reply, respond. *3 v.* to account or answer for. *4 v.* to profit from.

rakákámòn (rakákámònì-) *v.* to be gravelly, rocky. See also *ŋarʉ́dɔ̀n*.

ràm (ràmʉ̀-) *pl.* **rámíkw**[a]. *n.* pile of dry branches with grass growing up among them.

ramés (ramɛ́sɨ́-) *1 v.* to have multiples, more than one of. *2 v.* to marry polygamously.

ramɛtés (ramɛtésɨ́-) *v.* to attach, fix, join.

Raraan (Raraaní-) *n.* December: month of falling leaves. See also *Íbùbù*.

raraanón (raraanónì-) *1 v.* to fall gently (leaves, paper). *2 v.* to die off.

rárímetés (rárímetésí-) *v.* to decrease, diminish, downgrade.

rárímòn (rárímònì-) *v.* to decline, decrease, diminish, drop off.

ratatáɲón (ratatáɲónì-) *v.* to be droopy, saggy.

ràtòn (ràtònì-) *v.* to be at ground level.

rátsɛ́s (rátsɛ́sɨ̀-) *v.* to mend, patch, repair (by sewing).

rátsiés (rátsiesí-) *v.* to mend, patch, or repair repeatedly (by sewing).

rêb[a] (rébè-) *n.* finger millet. *Eleusine coracana*.

rɛ̀b[a] (rɛ̀bè-) *n.* light rain prolonged for hours after a heavy rain.

rébèmès (rébè-mèsè-) *n.* millet beer. See also *ŋamarʉwáy*[a].

rébès (rébèsì-) *v.* to deny, deprive, withhold from.

rébìmètòn (rébìmètònì-) *v.* to be denied, deprived, withheld from.

rébɔ̀n (rébɔ̀nì-) *v.* to be disruptive, interruptive.

rɛɓédɔ̀n (rɛɓédɔ̀nɨ̀-) *v.* to be tender (e.g. an egg or soft vegetable). See also *redédɔ̀n*.

rèɗᵋ (rèɗɛ̀) *ideo.* tenderly.

rɛɗédɔ̀n (rɛɗédɔ̀nɨ̀-) *v.* to be tender (e.g. an egg or soft vegetable). See also *rɛɓédɔ̀n*.

rɛɗɛɗánón (rɛɗɛɗánónì-) *v.* to crack, crackle, pop (like roasting maize, tree on fire, thunder, gunfire, or people talking angrily). See also *ɗɛɗɛanón*.

rɛɗés (rɛɗésɨ́-) *v.* to squash, squish (e.g. a louse or tick). See also *ɓirés*.

rɛ́és (rɛ́ésɨ̀-) *v.* to coerce, extort, force, pressure. See also *tɔrɛɛs*.

rɛɛtés (rɛɛtésɨ́-) *v.* to coerce, extort, force, pressure.

rɛfékɲɔ̀n (rɛfékɲɔ̀nɨ̀-) *v.* to flump down, plop down (often indecently exposing oneself).

régirégòn (régirégònì-) *v.* to talk all at once (of big crowds).

reídòn (reídònì-) *v.* to be egocentric, self-centered.

rékés (rékésɨ̀-) *v.* to scrape off (e.g. hair from a skin). See also *tʉkʉrɛs*.

rɛkéɲémɔ̀n (rɛkéɲémɔ̀nɨ̀-) *v.* to be scrawny, stunted.

reŋíónukotᵃ (reŋíónukotí-) *v.* to have seizures, seize frequently.

rèŋòn (rèŋònì-) *v.* to faint, go unconscious, pass out, swoon.

rèrrr (rèrrr) *ideo.* baa! (bleating sound of goats and sheep).

rès (rèsè) *ideo.* phoot! (sound made when a spear pierces an animal's body and comes out the other side). See also *pʉ̀ʉ̀tʉ*.

rès (rèsè) *ideo.* rattily, tattily.

rɛsédɔ̀n (rɛsédɔ̀nɨ̀-) *v.* to be rattty, tatty, worn out (e.g. old clothes).

rétítésúkotᵃ (rétítésúkotí-) *v.* to bend over.

rétón (rétónì-) *1 v.* to be bent or bowed over. *2 v.* to be deformed, distorted in shape.

rexúkúmòn (rexúkúmònì-) *v.* to be flabby, pudgy, tubby. See also *gerúsúmòn*.

ri (rié-) *n.* goat(s).

ríbiribánón (ríbiribánónì-) *1 v.* to be crooked, jagged. *2 v.* to be cross-eyed, strabismic.

riɓiríɓón (riɓiríɓónì-) *v.* to glimmer, shimmer (like a mirage).

rídziridzánón (rídziridzánónì-) *v.* to be ragged, tattered.

riɗés (riɗésɨ́-) *1 v.* to pinch, squeeze, squish, wedge. *2 v.* to clamp, clinch (e.g. in teeth).

riɗiesíkwàz (riɗiesí-kwàzà-) *pl.* **riɗiesíkwazíkᵃ**. *n.* cloth tied around the waist (either to bind the stomach when hungry or to act as a baby's diaper).

riɗímétòn (riɗímétònì-) *v.* to clamp shut, constrict, contract, narrow.

riébàr (rié-bàrɔ̀) *pl.* **riébaritín**. *n.* flock of goats.

rieím (rié-ímà-) *pl.* **riéwíkᵃ**. *n.* goat kid.

rieŋwa (rie-ŋwaá-) *n.* doe, nanny: female goat.

rieófúr (rié-ófúrí-) *pl.* **rieófúríkᵃ**. *n.* goat-leather bag.

ríínós (ríínósí-) *1 v.* to go or run after each other (as in children's play). *2 v.* to have an affair, pursue each other sexually.

ríjᵃ (ríjá-) *pl.* **ríjíkᵃ**. *n.* bush, forest, scrub, woods.

ríjáàkᵃ (ríjá-àkà-) *pl.* **ríjáakɨtɨ́n**. *n.* entrance to thick bush or forest.

ríjíkaajíkᵃ (ríjíka-ajíká-) *n.* bush country, scrubland, woodland. *Lit.* 'within the forests'.

ríjíkààm (ríjíkà-àmà-) *pl.* **ríjíkaik**ᵃ. *n.* bandit or vagabond in the bush.

ríjíkànànès (ríjíkànànèsì-) *n.* vagabondage, vagrancy (in the bush). See also *xikw*ᵃ.

rikíríkᵃ (rikíríkì-) *pl.* **rikíríkìk**ᵃ. *1 n.* granite. *2 n.* rocky outcrop.

rìkwᵃ (rìkò-) *pl.* **ríkwítín**. *n.* horizontal supporting pole.

rìƙòŋ (rìƙòŋò-) *pl.* **ríƙóŋik**ᵃ. *n.* big widemouth gourd used for brewing beer and storing water.

rɨmɛ́s (rɨmɛ́sɨ́-) *v.* to appeal to, find refuge in, shelter, take shelter in.

rɨmɛ́sá dìdìù *v.* to take shelter from rain.

rìmòn (rìmònì-) *v.* to melt away, shrink back (out of sight).

ripᵃ (ripá-) *pl.* **ripitɨ́n**. *1 n.* hole, hollow. *2 n.* grave, tomb.

ririanéton (ririanétònì-) *v.* to become blazing hot, sweltering.

ririanón (ririanónì-) *v.* to be blazing hot, sweltering.

rirís (rirísá-) *pl.* **rirísík**ᵃ. *n.* tree used for building and fencing.

rɨrrr (rɨrrr) *ideo.* hsss! (sound of a flame).

risés (risésí-) *v.* to affront, insult, offend.

rités (ritésí-) *v.* to move, push (e.g. flour into a sack, soil into a hole).

ritésúƙotᵃ (ritésúƙotí-) *v.* to move or push away.

ritetés (ritetésí-) *v.* to move or pull out (e.g. the small stick holding up a flat stone in a bird-trap).

ritídòn (ritídònì-) *v.* to be delicious, scrumptious.

rɨtsɛ́s (rɨtsɛ́sɨ̀-) *v.* to catch (up with), overtake.

rɨtsɨrɨtsánón (rɨtsɨrɨtsánónì-) *v.* to be ceaseless, constant, never-ending (e.g. one's supply of grain at home on a good year).

rìtⁱ (rìtì) *ideo.* kerplunk! (sound of falling heavily).

rìtⁱ (rìtì) *ideo.* deliciously.

rò (rò) *adv.* actually, exactly, indeed.

rɔam (rɔamá-) *1 n.* beads strung on a string. *2 n.* kabob, shish kebab, skewered meat. *Lit.* 'skewerable'.

róbiróbòn (róbiróbònì-) *v.* to absorb heat (e.g. from the sun).

róbɔdɔmɔ̀n (róbɔdɔmɔ̀nì-) *v.* to be crusted over, crusty, encrusted (e.g. eyes or ears).

ròɓᵃ (ròɓà-) *n.* folk, people.

ròɓà (ròɓà) *interj.* folks! people! (a term for addressing a group).

rɔɓᵃ (rɔɓá-) *pl.* **rɔɓɨtɨn**. *n.* animal collar, leash. Not to be confused with *ròɓᵃ*.

roɓa ni gúrítínía dayaákᵃ *n.* humanitarians, philanthropists. *Lit.* 'people with good hearts'.

roɓazeikᵃ (roɓa-zeiká-) *n.* adults, big people, leaders.

roɓazeikánánès (roɓazeikánánèsì-) *1 n.* adulthood (of many). *2 n.* leadership (of many).

rɔɓɔ (rɔɓɔ) *ideo.* gristlely, rubberily.

rɔɓɔ́dòn (rɔɓɔ́dònì-) *v.* to be cartilaginous, gristly, rubbery (when chewed).

rɔɗɛ́s (rɔɗɛ́sɨ́-) *v.* to perforate or pierce making a popping sound.

rɔ́ɛ́s (rɔ́ɛ́sɨ̀-) *1 v.* to string, thread (e.g. beads on a necklace, or meat on a string of bark for carrying). *2 v.* to skewer, spit.

Rɔ́gɛ̀hɔ̀ (Rɔ́gɛ̀-hòò-) *n.* name of a hill or mountain. *Lit.* 'reedbuck-hut'.

rɔ́gɛŋwa (rɔ́gɛ-ŋwaá-) *n.* female mountain reedbuck. *Redunca fulvorufula.*

rògìrògᵃ (rògìrògì-) *pl.* **rógìrògìk**ᵃ. *n.* tortoise shell (made into a musical rattle).

roiróón (roiróónì-) *v.* to be loose, unaffixed, unfastened (e.g. beads on a string, hoe on a handle). See also *dolódòn*.

rɔjᵒ (rɔ̀jɔ̀) *1 ideo.* squashily, squelchily, squishily. *2 ideo.* arthritically.

rɔjɔ́dɔ̀n (rɔjɔ́dɔ̀nɨ̀-) *1 v.* to be squashy, squelchy, squishy (like boiled pumpkin or mud). *2 v.* to be arthritic. See also *ɓirídòn*.

rɔ́ƙɛ́s (rɔ́ƙɛ́sɨ̀-) *v.* to install, mount, set up (a beehive).

rɔ́ƙɔ́ (rɔ́ƙɔ́ɔ̀-) *pl.* **rɔ́ƙɔ́ìk**ᵃ. *n.* tamarind tree whose sour fruits are eaten raw and whose seeds (*dɛ̂g*ᵃ) are fried, dried, and ground into flour; its leaves are crushed, infused, and sprayed over gardens as a pesticide. *Tamarindus indica.*

Rɔ́ƙɔ́dɛ̀ (Rɔ́ƙɔ́-dɛ̀à-) *n.* a sacred place with a tamarind tree at the foot of the escarpment where religious ceremonies used to be held. *Lit.* 'tamarind-foot'.

rɔ́ƙɔ́rɔƙánón (rɔ́ƙɔ́rɔƙánónì-) *1 v.* to be constricted, narrow, pressed. *2 v.* to be gruff, hoarse, husky. See also *kokórómòn*.

rómɔ́n (rómɔ́nɨ̀-) *v.* to be dense, impenetrable, thick (like an unburned thicket).

rɔɲɛ́s (rɔɲɛ́sɨ́-) *v.* to compress, force together (two non-fitting parts).

rɔɲɛ́sá asɨ́ (rɔɲɛ́sá asɨ́) *v.* to ingratiate, sidle up to, try to get close to.

rɔ́ŋ (rɔ́ŋó-) *n.* something wrong in any way: bad, foolish, incorrect.

Rɔ̀ŋɔ̀tᵃ (Rɔ̀ŋɔ̀tì-) *n.* name of a mountain in Turkanaland, Kenya, that the Ik used to frequent in search of food. Also called *Sɔ̀ŋɔ̀t*ᵃ.

rɔ́ɔ́s (rɔ́ɔ́sɨ̀-) *1 v.* to be strung, threaded. *2 v.* to be skewered.

rɔ̀r (rɔ̀rì-) *n.* tree whose seeds are boiled and eaten. *Acacia sp.* OR *Boscia salicifolia.*

rɔrɛ́s (rɔrɛ́sɨ́-) *v.* to sieve, sift, sort (e.g. grains or rice to find and remove small stones). See also *isalɛs*.

róróìɔkᵃ (róróì-ɔ̀kà-) *n.* upper hipbone, pelvis.

rɔ́rɔ́tɔ̀n (rɔ́rɔ́tɔ̀nɨ̀-) *v.* to stoop over (as when climbing a steep slope).

róróyᵃ (róróì-) *pl.* **róróìk**ᵃ. *n.* waist, waistline.

rɔtam (rɔtamá-) *n.* object or person under surveillance (like a camp of enemies or an animal trap that has been set). *Lit.* 'surveilable'.

rɔtɛ́ám (rɔtɛ́-ámà-) *pl.* **rɔtɛ́ík**ᵃ. *n.* scout, sleuth, spy.

rɔ́tɛ́s (rɔ́tɛ́sɨ̀-) *v.* to sleuth on, spy on, surveil.

rɔwᵃ (rɔwá-) *pl.* **rówíkw**ᵃ. *n.* field, flatland, flat meadow.

rɔwáám (rɔwá-ámà-) *n.* Turkana person. *Lit.* 'flatlander'.

rɔ̂gᵃ (rɔ́gɛ̀-) *n.* mountain reedbuck. *Redunca fulvorufula.*

rúbès (rúbèsì-) *v.* to aggravate, exacerbate, worsen.

rúbès (rúbèsɨ̀-) *v.* to hang by tucking, tuck up.

rúbɛsʉkɔtᵃ (rúbɛsʉkɔtɨ́-) v. to hang up by tucking, tuck up.

rúbètɔ̀n (rúbètɔ̀nɨ̀-) v. to germinate, sprout up. See also búrukúkón and xúbètòn.

rúbɔ̀n (rúbɔ̀nɨ̀-) v. to germinate, sprout. See also búrukúkón and xúbòn.

ruɓétón (ruɓétónɨ̀-) v. to collapse, fall, tumble (of buildings, fences, trees).

rúɓón (rúɓónɨ̀-) 1 v. to grunt in pain. 2 v. to hoot (of large owls).

ruɓonukotᵃ (ruɓonukotí-) v. to collapse, fall, tumble (of buildings, fences, trees).

ruɓutetés (ruɓutetésí-) v. to bring down, cut down, fell.

rúdzès (rúdzèsì-) v. to carry many of (e.g. things stuffed in pockets).

ruɗés (ruɗésí-) v. to perforate, punch a hole in, puncture (e.g. something hard like a gourd or jerrycan).

rués (ruesí-) v. to deracinate, extirpate, pull up, uproot. See also ɗués.

rúɛ́s (rúɛ́sɨ̀-) v. to box in, corner, trap.

Rúfa (Rúfaa-) n. personal name of an elder from Kamion.

rúgètsᵃ (rúgètsì-) pl. rúgètsìkᵃ. n. jut, protrusion, protuberance (e.g. in bone or rock).

rúgʉ̀ɗʉ̀mɔ̀n (rúgʉ̀ɗʉ̀mɔ̀nɨ̀-) v. to be hunched or stooped over (like a person or tree). See also mʉkʉ́rʉ́mɔ̀n.

rúgurugánón (rúgurugánónì-) v. to be ragged, rough, rugged.

rʉjanón (rʉjanónì-) v. to be creased, crinkled, wrinkled (like a woman's skin after birth). See also turújón and zamʉjánón.

rʉjés (rʉjésí-) v. to pull back, resile, retract. See also dolés.

rʉjɛtésá asɨ́ v. to pull oneself back, retract oneself (like a snake into a hole).

rʉjɛtón (rʉjɛtónì-) v. to duck, get down (e.g. to hide from danger).

rʉ̀jɔ̀n (rʉ̀jɔ̀nɨ̀-) v. to slouch, slump.

rʉjʉrújánón (rʉjʉrújánónì-) v. to be creased, wrinkled. See also turújón and zamʉjánón.

rʉkᵃ (rʉkú-) pl. rʉkɨtɨ́n. n. hump on animal's back (e.g. cow or camel).

rukûdzᵃ (rukúdzò-) pl. rukúdzìkᵃ. n. tree species whose black seeds are boiled and added to porridge as a medicine for chest infections, whose bark is decocted and drunk to treat meningitis, whose branching stems are used to make mingling sticks, and whose wicked hooked thorns deliver painful, poisonous scratches to the skin. *Zanthoxylum chalybeum*.

rukurúkón (rukurúkónì-) v. to be edgy, jittery, jumpy, nervous.

rúmánitésúkotᵃ (rúmánitésúkotí-) 1 v. to make fall, trip. 2 v. to fail, make fail.

rúmánòn (rúmánònì-) 1 v. to fall, stumble, trip. 2 v. to have an accident or mishap. 3 v. to fail, flunk, lose.

rúmánònà kàràtsʉ̀ v. to be overthrown, removed from office. Lit. 'to fall from the chair'.

rumetᵃ (rumetí-) n. downfall, failure, fall.

rumɛtón (rumɛtónì-) v. to retire, retreat (due to old age).

rumurúm (rumurúmá-) pl. rumurúmìkᵃ. n. sharp grass stub left after a fire.

rùròn (rùrònì-) v. to bruise, contuse.

rùs (rùsù) ideo. tenderly.

227

rusúdòn (rusúdònì-) *v.* to be tender (like young weeds or well-cooked meat). See also *xɛɓédɔ̀n*.

rùt[a] (rùtà-) *n.* pungently sweet fermented porridge.

rútɛ́s (rútɛ́sɨ̀-) *v.* to blow one's nose, exsufflate.

rutésúƙot[a] (rutésúƙotí-) *v.* to knife, thrust a knife into.

rutet[a] (rutetí-) *n.* hillside, mountainside.

rutet[o] *n.* along the side of a slope.

rʉtsɛ́s (rʉtsɛ́sɨ́-) *v.* to cram, jam, ram, stuff. See also *isìkɛs*.

rʉtsɛ́súƙot[a] (rʉtsɛ́súƙɔtɨ́-) *v.* to cram, jam, ram, stuff.

rùt[u] (rùtù) *ideo.* splitch! (sound of gouging or stabbing).

rutúdùm (rutúdùmà-) *n.* speckled pigeon. *Columba guinea.*

rutukuɲ (rutukuɲu) *ideo.* dying as many, in large numbers.

ruutésuƙot[a] (ruutésuƙotí-) *v.* to pull or tear out, uproot.

ruutetés (ruutetésí-) *v.* to pull out, tear out, uproot. See also *ɗuetés*.

S

sa (saí-) *pro.* some more, some other.

Sààŋìròàwª (Sààŋìrò-àwà-) *n.* name of a hill or mountain. *Lit.* 'Saŋiro's place'.

sáásò sɨ̀n *n.* yesterday.

sàbà (sàbàà-) *pl.* **sábàɨkª**. *n.* river. Not to be confused with *sábà*.

sábà (sábàɨ-) *pl.* **sábàɨkª**. *n.* intra-abdominal fat, organ fat, visceral fat. Not to be confused with *sàbà*.

Sabaa Damán *n.* name of a river. *Lit.* 'River Daman'.

sàbààƙwª (sàbà-àƙɔ̀-) *n.* riverbed, river bottom.

sàbàgwàs (sàbà-gwàsà-) *pl.* **sabagwasíkª**. *n.* black hammerstone obtained from riverbeds. *Lit.* 'river-stone'.

sábɨ̀rɨ̀rɔ̀n (sábɨ̀rɨ̀rɔ̀nɨ̀-) *v.* to stick out (e.g. the branches of a leafless tree, hair on cold skin, wet fur).

sáɓés (sáɓésì-) *v.* to kill, murder, slay (many). Compare with *cɛés*.

sáɓésìàm (sáɓésì-àmà-) *pl.* **sáɓésiikª**. *n.* killer, murderer, slayer (of more than one).

sáɓítetés (sáɓítetésí-) *v.* to cause to kill (more than one).

sáɓúmós (sáɓúmósí-) *v.* to kill each other.

ságoanón (ságoanónì-) *v.* to be entangled, entrapped, snared, tangled. See also *kòtsòn*.

ságòsìm (ságò-sìmà-) *pl.* **ságosimitín**. *n.* net trap, snare.

sàgwª (ságò-) *n.* net-trapping, snaring, trapping with snares.

ságwàràmòn (ságwàràmònì-) *v.* to be bare, shadeless.

ságwès (ságwèsì-) *1 v.* to ensnare, entangle, snare, trap with a net. *2 v.* to catch, corral, round up (as with a net). See also *kotsítésukotª*.

sáítòn (sáítònì-) *v.* to encroach, infiltrate, invade (e.g. of enemies or a sickness).

sakalúkª (sakalúká-) *n.* male *kodowª*: unidentified antelope species.

sakám (sakámá-) *pl.* **sakámíkª**. *n.* liver.

sakánámòn (sakánámònì-) *v.* to be bowl-shaped, concave. See also *tsukúlúmòn*.

sakátán (sakátánɨ̀-) *n.* thick, dry, unburned grass (which when it catches fire causes a hot, fast-burning blaze).

sakátánòn (sakátánònì-) *v.* to be dry, thick, and unburned (of grass).

sakɛin *n.* last year, a year ago.

Saloloŋ (Saloloŋó-) *n.* name of a river.

sáŋamátª (sáŋamátɨ̀-) *n.* crumbly sedimentary rock.

Saŋaŋ (Saŋaŋɨ́-) *n.* a personal name.

saŋáŋá (<saŋáŋóòn) *v.*

saŋáŋóòn (saŋaŋóónì-/saŋaŋá-) *v.* to be scaly, scurfy (e.g. the skin of a reptile or plucked bird).

Saŋar (Saŋarɨ́-) *n.* name of a river with an associated sacred place and its swarm of bees.

sarɨsar (sarɨsarɨ́-) *pl.* **sarɨ́sárɨkª**. *n.* bridge of nose, nasal bridge.

sarɨ́sárɨkª (sarɨ́sárɨkà-) *n.* grill of a vehicle.

sárón (sárónì-) *1 v.* to still be. *2 v.* to be not yet, not yet be.

sàsàr (sàsàrà-) *n.* beeswax that is chewed and spit out.

sátᵃ (sátá-) *pl.* **sátíkw**ᵃ. *n.* shallow pool on the surface of a rock. Compare with *mɔkɔr*.

sátíkócue (sátíkó-cué-) *n.* water from a pool on the surface of a rock.

saúkúmòn (saúkúmònì-) *v.* to be fuzzy, hairy, woolly.

sawatᵃ (sawatɔ́-) *pl.* **sáwátɨk**ᵃ. *n.* shoulder.

sawatɔ́ɔ́kᵃ (sawatɔ́-ɔ́kà-) *pl.* **sáwátikɔɔkɨtín**. *n.* shoulder bone, scapula.

sawátsámòn (sawátsámònì-) *v.* to be gangly, lanky, spindly (like tall grass or tall person).

sayó ɲásáàtɨkàᵋ *n.* sometimes (in terms of hours).

sè (sèà-) *n.* blood.

sèààm (sèà-àmà-) *pl.* **seaik**ᵃ. *n.* bloodthirsty person, killer, murderer. *Lit.* 'blood-person'.

seacɛmɛ́r (sea-cɛmɛrɨ́-) *n.* blood herb: vine species whose roots are crushed, soaked in water, and a) drunk by a woman having just given birth to stop her bleeding or b) sprinkled on weapons by a woman who having just given birth so her bleeding does not jeopardize the hunt's success.

seamucé (sea-mucéè-) *pl.* **seamucéìk**ᵃ. *n.* blood vessel, vein. *Lit.* 'blood-path'.

seátᵒ *n.* empty-handed, unrewarded.

séɓés (séɓésì-) *1 v.* to brush, sweep. *2 v.* to sand. *3 v.* to grade, level (roads).

séɓésìàm (séɓésì-àmà-) *pl.* **séɓésiik**ᵃ. *1 n.* sweeper. *2 n.* road grader.

séɓésuƙotᵃ (séɓésuƙotí-) *v.* to brush or sweep away/off.

séɓetés (séɓetésí-) *v.* to sweep up.

seɓuránón (seɓuránónì-) *v.* to be scarred up.

sêdᵃ (sédà-) *pl.* **sédìk**ᵃ. *n.* garden.

seekwᵃ (seekó-) *n.* bouillon, broth, soup.

sɛ́ɛ́s (sɛ́ɛ́sɨ̀-) *v.* to make a funeral sacrifice of a goat to prevent the deceased's ghost from disturbing the relatives (by stunting their growth and the yield of their crops). See also *ipúɲéés*.

sègᵃ (sègà-) *pl.* **ségitín**. *n.* umbrella thorn: long-thorned tree species whose bark fiber is used in building and whose seed-pods are eaten by goats. *Acacia tortilis*.

Sègààwᵃ (Sègà-àwà-) *n.* name of a place and a deserted village. *Lit.* 'umbrella thorn place'.

Segaikᵃ (Sega-icé-) *n.* traditional men's age-group with the Umbrella Thorn tree as its totem (#3 in the historical line). *Lit.* 'Umbrella Thorn Folk'.

seger (segerí-) *pl.* **ségèrìk**ᵃ. *n.* softwood tree whose roots and bark are pounded, soaked, and drunk for stomach ailments and whose bark, when removed from the wood, is used by children as a flue, air-gun (for shooting figs), or air-pump. *Steganotaenia araliacea*.

Segeríkwár (Segerí-kwárà-) *n.* name of a mountain. *Lit.* '*seger*-mountain'.

Séíkwàr (Séí-kwàrà-) *n.* name of a mountain. *Lit.* 'quartzite-mountain'.

seínení (seínenîi-) *n.* tree species whose branches are used for fencing. *Stereospermum kuntianum*.

Séítíníkokór (Séítíní-kokóró-) *n.* name of a hill or mountain. *Lit.* 'quartzite-ridge'.

Sɛkɛɗíáwᵃ (Sɛkɛɗí-áwà-) *n.* name of a hill or mountain and associated river. *Lit.* '*Sɛkɛɗ*'s place'.

sɛkɛmán (sɛkɛmání-) *n.* grain that falls to the ground through the drying platform.

sɛkɛ́s (sɛkɛ́sɨ́-) *v.* to scratch or scrub off.

sɛkɛ́súƙɔtᵃ (sɛkɛ́súƙɔtɨ́-) *v.* to scratch or scrub off.

Sɛkɛtᵃ (Sɛkɛté-) *n.* name of a river.

sɛkɔnʉƙɔtᵃ (sɛkɔnʉƙɔtɨ́-) *v.* to fade (of color). See also *kitsonuƙotᵃ*.

sekweres (sekweresí-) *v.* to scurry up, skitter up.

seƙelánón (seƙelánónì-) *v.* to be dessicated, dried out (like old wood).

sèlètᵋ (sèlètè) *ideo.* schlip! (sound of slipping). See also *jʉ́rʉ́tᵘ*.

sɛlɛ́tɛ́mɔ̀n (sɛlɛ́tɛ́mɔ̀nɨ̀-) *v.* to be slippy, slithery (e.g. a cat, snake, or spear in the air).

sɛlɛ́tɛ́tɔ̀n (sɛlɛ́tɛ́tɔ̀nɨ̀-) *v.* to slide or slip out (like paper from a printer).

sémédedánón (sémédedánónì-) *v.* to be inclined, sloped.

semélémòn (semélémònì-) *v.* to be elliptical, oval (e.g. cucumber, egg, or river stones).

sémɨ̀s (sémɨ̀sɨ̀-) *n.* Anglican, Protestant.

sɛ́rɛ́ƙɛkánón (sɛ́rɛ́ƙɛkánónì-) *v.* to be runty, shrimpy, stunted.

sɛrɛpɛs (sɛrɛpɛsɨ́-) *v.* to slip in, slip through (e.g. when hiding a stick in the grass).

sɛrɛ́pɛ́sʉƙɔtᵃ (sɛrɛ́pɛ́sʉƙɔtɨ́-) *v.* to slip into/through (e.g. pushing through a fence).

sèrèyᵃ (sèrèì-) *pl.* sereíkᵃ. *n.* gourd basin made from a large gourd cut in half.

serɨ́nà (serɨ́nàà-) *n.* sorghum variety with short stalks and purplish seeds.

sɛsɛanón (sɛsɛanónì-) *v.* to whisper.

sɛsɛanóniàm (sɛsɛanónì-àmà-) *pl.* sɛsɛanóniikᵃ. *n.* gossiper, whisperer.

sésèn (sésènì-) *n.* tree species from which bowls and stools are carved. *Hymenodictyon floribundum.*

Sɛʉsɛ́wᵃ (Sɛʉsɛ́ʉ-) *n.* nickname of a colonial British road engineer that worked near Ikland.

sèwᵃ (sèwà-) *pl.* séwɨ́tín. *n.* cane, club, stick.

séyᵃ (séí-) *pl.* séítín. *n.* quartzite.

sɨ̂bᵃ (sɨ́bɔ̀-) *n.* barm, leaven, yeast.

sɨbánón (sɨbánónì-) *v.* to be recently impregnated, pregnant (still in the first term when it cannot be seen).

sɨ́biónuƙotᵃ (sɨ́biónuƙotɨ́-) *v.* to stand around as a group.

sɨ́bitɛ́súƙɔtᵃ (sɨ́bitɛ́súƙɔtɨ́-) *v.* to make stand around.

sɨ́bɔn (sɨ́bɔnɨ̀-) *v.* to stand around.

sɨ̂dᵃ (sɨ́dà-) *n.* bee larva.

sɨ́dàhò (sɨ́dà-hòò-) *pl.* sɨ́dahoíkᵃ. *n.* bee larva chamber.

sɨ́dilé (sɨ́diléè-) *n.* terrapin, turtle. *Pelomedusa subrufa.*

sɨ́dɔ̀rɔ̀mɔ̀n (sɨ́dɔ̀rɔ̀mɔ̀nɨ̀-) *v.* to be slender, slim (e.g. person or tree).

sɨ́ɛ́s (sɨ́ɛ́sɨ̀-) *v.* to smear (with funerary goat dung soon after a death).

sìgìrìgìr (sìgìrìgìrì-) *pl.* sígìrìgìrìkᵃ. *n.* mane, ridge of hair.

Siitán (Siitánì-) *n.* devil, Lucifer, Satan.

sɨ́kɔ́ɔ́rɛ́s (sɨ́kɔ́ɔ́rɛ́sɨ́-) *v.* to winnow by pouring from a container to the ground.

sikusába (siku-sábàà-) *n.* tiger beetle larva. *Cicindelinae.*

sikwárámòn (sikwárámònì-) *v.* to be wimpy, wussy. See also *kalɛ́ɛ́tsɛránón*.

sikwés (sikwésí-) *v.* to braid, plait.

sikwetés (sikwetésí-) *1 v.* to braid or plait up. *2 v.* to afflict, bring calamity upon.

siƙᵃ (siƙá-) *n.* dew.

Siƙákᵉ *n.* name of a place. *Lit.* 'in the dew'.

Sìƙètìà (Sìƙètìàà-) *n.* Siƙetia (I & II): two of the Ik's twelve clans.

Sìƙètìààm (Sìƙètìà-àmà) *pl.* **Siƙetiaik**ᵃ. *n.* Siƙetia clan member.

siƙisiƙánétòn (siƙisiƙánétònì-) *v.* to become grainy, textured (like the *rágan* tuber or one's fingerprints).

síƙísíƙánón (síƙísíƙánónì-) *v.* to be grainy, textured (like the *rágan* tuber or one's fingerprints).

síƙón (síƙónì-) *1 v.* to sneeze, sternutate. *2 v.* to snort, whistle (e.g. the alarm call of antelopes).

sìƙwᵃ (sìƙwà-) *1 n.* sneeze, sternutation. *2 n.* snort, whistle (e.g. the alarm call of antelopes).

silaɓánón (silaɓánónì-) *v.* to be diluted, thinned out.

siláxɨŋ (siláxɨŋɨ-) *n.* cutting or slashing of grass.

sílím (sílímù-) *n.* HIV-AIDS. See also *lóɓúlukúɲ*.

silɔ́jɔ́mɔ̀n (silɔ́jɔ́mɔ̀nɨ̀-) *v.* to be bare, denuded, naked, unadorned. See also *tudúsúmòn*.

sílɔlɔ́jᵃ (sílɔlɔ́já-) *n.* slender mongoose. *Herpestes sanguineus*.

Silóyᵃ (Silóì-) *n.* a personal name.

sim (simá-) *pl.* **simitín**. *n.* cord, string, twisted fiber.

simááƙátᵃ (simá-áƙátí-) *pl.* **simááƙátík**ᵃ. *n.* knot. *Lit.* 'cord-nostril'.

simánón (simánónì-) *1 v.* to be fibrous, stringy (like sisal fiber). *2 v.* to be sinewy, wiry (e.g. when malnourished).

siméékwᵃ (simé-ékù-) *pl.* **simítíníekwitín**. *n.* center of a fiber-string snare (once it is set). *Lit.* 'cord-eye'.

símídídí (símídídíì-) *n.* mote, particle, speck.

simidímídés (simidímídésí-) *v.* to rub between fingers (e.g. dust, flour, or sand).

simiránón (simiránónì-) *v.* to be corroded, rusty.

simírɔn (simírɔnɨ-) *v.* to corrode, rust. See also *iróróòn*.

simísímàtᵃ (simísímàtɨ-) *n.* vine that grows as a weed, is tough to cut with hoe, and which climbs all over crops, dragging them down. *Neotonia wightii*.

sìn (=sìnà) *1 dem.* that (yesterday). *2 rel.* that/which (yesterday).

sìn (=sìnì) *1 dem.* those (yesterday, plural). *2 rel.* that/which (yesterday, plural).

sìnà (sìnà) *subordconn.* when ... (yesterday). The main verb follows this word takes the dummy pronoun.

sínés (sínésɨ-) *v.* to cover (a corpse with leaves and branches).

siŋíl (siŋílá-) *n.* small black ant species that causes pain if it gets in an eye. Also called *ɓáritson*.

siŋírón (siŋírónì-) *v.* to brood, fume, sulk.

sìŋòn (sìŋònì-) *v.* to be depressed, gloomy, sad.

Síɔ̀ɔ̀tᵃ (Síɔ̀ɔ̀tɔ̀-) *n.* name of a river. *Lit.* 'large-leaf albizia'.

síɔɔtᵃ (síɔɔtɔ-) *pl.* **síɔɔtík**ᵃ. *n.* large-leafed albizia: tree species from whose wood hoe handles, stools, spoons, and mingling sticks are carved. *Albizia grandibracteata.*

sír (síɾɨ̀-) *n.* dropsy, edema.

sír (síɾá-) *n.* early morning announcement or message of important information delivered by an elder to the whole village.

síráàm (síɾá-àmà-) *pl.* **síráik**[a]. *n.* announcer, herald (often a village elder).

síránòn (síránònì-) *v.* to announce, declare, herald.

Síré (Síréè-) *n.* a personal name.

sɨs (sɨsɨ́-) *n.* honey beer, mead: traditional grain beer with honey added right before drinking, making it potently alcoholic. See also *tsɔkam.*

sɨsɨβɛs (sɨsɨβɛsɨ́-) *v.* to bait or lure (bees by putting special leaves in or around a hive's grass entrances).

sɨsɨk[a] (sɨsɨká-) *pl.* **sɨsɨ́ɨ́kɨ̀n**. *n.* center, middle.

sɨsɨkáám (sɨsɨká-ámà-) *pl.* **sɨsɨkáík**[a]. *n.* middle child.

sɨsɨkák[ɛ] *n.* between, halfway, in the center/middle.

sɨsɨ́kêd[a] (sɨsɨ́kédè-) *n.* center, halfway point, middle.

síts'[a] (síts'á-) *pl.* **síts'ítín**. *n.* ritual killing, sacrifice.

síts'[a] (síts'á-) *1 n.* hair. *2 n.* termite wings.

síts'ádè (síts'á-dèà-) *pl.* **síts'ádɛík**[a]. *1 n.* hair follicle. *2 n.* skin bump. *Lit.* 'hair-foot'.

sits'és (sits'ésí-) *v.* to court, date, engage, woo.

síts'ímós (síts'ímósí-) *v.* to court, date, or engage each other.

sɔɓɔ́lɔ́mɔ̀n (sɔɓɔ́lɔ́mɔ̀nɨ̀-) *v.* to be overgrown, unkempt (e.g. a garden or home).

sɔ́gɛ̀kàk[a] (sɔ́gɛ̀-kàkà-) *n.* reed whose fruits are cooked as a vegetable. *Celosia schweinfurthiana.*

Sɔ́gɛsabá (Sɔ́gɛ-sabáà-) *n.* name of a river near *Rɔ̀ŋɔ̀t*[a]. *Lit.* 'reed-river'. Also called *Loteteleít*[a].

sɔk[a] (sɔkɔ́-) *pl.* **sɔkɨtín**. *1 n.* root. *2 n.* hoof. *3 n.* leg (of furniture).

sɔ́k[a] (sɔ́ká-) *pl.* **sɔ́kɨ́tɨ́n**. *1 n.* grooved spout of a gourd bowl (created by bisecting the gourd's stem). *2 n.* gutter, trough.

sɔka na ƙwázà[ɛ] *n.* bottom hem. *Lit.* 'root of the cloth'.

sɔkɛd[a] (sɔkɛdɛ-) *pl.* **sɔ̀kɨn**. *n.* root.

sokóɗómòn (sokóɗómònì-) *v.* to be hooked, hooklike (like a cane or umbrella). See also *lɔkɔ́ɗɔ́n.*

sokomet[a] (sokometí-) *n.* small worker ant or termite.

sokósɨ́ɨk[ɛ] *v.* quietly, softly.

Soƙogwááś (Soƙogwáásɨ̀-) *n.* name of a mountain in the east of Ikland. Also called *Lopokók*[a].

soƙolánón (soƙolánónì-) *v.* to be curved forward (of horns or trees).

sɔƙɔ́ɲɔ́mɔ̀n (sɔƙɔ́ɲɔ́mɔ̀nɨ̀-) *v.* to be clubfooted, clubhanded.

soƙóríties (soƙórítieś̨-) *v.* to claw, rake with nails, scratch with claws.

sòlɨsòl (sòlɨsòlɨ-) *n.* sharp-bladed grass species that can cut skin and is used for thatching and by children to make whistles. *Gramineae sp.*

Somálìà (Somálìàà-) *n.* Somalia.

sómomójón (sómomójónì-) *v.* to be covered in sores, rashy, scabby.

sɔn (sɔní-) *pl.* **sɔnitín**. *n.* clitoris.

sɔniíkᵃ (sɔní-íkà-) *n.* head or tip of the clitoris.

Sópìà (Sópìàà-) *n.* Abyssinia, Ethiopia. See also *Isópìà*.

sore (soreé-) *1 n.* boy. *2 n.* son.

soréím (soré-ímà-) *pl.* **soréwík**ᵃ. *1 n.* little boy. *2 n.* young son.

sɔrés (sɔrésí-) *v.* to pluck.

sɔs (sɔsá-) *1 n.* black beeswax, propolis. *2 n.* candle wax.

sosóbòs (sosóbòsì-) *n.* sausage tree: whose huge pods are used in fermenting beer or are cut into pieces as charms to stop rain; Dodoth bisect the pod and send a sick person through the halves to be healed; its parasitic plant is also applied to swellings. *Kigelia africana*.

sotés (sotésí-) *v.* to carve, sculpt.

sotetés (sotetésí-) *v.* to carve, sculpt.

sôgᵃ (sógè-) *n.* reed whose reddish stems are used to weave baskets.

súbɛs (súbɛsì-) *1 v.* to charm, influence, persuade, sway, tempt (for ill purposes). *2 n.* to politick, win the support of.

súbɛsìàm (súbɛsì-àmà-) *pl.* **súbɛsiik**ᵃ. *n.* charmer, influencer, tempter.

súbɛsukɔtᵃ (súbɛsukɔtí-) *v.* to charm, influence, persuade, sway, tempt (for ill purposes).

súbitésúkɔta así *v.* to seduce, tempt.

súbunɔs (súbunɔ́sí-) *v.* to influence each other (for ill purposes).

súɓánòn (súɓánònì-) *v.* to get ready or prepare to go.

súɓánònìàm (súɓánònì-àmà-) *pl.* **súɓánoniik**ᵃ. *n.* preparing traveler.

suɓés (suɓésí-) *v.* to bewitch, hex, jinx. See also *ipeɗes*.

suɓésìàm (suɓésí-àmà-) *pl.* **suɓésiik**ᵃ. *n.* bewitcher, hexer.

sùɓètᵃ (sùɓètì-) *n.* preparation for travel.

suɓétón (suɓétónì-) *v.* to get ready or prepare to go.

sùɗᵃ (sùɗà-) *pl.* **súɗitín**. *n.* last or lowest rib.

Suɗán (Suɗánì-) *n.* South Sudan.

Sugur (Sugurá) *n.* a personal name.

sugur (sugurá-) *pl.* **súgùrìk**ᵃ. *1 n.* air, air current, breeze, wind. *2 n.* spirit. *3 n.* fever, flu, malaria. *4 n.* cellular network. *5 n.* shrub whose root concoction is drunk as a remedy for the *sugur* sickness.

Sugura ná Dà *n.* Holy Spirit: third person in the Christian Trinity. *Lit.* 'spirit that is glorious'.

suguráɗáwᵃ (sugurá-ɗáò-) *pl.* **suguráɗáwítín**. *n.* fan or propeller blade.

súkés (súkésì-) *1 v.* to bypass, go around, overtake. *2 v.* to exceed, surpass, top. *3 v.* to win. See also *isukɛs*.

súkɔn (súkɔ́nì-) *v.* to itch.

súkúsuká (súkúsukáà-) *n.* plant species that causes painful itching when touched. *Tragia insuavis*.

súkúsukágwa (súkúsuká-gwaá-) *n.* bird species.

sùkùtèlà (sùkùtèlàà-) *n.* hard crystallized honey.

súkútés (súkútésí-) *v.* to brush, clean, scratch, scrub. See also *súútés*.

súkútésídàkwᵃ (súkútésí-dàkù-) *pl.* **súkútésídakwitín**. *n.* toothbrush. *Lit.* 'brush-stick'. See also *ɲáɓurás* and *tsitsín*.

súkútésítsirím (súkútésí-tsirímú-) *pl.* **súkútésítsirímík**[a]. *1 n.* metal hook used to scratch irritants like head lice. *2 n.* metal rod used to clean gun barrels. *Lit.* 'scratch-metal'.

sulútúmɔ̀n (sulútúmɔ̀nì-) *v.* to be oblong.

súm (súmá-) *n.* atmospheric haze.

sùp[a] (sùpà-) *pl.* **súpítín**. *1 n.* breath, exhalation, inhalation. *2 n.* spirit. *3 n.* vowel.

supaicíká ni isaák[a] *n.* 'heavy' vowels: vowels made with Advanced Tongue Root [+ATR].

supaicíká ni líîd[a] *n.* voiceless vowels.

supaicíká ni nesíbòs *n.* voiced vowels.

supaicíká ni ɔlɔ́daák[a] *n.* 'light' vowels: made without Advanced Tongue Root [-ATR]).

supaicíká tódà[o] *n.* vowels. *Lit.* 'breathings in speech'.

supétɔ́n (supétɔ́nì-) *v.* to breathe in, inhale.

súpɔ́n (súpɔ́nì-) *v.* to breathe, respire. See also *iéŋɔ́n*.

súpɔ́nukɔt[a] (súpɔ́nukɔtí-) *v.* to breathe out, exhale.

súr (súró-) *pl.* **súrítín**. *n.* shrub species used for firewood and eaten by livestock; it often provides shade for tobacco gardens; elders use its switches to ceremonially whip hunters before their departure on a hunt. *Cadaba farinosa.* See also *mét*[a].

surusúrɔ́n (surusúrɔ́nì-) *1 v.* to be straight. *2 v.* to be lanky.

sús (súsá-) *n.* plant stubble left over from the harvest of grains.

sùtòn (sùtònì-) *v.* to rally, respond as a group (e.g. in response to an alarm).

súútés (súútésí-) *1 v.* to brush, clean, scratch, scrub. *2 v.* to sand. See also *súkútés*.

súw[a] (súwá-) *pl.* **súwín**. *n.* beam, ray, or shaft of light. See also *bás*.

swèèè (swèèè) *ideo.* swish! (sound of brushing against something). The vowels of this word are pronounced silently.

t

tàà (tàà) *comp.* i.e., that (is).

táá (táá=) *adv.* next (time).

táábarats[a] (táábaratsó-) *n.* tomorrow (morning).

táábarats[o] *n.* tomorrow (morning).

taasámòn (taasámònì-) *v.* to be sweet-and-sour. See also *mitimítón*.

tààts[a] (tààtsà-) *n.* payment, remuneration.

taatsaama tódà[e] *n.* speaker, spokesperson.

taatsakabáɗ[a] (taatsa-kabáɗá-) *pl.* **taatsakabáɗík**[a]. *n.* payment slip, receipt, voucher.

taatses (taatsesí-) *1 v.* to pay, remunerate. *2 v.* to answer, reply, respond, retort.

taatsesá bùɗàmàk[e] *v.* to pay haphazardly (for what you did not do or take). *Lit.* 'to pay in the dark'.

taatsesa ɗoɗóbò[e] *v.* to show appreciation to one's caregivers (often by giving a gift of beer or honey). *Lit.* 'to pay for the baby-sling'.

taatsesa káwí *v.* to pay a fine unjustly (for a crime one did not commit). *Lit.* 'to pay for ashes'.

taatsesa ɲeutsúrù[i] *v.* to pay tax.

taatsesa tsam *v.* to pay in vain (for what one does not owe).

taatsésuƙot[a] (taatsésuƙotí-) *1 v.* to pay off, repay. *2 v.* to answer, reply, respond, retort.

taatsetés (taatsetésí-) *v.* to answer, reply, respond, retort.

tâb[a] (tábò-) *pl.* **tábitín**. *1 n.* shrub species whose berries and young roots are eaten raw, whose branches are used as fighting switches, and whose bark fibers are used to string beads. *2 n.* allium species: plant growing from a bulb and that produces a single large red flower worn by children as a hat. *Allium sp.*

tábaɨàm (tábaɨ-àmà-) *pl.* **tábaiik**[a]. *n.* westerner.

tábaixan (tábaɨ-xaná-) *dem.* westerly direction.

tabam (tabamá-) *n.* tangible, touchable.

taban (tabaní-) *pl.* **tábànɨk**[a]. *1 n.* wing. *2 n.* fin.

tábàr (tábàrɨ-) *pl.* **tábàrɨk**[a]. *n.* dam, pond, pool, waterhole.

tàbàrɨbàr (tàbàrɨbàrɨ-) *n.* cocktail acacia ant. *Crematogaster sp.*

tábaricue (tábari-cué-) *1 n.* pond water. *2 n.* African tea, milk tea.

tábàsànètòn (tábàsànètònì-) *v.* to be patched, spotted (with different colors). See also *komolánón* and *koríánètòn*.

tábày[a] (tábàɨ-) *n.* west.

tábès (tábèsì-) *1 v.* to feel, touch. *2 v.* to be about, concern, touch on. *3 v.* to move or stir emotionally.

tábitetés (tábitetésí-) *v.* to make touch.

tábodiés (tábodiesí-) *v.* to touch all over.

tábòlèt[a] (tábò-lètà-) *pl.* **táboletitín**. *n.* girl's loincloth made from the bark of the *tâb*[a] shrub.

tabúétòn (tabúétònì-) *v.* to fizz, foam, or froth up, seethe over.

tábunós (tábunósí-) *1 v.* to touch each other. *2 v.* to beat each other.

tabúón (tabúónì-) *1 v.* to fizz, foam, froth, seethe. *2 v.* to build up (the way termites build their mounds).

táburubúrɔ́n (táburubúrɔ́nì-) *v.* to be hot (of the ground).

taɓ[a] (taɓá-) *pl.* **taɓíkw**[a]. *n.* boulder, large rock.

taɓá (<taɓɛɛs) *v.*

taɓádè (taɓá-dèà-) *pl.* **táɓíkódɛ́ík**[a]. *n.* base or foot of a boulder.

taɓakés (taɓakésí-) *v.* to carry by hand or in one's arms.

Taɓákókór (Taɓá-kókóró-) *n.* name of a hill or mountain. *Lit.* 'boulder-ridge'.

taɓales (taɓalesí-) *v.* to despoil, loot, plunder, ransack.

taɓɛɛs (taɓɛɛsɨ́-/taɓá-) *v.* to extend, hold out (e.g. one's hands, palms-up, to catch something or as a gesture of begging).

taɓólón (taɓólónì-) *v.* to exult, gloat.

taɓolos (taɓolosí-) *v.* to be exultant, gleeful, gloating.

taɓóɲómòn (taɓóɲómònì-) *v.* to have flat buttocks.

taɗá (<taɗɛɛs) *v.*

taɗaɗáŋón (taɗaɗáŋónì-) *v.* to be slightly bitter but edible.

taɗaŋes (taɗaŋesí-) *v.* to abide, bear, endure, put up with, stand, tolerate.

taɗáŋón (taɗáŋónì-) *v.* to hang in there, keep on, persist, prevail.

tàɗàpààm (tàɗàpà-àmà-) *pl.* **taɗapaik**[a]. *n.* ambusher.

taɗapes (taɗapesí-) *1 v.* to mend, patch, repair. *2 v.* to ambush, waylay. See also *iɗaarés*.

taɗapetés (taɗapetésí-) *1 v.* to mend or patch up, repair. *2 v.* to ambush, waylay.

taɗápitetés (taɗápitetésí-) *v.* to construct or craft (a proverb, parable, riddle, etc.).

taɗápítotós (taɗápítotósí-) *pl.* **taɗápítotósíicík**[a]. *n.* parable, proverb, riddle, saying.

taɗapos (taɗaposí-) *v.* to be mended, patched, repaired.

taɗates (taɗatesí-) *v.* to break new ground by plowing. See also *túburés*.

taɗatsánón (taɗatsánónì-) *v.* to be deficient, lacking, insufficient.

taɗɛɛs (taɗɛɛsɨ́-/taɗá-) *v.* to overdo (e.g. a job, an amount of food, or even items a thief tries to steal).

tafakés (tafakésí-) *v.* to spread out under (e.g. a hide to catch falling flour).

tafakésá asɨ *v.* to sit immodestly (with legs spread apart).

taítayó (taítayóò-) *n.* dizziness, lightheadedness, vertigo.

tajakes (tajakesí-) *1 v.* to hold by the jaw or mouth (e.g. a person or a dog being given medicine by force). *2 v.* to remove the lower jaw (of a slain animal).

tajales (tajalesí-) *v.* to give up, let go of, relinquish, surrender.

tajálésukot[a] (tajálésukotí-) *v.* to give up, let go of, relinquish, surrender.

tajaletés (tajaletésí-) *v.* to give up, let go of, relinquish, surrender.

takaɗes (takaɗesí-) *v.* to despise, disdain, hate. See also *ts'áɓès*.

takánétòn (takánétònì-) *v.* to appear, show up, surface, turn up.

Takanikʉlɛ́ (Takani-kʉlɛ́ɛ̀-) *n.* name of a place where the Turkana found an old woman because her elbow was visible. *Lit.* 'appearing-elbow'.

237

takanités (takanitesí-) *v.* to detect, discover, find.

takánón (takánónì-) *1 v.* to be present, seen, visible. *2 v.* to be clear, evident, obvious.

takár (takárɨ-) *pl.* **takárɨk**[a]. *1 n.* forehead. *2 n.* face, visage.

takarêd[a] (takárɛ́dɛ̀-) *n.* face, front.

takátákánón (takátákánónì-) *v.* to be cracked, fissured, fractured (e.g. heated rock, dried out mud puddle). See also *médemedánón*.

tákés (tákésì-) *v.* to mean, mention, refer to.

takiés (takiesí-) *v.* to lift carefully (palm upward).

takwés (takwésí-) *v.* to step or tread on.

takwésá ɲamɨɨlɨɨ *v.* to pedal a bicycle.

takwiesúƙota dáŋá[e] *v.* to trample edible termites.

takwitakwiés (takwitakwiesí-) *v.* to step all over, trample.

taƙáá na ŋáɲós *n.* open-toed shoe.

taƙámón (taƙámónì-) *v.* to chance upon, come across, happen upon.

tàƙàt[a] (tàƙàtà-) *n.* call-and-response group prayer.

taƙates (taƙatesí-) *v.* to lead call-and-response group prayers.

taƙátésuƙot[a] (taƙátésuƙotí-) *v.* to pray against/away.

taƙáy[a] (taƙáí-) *pl.* **taƙáík**[a]. *n.* shoe.

talakes (talakesí-) *1 v.* to free, let go, release. *2 v.* to allow, permit. See also *hodés*.

tàlàlìdòm (tàlàlìdòmò-) *n.* small animal species that steals food from homes, especially from pots of food (possibly a type of mongoose).

talóón (talóónì-) *v.* to be nauseated, queasy.

tamá (<tamɛɛs) *v.*

tamáísánón (tamáísánónì-) *v.* to smile.

tamanɛs (tamanɛsí-) *v.* to circumvent, encircle, go around, skirt.

tamanɛtés (tamanɛtésí-) *v.* to circumvent, encircle, go around, skirt.

tamánɛ́tɔ̀n (tamánɛ́tɔ̀nì-) *v.* to go or wind around.

tamaniés (tamaniesí-) *v.* to circumvent, encircle, go around, or skirt repeatedly.

tamátámatés (tamátámatésí-) *v.* to consider, contemplate, mull over, ponder, think on. See also *tamɨ́támiés*.

Tamateeɓon (Tamateeɓonó-) *n.* name of a river.

tamɛɛs (tamɛɛsí-/tamá-) *1 v.* to adore, extol, laud, praise (e.g. one's spouse, a friend, or even an animal like a favorite ox; may involve complimentary words and affectionate physical touch). *2 v.* to give an admiring nickname to.

tamɛɛsɨêd[a] (tamɛɛsɨ́-édì-) *pl.* **tamɛɛsɨ́éditín**. *n.* affectionate nickname.

tamés (tamésí-) *v.* to think.

tamésɨ̀àm (tamésɨ́-àmà-) *pl.* **tamésɨ́ik**[a]. *n.* contemplative, thinker.

tamésúƙɔt[a] (tamésúƙɔtí-) *v.* to recall, recollect, remember, think back on.

tamɛtés (tamɛtésí-) *1 v.* to consider, imagine, ponder, think about. *2 v.* to recall, recollect, remember. See also *anɛtés*.

támɨ́nɔ́s (támɨ́nɔ́sɨ́-) *1 v.* to think about each other. *2 v.* to compare each other.

tamɨ́támiés (tamɨ́támiesí-) *v.* to consider, contemplate, mull over, ponder, think on. See also *tamátámatés*.

tamitɛtés (tamitɛtési-) *1 v.* to remind. *2 v.* to memorize. *3 v.* to record.

tàn (tànɨ-) *n.* a lot, plenty. Also used as the second word in a compound word, where the first word refers to that which is much or many.

taná (<tanɔ́ɔ́n) *v.*

tànàŋ (tànàŋà-) *n.* mud plaster.

tanaŋes (tanaŋesí-) *1 v.* to box, knock, punch, slug. *2 v.* to mud, plaster (with mud).

tanaŋínáŋesukot[a] (tanaŋínáŋesukotí-) *v.* to bang into repeatedly, knock around.

tanɔ́ɔ́n (tanɔ́ɔ́nɨ-/taná-) *v.* to be how many?

taɲálá (<taɲáléés) *v.*

taɲálá (<taɲálóòn) *v.*

taɲáléés (taɲáléésí-/taɲálá-) *v.* to divide, parcel, portion (e.g. food or tobacco).

taɲáléetés (taɲáléetésí-) *v.* to divide up, parcel out, portion out (e.g. food or tobacco).

taɲáléetésá asɨ *v.* to collapse, crumble, fall down (e.g. house, riverbank, wall).

taɲálóòn (taɲálóònì-/taɲálá-) *v.* to collapse, crumble, fall down (e.g. house, riverbank, wall). See also *ɲalámétòn*.

taɲɛɛs (taɲɛɛsí-) *1 v.* to enlarge, expand. *2 v.* to elaborate or expound on. See also *iɲɛɛs*.

taɲɛ́ɔ́n (taɲɛ́ɔ́nɨ-) *v.* to blow up, expand (e.g. balloon, cloud, fire). See also *xuanón*.

taŋáíkìn (taŋáíkìnì-) *pro.* co- (plural): cohorts, colleagues, comrades, etc.

tàŋàs (tàŋàsɨ-) *n.* marching orders (for hunting, patrolling, etc.).

taŋasɛs (taŋasɛsí-) *v.* to discharge, give marching orders to, order out (e.g. hunters or soldiers).

taŋates (taŋatesí-) *v.* to grab, snatch. See also *ŋusés* and *tokopes*.

taŋátésukot[a] (taŋátésukotí-) *v.* to grab or snatch away. See also *tokópésukot*[a].

taŋatsárón (taŋatsáróni-) *v.* to branch, fork, split. See also *tɛlɛ́tsɔ́n* and *toŋélón*.

taŋɛ́êd[a] (taŋɛ́ɛ́dè-) *pl.* **taŋáíkìn.** *pro.* co-: cohort, colleaque, comrade, etc.

táŋés (táŋɛ́sɨ-) *v.* to advise, counsel, dissuade (from wrongdoing).

taŋɛtés (taŋɛtésí-) *v.* to advise, counsel, dissuade (from wrongdoing).

táɲínɔ́s (táɲínɔ́sí-) *v.* to advise or counsel each other.

tapá (<tapɛɛs) *v.*

tapáínɔ́s (tapáínɔ́sɨ-) *v.* to accuse or blame each other falsely.

tapɛɛs (tapɛɛsí-/tapá-) *v.* to accuse or blame falsely.

tárábes (tárábesí-) *1 v.* to fondle or grope (as in a sexual encounter). *2 v.* to pat down, search (as in a security check). See also *idadamés*.

tárábiés (tárábiésí-) *1 v.* to fondle or grope all over (as in a sexual encounter). *2 v.* to pat down or search all over (as in a security check).

taráɗá (taráɗáà-) *1 n.* groundnut(s), peanut(s). See also *ɲépulé.* *2 n.* striped ground squirrel. *Xerus erythropus.*

taraŋés (taraŋésí-) *v.* to put or set nearby.

tarares (tararesí-) *v.* to gather, glean, harvest, reap (from the ground). See also *irárátés* and *irarɛs*.

tarates (taratesí-) *1 v.* to be naughty, behave badly. *2 v.* to abuse sexually, molest.

taratiés (taratiesí-) *v.* to be naughty, behave badly (as a habit).

taríɔ́n (taríɔ́nɨ-) *v.* to be pregnant.

tás (tásá-) *pl.* **tásítín**. *1 n.* grave, gravesite, tomb. *2 n.* ghost, ghoul, phantom, wraith. *3 n.* the deceased, departed, the late. *4 n.* mark, scar.

tasá (<tasɔ́ɔ́n) *v.*

tasá (<tasɛɛs) *v.*

tasaɓes (tasaɓesí-) *v.* to add on, increase, pile on.

tasaɓesa mɛnáᵋ *v.* to exaggerate, hyperbolize. *Lit.* 'to add on words'.

tasálétòn (tasálétònì-) *v.* to call off, cancel, forego (e.g. a meal or a journey).

tasáletona kíjáᵉ *1 n.* failure of a season (e.g. the harvest). *2 n.* apocalypse, end of the world.

tasálón (tasálónì-) *v.* to call off, cancel, forego (e.g. a meal or a journey).

tasápánitetés (tasápánitetésí-) *v.* to induct or initiate into a higher age-group.

tasapánón (tasapánónì-) *v.* to be inducted or initiated into the next age-group.

Tasapetíáwᵃ (Tasapetí-áwà-) *n.* name of a place. *Lit.* 'initiation-place'.

tasápétòn (tasápétònì-) *n.* to get inducted or initiated into the next age-group.

tasɛɛs (tasɛɛsɨ́-/tasá-) *v.* to bring up, raise, rear (children or animals).

tásêdᵃ (táséd ɛ-) *pl.* **tásɨn**. *1 n.* grave, gravesite, tomb . *2 n.* scar.

tasónón (tasónònì-) *v.* to be sad, sorrowful. See also *itásónòn*.

tasɔ́ɔ́n (tasɔ́ɔ́nɨ-/tasá-) *v.* to amble, promenade, stroll.

tatᵃ (tatí-) *n.* saliva, spit, spittle.

tátà (tátàà-) *pl.* **táta in**. *n.* my aunt (father's sister).

tátàèàkwᵃ (tátà-èàkwà-) *n.* my uncle (father's sister's husband).

tátàìm (tátà-ìmà-) *pl.* **tátawik**ᵃ. *n.* my cousin (father's sister's child).

tatanám (tatanámà-) *n.* so-and-so, whats-their-name.

tataɲes (tataɲesí-) *v.* to catch sight of suddenly.

tatatᵃ (tatatí-) *pl.* **tatatíkw**ᵃ. *1 n.* his/her aunt (father's sister). *2 n.* his/her cousin.

tatatíéákwᵃ (tatatí-éákwà-) *n.* his/her uncle (father's sister's husband).

tatatíím (tatatí-ímà-) *pl.* **tatatíwík**ᵃ. *n.* his/her cousin (father's sister's child).

tatés (tatésí-) *1 v.* to spit. *2 v.* to affront, disrespect, insult (e.g. by giving a small amount of food).

tatésúƙotᵃ (tatésúƙotí-) *v.* to spit out.

tatíájᵃ (tatí-ájɨ-) *n.* spit-pestle plant: species whose finger-sized roots are bitten and the juice is spat on the pestle used to pound termites.

tatiés (tatiesí-) *1 v.* to spit repeatedly. *2 v.* to bless. See also *imwaímwéés*.

tatiesíám (tatiesí-ámà-) *pl.* **tatiesíík**ᵃ. *1 n.* spitter (e.g. of morsels fed by a bereaved elder). *2 n.* blesser.

tatiésuƙotᵃ (tatiésuƙotí-) *v.* to spit out repeatedly (e.g. food as part of a funeral ceremony).

tatifíánón (tatifíánónì-) *v.* to be festering, suppurating (includes pus and dirtiness).

tatíón (tatíónì-) *v.* to drip (of rain).

tatiós (tatiosí-) *v.* to be blessed.

tatitésuƙotíám (tatitésuƙotí-ámà) *pl.* **tatitésuƙotíík**[a]. *n.* bereaved elder who feeds morsels to the family which they must then spit out on the ground.

tátó (tátóò-) *pl.* **tátóín.** *n.* your aunt (father's sister).

tátóéákw[a] (tátó-éákwá-) *n.* your uncle (father's sister's husband).

tátóím (tátó-ímá-) *pl.* **tátówík**[a]. *n.* your cousin (father's sister's child).

tàtòn (tàtònì-) *v.* to spit.

tatónón (tatónónì-) *v.* to sit dejectedly with one's chin in one's hand or on one's knees (due to coldness, depression, sadness, etc.).

tatsá (<tatsɔ́ɔ́n) *v.*

tatsáɗésuƙot[a] (tatsáɗésuƙotí-) *v.* to keep away/back, retain.

tatsáɗón (tatsáɗónì-) *v.* to break away, secede.

tatséétɔ̀n (tatséétɔ̀nɨ̀-) *n.* to clear off/up (e.g. weather).

tatsɔ́ɔ́n (tatsɔ́ɔ́nɨ̀-/tatsá-) *v.* to be bright, clear (e.g. of the sky or weather).

tatún (tatúná-) *pl.* **tatúník**[a]. *n.* chin, mentum.

táùn (táùnì-) *pl.* **táùnik**[a]. *n.* town, trading center. See also *ɲálaín.*

tawaɗes (tawaɗesí-) *v.* to dig (in search of water).

tawanes (tawanesí-) *v.* to afflict, harm, hurt.

tawanímétòn (tawanímétònì-) *v.* to be afflicted, badly off, suffering.

tawánìtetés (tawánítetésí-) *v.* to afflict, harm, hurt.

té (té) *interj.* oh! (an expression of surprise).

tɛ̀ (tɛ̀) *ideo.* snap! (sound of breaking firewood).

tebeleƙes (tebeleƙesí-) *pl.* **tebeléƙésìk**[a]. *n.* broken gourd ladle.

tébès (tébèsɨ̀-) *v.* to scoop, take up.

tébɛsiama jumwɨ *n.* digger, excavator.

tébɛsiama kíjá[e] *n.* curser of natural resources: sorcerer who takes soil or water from one place to make that area have a drought or a poor crop yield.

tébɛtaná bì *v.* welcome! (to one person).

tébɛtaná bìt[a] *v.* welcome! (to more than one person).

tébɛtés (tébɛtésɨ́-) *1 v.* to scoop out/up. *2 v.* to fetch, get. *3 v.* to receive, welcome.

tébinés (tébinésí-) *v.* to lean on (e.g. a walking stick).

tébitebiés (tébitebiesí-) *v.* to respond repeatedly (as in bird or animal calls).

Teɓur (Teɓurí-) *n.* Abim, Labwor.

teɓúránétòn (teɓúránétònì-) *1 v.* to lose reddish-brown color (of newborn Africans). *2 v.* to enter puberty, mature sexually.

teɓúsúmòn (teɓúsúmònì-) *v.* to be bloated, distended, inflated (e.g. a child's belly).

tɛɛmémòn (tɛɛmémɔ̀nɨ̀-) *v.* to be breakable, fragile.

tɛɛté (tɛɛtéè-) *n.* tree species whose stems are used as house poles and whose wood is carved into spoons.

téétɔ̀n (téétɔ̀nɨ̀-) *v.* to drop, fall.

tegeles (tegelesí-) *v.* to bar, barricade, block. See also *tokólésuƙot*[a].

tegelesa ɲerukuɗeé v. to block the road, make a roadblock.

téíètòn (téíètònì-) v. to fall down repeatedly.

tɛikɔ́tòn (tɛikɔ́tònɨ-) v. to drop, fall. Also pronounced as *tɔɔnʉkɔt*ᵃ.

tɛitésʉkɔtᵃ (tɛitésʉkɔtɨ́-) v. to drop, make fall.

tɛitɛtés (tɛitɛtésɨ-) v. to drop, make fall.

tékènìkɔ̀l (tékènìkɔ̀lɔ̀-) n. technical school, vocational school.

tɛkɛɲɛs (tɛkɛɲɛsɨ́-) v. to peek or peer through (e.g. eyelids or maize husks).

tekeɲiés (tekeɲiesí-) v. to peek or peer through repeatedly (e.g. eyelids or maize husks).

Tekó (Tekóò-) n. a personal name.

tékédèmɔ̀n (tékédèmɔ̀nɨ-) v. to be shallow. See also *tɛkézèmɔ̀n*.

tɛkɛram (tɛkɛramá-) n. soldier ant or termite.

tékézèmɔ̀n (tékézèmɔ̀nɨ-) v. to be shallow. See also *tɛkédèmɔ̀n*.

tɛlɛɛs (tɛlɛɛsɨ́-) v. to open up, spread apart (e.g. arms, legs, or wings).

Télékᵃ (Télékɨ-) n. Telek (I & II): two of the Ik's twelve clans.

Télékɨ̀àm (Télékɨ-àmà-) pl. **Télékiik**ᵃ. n. Telek clan member.

tɛlétsón (tɛlétsónɨ-) v. to branch, fork, split. See also *taŋatsárón* and *toŋélón*.

tèmùr (tèmùrà-) pl. **tɛmúrík**ᵃ. 1 n. beard, goatee. 2 n. pubic hair. See also *ɲépénɛk*ᵃ.

tenákᵃ (tenáa) adv. and yet, while (earlier today).

tènòkᵒ (tènòò) adv. and yet, while (a long time ago).

tènùs (tènùsè-) n. male Beisa oryx. *Oryx gazella beisa*.

tɛɲɛfɛs (tɛɲɛfɛsɨ́-) v. to harass, hassle.

tɛɲéfúnós (tɛɲéfúnósɨ́-) v. to harass or hassle each other.

tɛɲɛlɛs (tɛɲɛlɛsɨ́-) 1 v. to chip. 2 v. to excise (the two lower front teeth for culturally cosmetic purposes). See also *ŋɛlés*.

téŋér (téŋérɨ-) n. crime, lawbreaking, offense.

téŋérɨ̀àm (téŋérɨ-àmà-) pl. **téŋériik**ᵃ. n. criminal, lawbreaker, offender.

terêgᵃ (terégì-) pl. **terégiicík**ᵃ. 1 n. employment, job, task, work. 2 n. ministry, service.

teréga na kaúdzòᵉ n. work for pay.

tereganés (tereganésí-) v. to work. See also *ikásíés*.

teréganitetés (teréganitetésí-) v. to employ, hire, put to work, work. See also *ikásíitetés*.

terégìàm (terégì-àmà-) pl. **terégiik**ᵃ. n. employee, hired hand, worker.

terégiama awáᵉ n. domestic servant, house help.

Terégiicíká Dɛikaicé n. Acts of the Apostles: New Testament book.

terégikabáɗᵃ (terégi-kabáɗá-) pl. **terégikabáɗík**ᵃ. n. work contract.

térɛkékɛ (térɛkékɛé-) n. meningitis. See also *ɲétɛrɛkékɛ*.

tɛrɛkɛs (tɛrɛkɛsɛ) ideo. all night, the whole night, till morning.

terémétòn (terémétònì-) v. to part ways, separate, split up.

terémón (terémónì-) 1 v. to part ways, separate, split apart. 2 v. to divorce, separate, split up. 3 v. to rebel, rise up.

terémónuƙotᵃ (terémónuƙotí-) v. to divorce, separate, split up.

tɛrɛréɔ́n (tɛrɛréɔ́nɨ-) v. to be astringent. See also *ƙérikérɔ̀n*.

Terés (Terésí-) n. October. See also *Lɔlɔɓáy*ᵃ.

terés (terésí-) *1* v. to divide, separate, split. *2* v. to arbitrate, intercede, liaise, mediate.

térés (térésɨ-) v. to roam, rove, wander.

terésúƙota así v. to separate oneself, set oneself apart.

terétéránitésúƙotᵃ (terétéránitésúƙotí-) v. to divide up, separate out, split up (in groups or pieces).

terétéránón (terétéránónì-) v. to be divided up, separated out, split up (in groups or pieces).

tereties (teretiesí-) *1* v. to divide up, separate, split up (into groups). *2* v. to segregate, show favoritism, single out.

teretiesá ínóᵉ v. to divide up an animal into parts.

teretiinós (teretiinósí-) v. to be disunited with each other, divided amongst each other.

teretiós (teretiosí-) *1* v. to be divided up, separated, split up. *2* v. to be segregated, singled out.

térútsù (térútsù) adv. after, when already. See also *tórútsù*.

tès (tèsè) ideo. broken beyond repair.

tèsìn (tèsɨnà) adv. and yet, while (yesterday, recently).

tetíŋón (tetíŋónɨ-) v. to be thick (e.g. clothing or metal).

tɛtsés (tɛtsésí-) v. to kick.

tɛtsésá jéjèikàᵉ v. to kick hides or skins (in order to spread them out to dry).

tɛtsésá ɲéperétì v. to march in a parade, parade. *Lit.* 'to kick the parade'.

tetsítétsiés (tetsítétsiesí-) v. to kick repeatedly.

Tɛúsɔ̀ (Tɛúsɔ̀ɔ̀-) n. name given the Ik by the Ateker peoples.

tɛwɛɛs (tɛwɛɛsɨ́-) v. to broadcast, scatter (seeds), sow.

tèwèr (tèwèrà-) *pl.* **tɛwérík**ᵃ. n. bridge.

tɛwɛrɛs (tɛwɛrɛsɨ́-) v. to blacken, dye black (e.g. hair with ground ironstone or the seeds of *Pappea capensis*).

tézèɗɔ̀n (tézèɗɔ̀nɨ-) v. to be bent back (e.g. one's leg when sitting).

tézètɔ̀n (tézètɔ̀nɨ-) *1* v. to be all done, all gone, finished, out, used up. *2* v. to die, expire.

tíbɨɗésón (tíbɨɗésónɨ-) v. to be constipated.

tíbɨɗɨlɔ̀n (tíbɨɗɨlɔ̀nɨ-) v. to go head-over-heels, somersault.

tibɨ́étɔ̀n (tibɨ́étɔ̀nɨ-) *1* v. to bulge, protrude, stick out. *2* v. to be constipated.

tɨbɨ́ón (tɨbɨ́ónɨ-) v. to be bulging, protruding, sticking out.

tíbòlòkòɲ (tíbòlòkòɲɨ-) *pl.* **tíbòlòkòɲɨk**ᵃ. n. claw, nail (finger or toe), talon.

tɨɓᵃ (tɨɓɔ́-) n. tall grass species used for thatching and whose stalks are chewed for their sweet juice. *Gramineae sp.*

tɨɓⁱ (tɨɓɨ) ideo. tightly.

tígàkètòn (tígàkètònɨ-) v. to get down on all fours.

tígàkòn (tígàkònɨ-) v. to be on all fours.

tígàràmàtsᵃ (tígàràmàtsí-) *pl.* **tígàràmàtsɨk**ᵃ. n. eldest child, firstborn.

tɨ́ɨr (tɨ́ɨrɨ-) *pl.* **tɨ́ɨrɨk**ᵃ. n. tree species with long thorns and often used in fencing and whose wood is carved into stools and digging sticks. *Acacia sp.*

tíítiitíí (tíítiitíí) *ideo.* vreevreew! (sound of whistling).

tiits'ímɔ̀n (tiits'ímɔ̀nì-) *v.* to be narrow, small (of an opening, like an eye).

tikiɛtés (tikiɛtésí-) *v.* to hang up (e.g. seeds for next year's planting).

tikitetés (tikitetésí-) *v.* to scrape clean (e.g. bottom of a pan).

tikítíkona gúró[e] *v.* to feel faint or weak (from fear, high blood-sugar, etc.).

tíkòŋ (tíkòŋù-) *n.* shrub species whose berries are eaten and whose roots are chewed raw by one who swore not to go somewhere and then goes, the chewing protecting him/her from falling ill. *Lantana trifolia*.

tìkɔ̀r (tìkɔ̀rà-) *n.* hail, ice.

tikorotót[a] (tikorotótó-) *1 n.* aloe. *Aloe sp.* *2 n.* persistent beggar.

tìkɔ̀rɔ̀ts[a] (tìkɔ̀rɔ̀tsì-) *n.* scaly francolin. *Francolinus squamatus*.

tík[i] (tíkí) *ideo.* midnight black, pitch black.

tiƙódzòmòn (tiƙódzòmònì-) *v.* to be shallow. See also *tɛƙédèmɔ̀n* and *tɛƙézèmɔ̀n*.

tìl (tìlà-) *n.* vine species whose black seeds are worn as beads on girls' loincloths and whose parasitic plant (*tìlàlèz*) is used by boys as a charm to attract girls. *Cardiospermum corindum*.

tìlàlèt[a] (tìlà-lètà-) *pl.* tilaletitín. *n.* girls' small beaded loincloth made with the seeds of the *til* vine.

tìlàlèz (tìlà-lèzà-) *n.* plant that is parasitic to the *til* vine and which is used by boys as a charm to attract girls.

tílàŋ (tílàŋì-) *n.* buffalo thorn: tree species whose reddish-brown fruits are eaten raw and whose wood is used for building and fencing; a bark decoction is drunk to treat pain and snakebites. *Ziziphus mucronata*.

tiléŋ (tiléŋì-) *pl.* tiléŋik[a]. *n.* pupil of the eye.

tilímón (tilímónì-) *v.* to cease or stop (blowing or boiling).

tilíwɔ́n (tilíwɔ́nì-) *v.* to be pristine, pure, virginal.

tìlòkòts[a] (tìlòkòtsì-) *n.* African grey hornbill. *Tockus nasutus*.

tilóts'ómòn (tilóts'ómònì-) *v.* to be little in volume (a container, tree-hole, etc.).

Timatéw[a] (Timatéò-) *1 n.* Timothy. *2 n.* Timothy: New Testament book.

timél (timélí-) *pl.* timélík[a]. *1 n.* rafter stick (running vertically toward the center in the roof of a grass-thatched hut). *2 n.* small stick used in a bird snare to trigger the release of a large bent stick connected to a small string.

timiɗɛs (timiɗɛsí-) *v.* to lick clean, lick up (using one's fingers).

timóy[a] (timóí-) *pl.* timóík[a]. *n.* tail.

Tímumucé (Tímu-mucéè-) *n.* Timu Road.

tìmùɔz (tìmùɔzà-) *n.* alpha male baboon. See also *òliòt[a]*.

tìnòn (tìnònì-) *v.* to be opaquely thick.

tiɲíɲ (tiɲíɲí-) *n.* black flying ant species.

tiŋátiŋá (tiŋátiŋáà-) *n.* rat species.

tíɔ́ (tíɔ́) *interj.* now now! there there! (an expression of calming).

tíɔ jɔ́ɔ́ *interj.* now now! there there! (an expression of calming).

tìr (tìrì) *ideo.* very full.

tirés (tirésí-) *v.* to copulate, have sex, or mate with. Not to be confused with *tírés*!

tírés (tírésì-) *v.* to handle, have, hold. Not to be confused with *tirés*!

tírésa dzɔɗátɨ *v.* to be greedy. *Lit.* 'to hold the rectum'.

tirésíama ínó[e] *n.* bestialist.

tirésíama ts'óóniicé *n.* necrophilist.

tirésíàw[a] (tirésí-àwà-) *pl.* **tirésíawík**[a]. *n.* sexual rendezvous, tryst.

tírésìàw[a] (tírésì-àwà-) *pl.* **tírésiawík**[a]. *n.* grip, handgrip, handle, hold.

tirifɛs (tɨrifɛsɨ-) *v.* to check out, investigate, observe, peer at.

tirifɛtés (tɨrifɛtésɨ-) *v.* to check out, investigate, observe, peer at.

tirifɛtésɨàm (tɨrifɛtésɨ-àmà-) *pl.* **tirifɛtésíik**[a]. *n.* detective, investigator.

tirifiés (tirifiesí-) *v.* to check out thoroughly, investigate.

tirifiesíáma ɲápukánɨ *n.* government investigator or security officer.

tirifɨrífés (tirifɨrífésɨ-) *v.* to investigate, look around, snoop around.

Tɨríkɔl (Tɨríkɔlɨ-) *n.* name of a river near Lóɗwàr, Kenya.

tɨrɨkà (tɨrɨkàà-) *pl.* **tɨrɨkàìk**[a]. *n.* light striped blanket.

tirímós (tirímósí-) *v.* to copulate, have sex, mate with each other.

tírínós (tírínósí-) *v.* to hold each other (e.g. while holding hands or walking side-by-side).

tírínósá kwètɨkà[ᵓ] *v.* to hold hands.

tɨrirɨɲón (tɨrirɨɲónì-) *v.* to be fortunate, lucky.

tiritirikwáy[a] (tiritiri-kwáɨ-) *n.* vine species that is worn around the necks of age-group initiates' wives during the post-initiation ceremony of beer drinking and slaughtering a goat.

tiróŋ (tiróŋí-) *pl.* **tiróŋík**[a]. *n.* molar.

tisílón (tisílónì-) *1 v.* to be lonely, lonesome. *2 v.* to be calm, peaceful, placid, quiet.

titianón (titianónì-) *1 v.* to be piping hot, very hot. *2 v.* to be feverish. *3 v.* to be fashionable, smart, stylish.

titíj[a] (titíjɨ-) *pl.* **titíjɨk**[a]. *n.* heel.

titíjɨkòn (titíjɨ-kònì-) *n.* Achilles tendon.

titikes (titikesí-) *1 v.* to hold back, forestall, stall. *2 v.* to hold with teeth, sink teeth into (to prevent escape).

Titímá (Titímáà-) *n.* May: month of ripe grain. See also *Kɨnám*.

titímáiƙot[a] (<titímóonuƙot[a]) *v.*

titimɛs (titimɛsɨ-) *v.* to observe, study.

titímóonuƙot[a] (titímóonuƙotí-/titímáiƙot-) *v.* to near maturity (of grain) to the point where the seed-heads are about to open up.

titír (titírí-) *pl.* **titírík**[a]. *n.* forked pole.

titirés (titirésí-) *v.* to prop, support, undergird.

titirésígwàs (titirésí-gwàsà-) *pl.* **titirésígwasík**[a]. *n.* stone that supports grinding stones.

titiretés (titiretésí-) *1 v.* to hold up, prop up, support, undergird. *2 v.* to delay, hold up, prevent from doing.

titiritésíàw[a] (titiritésí-àwà-) *pl.* **titiritésíawík**[a]. *n.* brake pedal.

titisíánón (titisíánónì-) *v.* to ache (of lymph nodes in the groin).

Títò (Títòò-) *1 n.* Titus. *2 n.* Titus: book in the New Testament.

tits'ɛ́s (tits'ɛ́sɨ-) *1 v.* to block, dam, plug. *2 v.* to conceal, cover (a hole, the truth).

tits'ɛ́súƙot[a] (tits'ɛ́súƙotí-) *1 v.* to block, dam, or plug up. *2 v.* to conceal, cover up (a hole, the truth).

tits'ímétòn (tits'ímétònì-) *v.* to block, dam, or plug up.

tits'ɔ́sɨ́ (tits'ɔ́sɨ́-) *v.* to be blocked, dammed, plugged.

tɨw (tɨ̀wɨ̀) *ideo.* needle-thinly.

tiwídòn (tiwídònì-) *v.* to be needle-thin.

tóbìrìbìròn (tóbìrìbìrònì-) *v.* to ascend, climb, go up.

tɔbɔŋ (tɔbɔŋɔ́-) *pl.* **tɔ́bɔ̀ŋɨ̀k**ᵃ. *1 n.* mush (posho) made from boiling water and grain meal. *2 n.* bread.

tɔbɔŋɔ́ám (tɔbɔŋɔ́-ámà-) *pl.* **tɔbɔŋóík**ᵃ. *n.* Napore person. *Lit.* 'meal mush person'.

tɔbɔŋɔ́ɲɛ́ƙᵃ (tɔbɔŋɔ́-ɲɛ́kɛ̀-) *n.* hunger for meal mush (posho).

tɔɓéíón (tɔɓéíónì-) *v.* to be typically correct, right, or true.

tɔɓɛitɛtés (tɔɓɛitɛtésɨ́-) *1 v.* to aim, direct, guide, send straight to. *2 v.* to correct, make right, rectify. See also *tsírítɛtés*.

tɔɓɛlɛs (tɔɓɛlɛsɨ́-) *v.* to hunt, prey on.

tɔɓɛlɛs (tɔɓɛlɛsɨ́-) *v.* to split. See also *ɓɛlés*.

tɔɓélésuƙotaᵃ (tɔɓélésuƙotɨ́-) *v.* to split apart/up.

tɔɓéɲétòn (tɔɓéɲétònì-) *v.* to ask for, elicit, evoke, solicit.

tɔɓéɔ́n (tɔɓéɔ́nɨ̀-) *1 v.* to be direct, straight. *2 v.* to be correct, right, true. See also *tsírɔ́n*.

tɔɓés (tɔɓésɨ́-) *1 v.* to spear, strike. *2 v.* to attack, maraud, raid.

tɔɓésá asɨ́ *v.* to shoot or zip over (i.e. to move quickly).

tɔɓésá dakwí *v.* to spear a tree (as part of a marriage ceremony proving the ability of the groom to provide for his new family).

tɔɓésíàm (tɔɓésí-àmà-) *pl.* **tɔɓésíik**ᵃ. *n.* attacker, marauder, raider (esp. of livestock).

tɔɓésúƙotᵃ (tɔɓésúƙotɨ́-) *v.* to attack, pillage, plunder, raid.

tɔɓésúƙota ɓisáᵋ *v.* to throw a spear (to curse to death by violence).

tɔɓetés (tɔɓetésɨ́-) *v.* to pillage, plunder, raid (and bring back).

tɔɓilɛs (tɔɓilɛsɨ́-) *v.* to bend, fold.

tɔɓilɛsa asɨ́ *v.* to be bent or folded over.

tɔɓilɛtés (tɔɓilɛtésɨ́-) *v.* to fold up, roll up.

tɔɓítóɓiés (tɔɓítóɓiesɨ́-) *v.* to spear repeatedly.

tɔɓɔkᵃ (tɔɓɔkɔ́-) *pl.* **tɔ́ɓɔ́kɨ̀k**ᵃ. *n.* potsherd: piece of broken pottery.

tɔ́ɓɔ́kɨ̀kààm (tɔ́ɓɔ́kɨ̀kà-àmà-) *pl.* **tɔ́ɓɔ́kɨ̀kaik**ᵃ. *n.* Toposa person. *Lit.* 'potsherds-person'.

tɔɓɔ́rɔ́kánón (tɔɓɔ́rɔ́kánónì-) *v.* to sprout (of feathers, mushrooms, etc.).

tɔɓules (tɔɓulesɨ́-) *v.* to appall, horrify, shock.

tɔɓúlón (tɔɓúlónì-) *v.* to be appalling, astonishing, horrifying, shocking. See also *iɓálɔ́n*.

tɔɓwaɲes (tɔɓwaɲesɨ́-) *1 v.* to break up, disperse, scatter. *2 v.* to change, exchange (money). See also *iwéélés*.

tôdᵃ (tódà-) *pl.* **tódaicík**ᵃ. *n.* language, speech, talk, telling.

tóda ni buɗám *n.* muddled, obscure speech.

tódààm (tódà-àmà-) *pl.* **tódaik**ᵃ. *1 n.* speaker, talker, teller. *2 n.* representative, spokesperson.

tódèèkwᵃ (tódè-èkù-) *pl.* **tódeekwitín**. *n.* point, topic, word. *Lit.* 'speech-eye'. See also *mɛnéékw*ᵃ.

tódetés (tódetésí-) *1 v.* to speak or talk about. *2 v.* to state the verdict.

tódètòn (tódètònì-) *v.* to say, speak, tell.

tódinós (tódinósí-) *v.* to converse, speak or talk to each other, tell each other.

tódòn (tódònì-) *v.* to speak, talk, tell.

tódonuƙot[a] (tódonuƙotí-) *v.* to begin to speak.

tɔɗɛtɛs (tɔɗɛtɛsí-) *v.* to flick, flicker, flip, flitter.

tɔɗɛtɛsa asɨ́ *v.* to flicker, glint (of sunlight over the horizon).

tɔɗɛtɛsa ébà[ɛ] *v.* to fire a weapon (by pulling the trigger).

tɔɗétésuƙot[a] (tɔɗétésuƙotí-) *1 v.* to flick or flip away/off. *2 v.* to fire (a weapon by pulling the trigger). *3 v.* to exorcize (a sickness spirit).

toɗóánètòn (toɗóánètònì-) *v.* to be crescent-shaped (e.g. a horn or tooth).

tɔ́ɗɔ́n (tɔ́ɗɔ́nɨ-) *1 v.* to be contracted, deflated, shriveled, shrunk. *2 v.* to be miniature, miniscule, tiny.

tɔ́ɗɔ́nuƙot[a] (tɔ́ɗɔ́nuƙotí-) *v.* to contract, deflate, shrink, shrivel (e.g. a flat football).

toɗóón (toɗóónì-) *1 v.* to alight, land, touch down. *2 v.* to fall upon (in attack). *3 v.* to begin, start.

tɔɗɔ́pón (tɔɗɔ́pónɨ-) *v.* to butt, head-butt (esp. in dances that mimic bulls).

toɗúón (toɗúónì-) *1 v.* to blow up, burst, erupt, explode. *2 v.* to stop beating (of the heart from fear).

tɔɗúpón (tɔɗúpónɨ-) *v.* to file, move in single file. See also *torópón*.

toɗyakos (toɗyakosí-) *v.* illegal, unlawful.

tɔfɔ́ɗɔn (tɔfɔ́ɗɔ́nɨ-) *1 v.* to exude, ooze, seep (foul fluids). *2 v.* to spatter, splatter (thick liquids).

tɔfɔ́l (tɔfɔ́là-) *pl.* **tɔfɔ́lɨ́k**[a]. *n.* tree bark rope.

tofóróƙánón (tofóróƙánónì-) *v.* to compose and sing a song loudly while walking (a song often about the virtues of one's favorite ox).

tofóróƙétòn (tofóróƙétònì-) *v.* to break into a song one composes while walking (often a song about the virtues of one's favorite ox).

toíɗón (toíɗónì-) *v.* to have an S-shaped or scoliotic spine.

toíésuƙot[a] (toíésuƙotí-) *v.* to calm or settle down.

toikíkón (toikíkónì-) *1 v.* to be safe: calm, reserved, self-controlled. *2 v.* to be secure: cautious, thrifty, well-prepared.

tòìmèn (tòìmènà-) *n.* that, that is (to say).

toíónuƙot[a] (toíónuƙotí-) *v.* to get better, heal up, stop hurting. See also *iŋáléétòn* and *maráŋónuƙot*[a].

toipánón (toipánónì-) *v.* to be able-bodied, youthful (in middle-age).

toipánónìàm (toipánónì-àmà-) *pl.* **toipánóniik**[a]. *n.* able-bodied, youthful adult (age 40-50).

tóítetés (tóítetésí-) *v.* to draw out, elicit speech, get to talk. See also *iénítetés*.

tɔjɛmɛs (tɔjɛmɛsí-) *v.* to jeer, make fun of, mock, ridicule.

tɔjipɛs (tɔjipɛsí-) *v.* to nibble off one by one (e.g. kernels of sorghum). See also *iɲibɛs*.

tɔ̀k[a] (tɔ̀kà-) *pl.* **tókɨ́tín**. *n.* jugular or supersternal notch: soft indentation between collarbones.

tɔkééŕɛ́s (tɔkééŕɛ́sɨ́-) *v.* to cross, traverse.

tɔkɛtɛs (tɔkɛtɛsɨ́-) *v.* to extract, pull off/out. See also *tolés*.

tɔkétésʉkɔtᵃ (tɔkétésʉkɔtɨ́-) *v.* to extract, pull off/out, remove.

tɔkɛtɛtés (tɔkɛtɛtésɨ́-) *v.* to extract, pull out, remove. See also *toletés*.

tɔkɨ́ɔ́n (tɔkɨ́ɔ́nɨ̀-) *v.* to confess.

Tɔ̀kɔ̀bᵃ (Tɔ̀kɔ̀bà-) *n.* a personal name.

tɔ̀kɔ̀bᵃ (tɔ̀kɔ̀bà-) *v.* agriculture, cultivation, farming, plowing.

tɔ̀kɔ̀bààm (tɔ̀kɔ̀bà-àmà-) *pl.* tɔkɔbaikᵃ. *n.* agriculturalist, cultivator, farmer, plower.

tɔkɔbam (tɔkɔbamá-) *n.* arable, cultivatable, farmable, tillable.

tɔkɔbatsóyᵃ (tɔkɔba-tsóí-) *n.* farming season, plowing season.

tɔkɔ́bɛs (tɔkɔ́bɛsɨ́-) *v.* to cultivate, farm, plow, till, work.

tɔkɔ́bitɛtés (tɔkɔ́bitɛtésɨ́-) *v.* to make cultivate or plow (e.g. oxen).

tɔkɔ́bitɔtɔ́s (tɔkɔ́bitɔtɔ́sɨ́-) *v.* to be cultivated, plowed, tilled (usually by oxen).

tokódòn (tokódònì-) *v.* to be tightly tied down so as to be immovable.

tɔkɔɗɛs (tɔkɔɗɛsɨ́-) *v.* to grasp, hold by a handle.

tɔkɔɗɨ́kɔ́ɗɔn (tɔkɔɗɨ́kɔ́ɗɔ̀nɨ̀-) *v.* to cramp (abdominally).

tɔ̀kɔ̀n (tɔ̀kɔ̀nɨ̀-) *v.* to be slender, slim. See also *kaɗótsómòn* and *sɨ́dɔ̀rɔ̀mɔ̀n*.

tokopes (tokopesɨ́-) *v.* to grab, seize, snatch. See also *ikamɛs*, *iredɛs*, and *ŋusés*.

tokópésʉkɔtᵃ (tokópésʉkɔtɨ́-) *v.* to grab, seize, or snatch away. See also *taŋátésukotᵃ*.

tɔkɔrɛs (tɔkɔrɛsɨ́-) *1 v.* to dispense, disperse, distribute, divide out/up. *2 v.* to divide mathematically. See also *kisanes* and *kɨ́sés*.

tɔkɔ́résʉkɔtᵃ (tɔkɔ́résʉkɔtɨ́-) *v.* to dispense, disperse, distribute, divide out/up. See also *kisanes* and *kɨ́sés*.

tɔkɔ́rúkɔ́résʉkɔtᵃ (tɔkɔ́rúkɔ́résʉkɔtɨ́-) *v.* to dispense, disperse, distribute, divide out/up. See also *kisanes* and *kɨ́sés*.

tokúétòn (tokúétònì-) *v.* to react suddenly: crack, jerk, snap. See also *tokúréètòn*.

tokúréètòn (tokúréètònì-) *v.* to react suddenly: crack, jerk, snap. See also *tokúétòn*.

tɔkam (tɔkamá-) *n.* edible termites that are dewinged and dried.

tɔkɛrɛtés (tɔkɛrɛtésɨ́-) *v.* to light (fire).

tɔ́ƙɛ́s (tɔ́ƙɛ́sɨ̀-) *v.* to chip in, contribute, pay (e.g. toward a brideprice or fine).

toƙírá (<toƙíróòn) *v.*

toƙíróòn (toƙíróònì-/toƙírá-) *v.* to bear down, charge, react against, turn on (as if to attack).

toƙízà (<toƙízòòn) *v.*

toƙizeesá asɨ́ *v.* to move in, settle in, stay for a while.

toƙízèètòn (toƙízèètònì-) *v.* to move in, settle in (e.g. bad weather).

toƙízòòn (toƙízòònì-/toƙíza-) *v.* to hang around, stay a while, stick around (e.g. bad weather).

toƙólésʉkɔtᵃ (toƙólésʉkɔtí-) *v.* to bar, barricade, block off. See also *tegeles*.

tɔƙɔtɔƙᵃ (tɔƙɔtɔƙɔ́-) *n.* slug, snail.

tɔƙɔtɔƙáhò (tɔƙɔtɔƙá-hòò-) *pl.* tɔƙɔtɔƙáhoíkᵃ. *n.* snail shell.

tɔkʉmʉ́ƙʉ́més (tɔkʉmʉ́ƙʉ́mésɨ́-) *v.* to fire on, open fire on.

tɔléléɛtés (tɔléléɛtésɨ́-) *v.* to creep or sneak up on.

tɔléléɔ̀n (tɔléléɔ̀nɨ̀-) *v.* to dribble, trickle. See also *ipinɨ́pínɔ̀n*.

tolepetés (tolepetésí-) *v.* to drink or eat a lot of.

tolés (tolésí-) *v.* to extract, pull off/out. See also *tɔkɛtɛs*.

tolésìam (tolésí-àmà-) *pl.* **tolésiik**[a]. *n.* dentist.

toletés (toletésí-) *1 v.* to extract, pull off/out. *2 v.* to dislocate, dislodge. See also *tɔkɛtɛtés*.

tolíón (tolíónì-) *v.* to crawl, move on all fours (like a baby or chameleon). See also *akúkúrɔ̀n*.

tɔlɔɛs (tɔlɔɛsɨ́-) *v.* to lay or spread out (e.g. clothing or meat to dry).

tɔlɔɛsa mɛná[ɛ] *v.* to lay it out (e.g. feelings or issues).

tɔ̀lɔ̀k[a] (tɔ̀lɔ̀kà-) *n.* trapping.

tɔlɔkés (tɔlɔkésɨ́-) *v.* to trap.

tolómétòn (tolómétònì-) *1 v.* to come off/out, fall off/out. *2 v.* to become dislocated, dislodged.

tolotiés (tolotiesí-) *v.* to extract or pull off/out repeatedly.

tolótólánón (tolótólánónì-) *v.* to be (at the age of) losing teeth.

Tòlòyà (Tòlòyàà-) *n.* name of a mountain slope where the road from Kamion descends into Kenya.

toluétòn (toluétònì-) *v.* to betray, change allegiances, double-cross, turn against/on.

tɔlʉkɛs (tɔlʉkɛsɨ́-) *v.* to circle.

tɔlúkɛsʉkɔt[a] (tɔlúkɛsʉkɔtɨ́-) *1 v.* to circle. *2 v.* to cut out, exclude, isolate.

tɔlʉkɛtés (tɔlʉkɛtésɨ́-) *1 v.* to circle. *2 v.* to cut out a circle.

tɔlʉkúlúkés (tɔlʉkúlúkésɨ́-) *v.* to make circles in/on.

tɔlʉkúlúkɔ̀n (tɔlʉkúlúkɔ̀nɨ̀-) *v.* to have circles.

tolúónìam (tolúónì-àmà-) *pl.* **tolúóniik**[a]. *n.* betrayer, double-crosser, traitor.

tolúónʉkot[a] (tolúónʉkotí-) *v.* to betray, change allegiances, double-cross, turn against/on.

tolúúnós (tolúúnósí-) *v.* to betray or turn against/on each other.

tolúútésʉkot[a] (tolúútésʉkotí-) *v.* to change allegiances, turn against.

tòmàlàɗò (tòmàlàɗòò-) *n.* throat infection (with swelling of glands).

tɔmɛɛs (tɔmɛɛsɨ́-) *1 v.* to come/go via, follow. *2 v.* to stick with, support.

tɔméésʉkɔt[a] (tɔméésʉkɔtɨ́-) *v.* to follow, go via/by way of.

tɔmɛɛtés (tɔmɛɛtésɨ́-) *v.* to come by way of, come via, follow here. See also *iébɛtés*.

tɔmɛɛtésá tódà[ɛ] *v.* to spell it out. *Lit.* 'come via the speech'.

tɔméínós (tɔméínósɨ́-) *v.* to stand by or support each other. *Lit.* 'follow each other'.

tɔmɛrímérɔ̀n (tɔmɛrímérɔ̀nɨ̀-) *v.* to be bewildered, dazed, stupefied.

tɔminɛs (tɔminɛsɨ́-) *v.* to appeal to, attract, draw.

tɔmɔkɔrɛs (tɔmɔkɔrɛsɨ́-) *pl.* **tɔmɔ́kɔ́rɛ̀sɨ̀k**[a]. *n.* stick bent in a u-shape and stuck in the ground as part of a bird snare; another larger stick is bent over and hooked on this one and triggered with other sticks.

tɔ̀mɔ̀ràam (tɔ̀mɔ̀rà-àmà-) *pl.* tɔmɔraikᵃ. *n.* friend or neighbor with whom one shares in common.

tɔmɔram (tɔmɔramá-) *n.* share, shareable.

tɔmɔrɛs (tɔmɔrɛsɨ́-) *v.* to share.

tɔmɔ́rɨ́nɔ́s (tɔmɔ́rɨ́nɔ́sɨ́-) *v.* to share with each other.

tɔmɔ́tɔ́mánɨ̀am (tɔmɔ́tɔ́mánɨ̀-àmà-) *pl.* tɔmɔ́tɔ́mániikᵃ. *n.* scabby person.

tɔmɔ́tɔ́mánón (tɔmɔ́tɔ́mánónì-) *v.* to be covered in sores, scabby.

tɔmɔtsɔkánón (tɔmɔtsɔkánónì-) *v.* to be verrucose, warty.

tomuɲes (tomuɲesɨ́-) *v.* to break off small pieces or chunks of.

tɔmʉɲɛs (tɔmʉɲɛsɨ́-) *v.* to notch (ears). See also *topones*.

tɔnɛɛtés (tɔnɛɛtésɨ́-) *v.* to foist, impose.

tɔnɛɛtésá asɨ́ *v.* to foist or impose oneself.

tònì (tònì) *1 prep.* even. *2 subordconn.* even if, still if. If acting as a preposition, this word is followed by a noun in the oblique case.

toni naɓó *n.* furthermore, moreover.

tonokes (tonokesɨ́-) *v.* to lean or rest against. See also *ikɔɲɛs*.

tɔnʉpam (tɔnʉpamá-) *n.* believable, credible, trustworthy.

tɔnʉpɛs (tɔnʉpɛsɨ́-) *v.* to believe, have faith in, trust.

tɔnʉpɛsɨ́ám (tɔnʉpɛsɨ́-ámà-) *pl.* tɔnʉpɛsíikᵃ. *n.* believer, truster.

tonyámón (tonyámónì-) *v.* to prowl, stalk.

tonyámónukotᵃ (tonyámónukotɨ́-) *v.* to jump, pounce.

tɔɲɨ́lɨ́ɲɨ́lɛ́s (tɔɲɨ́lɨ́ɲɨ́lɛ́sɨ́-) *v.* to strip off or tear off in thin strips.

tɔɲimɛtés (tɔɲimɛtésɨ́-) *v.* to pinch or tweak off.

tɔŋɛɗɛs (tɔŋɛɗɛsɨ́-) *v.* to break, pull apart, cut, sever, tear (rope-like objects). See also *ikéŋéɗɛ́s*.

tɔŋɛ́ɛ́rɛ́s (tɔŋɛ́ɛ́rɛ́sɨ́-) *v.* to divide equally in two.

toŋélón (toŋélónì-) *v.* to branch, fork, split. See also *taŋatsárón* and *tɛlétsón*.

tɔŋɛtɛs (tɔŋɛtɛsɨ́-) *v.* to connect, join, link. See also *toropes* and *tɔrʉtsɛs*.

tɔŋétónʉkotᵃ (tɔŋétónʉkotɨ́-) *v.* to connect, join up, link up, rejoin.

tɔ̀ŋɔ̀làam (tɔ̀ŋɔ̀là-àmà-) *pl.* tɔŋɔlaikᵃ. *n.* butcher, slaughterer.

tɔŋɔlɛs (tɔŋɔlɛsɨ́-) *v.* to butcher, slaughter, slay. See also *hoés*.

toŋórómòn (toŋórómònì-) *v.* to be carinated, keeled, ridged (steep on both sides). See also *toróŋómòn*.

toomín (toomíní-) *n.* ten.

toomínékwà àɗᵉ *n.* thirty. Lit. 'ten-eye three'.

toomínékwa léɓètsᵉ *n.* twenty. Lit. 'ten-eye two'.

toomínékwa ts'agús *n.* forty. Lit. 'ten-eye four'.

toomínékwa tûdᵉ *n.* fifty. Lit. 'ten-eye five'.

toomínékwa túde ńdà kèɗɨ kɔ̀n *n.* sixty. Lit. 'ten-eye five and that one'.

toomínékwa túde ńdà kìɗɨ àɗᵉ *n.* eighty. Lit. 'ten-eye five and those three'.

toomínékwa túde ńda kiɗɨ léɓètsᵉ *n.* seventy. Lit. 'ten-eye five and those two'.

toomínékwa túde ńda kiɗi ts'agús *n.* ninety. *Lit.* 'ten-eye five and those four'.

toomíní ńdà kèɗɨ kɔ̀n *n.* eleven. *Lit.* 'ten and that one'.

toomíní ńdà kìɗi àɗᵉ *n.* thirteen. *Lit.* 'ten and those three'.

toomíní ńda kiɗi léɓètsᵉ *n.* twelve. *Lit.* 'ten and those two'.

toomíní ńda kiɗi ts'agús *n.* fourteen.

toomíní ńda kiɗi tûdᵉ *n.* fifteen.

toomíní ńda kiɗi túde ńdà kèɗɨ kɔ̀n *n.* sixteen. *Lit.* 'ten and those five and that one'.

toomíní ńda kiɗi túde ńdà kìɗi àɗᵉ *n.* eighteen. *Lit.* 'ten and those five and those three'.

toomíní ńda kiɗi túde ńda kiɗi léɓètsᵉ *n.* seventeen. *Lit.* 'ten and those five and those two'.

toomíní ńda kiɗi túde ńda kiɗi ts'agús *n.* nineteen. *Lit.* 'ten and those five and those four'.

tɔɔnᵾkɔtᵃ (tɔɔnᵾkɔtɨ́-) *v.* to go down or set (of the sun). See also *itsólóŋòn* and *tɔɔsɔ́ŋɔ́n*.

Tòòrwààkᵃ (Tòòrwà-àkà-) *n.* name of a hill or mountain and associated river.

tɔɔsétɔ̀n (tɔɔsétɔ̀nɨ̀-) *v.* to be available, common.

tɔɔsɔ́ŋɔ́n (tɔɔsɔ́ŋɔ́nɨ̀-) *v.* to go down in the afternoon (of the sun). See also *itsólóŋòn* and *tɔɔnᵾkɔt*ᵃ.

topéɗésuƙotᵃ (topéɗésuƙotí-) *1 v.* to be able to, can, capable of. *2 v.* to have authority.

topéɗésuƙotíám (topéɗésuƙotí-ámà-) *pl.* **topéɗésuƙotíík**ᵃ. *n.* person in authority.

tɔpéétɔ̀n (tɔpéétɔ̀nɨ̀-) *v.* to break away, escape, or skip out (and come).

tɔpéɔ́n (tɔpéɔ́nɨ̀-) *v.* to escape, get out of, skip out on.

tɔpéɔ́nᵾƙɔtᵃ (tɔpéɔ́nᵾƙɔtɨ́-) *v.* to break away, escape, or skip out (and go).

Topér (Topérí-) *n.* a personal name.

tɔpɛtɛs (tɔpɛtɛsí-) *v.* to spread out, unfurl, unroll (e.g. a mat).

topétésuƙotᵃ (topétésuƙotí-) *v.* to ablactate, wean.

tɔpétésᵾƙɔtᵃ (tɔpétésᵾƙɔtɨ́-) *v.* to spread out, unfurl, unroll.

tɔpétɔ́n (tɔpétɔ́nɨ̀-) *1 v.* to slant gradually outward (of animal horns). *2 v.* to be flat-topped.

topíánètòn (topíánètònì-) *v.* to endure, last, subsist, survive.

tɔpɨrɨ́pɨ́rɛ́s (tɔpɨrɨ́pɨ́rɛ́sɨ́-) *v.* to twirl, twist.

tɔpɨrɨ́pɨ́rɔ̀n (tɔpɨrɨ́pɨ́rɔ̀nɨ̀-) *v.* to swirl up, whirl around (e.g. smoke from a fire or a whirlwind).

topóɗón (topóɗónì-) *v.* to bemoan, bewail, deplore. See also *kɔ̀ɗɔ̀n*.

topones (toponesí-) *v.* to notch (animal ears). See also *tɔmᵾɲes*.

topues (topuesí-) *v.* to kill (an animal) to honor or please others. See also *ipéyéés*.

toputes (toputesí-) *v.* to copy, duplicate, replicate, reproduce.

toputetés (toputetésí-) *v.* to copy, duplicate, replicate, reproduce.

topútétòn (topútétònì-) *v.* to look like, match, resemble.

tɔpwaɲɨ́pwáɲés (tɔpwaɲɨ́pwáɲésɨ́-) *v.* to break up, crumble (e.g. soft rock).

topwatímétòn (topwatímétònì-) *1 v.* to become sated, satiated. *2 v.* to be cleared off, cleared out (like a path or riverbed).

topwátón (topwátónì-) *v.* to satisfy hunger (and thereby survive).

tɔ̀r (tɔ̀rɔ̀) *ideo.* compactedly.

toráƙádòs (toráƙádòsì-) *n.* non-governmental organization (NGO).

toreɓes (toreɓesí-) *1 v.* to spy on, surveil, watch. *2 v.* to abduct, snatch, take by force. See also *rótés*.

tɔrɛɛs (tɔrɛɛsí-) *v.* to coerce, extort, force, pressure. See also *réés*.

toreimétòn (toreimétònì-) *v.* to be coerced, extorted, pressured.

toremes (toremesí-) *1 v.* to heave, heft, shove. *2 v.* to mix (porridge with soaked beer mash). See also *pepɛrɛs*.

tɔrémúnɔs (tɔrémúnɔ́sí-) *v.* to falsely accuse each other.

tɔrés (tɔrésí-) *v.* to pitch, toss.

tɔrésúƙot[a] (tɔrésúƙotí-) *v.* to pitch or toss away.

tɔrɛtés (tɔrɛtésí-) *v.* to pitch or toss this way.

tòrìkààm (tòrìkà-àmà-) *pl.* **torikaik**[a]. *n.* guide, leader.

Torikaika Rié *n.* constellation of six stars. *Lit.* 'leaders of the goats'.

torikes (torikesí-) *v.* to guide, lead.

torikesíám (torikesí-ámà-) *pl.* **torikesíík**[a]. *n.* guide, leader.

toríkésuƙot[a] (toríkésuƙotí-) *v.* to guide away, lead away/off.

toriketés (toriketésí-) *v.* to guide or lead this way.

toríkínós (toríkínósí-) *v.* to move together.

torítéetés (torítéetésí-) *v.* to accumulate, amass. See also *idapɛtés*.

tɔ́rɔ́bɛs (tɔ́rɔ́bɛsí-) *1 v.* to gift, give gifts to, present (e.g. the family of newborn twins). *2 v.* to award, honor, reward.

tɔ́rɔ́bɛsa na íloɛsí *n.* award, reward, trophy. *Lit.* 'gifting of victory'.

toroɓ[a] (toroɓó-) *pl.* **tóróɓìk**[a]. *n.* breastbone, sternum. See also *gɔgɔm*.

toroɓóɔ́k[a] (toroɓó-ɔ́kà-) *n.* xiphoid process: bone below the sternum.

tɔrɔ́dɔ̀n (tɔrɔ́dɔ̀nì-) *v.* to be compacted, compressed, hard, packed down.

tɔ̀rɔ̀mɨ̀ɲ (tɔ̀rɔ̀mɨ̀ɲà-) *n.* North African crested porcupine. *Hystrix cristata*.

torónón (torónónì-) *v.* to fast, go hungry.

Tɔrɔŋɔ́ (Tɔrɔŋɔ́ɔ̀-) *n.* name of a steep ridge and deserted village near *Óríɓo*.

toróŋómòn (toróŋómònì-) *v.* to be carinated, keeled, ridged (steep on both sides). See also *toɲórómòn*.

toropes (toropesí-) *v.* to connect, join, link. See also *tɔɲɛtɛs* and *tɔrʉtsɛs*.

torópétòn (torópétònì-) *v.* to come successively, file in.

torópón (torópónì-) *v.* to file, move in single file. See also *tɔdʉ́pón*.

tɔrúɓón (tɔrúɓónì-) *1 v.* to grow back, regrow (of trees). *2 v.* to come back, happen again, recur, return.

tɔrʉtsɛs (tɔrʉtsɛsí-) *v.* to connect, join, link. See also *tɔɲɛtɛs* and *toropes*.

tórútsù (tórútsù) *adv.* after, when already. See also *térútsù*.

torwá (<torwóón) *v.*

torwáíƙot[a] (<torwóónuƙot[a]) *v.*

torwóón (torwóónì-/torwá-) *v.* to be relaxed, stretched out resting.

torwóónuƙotᵃ (torwóónuƙotí-/torwá-íƙot-) *v.* to relax, stretch out to rest.

toryáɓón (toryáɓónì-) *v.* to be in pain, have pain (e.g. during labor).

toryoŋes (toryoŋesí-) *v.* to sling over (e.g. a hoe on one's shoulder).

toryóŋón (toryóŋónì-) *v.* to curve backward (of horns).

tɔsɛɛtés (tɔsɛɛtésí-) *v.* to choose, elect, pick out, select. See also *ɲumɛtés* and *xóbɛtés*.

tɔsésón (tɔsésónɨ-) *v.* to err, make a mistake, sin.

tosipetés (tosipetésí-) *v.* to decelerate, slow down (e.g. from a run to a walk).

tosípón (tosípónì-) *v.* to start raining gently.

tɔsódókɔn (tɔsódókɔnɨ-) *v.* to congeal, gel, set up (e.g. cold posho or peanut paste). See also *ipúkákòn*.

tɔsuɓɛs (tɔsuɓɛsí-) *v.* to create, make. See also *idimɛtés* and *iroketes*.

tɔsuɓɛtésìam (tɔsuɓɛtésí-àmà-) *pl.* **tɔsuɓɛtésiik**ᵃ. *n.* creator, maker.

tɔtᵃ (tɔtó-) *n.* vine species whose bark is used for tying granaries, whose leaves are cooked as a vegetable, and which is dipped in water and sprinkled by elders to attract rain.

totírón (totíróni-) *v.* to ascend, climb, go up (a hill, slope).

totó (totóò-) *pl.* **totóin**. *n.* aunt (mother's sister).

tɔtɔanón (tɔtɔanónì-) *v.* to crash, rumble, thunder (while moving).

totóánonuƙotᵃ (totóánonuƙotí-) *1 v.* to get lost, go into exile. *2 v.* to fail, take a loss (e.g. in one's garden).

totóèàkwᵃ (totó-èàkwà-) *n.* uncle (mother's sister's husband).

totóìm (totó-ìmà-) *pl.* **totówik**ᵃ. *1 n.* cousin (mother's sister's child). *2 n.* my cousin child.

totores (totoresí-) *v.* to adopt (an animal as one's personal mascot, of which one can mimic and praise its attributes); have as a pet.

tototᵃ (tototí-) *pl.* **tototíkw**ᵃ. *n.* his/her aunt (mother's sister).

tototíéákwᵃ (tototí-éákwà-) *n.* his/her uncle (mother's sister's husband).

tototíím (tototí-ímà-) *pl.* **tototíwík**ᵃ. *n.* his/her cousin (mother's sister's child).

totsédón (totsédónì-) *v.* to creep, prowl, sneak.

totseres (totseresí-) *v.* to cope with, deal with, handle, manage.

totsérímós (totsérímósí-) *v.* to deal with or manage each other.

totsetes (totsetesí-) *v.* to check, mark, tick.

tɔtsóón (tɔtsóónɨ-) *1 v.* to be careful, beware, look out (beware). *2 v.* to be sensitive (e.g. to light).

tɔtsudɛs (tɔtsudɛsí-) *v.* to pluck, pull out (esp. feathers and fur). Also pronounced as *tutsudɛs*.

tóts'és (tóts'ésɨ-) *v.* to hammer, pound (esp. with a stone).

totues (totuesí-) *v.* to extract (evil charms from the body).

tɔtunɛs (tɔtunɛsí-) *v.* to embrace, hug.

tɔtúnúmós (tɔtúnúmósɨ-) *v.* to embrace or hug each other.

tɔtúpón (tɔtúpónɨ-) *v.* to be next, follow in line.

tòtwàrààm (tòtwàrà-àmà-) *pl.* **totwaraik**ᵃ. *n.* governor, ruler, sovereign. See also *ipúkéésìam*.

toukes (toukesí-) *1 v.* to fell (trees). *2 v.* to gag, retch.

touketés (touketésí-) *1 v.* to fell (trees). *2 v.* to gag, retch.

toúmón (toúmónì-) *v.* to be startled, taken off guard. The experiencer of this is marked with the dative case.

touríánòn (touríánònì-) *v.* to curl up to rest or sleep.

tɔúrúmɔ̀n (tɔúrúmɔ̀nɨ-) *1 v.* to incubate. *2 v.* to nurture (of a woman with a newborn). *3 v.* to hang round, linger, stay a while, tarry.

towá (<towóón) *v.*

towáíƙot[a] (<towóónuƙot[a]) *v.*

towates (towatesí-) *1 v.* to flick, sprinkle. *2 v.* to fling, toss. *3 v.* to spy on from afar.

towátésúƙot[a] (towátésúƙotí-) *v.* to fling or toss away/off.

towatetés (towatetésí-) *v.* to flick, sprinkle.

towoɗetés (towoɗetésí-) *v.* to scoop up (e.g. food in one's hand).

tɔ̀wɔ̀n (tɔ̀wɔ̀nɨ-) *v.* to leak.

towóón (towóónì-/towá-) *v.* to stand around (e.g. a fire).

towóónuƙot[a] (towóónuƙotí-/towáíƙot-) *v.* to stand around (e.g. a fire).

Tówotó (Tówotóò-) *n.* nickname of an old woman named *Matsú*.

towúryánòn (towúryánònì-) *v.* to oversleep, stay lying down.

tɔwútɔn (tɔwútɔnɨ-) *v.* to grow tall. See also *zikíbètòn*.

towutses (towutsesí-) *v.* to bulldoze, level, raze.

towútsóniàm (towútsónì-àmà-) *pl.* **towútsóniik**[a]. *n.* bulldozer.

toyeetés (toyeetésí-) *v.* to build, construct. See also *berés*.

toyeres (toyeresí-) *v.* to bump, glance, swipe. See also *iébès*.

tɔyɔ́ɔ́n (tɔyɔ́ɔ́nɨ-) *v.* to bleed, shed blood.

tù (tù) *ideo.* ptooey! (the sound of spitting).

túbès (túbèsì-) *v.* to follow.

túbèsìàm (túbèsì-àmà-) *pl.* **túbesiik**[a]. *n.* acolyte, devotee, follower.

túbesiama ámázeámà[e] *n.* government escort, member of an entourage.

túbesiama ɲápukánɨ *n.* government official (e.g. councillor or member of parliament).

túbesuƙot[a] (túbesuƙotí-) *v.* to follow away/off, go after.

túbunós (túbunósí-) *v.* to follow each other (e.g. sheep in a flock).

túbùr (túbùrà-) *pl.* **túbùrìk**[a]. *n.* newly broken ground, newly plowed garden.

túburés (túburesí-) *v.* to break new ground by plowing. See also *taɗates*.

tuɓunés (tuɓunésɨ-) *1 v.* to cover (an opening). *2 v.* to asphyxiate, smother, suffocate.

tuɓunímétòn (tuɓunímétònì-) *1 v.* to get covered (e.g. the opening of a container). *2 v.* to asphyxiate, suffocate.

tuɓutes (tuɓutesí-) *v.* to drop, lose, remove, shed, take off.

tuɓútésuƙot[a] (tuɓútésuƙotí-) *v.* to drop, lose, remove, shed, take off.

tuɓutetés (tuɓutetésí-) *v.* to extract, remove, take out.

tuɓútitésúƙot[a] (tuɓútitésúƙotí-) *v.* to fatten up, put weight on.

tuɓútónuƙot[a] (tuɓútónuƙotí-) *v.* to fatten up, gain weight. See also *zízonuƙot*[a].

tùdᵉ (tùdè) *num.* five.

tude ńdà kɛ̀ɗɨ kɔ̀n *num.* six. *Lit.* 'five and that one'.

tude ńdà kìɗɨ àɗᵉ *num.* eight. *Lit.* 'five and those three'.

tude ńda kiɗi lɛ́ɓɛ̀tsᵉ *num.* seven. *Lit.* 'five and those two'.

tude ńda kiɗi ts'agús *num.* nine. *Lit.* 'five and those four'.

tùdᵒ *num.* five times.

tùdòn (tùdònì-) *v.* to be five.

tùdᵘ (tùdù) *ideo.* boing! (sound made when a spear fails to penetrate an animal and bounces off).

tùɗᵃ (tùɗà) *ideo.* leatherily, toughly.

tuɗádòn (tuɗádònì-) *v.* to be leathery, tough (like a ratel's hide).

tuɗúlón (tuɗúlónì-) *v.* to be inverted, upside-down.

tuɗúlónìàm (tuɗúlónì-àmà-) *pl.* tuɗúlóniikᵃ. *1 n.* sorcerer who stops rain. *2 n.* Muslim.

tuɗúlútés (tuɗúlútésí-) *v.* to invert, turn upside-down.

tuɗúsúmòn (tuɗúsúmònì-) *v.* to be bare, exposed, naked, nude. See also *sɨlɔ́jɔ́mɔ̀n*.

tuɗɨtam (tuɗɨtamá-) *n.* meal mush stirred stiff. See also *ilɨram* and *tɔbɔŋ*.

tuɗɨtɛsɨ́dàkwᵃ (tuɗɨtɛsɨ́-dàkù-) *pl.* tuɗɨtɛsɨ́dakwitín. *n.* stick used to stir meal mush until it stiffens.

tuɗɨtɛtés (tuɗɨtɛtésí-) *v.* to stiffen by stirring (e.g. meal mush).

tuɗɨtɔs (tuɗɨtɔsɨ́-) *v.* to be stiff from being stirred (e.g. meal mush).

tùf (tùfà) *1 ideo.* bouncily, springily. *2 ideo.* bluntly, dully.

tufádòn (tufádònì-) *1 v.* to be bouncy, springy (like soil that a hoe cannot penetrate). *2 v.* to be blunt, dull. See also *tusúdòn*.

tùfɛ̀rɛ̀kᵃ (tùfɛ̀rɛ̀kɛ̀-) *n.* Black Jack: prolific weed species with yellow flowers and long, thin seeds that stick to clothing and fur, and whose pollen bees use to make honey. *Bidens pilosa*.

tɨfɛ́s (tɨfɛ́sɨ́-) *v.* to sew, stitch, tailor.

tɨfɛ́sɨ̀àm (tɨfɛ́sɨ́-àmà-) *pl.* tɨfɛ́siikᵃ. *n.* seamster, seamstress, tailor.

tufúl (tufúlá-) *n.* field rat species.

tùkᵃ (tùkà-) *pl.* túkítín. *n.* feather, plume.

tɨkán (tɨkánɨ́-) *n.* large lump of fat in an eland's abdomen, traditionally the delicacy of elders only.

tukéyᵃ (tukéí-) *n.* long-legged green fly species. *Dolichopodidae*.

tukuɗes (tukuɗesí-) *v.* to bend, crook.

tukúɗón (tukúɗònì-) *v.* to be bent, crooked.

tukúɗúkuɗánón (tukúɗúkuɗánónì-) *v.* to be curvy, winding, zigzagging.

tukukúɲón (tukukúɲònì-) *v.* to be aromatic, fragrant, sweet-smelling.

túkulétᵃ (túkulétí-) *pl.* túkulétíkᵃ. *1 n.* small round gourd used to hold beer, water, or grain. *2 n.* 1-liter jerrycan.

tukures (tukuresí-) *v.* to dig or scratch up. See also *tukutes*.

tɨkɨrɛs (tɨkɨrɛsɨ́-) *v.* to scrape off (e.g. sisal bark). See also *rékés*.

tukuretés (tukuretésí-) *v.* to dig or fish out, retrieve. See also *tukutetés*.

tukutes (tukutesí-) *v.* to claw, dig, or scratch up. See also *tukures*.

tukutesíáma ts'óóniicé *n.* body snatcher, graverobber.

tukutetés (tukutetésí-) *v.* to dig or fish out, retrieve. See also *tukuretés*.

túkútùk[a] (túkútùkù-) *n.* jigger, chigoe flea, sand flea. *Tunga sp.*.

tʉkʉtʉkán (tʉkʉtʉkánɨ-) *n.* vine species with round leaves and stems that are carved into tobacco pipes. *Ipomoea spathulata*.

tuƙúméton (tuƙúmétònì-) *v.* to erupt, flare up, ignite.

tʉlárɔ́y[a] (tʉlárɔ̀ɨ-) *n.* softwood tree species with inedible fruits and whose wood is used to make troughs; its roots may be pounded and scattered over fields as a pesticide. *Commiphora sp.*

tule (tuleé-) *n.* liquor, strong drink. See also *kombót*[a].

tùlèl (tùlèlì-) *pl.* **tulélík**[a]. *1 n.* Sodom apple: shrub with inedible yellow fruits whose juice is poured into infected ears, and whose roots may be chewed for stomach ailments. *Solanum incanum*. *2 n.* eggplant.

tulíánètòn (tulíánètònì-) *v.* to be white with black eye patches.

tulú (tulúù-) *n.* bunny, hare, rabbit.

tʉlʉŋes (tʉlʉŋɛsɨ-) *v.* to abhor, abominate, detest, loathe.

tʉlʉŋɛsa tɔsésónɨ *v.* to repent of sins.

tʉlúŋón (tʉlúŋónɨ-) *v.* to go in a rage, storm off.

tʉlúŋónʉkɔt[a] (tʉlúŋónʉkɔtɨ-) *v.* to go off in a rage, leave in disgust, storm off.

Tulútúl (Tulútúlù-) *n.* name of a place and associated human habitations on the edge of Timu Forest.

tʉmɛdɛ́ɛ́ *dem.* there: a place already known or mentioned.

tùmèè (tùmèè-) *n.* large number, many, multitude.

tʉmʉɗʉŋes (tʉmʉɗʉŋɛsɨ-) *v.* to crumple, enfold, enwrap.

tʉmʉɗʉŋetés (tʉmʉɗʉŋetésɨ-) *v.* to crumple up, enfold, enwrap.

tun (tuná-) *pl.* **tunitín**. *n.* huge leather sack made of calf or cow hide. Not to be confused with *tún*.

tún (túná-) *pl.* **túnítín**. *1 n.* flower bud. *2 n.* abscess, boil. Not to be confused with *tun*.

tʉnés (tʉnésɨ-) *v.* to pinch, tweak.

túnɨ́túnɨ́mɔ́s (túnɨ́túnɨ́mɔ́sɨ-) *v.* to pinch each other (as children do).

tʉnʉkɛs (tʉnʉkɛsɨ-) *v.* to bury, inhume, inter, lay to rest. See also *búdès* and *muɗés*.

tʉnʉkɛsíám (tʉnʉkɛsɨ́-ámà-) *pl.* **tʉnʉkɛsíík**[a]. *n.* gravedigger. See also *muɗésíàm*.

tʉnʉkitetés (tʉnʉkitetésɨ-) *v.* to make bury.

tʉnʉkɔs (tʉnʉkɔsɨ-) *v.* to be buried, interred, laid to rest.

tʉnʉ́tʉ́natés (tʉnʉ́tʉ́natésɨ-) *v.* to pinch all over.

tunútúniés (tunútúniesɨ-) *v.* to pinch flirtatiously.

tùr (tùrù-) *pl.* **túrítín**. *n.* huge tree species in whose shade tobacco is planted and in whose branches beehives are mounted.

Turakwareekw[a] (Tura-kware-ekú-) *n.* name of a river flowing from a mountain. *Lit.* 'tur mountain-eye'.

turues (turuesí-) *v.* to stone repeatedly, throw stones. Compare with *zébès*.

turuetés (turuetésí-) *v.* to stone repeatedly, throw stones.

turújón (turújónì-) *v.* to be creased, crinkled, wrinkled. See also *rʉjanón* and *zamʉjánón*.

turujúrújánón (turujúrújánónì-) *v.* to be creasy, crinkly, wrinkly.

túrúkukú (túrúkukúù-) *n.* red-eyed dove. *Streptopelia semitorquata*.

Tùrùmàràak[a] (Tùrùmàrà-àkà-) *n.* name of a river formed at the confluence of the *Nòf* and *Palú* rivers. *Lit.* 'Tùrùmàrà-mouth'.

turunet[a] (turunetí-) *pl.* **turúnétìk**[a]. *n.* carissa shrub: species whose red-to-black berries with milky sap are edible raw and can be used to make wine; the shafts of its stems are carved into tobacco pipes, an infusion of its leaves is medicinal, and its thorny branches are useful for fencing. *Calisa edulis*.

turúnétòn (turúnétònì-) *v.* to bow the head, look down.

turúnón (turúnónì-) *1 v.* to bow the head, look down. *2 v.* to grieve, mourn.

turúnóniàm (turúnónì-àmà-) *pl.* **turúnóniik**[a]. *n.* mourner, thinker (who bows the head).

tùs (tùsù) *ideo.* bouncily, springily.

tùs (tùsù) *ideo.* quish! (sound of flesh being punctured). See also *pìs*.

tús (túsí-) *n.* klipspringer. *Oreotragus oreotragus*.

tʉsés (tʉsésí-) *v.* to pinch up (granular substances like flour, soil, sugar).

túsídèr (túsí-dèrò-) *n.* klipspringer rat.

tusúdòn (tusúdònì-) *v.* to be bouncy, springy. See also *tufádòn*.

tusuketés (tusuketésí-) *v.* to curl, fold, or scrunch up.

tusúkón (tusúkónì-) *v.* to curl, fold, or scrunch up (e.g. in the fetal position).

Tutét[a] (Tutétí-) *n.* name of a hill or mountain.

tʉtsʉdɛs (tʉtsʉdɛsí-) *v.* to pluck, pull out (esp. feathers and fur). Also pronounced as *tɔtsʉdɛs*.

tʉtsʉɛs (tʉtsʉɛsí-) *v.* to squeeze, wring. See also *tʉtsʉɛs*.

tʉtsʉ́ɛsʉkɔt[a] (tʉtsʉ́ɛsʉkɔtí-) *v.* to squeeze or wring out.

tùtùf (tùtùfà-) *pl.* **tʉtúfík**[a]. *n.* tall tree species whose leaves are smoked over crops as a pesticide and whose branches are carved into pestles. *Combretium sp.*.

tutufánón (tutufánónì-) *v.* to go to seed (of millet or sorghum).

Tùtùk[a] (Tùtùkù-) *n.* five-star constellation in which the stars are crowded together.

tutukánón (tutukánónì-) *v.* to be crowded together; bunched, heaped or piled up.

tʉtukɛs (tʉtukɛsí-) *v.* to weave (e.g. the handle of a drinking gourd or the opening of a granary).

tutukesíáw[a] (tutukesí-áwà-) *pl.* **tutukesíáwík**[a]. *n.* bunch, heap, pile.

tutuketés (tutuketésí-) *v.* to bunch, heap, or pile up.

tùtùr (tùtùrù) *ideo.* to the end. See also *dùdùŋ*.

tuutes (tuutesí-) *v.* to extract, pull out, remove (e.g. the testicles).

tuutetés (tuutetésí-) *v.* to extract, pull out, remove (e.g. the testicles).

túw[a] (túwá-) *pl.* **túwítín**. *1 n.* praying mantis. *Mantis sp.*. *2 n.* stick insect, walking stick. *3 n.* food cooked first and given to elders.

tɨwétɔ́n (tɨwétɔ́nɨ-) *1 v.* to crop up, germinate, sprout. *2 v.* to expand, swell up (e.g. rice when cooked).

tùwɔ̀n (tùwɔ̀nɨ-) *1 v.* to crop up, germinate, sprout. *2 v.* to expand, swell (e.g. rice when cooked).

túzɨɗɛ́s (túzɨɗɛ́sɨ-) *v.* to plug, stop (e.g. exit holes of edible termites).

túzɨɗɛ́súƙɔt[a] (túzɨɗɛ́súƙɔtɨ́-) *v.* to plug or stop up (e.g. the exit holes of edible termites).

túzɨŋɛ́s (túzɨŋɛ́sɨ-) *v.* to carry on/over a shoulder.

túzùŋɔ̀n (túzùŋɔ̀nɨ-) *v.* to grow up and backwards (of horns).

túḿbàb[a] (túḿbàbà-) *n.* plant species whose inedible yam-like round tubers are cut and waved around to prevent rain from coming; tubers are also used as mock prey during spearing practice. *Dolichos kilimandscharicus*. Also pronounced as *túúbàb*[a].

ts

tsá (<tsóón) *v.*

tsábatsabánón (tsábatsabánónì-) *v.* to shudder, tremble (from fear or hunger).

tsábò (tsábò) *adv.* apparently, evidently, obviously.

tsáíkotᵃ (<tsóónukotᵃ) *v.*

tsaikótòn (tsaikótònì-) *v.* to dry up, evaporate. See also *tsóónukotᵃ*.

tsáítés (tsáítésí-) *v.* to dry.

tsáítésúkotᵃ (tsáítésúkotí-) *v.* to dry up/out.

tsàkᵃ (tsàkà) *ideo.* waterily.

tsakádòn (tsakádònì-) *v.* to be watery.

tsákàtsᵃ (tsákàtsɨ-) *n.* small plant species with white, inedible tubers.

tsakátsákánón (tsakátsákánónì-) *1 v.* to be pitted, pocked, pockmarked. *2 v.* to be insecure, unsafe (of an area).

tsakétón (tsakétónì-) *v.* to fall in numbers (like fruit from a tree).

tsákíètòn (tsákíètònì-) *v.* to fall continuously in numbers.

Tsakɨrɨkᵃ (Tsakɨrɨkɨ́-) *n.* name of a hill or mountain.

tsakitésúkotᵃ (tsakitésúkotí-) *v.* to drop in numbers (coins, seeds, etc.).

tsakûdᵃ (tsakúdè-) *pl.* **tsakúdìkᵃ**. *n.* firedrill: thin stick spun between both hands to create enough friction with a wooden board to start a fire. For the related verb, see *tsapés*.

Tsakúdèɓò (Tsakúdè-ɓòò-) *n.* name of a hill or mountain and associated river. *Lit.* 'firedrilll-escarpment'.

tsakúdècèkᵃ (tsakúdè-cèkì-) *n.* fireboard: soft wooden base in which a thin stick is drilled to create enough friction to light a fire. *Lit.* 'firedrill-woman'.

tsakúdèèàkwᵃ (tsakúdè-èàkwà-) *n.* firedrill: thin stick spun between both hands to create enough friction with a wooden board to start a fire. *Lit.* 'firedrill-man'.

tsákólómòn (tsákólómònì-) *v.* to be leggy, long-legged (like a gangly person, spider, or table, or when a porcupine raises up to avoid a snake). See also *tsɔ́gɔ̀rɔ̀mɔ̀n*.

tsàl (tsàlà-) *pl.* **tsálítín**. *n.* tree species whose seeds are roasted or boiled multiple times to remove toxins and provide food during a famine. *Capparaceae sp.*

tsalitsálɔ́n (tsalitsálɔ́nɨ-) *v.* to gleam or glimmer when wet (e.g. rocks or tarmac).

tsàm (tsamú-) *n.* costlessless, gratis, gratuitousness.

tsàm (tsàmù) *adv.* just, I guess, I suppose.

tsamɛ́s (tsamɛ́sɨ́-) *v.* to enjoy, like.

tsamɛtɛ́s (tsamɛtɛ́sɨ́-) *v.* to accept, acquiesce to, agree to.

tsamɛtɛsá ikóŋónì *v.* to swear or take an oath.

tsamɛ́tésa ɨ̀làmàᵋ *v.* to accept a curse (giving it power).

tsámúnɔ́s (tsámúnɔ́sɨ́-) *v.* to like each other.

tsámúnɔtɔ́s (tsámúnɔtɔ́sɨ́-) *v.* to agree with each other.

tsámúnɔtɔ́sɨ̀àm (tsámúnɔtɔ́sɨ́-àmà-) *pl.* **tsámúnɔtɔ́síik**[a]. *n.* friend or neighbor with whom you share understanding.

tsamʉya (tsamʉyaá-) *n.* small plant species with edible leaves and whose black, inedible berries can be fried, ground, and rubbed into cuts on the chest as a treatment for chest pain. *Chenopodium opulifolium.*

tsàŋ (tsàŋà-) *pl.* **tsáŋítín.** *n.* gap (in a mountain or in one's teeth).

tsáŋés (tsáŋésì-) *1 v.* to anoint, embrocate, inunct. *2 v.* to paint. *3 v.* to inaugurate. See also *kwɨ́rés.*

tsáŋésa mayaakóniicé *v.* to anoint the sick.

tsáŋós (tsáŋósì-) *1 v.* to be anointed. *2 v.* to be painted.

tsaórómòn (tsaórómònì-) *v.* to be see-through, transparent.

tsapés (tsapésí-) *1 v.* to twirl between both hands. *2 v.* to ignite or start (a fire by twirling a stick betweeen one's hands). *3 v.* to brew.

tsapésá mɛ̀sɛ̀ *v.* to brew beer. See also *waatésá mɛ̀sɛ̀.*

tsapetam (tsapetamá-) *n.* twirlable between one's hands.

tsàpòn (tsàpònì-) *v.* to be bored or drilled full of holes (e.g. wood bored by insects).

tsar (tsarɨ́-) *n.* useless or worthless thing. See also *pás.*

tsàr (tsàrà) *ideo.* carelessly, heedlessly.

tsarátán (tsarátánɨ̀-) *n.* cleft of a rock, rock crevice.

tsarɨ́nánès (tsarɨ́nánèsì-) *n.* uselessness, worthlessness. See also *pásìnànès.*

tsario (tsarió-) *n.* weaverbird. *Ploceus sp.*

tsarúk[a] (tsarúkú-) *n.* Beisa oryx. *Oryx gazella beisa.*

tsarúkúèb[a] (tsarúkú-ɛ̀bà-) *pl.* **tsarúkúɛbitín.** *n.* oryx horn.

tsaúdɔ̀n (tsaúdɔ̀nɨ̀-) *v.* to be dry and crumbly (like a dried out leaf).

tsaúɗɨmɔ̀n (tsaúɗɨmɔ̀nɨ̀-) *v.* to be petite, small-bodied, tiny.

tsàu (tsàù) *ideo.* crumbly-dryly.

tsè (<tsòòn) *v.*

tsɛɓɛ́kɛ́mɔ̀n (tsɛɓɛ́kɛ́mɔ̀nɨ̀-) *v.* to be cooked medium, half-cooked.

tsèf (tsèfà-) *pl.* **tséfítín.** *n.* patch of forest cleared for cultivation (cut branches are left to dry in the sun).

tsèfètsèf (tsèfètsèfè) *ideo.* gwuf gwuf (sound of an animal walking). The vowels of this word are pronounced silently.

tseiƙot[a] (<tsoonuƙot[a]) *v.*

tsèk[ɛ] (tsèkè) *ideo.* completely full.

tsekétón (tsekétónì-) *1 v.* to grow bushy, grow over. *2 v.* to grow furry or hairy.

tsekís (tsekísí-) *n.* brush, bush(es), thicket, thick vegetation.

tsekísíàƙw[a] (tsekísí-àƙɔ̀-) *n.* brush, bush(es), thicket, thick vegetation.

tsèkòn (tsèkònì-) *1 v.* to be bushy, overgrown, weedy. *2 v.* to be furry, hairy.

tsereɗeɗí (tsereɗeɗìi-) *n.* hardwood tree species used for building, fencing, and carving. *Osyris abyssinica.*

tsɛrék[a] (tsɛrékɨ́-) *pl.* **tsɛrékɨ́k**[a]. *n.* shinbone, tibia.

tsɛ́rɛkɛ́kɔ́n (tsɛ́rɛkɛ́kɔ́nɨ̀-) *1 v.* to be footsure, surefooted. *2 v.* to be rigid, stiff.

tsét[a] (tsétá-) *1 n.* serum, serous fluid (from wounds). *2 n.* cow urine.

tsètsèkwᵃ (tsètsèkù-) *1 n.* small tree species whose stems are used as house poles and whose bark is stripped into fiber used for making hunting nets. *Tarenna graveolens.* See also *tsɨkwᵃ*. *2 n.* either of the two upper ribs.

tsɨβil (tsɨβɨlà-) *n.* common bulbul. *Pycnonotus barbatus.* Also called *òtsɨβɨl*.

tsídzès (tsídzèsì-) *1 v.* to carry on the head. *2 v.* to ship, transport.

tsídzèsìàwᵃ (tsídzèsì-àwà-) *pl.* **tsídzesiawík**ᵃ. *n.* carrier, flatbed.

tsídzesuƙotᵃ (tsídzesuƙotí-) *1 v.* to carry away on the head. *2 v.* to ship or transport away/off.

tsídzètòn (tsídzètònì-) *1 v.* to flush or rush out (e.g. animals from thickets). *2 v.* to come to, startle awake, wake up suddenly.

tsídzitetés (tsídzitetésí-) *1 v.* to make carry on the head. *2 v.* to flush out, jump (e.g. animals from thickets).

tsídzonuƙotᵃ (tsídzonuƙotí-) *v.* to take or tear off (e.g. animals from thickets).

tsídⁱ (tsídɨ) *quant.* all, entire, whole.

tsídɨtsídⁱ (tsídɨtsídɨ) *quant.* all, entire, whole.

Tsígàkᵃ (Tsígàkà-) *n.* name of a mountain slope with a cattle trail.

tsígìmètòn (tsígìmètònì-) *v.* to climb down this way, come down, descend this way. Also pronounced as *kídzìmètòn*.

tsiir (tsɨɨrɨ́-) *pl.* **tsɨɨrík**ᵃ. *n.* broad base of a vertically oriented ridge.

tsíítés (tsíítésí-) *v.* to contemn, despise, disdain, scorn.

tsɨkòn (tsɨkònì-) *v.* to walk hesitantly (e.g. a criminal or a stranger).

tsɨkwᵃ (tsɨkɔ́-) *pl.* **tsɨkwɨtín**. *n.* small tree species whose stems are used as house poles and whose bark is stripped into fiber used for making hunting nets. *Tarenna graveolens.* See also *tsètsèkwᵃ*.

tsɨl (tsɨlɨ̀) *ideo.* all along the way.

Tsɨlá (Tsɨláà-) *n.* a personal name.

tsɨpɨtsɨpɔ́n (tsɨpɨtsɨpɔ́nɨ̀-) *1 v.* to condense, distill, form droplets (dew, sweat). *2 v.* to be spotted (like a leopard). See also *ikópíon*.

tsɨrim (tsɨrɨmú-) *pl.* **tsɨrɨmɨ́k**ᵃ. *n.* metal (of any kind or shape).

tsɨrɨmúdòm (tsɨrɨmú-dòmà-) *pl.* **tsɨrɨmúdomɨtín**. *n.* metal pot.

tsɨrɨtɛs (tsɨrɨtɛsɨ́-) *v.* to spit a long distance (esp. of those who dip tobacco and spit the juice, usually between the top front teeth).

tsɨ́rɨ́tɛtés (tsɨ́rɨ́tɛtésɨ́-) *1 v.* to erect, put or set upright. *2 v.* to aim, direct, guide. *3 v.* to correct, make right, rectify. See also *itsɨ́rɨ́tɛtés* and *tɔβɛitɛtés*.

tsɨ́rɔ́n (tsɨ́rɔ́nɨ̀-) *1 v.* to be erect, upright. *2 v.* to go directly, hit the target. *3 v.* to be correct, right, true. See also *itsɨ́rɔ́n*.

tsítsᵃ (tsítsɨ́-) *1 n.* honeyguide (lesser and possibly other species). *Indicator sp.* *2 n.* informant, intelligence officer. Not to be confused with *tsìtsᵃ*.

tsìtsᵃ (tsìtsà-) *n.* falcon, goshawk, hawk. Not to be confused with *tsítsᵃ*.

tsɨtsá na kwátsᵃ *n.* parish intelligence and security officer (PISO). *Lit.* 'lesser honeyguide'.

tsitsikes (tsitsikesí-) *v.* to roll.

tsitsikesa jɔté *v.* to roll the root of *jɔtᵃ* for spearing practice.

tsitsíkésuƙota asɨ *v.* to roll away.

tsitsiketésá asɨ *v.* to roll this way.

tsitsikiés (tsitsikiesí-) *v.* to roll repeatedly.

tsitsín (tsitsíná-) *pl.* **tsitsínik**[a]. *1 n.* stick for scraping honey from a container. *2 n.* toothbrush. *3 n.* paintbrush.

tsò (tsò) *1 adv.* in the distant future. *2 adv.* in the distant past.

tsóɗitsóno (tsóɗitsónoó-) *n.* bird species.

tsoe (tsoé-) *n.* wild hunting dog. *Lycaon pictus*.

tsóéàm (tsóé-àmà-) *n.* rain that comes to Ikland from the west.

tsɔ́gɔ̀rɔ̀mòn (tsɔ́gɔ̀rɔ̀mònɨ̀-) *v.* to be leggy, long-legged (like a gangly person, spider, or table, or when a porcupine raises up to avoid a snake). See also *tsákólómòn*.

tsoík[o] *n.* all night, the whole night, till morning.

tsokôb[a] (tsokóbè-) *n.* Abdim's stork. *Ciconia abdimii*.

tsòkòlòr (tsòkòlòrì-) *pl.* **tsokólórìk**[a]. *n.* oblong pumpkin.

tsokótsókánón (tsokótsókánóní-) *v.* to be a mixture of fat and meat.

tsól (tsólé-) *n.* black-winged red bishop. *Euplectes hordeaceus*.

tsɔlɨ́lɔ́n (tsɔlɨ́lɔ́nɨ̀-) *v.* to be liquid.

tsolólómòn (tsolólómònì-) *v.* to be amenable, compliant, willing.

tsòn (tsònì) *ideo.* blood red, crimson, ruby red, scarlet.

tsɔnitsɔnɔ́s (tsɔnitsɔnɔsɨ́-) *v.* to be restless or unsettled (shown by one's tendency to crouch instead of sit or move instead of settle).

tsɔnitsɔnɔsɨ́ám (tsɔnitsɔnɔsɨ́-ámà-) *pl.* **tsɔnitsɔnɔsíík**[a]. *n.* restless or unsettled person (who crouches instead of sits or moves around instead of settles).

tsɔ́nɔ́n (tsɔ́nɔ́nɨ̀-) *v.* to crouch, squat.

Tsɔŋɔ́rán (Tsɔŋɔ́ránɨ̀-) *n.* name of a hill or mountain.

tsòòn (tsòònì-/tse-) *v.* to dawn, rise (of the sun). See also *walámón*.

tsóón (tsóónì-/tsá-) *v.* to be dry.

tsóóna kíjá[e] *v.* drought.

tsoonuƙot[a] (tsoonuƙotí-/tseiƙot-) *v.* to dawn, rise (of sun).

tsóónuƙot[a] (tsóónuƙotí-/tsáíƙot-) *v.* to dry out/up, evaporate.

tsɔ́r (tsɔ́rá-) *n.* baboon. *Papio cynocephalus*.

Tsɔ́ráàw[a] (Tsɔ́rá-àwà-) *n.* name of a rocky outcropping in *Nòf*. Lit. 'baboon-place'.

tsɔ́ráɗoɗôb[a] (tsɔ́rá-ɗoɗóbà-) *n.* vine species used as a treatment for cracks in cows' skin on their legs and whose leaves are cooked and the decoction drunk for stomach ailments; baboons eat the whole plant. Lit. 'baboon baby-carrier'. *Cucumis dipsaceus*.

tsɔ́rákwèt[a] (tsɔ́rá-kwètà-) *n.* deformity of maize cobs in which the cob grows with several fingers resembling a baboon's hand. Lit. 'baboon-hand'.

tsɔ́ráŋwa (tsɔ́rá-ŋwaá-) *n.* female baboon.

tsɔrés (tsɔrésɨ́-) *v.* to bleed for drinking.

tsòrìàm (tsòrìàmà-) *n.* white-rumped swift. *Apus affinis/Apus caffer*.

tsòrìt[a] (tsòrìtì-) *pl.* **tsorítík**[a]. *n.* artery, blood vessel, capillary, vein.

tsorokoní (tsorokonîí-) *n.* small mosquito species.

tsɔ́tsɔ́n (tsɔ́tsɔ́nɨ̀-) *v.* to be keen, sharp (of eyesight).

tsówír (tsówírì-) *n.* speckled mousebird. *Colius striatus.*

tsowírímòn (tsowírímònì-) *v.* to be crested, plumed.

tsóyᵃ (tsóí-) *n.* season.

tsùbèɗᵋ (tsùbèɗɛ̀) *ideo.* crunch crunch (sound of walking).

tsúɓᵃ (tsúɓá-) *pl.* **tsúɓítín**. *n.* bird tail.

tsuɓáánètòn (tsuɓáánètònì-) *v.* to be pointy (like a girl's breasts or a pig's snout).

tsuɓɛ́s (tsuɓɛ́sɨ́-) *v.* to sip. See also *abutiés*.

tsuɓɛtɛ́s (tsuɓɛtɛ́sɨ́-) *v.* to sip, take a sip. See also *abutɛtɛ́s*.

tsúdòn (tsúdònì-) *v.* to raise one's buttocks (e.g. while lying face-down).

tsuɗutsuɗɔ́s (tsuɗutsuɗɔsɨ́-) *v.* to be jittery, jumpy (e.g. a mouse or a thief).

tsúkuɗúɗɔ́n (tsúkuɗúɗɔ́nì-) *1 v.* to be miserable, wretched (like animals in the cold or rain). *2 v.* to be concerned, worried (like when one moves through a dangerous area).

tsuƙúlúmòn (tsuƙúlúmònì-) *v.* to be bowl-shaped, concave. See also *sakánámòn*.

tsulátᵃ (tsulátɨ́) *pl.* **tsulátɨ́k**ᵃ. *n.* tuft, tussock (of hair or feathers).

tsum (tsumá-) *pl.* **tsumitín**. *n.* desert date: thorny tree species whose leaves are picked by women and eaten as a vegetable or spice, whose berries (*òwà*) are eaten raw or cooked, and whose resin is used as a glue; soap is made from its inner bark, and a root decoction is drunk for bone-pain or stomach ailments. *Balanites aegyptiaca.*

tsurúɗúmòn (tsurúɗúmònì-) *v.* to be bulging, convex.

tsùtᵃ (tsùtà-) *pl.* **tsútítín**. *n.* tip of a hut's roof where the last layer of thatching is brought together in a column and woven tightly in place.

tsútɔ̀ (tsútɔ̀) *adv.* completely, totally.

tsútsᵃ (tsútsá-) *n.* fly.

Tsùtsùkààwᵃ (Tsùtsùkà-àwà-) *n.* name of a deserted village. *Lit.* 'rubbing-place'.

tsutsukes (tsutsukesí-) *1 v.* to roll between hands, rub in hands (e.g. sorghum or millet to remove the seeds from the stems). *2 v.* to limber, supple (e.g. leather clothing).

tsutsukúmétòn (tsutsukúmétònì-) *v.* to grow limber or supple.

tsùtᵘ (tsùtù) *adv.* ever, never.

tsúúr (tsúúrà-) *pl.* **tsúúrɨk**ᵃ. *n.* white thorn acacia: a scrubby, plentiful tree species whose extremely hard wood is good for building and fencing; its resin is chewed and a bark decoction taken for bloating. *Acacia hockii.*

tsùwà (tsùwàà-) *1 v.* to run. *2 v.* to race.

tsuwa na iɓákɔ́nì *n.* race. *Lit.* 'running side-by-side'.

tsuwoós (tsuwoosí-) *v.* to be active, lively.

tswɨ́ɨtswɨ́ (tswɨ́ɨtswɨ́) *ideo.* squeak squeak! (sound made by rodents).

tswɨ́ɨtswɨ́ (tswɨ́ɨtswɨ̀-) *n.* cicada. *Cicadidae.*

ts'

ts'ábès (ts'ábèsì-) *1 v.* to despise, detest, hate. *2 v.* to not sit well with. See also *takaɗes*.

ts'ábunós (ts'ábunósí-) *v.* to despise, detest, or hate each other.

ts'aɗ[a] (ts'aɗí-) *n.* fire.

ts'aɗíák[a] (ts'aɗí-ákà-) *n.* flame. *Lit.* 'fire-mouth'.

Ts'aɗíáw[a] (Ts'aɗí-áwà-) *n.* name of a place where a village was burnt down. *Lit.* 'fire-place'.

ts'aɗícémèr (ts'aɗí-cémèrɨ-) *n.* fire herb: small blackish plant species found at the bases of boulders and whose leaves are charred, ground, and applied to burns. *Pellaea adiantoidea*.

ts'aɗídàkw[a] (ts'aɗí-dàkù-) *n.* firewood.

ts'aɗíékw[a] (ts'aɗí-ékù-) *pl.* **ts'aɗíékwítín**. *1 n.* fireplace, hearth. *2 n.* family. *Lit.* 'fire-eye'.

ts'aɗíój[a] (ts'aɗí-ójà-) *pl.* **ts'aɗíójɨtín**. *n.* burn. *Lit.* 'fire-wound'.

ts'àf (ts'àfù-) *pl.* **ts'áfɨtín**. *n.* chaw, plug, wad (of sth. chewable: honeycomb, sugarcane, or tobacco).

ts'àf (ts'àfù) *ideo.* unchewably, undigestibly.

ts'afés (ts'afésɨ-) *v.* to chew to extract juice (honey, sugar, tobacco).

ts'afúdòn (ts'afúdònɨ-) *v.* to be unchewable, undigestible (e.g. chewing tobacco or chewy maize).

ts'àg[a] (ts'ágà-) *pl.* **ts'ágitín**. *n.* crud, dirtiness, filth, filthiness, grime.

ts'ágààm (ts'ágà-àmà-) *pl.* **ts'ágaik**[a]. *n.* filthy person.

ts'ágòn (ts'ágònì-) *v.* to be cruddy, dirty, filthy, grimy. See also *itútsón*.

ts'agús (ts'agúsé) *num.* four.

ts'agusátìk[e] *v.* four-by-four.

ts'agús[o] *num.* four times.

ts'agúsón (ts'agúsónì-) *v.* to be four.

ts'ágwà (<ts'ágwòòn) *v.*

ts'ágwòòn (ts'ágwòònì-/ts'ágwa-) *v.* to be raw (uncooked or unripe).

ts'àl (ts'àlì) *ideo.* drenchedly, soppingly.

ts'álés (ts'álésì-) *v.* to remove, take out (as from a cooking pot).

ts'aletés (ts'aletésí-) *v.* to remove, take out (as from a cooking pot).

ts'alídòn (ts'alídònì-) *v.* to be drenched, soaked, sopping (with oil).

ts'álóbiés (ts'álóbiesí-) *1 v.* to finger out (food before it is served in dishes). *2 v.* to finger during sex.

ts'álúbòn (ts'álúbònì-) *v.* to slosh, splash.

ts'an (ts'anɨ-) *n.* louse, lice. *Pediculidae*.

ts'anán (ts'anánɨ-) *n.* small insect that eats sorghum seeds on the plant and makes its own honey.

ts'aráfón (ts'aráfónì-) *v.* to be dark brown, umber (of human skin, between the 'red' and 'black' tones).

ts'é (<ts'óón) *v.*

ts'ɛ̀ (ts'èà-) *pl.* **ts'ɛ́ɨtín**. *n.* hide, pelt, skin.

ts'ɛa na kwanɨ *n.* foreskin.

ts'édaikén (ts'édaikén) *dem.* there.

ts'édɛ́ɛ́ (ts'édɛ́-) *dem.* there: a place already known or mentioned.

ts'édɔ́ɔ́ kɔ̀nà *pro.* from there, then.

tsʼeiƙotᵃ (<tsʼoonuƙotᵃ) *v.*

tsʼéíƙotᵃ (<tsʼóónuƙotᵃ) *v.*

tsʼeites (tsʼeitesí-) *v.* to extinguish, put out, quench.

tsʼeitésuƙotᵃ (tsʼeitésuƙotí-) *1 v.* to extinguish, put out, quench. *2 v.* to switch or turn off electrically. *3 v.* to snuff out (i.e. kill, murder).

tsʼètà kònà *n.* likewise, in the same way.

tsʼíínáá (tsʼíínáá) *n.* all the time.

tsʼíínúó (tsʼíínúó) *n.* everywhere.

tsʼiƙᵃ (tsʼiƙá-) *1 n.* bee, honeybee. *Apis mellifera*. *2 n.* honey.

tsʼiƙábòtᵃ (tsʼiƙá-bòtà-) *pl.* **tsʼiƙábotitín**. *n.* swarm of bees on the move.

tsʼiƙáhò (tsʼiƙá-hòò-) *pl.* **tsʼiƙáhoíƙ**ᵃ. *n.* honeycomb. *Lit.* 'bee-house'. See also *dàdàhò*.

tsʼɨ̀n (tsʼɨ̀nɔ̀-) *n.* taboo against husbands of pregnant wives participating in any food-gathering activities such as hunting.

tsʼɨ̀nɔ̀àm (tsʼɨ̀nɔ̀-àmà-) *pl.* **tsʼinoik**ᵃ. *n.* husband prohibited from participating in food-gathering activities due to the pregnancy of his wife.

tsʼɨ̀nɔ̀n (tsʼɨ̀nɔ̀nɨ-) *v.* to be pregnant, with the result that one's husband is prohibited from participating in any food-gathering activities.

tsʼɨrítɔ̀n (tsʼɨrítɔ̀nɨ-) *v.* to spurt, squirt (e.g. blood or spit).

tsʼitsʼés (tsʼitsʼésɨ-) *v.* to track.

tsʼitsʼésà dèìkàᵋ *v.* to track footprints.

tsʼitsʼitésuƙotᵃ (tsʼitsʼitésuƙotí-) *v.* to make sharp, sharpen.

tsʼitsʼitetés (tsʼitsʼitetésɨ-) *v.* to make sharp, sharpen.

tsʼitsʼɔ́n (tsʼitsʼɔ́nɨ-) *1 v.* to be sharp. *2 v.* to be pointed. *3 v.* to be covetous, grabby, greedy. *4 v.* to have unprotected sex.

tsʼɔdites (tsʼɔditesɨ-) *v.* to prick, stick.

tsʼɔƙam (tsʼɔƙamá-) *n.* honey beer, mead made by mixing grain beer with honey. See also *sis*.

tsʼɔƙés (tsʼɔƙésí-) *v.* to brew or pitch (mead by mixing beer with honey).

tsʼɔƙɔ́m (tsʼɔƙɔ́má-) *n.* tree species whose yellow fruits are eaten raw, whose seeds are cracked, mashed, and fried to be eaten, and from whose wood stools and troughs are carved. *Sclerocarya birrea*.

tsʼolites (tsʼolitesí-) *v.* to administer in drops, dribble, drizzle.

tsʼolitésuƙotᵃ (tsʼolitésuƙotí-) *v.* to administer in drops, dribble, drizzle.

tsʼolitésuƙota séàᵉ *v.* to drain blood.

tsʼòlòn (tsʼòlònɨ-) *v.* to dribble, drip, drizzle. See also *idɔ́nɔ́n*.

tsʼɔ̀ɔ̀ (tsʼɔ̀ɔ̀) *1 adv.* now. *2 adv.* soon. *3 adv.* just recently.

tsʼóón (tsʼóónɨ-/tsʼé-) *v.* to die (of many).

tsʼóóniikᵃ (tsʼóóni-icé-) *n.* dead people.

tsʼoonuƙotᵃ (tsʼoonuƙotí-/tsʼeiƙot-) *1 v.* to die or go out (of fire or light). *2 v.* to switch or turn off (of electrically powered things). Not to be confused with *tsʼóónuƙot*ᵃ.

tsʼóónuƙotᵃ (tsʼóónuƙotí-/tsʼéíƙot-) *v.* to die off/out (of more than one). Not to be confused with *tsʼoonuƙot*ᵃ.

tsʼúbʉlátᵃ (tsʼúbʉlátɨ-) *pl.* **tsʼúbʉlátikw**ᵃ. *n.* plug or stopper made from grass or leaves. See also *tsʼûb*ᵃ.

tsʼûdᵃ (tsʼúdè-) *1 n.* smoke. *2 n.* exhaust, fumes. *3 n.* smoke signal. *4 n.* tobacco.

ts'údemucé (ts'úde-mucéè-) *pl.* **ts'ú-demucéík**[a]. *n.* exhaust pipe, muffler.

ts'udités (ts'uditésí-) *v.* to fumigate, smoke. See also *ipúréés* and *iwaɲíwáɲés*.

ts'ʉ̀fɔ̀n (ts'ʉ̀fɔ̀nɨ̀-) *v.* to peek or peep out from behind or inside.

ts'úgʉram (ts'úgʉramá-) *n.* shrub species that grows on rocky outcroppings and has big leaves which are used to treat scabies.

ts'ʉnés (ts'ʉnésí-) *v.* to kiss.

ts'únúnɔ́s (ts'únúnɔ́sɨ́-) *v.* to kiss each other.

ts'ʉts'ʉ (ts'ʉts'ʉ́-) *n.* garbage, refuse, rubbish, trash.

ts'ʉts'ʉ́áw[a] (ts'ʉts'ʉ́-áwà-) *pl.* **ts'ʉts'ʉ́áwík**[a]. *n.* garbage dump, rubbish pile.

ts'úts'útés (ts'úts'útésí-) *v.* to suck out/up (e.g. marrow or milk).

ts'ʉ́ʉ́tés (ts'ʉ́ʉ́tésí-) *1 v.* to suck out/up (e.g. marrow or milk). *2 v.* to make a sucking sound in derision. See also *kʉdés*.

ts'ʉ́ʉ́tɔnʉkɔt[a] (ts'ʉ́ʉ́tɔnʉkɔtɨ́-) *v.* to be absorbed, sucked dry, sucked up.

ts'ʉ̀wɔ̀n (ts'ʉ̀wɔ̀nɨ̀-) *v.* to come and go in bunches (like bees at a beehive).

ts'ûb[a] (ts'ûbà-) *pl.* **ts'úbitín**. *n.* plug or stopper made from grass or leaves. See also *ts'ûbʉlát*[a].

u/ʉ

ûd[a] (údè-) *n.* soft dry grass that is used as a mattress, a sponge for bathing, and a plug for granaries and beehives.

Ugánɗà (Ugánɗàà-) *n.* Uganda.

úgès (úgèsì-) *v.* to dig, excavate, unearth.

úgetés (úgetésí-) *v.* to dig out/up, excavate, unearth.

ugwam (ugwamá-) *pl.* **úgwamatikw**[a]. *1 n.* sibling-in-law (wife's siblings). *2 n.* sibling-in-law (brother's wife's sibling). *3 n.* brother-in-law (sister's husband). *4 n.* sister's husband's sibling.

Uláyà (Uláyàà-) *n.* Europe.

ún (únó-) *pl.* **únítín**. *n.* rope. See also *ŋún*.

upánón (upánònì-) *v.* to be inseparable (of close friends).

uré (uréì-) *pl.* **uréìk**[a]. *n.* mat made of *sɔ̂g*[a] reeds woven together with bark fiber and used to dry edible termites over fire in a hut when it starts to rain.

urém (urémá-) *n.* vine whose fruits and leaves are eaten raw or cooked. *Pentarrhinum insipidum*.

Úrù (Úrùù-) *n.* Independence Day of Uganda (October 9, 1962). From the Swahili word *uhuru* 'freedom'.

ùrùkùs (ùrùkùsù) *ideo.* abruptly, suddenly.

urúr (urúrá-) *pl.* **urúrík**[a]. *n.* gully or trench formed by running water. See also *ɲékúrumot*[a].

urúsáy[a] (ʉrúsáɨ-) *n.* large tree used for fencing and firewood, whose wood burns slowly and well, and whose leaves and roots are used as eye medicine. *Justicia sp.*

utés (utésí-) *v.* to clear a path, find or make a way through, penetrate.

utésúƙot[a] (utésúƙotí-) *v.* to clear a path, find or make a way through, penetrate.

útétòn (útétònì-) *v.* to find entrance to or a way into.

útɔ̀ (útɔ̀ɔ̀-) *n.* seed oil (e.g. simsim or sunflower).

ùtòn (ùtònì-) *v.* to escape, get away.

utonuƙot[a] (utonuƙotí-) *v.* to escape, get away/out/through.

ututetés (ututetésí-) *v.* to drive or force through, thrust. See also *xutés*.

ututiés (ututiesí-) *v.* to drive or force through repeatedly, thrust repeatedly.

ùwòò (ùwòò) *ideo.* completely open and visible.

Ʉzɛ̀t[a] (Ʉzɛ̀tɨ-) *n.* Uzet: one of the Ik's twelve clans.

Ʉzɛ̀tɨàm (Ʉzɛ̀tɨ-àmà-) *pl.* **Ʉzɛtiik**[a]. *n.* Uzet clan member.

W

wà (<wɔ́ɔ̀n) *v.*

wà (<weés) *v.*

wà (wàà-) *pl.* **waicík**[a]. *1 n.* greens, vegetables (planted or wild). *2 n.* fodder, grazing, pasture.

wààà (wààà) *ideo.* whoosh (sound of rushing water). The vowels of this word are pronounced silently.

wáák[a] (wáákà-) *pl.* **wáákaicík**[a]. *n.* game, play, sport.

wáák[a] (wáákà-) *v.* to play.

wááka dikwitíní *n.* dance with singing.

wááka na támɔtɔ́s *n.* drama, play, skit. *Lit.* 'play that is thought up'.

wáákààm (wáákà-àmà-) *pl.* **wáákaik**[a]. *n.* player.

wáákitetés (wáákitetésí-) *v.* to mess or play around with.

wáákós (wáákósí-) *v.* to be playful.

wààm (wà-àmà-) *pl.* **waik**[a]. *n.* forager, gatherer (of wild greens). See also *gaɗikamáám*.

wáán (wáánà-) *pl.* **wáánaicík**[a]. *1 n.* begging, soliciting, supplication. *2 n.* prayer. *3 n.* religious service, worship.

wáán (wáánà-) *1 v.* to beg, implore, solicit. *2 v.* to pray. *3 v.* to hold a religious service, worship.

wáána na muɗésíàmà[e] *n.* prayer for the gravedigger.

wáána na tɛ́zɛ̀tɔ̀nɪ̀ *n.* closing prayer.

wáánààm (wáánà-àmà-) *pl.* **wáánaik**[a]. *1 n.* beggar. *2 n.* one who prays, prayerful person.

wáánààm (wáánà-àmà-) *pl.* **wáániik**[a]. *n.* guest, visitor.

wáánàhò (wáána-hòò-) *pl.* **wáánahoík**[a]. *n.* church, house of prayer.

wáánɛtés (wáánɛtésí-) *1 v.* to ask for, request. *2 v.* to borrow. See also *iɗenetés*.

wáánɪ́nɔ́s (wáánɪ́nɔ́sɪ́-) *v.* to beg and borrow from each other.

wáánitɛtésíàm (wáánitɛtésí-àmà-) *pl.* **wáánitɛtésíik**[a]. *n.* worship leader.

waatés (waatésɪ́-) *v.* to brew, infuse, steep.

waatésá mèsè *v.* to brew beer (by soaking grist). See also *tsapésá mèsè*.

wádòn (wádònì-) *v.* to boil, simmer. See also *ígùlàjòn*.

waicíkásèd[a] (wa-icíká-sèdà-) *pl.* **waicíkásedík**[a]. *n.* vegetable garden.

waín (waínó-) *n.* hunters' call for help in carrying meat home.

waitésukota dakwí *v.* to make (a new bride) collect firewood for her new family.

waitetés (waitetésí-) *v.* to graze, pasture, take to pasture.

wakatiés (wakatiesí-) *v.* to break off or snap off in pieces.

wakáwákatés (wakáwákatésí-) *v.* to break off or snap off in pieces.

wakés (wakésí-) *1 v.* to break or snap off (e.g. a bone, tooth, or tree branch). *2 v.* to cock (a weapon). See also *pokés*.

wakésíàw[a] (wakésí-àwà-) *pl.* **wakésíawík**[a]. *n.* cocking lever.

walá (waláá-) *n.* sorghum variety with tall stalks and red or white seeds.

walámón (walámónì-) *1 v.* to dawn. *2 v.* to realize, see, understand. See also *tsòòn*.

waliwálɔ́n (walɨwálɔ́nɨ̀-) *v.* to be agitated, disturbed, perturbed (e.g. by heat or wind).

waŋádòn (waŋádònɨ̀-) *v.* to be charitable, generous, liberal (with one's belongings, etc.).

warɨwar (warɨwarɨ́-) *pl.* **warɨ́wárɨ̀k**[a]. *n.* tree species whose bark infusion can be drunk for fever and stomach ailments, and whose termite-resistant branches are used in building and fencing. *Dombeya quinqueseta*.

wàrɔ̀t[a] (wàrɔ̀tɔ̀-) *pl.* **warótíkw**[a]. *n.* termite colony at an inactive stage with small undeveloped mounds and few flying insects.

was (wasɔ́-) *1 n.* position, posture, stance. *2 n.* cessation, halting, stoppage, stopping. *3 n.* campaign, candidacy, nomination.

wasétɔ́n (wasétɔ́nɨ̀-) *v.* to balk, hesitate, refuse, waffle.

wasɨtɛs (wasɨtɛsɨ́-) *1 v.* to erect, stand up, support. *2 v.* to halt, stop. *3 v.* to arrest, take to court. *4 v.* to nominate for political office.

wasɨtɛsa iká[e] *1 v.* to raise the head. *2 v.* to be preoccupied.

wasɨ́tɛ́sʉkɔt[a] (wasɨ́tɛ́sʉkɔtɨ́-) *1 v.* to erect, stand up, support. *2 v.* to halt, stop. *3 v.* to arrest, take to court. *4 v.* to nominate for political office.

wasɔ́ám (wasɔ́-ámà-) *pl.* **wasóík**[a]. *n.* candidate, nominee.

wasɔ́áw[a] (wasɔ́-áwà-) *pl.* **wasɔ́áwík**[a]. *n.* stop (e.g. of a bus), stopover.

wàsɔ̀n (wàsɔ̀nɨ̀-) *1 v.* to stand (in general, but also for political office or trial). *2 v.* to be stationary, still, unmoving. *3 v.* to be stagnant. *4 v.* to be accountable, in charge, responsible.

wasɔna kúrúɓádù *v.* to be in charge of or responsible for things.

wasɔna ts'ír *v.* to stand still or upright.

wasɔnʉkɔt[a] (wasɔnʉkɔtɨ́-) *v.* to come to a stop, halt, stand still, stop.

wat[a] (waté-) *n.* rain.

watégwà (waté-gwàà-) *n.* bat species whose noctural cry predicts rain. *Lit.* 'rain-bird'.

wàtòn (wàtònɨ̀-) *v.* to rain.

watsóy[a] (wa-tsóí-) *n.* harvest, harvest time. See also *karɔŋ*.

wàts'w[a] (wàts'ɔ̀-) *pl.* **wáts'íkw**[a]. *n.* beehive found in a rock crevice.

wàx (wàxɨ̀-) *1 n.* ahead, front. *2 n.* before, earlier time.

wàxèd[a] (wàxèdè-) *n.* point of departure, starting point.

wàxɨ̀àm (wàxɨ̀-àmà-) *pl.* **waxiik**[a]. *1 n.* first person. *2 n.* firstborn.

wàxɨdòm (wàxɨ-dòmà-) *pl.* **waxɨdomɨtín**. *n.* first pot of edible termites to be cooked and eaten. See also *kɨ́túk*[a].

wàxɨ̀k[e] *n.* ahead, foreward, in front, onward.

wàxù *1 n.* ahead, in front. *2 n.* before, earlier, first.

wâz (wázò-) *pl.* **wázìkw**[a]. *n.* young female (human or non-human).

wɛ́dɔ̀n (wɛ́dɔ̀nɨ̀-) *v.* to detour, change course, take a diverson. See also *kekérón*.

wɛɗɨwɛ́ɗɔ́n (wɛɗɨwɛ́ɗɔ́nɨ̀-) *v.* to flap, flutter.

wɛ́ɛ́nòn (wɛ́ɛ́nɔ̀nɨ̀-) *v.* to be fast, quick, speedy. See also *itírónòn*.

weés (weésí-/wa-) *v.* to harvest, reap.

weesá dakwí *v.* to collect firewood.

weesa kíjá[e] *v.* to play the field (sexually), sleep around. *Lit.* 'reaping the land'.

wéésánón (wéésánónì-) *v.* to be lazy, slothful. See also *itátsámánón*.

weésíàm (weésí-àmà-) *pl.* **weésíik**ᵃ. *n.* harvester, reaper.

wɛ́ƙɛ́ƙᵃ (wɛ́ƙɛ́ƙì-) *n.* vine species once used as rope in thatching old-style granaries.

wèl (wèlà-) *pl.* **wélíkw**ᵃ. *n.* small opening, passageway, tunnel (e.g. made by an animal through thick grass, or by people to enter a hut or to pass between the sections of a homestead).

wèlèèkwᵃ (wèlè-èkù-) *n.* center of a small opening, passageway, or tunnel.

wèr (wèrè) *ideo.* totally naked.

wéreƙéƙón (wéreƙéƙónì-) *v.* to dawn with a cool breeze (during the transition between predawn darkness and early dawn).

wɛrɛƙɛs (wɛrɛƙɛs) *ideo.* immediately, instantly.

weretsᵃ (weretsí-) *n.* cry, outcry.

weretsíám (weretsí-àmà-) *pl.* **weretsíík**ᵃ. *n.* crier, spotter (one who keeps watch and alerts others of animals, enemies, or forbidden things).

werétsón (werétsónì-) *1 v.* to cry out (in alarm, fear, or pain). *2 v.* to bray, heehaw. See also *bɔ́rɔ́rɔ̀n*.

werétsónuƙotᵃ (werétsónuƙotí-) *v.* to cry out (in alarm, fear, or pain).

wetam (wetamá-) *n.* beverage, drink, drinkable, potable.

wetés (wetésí-) *1 v.* to drink, imbibe. *2 v.* to smoke, snuff.

wetésá cɛmɛ́ríkàᵋ *v.* to take medicine (traditional or modern).

wetésá kɔɨnáᵋ *v.* to catch a whiff, pick up a scent, smell.

wetésíàm (wetésí-àmà-) *pl.* **wetésíik**ᵃ. *n.* drinker, imbiber.

wetités (wetitésí-) *v.* to give drink, irrigate, water.

wetitésá cɛmɛ́ríkàᵋ *v.* to give medicine, treat.

wetitésíàm (wetitésí-àmà-) *pl.* **wetitésíik**ᵃ. *n.* herbalist, traditional healer. See also *cɛmɛ́ríkààm*.

wetitésuƙotᵃ (wetitésuƙotí-) *1 v.* to give drink, irrigate, water. *2 v.* to charge (electrically).

wɛts'ᵋ (wɛts'ɛ̀) *ideo.* breakably, brittlely.

wɛts'ɛ́dɔ̀n (wɛts'ɛ́dɔ̀nɨ-) *v.* to be breakable, brittle. See also *ɛɔmɔ́dɔ̀n* and *poƙódòn*.

wɛts'ɛ́mɔ́n (wɛts'ɛ́mɔ́nɨ-) *v.* to break or chip off.

wɛts'ɛ́s (wɛts'ɛ́sɨ-) *v.* to break of chip off, knap.

wɛts'ɛtɛ́s (wɛts'ɛtɛ́sɨ-) *v.* to break or chip off, knap.

wets'etiés (wets'etiesí-) *v.* to break or chip off in pieces.

wèwèès (wèwèèsè) *ideo.* leisurely, slowly, taking one's time.

wice ni *interj.* these kids, I tell you! (an expression of any positive or negative opinion of more than one object or person). *Lit.* 'these children'.

wicénánès (wicénánèsì-) *n.* childhood, childlikeness, childishness. *Lit.* 'being children'.

wîdzᵃ (wídzò-) *pl.* **wídzitín.** *n.* evening (roughly 5:00-7:00 p.m.).

wídzèèkwᵃ (wídzè-èkù-) *pl.* **wídzeekwitín.** *n.* evening near sunset (roughly 6:30-7:00). *Lit.* 'evening-eye'.

wîdzᵒ *n.* at evening time, during the evening.

wɨd¹ (wɨdɨ) *ideo.* vanishingly.

wɨdɨɗánón (wɨdɨɗánónɨ-) *v.* to clamp, clench, clinch (with the teeth). See also *kɨ́dzɨ̀kɔ̀ɔ̀n*.

wɨɗɨmɔ́nʉkɔtᵃ (wɨɗɨmɔ́nʉkɔtɨ́-) *v.* to disappear, vanish. See also *ɨ́ɗɔ́n*.

wɨ́ɗɨ́wɨɗánón (wɨ́ɗɨ́wɨɗánónɨ-) *v.* to clamp, clench, clinch (with teeth).

wikᵃ (wicé-) *n.* children, kids.

wɨl (wɨlɨ) *ideo.* injuredly, painfully.

wɨlɨmón (wɨlɨmónɨ-) *v.* to hurt (of an injury).

wɨlɨwɨl (wɨlɨwɨlɨ) *ideo.* injuredly, painfully.

wɨɲ (wɨɲɨ) *1 ideo.* richly in taste. *2 ideo.* gratifyingly.

wɨɲɨ́dɔ̀n (wɨɲɨ́dɔ̀nɨ-) *v.* to be rich (in taste), sensually gratifying (like beer or fatty food).

wɨɲɨwɨ́ɲón (wɨɲɨwɨ́ɲónɨ-) *v.* to be rich (in taste), sensually gratifying (like beer or fatty food).

wír (wírí) *ideo.* zoom! (sound of a swiftly moving object). See also *yír*.

wíránés (wíránésí-) *v.* to desire, long or wish for.

wíríwíránón (wíríwíránónì-) *v.* to be avoidant, circumventing, evasive, steering clear. See also *wíríwíránón*.

witsiwítsétòn (witsiwítsétònì-) *v.* to darken, get dark.

wɨù (wɨù) *ideo.* going for good, not looking back.

wízilés (wízilésí-) *v.* to squint. See also *ɨmʉɗʉ́mʉ́ɗɔ̀n*.

wízilɨ́lón (wízilɨ́lónì-) *v.* to be foul-smelling, rank, stinking. See also *ɨmʉ́sɔ́ɔ̀n*.

wízìlìmɔ̀n (wízìlìmɔ̀nì-) *v.* to be squinty, squinty-eyed (of babies or the elderly).

wíziwizatós (wíziwizatósí-) *v.* to be striped (like a zebra).

wíziwizetés (wíziwizetésí-) *v.* to scrawl, scribble.

wóí (wóí) *interj.* aah! (an expression of fear or pain).

wòò (wòò) *ideo.* cavernous, very deep.

wɔ̀ɔ̀n (wɔ̀ɔ̀nɨ-/wa-) *v.* to eat or drink too much.

wòròkòkᵒ (wòròkòkò) *ideo.* dryly.

wówójés (wówójésí-) *v.* to scrape (the flesh off of, e.g. a bone or a gourd).

wówójᵒ (wówójò) *ideo.* word used by honey-hunters for summoning bees to come colonize a newly placed hive.

wɔ̀x (wɔ̀xɔ̀) *ideo.* sounding like *sh-sh*.

wɔxɔ́dɔ̀n (wɔxɔ́dɔ̀nɨ-) *v.* to make a *sh-sh* sound (e.g. dry leaves, a paper bag, etc.).

wuɗétón (wuɗétónɨ-) *v.* to burn to ashes, incinerate (e.g. a body, food, wood).

wùɗòn (wùɗònɨ-) *v.* to be burnt to ashes, incinerated (e.g. a body, food, wood).

wúlù (wúlù) *1 interj.* wow! (an expression of amazement). *2 interj.* yikes! (an expression of having a close call). Also pronounced as *wúlú*.

wulúkúmɔ̀n (wulúkúmɔ̀nɨ-) *v.* to be squirmy, wriggly (like a baby trying to get out of its sling or a girl escaping from a suitor).

wùòò (wùòò) *ideo.* whoosh! (sound of a Euphorbia tree falling).

wúrukukánón (wúrukukánónì-) *1 v.* to have contractions. *2 v.* to be cowardly, faint-hearted, fearful.

Wús (Wúsé-) *n.* name of a place.

X

xàɓ^u (xàɓù) *ideo.* softly.

xaɓúdòn (xaɓúdònì-) *v.* to be soft (e.g. mattresses, ripe fruit, soil, etc.).

xáɓútés (xáɓútésí-) *v.* to slurp. See also *isɔ́rɔ́ɓɛ́s*.

xakútsúmòn (xakútsúmònì-) *v.* to be abyssal, bottomless, unfathomable.

xaƙarés (xaƙarésí-) *v.* to clear the throat, harrumph, hawk. See also *hákátòn*.

xáƙátòn (xáƙátònì-) *v.* to gag, heave, retch. See also *jaƙátós*.

xáƙw^a (xáƙú-) *pl.* **xáƙwítín**. *n.* dried flesh left on a skinned hide. Compare with *ɲɔpɔdɛ*.

xán (xáná-) *pl.* **xáín**. *1 n.* side. *2 n.* direction, location.

xàr (xàrà-) *pl.* **xárítín**. *n.* bladder.

xaramucé (xara-mucéè-) *pl.* **xárítínímucéík^a**. *n.* urethra.

xàtsòn (xàtsònɨ-) *v.* to go into exile, leave home.

xà^u (xàù) *ideo.* crackly, crunchily.

xaúdòn (xaúdònì-) *v.* to be crackly or crunchy (in sound, like wadded paper).

xawɨ́ɨ́ts'ⁱ (xawɨ́ɨ́ts'ɨ̀) *ideo.* burnt to ashes, incinerated.

xɛɓás (xɛɓásɨ́-) *n.* cowardice, fear, shyness, timidity.

xɛɓásɨ̀am (xɛɓásɨ́-àmà-) *pl.* **xɛɓásíik^a**. *n.* coward, shy or timid person.

xèɓ^ɛ (xèɓè) *ideo.* tenderly (of plants).

xɛɓédòn (xɛɓédònì-) *v.* to be tender (of new plant growth). See also *rusúdòn*.

xɛɓitɛs (xɛɓitɛsí-) *v.* to frighten, intimidate, scare.

xɛɓitésúƙɔt^a (xɛɓitésúƙɔtɨ́-) *v.* to frighten, intimidate, scare. See also *kitítésuƙot^a*.

xèɓɔ̀n (xèɓɔ̀nɨ̀-) *1 v.* to be afraid, cowardly, fearful. *2 v.* to be shy, timid. *3 v.* to honor, respect.

xɛɛ́s (xɛɛsɨ́-) *v.* to dust, sprinkle. See also *ízuzués*.

xɛɛsúƙɔt^a (xɛɛsúƙɔtɨ́-) *1 v.* to dust, sprinkle. *2 v.* to return a bride (to her home by sprinkling water on the gate of her parents' home).

xɛɛtés (xɛɛtésɨ́-) *v.* to dust, sprinkle.

xémétɔ̀n (xémétɔ̀nɨ̀-) *v.* to fall from up high (e.g. from a tree).

xɛmɔnʉ́ƙɔt^a (xɛmɔnʉ́ƙɔtɨ́-) *v.* to fall from up high (e.g. from a tree).

xèr (xèrà-) *n.* belch, burp.

xerétón (xerétónì-) *1 v.* to belch, burp. *2 v.* to disgorge, regurgitate.

xérón (xérónì-) *1 v.* to belch, burp. *2 v.* to bawl, bellow, roar.

xɛxánón (xɛxánónì-) *v.* to be bloated (from overeating or from eating certain gaseous foods).

xɨ́dɔ̀n (xɨ́dɔ̀nɨ̀-) *v.* to be verdant, very green. See also *kwɨxɨ́dɔ̀n*.

xɨ́dɔna ekwitíní *v.* jaundice of the eyes.

xɨkɛ́s (xɨkɛ́sɨ́-) *v.* to hang up.

xɨkɛ́súƙɔt^a (xɨkɛ́súƙɔtɨ́-) *v.* to hang up.

xɨkóám (xɨkó-ámà-) *pl.* **xɨkóík^a**. *n.* vagabond, vagrant of the wilderness (who may appear at your home, disheveled and in need of help).

xɨkw^a (xɨkó-) *n.* vagabondage, vagrancy in the wilderness. See also *rɨ́jɨ́kànànès*.

xíkón (xíkónì-) *v.* to hiccough, hiccup. See also *xíkwítòn*.

xìkwᵃ (xìkwà-) *n.* hiccough, hiccup.

xíkwítòn (xíkwítònì-) *v.* to hiccough, hiccup. See also *xíkón*.

xíkwítós (xíkwítósí-) *v.* to cry breathily, wheeze.

xiŋatᵃ (xiŋatí-) *pl.* **xiŋátíkwᵃ**. *n.* dusk, twilight (roughly 7:00-8:00 pm).

xiŋatétón (xiŋatétónì-) *v.* to be dusk, twilight.

xiŋatʼ *n.* at dusk, during twilight.

xɔ́bɛtɛ́s (xɔ́bɛtɛ́sɨ-) *v.* to choose, elect, pick, select. See also *ɲumɛtés* and *tɔsɛɛtés*.

xɔ́bɛtɛ́sá asɨ *v.* to enlist, enroll, join, sign up for.

xɔ́bɛtɛ́sá ɲápukánɨ *v.* to elect government officials.

xɔ́bɔtɔ́s (xɔ́bɔtɔ́sɨ-) *v.* to be choosen, elected, selected.

xɔ́dɔ̀n (xɔ́dɔ̀nì-) *v.* to be immaculate, perfect, pristine, pure, spotless, virginal. See also *xɔtánón*.

xɔ́dɔnʉkɔtᵃ (xɔ́dɔnʉkɔtɨ́-) *v.* to become better, improve, return to normal. See also *doonukotᵃ*.

xokómón (xokómónì-) *v.* to germinate, sprout (of grain).

xɔnɔ́ɔ́kɔn (xɔnɔ́ɔ́kɔnɨ-) *n.* half, part, portion.

xɔ́ŋɛ́s (xɔ́ŋɛ́sɨ-) *v.* to fix with a woven handle (e.g. a gourd).

xɔŋɔŋ (xɔŋɔŋɔ́-) *pl.* **xɔŋɔ́ŋɨkᵃ**. *n.* large animal-skin cloak worn mostly by old women.

xɔ̀r (xɔ̀rɔ̀) *ideo.* gooily, goopily, gunkily.

xɔrɔ́dɔ̀n (xɔrɔ́dɔ̀nɨ-) *v.* to be gooey, goopy, gunky.

xɔtánón (xɔtánónì-) *v.* to be immaculate, perfect, pristine, pure, spotless, virginal. See also *xɔ́dɔ̀n*.

xɔ́tsɛ́s (xɔ́tsɛ́sɨ-) *v.* to exchange, swap, trade. See also *ilókótsés* and *ixɔtsɛs*.

xɔ́tsɨ́nɔ́s (xɔ́tsɨnɔ́sɨ-) *v.* to trade with each other.

xoúxoú (xoúxoúù-) *1 n.* vine species whose roots are eaten raw and with which children play, pretending they are meat. *Asclepiadaceae sp.* *2 n.* plant disease that withers maize and sorghum leaves.

xóuxówòn (xóuxówònì-) *v.* to be whitish (typical of a crop disease which makes the plant infertile).

xuanón (xuanónì-) *v.* to blow up, expand, inflate, puff up, swell. See also *taɲéɔn*.

xúbètòn (xúbètònì-) *v.* to germinate, sprout. See also *búrukúkón* and *rúbètòn*.

xúbòn (xúbònì-) *v.* to germinate, sprout. See also *búrukúkón* and *rúbɔn*.

xukúmánòn (xukúmánònì-) *v.* to hang low with weight (e.g. a washline with many clothes).

xukúmétòn (xukúmétònì-) *v.* to break or collapse from weight.

xʉram (xʉramá-) *pl.* **xʉrámíkᵃ**. *n.* patch of unburned grass (left after a fire).

xúrɛ́s (xúrɛ́sɨ-) *v.* to do patchily or in patches (e.g. leaving patches in a cultivated garden, or fire leaving patches of brush).

xutés (xutésí-) *v.* to drive or force through, thrust. See also *ututetés*.

xutésúkotᵃ (xutésúkotí-) *1 v.* to drive or force through, thrust. *2 v.* to insert, put inside.

xuxuanitetés (xuxuanitetésí-) *v.* to blow up, fill with air, flex (muscles), inflate, puff up.

xuxuanón (xuxuanónì-) *v.* to blow up, expand, inflate, puff up, swell. See also *xuanón*.

xuxûb[a] (xuxúbò-) *pl.* **xuxúbìk**[a]. *n.* forest dombeya: tree species whose bark fibers and wood are used in building and whose twigs are used to make firedrills. *Dombeya goetzenii.*

Y

Yakóɓò (Yakóɓòò-) *1 n.* Jacob, James. *2 n.* James: New Testament book.

yàŋ (yàŋà) *ideo.* sludgily.

yáŋ (yáŋɨ̀-) *pl.* **yáŋín.** *1 n.* my mother. *2 n.* my aunt (father's brother's wife). *3 interj.* oh! wow! (an expression of amazement).

yaŋádòn (yaŋádònɨ̀-) *1 v.* to be sludgy, thick (like lava, porridge, or wet cement). *2 v.* to be loosely tied down. See also *hajádòn* and *lajádòn*.

yáŋìim (yáŋɨ̀-ìmà-) *pl.* **yáŋiwik**[a]. *n.* my cousin (father's brother's wife's child).

yáŋɨ̀ɲòt[a] (yáŋɨ̀-ɲòtà-) *n.* my mother-in-law (sibling's spouse's mother).

yáó (yáòò-) *pl.* **yáóín.** *n.* your sister.

yáóím (yáó-ímá-) *pl.* **yáówík**[a]. *n.* your niece or nephew (sister's child).

Yarán (Yaránɨ́-) *n.* a personal name.

yeá (yeáà-) *pl.* **yeáín.** *n.* my sister.

yeáìm (yeá-ìmà-) *pl.* **yeáwik**[a]. *n.* my niece or nephew (sister's child).

yeát[a] (yeatí-) *pl.* **yeatíkw**[a]. *n.* his/her/its sister.

yeatíím (yeatí-ímà-) *pl.* **yeatíwík**[a]. *n.* his/her niece or nephew (sister's child).

yeatínánès (yeatínánèsì-) *n.* sisterhood, sisterliness.

yeé' (yeé') *interj.* huh! (an expression of derision or disbelief). The apostrophe at the end represents a glottal stop, an abrupt end to the word's voicing.

yèl (yèlè) *ideo.* dryly.

Yɛlɨ́yél (Yɛlɨ́yélɨ̀-) *n.* June: month of full grain germination. See also *Nàmàkàr*.

yɛlɨ́yélɔ̀n (yɛlɨ́yélɔ̀nɨ̀-) *v.* to germinate fully (of grain seed-heads).

yɛ̀m (yɛ̀mɛ̀) *ideo.* delicately, fragilely.

yɛmɛ́dɔ̀n (yɛmɛ́dɔ̀nɨ̀-) *v.* to be delicate, fragile.

Yésù (Yésùù-) *n.* Jesus.

yír (yírí) *ideo.* zoom! (sound of a swiftly moving object). See also *wír*.

Yoánà (Yoánàà-) *1 n.* John. *2 n.* John: New Testament books by this name.

yóói (yóói) *interj.* uh-huh, sure! (an expression of humored disbelief).

yù (yùù) *ideo.* softly (of soil).

yʉanitetés (yʉanitetésí-) *v.* to lie, prevaricate. May also be spelled as *ywaanitetés*.

yʉanón (yʉanónì-) *v.* to be a liar, dishonest, lie, prevaricate. May also be spelled as *ywaanón*.

Yúdà (Yúdàà-) *n.* Jude: book in the New Testament.

yʉɛ (yʉɛ́-) *n.* falsehood, lie, prevarication, untruth.

yʉɛ́ám (yʉɛ́-ámà-) *pl.* **yuéík**[a]. *n.* liar.

yùm (yùmù) *ideo.* softly inside.

yumúdòn (yumúdònì-) *v.* to be soft inside, have a soft interior (food, soil, or wood).

yunivásìtì (yunivásìtìì-) *n.* college, university.

yús (yúsì-) *n.* young people, youth.

yuúdòn (yuúdònì-) *v.* to be soft (of soil).

Z

zaɓatiés (zaɓatiesí-) *v.* to switch or whip lightly. See also *ízabizabés*.

zadídímòn (zadídímònì-) *v.* to be arched or arch-backed (like a donkey or a stooped person).

zamʉjánón (zamʉjánónì-) *v.* to be creased, crinkled, wrinkled. See also *rʉjanón* and *turújón*.

zè (<zòòn) *v.*

zébès (zébèsì-) *v.* to stone, throw a stone. Compare with *turues*.

zébesuƙot[a] (zébesuƙotí-) *v.* to stone or throw a stone that way.

zébetés (zébetésí-) *v.* to stone or throw a stone this way.

zeetón (zeetónì-) *v.* to grow up.

zeikaakón (zeikaakónì-) *1 v.* to be big, huge, large (of many). *2 v.* to be broad, wide (of many). *3 v.* to be grown up, mature.

zeiƙot[a] (<zoonuƙot[a]) *v.*

zeís (zeísí-) *1 n.* bigness, greatness, largeness. *2 n.* age, maturity, oldness. *3 n.* importance, preeminence, superiority. *4 n.* position, rank, status. *5 n.* authority, might, power.

zeisêd[a] (zeísédè-) *n.* import, meaning, significance.

zeísíàm (zeísí-àmà-) *pl.* **zeísíik**[a]. *n.* authority, one in charge.

zeísínànès (zeísínànèsì-) *n.* position, rank, status.

zeites (zeitesí-) *1 v.* to enlarge, increase (size), make bigger. *2 v.* to develop, foster, grow, promote (e.g. plants or the economy). See also *iwanetés*.

zeitésuƙot[a] (zeitésuƙotí-) *1 v.* to enlarge, increase (size), make bigger. *2 v.* to develop, foster, grow, promote (e.g. plants or the economy).

zeket[a] (zeketí-) *pl.* **zekétík**[a]. *n.* crease, crimp, crinkle, raised line, ridge (e.g. that found inside a gourd or on the skin of a malnourished person's buttocks).

zɛƙɔ́am (zɛƙɔ́-ámà-) *pl.* **zɛƙóík**[a]. *n.* denizen, inhabitant, resident.

zɛƙɔ́aw[a] (zɛƙɔ́-áwà-) *pl.* **zɛƙɔ́awík**[a]. *1 n.* seat, sitting place. *2 n.* room, space (e.g. in a room or vehicle). *3 n.* abode, dwelling, habitation, home, residence. May also be spelled as *zɛƙwááw*[a].

zɛƙɔ́awa na maráŋ *1 n.* clean and orderly home. *2 n.* place of honor.

zɛƙɔ́awa ná zè *1 n.* big gathering. *2 n.* city, metropolis, urban center.

zɛƙw[a] (zɛƙɔ́-) *n.* daily life, existence.

zɛƙwa ná dà *1 n.* peaceful coexistence. *2 n.* high standard of living, prosperity, the good life.

zɛƙwétɔ́n (zɛƙwétɔ́nì-) *1 v.* to sit, sit down, take a seat. *2 v.* to alight, land. *3 v.* to move in, settle. *4 v.* to calm down, chill out, settle down.

zɛƙwitɛtés (zɛƙwitɛtésí-) *1 v.* to make sit, sit down. *2 v.* to calm down or settle down.

zɛ̀ƙwɔ̀n (zɛ̀ƙwɔ̀nì-) *1 v.* to be seated, sitting. *2 v.* to live, stay.

zɛƙwona karatsɔɔ jáká[e] *n.* taboo of sitting on the stools of elders.

zɛ̀ƙwɔ̀nà lìòò *v.* to sit alone, silently.

ziál (ziálá) *ideo.* laboriously (of movement, walking).

ziálámòn (ziálámònì-) *v.* to be beat, exhausted, spent, tuckered, wiped or worn out. See also *ziláámòn*.

zíbòn (zíbònì-) *v.* to go for a walk during one's free time, stroll.

zíbos (zíbosí-) *v.* to have free time to walk around.

ziɗát[a] (ziɗátá) *ideo.* whack! (sound of someone being beaten).

zììì (zììì) *ideo.* vroom! (sound of a vehicle).

zikam (zikamá-) *pl.* **zikámík**[a]. *n.* bunch, bundle, sheaf. *Lit.* 'tyable'.

zíkɛ́s (zíkɛ́sɨ-) *1 v.* to bind, fasten, tie. *2 v.* to apprehend, arrest. *3 v.* to imprison, incarcerate, jail.

zíkɛ́sà kɔ́ɓà[ɛ] *v.* to tie off the umbilical cord.

zíkɛ́sìàw[a] (zíkɛ́sɨ-àwà-) *pl.* **zíkɛ́sìawík**[a]. *n.* jail, penitentiary, prison. *Lit.* 'binding-place'.

zíkɛ́sʉƙot[a] (zíkɛ́sʉƙotí-) *1 v.* to bind or tie up. *2 v.* to apprehend, arrest. *3 v.* to imprison, jail, lock up.

zikɛtés (zikɛtésɨ-) *v.* to bind or tie up.

zikíbaakón (zikíbaakónì-) *1 v.* to be lengthy, long (of many). *2 v.* to be high, tall (of many).

zikíbàs (zikíbàsɨ-) *1 n.* distance, length. *2 n.* altitude, height, tallness.

zikíbètòn (zikíbètònì-) *1 v.* to grow long, lengthen, prolong. *2 v.* to grow high or tall.

zikíbitésúƙot[a] (zikíbitésúƙotí-) *1 v.* to extend, lengthen, prolong, protract. *2 v.* to extend up, make high or tall, raise.

zikíbòn (zikíbònì-) *1 v.* to be lengthy, long. *2 v.* to be high, tall.

zikíbonuƙot[a] (zikíbonuƙotí-) *1 v.* to lengthen: become longer, prolonged or protracted. *2 v.* to extend up, grow high or tall, rise.

zíkímétòn (zíkímétònì-) *v.* to be beat, exhausted, spent, tuckered, wiped or worn out. See also *ziláámètòn*.

zɨ́kɨ́zɨkánón (zɨ́kɨ́zɨkánónì-) *v.* to be bound or tied up together.

zíkɔ́s (zíkɔ́sɨ-) *1 v.* to be bound, fastened, tied. *2 v.* to be apprehend, arrested. *3 v.* to be behind bars, imprisoned, incarcerated, jailed, locked up.

ziláámètòn (ziláámètònì-) *1 v.* to become exhausted or worn out. *2 v.* to become flaccid (of the penis). See also *zíkímétòn*.

ziláámòn (ziláámònì-) *v.* to be beat, exhausted, spent, tuckered, wiped or worn out. See also *ziálámòn*.

zin (zinó-) *n.* zebra. *Hippotigris quagga (boehmi/granti)*.

Zináík[a] (Ziná-ícé-) *n.* traditional men's age-group with the zebra as its totem (#4 in the historical line). *Lit.* 'Zebra-Folk'.

zít[a] (zítá-) *pl.* **zítítín**. *n.* round winnowing basket.

zízès (zízèsɨ-) *v.* to menace, threaten, warn.

zízités (zízitésí-) *1 v.* to fatten. *2 v.* to fertilize (plants).

zízitésúƙot[a] (zízitésúƙotí-) *1 v.* to fatten up. *2 v.* to fertilize (plants).

zízòn (zízònì-) *1 v.* to be fat, healthy, plump, well-fed. *2 v.* to be fertile (of soil). *3 v.* to be meaningful, significant.

zízònìàm (zízònì-àmà-) *pl.* **zízoniik**[a]. *n.* fat, healthy, or plump person.

zízonuƙot[a] (zízonuƙotí-) *v.* to fatten up, gain weight, get healthy. See also *tuɓútónuƙot*[a].

zɔ́ɓès (zɔ́ɓèsɨ-) *v.* to fix, insert (e.g. rafters into a roof or sticks and thorny branches into a fence).

zòòn (zòònì-/ze-) *1 v.* to be big, huge, large. *2 v.* to be broad, wide. *3 v.* to be mature, old, of age. *4 v.* to be grand, great.

zoona terégù *v.* to be in charge of work.

zòònìàm (zòònì-àmà-) *pl.* **zooniik**[a]. *n.* person in charge.

zoonuƙot[a] (zoonuƙotí-/zeiƙot-) *1 v.* to become bigger, grow bigger. *2 v.* to broaden, widen. *3 v.* to age, grow in age, mature. See also *iwánétòn*.

zɔ̀t[a] (zɔ̀tà-) *pl.* **zɔ́tɨ́tɨ́n**. *1 n.* chain. *2 n.* spring mechanism of a weapon.

zɔ̀tɛ̀ɛ̀b[a] (zɔ̀tɛ̀-ɛ̀bà-) *pl.* **zɔtɛɛbɨtɨ́n**. *n.* belt-fed machine gun. *Lit.* 'chain-gun'.

zɔ́tɛ́tɔ̀n (zɔ́tɛ́tɔ̀nɨ-) *v.* to join, link up.

zɔ́tɔ́n (zɔ́tɔ́nɨ-) *v.* to be chained or linked (e.g. oxen or donkeys carrying a load).

zùk[u] (zùkù) *1 adv.* very. *2 adv.* especially.

Part III

English-Ik reversal index

a kɔ́nɨ́ɛn *pro.*
a bit kédìim *n.*
a few kínɨ́ɛn *pro.*
a fifth (be) kɔnɔna túdònù *v.*
a little bit kédiima kwáts\[a\] *n.*
a little while kédiima kwáts\[a\] *n.*
a long time dèŋ *ideo.*; kéda zikîb\[a\] *n.*; ódowicíká nì kòm *n.*
a long while kéda zikîb\[a\] *n.*; ódowicíká nì kòm *n.*
a lot mbáyà *adv.*; pʉ́n *ideo.*; tàn *n.*
a short time kédiima kwáts\[a\] *n.*; ódowicíká nì ƙwàd\[e\] *n.*
a short while ódowicíká nì ƙwàd\[e\] *n.*
a time kédìim *n.*
a while kédìim *n.*
a while ago nótsò *adv.*
a year ago sakɛin *n.*
aah! wóí *interj.*
aardvark ɲodôd\[a\] *n.*
aardwolf náƙɨ́rà *n.*
ab ɲákwálɨkwal *n.*
abandon góózés *v.*; góózesuƙot\[a\] *v.*
abandoned góózosuƙot\[a\] *v.*
abbattoir hoesího *n.*
abdomen bùbù *n.*
abdominal disease gɛf *n.*
abdominal muscle ɲákwálɨkwal *n.*
abduct iɛpɛtés *v.*; toreɓes *v.*
abhor tʉlʉŋɛs *v.*
abide nɛɛs *v.*; nɛɛsúƙɔt\[a\] *v.*; taɗaŋes *v.*
ability ɲapéɗór *n.*
Abim Teɓur *n.*
ablactate topétésuƙot\[a\] *v.*
able to topéɗésuƙot\[a\] *v.*
able-bodied (of middle age) toipánón *v.*

able-bodied adult toipánóniàm *n.*
abode aw\[a\] *n.*; zɛƙɔ́áw\[a\] *n.*
abominate tʉlʉŋɛs *v.*
abort iɲétséetés *v.*; iɲétsóòn *v.*; iyétséetés *v.*; iyétsóòn *v.*
abort repeatedly iyétséyeés *v.*
above nɔ́ɔ́ kwar\[ɔ\] *n.*
abruptly ŋàm *ideo.*; ùrùƙùs *ideo.*
abscess tún *n.*
absent-minded ɓotsódòn *v.*
absorb (attention) itúmúránitésúƙot\[a\] *v.*
absorb heat róbiróbòn *v.*
absorbed ts'ʉ́útɔnʉƙɔt\[a\] *v.*
absorbed (attention) itúmúránón *v.*
abstain (from food) ikáɲón *v.*
abuse ilarɛs *v.*; ilwarɛs *v.*
abuse sexually tarates *v.*
abuse verbally iyaŋes *v.*
Abutilon species ídòkàk\[a\] *n.*
abyssal xakútsúmòn *v.*
Abyssinia Isópìà *n.*; Sópìà *n.*
acacia (Gerrard's) ɓʉkúlá *n.*
acacia (gum) ɗerét\[a\] *n.*; lofílitsí *n.*
acacia (hook-thorn) kásɨ́t\[a\] *n.*
acacia (Naivaisha thorn) lɛ̀r *n.*
acacia (Nubian) gɔmɔr *n.*
acacia (scented-pod) kilɔ́rɨ́t\[a\] *n.*
acacia (wait-a-bit) kúrà *n.*
acacia (white thorn) tsúúr *n.*
Acacia brevispica kúrà *n.*
Acacia gerrardii ɓʉkúlá *n.*
Acacia hockii tsúúr *n.*
Acacia mellifera kásɨ́t\[a\] *n.*
Acacia nilotica kilɔ́rɨ́t\[a\] *n.*
Acacia nubica gɔmɔr *n.*
Acacia senegal ɗerét\[a\] *n.*; lofílitsí *n.*
Acacia species ròr *n.*; tɨ́ɨ́r *n.*

Acacia tortilis sèg^a *n.*
Acacia xanthophloea lɛ̀r *n.*
Acalypha fruticosa jɨjîd^a *n.*
accept tsamɛtés *v.*
accept a curse tsamétésa ɨ̀làmà^ɛ *v.*
accident (have an) rúmánòn *v.*
accompany iníámésuƙot^a *v.*
accompany away elánónuƙot^a *v.*
accompany here elánétòn *v.*
account ɲádís *n.*
account for rajetés *v.*
accountable wàsɔ̀n *v.*
accumulate ɨɗaɲɛtés *v.*; torítéetés *v.*
accumulate one-by-one ɨɗébɛtés *v.*
accuse ɨsɨ́ɨ́tés *v.*
accuse each other falsely kɛrɨ́nɔ́s *v.*; tapáɨ́nɔ́s *v.*
accuse falsely ipwáákés *v.*; kɛrés *v.*; tapɛɛs *v.*
accuser ɨsɨ́ɨ́tésɨ̀àm *n.*
accuser (false) kɛrɨ́nɔ́sɨ̀àm *n.*; lóliit^a *n.*
accustom ɨtalɛs *v.*; naɨ́nɛɛtés *v.*; naɨ́tésʉƙɔt^a *v.*
accustomed ɨtalɔs *v.*
acerbic ɓatsilárón *v.*
ache áts'ɛs *v.*; dódòn *v.*
ache (begin to) dódètòn *v.*
ache (of joints) ɨtɨlɨ́tɨ́lɔ̀n *v.*
ache (of lymph nodes) titisíánón *v.*
ache (of teeth) isálílòn *v.*
achieve enés *v.*
Acholi language Ŋíkátsolítôd^a *n.*
Acholi person Ŋíkátsolíám *n.*
acid reflux áts'ɛ́sa gúró^e *n.*
acne ŋ́kaŋók^a *n.*
acolyte túbèsìàm *n.*

acquaint naɨ́nɛɛtés *v.*; naɨ́tésʉƙɔt^a *v.*
acquainted (mutually) náɨ́nɔ́s *v.*
acquiesce to tsamɛtés *v.*
acquire iryámétòn *v.*
acquit ɨɛtɛ́sá ɨsɨ́ɨ́tésʉ́ *v.*
acrid ɓatsilárón *v.*
act iɲétsóòn *v.*; iyétsóòn *v.*
act falsely ipwáákés *v.*
act in sync ilíréètòn *v.*
act in unison ilíréètòn *v.*
actionable itíyéetam *n.*
active ɨkwɨɲɨ́kwɨ́ɲɔ́n *v.*; iona ńda sea ni itsúr *v.*; kʉrúkʉ́rɔ́s *v.*; kwɨɲɨ́dɔ̀n *v.*; tsuwoós *v.*
actively kwɨ̀ɲ *ideo.*
Acts of the Apostles Terégiicíká Dɛɨkaicé *n.*
actually károkó *adv.*; rò *adv.*
add ɗɔtsés *v.*; ɗɔtsésúƙɔt^a *v.*; ɨatɛs *v.*
add in ɗɔtsés *v.*; ɗɔtsésʉ́ƙɔt^a *v.*
add on tasaɓes *v.*
add on top iɗokes *v.*
add repeatedly ɨatiés *v.*; ɨatiésuƙot^a *v.*
add together ɗɔtsés *v.*; ɗɔtsésʉ́ƙɔt^a *v.*
add up ɗɔtsɛtés *v.*
add water to ɨlálátés *v.*; ɨlatɛs *v.*
added ɗɔtsɔ́s *v.*; ɨatímétòn *v.*; ɨatɔs *v.*
adder (dwarf) naréw^a *n.*
adder (puff) bɛf *n.*
Adenium obesum dɛréƙ^a *n.*; jɔt^a *n.*
adhere ƙɨ́dzɔn *v.*; nɔtsɔ́mɔ́n *v.*
adhere to ɨnɔtsɛs *v.*
adhesive nɔtsɔ́dɔ̀n *v.*
adhesively nɔ̀ts^ɔ *ideo.*
adipose tissue cɛím *n.*; ɛfás *n.*
adjacent ɨɓákɔ́n *v.*
adjacent to (move) ɨɓákɔ́nʉƙɔt^a *v.*

adjudicate   *agreeableness*

adjudicate ŋʉrés *v.*; ŋurutiés *v.*; ŋurutiesʉ́ƙotᵃ *v.*
adjudicated ŋurutiós *v.*
administer imɔlɛs *v.*
administer in drops ts'olites *v.*; ts'olítésʉƙotᵃ *v.*
administration ɲápukán *n.*; ɲeryaŋ *n.*
administrator imɔlɛsɨ́ám *n.*
admire isémeés *v.*; iséméetés *v.*
admirer mɨnɛ́sɨ̀àm *n.*
adopt (a mascot) totores *v.*
adore mɨnés *v.*; tamɛɛs *v.*
adorn daites *v.*; naƙwɨ́dɛtés *v.*
adornment ɲewale *n.*
adult ámáze *n.*
adulterer ɓúƙónìàm *n.*
adulteress ɓúƙónìàm *n.*
adulthood (of many) roɓazeikánánès *n.*
adults roɓazeikᵃ *n.*
advertise (attributes) kɔkɔanón *v.*
advice each other táɲɨ́nós *v.*
advise táɲés *v.*; taŋɛtés *v.*
adze lorokon *n.*
aerate iwúlákés *v.*
affair (have an) ríínós *v.*
affect kʉpés *v.*
affix mɨnés *v.*
afflict sikwetés *v.*; tawanes *v.*; tawánítetés *v.*
afflicted tawanímétòn *v.*
affluence ídzànànès *n.*
affront risés *v.*; tatés *v.*
aflutter kìtòn *v.*
afraid paupáwón *v.*; xèɓɔn *v.*
Africa Buɗámóniicékíɟᵃ *n.*
African buɗámónìàm *n.*

after jɨ̀rù *n.*; térútsù *adv.*; tórútsù *adv.*
after all jâbᵒ *adv.*
afterlife didigwarí *n.*
again naɓó *adv.*
age dunétón *v.*; zeís *n.*; zoonuƙotᵃ *v.*
age-group ɲanáƙɛ́tᵃ *n.*
age-group (Blood-Strugglers) Ŋɨ́mariɔkɔ́tᵃ *n.*; Ŋuésɨ̂ikà sèàᵉ *n.*
age-group (Buffalo) Gasaraikᵃ *n.*; Ŋíƙósowa *n.*
age-group (Eland) Basaúréikᵃ *n.*; Ŋɨ́wápɛtɔ *n.*
age-group (Elephant) Ŋitɔ́mɛ́ *n.*; Oŋoriikᵃ *n.*
age-group (Gazelle) Kodowíikᵃ *n.*; Ŋíɲóleɲaŋ *n.*
age-group (Giraffe) Gwaɨts'iikᵃ *n.*; Ŋkóryó *n.*
age-group (Leopard) Ŋisíráyᵃ *n.*; Nʉsíikᵃ *n.*
age-group (Lion) Máóikᵃ *n.*; Ŋíɲátuɲo *n.*
age-group (Ostrich) Leweɲiikᵃ *n.*; Ŋímérimoŋ *n.*; Ŋ́kaleesó *n.*
age-group (Umbrella Thorn) Ŋɨ́tɨ̵́ira *n.*; Segaikᵃ *n.*
age-group (Zebra) Ŋítúkoyᵃ *n.*; Zɨnáíkᵃ *n.*
age-set ɲanáƙɛ́tᵃ *n.*
aggravate iwɨwɨnés *v.*; rúbès *v.*
aggregate rock ɲékɔ́kɔ́té *n.*
agile pɔdɔ́dɔ̀n *v.*
agilely pɔ̀dᵒ *ideo.*
agitate ɨ́bɔbɔtsés *v.*; ɨ́bɔtsés *v.*; ilɔ́lɔ́ŋés *v.*
agitated ɨ́bɔtsɛ́sá asɨ́ *v.*; iƙúrúmós *v.*; walɨwálɔ́n *v.*
ago kwààkᵉ *n.*
agree to tsamɛtés *v.*
agree with each other tsámʉ́nɔtɔ́s *v.*
agreeableness daás *n.*

agreeble dòòn v.
agricultural course ágɨrɨkácà n.
agriculturalist tɔ̀kɔ̀bààm n.
agriculture tɔ̀kɔ̀bᵃ v.
ahead ɛ̀kwɔ̀n v.; wàx n.; wàxɨ̀kᵋ n.; wàxʉ̀ n.
aid ɨŋaarɛ́s v.
aided ɨŋaarímétòn v.
AIDS lóɓúlukúɲ n.; sɨlɨ́m n.
aim idɨ́rɔ́n v.; ɨtsɨ́rɨ́tɛtɛ́s v.; iyoes v.; tsɨ́rɨ́tɛtɛ́s v.; tɔɓɛɨtɛtɛ́s v.
aim for ɨpɨmɛs v.; iyoesa asɨ́ v.
air gwa n.; sugur n.
aircraft idɛ́kè n.
airfield ɲakwaanja n.
airplane idɛ́kè n.
airport ɲakwaanja n.
airstrip ɲakwaanja n.
ajar bɔrɔ́ɔ́n v.; ŋawɨ́ɔ́n v.
AK-47 ɲámakadá n.
alarm ɲakalo n.
albizia (large-leaf) sɨ́ɔ̀ɔ̀tᵃ n.
Albizia anthelmintica óbìjòɔ̀z n.
Albizia grandibracteata sɨ́ɔ̀ɔ̀tᵃ n.
alcohol craving mɛ̀sɛ̀ɲɛ̀kᶠᵃ n.
alcoholic ɛ́sáàm n.
alcoholism ɛ́s n.
alert gonɛ́s v.; itsópóòn v.; ɲɨ́zɛ̀s v.; ɲakalo n.
alien jalánón v.; kɨ́jɨ́kààm n.
alight todɔ́ɔ́n v.; zɛɦwɛ́tɔ́n v.
alive ɦyekes v.
all ɓutᵘ ideo.; botedᵒ n.; daɲɨdaŋ quant.; mùɲ quant.; mùɲùmùɲ quant.; pílɛ̀ ideo.; pítⁱ ideo.; tsɨdᶦ quant.; tsɨdɨtsɨdᶦ quant.

all day ódàtù n.
all done tɛ́zɛ̀tɔ̀n v.
all fours (get on) tígàkɛ̀tòn v.
all gone tɛ́zɛ̀tɔ̀n v.
all night tsoíkᵒ n.; tɛrɛkɛs ideo.
all the time àrɨ̀ŋàs adv.; jîkⁱ adv.; ts'íínáá n.
all the way to gònɛ̀ prep.; pákà prep.
allergic reaction (skin) nabêz n.
allergy (skin) nabêz n.
Allium species tâbᵃ n.
Allophylus species àdèɲèlìò n.
allot ɨmɔlɛs v.
allow talakes v.
allure ɨmɔdɛtɛ́s v.
almost ɦyɔtɔ́gɔ̀n v.
almost do bɛ́dɛ́s v.
aloe tikorotótᵃ n.
Aloe species tikorotótᵃ n.
alone ɛdá adv.; kɔ̀nɔ̀n v.
along the side rutetᵒ n.
along the way tsɨ̀l ideo.
alsatian (dog) ɲeryaɲíŋókᵃ n.
also jɨ̀kᶠ adv.
altar lɔpɨtá n.
alter ɨɓélɛ́ɛ́s v.
alternated idómíòn v.
altitude zikíbàs n.
aluminum ŋkwáɲáyᵃ n.
aluminum lip plug ŋkwáɲáyᵃ n.
always àrɨ̀ŋàs adv.; jîkⁱ adv.
amass idaɲɛtɛs v.; torítéetɛ́s v.
amass one-by-one idɛ́bɛtɛ́s v.
ambitious ɨkázànòòn v.
amble ɨpɛ́ɛ́ɲɛ́sá asɨ́ v.; tasɔ́ɔ́n v.
amblyopic pɨlɨ́rɨ́mɔ̀n v.
ambulatory ɓɛkɛsɔs v.

ambush

ambush iɗaarés *v.*; taɗapes *v.*; taɗapetés *v.*
ambusher tàɗàpààm *n.*
ameliorate maraŋités *v.*; maraŋítésuƙotᵃ *v.*
amenable tsolólómòn *v.*
America Amérìkà *n.*; Ɓets'oniicékíjᵃ *n.*
American Amérìkààm *n.*; ɓèts'ònìàm *n.*
amniotic fluid baúcùè *n.*
amuse fekitetés *v.*; imúmwárés *v.*
an kɔ́nɨ́ɛn *pro.*
anal sphincter ɔ́zàhò *n.*
analyze ŋʉrɛtés *v.*
anchor ɲólóitᵃ *n.*
ancient kɔ̀wɔ̀n *v.*
and ńdà *coordconn.*
and then náàtì *coordconn.*
and yet (earlier today) tenákᵃ *adv.*
and yet (long ago) tènòkᵒ *adv.*
and yet (yesterday) tèsɨ̀n *adv.*
Andropogon chinensis jan *n.*; jɛn *n.*
anemic dɛrédɔ̀n *v.*
anemically dɛ̀r *ideo.*
angel ɲɨ́malái̵kàn *n.*
anger gaánàs *n.*; gaanítésuƙotᵃ *v.*; ɲɛlil *n.*
Anglican sɛ́mɨ̀s *n.*
angry gaanón *v.*; ilɨ́lɨ́ɔ̀n *v.*; iŋóyáánón *v.*
angry (become) gaanónuƙotᵃ *v.*; ilɨ́lɨ́ɔnʉƙɔtᵃ *v.*
angry at each other ilɨ́lɨ́ɨnós *v.*
anguish itsanɨ́tsánɛs *v.*
animal (domestic) ínwá na awáᵉ *n.*
animal (wild) ínwá na rijááƙɔ̀ᵋ *n.*
animal bed dɨ́pɔ̀ *n.*; nakús *n.*
animal doctor ɗakɨtárɨama ínóᵉ *n.*

ant species (black flying)

animal species tàlàlìdòm *n.*
animal(s) ínwᵃ *n.*
animal-likeness ínónànès *n.*
animateness ínónànès *n.*
animism ɲakujíícíkᵃ *n.*
animist ɲakujíícíkáàm *n.*
ankle dɛámóróƙᵃ *n.*; kɔpɨkɔpᵃ *n.*
anklet (coiled) ɲéƙɨ́lɔɗa *n.*
anklet (gold) ɲámaritóítᵃ *n.*
anklet (metal) dɛɨkatsɨrɨ́m *n.*
Ankole cow Ŋíɲaŋkóléɦyɔ́ *n.*
annihilate iƙɔmɛs *v.*; kánɛs *v.*
annihilated kanímétòn *v.*
announce ɗoɗésúƙotᵃ *v.*; síránòn *v.*
announcement (morning) sír *n.*
announcer síráám *n.*
annoy gaanítésuƙotᵃ *v.*; itsanɛs *v.*
annoyance gaánàs *n.*; ɲɛlil *n.*
annoyed gaanón *v.*; ilɨ́lɨ́ɔ̀n *v.*; iŋóyáánón *v.*
annoyed (become) gaanónuƙotᵃ *v.*; ilɨ́lɨ́ɔnʉƙɔtᵃ *v.*
annoying fifòn *v.*; itsánánòn *v.*
anoint iɲóɲóés *v.*; kwɨ́rɛs *v.*; tsáɲés *v.*
anoint the sick tsáɲésa mayaakóniicé *v.*
anointed tsáɲós *v.*
another kɔn *pro.*
another day kónító ódòwì *n.*
answer rajés *v.*; rajetés *v.*; taatsɛs *v.*; taatsésuƙotᵃ *v.*; taatsetés *v.*
answer for rajetés *v.*
ant (cocktail acacia) tàbàrɨ̀bàr *n.*
ant (safari) ƙúduƙûdᵃ *n.*
ant (small worker) sokomɛtᵃ *n.*
ant (soldier) lókóƙᵃ *n.*; tɛkɛram *n.*
ant species (black biting) ɲémúkùɲ *n.*
ant species (black flying) amózà *n.*; tiɲɨ́ɲ *n.*

ant species (black) ɓáritson *n.*; ílegûgᵃ *n.*; siɲɨl *n.*
ant species (blackish flying) kwɛlɛ́ɗᵃ *n.*
ant species (red flying) kútúŋùdàdᵃ *n.*
ant species (sugar-eating) ɗɔ́gɨɗɔ̂gᵃ *n.*
antbear ɲoɗôdᵃ *n.*
anteater ɲoɗôdᵃ *n.*
antelope (male) sakalúkᵃ *n.*
antelope (roan) ɗorôgᵃ *n.*
antelope (whistling) ɲétíli *n.*
antenna (insect) êbᵃ *n.*
anthill kutútᵃ *n.*
anthill (holey) lòkòsòs *n.*
anthill chamber ɓarán *n.*
antler êbᵃ *n.*
ants species (singing) jɔrɔr *n.*
antsy kakáánón *v.*
anus kazɨtᵃ *n.*; ɔ́zààkᵃ *n.*
anvil (stone) ityakesígwàs *n.*
anxious alólóŋòn *v.*
any mùɲ *quant.*
apocalyse tasálétona kíjáᵉ *n.*
appall iɓálétòn *v.*; lilétón *v.*; toɓules *v.*
appalling iɓálɔ́n *v.*; toɓúlón *v.*
apparently ɨ́kwà *adv.*; ókò *adv.*; tsábò *adv.*
apparition kúrúkúr *n.*
appeal to rimɛ́s *v.*; tɔminɛs *v.*
appear lɛlɛmánétòn *v.*; lɛlétón *v.*; pɛlémétòn *v.*; takánétòn *v.*
appear randomly iɗotíɗótòn *v.*
appearing lɛlɛmánón *v.*
appearing suddenly pìrⁱ *ideo.*
appease ɨkanɛ́s *v.*; ɨkanɨ́kánɛ́s *v.*
appendage (arm-like) kwɛtᵃ *n.*
appendicitis lɔkapɛtᵃ *n.*

appendix lɔkapɛtᵃ *n.*
appetite (for meat) bisákᵃ *n.*
appetite (have an) ɨrɔ́rɔ́kánón *v.*
apply heat to ɨmaɗɛs *v.*; ɨmáɗɛ́sʉkɔtᵃ *v.*
apportion imɔlɛs *v.*
appreciate ilákásɨ́tɛ́sʉkɔtᵃ *v.*
appreciative ilákásɔ́nʉkɔtᵃ *v.*
apprehend ƙanetés *v.*; zɨ́kɛ́s *v.*; zɨ́kɛ́sʉkɔtᵃ *v.*; zɨ́kɔ́s *v.*
apprehensive ísánòn *v.*
apprehensive (become) ísánonuƙɔtᵃ *v.*
approach fiyɔtɔ́gètɔ̀n *v.*
approach (going) fiyɔtɔ́gɔnʉkɔtᵃ *v.*
approach death inunúmétòn *v.*
appropriate itémón *v.*
approximate fiyɔtɔ́gètɔ̀n *v.*; fiyɔtɔ́gɔ̀n *v.*
April Lomarukᵃ *n.*; Lɔmɔ́yᵃ *n.*
Arab Ŋímaraɓúìàm *n.*; Oríáé *n.*
Arabic language Múɗùgùrìtòdᵃ *n.*; Oríáénítòdᵃ *n.*
arable tɔkɔbam *n.*
arbitrate terés *v.*
arc ilúkúɗòn *v.*
arch-backed zaɗíɗímòn *v.*
arched zaɗíɗímòn *v.*
area ayᵃ *n.*; bácɨ́kᵃ *n.*; ɲétɛɛr *n.*
area (adjoining) nabɨɗɨtᵃ *n.*
argue nɛpɛƙánón *v.*
argue (of many) ilérúmùòn *v.*
argue with déƙwítetés *v.*
arguer nɛpɛ́ƙáàm *n.*
argument dèƙwᵃ *n.*; ɲelerum *n.*
argumentative deƙwideƙos *v.*
argumentative person nɛpɛ́ƙáàm *n.*
Arisaema ruwenzoricum ɓóéɗᵃ *n.*
Aristida adoensis ɲeɗuar *n.*
arithmetic ɲámára *n.*

arm kwɛtᵃ *n.*
arm (upper) cwɛtᵃ *n.*; ɲorótónitᵃ *n.*
arm bone (upper) ɲorótónitíɔ́kᵃ *n.*
armored vehicle gasoa na ilɨ́r *n.*
armpit bàbà *n.*
armpit muscle gufééḿ *n.*
arms kúrúɓáa ni cɛmáᵋ *n.*
army kéà *n.*
aromatic tukukúɲón *v.*
arouse iɓúrétɔ̀n *v.*
aroused iɓurímétòn *v.*
aroused sexually kwídikwidós *v.*
arrange idɔ́bès *v.*; idɔ́bɛtés *v.*; inábɛs *v.*; inábɛsʉ̀kɔ̀tᵃ *v.*; inábɛtés *v.*; itíbès *v.*; itíbesúkɔ̀tᵃ *v.*
arrange engagement idimésá ɨ̀ùmàᵋ *v.*
arrange marriage idimésá buƙúⁱ *v.*
arrest wasitɛs *v.*; wasitésʉkɔt ᵃ *v.*; zɨ́kɛ́s *v.*; zɨ́kɛ́sʉkɔtᵃ *v.*
arrested zɨ́kɔ́s *v.*
arrive (here) itétɔ́n *v.*
arrive in kùtɔ̀n *v.*
arrogant itúrón *v.*; ɨwɔ́kɔ́n *v.*
arrogant person ɨwɔ́kɔ́nɨ̀àm *n.*
arrow ɲámal *n.*; ɲécɨpɨtá *n.*
arrow hole ɲámalɨ́ákᵃ *n.*
arrow rings ilɨɲɨréśɨ̀àwᵃ *n.*
arrow shaft ɲámalɨ́dàkwᵃ *n.*
arrowhead naƙaf *n.*
arrowhead base ɓólóèdᵃ *n.*
artery tsòritᵃ *n.*
arthritic rɔjɔ́dɔ̀n *v.*
arthritically rɔ̀jɔ *ideo.*
articulation (anatomical) ɲékel *n.*
artifacts kúrúɓáà nùù kɔ̀wᵃ *n.*
artificial idimɔtɔ́sá ròɓº *v.*

artillery gun komótsɛ̀ɛ̀bᵃ *n.*
artist idiméśɨàm *n.*
as dɨ́tá *prep.*
as a whole botedº *n.*
as well jɨ̀kᵋ *adv.*
ascend tóbìrìbìròn *v.*; totírón *v.*
Asclepiadaceae species lócén *n.*; xoúxoú *n.*
ash(es) káwᵃ *n.*
ashamed kweelémòn *v.*
ashamed (become) iɛ́ɓétɔ̀n *v.*; iryámétona ɲiléétsìkᵉ *v.*
ask esetɛ́s *v.*; esetésúkɔtᵃ *v.*; esetetés *v.*
ask for tɔɓéɲétɔ̀n *v.*; wáánɛtés *v.*
asleep (limbs) isálílòn *v.*
Asparagus flagellaris kòkòròtsᵃ *n.*
asphyxiate tuɓunɛ́s *v.*; tuɓunímétòn *v.*
ass ɔ̀z *n.*
ass (donkey) dìdᵃ *n.*
assault iríɓeés *v.*
assault sexually itikiesúkɔtᵃ *v.*
assay ikatɛs *v.*
assemble irɨ́réésʉkɔtᵃ *v.*; irɨ́rɛetésá asɨ́ *v.*; iryámíryámètòn *v.*; itóyéés *v.*; itóyéésa asɨ *v.*; itsúnétɔ̀n *v.*; iʉdes *v.*; iʉdetés *v.*
assembly kur *n.*; ɲatúkɔtᵃ *n.*; ɲékíikò *n.*; ɲémítìŋ *n.*
assess esetɛ́s *v.*; iniŋes *v.*
assist iŋaarés *v.*
assistant iŋaarésɨàm *n.*; karan *n.*
assisted iŋaarímétòn *v.*
assort isɨ́ɨ́lɛs *v.*
assortment ɲalɨ́ɲalɨ́ *n.*
astonish iɓálétɔ̀n *v.*; lilétón *v.*
astonishing iɓálɔ́n *v.*; toɓúlón *v.*
astringent ƙeriƙérón *v.*; tɛrɛrɛón *v.*
at dawn ɲaɓáítɔ *n.*
at daytime ódòº *n.*

at dusk xiŋatᵒ *n.*
at night mukú *n.*
at once ikéé kɔ̀n *n.*; ɲásáàtɔ̀ kɔ̀n *n.*
at one time kédìè kɔ̀n *n.*; kédò kɔ̀n *n.*
at the same time ɲásáàtɔ̀ kɔ̀n *n.*
Ateso language Ŋítésótôdᵃ *n.*
atheist nɛpɛ́ƙáàm *n.*
atmosphere didigwarí *n.*
atom kiɗoɗotsᵃ *n.*
atone for iɓutes *v.*
attach ɗɔtsɛtés *v.*; ramɛtés *v.*
attached ɗɔtsɔ́s *v.*
attack iríɓeés *v.*; toɓés *v.*; toɓésúƙot *v.*
attacker toɓésíàm *n.*
attain enés *v.*
attempt ɨkatɛs *v.*
attempt repeatedly ɨkatɨ́kátés *v.*
attend to ewanes *v.*; ewanetés *v.*
attend to (garden) kɔés *v.*
attendant (garden) kɔɛsɨ̀àm *n.*
attention span (have a short) dᵾmɛ́ɗɛ́mɔ̀n *v.*
attentive itsópóòn *v.*
attest to itsáɗénés *v.*
attire (fine) ɲɛ́nɨs *n.*
attract itᵾ́lɛ́ɛtés *v.*; tɔminɛs *v.*
attractive dòòn *v.*
attractive person iɓᵾretésíàm *n.*
attribute (personal) ɲɛpɨtɛa ámáᵉ *n.*
auction ókísèn *n.*
August Diwamúce *n.*; Iɗátáŋɛ́r *n.*; Lósᵾ́ɓán *n.*
aunt (his/her father's brother's wife) ŋwáátᵃ *n.*
aunt (his/her father's sister) tatatᵃ *n.*

aunt (his/her mother's brother's wife) momotícékᵃ *n.*
aunt (his/her mother's sister) tototᵃ *n.*
aunt (mother's brother's wife) momócèkᵃ *n.*
aunt (mother's sister) totó *n.*
aunt (my father's brother's wife) yáŋ *n.*
aunt (my father's sister) tátà *n.*
aunt (your father's brother's wife) ŋɔ́ *n.*
aunt (your father's sister) tátó *n.*
authority zeís *n.*
authority (have) topéɗésuƙotᵃ *v.*
authority (person) zeísíàm *n.*
automobile ɲómotoká *n.*
avail bɨrɛ́s *v.*
available tɔɔsɛ́tɔ̀n *v.*
avenge ɲaŋés *v.*; ɲaŋésúƙotᵃ *v.*
average ŋwaniŋwánón *v.*
avert eyes kurukúrón *v.*
avocado ɲóvakáɗò *n.*
avoid eye contact kurukúrón *v.*
avoid repeatedly iwitíwítòn *v.*
avoidant firifíránón *v.*; wíríwíránón *v.*
avow ikóŋón *v.*
await kɔés *v.*; kɔɛtés *v.*
awake gonés *v.*
awake for sex gòkòn *v.*
awaken gonésétòn *v.*
award tɔrɔ́bɛs *v.*; tɔ́rɔ́bɛsa na ɨ́lɔɛsɨ́ *n.*
awkward betsínón *v.*; iɓaɲíɓaŋɔ̀n *v.*; pɔsɔ́kɔ́mɔ̀n *v.*
awl ɓɔtsɔ́tᵃ *n.*
axe dzibér *n.*
axe (modern) naniɲiniŋ *n.*; naɲiniŋin *n.*
axe (traditional) kuɲukúdzibér *n.*
axe-blessing ceremony dzíbèrìkàmès *n.*
axehead (modern) naniɲiniŋ *n.*; naɲiniŋin *n.*

baa! bèrrr *ideo.*; mɛ́ɛ̀ɛ̀ *ideo.*; rèrrr *ideo.*
babble íbìrìbìròn *v.*; imátôdᵃ *n.*
baboon tsɔ́r *n.*
baboon (alpha male) òlìòtᵃ *n.*; tìmùòz *n.*
baboon (female) tsɔ́ráŋwa *n.*
baboon (lone male) òrègèm *n.*
baboon troop kwaár *n.*
baby ɗiakᵃ *n.*; im *n.*
baby carrier ɗoɗôbᵃ *n.*
baby hair imásíts'ᵃ *n.*
baby primate kíɗɔlɛ́ *n.*
baby sling ɗoɗôbᵃ *n.*
baby talk imátôdᵃ *n.*
baby wipe ɲíɨ́ɗɛ̀sɨ̀kwàz *n.*
back jɨ̀r *n.*; jɨ̀rɨ̀kᵋ *n.*; kanɛdᵃ *n.*; ɔ́zɛ̀dᵃ *n.*
back (lower) ɲékɨpɛtɛ́tᵃ *n.*
back (upper) kan *n.*
back of hand kwɛtákán *n.*
back of leg búbuiem *n.*
back out isɨ́rɨ́mɔ̀n *v.*; rajánón *v.*
back part jɨ́rêdᵃ *n.*
back side namɛ́ɗɔ́ɛ̀dᵃ *n.*
back then ódowicíká kì nùù kì *n.*; ódowicíkó nùkᵘ *n.*
back up ikutúkútés *v.*; ikutúkútòn *v.*
backbone gògòròjòɔ̀kᵃ *n.*
backside ɔ́zɛ̀dᵃ *n.*; ɔ̂z *n.*
backward jɨ̀rɨ̀kᵋ *n.*
backyard bɔlɔl *n.*
bad gaanón *v.*
bad (make) gaanítésuƙotᵃ *v.*
bad (of many) gaanaakón *v.*
bad eye (have a) ɗooɲómòn *v.*
badger ilúlúés *v.*
badly gàànìkᵉ *v.*

badly off tawanímétòn *v.*
badness gaánàs *n.*
baffled iɓíléròn *v.*; icɔ́ɲáimetona ikáᵉ *v.*
bag ɲéɓɛ́kᵃ *n.*; ofur *n.*
bag (burlap) ɲéguniyá *n.*
bag (cloth) ɲáwárófúr *n.*
bag (goat-leather) riéófúr *n.*
bag (leather) èwᵃ *n.*
bag (plastic) ɲápaalí *n.*
baggage botitín *n.*
bagworm mɔɗɔ́dᵃ *n.*
bait imɔɗɛtés *v.*
bait (bees) sɨsɨɓɛs *v.*
bake jʉés *v.*
baked jʉɔ́s *v.*
balance iríánitetés *v.*; itátéés *v.*
Balanites aegyptiaca tsʉm *n.*
Balanites pedicellaris ɓòŋ *n.*
bald ŋoléánètòn *v.*
bald on top palórómòn *v.*
balefire ɲágaaɗi *n.*
balk kwérɛɗɛ́ɗɔ́n *v.*; wasétɔn *v.*
ball ɲépɨɨrá *n.*
ball field ɲakwaanja *n.*
ball up imúnúkukúón *v.*
ball-shaped ɨlʉ́lʉ́ŋɔ́s *v.*
ball-shaped (make) ɨlʉ́lʉ́ŋés *v.*
ballot kàbàdᵃ *n.*
bamboo (mountain) ɲégiróyᵃ *n.*
banana ɲómototó *n.*
bandage ɨmakɛs *v.*
bandit lotáɗá *n.*
bandit (bush) ríjíkààm *n.*
banditry lotáɗánànès *n.*; ŋirúkóìnànès *n.*

bang into ɨbaɗɛ́s *v.*
bang into repeatedly ɨbaɗiés *v.*; tanaɲínáŋesuƙotª *v.*
bang on ɨɗatɛs *v.*
bang! pààɗòkᵒ *ideo.*
bank ɓɔ́kɔɲ *n.*; kaɓéléɓelánón *v.*; ɲáɓaŋkª *n.*
bank check kaúdzokabáɗª *n.*
banquet írésiŋƙáƙª *n.*
bantam puusúmòn *v.*
bao (game) ɲékilelés *n.*
baptism ɓatísimú *n.*
baptismal certificate ɓatísimúkabáɗª *n.*
baptismal name ɓatísimúêdª *n.*
baptize iɓátíseés *v.*
bar ɲáɓá *n.*; tegeles *v.*; toƙólésuƙotª *v.*
bar (wooden) naƙólítª *n.*
barb omén *n.*
barbeque itɔlɛs *v.*
barbeque spot naƙɨ́rɨ́kɛ̀tª *n.*
barbequed itɔlɔs *v.*
barbet (ground) loyeté *n.*
bare ilérón *v.*; lemúánètòn *v.*; leŋúrúmòn *v.*; sɨlɔ́jɔ́mòn *v.*; tuɗúsúmòn *v.*
bare (of a patch) patsólómòn *v.*
bare (of a tree) ságwàràmòn *v.*
bare foot gɔ̀rɨgɔr *n.*
bare teeth kwɨ́ɲɨ́kɔ̀ɲ *v.*
barefoot gɔ́rɨ́gɔrɨ̀kᵓ *n.*
barf fiyɛnɛ́tón *v.*; fiyɛ̀nɔ̀n *v.*
bark bɔɗɔ́kª *n.*; ígòmòn *v.*
bark at doƙofiés *v.*
bark soap jaobɔɗɔ́kª *n.*
Barleria acanthoides ɲólíƙàf *n.*
barm sɨ̀bª *n.*

barrack ɲáɓáràkɨ̀s *n.*; ɲeryaɲíɓór *n.*
barrage with words ɨdʉrésá tódàᵉ *v.*
barrel (gun) moróƙêdª *n.*
barrel (large) ɲépípa *n.*
barrel (plastic) ɲékakúŋgù *n.*
barrel-shaped ɗatáɲámòn *v.*
barren iƙólípánón *v.*; osorosánón *v.*
barren (animal or person) ɲoƙólípª *n.*
barren person òsòròs *n.*
barricade tegeles *v.*; toƙólésuƙotª *v.*
barrier (thorny) ɲéríwi *n.*
base dɛ *n.*; dɛɛdª *n.*; dziŋ *n.*
base of a boulder taɓádɛ̀ *n.*
base of a fence marɨɲɨ́dɛ̀ *n.*
base of a mountain kwarádɛ̀ *n.*
base of beehive tree kànàxàdɛ̀ *n.*
base of ridge tsɨɨr *n.*
base of sacred tree lɔ́ƙɔ́ŋʉ̀dɛ̀ *n.*
Basella alba lòɓòlìà *n.*
bash inipes *v.*
basin ɲáɓáf *n.*; ɲéɓésèn *n.*
basin (gourd) sèrèyª *n.*
basket (winnowing) zítª *n.*
bastard ŋabɔ́bòìm *n.*
bat lɔ́péɗɛpéɗª *n.*
bat species watégwà *n.*
bateleur oromén *n.*
bath féíàwª *n.*
bathe féítetés *v.*; féón *v.*
bathing féyª *n.*
bathing stone gwasa na féí *n.*
bathroom féíàwª *n.*
bathtub itúɓª *n.*
batis (chin-spot) iwótsígwà *n.*; nàŋʉ̀ràmɓɔ̀ *n.*
battalion ɲéɓatál *n.*
batter ipuƙúpúƙés *v.*

battery gúr *n.*; gwas *n.*; ɲéɓeterí *n.*
bawl xérón *v.*
be (make) mititɛs *v.*
be (not) beníón *v.*; bɛnɔ́ɔ́n *v.*
be (some size) ítón *v.*
be (somehow) ìròn *v.*
be (someone or something) mɨ̀tɔ̀n *v.*
be (somewhere) iòn *v.*
be about tábès *v.*
be alone iònà ɗòkᵘ *v.*; iona ɛɗá *v.*
be doing cèmɔ̀n *v.*
be en route iona muceékᵉ *v.*
be in trouble iona ɲitsanɨ́kᵋ *v.*
be neighbors narúétinós *v.*
be not yet sárón *v.*
be on the way iona muceékᵉ *v.*
be solitary iònà ɗòkᵘ *v.*; iona ɛɗá *v.*
be the only iònà ɗòkᵘ *v.*
be with iona ńdà *v.*
bead iɗɛrɛs *v.*
bead (big white) lokoitᵃ *n.*
beaded iɗɛrɔs *v.*
beaded vest ɲáɓol *n.*
beads ŋabitᵃ *n.*
beads (strung) rɔam *n.*
beadwork ŋabitᵃ *n.*
beak aka gwaáᵉ *n.*; gwáákᵃ *n.*
beam of light bás *n.*; sɨ́wᵃ *n.*
bean (red) màràŋgwà *n.*
bean variety mariɲɨmórídᵃ *n.*
bean(s) mòrɨdᵃ *n.*
bear nɛɛ́s *v.*; nɛɛsɨ́ƙɔtᵃ *v.*; taɗaŋes *v.*
bear a child ƙwaatetés *v.*
bear down toƙíróòn *v.*
bear legs first ijɨlɛtés *v.*

bear prematurely isɔɛtés *v.*
bear twins imɨ́ítɛtés *v.*
bear witness to itsáɗénés *v.*
beard ɲépénɛkᵃ *n.*; tèmɨ̀r *n.*
beast (mythical) ɲaŋu *n.*
beast(s) ínwᵃ *n.*
beat inɔmɛs *v.*
beat (defeat) kurés *v.*; kurésúƙotᵃ *v.*
beat (heart) ƙádiƙádòn *v.*
beat (outdo) ilɔɛs *v.*; ilɔɛtés *v.*
beat (pulsate) dìkwòn *v.*
beat (rhythm) irɛɛsa dikwáᵉ *v.*
beat (tired) ilɔ́étòn *v.*; ilɔ́yɔ́n *v.*; ziálámòn *v.*; zíkímétòn *v.*; ziláámòn *v.*
beat (win) irɛɛs *v.*; kɔritɛtés *v.*
beat back iɗáfésɨƙɔtᵃ *v.*; iɗáfésɨƙɔta asɨ *v.*
beat down íbutsés *v.*; iɗáfésɨƙɔtᵃ *v.*; ilɔ́itésɨƙɔtᵃ *v.*
beat each other tábunós *v.*
beat off ipɨtɛs *v.*
beat out íbutsés *v.*
beautiful dòòn *v.*
beautify daites *v.*; ɨgwɨgwɨjés *v.*; naƙwɨ́dɛtés *v.*
beautify oneself daitetésá asɨ *v.*
beauty daás *n.*
because ikótéré *subordconn.*; kóteré *subordconn.*
because (of) ɗúó *pro.*
because of ikótéré *prep.*; kóteré *prep.*
Becium species ɔ́jɨ́tɨ́nɨ́cɛmɛ́r *n.*
become (some size) ítónuƙotᵃ *v.*
become (somehow) ironuƙotᵃ *v.*
become (someone/something) mitɔnɨƙɔtᵃ *v.*
become like ƙámétòn *v.*; ƙámónuƙotᵃ *v.*
bed ɲékɨtaɗa *n.*

bed (animal) ɗípɔ̀ *n*.; nakús *n*.
bedbugs ŋítúmɨ̀kᵃ *n*.
beddings kúrúɓáa ni epwí *n*.
bedlam ɲɔ́ŋɔtsán *n*.
bee ts'ɨkᵃ *n*.
bee (carpenter) dʉrʉdʉr *n*.
bee (ground) mɔ́dᵃ *n*.
bee (stingless) lɔwɨɲ *n*.
bee (sweat) lɔwɨɲ *n*.
bee (tree) múkás *n*.
bee (worker) naaseɲaŋ *n*.
bee eater kesenígwà *n*.
bee larva sɨ̀dᵃ *n*.
bee larva chamber sɨ́dàhò *n*.
bee queen lókílóróŋ *n*.; okílóŋór *n*.
bee scout páupáwᵃ *n*.
bee summoning wówójᵒ *ideo.*
bee swarm (mobile) ts'ɨkábòtᵃ *n*.
bee-eater coorígwà *n*.
beehive kànàxà *n*.
beehive (ground bee) kùkùsèn *n*.
beehive (in rock) wàts'wᵃ *n*.
beehive (in tree) hàbᵃ *n*.
beehive cover makúl *n*.
beehive hut Icéhò *n*.
beehive shell ɗòl *n*.
beer mɛ̀s *n*.
beer (bottled) ɲéɓía *n*.
beer (bottom layer) ɔ́zɛ̀dà mɛ̀sɛ̀ *n*.
beer (breakfast) lɔkátɔ́rɔ̀tᵃ *n*.
beer (for birth ceremony) mɛsa kwaaté *n*.
beer (for naming ceremony) mɛsa édì *n*.
beer (for sale) ɲékɨ̀ráɓᵃ *n*.
beer (honey) sɨs *n*.; ts'ɔkam *n*.

beer (leftover) cueina mésɛ̀ *n*.; mɛsɛcue *n*.
beer (millet) ŋamarʉwáyᵃ *n*.; rébèmɛ̀s *n*.
beer (stale) ɗìɗèkwàtsᵃ *n*.
beer (wedding) ɲalakʉtsᵃ *n*.
beer barm cúrúkà mèsɛ̀ *n*.
beer dregs ɗʉká *n*.; dàjᵃ *n*.
beer dregs (in a pot) dómóɔ̀zà mɛ̀sɛ̀ *n*.
beer head ikeda mésɛ̀ *n*.
beer hunger mɛ̀sɛ̀ɲèkᵃ *n*.
beer porridge rùtᵃ *n*.
beer pot mɛ̀sɛ̀dòm *n*.
beer yeast cúrúkà mɛ̀sɛ̀ *n*.
beeswax (black) sɔs *n*.
beeswax (chewed) sàsàr *n*.
beetle (brown jewel) dùràtsᵃ *n*.
beetle (bruchid) dʉmúná mòrìɗòᵉ *n*.
beetle (burrowing ground) lɔ́ŋɨ́zɨŋɨ̀z *n*.
beetle (dung) dʉmún *n*.
beetle (water) dʉɗɛ́r *n*.
beetle larva (tiger) sikusába *n*.
before ɗàmùs *subordconn.*; ɗèmùs *subordconn.*; kwààkᵉ *n*.; wàx *n*.; wàxʉ̀ *n*.
before dawn ɲaɓáɨ́tᵒ *n*.
beg itsenes *v*.; wáán *v*.
beg from each other wááníɲɔ́s *v*.
beg relentlessly itseniés *v*.
beg relentlessly (begin to) itsenietés *v*.
beggar wáánààm *n*.
beggar (persistent) tikorotótᵃ *n*.
begging wáán *n*.
begin iséétòn *v*.; isóón *v*.; itsyákétòn *v*.; toɗóón *v*.
beginning point itsyákétònìàwᵃ *n*.
behave badly tarates *v*.; taratiés *v*.
behavior ɲɛpɨ̀tɛ *n*.
behind jɨ̀r *n*.; jɨ̀rɨ̀kᵉ *n*.; jɨ̀rʉ̀ *n*.; kanɛdᵃ *n*.; kànèdèkᵋ *n*.; kanɨtɨ́nʉ́ *n*.

behind bars (jailed) zɨkós *v.*
being ɦyekes *n.*
belabor idɔtsɛs *v.*
belch xèr *n.*; xerétɔ́n *v.*; xérón *v.*
belief ɲanúpɨ́tᵃ *n.*
believable tɔnʉpam *n.*
believe tɔnʉpɛs *v.*
believer tɔnʉpɛsɨ́ám *n.*
bellicose cɛmɨcɛmɔs *v.*
bellow ábʉ̀bʉ̀ƙɔ̀n *v.*; béúrètòn *v.*; ikɨ́lɔ́n *v.*; xérón *v.*
belly bùbù *n.*; gwàjᵃ *n.*
belly (of a pot) bakútsêdᵃ *n.*
belly button ƙɔ̀ɓᵃ *n.*
bellyache áts'ɛ́sà bùbùì *n.*
belongings kúrúɓâdᵃ *n.*; kúrúɓáicíkᵃ *n.*
below kɔ́ɔ́ kíjᵒ *n.*; nɔ́ɔ́ kíjᵒ *n.*
belowground ɗis *n.*
belt ɲámisípᵃ *n.*; ɲémisípᵃ *n.*
belt (beaded) ɲátóè *n.*
bemoan ƙɔ̀ɗɔ̀n *v.*; topóɗón *v.*
bench ɲɛ́ɓɛ́ɲc *n.*; ɲófóm *n.*
bend itúkúɗètòn *v.*; itúkúɗòn *v.*; nɔkɨnɔ́ƙɔ́n *v.*; tɔɓɨlɛs *v.*; tukuɗes *v.*
bend over dʉ́gʉ̀mètòn *v.*; rétítésúƙotᵃ *v.*
bend sideways kwɛ́ɗɔ̀n *v.*
bendily lɛts'ᵋ *ideo.*; nàƙwᵃ *ideo.*; nàᵘ *ideo.*; nɔ̀kᵓ *ideo.*
bendy lɛts'édɔ̀n *v.*; naƙwádòn *v.*; naúdòn *v.*; nɔkɔ́dɔ̀n *v.*
benefit ikɛ́ɨtɛtɛs *v.*
bent dɔ́gɔ̀lɔ̀mɔ̀n *v.*; tukúɗón *v.*
bent back tɛ́zɛ̀ɗɔ̀n *v.*
bent forward koɗósón *v.*
bent over dʉ́gʉ̀mɔ̀n *v.*; ƙúzùmòn *v.*; rétón *v.*; tɔɓɨlɛsa asɨ *v.*

berate dɔxɛ́s *v.*; dɔxɛ́súƙotᵃ *v.*
Berchemia discolor ɗewen *n.*
beseech iƙenes *v.*
beside iɓákɔ̀n *v.*; ŋabérᵒ *n.*
beside (move) iɓákɔ́nʉƙotᵃ *v.*
besmear iɲóɲóés *v.*
bestialist tirésíama ɨ́nóᵉ *n.*
betray tolúétɔ̀n *v.*; tolúónuƙotᵃ *v.*
betray each other tolúúnós *v.*
betrayer ŋɨtúrumúám *n.*; tolúónɨ̀àm *n.*
better maraɲités *v.*; maraɲítésuƙotᵃ *v.*
better (get) doonuƙotᵃ *v.*; iɲáléètòn *v.*; maráŋónuƙotᵃ *v.*; toiónuƙotᵃ *v.*; xɔ́dɔnʉƙotᵃ *v.*
better (make a bit) ɓarɨɓárɔ́nʉƙotᵃ *v.*
better slightly ŋwanɨ́ŋwánɨtɛ́s *v.*
between sɨsikákᵉ *n.*
beverage wetam *n.*
bewail topóɗón *v.*
beware tɔtsɔ́ɔ́n *v.*
bewildered tɔmɛrɨ́mɛ́rɔ̀n *v.*
bewitch ipeɗes *v.*; sʉɓɛ́s *v.*
bewitch by pointing ɗóɗiés *v.*
bewitch by the evil eye idɛmɛs *v.*
bewitcher ipèɗààm *n.*; sʉɓɛ́sɨ̀àm *n.*
bhang ɲábaŋgí *n.*
Bible Ɲáɓáɨɓɔ̀l *n.*
bicep cwɛtééḿ *n.*
bicep/tricep ɲorótónitíém *n.*
bicker iƙúmúnós *v.*; iɲʉ́ɲʉ́rɔ̀n *v.*; ŋʉ́zʉmánón *v.*
bicycle ɲamɨɨli *n.*
biddy gwaŋwa *n.*
biddy (chick) ɲɔ́kɔkɔróím *n.*
Bidens pilosa tʉ̀fɛ̀rɛ̀ƙᵃ *n.*
big zòòn *v.*

big (become) ítónà dìdìkᵉ v.
big (of many) zeikaakón v.
big day ódowa ná zè n.
big man ámáze n.; ámázeám n.
big people roɓazeikᵃ n.
big person ámáze n.
bigger (become) iwánétòn v.; zoonukotᵃ v.
bigger (make a bit) ɓariɓarítésukɔt ᵃ v.
bigger (make) iwanetés v.; zeites v.; zeitésukotᵃ v.
bigness zeís n.
bike ɲamɨɨli n.
bile bɨɗᵃ n.
bill gwáákᵃ n.; kaúdzokabáɗᵃ n.
bill (monetary) ɲónótᵃ n.
billfold ɲópóc n.
billion ɗòlà kòn n.; ɲéɓìlìon n.
billow ipúróòn v.
billow up ipúréètòn v.
biltong ŋátɔɔsa n.
bind imakɛs v.; ɨriɗɛtés v.; zíkés v.
bind the stomach iriɗɛsá bùbùàᵉ v.
bind up zíkésukɔtᵃ v.; zikɛtés v.
bine iriɗɛs v.
binge iwótsóòn v.
binoculars ɲáɓaraɓɨn n.
bird gwa n.
bird (domestic) gwaa na awáᵉ n.
bird (female) gwaŋwa n.
bird (male) gwácúrúkᵃ n.
bird (nocturnal) mukúágwà n.
bird species àdènès n.; bíro n.; cicídè n.; ɗiitᵃ n.; dàbɨ̀jᵃ n.; dòɗɨdòɗɨgwà n.; fetígwà n.; firits'ár n.; itsól n.; jɨlɨfifɨ n.; kɨlòlòɓᵃ n.; kiyér n.; kólór n.; lorokonígwà n.; lotiwúótᵃ n.; napóɗè n.; ɲíkwaamwíyá n.; ɲókɔɗɔɔŋór n.; ɔ̀fàgwà n.; óƙírotᵃ n.; ɔríyɔ́ n.; súƙúsuƙágwa n.; tsóɗitsóno n.

bird tail tsúɓᵃ n.
bird-scarer kɔɛsɨàm n.
birdhouse gwáho n.
birth ƙwaátᵃ n.
birth relation ɦyeínósá na ƙóɓàᵋ v.
birthing complications ƙwaata ná gààn n.
biscuit (sweet) ɲéɓisikótᵃ n.
bisect ɨwáwáɗés v.; pakés v.
bishop ɲépiskóópì n.
bishop bird (black-winged red) tsól n.
bishop bird (red/yellow) loɓúrútùtᵃ n.
bitch ŋókíŋwa n.
bite áts'ɛs v.; ƙɨdzès v.
bite each other ƙɨdzinós v.
bite hard áts'ésukɔtᵃ v.
bite repeatedly ƙɨdzatiés v.
bitter fàɗon v.
bitter (but edible) taɗaɗáɲón v.
bitter (make) faɗites v.
bitter (slightly) ɓakɨɓákón v.
bitter thing kèrèmìdzᵃ n.
bivouac napérítᵃ n.; ɲákamɓí n.
blabber ilemílémòn v.
blabbermouth gáʒadiŋwa n.
black buɗámón v.
black (of many) buɗamaakón v.
black (very) cucᵘ ideo.; múɗèr ideo.; tíkⁱ ideo.
Black Jack tùfèrèƙᵃ n.
black person buɗámóniàm n.
black with white cheeks kɨɗapánètòn v.
black with white rump kedíánètòn v.
black-and-white kábìlànètòn v.

294

blackboard ɲáɓáo *n.*
blacken kɔrɛtés *v.*; kɔritɛtés *v.*; tɛwɛrɛs *v.*
blackened kɔrétɔ́n *v.*
blackmail iɲaalés *v.*
blacksmith ìtyàkààm *n.*
bladder xàr *n.*
bladder area hejú *n.*
blade ɗàwᵃ *n.*
blade (fan) suguráɗáwᵃ *n.*
blade (propeller) suguráɗáwᵃ *n.*
blame each other falsely tapáɨnɔ́s *v.*
blame falsely tapɛɛs *v.*
bland cucuéón *v.*; ɗèƙwɔ̀n *v.*; jɔ̀lɔ̀n *v.*; mujálámòn *v.*
blanket gubés *v.*; ɲéɓurankítᵃ *n.*
blanket (cotton) ɲákamariɗúkᵃ *n.*
blanket (light) tɨ́rɨ̀kà *n.*
blanket (Maasai style) lorwaneta *n.*
blanket over gubésúƙotᵃ *v.*
blaspheme éɓetiés *v.*
blather íɓìrìbìròn *v.*
blaze a trail ipútésuƙɔta muceé *v.*
bleb ɔ́jáìm *n.*
bleed tɔyɔ́ɔ́n *v.*
bleed for drinking tsɔrés *v.*
bleed for healing kɔ́és *v.*
bleed from nose ƙòlòn *v.*
blend iɗyates *v.*; iɲales *v.*; ìtsɔɓɨ́tsɔ́ɓés *v.*; itsulútsúlés *v.*
blend (grains) ikáɗóés *v.*
blended ìtsɔɓɨ́tsɔ́ɓɔ̀n *v.*; ìtsɔɓɨ́tsɔ́ɓɔ́s *v.*
bless ìmwaɨmwéés *v.*; tatiés *v.*
blessed tatiós *v.*
blesser tatiesíám *n.*
blind múɗúkánón *v.*

blink ɨ̀ɓèɗɨ̀bèɗɔ̀n *v.*; irwapírwápòn *v.*
blister buɓuxánónuƙotᵃ *v.*; ileɓíléɓòn *v.*; ɔ́jáìm *n.*
blistered buɓuxánón *v.*
bllgh bllgh (boiling) ƙwèjᵋ *ideo.*
bloated teɓúsúmòn *v.*
bloated from overeating xɛxánón *v.*
block ɗinés *v.*; iɓatɛs *v.*; iƙiɛs *v.*; ɲéɓulókᵃ *n.*; tegeles *v.*; tɨts'ɛ́s *v.*
block off toƙólésuƙotᵃ *v.*
block repeatedly iɓatíɓátés *v.*
block the road tegelesa ɲerukuɗeé *v.*
block up tɨts'ɛ́súƙotᵃ *v.*; tɨts'ímétòn *v.*
blocked ɗinɔ́s *v.*; tɨts'ɔ́s *v.*
blockheaded lɛrédɔ̀n *v.*
blood sè *n.*
blood (coagulated) ŋazul *n.*
blood covenant iɓólínósa na séàᵉ *v.*
blood herb seacɛmér *n.*
blood red tsòn *ideo.*
blood relation fiyeínósá na séàᵉ *v.*
blood vessel seamucé *n.*; tsɔ̀rìtᵃ *n.*
bloodthirsty person sèààm *n.*
bloom iɔ́kɔ́n *v.*
blossom iɔ́kɔ́n *v.*; ŋatur *n.*
blow fútés *v.*; fútón *v.*
blow (a projectile) ɗétés *v.*
blow (of breeze) ipiipíòn *v.*
blow (waste) eletiésuƙotᵃ *v.*; iɲekes *v.*; iɲékésuƙotᵃ *v.*; iɲekíɲékés *v.*
blow away fútésuƙotᵃ *v.*
blow nose rútés *v.*
blow off fútésuƙotᵃ *v.*
blow on gently borotsiés *v.*
blow up taɲéɔ́n *v.*; xuanón *v.*; xuxuanitetés *v.*; xuxuanón *v.*
blow up (explode) toɗúón *v.*
blubber ceím *n.*

blue-gray bósánòn *v.*; kábusubusánón *v.*
blunder (verbally) eletiesá mɛná⁼ *v.*
blunt duŋúlúmòn *v.*; líídòn *v.*; tufádòn *v.*
bluntly lì *ideo.*; tùf *ideo.*
blurt news eletiesá mɛná⁼ *v.*
blush ɓʉnʉ́mɔ́nà sèàᵉ *v.*
bluster ígòmòn *v.*
board ɲáɓao *n.*; otsés *v.*
boast ígòmòn *v.*; ɨwʉ́lón *v.*
boasting itúrónìtòdᵃ *n.*
boat itúɓᵃ *n.*
bob iupúúpòn *v.*
bodiliness nébùnànès *n.*
body nêbᵃ *n.*
body hair nébùsìts'ᵃ *n.*
body of water cúénêbᵃ *n.*
body part ɲekiner *n.*
body snatcher tukutesíáma ts'óóniicé *n.*
boggily fɔts'ᵓ *ideo.*
boggy fɔts'ɔ́dɔ̀n *v.*
bogus láŋ *n.*
boil féés *v.*; ígulajitetés *v.*; ígùlàjòn *v.*; itsúrítetés *v.*; itsúrón *v.*; ƙwɛɟédòn *v.*; ƙwɛɟɨ́ƙwéjòn *v.*; tún *n.*; wádòn *v.*
boil (large) ɲáɓús *n.*
boiling ƙwɛɟédòn *v.*; ƙwɛɟɨ́ƙwéjòn *v.*
boing! tùdᵘ *ideo.*
Bokora person mɔkɔrɔ́ám *n.*; Ŋíɓɔ́kɔráám *n.*
bolt carrier bùbùàƙwᵃ *n.*
boma ɓór *n.*
bombard ɨdʉrés *v.*
bombard with spears bɛrés *v.*
bombard with words ɨdʉrésá tódàᵉ *v.*
bombinate ilólués *v.*
bond nɔtsɔ́mɔ́n *v.*

bone ɔkᵃ *n.*
bone (cancellous) ɲéɲam *n.*
bone (costal) ŋabériɔ̀kᵃ *n.*
bone (inner ear) bòsìɔ̀kᵃ *n.*
bone (nasal) aƙatíɔ́kᵃ *n.*
bone (occipital) nàmèɗɔ̀ *n.*
bone (pubic) didisíɔ́kᵃ *n.*
bone (shoulder) sawatɔ́ɔ́kᵃ *n.*
bone (spongy) ɲéɲam *n.*
bone (supraorbital) ekúɔ́kᵃ *n.*
bone (temporal) bòsìɔ̀kᵃ *n.*
bone (zygomatic) aƙáƙúm *n.*
bone below sternum toroɓɔ́ɔ́kᵃ *n.*
bone marrow hègᵃ *n.*
boneheaded lɛrɛ́dɔ̀n *v.*
bonfire ɲágaaɗi *n.*
bony gɔ́gɔ̀rɔ̀mɔ̀n *v.*; iróƙóòn *v.*; itóƙóƙòòn *v.*; kwédekwedánón *v.*
book ɲáɓúkᵃ *n.*
book of prayers ɲáɓúka wáánàᵉ *n.*
boom ɗukuɗúkón *v.*
boom (voice) ɔ́bès *v.*
boom! pès *ideo.*
booster tower ɲébusitá *n.*
boot ɲáɓutús *n.*
border cíkóroyᵃ *n.*
bore ilɔ́étɔ̀n *v.*; ɨpɨrɨ́pɨ́rés *v.*; pulutiés *v.*
bored bɔ́rɔ́n *v.*; ilɔ́yɔ́n *v.*
bored (become) bɔrétɔ́n *v.*
bored (drilled) tsàpòn *v.*
borehole ɲatsʉʉma *n.*
borehole casing ɲatsʉʉmánêbᵃ *n.*
borehole footing ɲatsʉʉmádè *n.*
borehole handle ɲatsʉʉmáƙwétᵃ *n.*
borehole pipe ɲatsʉʉmáárɨ *n.*
borehole shaft ɲatsʉʉmáhò *n.*
borehole water ɲatsʉʉmácúé *n.*

boring

boring itópénòn *v.*; jɔ̀lɔ̀n *v.*
born again (religiously) hoɗetésá asɨ́ *v.*
born handless duŋúlúmòn *v.*
borrow iɗenes *v.*; iɗenetés *v.*; wáánɛtɛ́s *v.*
borrow from each other wáánɨ́nɔ́s *v.*
Boscia angustifolia ɓàjᵃ *n.*
Boscia coriacea gɛbɛjᵃ *n.*
Boscia salicifolia ròr *n.*
boss ámáze *n.*; ámázeám *n.*; ámázeáma terégì *n.*
botch hamʉjés *v.*
both gáí *quant.*
bothersome fifòn *v.*; ɨtsánánòn *v.*
bottle (glass) ɲetsúpa *n.*
bottle (plastic) ɲɛrɔɓɨrɔ́ɓᵃ *n.*
bottlecap game ŋ́karakocóyᵃ *n.*
bottom ɔ́zɛ̀dᵃ *n.*; ɔ̀z *n.*
bottom layer of beer ɔ́zɛ̀dà mɛ̀sɛ̀ *n.*
bottom of pot/pan dómóɔ̀z *n.*
bottomless xakútsúmòn *v.*
boubou (slate-colored) kukuɗetsᵃ *n.*
bough dakúkwɛ́tᵃ *n.*
bouillon seekwᵃ *n.*
boulder taɓᵃ *n.*
boulder (flat) gɨzá *n.*; lolataɓᵃ *n.*
boulder base taɓádɛ̀ *n.*
bounce íbotitésʉ́kotᵃ *v.*; íbotitetés *v.*; íbòtòn *v.*
bounce along ɨɲɔ́pɨ́sɔ̀ɔ̀n *v.*
bounce off iɗótón *v.*
bouncily tùf *ideo.*; tùs *ideo.*
bouncy tufádòn *v.*; tusúdòn *v.*
bound iɗótón *v.*; ɨ́gɔ̀rɔ̀bɔ̀n *v.*; ɨrɨɗɔs *v.*; zɨ́kɔ́s *v.*
bound up together zɨ́kɨ́zɨkánón *v.*

brand

boundaries (having) cíkóróìkànànès *n.*
boundary cíkóroyᵃ *n.*
boundary (garden) ɲókorimítᵃ *n.*
boundedness cíkóróìkànànès *n.*
bow (head) turúnétòn *v.*; turúnón *v.*
bow (weapon) ɲakawᵃ *n.*
bowed dɔ́gɔ̀lɔ̀mɔ̀n *v.*
bowed over rétón *v.*
bowel bùbùàƙwᵃ *n.*
bowl (gourd) kàɓàɲ *n.*
bowl (of child) imáƙɔ́fɔ *n.*
bowl-shaped saƙánámòn *v.*; tsuƙúlúmòn *v.*
box ɲásaɗukú *n.*; tanaŋes *v.*
box in rʉ́ɛ́s *v.*
boy ɲámal *n.*; sore *n.*
boy (baby) ɓɨs *n.*
boy (little) soréím *n.*
boy (teenage) ɲɨ́sɔ́rɔkɔ́ám *n.*
boys (teenage) ɲɨ́sɔ́rɔkᵃ *n.*; pànèès *n.*
bozo ɲɛ́ɛ́s *n.*
bra ɲákɨlááƙᵃ *n.*
brace íbunutsés *v.*; ɨrʉ́rʉ́ɓɛ́s *v.*; ƙaƙates *n.*
bracelet (coiled) ɲɛƙɨ́lɔɗa *n.*
bracelet (gold) ɲámaritóítᵃ *n.*
bracelet (white leather) ɲácáɗa *n.*
brag ígòmòn *v.*; ɨwʉ́lón *v.*
bragging itúrónìtòdᵃ *n.*
braid bɛrés *v.*; sikwés *v.*
braid up sikwetés *v.*
brain ɗam *n.*
brake pedal titiritésíàwᵃ *n.*
branch dakúkwɛ́tᵃ *n.*; kwɛtᵃ *n.*; taŋatsárón *v.*; tɛlɛ́tsón *v.*; toɲélón *v.*
branch pile (dry) ràm *n.*
brand imátsárés *v.*; itsʉŋes *v.*; ɲámátsar *n.*

brassiere ɲákɨláƙᵃ *n.*
brave itítíɲòn *v.*
bray werétsón *v.*
bread tɔbɔŋ *n.*
bread (flat) ɲécapatí *n.*
break badonuƙotᵃ *v.*; cɛɛ́s *v.*; cɛɛ́súƙɔtᵃ *v.*; ɗɛsɛ́mɔ́n *v.*; ɗusés *v.*; ɗusúmón *v.*; ɗusutes *v.*; iƙéŋéɗɛ́s *v.*; ŋʉrés *v.*; ŋʉrúmón *v.*; tɔŋɛɗɛs *v.*
break (make) badítésuƙotᵃ *v.*
break (of day) ɓelémón *v.*
break apart ɗɛsɛ́ɗɛ́sánón *v.*; ijʉƙújʉ́ƙɛ́s *v.*
break away tatsáɗón *v.*; tɔpéɔ́n *v.*
break away (and come) tɔpéɛ́tɔ̀n *v.*
break away (and go) tɔpéɔnʉƙɔtᵃ *v.*
break due to weight xuƙúmétòn *v.*
break into itúwéés *v.*
break into pieces ɓilíɓílɛ́s *v.*; iɓɛsíɓɛsɛ́s *v.*; itɛítéés *v.*; ŋilíŋílánón *v.*
break into song tofóróƙétòn *v.*
break new ground taɗates *v.*; túburés *v.*
break off ɗusésúƙotᵃ *v.*; iɓɛƙíɓéƙés *v.*; pɛsɛlɛs *v.*; pɛsɛ́métɔ̀n *v.*; pokés *v.*; poketés *v.*; pokómón *v.*; wakés *v.*; wɛts'ɛ́mɔ́n *v.*; wɛts'ɛ́s *v.*; wɛts'ɛtɛ́s *v.*
break off in groups ŋilíŋílánón *v.*; pókíetésá así́ɛ kédìè kɔ̀n *v.*
break off in pieces iwɛts'ɨwɛ́ts'ɛ́s *v.*; tomuɲes *v.*; wakatiés *v.*; wakáwákatés *v.*; wets'etiés *v.*
break out (of skin) iɲárúrètòn *v.*; morétón *v.*
break the law ŋʉrésá ɨtsɨ̀kàᵋ *v.*
break up ijʉƙújʉ́ƙɛ́s *v.*; ɨwɛ́ɛ́lɛ́s *v.*; tɔpwaɲɨ́pwáɲés *v.*
break up (a group) toɓwaŋes *v.*
break wind fenétón *v.*

breakable ɛɔmɔ́dɔ̀n *v.*; ŋʉɓúdɔ̀n *v.*; pokódòn *v.*; tɛɛmémɔ̀n *v.*; wɛts'édɔ̀n *v.*
breakably ɛ̀ɔm *ideo.*; ŋʉ̀ɓʉ *ideo.*; pòk° *ideo.*; wèts'ᵋ *ideo.*
breakage point ɗusutesíáwᵃ *n.*
breaker ŋʉrésɨ́am *n.*
breakfast ŋƙáƙá na baratsóᵉ *n.*
breast îdwᵃ *n.*
breast (area) bakutsᵃ *n.*
breast (cut of meat) làf *n.*
breast areola ídoeɗᵃ *n.*
breast milk ámàìdwᵃ *n.*
breast twitch lɔkɨsɨ́ná *n.*
breastbone gɔgɔm *n.*; toroɓᵃ *n.*
breastbone (of a chicken) bɨbijᵃ *n.*
breastfeed naƙwɛ́s *v.*; naƙwɛ́súƙɔtᵃ *v.*; naƙwɨtɛs *v.*
breastmilk (have) cèrɔ̀n *v.*
breath sʉ̀pᵃ *n.*
breathe ɨɛ́ŋɔ́n *v.*; súpɔ́n *v.*
breathe fitfully ɗɨ́ɗɨ́tɔ̀n *v.*
breathe heavily fúútòn *v.*
breathe in sʉpétɔ́n *v.*
breathe out súpɔ́nʉƙɔtᵃ *v.*
breeze sugur *n.*
brew otés *v.*; tsapés *v.*; waatés *v.*
brew (mead) ts'ɔƙɛ́s *v.*
brew beer tsapésá mèsè *v.*; waatésá mèsè *v.*
brewski mès *n.*
bribe ilʉŋúlʉ́ŋɛ́s *v.*
brick ɲéɓulókᵃ *n.*
bride bɔƙátɨn *n.*
bride (return a) xɛɛsúƙɔtᵃ *v.*
bridegroom bɔƙátɨ́nɨ̀èàkwᵃ *n.*
brideprice buƙᵃ *n.*
brideprice (extract) buƙitetés *v.*

brideprice gift bukotam *n.*
brideprice payer bukúám *n.*
bridge àrònìàwᵃ *n.*; ɲɔdɔrɔcá *n.*; tèwèr *n.*
bridge of nose sarɨsar *n.*
brigandry ŋirúkóìnànès *n.*
bright gwɛɲémɔ́n *v.*; ɨméɗɔ́n *v.*
bright (of sky) tatsɔ́ɔ́n *v.*
brilliant gwɛɲémɔ́n *v.*; ɨméɗɔ́n *v.*
bring detés *v.*; ɨakɛtés *v.*; ɨjʉkɛtés *v.*
bring all of ɨsʉɲɛtés *v.*
bring alongside ɨnapɛtés *v.*; napɛtés *v.*
bring back rajetés *v.*
bring beside ɨnapɛtés *v.*; napɛtés *v.*
bring down ruɓutetés *v.*
bring matters to a close kɔkɛtésá mɛnáᵋ *v.*
bring out pulutetés *v.*
bring slowly ɨɛmɛtés *v.*
bring to a boil ɨtsúrítetés *v.*
bring together ɨtóyéés *v.*
bring up ɨlímítés *v.*; tasɛɛs *v.*
bristling bʉlʉbʉlɔs *v.*
bristly bʉlʉbʉlɔs *v.*
British colonial government gɛrɛ́sà *n.*
brittle bɔɲɔ́dɔ̀n *v.*; ɛɔmɔ́dɔ̀n *v.*; ɨwɛléwélánón *v.*; ŋʉɓʉ́dɔ̀n *v.*; pɛsɛ́pɛ́sánón *v.*; pokódɔ̀n *v.*; wɛts'édɔ̀n *v.*
brittlely bɔɲ *ideo.*; ɛ̀ɔm *ideo.*; ŋʉ̀ɓʉ *ideo.*; pòkᵒ *ideo.*; wɛ̀ts'ᵋ *ideo.*
broad laɲɨrímɔ̀n *v.*; laɲɨrón *v.*; zɔ̀ɔ̀n *v.*
broad (of many) zeɨkaakón *v.*
broad-bladed fakádɔ̀n *v.*
broad-bladedly fàkᵃ *ideo.*
broadcast tɛwɛɛs *v.*
broaden zoonukotᵃ *v.*

broke (go) ŋʉrʉ́mɔ́n *v.*
broken bàdɔ̀n *v.*; ŋʉrɔ́s *v.*
broken (get) ŋʉrʉ́mɔ́n *v.*
broken beyond repair tɛ̀s *ideo.*
broken out (of skin) ɨɲárúrɔ̀n *v.*; katúrúturánón *v.*
broken up ŋʉrʉ́ŋʉ́ránón *v.*
brood kúkɨ́n *n.*; siɲírón *v.*
broom jan *n.*; jɛn *n.*
broomgrass jan *n.*; jɛn *n.*
broth ɲóɓɔ́ka *n.*; seekwᵃ *n.*
brother (his/her/its) leatᵃ *n.*
brother (my) ɛdɛ́ *n.*
brother (your) léó *n.*
brother-in-law (brother's wife's brother) ugwam *n.*
brother-in-law (her husband's brother) ntsínámúí *n.*
brother-in-law (his brother's wife's brother) ntsúgwám *n.*
brother-in-law (his wife's brother) ntsúgwám *n.*
brother-in-law (his/her child's spouse's father) ntsíɲótᵃ *n.*
brother-in-law (his/her sister's husband's brother) ntsúgwám *n.*
brother-in-law (husband's brother) námúí *n.*
brother-in-law (my brother's wife's brother) ɲcugwám *n.*
brother-in-law (my husband's brother) ɲcinamúí *n.*
brother-in-law (my sister's husband) ɲcugwám *n.*
brother-in-law (my wife's brother) ɲcugwám *n.*
brother-in-law (sister's husband's brother) ugwam *n.*

brother-in-law (sister's husband) ntsúgwám *n.*; ugwam *n.*

brother-in-law (wife's brother) ugwam *n.*

brother-in-law (your brother's wife's brother) bugwám *n.*

brother-in-law (your child's spouse's father) biɲót[a] *n.*

brother-in-law (your husband's brother) binamúí *n.*

brother-in-law (your sister's husband's brother) bugwám *n.*

brother-in-law (your sister's husband) bugwám *n.*

brother-in-law (your wife's brother) bugwám *n.*

brotherhood leatínánès *n.*

brotherliness leatínánès *n.*

brow bone ekúɔ́k[a] *n.*

brown muƙíánètòn *v.*; ɔŋɔ́ránètòn *v.*

brown (dark) kipɨ́ránètòn *v.*; ts'aráfón *v.*

brown-skinned ɗiwòn *v.*

brown-skinned person ɗiwòniàm *n.*

bruise ƙwár *n.*; rùròn *v.*

brush iƙwɛrɛs *v.*; séɓés *v.*; súƙɨ́tés *v.*; sɨ́útés *v.*; tsekís *n.*; tsekísiàƙw[a] *n.*

brush (scrub) ɲecaaƙo *n.*

brush (thick) môg[a] *n.*

brush aside ipalɨ́pálés *v.*

brush away séɓésuƙot[a] *v.*

brush off itútúés *v.*; itútúésuƙot[a] *v.*; séɓésuƙot[a] *v.*

brush out iƙwérésɨƙɔt[a] *v.*

brushed iƙwɛrɔs *v.*

brutal isɨlɨ́ánón *v.*

brute(s) ínw[a] *n.*

bubble ígùlàjòn *v.*

bubble (make) ígulajitetés *v.*

buck (dollar) ɲɔɗɔ́la *n.*

buck-toothed iɲísɨ́mɔ̀n *v.*

bucket ɲáɓákèt[a] *n.*; ɲéɓákèt[a] *n.*

bucket (metal) ɲépeelí *n.*

bud tún *n.*

buffalo gàsàr *n.*

buffalo bull eûz *n.*

buffalo calf gàsàràìm *n.*

buffalo cow gasaraŋwa *n.*

buffalo thorn tree tɨ́làŋ *n.*

bug ilúlúés *v.*; ƙɨts'[a] *n.*

bug-eyed ɓɛlɛ́rɛ́mɔ̀n *v.*

build bɛrés *v.*; toyeetés *v.*

build on the ground ikamɛtés *v.*

build up (of a termite mound) tabúón *v.*

builder bɛrɛ́sɨ̀àm *n.*; ɲífunɗíàm *n.*

building (modern) ɲeryaɲíhò *n.*

bulbous bulúƙúmòn *v.*; lɔrɔ́dɔ̀n *v.*

bulbously lɔ̀r *ideo.*

bulbul (common) òtsìɓìl *n.*; tsìɓìl *n.*

bulge tibɨ́étòn *v.*

bulging bulúƙúmòn *v.*; lɔrɔ́dɔ̀n *v.*; tsɨrɨ́ɗɨ́mɔ̀n *v.*; tibɨ́ón *v.*

bulgingly lɔ̀r *ideo.*

bulkily bɛ̀f *ideo.*

bulky ɓutúrúmòn *v.*; bɛfɨ́dɔ̀n *v.*; bɛfɨ́ƙɨ́mɔ̀n *v.*

bull cúrúk[a] *n.*

bulldoze towutses *v.*

bulldozer towútsóniàm *n.*

bullet bɨbɨn *n.*; eɗeɗ[a] *n.*; ɲámal *n.*

bullet hole ɲámalɨ́ák[a] *n.*

bullet wound bɨbɨnɔ́ɔ́j[a] *n.*

bullrush isɨ̀k[a] *n.*

bum lɛŋés *v.*; lɛŋésɨ̀àm *n.*; ɲakárámɨt[a] *n.*

bump

bump íbaɗɛ́s v.; íɓaɲɛs v.; iɛ́bès v.; iɛ́bɛtɛ́s v.; toyeres v.
bump (skin) síts'ádè n.
bump off (kill) iɗɛɛs v.; iɗɛ́ɛ́sʉk̗ɔtᵃ v.
bump repeatedly íbaɗiɛ́s v.
bumpy ƙumúƙúmánón v.
bumpy (of skin) katúrúturánón v.
bunch ɓòtòŋ n.; tutukesíáwᵃ n.; zɨkam n.
bunch (of bees) ɲénéne n.
bunch up tutukɛtɛ́s v.
bunched up tutukánón v.
bundle iɗɨlɛs v.; méyᵃ n.; zɨkam n.
bundle (of crops) ɲénéne n.
bungle hamʉjɛ́s v.
bunk iɓááŋàsɨtòdᵃ n.
bunny tulú n.
buoy ilélébètòn v.
burble ábʉ̀bʉ̀k̗ɔ̀n v.; ábʉ̀bʉ̀k̗ɔ̀n v.
burden botᵃ n.; inʉɛs v.; isites v.
burdensome ìsòn v.
burglar dzúám n.
burgle dzuesɛ́s v.; dzuesetɛ́s v.
buried tʉnʉkɔs v.
burlgary dzú n.
burn itsʉɲɛs v.; kʉpɛ́s v.; kʉpɛ́súk̗ɔtᵃ v.; ts'aɗíɔ́jᵃ n.
burn (blistered) ɲéleɓuléɓu n.
burn (of eyes) ŋaɓɨŋáɓɔ́n v.; ŋàɓɔ̀n v.
burn (of pain) ɓɛiɓɛ́ɔ́n v.
burn a little irɔɗɨ́rɔ́ɗɛ́s v.
burn around iɗɛiɗɛ́ɛ́s v.
burn off (land) irórobɛs v.
burn poorly ikáwɨ́lɔ̀n v.
burn to ashes wuɗetón v.
burn up itsúŋɛ́sʉk̗ɔtᵃ v.

butt

burnt to ashes wùɗòn v.; xawɨ́ɨ́ts'ⁱ ideo.
burp xèr n.; xerétón v.; xérón v.
burrow akᵃ n.
burst ɓilímón v.; toɗúón v.
bury búdès v.; búdesuk̗otᵃ v.; muɗɛ́s v.; tʉnʉkɛs v.
bury (make) tʉnʉkitɛtɛ́s v.
bury a bird muɗɛ́sá gwaáᵉ v.
bury a stink-bug muɗɛ́sá logeréɲoé v.
bury life of one's children muɗɛ́sá ɦyekesíé wicé v.
bury medicine muɗɛ́sá cɛmɛ́rɨ́kàᵋ v.
bus ɲáɓás n.
bush ríjᵃ n.
bush barbet kɔkɨ́rɨ́kɔkᵃ n.
bush country ríjíkaajíkᵃ n.
bush(es) tsekís n.; tsekísíàk̗wᵃ n.
bushbaby gwan n.
bushbuck kʉláɓᵃ n.
bushbuck (female) natsɨ́ɓɨlɨ́ n.
bushbuck (male) òɗòmòr n.
bushbuck leaf kʉláɓákàkᵃ n.
bushcamp napérítᵃ n.
bushpig bòròkᵃ n.
bushpig boar borokucúrúkᵃ n.
bushpig piglet bòròkùìm n.
bushpig sow borokuŋwa n.
bushy tsèkòn v.
business dzîgwᵃ n.
bustard hɔ́tɔ̀ n.
busy ígùjùgùjòn v.
but kòt° coordconn.
butcher hoɛ́s v.; hoesíàm n.; tɔ̀ŋɔ̀lààm n.; tɔŋɔlɛs v.
butchery hoesího n.
butt ɔ̂z n.; toɗɔ́pɔ́n v.

301

butt (of gun) dɛɛdᵃ *n.*
butt cheek komos *n.*
butt in íbʉbʉŋés *v.*; íbʉbʉŋésʉƙotᵃ *v.*
butter íbɔtsam *n.*
butter (seed) ɲówoɗí *n.*
butter flask ɲéɓur *n.*
butterfly béɗíbeɗú *n.*; bóɗíboɗú *n.*
buttock komos *n.*
buttock underside kwatsíém *n.*
buttocks (have flat) taɓóɲómòn *v.*
button ɲájaará *n.*
buy dzígwès *v.*; dzígwetés *v.*
buy off ilʉŋúlʉ́ŋés *v.*
buyer dzígwààm *n.*; dzígwèsìàm *n.*
buzz around ilólúés *v.*
buzzard (augur) alálá *n.*
by foot dèɨ̀kᵓ *n.*
by night mukú *n.*
by what path? ndayᵒ *n.*
bypass isʉkɛs *v.*; sʉ́kés *v.*
cabbage ɲákáɓìc *n.*
cabinet ɲákábàtᵃ *n.*
cache irwanes *v.*; laɓᵃ *n.*
cackle ikékémòn *v.*
cactus species ɲéɲɛwán *n.*
Cadaba farinosa métᵃ *n.*; súr *n.*
cadaver loukúétsᵎᵃ *n.*; ɲélɛl *n.*
cadaverous iróƙóòn *v.*; itóƙóƙòòn *v.*; kwédekwedánón *v.*
cadge lɛŋés *v.*
cadger lɛŋésɨ̀àm *n.*
café ɲéótèl *n.*
cage (trap) ɲáɓáo *n.*
cajole ɨmámɛɛ́s *v.*
calabash kàŋèr *n.*

calendar ɲákaléɲɗà *n.*
calf kɔrɔ́bᵃ *n.*
Calisa edulis turunetᵃ *n.*
call óés *v.*
call (of animals) ƙɔ̀ɗɔ̀n *v.*
call (in alarm) íbòfòn *v.*
call (name) óés *v.*
call continuously óísiés *v.*
call each other óímós *v.*
call for rain dʉbés *v.*
call here oetés *v.*
call off ŋɨ́ɨ́ɗésʉ́ƙotᵃ *v.*; tasálétòn *v.*; tasálón *v.*
call on the phone iwésúƙotᵃ *v.*; iwetés *v.*
call repeatedly óésés *v.*
call sweetly imámɛɛtés *v.*
callous ɓulúrúmòn *v.*
calm tisílón *v.*; toikíkón *v.*
calm down ijémɔ́nʉkɔtᵃ *v.*; itiketésá gúróe kíjákᵉ *v.*; toiésuƙotᵃ *v.*; zɛƙwétón *v.*; zɛƙwɨtɛtés *v.*
calm down the heart cucuéítésuƙota gúróᵉ *v.*
calm dowwn ɗipímón *v.*
calm person gúróàm *n.*
camel gwaɨ́tsᵎᵃ *n.*; ɲákáal *n.*
camp napérítᵃ *n.*; ɲákamɓí *n.*
camp (garden) ɲóɓóotᵃ *n.*
camp kitchen ŋkáƙáhò *n.*
campaign was *n.*
campaign ads ɲáɓás *n.*
can topéɗésuƙotᵃ *v.*
can (large) ɲéɗépe *n.*
can (metal) ɲékén *n.*
cancel ŋɨ́ɨ́ɗésʉ́ƙotᵃ *v.*; tasálétòn *v.*; tasálón *v.*
cancel (make) ŋɨ́ɨ́ɗɨtésʉƙotᵃ *v.*
candidacy was *n.*

candidate wasɔ́ám *n.*
candidiasis losúk[a] *n.*
candle wax sɔs *n.*
candy ɲátamɨtám *n.*
cane iɗitsɛs *v.*; inɔmɛs *v.*; kasɨ́r *n.*; sɛ̀w[a] *n.*
cane (hooked) ɲótooɗó *n.*
cane rat ŋʉr *n.*
canine tooth bàdìam *n.*
cannabis lɔ́tɔ́ɓa ná zè *n.*
cannibal áts'ɛsɨ̀àmà ròɓà[e] *n.*
cannon komótsɛ́ɛ̀ɓ[a] *n.*
canteen (gourd) nasɛmɛ́ *n.*
Canthium lactescens kómoló *n.*
Canthium species dodík[a] *n.*; kàrɛ̀ *n.*; milékw[a] *n.*
canvass (an area) ɨkáyɛ́ɛ́s *v.*
cap ɲákopiyá *n.*
cap (giraffe-tail) ɲɔ́tsɔ́ɓɛ *n.*
cap (human hair) ɲóɓókot[a] *n.*
cap (ignition) ɔ́zɛ̀ɗ[a] *n.*
capability ɲapéɗór *n.*
capable of topéɗésuƙot[a] *v.*
capillary tsòrìt[a] *n.*
Capparaceae species tsàl *n.*
Capparis tomentosa lókúɗukuɗét[a] *n.*
capture dúɓès *v.*; ɨkamɛ́sɨ́ƙɔt[a] *v.*
car kàèɩm *n.*; ɲómotoká *n.*
car (small) pɔ́ɗɛ̀ *n.*
caracal naɨtakɨ́pʉ́rat[a] *n.*
carbon black ɲémúɗets[a] *n.*; ɲémúɗuɗu *n.*
carcass ɗòl *n.*
card (identity) ɲákáɗ[a] *n.*
card (Kenyan ID) ɲekɨpanɗɛ *n.*
card (playing) ɲákáɗ[a] *n.*

cardboard (thin) ɲépáɨ̀l *n.*
Cardiospermum corindum tɩ̀l *n.*
cards (playing) ɲákáɗɨk[a] *n.*
care ɨkatsɛs *v.*; ɨmɨsɛs *v.*
care for bɔnɛ́s *v.*; ɨrɨtsɛ́s *v.*
care for (the sick) maɨtetɛ́s *v.*
care for oneself ɨrɨtsɛ́sá asɨ́ *v.*
care-free person ɨɓámɔ́nɨ̀àm *n.*
careful tɔtsɔ́ɔ́n *v.*
carefully hɨɨj[a] *adv.*; hɨɨj[ɔ] *adv.*
carelessly càc[i] *adv.*; fùts'àts'[a] *ideo.*; tsàr *ideo.*
caress ɨɓɔnɨ́ɓɔ́nɛ́s *v.*; ɨɓonɨ́ɓónɨés *v.*; ɨwáwɛ́ɛ́s *v.*
caretaker bɔnɛ́ám *n.*; ɨrɨtsɛ́sɨ̀àm *n.*; itelesíám *n.*
caretaking bɔn *n.*
cargo bot[a] *n.*; botɨtín *n.*
Carica papaya ɲápaɨpáy[a] *n.*
carinated toŋórómòn *v.*; toróŋómòn *v.*
carissa shrub turunet[a] *n.*
carnivore loúk[a] *n.*
carpenter ɲáɓáòɨkààm *n.*
carrier tsídzèsìàw[a] *n.*
carrion itam *n.*
carrot kárʉ̀ts'[a] *n.*
carry away on the head tsídzesuƙot[a] *v.*
carry by hand taɓakɛ́s *v.*
carry in arms taɓakɛ́s *v.*
carry many of rúdzès *v.*
carry on shoulder tʉ́zʉŋɛ́s *v.*
carry on the back édès *v.*
carry on the head tsídzès *v.*
carry on the head (make) tsídzitetɛ́s *v.*
carry together ilélébɛ́s *v.*
carry under ilʉkɛs *v.*
cartilage ŋɔrɔɓɔɓ[a] *n.*

cartilaginous rɔbɔ́dɔ̀n v.
cartridge ɲéburocó n.; ɲɛsɛpɛɗɛ n.
carve sotés v.; sotetés v.
case (legal) ɲékés n.
cash kaúdzà nì ɓèts'ᵃ n.
casing hò n.
casing (borehole) ɲatsʉʉmánêbᵃ n.
casing (shell) ɲéburocó n.; ɲɛsɛpɛɗɛ n.
cassava ɲómoŋgó n.
Cassia hildebrandtii ɲasal n.
Cassia singueana lɔ́kérʉ́ n.
cast góózés v.
cast (for divination) ipés v.
cast away góózesuƙotᵃ v.; hábatsésúƙotᵃ v.
cast down hábatsetés v.
cast sandals (in divination) ipésá taƙáíkàᵋ v.
cast stones (in divination) ipésá gwàsìkàᵉ v.
cast this way góózetés v.
castor-oil plant ɨmánán n.
castrate iƙélémés v.
casual faɗétón v.
cat púùs n.
cat's-tail ɨsɨkᵃ n.
catapult ɲapaaru n.
cataract kɛs n.
catch dúbès v.; ikamésúƙotᵃ v.; ikamɛtés v.; ságwès v.
catch (up with) rɨtsés v.
catch a whiff wetésá kɔɨnáᵋ v.
catch fire aeétón v.; léjétón v.
catch off guard bóges v.; itúúmés v.
catch one's breath iɨŋɔnʉƙotᵃ v.
catch scent of mídzatetés v.

catch sight of enésúƙotᵃ v.; tataɲes v.
catch the attention of itúlɛɛtés v.
catechism ɲákatékísìmù n.
catechist ŋíkatikisítààm n.
categorize isɨ́ɨ́lés v.
cater for ɨgɔɲés v.
Catha edulis ɲémurúŋgù n.
Catholic church Katólìkà n.
Catholic person Katólìkààm n.
Catholic priest páɗèr n.
Catholicism Katólìkà n.
cattle ɦyɔ̀ n.
cattle disease lɔlɛɛʉ́ n.
cattle herd ɦyɔ̀bàr n.
Caucasian ɓèts'ònìàm n.; ɲémúsukitᵃ n.
cause abdominal pain ɲimíɲímàtòn v.
cause pain áts'ɛs v.
cause problems buƙetésá mɛnáᵋ v.
cause problems for itsánɨtɛtés v.
cause torment for itsanɨtsánitɛtés v.
cauterize itsues v.
cautious toikíkón v.
cavalier faɗétón v.
cave pakwᵃ n.
cave (small) pàɗwᵃ n.
cave (vertical) ɲáɗúyᵃ n.
cave entrance pakóásákᵃ n.
cave interior pakóáƙwᵃ n.
caved in paɗókómòn v.
cavern (vertical) ɲáɗúyᵃ n.
cavernous wòò ideo.
cavity (abdominal) bùbùàƙwᵃ n.
cavity (oral) akᵃ n.
cease bɔlɔnʉƙotᵃ v.
cease (blowing or boiling) tilímón v.
ceaseless rɨtsɨritsánón v.
cedar (African pencil) asʉnán n.

ceiling (upper) lɔɓîz *n.*
celebrate inumúnúmɛ́s *v.*; inúnúmɛ́s *v.*; iyóómètòn *v.*
celebration ɲápáti *n.*
cellular network sugur *n.*
Celosia schweinfurthiana sɔ́gèkàk^a *n.*
cement ɲésímìt^a *n.*
census ɲɛkɨmar *n.*
cent ŋáɓɔ́ɔla *n.*; ŋásɛntáɨ̀èkw^a *n.*
center ekw^a *n.*; sɨsɨk^a *n.*; sɨsɨ́kêd^a *n.*
center of snare siméékw^a *n.*
center point ekw^a *n.*
centipede ƙɔ́dɔxɔ́ *n.*
central part bakútsêd^a *n.*
cents ŋásɛntáy^a *n.*
cereal ed^a *n.*
ceremonial meal írésiŋƙáƙ^a *n.*
ceremony (conduct a) írés *n.*
certainly kárɨká *adv.*
cervical vertebrae ɦyukumúɔ́k^a *n.*
cervix dòdìèkw^a *n.*
cessation was *n.*
cestode apéléle *n.*
chafed ɲɛdɛ́dɔ̀n *v.*
chafedly ɲèd^ɛ *ideo.*
chaff dust ŋawɨ́l *n.*
chaffs nakariɓ^a *n.*
chain zɔ̀t^a *n.*
chained zɔ́tɔ́n *v.*
chair kàràts^a *n.*
chairperson (of village) ámázeáma awá^e *n.*
chalk ɲécɔ́ka *n.*
chalkboard ɲáɓáo *n.*
chalky (dry) pʉrákámòn *v.*; pʉráɲámòn *v.*; pʉsélémɔ̀n *v.*

challenge (verbally) nɛpɛƙanitetés *v.*
chamber (bee larva) sɨ́dàhò *n.*
chameleon hɨ́ƙɔ́ *n.*
chance ŋawɨlɛs *v.*
chance upon taƙámón *v.*
change beníónuƙot^a *v.*; iɓéléés *v.*; iɓéléìmètòn *v.*; icéɲjeés *v.*; icéɲjèìmètòn *v.*; ilotses *v.*; ilotsímétòn *v.*
change (money) toɓwaɲes *v.*
change allegiences tolúétòn *v.*; tolúónuƙot^a *v.*; tolúútésuƙot^a *v.*
change course wɛ́dɔ̀n *v.*
change decisions ilotsesa mɛná^ɛ *v.*
change one's direction iɓéléésuƙota asɨ́ *v.*
change position isʉ́tɔ́n *v.*
change statements iɓelíɓélésa tódà^e *v.*
change the story iɓelíɓélésa tódà^e *v.*
change the subject ijʉlɛsa tódà^e *v.*
chaotic (beocome) iŋɔ́dyàimètòn *v.*
chapati ɲécapatí *n.*
chapeau ɲákakar *n.*
chapel ɲécápɔ̀l *n.*
chapped ɓɛlɛ́ɓélánón *v.*
chapter ɔ́dɔ̀k^a *n.*
char kɔrɛtés *v.*; kɔrɨtɛtés *v.*
charcoal leûz *n.*; ɲámakáy^a *n.*
charge (accuse) isɨ́ɨ́tɛ́s *v.*
charge (attack) toƙíróòn *v.*
charge (electrically) cɨɨtésuƙot^a *v.*; hábitésúƙot^a *v.*; ŋƙitɛtés *v.*; wetitésuƙot^a *v.*
charge (order) itsikɛs *v.*
Charismatic Ŋímorokóléìàm *n.*
charitable waŋádòn *v.*
charm súɓès *v.*; súɓɛsʉƙɔt^a *v.*
charmer súɓèsɨàm *n.*

charred kɔrétón v.
chase ifalífálés v.; ilɔŋɛs v.
chase after ilóŋésuƙɔtᵃ v.; irukes v.; irúƙésuƙɔtᵃ v.
chase away ikutses v.; ikútsésuƙɔtᵃ v.
chase down (the throat) itikes v.
chase off ikutses v.; ikútsésuƙɔtᵃ v.
chattily ɗɛm ideo.; pòx ideo.
chatty ɗɛmɨɗòn v.; ɗɛmɨɗémón v.; ikútúƙánón v.; poxóɗòn v.
chaw ts'àf n.
cheap batánón v.
cheat imɔɗɛs v.; imóɗésuƙɔtᵃ v.
check (bank) kaúdzokabáɗᵃ n.
check (mark) totsetes v.
check on ifátésuƙɔtᵃ v.; lágalagetés v.
check out gonés v.; ɦyeités v.; ifátésuƙɔtᵃ v.; isémeés v.; iséméetés v.; lágalagetés v.; tɨriɦɛs v.; tɨriɦɛtés v.
check out (here) gonetés v.
check out (there) gonésúƙɔtᵃ v.
check out thoroughly tɨrifiés v.
checkers néɗurápᵃ n.
cheek ɔbᵃ n.
cheek (butt) komos n.
cheekbone akáƙúm n.
cheep cheep! ƙíɛƙíɛƙíɛ ideo.
cheese néɗiol n.
cheetah nárará n.
chef kɔŋésɨàm n.
chemical cèmèr n.
Chenopodium opulifolium tsamuya n.
cherish mɨnés v.
chest bakutsᵃ n.
chest (inner) gúr n.
chest (storage) násaɗukú n.

chest disease neɗekea bákútsìkàᵉ n.
chest hair bakutsísíts'ᵃ n.
chew áts'ɛ́s v.; ináɗútés v.
chew (tobacco) imátáŋés v.; mataŋes v.
chew extractively ts'afés v.
chew on nɛbés v.
chew roughly ikaŋíkáŋés v.; iŋaɨŋɛɛ́s v.; iŋáŋɛɛ́s v.
chewily kàŋ ideo.; kwàⁱ ideo.
chewy dɨriŋíŋón v.; kaŋádòn v.; kwaíɗòn v.
chick gwáím n.; nókokoróím n.
chicken nókokor n.
chicken backbone neturuƙúƙu n.
chicken coop nókokoróhò n.
chickenpox nɛtunɛ n.; puurú n.
chide dɔxés v.; dɔxésúƙɔtᵃ v.
chief ámáze n.; ámázeám n.; nériósitᵃ n.
chief (crew) ámázeáma terégì n.
chief (parish) nékúŋutᵃ n.
chief (subcounty) nejákáɨtᵃ n.
chief elder ámázeáma awáᵉ n.; diyoama ná zè n.
child im n.
child (foreign) ɦyòim n.
child (his/her/its) ntsíím n.
child (my) ńcìim n.
child (of someone) ámáìm n.
child (your) biím n.
child's bowl imáƙófɔ n.
childhood imánánès n.; wicénánès n.
childishness imánánès n.; wicénánès n.
childless ikólípánón v.; osorosánón v.
childless person nokólípᵃ n.; òsòròs n.
childlikeness imánánès n.; wicénánès n.
children wikᵃ n.
children (young) kómósikaa ɓets'aakátìkᵉ n.

chill cucuéítésuƙotᵃ v.
chill (damp) cucue n.
chill out zɛƙwétɔ́n v.
chilly cucuéón v.
chin tatɨ́n n.
chinches ɲɨtúmɨkᵃ n.
chink against ɨ́gatsɨgatsɛ́s v.
chip ŋɛlɛ́s v.; pɛsɛlam n.; pésélamedᵃ n.; pɛsɛlɛs v.; tɛŋɛlɛs v.
chip (wood) kɨ́ɓézam n.
chip in tɔ́ƙés v.
chip off ŋɛlɛ́mɛ́tɔ̀n v.; pɛsémɛ́tɔ̀n v.; wɛts'émɔ́n v.; wɛts'ɛ́s v.; wɛts'ɛtɛ́s v.
chip off (bark) iɓóɓólés v.
chip off in pieces wɛts'ɛtiɛ́s v.
chip repeatedly ɨwɛts'ɨwɛ́ts'ɛ́s v.
chirp chirp! ƙɨɛƙɨɛƙɨɛ ideo.
choir ɲákwáya n.
choke ikɛtɛs v.; ikɛtiɛ́s v.
cholera kɔlérà n.
chomp iŋomes v.; ƙɨ́dzès v.
choose ɗɨmɛtɛ́s v.; iɗókóliɛ́s v.; iƙɛlɛs v.; iƙɛlɛtɛ́s v.; ɲɨmɛtɛ́s v.; tɔsɛɛtɛ́s v.; xóɓɛtɛ́s v.
choosen xóɓɔtɔ́s v.
chop in pieces ŋurutiɛ́s v.
chop up in pieces ŋurutiɛsúƙotᵃ v.
chop! pùà ideo.
chopped in pieces ŋurutiós v.
chopper naƙɨ́liƙɨ́l n.
chorus ɲákwáya n.
chosen ƙanotós v.
Christian Ŋíkiristóìàm n.
Christian name ɓatísimúêdᵃ n.
Christianity ŋíkiristóìnànès n.
Christlikeness ŋíkiristóìnànès n.

Christmas service nuélì n.
chronic kɔ̀wɔ̀n v.
chronically ill maimoos v.
chronically ill person maimoosíám n.
chubbily dèjᵋ ideo.
chubby dɛjɛ́dɔ̀n v.
chuckle gagaanón v.
chug gégès v.; ijɨ́ɨ́résʉƙotᵃ v.
chunk julam n.
chunk (small) julamáím n.
chunky ŋʉmúɲʉ́mánón v.
church ɲakujíhɔ̀ n.; ɲégelesíà n.; wáánàhò n.
churn ɨɓɔbɔtsɛ́s v.; ɨɓɔtsɛ́s v.; ɨɓɔtsésá asɨ́ v.; ɨgùlàjòn v.
chyme eyᵃ n.; gaɗár n.; ŋkújɨtᵃ n.
cicada tswɨ̈itswɨ̈ n.
cicatrix ƙwár n.
cigarette ɲɔsɔkatá n.
cinder bʉbʉn n.
cinema ɲévíɗyòhò n.
circle tɔlʉkɛs v.; tɔlúƙésʉƙotᵃ v.; tɔlʉkɛtɛ́s v.
circles in (make) tɔlʉkúlʉ́ƙés v.
circular ɗukúdòn v.
circularly ɗùkᵘ ideo.
circulate ilɔmɨ́lɔ́mɔ̀n v.; irímɛ́tɔ̀n v.; irímítɛtɛ́s v.; irímón v.
circulate in irimɛs v.
circumcise ilɨ́ɲɨ́rɛ́s v.; ilɨrɛs v.
circumcised lɛŋɛ́rɛ́mɔ̀n v.
circumvent tamanɛs v.; tamanɛtɛ́s v.
circumventing firifiránón v.; wiríwiránón v.
circumvolve ilɨrɛs v.
circumvolve repeatedly ilɨrɨ́lɨ́rɛ́s v.
Cissus rhodesiae bɛfácémér n.
Citrullus species nàdɛ̀kwɛ̀l n.

citrus fruit ɲámucúɲ̃ka̍ *n.*
city zɛkɔ́áwa ná zè *n.*
city (capital) awa ná zè *n.*
civet (African) mɨnɨ́t[a] *n.*
clack irɔjɨ́rɔ́jɛ́s *v.*
clamber ilɛ́pɔ́n *v.*
clamber down itsɔrɛtɛ́sá asɨ́ *v.*; itsɔ́rɔ́nʉkɔt[a] *v.*
clamber up ilɛ́pɛ́sʉkɔt[a] *v.*; itsɛ́tsɛ́ɛ́s *v.*
clamp riɗɛ́s *v.*; wɨɗɨɗánón *v.*; wɨ́ɗɨ̍wɨɗánón *v.*
clamp shut riɗímétòn *v.*
clan bònìt[a] *n.*
clan (Gaɗukuɲ) Gaɗukúɲ *n.*
clan (Ilɛŋ) Ilɛ́ŋ *n.*
clan (Komokua) Kòmòkùà *n.*
clan (paternal) ɔ́dɔ̀k[a] *n.*; àsàk[a] *n.*
clan (Siketia) Sìkètìà *n.*
clan (Telek) Tɛ́lɛ́k[a] *n.*
clan (Uzet) Ʉ́zɛ̀t[a] *n.*
clan (Ɲiɓoŋorona) Ɲɨ́ɓɔ́ŋɔrɔna *n.*
clan (Ɲiɗotsa) Ɲɨ́ɗɔ́tsa *n.*
clan (Norobat) Nɔrɔbat[a] *n.*
clan member (Gaɗukuɲ) Gaɗukúɲùàm *n.*
clan member (Ilɛŋ) Ilɛ́ŋíàm *n.*
clan member (Komokua) Kòmòkùààm *n.*
clan member (Siketia) Sìkètìààm *n.*
clan member (Telek) Tɛ́lɛ́kìàm *n.*
clan member (Uzet) Ʉ́zɛ̀tìàm *n.*
clan member (Ɲiɓoŋorona) Ɲɨ́ɓɔ́ŋɔrɔnáám *n.*
clan member (Ɲiɗotsa) Ɲɨ́ɗɔ́tsáám *n.*
clan member (Norobat) Nɔrɔbatíám *n.*
clap iɗafɛs *v.*
clap clap! rààràà̀rà *ideo.*
clap hands iɗafɛsa kwétɨ̀kà[ɛ] *v.*
clapping dance ɲókorot[a] *n.*
clarify enitetɛ́s *v.*
clash ikúmúnós *v.*
clasp mʉkʉtɛs *v.*
class ɲékɨlás *n.*; ɲókós *n.*
class (school) hò *n.*
classify isɨ́ɨ́lɛ́s *v.*
classroom ɲékɨlás *n.*
clavicle ɲálakamáàì̀tìɔ̀k[a] *n.*
claw sokɔ́rítɛs *v.*; tíbòlòkòɲ *n.*
claw up ikúkúrɛ́s *v.*; tʉkʉtɛs *v.*
clay (black) ŋɔra na buɗám *n.*
clay (colored) ŋɔr *n.*
clay (red) ŋɔra na ɗíw[a] *n.*
clay (smear with) ŋɔritɛtɛ́s *v.*
clay pot (blackened) dómá na buɗám *n.*
clay pot (small) ɲekulu *n.*
clean ɓɛts'òn *v.*; fítɛ́s *v.*; kɨlɨwɨ́tánón *v.*; ɲɨ́ɨ́ɗɛ́s *v.*; súkútɛ́s *v.*; sʉʉtɛ́s *v.*
clean (a surface) ikʉlɛs *v.*; ikwalɛs *v.*; iliwɛs *v.*
clean off ɲɨ́ɨ́ɗɛ́sʉ́kɔt[a] *v.*
clean off (a surface) ikʉ́lɛ́sʉkɔt[a] *v.*; iliwɨ́lɨ́wɛtɛ́s *v.*
clean up ɲɨ́ɨ́ɗetɛ́s *v.*
clean up (a surface) ikʉletɛ́s *v.*
cleaned off iliwɨ́lɨ́wós *v.*
cleaning rod súkútɛ́sítsirɨ́m *n.*
clear ɓɛts'òn *v.*; bótsón *v.*; fotólón *v.*; iɛtɛ́sá isɨ́ɨ́tɛ́sʉ́ *v.*; kánɔ́n *v.*; kɨlɨwɨ́tánón *v.*; takánón *v.*
clear (a surface) ikʉlɛs *v.*; ikwalɛs *v.*; iliwɛs *v.*
clear (grass) ɨ́ɛ́s *v.*; irɛɲɛs *v.*
clear (of a path) kɔlánétòn *v.*
clear (of many) ɓɛts'aakón *v.*

clear (of mind) bótsóna iká̱ᵉ *v.*
clear (of weather) tatsɔ́ɔ́n *v.*
clear (the throat) hákátòn *v.*; xaƙarés *v.*
clear (visually) isólólòòn *v.*
clear a path in idɨdɨwɛ́s *v.*
clear a path through utés *v.*; utésúƙɔtᵃ *v.*
clear away (grass) irɛɲésuƙɔtᵃ *v.*
clear off (a surface) iƙúlésuƙɔtᵃ *v.*; iliwɨlɨwɛtés *v.*
clear off (brush) iɓúɓués *v.*
clear off (visually) isólólòètòn *v.*
clear off/up tatsɛ́ɛ́tɔ̀n *n.*
clear out bulútésuƙɔtᵃ *v.*
clear out (brush) iɓúɓués *v.*
clear up (a surface) iƙulɛtés *v.*
clear up (of sickness) iɛ́ɓɔ́nuƙɔtᵃ *v.*
clear up (visually) isólólòètòn *v.*
clearable area kawam *n.*
cleared (of grass) ɨ́ɔ́s *v.*
cleared forest tsɛ̀f *n.*
cleared off iliwɨlɨwɔ́s *v.*; topwatímétòn *v.*
clearing ɓɔdᵃ *n.*; dɨ́pɔ̀ *n.*
cleft (rock) tsarátán *n.*
cleft palate akáts'ɛa na paƙós *n.*
cleg ɲópɔdɔƙɨ *n.*
cleg (black) lɔŋizɛtᵃ *n.*
clench imúnúkukúón *v.*; itɔkɔdɛs *v.*; mukutɛs *v.*; wɨdɨdánón *v.*; wɨdɨwɨdánón *v.*
clench buttocks iídón *v.*
clench teeth ƙɨdzɨkɔ̀ɔ̀n *v.*
clench up mukutɛtés *v.*
clever nɔɔsánón *v.*
clever person nɔɔsáàm *n.*

cleverness nɔɔ́s *n.*
click disapprovingly itswɛtɨtswétɔ̀n *v.*
cliff chat (bird) akɔ́ŋikɔŋ *n.*
clifflike fujúlúmòn *v.*
cliffy fujúlúmòn *v.*
climb otsés *v.*; tóbìrìbìròn *v.*; totírón *v.*
climb down (that way) kídzimonuƙɔtᵃ *v.*
climb down (this way) kídzìmètòn *v.*; tsígìmètòn *v.*
climb on otsésúƙɔtᵃ *v.*
climb up otsésúƙɔtᵃ *v.*
climb with gear itséƙéés *v.*; itséƙóòn *v.*
clinch rɨdɛs *v.*; wɨdɨdánón *v.*; wɨdɨwɨdánón *v.*
cling dɛlémɔ́n *v.*; ƙɨdzɔ̀n *v.*
cling to inɔtsɛs *v.*; irumɛs *v.*; ŋɔtsés *v.*
clinic dakɨtár *n.*
clink against ɨgatsɨgatsés *v.*
clink! ƙwɨ́l *ideo.*
clip irɛɓɛs *v.*
clip (of a gun) ɲókópo *n.*
clip off irɛ́ɓésuƙɔtᵃ *v.*
clique kábùn *n.*
clitoris sɔn *n.*
clitoris head sɔnííƙᵃ *n.*
clitoris tip sɔnííƙᵃ *n.*
cloak ɲáléso *n.*; ɲáwáro *n.*
cloak (leather) xɔŋɔŋ *n.*
clobber ipukúpúkés *v.*
clock fɛtᵃ *n.*
clogged firímón *v.*
close ɦyɔtɔ́gɔ̀n *v.*; ikóóbés *v.*; ikóóbetés *v.*; kɔkés *v.*; kɔkɛtés *v.*; kokímétòn *v.*; muts'utɛs *v.*
close (make) kɔkɨtɛtés *v.*
close by ɦyàtàkᵃ *n.*
close the eyes múdúkánón *v.*

close to each other ɦyɔtɔ́gɨmɔ́s v.
close up muts'útésukɔtᵃ v.
close up repeatedly muts'utiesúkotᵃ v.
closing prayer wáána na tézɛ̀tɔ̀nɨ̀ n.
clot iɗíkétòn v.; iɗikitetés v.
cloth (small) ƙwàzàìm n.
cloth (waist-) riɗiesíƙwàz n.
cloth(es) ƙwàz n.
clothing ƙwàz n.
clothing (leather) ínóƙwàz n.
clothing (sheep-leather) ɗóɗòƙwàz n.
clotted iɗíkón v.
cloud gìdᵃ n.; ɲáɗís n.
cloud (dark) gida ná buɗám n.
cloud (white) gìdà nà ɓèts'ᵃ n.
cloud cover kùpᵃ n.
cloud over/up gobétón v.; kupétón v.; kupukúpón v.; mɔkɨmɔ́ƙón v.
cloudiness kùpᵃ n.; kùpààƙwᵃ n.
cloudless kánɔ́n v.
cloudy kùpòn v.
club sèwᵃ n.
club (group) ɲégurúf n.
clubfooted ƙɔɔlɔ́mɔ̀nà dè̠kà̠ᵋ v.; sɔƙɔ́ɲɔ́mɔ̀n v.
clubhanded sɔƙɔ́ɲɔ́mɔ̀n v.
cluck at iƙɛnɨƙénés v.
cluck disapprovingly ɨtswɛtɨ́tswétɔ̀n v.
cluck! ƙútᵘ ideo.
clump ɓòtòŋ n.
clumsy ɨɓaŋɨ́ɓáɲòn v.; pɔsɔ́kɔ́mɔ̀n v.
clunky pɔsɔ́kɔ́mɔ̀n v.
cluster ɓòtòŋ n.
co- (my) ɲ́citaŋá n.
co- (plural) taŋái̠kɨ̠n pro.

co- (singular) taŋéêdᵃ pro.
co- (your) bitáŋá n.
co-op ɲégurúf n.
co-wife ɛán n.
coagulate iɗíkétòn v.; iɗikitetés v.
coagulated iɗíkón v.
coal bʉbʉn n.
coarse gwɛrɛ́jɛ́jòn v.
coat ɲókóti n.
coax ɨmáméés v.
coax into coming ɨmáméɛtés v.
cobra loúpal n.
cobweb abûbᵃ n.
cock gwácúrúkᵃ n.
cock (weapon) wakés v.
cocking lever wakésìàwᵃ n.
cockle-doodle-doo! kʉkúúkᵘ ideo.
cockroach lɔmɛ́jɛ́kɛlɛ́ n.
cocky ɨwɔ́ƙɔ́n v.
cocky person ɨwɔ́ƙɔ́nɨ̀àm n.
cocoon mɔɗɔ́ɗᵃ n.
cocoon opening mɔɗɔ́ɗɔ̀ékwᵃ n.
coerce réés v.; rɛɛtés v.; tɔrɛɛs v.
coerced toreimétòn v.
coexistence (peaceful) zɛƙwa ná dà n.
coffee ɲákáwa n.
cohort taŋéêdᵃ pro.
cohort (your) bitáŋá n.
cohorts taŋái̠kɨ̠n pro.
coil ilúƙúretés v.; ɨnɔɛs v.
coil around ɨnɔɛtés v.
coil up ilúƙúrètòn v.
coiled iyérón v.
coiled loosely ŋarúxánòn v.
coiled up ilúƙúròn v.

coin kaúdzèèkwᵃ *n.*; ŋárɔpɨyéékwᵃ *n.*; ɲésimón *n.*; ɲókóìn *n.*

coinhabit ínínós *v.*

cold ɨɛ́ɓɔ́n *v.*

cold (become) ɨɛ́ɓétɔ̀n *v.*; ɨɛ́ɓɔ́nʉkɔt ᵃ *v.*

cold (make) ɨɛ́ɓɨ́tɛ́sʉkɔtᵃ *v.*

cold (virus) ɲarʉ́kʉ́m *n.*

cold weather ɨɛ́ɓɔ́na kɨ́já ᵉ *v.*

collaborate on iŋáɲárɛtɛ́s *v.*

collapse baɗonuƙotᵃ *v.*; lajámétòn *v.*; ɲalámétòn *v.*; ɲalámónuƙotᵃ *v.*; ruɓétón *v.*; ruɓonuƙotᵃ *v.*; taɲáléetésá asɨ́ *v.*; taɲálóòn *v.*

collapse due to weight xukúmétòn *v.*

collapsed paɗókómòn *v.*

collar ɦiyʉkʉma ƙwázà ᵉ *n.*; ikeda ƙwázà ᵉ *n.*

collar (animal) rɔɓᵃ *n.*

collarbone ɲálaƙamááìtìɔkᵃ *n.*

colleague taŋɛ́êɗᵃ *pro.*

colleague (my) ńcitaɲá *n.*

colleague (your) bitáɲá *n.*

colleagues taŋáɨ́kɨ̀n *pro.*

collect ikóóbés *v.*; ikóóbetés *v.*; irɨ́rɛ́ɛs *v.*; irɨ́rɛ́ɛsʉƙotᵃ *v.*; itsʉnɛs *v.*; itsʉnɛtés *v.*; iʉɗɛs *v.*; iʉɗɛtés *v.*

collect (contributions) bɔsɛtés *v.*

collect a debt amʉtsanés *v.*

collect firewood weesá dakwí *v.*

collect rubbish ɲaɗaɗés *v.*

college ɲésukúl *n.*; yunivásìtì *n.*

colloquium ɲésémìnà *n.*

colonize ínésuƙotᵃ *v.*

color ŋɔr *n.*

colored soil ɲálámʉɲena *n.*

Colossians (biblical) Ŋíkolosáikᵃ *n.*

colossus kébàdà *n.*; nábàdà *n.*; nébàdà *n.*

colostrum ɲóɗós *n.*

coma (be in a) bàdòn *v.*

comatose ifáfúkós *v.*

comb iƙwɛrɛs *v.*; ɲɛkésétᵃ *n.*

comb out iƙwɛ́résʉƙotᵃ *v.*

combatant cɛmáám *n.*

combative cɛmɨcɛmɔs *v.*

combed iƙwɛrɔs *v.*

combine ɗɔtsɛ́s *v.*; ɗɔtsɛ́súƙotᵃ *v.*; ɗɔt-sɛtés *v.*; iɗyates *v.*; iɲales *v.*

combine (grains) ikáɗóés *v.*

Combretium species tùtùf *n.*

come àtsòn *v.*; ɨnapɛtésá asɨ́ *v.*

come (get to) isúɲúrɛ́s *v.*

come across bunétón *v.*; bùnòn *v.*; it-sɔŋɛtés *v.*; ŋawɨlɛs *v.*; taƙámón *v.*

come after elánétòn *v.*

come alongside nápón *v.*

come and go in bunches ts'ʉ̀wɔ̀n *v.*

come apart ɗɛsɛ́ɗɛ́sánón *v.*; ɗusúmón *v.*

come around ilɔ́ɗétɔ̀n *v.*; irímétòn *v.*

come back iɓóɓóŋètòn *v.*; itétón *v.*; tɔrʉ́ɓɔ́n *v.*

come back around iƙʉlúƙúlɔ̀n *v.*

come back to life ɦiyekétón *v.*

come beside nápón *v.*

come by iɛ́ɓɛtés *v.*

come by way of tɔmɛɛtés *v.*

come close ɦiyɔtɔ́gètòn *v.*

come down kídzìmètòn *v.*; tsígìmètòn *v.*

come early isókétón *v.*

come edging itsoɗiétòn *v.*

come for a visit ɨlɛ́ɛ́tɔ̀n *v.*

come free hoɗómón *v.*

come in (of teeth) morétón *v.*

come in convoy itɨ́létòn v.
come in procession itɨ́létòn v.
come inching itsoɗiétòn v.
come into view lɛlɛmánétòn v.; lɛlétɔ́n v.; pɛlémétɔ́n v.
come late íbànètòn v.; irípétòn v.
come of age iriétòn v.
come off hoɗómón v.; tolómétòn v.
come out pulúmétòn v.; tolómétòn v.
come out (of stars) jʉ́étòn v.
come quickly ikómééton v.
come successively torópétòn v.
come to (wake) tsídzètòn v.
come to a consensus bɛrɛtésá mɛná^e v.
come to a stop wasɔnʉƙɔt^a v.
come together ikóóbetésá asɨ v.
come undone hoɗómón v.
come uninvitedly imíŋóòn v.
come via tɔmɛɛs v.; tɔmɛɛtés v.
come with elánétòn v.
coming into view lɛlɛmánón v.
commander itsikɛsíám n.
commandment (divine) itsikɛsa Ɲákují v.
Commelina species gùj^a n.
commence iséétòn v.; isóón v.; itsyákétòn v.
commerce dzîgw^a n.
commerce (do) dzígwès v.
comminge itsulútsúlés v.
commingle ídulés v.; íduludulés v.; itsɔɓɨtsɔ́ɓɛ́s v.
commingled itsɔɓɨtsɔ́ɓɔ̀n v.; itsɔɓɨtsɔ́ɓɔ́s v.
Commiphora africana ibét^a n.
Commiphora campestris lɔ́lɔwɨ n.

Commiphora species tʉlárɔ́y^a n.
commit adultery ɓúƙón v.
commit oneself imíɗɨtsɛ́sa asɨ v.
commix ídulés v.; íduludulés v.
commodities kúrúɓaicík^a n.
commodity dzígwam n.; dzígwetam n.; dzííƙotam n.
common tɔɔsétɔ̀n v.
Communion Ŋƙáƙá Komúnió^e n.
community narúét^a n.
compacted ɗɔtsánón v.; ɗɔtsɔ́s v.; dirídòn v.; tɔrɔ́dɔ̀n v.
compactedly dìr ideo.; tɔ̀r ideo.
companion itumetésíàm n.
company itumetésíàm n.; itúmétòn v.
company of girls ɲèràaƙw^a n.
compare iríánitetés v.; ƙámítetés v.
compare each other támɨnɔ́s v.
compel itiŋɛs v.
compete ikátɨnɔ́s v.; ilɔ́ɨmɔ́s v.; ilɔ́ɨnɔ́s v.
complain iŋʉrúŋúrɔ̀n v.; ƙɔ̀ɗɔ̀n v.
comple itɨŋɛ́ɛ́s v.
complete ŋábesʉƙɔt^a v.
completed ŋábɔnʉƙɔt^a v.; nábɔnʉƙɔt^a v.
completely jikî adv.; kɔ́nɨ́tiák^e pro.; píle ideo.; tsʉ́tɔ̀ adv.
compliant tsolólómòn v.
compose (music) iroketés v.
compound awááƙw^a n.
comprehend nesíbes v.
compress iriɗɛtés v.; rɔŋɛ́s v.
compressed iriɗɔs v.; tɔrɔ́dɔ̀n v.
computer ɲókompyútà n.
comrade taŋééd^a pro.
comrades taŋáɨƙɨn pro.
con imɔɗɛs v.
concave saƙánámòn v.; tsuƙúlúmòn v.

concave (flatly) ɓɛtélémɔ̀n *v.*; fɛtélémɔ̀n *v.*

conceal búdès *v.*; búdesuƙotᵃ *v.*; idɛɛs *v.*; idéésʉƙɔtᵃ *v.*; ipáŋwéés *v.*; tɨts'ɛ́s *v.*; tɨts'ésʉ́ƙɔtᵃ *v.*

conceal matters kɔkɛ́sá mɛnáᵋ *v.*

conceal oneself budɛ́s *v.*

concealed budésón *v.*; búdòs *v.*

concede ógoés *v.*

conceited itúrón *v.*

concern (topic) tábès *v.*

concerned ɨ́sánòn *v.*

concerned (become) ɨ́sánonuƙotᵃ *v.*

conciliate isɨ́lɨ́tésʉƙɔtᵃ *v.*

conclude matters kɔkɛtésá mɛnáᵋ *v.*

conclusion ɲémíso *n.*

condense (of water) ikópíòn *v.*

condense (water) tsɨpɨtsɨ́pón *v.*

cone of tobacco bɔrɔkɔƙᵃ *n.*; lɔ́tɔ́ɓabɔrɔkɔ́ƙᵃ *n.*

confess tɔkɨ́ón *v.*

confine iƙalɨ́ƙálɛ́s *v.*; ɨridɛs *v.*; ɨridɛtɛ́s *v.*

confirm ninɛtɛ́s *v.*

confirm the case enɛ́sá mɛnáᵋ *v.*

confirmation (religious) ɲékipeyés *n.*

Confirmation (Confirmation) koferemáásìò *n.*

conflagration kómɛ́ts'àdᵃ *n.*

conflate itsɔɓɨtsɔ́ɓɛ́s *v.*; itsulútsúlɛ́s *v.*

conflated itsɔɓɨtsɔ́ɓɔ̀n *v.*; itsɔɓɨtsɔ́ɓɔ́s *v.*

conflict ɲékúruƙur *n.*; ɲépɨ́dipɨdᵃ *n.*

conflict (cause) irémóòn *v.*

confound iƙures *v.*

confounded iƙúrúmétona iƙáᵉ *v.*

confuse iƙures *v.*; ilotses *v.*

confused iɓíléròn *v.*; ɨcɔ́ŋáimetona iƙáᵉ *v.*; iƙúrúmétona iƙáᵉ *v.*; lɔŋɔanón *v.*

confused (become) lɔŋɔanónuƙotᵃ *v.*

congeal idíkétòn *v.*; idikitetés *v.*; tɔsɔ́dɔ́kɔ̀n *v.*

congeal when cooled ipúkákòn *v.*

congealed idíkón *v.*

congested (nasally) dɨnɔ́s *v.*

Congo Kóŋgò *n.*

congregate ikóóbetésá asɨ́ *v.*; ɨrɨ́rɛɛtésá asɨ́ *v.*; iryámíryámètòn *v.*; itóyéésa asɨ́ *v.*; itsúnétòn *v.*; itukánón *v.*

congregation ɲatúkɔ́tᵃ *n.*

connect dɛsémón *v.*; imánétòn *v.*; imánónuƙotᵃ *v.*; tɔŋɛtɛs *v.*; tɔŋétónuƙotᵃ *v.*; toropes *v.*; tɔrʉtsɛs *v.*

conserve imɨnɨmɨ́nɛ́s *v.*

consider tamátámatés *v.*; tamɛtɛ́s *v.*; tamɨ́támiés *v.*

consonant ŋurutiesá tódàᵒ *n.*

constant rɨ́tsɨ́ritsánón *v.*

constellation (five-star) Ɲerawikᵃ *n.*; Tùtùkᵃ *n.*

constellation (seven-star) Lorokonídàkwᵃ *n.*

constellation (six-star) Torikaika Rié *n.*

constellation (Southern Cross) Ɲémusaláɓà *n.*

constipated firímón *v.*; tɨ́ɓidɛ́són *v.*; tɨɓɨ́étòn *v.*

constrained iridɔs *v.*

constrict ɨridɛs *v.*; ɨridɛtɛ́s *v.*; ridímétòn *v.*

constricted iridɔs *v.*; rɔ́kɔ́rɔkánón *v.*

construct bɛrɛ́s *v.*; toyeetɛ́s *v.*

construct (a saying) tadápítetɛ́s *v.*

consume dádítɛ́s *v.*; iɓalɨ́ɓálɛ́s *v.*; ŋƙáƙɛ́s *v.*; ŋƙɛ́s *v.*

contain ɨrɨtsɛ́s *v.*
container (big) kúbùr *n.*
contemn tsíítés *v.*
contemplate ɲɛɓés *v.*; tamátámatés *v.*; tamɨ́támiés *v.*
contemplative tamɛ́sɨ̀àm *n.*
contend ɨlɔ́ɨ́mɔ́s *v.*; ɨlɔ́ɨ́nɔ́s *v.*; kóríètòn *v.*
contentious deƙwideƙos *v.*
continue itemes *v.*; itemetés *v.*
contort imákóitetés *v.*
contorted imákóòn *v.*
contorted (become) imákwèètòn *v.*
contract rɨɗímétòn *v.*; tɔ́ɗɔ́nʉƙɔtᵃ *v.*
contract (cramp) ɨtɨɓɨ́tɨ́ɓɔ̀n *v.*
contract (work) kabaɗa na terégì *n.*; terégikabáɗᵃ *n.*
contracted tɔ́ɗɔ́n *v.*
contradict deƙwítetés *v.*; nɛpɛƙanitetés *v.*
contribute tɔ́ƙɛ́s *v.*
contribute resources ɗɔtsɛ́sá ɦyekesí *v.*
contributions (extract) bɔsɨtetés *v.*
contuse rùròn *v.*
contusion ƙwár *n.*
convene iƙíƙóanón *v.*; itukánón *v.*
converge itóyéésa asɨ́ *v.*
conversation ɲékukwá *n.*
converse ɨɛnón *v.*; tódinós *v.*
convex tsʉrúɗúmɔ̀n *v.*
convulse ɨmɨ́mɨ́jés *v.*
Conyza species ɲéʉrʉmɛmɛ́ *n.*
coo (of infants) iɲɨnɨ́ɲɨ́nɔ̀n *v.*
cook itiŋés *v.*; kɔŋɛ́sɨ̀àm *n.*
cook by boiling féés *v.*
cook by stirring kɔŋés *v.*
cook for friends féésa íditíní *v.*

cook out (poison) natsɛ́s *v.*
cook quickly hataikánón *v.*
cook up ɨɗɔ́ɗɔ́és *v.*
cooked well ɗʉmʉ́dɔ̀n *v.*
cooked medium tsɛɓɛ́ƙɛ́mɔ̀n *v.*
cooked tough haʉ́dɔ̀n *v.*
cooked very tough hàᵘ *ideo.*
cooker ɲɛsiŋƙiri *n.*
cookie ɲɛ́ɓisikótᵃ *n.*
cooking hut ɲéjigón *n.*
cooking place itiŋésíàwᵃ *n.*
cooking stick kɔŋɛ́sɨ́dàkwᵃ *n.*
cooking stone caál *n.*
cool cucuéón *v.*
cool down cucuéétòn *v.*; cucuéítésuƙotᵃ *v.*; cucuéónuƙotᵃ *v.*; ɗipímón *v.*
cool down (emotionally) iɛɓɨ́tésʉƙɔta gúróᵉ *v.*
cool down (food) iƙaʉ́tés *v.*
cool down the heart cucuéítésuƙota gúróᵉ *v.*
cool off cucuéétòn *v.*; cucuéónuƙotᵃ *v.*
coop (chicken) ɲɔ́kɔkɔrɔ́hò *n.*
cooperate ɗɔtsánón *v.*; ɗɔtsánónuƙotᵃ *v.*
cooperate on iɲáɲárɛtés *v.*
coordinate ilíráitetés *v.*
coordinated ilíróòn *v.*
cope with totseres *v.*
coppice (round) ɲalúƙétᵃ *n.*
copulate with tirés *v.*
copy iɲitiés *v.*; toputes *v.*; toputetés *v.*
cord sim *n.*
Cordia sinensis ɲóɗomé *n.*
cordon-bleu (red-cheeked) ŋíkaɗiidí *n.*
core ekwedᵃ *n.*
core out iɓóɓórés *v.*
cored out iɓóɓórós *v.*

Corinthians (biblical) ŋíkoríntoikᵃ n.
corn màlòr n.; màlòrièdᵃ n.; ɲaɓʉra n.
corncob ɲaɓʉraɨ́dàkwᵃ n.
corncobs (leftover) iraɲ n.
corner ɲɔkɔɔna n.; rʉ́ɛ́s v.
corner of the eye ɗoɗékwᵃ n.
corpse loukúéts'ᵃ n.; ɲélɛl n.
corral ɓór n.; ikoŋetés v.; ɨkwɛtɨ́kwétés v.; ƙalɨ́ƙálés v.; ságwès v.
correct itsɨ́rɨ́tɛtés v.; itsɨrɔ́n v.; iyóón v.; tsɨ́rɨ́tɛtés v.; tsɨrɔ́n v.; tɔɓɛitɛtés v.; tɔɓéɔ́n v.
correct (typcially) toɓéión v.
corridor bácɨ́kᵃ n.
corroborate ninɛtés v.
corrode irórôòn v.; simɨrɔ́n v.
corroded simiránón v.
corrupt iƙurúƙúròn v.; ilʉŋúlʉ́ŋés v.; iráŋʉ́nánón v.
corruption ɲéƙúruƙur n.
cosmos kíjᵃ n.
cost ɲéɓéyᵃ n.
costlessness tsàm n.
cot ɲékɨ́taɗa n.
coterie kábùn n.
cotton ɲápáma n.
coucal múɗuɗú n.
cough ɔf n.; ɔfɔn v.
councillor ŋurutiesíama mɛná ᵋ n.; ɲákáńsɔ̀là n.
counsel táŋés v.; taŋetés v.
counsel each other táŋɨnɔ́s v.
count imaarés v.
counterfeit láŋ n.
country kíjᵃ n.
county ɲákáúńtì n.

courageous itítíŋòn v.
courgette lomuƙe n.
courier dɛáám n.
course isépón v.; ɲókós n.
court ɲókótᵃ n.; sits'és v.
court each other síts'ímós v.
court fee kárátsɨ̀kᵃ n.
courthouse ɲókótᵃ n.
cousin (his/her father's brother's child) babatíím n.
cousin (his/her father's brother's son) leatᵃ n.
cousin (his/her father's sister's child) tatatíím n.
cousin (his/her mother's brother's child) momotíím n.
cousin (his/her mother's sister's child) tototíím n.
cousin (mother's brother's child) momóìm n.
cousin (mother's sister's child) totóìm n.
cousin (my father's brother's child) ŋgóím n.
cousin (my father's brother's son) ɛdɛ́ n.
cousin (my father's brother's wife's child) yáŋììm n.
cousin (my father's sister's child) tátàìm n.
cousin (your father's brother's child) bábòìm n.
cousin (your father's brother's son) léó n.
cousin (your father's sister's child) tátóím n.
covenant iɓoletés v.

cover gubés *v.*; kɔkés *v.*; kɔkɛtés *v.*; títs'ɛ́s *v.*
cover (a corpse) sɨ́nɛ́s *v.*
cover (an area) idɛŋɛs *v.*; ikáyɛ́ɛ́s *v.*
cover (an opening) tʉɓʉnɛ́s *v.*
cover (flat) ɲápár *n.*
cover (termites) mɔkɛ́s *v.*
cover oneself kɔkɛ́sá asɨ *v.*
cover up bukúrésuƙotᵃ *v.*; gubésúƙotᵃ *v.*; tits'ésúƙotᵃ *v.*
cover up issues kɔkɛ́sá mɛnáᵋ *v.*
coverall (leather) kɔ́lɔ́tsᵃ *n.*
covered idéɲímètòn *v.*
covered (get) tuɓunímétòn *v.*
covered in sores sómomójón *v.*; tɔmɔ́tɔ́mánón *v.*
covert búdòs *v.*
covetous ts'ɨ́ts'ɔ́n *v.*
cow fiyɔŋwa *n.*
cow (Ankole) Ŋíɲaŋkóléfiyɔ́ *n.*
cow (elephant) oŋoriŋwa *n.*
cow leather fiyɔjejé *n.*
cow milk fiyòìdwᵃ *n.*
cow udder fiyòìdwᵃ *n.*
cow urine tsétᵃ *n.*
cow(s) fiyɔ̀ *n.*
cow-leather shoe fiyɔtaƙáyᵃ *n.*
coward xɛɓásɨ̀àm *n.*
cowardice xɛɓás *n.*
cowardly jàƙwᵃ *ideo.*; jaƙwádòn *v.*; wúrukukánón *v.*; xèɓɔ̀n *v.*
cowbell ɲákáádoŋotᵃ *n.*
cowdung fiyɔ̀èts'ᵃ *n.*; ŋɔtᵃ *n.*
cowfly lótsótsᵃ *n.*
cowherd còòkààm *n.*
cowhide fiyɔjejé *n.*

cowpea leaves Icémórídókàkᵃ *n.*
cowpeas Icémórídᵃ *n.*
cowskin fiyɔjejé *n.*
crack ɓɛlɛ́s *v.*; ɓɛlɛtɛ́s *v.*
crack (react) tokúétòn *v.*; tokúréètòn *v.*
crack (sound) dɛdɛanón *v.*; irɔjɨ́rɔ́jɛ́s *v.*; rɛdɛdánón *v.*
crack apart itotoles *v.*
crack in pieces iráráƙɛ́s *v.*
crack knuckles irɔjɨrɔ́jɛ́sá kɔrɔ́kɨ́kàᵋ *v.*
crack open ɓɛlémón *v.*; iƙéƙɛ́ɛ́s *v.*
crack open (bones) ikokes *v.*
crack slightly beemón *v.*
crack! fiyòm *ideo.*
cracked ɓaaɓánón *v.*; ɓɛlɛ́ɓɛ́lánón *v.*; ɓɛlɔ́s *v.*; médemedánón *v.*; takátákánón *v.*
cracked skin (on feet) ɲaɓaɓa *n.*
cracker ɲéɓisikótᵃ *n.*
crackle dɛdɛanón *v.*; rɛdɛdánón *v.*
crackly xàᵘ *ideo.*
crackly (in sound) xaúdòn *v.*
craft bɛrɛtɛ́s *v.*
craft (a saying) tadápítetés *v.*
craftiness nɔɔ́s *n.*
crafty nɔɔsánón *v.*
crag ɲéɛ́sɛ *n.*
Craibia laurentii kaûdzᵃ *n.*
cram isɨkɛs *v.*; rʉtsɛ́s *v.*; rʉtsɛ́súƙɔtᵃ *v.*
cramp itiɓítíɓɔ̀n *v.*
cramp (abdominally) tɔkɔdɨ́kɔ́dɔ̀n *v.*
cramp up imúnúkukúón *v.*
cranium ikɔ́ɔ́kᵃ *n.*; ɔka ikáᵉ *n.*
crap nts'áƙón *v.*
crash (sound) tɔtɔanón *v.*
crash through brush dádítésa ríjáᵉ *v.*
Crataeva adansonii ɲéyoroeté *n.*

craving (have a) ɨrɔ́rɔ́kánón *v.*
craw gwà *n.*
crawl akúkúròn *v.*; tolíón *v.*
crawl up ikókórés *v.*
crawl up this way ikókóretés *v.*
craziness legé *n.*; lejé *n.*; lejééd^a *n.*; lejénánès *n.*; ŋkérép^a *n.*
crazy iworós *v.*
crazy (go) dojánónuƙot^a *v.*
crazy person lejéàm *n.*
cream off ijɨlɛtés *v.*
crease zeket^a *n.*
creased rɨjanón *v.*; rɨjɨrɨ́jánón *v.*; turújón *v.*; zamɨjánón *v.*
creasy turujúrújánón *v.*
create idimɛtés *v.*; iroketés *v.*; tɔsɨɓɛs *v.*
create peace fitésa kíjá^e *v.*; ilɔ́tésɨƙɔta kíjá^e *v.*
created idimɔtós *v.*
creation kíjá na idimɔtós *n.*
creator idiméstàm *n.*; idimɛtéstàm *n.*; tɔsɨɓɛtéstàm *n.*
creature idimɔtós *n.*
credible tɔnɨpam *n.*
credit idenes *v.*; idenetés *v.*; kál *n.*
creek ɨ̀àwɨ̀àw^a *n.*
creep akúƙúròn *v.*; ƙɨts'áám *n.*; totsédón *v.*
creep up ɨ̀bèdɨ̀bèdɔn *v.*
creep up on tɔléléɛtés *v.*
creeper ɲélɔ́kɨlɔk^a *n.*
crescent-shaped todóánètòn *v.*
crest (bird) ɲálem *n.*
crested tsowírímòn *v.*
crevice (rock) tsarátán *n.*
crew ɲájore *n.*

cricket jòrìjòr *n.*
cricket (armoured) ikɔ́kɔ́yà *n.*
crier weretsíám *n.*
crime téɲér *n.*
criminal ɲɔ́mɔkɔsáàm *n.*; téɲérɨ̀àm *n.*
crimp zeket^a *n.*
crimson tsòn *ideo.*
cringe ŋaxétɔ́n *v.*
crinkle zeket^a *n.*
crinkled rɨjanón *v.*; turújón *v.*; zamɨjánón *v.*
crinkly turujúrújánón *v.*
cripple ŋwàxɔ̀nɨ̀àm *n.*
crippled ŋwàxɔ̀n *v.*
crock (soot) ɲémúdets^a *n.*; ɲémúdudu *n.*
crocodile ɲetíɲáŋ *n.*
crombec (woodland) natúdusé *n.*
crook itúkúdètòn *v.*; itúkúdòn *v.*; tukudes *v.*
crook (cane) ɲótoodó *n.*
crook (climbing) ƙɔ̀dɔ̀t^a *n.*
crook (staff) ɲéseeɓɔ́ *n.*
crooked gɔ́lɔ́gɔlánón *v.*; ríbiribánón *v.*; tukúdón *v.*
crooked (corrupt) iƙurúƙúròn *v.*
crooked neck (have a) lɔkɔdɨ́kɔ́dɔ̀n *v.*
crop gwà *n.*; isésélés *v.*
crop up tɨwétɔ́n *v.*; tɨwɔ̀n *v.*
crops (nearly ripe) porór *n.*
cross kámáránón *v.*; kámárányuƙot^a *v.*; ŋɨrés *v.*; ɲémusalába *n.*; tɔkéérés *v.*
cross over górés *v.*; ígorés *v.*; ígorésúƙot^a *v.*
cross over a spear góriésá ɓɨsá^ɛ *v.*
cross repeatedly góriés *v.*; ígoriés *v.*
cross to that side aronuƙot^a *v.*
cross to this side arétón *v.*
cross-eyed kámáránón *v.*; ríbiribánón *v.*

crossing àrònìàwᵃ *n.*
crossing (river) ôdᵃ *n.*; ódèèkwᵃ *n.*
crossroad bézèkètìkìn *n.*
Crotalaria lachnocarpoides iɛƙiɛƙᵃ *n.*
crotch lɔkɔ́r *n.*
crotch of a tree bɔ̀kᵃ *n.*; bɔ̀kèdᵃ *n.*
Croton dichogamus ɓólìs *n.*
crouch dɛ́gɛ̀mɔ̀n *v.*; rábʉ̀xɔ̀n *v.*; tsɔ́nɔ́n *v.*
crow ikwóón *v.*
crow (pied) kʉ́ràkᵃ *n.*
crowbar ɲotolim *n.*
crowd itsuɗútsúɗés *v.*; ituɗútúɗés *v.*; ɲéɓúku *n.*; ɲerípírìpᵃ *n.*; òdìòs *n.*
crowded together lolotánón *v.*; tutukánón *v.*
crown (bird) ɲálem *n.*
crown of head ikágwarí *n.*
crud ts'âgᵃ *n.*
cruddy itútsón *v.*; ts'ágòn *v.*
crumble ɗukúmétòn *v.*; ɗukúmón *v.*; ɲalámétòn *v.*; ɲalámónuƙotᵃ *v.*; taɲáléetésá asɨ *v.*; taɲálóòn *v.*; tɔpwaɲɨpwáɲés *v.*
crumble off pɛsémétòn *v.*
crumbly bùɲ *ideo.*; buɲádòn *v.*; ɨwɛléwélánón *v.*; pɛsépésánón *v.*
crumbly dry tsaʉ́dɔ̀n *v.*
crumbly substance búɲèn *n.*
crumbly-dryly tsàᵘ *ideo.*
crumby ɲʉmʉ́ɲʉ́mánón *v.*
crumple lajámétòn *v.*; tʉmʉɗʉɲɛs *v.*
crumple up tʉmʉɗʉɲɛtés *v.*
crunch ɨʉmʉ́ɨ́ʉ́més *v.*
crunch (food) iruɓes *v.*
crunch (sound) ɨrɔjɨrɔ́jɛ́s *v.*
crunch crunch ƙɛ̀ƙᵋ *ideo.*; tsʉ̀bɛ̀dᵋ *ideo.*

crunchily xàᵘ *ideo.*
crunchy karúts'ʉ́mɔ̀n *v.*
crunchy (in sound) xaúdòn *v.*
crush iɗoses *v.*; iƖɛɗɛs *v.*; itsakɛs *v.*
crush (win) kɔritɛtés *v.*
crush into powder itsomes *v.*
crush up itsakɨtsákɛ́s *v.*
crust ɔmɔ́x *n.*
crusted over rɔ́bɔ̀ɗɔ̀mɔ̀n *v.*
crusty rɔ́bɔ̀ɗɔ̀mɔ̀n *v.*
cry ƙɔ̀ɗɔ̀n *v.*; werɛtsᵃ *n.*
cry (make) ƙɔɗitɛs *v.*
cry breathily xíƙwítós *v.*
cry easily dzálón *v.*; iɲɛ́ɛ́mɔ̀n *v.*
cry out bɔ́rɔ́rɔ̀n *v.*; werétsón *v.*; werétsónuƙotᵃ *v.*
crystallize ɲaʉ́dɔnʉƙotᵃ *v.*
crystallized ɲaʉ́dɔ̀n *v.*
crystallizedly ɲàᵘ *ideo.*
cucumber kɔlil *n.*
cucumber grass kɔliƖɨ́kú *n.*
cucumber juice kɔliƖɨ́cúé *n.*
cucumber seed kɔliƖɨ́ékwᵃ *n.*
Cucumis dipsaceus tsɔ́ráɗoɗôbᵃ *n.*
Cucumis figarei loɗeɗᵃ *n.*
cultivatable tɔkɔbam *n.*
cultivate tɔkɔ́bɛs *v.*
cultivate (make) tɔkɔ́bitɛtés *v.*
cultivate early iɗɔ́rɛʉƙotᵃ *v.*
cultivated tɔkɔ́bitɔtɔ́s *v.*
cultivation tɔkɔ̀bᵃ *v.*
cultivation (early) ɨɗɔr *n.*
cultivator tɔkɔ̀bààm *n.*
cumbersome pɔsɔ́kɔ́mɔ̀n *v.*
cuneal likɛ́ɗɨ́mɔ̀n *v.*
cunning nɔɔ́s *n.*; nɔɔsánón *v.*
cup ɲókópo *n.*

cupboard ɲákábàtᵃ n.
Cupressus lusitanica asʉnán n.
cure maraɲítésuƙotᵃ v.; mɨ́nés v.
curl ilúƙúretés v.
curl around imanímánés v.
curl up ilúƙúrètòn v.; tusuketés v.; tusúkón v.
curl up (to rest) touríánòn v.
curled up ilúƙúròn v.
current issues kíjámèn n.
current of air sugur n.
curse ébetiés v.; ɨ̀làm n.; ilamɛs v.; itsenes v.; kótés v.
curse with a difficult birth ikɛɗɛs v.
cursed ɨlamɔs v.
cursed (of a birth) ikɛɗɔs v.
curser of natural resources tébɛsɨama kíjáᵉ n.
curses ɲítsen n.
curtain (doorway) ɲétiriƙá n.
curve ilúƙúɗòn v.
curve backward (of horns) toryóɲón v.
curved forward soƙolánón v.
curvy tukúɗúkuɗánón v.
cushion ɲápalís n.; ɲápalís n.
cuspid bàdìam n.
cuss out ébetiés v.; kótés v.
Cussonia arborea boxoƙorétᵃ n.
custom ɲatal n.; ɲeker n.
customer dzígwààm n.; dzígwèsìam n.
cut ɗesémón v.; ɗusúmón v.; ɗusutes v.; hoés v.; ikéɲéɗés v.; ŋʉrés v.; ŋʉrós v.; tɔŋɛɗɛs v.
cut (of meat) ɲekiner n.
cut (vegetation) iɗɛtɛs v.; irɛjɛs v.
cut a circle tɔlʉkɛtés v.

cut a ring in ilɨɲɨrɛ́s v.
cut across piɗés v.
cut around ilɨɲɨrɛ́s v.; ilɨrɛs v.
cut away iƙémíƙémés v.; ŋʉrésúƙɔtᵃ v.
cut bluntly ifitífités v.
cut down ruɓutetés v.
cut dully iɲulúŋúlés v.
cut in (verbally) itoɓes v.
cut in chunks julés v.
cut in conversation itoɓítóɓésa tóɗàᵉ v.
cut in pieces ŋurutiés v.; ŋurutiós v.
cut in slices írés v.; irikíríkés v.
cut in strips iɗiɗɛs v.
cut in two iwáwáɗés v.
cut into hoetés v.
cut noisily iwɔxɨwɔ́xés v.
cut off ŋʉrésúƙɔtᵃ v.; ŋurúmétòn v.
cut off (branches) iteɗes v.
cut off (verbally) iƙofes v.
cut off completely fùtᵘ ideo.
cut out ɓilés v.; hoetés v.
cut out (exlude) tɔlúkésʉƙɔtᵃ v.
cut out respiratory organs itórópés v.
cut short ŋurúmétòn v.
cut through ɓʉ́nés v.; ɓʉnɛtés v.
cut up hoetés v.; ŋʉrɛtés v.; ŋʉrúŋʉránón v.
cut up in pieces iɲilɨɲílánón v.; iɲilɨɲílés v.; ŋurutiesúƙɔtᵃ v.
cut with a blade kawés v.
cuttable ɓʉnɛtam n.
cutting of grass sɨláxɨŋ n.
cycle irɔmɛs v.
cylindrical ɗatáɲámòn v.
Cynachium species ɲákamóɲɔ n.
Cynodon dactylon mʉrɔn n.
Cyperus alternifolius bùsùbùs n.

Cyperus distans gòmòjòjᵃ *n.*
Cyphostemma junceum ɲɛcaal *n.*
daily life zɛkwᵃ *n.*
dam tábàr *n.*; tɨts'és *v.*
dam up itékélés *v.*; tɨts'ésʉƙɔtᵃ *v.*; tɨts'-imétòn *v.*
damage kwɛts'és *v.*
damaged (get) kwɛts'émɔ́n *v.*
dammed tɨts'ɔ́s *v.*
damn ɨlamɛs *v.*
damned ɨlamɔs *v.*
damn! ɗʉ̀rʉ̀ *n.*
damp ɗɔ́ƙɔ̀n *v.*
damp (become) ɗɔkɔnʉƙɔtᵃ *v.*
dampen ɗɔƙítésʉƙɔtᵃ *v.*
dance dikwᵃ *n.*; dikwétón *v.*
dance (clapping) ɲókorotᵃ *n.*
dance (ecstatic) jàkàlʉ̀kà *n.*
dance (like to) dikwidikos *v.*
dance (stork-style) dikwa na tsokóbè *n.*
dance (style of) ɲélɛmá *n.*
dance and sing óìdìkwòn *v.*
dance at danceground dikwétóna ŋabɔ́bɔ̀ɔ *v.*
dance hall dikwáhò *n.*
dance toward ilépón *v.*
dance with singing wááka dikwitíní *n.*
dance with stomping ɨpàs *n.*
dance-walk ɨpásétòn *v.*
danceground ŋabɔ́bɔ̀ *n.*
dancing ɲaɓolya *n.*
danger gaánàs *n.*; ɲárém *n.*
dangerous gaanón *v.*
dangle alólóánitetés *v.*; alólóánón *v.*; alólóés *v.*
dapple ɨtsɔɓɨ́tsɔ́ɓɛ́s *v.*

dappled ɨtsɔɓɨ́tsɔ́ɓɔ̀n *v.*; ɨtsɔɓɨ́tsɔ́ɓɔ́s *v.*
dark buɗámón *v.*
dark (of many) buɗamaakón *v.*
darken kaikóón *v.*; kurukúrétòn *v.*; witsiwítsétòn *v.*
darkness bùɗàm *n.*
darkness (pitch) ɲákámus *n.*
dart ɓɨsáím *n.*; ɨrʉtsɛsa asɨ *v.*
dart away ɨpúmɔ́nʉƙɔtᵃ *v.*
dart off ɨpúmɔ́nʉƙɔtᵃ *v.*
dart out ɨpúmétòn *v.*
dash dzèrɔ̀n *v.*
dash away ɨpúmɔ́nʉƙɔtᵃ *v.*
dash off ɨpúmɔ́nʉƙɔtᵃ *v.*
dash out ɨpúmétòn *v.*
dassie kwɨnɨƙᵃ *n.*
date sɨts'és *v.*
date (desert) òwà *n.*
date each other sɨ́ts'ímós *v.*
Datura stramonium lɔmɔ́yᵃ *n.*
daub ɨwarɛs *v.*
daubed ɨwarɔs *v.*
daughter jàgwᵃ *n.*; ɲàràm *n.*
daughter (his/her) jágwèdᵃ *n.*
daughter-in-law bɔkátɨ́n *n.*; imácékᵃ *n.*
daughters ɲèr *n.*
dauntless itítíŋòn *v.*
dawn ɓelémón *v.*; ítóna kɨ́jée ts'ɛɛ *v.*; pɛlémɔ́na fetí *v.*; tsòòn *v.*; tsoonuƙotᵃ *v.*; walámón *v.*
dawn cooly wéreƙéƙón *v.*
dawn red ɨpɨrɨ́pɨ́rɛ̀tɔ̀n *v.*
day ódòwᵃ *n.*
day after tomorrow kétsóibaráts *n.*
day before yesterday nótsóò nòkᵒ *n.*
daybreak pɛlémɔ́na fetí *v.*
daze ɨrakɛs *v.*; ɨrákésʉƙɔtᵃ *v.*

dazed *dejected*

dazed ijárɔ́n *v.*; jarámétòn *v.*; tɔmɛrímérɔ̀n *v.*
deacon iritsɛ́sɨ̀àm *n.*
dead (almost) inunúmónuƙotᵃ *v.*
dead people ts'óóniikᵃ *n.*
dead person bàdònìàm *n.*
deaf ilios *v.*; mɨ̀ɲɔ̀n *v.*
deaf person ámá nà mɨ̀ɲ *n.*; bositíníàm *n.*
deal out imɔlɛs *v.*
deal with nɛɛ́s *v.*; nɛɛsɨ́ƙɔtᵃ *v.*; totseres *v.*
deal with each other totsérímós *v.*
death (natural) badona ná jèjèⁱ *n.*
debate nɛpɛƙánón *v.*
debile bɨlájámɔ̀n *v.*; daƙwádòn *v.*
debt amɨ́tsᵃ *n.*; kál *n.*
debtor amɨtsáàm *n.*; amɨtsáàm *n.*
decay ɗutɨ́ɗɨtánónuƙotᵃ *v.*; lolómónuƙotᵃ *v.*; masánétòn *v.*; mɨsánétòn *v.*
decayed ɗatáɗátánón *v.*; ɗutúdòn *v.*
decayed (very) ɗùtᵘ *ideo.*
decaying ɗutɨ́ɗɨtánón *v.*
decease irɨ́ɗétɔ̀n *v.*
deceased bàdònìàm *n.*; tás *n.*
deceive imɔɗɛs *v.*
decelerate tosipetés *v.*
December Ibùɓù *n.*; Raraan *n.*
decide on ɲɨmɛtés *v.*
decked out naƙwɨ́dòn *v.*
declare sírànòn *v.*
decline míjés *v.*; rárímòn *v.*
decompose ɗutɨ́ɗɨtánónuƙotᵃ *v.*; mɨsánétòn *v.*
decomposed ɗatáɗátánón *v.*; ɗutúdòn *v.*
decomposing ɗutɨ́ɗɨtánón *v.*

decorate isires *v.*; naƙwɨ́dɛtés *v.*
decorate with beads idɛrɛs *v.*
decorated isiros *v.*
decorated with beads idɛrɔs *v.*
decoration ŋásír *n.*; ɲewale *n.*
decrease rárímetés *v.*; rárímòn *v.*
decrease in number ƙwaɗonuƙotᵃ *v.*
decrease in size kwátsónuƙotᵃ *v.*
decrease size kwatsítésuƙotᵃ *v.*
decreased bɨráɨ́tɔ̀n *v.*
decrepit gɔ́gɔ̀rɔ̀mɔ̀n *v.*
decrepitly gɔ̀gɔ̀r *ideo.*
deep ɓòɓòn *v.*
deep (very) wòò *ideo.*
deep asleep nɨsɨ́dɔ̀n *v.*
deepen ɓoɓonuƙotᵃ *v.*
deeper (become) ɓoɓonuƙotᵃ *v.*
deeply dùù *ideo.*
defame itúrúmés *v.*
defeat ilɔɛs *v.*; ilɔɛtés *v.*; ipíyéésuƙotᵃ *v.*; kurés *v.*; kurésúƙotᵃ *v.*
defeated iloimétòn *v.*
defecate nts'áƙón *v.*
defecate often iɓutɨ́ɓɨ́tɔ̀n *v.*
defecation spot nts'áƙáàwᵃ *n.*
defend cookés *v.*; iɛtés *v.*
defender còòkààm *n.*; iɛtésɨ̀àm *n.*
deficient idáƙón *v.*; taɗatsánón *v.*
deflate ɓilímón *v.*; tɔ́ɗɔ́nɨƙotᵃ *v.*
deflated fɔrɔ́ts'ɔmɔ̀n *v.*; tɔ́ɗɔ́n *v.*
deflect iɓatɛs *v.*; iƙɨɛs *v.*
deflect repeatedly iɓatɨ́ɓátés *v.*
deformed rétón *v.*
deformed (of an eye) ɗooɲómòn *v.*
degree kêdᵃ *n.*
dejected isɔ́nɛ́sɔ̀n *v.*

delay asínón *v.*; inípónítésúkotᵃ *v.*; ɨtɨ́ɔ́n *v.*; itúmésukotᵃ *v.*; titiretés *v.*
delegate irotes *v.*
deliberate iyótsóós *v.*
delicacy gwadam *n.*; ɲɛmʉna *n.*
delicate yɛmɛ́dɔ̀n *v.*
delicate (thin) bɛɗɛ́dɔ̀n *v.*
delicately yèm *ideo.*
delicious ritídòn *v.*
deliciously rìtⁱ *ideo.*
delight ɨlákásɨ́tɛ́sʉkɔt ᵃ *v.*; ɨmúmúɨtɛtés *v.*
deliver a child kwaatetés *v.*
demolish ipáríés *v.*; itɔ́tɔ́és *v.*
demon ɲɛkɨ́pyɛ́ *n.*
demon possession legé *n.*; lejé *n.*; lejééd ᵃ *n.*; lejénánès *n.*; ŋkérép ᵃ *n.*
demon-possessed person lejéàm *n.*
demons ɲɨ́pyɛn *n.*
demonstrate ɗoɗésúkot ᵃ *v.*; itétémés *v.*
den ak ᵃ *n.*
denied rébìmètòn *v.*
denigrate itúrúmés *v.*
denizen zɛkɔ́ám *n.*
denomination (religious) ɲéɗíni *n.*
dense rɔ́mɔ́n *v.*
dense (become) mogánétòn *v.*
dense (of a thicket) mogánón *v.*
dense (of undergrowth) bòmòn *v.*
dent luɗés *v.*; rábaɗamitésúkot ᵃ *v.*
dented luɗúmón *v.*; rábàɗàmòn *v.*
dented (get) rábaɗamonukot ᵃ *v.*
dentifrice ɲókólíkèt ᵃ *n.*
dentist tolésíàm *n.*
denuded sɨlɔ́jɔ́mɔ̀n *v.*
deny dimés *v.*; rébès *v.*

departed (dead) tás *n.*
depend on ikɔŋɛs *v.*
dependable ikékéɲòn *v.*
dependant fiyekesíám *n.*
dependence bɔnánés *n.*
dependent bɔnán *n.*
depict iwetés *v.*
depleted ikarímétòn *v.*
deplore topóɗón *v.*
deploy eréges *v.*
depraved ɨráŋúnánón *v.*
depress luɗés *v.*
depressed isɔ́nɛ́sɔ̀n *v.*; sìŋòn *v.*
deprive rébès *v.*
deprived rébìmètòn *v.*
deracinate ɗués *v.*; ɗuetés *v.*; rués *v.*
deranged iworós *v.*
derelict kɔlɔlánón *v.*
deride with a sucking sound ts'úútés *v.*
descend ɗipímón *v.*; kídzìmòn *v.*
descend (out of sight) lakámétòn *v.*; lakámón *v.*
descend (that way) kídzimonukot ᵃ *v.*
descend (this way) kídzìmètòn *v.*; tsígìmètòn *v.*
descend into chaos iɲóɗyáìmètòn *v.*
desert góózés *v.*; góózesukot ᵃ *v.*; nalɔŋɨzat ᵃ *n.*
desert date tsʉm *n.*
desert date (fruit) òwà *n.*
desert dated (ripe) kwɨ́lɨlɨ *n.*
desert rose dɛrɛ́k ᵃ *n.*; jɔt ᵃ *n.*
deserted góózosukot ᵃ *v.*
designs ɲákɨran *n.*
desire kanetés *v.*; wíránés *v.*
desist bɔlɔnʉkot ᵃ *v.*
desk ɲéméza na ɨ́kɨ̀rà ᵋ *n.*

despise ilɛ́lɛ́ɛ́s v.; ts'ábès v.; tsíítés v.; takaɗes v.

despise each other ilɛ́lɛ́imós v.; ts'ábunós v.

despoil taɓales v.

dessicated seƙelánón v.

destitute iƙúrúfánón v.; iɓúlíánón v.

destitute person iɓúlíánóníàm n.; iƙúrúfánóníàm n.

destroy ináƙúés v.; ináƙúetés v.; ipáríés v.; itɔ́tɔ́és v.

destroy violently gaɗés v.

destroyed ináƙúós v.; ináƙúotós v.

detachment (military) ɲéɗitác n.

detain itúmésuƙotᵃ v.

detect takanités v.

detective tirifɛtésíàm n.

detergent ɲásaɓuní n.

detergent (laundry) hómò n.; ɲéómò n.

determined iƙázànòòn v.; imúƙáánón v.

detest ilɛ́lɛ́ɛ́s v.; ts'ábès v.; tuluɲɛs v.

detest each other ts'ábunós v.

detour wédɔ̀n v.

detour widely ƙeƙérón v.

devastate isíłánitɛtés v.

develop bɛrés v.; zeites v.; zeitésuƙotᵃ v.

developed ikeimétòn v.

deviate imámáɗós v.; itípéés v.; iwitités v.

devil Siitán n.

devilry badirétᵃ n.

devise iroketés v.

devote onself imíɗitsésa así v.

devotee mínésìàm n.; túbèsìàm n.

devour ɗáɗítés v.; ŋƙáƙésuƙotᵃ v.

devout person ɲakujíám n.

dew siƙᵃ n.

dewlap ɓòlíɓòl n.

Dhaasanac people Ŋíɗóŋiro n.

diagnose ipimɛs v.

diaper ets'íƙwâz n.

diaphragm kàɓᵃ n.

diarrhate harítɔ́n v.

diarrhea hár n.

diarrhea (chunky) hárá na gwɛrɛjɛ́jᵃ n.

diarrhea (have explosive) ifulúfúlòn v.

diarrhea (have liquidy) harítɔ́na pìɔ v.

diarrhea (have) harítɔ́n v.

diarrhea (liquid) hárá na tíłiwᵃ n.

diarrhea (severe) hárá ná zè n.

diarrheal dulúmón v.

diarrheal mucus hárígaɗár n.

dice ŋurutiés v.

dice up ŋurutiesúƙotᵃ v.

diced ŋurutiós v.

Dichrostachys cinerea gùr n.

dictionary ɲéɗíkìxònàrì n.

did not máa adv.

Didinga language Ŋíídìɲátôdᵃ n.

Didinga man kéxésìàm n.

Didinga person lɔ́tɔ́bààm n.; Ŋíídìŋáám n.; ɲémurúŋgùàm n.

die bàdòn v.; badonuƙotᵃ v.; tézètɔ̀n v.

die (make) baɗítésuƙotᵃ v.

die (of many) ts'óón v.

die down ɗipímón v.

die off bulonuƙotᵃ v.; raraanón v.

die off (of many) ts'óónuƙotᵃ v.

die out bulonuƙotᵃ v.

die out (of fire) ts'oonuƙotᵃ v.

die out (of many) ts'óónuƙotᵃ v.

die suddenly itúlésuƙɔta así v.

diesel ceím n.

differ jalánónuƙotª v.
different jalájálánón v.; jalánón v.
different (become) jalánónuƙotª v.
differentiate jalanites v.
difficult imákóòn v.; itíónòn v.
difficult (become) imákwéètòn v.; kurósúƙotª v.
difficult (make) imákóitetés v.
difficulty ŋátíónis n.
dig úgès v.
dig (for water) tawaɗes v.
dig by scratching ikúkúrés v.
dig out ikuɗúkúɗés v.; tukuretés v.; tukutetés v.; úgetés v.
dig randomly ɨtsɛɗɨtsɛ́ɗés v.
dig up tukures v.; tukutes v.; úgetés v.
digest ŋɔ́és v.
digested ŋɔ́ɔ́s v.
digger ɲétɛrɛƙitaa na kwɛtáᵋ n.; tébɛsiama jʉmwɨ n.
digging stick fen n.
digit kɔrɔ́kª n.
digit (number) ɲánambá n.
digress hakonuƙotª v.; iɓátésʉƙɔta mɛnáᵋ v.
dik-dik (Gunther's) ɲól n.
dik-dik mushroom ɲolíkɨnám n.
dik-dik thornbush ɲólíkàf n.
dilapidated kɔlɔlánón v.
dilate imiɗɨmɨɗés v.
diluted silaɓánón v.
dim kaikóón v.
dim (in intellect) buɗámón v.
dim (of eyesight) buɗámón v.
dim (of many) buɗamaakón v.
diminish rárímetés v.; rárímòn v.

ding rábaɗamitésúƙotª v.
dinged rábàɗàmòn v.
dinged (get) rábaɗamonuƙotª v.
dining area ŋƙáƙáàyª n.
dinner ŋƙáƙá na wídzòᵉ n.
Dioscorea species ewêdª n.
Diospyros scabra godiywª n.
dip ilumes v.; ilúmésuƙotª v.; iúpón v.
dip away iúpónuƙotª v.
dip down iúpétòn v.
dip into iɗipes v.
dip out (liquid) ábʉbʉƙɛ́s v.
dipper ƙór n.
dipteran dililits'ª n.
direct itsɨrítɛtés v.; iyoes v.; tsɨrítɛtés v.; tɔɓɛitɛtés v.; tɔɓɛ́ón v.
direction xán n.
dirt jʉm n.
dirt (red) boŋórén n.
dirt mixed with grain bɔɗájʉ́m n.
dirt-poor iɓúlíánón v.
dirt-poor person iɓúlíánóniàm n.
dirtiness ts'âgª n.
dirty buɗámón v.; ɨráɲúnánón v.; kaɓúrútsánón v.; ŋɔrɔ́ɲɔ́mɔ̀n v.; ɲɔŋɔ́rómòn v.; ts'ágòn v.
dirty (of many) buɗamaakón v.
disability ŋwaxás n.
disabled ŋwàxɔ̀n v.
disabled person ámá nà ŋwàx n.; ŋwàxɔ̀nɨàm n.
disagree nɛpɛƙánón v.
disappear buanónuƙotª v.; ɨɨɗɔ́n v.; kúbonuƙotª v.; wiɗɨmɔ́nʉƙɔtª v.
disappear (make) buanítésuƙotª v.; iwítésuƙotª v.
disappeared buanón v.
disc (aluminum) ɲépéɗe n.

discard

discard hábatsésúkotᵃ v.; hábatsetés v.
discern ɦyeités v.
discharge ɓóri̱tòn v.; ídzès v.; ídzesukotᵃ v.; ídzòn v.; taŋasɛs v.
discharge (mucupurulent) dɔx n.
discharge continuously ídziidziés v.
disciple dɛáám n.
disclose ilééránitetés v.
disco dikwáhò n.
discontent lɔlɔanón v.
discord ɲékúrukur n.; ɲépi̱ɗi̱pi̱ɗᵃ n.
discourage faɗites v.; ikarɛtés v.; ilɔ́ítésu̱kɔtᵃ v.
discover enés v.; takanités v.
discovery nòìn n.
discriminate ilɔ́ɗi̱ŋés v.
discrimination ɲoloɗiŋ n.
discriminatory ilɔ́ɗi̱ŋánón v.
discuss i̱ɛnétòn v.; i̱ɛnón v.
discuss details ituetésá tódàᵉ v.
discuss matters (as a group) itukanetésá mɛnáᵋ v.
discussion ɲékukwá n.
disdain ilɛ́ɛɛs v.; tsíítés v.; takaɗes v.
disease màywᵃ n.; ɲeɗeke n.
disease (liver) ɲeɗekea sakámáᵉ n.
disease (mild) ɲeɗekéím n.
disease of chest ɲeɗekea bákútsìkàᵉ n.
disembowel ɓilésúkotᵃ v.
disgorge xerétón v.
disgrace iryámítetésá ŋiléétsìkᵉ v.; ŋiléétsᵃ n.
disgraced (become) iryámétona ŋiléétsìkᵉ v.
disgracefulness ŋiléétsìnànès n.
disgust ilɛ́lɛ́i̱tɛtés v.

displease

dish out gárés v.; i̱mɔlɛs v.
dish up gárés v.
dish-rack lɔpi̱táá na kófóikóᵉ n.
dishevel imóɲíkees v.; imóɲíkeetés v.
dishonest yu̱anón v.
disintegrate ɗukúmétòn v.; ɗukúmón v.
disintegrating i̱ɲili̱ɲi̱lánón v.
dislocate toletés v.
dislocate (joint) kwi̱jɛ́s v.
dislocated kwi̱ji̱mɔ́n v.
dislocated (become) tolómétòn v.
dislocated (get) ɓuumón v.
dislodge iloílóés v.; toletés v.
dislodged (become) tolómétòn v.
dismantle iju̱kújukɛ́s v.
disobedience ɲésɛ́kɔ n.
disobedient isɛ́kɔ́ánón v.
disobedient person ɲésɛ́kɔ́ám n.
disorderly lɔŋɔanón v.
disorderly (become) lɔŋɔanónukotᵃ v.
disorientation (topographical) ɲíjokopí n.
dispel itwares v.
dispense kisanes v.; kísés v.; tɔkɔrɛs v.; tɔkɔ́résu̱kɔtᵃ v.; tɔkɔ́rúkɔ́résu̱kɔtᵃ v.
disperse alámááránón v.; ɓunúmón v.; ɓunutés v.; ilámááránón v.; itwares v.; iwɛ́ɛlánón v.; iwɛ́ɛlɛ́s v.; iwɛ́ɛlɛ́su̱kotᵃ v.; iwɛ́ɛletés v.; kisanes v.; kísés v.; toɓwaŋes v.; tɔkɔrɛs v.; tɔkɔ́résu̱kɔtᵃ v.; tɔkɔ́rúkɔ́résukotᵃ v.
dispersed iwɛ́ɛlós v.
dispersion kís n.
displace dzukɛ́s v.; ilójésukotᵃ v.; ilɔ́li̱ɛ́s v.
displace away dzukésúkotᵃ v.
displace this way dzukɛtés v.
displease i̱gaɗɛs v.

325

disprove isalɛs v.; isalɛtés v.; isalités v.
disproven isálímétòn v.
disputation ɲelerum n.
dispute dèƙwᵃ n.
dispute (of many) ilérúmùòn v.
disregard bálábálatés v.; balés v.; balɛtés v.
disrespect tatés v.
disrupt ibubuŋés v.; ibubuŋésúƙotᵃ v.
disruptive rébòn v.
dissatisfied lɔlɔanón v.
dissatisfy ígadés v.
dissect pakés v.
dissimilar jalánón v.
dissipate alámááránón v.; ilámááránón v.; iwéélánón v.; iwéélésuƙotᵃ v.; iwéélɛtés v.
dissipated iwéélós v.
dissolve ilɔkɛs v.; lajámétòn v.
dissolve (in mouth) inuƙúnúƙwés v.
dissuade táɲés v.; taɲetés v.
distance iɛkás n.; iɛƙítésuƙotᵃ v.; zikíbàs n.
distance (in miles) máirɔ̀edᵃ n.
distant ìɛ̀ƙòn v.
distant (slightly) iɛƙíéƙòn v.
distended teɓúsúmòn v.
distill tsipitsípón v.
distinguish jalanites v.
distort imáƙóitetés v.
distort (truth) isudes v.; isudetés v.
distorted imáƙóòn v.; rétón v.
distorted (become) imáƙwéètòn v.
distract gwelítésuƙotᵃ v.; hakaikitetés v.; itúmúránitésúƙotᵃ v.
distracted itúmúránón v.

distractible duméɗémòn v.
distressed (become) ilárímétòn v.; ilwárímétòn v.
distribute kisanes v.; kísés v.; tɔkɔrɛs v.; tɔkɔrésuƙotᵃ v.; tɔkɔ́rúkɔ́résuƙotᵃ v.
distribution kís n.
distributor kísáàm n.; kisanesíám n.
district ɲédísítùrìkᵃ n.
District Commissioner diisí n.
disturb itsanɛs v.
disturbed waliwálón v.
disunited with each other teretiinós v.
ditch cúémúcè n.; hábatsésúƙotᵃ v.; hábatsetés v.
diverse jalájálánón v.
diversionary tactic ɲépípa n.
divert itípées v.; iwitités v.
divide pakés v.; taɲáléés v.; terés v.
divide in two tɔŋéérés v.
divide mathematically tɔkɔrɛs v.
divide out kisanes v.; kísés v.; tɔkɔrɛs v.; tɔkɔrésuƙotᵃ v.; tɔkɔ́rúkɔ́résuƙotᵃ v.
divide up hoetés v.; kisanes v.; kísés v.; taɲáléetés v.; terétéránitésúƙotᵃ v.; tereties v.; tɔkɔrɛs v.; tɔkɔrésuƙotᵃ v.; tɔkɔ́rúkɔ́résuƙotᵃ v.
divide up an animal teretiesá ínóᵉ v.
divided amongst each other teretiinós v.
divided in pieces ŋurutiós v.
divided up terétéránón v.; teretiós v.
divination fadás n.
divine fàdòn v.
diviner fàdònìàm n.
divinity ɲakujínánès n.
division (military) ɲédivíxìon n.
division (space) naƙúlé n.

divorce hoɗés v.; terémón v.; terémónuƙotᵃ v.
divulge kwɛts'ɛ́s v.
divulged kwɛts'ɛ́món v.
divvy up hoetés v.
dizziness taítayó n.
dizzy imáúròn v.
do itíyéés v.; itíyéetés v.
do again iɓóŋón v.; iɲaƙes v.; iɲoƙes v.; iɲóƙésuƙotᵃ v.
do aimlessly ipɛ́ipɛ́ɛ́s v.
do away with guts'urɛs v.; guts'uriés v.; itsúrúés v.
do business dzígwès v.; itsúrútseés v.
do faster imúmúrɛ́s v.
do in itsútésuƙɔtᵃ v.
do in patches xúrés v.
do like iretes v.
do not ejá adv.; máa adv.
do partially iliŋɛs v.
do patchily xúrés v.
do poorly itáƙálés v.
do properly iyomes v.
do quickly iɓurúɓúròn v.
do streakily iliŋɛs v.
do wrongly hamujés v.
do(es) not ńtá adv.
do-nothing ɲakárámitᵃ n.
doable ikásíetam v.; itíyéetam n.
doctor ɗakitáriàm n.
doctor (animal) ɗakitáriama ínóᵉ n.
document kàbàɗᵃ n.; ɲákaratás n.
doddering kamudurudádòn v.
doddery dúnésòn v.; itúléròn v.
doddery (become) itúléronuƙotᵃ v.
dodge kiɗonuƙɔtᵃ v.

dodge repeatedly iwitíwítòn v.
Dodoth County Dàsòƙᵃ n.
Dodoth dialect Gwágwaicétôdᵃ n.
Dodoth people Cɔ́ƙɔ́tɔ̀m n.
Dodoth person Cɔ́ƙɔ́tɔ̀mèàm n.; Gwágwààm n.
doe (goat) rieŋwa n.
dog ŋókᵃ n.
dog (female) ŋókíŋwa n.
dog (male) ŋókícikwᵃ n.
dog (wild hunting) tsoe n.
dog poop ŋókíèts'ᵃ n.
dogfly ŋókítsùtsᵃ n.
dole out iɲɨ́ɲínɛ́s v.
Dolichos kilimandscharicus túḿbàbᵃ n.
Dolichos oliveri dàlìs n.
dollar ɲoɗɔ́la n.
Dombeya goetzenii xuxûbᵃ n.
Dombeya quinqueseta wariwar n.
domestic animal ínwá na awáᵉ n.
domestic violence gaɗᵃ n.
domesticate bɔnés v.
domical loŋórómòn v.
dominate ɔ́bès v.
donate dónés v.; dónésuƙotᵃ v.
donate sporadically donitiésuƙotᵃ v.
done itíyáìmètòn v.
done (finished) ɲábɔnuƙɔtᵃ v.; nábɔnuƙɔtᵃ v.
done (get) itíyéetés v.
donkey ɗiɗᵃ n.
donkey (female) ɗiɗeŋwa n.
donkey (male) ɗiɗecúrúkᵃ n.
donkey (young) ɗiɗèim n.
donor dónésiàm n.
doomed ilamɔs v.
door àsàkᵃ n.

door body àsàkànèbᵃ *n.*
doorframe ɲɛ́fɨrɛ́m *n.*
doorstep lòkìtòŋ *n.*; lòrìòŋòn *n.*
doorway àsàkᵃ *n.*
dormouse ɲáaɲún *n.*
dot bàsɔ̀n *v.*; iɗolíɗólés *v.*
dotted iɗolíɗólòn *v.*; merixánón *v.*
double-crosser tolúónìàm *n.*
doubt iɲáyéés *v.*; itóŋóòn *v.*
doubt matters itóŋóiesá mɛnáᵋ *v.*
doubtful ikókós *v.*
dough dɨbam *n.*
doughily nɨ̀r *ideo.*
doughy nɨrɨ́dɔ̀n *v.*
douse ɨɛ́ɓɨtɛtés *v.*
dove bîbᵃ *n.*
dove (red-eyed) túrúkukú *n.*
down gígìròkᵉ *n.*; kíjákᵉ *n.*; kɔ́ɔ́ kíjᵒ *n.*; nɔ́ɔ́ kíjᵒ *n.*
down (drink) ijɨ́ɨ́résɨkotᵃ *v.*
down (food) lakatiés *v.*; lukutiés *v.*
down (gulp) itúlákáɲés *v.*
down-striped ikwɛrɔs *v.*
downcast ijúrúròn *v.*; ɨsónɛ́sɔ̀n *v.*
downcast (of eyes) ijúrújúròn *v.*
downfall rumetᵃ *n.*
downgrade rárímetés *v.*
downward gígìròkᵉ *n.*; ijúrúròn *v.*; kɔ́ɔ́ kíjᵒ *n.*
downward (gaze) ijúrújúròn *v.*
downward place gígìr *n.*
doze off ɨlúzètòn *v.*
draff ɗɨká *n.*; dàjᵃ *n.*
drag fɔ́fɔ́tés *v.*; ifɔɛs *v.*
drag along béberiés *v.*

drag away béberésúkotᵃ *v.*
drag off béberésúkotᵃ *v.*
drag oneself ifɔɛsa asɨ *v.*
dragonfly ɗàɗàgwà *n.*
drain ɨ́dzòn *v.*
drain blood tsʼolítésukota séàᵉ *v.*
drainage area ɲɛrétᵃ *n.*
drama wááka na támɔtɔ́s *n.*
drape ilɔ́gɔtsés *v.*
draw eminés *v.*; ikɛrɛs *v.*; iwetés *v.*
draw (attract) tɔminɛs *v.*
draw (signs) ikɨrɛs *v.*
draw apart eminiés *v.*
draw away eminésúkotᵃ *v.*
draw back isúrúmɔ̀n *v.*
draw near ɦyɔtɔ́gètòn *v.*
draw off eminésúkotᵃ *v.*
draw out béberés *v.*; eminetés *v.*
draw out speech ɨɛ́nɨ́tɛtés *v.*; tóítetés *v.*
draw saliva imɨjúmɨ́jɔ̀n *v.*
draw up eminetés *v.*
DRC Kóŋgò *n.*
dread paupáwón *v.*
dream asínítòn *v.*
dreamer asínítònìàm *n.*
dregs ɗɨká *n.*; dàjᵃ *n.*
drenched tsʼalídòn *v.*
drenchedly tsʼàl *ideo.*
dress ŋábès *v.*; ɲékiteitéyᵃ *n.*
dress up ŋábitetés *v.*; nakwɨ́dɛtés *v.*
dressed (get) ŋábitetés *v.*
dressed up nakwɨ́dɔ̀n *v.*
dressed up (very) nàkwⁱ *ideo.*
dresser (fine) ɲásírìàm *n.*

dribble

dribble iɗɔ́nɔ́n *v.*; imilɛtés *v.*; ipinípínɔ̀n *v.*; ts'olites *v.*; ts'olítésuƙotᵃ *v.*; ts'òlòn *v.*; tɔlɛ́lɛ́ɔ̀n *v.*
dried out mɔ̀sɔ̀n *v.*; seƙelánón *v.*
dried up kɔlɔlánón *v.*
drift ilɔ́líɛ́sá así *v.*
drift away ilélébonuƙotᵃ *v.*
drift off hakonuƙotᵃ *v.*
drifter botibotosíám *n.*
drill ipirípírɛs *v.*; pulutiés *v.*
drilled tsàpòn *v.*
driller pulutiesíàm *n.*
Drimia altissima bulubulátᵃ *n.*
drink wetam *n.*; wetés *v.*
drink (carbonated) ɲɔsɔ́ɗa *n.*
drink (give) wetités *v.*; wetitésuƙotᵃ *v.*
drink (orange) ɲékwiɲcá *n.*
drink (strong) kombótᵃ *n.*; tule *n.*
drink a lot of tolepetés *v.*
drink like a cow bútés *v.*
drink slowly iwɛtɛs *v.*
drink to last drop ijɨ́ɨ́rɛ́suƙotᵃ *v.*
drink too much wɔ̀ɔ̀n *v.*
drink with a straw ɓiɓítɛs *v.*
drinkable wetam *n.*
drinker wetésíàm *n.*
drinking straw ɲálamorú *n.*
drip iƙiliƙílɔ̀n *v.*; ilimɛsa así *v.*; ilɨ́mɔ́n *v.*; imilɛtés *v.*; itáɓóòn *v.*; ts'òlòn *v.*
drip (of rain) tatíón *v.*
drip continuously iɗɔ́nón *v.*
drive ifalífálɛ́s *v.*
drive (a vehicle) hɔnés *v.*
drive (animals) hɔ́nés *v.*
drive away hɔnésúƙotᵃ *v.*
drive off hɔnésúƙotᵃ *v.*

drunkard

drive out (here) hɔnɛtés *v.*
drive out animals hɔnɛtésá ínóᵉ *v.*
drive through ututetés *v.*; xutés *v.*; xutésúƙotᵃ *v.*
drive through repeatedly ututiés *v.*
driven imúkáánón *v.*
driver ɲíɗɛrɛpáìàm *n.*
driver's license kabaɗa na hɔnésɨ̀ɛ̀ kàèè *n.*
driving permit kabaɗa na hɔnésɨ̀ɛ̀ kàèè *n.*
drizzle ilimɨ́lɨ́mɔ̀n *v.*; isɨ́ɨ́sɛ́ɔ̀n *v.*; itáɓóòn *v.*; ɲélɨ́milim *n.*; ts'olites *v.*; ts'olítésuƙotᵃ *v.*; ts'òlòn *v.*
drongo (fork-tailed) bèùr *n.*; mèùr *n.*
drool ijókón *v.*
droop iƙɔ́nɔ́nɔ̀ɔ̀n *v.*
droop (of eyelids) irwápón *v.*
droopy ratatáɲón *v.*
drop ɗaɗátésuƙotᵃ *v.*; imilɛtés *v.*; tɛ́ɛ́tɔ̀n *v.*; tɛiƙɔ́tɔ̀n *v.*; tɛitésuƙotᵃ *v.*; tɛitetés *v.*; tuɓutes *v.*
drop down iɗíón *v.*
drop in numbers tsakitésúƙotᵃ *v.*
drop into iɗoes *v.*
drop off rárímòn *v.*
drop-off látsó *n.*
droppings ets'ᵃ *n.*
dropsy sɨ́r *n.*
drought ɲɔrɔn *n.*; tsóóna kíjáᵉ *v.*
drowsy ilúzɔ̀n *v.*; iyalíyálòn *v.*
drug cèmèr *n.*
drum iwótsᵃ *n.*; ɲéɓur *n.*
drum (large) ɲépípa *n.*
drum (plastic) ɲékakúŋgù *n.*
drum (talking) ɲéɗɨ̈itᵃ *n.*
drunk ɛ́sáàm *n.*; ɛsánón *v.*
drunkard ɛ́sáàm *n.*

drunken talk ɛ́sátòdᵃ *n.*
drunkenness ɛ́s *n.*
dry tsáítɛ́s *v.*; tsóón *v.*
dry (partially) mɔsɨ́mɔ́sɔ̀n *v.*
dry and crumbly tsaɨ́dɔ̀n *v.*
dry and dusty puɗádɔ̀n *v.*
dry and thick (of grass) sakátánɔ̀n *v.*
dry by cooking kɛ́xɛ́s *v.*
dry out lolómónuƙotᵃ *v.*; mɔsɔnʉƙɔtᵃ *v.*; tsáítɛ́súƙotᵃ *v.*; tsóónuƙotᵃ *v.*
dry over fire ilɨ́lɨ́ɛ́s *v.*
dry season ôdzᵃ *n.*; ódzatsóyᵃ *n.*
dry season leaves ódzàkàkᵃ *n.*
dry season rain ódzadidí *n.*
dry up tsaiƙótòn *v.*; tsáítɛ́súƙotᵃ *v.*; tsóónuƙotᵃ *v.*
drying rack lɔɓaɓal *n.*
dryly ɗàkᵃ *ideo.*; wòròƙòƙᵒ *ideo.*; yɛ̀l *ideo.*
dryly as dust pùɗᵃ *ideo.*
dubious iƙóƙós *v.*
duck iúpón *v.*; ɲáɓata *n.*; rʉjétón *v.*
duck away iúpónuƙotᵃ *v.*
duck down dégèmɔ̀n *v.*; iúpétòn *v.*
duck up and down iupúúpòn *v.*
dude ɲɛ́ɛ́s *n.*
due to ikótɛrɛ́ *prep.*; kótɛrɛ́ *prep.*
due to (the fact that) ɗúó *pro.*
due to the fact that ikótɛrɛ́ *subordconn.*; kótɛrɛ́ *subordconn.*
duel ɲèùrìà *n.*; ɲeuríétòn *v.*
duiker (common) ŋamur *n.*
dull duŋúlúmòn *v.*; ijíɲáánón *v.*; líídòn *v.*; tufádòn *v.*
dull (boring) itópɛnòn *v.*; jɔ̀lɔ̀n *v.*
dull (in intellect) buɗámón *v.*

dull (of blades) fitídòn *v.*
dully lì *ideo.*; tùf *ideo.*
dully (of blades) fitⁱ *ideo.*
dumb iɓááɲɔ̀n *v.*; miɲɔna íkèdè *v.*
dump ƙúdès *v.*
dump (garbage) bɔlɔl *n.*
dump out iɓutúɓútés *v.*; ixóxóƙés *v.*; ixuƙúxúƙés *v.*; ixúxúƙés *v.*; ƙúdesuƙotᵃ *v.*; ƙúdetés *v.*
dump over bukúrésuƙota asɨ́ *v.*
dump truck ƙúdèsìam *n.*; ɲétípa *n.*
dung etsˀa *n.*
dung (cow) fiyɔ̀ètsˀᵃ *n.*; ŋɔtᵃ *n.*
dunk (baptize) iɓátíseés *v.*
duplicate toputes *v.*; toputetés *v.*
duramen gúréda dakwí *n.*
during the day ódòᵒ *n.*
during the evening wîdzᵒ *n.*
during the night mukú *n.*
during twilight xiŋatᵓ *n.*
dusk xiŋatᵃ *n.*; xiŋatétón *v.*
dusky mígirigíránón *v.*
dust bur *n.*; ízuzuɛ́s *v.*; kabas *n.*; kábàsìn *n.*; xɛɛs *v.*; xɛɛsúƙɔtᵃ *v.*; xɛɛtɛ́s *v.*
dust (airborn) bú *n.*
dust (of chaff) ŋawɨ́l *n.*
dust bath (of birds) bùtsᵃ *n.*
dust cloud bú *n.*
dust devil lòtàbùsèn *n.*
dust off itútúɛ́s *v.*; itútúésuƙotᵃ *v.*
duster ɲáɗasɨtá *n.*
dusty-dry puɗádòn *v.*
duty (work) ɲetitsᵃ *n.*
dwarfish puusúmòn *v.*
dwelling zɛƙɔ́áwᵃ *n.*
dye black tɛwɛrɛs *v.*

dying inunúmétòn *v.*; inunúmónuƙotᵃ *v.*
dying in numbers rutukuɲ *ideo.*
dynamite ɲáɓarútᵃ *n.*
dyspepsia dimésá bubue ŋɔɛsɨ *n.*
each one kéŋán *n.*; kɨnɨŋàn *n.*; ŋàn *pro.*
eager olódòn *v.*
eagle loƙól *n.*
eagle (long-crested) kɨlɨkɨliká *n.*
ear bòs *n.*
ear hair bòsìsìts'ᵃ *n.*
ear hole bòsìèkwᵃ *n.*
ear infection ɲɛmɨdimidᵃ *n.*
earler wàxʉ *n.*
earlier ŋɔ́rɔ́n *v.*
earlier time wàx *n.*
earlier today nákᵃ *adv.*
earlobe scar ɲétɨlitɛl *n.*
early ɛ̀kwɔ̀n *v.*
earn a living bɛ́ɗésa fiyekesɨ *v.*
earring ɲétɨlitil *n.*
earth jʉm *n.*; kɨjᵃ *n.*
earth (scorched) kàròƙᵃ *n.*
earthquake ɲéríkirikᵃ *n.*
earthworm ídèmèim *n.*
earwax ŋókìɛts'ᵃ *n.*; ɲéɗípor *n.*
earwig natélétsìò *n.*
ease (in place) iɛpɛs *v.*
ease down iɛpɛtés *v.*
ease off iɛpésʉƙɔta asɨ *v.*; iɛpónʉƙɔtᵃ *v.*
ease off with iɛpésʉƙɔtᵃ *v.*
ease over iɛpɛsa asɨ *v.*
ease up iŋáléètòn *v.*; iwɔ́ɔ́nʉƙɔtᵃ *v.*
ease up on someone iɛpɛsa asɨɛ ámákᵉ *v.*
east fetíékwᵃ *n.*
easterly direction fetíékuxan *dem.*

easterner fetíékùam *n.*
easy batánón *v.*; ɔfɔ́dòn *v.*
easy (to seduce) batánón *v.*
easy to manage olódòn *v.*
eat ŋƙáƙés *v.*; ŋƙés *v.*
eat a lot of tolepetés *v.*
eat all áts'ɛsʉƙɔtᵃ *v.*
eat gingerly ɨláláŋés *v.*
eat live termites ƙɨdzɛsa dáŋáᵉ *v.*
eat too much wɔ̀ɔ̀n *v.*
eat up áts'ɛsʉƙɔtᵃ *v.*; ŋƙáƙésuƙɔtᵃ *v.*
eatable ŋƙam *n.*
eatery ɲéótèl *n.*
eating ŋƙáƙᵃ *n.*
eating place ŋƙáƙáàyᵃ *n.*
eclipse (lunar) badona arágwanɨ *n.*
eclipse (solar) badona fetí *n.*
economize imɨnɨmɨnɛs *v.*
ecstasy (be in) iráƙésʉƙɔta asɨ *v.*
ecstatic (become) ɛfɔnʉƙɔtᵃ *v.*
edema sɨr *n.*
edge itsóɗón *v.*; kwaywᵃ *n.*; kweedᵃ *n.*; ɲimanitésìàwᵃ *n.*
edge (cliff) látsó *n.*
edge over here itsoɗiétòn *v.*
edges kwàin *n.*
edgy rukurúkón *v.*
edible ŋƙam *n.*
educate isómáitetés *v.*
education ɲósomá *n.*
effloresce ɲaʉ́dɔnʉƙɔtᵃ *v.*
egg ɓiɓᵃ *n.*
egg on isʉ́sʉ́és *v.*; itsótsóés *v.*
egg yolk ɗukes *n.*
eggplant tùlèl *n.*
eggsack ɓiɓáhò *n.*
eggshell ɔfɔrɔƙᵃ *n.*

egocentric reídòn *v.*
egress pulúmétòn *v.*
egret ɲɛɓɔŋ *n.*
Egyptian thorn kɨlɔ́rɨ́tᵃ *n.*
eight tude ńdà kìɗì àɗᵉ *num.*
eight o'clock ɲásáatɨkaa leɓetsátìkᵉ *n.*
eighteen toomíní ńda kiɗì túde ńdà kìɗì àɗᵉ *n.*
eighty toomínékwa túde ńdà kìɗì àɗᵉ *n.*
either ... or ... mɨ́si ... mɨ́si ... *coordconn.*
ejaculate kúdetésá ɗíróᵉ *v.*
elaborate imiɗímíɗésa mɛnáᵋ *v.*
elaborate on iɲɛɛs *v.*; taɲɛɛs *v.*
eland basaúr *n.*
eland (female) dzàbùl *n.*
eland (male) karám *n.*
eland visceral fat tʉkán *n.*
elbow kʉlɛ́ *n.*
elder dìyòàm *n.*; jákám *n.*; ŋurutiesíama tódàᵉ *n.*
elder (chief) ámázeáma awáᵉ *n.*; diyoama ná zè *n.*
elder who judges bɨlamʉ́sɨ̀àm *n.*
elder's first food túwᵃ *n.*
elderliness jákámànànès *n.*
elderly dúnésòn *v.*
elderly (of many) dunaakón *v.*
elderly (the) dunaakóniikᵃ *n.*
elderly person dúnésìàm *n.*
elders jákᵃ *n.*
elders (obese) ijʉkɛsííka búbùikàᵉ *n.*
eldership jákámànànès *n.*
eldest child tígàràmàtsᵃ *n.*
elect kanotós *v.*; tɔsɛɛtés *v.*; xɔ́bɛtés *v.*
elect government officials xɔ́bɛtésá ɲápukánɨ *v.*

elected xɔ́bɔtɔ́s *v.*
elephant òŋòr *n.*
elephant (female) oŋoriŋwa *n.*
elephant bull kɨ́lɨ́ɲɨ̀tᵃ *n.*
elephant grass òŋòrìkù *n.*
elephant gun ɲáturugéyᵃ *n.*
elephant trunk gìgᵃ *n.*; òŋòrìkwɛ̀tᵃ *n.*
elephant tusk òŋòrìkwàywᵃ *n.*
Eleusine coracana rêbᵃ *n.*
elevate ɓukés *v.*; íbokés *v.*; ikɛ́ɛ́sʉkɔtᵃ *v.*; ikɛɛtés *v.*
elevate (make) ikɛ́ɨ́tɛtés *v.*
elevated ikɔɔtɔ́s *v.*
eleven ńda nébèè kɔ̀n *n.*; toomíní ńda kèɗɨ kɔ̀n *n.*
eleven o'clock ɲásáatɨkaa tudátìkᵉ *n.*
elicit tɔɓéɲétɔ̀n *v.*
elicit speech iɛ́nítɛtés *v.*; tóítetés *v.*
elliptical semélémòn *v.*
elude iɓʉtsɛs *v.*; iɓʉtsɛtésá asɨ́ *v.*
emaciated irókóòn *v.*; itókókòòn *v.*; lotímálèmòn *v.*
embankment ɓɔ́kɔ̀n *n.*
embarrass ɓets'itetés *v.*; iryámítetésá ŋiléétsìkᵉ *v.*
embarrassed kweelémòn *v.*
embarrassed (become) iɛ́ɓétɔ̀n *v.*; iryámétona ŋiléétsìkᵉ *v.*
embellish daites *v.*; ɨgwɨgwɨjés *v.*; isires *v.*
embellished isiros *v.*
ember bʉbʉn *n.*
embitter faɗites *v.*
emblems ŋákɨran *n.*
embodiment nébùnànès *n.*
embrace irʉmɛs *v.*; tɔtʉnɛs *v.*
embrace each other irúmúnɔ́s *v.*; tɔtúnʉ́mɔ́s *v.*

embrocate kwɨrɛ́s *v.*; tsáŋés *v.*
embroider isires *v.*
embroidered isiros *v.*
embryo edˈedᵃ *n.*
emerge lɛlɛmánétòn *v.*; lɛlétón *v.*; pɛléméton *v.*; pulúmétòn *v.*
emerge (of termites) kɨ́dzɔ̀n *v.*
emerging lɛlɛmánón *v.*
emissary erégesíám *n.*
emit bɔ́rɨ́tòn *v.*; ídzès *v.*; ídzesukotᵃ *v.*; ídzòn *v.*; itsues *v.*; itsuetés *v.*
emit continuously ídziidziés *v.*
emit nocturnally (semen) kúdesa dˈíróe asɨ́ *v.*
employ bukɨtésukotᵃ *v.*; eréges *v.*; ikásíitetés *v.*; teréganitetés *v.*
employee ɲákásìàm *n.*; terégìàm *n.*
employer ámázeáma terégì *n.*; bukɨtésukotíám *n.*
employment ɲákási *n.*; terêgᵃ *n.*
empty bótsón *v.*; bùlòn *v.*
empty by shaking iwɔkɛs *v.*
empty out bulonukotᵃ *v.*; bulútésukotᵃ *v.*
empty sound fùù *ideo.*
empty-handed kwɛtɨkɨnᵓ *n.*; seátᵒ *n.*
empty-handedly gwèlèjᵉ *ideo.*
emulate iɲitiés *v.*
emulsify ilɔkɛs *v.*
en route múkò *n.*
encampment ɲákambɨ́ *n.*
encircle irikɛs *v.*; irɨkɛ́sukotᵃ *v.*; irikɛtɛ́s *v.*; tamanɛs *v.*; tamanɛtɛ́s *v.*
encircle repeatedly tamaniés *v.*
enclose ipúpúɲɛs *v.*; ipúpúɲɛtɛ́s *v.*
enclose (termites) mɔkɛ́s *v.*

encounter imánétòn *v.*; imánónukotᵃ *v.*; ŋimánétòn *v.*; ɲimánétòn *v.*; ɲimánón *v.*
encourage imúkáitetés *v.*
encroach sáitòn *v.*
encrusted rɔ́bɔ̀dˈɔ̀mɔ̀n *v.*
encumber inʉɛs *v.*; isites *v.*
end ŋurúmétòn *v.*; ɲémíso *n.*
end of the world tasálétona kíjáᵉ *n.*
ending ɲémíso *n.*
endure imúkɔ́ɔ̀n *v.*; nɛɛ́s *v.*; nɛɛsʉ́kɔtᵃ *v.*; tadˈaɲɛs *v.*; topíánètòn *v.*
enemies lɔŋɔ́tᵃ *n.*
enemy lɔŋɔ́tɔ́m *n.*
energetic ibɛ́rɔ́ánón *v.*; ikwiɲɨ́kwɨ́ɲɔ́n *v.*; iona ńda sea ni itsúr *v.*; kʉrúkʉ́rɔ́s *v.*; kwiɲɨ́dɔ̀n *v.*
energetically kwìɲ *ideo.*
enfold tʉmʉdˈʉɲɛs *v.*; tʉmʉdˈʉɲɛtɛ́s *v.*
engage sitsˈés *v.*
engage each other sítsˈímós *v.*
engagement ɨʉ̀m *n.*
engine gúr *n.*
English language Betsˈoniicétôdᵃ *n.*; Ŋímusukúitòdᵃ *n.*
enhaloed itówóòn *v.*
enhance maraŋités *v.*; maraŋítésukotᵃ *v.*
enjoy iyóómètòn *v.*; tsamɛ́s *v.*
enlarge iɲɛɛs *v.*; iwanetɛ́s *v.*; iwánétòn *v.*; taɲɛɛs *v.*; zeites *v.*; zeitésukotᵃ *v.*
enlarge (a hole) ikúkúrɛ́s *v.*
enlarge (a small hole) imɨdˈɨ́mɨ́dˈɛ́s *v.*
enlarge slightly baribárɨ́tésʉkɔtᵃ *v.*; baribárɔ́nʉkɔtᵃ *v.*
enlist xɔ́bɛtɛ́sá asɨ́ *v.*
enmity lɔŋɔ́tánànès *n.*

enough itémón *v.*; ŋábɔnʉkɔtᵃ *v.*; nábɔnʉkɔtᵃ *v.*
enrich barɨ́tésʉkɔtᵃ *v.*
enroll xɔ́bɛtésá asɨ́ *v.*
ensared (become) kotsonuƙotᵃ *v.*
enshroud ikáburés *v.*
enslavement ɲilébúìnànès *n.*; ɲipɔ́táɨnànès *n.*
ensnare kotsítésuƙotᵃ *v.*; ságwès *v.*
ensnared kòtsòn *v.*
entangle ságwès *v.*
entangled ságoanón *v.*
enter bukéton *v.*; bukítésuƙotᵃ *v.*; bùƙòn *v.*; buƙonuƙotᵃ *v.*; ilumetésá asɨ́ *v.*
enter (make) bukítésuƙotᵃ *v.*
entertain fekitetés *v.*; imúmwárés *v.*
entertaining èfɔ̀n *v.*
enthusiastic olódòn *v.*
entice imɔɗɛtés *v.*; ɨsʉ́ŋʉ́rés *v.*
entire ɗàŋɨ̀ɗàŋ *quant.*; mùɲ *quant.*; mùɲùmùɲ *quant.*; tsɨ́ɗⁱ *quant.*; tsɨ́ɗitsɨ́ɗⁱ *quant.*
entirely butᵘ *ideo.*; botedᵒ *n.*
entities kúrúbâdᵃ *n.*
entity kɔ́rɔ́bâdᵃ *n.*
entourage member túbesiama ámázeámàᵉ *n.*
entrails (inspect) fiyeitésá arɨ́ɨ̀kàᵋ *v.*
entrance akᵃ *n.*
entrap kotsítésuƙotᵃ *v.*
entrapped kòtsòn *v.*; ságoanón *v.*
entrapped (become) kotsonuƙotᵃ *v.*
entreat iƙenes *v.*
enumerate ɨmaarés *v.*
envelope ɲábaasá *n.*
envious ɨrákáánón *v.*

envious (make oneself) ɨrakɛsa asɨ́ *v.*
environment kíjᵃ *n.*
envision asínítòn *v.*
envoy erégesíám *n.*
envy ɨrákáánás *n.*
enwrap ikáburés *v.*; tʉmʉɗʉɲɛs *v.*; tʉmʉɗʉɲɛtés *v.*
Ephesians (biblical) Ŋíepesóíkᵃ *n.*
epicardium máxìŋ *n.*
epistle ɲábáruwa *n.*
equal iríánòn *v.*
equal (become) iríánonuƙotᵃ *v.*
equal (make) iríánitetés *v.*
equalize ikwáánitetés *v.*; iríánitetés *v.*
equate ikwáánitetés *v.*; iríánitetés *v.*; iríánonuƙotᵃ *v.*
eradicate bulútésuƙotᵃ *v.*
Eragrostis braunii fiyɔ̀jàn *n.*
Eragrostis superba ɲamaɗaŋɨ́kú *n.*
erase iɲiɲiés *v.*
eraser ɲárába *n.*
eraser (chalkboard) ɲáɗasitá *n.*
erect itsɨ́rɨ́tɛtés *v.*; itsɨ́rɔ́n *v.*; tsɨ́rɨ́tetés *v.*; tsɨ́rɔ́n *v.*; wasitɛs *v.*
erection (have an) kwídètòn *v.*; kwídòn *v.*
erode iƙúƙúrés *v.*
erosion bɔrɔ̀tsᵃ *n.*; dìdìàkᵃ *n.*
err hakonuƙotᵃ *v.*; tɔséssɔ́n *v.*
errand-runner erégesíám *n.*
error ɲasécón *n.*; ɲɔ́mɔkɔsá *n.*
erudite nɔɔsánón *v.*
erudition nɔɔ́s *n.*
erupt bilímón *v.*; dulúmón *v.*; toɗúón *v.*; tuƙúmétòn *v.*
erupt (in flames) léjétɔ́n *v.*
Erythrina abyssinica itɨ́tɨ *n.*
escalate iɗíkétòn *v.*; iɗikitetés *v.*

escape

escape iɓutsúmétòn *v.*; iwálílòn *v.*; tɔpéɔ́n *v.*; ùtòn *v.*; utonuƙotᵃ *v.*
escape (and come) tɔpéétòn *v.*
escape (and go) tɔpéɔ́nʉƙɔtᵃ *v.*
escarpment ɓo *n.*
escarpment edge ɓóákᵃ *n.*
escort iníámésuƙotᵃ *v.*
escort (government) túbesiama ámázeámàᵉ *n.*
esophagus moróká na kwátsᵃ *n.*
especially zùkᵘ *adv.*
essence ekwedᵃ *n.*
etchings ɲáƙɨran *n.*
Ethiopia Isópìà *n.*; Sópìà *n.*
ethnic group dìywᵃ *n.*; ɲákaɓɨlá *n.*
Ethur language Ŋítéɓurítôdᵃ *n.*
eucalypt ɲépɔrésɨ̀tà *n.*
Eucalyptus species ɲépɔrésɨ̀tà *n.*
Euclea schimperi èmùsìà *n.*
Euphorbia bussei isókóyᵃ *n.*
Euphorbia candelabrum mùs *n.*
Euphorbia prostrata lódíkórócɛmɛ́r *n.*
Euphorbia tirucalli ɨnwᵃ *n.*
Europe Bets'oniicékíjᵃ *n.*; Uláyà *n.*
European ɓèts'ònìàm *n.*; ɲémúsukitᵃ *n.*
European language Bets'oniicétôdᵃ *n.*; Ŋímusukúìtòdᵃ *n.*
evade iɓʉtsɛs *v.*; iɓʉtsɛtésá asɨ *v.*; iɓutsúmétòn *v.*
evade repeatedly iwitíwítòn *v.*
evaluate inìɲes *v.*
evangelist itátámésɨ̀am *n.*
evangelize itátámés *v.*
evaporate buanónuƙotᵃ *v.*; ipúréètòn *v.*; tsaiƙótòn *v.*; tsóónuƙotᵃ *v.*
evasive firifíránón *v.*; wíríwíránón *v.*

exchange words

even iƙʉlɛs *v.*; iƙwalɛs *v.*; nááƙwa *n.*; tònì *prep.*
even if átà *subordconn.*; tònì *subordconn.*
even out iƙʉlɛtés *v.*
evening wîdzᵃ *n.*
evening near sunset wídzèèkwᵃ *n.*
evening time wîdzᵒ *n.*
ever tsʉ̀tᵘ *adv.*
every person kéám *n.*; nɨ́am *n.*
everywhere ts'íínúó *n.*
evidence ɲekísíɓitᵃ *n.*
evident takánón *v.*
evidently tsábò *adv.*
evil gaánàs *n.*; gaanón *v.*
evil (of many) gaanaakón *v.*
evil eye (having the) ekúnánès *n.*
evil-eye gazer ekúám *n.*
eviscerate ɓilésúƙotᵃ *v.*
evoke tɔɓéɲétòn *v.*
Evolvus alsinoides ídocɛmɛ́r *n.*
ewe ɗóɗoŋwa *n.*
exacerbate rúbès *v.*
exactly dàn *adv.*; rò *adv.*
exaggerate imiɗɨ́mɨ́ɗɛ́sa mɛná*ᵋ v.*; tasaɓesa mɛnáᵋ *v.*
exalt itúrútés *v.*
examination ɲétésɨ̀tᵃ *n.*
examination room ɦiyeítésihò *n.*
exasperate iwɨ́wɨ́nɛs *v.*
excavate úgès *v.*; úgetés *v.*
excavator ɲétɛrɛƙitaa na kwɛtáᵋ *n.*; òɲòrìkwètᵃ *n.*; tébɛsiama jʉmwɨ *n.*
exceed ilɔɛs *v.*; isʉkɛs *v.*; súkɛ́s *v.*
exchange ilókótsés *v.*; ixɔtsɛs *v.*; xɔ́tsɛ́s *v.*
exchange (money) toɓwaɲes *v.*
exchange words bezekanitetésá tódàᵉ *v.*; ilókótsésa mɛnáᵋ *v.*

335

excise ɓilés *v.*
excise (teeth) tɛŋɛlɛs *v.*
exclude tɔlúkésʉkɔtᵃ *v.*
excrement etsʼᵃ *n.*
excuse ógoés *v.*
excused ógoós *v.*
exempt ógoés *v.*; ógoós *v.*
exercise itétémés *v.*
exercise (the body) kɔƙatés *v.*
exhalation sùpᵃ *n.*
exhale súpónʉƙɔtᵃ *v.*
exhaust tsʼûdᵃ *n.*
exhaust pipe tsʼúdemucé *n.*
exhausted bitsétón *v.*; ikarímétòn *v.*; ziálámòn *v.*; zíkímétòn *v.*; ziláámòn *v.*
exhausted (become) ziláámètòn *v.*
exhaustion baƙáíƙᵃ *n.*; ɲékɨ́tɔ́wɔ́ *n.*
exhibit ɲekísíɓitᵃ *n.*
existence ɦyekes *n.*; zɛƙwᵃ *n.*
exit pulúmón *v.*
exonerate iɛtésá isɨ́ɨtésʉ́ *v.*
exorbitant, high in price itíónòn *v.*
exorcist kɔ́tésɨ̀am *n.*
exorcize hɔnɛ́súƙɔtᵃ *v.*; kɔ́tés *v.*; tɔdétésʉƙɔtᵃ *v.*
exorcize spirits kɔ́tésa súgùrìkàᵉ *v.*
expand iɲɛɛs *v.*; iwanetés *v.*; iwánétòn *v.*; taɲɛɛs *v.*; taɲéɔ́n *v.*; tʉwétón *v.*; tʉ̀wɔ̀n *v.*; xuanón *v.*; xuxuanón *v.*
expand on the issues imɨdɨ́mɨdésa mɛnáᵋ *v.*
expanded iatɔs *v.*
expect kɔés *v.*; kɔɛtés *v.*
expedition ɲásápari *n.*
expel ídzès *v.*; ídzesuƙɔtᵃ *v.*; ilɔ́lɨ́és *v.*
expel continuously ídziidziés *v.*

expend isítíyeés *v.*
expense ɲéɓéyᵃ *n.*
expensive itíónòn *v.*; ŋɨ̀xɔ̀n *v.*
experience (gain) nɔɔsánétòn *v.*
expiate iɓutes *v.*
expire bitsétón *v.*; ɨrɨ́détòn *v.*
expire (die) tézètòn *v.*
explain enitetés *v.*
explode ɓilímón *v.*; toɗúón *v.*
exploit inɔmɛtés *v.*
expose ɗoɗésúƙɔtᵃ *v.*; iléérànitetés *v.*; ilététaitetés *v.*
exposed iléérànón *v.*; ilététòòn *v.*; tuɗúsúmòn *v.*
expound on iɲɛɛs *v.*; taɲɛɛs *v.*
exsufflate rútés *v.*
extend zikíbitésúƙɔtᵃ *v.*
extend (hands) taɓɛɛs *v.*
extend up zikíbitésúƙɔtᵃ *v.*; zikíbonuƙɔtᵃ *v.*
extensor (muscle) ɲépísikitíém *n.*
exterminate kánés *v.*
extinct (go) bulonuƙɔtᵃ *v.*; kanímétòn *v.*
extinguish tsʼeites *v.*; tsʼeítésuƙɔtᵃ *v.*
extirpate ɗués *v.*; ɗuetés *v.*; rués *v.*
extol itúrútés *v.*; tamɛɛs *v.*
extort réés *v.*; rɛɛtés *v.*; tɔrɛɛs *v.*
extorted toreimétòn *v.*
extra iɓámón *v.*; jɛjétón *v.*
extract béberés *v.*; faɗetés *v.*; tɔkɛtɛs *v.*; tɔkétésʉƙɔtᵃ *v.*; tɔkɛtɛtés *v.*; tolés *v.*; toletés *v.*; tuɓutetés *v.*; tuutes *v.*; tuutetés *v.*
extract (evil charms) totues *v.*
extract brideprice buƙitetés *v.*
extract repeatedly tolotiés *v.*
extremity (arm-like) kwɛtᵃ *n.*
exude tɔfɔ́dɔ́n *v.*

exult iwóŋón *v.*; taɓólón *v.*
exultant taɓolos *v.*
exuviate fòlòn *v.*
eye ekwᵃ *n.*; iséméés *v.*; iséméetés *v.*
eye disease lokiyo *n.*
eye jaundice xɨdɔna ekwitíní *v.*
eyeball gɔ̀kᵃ *n.*
eyebrow ekúkɔ́ɔ́kwarósíts'ᵃ *n.*; ekúsíts'ᵃ *n.*
eyeglasses ɲékiyóìkᵃ *n.*
eyelash ekúsíts'ᵃ *n.*
eyelid gɔrɔ́x *n.*
eyesight (have poor) múɗúkánón *v.*; ŋwaxɔna ekwitíní *v.*
fable (animal) emuta ínóᵉ *n.*
face takár *n.*; takárêdᵃ *n.*
face back to back ƙuƙɨmánón *v.*
face each other maímós *v.*
face in one direction itɛ́ɛritɛtɛ́s *v.*
face one direction itɛ́ɛ́rɔ̀n *v.*
facial incisions (make) dzeretiés *v.*
fade buanónuƙotᵃ *v.*
fade (of color) kitsonuƙotᵃ *v.*; sɛkɔnɨƙɔtᵃ *v.*
Fadigura species fàdìgùr *n.*
fail ilajɨlájɛ́s *v.*; iɲétsóòn *v.*; iyétsóòn *v.*; rúmánitésúƙotᵃ *v.*; rúmánòn *v.*; totóánonuƙotᵃ *v.*
fail (make) rúmánitésúƙotᵃ *v.*
fail to cross paths bezekánón *v.*
fail to get fàlòn *v.*
fail to meet bezekánón *v.*
failure rumetᵃ *n.*
failure of a season tasálétona kɨ́jáᵉ *n.*
faint iɲɨɲɨánón *v.*; rèŋòn *v.*

faint-hearted jaƙwádòn *v.*; wúrukukánón *v.*
fair dòòn *v.*
fairy kíjáìm *n.*
faith ɲanɨpɨ́tᵃ *n.*
faith (religion) ɲéɗíní *n.*
faith in (have) tɔnɨpɛs *v.*
fake itsárɨánón *v.*; láŋ *n.*
falcon tsìtsᵃ *n.*
fall ruɓétón *v.*; ruɓonuƙotᵃ *v.*; rúmánòn *v.*; rumetᵃ *n.*; tɛ́ɛ́tɔ̀n *v.*; tɛiƙɔ́tɔ̀n *v.*
fall (make) rúmánitésúƙotᵃ *v.*; tɛitésɨƙotᵃ *v.*; tɛitɛtɛ́s *v.*
fall apart ɗukúmétòn *v.*; ɗukúmón *v.*
fall back isíɗéètòn *v.*; maɗámón *v.*
fall behind isíɗéètòn *v.*
fall continuously in numbers tsákìètòn *v.*
fall down lajámétòn *v.*
fall down (crumble) ɲalámétòn *v.*; ɲalámónuƙotᵃ *v.*; taɲáléetésá asɨ *v.*; taɲálóòn *v.*
fall down repeatedly téíètòn *v.*
fall for (in love) isémúreés *v.*
fall from up high xɛ́métòn *v.*; xɛmɔnɨƙotᵃ *v.*
fall gently raraanón *v.*
fall in love with isémúreés *v.*
fall in numbers tsakétón *v.*
fall off tolómétòn *v.*
fall out tolómétòn *v.*
fall sick meetón *v.*
fall upon (attack) toɗóón *v.*
falling apart iɲilɨɲɨ́lánón *v.*
falling sound hyeaa *ideo.*
falls látsóìkᵃ *n.*

false information isuɗam *n.*
falsehood yʉɛ *n.*
falsely accuse each other tɔrémʉ́nɔ́s *v.*
falsify isuɗes *v.*; isuɗetés *v.*
familiarize naɨ́nɛɛtés *v.*; naɨ́tésʉkɔtª *v.*
familiarize oneself with ɦyeités *v.*
family ts'aɗíékwª *n.*
famine ɲɔrɔkɔ *n.*
famished ɲɛƙánón *v.*
famous arútón *v.*; ɦyoós *v.*
fan ipukes *v.*
fancy ɨmáráɗaɗòòn *v.*
fang ƙɨdzèsɨkwàywª *n.*
fang (snake) ídèmèkwàywª *n.*
far ɨ̀ɛ̀ƙɔ̀n *v.*
far (a bit) ɦyàƙàtàkª *n.*
far (slightly) ɨɛƙɨ́éƙɔ̀n *v.*
far from each other ɨɛ́ƙɨmɔ́s *v.*
faraway ɦyàƙàtàkª *n.*
farm tɔkɔ́bɛs *v.*
farmable tɔkɔbam *n.*
farmer tɔ̀kɔ̀bààm *n.*
farming tɔ̀kɔ̀bª *v.*
farming season tɔkɔbatsóyª *n.*
farmland ɲámanikór *n.*
farness ɨɛƙás *n.*
fart fèn *n.*; fenétón *v.*
fashionable titianón *v.*
fashionista ɲásírìàm *n.*
fast ɗàmʉ̀s *adv.*; ɗèmʉ̀s *adv.*; ɨkáɲón *v.*; itírónòn *v.*; torónón *v.*; wɛ́ɛ́nɔ̀n *v.*
fasten iwetés *v.*; zɨ́ƙés *v.*
fastened zɨ́ƙɔ́s *v.*
fastened tightly ŋɔ̀tsɔ̀n *v.*
faster (be) ɨmʉ́mʉ́rɔ̀n *v.*
faster (do) ɨmʉ́mʉ́rés *v.*
fat ceím *n.*; ɛfás *n.*; zízòn *v.*
fat (congealed) gwadam *n.*
fat (epicardial) máxɨŋ *n.*
fat (intra-abdominal) sábà *n.*
fat (organ) sábà *n.*
fat (visceral) sábà *n.*
fat person zízònìàm *n.*
fat slug bébam *n.*
fat-ass bébam *n.*
father (his/her/its) babatª *n.*
father (my) abáɲ *n.*
father (your) bábò *n.*
father-in-law (her) bɔbatª *n.*
father-in-law (his) ntsíemetá *n.*
father-in-law (his/her sibling's spouse's father) babatíɲótª *n.*
father-in-law (my sibling's spouse's father) abáɲɨ̀ɲòtª *n.*
father-in-law (my, of men) ɲ́ciemetá *n.*
father-in-law (my, of women) bɔbá *n.*
father-in-law (of men) emetá *n.*
father-in-law (your sibling's spouse's father) báboɲótª *n.*
father-in-law (your, of men) biemetá *n.*
father-in-law (your, of women) bɔ́bɔ̀ *n.*
fatherhood babatínánès *n.*
fatherliness babatínánès *n.*
fatigue (extreme) ɲɛƙɨtɔ́wɔ́ *n.*
fatso bébam *n.*
fatten zízités *v.*
fatten up tuɓútitésúkotª *v.*; tuɓútónuƙotª *v.*; zízitésúƙotª *v.*; zízonuƙotª *v.*
fault ɲɔ́mɔkɔsá *n.*
fear mòròn *v.*; xɛɓás *n.*
fearful jaƙwádòn *v.*; wúrukukánón *v.*; xɛ̀ɓɔ̀n *v.*
fearfully jàƙwª *ideo.*

fearless itítíŋòn v.
feasible ikásíetam v.; itíyéetam n.
feast írésiŋḱáḱᵃ n.
feather tùkᵃ n.
February Ɓèts'òn n.; Lokwaŋ n.
feces ets'ᵃ n.
feces (loose) eruxam n.
feces (Rhus natalensis) mɨsáɨ̀ets'ᵃ n.
feckless ɨkálájaránón v.
feeble dɛrédòn v.; ɨpáláḱòn v.; juódòn v.
feebly dɛr ideo.; jùᵒ ideo.
feed bɔnés v.; ŋḱáḱítetés v.; ŋḱitetés v.
feed (fire) iríréés v.; iríréetés v.
feed nocturnally aúgòn v.
feeding ŋḱáḱᵃ n.
feel enés v.; imínímínés v.; mínímínatés v.; tábès v.
feel around ɨtapɨ́tápòn v.
feel bad (make) ɓaritès v.; ɓarítésuḱotᵃ v.
feel faint tikítíkona gúróᵉ v.
feel mercy cucuéétòn v.
feel weak tikítíkona gúróᵉ v.
feign iɲétsóòn v.; iyétsóòn v.
fell ruɓutetés v.
fell (trees) toukes v.; toukétes v.
fellow ɛbam n.
felt (on the skin) fiifíón v.
felted kémúsánón v.
female (animal) ŋwa n.
female (young) wâz n.
femininity cekínánès n.
femur gubesíóḱᵃ n.
fence iriwes v.; mɛtsés v.
fence (outer thorny) ɲéríwi n.

fence (wooden) mariŋ n.
feral ɨsɨlɨ́ánón v.
ferment ɓaronuḱotᵃ v.
ferocious ɦyɛtɨɦyɛtɔs v.; ɦyɛ̀tòn v.
ferocity ɦyɛtás n.
ferry iríítés v.
fertile bòmòn v.; ɨ́ḱón v.
fertile (of soil) zízòn v.
fertile soil juma na zîz n.
fertilize (plants) zízités v.; zízitésúḱotᵃ v.
festering tatifiánón v.
fetch tébɛtés v.
fetch (water) kotsés v.; kotsetés v.
fetid ɗɛtsɨɗétsón v.
fetidly ɗɛtsᵋ ideo.
fetus ɗúr n.
fever hábona nébwì n.; sugur n.
fever tree lɛ̀r n.
feverish titianón v.
few ɨmaarós v.; ḱwàdᵉ quant.; ḱwàɗòn v.
fewer ḱwaɗiḱwáɗón v.
fewer (become) ḱwaɗonuḱotᵃ v.
fiber ŋɨ́sil n.
fiber (twiste) sim n.
fibrous simánón v.
fickle at work ɨpáláḱòn v.
Ficus ingens namúɗitᵃ n.
Ficus platyphylla baratᵃ n.
Ficus species náɨnɛné n.; ɲákáratᵃ n.; ɲékerum n.
Ficus sycomorus áts'ᵃ n.
fiddle ɲakawᵃ n.
fiddle with ígujugujés v.
fidgety kakáánón v.

field rɔwᵃ *n.*
field (ball) ɲakwaanja *n.*
field (large) ɲámanikór *n.*
field glasses ɲáɓaraɓɨ́n *n.*
fierce fiyɛtifiyɛtɔs *v.*; fiyètɔ̀n *v.*; iɲɛ́ɛ́mɔ̀n *v.*
fierceness fiyɛtás *n.*
fifteen toomíní ńda kiɗi tûdᵉ *n.*
fifth (one) ɗa túdònì *pro.*
fifty toomínékwa tûdᵉ *n.*
fig tree base baratídè *n.*
fig tree species áts'ᵃ *n.*; baratᵃ *n.*; náíɲɛnɛ́ *n.*; namúɗitᵃ *n.*; ɲákáratᵃ *n.*; ɲékerum *n.*
fight cɛmɔ̀n *v.*; déƙwítetés *v.*; iƙaíƙɛ́ɛ́s *v.*; iƙáƙɛ́ɛ́s *v.*; iƙáƙɛɛtés *v.*; iƙúmúnós *v.*
fighter cɛmáám *n.*
fighter (be a) cɛmɛkánón *v.*
figs (dried out) kòsòwᵃ *n.*
figure out hoetés *v.*
filch itíɗíɗés *v.*
file tɔɗúpón *v.*; torópón *v.*
file in torópétòn *v.*
filiariasis ɲɛkwɨ *n.*
fill ciitésuƙɔtᵃ *v.*; éétòn *v.*; imíɗítsɛ́s *v.*
fill completely lujulújés *v.*
fill in imetsités *v.*
fill in for imetsés *v.*
fill mouth aukes *v.*
fill up éítésuƙotᵃ *v.*; éítetés *v.*; ilílíés *v.*; ilujúlújés *v.*; jɨrɨ́jɨ́rètɔ̀n *v.*; jɨrɨ́jɨ́rɔ̀n *v.*
fill with air xuxuanitetés *v.*
fillet iƙémíƙémés *v.*
film (movie) kúrúkúríka ni ɓɛƙɛ́s *n.*; ɲévíɗyo *n.*
filter ijiwɛs *v.*; itiwɛs *v.*
filth ts'âgᵃ *n.*

filthiness ts'âgᵃ *n.*
filthy itútsón *v.*; ŋorótsánón *v.*; ts'ágòn *v.*
filthy person ts'ágààm *n.*
fin taban *n.*
final to arrive irúpóòn *v.*
final to come irúpéètòn *v.*
finance kaúdzòmèn *n.*
financial matters kaúdzòmèn *n.*
find itétón *v.*; itɔ́ɔ́n *v.*; nòìn *n.*; takanités *v.*
find a way into útétòn *v.*
find a way through utés *v.*; utésúƙotᵃ *v.*
find an entrance to útétòn *v.*
find each other missing ítínós *v.*
find missing ítés *v.*
find proof enésá mɛná*ᵉ* *v.*
find refuge in rimɛ́s *v.*
find remains of ítés *v.*
fine dòòn *v.*; ɲáfaɨ́n *n.*
fine for impregnation itsúlítetés *v.*; fine (impregnation) ɲɛkitsul *n.*
fine (marital) ɲápaín *n.*
fine for sexual misconduct kasurúɓé *n.*
fine! maráŋ *interj.*
finger iminɨmɨ́nɛ́s *v.*; kɔrɔ́kᵃ *n.*; minɨ́mɨ́natés *v.*
finger bone kɔrɔ́kɔ́ɔ̀kᵃ *n.*
finger out (food) ts'álóbiés *v.*
finger sexually ts'álóbiés *v.*
fingernail tíbòlòkòɲ *n.*
fingers (extra) ɲéɗónɨɗon *n.*
finish iríƙésuƙɔtᵃ *v.*; ɲáɓɛsuƙɔtᵃ *v.*
finish off imúɲésuƙɔtᵃ *v.*; imuɲetés *v.*; iɲóɗésuƙɔtᵃ *v.*; iríƙésuƙɔtᵃ *v.*; itsutɛs *v.*; itsútésuƙɔtᵃ *v.*
finish off (crops) iróríƙés *n.*

finished ŋábɔnʉƙɔtᵃ v.; nábɔnʉƙɔtᵃ v.; tézètɔ̀n v.

finished (totally) kwèrèt̚ᵉ ideo.

finished off ɨmúɲúmétòn v.; ɨt-sútúmétòn v.

fire hoɗésúƙotᵃ v.; ídzès v.; ídzesuƙotᵃ v.; ɨtsʉŋɛs v.; ts'aɗᵃ n.

fire (a weapon) tɔɗétésʉƙɔtᵃ v.

fire a weapon tɔɗɛtɛsa ɛ́bàᵋ v.

fire herb ts'aɗícɛ́mɛ̀r n.

fire lily bʉlʉbʉlátᵃ n.

fire on ɗamatés v.; tɔƙʉmúƙʉmɛ́s v.

fire repeatedly ídziidziés v.

firearm ɛ̂bᵃ n.

fireboard tsakúdècèkᵃ n.

firebreak (make a) ɨɗɛiɗɛ́ɛ́s v.

firedrill tsakûɗᵃ n.; tsakúdèèàkwᵃ n.

firefinch lòtsòr n.

firefly lɔ́ɗʉ́mɛ́l n.

fireplace ts'aɗíékwᵃ n.

firewood dakwᵃ n.; gamam n.; ts'aɗídàkwᵃ n.

firing pin mʉtʉ n.

firmament lúl n.

first èkwɔ̀n v.; wàxʉ̀ n.

first (be the) mɨtɔna ɗɨ́ɛ́ wàxɨ v.

first (one) ɗa kɔ́nɔ̀nɨ̀ pro.; ɗa wáxɨ pro.

first person wàxɨ̀am n.

firstborn tígàràmàtsᵃ n.; wàxɨ̀am n.

fiscal bílɔɔrɔ́ n.

fish ŋkɔ́lɨ́a n.

fish out tukuretés v.; tukutetés v.

fissured médemedánón v.; takátákánón v.

fist ɨlʉlʉŋam n.; mʉkʉtam n.

fistful ɨlʉlʉŋam n.

fit ɗoxóɗòn v.

fit (physically) ɨtsyátón v.

fitly ɗòx ideo.

fitting ɨtémón v.

five tùɗᵉ num.; tùɗòn v.

five o'clock ɲásáatɨkaa mɨtátie toomíní ńdà kèɗɨ kɔ̀n n.

five times tùɗᵒ num.

fix ɨɗɨmés v.; ɨɗɨmésúƙɔtᵃ v.; ɨɗɨmɛtés v.; ramɛtés v.; zɔ́bès v.

fix a handle on xɔ́ŋɛ́s v.

fix on mɨnɛ́s v.

fixed ɨɗɨmɔ́s v.

fixer ɨɗɨmɛ́sɨ̀am n.

fixture (tool) mɨnɛ́sɨ̀awᵃ n.

fizz tabúón v.

fizz up tabúétòn v.

flabbily lùjᵘ ideo.

flabby gerúsúmòn v.; lujúdòn v.; rexúkúmòn v.

flaccid lujúdòn v.

flaccid (become, of the penis) ziláámètòn v.

flaccidly lùjᵘ ideo.

flag ɨwɔ́ɔ́nʉƙɔtᵃ v.; ɲébendʼéra n.

flagging ɨwɔ́ɔ́n v.

flake (wood) kɨ́ɓézam n.

flame arír n.; ts'aɗíákᵃ n.

flame tree ɨtɨ́tɨ́ n.

flank ɲábèrèɗᵃ n.

flap ɨpukúpúkɛ́s v.; ɨwakúwákòn v.; wɛɗɨwɛ́ɗón v.

flapping pɛɗɛ́pɛ́ɗánón v.

flare ɨmɛ́ɗón v.

flare up dulúmón v.; ɨmɛ́ɗétòn v.; tuƙúmétòn v.

flare up (of skin) ɨɲárúrètòn v.

flared up (of skin) ɨɲárúròn v.

flash ɨmɛɗɛ́tòn v.; ɨmɛɗɔ́n v.; itweɲítwɛ́ɲòn v.
flash! lɛ́jᵋ ideo.
flashlight ɲótótsᵃ n.
flashy ɨmáráɗàɗòòn v.
flask (butter) ɲɛ́bur n.
flask (gourd) nasɛmɛ́ n.; ɲekúrúm n.
flask (small gourd) ɲékútàm n.
flat ɨpáɗaɲɔ̀n v.; pùnùkᵘ ideo.
flat (deflated) fɔrɔ́ts'ɔ́mɔ̀n v.
flat (of an area) kalápátánón v.
flat (of land) dàsòn v.
flat (of objects) ɗapálámɔ̀n v.
flat area lopem n.
flat buttocks (have) taɓóɲómòn v.
flat-topped tɔpɛ́tɔ́n v.
flatbed tsídzèsìàwᵃ n.
flatland rɔwᵃ n.
flatly ɓɛlɛlɛtsᵋ ideo.; ɗèɲ ideo.
flatly concave ɓɛtélémɔ̀n v.; fɛtélémɔ̀n v.
flatten epitésúkòtà ɗèɲ v.; ɨɲíkéésukotᵃ v.; ɲaɗés v.
flatten out kalápátánitetés v.; ɲaɗésúkotᵃ v.
flatten out (an area) kalápátánónukotᵃ v.
flatten repeatedly ɲaɗíés v.
flatulence fèn n.
flatulent fɛnɛ́ɗòn v.
flatulently fèn ideo.
flaunt kɔkɔanón v.
flavor ɛfites v.; ɨbutsurés v.; iwéwérés v.
flavorful ɛ̀fɔn v.
flavorful (become) ɛfɔnʉkɔtᵃ v.
flavoring ɲɛ́ɓisár n.

flavorless ɗɛ̀kwòn v.; jɔ̀lɔ̀n v.; mujálámòn v.
flea (chigoe) túkútùkᵃ n.
flea (sand) túkútùkᵃ n.
flea(s) naɗɛ́pᵃ n.
fleas ɲɨkaɗɛpɨ́ɗɛ́pᵃ n.
fleck bàsɔ̀n v.
flecked ɨlɨmɨ́lɨ́mɔ̀n v.
flecked with fat káɓìlànètòn v.
flee dukésúkota mòràᵉ v.; moronukotᵃ v.
flee (of many) iɗúzòn v.
fleece ɗóɗòsìts'ᵃ n.
flesh em n.
flesh dried on hide xákwᵃ n.
flesh left on hide ɲɔpɔɗɛ n.
flex itúkúɗètòn v.; itúkúɗòn v.; nɔkɨnɔ́kɔ́n v.
flex (muscles) xuxuanitetés v.
flexible nakwádòn v.; naúdòn v.; nɔkɔ́dɔ̀n v.
flexibly nàkwᵃ ideo.; nàᵘ ideo.; nɔ̀kɔ̀ ideo.
flexor (muscle) ɲépísikitíém n.
flick tɔɗɛtɛs v.; towates v.; towatetés v.
flick away tɔɗɛ́tɛ́sʉkɔtᵃ v.
flick off tɔɗɛ́tɛ́sʉkɔtᵃ v.
flicker ɨmɛɗɨ́mɛ́ɗɔ̀n v.; ɨmɛlɛs v.; itweɲítwɛ́ɲòn v.; tɔɗɛtɛs v.
flicker (of light) tɔɗɛtɛsa asɨ́ v.
flinch ŋaxɛ́tɔ́n v.
flinch (make) ininínɨ́ɲés v.
fling ɨpákésʉkɔtᵃ v.; ɨrʉtsɛs v.; towates v.
fling away towátésúkotᵃ v.
fling off towátésúkotᵃ v.
fling water ɨpakɛsa cué v.
flip ɨjʉlɛs v.; ɨjʉlɛtés v.; tɔɗɛtɛs v.
flip away tɔɗɛ́tɛ́sʉkɔtᵃ v.

flip off tɔɗɛ́tɛ́sʉ̄kɔtᵃ *v.*
flip over aɓúlúkánón *v.*
flipped ijʉlɔs *v.*
flit ikaikɛ́ɛ́s *v.*
flit around ipɛrɨ́pɛ́rɔ̀n *v.*
flitter imɛlɛs *v.*; ipɛrɨ́pɛ́rɔ̀n *v.*; iwolíwólòn *v.*; tɔɗɛtɛs *v.*
flitter (of termites) érítòn *v.*
float ilélébètòn *v.*
float away ilélébonukotᵃ *v.*
flock bàr *n.*
flock (small) bàròìm *n.*
flock of birds gwábàr *n.*
flock of goats riébàr *n.*
flock of sheep ɗóɗòbàr *n.*
flocks ɲɨ́ɓarɛn *n.*
flog iɓúɲéés *v.*
flood íswᵃ *n.*
flood rubbish ɲérímama *n.*
floodplain ɲéɓúruɓur *n.*
floor dziŋ *n.*; kíjᵃ *n.*
flop! kùm *ideo.*
flour kabas *n.*
flour (dry) ŋápʉpᵃ *n.*
flour (moist) ŋámɨ́rɔ *n.*
flourish iɔ́kɔ́n *v.*
flourish (of plants) gáruɓúɓón *v.*; karuɓúɓón *v.*
flow isépón *v.*
flow (menses) iona arágwanɨ́kᵋ *v.*
flow away isépónukotᵃ *v.*
flow in waves ídulumona cué *v.*
flower iɔ́kɔ́n *v.*; ŋátur *n.*
flower (sorghum) ƙádetésá kadɨxáᵋ *v.*
flower bud tún *n.*

flu ɲarúkúm *n.*; sugur *n.*
fluctuate iɲikétòn *v.*; iɲikiétòn *v.*; iɲikíɲíkòn *v.*; iɲíkón *v.*
fluid cuanón *v.*
flump down rɛfɛ́kɛ́ɲɔ̀n *v.*
flunk rúmánòn *v.*
flush ɓʉnúmɔ́nà sèàᵉ *v.*
flush out tsídzètòn *v.*; tsídzitetés *v.*
flushed iyaɲíyáŋòn *v.*
flustered iyaɲíyáŋòn *v.*
flute ɲálamorú *n.*
flutter ipukúpúkés *v.*; iwolíwólòn *v.*; pɛɗɛpɛ́ɗón *v.*; wɛɗɨwɛ́ɗón *v.*
flutter (of termites) érítòn *v.*
fluttering pɛɗɛ́pɛ́ɗánón *v.*
fly bʉrétɔ́n *v.*; bʉ̀rɔ̀n *v.*; iwálílòn *v.*; tsútsᵃ *n.*
fly (biting) lɔŋɨzɛtᵃ *n.*; lótsótsᵃ *n.*; ɲɔ́pɔɗɔkʉ́ *n.*
fly (flee, of many) iɗúzòn *v.*
fly (tsetse) ɲɛ́ɗɨitᵃ *n.*
fly away bʉrɔnʉkɔtᵃ *v.*
fly off bʉrɔnʉkɔtᵃ *v.*
fly species (green) tukéyᵃ *n.*
flycatcher (paradise) iboboyᵃ *n.*
foal ɗiɗèim *n.*
foal (female) ɗiɗèwàz *n.*
foam guf *n.*; tabúón *v.*
foam up tabúétòn *v.*
fodder wà *n.*
foe lɔŋɔ́tɔ́m *n.*
foes lɔŋɔ́tᵃ *n.*
fog góʒòwᵃ *n.*
foil kwaɲés *v.*; kwaɲésʉ́kɔtᵃ *v.*
foist tɔnɛɛtés *v.*
foist oneself tɔnɛɛtésá asɨ *v.*
fold iwoles *v.*; tɔɓɨlɛs *v.*
fold in half ikóóbés *v.*; ikóóbetés *v.*

fold over   *forceps*

fold over iwoletés *v.*
fold up ikóóbés *v.*; ikóóbetés *v.*; tɔɓiletés *v.*; tusuketés *v.*; tusúkón *v.*
folded over tɔɓilɛsa asɨ *v.*
folk ròɓᵃ *n.*
folks! òɓà *interj.*; ròɓà *interj.*
follicle (hair) síts'ádè *n.*
follow idupes *v.*; tɔmɛɛs *v.*; tɔmɛ́ɛ́sʉkɔtᵃ *v.*; túbès *v.*
follow (in doing) itákúòn *v.*
follow after elánónukotᵃ *v.*
follow away túbesukotᵃ *v.*
follow each other túbunós *v.*
follow here tɔmɛɛtés *v.*
follow in line tɔtúpón *v.*
follow off túbesukotᵃ *v.*
follower dɛáám *n.*; túbèsìàm *n.*
folly iɓááŋàs *n.*
fondle ɨdadamɛ́s *v.*; iwáwɛ́ɛ́s *v.*; tárábes *v.*
fondle all over tárábiés *v.*
fontanelle badibadas *n.*; bɔdibɔdɔs *n.*
food ŋkákᵃ *n.*
food (for elders first) túwᵃ *n.*
food (give) ŋkákitetés *v.*; ŋkitetés *v.*
food (gnawable) ats'am *n.*
food (peelable) isɨmam *n.*
food (ready) aeam *n.*
food (ripe) aeam *n.*
food (sippable) abutiam *n.*
food (slurpable) isɔrɔɓam *n.*
food residue ɲédúrudur *n.*
food slices (dried) iram *n.*
fool! dúrʉdɔ́ɔ *interj.*
fool's gold ɲésiɓalitútu *n.*
foolish iɓááŋɔ̀n *v.*

foolishness iɓááŋàs *n.*
foot dɛ *n.*; dɛɛdᵃ *n.*
foot (non-animal) dɛ *n.*; dɛɛdᵃ *n.*; dziŋ *n.*
foot of a boulder taɓádè *n.*
foot of a fence mariŋɨdè *n.*
foot of a mountain kwarádè *n.*
foot of a tree dakúdè *n.*
football ɲépɨɨrá *n.*
footer dèèdà hòᵉ *n.*
footfall kɨmátsᵃ *n.*
footing of a borehole ɲatsʉʉmádè *n.*
footman dɛáám *n.*
footpath (fresh) fɨfɨtᵃ *n.*
footprint dɛ *n.*
footstep kɨmátsᵃ *n.*
footsure tsɛ́rɛkɛ́kɔ́n *v.*
for good kìŋ *ideo.*
for nothing ŋálàkᵃ *ideo.*
for the reason that ikóteré *subordconn.*; kóteré *subordconn.*
for what? isiɛnɨ́kᵋ *n.*
forager gadikamáám *n.*
forager (of greens) wààm *n.*
foraging gadikam *n.*
foraging in the valleys fátáràakànànès *n.*
forbid dimités *v.*; dimitetés *v.*; itáléés *v.*
forbidden itáléánón *v.*; itálóós *v.*
force itɨ́ŋɛ́ɛ́s *v.*; itiŋes *v.*; réés *v.*; rɛɛtés *v.*; tɔrɛɛs *v.*
force oneself itiŋɛsa asɨ *v.*
force out ilɔ́lɨ́és *v.*
force through ututetés *v.*; xutés *v.*; xutésúkotᵃ *v.*
force through repeatedly ututiés *v.*
force together rɔŋés *v.*
forceps ɲɔkɔ́ɲétᵃ *n.*

ford àrònìàwᵃ *n.*; ôdᵃ *n.*; ódèèkwᵃ *n.*
forearm k̂ódɔ̀l *n.*; ɲepísíkitᵃ *n.*
forearm muscle ɲépísikitiém *n.*
forego bɔlɛ́súk̂ɔtᵃ *v.*; tasálétòn *v.*; tasálón *v.*
forehead takár *n.*
foreign jalánón *v.*
foreign child fiyòìm *n.*
foreign language fiyɔɛn *n.*; fiyɔ̀tòdᵃ *n.*
foreign woman fiyɔ̀cèkᵃ *n.*
foreigner ámá na biyáᵉ *n.*; fiyɔ̀àm *n.*; kíjíkààm *n.*; ɲíɓúkúìàm *n.*; ɲeɓúkúitᵃ *n.*
foreleg ɲepísíkitᵃ *n.*
foreleg muscle ɲépísikitiém *n.*
foreman ámázeáma terégì *n.*
foremilk ɲódós *n.*
foreskin kwanɨ́ts'ɛ́ *n.*; ts'ɛa na kwanɨ́ *n.*
forest dakúák̂wᵃ *n.*; fɔrɔ́sɨ̀tà *n.*; ríjᵃ *n.*
forest (cleared) tsɛ̀f *n.*
forest (dense) lolítsᵃ *n.*
forest (planted) ɲépɔrɛ́sɨ̀tà *n.*
forest dombeya xuxûbᵃ *n.*
forest entrance ríjáàkᵃ *n.*
forestall titikes *v.*
forever jikɨ̂ *adv.*; mùkà *adv.*; pákà *adv.*
forever and ever kaɨ́nɨ́ka ńda kaɨ́nɨ́kᵃ *n.*
forfeit kuritésúk̂ota asɨ́ *v.*
forge ityakes *v.*
forger ìtyàkààm *n.*
forget hakaikés *v.*
forget (make) gwelítésuk̂otᵃ *v.*; hakaikitetés *v.*
forgetful imáɗíɲánón *v.*
forging stone ityakesígwàs *n.*
forgive ik̂enes *v.*; ógoés *v.*

forgotten gwèlòn *v.*; hakaikós *v.*; hakonuk̂otᵃ *v.*; iɓíléròn *v.*
forgotten (become) iɓíléronuk̂otᵃ *v.*
fork ɲácak̂warátᵃ *n.*; ɲɔ́fɔ́kᵃ *n.*; taŋatsárón *v.*; tɛlɛ́tsón *v.*; toŋélón *v.*
fork (of a tree) bɔ̀kɛ̀dᵃ *n.*
fork of a tree bɔ̀kᵃ *n.*
form bɛrɛtés *v.*; itues *v.*; ituetés *v.*; ituetésá asɨ́ *v.*
form droplets tsɨpɨtsɨ́pón *v.*
form rainclouds mɔk̂imɔ́k̂ón *v.*
forsake góózés *v.*; góózesuk̂otᵃ *v.*
forsake each other góózinósúk̂otᵃ *v.*
forsaken góózosuk̂otᵃ *v.*
fortify ŋixɨ́tésuk̂otᵃ *v.*
fortunate tɨrirɨ́ŋón *v.*
fortune muce *n.*; ɲaɓáátᵃ *n.*
fortune (decent) mucea na ɓáriɓár *n.*
fortune (good) mucea na títìan *n.*; ɲarérɛŋ *n.*
fortune (ill) mucea ná jɔ̀l *n.*
fortune (terrible) mucea na inák̂úós *n.*
forty toomínékwa ts'agús *n.*
forward wàxɨ̀kᵋ *n.*
foster zeites *v.*; zeitésuk̂otᵃ *v.*
foul ɗetsɨɗétsón *v.*; imúsɔ́ɔ̀n *v.*
foul (become) imúsɛ́ɛ̀tòn *v.*
foul-smelling wɨzilɨ́lón *v.*
foully ɗɛtsᵋ *ideo.*
foundation dɛ̀ɛ̀dà hòᵉ *n.*
fountain ɲɛitánitᵃ *n.*
four ts'agús *num.*; ts'agúsón *v.*
four o'clock ɲásáatikaa mɨtátie toomín *n.*
four times ts'agúsᵒ *num.*

four years ago kaɨnɔ nɔɔ kɛ *n.*; nɔkɛɨna kenóó ke *n.*
four-by-four tsʼagusátìkᵉ *v.*
fourteen toomíní ńda kiɗi tsʼagús *n.*
fourth (be a) kɔnɔna tsʼagúsónù *v.*
fourth (one) ɗa tsʼagúsónì *pro.*
fowl ɡwa *n.*
fox (bat-eared) bùràtsᵃ *n.*
fractured takátákánón *v.*
fragile tɛɛmémɔ̀n *v.*; yɛmédɔ̀n *v.*
fragilely yèm *ideo.*
fragment gúɗúsam *n.*
fragrant tukukúɲón *v.*
frail dɛrédɔ̀n *v.*; ɨpáláƙɔ̀n *v.*; ʝuódòn *v.*
frailly dèr *ideo.*; ʝùᵒ *ideo.*
frame (door) ɲéfɨrém *n.*
francolin (crested) bɨlɨ́kɛrɛté *n.*
francolin (Jackson's) kwɨtsɨ́ladidí *n.*
francolin (scaly) tɨkɔ̀rɔ̀tsᵃ *n.*
frayed ɲɛɗédɔ̀n *v.*
frayedly ɲèɗᵋ *ideo.*
freak ƙʉtsʼáám *n.*
freak out doʝánónuƙotᵃ *v.*
free ɓàŋɔ̀n *v.*; bùlòn *v.*; hoɗés *v.*; hoɗésúƙotᵃ *v.*; hoɗetés *v.*; ɨɓámón *v.*; talakes *v.*
free of charge ɨɓámón *v.*
free oneself hoɗetésá asɨ *v.*
free to walk zíbos *v.*
freeload lɛŋɛ́s *v.*
freeloader lɛŋɛ́sɨ́àm *n.*
freeloading olíɓó *n.*
freer hoɗetésíàm *n.*
fresh erútsón *v.*
fret alólóŋòn *v.*
friar purutél *n.*

Friday Ɲákásíá tùdìkᵉ *n.*
friend (agreer) tsámúnɔtɔ́sɨ́àm *n.*
friend (foreign) ɲòtᵃ *n.*
friend (his/her foreign) ntsíɲótᵃ *n.*
friend (in-group) ɛbam *n.*
friend (my foreign) ńcìɲòtᵃ *n.*
friend (my) nádzàƙᵃ *n.*
friend (sharer) tɔ̀mɔ̀rààm *n.*
friend (your foreign) bɨɲótᵃ *n.*
friendliness (in-group) ɛbamánánès *n.*
friendliness (out-group) ɲotánánès *n.*; ɲótíkónánès *n.*
friends (make foreign) ɲotánónuƙotᵃ *v.*
friendship (in-group) ɛbamánánès *n.*
friendship (out-group) ɲotánánès *n.*; ɲótíkónánès *n.*
frighten kitítésuƙotᵃ *v.*; ŋaxɨtetés *v.*; xɛɓɨtes *v.*; xɛɓɨtésúƙɔtᵃ *v.*
frighten away irɛmɛs *v.*
frighten off irɛmɛs *v.*
frightened ŋaxétón *v.*
frigid (sexually) ɨɛ́ɓón *v.*
fringe kwaywᵃ *n.*; kweedᵃ *n.*
frog ƙwaátᵃ *n.*
from nàpèì *prep.*; nɛ́ɛ́ *prep.*; ɲàpèì *prep.*
from the heart gúróénᵓ *n.*
from there tsʼédɔ́ɔ́ kɔ̀nà *pro.*
from when nàpèì *subordconn.*; ɲàpèì *subordconn.*
from where? ndéé *n.*
front takárêdᵃ *n.*; wàx *n.*
frontal bone (upper) matáɲɨ́gwarí *n.*
froofy bʉlʉbʉlɔs *v.*
froth guf *n.*; tabúón *v.*
froth up tabúétòn *v.*
frown iɲíkón *v.*
frowning (begin) iɲíkétòn *v.*

frozen (in fear)   *garden*

frozen (in fear) dodimórón *v.*
frozen (still) lɛrédɔ̀n *v.*
fruit of *ts'ɔkɔm* fɔfɔ́jᵃ *n.*; ŋalúɓᵃ *n.*
fruit(s) eɗin *n.*
fruit-laden bɔ́ŋɔ́n *v.*
fruitless (become) ɨkárímétòn *v.*
frustrate ɨkarɛtés *v.*; ɨlɔ́ɨtésʉkɔtᵃ *v.*
fry kɛ́xɛ́s *v.*
fryer kɛ́xɛ́sɨ̀am *n.*
fuck ɨtɛpɛs *v.*
fuel ceím *n.*
fuel (fire) iríréés *v.*; iríréetés *v.*
Fuerstia africana kʉláɓákàkᵃ *n.*
fulfill ɨrɨ́kɛ́sʉkɔtᵃ *v.*
full cɨ̀ɔn *v.*; eódòn *v.*
full (become) cɨɔnʉkɔtᵃ *v.*; éétòn *v.*
full (completely) tsɛ̀kᵋ *ideo.*
full (very) pɨ̀c *ideo.*; tìr *ideo.*
full completely lʉjʉlújón *v.*
full of it (lying) isuɗesa mɛnáᵋ *v.*
fully fɨr *ideo.*
fumble around ɨtapɨ́tápɔ̀n *v.*
fume ipúróòn *v.*
fume (angrily) siɲírón *v.*
fumes ts'ûdᵃ *n.*
fumigate ipúréés *v.*; iwaɲíwáɲés *v.*; ts'u-dités *v.*
fun ɛ̀fɔ̀n *v.*
fun (become) ɛfɔnʉkɔtᵃ *v.*
fun (have) iyóómètòn *v.*
fun (make) ɛfɨtɛs *v.*
function ɲákásìèdᵃ *n.*
funerary goat kɔ̀pᵃ *n.*; ɲépúɲa *n.*
funerary-goat killer ɲépúɲáám *n.*
funny ɛ̀fɔ̀n *v.*

funny (become) ɛfɔnʉkɔtᵃ *v.*
funny (make) ɛfɨtɛs *v.*
fur ínósìts'ᵃ *n.*
furnace (brick) ɲéripipí *n.*
furrow ɲépélʉ *n.*
furry tsèkòn *v.*
furthermore naɓó *coordconn.*; toni naɓó *n.*
fury gaánàs *n.*; ɲɛlɨl *n.*
fuse iɲales *v.*
futile (become) ɨkárímétòn *v.*
future fàr *adv.*
future (distant) tsò *adv.*
fuzzy saúkúmòn *v.*
gabby mɔɲɨmɔɲɔs *v.*
gag jakátós *v.*; toukes *v.*; touketés *v.*; xákátòn *v.*
gain ground on iɗiles *v.*
gain weight tuɓútónukɔtᵃ *v.*; zízonukɔtᵃ *v.*
galago (lesser) gwan *n.*
Galatians (biblical) Ŋígalatíaikᵃ *n.*
gall bɨ̀ɗᵃ *n.*
gallbladder bɨ̀ɗᵃ *n.*; bɨ̀ɗàhò *n.*
game ɲaɓolya *n.*; wáákᵃ *n.*
game (Ludo) ɲélúɗo *n.*
gang ɲájore *n.*
gang up on ɨɲáŋarɛtés *v.*
gangly sawátsámòn *v.*
gap ɨkálámɛ́s *v.*; tsàŋ *n.*
gaping hádòlòmòn *v.*; laɓáɲámòn *v.*; lafárámòn *v.*
gappy (teeth) ɲaŋálómòn *v.*
garbage ts'ʉts'ʉ *n.*
garbage dump ts'ʉts'úáwᵃ *n.*
garble kʉjúɗòn *v.*
garble speech iŋolíŋólésa tódàᵋ *v.*
garden sêdᵃ *n.*

347

garden (multi-year) ŋwan *n.*
garden (newly cleared) kiwɨ́l *n.*
garden (newly plowed) túbùr *n.*
garden (tiny) fɔ́ɗᵃ *n.*
garden (vegetable) waicíkásèdᵃ *n.*
garden boundary ɲókorimɨ́tᵃ *n.*
garden camp ɲóɓóotᵃ *n.*
garden edge lɔkiram *n.*
garden rain shelter lɔtɔ́ƙᵃ *n.*
garment ƙwàz *n.*
gas (intestinal) fèn *n.*
gas (petrol) ceím *n.*
gas (propane) ɲágás *n.*
gash dzɛrés *v.*
gasoline ɲépetorón *n.*
gassily fèn *ideo.*
gassy fɛnɛ́dɔ̀n *v.*
gate ɔ́dɔ̀kᵃ *n.*
gateway ɔ́dɔ̀kᵃ *n.*
gather ikóóbés *v.*; ɨrɨ́rɛ́ɛ́s *v.*; ɨtsʉnɛs *v.*; ɨtsʉnɛtés *v.*; ɨtsʉ́nétɔ̀n *v.*; itukánón *v.*; itukes *v.*; ɨʉɗɛs *v.*; ɨʉɗɛtés *v.*
gather (contributions) bɔsɛtés *v.*
gather (glean) ɨrárátés *v.*; irarɛs *v.*; tarares *v.*
gather and move ɲʉɲés *v.*
gather and remove ɲʉɲésʉƙɔtᵃ *v.*
gather oneselves ɗɔtsɛtésá asɨ *v.*; ɨrɨ́rɛ́ɛtésá asɨ *v.*
gather saliva imʉjʉ́mʉ́jɔ̀n *v.*
gather socially ɨtsʉnɛtésá asɨ *v.*
gather up ikóóbetés *v.*; ɨrɨ́rɛ́ɛsʉƙɔtᵃ *v.*; ituketés *v.*
gather up and move ɲʉɲɛtés *v.*
gatherer (of greens) wààm *n.*
gathering kur *n.*; ɲatúkɔ́tᵃ *n.*

gathering (big) zɛƙɔ́áwa ná zè *n.*
gauche betsínón *v.*
gaudy ɨmárádàɗòòn *v.*
gaunt ikárɔ́n *v.*; kɔrɔ́ɗɔ́mɔ̀n *v.*; lotímálèmòn *v.*
gaze at emptily itelesa bàrìrrr *v.*
gazelle kodowᵃ *n.*
gearshift cɛbɛn *n.*; ɲésɛɛɓɔ́ *n.*
gearstick cɛbɛn *n.*; ɲésɛɛɓɔ́ *n.*
gecko lókíɓoɓó *n.*
gecko (dwarf) kíɓíɓɨtᵃ *n.*
gecko species? lédᵃ *n.*; ɲámɨliɔŋɔ́r *n.*
gel tɔsɔ́ɗɔ́kɔ̀n *v.*
gelatinous milílón *v.*
generosity daás *n.*
generous dòòn *v.*; waŋádòn *v.*
generous person dòònìàm *n.*
genet lɔrɨ́ƙɨ̀là *n.*
genitalia (female) didis *n.*
gentle batánón *v.*
genuflect kutúɲétòn *v.*
germ ƙʉtsʼᵃ *n.*
German shepherd ɲeryaɲíŋókᵃ *n.*
germinate ɓúrukúkón *v.*; morétón *v.*; rúbètɔ̀n *v.*; rúbɔ̀n *v.*; tʉwétón *v.*; tʉ̀wɔ̀n *v.*; xúbètòn *v.*; xúbòn *v.*
germinate (of grain) xokómón *v.*
germinate fully (of grain) yɛlɨyélɔ̀n *v.*
get iryámétòn *v.*; ɨtétɔ́n *v.*; ɨtɔ́ɔ́n *v.*; ƙanetés *v.*; tébetés *v.*
get (cause to) ƙanitetés *v.*
get (water) kotsés *v.*; kotsetés *v.*
get a rise out of ɨtɔ́ŋɔ́és *v.*
get away iɓutsúmétòn *v.*; iwálílòn *v.*; ùtòn *v.*; utonuƙotᵃ *v.*
get away (from home) ipéérɔ̀n *v.*
get away from iɓutsɛs *v.*; iɓutsɛtésá asɨ *v.*

get close to rɔɲésá asɨ́ v.
get cloudy kupétón v.; kupukúpón v.
get dark witsiwítsétòn v.
get down rʉjétón v.
get going ɗóɗésa muceé v.
get here itaitɛtés v.
get light (of sun) ítóna kíjée ts'ɛɛ v.
get lost hakonuƙotᵃ v.
get on otsés v.; otsésúƙotᵃ v.
get out tɔpéón v.; utonuƙotᵃ v.
get out of the way ècòn v.; èkòn v.
get payback ɲaŋés v.
get ready to go súɓánòn v.; suɓétón v.
get rid of gʉts'ʉrɛs v.; guts'uriés v.; itsúrúés v.
get rid of (kill) iɗɛɛs v.; iɗéésʉƙɔtᵃ v.
get saved hoɗetésá asɨ́ v.
get shady kurukúrétòn v.
get sick meetón v.
get there itaités v.
get through utonuƙotᵃ v.
get to know ɦyeités v.
get together itsʉnɛtésá asɨ́ v.
get up ŋkáítetés v.; ŋkéétòn v.; ŋkóón v.
get up (of many) ŋkaíón v.
ghost kúrúkúr n.; lopéren n.; tás n.
ghoul lopéren n.; tás n.
giant bàdᵃ n.; kébàdà n.; nábàdà n.; nébàdà n.
gift meetam n.; tɔ́rɔ́bɛs v.
gifts meetésíicíkᵃ n.
giggle gagaanón v.
giggly fekifekos v.
gimp isɛ́pón v.; itɔ́ƙɔ́ɔ̀n v.; itsúkúkòn v.
gimpily itsúkúkᵘ ideo.

gimpy ŋoɗólómòn v.
gin (Sunny) ɲásáníjìn n.
gingiva dirijijᵃ n.
giraffe gwaɨts'ᵃ n.
giraffe bull gwaɨts'ɨcikwᵃ n.
giraffe calf gwaɨts'îim n.
giraffe cow gwaɨts'ɨŋwa n.
giraffe-tail cap ɲɔ́tsɔ́ɓɛ n.
girl ɲàràm n.
girl (baby) cue n.
girl (little) ɲàràmàim n.
girls' company ɲèràaƙwᵃ n.
girl-crazy iɲéráánón v.
girlfriend ɲàràm n.
girls ɲèr n.
girls (little) ɲerawikᵃ n.
girls' grass ɲèràkù n.
give bɨrés v.; ijokes v.; ijókésuƙotᵃ v.; meés v.; meetés v.
give (chewing tobacco) mátáŋitɛtés v.
give a ride to iɛ́ɓès v.; iɛ́ɓɛsʉƙɔtᵃ v.; iɛ́ɓɛtés v.
give across ígorésúƙotᵃ v.
give away maƙésúƙotᵃ v.
give back rajésúƙotᵃ v.; rajetés v.
give birth ƙwaatón v.
give birth (help) ƙwaatítetés v.
give birth to ƙwaatetés v.
give birth to prematurely isɔɛtés v.
give chace irúkésuƙotᵃ v.
give drink wetités v.
give each other maímós v.
give food relief bɔnés v.
give gifts to tɔ́rɔ́bɛs v.
give in kuritésúƙota asɨ́ v.

give marching orders to taŋasɛs *v.*
give medicine wetitésá cɛmérı́kàᵋ *v.*
give off itsues *v.*; itsuetés *v.*
give oneself away makésúkota asɨ́ *v.*
give out dónés *v.*; dónésukotᵃ *v.*; makésúkotᵃ *v.*
give over ígorésúkotᵃ *v.*
give rectally iturɛs *v.*
give suck to nakwitɛs *v.*
give up bɔlésúkɔtᵃ *v.*; kuritésúkota asɨ́ *v.*; tajales *v.*; tajálésukotᵃ *v.*; tajaletés *v.*
given moós *v.*
giver meesíám *n.*
giving birth kwaátᵃ *n.*
gizzard ŋìl *n.*
glad ɨlákásɔ̀n *v.*
glad (become) ɨlákásɔ́nukɔt *v.*
glade ɓɔdᵃ *n.*; dɨ́pɔ̀ *n.*
glance iɛ́bɛ̀s *v.*; iɛ́bɛsukɔtᵃ *v.*; iɛ́bɛsukɔtᵃ *v.*; iɛ́bɛtés *v.*
glance (bump) toyeres *v.*
glance off idótón *v.*
glance sidelong at iŋɔ́ɓélés *v.*
gland kùts'àts'ᵃ *n.*
glandular swelling lɔ́mɨ́limɨ́l *n.*
glans penis edɛdᵃ *n.*; kwanɨ́edᵃ *n.*
glare irɨ́rɔ́n *v.*
glare at ŋɔ́zès *v.*; ŋóziés *v.*
glare at each other ŋɔ́zɨnɔ́s *v.*
glarer ŋɔ́zɛ̀sɨ̀àm *n.*
glasses ɲékiyóìkᵃ *n.*
gleam parɨpárɔ́n *v.*; pirɨpírón *v.*
gleam when wet tsalɨtsálɔ́n *v.*
gleaming ɓalɨ́dɔ̀n *v.*; pirídòn *v.*
glean ɨrárátés *v.*; ɨrarɛs *v.*; tarares *v.*
gleeful taɓolos *v.*

glide ifɛlɛsa asɨ́ *v.*; ifélɔ́nukɔtᵃ *v.*; iɔ́ɔ́rés *v.*; iɔ́ɔ́rɔ̀n *v.*
glide through isélɛ́tésukɔta asɨ́ *v.*
glimmer riɓiríɓón *v.*
glimmer when wet tsalɨtsálɔ́n *v.*
glint tɔdɛtɛsa asɨ́ *v.*
glisten parɨpárɔ́n *v.*; piripírón *v.*
glistening ɓalɨ́dɔ̀n *v.*
glitter imɛdɨ́médɔ̀n *v.*
glitterily mìl *ideo.*
glittery milɨ́dɔ̀n *v.*
gloat taɓólón *v.*
gloating taɓolos *v.*
globe kíjᵃ *n.*
gloomy sìŋòn *v.*
glorious dòòn *v.*
glory daás *n.*
glow (of fire) lɔɔrán *n.*
glue ɲágám *n.*
gluey dɔmɔ́dɔ̀n *v.*; irɨ́ɨ́tánón *v.*
gluily dɔ̀m *ideo.*
glut iwótsóòn *v.*
glutton lòkòdòŋìròàm *n.*; lokɛkɛs *n.*
gluttonousness lokodoŋironánés *n.*
gluttony aeásá bùbùì *n.*; lòkòdòŋìrò *n.*
gnarled lɛrékémɔ̀n *v.*
gnat dililits'ᵃ *n.*
gnaw áts'és *v.*
Gnidia subcordata misɨ́ás *n.*
go kòòn *v.*
go [a sound] kùtɔ̀n *v.*; kutɔnukɔtᵃ *v.*
go across górés *v.*; ígorés *v.*; ígorésúkotᵃ *v.*; kámáránón *v.*; kámáránónukotᵃ *v.*
go across repeatedly góriés *v.*; ígoriés *v.*
go after ilɔŋɛs *v.*; ilɔ́ŋésukotᵃ *v.*; túbesukotᵃ *v.*
go after each other ríínós *v.*

go ahead ƙoona wáxɨ̀kᵋ *v.*
go along the side ƙoona rutet° *v.*
go around ilɔ́ɗɔ́nʉƙɔtᵃ *v.*; iɛsʉƙɛs *v.*; sʉ́ƙɛ́s *v.*; tamanɛs *v.*; tamanɛtɛ́s *v.*; tamánɛ́tɔ̀n *v.*
go around in irimes v.
go around repeatedly tamaniɛ́s *v.*
go around restlessly ɗotíɗótòn *v.*
go asleep (of limbs) isálílètòn *v.*
go astray hakonʉƙotᵃ *v.*; itwáŋón *v.*
go at dawn ifúlón *v.*
go away forever ƙòònà jɨ̀r *v.*
go back iɓóɓóŋòn *v.*; itéón *v.*; itíón *v.*; ƙoona jɨ́rɨ̀kᵋ *v.*
go behind ƙoona jɨ́rɨ̀kᵋ *v.*
go behind clouds ƙooná gìdààƙɔ̀kᵋ *v.*
go bring ƙáidetɛ́s *v.*
go broke ŋʉrúmón *v.*
go by iɛ́bɛs *v.*; iɛ́bɛsʉƙɔtᵃ *v.*; ilúɲón *v.*; ilúɲónʉƙotᵃ *v.*
go by way of tɔmɛ́ɛ́sʉƙɔtᵃ *v.*
go crazy dojánónʉƙotᵃ *v.*; itwáŋón *v.*
go directly itsɨ́rɔ́n *v.*; iyoesa asɨ́ *v.*; tsɨ́rɔ́n *v.*
go down ƙoona gígìròkᵋ *v.*; kídzimonʉƙotᵃ *v.*; rajámón *v.*; rajánón *v.*
go down (of sun in afternoon) tɔɔsɔ́ŋón *v.*
go down (of sun) itsólóŋòn *v.*; tɔɔnʉƙɔtᵃ *v.*
go down (out of sight) lakámɛ́tòn *v.*; lakámón *v.*
go down low ɗipímón *v.*
go early isókón *v.*
go extinct bulonʉƙotᵃ *v.*
go for a visit ilɔ́ɔ́n *v.*; ilɔ́ɔ́nʉƙɔtᵃ *v.*; ipásóòn *v.*

go for a walk iɗámón *v.*; zíbòn *v.*
go get ƙáidetɛ́s *v.*
go head-over-heels tɨ́bɨ̀ɗɨ̀lɔ̀n *v.*
go horizontally kámáránónʉƙotᵃ *v.*
go hungry torónón *v.*
go in ɓʉƙétón *v.*; ɓùƙòn *v.*; ɓʉƙonʉƙotᵃ *v.*
go in a rage tʉlúŋón *v.*
go in convoy itɨ́lɔ́nʉƙɔtᵃ *v.*
go in front ƙoona wáxɨ̀kᵋ *v.*
go in procession itɨ́lɔ́nʉƙɔtᵃ *v.*
go into exile totóánonʉƙotᵃ *v.*; xàtsɔ̀n *v.*
go late íbànòn *v.*; irípón *v.*
go near ɦyɔtɔ́gɔnʉƙɔtᵃ *v.*
go off (rot) masánɛ́tòn *v.*; mʉsánɛ́tòn *v.*
go off course kwɛ́dɔ̀n *v.*
go off in a rage tʉlúŋónʉƙɔtᵃ *v.*
go off one-by-one kónionúƙotᵃ *v.*
go off topic hakonʉƙotᵃ *v.*
go off track imámáɗós *v.*
go on pórón *v.*
go on (to do) itáƙúon *v.*
go on a trip ilɔ́ɔ́nʉƙɔtᵃ *v.*
go out pulúmón *v.*
go out (of fire) ts'oonʉƙotᵃ *v.*
go out of sight kúbonʉƙotᵃ *v.*
go over górɛ́s *v.*; ígorɛ́s *v.*; ígorɛ́súƙotᵃ *v.*
go over matters bɛrɛ́sá mɛná*ᵋ v.*
go past bʉnɔnʉƙotᵃ *v.*
go quickly ikómóonʉƙotᵃ *v.*
go round and round ilɔɗɨ́lɔ́ɗɔ̀n *v.*
go straight isɛ́rɛ́rèòn *v.*
go through ilámɔ́n *v.*; piɗɛ́s *v.*; pʉtúmón *v.*
go to seed egɛ́sá ekwí *v.*; tutufánón *v.*
go to sleep eponʉƙotᵃ *v.*
go under (water) ɓʉƙonʉƙotᵃ *v.*

351

go up ƙooná dìdìkᵉ *v.*; tóbìrìbìròn *v.*; totírón *v.*
go via tɔmɛɛs *v.*; tɔmɛ́ɛsʉƙɔtᵃ *v.*
go with elánónuƙotᵃ *v.*
go-away bird (white-bellied) ƙwáaƙwá *n.*
goad ijʉkʉ́jʉ́kɛ́s *v.*
goat (female) rieŋwa *n.*
goat (funerary) kɔ̀pᵃ *n.*; ɲépúɲa *n.*
goat flock riébàr *n.*
goat kid riéím *n.*
goat(s) ri *n.*
goat-leather bag riéófúr *n.*
goatee ɲépénɛkᵃ *n.*; tèmʉ̀r *n.*
gobble down ifáfúkés *v.*; ŋɔfés *v.*
gobbler (of food) lòkòdòɲìròàm *n.*; loƙeƙes *n.*
gobbling (of food) lòkòdòɲìrò *n.*
God áméda kíjáᵉ *n.*; didigwarí *n.*; Ɲakujᵃ *n.*
god Ɲakujᵃ *n.*
godhood ɲakujínánɛs *n.*
godly person ɲakujíám *n.*
gods ɲakujíícíkᵃ *n.*
goer ƙòòníàm *n.*
going for good wɨ̀ʉ̀ *ideo.*
goiter ɓòlìɓòl *n.*
gold gólɨdᵃ *n.*
gold dust ɲéɲiɲɨ *n.*
gold flecks ŋkadɛɛdɛ́yᵃ *n.*
golden earring ɲámaritóitᵃ *n.*
goliath bàdᵃ *n.*
Gomphocarpus fruticosus lɔsalátᵃ *n.*
goo gadár *n.*
good maráŋón *v.*
good (become) maráŋónuƙotᵃ *v.*
good (make) maraŋités *v.*; maraŋítésuƙotᵃ *v.*
good (of many) dayaakón *v.*; maráŋaakón *v.*
good person maráŋónìàm *n.*
good! maráŋ *interj.*
good-looking dòòn *v.*
goodness maráŋás *n.*
goods kúrúɓâdᵃ *n.*; kúrúɓáicíkᵃ *n.*
gooey dɔmódɔ̀n *v.*; nɨrɨ́dɔ̀n *v.*; xɔrɔ́dɔ̀n *v.*
gooily dɔ̀m *ideo.*; nɨ̀r *ideo.*; xɔ̀r *ideo.*
goop gadár *n.*
goopily xɔ̀r *ideo.*
goopy ɓɔrɔ́tɔ́mɔ̀n *v.*; bɔrɔ́tsɔ́mɔ̀n *v.*; xɔrɔ́dɔ̀n *v.*
goose ɲáɓata *n.*
gorge fòtsᵃ *n.*; ɲɔ́kɔ́pɛ̀ *n.*
gorged itéɓúkòn *v.*
goshawk tsìtsᵃ *n.*
gossamer bɛdɛ́dɔ̀n *v.*
gossip about mɔ́ɲɛ́s *v.*
gossiper gáʒadiŋwa *n.*; sɛsɛanóníàm *n.*
gossipy mɔɲɨmɔɲɔs *v.*
gourd kàŋɛr *n.*
gourd (big oblong) ɲátúdu *n.*
gourd (big round) ɓoló *n.*; ɲápadɛr *n.*
gourd (bitter) óbìjòkwàtsᵃ *n.*
gourd (broken) ƙwɛsɛ́ *n.*
gourd (butter) dɛ̀kᵃ *n.*
gourd (cracked) naturutur *n.*
gourd (dried) iƙòlòtᵃ *n.*
gourd (edible) lomuƙe *n.*; lɔ́pʉ́l *n.*
gourd (flask) ɲekúrúm *n.*
gourd (funnel-stemmed) lɔkʉtúr *n.*
gourd (milking) ɲelépítᵃ *n.*
gourd (round) ƙɔfɔ́ *n.*
gourd (small round) dúlúƙuƙú *n.*; ƙɔfóìm *n.*; túkulétᵃ *n.*

gourd (small-mouthed) loƙú n.
gourd (wide-bottom) ɗùtᵃ n.
gourd (wide-mouthed) ƙoƙó n.; rìƙòŋ n.
gourd basin sèrèyᵃ n.
gourd bowl ƙɔfɔ́ n.
gourd enema bulukétᵃ n.
gourd flask bòrèn n.; nasɛmɛ́ n.
gourd flask (small) ɲékútàm n.
gourd flesh ɗɔxɔ̀ƙᵃ n.
gourd ladle (broken) tebeleƙes n.
gourd leaves ɲátuɓe n.
gourd plug akatɛ́tᵃ n.
gourd pulp ɗɔxɔ̀ƙᵃ n.
gourd rattle ɲɛ́ɛ́ƙiɛ́ƙᵃ n.
gourd scoop ɓòlòkòtsᵃ n.
gourd seed kàŋèrèèkwᵃ n.
gourd spout sɔ́kᵃ n.
gourmand lòkòɗòŋìròàm n.; loƙeƙes n.
govern ipúkéés v.
government ɲápukán n.; ɲeryaŋ n.
government (British colonial) gɛrésà n.
government employee ɲápukáníàm n.
government official ámázeáma ɲápukaní n.; túbesiama ɲápukání n.
governor ipúkéésíàm n.; tòtwàrààm n.
gown ɲékiteitéyᵃ n.
grab ídadamɛ́s v.; ikamɛ́súƙɔtᵃ v.; ikamɛtɛ́s v.; irɛɗɛs v.; ŋusés v.; ŋusésúƙotᵃ v.; taŋates v.; tokopes v.
grab away taŋátésuƙotᵃ v.; tokópésuƙotᵃ v.
grab repeatedly ikamíkámɛ́s v.
grabbiness dzɔɗátínànès n.
grabby itɔ́kɔ́ánòn v.; tsʼíts'ɔ́n v.
grace (Catholic) ɲégirasíà n.
grade (roads) séɓés v.

grade (school) hò n.
grader (of roads) séɓésìàm n.
grain eɗᵃ n.
grain (fallen) sɛkɛmán n.
grain (new) eɗa ni erútsᵃ n.
grain (regrown) lɔ́jɔjɔ́ n.; ɲópoté n.
grain beer eɗímɛ́s n.
grain disease lɔɓɛlɛɲ n.
grain harvest (first) ƙɔfɔ́èɗᵃ n.
grain thief lokoɓél n.
grain-filled dirt ɓɔɗájúm n.
grainy siƙisíƙánétòn v.; síƙísiƙánón v.
Gramineae species jayᵃ n.; kɔliliƙú n.kwiniƙíƙú n.; ; lɔ̀tàfàr n.; máyákù n.; miłár n.; ɲálaajáítᵃ n.; ɲámá n.; ɲèràkù n.; ɲokoɗopeyᵃ n.; sòlìsòl n.; tiɓᵃ n.
granary loɗúrú n.
granary (small) lɔkúɗᵃ n.
granary base loɗúrúdè n.
granary cover ɲésóto n.; ɲósóto n.
granary reed loɗúrúkɔ̀kᵃ n.
granary reed (vertical) ɲétémetsᵃ n.
grand zòòn v.
grandchild lobá n.
grandchild (his/her) ntsílóbà n.
grandchild (my) ɲcilobá n.
grandchild (your) bilóbà n.
grandfather (his/her) bɔbatᵃ n.
grandfather (my) bɔbá n.
grandfather (your) bɔ́bɔ̀ n.
grandmother (his/her) dádàtᵃ n.
grandmother (my) dadáŋ n.
grandmother (your) dádò n.
granite rikíríkᵃ n.
grapes ɲéviiní n.
grasp ŋɔtsés v.; tɔkɔɗɛs v.
grasping itɔ́kɔ́ánòn v.

grass

grass kù *n.*
grass (cow-broom) fiyɔ̀jàn *n.*
grass (matted) kémús *n.*
grass (soft) ûdᵃ *n.*
grass (thick dry) sakátán *n.*
grass hut ɲérwám *n.*
grass patch xʉram *n.*
grass shelter ɲɛ́kɪsakátᵃ *n.*
grass species fàɗìgùr *n.*; jayᵃ *n.*; kaxɨtᵃ *n.*; kwɪnɪkɨ́kú *n.*; loiɓórȍkᵃ *n.*; lɔ́mɔ́ɗaátᵃ *n.*; lɔ̀tàfàr *n.*; lɔ́tɨ́lɪtɨ́l *n.*; lɔtsɔ́gɔ̀m *n.*; máyákù *n.*; mèlètᵃ *n.*; mɪlɨ́ár *n.*; mʉrɔn *n.*; ɲálaajáɨ́tᵃ *n.*; ɲámá *n.*; ɲamaɗaɲɨ́kú *n.*; ɲaɲɛnɨjɛ́n *n.*; ɲeɗuar *n.*; ɲèràkù *n.*; ɲéuɗuúɗu *n.*; ɲokoɗopeyᵃ *n.*; ɔlɨ́ *n.*; ò ŋòrìkù *n.*; sòlìsòl *n.*; tiɓᵃ *n.*
grass stub rumurúm *n.*
grasshopper kɛkɛ́r *n.*
grassland dús *n.*
grate fɔ́fɔ́tés *v.*; ifɔɛs *v.*
gratifyingly wɨ̀ɲ *ideo.*
gratifying (sensually) wɨɲɨ́dɔ̀n *v.*; wɨɲiwɨ́ɲɔ́n *v.*
gratis tsàm *n.*
gratuitousness tsàm *n.*
grave ripᵃ *n.*; tás *n.*; tásêdᵃ *n.*
grave (pile of stones) gwàsìkàkìtsᵃ *n.*
gravedigger muɗésíàm *n.*; tʉnʉkɛsɨ́ám *n.*
gravedigger prayer wáána na muɗésíàmàᵉ *n.*
gravel aŋaras *n.*
gravelly ŋàr *ideo.*; ŋarʉ́dɔ̀n *v.*; rakákámòn *v.*
gravelly area aŋarasáákwᵃ *n.*
graverobber tukutesíáma ts'óóniicé *n.*
gravesite tás *n.*; tásêdᵃ *n.*

grime

gravitate irídòn *v.*
gravy ɲóɓɔ́ka *n.*
gray ɔŋɔ́ránètòn *v.*
gray (of weather) kùpòn *v.*
gray-brown ɔŋɔ́ránètòn *v.*
gray-haired kwɛrɛ́xɔ́n *v.*
graze waitetés *v.*
grazing wà *n.*
grease ŋiites *v.*
grease up ŋiitésúkotᵃ *v.*
greasy kùx *ideo.*
great zòòn *v.*
greatness zeís *n.*
greediness dzɔɗátɨ́nànès *n.*
greedy ts'ɨ́ts'ɔ́n *v.*; tírésa dzɔɗátɨ *v.*
greedy person kìɓèɓèàm *n.*
greedyguts loúkᵃ *n.*
Greek language Ŋígirɨ́kɨ̀tòdᵃ *n.*
Greek person Ŋígirɨ́kɨ̀àm *n.*
green ilɨ́ɓɔ́n *v.*
green (of many) iliɓaakón *v.*
green (turn) ilɨ́ɓɔ́nʉkɔtᵃ *v.*
green (turn, of many) iliɓaakónuкotᵃ *v.*
green (very) kwɪxɨ́dɔ̀n *v.*; xɨ́dɔ̀n *v.*
greenly kwɨx *ideo.*
greens wà *n.*
greet ɪmáxánés *v.*
greet each other ɪmáxánɨ́nɔ́s *v.*
Grewia bicolor jàwᵃ *n.*
Grewia tenax alárá *n.*; ɔgɔn *n.*
Grewia villosa mɔ̀z *n.*
grieve turúnón *v.*
grill itɔlɛs *v.*
grill (of vehicle) sarɨ́sárɨ̀kᵃ *n.*
grilled itɔlɔs *v.*
grimace iɲéɓɛ́rés *v.*
grime ts'âgᵃ *n.*

354

grimy   *growl*

grimy ts'ágòn *v.*
grin ɨmúmúɔ̀n *v.*
grind ŋɔ́ɛs *v.*
grind (make) ŋɔ́ɨtɛ́sʉkɔtᵃ *v.*
grind again iɲáɓúkɛ́s *v.*
grind coarsely ikaŋɨkáɲɛ́s *v.*; iɲáámɛ́s *v.*; iɲaɨŋɛ́ɛ́s *v.*; iɲáɲɛ́ɛ́s *v.*
grind finely iwɨɗɛs *v.*
grind quickly ipʉnɛs *v.*
grind well hamʉjɛ́s *v.*
grindable ŋɔam *n.*
grinding mill ŋɔɛsɨ́gwàs *n.*; ɲámasín *n.*
grinding stone gwas *n.*; ŋɔɛsɨ́gwàs *n.*
grinding stone (hand-held) imeda gwasáᵉ *n.*; kɨnata *n.*
grinding stone (lower) ŋwááteda gwasáᵉ *n.*
grip ikamɛs *v.*; ikamɛ́sʉ́kɔtᵃ *v.*; ikamɛtɛ́s *v.*; itɔkɔɗɛs *v.*; tírésìàwᵃ *n.*
grip repeatedly ikamɨ́kámɛ́s *v.*
grist kabas *n.*
grist (dry) ɲápʉpᵃ *n.*
grist (moist) ɲámɨrɔ̀ *n.*
gristle ŋɔrɔɓɔɓᵃ *n.*
gristlely rɔ̀ɓɔ̀ *ideo.*
gristly rɔɓɔ́dɔ̀n *v.*
gritty gwɛréjéjòn *v.*
grizzly kwɛréxɔ́n *v.*
groan éɓútòn *v.*; émɨ́tòn *v.*; émúròn *v.*
groggy mususánón *v.*
groin lɔkɔ́r *n.*
groom bɔk̓atɨ́nɨ̀èàkwᵃ *n.*
grope ɨdadamɛ́s *v.*
grope (sexually) tárábes *v.*
grope all over tárábiés *v.*
groping ɨdadamɔ́s *v.*

grouchy gaƙúrúmòn *v.*; ɲɨ́zɨ̀mɔ̀ɔ̀n *v.*
ground jʉm *n.*; ŋɔ́ɔ́s *v.*
ground (anchor) ɲólóitᵃ *n.*
ground (burnt) kàròƙᵃ *n.*
ground (newly broken) túbùr *n.*
ground bee mɔ́ɗᵃ *n.*
ground bee species ɲásaɲáɲo *n.*; ɲésîitᵃ *n.*
ground beehive kùkùsèn *n.*
ground finely iwɨɗɔs *v.*
ground level (be at) ràtòn *v.*
groundnut(s) ɲépulé *n.*; taráɗá *n.*
grounds awáákwᵃ *n.*
groundwater jʉmúcúé *n.*
groundwork dèèdà hòᵉ *n.*
group ɲájore *n.*; ɲégurúf *n.*
group (social) kábùn *n.*
group discussion natúkᵃ *n.*
grove gwi *n.*
grow ɨatímétòn *v.*; morétón *v.*; zeites *v.*; zeitésuƙotᵃ *v.*
grow back jɔɓɛ́tɔ́n *v.*; tɔrʉ́ɓɔ́n *v.*
grow bigger zoonuƙotᵃ *v.*
grow bushy tsekétón *v.*
grow furry tsekétón *v.*
grow hairy tsekétón *v.*
grow high zikíbètòn *v.*
grow in age zoonuƙotᵃ *v.*
grow limber tsutsukúmétòn *v.*
grow long zikíbètòn *v.*
grow old dunétón *v.*
grow over tsekétón *v.*
grow supple tsutsukúmétòn *v.*
grow tall tɔwʉ́tón *v.*; zikíbètòn *v.*
grow up iríétòn *v.*; zeetón *v.*
grow up and back (of horns) tʉ́zʉ̀ŋɔ̀n *v.*
growl ŋɔ́rɔ́ròn *v.*

growl (of stomach) ɗuɗuanón v.
grown underground ijéélɔ̀n v.
grown up (of many) zeikaakón v.
grown-up ámáze n.
grub ƙʉts'ᵃ n.
grub (food) ŋƙáƙᵃ n.
grub (rhinocerus beetle) lóɓúlukúɲ n.
gruel ɲáítɔ̀ n.; ɲéúji n.
gruff (of voice) ƙokórómòn v.; rɔ́ƙɔ́rɔƙánón v.
grumble iŋʉrúŋúrɔ̀n v.
grumble (of stomach) ɗuɗuanón v.
grumble to oneself ɲɛɓésá tódàᵉ v.
grume ŋazul n.
grumpy gaƙúrúmòn v.; ŋɨ́zɨ̀mɔ̀ɔ̀n v.
grunt iɗɨɲón v.
grunt in pain rúɓón v.
guard còòkààm n.; cookés v.; iritsés v.; ŋasɨ́ƙáárìàm n.
guard (local council) ŋɨ́ɲampáràyàm n.
guard (prison) cookaama zɨ́ƙésiicé n.
guarded cookotós v.
guardian còòkààm n.
guava ɲógóva n.
guest wáánààm n.
guest (long-term) fiyekesíám n.
guide itsɨrítɛtés v.; tsɨrítɛtés v.; tɔɓɛitɛtés v.; tòrìkààm n.; torikes v.; torikesíám n.
guide away toríkésuƙotᵃ v.
guide this way toriketés v.
guile nɔɔ́s n.
guileful nɔɔsánón v.
guineafowl (helmeted) jáɓúgwà n.
guitar ɲégitá n.
gullet moróká na kwátsᵃ n.
gully ɲéƙúrumotᵃ n.; urúr n.

gulp ágʉjés v.; gégès v.; itúláƙáɲés v.
gulp down lakatiés v.; lukutiés v.
gulp! gùlùjᵘ ideo.
gum ɲágám n.
gum (chewing) ɗɔtɔ́ n.
gum (food) iŋulúŋúlés v.
gum (of mouth) dirijijᵃ n.
gum (of trees) ɗòs n.
gum (rubbery) ɗɔtɔ́ n.
gummily ɗɔ̀s ideo.
gummy ɗɔsɔ́dɔ̀n v.; mɨnɨ́ƙɨmɔ̀n v.
gun ɛ̀bᵃ n.
gun (homemade) ɲamatiɗa n.
gun (large-bore) ɲáturugéyᵃ n.
gun (long-barreled) ɲépɛn n.
gun sight ɲélɨmɨrá n.
gun type ɲáɗúle n.
gunkily xɔ̀r ideo.
gunky ɓorɔ́tómòn v.; xɔrɔ́dɔ̀n v.
gunny sack ɲéɗɛpiɗɛ́pᵃ n.; ɲéguniyá n.
gunny sack (large) lomóŋin n.; ɲáwaawá n.
gunpowder leúzìn n.
gunstock ɛ́bàdɛ̀ n.
gurgle áɓùɓùƙɔ̀n v.
gurgle (of stomach) ɗuɗuanón v.
gut ɓilésúƙotᵃ v.; bùbù n.; bùbùàƙwᵃ n.
gutter sɔ́kᵃ n.
guy ɲéés n.
guzzle ágʉjés v.; gégès v.; ɨ́gʉjés v.
gwuf gwuf tsèfètsèf ideo.
habit ɲɛpitɛ n.
habitation zɛƙɔ́áwᵃ n.
habituate italɛs v.; naɨ́nɛɛtés v.; naɨ́tésuƙotᵃ v.
habituated italɔs v.
hacksaw ɲémʉsʉmén n.

haggard ikárɔ́n v.; kɔrɔ́ɗɔ́mɔ̀n v.
hail tɨkɔ̀r n.
hair síts'ᵃ n.
hair (of a baby) imásíts'ᵃ n.
hair (of head) ikásíts'ᵃ n.
hair (pubic) didisísíts'ᵃ n.; ɔ́zàsìts'ᵃ n.; tèmừr n.
hair (stiff) ɲégetsᵃ n.
hair column ɲotókósitᵃ n.
hair follicle síts'áɗè n.
hair jewelry ɲéméle n.
hair ridge sìgìrìgìr n.
hair-patch (styled) nàɗɨ̀àkᵃ n.
hairstyle ɲékiɲés n.
hairy saúkúmòn v.; tsèkòn v.
half ɲénɨ́s n.; xɔnɔ́ɔ́kɔn n.
half (be a) kɔnɔna leɓétsónù v.
half-asleep state mɔɗɔ́ɗɔ̀ekwᵃ n.
half-awake state mɔɗɔ́ɗɔ̀ekwᵃ n.
half-cooked tsɛɓékémɔ̀n v.
half-striped ŋurutiós v.
halfway sisɨkákᵉ n.
halfway point sisɨkêdᵃ n.
halt wasɨtes v.; wasɨtésɨkɔtᵃ v.; wasɔnɨkɔtᵃ v.
halting was n.
hammer ityakes v.; ɲéɲɔnɗɔ́ n.; tɔ́ts'és v.
hammerstone (black) sàbàgwàs n.
hamper iɓates v.
hamper repeatedly iɓatɨɓatés v.
hampered iɓatɨɓatɔ̀n v.
hand ikɔɓɛs v.; kwɛtᵃ n.
hand (left) betsínákwètᵃ n.
hand over here ikɔɓɛtés v.
hand over there ikɔ́ɓɛsɨkɔtᵃ v.

hand-crafted iɗimɔtɔ́sá kwètɨkᵓ v.
hand-held radio dɨrɨdɨra na tímoí n.
handbag ɲánɨ́ɓàkᵃ n.
handful ilɨlɨŋam n.
handgrip ɲɔkɔ́ɗɛ́tᵃ n.; tírésìàwᵃ n.
handgun ɲépɨ́sɨ́tɔ̀l n.
handicap iɓatɛs v.; ŋwaxás n.
handicap repeatedly iɓatɨɓatés v.
handicapped iɓatɨɓatɔ̀n v.; ŋwàxɔ̀n v.
handicapped person ŋwàxɔ̀nɨ̀am n.
handkerchief ɲákitamɓára n.
handle dɛɛɗᵃ n.; ikamɛs v.; ɲɔkɔ́ɗɛ́tᵃ n.; tírés v.; tírésìàwᵃ n.
handle (borehole) ɲatsɨɨmákwɛ́tᵃ n.
handle (hoe) ɲémɛlɛkɨ́dàkwᵃ n.
handle (manage) totseres v.
handle carefully iɓáɓɛ́ɛ́s v.
handmade iɗimɔtɔ́sá kwètɨkᵓ v.
handmade object kwɛtákɔ́rɔ́ɓáɗᵃ n.
handsaw ɲékirikɨ́r n.
handsome dòòn v.
handsomeness daás n.
handyman ɲifunɗíàm n.
hang (kill) ikɛtɛs v.
hang around tokɨ́zòòn v.; tɔúrúmɔ̀n v.
hang back isíɗóòn v.
hang by tucking rɨ́bɛ̀s v.
hang freely alólóánón v.
hang in there taɗáŋón v.
hang low with weight xukúmánòn v.
hang on to iritsés v.
hang oneself ikɛtɛsa asɨ́ v.
hang out itémɔ́ɔ̀n v.; itúmétòn v.
hang up inénéés v.; inénéésɨkɔtᵃ v.; xikɛ́s v.; xikɛ́súkɔtᵃ v.

hang up (in storage) tikiɛtés v.
hang up by tucking rúbɛsʉkɔtᵃ v.
hankering (have a) ɨrɔ́rɔ́kánón v.
Haplocoelum foliolosum ŋʉrúsá n.
happen ikásîimètòn v.; itíyáimètòn v.
happen again tɔrúɓɔ́n v.
happen quickly ɗoriɗórón v.
happen upon bunétón v.; bùnòn v.; ŋawɨlɛs v.; takámón v.
happiness ɲalakas n.
happy eaŋanes v.; ɨlákásɔ̀n v.
happy (become) ɨlákásɔ́nʉkɔtᵃ v.
happy (make) ɨlákásɨtésʉkɔtᵃ v.
harass isyees v.; tɛɲɛfɛs v.
harass each other tɛɲéfʉ́nɔ́s v.
hard ŋɨxɔ̀n v.; tɔrɔ́dɔ̀n v.
hard (difficult) itíónòn v.
hard (filled) dirídòn v.
hard (impenetrably) gɔɓɔ́dɔ̀n v.
hard (make) ŋixɨ́tésʉkɔtᵃ v.
hard (of wood) dèwòn v.
hard (of a substance) lɛrédɔ̀n v.
hard-of-hearing ilios v.
hard-working iɓɛ́rɔ́ánón v.
harden ŋixɨ́tésʉkɔtᵃ v.; ŋixɔnʉkɔtᵃ v.
harder (become) ŋixɔnʉkɔtᵃ v.
hardheadedness ŋixɔna iká́ᵉ v.
hardly gɔ̀ɓɔ ideo.; lèr ideo.
hardship ŋɨtsan n.
hare tulú n.
hare nickname bositíníàm n.
harm tawanes v.; tawánitetés v.
harmfulness kʉts'ánánès n.
harmonious isɨ́lɔ́n v.
harmonize isɨ́lɨ́tésʉkɔtᵃ v.

Harrisonia abyssinica kèlèrwᵃ n.
harrumph hákátòn v.; xakarés v.
harry isyees v.
haruspicate fiyeitésá arɨ́ɨ́kàᵋ v.
harvest ɨrárátés v.; ɨrarɛs v.; karɔŋ n.; tarares v.; watsóyᵃ n.; weés v.
harvest (honey) ɗusés v.
harvest (wild food) hakwés v.
harvest bountifully cɛɛtés v.
harvest millet ɨrábɛs v.
harvest of new grain eɗa ni erútsᵃ n.
harvest termites hakwésá dáɲáᵉ v.
harvest time karɔŋ n.; watsóyᵃ n.
harvester weésíàm n.
has not máa adv.
hassle tɛɲɛfɛs v.
hassle each other tɛɲéfʉ́nɔ́s v.
hasten iɓʉrúɓʉ́rɔ̀n v.; ikómóòn v.
hasten here ikóméètòn v.
hasten there ikómóonʉkɔtᵃ v.
hat ɲákopiyá n.
hat (wide-brim) ɲákakar n.
hatch (of chicks) ɓekétɔ́n v.; iɓɛ́ɓɔ́ɔ̀n v.
hatch out (of chicks) iɓɛ́ɓɛ́ètòn v.
hatchet dzibér n.
hatchet (traditional) kuɲukúdzibér n.
hate ts'ábès v.; takaɗes v.
hate each other dɛɲʉ́ɲʉ́nɔ́s v.; ts'ábunɔ́s v.
have girés v.; iona ńdà v.; tírés v.
have been around kɔ̀wɔ̀n v.
have circles tɔlʉkʉ́lʉ́kɔ̀n v.
have contractions wúrukukánón v.
have free time ipásóòn v.
have fun iyóómètòn v.

have hidden motives dzolugánón *v.*
have mercy on iƙenes *v.*
have multiples ramɛ́s *v.*
have not máa *adv.*
have pain toryáɓón *v.*
have problems iona ŋɨ́tsaníkᵋ *v.*
have sex èpòn *v.*
have sex (frequently) ɓútánés *v.*
have sex with tirɛ́s *v.*
have sex with each other tirímós *v.*
have time to walk around zíbos *v.*
have unprotected sex ts'ɨ́ts'ɔ́n *v.*
hawk hákátòn *v.*; tsìtsᵃ *n.*; xaƙarés *v.*
hawker ŋímutsurúsìàm *n.*
hawker (being a) ŋímutsurúsìnànès *n.*
haze (atmospheric) súm *n.*
hazy imítíròn *v.*
he ntsᵃ *pro.*
head iƙᵃ *n.*; iƙeɗᵃ *n.*
head of beer iƙeda mɛ́sè *n.*
head of trail mucédè *n.*
head honcho ámáze *n.*; ámázeám *n.*
head-butt tɔɗɔ́pón *v.*
head-pad ɨƙitᵃ *n.*
headband (beaded) ɲɛ́wakɔ́l *n.*
headband (men's) ɲɛcáátᵃ *n.*
heading iƙeɗᵃ *n.*
headlight ɲómotokéèkwᵃ *n.*
headmaster ámázeáma ɲɛ́sukúluⁱ *n.*
headrest diƙwam *n.*; kàràtsᵃ *n.*
headstart (get a) iɗílón *v.*
headway on (make) iɗiles *v.*
heal maraɲítésuƙotᵃ *v.*; maráŋónuƙotᵃ *v.*; mɨ́nɛ́s *v.*
heal up iɲálèètòn *v.*; toíónuƙotᵃ *v.*

healer (traditional) cɛmɛ́ríƙààm *n.*; irésíàm *n.*; ŋƙwa *n.*; wetitésíàm *n.*
health center ɗakɨtár *n.*
healthily ɗòx *ideo.*
healthy ɗoxódòn *v.*; iɲáléòn *v.*; nɛsɛƙánón *v.*; zízòn *v.*
healthy (get) zízonuƙotᵃ *v.*
healthy (keep) iritsɛ́sá ɲeɗekéícíƙáᵒ *v.*
healthy person zízònìàm *n.*
heap inʉƙʉ́nʉ́ƙés *v.*; itukes *v.*; kìtsᵃ *n.*; ɲatúkítᵃ *n.*; tutukesíáwᵃ *n.*
heap on iɗóɗókés *v.*
heap up iruƙetés *v.*; ituƙetés *v.*; kitsetés *v.*; tutuƙetés *v.*
heaped up iɗóɗókánón *v.*; tutukánón *v.*
hear nesés *v.*; nesíbes *v.*
heart (physical) gúróèɗᵃ *n.*
heart (soul) gúr *n.*
heart fat máxìŋ *n.*
heart-rot (have) ɓʉɓʉsánón *v.*
heartache áts'ɛ́sa gúróᵉ *n.*
heartburn áts'ɛ́sa gúróᵉ *n.*; kɨ́ɓɔ́ɔz *n.*
hearth ts'aɗíékwᵃ *n.*
hearthstone caál *n.*
heartsick moona gúróᵉ *v.*
heartwood gúréda dakwí *n.*
heat imaɗɛs *v.*
heat up hábètòn *v.*; hábitésúƙotᵃ *v.*; hábonuƙotᵃ *v.*; imáɗɛ́sʉƙotᵃ *v.*; imɔ́lɔ́ŋɛtés *v.*
heated (angry) ilɨ́lɨ́òn *v.*
heated (become) ilɨ́lɨ́ɔnʉƙɔtᵃ *v.*
heathen ŋɨ́kafɨ̀rìàm *n.*
heave jaƙátós *v.*; ɲɛɲɛrɛs *v.*; toremes *v.*; xáƙátòn *v.*
heave away itsɔ́résʉƙɔtᵃ *v.*

Heaven awa ná zè *n.*; awa Ɲákují *n.*; didigwarí *n.*; gìdòɔ̀kª *n.*
heavens lúl *n.*
heavily lìr *ideo.*
heavy ìsòn *v.*
heavy (make) inúítɛ́súƙɔtª *v.*; isites *v.*
heavy-laded iúƙón *v.*
Hebrew language Ŋíyuɗáítòdª *n.*
Hebrew person Ŋíyuɗáìàm *n.*
Hebrews (biblical) Ŋíeɓuráiikª *n.*
hedge itsóɗón *v.*
hedgehog (four-toed) náabús *n.*
hedging in (of prey) nakítsòɗª *n.*
hee-haw werétsón *v.*
heed nesíbes *v.*
heedlessly càcⁱ *adv.*; fùts'àts'ª *ideo.*; tsàr *ideo.*
heel titíjª *n.*
heft ɲɛɲɛrɛs *v.*; toremes *v.*
heftily bɛ̀f *ideo.*
hefty bɛfúɗɔ̀n *v.*; bɛfúƙúmɔ̀n *v.*
height zikíbàs *n.*
heir irìtsɛ́sɨ́àm *n.*
heist imɔ́ɗɛ́súƙɔtª *v.*
Helianthus species ɲékiɗɛkiɗɛ́ *n.*; ɲétɔɔkíɗɛ́ *n.*
Helichrysum odoratissimum ɲéúlam *n.*
helicopter naƙɨ́lɨƙɨ́l *n.*
help bɨ́rɛ́s *v.*; iɲaarɛ́s *v.*
help each other iɲáárɨ́nɔ́s *v.*
help give birth iɲaarɨ́nɔ́sá ƙwaatɛ́° *v.*
helped iɲaarímétòn *v.*
helper iɲaarɛ́sɨ̀àm *n.*
hem kweeda ƙwázàᵉ *n.*
hem (bottom) sɔka na ƙwázàᵋ *n.*
hemispherical loŋórómòn *v.*

hemp ɲábaŋgí *n.*
hen gwaŋwa *n.*
henhouse ɲókɔkɔrɔ́hò *n.*
her ntsª *pro.*
herald síráàm *n.*; síránòn *v.*
herb (medicinal) cɛmɛ̀r *n.*
herbalist cɛmɛ́rɨ́kààm *n.*; wetitɛ́síàm *n.*
herd bàr *n.*
herd (small) bàròìm *n.*
herd of cattle fiyɔ̀bàr *n.*
herds ɲɨ́ɓarɛn *n.*
here naíkɛ́ *dem.*; náíta na *dem.*; nayá *n.*; nayɛ́ *dem.*; nayɛ́ na *dem.*; nɔ́ɔ́ *dem.*
here you go! ne *interj.*
here! ne *interj.*
hermitic iɓóótánón *v.*
herniate itsúbùɗòn *v.*
herniated itsúbùɗùmɔ̀n *v.*
herpes (of lips) ɲótótsª *n.*
hers ntsɛ́n *pro.*
herself nébèdª *n.*; ntsínêbª *n.*
hesitate imɔ́métɔ̀n *v.*; isíƙóòn *v.*; itóŋóòn *v.*; mɔ́métɔ̀n *v.*; wasɛ́tɔ́n *v.*
hex ipeɗes *v.*; suɓɛ́s *v.*
hexer ipèɗààm *n.*; suɓɛ́sɨ̀àm *n.*
hey! hèz *interj.*
hibernate itáƙálɛ́sá asɨ *v.*
Hibiscus cannbinus ɔ́bɛr *n.*
Hibiscus esculentus ɲɔlɔlɔtª *n.*
hiccough xíƙón *v.*; xìƙwª *n.*; xíƙwítòn *v.*
hiccup xíƙón *v.*; xìƙwª *n.*; xíƙwítòn *v.*
hidden buɗésón *v.*; búɗòs *v.*
hidden (become) buɗésónuƙotª *v.*
hide buanítesuƙotª *v.*; búdès *v.*; búdesuƙotª *v.*; iɗɛɛs *v.*; ipáŋwéés *v.*; ts'ɛ̀ *n.*
hide away iɗɛ́ɛ́suƙotª *v.*; iwítésuƙotª *v.*

hide oneself ɓudés *v.*
hide poorly itárákáɲés *v.*
hide repeatedly iɗaiyes *v.*
hideous itópénòn *v.*; làlòn *v.*
high zikíbòn *v.*
high (get oneself) irákésʉƙɔta asɨ́ *v.*
high (grow) zikíbonuƙotᵃ *v.*
high (make) zikíbitésúƙotᵃ *v.*
high (of many) zikíbaakón *v.*
high-pitched ɓòɓòn *v.*
higher than ileŋes *v.*
highway ɲerukuɗe *n.*
hill kùɓᵃ *n.*
hillside rutetᵃ *n.*
hillside (unseen) kûbᵃ *n.*
hilltop kuɓagwarí *n.*
hilltop (flat) kùɓààƙwᵃ *n.*
hilly ƙumúƙúmánón *v.*
him ntsᵃ *pro.*
himself nébèdᵃ *n.*; ntsínêbᵃ *n.*
hind-apron (leather) dekᵃ *n.*
hinder iɓatɛs *v.*; itítírés *v.*
hinder repeatedly iɓatɨ́ɓátés *v.*
hindered iɓatɨ́ɓátɔ̀n *v.*
hindleg (right) ɲálán *n.*
hinge ɲépɛtá *n.*
hip obólén *n.*
hip joint socket loŋóléhò *n.*
hipbone (lower) obólénìɔ̀kᵃ *n.*
hipbone (upper) róróìɔ̀kᵃ *n.*
hippo ɲépírìà *n.*
Hippocratea africana mɨ́ʒɨ̀ʒ *n.*
hippopotamus ɲépírìà *n.*
hire ɓuƙítésuƙotᵃ *v.*; ikásíitetés *v.*; ipáŋƙeés *v.*; teréganitetés *v.*

hire temporarily ilɛjɨ́léjɨtɛtés *v.*
hired hand terégìàm *n.*
hirer ɓuƙítésuƙotíám *n.*
his ntsᵃ *pro.*; ntsɛ́n *pro.*
his/her cousin tatatᵃ *n.*
hiss fúútòn *v.*
history emutíká nùù kɔ̀wᵃ *n.*
hit ɗálútés *v.*; ɨɓaɗés *v.*; iwés *v.*; iwésuƙotᵃ *v.*
hit (exploit) inɔmɛtés *v.*
hit from behind kɔnɨtɛtés *v.*
hit repeatedly ɨɓaɗiés *v.*; ɨramɨ́rámés *v.*
hit the target itsɨrɔ́n *v.*; tsɨrɔ́n *v.*
HIV lóɓúlukúɲ *n.*; sílím *n.*
hive kànàxà *n.*
hoard irwanes *v.*
hoarse ƙoƙórómòn *v.*; rɔ́ƙɔ́rɔƙánón *v.*
hoary kwɛréxɔ́n *v.*
hobble isɛpón *v.*; itɔ́ƙɔ̀n *v.*; itsúƙúkòn *v.*
hobbling ŋoɗólómòn *v.*
hobblingly itsúƙúkᵘ *ideo.*
hodgepodge ɲótsɔ́ɓɨtsɔɓᵃ *n.*
hoe ɲákakurá *n.*; ɲɛmɛlɛkɨ́ *n.*
hoe (push type) kúɓèl *n.*
hoe handle ɲɛmɛlɛkɨ́dàkwᵃ *n.*
hoe up (grass) ɨ́ɛ́s *v.*; ireɲes *v.*
hoed up (of grass) ɨ́ɔ́s *v.*
hog ɲéguruwé *n.*
hog-tie itʉsɛtés *v.*
hogwash iɓááɲàsɨ̀tɔ̀dᵃ *n.*
hold ikamɛs *v.*; tírés *v.*; tírésìàwᵃ *n.*
hold back iƙalɨ́ƙálés *v.*; isíƙeés *v.*; ititíƙés *v.*; itítíƙetés *v.*; rajés *v.*; titikes *v.*
hold by handle tɔkɔɗes *v.*
hold by the mouth tajakes *v.*

hold down ɗaɗátésuƙotᵃ v.; itikes v.
hold each other tírínós v.
hold fast itííròòn v.
hold hands tírínósá kwètɨ̀kàˀ v.
hold in iƙalíƙálɛ́s v.
hold inside ipáŋwéés v.
hold off rajés v.
hold onto ikamɨ́kámɛ́s v.; ŋɔtsés v.
hold out (hands) taɓɛɛs v.
hold religious service wáán v.
hold up alólóés v.; iƙaŋɛs v.; itúmésuƙotᵃ v.; titiretés v.
hold with teeth titikes v.
hole aƙᵃ n.; iɓólóɲés v.; itoɓes v.; ripᵃ n.
hole (in river) ɲétsúur n.
hole (in tree) kotím n.
hole repeatedly itoɓítóɓés v.
hole up (hide) itáƙálésá asɨ v.
holiday ɲákarám n.
holiday (national) ɲésukukú n.; ódowa ná zè n.
holiness daás n.
holler iƙɨ́lɔ́n v.; iƙúétòn v.; iƙúón v.; iƙúónuƙotᵃ v.
hollow bótsón v.; ripᵃ n.
hollow (in tree) kotím n.
hollow out iɓóɓórés v.; irórókés v.
hollowed out iɓóɓórós v.
holy ɓèts'òn v.; dòòn v.
Holy Communion Ŋƙáƙá Komúnióᵉ n.
holy ground ɲɛkɨ́wɔ́rɨ̀tᵃ n.
Holy Spirit Sugura ná Dà n.
home awᵃ n.; zɛƙɔ́áwᵃ n.
home (big) awa ná zè n.
home (clean, orderly) zɛƙɔ́áwa na maráŋ n.

home life awááƙwᵃ n.
homebody awáám n.
homeless person tsɔnɨtsɔnɔsɨ́ám n.
homestead awᵃ n.
homestead (abandoned) ɲóɓóotᵃ n.; on n.; oníáwᵃ n.
honest person easíám n.
honesty eas n.
honey ɗàɗᵃ n.; ts'ɨƙᵃ n.
honey (crystallized) sùƙùtèlà n.
honey (liquid) lɛ̀ɓᵃ n.
honey badger lɛŋ n.
honey bag ɗàɗèèwᵃ n.; èwᵃ n.
honey beer sɨs n.; ts'ɔƙam n.
honey hunter lɛŋésɨ́am n.
honeybee ts'ɨƙᵃ n.
honeycomb ɗàɗàhò n.; ts'ɨƙáhò n.
honeycomb (crystallized) dòkìr n.
honeycomb (dry) ɔfɔrɔƙᵃ n.
honeycomb (new) lòmìl n.
honeycomb (old black) bɔkɔ́ƙᵃ n.
honeyguide tsɨ́tsᵃ n.
honor tɔ́rɔ́bɛs v.; xèɓɔ̀n v.
hood (of a snake) ɓòlìɓòl n.
hoof gɔ̀rɨ̀gɔ̀r n.; sɔƙᵃ n.
hook (metal) súƙútésɨ́tsɨrɨ́m n.
hook-shaped lɔkɔ́ɗɔ́n v.
hooked lɔkɔ́ɗɔ́n v.; sokóɗómòn v.
hooklike sokóɗómòn v.
hoopoe (green wood-) ƙáraƙár n.
hoot (of owls) rúɓón v.
hop iɗótón v.
hop along iɗotíɗótòn v.
hop on one leg itsóɗóƙɔ̀n v.
hope ítánòn v.
hope for ítánésuƙotᵃ v.
hopscotch cédicedí n.

horizontal kámáránón *v.*
horizontalize kámáriés *v.*; kámáriésúkot^a *v.*
horizontalized kámáriós *v.*
horn êb^a *n.*
horn (musical) êb^a *n.*; ɲɛrʉpɛpɛ́ *n.*
horn (oryx) tsarʉ́kʉ́ɛ̀b^a *n.*
horn (voice-amplifying) ɲárʉpɛpɛ́ *n.*
hornbill (African grey) tìlòkòts^a *n.*
hornbill (red-billed) kɔ̀kɔ̀t^a *n.*
hornet dɛrɛ́k̔^a *n.*
hornless lemúánètòn *v.*
horny (sexually) kwídikwidós *v.*
horrify iɓálétòn *v.*; lilétón *v.*; toɓules *v.*
horrifying iɓálɔ́n *v.*; toɓúlón *v.*
horse ɲaŋólé *n.*
Hoslundia opposita ɲérikɨrɨ́k^a *n.*
hospital ɗakɨtár *n.*
hospital ward mayaakóniicéhò *n.*
hostel epúáw^a *n.*; ɲólój^a *n.*
hostility lɔŋɔ́tánànès *n.*
hot hábòn *v.*
hot (become blazing) ririanétòn *v.*
hot (become) hábètòn *v.*; hábonukot^a *v.*
hot (blazing) ririanón *v.*
hot (make) hábitésúkot^a *v.*
hot (of the ground) tábʉrʉbʉ́rɔ́n *v.*
hot (piping) titianón *v.*
hot (very) pɨ̀rrr *ideo.*; titianón *v.*
hot weather hábona kíjá^e *n.*
hot-tempered gúránòn *v.*; gúránòn *v.*; gúránós *v.*; gúránós *v.*
hot-tempered person gúróàm *n.*
hotel epúáw^a *n.*; ɲólój^a *n.*
hothead gúróàm *n.*

hotheaded gúránòn *v.*; gúránós *v.*
hour ɲásáat^a *n.*
house hò *n.*
house help terégiama awá^e *n.*
house of prayer wáánàhò *n.*
house of worship itúrútésiho *n.*; ɲakujíhò *n.*
house rat ɗérá na áwìkà^e *n.*
housecat púùs *n.*
housewarming (host a) fáídomés *v.*
housing hò *n.*
how (it is) naɨ́tá *subordconn.*
how many? tanɔ́ɔ́n *v.*
how? ńtí *adv.*
howitzer ɲómóta *n.*
howl ikúétòn *v.*; ikúón *v.*; ikúónukot^a *v.*; irúrúmòòn *v.*
hsss! rɨrrr *ideo.*
hug irʉmɛs *v.*; tɔtʉnɛs *v.*
hug each other irʉ́mʉ́nɔ́s *v.*; tɔtʉ́nʉ́mɔ́s *v.*
huge zòòn *v.*
huge (of many) zeikaakón *v.*
huh! yeé' *interj.*
hulky ɓutúrúmòn *v.*
human being buɗámóniàm *n.*
humanitarian lɔjɔkɔtáw^a *n.*
humanitarians roɓa ni gúrítínía dayaák^a *n.*
humanness ámánànès *n.*
humble batánón *v.*
humble oneself kwatsitésúkota asɨ *v.*
humerus ɲorótónitiɔ́k^a *n.*
humiliate ɓets'itetés *v.*
humiliated kweelémòn *v.*
humor cɛ́ŋ *n.*
hump (animal) rʉk^a *n.*
hunch over dúgùmètòn *v.*

hunched mɨkɨrɨmɔ̀n *v.*
hunched over dɨ́gɨ̀mɔ̀n *v.*; gɨ́gɨ̀rɔ̀n *v.*; rɨ́gɨ̀dɨ̀mɔ̀n *v.*
hundred ŋamɨ́á *n.*
hunger ɲɛ̀ƙᵃ *n.*
hunger for meal mush tɔbɔŋɔ́ɲɛ́ƙᵃ *n.*
hunger for meat bisákᵃ *n.*
hungover mususánón *v.*
hungriness ɲɛ̀ƙᵃ *n.*
hungry (be quickly) hɔɓɔ́mɔ́n *v.*
hunker rábɨ̀xɔ̀n *v.*
hunt ƙàƙᵃ *n.*; ƙaƙés *v.*; tɔɓɛlɛs *v.*
hunt (honey) lɛŋés *v.*
hunter ƙàƙààm *n.*
hunters' call for help waín *n.*
hunting ƙàƙᵃ *n.*
hunting ground itsóɗóniàwᵃ *n.*
hunting with ropes ƙaƙa ŋúnítínº *n.*
hurdle itúlúmòòn *v.*
hurl imasɛs *v.*; irɨtsɛs *v.*
hurl (vomit) ɦyɛnɛ́tɔ́n *v.*; ɦyɛ̀nɔ̀n *v.*; ilɔ́ɓɔ́tɛtɛ́s *v.*
hurl away imásɛ́sɨƙɔtᵃ *v.*
hurl this way imasɛtɛ́s *v.*
hurry iɓɨ́ɲɔ́n *v.*; iɓɨrɨ́ɓɨ́rɔ̀n *v.*; ikirɨ́kɨ́rɔ̀n *v.*; ikómóòn *v.*
hurry over there ikómóonɨƙɔtᵃ *v.*
hurry this way ikómèètòn *v.*; ŋusetésá asɨ́ *v.*
hurt áts'ɛ́s *v.*; dódòn *v.*; irɨ́ɗɔ́n *v.*; tawanes *v.*; tawánítetés *v.*
hurt (begin to) dódètòn *v.*
hurt (in the chest) iláfúkòn *v.*
hurt (of an injury) wilɨ́mɔ́n *v.*
hurt (of teeth) isálílòn *v.*; itóɲílés *v.*
hurt intermittently áts'ietés *v.*

husband eakwᵃ *n.*
husband (her) ntsiéákwᵃ *n.*
husband (my) ɲcièàkwᵃ *n.*
husband (of my wife's sister) kɨɓá *n.*
husband (tabooed) ts'ɨ̀nɔ̀àm *n.*
husband (your) biéákwᵃ *n.*
husbands ɲɔtᵃ *n.*
hush ɦyakwés *v.*; ijémɨ́tésɨƙɔtᵃ *v.*
hush up ijémɔ́nɨƙɔtᵃ *v.*
hushed ijémɔ́n *v.*
hushedly jɨ̀r *ideo.*
husk bɔɗɔ́kᵃ *n.*; poɗés *v.*; poɗetés *v.*
husks nakariɓᵃ *n.*
husky (of voice) ƙokórómòn *v.*; rɔ́ƙɔ́rɔƙánón *v.*
hussy dekitíníàm *n.*
hut hò *n.*
hut (grass) ɲérwám *n.*
hut (Toposa) Kɔrɔmɔtáhó *n.*
hyena haú *n.*
hyena (spotted) atɔŋ *n.*; natiŋá *n.*
hyena (striped) ɲetutu *n.*
hyena rider otsésíama haúùⁱ *n.*
hyena species oyóŋ *n.*
hygienic nɛsɛƙánón *v.*
Hymenodictyon floribundum sésèn *n.*
hyperbolize imiɗɨ́mɨ́ɗésa mɛnáᵋ *v.*; tasaɓesa mɛnáᵋ *v.*
hypocritical itsárɨ́ánón *v.*
Hypoxis obtusa ɲésɨ́tè *n.*
hyrax kwɨniƙᵃ *n.*
hyrax (bush) ɔlɨ́r *n.*
hyrax (rock) barís *n.*
hyrax grass kwɨniƙɨ́kú *n.*
hyrax half irutumén *n.*
hyrax nickname lotúɗuzé *n.*
I ŋ́kᵃ *pro.*

I guess tsàm *adv.*
I suppose tsàm *adv.*
I.D. ɓɛƙɛsɨ́kabádᵃ *n.*
i.e. tàà *comp.*
ice tɨ̀kɔ̀r *n.*
ichneumon mútètsᵃ *n.*
identification card (Kenyan) ɲɛkɨpandɛ *n.*
identity car ɓɛƙɛ́sɨ́kabádᵃ *n.*
idiocy ɨɓááŋàs *n.*
idiot bóx *n.*; ɨɓááŋàsɨ̀àm *n.*
idiot! ɗúrʉɗɔ́ɔ̀ *interj.*
idiotic ɨɓááŋɔ̀n *v.*
idle ɨlárón *v.*; ɨlwárón *v.*
idler ɲakárámɨtᵃ *n.*
idol kúrúkúr *n.*
if mísɨ *subordconn.*; na *subordconn.*
if ... had (a while ago) nànòò *subordconn.*
if ... had (earlier) nanáá *subordconn.*
if ... had (yesterday) nábèè *subordconn.*
if ... would naƙánàkᵃ *subordconn.*
if ... would have (a while ago) naƙánòkᵒ *subordconn.*
if ... would have (earlier) naƙánàkᵃ *subordconn.*
if ... would have (yesterday) naƙásàm *subordconn.*
ignite dulúmón *v.*; lɛ́jɛ́tɔ́n *v.*; tsapés *v.*; tuƙúmétòn *v.*
ignition aeitetésíàwᵃ *n.*
ignore bálábálatés *v.*; balɛ́s *v.*; balɛtés *v.*
Ik country Icékíjᵃ *n.*
Ik county Icékíjᵃ *n.*
Ik dance Icédìkwᵃ *n.*
Ik day Icéódòwᵃ *n.*
Ik language Icéɛ́n *n.*; Icénáƙáf *n.*; Icétôdᵃ *n.*
Ik people Ikᵃ *n.*; Tɛʉ́sɔ̀ *n.*
Ik person Icéám *n.*
Ik tobacco kwɨ́lilɨ́ *n.*
Ik tribe Icédìywᵃ *n.*
Ikland Icékíjᵃ *n.*
Iklikeness Icénánès *n.*
Ikness Icénánès *n.*
ill mòòn *v.*
ill (make) inʉɛs *v.*
ill (nauseated) iláƙízòn *v.*
ill (of many) mayaakón *v.*
ill-fitting nalójón *v.*
illegal toɗyakos *v.*
illegitimate child ŋabɔ́bòìm *n.*
illiteracy ɨɓááŋàs *n.*
illiterate ɨɓááŋɔ̀n *v.*
illness màywᵃ *n.*; ɲeɗeke *n.*
illness (mental) lejénánès *n.*
illness (mild) ɲeɗekéím *n.*
illusion of movement lɔ́wɨ́rɨwɨ́r *n.*
illustrate ɗoɗésúƙotᵃ *v.*; itétémés *v.*
imagine tamɛtés *v.*
imbecile ɨɓááŋàsɨ̀àm *n.*
imbibe béberetés *v.*; wetés *v.*
imbiber wetésíàm *n.*
imitate iɲitiés *v.*
immaculate xɔ́dɔ̀n *v.*; xɔtánón *v.*
immediately wɛrɛkɛs *ideo.*
immerse ilumes *v.*; ilúmésuƙotᵃ *v.*
immerse oneself ilumetésá asɨ́ *v.*
immigrant botáám *n.*
immovable diriɓóón *v.*
immunize itsɨpɨ́tsɨ́pɛ́s *v.*
imp kíjáìm *n.*
impede ɨɓatɛs *v.*

impede repeatedly ɨbatɨ́bátɛ́s *v.*
impel ɨfalɨ́fálɛ́s *v.*
impenetrable rɔ́mɔ́n *v.*
impervious itsyátón *v.*
impetuous ɨɓéléánón *v.*; ɨɓélɔ́ɔ̀n *v.*
impliable gɔkɔ́dɔ̀n *v.*
implore wáán *v.*
import zeísêd[a] *n.*
importance zeís *n.*
important itíónòn *v.*
impose tɔnɛɛtés *v.*
impose oneself tɔnɛɛtésá asɨ́ *v.*
impoverishment ŋókínànɛ̀s *n.*
imprecate ɨlamɛs *v.*
imprecation ɨ̀làm *n.*
impregnated (recently) sɨbánón *v.*
imprison egésá hòòk[e] *v.*; egésá zɨ́késɨ̀k[ɛ] *v.*; zɨ́kés *v.*; zɨ́késʉkɔt[a] *v.*
imprisoned zɨ́kɔ́s *v.*
improve doonʉkɔt[a] *v.*; iŋáléètòn *v.*; maraŋités *v.*; maraŋítésʉkɔt[a] *v.*; maráŋónʉkɔt[a] *v.*; xɔ́dɔnʉkɔt[a] *v.*
improve slightly ŋwanɨ́ŋwánítés *v.*
impudent ɲɔmɔránón *v.*
impulsive ɨɓéléánón *v.*; ɨɓélɔ́ɔ̀n *v.*
in addition jɨ̀k[ɛ] *adv.*
in charge wàsɔn *v.*; zeísíàm *n.*; zòònìàm *n.*
in charge of things wasɔna kúrúɓádù *v.*
in charge of work zoona terégù *v.*
in concert ikéé kɔ̀n *n.*
in flux iɲíkón *v.*
in front ɛ̀kwɔ̀n *v.*; wàxɨ̀k[ɛ] *n.*; wàxʉ̀ *n.*
in labor koríón *v.*
in labor (difficult) imákóòn *v.*

in large denominations (of cash) ɗukúdòn *v.*
in order that ikóteré *subordconn.*; kánɨ *subordconn.*; kánɨ náa táa *subordconn.*; kóteré *subordconn.*
in order that ... not kánɨ mookóo *subordconn.*
in pain toryáɓón *v.*
in shape ɗoxódòn *v.*; itsyátón *v.*
in shock ɨjárɔ́n *v.*; jarámétòn *v.*
in shreds dzérédzɛránón *v.*
in that direction kɔ́ɔ́ kɛ *dem.*
in the back jɨ̀rʉ̀ *n.*
in the center sɨsɨkák[ɛ] *n.*
in the future fàr *adv.*
in the hell! ɲák[a] *adv.*
in the middle sɨsɨkák[ɛ] *n.*
in the morning barats[o] *n.*
in the rear jɨ̀rʉ̀ *n.*
in the same way ts'ɛ̀tà kɔ̀nà *n.*
in the world! ɲák[a] *adv.*
in this direction nɔ́ɔ́ *dem.*; nɔ́ɔ́ na *dem.*
in three years nakaɨna far *n.*
in two years nakaɨna tso *n.*
in twos leɓetsíón *v.*
in unison ilíróòn *v.*
in vain ŋálàk[a] *ideo.*
in-law ceŋetiám *n.*
in-law (my child's spouse's parent) ńcɨɲòt[a] *n.*
in-law (parent) emetá *n.*
in-law (removed) ɲòt[a] *n.*
in-laws (being) ceŋetínánɛ̀s *n.*
inactive ɨlárón *v.*; ɨlwárɔ́n *v.*
inadequate lʉkáámòn *v.*
inadequate (make) lʉkáámitésʉ́kɔt[a] *v.*

inattentive ɓotsódòn v.
inaugurate tsáŋés v.
inaugurate (new year) itówéés n.
inbreeder kɔ́nɨ́sɨ̀àm n.
inbreeding kɔ́nɨ́s n.
incarcerate zɨ́kɛ́s v.
incarcerated zɨ́kɔ́s v.
incest kɔ́nɨ́s n.
incestuous person kɔ́nɨ́sɨ̀àm n.
inch itsóɗón v.
inch over here itsoɗiétòn v.
incinerate wuɗétón v.
incinerated wùɗòn v.; xawɨ́ɨts'ⁱ ideo.
incisor ƙɨ́dzɛ̀sɨ̀kwàywᵃ n.
incite ɓɛkɛtés v.; ɨsúsúés v.; itsótsóés v.
incite (verbally) itɔ́ŋɔ́és v.
incite desire iɓúrétòn v.
incited iƙúrúmós v.
incitement ɓɛkam n.
incitive ɓɛkánón v.
inclined sémédedánón v.
inclose ɨɓuɓuŋés v.; ɨɓuɓuŋésuƙɔtᵃ v.
include ɓuƙítésuƙɔtᵃ v.
including nááƙwa n.
incorrectly kèɗè adv.
increase bɨtétón v.; bɨtɨtam n.; bɨtɨtɛtés v.; ɨatɛs v.; ɨatímétòn v.; komítésuƙɔtᵃ v.; tasaɓes v.
increase (size) zeites v.; zeitésuƙɔtᵃ v.
increased ɨatɔs v.
incubate tɔúrúmòn v.
indeed rò adv.
indefinitely páƙà adv.
indent luɗés v.
indented luɗúmón v.

indentureship ŋiléɓúìnànès n.
Independence Day Úrù n.
Indian Ŋímiiɗìàm n.
Indian jujube ɨláŋ n.
Indian jujube grove ɨláŋɨgwì n.
indicate ɗóɗés v.; ɗoɗésuƙotᵃ v.
indigestion dimésá bubue ŋɔɛsɨ́ n.
Indigofera arrecta ɲɛʉrʉlatsᵃ n.
indistinct (visibly) imítíròn v.
indolent ɓuɓusánón v.
induct tasápánitetés v.
inducted tasapánón v.
inducted (get) tasápétòn n.
industrious ɨɓɛ́rɔ́ánón v.
inebriated ɛsánón v.
inebriation ɛ́s n.
inept betsínón v.; hádaadánón v.; iƙálájaránón v.
infant ɗiakᵃ n.
infection (urinary) lɔrɨ́ɗᵃ n.
inferno kómɛ́ts'àɗᵃ n.
infertile iƙólípánón v.; osorosánón v.
infertile (animal or person) ɲokólípᵃ n.
infertile person òsòròs n.
infiltrate sáítòn v.
infirmary ɗakɨtár n.
infix otés v.
inflammatory ɓɛkánón v.
inflate ɨsɨkɛs v.; xuanón v.; xuxuanitetés v.; xuxuanón v.
inflated teɓúsúmòn v.
inflexible ɓotsódòn v.; kɛtérémòn v.
influence ɲɛsʉpᵃ n.; súbès v.; súbɛsʉƙɔtᵃ v.
influence each other súbʉnɔ́s v.
influencer súbèsɨ̀àm n.

inform ɦyeitésúkotᵃ *v.*; ɦyeitetés *v.*
informant tsɨ́tsᵃ *n.*
information emutᵃ *n.*; emútíkᵃ *n.*
infrequent búúbuanón *v.*
infuse waatés *v.*
ingest béberetés *v.*
ingratiate rɔɲésá asɨ́ *v.*
inhabit ínés *v.*; ínésukotᵃ *v.*
inhabitant zɛkɔ́ám *n.*
inhalation sʉ̀pᵃ *n.*
inhale sʉpétɔ́n *v.*
inhale (food) ɗáɗítés *v.*; lakatiés *v.*; lukutiés *v.*
inherit imetsés *v.*
inheritor irɨtsésɨ́àm *n.*
inhume búdès *v.*; muɗés *v.*; tʉnʉkɛs *v.*
initiate tasápánitetés *v.*
initiate (a dance) iwees *v.*
initiated tasapánón *v.*
initiated (get) tasápétòn *n.*
initiation ɲékipeyés *n.*
inject ilúkútsés *v.*
injuredly wɨl *ideo.*; wɨ̀lɨwɨ̀l *ideo.*
injury ɲárɨ́má *n.*
ink ɲéwiinó *n.*
inkpad ɲezeí *n.*
inn epúáwᵃ *n.*; ɲólójᵃ *n.*
inner ear bone bòsìɔ̀kᵃ *n.*
innocence iɓááŋàs *n.*
innocent iɓááŋɔ̀n *v.*
inquire esetés *v.*; esetésúkotᵃ *v.*; esetetés *v.*
inquiry esetés *n.*
insane talk lejétòdᵃ *n.*
insanity legé *n.*; lejé *n.*; lejéèdᵃ *n.*; lejénánès *n.*

insect kʉts'ᵃ *n.*
insect (cloth-eating) kurukur *n.*
insect (wood-boring) lɔ́pɨ́rɨpɨ́r *n.*
insect species ts'anán *n.*
insecticide kʉts'ácɛ́mɛr *n.*
insecure (of an area) tsakátsákánón *v.*
insecurity ɲárém *n.*
insecurity (create) irémóòn *v.*
inseminate itɛpɛs *v.*
insensitive ilɛtɨ́létɔ̀n *v.*; ilɛ́tʉ́ránón *v.*
inseparable upánón *v.*
insert ɨɓʉɓuɲés *v.*; ɨɓʉɓuɲésúkotᵃ *v.*; iwoɗiwóɗés *v.*; otés *v.*; zɔ́bès *v.*
inside akwᵃ *n.*; ákwêdᵃ *n.*
inside (a house) hoakwᵃ *n.*
insincere itsárɨ́ánón *v.*
insolent dirídòn *v.*; ɲɔmɔránón *v.*
insomnia gòkᵃ *n.*
insomnia (have) gòkòn *v.*
inspect gonés *v.*; ɨpɨ́jɨ́kés *v.*; isémeés *v.*; iséméetés *v.*
inspect (here) gonetés *v.*
inspect (there) gonésúkotᵃ *v.*
inspect entrails ɦyeitésá arɨ́ɨ́kàᵋ *v.*
install (a beehive) rɔ́kɛ́s *v.*
instantly wɛrɛkɛs *ideo.*
instead (of) àkɨ̀lɔ̀ *prep.*
institute (educational) ɲésukúl *n.*
instruct itátámés *v.*; itsɨkɛs *v.*; nɔɔsanitetés *v.*
instructor itátámésɨ̀am *n.*; ŋímaalímùàm *n.*
instrument (stringed) aɗúŋkú *n.*
insubordinate isɛ́kɔ́ánón *v.*
insubordination ɲɛ́sɛ́kɔ *n.*
insufficient gàdɔ̀n *v.*; iɗákɔ́n *v.*; lukáámòn *v.*; taɗatsánón *v.*
insufficient (make) lukáámitésúkotᵃ *v.*

insult

insult iyaŋes *v.*; risés *v.*; tatés *v.*
integrity eas *n.*
intelligence akɨlɨkᵃ *n.*; nɔɔ́s *n.*
intelligence officer tsɨ́tsᵃ *n.*
intelligent nɔɔsánón *v.*
intelligent person nɔɔsáàm *n.*
intend (to do) bɛ́ɗɛ́s *v.*; ɨwɔ́ŋón *v.*
intend to do kùtɔ̀n *v.*
intense iɗíkón *v.*
intensify iɗíkétòn *v.*; iɗikitetés *v.*
intentional iyótsóós *v.*
inter búdès *v.*; muɗés *v.*; tʉnʉkɛs *v.*
intercede terés *v.*
intercourse (sexual) epᵃ *n.*
interesting èfɔ̀n *v.*
interfere ɨbʉbʉŋés *v.*; ɨbʉbʉŋésʉ́ƙɔtᵃ *v.*
interior aƙwᵃ *n.*; áƙwêdᵃ *n.*
interject ilúkútsés *v.*
interlace ilɔ́ƙérɛ́s *v.*
interlock ilɔ́ƙérɛ́s *v.*
interpose ilúkútsés *v.*
interpret ŋʉrɛtés *v.*
interred tʉnʉkɔs *v.*
interrogate esetiés *v.*; ɨnɨnés *v.*
interrupt iƙofes *v.*; itoɓes *v.*
interrupt conversation itoɓítóɓésa tódàᵉ *v.*
interruptive rébɔ̀n *v.*
interspace ilores *v.*
intersperse iɗomes *v.*
interspersed iɗómíòn *v.*
intertwine ɨmójɨrés *v.*
intervals (do in) iɗomes *v.*
interweave ilɔ́ƙérɛ́s *v.*
intestine nasoroɲ *n.*

it

intestine (large) bɔ̀ *n.*; ɲétenús *n.*
intestine (small) arɨ *n.*
intimidate iɔ́ɓɔ́rɛ́s *v.*; kitítésʉƙɔtᵃ *v.*; xɛɓites *v.*; xɛɓitésʉ́ƙɔtᵃ *v.*
intoxicated ɛsánón *v.*
intravenous drip ɲéɗʉrɨ́pᵃ *n.*
intrepid itítíɲòn *v.*
introduce ɗoɗésúƙɔtᵃ *v.*
inunct kwɨrés *v.*; tsáŋés *v.*
invade sáitòn *v.*
invent iroketés *v.*
inventor iɗimɛ́sɨ̀àm *n.*
invert itsúbùɗɔ̀n *v.*; tuɗúlútés *v.*
inverted itsúbùɗùmɔ̀n *v.*; tuɗúlón *v.*
investigate esetiés *v.*; ɨpɨjɨkɛ́s *v.*; tirifɛs *v.*; tirifɛtɛs *v.*; tirifiɛ́s *v.*; tirifɨrɨ́fɛ́s *v.*
investigator tirifɛtésɨ̀àm *n.*
investigator (government) tirifiesíáma ɲápukánɨ *n.*
invisible kúbòn *v.*
invite óés *v.*
Ipomoea spathulata tʉkʉtʉkán *n.*
Ipomoea wightii kapʉratᵃ *n.*
irascible gúránòn *v.*; gúránós *v.*
iron disulfide ɲésiɓalitútu *n.*
iron sheets kua ni ɲeryaɲi *n.*
ironstone ŋarɨ́àm *n.*
irresponsible ikálájaránón *v.*
irrigate wetités *v.*; wetitésʉƙɔtᵃ *v.*
irritate itsanɛs *v.*
irritating fifòn *v.*; ɨtsánánòn *v.*
Islam Ŋɨsilám *n.*
isolate ilɔ́ɗɨŋés *v.*; ɨpátsɛ́sʉƙɔtᵃ *v.*; tɔlúkésʉƙɔtᵃ *v.*
isolate oneself ɨpátsɛ́sʉƙɔta asɨ *v.*
issue pulutetés *v.*
issues mɛn *n.*
it ntsᵃ *pro.*

it seems

it seems ɨ́kwà *adv.*; ókò *adv.*
it's likely ntsúó ts'ɔɔ *pro.*
itch súƙɔ́n *v.*
item kɔ́rɔ́ɓâdᵃ *n.*
items kúrúɓâdᵃ *n.*
its ntsᵃ *pro.*; ntsɛ́n *pro.*
itself nébèdᵃ *n.*; ntsínêbᵃ *n.*
ivory òŋòrìkwàywᵃ *n.*
jab gafarɛs *v.*; gɛfɛrɛs *v.*; iɓaɲɛs *v.*; iƙumes *v.*
jab repeatedly gafariés *v.*
jabber ilemílémòn *v.*
jack ɗiɗecúrúkᵃ *n.*
jackal isér *n.*
jackal (golden) ɲekiliriŋ *n.*
jacket ɲɛ́jákɛ̀tᵃ *n.*
Jacob Yakóɓò *n.*
jagged ríbiribánón *v.*
jail egésá hòòkᵉ *v.*; egésá ɲájálaákᵉ *v.*; egésá zɨ́kɛ́sɨ̀kᵋ *v.*; lɔjála *n.*; ɲájála *n.*; zɨ́kɛ́s *v.*; zɨ́kɛ́sɨ̀awᵃ *n.*; zɨ́kɛ́suƙɔtᵃ *v.*
jailed zɨ́kɔ́s *v.*
jam iɗilɛs *v.*; iɗɔ́tsɔ́n *v.*; rutsés *v.*; rutsésuƙɔtᵃ *v.*
jam into ipúkútsésuƙotᵃ *v.*
James Yakóɓò *n.*
James (biblical) Yakóɓò *n.*
jammed together lolotánón *v.*
January Kùpòn *n.*; Lomukᵃ *n.*
jar kurétón *v.*
jaundice ɲaŋáánètòn *v.*
jaundice (of eyes) xɨ́dɔna ekwitíní *v.*
jaw ƙálíts'ᵃ *n.*
jawbone ƙálíts'ɔ̀kᵃ *n.*
jawbone corner ƙakúŋ *n.*
jealous ɨrákáánón *v.*

join

jealous (make oneself) ɨrakɛsa asɨ́ *v.*
jealousy ɨrákáánás *n.*
jeer tɔjɛmɛs *v.*
jelly-like milílón *v.*
jenny ɗiɗeŋwa *n.*
jerk iɓwates *v.*; ilikɨ́lɨ́kɛ́s *v.*; ipoles *v.*
jerk (react) tokúétòn *v.*; tokúréètòn *v.*
jerk out ipoletés *v.*
jerk up ipoletés *v.*
jerky ŋátɔɔsa *n.*
jerrycan ɲɛ́jɨrɨkán *n.*
jerrycan (1-liter) túkulétᵃ *n.*
jerrycan (half) ɲéɓukuɓúkᵃ *n.*
Jesus Yésù *n.*
jet (plane) loɗúwa *n.*
Jew Ŋíyuɗáíàm *n.*
jewelry (hair) ɲéméle *n.*
Jie dialect Fetíícétôdᵃ *n.*
Jie person Fetíám *n.*
jigger túkútùkᵃ *n.*
jiggily lòkᵒ *ideo.*
jiggle iɓokes *v.*; ilikɨ́lɨ́kɛ́s *v.*; iyɔŋɨ́yɔ́ŋés *v.*
jiggly lokódòn *v.*
jinx ipeɗes *v.*; suɓés *v.*
jinxed iɲuɲúánón *v.*
jinxer ipèɗààm *n.*
jittery rukurúkón *v.*; tsuɗutsuɗɔ́s *v.*
job ɲákási *n.*; ɲetitsᵃ *n.*; terêgᵃ *n.*
jobless ilwárɔ́na terégù *v.*
jog isipísípòn *v.*; isɔƙɨ́sɔ́ƙòn *v.*; isumúsumòn *v.*
John Yoánà *n.*
John (biblical) Yoánà *n.*
join ɗesémón *v.*; ɗotsés *v.*; ɗotsésuƙɔtᵃ *v.*; ɗotsɛtés *v.*; ɲimanites *v.*; ramɛtés *v.*; tɔŋɛtes *v.*; toropes *v.*; tɔrutsɛs *v.*; xɔ́bɛtésá asɨ́ *v.*

join end-to-end ƙɨ́dzitɛtés *v.*
join in ɓukonuƙotᵃ *v.*
join together ɗɔtsánónuƙotᵃ *v.*
join up imánónuƙotᵃ *v.*; tɔŋétónʉƙɔtᵃ *v.*; zɔ́tétɔ̀n *v.*
joined ɗɔtsós *v.*
joined together ɗɔtsánón *v.*; kumutsánón *v.*
joint ɲékel *n.*; ɲimanitésíàwᵃ *n.*
joint (costovertebral) ŋábèrìkàdè *n.*
joke céŋ *n.*
joke around ceŋánón *v.*
joker céŋáàm *n.*
jokester céŋáàm *n.*
joking céŋ *n.*
jolt kurétón *v.*
jounce íbotitésúƙotᵃ *v.*; íbotitetés *v.*
journey ɲásápari *n.*
jowl bòkìbòkᵃ *n.*
joyful eaɲanes *v.*
Jude (biblical) Yúdà *n.*
judge ŋʉrés *v.*; ŋʉrɛtés *v.*; ŋʉrɛtesɨ́àm *n.*; ŋurutiés *v.*; ŋurutiesíàm *n.*; ŋurutiesúƙotᵃ *v.*
judge (pardoning) ógoesíám *n.*
judged ŋurutiós *v.*
judging elder bilamúsɨ́àm *n.*
jug ɲéjá *n.*
jug (wooden) ɲɛkʉlʉmɛ *n.*
juice ɲéjúùs *n.*
juicily kwìtsⁱⁱ *ideo.*
juicy kwits'ídòn *v.*
juicy (of meat) duláts'ámòn *v.*
July Ilɨ́ɲéètsʼᵃ *v.*; Lomoɗokogéc *n.*
jumble up imɔrɨ́mɔ́rés *v.*
jumbled lɔŋɔanón *v.*
jumbled up imɔrɨ́mɔ́rós *v.*
jumbled up (become) lɔŋɔanónuƙotᵃ *v.*
jump íbòtòn *v.*; iɗótón *v.*
jump (attack) tonyámónuƙotᵃ *v.*
jump (make) íbotitésúƙotᵃ *v.*; íbotitetés *v.*
jump (startle) tsídzitetés *v.*
jump down apííròn *v.*; ipííròn *v.*
jump excitedly ɗamɨɗámɔ́n *v.*
jump off apííròn *v.*; ipííròn *v.*
jump rope ígoriesá simáᵉ *v.*
jump to it apííròn *v.*; ipííròn *v.*
jump up iɗéétòn *v.*; iɗéétòn *v.*
jumping out iɗéón *v.*
jumping up iɗéón *v.*
jumpy rukurúkón *v.*; tsʉɗʉtsʉɗós *v.*
junction bézèkètìkìn *n.*
June Nàmàkàr *n.*; Yɛlɨ́yél *n.*
jungle lolítsᵃ *n.*
jury member kárátsɨ̀kààm *n.*
just já *adv.*; ɲákᵃ *adv.*; tsàm *adv.*
just there néda ne *dem.*; néíta ne *dem.*
Justicia species ʉrúsáyᵃ *n.*
jut rúgètsᵃ *n.*
Kaabong Road Kaaɓóŋimucé *n.*
Kaabong town Kaaɓóŋ *n.*
Kaakuma town Káákuma *n.*
kabob rɔam *n.*
kaboom! pààɗòkᵒ *ideo.*
kalah (game) ɲékilelés *n.*
Kamion Kámíón *n.*
Kamion Road Kámíónomucé *n.*
Kathile town Kàsìlè *n.*
keeled toŋórómòn *v.*; toróŋómòn *v.*
keen (of eyesight) tsótsón *v.*
keep girés *v.*; iritsés *v.*
keep an eye on ifátésʉƙɔtᵃ *v.*

keep aside ógoɗés v.; ógoɗésúƙotᵃ v.; oƙésúƙotᵃ v.
keep away tatsáɗésuƙotᵃ v.
keep back itúmésuƙotᵃ v.; tatsáɗésuƙotᵃ v.
keep calling óísiés v.
keep company itúmétòn v.
keep going pórón v.
keep on itemes v.; itemetés v.; taɗáŋón v.
keep one's mouth shut iɓótóŋésá akáᵉ v.
keep the beat irɛɛsa dikwáᵉ v.
keep the law girésá ɨtsɨkàᵋ v.
keep thoughts secret girésá mɛnáᵋ v.
keep to oneself girésá asɨ v.
keep waiting ilaritɛtés v.; ilwaritɛtés v.
keeper iritsésɨàm n.
keloid ɲépóros n.
Kenya Kéɲà n.
kernel eɗedᵃ n.; **kernel** ekwedᵃ n.
kernels (hollowed) dololoƙᵃ n.; dololots'ᵃ n.
kerosene ceím n.
kerplunk! rìtⁱ ideo.
key ɲófuŋƙúwo n.
khat ɲémurúŋgù n.
khat-chewer ɲémurúŋgùàm n.
kick tɛtsés v.
kick hides tɛtsésá jéjèìkàᵉ v.
kick off (a dance) iwees v.
kick off (new year) itówéés n.
kick repeatedly tetsítétsiés v.
kid (child) im n.
kid (goat) riéím n.
kidnap iɛpɛtés v.
kidney ɲaŋalúr n.

kids wikᵃ n.
Kigelia africana sosóbòs n.
kill (many) sáɓés v.
kill (singly) cɛɛs v.; cɛɛsúƙɔtᵃ v.
kill each other sáɓúmós v.
kill for ipéyéés v.; topues v.
kill for (make) ipéyéitésúƙotᵃ v.
kill more than one (make) sáɓítetés v.
kill off iɗɛ́ɛsʉƙɔtᵃ v.
kill serially ikɛɲɨ́kɛ́ɲés v.
kill time ipásóòn v.
killed (pay to have) ilʉŋúlʉ́ŋés v.
killer sèààm n.
killer (of many) sáɓésìàm n.
killer (serial) ikɛɲɨ́kɛ́ɲésɨàm n.
killer (singly) cɛɛsɨám n.
killing one-by-one kèɲ ideo.
kiln ɲéripipí n.
kin ɦyeímós v.; ɦyeínós v.
kind batánón v.; bònìtᵃ n.; maráŋón v.; ɲákaɓílá n.
kind person maráŋónìàm n.
kindle games v.
kindle a fire gamésá ts'aɗí v.
kindling gamam n.; lúulú n.
kindling (small) ɗɛ̀rètsᵃ n.
king ɲéríósitᵃ n.
kingfisher kílootór n.
kinship by birth ɦyeínósá na ƙóɓàᵋ v.
kinship by blood ɦyeínósá na séàᵉ v.
kiosk ɗʉkán n.; ɲáɗʉkán n.
kiss ts'ʉnés v.
kiss each other ts'ʉ́nʉ́nós v.
kitchen itiŋésíàwᵃ n.; ɲéjigón n.
kitchen (camp) ŋƙáƙáhò n.
kite (black) jolíl n.

Kleinia species kɨmɔdɔrɔtsᵃ *n.*; loɓóɲiɓóŋ *n.*
kleptomania kɔrɔ́kɨ́kànànès *n.*
kleptomaniac kɔrɔ́kɨ́kààm *n.*
klipspringer tɨ́s *n.*
klipspringer rat tɨsɨ́ɗèr *n.*
klop klop kùr *ideo.*
knap pɛsɛlɛs *v.*; wɛtsʼɛ́s *v.*; wɛtsʼɛtɛ́s *v.*
knap repeatedly ɨwɛtsʼɨwɛ́tsʼɛ́s *v.*
knead dɨbɛ́s *v.*; iɗaɲíɗáɲɛ́s *v.*
knee kútúŋ *n.*
knee (posterior) ƙór *n.*
kneecap bùrùkùtsᵃ *n.*
kneel kutúŋétòn *v.*
kneeling kutúŋón *v.*
knife ɗàwᵃ *n.*; rutésúƙotᵃ *v.*
knife (wrist) ɲáɓaarátᵃ *n.*
knitting needle ɲésɨlíɓá *n.*
knobby lɛrɛ́kɛ́mɔ̀n *v.*
knock ɨbaɗɛ́s *v.*; ɨɲatɛs *v.*; tanaŋes *v.*
knock around tanaɲínáŋesuƙotᵃ *v.*
knock back ɨɓatɛs *v.*
knock back repeatedly ɨɓatɨ́ɓátɛ́s *v.*
knock down ɨbatɛs *v.*; ɨbatɛtɛ́s *v.*; ɨpɨtɛs *v.*
knock down repeatedly ɨbatiés *v.*
knock off ɨpɨtɛs *v.*
knock on iɗɔŋɨ́ɗɔ́ŋɛ́s *v.*; ikoŋíkóŋɛ́s *v.*
knock over ɨbatɛs *v.*; ɨbatɛtɛ́s *v.*
knock over repeatedly ɨbatiés *v.*
knock repeatedly ɨbaɗiés *v.*; ɨɲatiés *v.*
knot simááƙátᵃ *n.*
knot (in wood) gɔ̀ɓᵃ *n.*; ɔ́jᵃ *n.*
know enɛ́s *v.*; ɦyeés *v.*; íyeés *v.*
know (come to) ɦyeésúƙotᵃ *v.*

knowledge nɔɔ́s *n.*
knowledgeable nɔɔsánón *v.*
known ɦyoós *v.*
kob máyá *n.*
kob grass máyákù *n.*
kraal ɓór *n.*
kudu (female greater) kòtòbᵃ *n.*
kudu (greater) akɨ́n *n.*
kudu (lesser) àbɛ̀tᵃ *n.*
kudu (male greater) anás *n.*
Kuliak people Ŋkúlákᵃ *n.*
label imátsárɛ́s *v.*
labia (vulval) kwàìn *n.*
labor (be in) koríón *v.*
labor (difficult) ƙwaata ná gààn *n.*
laboriously ziál *ideo.*
labret gwalátᵃ *n.*
labret combo ɲétépes *n.*
Labwor Teɓur *n.*
Labworian Ŋítéɓuriám *n.*
lack bɨrɔ́ɔ́nɨ̀mɛ̀n *n.*; iɗakɛ́s *v.*
lacking bɨrɔ́ɔ́n *v.*; gàɗɔ̀n *v.*; iɗákɔ́n *v.*; luƙáámòn *v.*; taɗatsánón *v.*
lacking (make) luƙáámitésúƙotᵃ *v.*
lackluster jɔ̀lɔ̀n *v.*
ladder ɲáláɗa *n.*
ladle ƙór *n.*
ladle (broken) tebeleƙes *n.*
lag isíɗèètòn *v.*; isíɗóòn *v.*
Lagenaria species lomuƙe *n.*; lɔ́púl *n.*
Lagenaria sphaerica óbijoetsʼᵃ *n.*
laid flat fatsámánòn *v.*
laid to rest tɨnɨkɔs *v.*
lair akᵃ *n.*
lake ɲánam *n.*

lamb ɗóɗòìm n.
lame ŋwàxɔ̀n v.
lame person ŋwàxɔ̀nɨ̀àm n.
lameness ŋwaxás n.
lament itseniés v.; kɔ̀ɗɔ̀n v.
lamp (oil) ɲɔ́tɔɗɔpá n.
land kíjᵃ n.; toɗóón v.; zɛkwétɔ́n v.
land deed jɨmúkábaɗᵃ n.
land title jɨmúkábaɗᵃ n.
land transformation beniitesa kíjáᵉ n.
landowner áméda kíjáᵉ n.
landslide bɔ̀rɔ̀tsᵃ n.; dìdìàkᵃ n.
language naƙaf n.; tôdᵃ n.
language (European) Ɓets'oniicétôdᵃ n.; Ŋímusukúìtòdᵃ n.
language (foreign) fiyɔɛn n.; fiyɔ̀tòdᵃ n.
lanky sawátsámòn v.; sɨrɨsɨ́rɔ́n v.
Lannea schimperi ekoɗitᵃ n.; meleke n.
Lantana trifolia tíkòŋ n.
lantern ɲátaayá n.
lap up ijaƙɨjáƙɛs v.
lappet ɲétélɨtɛl n.
larceny dzú n.
large zòòn v.
large (of many) zeikaakón v.
large numbers (in) ɓɨlɛs ideo.
large tin can ɲákaɓurúr n.
largeness zeís n.
larva (bee) sîdᵃ n.
larva (tiger beetle) sikusába n.
larynx gɔ̀kᵃ n.
lash iɓúŋéés v.; iɗitsɛs v.
last topíánètòn v.
last (be the very) its'iɗéètòn v.
last (be the) mitɔna ɗɨ́ɛ́ jɨrɨ v.

last (one) ɗa jɨrɨ pro.
last (unit of time) bàtsᵉ adv.
last born (being the) eŋúnúnànès n.
last person jɨrɨ̀àm n.
last to show up irúpéètòn v.; irúpóòn v.
last year kainɔ sɨn n.; nótso kainɔ sɨn n.; sakɛin n.
lastborn eŋún n.; jɨrɨ̀àm n.
late (dead) tás n.
later jɨrù n.
latest person jɨrɨ̀àm n.
latrine ets'íhò n.; ɲótsorón n.
laud tamɛɛs v.
laugh fèkòn v.
laugh (make) fekitetés v.
laugh a lot fekifekos v.
laugh uproariously ɗɛtɛ́ɗɛ́tánón v.
launch iɗéètòn v.; itówéés n.
law itsɨkɛs n.
law of God itsɨkɛsa Ŋákují v.
lawbreaker téŋérɨ̀àm n.
lawbreaking téŋér n.
lawful order ɲíkísila n.; ɲɛkɨsɨl n.
laws (local) itsɨkɛsíícíká kíjáᵉ v.
laws of the land itsɨkɛsíícíká kíjáᵉ v.
lay (eggs) iɓɛ́ɓɛɛsɨƙotᵃ v.
lay down epítésuƙotᵃ v.
lay flat epitésúƙòtà ɗèŋ v.
lay it out (issues) tɔlɔɛsa mɛnáᵋ v.
lay loosely lajetés v.
lay out ipépétés v.; tɔlɔɛs v.
lay over ilɔ́gɔtsés v.
lay prostrate bukites v.
lay to rest búdɛs v.; muɗés v.; tɨnɨƙɛs v.
lay waste to isɨlɨ́ánitɛtés v.

laying of eggs ƙwaata ɓíɓàᵉ *n.*
lazy ɨtátsámánón *v.*; karámóòn *v.*; wéésánón *v.*
lazy eye (have a) pɨlɨ́rɨ́mɔ̀n *v.*
LCI ámázeáma na kɔ́nɔ̀nɨ *n.*; arasí *n.*
lead torikes *v.*
lead astray hakítésuƙotᵃ *v.*; itwáɲítésúƙotᵃ *v.*
lead away toríkésuƙotᵃ *v.*
lead group prayers taƙates *v.*
lead off toríkésuƙotᵃ *v.*
lead slowly ɨɛmɛs *v.*
lead this way toriketés *v.*
leader tòrɪkààm *n.*; torikesíám *n.*
leaders roɓazeikᵃ *n.*
leadership (of many) roɓazeikánánès *n.*
leaf kakᵃ *n.*
leaflike katálámòn *v.*
leak ipinɨ́pɨ́nɔ̀n *v.*; tɔ̀wɔ̀n *v.*
lean liƙés *v.*
lean against iƙɔ́ɲɨtés *v.*; iƙɔ́ɲɨ́tésuƙotᵃ *v.*; tonokes *v.*
lean on iƙɔŋɛs *v.*; tébinés *v.*
lean over íboɗolés *v.*
leaned against iƙɔ́ɲɨtɔ́s *v.*
leaned on iƙɔ́ɲɨtɔ́s *v.*
leap íbòtòn *v.*; iɗótón *v.*; ɨ́gɔ̀rɔ̀bɔ̀n *v.*
leap into action ipííròn *v.*
leapfrog ɨ́goriés *v.*
learn ɦyeésúƙotᵃ *v.*; nɔɔsánétòn *v.*
lease ipáŋƙeés *v.*
leash rɔɓᵃ *n.*
leather jèjè *n.*
leather (cow) ɦyɔjejé *n.*
leather brassiere ɲákɨlaƙᵃ *n.*
leather cloak xɔŋɔŋ *n.*
leather clothing ínóƙwàz *n.*
leather leggings ŋapokóyᵃ *n.*
leather mat jèjè *n.*
leather shawl xɔŋɔŋ *n.*
leather shoe ɲáɓʉʉrá *n.*
leather strap ƙɨ́wᵃ *n.*
leather strips ŋamɔ́lɔ́l *n.*
leather tassel ƙɨ́ítɨ́nísɔ̀kᵃ *n.*
leatherily tùɗᵃ *ideo.*
leathery tuɗáɗòn *v.*
leave ógoés *v.*
leave (go) ƙòòn *v.*
leave a mess nts'áƙóna sèrèìkᵉ *v.*
leave aside ɨnápésʉƙɔtᵃ *v.*
leave behind ilaŋés *v.*
leave early gáƙón *v.*
leave gaps in ɨkálámɛs *v.*
leave home xàtsɔ̀n *v.*
leave in a huff gwaitón *v.*; ɨ́gwɨ̀jɨ̀rɔ̀n *v.*
leave in the open ilététaitetés *v.*
leave one's memory hakonuƙotᵃ *v.*
leave open ɨɲáɓólés *v.*
leave to ijokes *v.*; ijókésuƙotᵃ *v.*
leaven sîɓᵃ *n.*
leaves (dry) ódzàkàkᵃ *n.*
leaves (Hibiscus cannabinus) óbèràkàkᵃ *n.*
leech kɔ́ɛs *v.*
left ógoós *v.*
left alone ɗòwòn *v.*
left hand betsínákwètᵃ *n.*
left in the open ilététòòn *v.*
left rib betsínáŋabér *n.*
left-handed betsínón *v.*
leftover jɛjétón *v.*; jɨrêdᵃ *n.*; ógoɗesam *n.*
leftovers jɨrɨn *n.*; ɲomokojo *n.*
leg dɛ *n.*; dɛɛdᵃ *n.*

leg (of furniture) sɔkᵃ *n.*
leg-meat taboo dɛ *n.*
leggings (leather) ŋapokóyᵃ *n.*
leggy tsákólómòn *v.*; tsɔ́gɔ̀rɔ̀mòn *v.*
legible isómáìmètòn *v.*
legion mikídòn *v.*
leisure ɲɛ́tɛmá *n.*
leisure (be at) itɛ́mɔ́ɔ̀n *v.*
leisurely wɛ̀wɛ̀ɛ̀s *ideo.*
lemon ɲámucúŋkà *n.*
length zikíbàs *n.*
lengthen zikíbètòn *v.*; zikíbitésúƙotᵃ *v.*; zikíbonuƙotᵃ *v.*
lengthy zikíbòn *v.*
lengthy (of many) zikíbaakón *v.*
lentils ɲɔ́ɓɔɔ́ *n.*
Leonotis species ɲɛtúlerú *n.*
leopard gʉɓér *n.*
leopard (male) nʉs *n.*
less bɨráʉ́tɔ̀n *v.*
less than ilɔɛs *v.*
less-than-full kíón *v.*
lest náa táà *subordconn.*
let ógoés *v.*; ógoós *v.*
let down iyolíyólés *v.*
let down (milk) cèrɔ̀n *v.*
let go talakes *v.*
let go of tajales *v.*; tajálésuƙotᵃ *v.*; tajaletés *v.*
let know ɦyeitésúƙotᵃ *v.*; ɦyeitetés *v.*
let loose itsues *v.*; itsuetés *v.*
let not ejá *adv.*
let oneself be known ɗóɗítetésá asɨ́ *v.*
let out itsues *v.*; itsuetés *v.*
let out (secret) kwɛts'ɛ́mɔ́n *v.*; kwɛts'ɛ́s *v.*
let slide isɔɛs *v.*; isɔɛtés *v.*
let slip isɔɛs *v.*; isɔɛtés *v.*
letter béɗíbeɗú *n.*; bóɗíboɗú *n.*; ɲáɓáruwa *n.*
letter (alphabetical) ɲégutá *n.*; ɲéɲugutá *n.*
level ɗàsòn *v.*; ɨpáɗáɲɔ̀n *v.*; lopem *n.*; ɲaɗés *v.*; ɲolókér *n.*; towutses *v.*
level (of an area) kalápátánón *v.*
level (roads) séɓés *v.*
level (school) hò *n.*
level out kalápátánitetés *v.*; ɲaɗésúƙotᵃ *v.*
level out (an area) kalápátánónuƙotᵃ *v.*
level repeatedly ɲaɗiés *v.*
levy ɲéutsúr *n.*
lexicon ɲéɗíkìxònàrì *n.*
liaise terés *v.*
liar yʉɛ́ám *n.*
liar (be a) yʉanón *v.*
liberal waŋádòn *v.*
liberate hoɗés *v.*; hoɗésúƙotᵃ *v.*; hoɗetés *v.*
lice ts'an *n.*
lice egg(s) inakᵃ *n.*
lick kánés *v.*
lick (of flames) inɛpɨ́nɛ́pɔ̀n *v.*
lick clean timɨɗes *v.*
lick up timɨɗes *v.*
lid (flat) ɲápár *n.*
lie isuɗam *n.*; isuɗesa mɛná[ɛ] *v.*; itoŋetésá tódà[e] *v.*; yʉanitetés *v.*; yʉanón *v.*; yʉɛ *n.*
lie (legs straight) itɛ́ɛ́lòn *v.*
lie around flat fatsifatsos *v.*
lie down eponuƙot *v.*; itsólóŋòn *v.*
lie down prostrate bukonuƙotᵃ *v.*
lie face-up fátsón *v.*

lie in wait for ɨɗaarɛ́s *v.*
lie on the back fátsón *v.*; ɨɗɛ́ɗɔ̀ɔ̀n *v.*
lie on the side epona ŋabérᵒ *v.*
lie prostrate bùkòn *v.*; bukukánón *v.*
life ɦyekes *n.*
life (daily) zɛƙwᵃ *n.*
lift ɓuƙés *v.*
lift (make) ikɛ́ɨ̀tɛtɛ́s *v.*
lift (steal) ɨtɨ́ɗɨ́ɗɛ́s *v.*
lift carefully takiés *v.*
lift off ɓuƙetés *v.*
lift together ilélébés *v.*
lift up ikɛ́ɛ́sʉƙɔtᵃ *v.*; ikɛɛtɛ́s *v.*
lifted ikeimétòn *v.*
lifted up ikɔɔtɔ́s *v.*
ligament kon *n.*
ligament (iliolumbar) ɛkɛwᵃ *n.*
light aeitetés *v.*
light (fire) gamés *v.*; tɔkɛrɛtés *v.*
light in color bɛɗéɗòn *v.*; ɓèts'òn *v.*
light (in color, of many) ɓets'aakón *v.*
light (slightly) ɓèts'ɨɓèts'òn *v.*
light a fire gamésá ts'aɗí *v.*
light up aeétón *v.*; iléúrés *v.*; inwakes *v.*
lightbeam bás *n.*; súwᵃ *n.*
lightheaded imáúròn *v.*
lightheadedness taítayó *n.*
lightly (in color) bɛ̀dᶓ *ideo.*
lightning ɨmɛ́ɗɔ́nà dìdìì *n.*
lightweight fɔkɔ́ɗòn *v.*; ɔfɔ́ɗòn *v.*; olóɗòn *v.*
lightweightly fɔ̀kɔ̀ *ideo.*
like ɗɨ́tá *prep.*; ƙámón *v.*; tsamɛ́s *v.*
like (a lot) gaanón *v.*
like (it is) naɨ́tá *subordconn.*

like (to do) itáŋátɔ̀n *v.*
like each other tsámʉ́nɔ́s *v.*
like that! ńtí *interj.*; ńtíà jà *adv.*; ńtía jikɨ̀ *adv.*
like this ƙámónà ts'ɛ̀ɛ̀n *v.*
like this! ńtí *adv.*
liken ƙámítetés *v.*
likewise ts'ɛ̀tà kɔ̀nà *n.*
lily (fire) bʉlʉbʉlátᵃ *n.*
limb (of a tree) dakúkwɛ́tᵃ *n.*
limber gwidíɗòn *v.*; tsutsukes *v.*
limberly gwìdⁱ *ideo.*
limbless ŋʉɗʉ́sʉ́mòn *v.*
limit cíkóroyᵃ *n.*; ɨrɨɗɛs *v.*; ɨrɨɗɛtɛ́s *v.*
limited ɨrɨɗɔs *v.*
limp itsóɗón *v.*
line ɲálaín *n.*; ɲérɨŋkís *n.*
line (furrow) ɲɛ́pɛ́lʉ *n.*
line (level) ɲolókér *n.*
line (raised) zeketᵃ *n.*
linger ɓaɓaránón *v.*; tɔúrúmòn *v.*
link tɔŋɛtɛs *v.*; toropes *v.*; tɔrʉtsɛs *v.*
link up tɔŋɛ́tɔ́nʉƙɔtᵃ *v.*; zɔ́tɛ́tɔ̀n *v.*
linked zɔ́tɔ́n *v.*
lion máwᵃ *n.*
lip akákwáywᵃ *n.*
lip herpes ɲótótsᵃ *n.*
lip plug gwalátᵃ *n.*
lip plug (combo) ɲétépes *n.*
liquid cuanón *v.*; cue *n.*; tsɔlɨ́lɔ́n *v.*
liquid (become) cuanónuƙɔtᵃ *v.*
liquify cuanónuƙɔtᵃ *v.*
liquor kombótᵃ *n.*; tule *n.*
list ɗɔtsɛtɛ́s *v.*
list of names éditíníkabáɗᵃ *n.*
listen nesíbes *v.*
listener nesíbesíám *n.*

lit àèòn v.
literacy nɔɔ́s n.
literate nɔɔsánón v.
lithe gwidídòn v.
lithely gwìdⁱ ideo.
litter ƙuƙɨ́n n.
little (become) kwátsónuƙotᵃ v.
little (of many) kwátsíkaakón v.
little in amount ƙwàɗòn v.
little in size kwátsón v.
little in volume tilóts'ómòn v.
live ɦyekes v.; zèƙwɔ̀n v.
live in ínés v.
live long ikoɲíkóɲòn v.
live on jèjòn v.
live solitarily iɓóótánón v.
live through pùrɔ̀n v.
live together ínínós v.
livelihood ɦyekes n.
lively tsuwoós v.
liver sakám n.
liver disease ɲeɗekea sakámáᵉ n.
livestock ŋɨ́ɓarɛn n.
livestock pen ɓór n.
living ɦyekes n.
lizard pɔ̀pɔ̀s n.
lizard (Nile monitor) náganâgᵃ n.
lizard sp. lúulú n.
load botᵃ n.
load a load ɓuƙésá botáᵉ v.
loaded down ɨ́uƙón v.
loader ŋiɓóóìàm n.
loafer ɲakárámɨtᵃ n.
loan kál n.
loathe tɨlɨŋɛs v.

local áméda kíjáᵉ n.
Local Councillor I ámázeáma na kónɔ̀nɨ̀ n.; arasí n.
locality ɲétɛɛr n.
location ayᵃ n.; gwarí n.; kíjᵃ n.; xán n.
lock iɓótóɲés v.; iwetés v.; ɲékifúl n.
lock up egésá hòòkᵉ v.; egésá zɨ́késɨ̀kᵉ v.
lock up (imprison) zɨ́késɨkɔtᵃ v.
locked up (imprisoned) zɨ́kós v.
lockjaw ɲeɗekea na itɛnɨ́túƙɔta ámákᵃ n.
locust girú n.
locust (milkweed) ɓɔlɔrɔtsᵃ n.
lodge epúáwᵃ n.; ɲólójᵃ n.
Lodwar town Lóɗwàr n.
log ƙúl n.
log (door-barring) naƙólítᵃ n.
loincloth fóɗᵃ n.
loincloth (beaded) lètᵃ n.; tìlàlètᵃ n.
loincloth (tâb-shrub) tábòlètᵃ n.
loincloth (women's) ɲákáɗeŋo n.
loiter ɓaɓaránón v.
Lokichokio town Lokicókio n.
lonely tisílón v.
lonesome tisílón v.
long ítánòn v.; zikíbòn v.
long (of many) zikíbaakón v.
long ago kaɨnɨ́kò nùkᵒ n.; kɔ̀wè nòkᵒ v.; nòkᵒ adv.; ódowicíká kɨ nùù kɨ n.; ódowicíkó nùkᵘ n.
long for ítánésuƙotᵃ v.; wíránés v.
long since kwààkè nòkᵒ n.
long-legged tsáƙólómòn v.; tsɔ́gɔ̀rɔ̀mòn v.
long-necked loƙózòmòn v.
longer (become) zikíbonuƙotᵃ v.
look around tirifɨrɨ́fés v.
look around cautiously imwáɲón v.
look at gonés v.

look at (here) gonetés *v.*
look at (there) gonésukotᵃ *v.*
look at each other gónímós *v.*
look down turúnétòn *v.*; turúnón *v.*
look for bédés *v.*; bedɛtés *v.*; ikʉjɛs *v.*
look like topútétòn *v.*
look out tɔtsɔ́ɔ́n *v.*
look over isémeés *v.*; iséméetés *v.*
looking great nakwídɔ̀n *v.*
looking very good nàkwⁱ *ideo.*
lookout dìywᵃ *n.*
loop inɔɛs *v.*
loop around inɔɛtés *v.*
loose ɓàŋɔ̀n *v.*; dolódòn *v.*; iɓámón *v.*; lokilókón *v.*; lokódòn *v.*; nalójón *v.*; roiróón *v.*
loose (of stool) dulúmón *v.*; erúxón *v.*
loose (sexually) imáláánón *v.*
loosely dòl *ideo.*; hàjᵃ *ideo.*; làjᵃ *ideo.*; lòkᵒ *ideo.*
loosely tied hajádòn *v.*
loosely tied down lajádòn *v.*; yaŋádòn *v.*
loosen hodómón *v.*; ilajɨlájés *v.*; iloílóés *v.*; inɔinɔés *v.*
loosen (soil) iwúlákés *v.*
looseness ɓaŋás *n.*
loot taɓales *v.*
lop iséséles *v.*
lop off (branches) itedes *v.*
lope isipísipòn *v.*; isɔkɨ́sɔ́kɔ̀n *v.*; isʉmúsúmɔ̀n *v.*
lord ámáze *n.*; ámázeám *n.*
Lord's Prayer Ɲakujíwáán *n.*
lorry lóórì *n.*; ɲolórì *n.*
lose buanítésukotᵃ *v.*; góózesukotᵃ *v.*; iloimétòn *v.*; rúmánòn *v.*

lose (drop) tuɓutes *v.*; tuɓútésukotᵃ *v.*
lose (sth. valuable) iɲekes *v.*; iɲékésukotᵃ *v.*
lose interest bɔrétɔ́n *v.*; kitsonukotᵃ *v.*
lose one's mind itwáŋón *v.*
lose red-brown color teɓúránétòn *v.*
lose the way hakonukotᵃ *v.*; itwáŋón *v.*
losing teeth tolótólánón *v.*
loss (take a) totóánonukotᵃ *v.*
lost buanón *v.*; góózosukotᵃ *v.*; totóánonukotᵃ *v.*
lost (get) buanónukotᵃ *v.*; itwáŋón *v.*; totóánonukotᵃ *v.*
lot muce *n.*; ɲaɓáátᵃ *n.*
lots kom *n.*
loud bɔrɔ́ɔ́n *v.*; ilélémùòn *v.*
loud person nɔ̀sààm *n.*
lounge iríkímánón *v.*
louse ts'an *n.*
lousiness pásìnànès *n.*
lousy pás *n.*
love mínés *v.*
love (make) èpòn *v.*
love child ŋabɔ́bòim *n.*
love each other mínínós *v.*
love of neighbors mínínósá na áwìkàᵉ *v.*
love that is feigned mínínósá na iɓám *v.*
loveliness daás *n.*
lovely dòòn *v.*
lovely (make) daites *v.*
lover epúám *n.*; mínésìàm *n.*; mínínósìàm *n.*
lover of sleep epúám *n.*
low kúdón *v.*; ŋʉdúsúmɔ̀n *v.*; ŋʉsúlúmɔ̀n *v.*
low (of cows) erutánón *v.*
low (of many) kúdaakón *v.*

lower ɓuƙetés *v.*; iyolíyólés *v.*
lower oneself iyééseetésá asɨ́ *v.*
lowland gígìr *n.*
lowland living dziŋánànès *n.*
lowness kuɗás *n.*
lubricant ceím *n.*
lubricate ŋiites *v.*; ŋiitésúƙot[a] *v.*
Lucifer Siitán *n.*
luck muce *n.*; ɲaɓáát[a] *n.*
luck (average) mucea na ɓárɨɓár *n.*
luck (awful) mucea na ináƙúós *n.*
luck (bad) mucea ná jɔ̀l *n.*
luck (good) mucea na títìàn *n.*; ɲarérɛ́ŋ *n.*
lucky tɨrirɨ́ŋón *v.*
Ludo (game) ɲélúɗo *n.*
Luganda Ŋɨmúgandáétòd[a] *n.*
luggage botitín *n.*
Luke Lúkà *n.*
Luke (biblical) Lúkà *n.*
lukewarm mujálámòn *v.*
lunar eclipse badona arágwanɨ *n.*
lung gàfɨgàf *n.*
lurch gakímón *v.*; nɛ́rɨnɛ́rón *v.*
lurch (of heart) mulúráŋòn *v.*
lure imɔɗɛtés *v.*; isɨ́ŋɨ́rés *v.*
lure (bees) sɨsɨɓɛs *v.*
luxate ƙwijɛ́s *v.*
luxated ƙwijɨ́món *v.*
Lycopersicon esculentum ɲéɲaaɲá *n.*
lying down èpòn *v.*
lymph node ƙùts'àts'[a] *n.*
machete ɲápaŋká *n.*
machine ɲámasín *n.*
machine gun (belt-fed) zɔ̀tɛ̀ɛ̀b[a] *n.*

mad person lejéàm *n.*
made iɗimɔ́s *v.*; iɗimɔtɔ́s *v.*
madness legé *n.*; lejé *n.*; lejèèd[a] *n.*; ŋkérép[a] *n.*
Maerua angolensis lóɗɨwé *n.*
Maerua pseudopetalosa gomóí *n.*
Maerua triphylla iroroy[a] *n.*
magazine (of a gun) ɲókópo *n.*
magnanimity daás *n.*
magnanimous dòòn *v.*
magnanimous person dòònìàm *n.*
maiden ɲàràm *n.*
maidens ɲèr *n.*
maintain isáɓɨsiŋɛés *v.*
maintain poorly isɔ́ɓɔ́lés *v.*
maize màlòr *n.*; màlòrìèd[a] *n.*; ɲaɓʉra *n.*
maize (unripe) ígùm *n.*; káruɓú *n.*; ɲaɲárɨ́tɛ̀ *n.*
maize cob ɲaɓʉraɨ́dàkw[a] *n.*
maize deformity ŋƙwa *n.*; tsɔ́rákwɛ̀t[a] *n.*
maize kernels (milky) îdw[a] *n.*
maize kernels (tough) lúgùm *n.*
maize variety ágirikácà *n.*; arágwànà kɔ̀n *n.*; ɲóɗòmòŋòlè *n.*
maize variety (black and white) ɔkɨ́rɨ́ɗɨɗɨ *n.*
maize variety (multicolored) katólìkà *n.*
maize variety (white) katʉmán *n.*; nakatʉmán *n.*
make bɛrés *v.*; iɗimés *v.*; iɗimésúƙot[a] *v.*; iɗimɛtés *v.*; itues *v.*; ituetés *v.*; tɔsʉɓɛs *v.*
make a *sh-sh* sound wɔxɔ́dɔ̀n *v.*
make a hole in iɓólóɲés *v.*; itoɓes *v.*
make a mistake hakonuƙot[a] *v.*; tɔsɛ́sɔ́n *v.*
make a racket nɔsátón *v.*

make a way through utés *v.*; utésúƙotᵃ *v.*
make blocks iwésá ɲéɓulókìkàᵉ *v.*
make bricks iwésá ɲéɓulókìkàᵉ *v.*
make excellently iyomes *v.*
make fun of tɔjɛmɛs *v.*
make hole in pulés *v.*
make holes in repeatedly itoɓítóɓés *v.*
make ill inʉɛs *v.*
make into one kɔnɨ́tésʉƙɔtᵃ *v.*
make into porridge iújietés *v.*
make like iretes *v.*
make money itsúrútseés *v.*
make noise arútón *v.*; fútón *v.*
make oneself look good daitetésá asɨ́ *v.*
make peace apápánèètɔ̀n *v.*; apápánɔ̀ɔ̀n *v.*
make plans ipáŋƙeés *v.*
make poorly itáƙálɛ́s *v.*
make roadblock tegelesa ɲerukuɗeé *v.*
make to collect firewood waitésuƙota dakwí *v.*
make trouble for itsánɨ́tɛtés *v.*
make up (invent) iroketés *v.*
make up (lies) isuɗes *v.*; isuɗetés *v.*
make use of eréges *v.*
maker iɗimɛtésɨ́àm *n.*; tɔsʉɓɛtésɨ́àm *n.*
maladroit hádaadánón *v.*
malady màywᵃ *n.*
malar akáƙúm *n.*
malaria sugur *n.*
male cúrúkᵃ *n.*
male animal cikwᵃ *n.*
malediction ɨ̀làm *n.*
malicious person ɲékɨsɨránɨ̀am *n.*
maliciousness ɲékɨsɨrán *n.*

malleable lumúdòn *v.*
malleably lùm *ideo.*
malnourished child dódòkᵃ *n.*
malt ɨ̀kɔ̀ŋ *n.*
mamba mɨ́ɔ̀kᵃ *n.*
man eakwᵃ *n.*
man (old) jákám *n.*
man (young) ŋɨ́mɔ́kɔkáám *n.*; ɲɨsɔ́rɔkɔ́ám *n.*
manage ɨritsés *v.*; totseres *v.*
manage each other totsérímós *v.*
manageable ɔfɔ́dɔ̀n *v.*; olódòn *v.*
manager ɨritsésɨ̀am *n.*
mancala (game) ɲékilelés *n.*
mandible ƙálíts'ᵃ *n.*
mandibular angle ƙaƙúŋ *n.*
mandibular bone ƙálíts'ɨ̀ɔ̀kᵃ *n.*
mane sìgìrìgìr *n.*
maneuver (manually) ƙɔxés *v.*
mange ɲéƙúrara *n.*
manger itúɓᵃ *n.*
Mangifera indica ɲémɨɛ́ḿɓè *n.*
mangle ɨɛmɨ́ɛmɛ́s *v.*
mango ɲémɨɛ́ḿɓè *n.*
manhood eakwánánès *n.*
Manihot species ɲómoŋgó *n.*
manioc ɲómoŋgó *n.*
manipulate (manually) ƙɔxés *v.*
manliness eakwánánès *n.*
manmade iɗimɔtɔ́sá ròɓº *v.*
manner ɲɛpɨtɛ *n.*
manure ɦiyɔ̀ètsˈᵃ *n.*; ŋɔtᵃ *n.*
many kom *n.*; kòm *quant.*; kòmòn *v.*; tùmèè *n.*
many (become) ítónà dìdìkᵉ *v.*; komonuƙotᵃ *v.*
manyatta awᵃ *n.*

manyness komás *n.*
map ɲámáp[a] *n.*
maraud toɓés *v.*
marauder toɓésíàm *n.*
march iríánònà dèìkà[ɛ] *v.*; ɲéperét[a] *n.*; tɛtsɛ́sá ɲéperétì *v.*
March Dáŋ *n.*; Lɔɗúɲɛ *n.*
marching orders tàŋàs *n.*
marginalization ɲoloɗiŋ *n.*
marginalize ilɔ́ɗɨŋɛ́s *v.*
marginalizing ilɔ́ɗɨŋánón *v.*
marijuana lɔ́tɔ́ɓa ná zè *n.*
Mark Máríkò *n.*
mark ikɛrɛs *v.*; imátsárɛ́s *v.*; isɛɓɛs *v.*; itwelítwélés *v.*; iwetés *v.*; ɲámátsar *n.*; totsetes *v.*
Mark (biblical) Máríkò *n.*
mark (on skin) tás *n.*
mark (signs) ikɨrɛs *v.*
marked isɛɓɔs *v.*; itwelítwélós *v.*
market dzígwààw[a] *n.*; ɲámákèt[a] *n.*
market (Kenyan) ɲɛ́fɨl *n.*
market (open air) ɗɨ́pɔ̀ *n.*
maroon kɨpúránètòn *v.*
married (of a bride) buƙós *v.*
marrow hèg[a] *n.*
marry by taking ɨʉmɛs *v.*
marry by taking away ɨʉmɛ́sʉƙɔt[a] *v.*
marry polygamously ramɛ́s *v.*
marsh ɲéjem *n.*
marsh (seasonal) ɲɛkɨ́pɔ́r *n.*; ɲotóbòr *n.*
marshily fɔts'ɔ *ideo.*
marshy fɔts'ɔ́dòn *v.*
masculinity eakwánánès *n.*
mash (grist) mʉrɛ́s *v.*
mash (sour) ɓaram *n.*

massacre giɟɛtɛ́s *v.*
massage jʉ́rɛ́s *v.*
massage out jʉ́rɛ́sʉƙɔt[a] *v.*; jʉrɛtɛ́s *v.*
massager jʉ́rɛ́sɨ̀àm *n.*
masseuse jʉ́rɛ́sɨ̀àm *n.*
master ámáze *n.*; ámázeám *n.*
masterpiece iyomam *n.*
masticate iɲáɗʉ́tɛ́s *v.*
masticate (tobacco) imátáŋɛ́s *v.*; mataŋɛs *v.*
mastitis ídoɲeɗeké *n.*
masturbate ijɔkɨjɔ́ƙɛ́sá kwanɨ *v.*
mat ɲámát[a] *n.*
mat (leather) jèjè *n.*
mat (small leather) ɗɛ́f *n.*
mat (termite-drying) uré *n.*
match ɲékiɓirít[a] *n.*; topútétòn *v.*
matchstick ɲékiɓirít[a] *n.*
mate with tirɛ́s *v.*
mate with each other tirímós *v.*
math ɲámára *n.*
mathematics ɲámára *n.*
matted kémúsánón *v.*
matted hair kémús *n.*
matters mɛn *n.*
Matthew Matéò *n.*
Matthew (biblical) Matéò *n.*
mattress ɲápalís *n.*
mature iríétòn *v.*; kɔkɔsánón *v.*; zòòn *v.*; zoonuƙot[a] *v.*
mature (of many) zeikaakón *v.*
mature sexually teɓúránètòn *v.*
mature sexually (of boys only) iɓʉyákòn *v.*
maturity zeís *n.*
May Kɨnám *n.*; Titímá *n.*
may ... kój[a] *adv.*

maybe

maybe ƙámá kiɗíé *v.*; ndóó fiyè *n.*
Maytenus undata múrotsíò *n.*
mbira lokemú *n.*
me ŋkᵃ *pro.*
mead sɨs *n.*; ts'ɔƙam *n.*
meadow (flat) rɔwᵃ *n.*
meal mush ilɨram *n.*; tɔbɔŋ *n.*; tʉɗʉtam *n.*
meal mush (solid) lúgùm *n.*
meal mush (watery) ɓɔtɨ́ *n.*
mealy gwɛrɛ́jɛ́jɔ̀n *v.*
mean fiyɛtifiyɛtɔs *v.*; fiyètɔ̀n *v.*; tákés *v.*
mean to do ɨwɔ́ŋɔ́n *v.*
mean talker hákátònìam *n.*
meander iƙɔɗɨ́ƙɔ́ɗɔ̀n *v.*; iƙulúƙúlòn *v.*;
meander/weave lúkúɗukuɗánón *v.*
meaning zeɨ́sêdᵃ *n.*
meaningful zízòn *v.*
meaningless buɗámón *v.*
meanness fiyɛtás *n.*
measles púrurú *n.*
measure ipɨmɛs *v.*; kêdᵃ *n.*
measure words ízɨɗesa tódaᵉ *v.*
meat em *n.*
meat (charred) kɔr *n.*
meat (dried) ŋátɔɔsa *n.*
meat (rib) ŋábèrìkèèm *n.*
meat (skewered) rɔam *n.*
meat dried on hide xáƙwᵃ *n.*
meat hunger bɨsákᵃ *n.*
meat hunger (satisfy) itsɔ́ɨ́tɛ́sʉƙɔtᵃ *v.*; itsɔ́ɔ́nʉƙɔtᵃ *v.*
meat-carrying call waín *n.*
mechanic iɗɨmɛ́sɨ̀àm *n.*; ŋífunɗíàm *n.*
medal gwas *n.*

mend with mud

mediate terés *v.*
medicate irés *v.*
medicine cèmèr *n.*
mediocre ŋwanɨŋwánɔ́n *v.*
medium-sized ɓarɨɓárɔ́n *v.*; jɔ̀ƙɔ̀n *v.*; lerúkúmòn *v.*
medulla spinalis lɔ́ɓɨ́rɨɓɨ́r *n.*
meek ɨɛ́ɓɔ́n *v.*
meet ikíkóanón *v.*; imánétòn *v.*; itóyéésa asɨ́ *v.*; itsʉnɛtɛ́sá asɨ́ *v.*; itsʉ́nétɔ̀n *v.*; itukánón *v.*; ɲimánétòn *v.*; ɲimánétòn *v.*; ɲimánón *v.*
meet together ɗɔtsánónuƙotᵃ *v.*; iryámíryámètòn *v.*
meet up imánónuƙotᵃ *v.*
meet while dancing ilépón *v.*
meet with iryámétòn *v.*
meeting kur *n.*; ɲékɨ̂ikò *n.*; ɲémítìŋ *n.*
melange ɲalɨ́ɲalɨ *n.*; ɲɔ́tsɔ́ɓitsɔɓᵃ *n.*
melon species nàdèkwèl *n.*
melt cuanónuƙotᵃ *v.*; lajámétòn *v.*
melt (in mouth) inʉƙʉ́nʉ́ƙwés *v.*
melt away rìmòn *v.*
memorize tamɨtetés *v.*
memory (have a good) ipɨ́ɨ́rɨánón *v.*
men ɲɔtᵃ *n.*
men (old) jákᵃ *n.*
men (young) karatsúna *n.*; ŋɨ́mɔ́kɔka *n.*; ŋɨsɔ́rɔkᵃ *n.*; pànèès *n.*
men-crazy iɲɔ́táánón *v.*
menace zízès *v.*
mend ɲimanites *v.*; rátsés *v.*; taɗapes *v.*
mend repeatedly rátsiés *v.*
mend up taɗapetés *v.*
mend with fire itsʉŋes *v.*
mend with mud nutsés *v.*

mended taɗapos *v.*
mendicant purutél *n.*
Mening language Ŋímeniɲítôdᵃ *n.*
Mening person Ŋímeniɲíám *n.*
meningitis ɲétɛrɛkékɛ *n.*; térɛkékɛ *n.*
menopause ŋʉrúmɔ́na ƙwaatéᵒ *v.*
menstruate iona arágwanɨ́kᵋ *v.*; itáléés *v.*
mental illness legé *n.*; lejé *n.*; lejééd ᵃ *n.*; lejénánès *n.*; ŋkérépᵃ *n.*
mention ilímítés *v.*; tákés *v.*
mentum tatún *n.*
merchandise dzígwam *n.*; dzígwetam *n.*; dzííƙotam *n.*
merciful isyónón *v.*
merciful (become) isyónónuƙotᵃ *v.*
mercy on (have) isyones *v.*
mesh ilɔ́ƙérés *v.*; ƙɨ́dzatiés *v.*
mess up hamʉjés *v.*; imɔ́ɲíkees *v.*; imɔ́ɲíkeetés *v.*
mess with (in fun) wáákitetés *v.*
message ɲéripótᵃ *n.*
message (morning) sír *n.*
message (send out a) mɛnɔnʉƙɔtᵃ *v.*
messenger dɛáám *n.*
metabolism (have a high) hɔbɔ́mɔ́n *v.*
metal tsɨrɨm *n.*
metal pot tsɨrɨmʉ́dòm *n.*
metal ringlet àgɨtᵃ *n.*
metalworker ìtyàkààm *n.*
mete out iɲɨ́ɲínés *v.*
meteor dɔ́xɛatá na tsúwà *n.*
meter ɲémíta *n.*; ɔkɔ́tsᵃ *n.*
method muce *n.*; ɲepɨtɛ *n.*
metropolis zɛƙɔ́awa ná zè *n.*
mewl iɲiiɲɨ́ɔ̀n *v.*; iɲɨ́ɲɨ́ɔ̀n *v.*
Meyna tetraphylla lòŋìr *n.*

microbe ƙʉts'ᵃ *n.*
midday ikágwaríìkᵋ *n.*; ódoo birɨr *n.*
middle sɨsɨkᵃ *n.*; sɨsɨ́kêdᵃ *n.*
middle child sɨsɨkáám *n.*
middle of path mucéákᵃ *n.*; mucéékwᵃ *n.*
middle part bakútsêdᵃ *n.*
midget puusúmòn *v.*
midnight mukúásɨ́sɨ́kᵃ *n.*
midrib gògòròjᵃ *n.*
midriff kàɓᵃ *n.*
midwife jʉ́résɨ̀àm *n.*; ƙwaatítetés *v.*; ƙwaatítetésíàm *n.*
might zeís *n.*
migraine headache iɗɨ́ɔ́na iká*ᵋ v.*
migrant botáám *n.*; botibotosíám *n.*
migrate bòtòn *v.*; ilotsesa zɛƙɔ́ᵋ *v.*
migrate away botonuƙotᵃ *v.*
migrate this way botétón *v.*
migration botᵃ *n.*
migratory botibotos *v.*
mild ɨɛ́ɓɔ́n *v.*
mildew lóburujᵃ *n.*; ɲóróiroyᵃ *n.*
mile máɨ̀rɔ̀ *n.*
mileage máɨ̀rɔ̀èdᵃ *n.*
milk îdwᵃ *n.*; jʉ́tés *v.*
milk (cow) ƙiyòidwᵃ *n.*
milk (fresh) ŋalépán *n.*
milk (from breast) ámáìdwᵃ *n.*
milk (sour) ídwà nì ɓàr *n.*
milk bush inwᵃ *n.*
milk tea tábarɨcue *n.*
milk tooth ídòkwàywᵃ *n.*
milk-leaf ídòkàkᵃ *n.*
milking gourd ɲelépítᵃ *n.*
mill ŋɔ́és *v.*; ŋɔɛsɨ́gwàs *n.*; ɲámasín *n.*
mill (gastric) ŋìl *n.*
milled ŋɔ́ɔ́s *v.*

millet (brown) ŋɔtᵃ *n.*
millet (finger) rêbᵃ *n.*
millet (harvest) irábɛs *v.*
millet beer ŋamaruwáyᵃ *n.*; rébèmès *n.*
millet left in field kírérebú *n.*
million dakwa kɔn *n.*; ɲémílìòn *n.*
millipede iƙórú *n.*
Mimusops kummel lokum *n.*
mind akɨ́lɨ̀kᵃ *n.*; ikatsɛs *v.*; imɨsɛs *v.*; ŋátámɛta *n.*
mine ɲjɛ́n *pro.*
mingle in íburuburés *v.*
mingle until stiff tuɗutɛtés *v.*
mingled stiff tuɗutɔs *v.*
mingling stick tuɗutɛsɨ́dàkwᵃ *n.*
mingling stick (pronged) ŋɛ́r *n.*
miniature tɔ́ɗɔ́n *v.*
miniscule dununúòn *v.*; tɔ́ɗɔ́n *v.*
minister pásɨ̀tà *n.*
ministry terêgᵃ *n.*
mira ɲémurúŋ̀gù *n.*
miracle (perform a) ikújíánón *v.*
miracles itíónàs *n.*
miracles (do) itíónòn *v.*
mirage ɲéríɓiriɓᵃ *n.*
mire dɔ́bᵃ *n.*
mirror ɲégɨlás *n.*; ɲérúɛ́tᵃ *n.*
misbehave imákwéètòn *v.*
misbehave (get to) imákóitetés *v.*
misbehaving imákóòn *v.*
miscarry iɲétséetés *v.*; iyétséetés *v.*; ƙúdetés *v.*; otés *v.*; otetés *v.*
miscreant ɲárásɨ́ám *n.*
miserable tsúkuɗúɗón *v.*
mishap (have a) rúmánòn *v.*

mishmash ɲɔ́tsɔ́ɓɨtsɔ́ɓᵃ *n.*
mislay ɨtáƙálɛ́s *v.*
mislead hakítésuƙotᵃ *v.*; itwáɲítésúƙotᵃ *v.*
misplace buanítésuƙotᵃ *v.*; góózesuƙotᵃ *v.*; ɨtáƙálɛ́s *v.*
misplaced buanón *v.*; góózosuƙotᵃ *v.*; iɓíléròn *v.*
misplaced (become) iɓíléronuƙotᵃ *v.*
miss fàlòn *v.*; ɨɗakɛ́s *v.*
miss (a shot) isɛɛs *v.*
miss narrowly iwitses *v.*
miss out on fàlòn *v.*
miss repeatedly isaɨsáyées *v.*
miss the point isɛɛsa mɛnáᵋ *v.*
misscary repeatedly iyétséyeés *v.*
missing (of an eye) ɗooɲómòn *v.*
mission ɲémíxòn *n.*
missionary lɔjɔkɔtáwᵃ *n.*
missive béɗíbeɗú *n.*; bóɗíboɗú *n.*; ɲáɓáruwa *n.*
mist gózòwᵃ *n.*
mistake ɲasécón *n.*; ɲɔ́mɔkɔsá *n.*
mistake (make a) hakonuƙotᵃ *v.*
mistake for ilotses *v.*
mistakenly kèɗè *adv.*
mister ámázeám *n.*
mistletoe lêz *n.*
misuse iɓalɨ́ɓálɛ́s *v.*; ilarɛs *v.*; ilwarɛs *v.*
mix iɗyates *v.*; iɲales *v.*; ɨtsɔɓɨtsɔ́ɓɛ́s *v.*; itsulútsúlɛ́s *v.*
mix (grains) ikáɗóés *v.*
mix (honey and termites) ƙéƙérɛ́s *v.*
mix (porridge and mash) toremes *v.*
mix in ɗɔtsɛ́s *v.*; ɗɔtsɛ́súƙɔtᵃ *v.*; ídulɛ́s *v.*; íduludulɛ́s *v.*

mix up

mix up imɔrɨmɔ́rɛ́s v.
mix up (confuse) ilotses v.
mixed itsɔɓɨ́tsɔ́ɓɔ̀n v.; itsɔɓɨ́tsɔ́ɓɔ́s v.
mixed up imɔrɨmɔ́rɔ́s v.
mixture ɲalɨ́ɲalɨ́ n.
mixture of fat and meat (be a) tsokó-tsókánón v.
moan éɓútòn v.; ɛ́mɨ́tɔ̀n v.; émúròn v.
mob ɲéɓúku n.
mobile ɓɛkɛsɔs v.
mobile phone dʉrʉdʉr n.; ɲásím n.
mobilize irɨ́réetés v.
mobilizer ɨ̀ʉɗààm n.
mock tɔjɛmɛs v.
model ikwáánitetés v.
modern building ɲeryaɲíhò n.
modern society ɲeryaŋ n.
modernity ɲeryaŋ n.
moist ɗɔ́kɔ̀n v.
moist (become) ɗɔkɔnʉkɔtᵃ v.
moisten ɗɔkɨ́tésʉkɔtᵃ v.; ɨpápɛ́ɛ́s v.
moisture-resistant pʉrákámòn v.; pʉráŋámòn v.; pʉsélémòn v.
moisturize (skin) ɨwasɛs v.
molar tiróŋ n.
mold lóburujᵃ n.; ɲóróiroyᵃ n.
mole ɲénʉkʉnúkʉ n.
molecule kiɗoɗotsᵃ n.
molest tarates v.
molt fòlòn v.
molting ɗaráɗáránón v.
Monday Ɲáɓarásà n.; Ɲákásíá kɔ̀nɨ̀kᵋ n.
money kaûdzᵃ n.; ŋárɔpɨyá n.
money tree kaûdzᵃ n.
mongoose (dwarf) múɗèr n.

moron

mongoose (Egyptian) mútètsᵃ n.
mongoose (gray) mútètsᵃ n.
mongoose (slender) sɨlɔlɔ́jᵃ n.
mongoose (white-tailed) lóɓíliwás n.
moniliasis losúkᵃ n.
monitor ifátésʉkɔtᵃ v.
monkey (colobus) ɲécʉma n.
monkey (female) ɔgɛraŋwa n.
monkey (male) ɔ̀gɛ̀r n.
monkey (patas) kolimɛ́wᵃ n.
monkey (vervet) kaɗokóyᵃ n.
monocular vision (have) ɗooɲómòn v.
monotonous itópénòn v.
monster ɲaɲu n.
monster (of a) kéɓàdà n.; nábàdà n.; néɓàdà n.
month arágwan n.
month of bad honey Lotséto n.
month of honey Nakaɓinín n.
month of weeding Lɔɓalɛl n.
moo erutánón v.
moo! buúù ideo.
mooch lɛŋés v.
moocher lɛŋésɨ̀àm n.
mooching olíɓó n.
moody kwits'íkwíts'ánón v.
moon arágwan n.
moon (full) arágwanɨ́ékwᵃ n.
moon (new) arágwanɨ́éɓitɨ́n n.
more kúbam n.; sa pro.
more than ilɔɛs v.
moreover naɓó coordconn.; toni naɓó n.
morning baratsᵃ n.
morning glory lòɓòlìà n.
moron bóx n.; iɓááŋàsɨ̀àm n.

386

morrow baratsᵃ *n.*
mortar iwótsᵃ *n.*; ɲómóta *n.*
mortar bottom iwótsíɔz *n.*
mortar mouth iwótsíàkᵃ *n.*
mosquito kɨmúr *n.*
mosquito (small) tsorokoní *n.*
most likely kárɨká *adv.*
mote símíɗíɗí *n.*
motel epúáwᵃ *n.*
mother (his/her/its) ŋwáátᵃ *n.*
mother (my) yáŋ *n.*
mother (your) ŋɔ́ *n.*
mother-in-law (her) dádàtᵃ *n.*
mother-in-law (his) ntsíémetá *n.*
mother-in-law (his/her sibling's spouse's mother) ŋwáátìɲòtᵃ *n.*
mother-in-law (my sibling's spouse's mother) yáɲɨɲòtᵃ *n.*
mother-in-law (my, of men) ɲciemetá *n.*
mother-in-law (my, of women) dadáŋ *n.*
mother-in-law (of men) emetá *n.*
mother-in-law (your sibling's spouse's mother) ŋɔ́ɲótᵃ *n.*
mother-in-law (your, of men) biemetá *n.*
mother-in-law (your, of women) dádò *n.*
motherhood ŋwáátìnànès *n.*
motherliness ŋwáátìnànès *n.*
motor gúr *n.*
mottle ɨtsɔɓɨtsɔ́ɓɛ́s *v.*
mottled ɨtsɔɓɨtsɔ́ɓɔ̀n *v.*; ɨtsɔɓɨtsɔ́ɓɔ́s *v.*
mould bɛrɛ́s *v.*
mound ɨnɨkɨ́nɨ́kɛ́s *v.*; kìtsᵃ *n.*; ɲatúkítᵃ *n.*

mount otsés *v.*
mount (a beehive) rɔ́ƙɛ́s *v.*
mount an offensive iríɓéés *v.*
mount up otsésúƙotᵃ *v.*
mountain kwar *n.*
mountain dweller kwàrìkààm *n.*
mountain saddle kwaréékwᵃ *n.*
mountainside rutetᵃ *n.*
mountaintop kwarágwarí *n.*
mourn ilúrón *v.*; turúnón *v.*
mourner turúnóniàm *n.*
mouse ɗér *n.*
mouse species naɓálámorú *n.*
mousebird (speckled) tsówír *n.*
mouth akᵃ *n.*; akɛdᵃ *n.*
mouth cover ɲákáparatᵃ *n.*
move ɓɛƙɛ́s *v.*; dzuƙɛ́s *v.*; ilɔpɛs *v.*; ilotsesa zɛƙɔ́ᵋ *v.*; ɨsútón *v.*; rités *v.*
move (an object) ɨsɨtɛs *v.*
move (emotionally) tábès *v.*
move (migrate) bòtòn *v.*
move after dark buɗamés *v.*
move around ilɨrɛs *v.*; ilɔmɨlɔ́mɔ̀n *v.*; irímón *v.*; ɨwarɨwárɛ́s *v.*
move around in ilɔpɨlɔ́pɛ́s *v.*
move around repeatedly ilɨrɨ́lɨ́rɛ́s *v.*
move aside ècòn *v.*; èkòn *v.*
move away botonuƙotᵃ *v.*; dzuƙésúƙotᵃ *v.*; ɨsútésɨƙotᵃ *v.*; ritésúƙotᵃ *v.*
move away on buttocks dɔ́dɔrɔnɨƙɔtᵃ *v.*
move back rajánón *v.*
move blindly ɓɛƙɛ́sá buɗamíkᵉ *v.*
move down kídzìmòn *v.*
move emotionally kɨpɛ́s *v.*
move in ínésuƙotᵃ *v.*; toƙízeesá asɨ *v.*; toƙízèètòn *v.*; zɛƙwɛ́tɔ́n *v.*

move in single file ijɨ́lɔ̀n *v.*; tɔdúpón *v.*; torópón *v.*
move off isútésukɔtᵃ *v.*
move on all fours tolíón *v.*
move on buttocks dódɔ̀rɔ̀n *v.*
move oneself rhythmically itinɨ́tɨ́nésá asɨ́ *v.*
move out ritetés *v.*
move past 6ùnɔ̀n *v.*
move quickly ikómóòn *v.*
move rhythmically itinɨ́tɨ́nés *v.*
move slowly inípónòn *v.*
move straight idɨ́rɨ́rɔ̀n *v.*
move this way botétón *v.*; dzuketés *v.*; isutɛtés *v.*
move to a point irídòn *v.*
move together toríkínós *v.*
move up and down alternately iyopíyópòn *v.*
movement (migration) botᵃ *n.*
movie kúrúkúríka ni 6ɛkés *n.*; ɲévídyo *n.*
mow idɛtɛs *v.*; irɛjɛs *v.*
much iru6es *v.*
muchomo kɔr *n.*
mucilage dòs *n.*
muck dɔ́bᵃ *n.*
muck things up nts'ákóna sèrèikᵉ *v.*
mucus dɔ́kɔ̀n *n.*; ɲarúkɨm *n.*
mucus (cervical) gadár *n.*
mucus (dried) dɔ̀x *n.*
mud dɔ́bᵃ *n.*
mud (plaster) tanaɲes *v.*
muddled talk dɔ́bàtòdᵃ *n.*
mudflap fɔ́dᵃ *n.*
mudslide bɔ̀rɔ̀tsᵃ *n.*; dìdìàkᵃ *n.*
muffler ts'údemucé *n.*

mug ɲámákᵃ *n.*
Muganda Ŋímúgandáeàm *n.*
mull over ɲɛ6és *v.*; tamátámatés *v.*; tamɨ́támiés *v.*
multi-patterned mɛrimɛránètòn *v.*
multiplicity komás *n.*
multiply bitétón *v.*; bititetés *v.*; komítésukotᵃ *v.*
multiply oneselves komitésá asɨ́ *v.*
multitude kom *n.*; ɲerípírìpᵃ *n.*; òdìòs *n.*; tùmèè *n.*
multitudinous kòmòn *v.*
mumble (food) iɲulúɲúlés *v.*
munch happily ilumulumés *v.*
munchy haúdɔ̀n *v.*
murder idɛɛs *v.*
murder (many) sá6és *v.*
murder (singly) cɛɛ́s *v.*; cɛɛ́súkɔtᵃ *v.*
murder each other idáinós *v.*
murder repeatedly idaiyes *v.*
murderer sèààm *n.*
murderer (of many) sá6ésìàm *n.*
murderer (singly) cɛɛsɨ́ám *n.*
murky ka6úrútsánón *v.*
murmur idulidulésa tódàᵉ *v.*; iɲurúɲúrɔ̀n *v.*
Musa species ɲómototó *n.*
muscle em *n.*
muscle (abdominal) ɲákwálikwal *n.*
muscle (cowl) ɲalakamáitᵃ *n.*
muscle (external oblique) ɲɔpɔl *n.*
muscle (intercostal) kilele6ú *n.*
muscle (mylohyoid) mukétᵃ *n.*
muscle (perineal) ɲalamatsar *n.*; ɲekidoɲitᵃ *n.*
muscle (plantaris) kóróèm *n.*
muscle (rhomboid) ɲésɨ́lisil *n.*
muscle (sacral) ɲɛtsir *n.*

muscle twitching bàdᵃ *n.*
mush (meal) ɨlɨram *n.*; tɔbɔŋ *n.*; tʉɗʉtam *n.*
mushily bùr *ideo.*; dàbᵘ *ideo.*; dùl *ideo.*; dùx *ideo.*
mushroom kɨnám *n.*
mushroom (dik-dik) ɲólíkɨnám *n.*
mushroom (elephant) oŋorikɨnám *n.*
mushroom species lɔmɔ́yᵃ *n.*; ŋɨɓalɛl *n.*; ŋits'e *n.*
mushy burádòn *v.*; dabúdòn *v.*; dulúdòn *v.*; duxúdòn *v.*
Muslim tuɗúlónìàm *n.*
must ɨtámáánón *v.*
must have ... (earlier today) nábàtsᵉ *adv.*
must have ... (long ago) nánòkᵒ *adv.*
must have ... (yesterday) násàm *adv.*
muster iríréetés *v.*
mute mɨɲɔ̀n *v.*
mutilate ɨɛmɨ́émés *v.*
mutter ɨdʉlidʉlɛ́sa tódàᵉ *v.*
mutton ɗóɗòèm *n.*
muzzle (of weapon) akɛdᵃ *n.*
my ŋkᵃ *pro.*
my cousin child totóìm *n.*
my friend nádzàƙᵃ *n.*
myopic mumúánón *v.*
myself ɲcìnèbᵃ *n.*
mythical beast ɲaɲu *n.*
nah ńtóodó *interj.*; ńtóondó *interj.*
nail gógès *v.*; ɲɔ́sʉmár *n.*
nail (finger) tíbòlòkòɲ *n.*
nailrod ɨsɨkᵃ *n.*
naive iɓááŋɔ̀n *v.*
naivete iɓááŋàs *n.*

naked ilérón *v.*; lemúánètòn *v.*; leŋúrúmòn *v.*; sɨlɔ́jɔ́mɔ̀n *v.*; tuɗúsúmòn *v.*
naked (totally) wɛ̀r *ideo.*
name êdᵃ *n.*; kʉ̀tɔ̀n *v.*; óés *v.*
name (hill/mountain) Aŋatár *n.*; Aŋolekókᵃ *n.*; Cùcùèìkᵃ *n.*; Curukᵃ *n.*; Curukúdè *n.*; Ɗʉmánámérɨx *n.*; Dɨ́mánɨ̀àkᵃ *n.*; Dúnémorókᵃ *n.*; Gàlàtsᵃ *n.*; Gomóìàwᵃ *n.*; Gózòwìkᵃ *n.*; Ìmɛ̀r *n.*; Iwar *n.*; Kaacikóyᵃ *n.*; Kaakámár *n.*; Kaatíríám *n.*; Kaɓʉ́tákurí *n.*; Kádzàn *n.*; Kakaɗᵃ *n.*; Kàkʉ̀tà *n.*; Kàlèànàŋìrò *n.*; Kàlèwɛ̀r *n.*; Kalɔbɛɲɛ́ɲ *n.*; Kaloŋoléárɛ́ɲan *n.*; Kamɔ́rɔ́mɔrátᵃ *n.*; Kanamútó *n.*; Kanatárúkᵃ *n.*; Kàpɛtà *n.*; Kapɛtapʉ́s *n.*; Karéɲaŋ *n.*; Karʉmɛmé *n.*; Kátárʉkɔ́tᵃ *n.*; Katsakól *n.*; Katsolé *n.*; Kàxɨ̀ɛrà *n.*; Keepákᵃ *n.*; Kétél *n.*; Kilóróŋ *n.*; Kɔ́cɔ́kɨɔ *n.*; Kocom *n.*; Kòfòè *n.*; Kókósowa *n.*; Kɔpàkwàr *n.*; Kotorúbé *n.*; Kùɓààwᵃ *n.*; Kʉráhò *n.*; Laatso *n.*; Lɔbɛɛ́l *n.*; Lɔcáráƙwatᵃ *n.*; Locom *n.*; Lɔcɔ́rɨ̀àlɔ̀sɨ̀à *n.*; Lɔ́ɗɔ́wɔ̀n *n.*; Lɔɗʉ́r *n.*; Lɔkaaƙɨlɨtᵃ *n.*; Lòkìlè *n.*; Lokinéne *n.*; Lokipáka *n.*; Lɔkɨtɔ́yᵃ *n.*; Lɔkwakaramɔ́yᵃ *n.*; Lɔ́méjᵃ *n.*; Lomérɨ́ɗok *n.*; Lɔmɨ́jᵃ *n.*; Lɔ́mɨl *n.*; Lomoɗóɲ *n.*; Lɔɲákwᵃ *n.*; Lɔ́ŋʉ́sʉl *n.*; Loocíkwa *n.*; Lɔɔɗɨ́ŋ *n.*; Lòòɗòs *n.*; Looɗóyᵃ *n.*; Lopéɗó *n.*; Lɔpétᵃ *n.*; Lopokókᵃ *n.*; Lopúwà *n.*; Lɔ̀sɛ̀rà *n.*; Lósíl *n.*; Lòsòlìà *n.*; Lotim *n.*; Lotíyá *n.*; Lòtsòròɓò *n.*; Loukómor *n.*; Lowákujᵃ *n.*; Mɔkɔrɔ́gwàs *n.*; Morúaŋáo *n.*; Moruaŋákiné *n.*; Morúaŋápiɔn *n.*; Moruaŋípi *n.*; Morúaŋìtà *n.*; Morúapólón *n.*; Morúárɛ́ɲán *n.*; Morúatapᵃ *n.*; Morúédikayᵃ *n.*; Morúéris *n.*; Morukoyan *n.*; Morúlem *n.*; Morúɲaŋ *n.*; Morúɲole *n.*; Mùƙè *n.*; Ŋasɛpᵃ *n.*; Ŋusuman *n.*; Náápoŋo *n.*; Nagomocóm *n.*; Naidɨ́ɗᵃ *n.*; Náɨ̀tà *n.*;

name (personal)   *name (place)*

Náitáyᵃ *n.*; Nakaɗapaláɨtᵃ *n.*; Nakalalé *n.*; Nakɨ́rɨ́kɛ̀tᵃ *n.*; Nàkòrìtààwᵃ *n.*; Nakɔrɔɗɔ́ *n.*; Naŋólébokᵃ *n.*; Napitiro *n.*; Napóroto *n.*; Narúkyeŋ *n.*; Nasurukéɲ *n.*; Natípem *n.*; Natsíátà *n.*; Naʉratᵃ *n.*; Nawáɗowᵃ *n.*; Ɲakwácᵃ *n.*; Ɲèràdzògᵃ *n.*; Ɲèràtàɓᵃ *n.*; Ɔrɔ́m *n.*; Ɔpʉs *n.*; Paalakán *n.*; Páɗɛ̀rɛ̀hò *n.*; Palúùkùɓᵃ *n.*; Pɨ́lɨ́kɨ̀tsᵃ *n.*; Pútá *n.*; Rɔ́gɛ̀hò *n.*; Ròŋòtᵃ *n.*; Sààŋìròàwᵃ *n.*; Segeríkwár *n.*; Séíkwàr *n.*; Séítíníkokór *n.*; Sɛkɛɗɨ́áwᵃ *n.*; Soƙogwáás *n.*; Tsakɨrɨkᵃ *n.*; Tsakúdèɓò *n.*; Tsígàkᵃ *n.*; Tsɔŋɔ́rán *n.*; Tsɔ́ráàwᵃ *n.*; Taɓákókór *n.*; Tòlòyà *n.*; Tòòrwààkᵃ *n.*; Tutétᵃ *n.*

name (personal) Acókᵃ *n.*; Acúkwa *n.*; Àɗùpà *n.*; Aemun *n.*; Akaɗéérótᵃ *n.*; Akɔl *n.*; Akóóro *n.*; Akúɗúkori *n.*; Apáálokiɓúkᵃ *n.*; Apáálokúkᵃ *n.*; Apáálomúkɨ́ᵃ *n.*; Apáálòŋìrò *n.*; Apáásiá *n.*; Apérítᵃ *n.*; Apʉs *n.*; Aramasán *n.*; Aríkó *n.*; Áryánkòrì *n.*; Asiróyᵃ *n.*; Cegem *n.*; Ɗɔan *n.*; Dakáyᵃ *n.*; Ɇ́kɨ̀tɛ̀là *n.*; Erupe *n.*; Gutí *n.*; Ɨ́jéekwᵃ *n.*; Ilʉ́kɔ́l *n.*; Irwátà *n.*; Itírá *n.*; Ɨ̀ʉɗà *n.*; Kali *n.*; Kalɨmapʉ́s *n.*; Kalɔyáŋ *n.*; Kawes *n.*; Kinimé *n.*; Kocí *n.*; Kɔés *n.*; Kɔkɔ́ *n.*; Kokóyᵃ *n.*; Koríye *n.*; Koroɓé *n.*; Koryaŋ *n.*; Kɔsɔŋ *n.*; Kúrúlè *n.*; Kʉsɛ́m *n.*; Kʉwám *n.*; Lemú *n.*; Loɓúɓúwo *n.*; Lɔcám *n.*; Lɔcápᵃ *n.*; Lociyo *n.*; Locóm *n.*; Locómín *n.*; Lɔgyél *n.*; Loíkí *n.*; Lójèrè *n.*; Lokapel *n.*; Lɔ̀kàtsᵃ *n.*; Lokauwa *n.*; Lokéɲéríɓɔ *n.*; Lɔkɨ̀jʉká *n.*; Lókírù *n.*; Lɔkɔl *n.*; Lɔ̀kʉ̀ɗà *n.*; Lɔkʉwám *n.*; Lokwaŋ *n.*; Lolém *n.*; Lɔmér *n.*; Lomoɲin *n.*; Lɔmɔ́yᵃ *n.*; Lɔmʉ́ɲén *n.*; Lómúrìà *n.*; Lomutsú *n.*; Loɲá *n.*; Loɲáɲálem *n.*; Lɔ̀ɲàŋàsʉ̀wà *n.*; Loŋóle *n.*; Lòŋòlè *n.*; Loŋólépalɔ́r *n.*; Loŋòlì *n.*; Lopeleméri *n.*; Lopéyókᵃ *n.*; Lopìè *n.*; Lopúsór *n.*; Lópúwà *n.*; Lorukuɗe *n.*; Losíke *n.*; Losíroyᵃ *n.*; Lotsul *n.*; Lɔ̀tʉ̀ɗɔ́ *n.*; Lotukᵃ *n.*; Lotukéyᵃ *n.*; Lotyaŋ *n.*; Lourien *n.*; Loyaŋorokᵃ *n.*; Lúkà *n.*; Maarʉkᵃ *n.*; Mamʉkíria *n.*; Máríkò *n.*; Matéò *n.*; Matsú *n.*; Moɗɨŋ *n.*; Moɗó *n.*; Ŋiriko *n.*; Ŋoya *n.*; Nacapíò *n.*; Naɗóóɲ *n.*; Nàdù *n.*; Nakɨ́ɲa *n.*; Nákírù *n.*; Nakɔŋ *n.*; Nakyéɲ *n.*; Namɔ́yᵃ *n.*; Naŋetéɓᵃ *n.*; Náɲòlì *n.*; Nápíyò *n.*; Napoliso *n.*; Narótᵃ *n.*; Nátɔmé *n.*; Natsapúó *n.*; Natsíámu *n.*; Nàwà *n.*; Nayaón *n.*; Ɲáɓátsᵃ *n.*; Ɲáɓoligúr *n.*; Ɲakalees *n.*; Ɲákamʉ *n.*; Ɲákáyᵃ *n.*; Ɲálem *n.*; Ɲaŋasir *n.*; Ɲaŋorokᵃ *n.*; Nékuɗuɗᵃ *n.*; Ɲéléle *n.*; Ɲɛlɛtsa *n.*; Némʉkᵃ *n.*; Ɲɛpʉlɔ *n.*; Ɲétayoŋ *n.*; Nókoɗós *n.*; Noŋoleɓókᵃ *n.*; Nɔ́rɔ́cɔm *n.*; Océn *n.*; Ɔŋɔr *n.*; Pelén *n.*; Píipí *n.*; Pʉlʉkɔ́l *n.*; Rúfa *n.*; Saŋaɲ *n.*; Sɛʉséwᵃ *n.*; Silóyᵃ *n.*; Síré *n.*; Sugur *n.*; Tsɨlá *n.*; Tekó *n.*; Timatéwᵃ *n.*; Títo *n.*; Tɔ̀kɔ̀bᵃ *n.*; Topér *n.*; Tówotó *n.*; Yakóɓò *n.*; Yarán *n.*; Yoánà *n.*

name (place) Árápííjí *n.*; Ɓèlèkwᵃ *n.*; Ɓets'oniicékíjᵃ *n.*; Bɔ̀rɔ̀tsààkᵃ *n.*; Buɗámóniicékíjᵃ *n.*; Burukáyᵃ *n.*; Caalíím *n.*; Dàsòkᵃ *n.*; Dìdèàwᵃ *n.*; Dómòkᵃ *n.*; Dɨ́mán *n.*; Gàràjɨ̀àwᵃ *n.*; Icékíjᵃ *n.*; Ilúúkori *n.*; Irikakokor *n.*; Isókòìàƙwᵃ *n.*; Ɨ́wá *n.*; Ɨ́wɔlɔ́ *n.*; Jàòàwᵃ *n.*; Kaaɓɔŋ *n.*; Káákuma *n.*; Kaaláɓè *n.*; Kaehɨ́kɔ́ *n.*; Kaikɛm *n.*; Kaikóɓà *n.*; Kámíón *n.*; Kanarɔ́ *n.*; Kapalú *n.*; Kapísima *n.*; Kàsìlè *n.*; Kawalakɔl *n.*; Kiɓícᵃ *n.*; Koror *n.*; Kʉ́ràɨ̀àƙwᵃ *n.*; Kùrùmò *n.*; Kwarikabubuíkᵃ *n.*; Lèrààkwᵃ *n.*; Lɔɓʉrákᵃ *n.*; Locóto *n.*; Lóɗwàr *n.*; Lòìtà *n.*; Lokicókio *n.*; Lɔkɨɲɔ́l *n.*; Lɔkɨtɛléélɔɓᵃ *n.*; Lɔ́kɔ̀l *n.*; Lòkòrìkìpì *n.*; Lɔ́kʉ́rʉ́kᵃ *n.*; Loƙúm *n.*; Lɔlɛ́łɨ̀à *n.*; Lolítsìàƙwᵃ *n.*; Lɔmálér *n.*; Lomataŋaáwᵃ *n.*; Lɔpɛlɨpɛl *n.*; Loporukɔlɔ́ŋ *n.*; Lɔrɛŋ *n.*; Loriɓóɓó *n.*; Losíroiáwᵃ *n.*; Losor *n.*; Lotíɲam *n.*;

Lotirém *n.*; Lɔtɔ́kɨ́kààwᵃ *n.*; Lɔtɔlér *n.*; Loúsúnà *n.*; Loyóro *n.*; Morícoro *n.*; Móróɗᵃ *n.*; Ŋʉrakᵃ *n.*; Náápoŋo *n.*; Nacákʉ́nɛtᵃ *n.*; Nakalelé *n.*; Naɔyakɨ́ŋɔ́l *n.*; Natɔ́rɔ́kɔkɨ́tɔ́ *n.*; Nayapan *n.*; Ɲálámʉɲɛna *n.*; Òŋòrìàwᵃ *n.*; Òŋòrìpàkwᵃ *n.*; Píré *n.*; Rɔ́kɔ́dè *n.*; Sègààwᵃ *n.*; Sikákᵉ *n.*; Ts'aɗíáwᵃ *n.*; Tsùtsùkààwᵃ *n.*; Takanikʉlé *n.*; Tasapetíáwᵃ *n.*; Teɓur *n.*; Tɔrɔŋɔ́ *n.*; Tulútúl *n.*; Wús *n.*

name (river) Cakalatɔ́m *n.*; Cerûbᵃ *n.*; Ɗóɗò *n.*; Dìdiàkᵃ *n.*; Dɨ́mánɨ̀àkᵃ *n.*; Dɔ́ɗɔ̀f *n.*; Dúlél *n.*; Gɔris *n.*; Íɓotokokᵃ *n.*; Iraf *n.*; Iryɔ́kɔ́ *n.*; Ísɛ́ *n.*; Iwam *n.*; Kolomúsábá *n.*; Kàkòlò *n.*; Kàlɔ̀jɔ̀kèès *n.*; Kalɔtúkɔ́ *n.*; Kaloturum *n.*; Kalouwan *n.*; Kámíónòakᵃ *n.*; Kanaɗápᵃ *n.*; Kanákérɛtᵃ *n.*; Kaɲɨ́kààl *n.*; Kàrèŋà *n.*; Katoposiɲaŋ *n.*; Kátɔ́rɔ̀sà *n.*; Katsakól *n.*; Kátsápeto *n.*; Kàwàlèès *n.*; Kéékoŋa *n.*; Kerûbᵃ *n.*; Kiɗorinamótᵃ *n.*; Kɔ́cɔ́kɨɔ *n.*; Kumetᵃ *n.*; Lɔɓɔsɔɔŋɔ́r *n.*; Lɔcɔ́rɨ́àlɔ̀sɨ̀à *n.*; Lɔɗúr *n.*; Lɔisɨ́ká *n.*; Lɔitánɨtᵃ *n.*; Lòkààpèlòtᵃ *n.*; Lɔkasaŋaté *n.*; Lòkìlè *n.*; Lokipáka *n.*; Lɔkɨtɔ́yᵃ *n.*; Lokúma *n.*; Lóloyᵃ *n.*; Lɔmaanɨ́kɔ *n.*; Lɔmacarɨwárɛtᵃ *n.*; Lómìl *n.*; Lɔŋása *n.*; Lɔɔsɔ́m *n.*; Loteteleítᵃ *n.*; Lòtsòròɓò *n.*; Meletisabá *n.*; Mɔkɔ́rɨ́kᵃ *n.*; Mukulitᵃ *n.*; Mʉtúnan *n.*; Nakamemeotᵃ *n.*; Nakoɗíle *n.*; Nàkwàɲà *n.*; Namerí *n.*; Namétúròn *n.*; Namórú *n.*; Naŋóléɓokᵃ *n.*; Napitiro *n.*; Natɔkɔ́ɔ́ŋor *n.*; Natsukúl *n.*; Natʉrʉkan *n.*; Nòf *n.*; Ɲerasabá *n.*; Ɲɔrɔbatᵃ *n.*; Oŋorisabá *n.*; Oŋóriz *n.*; Óríɓò *n.*; Óríɓosabá *n.*; Pakósábà *n.*; Palú *n.*; Popá *n.*; Puɗápúɗᵃ *n.*; Sabaa Damán *n.*; Saloloŋ *n.*; Saŋar *n.*; Sɛkɛɗíáwᵃ *n.*; Sɛkɛtᵃ *n.*; Sɨ́ɔ̀ɔ̀tᵃ *n.*; Sɔ́gɛsabá *n.*; Tsakúdèɓò *n.*; Tamateeɓon *n.*; Tɨ́rɨ́kɔ̀l *n.*; Tòòrwààkᵃ *n.*; Turakwareekwᵃ *n.*;

Tùrùmàrààkᵃ *n.*
name a newborn óésa édie imáᵉ *v.*
name of honor éda na moranâdᵉ *n.*
nanny (goat) rieŋwa *n.*
nape (of neck) fètìfètᵃ *n.*
nape of neck (fatty) nɨ̀tsɨ̀nɨ̀tsᵃ *n.*
Napore person Kàrèŋààm *n.*; Ŋɨ́kátapʉ́ám *n.*; Nàpɔ̀rèààm *n.*; tɔɓɔŋɔ́ám *n.*
nappy ets'íkwâz *n.*
narrate isíséés *v.*
narrative emutᵃ *n.*; ɲáɗís *n.*
narrator emútíkààm *n.*; isíséésíàm *n.*
narrow iɗɨŋón *v.*; irɨɗɔs *v.*; riɗɨmétòn *v.*; rɔ́kɔ́rɔkánón *v.*
narrow (of an opening) tɨits'ɨ́mɔ̀n *v.*
nasal bridge sarisar *n.*
nasty itútsón *v.*; ŋorótsánón *v.*
nation kíjᵃ *n.*
native áméda kíjáᵉ *n.*
nature kíjᵃ *n.*
naughty tarates *v.*
naughty (habitually) taratiés *v.*
nauseated ilákízòn *v.*; taloón *v.*
navel kɔ́ɓᵃ *n.*
navel hair kɔ́ɓàsìts'ᵃ *n.*
near ɦiyɔtógòn *v.*; ɨtómón *v.*
near death inunúmétòn *v.*
near maturity (of grain) titímóonukotᵃ *v.*
near to each another ɦiyɔtógɨmɔ́s *v.*
nearby ɦiyàtàkᵃ *n.*
nearly ripe bɔ́ŋón *v.*
neb loɓôz *n.*
necessary itámáánón *v.*
neck ɦiyʉkʉm *n.*
neckband ɦiyʉkʉma kwázàᵉ *n.*
neckbone bɔkɔ́s *n.*; ɦiyʉkʉmúɔ́kᵃ *n.*

neckrest kàràtsᵃ *n.*
neckring (metal) ɦyʉƙʉmútsɨrɨm *n.*
necktie ɲátáyᵃ *n.*
necktie (money-keeping) ɲɛƙɨl *n.*
necrophilist tirésíama ts'óóniicé *n.*
necrotize iɗéɗéŋés *v.*
nectar iɔkᵃ *n.*
need bɛ́ɗés *v.*
needle mʉtʉ *n.*; ɲɛ́sɨnɗán *n.*
needle (knitting) ɲɛ́silɨɓá *n.*
needle-thin tɨwɨ́ɗɔ̀n *v.*
needle-thinly tɨw *ideo.*
neglect balɛ́s *v.*; balɛtés *v.*; hakaikés *v.*; ilajɨ́lájɛ́s *v.*
neglect (property) isɔ́ɓɔ́lɛ́s *v.*
neglect oneself balɛ́sá asɨ *v.*
neglected hakaikós *v.*
negligent itátsámánón *v.*
negotiate ɗɔtsɛtésá tódàᵉ *v.*
neighbor itɔ́mɔ́nɨ̀àm *n.*; ŋƙáƙínósíàm *n.*; narúétìàm *n.*
neighbor (agreer) tsámʉ́nɔtɔ́sɨ̀àm *n.*
neighbor (close) ɦyɔtɔ́gɔ̀nɨ̀àm *n.*
neighbor (sharer) tɔ̀mɔ̀rààm *n.*
neighbor each other narúétinós *v.*
neighborhood narúétᵃ *n.*
neighbors (be) itɔ́mʉ́nɔ́s *v.*
Neotonia wightii simísímàtᵃ *n.*
nephew (her husband's sibling's son) ntsínámúîìm *n.*
nephew (his brother's son) ntsíím *n.*
nephew (his/her brother's son) leatíím *n.*
nephew (his/her sister's son) yeatíím *n.*
nephew (my brother's son) ɛdèìm *n.*; ɲcììm *n.*

nephew (my husband's sibling's son) ɲcinamúîìm *n.*
nephew (my sister's son) yeàìm *n.*
nephew (sororal) momó *n.*
nephew (your brother's son) biím *n.*; léóím *n.*
nephew (your husband's sibling's son) binamúîìm *n.*
nephew (your sister's son) yáóím *n.*
nephew-in-law (his/her child's spouse's brother) ntsíɲótàìm *n.*
nephew-in-law (my child's spouse's brother) ɲcìɲòtàìm *n.*
nephew-in-law (your child's spouse's brother) biɲótàìm *n.*
nerve ɲɨ́sil *n.*
nervous rukurúkón *v.*
nest gwáɦo *n.*
net (trap) ságòsìm *n.*
net-trapping sâgwᵃ *n.*
network (cellular) ɲénétìwàkᵃ *n.*; sugur *n.*
never jɨkɨ̂ *adv.*; mùkà *adv.*; tsʉ̀tᵘ *adv.*
never-ending rɨ́tsɨ́rɨtsánón *v.*
new erútsón *v.*
new (of foliage) ilɨɓɔ́n *v.*
new (plant growth) lɨ̀tɔ̀n *v.*
new thing ɲɨ́pyà *n.*
news emutᵃ *n.*; emútíkᵃ *n.*; ɲéripótᵃ *n.*
next tɔtʉ́pɔ́n *v.*
next (be the) mɨtɔna ɗɨ́ɛ́ tûbᵃ *v.*
next (time) táá *adv.*
next to iɓákɔ́n *v.*; itɔ́mɔ́n *v.*
next to (move) iɓákɔ́nʉƙɔtᵃ *v.*
next to each other iɓákɨ́nɔ́s *v.*; itɔ́mʉ́nɔ́s *v.*
next year kaɨnɔ na táá *n.*; kɛɨnatsᵃ *n.*

NGO (non-governmental organization) lɔjɔkɔtáwᵃ *n.*; toráƙádòs *n.*
nibble iɲibɛs *v.*; ɲéɲés *v.*
nibble off tɔjɨpɛs *v.*
nice dòòn *v.*
nice (make) daites *v.*
nice (of many) dayaakón *v.*
nicely maráɲíkᵉ *v.*
niceness daás *n.*
nick itɛɓɛs *v.*
nickname tamɛɛs *v.*
nickname (affectionate) tamɛɛsɨêdᵃ *n.*
nictate ɨ̀bɛ̀dɨ̀bɛ̀dɔ̀n *v.*; irwapírwápòn *v.*
niece (her husband's sibling's daughter) ntsínámúîim *n.*
niece (his brother's daughter) ntsiím *n.*
niece (his/her brother's daughter) leatiím *n.*
niece (his/her sister's daughter) yeatiím *n.*
niece (my brother's daughter) ɛdéìm *n.*; ɲcìim *n.*
niece (my husband's sibling's daughter) ɲcinamúîim *n.*
niece (my sister's daughter) yeáim *n.*
niece (your brother's daughter) biím *n.*; léóím *n.*
niece (your husband's sibling's son) binamúîim *n.*
niece (your sister's daughter) yáóím *n.*
niece-in-law (his/her child's spouse's sister) ntsíɲótàim *n.*
niece-in-law (my child's spouse's sister) ɲcìɲòtàìm *n.*
niece-in-law (your child's spouse's sister) biɲótàim *n.*
night mukú *n.*

night-walker ɓɛƙésɨama mukú *n.*
nightjar bóx *n.*
nighttime mukú *n.*
nighty-night! bubú *nurs.*
nimble pɔɗɔ́dɔ̀n *v.*
nimbly pɔ̀ɗᵒ *ideo.*
nine tude ńda kiɗi ts'agús *num.*
nine o'clock ɲásáatɨkaa aɗátɨkᵉ *n.*
nineteen toomíní ńda kiɗi túde ńda kiɗi ts'agús *n.*
ninety toomínékwa túde ńda kiɗi ts'agús *n.*
nipple ídòkàtsᵃ *n.*
nit(s) inakᵃ *n.*
no ńtóodó *interj.*; ńtóondó *interj.*
no-no! kɔkɔ́ *nurs.*
nocturnal emission ɗír *n.*
nod itéƙítéƙés *v.*
nod off ɨlúzètɔ̀n *v.*
noise nɔ̀s *n.*
noise (make a) arútónuƙotᵃ *v.*
noise (make) arútón *v.*
noise (make, of a vehicle) fútón *v.*
noisy ilélémùòn *v.*
nomad botibotosíám *n.*
nomadic botibotos *v.*
nominate for office wasitɛs *v.*; wasɨtésuƙɔtᵃ *v.*
nomination was *n.*
nominee wasɔ́ám *n.*
non-governmental organization lɔjɔkɔtáwᵃ *n.*; toráƙádòs *n.*
nonchalant faɗétón *v.*
nonsense dɔ́bàtòdᵃ *n.*; ɨɓááŋàsɨtòdᵃ *n.*
noon ikágwaríikᵉ *n.*; ódoo birir *n.*
normal (return to) xɔ́dɔnuƙɔtᵃ *v.*
north kɔ́ɔ́ kwarᵓ *n.*; nɔ́ɔ́ kwarᵓ *n.*

North America Amérìkà n.; ɓets'oniicékíjᵃ n.
northerly direction gwárixan dem.
northerner kɔ́ɔkwarɔ́ám n.
northward kɔ́ɔ kwarᵓ n.
nose aƙatᵃ n.
nosebleed (have a) ƙòlòn v.
nosebone aƙatíɔ́kᵃ n.
nostril aƙatᵃ n.; aƙatiékwᵃ n.
not ejá adv.; máa adv.; mòò adv.; ńtá adv.
not be beníón v.; bɛnɔ́ɔ́n v.
not be (somewhere) bɨrɔ́ɔ́n v.
not enough gàɗɔ̀n v.
not full kíón v.
not make sense ɗɛ̀ƙwɔ̀n v.
not sit well ts'ábès v.
not there bɨrɔ́ɔ́n v.
not yet be sárón v.
notch isɛɓɛs v.; itɛɓɛs v.
notch (ears) tɔmʉɲɛs v.; topones v.
notch (jugular) tɔ̀kᵃ n.
notched isɛɓɔs v.
note (monetary) kaúdzokabáɗᵃ n.; ɲónótᵃ n.
notice ewanes v.; ewanetés v.
novelty ɲɨ́pyà n.
November Kawés n.; Loipo n.
now nápáka na adv.; názɛ̀ƙwà n.; ts'ɔ́ɔ adv.
now now! tɨ́ɔ interj.; tɨ́ɔ jɔ́ɔ interj.
nowadays ódowicíkó nì n.; ódowicíkó nì kɔ̀nà n.
nude ilérón v.; lemúánètòn v.; leŋúrúmòn v.; tuɗúsúmòn v.
nugget gwas n.
numb (of body parts) imúnúkʉ̀kʉ̀ɔ̀n v.

number imaarés v.; ɲánamɓá n.
number (large) tʉ̀mɛ̀ɛ̀ n.
numbered imaarɔ́s v.
numbness (of body) ɲémʉnʉkʉ́ n.
numerous miƙídòn v.
numerously mìƙⁱ ideo.
nun ɓɨ́kɨ̀rà n.
nurse ɗakɨtárɨ̀àm n.
nurse (the sick) maitetés v.
nurture (newborn) tɔʉ́rʉ́mɔ̀n v.
Nyangatom people Ŋíóyatom n.
Nyangatom person Ŋísaakɔ́lɨ̀àm n.
Nyang'ia language Ŋɨ́ɲaɲɨ́yátòdᵃ n.
Nyang'ia person Ŋɨ́ɲaɲɨ́yáàm n.
nylon náìlòn n.
obese iɓutúɓútòn v.
obey nesíbes v.
obey (habitually) nesíbiés v.
object kɔ́rɔ́ɓâdᵃ n.
object (large) òrìkìrìkᵃ n.
object (surveiled) rɔtam n.
objects kúrúɓâdᵃ n.
obligation amútsᵃ n.
obliquely ŋabérᵒ n.
obliterate iƙɔmɛs v.
oblong sʉlʉ́túmɔ̀n v.
obscure iɲúɲúánón v.
observatory dìywᵃ n.
observe tɨrifɛs v.; tɨrifɛtés v.; titimɛs v.
observe (ceremony) inʉmʉ́nʉ́més v.; inʉ́nʉ́més v.
obsessed with girls iɲéráánón v.
obsessed with men iɲɔ́táánón v.
obstinate iɗɨ́kɨ́lɔ̀n v.
obstruct ɗinɛs v.; itítírés v.
obstructed ɗinɔ́s v.
obvious takánón v.

obviously tsábò *adv.*
occupy ɔ́bɛ̀s *v.*
occur ikásîimètòn *v.*; itíyáimètòn *v.*
ocean ɲánam *n.*
ocher ŋɔr *n.*
Ochna species ɲéleɓuléɓu *n.*
October Lɔlɔɓáyᵃ *n.*; Terés *n.*
odd jobs ɲéléjɨlɛjᵃ *n.*
odd jobs (do) ɨlɛjɨléjés *v.*
odds with each other (be at) ɗúlúnós *v.*
odor ɔn *n.*; ɔnɛdᵃ *n.*
Oenanthe palustris ŋálómóyá *n.*
of age zòòn *v.*
off (kill) ɨdɛɛs *v.*
off (rotten) masánón *v.*
off limits itáléánón *v.*; itálóós *v.*
offend risés *v.*
offender ɲómɔkɔsáàm *n.*; téŋérɨ̀àm *n.*
offense téŋér *n.*
offering (animal) ɲapʉ́ɔ́tᵃ *n.*
offerings meetésíicíkᵃ *n.*
office ɲápís *n.*
officer ŋurutiesíama tódàᵉ *n.*
official ŋurutiesíama mɛnáᵋ *n.*
official (government) ámázeáma ɲápukanɨ́ *n.*; túbesiama ɲápukánɨ́ *n.*
offload a load ɓuƙetésá botáᵉ *v.*
offspring kwatsᵃ *n.*
oh my God! Ɲakujᵃ *interj.*
oh my goodness hóítá kwí *interj.*
oh my word! hóítá kwí *interj.*
oh! ábaŋ *interj.*; té *interj.*; yáŋ *interj.*
oh, I see nés *adv.*
oh, you mean nés *adv.*
oil ceím *n.*

oil (seed) útɔ́ *n.*
oily kùx *ideo.*
okay! maráŋ *interj.*
okra ɲɔlɔlɔtᵃ *n.*
old dúnésòn *v.*; kɔ̀wɔ̀n *v.*; zòòn *v.*
old (of many) dunaakón *v.*
old man jákám *n.*
old men jákᵃ *n.*
old people dunaakóniikᵃ *n.*
old person dúnésìàm *n.*
old woman dúnéìm *n.*
old-fashioned kɔ̀wɔ̀n *v.*
oldness zeís *n.*
Olea europaea (africana) dèmìywᵃ *n.*
Olinia rochetiana ɓets'akáwᵃ *n.*
omasum ɲémékweɲ *n.*
on gwaríédekᵉ *n.*
on all fours tígàkòn *v.*
on empty stomach kùkᵘ *ideo.*
on foot dèɨkɔ *n.*
on that day ódeedóó *n.*
on the feet dèɨkàᵓ *n.*
on the legs dèɨkàᵓ *n.*
on the move ɓɛƙɛsɔs *v.*
on the way múkò *n.*
on top gwaríédekᵉ *n.*
once kɔnᵓ *num.*
once and for all kónɨ́tɨákᵉ *pro.*
once upon a time kónító ódòwì *n.*
one kɔ̀n *num.*; kɔ̀nɔ̀n *v.*
one (make into) kɔnɨ́tésʉƙɔtᵃ *v.*
one at a time kóníátìkᵉ *v.*; kónión *v.*
one day kónító ódòwì *n.*; na tsóíta kɔnɨ́ *n.*
one o'clock ɲásáatikaa tudátie ńda kiɗì léɓetsᵉ *n.*

one time kɔnɔ̀ *num.*
one-by-one kóníátìkᵉ *v.*; kóníón *v.*
onion ɲékuduŋƙúru *n.*
only ɛɗá *adv.*
onward wàxɨ̀kᵋ *n.*
ooze tɔfɔ́ɗɔ́n *v.*
opaque (thick) tìnòn *v.*
open bɔrɔ́ɔ́n *v.*; bótsón *v.*; fotólón *v.*; ŋáɲámòn *v.*; ŋáɲɛ́s *v.*; ŋáɲɔ́s *v.*; ŋawɨ́ɔ́n *v.*
open (completely) ùwòò *ideo.*
open fire on ɗamatés *v.*; tɔƙʉmʉ́ƙʉ́mɛ́s *v.*
open up tɛlɛɛs *v.*
open up (that way) ŋáɲɛ́sʉƙɔtᵃ *v.*
open up this way ŋaɲɛtés *v.*
open wide hádoletés *v.*
open-topped lɛɓéɲémɔ̀n *v.*
opening akᵃ *n.*; akɛdᵃ *n.*
opening (center) wɛ̀lèèkwᵃ *n.*
opening (small) wɛ̀l *n.*
operate on hoés *v.*; hoetés *v.*
operating room hoesího *n.*
operation (conduct an) iríɓéés *v.*
operation (military) ɲériɓá *n.*
operator ŋíɗɛrɛpáɨ̀àm *n.*
oppose iƙaíƙéés *v.*; iƙáƙéés *v.*; iƙáƙɛɛtés *v.*
opposite side jíjè *n.*
or kèɗè *coordconn.*; kòrì *coordconn.*
OR (operating room) hoesího *n.*
oracle ɲakujíícíkáàm *n.*
orange ɲámucúɲƙà *n.*
orange drink ɲékwɨ̞ɲcá *n.*
orbit irɨ́ŋɔ́n *v.*
orchestrate itukanitetés *v.*

order iɗɔ́ɓɛ̀s *v.*; iɗɔ́ɓɛtés *v.*; inábɛs *v.*; inábɛtés *v.*; itíɓès *v.*; itíɓesúƙotᵃ *v.*; itsɨƙɛs *v.*
order out taŋasɛs *v.*
orders (for marching) tàŋàs *n.*
organ fat sábà *n.*
organization máɗíŋ *n.*; ɲéguruf *n.*
organize iɗimés *v.*; iɗimésúƙotᵃ *v.*; iɗimiés *v.*; iɗimiesúƙotᵃ *v.*; ipáŋƙeés *v.*; itukanitetés *v.*
organized iɗimɔ́s *v.*
organizer iɗimiesíàm *n.*; ɨ̀ʉɗààm *n.*
organs (ritual) ɲorópúò *n.*
orgasm (have an) irákɛ́sʉƙɔta asɨ́ *v.*
orgasmic (become) ɛfɔnʉƙotᵃ *v.*
oribi kɔtɔ́r *n.*
origin itsyákétònìàwᵃ *n.*
Ormocarpum trichocarpum mozokoɗᵃ *n.*
orphan bɔnán *n.*
orphaned ikókíánón *v.*
orphanhood bɔnánés *n.*
oryx (Beisa) tsarúkᵃ *n.*
oryx (male) tènùs *n.*
oryx horn tsarúkʉ́ɛ̀ɓᵃ *n.*
os temporale bòsìɔ̀kᵃ *n.*
oscillate iŋolíŋólés *v.*
ostrich lèwèŋ *n.*
Osyris abyssinica tsereɗeɗí *n.*
other(s) kiɗíása *pro.*
otherwise náa táà *subordconn.*
ouch! aaii *interj.*; áí *interj.*
ought itámáánón *v.*
our (exclusive) ŋgwᵃ *pro.*
our (inclusive) ɲjín *pro.*
ours (exclusive) ŋgóén *pro.*
ours (inclusive) ɲjíníèn *pro.*
ourselves (exclusive) ŋgónébitín *n.*

ourselves (inclusive) ɲjínínebitín *n.*
oust ilɔ́lɨ́ɛs *v.*
out (finished) tɛ́zɛ̀tɔ̀n *v.*
out (of stars) jɨ̀ɔ̀n *v.*
out of sight kúbòn *v.*; lwàŋ *ideo.*
out of work ɨlwárɔ́na terégù *v.*
out-of-joint (get) ɓuumón *v.*
outbuilding ɲésitó *n.*
outcrop rikírík[a] *n.*
outcropping kúc[a] *n.*
outcry werets[a] *n.*
outdo ilɔɛs *v.*; ilɔɛtés *v.*; ipíyéésuƙot[a] *v.*
outer part kanɛd[a] *n.*
outer stomach kɨrarap[a] *n.*
outfit ɲéyúnìfòm *n.*
outhouse ets'íhò *n.*; ɲótsorón *n.*
outlaw mɛnáám *n.*
outmoded kɔ̀wɔ̀n *v.*
outside biy[a] *n.*; biyáxán *n.*; kànɛ̀dɛ̀k[ɛ] *n.*
outsider ámá na biyá[e] *n.*; ɦyɔ̀àm *n.*; kíjíkààm *n.*; ɲíɓúkúìàm *n.*; ɲeɓúkúit[a] *n.*
oval semélémòn *v.*
ovary ɓiɓáhò *n.*
over here nɔ́ɔ́ na *dem.*
over there kéda ke *dem.*; kéita ke *dem.*; kɨ́xána ke *n.*; kɔ́ɔ́ kɛ *dem.*
overabundance (here) níbàdà *n.*
overabundance (there) kíbàdà *n.*
overall (skin) kɔ́lɔ́ts[a] *n.*
overcast kùpòn *v.*
overcast (become) gobétón *v.*
overcast weather kùpààƙw[a] *n.*
overcome iloimétòn *v.*; ipíyéésuƙot[a] *v.*
overcrowd ƙɨ́dzɛ̀s *v.*
overdo taɗɛɛs *v.*

overeat iwótsóòn *v.*; ɲaɗésá ŋƙáƙá[e] *v.*; wɔ̀ɔ̀n *v.*
overflow ɨlápétɔ̀n *v.*
overfull isúwɔ́ɔ̀n *v.*
overgrown sɔɓɔ́lɔ́mɔ̀n *v.*; tsèkòn *v.*
overlook hakaikés *v.*; ɨlajɨ́lájɛs *v.*
overlooked hakaikós *v.*
overpower itikɛs *v.*
override ilotsesa mɛná[ɛ] *v.*
overrun ƙɨ́dzɛ̀s *v.*
oversee irɨtsés *v.*
oversleep towúryánòn *v.*
overtake ilaŋés *v.*; isɨkɛs *v.*; rɨ́tsés *v.*; sɨ́kés *v.*
overthrown rúmánònà kàràtsɨ̀ *v.*
overturn bukures *v.*; buƙúrésuƙot[a] *v.*; buƙúrésuƙota asɨ́ *v.*; buƙusítésuƙot[a] *v.*; iɓéléés *v.*; iɓéléetés *v.*; iɓéléìmètòn *v.*; iɓélúkáìmètòn *v.*; iɓélúkéés *v.*; pukés *v.*; puketés *v.*
overturn away pukésúƙot[a] *v.*
overweight iɓutúɓutòn *v.*
overwhelm kurés *v.*; kurésúƙot[a] *v.*
overwhelming (become) kurósúƙot[a] *v.*
ovum ɓìɓ[a] *n.*
ow! aaii *interj.*; áí *interj.*
oware (game) ɲékilelés *n.*
owl (African scops-) ƙórór *n.*
owl (eagle-) lófúk[a] *n.*
owner ámêd[a] *n.*
owner (of land) améda kíjá[e] *n.*
ox râgw[a] *n.*
ox name rágòèd[a] *n.*
ox plow ɲémɛlɛkɨ́à nà ɦyɔ̀ɔ̀[ɛ] *n.*
ox song rágòdìkw[a] *n.*
oxpecker (red-billed) dzàr *n.*

Ozoroa insignis (reticulata) mókol *n.*
pace off ɨmaarɛ́sá dèɨ̀kàᵋ *v.*
Pachycarpus schweinfurthii lóúpè *n.*
pacify ɨkanɛ́s *v.*; ɨkanɨ́kánɛ́s *v.*
pack ɨdɨlɛs *v.*; ɨsɨkɛs *v.*
pack down ɨdɛŋɛs *v.*
pack down personally ɨdɛŋɨdɛ́ŋɛ́s *v.*
package méyᵃ *n.*
packed down tɔrɔ́dɔ̀n *v.*
packed down (become) ɨdɛ́ŋɨ́mètòn *v.*
packet méyᵃ *n.*
paddle ɨƙures *v.*
paddle (spank) ɨpíkéés *v.*
padlock ɲékifúl *n.*
pagan ŋɨ́kafɨ̀rɨ̀àm *n.*
pail ɲáɓákèt^a *n.*; ɲéɓákèt^a *n.*
pail (metal) ɲépeelí *n.*
pain (cause sharp) ɨrɛɓɨ́rɛ́ɓɛ́s *v.*
painful dódòn *v.*
painfully wɨ̀l *ideo.*; wɨ̀lɨ̀wɨ̀l *ideo.*
paint ŋɔrɨtɛtɛ́s *v.*; ɲáraŋí *n.*; tsáŋɛ́s *v.*
paintbrush tsɨtsɨ́n *n.*
painted tsáŋɔ́s *v.*
palate aƙár *n.*
palate (cleft) aƙáts'ɛa na paƙɔ́s *n.*
palm (African fan) ŋɨ́ɗɨkan *n.*
palm (African wild date) lɔ̀kàtàt^a *n.*
palm (Borassus) ŋɨ́ɗɨkan *n.*
palm (of hand) kwɛtááƙwᵃ *n.*
palm tree species ɲétenɗé *n.*
palpebra gɔrɔ́x *n.*
palpitate dìkwòn *v.*
pan dóm *n.*; ɨlaƙɛs *v.*; ɨlaƙɨ́láƙɛ́s *v.*; ɨláláƙɛ́s *v.*; ɲákalááṭᵃ *n.*
pan (metal) ɲásipiryá *n.*; ɲésipiriyá *n.*

pan (small) dómáɨ̀m *n.*
pan bottom dómóɔ̀z *n.*
pancreas lópeyᵃ *n.*
pandemonium ɲóŋɔtsán *n.*
pandemonium (go into) dojánónuƙot^a *v.*; lɔŋɔanónuƙot^a *v.*
panel (solar) ɲósóla *n.*
panga ɲápaŋká *n.*
pangolin mɛkɛmɛkán *n.*
panic dojánónuƙot^a *v.*; lɔŋɔanónuƙot^a *v.*; ɲóŋɔtsán *n.*
Panicum maximum òŋòrɨ̀kù *n.*
panties (pair of) ɲekúrúm *n.*
pants (pair of) ɲétorós *n.*; ɲótorós *n.*
papaya ɲápaɨpáyᵃ *n.*
paper kàbàd^a *n.*; ɲákaratás *n.*
paper (file) ɲépáɨ̀l *n.*
Pappea capensis dzôgᵃ *n.*
parable taɗápítotós *n.*
parade ɲéperét^a *n.*; tɛtsɛ́sá ɲéperétì *v.*
parade about inésóòn *v.*
paraffin ceím *n.*
paralyzed (from fear) dodimórón *v.*
parasite ƙɨts'ᵃ *n.*
parasitic plant lêz *n.*
parasitic plant species ɲáɓús *n.*; tɨlàlɛ̀z *n.*
parcel taɲáléés *v.*
parcel out ɨɲɨɲínɛ́s *v.*; taɲáléetɛ́s *v.*
parch mɔsɔnʉƙot^a *v.*
parched mɔ̀sɔ̀n *v.*; paupáwón *v.*
parched (lightly) mɔsɨ́mɔ́sɔ̀n *v.*
pardon iƙenes *v.*; ógoés *v.*
pare ɨlimes *v.*; ɨpɛles *v.*
pare down ɨlimɛtɛ́s *v.*
parent ƙwaatetɛ́síàm *n.*

parent-in-law / *patch up*

parent-in-law emetá *n.*
parent-in-law (his) ntsíemetá *n.*
parent-in-law (my, of men) ɲciemetá *n.*
parent-in-law (your, of men) biemetá *n.*
parenthesia (be in) isálílòn *v.*
paresthesia (go into) isálílètòn *v.*
parish ɲápárìx *n.*
parish chief ámázeáma ɲépárìxì *n.*; ɲékúɲut^a *n.*
parish security officer tsɨ́tsá na kwáts^a *n.*
parking place ɨnábèsɨ̀àw^a *n.*
parrot loki *n.*
parry ɨɓatɛs *v.*
parry repeatedly ɨɓatɨ́ɓátés *v.*
part bácɨ́k^a *n.*; xɔnɔ́ɔ́kɔn *n.*
part (back) jɨ́rêd^a *n.*
part (body) ɲekiner *n.*
part (inner) ákwêd^a *n.*
part (middle) bakútsêd^a *n.*
part (straight, middle) gògòròj^a *n.*
part (top) gwaríêd^a *n.*; iked^a *n.*
part ways terémétòn *v.*; terémón *v.*; terémónukot^a *v.*
participate ɓukonukot^a *v.*
particle kiɗoɗots^a *n.*; símíɗiɗí *n.*
partition naƙúlé *n.*
party iyóómètòn *v.*; ɲápáti *n.*
pass ɨkɔɓɛs *v.*; ɨlámón *v.*; ilaŋés *v.*; ilúɲón *v.*; ilúɲónukot^a *v.*
pass (a test) górés *v.*
pass (time) dzuƙés *v.*
pass a law egésá itsikɛsɨ́ *v.*
pass along here ikɔɓɛtés *v.*
pass along there ikɔ́ɓɛ́sʉƙɔt^a *v.*
pass away bitsétón *v.*

pass by ɓʉ̀nɔ̀n *v.*; ilúɲón *v.*; ilúɲónukot^a *v.*
pass by going ɓʉnɔnʉƙɔt^a *v.*
pass gas fenétón *v.*
pass here via ɨɛ́bɛtɛ́s *v.*
pass off ijokɛs *v.*; ijókésuƙot^a *v.*
pass on ijokɛs *v.*; ijókésuƙot^a *v.*
pass on here ikɔɓɛtɛ́s *v.*
pass on problems ijokɛsa mɛná^ɛ *v.*
pass on there ikɔ́ɓɛ́sʉƙɔt^a *v.*
pass out rèŋòn *v.*
pass over górés *v.*; ígorés *v.*; ígorésúƙot^a *v.*
pass over a spear góriesá ɓɨsá^ɛ *v.*
pass over repeatedly góriés *v.*; ígoriés *v.*
pass round to each other ikɔ́ɓɨ́nɔ́s *v.*
pass through ɓuƙonukot^a *v.*; pʉtʉ́món *v.*
pass time ɨtɛ́mɔ́ɔ̀n *v.*
pass via ɨɛ́ɓɛ̀s *v.*; ɨɛ́ɓɛsʉƙɔt^a *v.*
passageway wɛ̀l *n.*
passageway (center) wɛ̀lèèkw^a *n.*
passport ɓɛƙɛ́sɨ́kabáɗ^a *n.*; kabaɗa na ɓɛƙɛ́sɨ́ *n.*
past (distant) tsò *adv.*
paste ilies *v.*; iliílíés *v.*
pasted iliílíós *v.*; ilios *v.*
pastor pásɨ̀tà *n.*
pasture wà *n.*; waitetés *v.*
pat iturútúrés *v.*
pat down ɨnatsɨ́nátsɛ́s *v.*; tárábes *v.*; tárábiés *v.*
patch rátsɛ́s *v.*; taɗapes *v.*
patch (bare) ɲapatsole *n.*
patch (hard) ɲapáyál *n.*
patch of cleared forest tsɛ̀f *n.*
patch of grass xʉram *n.*
patch repeatedly rátsiés *v.*
patch up taɗapetés *v.*

399

patched

patched komolánón *v.*; koríánètòn *v.*; tábàsànètòn *v.*; taɗapos *v.*
pate ikágwarí *n.*
patella bùrùkùts[a] *n.*
path muce *n.*
pathetic pás *n.*
patheticness pásìnànès *n.*
patients mayaakóniik[a] *n.*
patriclan àsàk[a] *n.*; ɔ́dɔ̀k[a] *n.*
paunch gwàj[a] *n.*
paunchy heɓúlúmòn *v.*
pause ɨmɔ́mɛ́tɔ̀n *v.*; isíƙóòn *v.*; mɔ́mɛ́tɔ̀n *v.*
pawpaw ɲápaɨpáy[a] *n.*
pay taatses *v.*
pay (tax) ƙúdès *v.*
pay a fine unjustly taatsesa káwí *v.*
pay brideprice buƙés *v.*; buƙetés *v.*
pay fine (for impregnation) ɨtsʉlɛs *v.*
pay haphazardly taatsesá bùɗàmàk[e] *v.*
pay in vain taatsesa tsam *v.*
pay off ɨlʉŋʉ́lʉ́ŋés *v.*; taatsésuƙot[a] *v.*
pay out brideprice buƙésúƙot[a] *v.*
pay tax taatsesa ɲéutsúrù[i] *v.*
pay toward tɔ́ƙés *v.*
payback (get) ɲaŋésúƙot[a] *v.*
payment tààts[a] *n.*
payment slip taatsakabáɗ[a] *n.*
peace ŋíkísila *n.*; ɲɛkɨsɨl *n.*
peace (make) isɨ́lɨ́tésʉƙɔt[a] *v.*
peaceful isɨ́lɔ́n *v.*; tisílón *v.*
peaceful (become) isɨ́lɔ́nʉƙɔt[a] *v.*
peaceful person isɨ́lɔ́nɨ̀àm *n.*
peak kwarágwarí *n.*
peanut(s) ɲépulé *n.*; taráɗá *n.*

pencil

pebble gwas *n.*
pec làf *n.*
peck itoɗítóɗés *v.*; ɨtɔ́tɔ́ŋés *v.*
pectoral muscle làf *n.*
pectus bakuts[a] *n.*
pedal a bicycle takwésá ɲamɨɨlɨ́ɨ *v.*
peddler ŋímutsurúsìàm *n.*
peddler (being a) ŋímutsurúsìnànès *n.*
pedestrian ɓɛƙésɨ̀àm *n.*
pee kʉtsáƙón *v.*; kwats[a] *n.*
pee-pee kwàà *nurs.*
peek at ikórímés *v.*; ilóíkés *v.*
peek out ts'ʉ̀fɔ̀n *v.*
peek through tɛkɛɲɛs *v.*
peek through repeatedly tekeɲiés *v.*
peel ɨpɛlɛs *v.*; ɔmɔ́x *n.*; poxés *v.*
peel off ɨwalɛtés *v.*; moxés *v.*; poxésúƙot[a] *v.*
peel with teeth ɨsɨmɛs *v.*
peelable food ɨsɨmam *n.*
peeling ɨpɛlɛtam *n.*
peep at ikórímés *v.*; ilóíkés *v.*
peep out ts'ʉ̀fɔ̀n *v.*
peer at tɨrɨfɛs *v.*; tɨrɨfɛtés *v.*
peer at over ɨrɨnɛs *v.*
peer through tɛkɛɲɛs *v.*
peer through repeatedly tekeɲiés *v.*
peg gógès *v.*; kìnòròt[a] *n.*
Pellaea adiantoidea ts'aɗícémèr *n.*
pelt ɨdʉrés *v.*; ínósìts'[a] *n.*; ts'ɛ̀ *n.*
pelvis róróìɔ̀k[a] *n.*
pen ɲákalám *n.*
penalty (financial) ɲáfaɨ́n *n.*
penance (Catholic) penitésìyà *n.*
pencil ɲépɨ́nɨ́sɨ̀l *n.*

penetrate (area) utés v.; utésúkotᵃ v.
penile shaft ɲέsεεɓɔ́ n.
penis kwan n.
penis hole kwanɨ́ékwᵃ n.
penitentiary zɨ́kέsɨ̀àwᵃ n.
penny ɲáɓɔ́ɔla n.
Pentarrhinum insipidum urém n.
Pentecost pεntεkɔ́stὲ n.
Pentecostal Ŋímorokóléìàm n.
people ròɓᵃ n.
people (tribe) dìywᵃ n.; ɲákaɓɨlá n.
people! òɓà interj.; ròɓà interj.
pepper ɲépilipíli n.
pepper (red) ɲákamʉlára n.
perceive enés v.
perch itséléléòn v.
perfect xɔ́dɔ̀n v.; xɔtánón v.
perforate ɓεkés v.; ɓεkεtés v.; húbutés v.; pulés v.; ruɗés v.
perforate (with a tool) gógès v.
perforate noisily rɔɗés v.
perforate repeatedly pulutiés v.
perform a miracle ikújíánón v.
perfume (natural) ɓúɓús n.
perhaps kámá kiɗíé v.; ndóó ɦiyè n.
peril gaánàs n.
perilous gaanón v.; ɨpárɨɲánón v.
perineal muscle ɲalamatsar n.; ɲekiɗoŋitᵃ n.
peripheral vision ɗoɗékwᵃ n.
perish bitsétón v.; ɨrɨ́ɗétɔ̀n v.
perjure isuɗes v.; isuɗetés v.
perjury ɲɔ́pɔkɔca n.
permanently kìŋ ideo.
permit talakes v.

perplexed iɓíléròn v.; ɨcɔ́ɲáimetona iká́ᵉ v.
Persea americana ɲóvakáɗò n.
persevere iɗaɲɨ́ɗáŋɔ̀n v.; ɨmʉ́kɔ́ɔ̀n v.
persist iɗaɲɨ́ɗáŋɔ̀n v.; taɗáŋón v.
person ám n.
person (indigenous) améda kɨ́já́ᵉ n.
person (surveiled) rɔtam n.
person in authority topéɗésukotíám n.
person who prays wáánààm n.
personal item ámákɔrɔ́ɓâdᵃ n.
personal property ámákɔrɔ́ɓâdᵃ n.
personhood ámánànès n.
perspiration kirotᵃ n.
perspire kirotánón v.
persuade súbὲs v.; súbεsʉkɔtᵃ v.
perturbed walɨwálɔ́n v.
pervert ɲárásɨám n.
pester ilúlúés v.
pestilence koɗó n.
pestle àjᵃ n.; iwótsídàkwᵃ n.; kuɲukᵃ n.
pet (have as a) totores v.
Peter Pétèrò n.
Peter (biblical) Pétèrò n.
petite tsaʉ́ɗɨ̈mɔ̀n v.
petrol ceím n.; ɲépetorón n.
phallus kwan n.
phantom lopéren n.; tás n.
philanthropic dòòn v.
philanthropist dónésìàm n.; lɔjɔkɔtáwᵃ n.
philanthropists roɓa ni gúrítínía dayaákᵃ n.
philanthropy daás n.
Philemon (biblical) Pɨlεmɔ́nὲ n.
Philippians (biblical) Pilípoikᵃ n.

401

phlebotomize kɔ́és v.
phlegm dɔ̀kɔ̀n n.; ɲarúkúm n.
phlegm (newborn) kɨ́ɓɔ́ɔ̀z n.
Phoenix reclinata lɔ̀kàtàtᵃ n.
phone dɨrɨdɨr n.; ɲásím n.
phone in iwetés v.
phone out iwésúƙotᵃ v.
phony ɨtsárɨánón v.; láŋ n.
phoot! pʉ̀ʉ̀tᵘ ideo.; rès ideo.
photo(graph) kúrúkúr n.; ɲépɨ́tsa n.
photograph iwetés v.
Phymateus species ɓɔlɔrɔtsᵃ n.
physical therapist jʉrésɨ̀àm n.
physically fit itsyátón v.
physician ɗakɨtárɨ̀àm n.
pick ɗʉmɛtés v.; iɗókóliés v.; ɲésurúr n.
pick (choose) xɔ́bɛtés v.
pick (nibble) ɲéɲés v.
pick (teeth) mɨnés v.
pick at itoɗɨ́tóɗés v.
pick categorically isɨ́ɨ́lɛtés v.
pick clean iúréés v.
pick fight with itojiés v.
pick off ikáábɛs v.; ikákápés v.; moxés v.
pick out ikuɗúkúɗés v.; iƙɛlɛs v.; iƙɛlɛtés v.; ƙélés v.; tɔsɛɛtés v.
pick up ɗʉmés v.; ɗʉmɛtés v.; iɗɛpɛs v.; iɗɛpɛtés v.
pick up (multiply) iɗɛpɨ́ɗépés v.; iɗɛpɨ́ɗépɛtés v.
pick up a scent wetésá kɔɨnáᵋ v.
pick up and bring iɛ́bɛtés v.
pick up and take iɛ́bɛsʉƙotᵃ v.
pick-pocket ɗɨ́ɗɨ́tésʉƙotᵃ v.; ɗɨ́ɗɨ́tɛtés v.
pickaxe ɲésurúr n.
picked (chosen) xɔ́bɔtós v.

picture kúrúkúr n.; ɲépɨ́tsa n.
piece julam n.
piece (small) julamáím n.; pɛsɛlam n.; pésélamedᵃ n.
piece of junk ƙwɛsɛ́ n.
pierce itsumés v.; pulés v.
pierce noisily rɔɗés v.
pierce repeatedly pulutiés v.
piercer pulutiesíàm n.
pig ɲéguruwé n.
pig out iwótsóòn v.; ɲaɗésá ŋƙáƙáᵉ v.
pigeon bîbᵃ n.
pigeon (green) orómó n.
pigeon (olive) lótúrum n.
pigeon (speckled) rutúdùm n.
pigment ɲáraŋgí n.
pile inʉkúnʉ́kés v.; itukes v.; kɨtsᵃ n.; ɲatúkítᵃ n.; tutukesíáwᵃ n.
pile (of dry branches) ràm n.
pile on iɗóɗókés v.
pile on (add) tasaɓes v.
pile up iruketés v.; ituketés v.; kitsetés v.; tutuketés v.
piled up iɗóɗókánón v.; tutukánón v.
pilfer itɨ́ɗɨ́ɗés v.
pill cɛ̀mɛ̀rɨ̀ɛ̀kwᵃ n.
pillage toɓésúƙotᵃ v.
pillage and bring toɓetés v.
pillow dɨkwam n.
pimples ŋkaŋókᵃ n.
pin mʉtʉ n.
pin (safety) ɲákwác n.
pinch rɨɗés v.; tʉnés v.
pinch all over tʉnútʉ́natés v.
pinch each other túnɨ́túnɨmɔ́s v.
pinch flirtatiously tunútúniés v.
pinch off ƙités v.; tɔɲɨmɛtés v.

pinch up (granules)

pinch up (granules) tɨsés v.
pinkish-red ɗiwiɗíwón v.
pinnacle (of hut) lómoloró n.
pinpoint ɗóɗiés v.
pinworms lɔkɨtɨ́r n.
pipe (borehole) ɲatsʉʉmáárɨ́ n.
pipe (tobacco) làr n.
pipe-stem laradakwᵃ n.
piquant ɓariɓárón v.; ɓarikíkón v.
PISO (parish intelligence and security officer) tsɨtsá na kwátsᵃ n.
pissed off ilɨ́lɨ́ɔn v.
pissed off (become) ilɨ́lɨ́ɔnʉkɔtᵃ v.
pistol ɲɛpɨ́sɨ́tɔl n.
pistol grip kɔɓᵃ n.
pit (trapping) ɲɔ́sɔ́ɔ́katᵃ n.
pitch tɔrés v.
pitch (mead) ts'ɔkɛ́s v.
pitch (soccer) ɲakwaanja n.
pitch away tɔrésúkɔtᵃ v.
pitch this way tɔrɛtés v.
pitcher ɲewatajá n.
pitcher (wooden) ɲɛkʉlʉmɛ n.
pitcherful ɲewatajá n.
pitfall trap ɲɔ́sɔ́ɔ́katᵃ n.
pitted tsakátsákánón v.
Pittosporum viridiflorum ɲékwaɲa n.
pity (have) isyónón v.
pity on (take) isyones v.
placate ikanɛ́s v.; ikanɨ́kánɛ́s v.
place awᵃ n.; bácɨ́kᵃ n.; egés v.; egetés v.; kíjᵃ n.
place of honor zɛkɔ́áwa na maráŋ n.
placenta ŋaxɔ̂bᵃ n.
placid tisílón v.

plastered

plague koɗó n.
plain ɓàŋɔ̀n v.; dús n.; ɨɓámɔ́n v.
plainness ɓaŋás n.
plait bɛrés v.; sikwés v.
plait up sikwetés v.
plan iɗimiés v.; iɗimiesúkɔtᵃ v.; ipáŋkeés v.
plan a time hoetésá ɲásáatɨ v.
plane (air-) iɗékè n.
plane (even) ikʉlɛs v.; ikʉlɛtés v.; ikwalɛs v.
plane off ikúlésʉkɔtᵃ v.
plank ɲáɓáo n.
plant dakwᵃ n.; ɨbités v.
plant (unknown) kɔ́rɔ́ɓáidàkwᵃ n.
plant disease xoúxoú n.
plant species bɛfácémɛ́r n.; bʉlʉbʉláta na sábàìkàᵉ n.; bùsùbùs n.; dàlìs n.; dodíkᵃ n.; gàsàràkwàtsᵃ n.; gòmòjòjᵃ n.; gùjᵃ n.; ídemɛcémɛ́r n.; íɗɛmèdàkwᵃ n.; íɗocɛmɛ́r n.; iɗakᵃ n.; jáláts n.; jijɨ̀ɗᵃ n.; jùjù n.; kèlèrwᵃ n.; kɨmɔ̀ɗɔ̀rɔ̀tsᵃ n.; kòkòròtsᵃ n.; kɔmɔ́m n.; komótsᵃ n.; loɓóŋiɓóŋ n.; lomerúkᵃ n.; lɔmɔ́yᵃ n.; lɔsalátᵃ n.; mɛ́rɛ́ɗɛɗɛ́ n.; múmùtᵃ n.; ɲálómóyá n.; ɲɨ́máarɔyᵃ n.; ɲɨ́tésʉrɔ n.; ɲáɓáɓú n.; ɲálamorú n.; ɲápatᵃ n.; ɲasal n.; ɲɛcaɓoyᵃ n.; ɲɛɛkɨmá n.; ɲɛkilitón n.; ɲesʉkuru n.; ɲɛsɨ́tɛ̀ n.; ɲétúlerú n.; ɲéúɗe n.; ɲéúlam n.; ɲɛʉrʉlatsᵃ n.; ɲɛʉrʉmɛmɛ́ n.; ɲoɗokole n.; ɔ́bèr n.; ɔ́jɨ́tɨ́nɨ́cɛmɛ́r n.; òŋòrìkwàtsᵃ n.; rágàn n.; súkʉ́sʉká n.; ts'aɗícɛ́mɛ̀r n.; tsákàtsᵃ n.; tsamʉya n.; tâbᵃ n.; túḿbàbᵃ n.
plantain ɲómototó n.
plaster ilɔɓɨ́lɔ́ɓés v.; ipʉtsɛs v.; ɨwarɛs v.
plaster (mud) tànàŋ n.
plaster (with mud) tanaŋes v.
plastered ɨwarɔs v.

plate ɲásaaní *n.*
plateau lopem *n.*
platform lɔpɨtá *n.*
platform (make a) ipɛ́tɛ́ɛ́s *v.*
platoon ɲépalatún *n.*
play ɲaɓolya *n.*; wáák^a *n.*; wáák^a *v.*
play (dramatic) wááka na támɔtɔ́s *n.*
play around with wáákitetés *v.*
play the field (sexually) weesa kíjá^e *v.*
play with iminímɨnɛ́s *v.*; minímɨnatés *v.*
player wáákààm *n.*
playful wáákós *v.*
plead with iƙenes *v.*
pleasant dòòn *v.*
pleasantness daás *n.*
please ilákásɨtɛ́suƙɔt^a *v.*; imúmúitetés *v.*; kój^a *adv.*
Plecthranthus species gàsàràkwàts^a *n.*
plentitude (here) níbàdà *n.*
plentitude (there) kíbàdà *n.*
plenty ɲábɔnuƙɔt^a *v.*; nábɔnuƙɔt^a *v.*; tàn *n.*
pliable lumúdòn *v.*
pliably lùm *ideo.*
pliers ɲɔkɔ́ɲɛ́t^a *n.*
plop down rɛfɛ́kɛ́ɲɔ̀n *v.*
plop! pùs *ideo.*
plot (owned) ɲeɗúkór *n.*
plot against imanɛs *v.*
plow tɔkɔ́bɛs *v.*
plow (make to) tɔkɔ́bɨtetés *v.*
plow (ox-) ɲɛmɛlɛkúà nà ɦiyɔ̀ɔ̀^ɛ *n.*
plowed tɔkɔ́bɨtɔtɔ́s *v.*
plower tɔ̀kɔ̀bààm *n.*
plowing tɔ̀kɔ̀b^a *v.*

plowing season tɔkɔbatsóy^a *n.*
pluck sɔrɛ́s *v.*; tɔtsʉɗɛs *v.*; tʉtsʉɗɛs *v.*
pluck off ɓotsetés *v.*
pluck off repeatedly ɓotsotiés *v.*
plug imɨɗɨtsés *v.*; ts'úbʉlát^a *n.*; ts'ûb^a *n.*; tɨts'ɛ́s *v.*; túzʉɗɛ́s *v.*
plug (chewable) ts'àf *n.*
plug (lip) gwalát^a *n.*
plug oneself in imɨɗɨtsɛ́sa asɨ́ *v.*
plug up tɨts'ɛ́súƙɔt^a *v.*; tɨts'ímétòn *v.*; túzʉɗɛ́súƙɔt^a *v.*
plugged tɨts'ɔ́s *v.*
plume tùk^a *n.*
plumed tsowírímòn *v.*
plump dɛjɛ́dɔ̀n *v.*; zízòn *v.*
plump person zízòniàm *n.*
plumply dèj^ɛ *ideo.*
plunder iɓolíɓólés *v.*; iɓolíɓólésuƙot^a *v.*; taɓales *v.*; toɓésúƙot^a *v.*
plunder and bring toɓetés *v.*
plural kòmòn *v.*
plurality komás *n.*
pneumonia ɲeɗekea bákútsìkà^e *n.*
pock itwelítwélés *v.*
pocked itwelítwélós *v.*; tsakátsákánón *v.*
pocket ofur *n.*
pocket (back) ofura na jɨ́rɨ *n.*
pocket (front) ofura na wáxɨ *n.*
pockmarked tsakátsákánón *v.*
podium lɔpɨtá *n.*
point ekw^a *n.*; ekwed^a *n.*; náƙáfèd^a *n.*
point (topic) mɛnéékw^a *n.*
point (word) tódèèkw^a *n.*
point at ɗóɗés *v.*; ɗoɗésúƙot^a *v.*
point at sunset ɗóɗiesá tsòòni *v.*
point backward kámáránón *v.*
point downward (of horns) ilúkánètòn *v.*

point of departure wàxèdᵃ *n.*
point out ɗóɗés *v.*; ɗoɗésúƙotᵃ *v.*
point to ɗóɗés *v.*; ɗoɗésúƙotᵃ *v.*
point to secretly ɗóɗiés *v.*
pointed ɨwɨtsón *v.*; ts'ɨts'ɔ́n *v.*
pointless buɗámón *v.*
pointless talk ɨɓámɔ́nɨtòdᵃ *n.*
points áƙátìkìn *n.*; ekwin *n.*
pointy tsuɓáánètòn *v.*
poison cèmèr *n.*; iɲaalés *v.*; ɲekísórìtᵃ *n.*
poisoner iɲaalésɨàm *n.*
poke iƙumes *v.*; itsemes *v.*
poke around on itsemítsémés *v.*
Pokot person Ŋúupéám *n.*
pole (forked) titír *n.*
pole (horizontal) rìkwᵃ *n.*
pole (wooden) dakwᵃ *n.*
polecat ɲewuruŋorokᵃ *n.*
police pólìs *n.*
police post ɲépɔ́sɨtᵃ *n.*
polish iríƙéés *v.*
politick súbès *n.*
pollen ɗukes *n.*; iɔkᵃ *n.*
polling station góózésìàwᵃ *n.*
pollywog ŋúɗúŋúɗᵃ *n.*
polydactyly ɲéɗɔ́niɗon *n.*
pond tábàr *n.*
pond water tábarɨcue *n.*
ponder ɲeɓés *v.*; tamátámatés *v.*; tamɛtés *v.*; tamɨtámiés *v.*
poo-poo! dɨ *nurs.*
pooched out ɓotólómòn *v.*
poofy bʉlʉbʉlɔs *v.*
pool imɨlɨmɨlòn *v.*; tábàr *n.*
pool (riverbed) ɲéɓwál *n.*

pool (rock) sátᵃ *n.*
poop ets'ᵃ *n.*; nts'áƙón *v.*
poor bùlòn *v.*; ikúrúfánón *v.*
poor as a dog iŋókíánón *v.*
poor eyesight (have) múɗúkánón *v.*; ŋwaxɔna ekwitíní *v.*
poor person ikúrúfánóníàm *n.*; ŋókᵃ *n.*
poorly gààniƙᵉ *v.*
pop (soda) ɲɔ́sɔ́ɗa *n.*
pop (sound) ɗɛɗɛanón *v.*; rɛɗɛɗánón *v.*
pop out ipɨrɨsɛtés *v.*
pop! pɨrɨs *ideo.*
pope abáŋ *n.*; pápà *n.*
populate ínésuƙotᵃ *v.*
population ɲekɨmar *n.*
porch hodzíŋ *n.*
porcupine tɔrɔ̀mɨ̀ŋ *n.*
porridge ŋáɨtɔ̀ *n.*; ɲéúji *n.*
porridge (fermented) rùtᵃ *n.*
porridge (thick) ízotam *n.*
portion taɲáléés *v.*; xɔnɔ́ɔ́kɔn *n.*
portion (best) ɲopol *n.*
portion (first) ɲopol *n.*
portion (of meat) ɲekiner *n.*
portion out taɲáléetés *v.*
Portulaca quadrifida iɗakᵃ *n.*
posho tɔbɔŋ *n.*
posho (solid) ilɨram *n.*; lúgùm *n.*
posho (stiff) tʉɗʉtam *n.*
posho (watery) ɓɔtɨ́ *n.*
position was *n.*
position (social) zeís *n.*; zeísínànès *n.*
possess girés *v.*
possession (demonic) lejénánès *n.*
possessions ɲámáli *n.*
possible itíyéetam *n.*
post (police) ɲépɔ́sɨtᵃ *n.*

postpone íbokés *v.*
postpone repeatedly dzúkudzukiés *v.*; irotírótés *v.*
posture was *n.*
pot dóm *n.*
pot (metal) ɲásipiryá *n.*; ɲésipiriyá *n.*; tsɨrɨmʉ́dòm *n.*
pot (of beer) mɛ̀sèdòm *n.*
pot (small clay) ɲekulu *n.*
pot (small) dómáìm *n.*
pot bottom dómóɔ̀z *n.*
pot of edible termites (first) wàxɨdòm *n.*
pot-belly gwàjᵃ *n.*
pot-holed kumúkúmánón *v.*
potable wetam *n.*
potato (wild) keîdzᵃ *n.*
potato(es) ɲɛɓɨás *n.*
potbellied heɓúlúmòn *v.*
potsherd tɔɓɔkᵃ *n.*
potter bɛrɛ́sɨama dómítíní *n.*
pottery (broken) tɔɓɔkᵃ *n.*
pouch ofur *n.*
poultry ɲókɔkɔr *n.*
pounce tonyámónukotᵃ *v.*
pound dúlútés *v.*; ɨdatɛs *v.*; idoses *v.*; tóts'és *v.*
pound (in a mortar) iwotses *v.*
pound (with a pestle) íɲés *v.*
pound repeatedly itsomítsómés *v.*
pounded (with a pestle) íɲós *v.*
pour kɨdɨkɨdòn *v.*; kúdès *v.*
pour down iyééseetés *v.*
pour from small opening ádʉdʉkɛ́s *v.*
pour into itʉrɛs *v.*; otés *v.*; otésúkotᵃ *v.*
pour out furúdòn *v.*; iyééseetés *v.*; kúdesukotᵃ *v.*; kúdetés *v.*

pour out (noisily) ɨdʉlɨdʉlés *v.*
pour out into otetés *v.*
pour out to last drop ijɨ́ɨ́résʉkɔtᵃ *v.*
pour to last drop ijɨ́ɨ́rɛs *v.*
pout iɓútɨ́ŋɔ̀n *v.*; imutúmútòn *v.*
pouty imʉtʉ́mʉ́tɔ́s *v.*
poverty ŋókínànès *n.*
poverty-stricken ikúrúfánón *v.*
poverty-stricken person ikúrúfánóníàm *n.*
powder kabas *n.*; kábàsìn *n.*
powderily lyàm *ideo.*
powdery iwɨdɔs *v.*; lyamádòn *v.*
power ŋgúf *n.*; ŋɨxás *n.*; ɲapédór *n.*; zeís *n.*
powerful ŋɨ̀xɔ̀n *v.*
practice itétémés *v.*
praise itúrútés *v.*; tamɛɛs *v.*
praise oneself itúrútésá asɨ *v.*
prattle ilemílémòn *v.*
pray wáán *v.*
pray (call-and-response) takates *v.*
pray against takátésukotᵃ *v.*
pray away takátésukotᵃ *v.*
prayer wáán *n.*
prayer (call-and-response) tàkàtᵃ *n.*
prayer (closing) wáána na tézètɔ̀nɨ *n.*
prayer book ɲaɓúka wáánàᵉ *n.*
prayer for gravedigger wáána na mudésíàmàᵉ *n.*
prayerful person wáánààm *n.*
praying mantis tʉ́wᵃ *n.*
preach itátámés *v.*
preacher itátámɛ́sɨ̀àm *n.*
precarious ipárɨ́ɲánón *v.*
precipice látsó *n.*
precipitation dìdì *n.*

precipitous iwósétòn v.; kúbèlèmòn v.
precisely dàn adv.
predator loúk[a] n.
predawn eúzòn v.; ɲaɓáɨ́t[a] n.
preeminence zeís n.
pregnancy taboo ts'ɨ̀n n.
pregnant tarɨ́ón v.
pregnant (newly) ƙeɗétón v.
pregnant (prohibitively) ts'ɨ̀nɔ̀n v.
pregnant (recently) sɨbánón v.
premeditate iwɔ́ŋɔ́n v.
preoccupied ígùjùgùjòn v.; itúmúránón v.; wasɨtɛsa iká[e] v.
preoccupy itúmúránitésúƙot[a] v.
preparation (for travel) sùɓèt[a] n.
prepare iɗimés v.; iɗimésúƙot[a] v.; iɗimiés v.; iɗimiesúƙot[a] v.; itemités v.
prepare (food) itiŋés v.
prepare oneself iɗimiesá asɨ́ v.
prepare to go súɓánòn v.; suɓétón v.
prepared iɗiméson v.
presence gwarí n.
present dónés v.; dónésuƙot[a] v.; takánón v.; tɔ́rɔ́bɛs v.
presently nápáka na adv.
press bízès v.; iɗɔtsɛs v.; isɨkares v.
press all over bízibizatés v.
press for details inɨnés v.
press on iɗaɲíɗáŋɔ̀n v.; ɨmúƙɔ́ɔ̀n v.; júrés v.
press out bízetés v.; júrésuƙot[a] v.; jʉrɛtés v.
press repeatedly iɗaɲíɗáɲés v.
pressed rɔ́ƙɔ́rɔkánón v.
pressure isɨkares v.; rɛ́ɛ́s v.; rɛɛtés v.; tɔrɛɛs v.

pressured toreimétòn v.
pressurize isɨkares v.
pretend iɲétsóòn v.; iyétsóòn v.
prettiness daás n.
pretty dòòn v.
prevail taɗáŋón v.
prevaricate isuɗesa mɛná[ɛ] v.; itoŋetésá tódà[e] v.; yʉanitetés v.; yʉanón v.
prevarication yʉɛ n.
prevent irɛtɛs v.; isíƙéés v.; itítírés v.
prey on tɔɓɛlɛs v.
price dzîgw[a] n.; dzígwèsèd[a] n.; ɲéɓéy[a] n.
prick ts'ɔɗɨtɛs v.
priest (Catholic) páɗɛ̀r n.
primate (female) ɔgɛraŋwa n.
primate (half-grown) kukát[a] n.
primate (male) ɔ̀gɛ̀r n.
primate infant kíɗɔlɛ́ n.
primer (ignition) ɔ́zɛ̀d[a] n.
principal ámázeáma ɲésukúlu[i] n.
print ipírintiŋeetés v.
print a book iwetésá ɲáɓúkwì v.
prison zíƙésɨ̀àw[a] n.
prison guard cookaama zíƙésiicé n.
prisoner ɲímamɓúsɨ̀àm n.
pristine ɗòwòn v.; tɨlɨ́wón v.; xɔ́dɔ̀n v.; xɔtánón v.
private búdòs v.
probably káríká adv.; ntsúó ts'ɔɔ pro.
probe inɨnés v.
problems mɛn n.; ɲítsan n.
proboscis (elephant) òɲòrìkwèt[a] n.
procedure ɲɛpɨtɛ n.
proceed pórón v.
proceed (to do) itáƙúòn v.

407

process issues bɛrɛ́sá mɛná$^\varepsilon$ v.
procession ɲɛɗʉpɛ n.
prod iƙumes v.; itsemes v.
produce ƙwaatítetés v.; pulutetés v.
produce a lot of cɛɛtés v.
produce seeds egésá ekwí v.
product dzígwam n.; dzígwetam n.; dzíiƙotam n.
profit bɨtɨtam n.; ɨkɛ́ɨtɛtɛ́s v.
profit from rajetés v.
progeny kwats^a n.
prohibit dimités v.; dimitetés v.; itáléés v.
prohibited itáléánón v.; itálóós v.
prohibition ɲatal n.
project irʉtsɛs v.; ɲɛprɔ́jɛ̀kɨ̀t^a n.
project anorectum doletésá ɔ́zà$^\varepsilon$ v.
prolapse ɨtsʉ́bʉ̀ɗɔ̀n v.
prolapsed ɨtsʉ́bʉ̀ɗʉ̀mɔ̀n v.
prolific bòmòn v.
prolong zikíbètòn v.; zikíbitésʉ́ƙot^a v.
prolonged (become) zikíbonuƙot^a v.
promenade tasɔ́ɔ́n v.
promiscuous (sexually) furés v.; ɨmáláánón v.
promise iɓoletés v.
promise each other iɓólínós v.
promote zeites v.; zeitésuƙot^a v.
pronely ɓɛlɛlɛts$^\varepsilon$ ideo.
pronounce kʉtɔnʉƙɔt^a v.
prop iƙɔŋɛs v.; titirés v.
prop (the head) díƙwɛ́s v.
prop against iƙɔ́ɲɨtɛ́s v.; iƙɔ́ɲɨtɛ́sʉƙɔt^a v.
prop on iƙɔ́ɲɨtɛ́s v.; iƙɔ́ɲɨtɛ́sʉƙɔt^a v.
prop up iƙaŋɛs v.; titiretés v.
propane gas ɲágás n.

propeller blade ɗàw^a n.; suguráɗáw^a n.
proper itémón v.
proper (of many) dayaakón v.
property kíj^a n.; ɲámáli n.
prophecy faɗás n.
prophesy fàɗòn v.; ikújíánón v.
prophet fàɗònìam n.; ɲakujíícíkáàm n.
propolis sɔs n.
propped against iƙɔ́ɲɨtɔ́s v.
propped on iƙɔ́ɲɨtɔ́s v.
proprietor ámêd^a n.
proscribe dimités v.; dimitetés v.
prosecutor isɨ́ɨ́tɛ́sɨ̀am n.
prospect fiyeités v.
prosperity ídzànànès n.; zɛƙwa ná dà n.
prostitute ɲamáláɨt^a n.
prostrate bùkòn v.; bukukánón v.
Protea gaguedi ɲícwéɲé n.
protect cookés v.
protected cookotós v.
protector còòkààm n.
protest nɛpɛƙánón v.
Protestant sémɨ̀s n.
protract zikíbitésuƙot^a v.
protracted (become) zikíbonuƙot^a v.
protrude tɨbɨ́ɛ́tɔ̀n v.
protrude (of ears) kweelémòn v.
protruding ɓotólómòn v.; tɨbɨɔ́n v.
protrusion rúgèts^a n.
protuberance rúgèts^a n.
proud itúrón v.
proverb taɗápítotós n.
provide for bɔnés v.; ɨgɔɲés v.
provider bɔnéám n.
provision bɔn n.
provocation ɓɛkam n.
provocativeness jʉ́ránànès n.

provoke

provoke ɓɛkɛtés *v.*; isúsúés *v.*; itsemes *v.*; itsótsóés *v.*

provoke (verbally) itɔ́ŋɔ́és *v.*

provoking ɓɛkánón *v.*; júránòn *v.*

prowl tonyámón *v.*; totséɗón *v.*

prune ikwákwárɛ́s *v.*; isésélés *v.*

pry apart ɓerepiés *v.*

pry bar ɲotolim *n.*

pry open ɓerepiés *v.*

pseudo- láŋ *n.*

Pseudocedrela species ɲókotit[a] *n.*

Psidium guajava ɲógóva *n.*

psyche gúr *n.*

ptooey! tù *ideo.*

puberty (enter) teɓúránétòn *v.*

puberty (enter, of boys) iɓɨyákòn *v.*

pubic area didis *n.*

pubic bone didisíɔ́k[a] *n.*

pubic hair didisísíts'[a] *n.*; ɔ́zàsìts'[a] *n.*; tèmùr *n.*

pubis didisíɔ́k[a] *n.*

public ɲáɲɔ́s *v.*

publish a book iwetésá ɲáɓúkwì *v.*

puddle imilɨmɨlɔ̀n *v.*

pudendum didis *n.*

pudgily lèɓᵘ *ideo.*

pudgy gerúsúmòn *v.*; leɓúdòn *v.*; rexúkúmòn *v.*

puff adder bɛf *n.*

puff up xuanón *v.*; xuxuanitetés *v.*; xuxuanón *v.*

puffily bɔ̀f *ideo.*; lèɓᵘ *ideo.*

puffy bɔfɔ́dɔ̀n *v.*; bʉlʉbʉlɔs *v.*; dúduránón *v.*; leɓúdòn *v.*

puke fiyɛnétɔ́n *v.*; fiyènɔ̀n *v.*

pummel

pull béberés *v.*; eminés *v.*; iɓwates *v.*; ijʉkɛtés *v.*; ipoles *v.*; itsɔrɛtés *v.*

pull (make) ijúkɨ́tɛtɛs *v.*

pull along béberiés *v.*

pull apart ɗusés *v.*; ɗusésúƙot[a] *v.*; ɗusutes *v.*; eminiés *v.*; ikéŋéɗés *v.*; tɔŋeɗɛs *v.*

pull away béberésúƙot[a] *v.*; eminésúƙot[a] *v.*

pull back dolés *v.*; doletés *v.*; rʉjés *v.*

pull back foreskin doletésá kwanɨ *v.*

pull down inietés *v.*; lɔkɔɗɛtés *v.*

pull forcefully iɓwatetés *v.*

pull in béberetés *v.*

pull off ɓotsetés *v.*; eminésúƙot[a] *v.*; tɔkɛtɛs *v.*; tɔkétésʉƙɔt[a] *v.*; tolés *v.*; toletés *v.*

pull off (bark) iɓóɓólés *v.*

pull off repeatedly ɓotsotiés *v.*; tolotiés *v.*

pull on ɗúrés *v.*; ɗʉtés *v.*

pull oneself away kɛlɛtésá asɨ *v.*

pull oneself back rʉjɛtésá asɨ *v.*

pull out ɗurɛtés *v.*; ɗʉtɛtés *v.*; eminetés *v.*; faɗetés *v.*; ipoletés *v.*; ritetés *v.*; ruutésuƙot[a] *v.*; ruutetés *v.*; tɔkɛtɛs *v.*; tɔkétésʉƙɔt[a] *v.*; tɔkɛtɛtés *v.*; tolés *v.*; toletés *v.*; tɔtsʉɗɛs *v.*; tʉtsʉɗɛs *v.*; tuutes *v.*; tuutetés *v.*

pull out repeatedly tolotiés *v.*

pull over itilɛtés *v.*

pull this way béberetés *v.*

pull up ɗués *v.*; ɗuetés *v.*; eminetés *v.*; ipoletés *v.*; rués *v.*

pulsate dìkwòn *v.*; ƙádiƙádòn *v.*

pulse ƙádiƙádòn *v.*

pulverize itsomes *v.*

pummel ɗúlútés *v.*

pump

pump íɲés *v.*
pump up ɨsɨkɛs *v.*
pumpkin kaiɗeyᵃ *n.*
pumpkin (oblong) naperorwá *n.*; tsòkòlòr *n.*
pumpkin (small unripe) ɗɔ́l *n.*
pumpkin (unripe) ɲɨ́kalʉtʉ́rɔ *n.*
pumpkin juice kaiɗeícúé *n.*
pumpkin piece kaiɗeíbɔrɔkɔ́ƙᵃ *n.*
pumpkin ring ɨbɔtᵃ *n.*
pumpkin seed kaiɗeíékwᵃ *n.*
pumpkin stem base kaiɗeíáƙátᵃ *n.*
punch tanaŋes *v.*
punch (a hole) húbutés *v.*; pulés *v.*; ruɗés *v.*
puncture ɓɛkés *v.*; ɓɛkɛtés *v.*; itsumés *v.*; pulés *v.*; ruɗés *v.*
puncture repeatedly pulutiés *v.*
punish iɗoŋes *v.*
puny gɔɗɨ́rɨ́mɔ̀n *v.*
pupil isóméésíàm *n.*; ɲósomáám *n.*
pupil (of eye) tiléŋ *n.*
puppy ŋókɨ̀im *n.*
pure ɓèts'òn *v.*; tɨlɨ́wɔ́n *v.*; xɔ́dɔ̀n *v.*; xɔtánón *v.*
purity (of food) lɛtsékɛ́ɛdᵃ *n.*
purplish-red kɨpúránètòn *v.*
purpose ɲákásìèdᵃ *n.*
purr ŋɔ́rɔ́rɔ̀n *v.*
purse ɲánɨ́bàkᵃ *n.*
pursue ilɔŋɛs *v.*; imɨ́tɨ́ŋɛés *v.*
pursue after ilɔ́ŋésʉƙɔtᵃ *v.*
pursue each other sexually ríínós *v.*
pus báts'ᵃ *n.*
push iɗɔtsɛs *v.*; ijʉkɛs *v.*; ipʉnɛs *v.*; rités *v.*

put on

push along ijʉkújʉ́kɛ́s *v.*
push aside repeatedly ijúkúmiés *v.*
push away ijʉ́kɛ́sʉƙɔtᵃ *v.*; ritésúƙɔtᵃ *v.*
push buttons (provoke) itsemes *v.*
push down ɗaɗátésʉƙɔtᵃ *v.*
push in and out irúrúƙés *v.*
push into ipúkútsésʉƙɔtᵃ *v.*; lakates *v.*
push into repeatedly lakatiés *v.*
push near to bɨɲés *v.*
push on bízès *v.*
push over itɨ́lɛ́sʉƙɔtᵃ *v.*
push over side lakates *v.*
push over side repeatedly lakatiés *v.*
pushing jʉ́ránòn *v.*
put egés *v.*; egetés *v.*
put ahead ɛkwɨtɛs *v.*; ɛkwɨ́tésʉƙɔtᵃ *v.*
put alongside inapɛs *v.*
put aside inápésʉƙɔtᵃ *v.*; iɲáɗéés *v.*; iɲáɗéésʉƙɔtᵃ *v.*; ógoɗés *v.*; ógoɗésúƙɔtᵃ *v.*; oƙésúƙɔtᵃ *v.*
put away ógoɗés *v.*; ógoɗésúƙɔtᵃ *v.*; oƙésúƙɔtᵃ *v.*
put back rajésúƙɔtᵃ *v.*; rajetés *v.*
put beside inapɛs *v.*
put in ɓuƙítésʉƙɔtᵃ *v.*; imetsités *v.*
put in a sling ɨbatalés *v.*
put in front ɛkwɨtɛs *v.*; ɛkwɨ́tésʉƙɔtᵃ *v.*
put in jail egésá ɲájálaáƙᵉ *v.*
put in order inábèsùƙɔtᵃ *v.*; itíbès *v.*; itíbesúƙɔtᵃ *v.*
put in twos leɓetsítésuƙɔtᵃ *v.*
put inside xutésúƙɔtᵃ *v.*
put nearby taraŋés *v.*
put off íboƙés *v.*
put off odor mídzòn *v.*
put off repeatedly dzúƙudzuƙiés *v.*; irotírótés *v.*
put on iwales *v.*; ŋábès *v.*

put on (beads) otés *v.*
put on a feather iwalesa túkà^e *v.*
put out ts'eites *v.*; ts'eítésuƙot^a *v.*
put to sleep epítésuƙot^a *v.*
put to work ikásíitetés *v.*; teréganitetés *v.*
put together itóyéés *v.*
put two-by-two leɓetsítésuƙot^a *v.*
put up íbokés *v.*
put up with taɗaɲes *v.*
put upright itsírítetés *v.*; tsírítetés *v.*
put weight on tuɓútitésúƙot^a *v.*
put in otés *v.*
putrefy múmútètòn *v.*
putrid múmútòn *v.*; ŋorótsánón *v.*
pyrosis kíɓɔ́ɔz *n.*
python ɲomórótòt^a *n.*
python tail-tip ɲégets^a *n.*
quaff itúlákáɲés *v.*
quail ɲelúru *n.*
quake irikíríkòn *v.*; kwalíkwálòn *v.*; ɲeríkirik^a *n.*
quaking sound ɓulʉɓʉl *ideo.*
qualms (have) paupáwón *v.*
quarrel dèƙw^a *n.*
quarrel (of many) ilérúmùòn *v.*
quarrel with (start a) déƙwítetés *v.*
quarreler deƙwideƙosíám *n.*
quarreling ɲelerum *n.*
quarrelsome deƙwideƙos *v.*
quarter (area) nabiɗit^a *n.*
quartzite séy^a *n.*
queasy iláƙízòn *v.*; itikítíkòn *v.*; talóón *v.*
queen bee lókílórón *n.*; okílóɲór *n.*
queen termite dádata dáɲá^e *n.*; dáɲádadát^a *n.*; ŋwááta dáɲá^e *n.*

quelea (red-billed) kimír *n.*
quench ts'eites *v.*; ts'eítésuƙot^a *v.*
question esetés *n.*; esetiés *v.*; iŋáyéés *v.*
question things itóŋóiesá mɛná^ɛ *v.*
quibble iɲúɲúròn *v.*
quick itírónòn *v.*; wéénòn *v.*
quickly ɗàmʉ̀s *adv.*; ɗɛ̀mʉ̀s *adv.*
quiet ijémɔ́n *v.*; líídòn *v.*; tisílón *v.*
quiet down ijémítésuƙot^a *v.*; ijémɔ́nuƙɔt^a *v.*
quietly jʉ̀r *ideo.*; lì *ideo.*; sokósíìk^e *v.*
quish! pìs *ideo.*; tùs *ideo.*
quit kuritésúƙota así *v.*
quiver kìtòn *v.*; kwalíkwálòn *v.*; nérinérón *v.*
quiver (begin to) kitétón *v.*
quiver (make) kitítésuƙot^a *v.*
rabbit tulú *n.*
rabbit nickname bositíníàm *n.*
race irʉtsɛsa así *v.*; tsùwà *v.*; tsuwa na iɓákɔ́nɨ *n.*
rack (drying) lɔpɨtá *n.*
racket nòs *n.*
racket (make a) ilélémùòn *v.*
radiance daás *n.*
radiant dòòn *v.*
radiator gàfigàf *n.*
radio dʉrʉdʉr *n.*; ɲéréɗi *n.*
rafter stick tɨmél *n.*
rag kàbàɗ^a *n.*
rage gaánàs *n.*; ilɛ́ɔ́n *v.*; ɲɛlil *n.*
ragged ikárɔ́n *v.*; kɔrɔ́ɗɔ̀mɔ̀n *v.*; rídziridzánón *v.*; rúgurugánón *v.*
raid toɓés *v.*; toɓésúƙot^a *v.*
raid and bring toɓetés *v.*
raider toɓésíàm *n.*
rain dìdì *n.*; wat^a *n.*; wàtòn *v.*

411

rain (drizzling) ɲélɨ́mɨlɨm *n.*
rain (dry season) ódzadidí *n.*
rain (gentle) déródɛɨ́k^a *n.*
rain (light) kúf *n.*; rɛ̀b^a *n.*
rain elsewhere itsέέrɔ̀ɔ̀n *v.*
rain from the west tsóéàm *n.*
rain sickness didiɲedeké *n.*
rain-stopper tudúlóniàm *n.*
rainbow nàtɔ̀lɔ̀kà *n.*
rains (eastern) obólén *n.*
rains (intermittent) ɲerupe *n.*
rainy season diditsóy^a *n.*; ɔtáy^a *n.*
raise bukés *v.*; ŋkáítetés *v.*; tasɛɛs *v.*; zikíbitésúƙot^a *v.*
raise (make) ikéítɛtés *v.*
raise buttocks tsúdòn *v.*
raise the head wasitɛsa iká^e *v.*
raise to kick dɛŋɛlɛs *v.*
raise up ikéésuƙot^a *v.*; ikɛɛtés *v.*
raise up (develop) bɛrés *v.*
raised up ikeimétòn *v.*; ikɔɔtós *v.*
rake ikwɛrɛs *v.*; ɲírés *v.*; ɲakwárét^a *n.*
rake (with nails) soƙóríties *v.*
rally iríréetés *v.*; sùtòn *v.*
ram rutsés *v.*; rutsésúƙot^a *v.*
ram (goat) bɔfɔkɔr *n.*
ram (sheep) dódocurúk^a *n.*
ram (young goat) kɔl *n.*
ram into ipúkútsésuƙot^a *v.*
rampage iléón *v.*
ramshackle kɔlɔlánón *v.*
ranger (game) lɔgέm *n.*
rank dɛtsidétsón *v.*; imúsɔ́ɔ̀n *v.*; múmútɔ̀n *v.*; wɨ́zilɨ́lón *v.*; zeís *n.*; zeísínànès *n.*
rank (become) imúsέètɔ̀n *v.*

rankle bɛkɛtés *v.*
rankling bɛkánón *v.*
ransack ibolíbólés *v.*; ibolíbólésuƙot^a *v.*; tabales *v.*
rap on idɔŋidɔ́ŋés *v.*; ikoŋíkóŋés *v.*; itɔ́tɔ́ŋés *v.*
rap on repeatedly ilɛrílérés *v.*
rap repeatedly idɛidɛ́ɛ́s *v.*
rapaciousness lokodoŋironánés *n.*
rape itikiesúƙot^a *v.*
rapturous (become) ɛfɔnuƙot^a *v.*
rare búúbuanón *v.*
rashy katúrúturánón *v.*; sómomójón *v.*
rat dér *n.*
rat (giant Gambia) lòlòt^a *n.*
rat (house) dérá na áwìkà^e *n.*
rat (striped ground) nàtsèr *n.*
rat poison dérócɛmér *n.*
rat species natélewá *n.*; tiɲátiɲá *n.*; tufúl *n.*; túsɨdèr *n.*
ratel lɛŋ *n.*
ration iminɨ́mɨ́nés *v.*
rattily rès *ideo.*
rattle (animal-hoof) lots'ilots'^{a} *n.*
rattle (gourd) ɲέέkɨ́ɛ́k^a *n.*
rattle (leg) coór *n.*
ratty rɛsédɔ̀n *v.*
ravage isɨlɨ́ánitɛtés *v.*
raven (fan-tailed) kúràk^a *n.*
ravine fòts^a *n.*; ɲókópè *n.*
ravine (river) ɔrɔr *n.*
raw ts'águ̯òòn *v.*
ray of light bás *n.*; súw^a *n.*
raze gijɛtés *v.*; ɲadésúƙot^a *v.*; towutses *v.*
razor (handmade) gìjìt^a *n.*
razorblade ɲóŋɔmbέ *n.*

reach (a destination) itɔ́ɔ́n v.
reach (make) itaités v.
reach a consensus ɗɔtsɛtésá tódàᵉ v.
reach and pull down likiɗes v.
reach here (make) itaitɛtés v.
react against tokíróòn v.
react suddenly tokúétòn v.; tokúréètòn v.
read isóméés v.
read (teach to) isómáitetés v.
readable isómáìmètòn v.
reader isóméésíàm n.
readings ɲósomáicíkᵃ n.
ready iɗimés v.; iɗimésɔ́n v.; iɗimésʉ́ƙɔtᵃ v.; iɗimiés v.; iɗimiesúƙɔtᵃ v.; itemités v.
ready (make) itemités v.
ready (to eat) àèòn v.
ready oneself iɗimiesá asɨ́ v.
ready to eat (become) aeonuƙɔtᵃ v.
ready to fight iríríkòn v.
ready to go (get) súɓánòn v.; suɓétón v.
ready, set, go! mérímeritsìò interj.
readying for harvest (of gardens) aeonuƙota kíjáᵉ n.
real estate kíjᵃ n.
realize walámón v.
really easíkᵉ n.; kárɨká adv.; mʉ̀kà adv.
really (much) pʉ́n ideo.
ream out irúútés v.
reanimate fiyekitetés v.
reap irárátés v.; irarɛs v.; tarares v.; weés v.
reaper weésíàm n.
rear jɨ̀r n.; kanɛdᵃ n.; ɔ́zèdᵃ n.; ɔ́z n.; tasɛɛs v.

rear end jɨ́rêdᵃ n.; ɔ́zèdᵃ n.
reassign ilɔpɛs v.
rebel mɛnáám n.; ɲɛkɛsʉpan n.; terémón v.
rebels (Sudanese) Ŋiɲéɲéyᵃ n.
rebound íɓòtòn v.; iɗótón v.
rebuff imɛ́ɗélés v.
rebuke dɔxés v.; dɔxésúƙɔtᵃ v.
recall anɛ́súƙɔtᵃ v.; anɛtés v.; tamésúƙɔtᵃ v.; tamɛtés v.
recall repeatedly aniesúƙɔtᵃ v.
recce irimírímés v.
recede rajámón v.; rajánón v.
receipt taatsakabáɗᵃ n.
receive tɛ́ɓɛtés v.
recent erútsón v.
recently ts'ɔ̀ɔ̀ adv.
reclaim irapɛs v.; irápɛ́sʉƙɔtᵃ v.
recline eponuƙɔtᵃ v.; iɗɛ́ɗɔ́ɔ̀n v.; itsólóŋòn v.
recognize fiyeités v.
recoil from itírákés v.
recollect anɛtés v.; tamésúƙɔtᵃ v.; tamɛtés v.
reconcile apápánèètɔn v.; apápánɔ̀ɔ̀n v.; isɨ́lɨ́tésʉƙɔtᵃ v.
reconnoiter irimírímés v.
record irékɔ́ɗiŋeés v.; tamitɛtés v.
record of attendance éditíníkabáɗᵃ n.
recorded (on paper) iƙirɔs v.
recount isíséés v.
recover irapɛs v.; irápɛ́sʉƙɔtᵃ v.; irapɛtés v.; irapɛtés v.
rectify itsɨ́rɨ́tɛtés v.; tsɨ́rɨ́tɛtés v.; tɔɓɛitɛtés v.
rector pásɨ̀tà n.
rectum dzɔɗátᵃ n.
recur tɔrúɓɔ́n v.

recycle ɨrɔmɛs v.
red ɗìwòn v.
red (become) ɗiwonuƙotᵃ v.
red (make) ɗiwítésuƙotᵃ v.
red (of many) ɗiwaakón v.
red (very) tsòn ideo.
red-pod terminalia gáʒàdᵃ n.
redden ɗiwítésuƙotᵃ v.; ɗiwonuƙotᵃ v.
reddish-brown bɔibɔ́ɔ́n v.
redeemer hoɗetésíàm n.
redo ɨɲaƙes v.; ɨɲoƙes v.; ɨɲóƙésuƙotᵃ v.
reduce rajámón v.; rajánón v.
reed kɛ̀ɗᵃ n.
reed (granary) ɲétémetsᵃ n.
reed ring nàtsìkwᵃ n.
reed species sɔ́gɛ̀kàkᵃ n.; sôgᵃ n.
reed wreath nàtsìkwᵃ n.
reedbuck (Bohor) ɲeɓuri n.
reedbuck (female mountain) rɔ́gɛŋwa n.
reedbuck (male mountain) cúkúɗùm n.
reedbuck (mountain) rɔ̂gᵃ n.
reedmace ɨsɨ̀kᵃ n.
reeds (small) kɔ̀kᵃ n.
reek ilíánòn v.; mídzona ɗɛtsɨɗɛ́tsɨ́kᵉ v.; mídzònà ɗùkᵘ v.
reel ɡakímón v.; ɨtɛrɨ́tɛ́rɔ̀n v.
reenact ɨɲites v.
refer to tákés v.
reflection kúrúkúr n.
reform cicianón v.
refuse dimés v.; ts'ʉts'ʉ n.; wasétón v.
refuse treatment béberésuƙota asɨ́ v.
refute ɨsales v.; ɨsaletés v.; ɨsalɨtés v.
refuted ɨsálímétòn v.
regale ɨmúmwárés v.

regalia ɲɛ́nɨs n.
regime ɲápukán n.
region ɲétɛɛr n.
regress rajánón v.
regret anɛ́súƙotᵃ v.
regrind iɲáɓúƙés v.
regrow jɔɓɛ́tɔ́n v.; tɔrʉ́ɓɔ́n v.
regrow (of hair) ŋʉrʉrʉ́ɲón v.
regrowing jɔ́ɓɔ̀n v.
regurgitate ɦyɛnɛ́tɔ́n v.; ɦyɛ̀nɔ̀n v.; xerétón v.
reign over ipúkéés v.
reject dimés v.; ɨmɛ́ɗélɛ́s v.; míjés v.
rejoin ɗɛsɛ́mɔ́n v.; tɔɲɛ́tɔ́nʉƙotᵃ v.
rekindle (with breath) fúts'iés v.
related ɦyeímós v.; ɦyeínós v.
related by birth ɦyeínósá ƙwaatéᵒ v.
related by marriage ɦyeínósá sits'ésú v.; ɲotánánès n.
relations (sexual) epᵃ n.
relax torwóónuƙotᵃ v.
relaxed torwóón v.
relay ilotses v.
relay tower ɲéɓusitá n.
release hoɗés v.; hoɗésúƙotᵃ v.; hoɗetés v.; itsues v.; itsuetés v.; talakes v.
releaser hoɗetésíàm n.
reliable ikékéɲòn v.
religion ɲéɗíni n.
religious matters ɲakujímɛ́n n.
relinquish bɔlɛ́súƙotᵃ v.; tajales v.; tajálésuƙotᵃ v.; tajaletés v.
relocate dzuƙés v.; ilójésuƙotᵃ v.
relocate away dzuƙésúƙotᵃ v.
relocate one's home ilotsesa zɛƙɔ́ᵋ v.
relocate this way dzuƙetés v.
rely on ɨƙɔŋes v.
remain jɛjɛ́tɔ́n v.; jɛ̀jɔ̀n v.

remain behind maɗámón *v.*
remainder jɨ́rêdᵃ *n.*; ógoɗesam *n.*
remainder (of food) ɲomokojo *n.*
remainders jɨ́rɨ́n *n.*
remains (find) ítés *v.*
remember anɛsúƙɔtᵃ *v.*; anɛtés *v.*; tamɛsúƙɔtᵃ *v.*; tamɛtés *v.*
remember clearly ipɨ́ɨ́rɨ́ánón *v.*
remember often aniesúƙotᵃ *v.*
remind tamɨtɛtés *v.*
remove hoɗésúƙotᵃ *v.*; hoɗetés *v.*; ƙanésúƙotᵃ *v.*; ƙanetés *v.*; ts'álés *v.*; ts'aletés *v.*; tɔkɛ́tésuƙɔtᵃ *v.*; tɔkɛtɛtés *v.*; tuɓutes *v.*; tuɓútésuƙotᵃ *v.*; tuɓutetés *v.*; tuutes *v.*; tuutetés *v.*
remove a bird ƙanésúƙota gwaáᵉ *v.*
remove gingerly dɨ́tés *v.*; dɨ́tésuƙɔtᵃ *v.*
remove shoes hoɗetésá taƙáɨ́ƙàᵋ *v.*
remove the jaw of tajakes *v.*
removed from office rúmánònà kàràtsu̱ *v.*
remunerate taatses *v.*
remuneration tààtsᵃ *n.*
rend dzɛrɛ́s *v.*
render ikɔɓɛs *v.*
rendezvous (sexual) tirésíàwᵃ *n.*
renounce claim over ógoés *v.*
rent ipáɲƙeés *v.*
rent (torn) dzɛrɔ́sɔ́n *v.*
repair iɗimɛ́s *v.*; iɗimɛ́súƙɔtᵃ *v.*; iɗimɛtés *v.*; ɲimanites *v.*; rátsɛ́s *v.*; taɗapes *v.*; taɗapetés *v.*
repair repeatedly rátsiés *v.*
repaired iɗimɔ́s *v.*; taɗapos *v.*
repay taatsésuƙotᵃ *v.*
repeat iɓóŋón *v.*; iɲaƙes *v.*; iɲoƙes *v.*; iɲóƙésuƙotᵃ *v.*

repeat endlessly ígujugujésa tódàᵉ *v.*
repel iɗáfɛ́su̱ƙɔtᵃ *v.*; itɨ́ɨ́lɛ́s *v.*
repelled iɗáfɛ́su̱ƙɔta asɨ́ *v.*
repent cicianón *v.*; fɨtésuƙota gu̱róᵉ *v.*
repent of sins tu̱lu̱ŋɛsa tɔsɛsónɨ̱ *v.*
replace imetsés *v.*; imetsités *v.*
replant (a garden) iɓures *v.*
replicate toputes *v.*; toputetés *v.*
reply rajés *v.*; rajetés *v.*; taatses *v.*; taatsésuƙotᵃ *v.*; taatsetés *v.*
report ɗoɗésúƙotᵃ *v.*; ɲéripótᵃ *n.*
repose iɗéɗɔ̀n *v.*
representative tódààm *n.*
reprimand dɔxɛ́s *v.*; dɔxɛ́súƙɔtᵃ *v.*
reprobate ɲárásɨ́ám *n.*
reproduce (copy) toputes *v.*; toputetés *v.*
repulse ilɛ́lɛ́ɨtɛtés *v.*; itɨ́ɨ́lɛ́s *v.*
repulse each other gu̱ts'u̱rɨ́nɔ́s *v.*
reputed fiyoós *v.*
request wáánɛtés *v.*
rescue iɛtés *v.*
rescuer iɛtésɨ́àm *n.*
resect ɓilés *v.*
resemble ikwáánòn *v.*; ƙámón *v.*; toputétòn *v.*
reserved toikíkón *v.*
residence zɛƙɔ́áwᵃ *n.*
resident zɛƙɔ́ám *n.*
residue (beer) ɗu̱ká *n.*; dàjᵃ *n.*
residue (food) ɲéɗúruɗur *n.*
resile ru̱jés *v.*
resilient itsyátón *v.*
resist iƙaɨ́ƙɛ́és *v.*; iƙáƙɛ́és *v.*; iƙáƙɛɛtés *v.*; irɛtɛs *v.*; kwɛ́rɛɗɛ́ɗɔ́n *v.*; rajés *v.*
resistant nikwɨ́dɔ̀n *v.*
resistantly nìkwⁱ *ideo.*
resistent itsyátón *v.*

resolve itemités *v.*
resolve an issue epitésuƙota tódàᵉ *v.*
resound arútón *v.*
respect mòròn *v.*; xèɓòn *v.*
respect each other mórímós *v.*
respire ɨɛ́ŋón *v.*; sʉ́pón *v.*
resplendent dòòn *v.*
respond rajés *v.*; rajetés *v.*; taatses *v.*; taatsésuƙotᵃ *v.*; taatsetés *v.*
respond as a group sùtòn *v.*
respond repeatedly tébitebiés *v.*
responsible âmêdᵃ *n.*; wàsɔ̀n *v.*
responsible for things wasɔna kúrúɓádù *v.*
resprout jɔɓétón *v.*
resprouting jɔ́ɓòn *v.*
rest ɨɛ́ŋón *v.*
rest (the head) díƙwés *v.*
rest against iƙɔŋɛs *v.*; iƙɔ́ɲítés *v.*; iƙɔ́ɲítésʉƙotᵃ *v.*; tonokes *v.*
rest on iƙɔŋɛs *v.*; iƙɔ́ɲítés *v.*; iƙɔ́ɲítésʉƙotᵃ *v.*
rest up ɨɛ́ŋónʉƙotᵃ *v.*
restaurant ŋƙáƙáhò *n.*; ɲéótèl *n.*
rested against iƙɔ́ɲítɔ́s *v.*
rested on iƙɔ́ɲítɔ́s *v.*
resting place ɨ̀ɛŋààwᵃ *n.*
restless ɗɛɲiɗɛɲɔs *v.*
restless (unsettled) tsɔnitsɔnɔ́s *v.*
restrain iƙalíƙálɛs *v.*; isíƙéés *v.*; itítíƙés *v.*; itítíƙetés *v.*
restrict iriɗɛs *v.*; iriɗɛtés *v.*
restricted iriɗɔs *v.*
resurrect ɦyekétón *v.*; ɦyekitetés *v.*
resuscitate fúts'iés *v.*; ikwárétòn *v.*

retain itítíƙés *v.*; itítíƙetés *v.*; tatsáɗésuƙotᵃ *v.*
retaliate ɲaɲés *v.*; ɲaɲésúƙotᵃ *v.*
retard inípónítésúƙotᵃ *v.*
retch jaƙátós *v.*; toukes *v.*; touketés *v.*; xáƙátòn *v.*
retell iɲitɛs *v.*
retire rumétón *v.*
retort taatses *v.*; taatsésuƙotᵃ *v.*; taatsetés *v.*
retrace one's steps iƙʉlúƙʉ́lɔ̀n *v.*
retract dolés *v.*; doletés *v.*; rʉjés *v.*
retract foreskin doletésá kwanɨ *v.*
retract oneself rʉjɛtésá asɨ *v.*
retreat ipɛ́ɛ́rɔ̀n *v.*; rajánón *v.*; rumétón *v.*
retrieve tukuretés *v.*; tukutetés *v.*
retrieve (food) lɛkés *v.*
retriever (of food) lɛkésɨ̀àm *n.*
return iɓóɓóŋòn *v.*; rajés *v.*; rajésúƙotᵃ *v.*; rajetés *v.*; tɔrúɓón *v.*
return bride xɛɛsúƙotᵃ *v.*
return here itétón *v.*
return there itéón *v.*; itíón *v.*
return this way iɓóɓóɲètòn *v.*
return to normal xɔ́dɔnʉƙotᵃ *v.*
reveal ɗoɗésúƙotᵃ *v.*; ɗóɗítetés *v.*; enitésúƙotᵃ *v.*; enitetés *v.*; iléérániteés *v.*; kwɛts'és *v.*
revealed kwɛts'émón *v.*
Revelation (biblical) Enitetés *n.*
revenge ɲaɲés *v.*; ɲaɲésúƙotᵃ *v.*
revere itúrútés *v.*; mòròn *v.*
reverse ikutúƙútés *v.*; ikutúƙútòn *v.*
revert rajánón *v.*
revive fúts'iés *v.*; ɦyekétón *v.*; ɦyekitetés *v.*; ikwárétòn *v.*

revolt ilɛ́lɛ́ɪ̀tɛtɛ́s v.
revolve irɨ́ŋɔ́n v.
reward tɔ́rɔ́bɛs v.; tɔ́rɔ́bɛsa na ɨ́lɔɛsɨ́ n.
rheum (dried) dɔ̀x n.
rhinoceros (black) óbìjᵃ n.
rhomboid muscle ɲésɨ́lɨsil n.
Rhus natalensis mɨsá n.
Rhynchosia hirta ɲéŋéso n.
rib ŋabér n.
rib (lefthand) betsínáŋabér n.
rib (lowest) sʉ̀dᵃ n.
rib (meat) kileleɓú n.
rib (righthand) ŋƙáƙáŋabér n.
rib (upper) tsètsèkwᵃ n.
rib bone ŋabérɨ́ɔkᵃ n.
rib meat ŋáberìkèèm n.
rich bàrɔ̀n v.; ijákáánón v.
rich (get) bárɛ́tɔ̀n v.; barɔnʉƙɔtᵃ v.
rich (in taste) wiɲɨ́dɔ̀n v.; wɨɲiwɨ́ɲón v.
rich (make) barɨ́tɛ́sʉƙɔtᵃ v.
rich person bàrɔ̀am n.; bàrɔ̀nɨ̀am n.
riches bàr n.
richly in taste wɨɲ ideo.
Ricinus communis imánán n.
rickety ɗɔxɔ́dɔ̀n v.; gɔ́gɔ̀rɔ̀mɔ̀n v.
ricochet iɗótón v.
rid oneself of gʉts'ʉrɛs v.; itsúrúés v.
riddle taɗápítotós n.
ride otsés v.
ride (a bicycle/motorcycle) hɔnɛ́s v.
ridge gògòròjᵃ n.; itórójɲés v.; kokór n.; zeketᵃ n.
ridge (of hair) sìgìrìgìr n.
ridge (vertical) fátár n.; ɲɔdɔ́kɛ́tᵃ n.
ridge base tsɨɨr n.

ridged toŋórómòn v.; toróŋómòn v.
ridges in (make) itórójɲés v.
ridgetop (vertical) fátáràakᵃ n.
ridicule tɔjɛmɛs v.
rifle (bolt-action) lomucir n.
rifle (short bolt-action) ɲápaŋƙaláɨ́tᵃ n.
rifle through iɓolíɓólés v.; iɓolíɓólésuƙotᵃ v.
rifled iyérón v.
right itsɨ́rɔ́n v.; iyóón v.; tsɨ́rɔ́n v.; tɔɓɛ́ɔ́n v.
right (make) itsɨ́rɨ́tɛtɛ́s v.; tsɨ́rɨ́tɛtɛ́s v.; tɔɓɛitɛtɛ́s v.
right (typically) toɓéíón v.
right away dɨr adv.
right hand ŋƙáƙákwɛ̀tᵃ n.
right here nayé kɔ̀nà dem.
right hindleg ɲálán n.
righthand rib ŋƙáƙáŋabér n.
rigid ɓotsódòn v.; kɛtérémòn v.; tsérekékón v.
rigidly ɓòtsᵒ ideo.
rind bodɔ́kᵃ n.
ring ilɨ́ɲɨ́rés v.; ilɨrɛs v.
ring (a bell) iwés v.
ring (finger) ɲákaɓɔɓwáátᵃ n.
ring (of ears) iwákón v.
ring (stick) ɲókokor n.; ɲɔkɔlɔɓɛr n.
ring hollow ɗɛʉɗéwɔ́n v.
ring of reeds nàtsìkwᵃ n.; ɲéleƙeré n.
ring-beam ɲolóɗo n.
ring-tone dikwᵃ n.
ringed itówóòn v.
ringlet (metal) àgɪ̀tᵃ n.
ringworm aɗáɗá n.
rinse ilailéés v.; ilɔ́lɔ́tsés v.
rinse (mouth) ígʉjʉgʉjés v.; imúmújés v.
rip dzɛrés v.

rip off (cheat) imɔɗɛs *v.*; imɔ́ɗɛ́sʉkɔtᵃ *v.*
ripe àèòn *v.*
ripe (nearly) its'ɔ́ƙɔ́n *v.*
ripen aeonuƙotᵃ *v.*; ƙádòn *v.*
ripen quickly hataikánón *v.*
ripen up aeétón *v.*
ripening kɔ̀ɓɔ̀n *v.*
ripped dzɛrɔ́sɔ́n *v.*; láládziránón *v.*
rise ŋkéétòn *v.*; ŋkóón *v.*; zikíbonuƙotᵃ *v.*
rise (of sun) tsòòn *v.*; tsoonuƙotᵃ *v.*
rise (of voice) ɔ́bɛ̀s *v.*
rise up (rebel) terémón *v.*
risk ɡaánàs *n.*
risky ɡaanón *v.*
ritual (do a) írés *n.*
ritual killing síts'ᵃ *n.*
river sàbà *n.*
river (small) ɔrɔr *n.*
river basin ɲɛrétᵃ *n.*
river bottom sàbààƙwᵃ *n.*
riverbank (opposite) ƙìròtᵃ *n.*
riverbed sàbààƙwᵃ *n.*
riverbed pool ɲéɓwál *n.*
roach lɔmɛ́jɛ́kɛlɛ́ *n.*
road muce *n.*; ɲerukuɗe *n.*
road grader séɓésìam *n.*
roam iwórón *v.*; térés *v.*
roamer ɓɛƙɛsɔsíám *n.*; irimesíám *n.*; iwóróníàm *n.*
roar ábʉ̀bʉ̀ƙɔ̀n *v.*; béúrètòn *v.*; erutánón *v.*; irúrúmòòn *v.*; xérón *v.*
roast jʉés *v.*
roast lightly iɔ́ɓɔ́rés *v.*
roasted jʉɔ́s *v.*
roasting ground naki̟ri̟kɛ̀tᵃ *n.*

robber lotáɗá *n.*; ŋuésíàm *n.*
robbery lotáɗánànès *n.*
robe ɲákaasó *n.*
robin-chat loƙírotᵃ *n.*
rock (crumbly) lɔkabʉ́ás *n.*
rock (large) taɓᵃ *n.*
rock (sedimentary) sáɲamátᵃ *n.*
rock (small) ɡwas *n.*
rock (soft) ɲékúkuse *n.*; sáɲamátᵃ *n.*
rock (table) ɡi̟zá *n.*
rock back and forth iikííkés *v.*; iukúúkés *v.*
rock crevice tsarátán *n.*
rock pool sátᵃ *n.*
rock pool water sátíkócue *n.*
rock well mɔƙɔr *n.*
rock well water mɔƙɔrɔ́cúé *n.*
rockily ɡàtsᵃ *ideo.*; ŋàr *ideo.*
rocky ɡatsádòn *v.*; ŋarʉ́dɔ̀n *v.*; rakákámòn *v.*
rocky outcrop kúcᵃ *n.*; riki̟ríkᵃ *n.*
rod jʉrʉm *n.*
rod (cleaning) súƙʉ́tési̟tsiri̟m *n.*
roil i̟bɔtsɛ́sá asi̟ *v.*; íɡùlàjòn *v.*
roll kaɓéléɓelánón *v.*; tsitsikes *v.*
roll a root tsitsikesa jɔtɛ́ *v.*
roll around aɓi̟ɓi̟lánón *v.*
roll around (in mouth) iɲɔ́lɔ́ɓɔ́ɲés *v.*
roll away tsitsíkésuƙota asi̟ *v.*
roll between hands tsutsukes *v.*
roll over iɓéléés *v.*; iɓéléìmètòn *v.*
roll repeatedly tsitsikiés *v.*
roll this way tsitsiketésá asi̟ *v.*
roll up i̟pɔ́pi̟rés *v.*; kaki̟rés *v.*; tɔɓi̟lɛtés *v.*
rolling sound dèrèdèr *ideo.*; kùrùkùr *ideo.*
Romans (biblical) Ŋi̟rɔmánɔ́niikᵃ *n.*

roof hogwarí *n.*
roof (of mouth) aƙár *n.*
roof ring (of reeds) ɲeleƙeré *n.*
roof tip (woven) tsùtᵃ *n.*
roofing sheet ɲámaamɓátᵃ *n.*
rooftop (inner) lɔɓîz *n.*
room naƙúlɛ́ *n.*
room (space) zɛƙɔ́áwᵃ *n.*
roomy ilɔ́lɔ́mɔ̀n *v.*; lalʉ́jɔ́n *v.*
roost itsélélèon *v.*
rooster gwácúrúkᵃ *n.*
root dakúsɔ́kᵃ *n.*; sɔkᵃ *n.*; sɔkɛdᵃ *n.*
root (of a tooth) kwayɔ́ɔ́kᵃ *n.*
rope ŋún *n.*; ún *n.*
rope (braided) natiɓᵃ *n.*
rope (tree bark) tɔ̀fɔ̀l *n.*
rot ɗutúɗutánónuƙotᵃ *v.*; masánétòn *v.*; mʉsánétòn *v.*
rotate ilɨrɛs *v.*; irímétòn *v.*; irímítetés *v.*; irímón *v.*
rotate around in irimes *v.*
rotate repeatedly ilirɨ́lɨ́rés *v.*
rotted ɗatáɗatánón *v.*
rotten ɗutúdòn *v.*; masánón *v.*
rotten (very) ɗùtᵘ *ideo.*
rotten at core ɓʉɓʉsánón *v.*
rotting ɗutúɗutánón *v.*
rotund pʉŋʉ́rʉ́mɔ̀n *v.*
rough ƙumúƙúmánón *v.*; rúgurugánón *v.*
rough (of a road) ƙumúƙúmánón *v.*
rough (of a surface) ŋaráɓámòn *v.*
roughen cɛ́ɓɛs *v.*
roughly gwèjᵋ *ideo.*
round ɗukúditésúƙotᵃ *v.*; ɗukúdòn *v.*; ilʉ́lʉ́ŋɔ́s *v.*; ɲásápari *n.*

round (and thick) baƙúlúmòn *v.*
round (make) ɗukúditésúƙotᵃ *v.*; ilʉ́lʉ́ŋɛ́s *v.*
round up ikoŋetés *v.*; ikwɛtɨ́kwétés *v.*; ƙalɨ́ƙálés *v.*; ságwès *v.*
roundly ɗùkᵘ *ideo.*
roused iƙúrúmós *v.*
rove tɛ́rɛs *v.*
rover ɓɛƙɛsɔsɨám *n.*; irimesíám *n.*
row iƙures *v.*
rub iríƙéés *v.*; jʉ́rɛs *v.*; ŋɨ́ɨ́ɗɛ́s *v.*
rub around iwulúwúlés *v.*
rub between fingers simiɗɨ́mɨ́ɗɛ́s *v.*
rub down/out jʉ́rɛ́sʉƙɔtᵃ *v.*; jʉrɛtés *v.*
rub in hands tsutsukɛs *v.*
rub off iɲiɲiés *v.*; ŋɨ́ɨ́ɗɛ́súƙɔtᵃ *v.*
rub vigorously ɨdʉlidʉlés *v.*
rubber ɗɔtɔ́ *n.*
rubber (eraser) ɲáráɓa *n.*
rubberily rɔ́ɓɔ *ideo.*
rubbery rɔɓɔ́dɔ̀n *v.*
rubbish tsʼʉtsʼʉ *n.*
rubbish pile tsʼʉtsʼʉ́áwᵃ *n.*
rubeola púrurú *n.*
ruffle dʉbɛ́s *v.*
rugged rúgurugánón *v.*
ruin imóɲíkees *v.*; imóɲíkeetés *v.*; ináƙúés *v.*; ináƙúetés *v.*; iraŋɛs *v.*; iraŋɛtés *v.*
ruined ináƙúós *v.*; ináƙúotós *v.*; iraŋɔs *v.*; iráŋúnánón *v.*
ruined (become) iraŋímétòn *v.*
ruinousness ƙʉts'ánánès *n.*
rule ipúƙéés *v.*; itsikɛs *n.*
ruler ipúƙéésíám *n.*; tòtwàrààm *n.*
rumble ɗukuɗúkón *v.*; iƙɨ́lɔ́n *v.*; tɔtɔanón *v.*
rumble off itíƙíròòn *v.*; itíríƙòòn *v.*

rumen ɲépʉnʉkᵃ n.
ruminate iɲáɗʉ́tés v.; ɲɛɓés v.
rumple imóɲíkees v.
rumple up imóɲíkeetés v.
run tsùwà v.
run (a direction) ŋàtɔ̀n v.
run (multiply) ŋatíón v.
run after irukes v.; irúkésukotᵃ v.
run after each other ríínós v.
run away duƙésúƙota mòràᵉ v.; moronuƙotᵃ v.; ŋatɔnʉƙɔtᵃ v.
run away (of many) iɗúzòn v.
run cold (of blood) ɓʉnʉ́mɔ́nà sèàᵉ v.
run hot (of blood) ɓʉnʉ́mɔ́nà sèàᵉ v.
run into ɨbaɗés v.; imánónuƙotᵃ v.; ɲimánétòn v.
run into (meet) imánétòn v.
run into repeatedly ɨbaɗiés v.
run off ikutses v.; ikútsésuƙotᵃ v.; ŋatɔnʉƙɔtᵃ v.
run out ídzòn v.
run this way ŋatétɔ́n v.
run-down kɔlɔlánón v.
running (send off) ŋatɨ́tésʉƙɔtᵃ v.
running jump (get a) itseɗítséɗòn v.
running naked lèdèr ideo.
running water lɔkájʉ́ n.
runt ƙʉ́ƙᵃ n.
runty séréƙeƙánón v.
rush iɓʉ́ŋón v.; ikɨrɨ́kɨ́rɔ̀n v.
rush into things ŋamiŋámón v.
rush off ipʉ́tésʉƙɔta así v.
rush out tsídzètòn v.
rust iróróòn v.; simɨ́rɔ́n v.
rustle ɓɛkɨɓékón v.
rustle up (food) iɗɔ́ɗɔ́és v.

rusty simɨránón v.
rusty (get) iɗolíɗólòn v.
Saba comorensis ɲamalil n.
sack hoɗésúƙotᵃ v.
sack (gunny) ɲéɗɛpiɗɛ́pᵃ n.; ɲéguniyá n.
sack (huge leather) tun n.
sack (large gunny) lomóŋin n.; ɲáwaawá n.
sack (leather) lokóoɗo n.
sack (nylon) ɲékisɛsɛ́ n.
sack (small plastic) ɲápaalí n.
sacrament ɲásakaraméntù n.
sacred place ɲekɨ́wɔ́rɨtᵃ n.
sacrifice síts'ᵃ n.
sacrifice against enemies loŋɔ́tásìts'ᵃ n.
sacrifice (funeral goat) ipúɲéés v.; sɛ́és v.
sacrifice (wedding) ɲékɨ́lama n.; ɲekʉma n.
sacrifice a goat cɛɛsá rié sàbàkᵉ v.
sacrum ɲɛtsir n.; ɲɛtsɨrɨɔ́kᵃ n.
sad itásónòn v.; sìŋòn v.; tasónón v.
saddle (donkey) ɲásaajᵃ n.
saddle (of a mountain) kwaréékwᵃ n.
safari ant kúduƙûdᵃ n.
safe ɲébeŋgí n.; toikíkón v.
safe-box ɲébeŋgí n.
safety (gun) bɔɗɔ́kᵃ n.; ŋáɲésɨ̀àwᵃ n.
safety pin ɲákwác n.
sag iƙɔ́nɔ́nɔ̀ɔ̀n v.
sag (of eyelids) irwápón v.
saggy ratatáɲón v.
sail iɔ́ɔ́rés v.; iɔ́ɔ́rɔ̀n v.
saintly dòòn v.
saliva tatᵃ n.
salivary glands ƙuts'átsʼíka ni tatí n.
salivate mʉ́lʉƙʉ́ƙɔ́n v.

saloon

saloon ɲáɓá *n.*
salt didigwarí *n.*; ɲémíli *n.*
Salvadora persica ɓaláŋ *n.*
same iríánòn *v.*
same (be the) ikwáánòn *v.*
sample kaites *v.*
sample from isɨkɨsékés *v.*; isésékés *v.*
sample many hamomos *v.*
sanctity daás *n.*
sand jɨmɨjɨmás *n.*; séɓés *v.*; sɨ́ɨ́tés *v.*
sand spring ɲakújá *n.*
sandal ŋaɗɛ́tá *n.*
sandal (rubber) ɲásánɗɔ̀l *n.*
Sansevieria robusta màlòr *n.*
Sansevieria species barat[a] *n.*; jɔ̂d[a] *n.*
sanza lokemú *n.*
sapless bɨlájámɔ̀n *v.*; daƙwádòn *v.*
Satan Siitán *n.*
sate cɨɨtésɨƙɔt[a] *v.*
sated cɨ̀ɔn *v.*
sated (become) cɨɔnɨƙɔt[a] *v.*; topwatíméton *v.*
satellite ɗɔxɛatá na ɓɛƙés *n.*
satiate cɨɨtésɨƙɔt[a] *v.*
satiated cɨ̀ɔn *v.*
satiated (become) cɨɔnɨƙɔt[a] *v.*; topwatíméton *v.*
satisfied cɨ̀ɔn *v.*
satisfy cɨɨtésɨƙɔt[a] *v.*
satisfy hunger topwátón *v.*
satisfy meat hunger itsɔ́ɨtésɨƙɔt[a] *v.*; itsɔ́ɔ́n *v.*; itsɔ́ɔ́nɨƙɔt[a] *v.*
saturated ilébìlèbètòn *v.*
Saturday Nárámɨram *n.*
Satureja species òŋòrìkwàts[a] *n.*

scar (big)

saucepan dóm *n.*; ɲásipiryá *n.*; ɲésipiriyá *n.*
saucepan (small) dómáɨm *n.*
saucer ɲásaaní *n.*
saunter ɨpɛ́ɛ́ɲésá asɨ́ *v.*
sausage tree sosóɓòs *n.*
savage ɦyɛtiɦyɛtɔs *v.*; ɦyɛ̀tɔ̀n *v.*; iɲɛ́ɛ́mɔ̀n *v.*; isɨ́lɨ́ánón *v.*
savagery ɦyɛtás *n.*
savannah dús *n.*
save girés *v.*; iɛtés *v.*
save (spiritually) hoɗetés *v.*
save oneself iɛtɛsá asɨ́ *v.*
saved (get) hoɗetésá asɨ́ *v.*
savior hoɗetésíam *n.*; iɛtɛ́sɨam *n.*
saw irikíríƙés *v.*; ɲéƙirikɨr *n.*
saw away at ifitífités *v.*
say kɨ̀tɔ̀n *v.*; kɨtɔnɨƙɔt[a] *v.*; tódètòn *v.*
say hello to ɨmáxánɛs *v.*
saying taɗápítotós *n.*
scab ɔmɔ́x *n.*
scabby sómomójón *v.*; tɔmɔ́tɔ́mánón *v.*
scabby person tɔmɔ́tɔ́mánɨ̀am *n.*
scabies kɔ́ts[a] *n.*
scaffolding (make) ɨpétéés *v.*
scald kɨpés *v.*; kɨpésɨƙɔt[a] *v.*
scale fâd[a] *n.*; ikókórés *v.*; kɔmɔ́m *n.*
scale (weighing) ɲeratíl *n.*
scale this way ikókóretés *v.*
scales ɲeratíl *n.*
scaly saŋaŋóòn *v.*
scamper up ɨtsɛ́tsɛɛ́s *v.*
scapula sawatɔ́ɔ́k[a] *n.*
scar ƙwár *n.*; ɔ́játàs *n.*; tás *n.*; tásêd[a] *n.*
scar (big) ɲepóros *n.*

scarce búúbuanón *v.*
scare kitítésuƙotᵃ *v.*; xɛɓites *v.*; xɛɓitésúƙɔtᵃ *v.*
scare away iremɛs *v.*
scare off iremɛs *v.*
scarified isɛɓɔs *v.*
scarify ɓunutiés *v.*; isɛɓɛs *v.*; isɛɓísɛ́ɓɛ́s *v.*
scarlet tsòn *ideo.*
scarred ɓulúrúmòn *v.*
scarred up seɓuránón *v.*
scat etsꞌᵃ *n.*
scatter ɓunúmón *v.*; ɓunutés *v.*; iɗɛrɛs *v.*; itwares *v.*; iwɛ́ɛ́lánón *v.*; iwɛ́ɛ́lɛ́s *v.*; iwɛ́ɛ́lɛ́suƙɔtᵃ *v.*; iwɛ́ɛ́lɛtés *v.*; toɓwaŋes *v.*
scatter (seeds) tɛwɛɛs *v.*
scatter around iɗɛríɗérɛ́s *v.*
scattered iɗɛrɔs *v.*; iwɛ́ɛ́lɔ́s *v.*; kazaanón *v.*
scattered around apɛ́tɛ́pɛ́tánón *v.*; iɗɛríɗérɔ́s *v.*
scavenge furés *v.*; iúréés *v.*
scavenger furésíàm *n.*
scent kɔ́ɪ́n *n.*
schlip! júrútᵘ *ideo.*; sɛ̀lɛ̀tᵋ *ideo.*
school ɲésukúl *n.*
school (technical) tékènɨkɔ̀l *n.*
school (vocational) tékènɨkɔ̀l *n.*
schooling ɲósomá *n.*
schunk! pùrùs *ideo.*
science ɲésɛ́ànɨ̀s *n.*
scissors ɲámakás *n.*
Sclerocarya birrea tsꞌɔkɔ́m *n.*
scold dɔxés *v.*; dɔxɛ́súƙɔtᵃ *v.*
scoliosis (have) toíɗón *v.*

scoop cɛɓɛn *n.*; tɛ́ɓɛs *v.*
scoop off ilaɓɛtɛ́s *v.*
scoop out (water) ɗalés *v.*
scoop out/up tɛ́ɓɛtɛ́s *v.*
scoop up cɛɓɛ́s *v.*; towoɗɛtɛ́s *v.*
scoop with fingers gafariés *v.*
scoot bɛ́berɛ́suƙota asɨ́ *v.*
scorch kɔrɛtɛ́s *v.*; kɔritɛtɛ́s *v.*
scorched kɔrɛ́tɔ́n *v.*
score isɛɓɛs *v.*
score (a goal) iƙólésuƙotᵃ *v.*
scored isɛɓɔs *v.*
scorn míjɛ́s *v.*; tsíítés *v.*
scorpion lóɗíkór *n.*
scorpion (water) lòcòrò *n.*
scorpion herb lóɗíkórócɛmɛ́r *n.*
scour (an area) iɗɛŋɛs *v.*
scoured iɗɛ́ŋímètòn *v.*
scourge iɓúŋéés *v.*
scout irimɛsíàm *n.*; rɔtéàm *n.*
scout bee páupáwᵃ *n.*
scout out irimírímés *v.*
scowl iɲíkón *v.*
scowling (begin) iɲíkétòn *v.*
scraggy gɔ́gɔ̀rɔ̀mɔ̀n *v.*
scramble ifáfáɲés *v.*; ilɛ́pón *v.*
scramble down kukuanón *v.*
scramble up ifɛ́ɗɛ́lɛ́s *v.*; ilɛ́pɛ́suƙɔtᵃ *v.*; imɔrímɔ́rɛ́s *v.*
scrambled up imɔrímɔ́rɔ́s *v.*
scrap ƙwɛsɛ́ *n.*
scrap metal (piece of) ɲɛpɛlɛrɛŋ *n.*
scrape fɔ́fɔ́tɛ́s *v.*; ifɔɛs *v.*; wówójɛ́s *v.*
scrape clean tikitɛtɛ́s *v.*
scrape off bátsɛ́s *v.*; iwalɛtɛ́s *v.*; rɛ́kɛ́s *v.*; tukurɛs *v.*

scratch gwegweritiés v.; súƙútés v.; súútés v.
scratch (with claws) soƙoríties v.
scratch off sɛkés v.; sɛkésúƙɔtᵃ v.
scratch up ikúkúrés v.; tukures v.; tukutes v.
scratch vigorously koxésúƙotᵃ v.
scratched gwegweritiós v.
scrawl gwegweritiés v.; wíziwizetés v.
scrawled gwegweritiós v.
scrawny kalɛ́ɛ́tsɛránón v.; rɛƙéɲémɔ̀n v.
scream ikwɨ́lɨ́lɔ̀n v.
screech iyíyéés v.
screw around on errand ɗipímón v.
screw up hamʉjés v.
scribble gwegweritiés v.; wíziwizetés v.
scribbled gwegweritiós v.
scripture (Christian) Ɲábáɨ́ɓɔ̀l n.
scrotal swelling ɲɛkwɨ n.
scrounge for furés v.
scrub ríjᵃ n.; súƙútés v.; súútés v.
scrub brush ɲecaaƙo n.
scrub off sɛkés v.; sɛkésúƙɔtᵃ v.
scrubby kalɛ́ɛ́tsɛránón v.
scrubland ɲáɓwa n.; ríjíkaajíkᵃ n.
scruff fɛ̀tìfɛ̀tᵃ n.
scruff (fat) nɨ̀tsɨnɨ̀tsᵃ n.
scrumptious ɗɔkɔ́dɔ̀n v.; ritídòn v.
scrumptiously ɗɔ̀kɔ ideo.
scrunch ɨ̀mɨ̀ɨ́ɨ́més v.
scrunch up ɨtʉsɛtés v.; tusuketés v.; tusúkón v.
scrutinize ipɨ́jɨ́kés v.
sculpt bɛretés v.; sotés v.; sotetés v.
scum kɨrarapᵃ n.
scurf kɔmɔ́m n.
scurfy saŋáŋóòn v.
scurry up ɨfɛɗɛ́lɛ́s v.; sekweres v.
sea ɲánam n.
seal ilies v.; iliíliés v.
sealed iliílíós v.; ilios v.
seamless iliílíós v.
seamster tʉfésɨ̀àm n.
seamstress tʉfésɨ̀àm n.
sear iɓues v.
search (an area) iɗɛŋɛs v.
search (pat down) tárábes v.
search all over (pat down) tárábiés v.
search for bɛɗés v.; bɛɗetés v.; ikʉjɛs v.
search in vain irójiés v.
searched over iɗéɲímètòn v.
season ɛfitɛs v.; íbutsurés v.; iwéwérés v.; tsóyᵃ n.
season (dry) ôdzᵃ n.; ódzatsóyᵃ n.
season (rainy) diditsóyᵃ n.; ɔtáyᵃ n.
seasoning ɲéɓisár n.
seat kàràtsᵃ n.; zɛƙɔ́áwᵃ n.
seated zɛ̀ƙwɔ̀n v.
seated (of many) góƙón v.
sebum îdwᵃ n.
secede tatsáɗón v.
seclude ipátsésʉƙotᵃ v.
seclude oneself ipátsésʉƙɔta asɨ́ v.
second (be the) mitɔna ɗɨ́ɛ́ lɛɓétsóni v.
second (one) ɗa lɛɓétsóni pro.
secret búdòs v.
secretary karan n.
secrete ɓɔ́rɨ́tɔ̀n v.
secretor ƙùts'àts'ᵃ n.
section bácɨ́kᵃ n.; itiɓes v.; itiɓítíɓés v.; julés v.; ƙɔ́dɔ̀l n.
section (area) nabɨdɨtᵃ n.
section (military) ɲésékíxìòn n.

section (plant) ɲékel *n.*
section (space) naƙúlɛ́ *n.*
secure toikíkón *v.*
Securinega virosa ɲalakas *n.*
security ŋíkísila *n.*; ɲɛkɨsɨl *n.*
security officer (government) tirifiesíáma ɲápukánɨ́ *n.*
seduce súbɨtɛ́súƙɔta asɨ́ *v.*
see enɛ́s *v.*; enésúƙotᵃ *v.*; walámón *v.*
see stars ɨmɛ́ɗɛ́tɔna ekwí *v.*
see-through tsaórómòn *v.*
seed eɗeɗᵃ *n.*; egésá ekwí *v.*; ekwᵃ *n.*; ekweɗᵃ *n.*; iŋárúrètòn *v.*
seed butter ɲówoɗí *n.*
seed mixture (nuptial) loŋazutᵃ *n.*
seed oil útɔ̀ *n.*
seed(s) kiɲom *n.*
seedeater (yellow-rumped) jɨlɨ́wᵃ *n.*
seeded iŋárúròn *v.*
seeds ekwin *n.*
seeds (have) iŋárúròn *v.*
seeds of jàwᵃ ílekó *n.*
seeing as how naɨ́tá *subordconn.*
seek bɛ́ɗɛ́s *v.*; bɛɗɛtɛ́s *v.*; ɨkʉjɛs *v.*; ɨmɨ́tɨ́ŋɛɛ́s *v.*
seemingly ɨ́kwà *adv.*; ókò *adv.*
seen lélɔ́n *v.*; takánón *v.*
seen (make) kɛtɛ́lɨtɛtɛ́s *v.*
seen clearly ilééránón *v.*; kɛtélɔ́n *v.*
seen dimly misimísón *v.*
seen faintly misimísón *v.*
seep tɔfɔ́ɗɔ́n *v.*
seer ɲakujíícíkáàm *n.*
seesaw iyopíyópòn *v.*
seethe tabúón *v.*
seethe over tabúétòn *v.*

segment itiɓes *v.*; itiɓítíɓés *v.*; julam *n.*; julés *v.*
segment (plant) ɲékel *n.*
segment (small) julamáím *n.*
segregate ilɔ́ɗɨ́ŋɛ́s *v.*; tereties *v.*
segregated teretiós *v.*
segregation ɲoloɗiŋ *n.*
segregative ilɔ́ɗɨ́ŋánón *v.*
seism ɲeríkirikᵃ *n.*
seize ɛ́nɛ́sʉƙɔtᵃ *v.*; ɨkamɛ́súƙɔtᵃ *v.*; ɨrakiesúƙota asɨ́ *v.*; ɨrákímétòn *v.*; ɨrɛɗɛs *v.*; tokopes *v.*; tokópésuƙotᵃ *v.*
seize frequently reɲíónuƙotᵃ *v.*
seizure (have a) ɨrákímétòn *v.*
seizures (have) ɨrakiesúƙota asɨ́ *v.*; reɲíónuƙotᵃ *v.*
Selaginella phillipsiana múmùtᵃ *n.*
select ɗumɛtɛ́s *v.*; iɗókóliés *v.*; iƙɛ́ƙɛ́ɛ́s *v.*; iƙɛlɛs *v.*; iƙɛlɛtɛ́s *v.*; ƙélɛ́s *v.*; tɔsɛɛtɛ́s *v.*; xɔ́bɛtɛ́s *v.*
select categorically isɨ́ɨ́lɛtɛ́s *v.*
select iteratively ƙélíetés *v.*
selected xɔ́bɔtɔ́s *v.*
self as *pro.*; nêbᵃ *n.*
self-centered reíɗòn *v.*
self-cleanse fɨtésuƙota gúróᵉ *v.*
self-controlled ɨritsésá asɨ́ *v.*; toikíkón *v.*
self-important iwɔ́ƙɔ́n *v.*
selfish hábòn *v.*
selfish person kiɓèɓèàm *n.*
selfishness hábàs *n.*
sell dzígwès *v.*; dzígwesuƙotᵃ *v.*
seller dzígwesuƙotiám *n.*
semen ɗír *n.*
semester ɲátám *n.*
seminar ɲésémìnà *n.*
send eréges *v.*
send back rajésúƙotᵃ *v.*

send early isókítésuƙotᵃ *v.*
send in a message mɛnétón *v.*
send off running ŋatɨ́tɛ́sʉƙɔtᵃ *v.*
send out a message mɛnɔnʉƙɔtᵃ *v.*
send soaring ɨɔ́ɔ́rɛ́s *v.*
send straight to tɔɓɛitɛtɛ́s *v.*
senile dúnésòn *v.*; itúléròn *v.*; kamudurudádòn *v.*
senile (become) itúléronuƙotᵃ *v.*
sense ƙanɛtɛ́s *v.*
sensitive (to light) tɔtsɔ́ɔ́n *v.*
sentry itelesíám *n.*; itelesíáma kíjáᵉ *n.*
separate ɗusɛ́s *v.*; ɗusɛ́súƙotᵃ *v.*; terémétòn *v.*; terémón *v.*; terémón *v.*; terémónuƙotᵃ *v.*; terɛ́s *v.*; teretíes *v.*
separate by shaking ɨkákɛ́ɛ́s *v.*
separate oneself terɛ́súƙota asɨ *v.*
separate out terétéránitɛ́súƙotᵃ *v.*
separate out by shaking ɨkákɛ́ɛ́sʉƙɔtᵃ *v.*
separated teretíós *v.*
separated out terétéránón *v.*
September Lotyakᵃ *n.*; Nakariɓᵃ *n.*
sequester ɨpátsɛ́sʉƙɔtᵃ *v.*
sequester oneself ɨpátsɛ́suƙɔta asɨ *v.*
serial killer ɨkɛɲɨkɛ́ɲɛ́sɨ̀am *n.*
serious (be) mitɔna síriàs *v.*
seriously ɓaᵘ *ideo.*
serous fluid tsétᵃ *n.*
serpent ídèm *n.*
serum tsétᵃ *n.*
serval ɲálukutúju *n.*
servant ŋípáƙásìam *n.*
servant (domestic) terégiama awáᵉ *n.*
servant (indentured) ŋiléɓúìam *n.*
serve (food) gárés *v.*
service ɨsáɓɨ́sɨŋɛɛ́s *v.*; terêgᵃ *n.*

service (religious) wáán *n.*
sesame kaɲʉm *n.*
Sesamum indicum kaɲʉm *n.*
set (joint) rajés *v.*
set (of sun) itsólóŋòn *v.*; tɔɔnʉƙɔtᵃ *v.*
set agape hádoletés *v.*
set aside ɨŋáɗɛ́ɛ́s *v.*; ɨŋáɗɛ́ɛ́sʉƙɔtᵃ *v.*
set fire to ɗamatés *v.*
set free hoɗɛ́s *v.*; hoɗɛ́súƙotᵃ *v.*; hoɗetés *v.*
set loose itsues *v.*; itsuetés *v.*
set nearby taraŋɛ́s *v.*
set oneself apart ƙɛ́lɛ́sʉƙota asɨ *v.*; terɛ́súƙota asɨ *v.*
set out ɗóɗésa mucɛɛ́ *v.*
set record straight ɨténitɛtɛ́sá tódàᵉ *v.*
set straight ɨténitɛtɛ́s *v.*
set up ɨnábɛtɛ́s *v.*
set up (a beehive) rɔ́ƙɛ́s *v.*
set up (gel) tɔsɔ́ɗɔ́kɔ̀n *v.*
set upright itsɨrɨ́tɛtɛ́s *v.*; tsɨ́rɨ́tɛtɛ́s *v.*
settle ínésuƙotᵃ *v.*; zɛƙwétón *v.*
settle a dispute epitésúƙota tódàᵉ *v.*
settle down ɗipímón *v.*; epítésuƙotᵃ *v.*; toíésuƙotᵃ *v.*; zɛƙwétón *v.*; zɛƙwitɛtɛ́s *v.*
settle in toƙízeesá asɨ *v.*; toƙízèètòn *v.*
settle on ɲʉmɛtɛ́s *v.*
seven tude ńda kiɗi léɓɛtsᵉ *num.*
seven o'clock ɲásáatɨ́á kɔ̀nɨ̀kᵉ *n.*
seventeen toomíní ńda kiɗi túde ńda kiɗi léɓɛtsᵉ *n.*
seventy toomínékwa túde ńda kiɗi léɓɛtsᵉ *n.*
sever ɗusɛ́s *v.*; ɗusɛ́súƙotᵃ *v.*; ɗusutes *v.*; ɨkɛ́ɲɛ́ɗɛ́s *v.*; tɔŋɛɗes *v.*
several jalájálánón *v.*
sew tʉfɛ́s *v.*
sewing machine ɲájarán *n.*

sex epᵃ *n.*
sex (have frequent) ɓútánés *v.*
sex (have unprotected) tsʼɨtsʼɔ́n *v.*
sex (have) èpòn *v.*
sexual afterglow (feel) irákímétòn *v.*
sexual intercourse epᵃ *n.*
sexual relations epᵃ *n.*
sexually insatiable (of a woman) ɓòɓòn *v.*
sexually-transmitted disease ɲamakaje *n.*
shade kur *n.*; kúrúkúr *n.*
shadeless ságwàràmòn *v.*
shades (glasses) ɲékiyóika ni fetí *n.*
shadow ikókótés *v.*; kúrúkúr *n.*
shaft morókᵃ *n.*
shaft (arrow) ɲámalɨ́dàkwᵃ *n.*
shaft (borehole) ɲatsʉʉmáhò *n.*
shaft (penile) ɲésɛɛɓɔ́ *n.*
shaft of light bás *n.*; sʉ́wᵃ *n.*
shaggy gaúsúmòn *v.*
shake iɓokɛs *v.*; kìtòn *v.*; kwalɨ́kwálòn *v.*
shake (begin to) kitétón *v.*
shake (make) kitítésʉƙotᵃ *v.*
shake back and forth ilɨ́lɨ́ŋés *v.*; iliŋɨ́lɨ́ŋés *v.*; ilitsílítsés *v.*
shake in a pan ilaƙɛs *v.*; ilaƙɨ́láƙés *v.*; iláláƙés *v.*
shake off iɓókésʉƙotᵃ *v.*; ilílítsés *v.*; iwatíwátés *v.*
shake out iɓutúɓútés *v.*; ilílítsés *v.*; ixóxóƙés *v.*; ixʉƙúxúƙés *v.*; ixúxúƙés *v.*
shake out noisily ixaxɛɛs *v.*
shake side to side ilitsílítsés *v.*
shake to separate ikákéɛ́s *v.*; ikákéɛ́sʉƙotᵃ *v.*

shake up and down itéƙítéƙés *v.*
shake vigorously ɨbɔbɔtsés *v.*; ɨbɔtsés *v.*
shaking sound ɓʉlʉɓʉl *ideo.*
shallow tɛƙɛ́dɛ̀mɔ̀n *v.*; tɛƙɛ́zɛ̀mɔ̀n *v.*; tiƙódzòmòn *v.*
shallowly concave ɓɛtélémɔ̀n *v.*; fɛtélémɔ̀n *v.*
shame ɓetsʼitetés *v.*; iryámítetésá ŋiléétsìkᵉ *v.*; ŋiléétsᵃ *n.*
shameful person ŋiléétsìàm *n.*
shamefulness ŋiléétsìnànès *n.*
shape bɛrɛtés *v.*; itues *v.*; ituetés *v.*
shape (with a blade) bɔ́tés *v.*
shard gúɗúsam *n.*
share tɔmɔram *n.*; tɔmɔrɛs *v.*
share with each other tɔmɔ́rɨ́nɔ́s *v.*
shareable tɔmɔram *n.*
sharp tsʼɨtsʼɔ́n *v.*
sharp (of eyesight) tsɔ́tsɔ́n *v.*
sharp (make) tsʼɨtsʼɨ́tésʉƙotᵃ *v.*; tsʼɨtsʼɨ́tɛtɛ́s *v.*
sharp in taste ɓariɓárón *v.*; ɓárikíkón *v.*
sharpen banés *v.*; tsʼɨtsʼɨ́tésʉƙotᵃ *v.*; tsʼɨtsʼɨ́tɛtɛ́s *v.*
shart iɓɨ́ɔ́n *v.*
shatter ɓilíɓílés *v.*; kwɛtsʼés *v.*
shattered (get) kwɛtsʼémón *v.*
shave bɔ́tés *v.*; ipɛlɛs *v.*
shave (even) ikʉlɛs *v.*; ikʉlɛtés *v.*; ikwalɛs *v.*
shave (hair) gɨ́jés *v.*
shave off iƙwéƙwérés *v.*
shave off (hair) gijɛtés *v.*
shaving ipɛlɛtam *n.*
shaving (wood) bɔtɛtam *n.*
shawl ɲáléso *n.*; ɲáwáro *n.*
shawl (cotton) ɲákamariƙán *n.*
shawl (leather) xɔŋɔŋ *n.*

sheaf zɨkam *n.*
sheaf (of crops) ɲénéne *n.*
sheath nakɨrɔ́r *n.*; ɲaɓúrɛ́t[a] *n.*
shed fòlòn *v.*; ɲésitó *n.*; tuɓutes *v.*; tuɓútésuƙot[a] *v.*
shed blood tɔyɔ́ɔ́n *v.*
shedding ɗáráɗáránón *v.*
sheep ɗóɗò *n.*
sheep tail ɗóɗotimóy[a] *n.*
sheep-leather clothing ɗóɗòƙwàz *n.*
sheep-leather skirt ɗóɗòƙwàz *n.*
sheet of paper kàbàɗ[a] *n.*
sheet of roofing ɲámaamɓát[a] *n.*
shell fâd[a] *n.*
shell (casing) ɲéɓurocó *n.*; ɲɛsɛpɛɗɛ *n.*
shell (of a beehive) ɗòl *n.*
shell (snail) irex *n.*; tɔkɔtɔƙáhò *n.*
shell (tortoise) ròɡìròɡ[a] *n.*
shelter kur *n.*; rɨmés *v.*
shelter (grass) ɲékɨsakát[a] *n.*
shelter from rain rɨmésá dìdìù *v.*
shepherd còòkààm *n.*; cookés *v.*
shield iƙɨɛs *v.*; kesen *n.*
shift ɨméérés *v.*; irotes *v.*; ɨsútón *v.*
shift (position) ɨsɔ́sɔ́ŋɔ́s *v.*
shift repeatedly irotírótés *v.*
shilling kaúdzèèkw[a] *n.*; ŋásɛntáɨ̀èkw[a] *n.*
shillings ŋásɛntáy[a] *n.*
shimmer riɓiríɓón *v.*
shin ɓɔ́l *n.*
shinbone tsɛrɛ́k[a] *n.*
shindig ɲápáti *n.*
shine ɨwɨrón *v.*
shine (begin to) ɨwɨrɛ́tòn *v.*
shine brightly ɨraɨ́rɔ̀n *v.*

shine forth (of heavenly bodies) júétɔ̀n *v.*
shinny up ifɛ́ɗɛ́lɛ́s *v.*
shiny pirídòn *v.*
ship irotes *v.*; tsídzès *v.*
ship away tsídzesuƙot[a] *v.*
ship off tsídzesuƙot[a] *v.*
ship repeatedly irotírótés *v.*
shirt ɲásáti *n.*
shish kebab rɔam *n.*
shit nts'áƙón *v.*
shit! ɗùrù *n.*
shiver kìtòn *v.*; kwalɨ́kwálɔ̀n *v.*
shiver (begin to) kitétón *v.*
shiver (make) kitítésuƙot[a] *v.*
shock iɓálétòn *v.*; lilétón *v.*; toɓules *v.*
shocking iɓálɔ́n *v.*; toɓúlón *v.*
shoe taƙáy[a] *n.*
shoe (cow-leather) fiyɔtaƙáy[a] *n.*
shoe (elephant leather) oŋoritaƙáy[a] *n.*
shoe (leather) ŋáɓʉʉrá *n.*
shoe (open-toed) taƙáá na ɲáɲós *n.*
shoe (tire rubber) ɲómotokátáƙáy[a] *n.*
shoe-strap lɔkaapɨ́n *n.*
shoelace lɔkaapɨ́n *n.*
shoot ídzès *v.*; ídzesuƙot[a] *v.*; ƙádès *v.*; ƙádesuƙot[a] *v.*
shoot across ídzesa asɨ́ *v.*
shoot over ídzesa asɨ́ *v.*; toɓésá asɨ́ *v.*
shoot repeatedly ídziidziés *v.*; ƙádiƙadiés *v.*
shop ɗʉkán *n.*; ɲáɗʉkán *n.*
short kúɗon *v.*; ŋʉɗúsʉ́mɔ̀n *v.*; ŋʉsúlʉ́mɔ̀n *v.*
short (make) kuɗítésuƙot[a] *v.*
short (of many) kúɗaakón *v.*
shorten kuɗítésuƙot[a] *v.*
shortness kuɗás *n.*

shorts ɲosoƙoloké *n.*
shorts (pair of) ɲésiriwáli *n.*
shortsighted mumúánón *v.*
should ɨtámáánón *v.*
shoulder sawat^a *n.*
shoulder bone sawatɔ́ɔ́ƙ^a *n.*
shout bofétón *v.*; bófón *v.*; iƙɨ́lɔ́n *v.*; iƙúétòn *v.*; iƙúón *v.*; iƙúónuƙot^a *v.*; nɔsátón *v.*
shout at ɨyáyɛ́ɛ́s *v.*
shout triumphantly iwóŋón *v.*
shouter nɔ̀sààm *n.*
shouting nɔ̀s *n.*
shove ɲékitiyó *n.*; ɲɛɲɛrɛs *v.*; toremes *v.*
shove away iɓwátésuƙot^a *v.*; itsɔ́résʉƙɔt^a *v.*
shovel (power-) ɲétɛrɛƙitaa na kwɛtá^ɛ *n.*
show ɗóɗés *v.*; ɗoɗésúƙot^a *v.*; ɗóɗítetés *v.*; enitésúƙot^a *v.*; enitetés *v.*; iléérániteté *v.*; itétémés *v.*
show appreciation to caregiver(s) taat-sesa ɗoɗóɓò^e *v.*
show favoritism tereties *v.*
show hospitality to ewanes *v.*; ewanetés *v.*
show off inésóòn *v.*
show oneself ɗóɗítetésá asɨ *v.*
show to be wrong isalɨtés *v.*
show up takánétòn *v.*
show up unwelcomely imɨŋóòn *v.*
shower féíàw^a *n.*; féón *v.*
shower (bombard) ɨdʉrɛ́s *v.*
showering féy^a *n.*
shred dzɛrɛ́s *v.*; dzeretiés *v.*; dzeretiésuƙot^a *v.*; kàbàɗ^a *n.*
shredded dzɛ́rɛ́dzɛránón *v.*; dzɛrɔ́sɔ́n *v.*; láládziránón *v.*

shrew ɗɔ́f *n.*
shrewd nɔɔsánón *v.*
shrewdness nɔ́ɔ́s *n.*
shriek ɨkwɨ́lɨ́lɔ̀n *v.*; iyíyéés *v.*
shrike bɨ́lɔɔrɔ́ *n.*
shrike (white-crested) kɨ́yɔɔrɔ́ *n.*
shrill ɓòɓòn *v.*
shrimpy sɛ́rɛ́ƙɛƙánón *v.*
shrink kiɗɔnʉƙɔt^a *v.*; tɔ́ɗɔ́nʉƙɔt^a *v.*
shrink back rìmòn *v.*
shrink back from itírákés *v.*
shrink down kwatsítésuƙot^a *v.*; kwátsónuƙot^a *v.*
shrink up hɛɗɔ́nʉƙɔt^a *v.*
shrivel kiɗɔnʉƙɔt^a *v.*; tɔ́ɗɔ́nʉƙɔt^a *v.*
shrivel up hɛɗɔ́nʉƙɔt^a *v.*; lolómónuƙot^a *v.*
shriveled bɔrɔ́ɗɔ́mɔ̀n *v.*; ƙɔ́rɔmɔmɔ́n *v.*; mitɨrɨmɔ̀n *v.*; tɔ́ɗɔ́n *v.*
shrub dakw^a *n.*
shrub species alárá *n.*; ɓets'akáw^a *n.*; ɓóéɗ^a *n.*; dìdì *n.*; gɛbɛj^a *n.*; gomói *n.*; ikitínicɛmɛ́r *n.*; jàw^a *n.*; lócén *n.*; lojeméy^a *n.*; lorít^a *n.*; lóúpè *n.*; marúƙúcɛmɛ́r *n.*; mét^a *n.*; milékw^a *n.*; misá *n.*; misɨ́ás *n.*; mɔ̀z *n.*; múrotsiò *n.*; ɲérɨkirɨ́k^a *n.*; ɲónomokére *n.*; ɔgɔn *n.*; sugur *n.*; súr *n.*; ts'ʉgʉram *n.*; tâb^a *n.*; tíkòŋ *n.*; turunet^a *n.*
shrug imɨ́mɨ́jés *v.*
shrunk tɔ́ɗɔ́n *v.*
shrunken bɔrɔ́ɗɔ́mɔ̀n *v.*
shuck poɗés *v.*; poɗetés *v.*
shudder nérɨnɛ́rɔ́n *v.*; tsábatsabánón *v.*
shuffle iyaŋíyáŋés *v.*
shush fiyakwés *v.*
shut kɔkés *v.*; kɔkɛtés *v.*; kokimétòn *v.*; mʉts'ʉtɛs *v.*
shut (make) kɔkitɛtés *v.*

shut down kɔkɛtés v.
shut oneself in kɔkɛ́sá asɨ́ v.
shut out kɔkɛ́súƙɔtᵃ v.
shut up iɓótóŋésá akáᵉ v.; ijɛ́mɨ́tésʉƙɔtᵃ v.; ijɛ́mɔ́nʉƙɔtᵃ v.; mʉts'ʉ́tésʉƙɔtᵃ v.
shut up (lock) iɓótóŋés v.
shut up repeatedly mʉts'ʉtiesúƙɔtᵃ v.
shy xɛ̀ɓɔ̀n v.
shy person xɛɓásɨ̀àm n.
shyness xɛɓás n.
sibling ŋgóím n.
sick mòòn v.
sick (of many) mayaakón v.
sick (queasy) itikítíkòn v.
sickle bush gùr n.
sickness màywᵃ n.; ɲeɗeke n.
sickness (kind of) loɓáyᵃ n.
sickness (mild) ɲeɗekéím n.
sickness spirit ɲeɗekéím n.
side ayᵃ n.; kwaywᵃ n.; kweedᵃ n.; xán n.
side (of hill or mountain) rutetᵃ n.
side of clothing ŋabérá ƙwàzàᵉ n.
side part ŋábèrèdᵃ n.
side-striped kámáriós v.
sidearm ɲɛpɨ́sɨ́tɔ̀l n.
sides kwàin n.
sidestep kiɗɔnʉƙɔtᵃ v.
sideswipe iɛ́bès v.
sidetrack a discussion iɓátésʉƙɔta mɛnáᵋ v.
sideways ŋabérᵒ n.
sidle up to rɔɲésá asɨ́ v.
sieve isalɛs v.; isalɛtés v.; ɲékeikéyᵃ n.; rɔrés v.
sieve (make) isalɨtés v.
sift isalɛs v.; isalɛtés v.; rɔrés v.

sift (make) isalɨtés v.
sight (front, of a weapon) ɲeteeɗe n.
sight (weapon) ɲɛ́lɨmɨrá n.
sign egésá kwetáᵋ v.; isáániŋeés v.; iwetés v.; ɲámátsar n.
sign the cross iwésá ɲémusaláɓàᵉ v.
sign up for xɔ́ɓɛtésá asɨ́ v.
signal ɲɨ́zès v.
signal (smoke) ts'ûdᵃ n.
significance zeísêdᵃ n.
significant itíónòn v.; zízòn v.
silence ijɛ́mɨ́tésʉƙɔtᵃ v.
silent ijɛ́mɔ́n v.; líídòn v.
silently jɨ̀r ideo.; lì ideo.
silk ɲɨ́sɨl n.
silkily jàm ideo.
silky-smooth jamúdòn v.
similar ikwáánòn v.
simmer wádòn v.
simple ɓàɲɔ̀n v.; batánón v.; iɓámɔ́n v.
simplicity ɓaɲás n.
simsim kaɲʉm n.
simulate ikwáánitetés v.
simultaneously ikéé kɔ̀n n.
sin ɲasécón n.; tɔsɛ́sɔ́n v.
since kwààkᵉ n.; naɨ́tá subordconn.; nàpèì subordconn.; ɲàpèì subordconn.
since earlier today kwaake nákᵃ n.
since long ago kwààkè nòkᵒ n.
since yesterday kwààkè sɨ̀n n.
sincerely gúróɛ́nᵓ n.
sinew kon n.
sinewy simánón v.
sing irúkón v.
sing and dance òidìkwòn v.
sing while walking tofóróƙánón v.
singe iwííɲés v.

singer ìrùkààm *n.*; irukósíam *n.*
singing ìrùk[a] *n.*
singing ants jɔrɔr *n.*
singing hall ìrùkàhò *n.*
single file ƙɨ́dzinós *v.*
single out tereties *v.*
singled out teretiós *v.*
sinistral betsínón *n.*
sink ɓuƙonuƙot[a] *v.*
sink (of heart) mulúráŋòn *v.*
sink teeth into titikes *v.*
sip abᵾtɛtés *v.*; ɨwɛtɛs *v.*; tsᵾɓés *v.*; tsᵾɓɛtés *v.*
sip continually abutiés *v.*
sippable food abutiam *n.*
sir ámáze *n.*; ámázeám *n.*
sire cúrúk[a] *n.*
sire (dog) ŋókícikw[a] *n.*
sisal rope baratɨsím *n.*; màlòr *n.*
sisal species bàdònìsìm *n.*; barat[a] *n.*; jɔ́d[a] *n.*; màlòr *n.*
sister (Catholic) ɓɨ́kɨ̀rà *n.*
sister (his/her/its) yeát[a] *n.*
sister (my) yeá *n.*
sister (your) yáó *n.*
sister's husband's sibling (my) ɲ́cugwám *n.*
sister-in-law (brother's wife's sister) ugwam *n.*
sister-in-law (brother's wife) námúí *n.*
sister-in-law (her husband's sister) ntsínámúí *n.*
sister-in-law (his brother's wife's sister) ntsúgwám *n.*
sister-in-law (his brother's wife) ntsínámúí *n.*
sister-in-law (his wife's sister) ntsúgwám *n.*
sister-in-law (his/her child's spouse's mother) ntsíɲót[a] *n.*
sister-in-law (his/her sister's husband's sister) ntsúgwám *n.*
sister-in-law (husband's brother's wife) ɛán *n.*
sister-in-law (husband's sister) námúí *n.*
sister-in-law (my brother's wife's sister) ɲ́cugwám *n.*
sister-in-law (my brother's wife) ɲ́cinamúí *n.*
sister-in-law (my husband's sister) ɲ́cinamúí *n.*
sister-in-law (my wife's sister) ɲ́cugwám *n.*
sister-in-law (my) ɛdécèk[a] *n.*
sister-in-law (sister's husband's sister) ugwam *n.*
sister-in-law (wife's sister) ugwam *n.*
sister-in-law (your brother's wife's sister) bugwám *n.*
sister-in-law (your brother's wife) binamúí *n.*
sister-in-law (your child's spouse's mother) biɲót[a] *n.*
sister-in-law (your husband's sister) binamúí *n.*
sister-in-law (your sister's husband's sister) bugwám *n.*
sister-in-law (your wife's sister) bugwám *n.*
sisterhood yeatínánès *n.*
sisterliness yeatínánès *n.*
sit zɛƙwétón *v.*
sit (legs straight) ɨtéélòn *v.*

sit (make) zɛƙwitɛtés v.
sit alone (silently) zɛ̀ƙwɔ̀nà lìòò v.
sit around iríƙímánón v.
sit decently iɗimésá asɨ́ v.
sit dejectedly tatónón v.
sit down zɛƙwétón v.; zɛƙwitɛtés v.
sit down (of many) goƙaakétòn v.
sit indecently iŋáúánón v.; tafakésá asɨ́ v.
sit legs apart iŋátsátsóòn v.
sit on a stool iƙáráròn v.
sit on the ground ipájón v.
sitting zɛ̀ƙwɔ̀n v.
sitting (of many) góƙón v.
sitting as a group góƙᵃ n.
sitting place dìywᵃ n.; góƙáàwᵃ n.; zɛƙɔ́áwᵃ n.
sitty-sit! dᵾᵾdú nurs.
six tude ńdà kèɗɨ kòn num.
six o'clock ɲásáatikaa mitátie toomíní ńda kiɗi lébètsᵉ n.
sixteen toomíní ńda kiɗi túde ńdà kèɗɨ kòn n.
sixty toomínékwa túde ńdà kèɗɨ kòn n.
skeletal iróƙóòn v.; itóƙóƙòòn v.; kwédekwedánón v.; lotímálèmòn v.
skeleton ɔkitín n.
skewer rɔ́és v.
skewered rɔ́ɔ́s v.
skid béberésuƙota asɨ́ v.; iféĺɔ́nᵾƙɔtᵃ v.
skill akɨ́lɨ̀kᵃ n.
skim off iƙáábɛs v.; iƙákápés v.; iƙááĺes v.; ilabɛtés v.; iripetés v.
skin hoés v.; poxés v.; tsʼɛ̀ n.
skin (cracked) kɔmɔ́m n.
skin (plant) ɔmɔ́x n.

skin bump síts'ádè n.
skin off poxésúƙotᵃ v.
skin on milk kɨrarapᵃ n.
skink lɔ́milɨ́ n.
skip out tɔpéɔ́n v.
skip out (and come) tɔpéétòn v.
skip out (and go) tɔpéɔ́nᵾƙɔtᵃ v.
skip rope ígoriesá simáᵉ v.
skirmish iƙúmúnós v.
skirt itsóɗón v.; ɲémɨrɨ́ńɗà n.; tamanɛs v.; tamanɛtés v.
skirt (sheep-leather) ɗóɗòƙwàz n.
skirt repeatedly tamaniés v.
skit wááka na támɔtɔ́s n.
skitter up sekwerɛs v.
skull ikóɔ́kᵃ n.; ɔka ikáᵉ n.
skullcap (nylon) nàɗɨàkᵃ n.
skunk-like animal ɲókᵾɗɔmᵾ́tᵾ̀ n.
sky didigwarí n.; gwa n.; lúl n.
sky (clear) dìdìɔ̀kᵃ n.; gìdòɔ̀kᵃ n.
slab (stone) lalatíbón n.
slack bàŋɔn v.; ɨtátsámánón v.
slack off ɨwɔ́ɔ́nᵾƙɔtᵃ v.
slacker ɲakárámɨtᵃ n.
slacking ɨwɔ́ɔ́n v.
slackness baŋás n.
slander itúrumés v.
slanderer ɲítúrumúám n.
slant outward (horns) tɔpétón v.
slap iɗafɛs v.; iɗáfésᵾƙɔtᵃ v.
slap around iɗafiés v.
slap the shoulders iɗafesa sáwátɨ̀kàᵋ v.
slash dzɛrés v.
slash (vegetation) iɗetɛs v.; irɛjɛs v.
slash firebreak ikɛbɨ́ƙébésa ts'aɗí v.
slasher ɲésilax n.
slashing of grass siláxɨ̀ŋ n.

slather ɨmɔdɨ́mɔ́dɛ́s *v*.; ɨmɔ́mɔ́dɛ́s *v*.
slaughter hoés *v*.; tɔŋɔlɛs *v*.
slaughterer tɔ̀ŋɔ̀làam *n*.
slaughterhouse hoesího *n*.
slave ŋɨpákásìam *n*.; ŋɨpɔ́táɨ̀am *n*.; ɲɔpɔ́táy[a] *n*.
slavery ŋɨlébúɨ̀nànès *n*.; ŋɨpɔ́táɨ̀nànès *n*.
slay tɔŋɔlɛs *v*.
slay (many) sábés *v*.
slay (singly) cɛɛ́s *v*.
slayer (of many) sábésìam *n*.
sleek ɨpɛlɨ́pélɔ̀n *v*.; mɨlɔ́dɔ̀n *v*.; pɨ́dɨ́dɔ̀n *v*.
sleekly mɨ̀l *ideo*.; pɨ̀d[i] *ideo*.
sleep ep[a] *n*.; èpòn *v*.; mɔdɔ́d[a] *n*.
sleep (of many) barájónʉkot[a] *v*.
sleep (put to) epítésʉkot[a] *v*.
sleep a lot epopos *v*.
sleep around (sexually) epopos *v*.; weesa kɨ́já[e] *v*.
sleeper epúám *n*.
sleeping èpòn *v*.
sleeping deeply nʉ̀s *ideo*.; nʉsɨ́dɔ̀n *v*.
sleeping place epúáw[a] *n*.
sleeping skin jèjè *n*.
sleepless gòkòn *v*.
sleepnessness gòk[a] *n*.
sleepy ɨlʉ́zɔ̀n *v*.; iyalíyálòn *v*.
sleeve kwɛt[a] *n*.
slender kadótsómòn *v*.; kɨdɨ́wɨ́tsánón *v*.; sɨ́dɔ̀rɔ̀mɔ̀n *v*.; tɔ̀kɔ̀n *v*.
slenderly kadóts[o] *ideo*.
sleuth rɔtéám *n*.
sleuth on rɔ́tés *v*.
slice hoés *v*.; írés *v*.
slice away ɨkémɨ́kémés *v*.
slice up irikɨ́rɨ́kés *v*.

sliced food (dry) iram *n*.
slick dɔrɔ́dɔ̀n *v*.; ɨpɛlɨ́pélɔ̀n *v*.; jʉrʉ́tʉ́mɔ̀n *v*.; jʉrʉtʉ́tɔ́n *v*.; kwirídòn *v*.; ŋìòn *v*.; pɛlédɔ̀n *v*.; pɨdɨ́dɔ̀n *v*.; pɔtɔ́dɔ̀n *v*.
slickly dɔ̀r *ideo*.; kwìr *ideo*.; pɛ̀l *ideo*.; pɨ̀d[i] *ideo*.; pɔ̀t[ɔ] *ideo*.
slide ɨfɛlɛsa asɨ́ *v*.; ɨfélɔ́nʉkot[a] *v*.; ɨsɔɛs *v*.; ɨsɔɛtés *v*.
slide off darámɔ́n *v*.
slide oneself through ɨsɔɛtésá asɨ́ *v*.
slide out sɛlététɔ̀n *v*.
slide through ɨsélétésʉkota asɨ́ *v*.
slight kɨdɨ́wɨtsánón *v*.
slight (with food) itáósés *v*.
slightly numerous komɨkómón *v*.
slim kadótsómòn *v*.; kɨdɨ́wɨ́tsánón *v*.; sɨ́dɔ̀rɔ̀mɔ̀n *v*.; tɔ̀kɔ̀n *v*.
slime gadár *n*.; kɨrarap[a] *n*.
slimly kadóts[o] *ideo*.
sling ɨbatalés *v*.; ɲapaaru *n*.
sling over toryoŋes *v*.
slingshot ɲapaaru *n*.; ɲépɨ̀ɨ́rá *n*.
slink ɨtɨ́dɨ́désá asɨ́ *v*.
slink away/off nʉ́nʉ́tɔ̀n *v*.
slip ɨfɛlɛsa asɨ́ *v*.; ɨsɔɛs *v*.; ɨsɔɛtés *v*.
slip away ɨfɛlɛsa asɨ́ *v*.
slip in sɛrɛpɛs *v*.
slip into ɨbʉbʉŋés *v*.; ɨbʉbʉŋésʉ́kot[a] *v*.; sɛrépésʉkot[a] *v*.
slip off ɨfɛlɛsa asɨ́ *v*.
slip oneself through ɨsɔɛtésá asɨ́ *v*.
slip out sɛlététɔ̀n *v*.
slip through ɨsélétésʉkota asɨ́ *v*.; sɛrɛpɛs *v*.; sɛrépésʉkot[a] *v*.
slipknot lɔ̀jʉ̀rʉ̀tà *n*.
slipper ŋadétá *n*.
slipperily dɔ̀r *ideo*.; kwìr *ideo*.; pɛ̀l *ideo*.; pɔ̀t[ɔ] *ideo*.

slippery ɗɔrɔ́dɔ̀n *v.*; jʉrʉ́tʉ́mɔ̀n *v.*; jʉrʉtʉ́tɔ́n *v.*; kwirídòn *v.*; pɛlɛ́dɔ̀n *v.*; pɔtɔ́dɔ̀n *v.*
slippy kwirídòn *v.*; sɛlɛ́témɔ̀n *v.*
slither lúkúɗukuɗánón *v.*
slithery sɛlɛ́témɔ̀n *v.*
slitted mijɨ́límɔ̀n *v.*
slope ɓɔ́kɔ̀ɲ *n.*
sloped sémédedánón *v.*
slosh ipɔkɛs *v.*; ts'álúbòn *v.*
slosh through water íbuɗésá cué *v.*
slothful ɓʉɓʉsánón *v.*; wéésánón *v.*
slouch rùjɔ̀n *v.*
slough off ɗarámɔ́n *v.*
slow inípónòn *v.*
slow (mentally) miɲɔna íkèdè *v.*
slow down inípónítésúƙotᵃ *v.*; ɨwɔ́ɔ́nʉƙotᵃ *v.*; tosipetés *v.*
slowing ɨwɔ́ɔ́n *v.*
slowly hɨɨjᵃ *adv.*; hɨɨjɔ *adv.*; kédie kwátsᵃ *n.*; wèwèès *ideo.*
slowly (very) pààì *ideo.*
sludgily yàŋ *ideo.*
sludgy bɔrɔ́tsɔ́mɔ̀n *v.*; yaŋádòn *v.*
slug tanaŋes *v.*; tɔƙɔtɔƙᵃ *n.*
slug (bullet) ɓʉɓʉn *n.*
sluggish ijíŋáánón *v.*
slumber epᵃ *n.*; èpòn *v.*; mɔɗɔ́ɗᵃ *n.*
slump rùjɔ̀n *v.*
slur ɗáƙón *v.*; iŋájápánón *v.*
slurp isɔ́rɔ́ɓɛs *v.*; xáɓútés *v.*
slurp continually. abutiés *v.*
slurpable food isɔrɔɓam *n.*
smack ídirés *v.*
small kwátsón *v.*
small (become) kwátsónuƙotᵃ *v.*
small (of many) kwátsíkaakón *v.*
small (opening) tɨɨts'ɨ́mɔ̀n *v.*
small-bodied tsaʉ́ɗɨ́mɔ̀n *v.*
smaller (make) kwatsítésuƙotᵃ *v.*
smash ilɛɗɛs *v.*; ɨtsakɛs *v.*
smash up ɨtsakɨtsákɛ́s *v.*
smear ilɔ́lɔ́rés *v.*; imɔɗɨ́mɔ́ɗés *v.*; imɔ́mɔ́ɗés *v.*
smear (goat dung) sɨ́ɛs *v.*
smear (reputation) itúrúmés *v.*
smear with clay ŋɔritɛtés *v.*
smell mídzatés *v.*; mídzatetés *v.*; mídzòn *v.*; ɔn *n.*; ɔnɛdᵃ *n.*; wetésá kɔɨnáᵋ *v.*
smell fetid mídzona ɗɛtsɨɗɛ́tsɨ́kᵋ *v.*
smell rotten mídzònà ɗùkᵘ *v.*
smell to death mídzatés *v.*
smelly ɨmúsɔ́ɔ̀n *v.*
smelly (become) ɨmúsɛ́ɛ̀tɔ̀n *v.*
smelly (make) mídzitésúƙotᵃ *v.*
smelly (very) ɗùkᵘ *ideo.*
smile ɨmúmúɔ̀n *v.*; tamáísánón *v.*
smile (make) ɨmúmúɨtɛtés *v.*
smock (leather) kɔ́lɔ́tsᵃ *n.*
smoke ipúróòn *v.*; iwaŋíwáŋés *v.*; ts'ûdᵃ *n.*; ts'uditɛ́s *v.*; wetés *v.*
smoke (a cigarette) isɔ́kɔ́teés *v.*
smoke (begin to) ipúréètòn *v.*
smoke (ritually) ipúréés *v.*
smoke out ipúréés *v.*
smoke signal ts'ûdᵃ *n.*
smolder iɲipíɲípòn *v.*
smooth lɨwɨdòn *v.*; pɨlɔ́dɔ̀n *v.*
smooth (make) pɨlɔ́ditésúƙotᵃ *v.*
smoothen ipiipíyeés *v.*
smoothen (with water) iláɓués *v.*
smoothen out pɨlɔ́ditésúƙotᵃ *v.*
smoothly jàm *ideo.*; lɨw *ideo.*; pɨl *ideo.*

smother tʉɓʉnɛ́s *v.*
smudge ɨlɔ́lɔ́rɛ́s *v.*
smuggle iɛpɛtɛ́s *v.*
smut fungus lósínákᵃ *n.*
snail tɔkɔtɔkᵃ *n.*
snail shell irex *n.*; tɔkɔtɔkáhò *n.*
snake ídèm *n.*
snake (blind) lokaliliŋ *n.*
snake (rufous beaked) oŋerepᵃ *n.*
snake (sand) nakɔlitákᵃ *n.*
snake (small green) ílebéɗᵃ *n.*
snake fang ídèmèkwàywᵃ *n.*
snake venom ídèmètàtᵃ *n.*
snake-bite ídemekɨdzɛ́s *n.*
snap ɗusúmón *v.*
snap (react) tokúétòn *v.*; tokúréètòn *v.*
snap (snarl) iɲɛ́ɛ́mɔ̀n *v.*
snap a photo iwetésá ɲépítsaáᵋ *v.*
snap a photo of iwetés *v.*
snap off iɓɛkɨɓékɛ́s *v.*; wakés *v.*
snap off in pieces wakatiés *v.*; wakáwákatés *v.*
snap! ɓɛkᵋ *ideo.*; ɗɨ *ideo.*; tɛ̀ *ideo.*
snapshot kúrúkúr *n.*; ɲépɨ́tsa *n.*
snare kotsítésukotᵃ *v.*; ságòsìm *n.*; ságwès *v.*
snare (neck) ɲákol *n.*
snare (wire neck) ɲáwáya *n.*
snare rope lozikinetᵃ *n.*; lozikitᵃ *n.*
snare spring kàswᵃ *n.*
snare stick tɨmél *n.*
snare stick (bent) tɔmɔkɔrɛs *n.*
snare trigger kwanɛdᵃ *n.*
snared kòtsòn *v.*; ságoanón *v.*
snared (become) kotsonukotᵃ *v.*

snaring sâgwᵃ *n.*
snarl iɲɛ́ɛ́mɔ̀n *v.*
snatch irɛɗɛs *v.*; ŋusés *v.*; ŋusésúkotᵃ *v.*; taŋates *v.*; tokopes *v.*; toreɓes *v.*
snatch away taŋátésukotᵃ *v.*; tokópésukotᵃ *v.*
sneak dɨdɨ́tésukotᵃ *v.*; dɨdɨtɛtɛ́s *v.*; isúmón *v.*; itɨdɨ́dɛ́s *v.*; itɨdɨ́dɛ́sá asɨ *v.*; totséɗón *v.*
sneak away dzuesésúkota asɨ *v.*; ifɛlɛsa asɨ *v.*
sneak off dzuesésúkota asɨ *v.*; ifɛlɛsa asɨ *v.*; isúmónukotᵃ *v.*
sneak up ɨ̀bɛ̀dɨ̀bɛ̀dɔ̀n *v.*; isúmétɔ̀n *v.*
sneak up on tɔléléɛtɛ́s *v.*
sneaky iɗásón *v.*
sneeze síkón *v.*; sìkwᵃ *n.*
sniff mídzatés *v.*
sniff (tobacco) júrɛ́s *v.*
snip iɲipes *v.*; irɛɓɛs *v.*
snip off irɛ́ɓɛ́sukotᵃ *v.*
snitch dɨdɨ́tésukotᵃ *v.*; dɨdɨtɛtɛ́s *v.*
snitch on ilíítés *v.*
snoop around tɨrifɨrífɛ́s *v.*
snore ŋɔ́rɔ́rɔ̀n *v.*
snort síkón *v.*; sìkwᵃ *n.*
snort at ifúkúfukɛ́s *v.*
snot ɗɔ̀kɔ̀n *n.*; ɲarúkʉ́m *n.*
snout loɓôz *n.*
snub iméɗélɛ́s *v.*
snub (with food) itáósés *v.*
snuff wetɛ́s *v.*
snuff (tobacco) júrɛ́s *v.*; júrɛ́sukotᵃ *v.*
snuff container ɲeɓuryaŋ *n.*
snuff out (life) ts'eítésukotᵃ *v.*
snuffle at ifúkúfukɛ́s *v.*
so kòtᵒ *coordconn.*

so that ikóteré *subordconn.*; kánɨ *subordconn.*; kánɨ náa táa *subordconn.*; kóteré *subordconn.*
so that ... not kánɨ mookóo *subordconn.*
so then ɓàz *interj.*; kɨ́ná *coordconn.*
so there! ɓàz *interj.*
so-and-so tatanám *n.*
so-so ŋwanɨŋwánón *v.*
soak ɨɛɓɨ́tɛtɛ́s *v.*
soak (grist) mʉrés *v.*
soaked ts'alídòn *v.*
soap dàlìs *n.*; ɲásaɓuní *n.*
soap (laundry) hómò *n.*; ɲéómò *n.*
soar ɨɔ́ɔ́rɔ̀n *v.*
sober (not drunk) bótsóna iká^e *v.*
soccer ɲépɨɨrá *n.*
sock ɲósóƙis *n.*
soda ɲósóɗa *n.*
soda ash ɲaɓáláŋit^a *n.*; ɲámakaɗí *n.*
sodium carbonate ɲaɓáláŋit^a *n.*; ɲámakaɗí *n.*
Sodom apple tùlèl *n.*
soft bubuxánón *v.*; buɗúdòn *v.*; burádòn *v.*; dabúdòn *v.*; heɓúdòn *v.*; jaulímòn *v.*; ɲipídòn *v.*; xaɓúdòn *v.*
soft (become) bubuxánónuƙot^a *v.*
soft (make) buɗúditésúƙot^a *v.*
soft (of metal) lumúdòn *v.*
soft (of soil) yuúdòn *v.*
soft (powdery) ɲapíɗímòm *v.*
soft and tender dabúdòn *v.*
soft inside yumúdòn *v.*
soft spot baɗibaɗas *n.*; bɔɗibɔɗɔs *n.*
soften bubuxánónuƙot^a *v.*
soften (emotionally) isyónónuƙot^a *v.*
soften up buɗúditésúƙot^a *v.*

softly bùd^u *ideo.*; dàb^u *ideo.*; hèɓ^u *ideo.*; lùm *ideo.*; ɲìpⁱ *ideo.*; sokósîik^e *v.*; xàɓ^u *ideo.*
softly (of soil) yù *ideo.*
softly inside yùm *ideo.*
soggy fɔts'ɔ́dɔ̀n *v.*
soil jʉm *n.*
soil (colored) ɲálámʉɲɛna *n.*
soil (fertile) jʉma na zîz *n.*
soil (red) boŋórén *n.*; ɲapala *n.*
soiled ɨráɲʉ́nánón *v.*; ŋɔrɔ́ɲɔ́mɔ̀n *v.*; ɲɔŋɔ́rɔ́mɔ̀n *v.*
Solanum incanum tùlèl *n.*
solar eclipse badona fetí *n.*
solar panel ɲósɔ́la *n.*
soldier jɔrɔrɔ́ám *n.*; kéàam *n.*
soldier ant lókók^a *n.*
soldier termite lókók^a *n.*
soldiers dìdì *n.*; jɔrɔr *n.*
sole ɗòk^u *adv.*
sole (of foot) dɛááƙw^a *n.*
solely ɛɗá *adv.*
solicit tɔɓéɲétɔ̀n *v.*; wáán *v.*
soliciting wáán *n.*
solidified iɗíkón *v.*
solidify iɗíkétòn *v.*; iɗikitetés *v.*
solitary ɗòk^u *adv.*
solvable problem itémítuƙotam *n.*
solve hoetés *v.*; itemités *v.*; ŋurutiés *v.*; ŋurutiesúƙot^a *v.*
solved ŋurutiós *v.*
Somali Oríáé *n.*
Somali language Ŋísʉmálɨtòd^a *n.*; Oríáénítòd^a *n.*
Somali person Ŋísʉmálɨ̀àm *n.*
Somalia Somálià *n.*
some (plural) kíníén *pro.*
some (singular) kónɨén *pro.*

some more sa *pro.*
some other sa *pro.*
some other (sg.) kɔn *pro.*
somebody kɔ́nɛ́ɛ́ná ámáᵉ *n.*
someone kɔ́nɛ́ɛ́ná ámáᵉ *n.*; kɔnɨ́ám *pro.*
somersault aɓúlúkánón *v.*; tɨ́bɨ̀dɨ́lɔ̀n *v.*
something kɔ́nɛ́ɛ́ná kɔ́rɔ́ɓádì *n.*
sometimes (hours) sayó ɲásáàtɨ̀kàᵉ *n.*
somewhere else kɔ́náyᵃ *pro.*
son dzàƙᵃ *n.*; sore *n.*
son (his/her) dzàƙèdᵃ *n.*
son (of my father) abáɲɨ́dzàƙᵃ *n.*
son (young) soréím *n.*
song dikwᵃ *n.*; ìrùkᵃ *n.*
Soo language Ŋítépesítôdᵃ *n.*
Soo people Ŋítépes *n.*
soon názèƙwà *n.*; ts'ɔ̀ɔ̀ *adv.*
soot ɲémúɗetsᵃ *n.*; ɲémúɗuɗu *n.*
soot (tobacco) ɲéɗɨ́por *n.*
sooty imɔ́ɗɔ́rɔ̀n *v.*
sopping ts'alídòn *v.*
soppingly ts'àl *ideo.*
sorcerer bàdiàm *n.*
sorcerer (who stops rain) tuɗúlónìam *n.*
sorcery badirétᵃ *n.*; badirétínànès *n.*; ƙɨ̵t- s'ánánès *n.*
sore ɔ́jᵃ *n.*
sore (small) ɔ́jáìm *n.*
sorghum ŋám *n.*
sorghum flowers kadɨx *n.*
sorghum variety (black) ŋámá na buɗám *n.*
sorghum variety (brownish-gray) dɨɗèŋàm *n.*
sorghum variety (droopy) lojúulú *n.*
sorghum variety (hairy) ɲákaɓír *n.*

sorghum variety (purplish) serɨ́nà *n.*
sorghum variety (red) ŋámá nà ɗiwᵃ *n.*; ɲɛmɛrayᵃ *n.*
sorghum variety (round-headed) nalɨ́ɨlɨ́ *n.*
sorghum variety (Toposa) Kɔrɔmɔtáŋám *n.*
sorghum variety (Turkana) ɲékimyétᵃ *n.*; Pakóicéŋám *n.*
sorghum variety (white) ŋámá nà ɓèts'ᵃ *n.*
sorghum variety (yellow) ɗókótsᵃ *n.*; natéɓᵃ *n.*; oɲaŋ *n.*
sorghum varity (tall) walá *n.*
sorrowful itásónòn *v.*; tasónón *v.*
sort isalɛs *v.*; isalɛtés *v.*; rɔrés *v.*
sort (make) isalités *v.*
soul gúr *n.*
sound arútón *v.*
sound an alarm iwákón *v.*
sound empty ɗɛɨ̵ɗéwɔ́n *v.*
sound out arútónuƙotᵃ *v.*
sounding alarm iwáákós *v.*
sounding like *sh-sh* wɔ̀x *ideo.*
soup seekwᵃ *n.*
sour ɓàròn *v.*
sour (become) ɓaronuƙotᵃ *v.*
sour (make) ɓarites *v.*; ɓarítésuƙotᵃ *v.*
sour (of malt) mɨ̵ránón *v.*
sour mash ɓaram *n.*
source itsyákétònìawᵃ *n.*
source of water cuáákᵃ *n.*
souse iéɓɨ́tɛtés *v.*
south kɔ́ɔ́ kíjᵒ *n.*; nɔ́ɔ́ kíjᵒ *n.*
South Sudan Sɨ̵ɗán *n.*
southerly direction gígiroxan *dem.*
Southern Cross Ɲémusaláɓà *n.*
southerner kɔ́ɔ́kíjóàm *n.*

southward kɔ́ɔ́ kíjº *n.*
sovereign ipúkéésíàm *n.*; tòtwàrààm *n.*
sow íbités *v.*; tɛwɛɛs *v.*
space ilɔ́lɔ́kés *v.*; ilores *v.*; zɛkɔ́áwᵃ *n.*
space (outer) didigwarí *n.*
space too closely itsuɗútsúɗés *v.*; ituɗútúɗés *v.*
spacious ilɔ́lɔ́mɔ̀n *v.*; lalʉ́jɔ́n *v.*
spade ɲakáɓétᵃ *n.*; ɲékitiyó *n.*
spade (wooden) nakútᵃ *n.*
spank ipíkéés *v.*
spar ɲèurià *n.*; ɲeuríétòn *v.*
spare iɓámɔ́n *v.*
sparklely mɨ̀l *ideo.*
sparkly milɨ́dɔ̀n *v.*
sparks ŋkaɗɛɛɗéyᵃ *n.*
sparrow (parrot-billed) midikᵃ *n.*
spatter iratɨ́rátés *v.*; irwaírwéés *v.*; irwates *v.*; iwéélánón *v.*; tɔfɔ́ɗɔ́n *v.*
spatula (wooden) cɛbɛn *n.*; ɲémiikó *n.*
speak iɛ́nɔ́n *v.*; tódètòn *v.*; tódòn *v.*
speak (begin to) tódonukotᵃ *v.*
speak about tódetés *v.*
speak eloquently isiresa akáᵉ *v.*
speak harshly ɡuts'uriesá tódàᵉ *v.*
speak harshly to dokofiés *v.*
speak indistinctly ɗákón *v.*; iɲájápánón *v.*
speak meanly ɡuts'uriesá tódàᵉ *v.*
speak pointlessly ipɛípɛ́ɛsá tódàᵉ *v.*
speak slowly ízɨdòn *v.*
speak to each other tódinós *v.*
speak vaguely iɲaiɲéésa tódaᵉ *v.*
speaker taatsaama tódàᵉ *n.*; tódààm *n.*
spear ɓis *n.*; toɓés *v.*
spear (long-headed) ɲátúm *n.*
spear (of many) bɛrés *v.*
spear (sharpened stick) jɨrɔ̀kᵃ *n.*
spear a tree toɓésá dakwí *v.*
spear bluntly iɲulúɲúlés *v.*
spear from afar itsɛ́tsɛ́ɛ́s *v.*
spear repeatedly toɓítóɓiés *v.*
spear shaft (long) narwá *n.*
spear shaft (short) erumén *n.*
spear through ɲéɲés *v.*
spearhead ɓisáákᵃ *n.*
spearhead (long-necked) ɲɛlɨrátᵃ *n.*
spearhead (short-necked) ɲéɓɨ́tɨ *n.*
spearhead neck ɓisáɓóló *n.*
speartip (rear) ɲérʉ́matsᵃ *n.*
special kanotós *v.*
specialty ɲɛmʉna *n.*
species bònìtᵃ *n.*; ɲákaɓilá *n.*
speck kiɗoɗotsᵃ *n.*; símíɗiɗí *n.*
speckle iɗolíɗólés *v.*; itwelítwélés *v.*
speckled iɗolíɗólòn *v.*; itwelítwélós *v.*
spectacles ɲékiyóìkᵃ *n.*
spectator enésúkotiám *n.*
specter kúrúkúr *n.*
speech tôdᵃ *n.*
speech (careless) múɗúkánónìtòdᵃ *n.*
speech (muddled) tóda ni buɗám *n.*
speed irʉtsɛsa asɨ́ *v.*; ɲésipíɗᵃ *n.*
speedy itírónòn *v.*; wéénòn *v.*
spell it out tɔmɛɛtésá tódàᵉ *v.*
spend the day iríóonukotᵃ *v.*
spend time iríóòn *v.*; iríóonukotᵃ *v.*
spend wildly ikwarɨ́kwárés *v.*
spent (tired) ziálámòn *v.*; zíkímétòn *v.*; ziláámòn *v.*
sperm ɗír *n.*
spew ilɔ́ɓɔ́tɛtɛs *v.*
sphenoid bone matáɲɨ̀ɔ̀kᵃ *n.*

spherical ilúlúŋɔ́s *v.*
spherical (make) ilúlúŋés *v.*
sphincter (anal) ɔ́zàhò *n.*
spice ɛfitɛs *v.*
spice up ɛfitɛs *v.*
spider abûbᵃ *n.*
spiderweb abûbᵃ *n.*
spike omén *n.*
spill ɗaɗatésukotᵃ *v.*; kúdès *v.*; kúdesukotᵃ *v.*; kúdetés *v.*
spill all over itsúrútsúrés *v.*; itsúrútsúrésúkɔtᵃ *v.*
spill over bukúrésukota así *v.*; ilápétɔ̀n *v.*
spin irímítetés *v.*; irímón *v.*; iríɲítés *v.*; iríɲón *v.*
spinach ɲásalàtà *n.*
spinal cord lɔ́bɨ́riɓɨ́r *n.*
spindly sawátsámòn *v.*
spine gògòròjᵃ *n.*; gògòròjɔ̀ɔ̀kᵃ *n.*
spiral ilúkúretés *v.*; iyérónukotᵃ *v.*
spiraled iyérón *v.*
spirit sugur *n.*; sùpᵃ *n.*
spirit (earth) ɲɛkɨ́pyɛ́ *n.*
spirit (evil) ɲɛkɨ́pyɛ́ *n.*
spirit (sickness-causing) ɲeɗekéim *n.*
spirit dance jàkàlùkà *n.*
spirits (earth) ŋɨ́pyɛn *n.*
spirits (evil) ŋɨ́pyɛn *n.*
spit tatᵃ *n.*; tatés *v.*; tàtòn *v.*
spit (skewer) rɔ́és *v.*
spit far tsiritɛs *v.*
spit on ɨmwaɨmwéés *v.*
spit out tatésúkotᵃ *v.*
spit out repeatedly tatiésukotᵃ *v.*
spit repeatedly tatiés *v.*

spit-inducer tatitésukotíám *n.*
spit-pestle plant tatíájᵃ *n.*
spiteful person ɲékisiránìàm *n.*
spitefulness ɲékisirán *n.*
spitter tatiesíám *n.*
spittle tatᵃ *n.*
splash ts'álúbòn *v.*
splash! bùlùkᵘ *ideo.*
splat! pɨ̀ɔ *ideo.*
splatter iratɨ́rátés *v.*; iwéélánón *v.*; tɔfɔ́ɗɔ́n *v.*
spleen máɗíŋ *n.*
splendid dòòn *v.*
splendor daás *n.*
splint íbunutsés *v.*
splish-splash! calúɓᵘ *ideo.*
split ɓɛlés *v.*; ɓɛlɛtés *v.*; ɓɛlɔ́s *v.*; taŋatsárón *v.*; tɛlétsɔ́n *v.*; terés *v.*; tɔɓɛlɛs *v.*; toŋélón *v.*
split apart ɓéɓélés *v.*; ɓéɓélɔ́s *v.*; itotoles *v.*; terémón *v.*; tɔɓélésukota ᵃ *v.*
split apart multiply ɓeletiés *v.*
split in pieces iɓéɓélés *v.*
split in two pakámón *v.*; pakés *v.*
split multiply pakatiés *v.*
split open ɓéɓélés *v.*; ɓéɓélɔ́s *v.*; ɓɛlɛ́ɓélánón *v.*; ɓelémón *v.*
split open (of pods) kwɛ́dɔ̀n *v.*
split up terémétòn *v.*; terémón *v.*; terémónukotᵃ *v.*; terétéránitésúkotᵃ *v.*; terétéránón *v.*; tereties *v.*; teretiós *v.*; tɔɓélésukotaᵃ *v.*
splitch! rùtᵘ *ideo.*
splosh ipɔkɛs *v.*
spoil imóɲíkees *v.*; imóɲíkeetés *v.*; iraŋɛs *v.*; iraŋɛtés *v.*; masánétòn *v.*
spoil everything nts'ákóna sèrèikᵉ *v.*

spoiled

spoiled ɨraɲɔs *v*.; ɨráŋʉ́nánón *v*.; masánón *v*.
spoiled (become) ɨraɲímétòn *v*.
spokesperson taatsaama tódàᵉ *n*.; tódààm *n*.
sponge lɛŋɛ́s *v*.; lɛŋɛ́sɨ̀àm *n*.
spongily bùf *ideo*.
sponging olíɓó *n*.
spongy bufúdòn *v*.
spongy bone ɲéɲam *n*.
spooky thing bàdìàm *n*.
spoon (metal) ɲékijikó *n*.
spoon (wooden) ƙolom *n*.
spoot! pɨ̀ɔ *ideo*.
sport ɲaɓolya *n*.; wáákᵃ *n*.
spot bàsɔ̀n *v*.; ɨtsɔɓɨtsɔ́ɓɛ́s *v*.
spot (bare) ɲapatsole *n*.
spot (claimed) ɲeɗúkór *n*.
spot (hard) ɲapáyál *n*.
spot (place) bácɨ́kᵃ *n*.
spotless xɔ́dòn *v*.; xɔtánón *v*.
spotted iɗolíɗólòn *v*.; ɨtsɔɓɨtsɔ́ɓɔ́s *v*.; komolánón *v*.; merixánón *v*.; tsɨpɨtsɨ́pɔ́n *v*.; tábàsànètòn *v*.
spotted (black-and-white) ŋorokánón *v*.; ŋorókón *v*.
spotter weretsíám *n*.
spotty ɨtsɔɓɨtsɔ́ɓɔ̀n *v*.
sprawl ɨpɛ́pɛ́tánón *v*.
sprawl out ɨpɛ́pɛ́tánónuƙotᵃ *v*.
spray bɨ́tɛ́s *v*.
spray (bombard) ɨ́dʉrɛ́s *v*.
spread imɔɗɨ́mɔ́ɗɛ́s *v*.; imɔ́mɔ́ɗɛ́s *v*.; ɨwɛ́ɛ́lɛ́s *v*.
spread (legs) apart dɛŋɛlɛs *v*.
spread about ɨpɛ́pɛ́tɛ́s *v*.

sprout (of leaves)

spread apart tɛlɛɛs *v*.
spread around ɓátsɛ́s *v*.; ikwákwárɛ́s *v*.; ikwarɨ́kwárɛ́s *v*.; ikwarɨ́kwarɔ́s *v*.; irɨ́ríjɛ́s *v*.; iwies *v*.
spread circularly imalɨ́málɛ́s *v*.
spread oneself open ɓátsɛ́sa asɨ́ *v*.
spread out ɨwɛ́ɛ́lánón *v*.; ɨwɛ́ɛ́lɛ́sʉƙotᵃ *v*.; ɨwɛ́ɛ́lɛtɛ́s *v*.; ɨwɛ́ɛ́lɔ́s *v*.; tɔlɔɛs *v*.; tɔpɛtɛs *v*.; tɔpɛ́tɛ́sʉƙotᵃ *v*.
spread out under tafakɛ́s *v*.
spread over (an area) ikáyɛ́ɛ́s *v*.
spread soil ɨwɛ́ɛ́lɛ́sá jʉmwɨ́ *v*.
spring íbòtòn *v*.; iɗɛ́ɛ́tɔ̀n *v*.; iɗótón *v*.; ɨgɔ̀rɔ̀bɔ̀n *v*.
spring (feather-holding) ɲeteeɗe *n*.
spring (of a trap) iɗálɛ́sʉƙota asɨ́ *v*.
spring (in sand) ɲakújá *n*.
spring (a trap) iɗalɛs *v*.
spring (of water) ɲeɨtánitᵃ *n*.; ɲɛlɛ́lyá *n*.
spring mechanism (of weapons) zɔ̀tᵃ *n*.
springily tùf *ideo*.; tùs *ideo*.
springing iɗɛ́ɔ́n *v*.
springy tufádòn *v*.; tusúdòn *v*.
sprinkle irwaírwɛ́ɛ́s *v*.; irwates *v*.; iyikes *v*.; towates *v*.; towatetɛ́s *v*.; xɛɛ́s *v*.; xɛɛsʉ́ƙotᵃ *v*.; xɛɛtɛ́s *v*.
sprinkle (granulates) ízuzués *v*.
sprinkle (rain) kʉ́f *n*.
sprinkle ashes on paths ƙúdesa káúe mucéíkàkᵉ *v*.
sprite kíjàim *n*.
spritz iyikes *v*.
sprout ɓúrukúkón *v*.; morétón *v*.; rúbɔ̀n *v*.; tɔɓɔ́rɔ́kánón *v*.; tʉwétón *v*.; tʉ̀wɔ̀n *v*.; xúbètòn *v*.; xúbòn *v*.
sprout (of grain) xokómón *v*.
sprout (of leaves) ŋʉrʉrúɲón *v*.

439

sprout (of maize cobs) isínákòn *v.*
sprout up ŋɯrɯ́ɲɯ́ɲètòn *v.*; rɯ́bètɔ̀n *v.*
spry pɔdɔ́dɔ̀n *v.*
spryly pɔ̀dᵓ *ideo.*
spud ɲéɓɨás *n.*
spur iɟɯkɯ́jɯ́kés *v.*; ɲégetsᵃ *n.*
spur on imɯ́káitetés *v.*
spurfowl (yellow-necked) kɔ̀dzᵃ *n.*
spurn imédélés *v.*
spurt tsʼɨrɨ́tɔ̀n *v.*
sputum dɔ́kɔ̀n *n.*; ɲarɯ́kɯ́m *n.*
spy irimesíám *n.*; rɔtéám *n.*
spy on lágalagetés *v.*; rɔ́tés *v.*; toreɓes *v.*
spy on from afar towates *v.*
spy out lágalagetés *v.*
squabble ikúmúnós *v.*; iɲɯ́ɲɯ́rɔ̀n *v.*; ŋɯ́zɯmánón *v.*
squander eletiésukotᵃ *v.*; iɲekes *v.*; iɲékésukotᵃ *v.*; iɲekíɲékés *v.*
squash ɓirés *v.*; ɓirítésukotᵃ *v.*; iledes *v.*; lomuke *n.*; lɔ́pɯ́l *n.*; redés *v.*
squashed (get) ɓirímón *v.*
squashily ɓìr *ideo.*; ɲàl *ideo.*; rɔ̀jᵓ *ideo.*
squashy ɓirídòn *v.*; ɲalídòn *v.*; rɔjɔ́dɔ̀n *v.*
squat tsɔ́nɔ́n *v.*
squeak squeak! tswɨ́ɨtswɨ́ *ideo.*
squeaky voice (have a) isirɨ́sɨrɔ́n *v.*
squeezable heɓúdòn *v.*
squeezably hèɓᵘ *ideo.*
squeeze bízès *v.*; iridɛs *v.*; iridetés *v.*; jɯtés *v.*; ridés *v.*; tɯtsɯes *v.*
squeeze all over bízibizatés *v.*
squeeze out bízetés *v.*; ipɨ́rɨsetés *v.*; jɯtésukɔtᵃ *v.*; tɯtsɯ́ésukɔtᵃ *v.*
squeezy heɓúdòn *v.*
squelchily rɔ̀jᵓ *ideo.*

squelchy rɔjɔ́dɔ̀n *v.*
squiggle ŋɯdɯŋɯ́dᵓn *v.*
squint imɯdɯ́mɯ́dᵓn *v.*; wɨ́zɨlés *v.*
squint at katsés *v.*
squinted pelérémòn *v.*
squinty pelérémòn *v.*; wɨ́zɨlɨ̀mɔ̀n *v.*
squinty-eyed wɨ́zɨlɨ̀mɔ̀n *v.*
squirm away gwɨ̀rɔ̀n *v.*
squirmy wɯlɯ́kɯ́mɔ̀n *v.*
squirrel (striped ground) tarádá *n.*
squirrel (tree) lukᵃ *n.*
squirt tsʼɨrɨ́tɔ̀n *v.*
squish ɓirés *v.*; ɓirítésukotᵃ *v.*; rɛdɛ́s *v.*; ridɛ́s *v.*
squished (get) ɓirímón *v.*
squishily ɓìr *ideo.*; ɲàl *ideo.*; rɔ̀jᵓ *ideo.*
squishy ɓirídòn *v.*; dulúdòn *v.*; duxúdòn *v.*; ɲalídòn *v.*; rɔjɔ́dɔ̀n *v.*
stab gafarɛs *v.*; gɛfɛrɛs *v.*
stab repeatedly gafariés *v.*
stabile diriɓóón *v.*
stability ɲíkísila *n.*; ɲɛkɨsil *n.*
stabilize irɯ́rɯ́ɓɛs *n.*; isɨlɔ́nɯkɔtᵃ *v.*; kakates *n.*
stable ikékéɲòn *v.*
stack up inábèsɯ̀kɔ̀tᵃ *v.*; inábɛtɛ́s *v.*
stack up on idɔ́dɔ́kés *v.*
stacked up idɔ́dɔ́kánón *v.*
staff jɯrɯm *n.*
staff (hook-necked) ɲésɛɛɓɔ́ *n.*
stagger gakímón *v.*; itɛrɨ́térɔ̀n *v.*; nérinérón *v.*
stagnant wàsɔ̀n *v.*
stair lopemúím *n.*
stake kìnɔ̀rɔ̀tᵃ *n.*
stale cucuéón *v.*
stalk arɯ́rɯ́bɔ̀n *v.*; kasɨ́r *n.*; morókᵃ *n.*; tonyámón *v.*

stall titikes *v.*
stammer ɗɔkɔ́lɔ́mɔ̀n *v.*; i̶k̶u̶j̶ú̶k̶ú̶j̶ɔ̀n *v.*
stammering gajádòn *v.*; kaɲádòn *v.*
stammering speech gajádònìtòd[a] *n.*
stammeringly gàj[a] *ideo.*
stamp itirítírés *v.*
stamp down iɲíkéésuƙot[a] *v.*
stamp pad ɲezeí *n.*
stance was *n.*
stand taɗaŋes *v.*; wàsɔ̀n *v.*
stand (for nomination) bɛ́ɗɛ́sa wasɔ́[ɛ] *v.*
stand (of many) gwámón *v.*
stand (of trees) gwi *n.*
stand apart iwásíòn *v.*
stand around si̶bɔ̀n *v.*; towóón *v.*; towóónuƙot[a] *v.*
stand around (make) si̶bi̶tésúƙɔt[a] *v.*
stand around as a group síbiónuƙot[a] *v.*
stand by each other tɔméɨ́nɔ́s *v.*
stand firm itííròòn *v.*
stand out kɛtélɔ́n *v.*
stand still wasɔna ts'ír *v.*; wasɔnuƙot[a] *v.*
stand up ŋkáítetés *v.*; ŋkéétòn *v.*; ŋkóón *v.*; wasitɛs *v.*; wasítésuƙot[a] *v.*
stand up (of many) gwamétón *v.*
stand upright wasɔna ts'ír *v.*
standard of living (high) zɛƙwa ná dà *n.*
star ɗɔ́xɛát[a] *n.*
star (evening) Dɔ́xɛatá xɨ̀ŋàtà[e] *n.*
star (morning) Dɔ́xɛatá na baratsó[e] *n.*; Dɔ́xɛatá tsòònì *n.*
star (shooting) ɗɔ́xɛatá na tsúwà *n.*
stare at ŋɔ́zɛ̀s *v.*; ŋóziés *v.*
stare at each other ŋɔ́zi̶nɔ́s *v.*
stare at emptily itelesa bàrìrrr *v.*
starer ŋɔ́zɛ̀si̶àm *n.*

starling (blue-eared) lɔɔmúyá *n.*
start iséétòn *v.*; isóón *v.*; itsyákétòn *v.*; toɗóón *v.*
start (fire) gamés *v.*; tsapés *v.*
start a fight with itojiés *v.*
start a fire gamésá ts'aɗí *v.*
start early ɛkwétɔ́n *v.*
start first ɛkwétɔ́n *v.*
start off (a dance) iwees *v.*
start raining tosípón *v.*
starting point wàxèd[a] *n.*
startle iniɲíniɲés *v.*; ŋaxitɛtés *v.*
startle awake tsídzètòn *v.*
startled ŋaxétɔ́n *v.*; toúmón *v.*
starvation ɲɔrɔkɔ *n.*
starving ɲɛƙánón *v.*
stash irwanes *v.*; laɓ[a] *n.*
stash (small) papaɗós *n.*
state kíj[a] *n.*
state the verdict tódetés *v.*
Stathmostelma peduncalatum ɲɨ́máarɔy[a] *n.*
station (missionary) ɲémíxòn *n.*
stationary diriɓóón *v.*; wàsɔ̀n *v.*
status zeís *n.*; zeísínànès *n.*
stay jèjɔ̀n *v.*; zɛƙwɔ̀n *v.*
stay a while toƙízeesá así̶ *v.*; toƙízòòn *v.*; tɔúrɨ́mɔ̀n *v.*
stay behind isíɗóòn *v.*
stay in ínés *v.*
stay lying towúryánòn *v.*
stay on jɛjétón *v.*
stay put iɗúkóós *v.*
stay together inínós *v.*
stay-at-home person awáám *n.*
STD ɲamakaje *n.*
steadily ɓa[u] *ideo.*

steady ikékéɲòn v.
steal dzuesés v.; dzuesetés v.
stealer dzúám n.
stealthy iɗásón v.
steam lɔkapʉ́r n.
steep iɔ́lɔ́lɔ̀n v.; kʉ́bɛ̀lɛ̀mɔ̀n v.; waatés v.
steep (dangerously) iwósétòn v.
steer (a vehicle) aɲires v.
steer clear ƙeƙérón v.
steering clear firifiránón v.; wíríwírá- nón v.
steering wheel ɲókokor n.
Steganotaenia araliacea seger n.
stench ɔn n.; ɔnɛdᵃ n.
step kɨ́mátsᵃ n.; lopemúím n.; ɔkɔ́tsᵃ n.
step all over takwitakwiés v.
step off (measure) ɨmaarésá dɛ̀ɨ̀kà ᵋ v.
step on takwés v.
Sterculia stenocarpa gàràjᵃ n.
Stereospermum kuntianum seínení n.
sterile ikólípánón v.; ɨsʉ́wɔ́ɔ̀n v.; os- orosánón v.
sterile (animal or person) ɲokólípᵃ n.
sterile person òsòròs n.
sternum gɔgɔm n.; toroɓᵃ n.
sternutate sɨƙón v.
sternutation sɨƙwᵃ n.
stich tʉfés v.
stick ɗɛlémɔ́n v.; dakwᵃ n.; iɗɔ́tsón v.; ɨnábɛs v.; jʉrʉm n.; ƙɨ́dzòn v.; nɔtsɔ́món v.; pokés v.; sɛ̀wᵃ n.; ts'ɔɗitɛs v.
stick (climbing) ƙɔ̀ɗɔ̀tᵃ n.
stick (honey) tsɨtsɨ́n n.
stick (hooked) lɔkɔ́dᵃ n.
stick (long digging) ɲédɨŋ n.
stick (metal-tipped) ɲákálɨrɨkɨtᵃ n.

stick (mingling) tʉɗʉtɛsɨ́dàkwᵃ n.
stick (net-holding) naƙwɨ́n n.
stick (round-headed) ɲéɓiró n.
stick (small hooked) pòròtᵃ n.
stick around iɗúkóós v.; toƙízòòn v.
stick in and out ɨjɔƙɨjɔ́ƙɛ́s v.
stick insect túwᵃ n.
stick out sábʉ̀rʉ̀rɔ̀n v.; tiɓɨ́étòn v.
stick out (of ears) kweelémòn v.
stick out of sight ikɨ́ɗɨ́tsɛ́s v.
stick out/up lɛɛmétòn v.
stick ring ɲókokor n.; ɲɔkɔlɔɓɛr n.
stick to iɗupes v.; ɨnɔtsɛs v.
stick to (keep on) ɗɛlémɔ́n v.
stick with tɔmɛɛs v.
stick with (keep on) ɗɛlémɔ́n v.
sticker kàf n.
stickily nɔ̀tsᵓ ideo.
sticking out tibɨ́ón v.
sticky irɨ̈tánón v.; minɨ́kɨmɔ̀n v.; nɔt- sɔ́dɔ̀n v.
stiff ɓotsódòn v.; gɔkɔ́dòn v.; kɛtɛrémòn v.; tsɛrɛkékón v.
stiffen by stirring tʉɗʉtetés v.
stiffly ɓòtsᵒ ideo.; gɔ̀kᵓ ideo.
stifling (weather) laŋádòn v.
still ijémón v.; lɛrédòn v.; wàsòn v.
still (become) ijémónʉƙɔtᵃ v.
still be sárón v.
still if tònì subordconn.
stimulate digitally ikɛɗɨ́ƙéɗés v.; ikwatɨ́kwátés v.
sting áts'ɛ́s v.; ƙɨ́dzɛs v.
sting (of pain) ɓɛɨɓɛ́ón v.
sting thoroughly áts'ɛ́sʉƙɔtᵃ v.
stinger kwan n.
stinginess hábàs n.

stingy hábòn *v.*; mɨnɨ́kɨ́mɔ̀n *v.*
stink ilíánòn *v.*; mídzòn *v.*; mídzona ɗɛtsɨɗɛ́tsɨ́kᵋ *v.*; mídzònà ɗùkᵘ *v.*
stink bug (green) logeréɲo *n.*
stinking wɨ́zɨlɨ́lɔ́n *v.*
stinky ɨmúsɔ́ɔ̀n *v.*
stinky (become) ɨmúsɛ́ɛ̀tɔ̀n *v.*
stinky (very) ɗùkᵘ *ideo.*
stipple iɗolíɗólés *v.*
stir iƙures *v.*; ɨlɔ́lɔ́ŋés *v.*
stir (emotionally) tábès *v.*
stir (restlessly) ɨsɔ́sɔ́ŋɔ́s *v.*
stir around ɨ́fáfáɲés *v.*
stir in íburubures *v.*
stirred stiff tɨɗɨtɔs *v.*
stirred up iƙúrúmós *v.*
stock (gun) ɛ́bàdɛ̀ *n.*
stock-still lɛrédòn *v.*
stocky kikímón *v.*
stomach ɡwà *n.*
stomach (first, of ruminants) ɲépɨnɨkᵃ *n.*
stomach (third, of ruminants) ɲémékweɲ *n.*
stomach ache áts'ɛ́sà bùbùì *n.*
stomach contents eyᵃ *n.*
stomach fluid (elephant) lɔpɔ́tsᵃ *n.*
stomp itirítírés *v.*
stone ɡwas *n.*; zébès *v.*
stone (cooking) caál *n.*
stone (flat) lalatíɓon *n.*
stone (hard black) lokítoɲí *n.*
stone (sharpening) lósùaɲ *n.*
stone (supporting) caál *n.*; titirésígwàs *n.*
stone repeatedly turues *v.*; turuetés *v.*

stone that way zébesuƙotᵃ *v.*
stone this way zébetés *v.*
stone-deaf ɗinɔ́s *v.*
stone-still lɛrédòn *v.*
stonily ɡàtsᵃ *ideo.*
stony ɡatsádòn *v.*
stool kàràtsᵃ *n.*
stool (fecal) ets'ᵃ *n.*
stool (loose) eruxam *n.*
stool (three-legged) dɛ̀ɨ̀kà àɗᵉ *n.*; lɔ̀cègèr *n.*
stool (two-legged) dɨ̂ɗèsɔ̀kᵃ *n.*; ɲámakukᵃ *n.*
stool carver kárátsɨ̀kààm *n.*
stoop over rɔ́rɔ́tòn *v.*
stooped mɨkɨ́rɨ́mɔ̀n *v.*
stooped over ɡɨ́ɡɨ̀rɔ̀n *v.*; rɨ́ɡɨ̀ɗɨ̀mɔ̀n *v.*
stop bɔlitésɨ́ƙɔtᵃ *v.*; imɔ́métòn *v.*; mɔ́métòn *v.*; wasɨtɛs *v.*; wasɨ́tésɨkɔtᵃ *v.*; wasɔ́áwᵃ *n.*; wasɔnɨkɔtᵃ *v.*
stop (blowing or boiling) tilímón *v.*
stop (plug) túzɨɗɛ́s *v.*
stop beating toɗúón *v.*
stop doing bɔlɔnɨƙɔtᵃ *v.*
stop hurting toíónuƙotᵃ *v.*
stop swarming (of termites) ɡwɛ́ɛ́ts'émɔ̀n *v.*
stop up ɗinɛ́s *v.*; imɨ́ɗɨtsés *v.*; túzɨɗɛ́sɨ́ƙɔtᵃ *v.*
stopover wasɔ́áwᵃ *n.*
stoppage was *n.*
stopped up ɗinɔ́s *v.*
stopper ts'úbɨlátᵃ *n.*; ts'ɨ̂bᵃ *n.*
stopping was *n.*
storage hole kùkùsèn *n.*
storage place ɡirésíàwᵃ *n.*
store ɗɨkán *n.*; ɡirés *v.*; ɡirésíàwᵃ *n.*; ɲáɗɨkán *n.*; ɲésitó *n.*; óɡoɗés *v.*

store away ógoɗésúkotᵃ v.; okésúkotᵃ v.
storehouse loɗúrú n.; lótsúm n.
storeroom ɲésitó n.
storey lopem n.
stork (Abdim's) tsokôbᵃ n.
stork-style dance dikwa na tsokóbè n.
storm itúúmés v.
storm (attack) bógès v.
storm off gwaitón v.; ɨgwɨjɨ̀rɔ̀n v.; tʉlúɲón v.; tʉlúɲónʉkɔtᵃ v.
story emutᵃ n.; ɲáɗís n.
storyteller emútíkààm n.; isíséésíàm n.
storytelling emútíkᵃ n.
stout laɲírímòn v.; laɲírón v.
stove (cooking) ɲesiŋkiri n.
strabismic kámáránón v.; ríbiribánón v.
straddle dɛŋɛlɛsá dɛáᵋ v.
straight iɗɨrón v.; iténón v.; sʉrʉsʉ́rón v.; tɔβéón v.
straight (horizontally) isérérèòn v.
straight (set) iténitɛtés v.
straight (vertically) isérérón v.
straight away dɨr adv.
straight part gògòròjᵃ n.
straighten iɗɨrítésʉkɔtᵃ v.; iténitɛtés v.; kɔés v.; kɔkatés v.
strain iɗɨɲón v.; ijiwɛs v.; itiwɛs v.
strain (muscles) ɗukés v.
strainer ɲékeikéyᵃ n.
strange talk kínítòdᵃ n.
stranger kónóm n.
strangers kíníám n.
strangle iketiés v.
strap kɨwᵃ n.
strap across ízokomés v.
strasbismal pɨlɨrɨmɔ̀n v.

straw (drinking) ɲálamorú n.; ɲeɓune n.
stray iwórón v.; iwóróniàm n.
stray off hakonukotᵃ v.
streaked ilɨɲánètòn v.; ilɨŋón v.
stream kɨdikɨdɔ̀n v.
stream (large) ɔrɔr n.
stream (small) ɨ̀àwɨ̀àwᵃ n.
stream out furúdòn v.
streaming out fùr ideo.
streamlined milódɔ̀n v.
strength ŋgúf n.; ɲixás n.; ɲakókóŋ n.
strengthen ɲixítésʉkɔtᵃ v.; ɲixɔnʉkɔtᵃ v.
stressed out (become) ilárímétòn v.; ilwárímétòn v.
stretch eminiés v.; kɔés v.; kɔkatés v.; kɔkɔanón v.
stretch across ikámárés v.
stretch out (to rest) torwóónukotᵃ v.
stretched out (resting) torwóón v.
strew iɗɛrɛs v.
strew about iɗɛríɗérés v.
strewn iɗɛrɔs v.; kazaanón v.
strewn about apétépétánón v.; ɗɛtéɗétánón v.; iɗɛríɗérós v.
stride dɛŋɛlɛsá dɛáᵋ v.; ɔkɔ́tsᵃ n.
strife ɲékúrukur n.; ɲépíɗipiɗᵃ n.
strike ɗálútés v.; iwés v.; iwésúkotᵃ v.; toɓés v.
strike (a match) dzɛrés v.
striking iɗéón v.
string róés v.; sim n.
string (nylon) ɲákol n.
stringy simánón v.
strip dzeretiés v.; dzeretiésukotᵃ v.; itakɛs v.
strip off iɓólótsés v.; iɓɔtes v.; itákésʉkɔtᵃ v.; tɔɲilɨɲilés v.
stripe dzeretiés v.

striped   *sucked up*

striped gwegweritiós *v.*; ikiros *v.*; ilíŋánètòn *v.*; ilíŋón *v.*; wíziwizatós *v.*
striped down the spine kɔlánétòn *v.*
stroke iwáwέέs *v.*
stroke affectionately iɓɔníɓónés *v.*; iɓoníɓóniés *v.*
stroll itémɔ́ɔ̀n *v.*; tasɔ́ɔ́n *v.*; zíɓòn *v.*
strong ŋɨ̀xɔ̀n *v.*
stronger (become) ŋɨxɔnʉkɔtᵃ *v.*
struggle kóríètòn *v.*; kɔrɔanón *v.*
struggle against cὲmɔ̀n *v.*
struggle for ŋués *v.*
struggle into iɓitsɨ́ɓɨtsés *v.*
struggle over ŋués *v.*
strung rɔ́ɔ́s *v.*
strut ikɔ́ɔ́résá asɨ *v.*; kɔ̀rɔ̀n *v.*
stub (grass) rumurúm *n.*
stubble (plant) sús *n.*
stubborn idɨ́kɨ́lɔ̀n *v.*
stubby ŋiríɓɨ́mɔ̀n *v.*; poŋórómòn *v.*
stubby-toothed ŋiríɓɨ́mɔ̀n *v.*
stuck ipɔ́kɔ́n *v.*
stuck (become) bokímón *v.*
stud cúrúkᵃ *n.*
student isómééσìàm *n.*; ɲósomáám *n.*
studies ɲósomá *n.*
study isómées *v.*; titimεs *v.*
stuff isikεs *v.*; kúrúɓáicíkᵃ *n.*; mεnáicíkᵃ *n.*; rʉtsés *v.*; rʉtsésʉ́kɔtᵃ *v.*
stuffed itéɓúkòn *v.*
stumble rúmánòn *v.*
stumble (make) ilέkwérés *v.*; ilέkwérεtés *v.*
stumble ahead ɓεkésá turúùkᵉ *v.*
stumble repeatedly iɲatiesá kíjáᵉ *v.*
stump gɔn *n.*

stun ɨrakεs *v.*; ɨrákésʉkɔtᵃ *v.*
stunned ɨjárɔ́n *v.*; jarámétòn *v.*
stunted rεkέɲémòn *v.*; sέrέkεkánón *v.*
stunted growth lɔɓúkεjén *n.*
stupefied tɔmεrɨmérɔ̀n *v.*
stupid iɓááŋɔ̀n *v.*
stupid person bóx *n.*; iɓááŋàsìàm *n.*
stupidity iɓááŋàs *n.*
sturdy ikékéɲòn *v.*
stutter ɗɔkɔ́lɔ́mɔ̀n *v.*; ikʉjúkújɔ̀n *v.*
stuttering gajádòn *v.*; kaŋádòn *v.*
stutteringly gàjᵃ *ideo.*
stylish titianón *v.*
stymie iɓatεs *v.*
stymie repeatedly iɓatɨ́ɓátés *v.*
subcounty ɲásáɓúkáúntì *n.*
subdue iɗáfésʉkɔtᵃ *v.*; itikεs *v.*
subdued iɗáfésʉkɔta asɨ *v.*
submerge ilumεs *v.*; ilúmésʉkɔtᵃ *v.*
subparish ɲásáɓúpárìx *n.*
subsist topíánètòn *v.*
substitute imetsités *v.*
substitute for imetsés *v.*
subtract kanésúkɔtᵃ *v.*
subversion ɲékúrukur *n.*
subverter ɲεkεsʉpan *n.*
succeed ilámɔ́n *v.*
success ídzànànès *n.*
succession ɲεɗʉpε *n.*
suck kʉɗés *v.*
suck on kʉɗés *v.*
suck on each other kʉɗʉ́nɔ́s *v.*
suck out kʉɗεtés *v.*; ts'ʉ́ts'ʉ́tés *v.*; ts'ʉ́ʉ́tés *v.*
suck up ts'ʉ́ts'ʉ́tés *v.*; ts'ʉ́ʉ́tés *v.*
sucked dry ts'ʉ́ʉ́tɔnʉkɔtᵃ *v.*
sucked up ts'ʉ́ʉ́tɔnʉkɔtᵃ *v.*

suckle naƙwɛ́s v.; naƙwɛ́súƙɔtᵃ v.; naƙwitɛs v.
suckling ɗiakᵃ n.
Sudan (South) Sʉɗán n.
Sudan gum arabic ɗerétᵃ n.; lofílitsí n.
Sudanese rebels Ŋiɲéɲéyᵃ n.
suddenly ŋàm ideo.; ùrùƙùs ideo.
suffer irɨɗón v.
suffer internally ɗuƙúkón v.
suffer quietly ɗuƙúkón v.
suffering tawanímétòn v.
sufficient nábɔnʉƙɔtᵃ v.; nábɔnʉƙɔtᵃ v.
suffocate tʉɓʉnɛ́s v.; tuɓunímétòn v.
sugar ɲósukarí n.
sugar ant ɗɔ́gɨɗɔ̂gᵃ n.
sugar bush ɲícwéɲé n.
sugary diridírón v.
suit (legal) ɲékés n.
suitable itémón v.
Suk person Ŋúupéám n.
sulk iɓʉ́túŋɔ̀n v.; imutúmútòn v.; siɲírón v.
sulky imʉtúmʉ́tɔ́s v.
sultry (weather) laŋádòn v.
sum up bɔsɛtés v.; ɗɔtsɛ́súƙɔta mɛnáᵋ v.
summarize bɔsɛtés v.; ɗɔtsɛ́súƙɔta mɛnáᵋ v.; itsʉnɛtés v.
summit kwarágwarí n.
summon iríréetés v.; óés v.
summon by whistling iwéwérés v.; iwówórés v.
summon here oetés v.
sun fetᵃ n.
sun range fetího̱ n.
sun watcher itelesíáma fetí n.
sun-watching point itelesíáwa fetí n.

sunbeam fetíbàs n.
sunbird itsókᵃ n.
Sunday Ɲásaɓétᵃ n.
sunflower ɲékiɗɛkiɗɛ́ n.; ɲétɔɔkɨɗɛ́ n.
sunglasses ɲékiyóika ni fetí n.
sunray fetíbàs n.
sunrise pɛlɛ́mɔ́na fetí v.
superiority zeís n.
supervise iritsɛ́s v.
supper ŋƙáƙá na wídzòᵉ n.
supple jaulímòn v.; tsutsukes v.
supplication wáán n.
supply ɨgɔɲɛ́s v.
support iƙaɲɛs v.; titirés v.; titiretés v.; tɔmɛɛs v.; wasitɛs v.
support each other tɔméɨnós v.
suppress iɗáfɛ́súƙɔtᵃ v.; itikes v.
suppressed iɗáfɛ́súƙɔta asɨ́ v.
suppurating tatifiánón v.
suppuration báts'ᵃ n.
suprapubic area hejú n.
surefooted tsɛ́rɛkéƙón v.
surface takánétòn v.
surgeon hoesíàm n.
surgery hoesího n.
surgery (perform) hoés v.; hoetés v.
surpass ilɔɛs v.; ilɔɛtés v.; isʉkɛs v.; súƙés v.
surpass in height ileŋes v.
surprise bógès v.; itúúmés v.
surrender tajales v.; tajálésuƙotᵃ v.; tajaletés v.
surround irikɛs v.; irɨƙɛ́súƙɔtᵃ v.; irikɛtés v.; itsóɗón v.
surrounding (of prey) nakítsòɗᵃ n.
surveil rɔ́tés v.; toreɓes v.
survey fiyeités v.
survival fiyekes n.

survive jɛ̀jɔ̀n *v.*; pùrɔ̀n *v.*; topíánètòn *v.*
survive (a mishap) isɛɛs *v.*
suspect each other ipɨ́jɨ́kimɔ́s *v.*
suspend in air alólóánitetés *v.*; alólóés *v.*
swagger ikɔ́ɔ́résá así *v.*; kɔ̀rɔ̀n *v.*
Swahili language ŋákiswahílìtòdᵃ *n.*
swallow lukés *v.*
swallow (bird) loménio *n.*
swamp ɲéjem *n.*
swamp (seasonal) ɲɛkɨ́pɔ́r *n.*; ɲotóbòr *n.*
swampily fɔ̀ts'ɔ *ideo.*
swampy fɔts'ɔ́dɔ̀n *v.*
swap ilókótsés *v.*; ixɔtsɛs *v.*; xɔ́tsés *v.*
swarm of bees (mobile) ts'ikábòtᵃ *n.*
swarm over iwówéés *v.*
sway ɲɛsʉpᵃ *n.*; súbès *v.*; súbɛsʉkɔtᵃ *v.*
sway gently jikijíkón *v.*
swear ikóŋón *v.*
swear (make) ikóŋítetés *v.*
swear an oath tsamɛtésá ikóŋóni *v.*
sweat kirotᵃ *n.*; kirotánón *v.*
sweep sébés *v.*
sweep aside ipalɨ́pálɛs *v.*
sweep away sébésukotᵃ *v.*
sweep off sébésukotᵃ *v.*
sweep up sébetés *v.*
sweeper sébésìàm *n.*
sweet diridírón *v.*; gwéts'ón *v.*; ɲátamɨtám *n.*
sweet (slightly) nɨkwɨ́dɔ̀n *v.*
sweet potato ɲakaɨ́ta *n.*
sweet potato leaves ɲakaɨ́tákákᵃ *n.*
sweet-and-sour mɨtimɨ́tɔ́n *v.*; taasámòn *v.*
sweet-smelling tukukúɲón *v.*

sweet-talk imámɛ́ɛ́s *v.*
sweeten ɛfitɛs *v.*
sweetly nɨ̀kwⁱ *ideo.*
swell èmòn *v.*; itébúkòn *v.*; tùwɔ̀n *v.*; xuanón *v.*; xuxuanón *v.*
swell (make) emites *v.*
swell (of many) emitaakón *v.*
swell up jɨrɨ́jɨ́rètòn *v.*; jɨrɨ́jɨ́rɔ̀n *v.*; tʉwétɔ́n *v.*
sweltering ririanón *v.*
sweltering (become) ririanétòn *v.*
swerve iwítón *v.*
swerve repeatedly aɲiriesón *v.*; iwitíwítòn *v.*
swift (bird) loménio *n.*
swift (white-rumped) tsòriàm *n.*
swim ilʉ́lʉ́mʉ̀ɔ̀n *v.*
swindle imɔdɛs *v.*
swine ɲéguruwé *n.*
swing akóláánón *v.*; lókólíl *n.*
swing by iɛ́bès *v.*; iɛ́bɛsʉkɔtᵃ *v.*; iɛ́bɛtés *v.*
swing side to side iŋolíŋólés *v.*
swipe iɛ́bɛsʉkɔtᵃ *v.*; iɛ́bɛtés *v.*; ipakɛs *v.*; toyeres *v.*
swipe away ipákésʉkɔtᵃ *v.*
swipe clean ikʉ́ʉ́lés *v.*
swipe off ipákésʉkɔtᵃ *v.*
swirl iwarɨwárés *v.*
swirl up tɔpirɨ́pírɔ̀n *v.*
swish idɨ̆ɨ̆dɛs *v.*
swish (mouth) íguyjʉguyjés *v.*; imúmújés *v.*
swish swish kòrrr *ideo.*
swish! swèèè *ideo.*
switch aeitetésíàwᵃ *n.*; ijʉlɛs *v.*; ijʉlɛtés *v.*; kíxwᵃ *n.*

switch (whip) ɨzaɓizaɓés *v.*; zaɓatiés *v.*
switch off (electrically) ts'eítésuƙotᵃ *v.*
switch off (of electricity) ts'oonuƙotᵃ *v.*
switch on (electrically) aeitetés *v.*
switch on (of electricity) aeétón *v.*
switch! dɨ *ideo.*
switched ijʉlɔs *v.*
swollen dúduránón *v.*; itéɓúkòn *v.*
swoon rèŋòn *v.*
swoosh ɨdɨɨdɛ́s *v.*
symmetrical ikwáánòn *v.*
sympathize cucuéétòn *v.*
synchronize ilíráitetés *v.*
synchronized ilíróòn *v.*
table ɲeméza *n.*
tableland lopem *n.*
tablet cèmèrɨèkwᵃ *n.*
tabletop ɲemézagwarí *n.*
taboo itáléánón *v.*; itálóós *v.*; ɲatal *n.*
taboo (make) itáléés *v.*
taboo of eating first isóón *n.*
taboo of eating prematurely ifófóés *n.*
taboo of leg meat dɛ *n.*
taboo of sitting on elders' stools zɛƙwɔna karatsɔɔ jáƙáᵉ *n.*
taboo of watching mother-in-law itelesa ceŋetíámàᵉ *n.*
taboo of water cue *n.*
tadpole ŋúɗúŋúɗᵃ *n.*
tag pilís *n.*
tahini ɲówoɗí *n.*
tail ikókótés *v.*; timóyᵃ *n.*
tail (chicken) bòrèn *n.*
tail (of a bird) tsúɓᵃ *n.*
tail-hair lɔ̀dᵃ *n.*
tail-tip (of a python) ɲégetsᵃ *n.*
tailor tʉfés *v.*; tʉfésɨam *n.*
take (somewhere) duƙésúƙotᵃ *v.*
take (swallow) béberetés *v.*
take a break ɨéŋónʉƙɔt ᵃ *v.*; imɔ́métɔ̀n *v.*; mɔ́métɔ̀n *v.*
take a diversion wédɔ̀n *v.*
take a loss totóánonuƙotᵃ *v.*
take a picture iwetésá ɲépítsaáᵋ *v.*
take a picture of iwetés *v.*
take a seat zɛƙwétón *v.*
take a shot at ɨ́dzesuƙotᵃ *v.*
take a sip abʉtɛtés *v.*; tsʉɓɛtés *v.*
take a trip ilɔ́ɔ́n *v.*
take advantage of inɔmɛtés *v.*
take aim iɗɨrɔ́n *v.*
take all of isʉɲɛs *v.*
take an oath ikóŋón *v.*; tsamɛtésá ikóŋóni *v.*
take apart ijʉƙújʉ́ƙɛ́s *v.*
take away ɨáƙésʉƙotᵃ *v.*; ƙanésúƙotᵃ *v.*
take away all of isúɲésʉƙɔtᵃ *v.*
take away gingerly ɗɨtésʉƙɔtᵃ *v.*
take back rajésúƙotᵃ *v.*
take by force ɛ́nɛ́suƙotᵃ *v.*; toreɓes *v.*
take by surprise bógès *v.*; itúúmés *v.*
take care of irɨtsés *v.*
take far away ɨɛƙɨ́tésʉƙɔtᵃ *v.*
take flight bʉrétón *v.*
take for a walk iláɨtésʉƙotᵃ *v.*; ɨtátéés *v.*
take form ituetésá asɨ *v.*
take gingerly ɗɨtés *v.*
take hold of ikamésúƙɔt ᵃ *v.*; ikamɛtés *v.*; ƙanetés *v.*; ŋusés *v.*; ŋusésúƙotᵃ *v.*
take hold of each other ikámúɲɔ́súƙotᵃ *v.*
take in ɓuƙítésuƙotᵃ *v.*
take in hand ƙanés *v.*

take medicine wetésá cɛmérɨ́kàᵋ *v.*
take nearly all kɔnitɛtés *v.*
take note of ewanetés *v.*
take note off ewanes *v.*
take off ɗóɗésa muceé *v.*; hoɗésúƙotᵃ *v.*; hoɗetés *v.*; lajetés *v.*; tuɓutes *v.*; tuɓútésuƙotᵃ *v.*
take off (running) ipʉ́tɛ́sʉƙɔta asɨ *v.*; tsídzonuƙotᵃ *v.*
take off flying bʉrétɔ́n *v.*; bʉrɔnʉƙɔtᵃ *v.*
take off hopping itseɗítséɗòn *v.*
take off shoes hoɗetésá taƙáɨ̀kàᵋ *v.*
take office itsyákétòn *v.*
take on credit iɗenes *v.*; iɗenetés *v.*
take out ƙanetés *v.*; pulúmítésúƙotᵃ *v.*; ts'álés *v.*; ts'aletés *v.*; tuɓutetés *v.*
take over for imetsés *v.*
take place ikásîimètòn *v.*; itíyâimètòn *v.*
take shape ituetésá asɨ *v.*
take shelter in rɨmɛs *v.*
take time iríòòn *v.*
take to court wasitɛs *v.*; wasɨ́tésʉƙɔtᵃ *v.*
take to pasture waitetés *v.*
take up tɛ́bɛ̀s *v.*
taken off guard toúmón *v.*
tale emutᵃ *n.*
talent akɨ́lɨ̀kᵃ *n.*
talk iɛ́nétɔ̀n *v.*; iɛ́nɔ́n *v.*; tôdᵃ *n.*; tódòn *v.*
talk (get to) iɛ́nɨ́tɛtɛ́s *v.*; tóítetés *v.*
talk (reckless) múɗúkánónìtòdᵃ *n.*
talk about mɔ́ɲɛs *v.*; tódetés *v.*
talk at once (crowds) régirégòn *v.*
talk foreignly iɗɨ́món *v.*
talk straight to the issue iténitɛtésá tódàᵉ *v.*
talk to each other tódinós *v.*

talkative ɗɛmɛ́ɗɔ̀n *v.*; ɗɛmɨɗɛ́món *v.*; ikútúkánón *v.*; poxóɗòn *v.*
talkatively ɗɛ̀m *ideo.*; pòx *ideo.*
talker akááḿ *n.*; tóɗààm *n.*
tall zikíɓòn *v.*
tall (grow) tɔwútɔ́n *v.*; zikíɓonuƙotᵃ *v.*
tall (make) zikíɓitésúƙotᵃ *v.*
tall (of many) zikíɓaakón *v.*
tall anthill kìtsᵃ *n.*
tallness zikíɓàs *n.*
tallow ɲéɗíol *n.*
talon tíɓòlòkòɲ *n.*
tamarind rɔ́ƙɔ́ *n.*
tamarind seeds ɗêgᵃ *n.*
Tamarindus indica rɔ́ƙɔ́ *n.*
tame bɔnɛ́s *v.*
tamp iɗɛɲɛs *v.*; itirítírés *v.*
tamp repeatedly iɗɛɲɨɗɛɲɛ́s *v.*
tamped down (become) iɗéɲímètòn *v.*
tan ɲirotsánón *v.*
tangible tabam *n.*
tangle imóɲíkees *v.*
tangle up imóɲíkeetés *v.*
tangled ságoanón *v.*
tangy mázɨmázɔ̀n *v.*
tank (military) gaso *n.*
tap on itɔ́tɔ́ɲɛ́s *v.*
tap out itɔɲítɔ́ɲɛ́s *v.*
tap repeatedly iɗɛiɗɛ́ɛ́s *v.*
tapeworm apéléle *n.*
Tarenna graveolens tsètsèkwᵃ *n.*; tsɨkwᵃ *n.*
target ipɨmɛs *v.*
tarp ɲéema *n.*
tarry tɔúrúmòn *v.*

tart ɓariɓárón *v.*; ɓárikíkón *v.*; ɓàròn *v.*; mázɨmázɔ̀n *v.*
task ɲákási *n.*; ɲetits[a] *n.*; terêg[a] *n.*
tassel (animal-tail) lɔ̀d[a] *n.*
tassel (giraffe-tail) gwaɨts'ɨ́lɔ̀d[a] *n.*
tassel (of maize) kâʒw[a] *n.*
taste kaites *v.*
tasteless ɗɛ̀ƙwɔ̀n *v.*; jɔ̀lɔ̀n *v.*; mujálámòn *v.*
tasty èfɔ̀n *v.*; gwéts'ón *v.*
tasty (become) ɛfɔnʉƙɔt[a] *v.*
tattered rídziridzánón *v.*
tattily rɛ̀s *ideo.*
tattle on ilíítés *v.*
tattoo itsɨpɨ́tsɨpés *v.*
tatty rɛsédɔ̀n *v.*
tawny ŋirotsánón *v.*
tax ɲéutsúr *n.*
tax collector ɲéútsuríám *n.*
tchagra kɨ́ɗɔ̀ *n.*
tea ɲécáy[a] *n.*
tea (African) tábarɨcue *n.*
tea (black) kotímácùè *n.*
tea (milk) tábarɨcue *n.*
teach ɨtátámés *v.*; nɔɔsanitetés *v.*
teach to read isómáitetés *v.*
teacher ɨtátámésɨ̀àm *n.*; ɲímaalímùàm *n.*
teacher (head) ámázeáma ɲésukúlu[i] *n.*
team ɲétím *n.*
tear ɗusés *v.*; ɗusúmón *v.*; ɗusutes *v.*; dzɛrɛ́s *v.*; ɨkéɲéɗés *v.*; tɔɲɛɗes *v.*
tear off ɗusésúƙot[a] *v.*; dzeretiés *v.*; dzeretiésuƙot[a] *v.*; dzɛ̀ròn *v.*
tear off (running) tsídzonuƙot[a] *v.*
tear off in strips tɔɲɨ́lɨ́ɲɨ́lés *v.*
tear out ruutésuƙot[a] *v.*; ruutetés *v.*

teardrop rain ekúcúédidí *n.*
tears ekúcé *n.*
tease ceŋánón *v.*
teaser céŋàam *n.*
teat îdw[a] *n.*
technical school tékènɨkɔl *n.*
teclea (small fruited) kɛ́láy[a] *n.*; ɲɛmaɨlɔŋ *n.*
Teclea nobilis kɛ́láy[a] *n.*; ɲɛmaɨlɔŋ *n.*
teem ƙɨdɨƙɨdɔ̀n *v.*
teem around iwówéés *v.*
teetering nɛrédɔ̀n *v.*
teeteringly nèrè *ideo.*
telephone ɲásím *n.*
television kúrúkúríka ni ɓɛƙɛ́s *n.*; ɲévíɗyo *n.*
tell fiyeitésúƙot[a] *v.*; fiyeitetés *v.*; isíséés *v.*; tódèton *v.*; tódòn *v.*
tell apart fiyeités *v.*
tell each other tódinós *v.*
tell on ilíítés *v.*
tell the time ɗoɗésúƙota ɲásáatɨ *v.*; itelesa fetí *v.*
tell the truth itsɨróna tódàk[e] *v.*
teller tódààm *n.*
telling tôd[a] *n.*
temperature (high) hábona nébwì *n.*
tempermental kwɨts'íkwɨts'ánón *v.*
temple area (of head) matáŋ *n.*
temple area (upper) matáŋɨ́gwarí *n.*
temple bone matáŋɨ̀ɔk[a] *n.*
tempt súbɛ̀s *v.*; súbɛsʉƙɔt[a] *v.*; súbɨtésúƙota asɨ́ *v.*
tempter súbèsɨ̀àm *n.*
ten toomín *n.*
ten o'clock ɲásáatikaa ts'agúsátɨk[e] *n.*
tenacious ɨkázànòòn *v.*
tend (garden) kɔés *v.*

tend (livestock)   *that*

tend (livestock) cookés *v.*
tend (to do) itáŋátòn *v.*
tended cookotós *v.*
tender rɛɓédòn *v.*; rɛdédòn *v.*; rusúdòn *v.*
tender (of plants) xɛɓédòn *v.*
tenderly dàbᵘ *ideo.*; rèdᵋ *ideo.*; rùs *ideo.*
tenderly (of plants) xèɓᵋ *ideo.*
tendon kon *n.*
tendon (Achilles) titíjɨkòn *n.*
tent ɲéema *n.*
tenth (be a) kɔnɔna toomínú *v.*
Tepeth language Ŋítépesítôdᵃ *n.*
Tepeth people Ŋítépes *n.*
tercel gwácúrúkᵃ *n.*
teres major guféém *n.*
term (school) ɲátám *n.*
term of endearment mínɛsɨèdᵃ *n.*
Terminalia brownii gáʒàdᵃ *n.*
terminate hoɗésúkotᵃ *v.*; iɲétséetés *v.*; iyétséetés *v.*
termite (early-flying) erún *n.*
termite (edible noctural) mukúádaŋ *n.*
termite (edible) dáŋ *n.*
termite (first eaten portion) kútúkᵃ *n.*
termite (small worker) sokometᵃ *n.*
termite (soldier) lókókᵃ *n.*; tɛkɛram *n.*
termite (tiny) létsᵃ *n.*
termite colony (active) abér *n.*
termite colony (inactive) wàrɔ̀tᵃ *n.*
termite column dáŋámorókᵃ *n.*
termite dirt dáŋájɨm *n.*
termite housing dáŋáhò *n.*
termite mound kutútᵃ *n.*
termite mound (holey) lòkòsòs *n.*
termite mound (old) dáŋákìtsᵃ *n.*

termite mound base dáŋádɛ̀ *n.*
termite mound chamber ɓarán *n.*
termite opening dáŋáàkᵃ *n.*
termite outlet dáŋéèkwᵃ *n.*
termite paste (edible) másálúkᵃ *n.*
termite queen dádata dáŋᵃᵉ *n.*; dáŋádadátᵃ *n.*; ŋwááta dáŋᵃᵉ *n.*
termite rain dáŋádidí *n.*
termite season dáŋátsóyᵃ *n.*
termite soil kerets'ᵃ *n.*
termite trap akarér *n.*
termite wings síts'ᵃ *n.*
termite worker nateɓú *n.*
termite(s) ɛs *n.*
termite-and-honey dish kɛkɛram *n.*
termite-drying mat uré *n.*
termites (dried, wingless) tɔkam *n.*
termites (first pot eaten) wàxɨdòm *n.*
termites (late-flying) ɓɛjékwᵃ *n.*
termites (pounded) iwótsíɔ̀z *n.*
terrapin sídilé *n.*
Teso person Ŋítésóàm *n.*
test esetés *v.*; iniŋes *v.*; ɨpɨmɛs *v.*; kaites *v.*; ɲétésɨtᵃ *n.*
testicle mɨ́ts'ᵃ *n.*
testify to itsáɗénés *v.*
testimony (false) ɲópɔkɔca *n.*
testis mɨ́ts'ᵃ *n.*
tetanus ɲeɗekea na itenɨ́túkɔta ámákᵃ *n.*
Teuso Tɛʉ́sɔ̀ *n.*
textured sɨkɨsɨ́kánétòn *v.*; sɨ́kɨsɨkánón *v.*
thank ilákásɨ́tésʉkɔtᵃ *v.*
thank (with grain) otés *v.*
thankful ilákásónʉkɔtᵃ *v.*
that tòìmèn *n.*

that (a while ago) nótsò *dem.*; nótsò *rel.*
that (a while ago, pl.) nútsù *rel.*
that (already known) déé *dem.*
that (earlier) nák^a *dem.*; nák^a *rel.*
that (earlier, pl.) níkⁱ *rel.*
that (is) tàà *comp.*
that (just there) ne *dem.*
that (long ago) nòk^o *dem.*; nòk^o *rel.*
that (long ago, pl.) nùk^u *rel.*
that (over there) ke *dem.*
that (plural) ni *rel.*
that (singular) na *rel.*
that (yesterday) sɨ̀n *dem.*; sɨ̀n *rel.*
that (yesterday, pl.) sìn *rel.*
that direction kɛ́xána kɛ *dem.*
that is (to say) tòìmɛ̀n *n.*
that one ɗa ne *pro.*
that one (just there) kɛɗá *pro.*
that one (over there) kɛɗa *pro.*
that way kɛ́xána kɛ *dem.*; kɨ́xána ke *n.*
that way! ńtía jikɨ̀ *adv.*
that way! ńtía jà *adv.*
thatch dosés *v.*
thatching (first layer) ɲáɓarasán *n.*
thatching layer kerêb^a *n.*
the coming year kɛinats^a *n.*
the good life zɛkwa ná dà *n.*
the others kiɗíása *pro.*
the very person/thing nébèd^a *n.*
the whole day ódàtù *n.*
the whole night tsoík^o *n.*; tɛrɛkɛs *ideo.*
theater (movie) ɲévíɗyòhò *n.*
theater (surgery) hoesího *n.*
theft dzú *n.*
their ńt^a *pro.*
theirs ńtíɛ̀n *pro.*
them ńt^a *pro.*
themselves ńtínebitín *n.*
then ɓàz *interj.*; já *adv.*; kɨ́ná *coordconn.*; kòt^o *coordconn.*; ts'ɛ́dɔ́ɔ́ kɔ̀nà *pro.*
theology ɲakujímɛ́n *n.*
there ƙɛ́daikɛ́n *dem.*; kɔ́ɔ́ *dem.*; ts'ɛ́daikɛ́n *dem.*
there (already known) ts'ɛ́dɛ́ɛ́ *dem.*; tʉmɛdɛ́ɛ́ *dem.*
there (far) kéda ke *dem.*; kéíta ke *dem.*; kɔ́ɔ́ kɛ *dem.*
there (near) nayé ne *dem.*; nédà *dem.*; néda ne *dem.*; néíta ne *dem.*
there there! tɨ́ɔ *interj.*; tɨ́ɔ jɔ́ɔ́ *interj.*
therefore kòt^o *coordconn.*
thermometer ɲátamóómìtà *n.*
these ni *dem.*
these areas/places niyá ni *dem.*
these days ódowicíkó nì *n.*
these guys, I tell you! ɲɔto ni *interj.*
these kids, I tell you! wice ni *interj.*
these ones ɗa *pro.*; ɗa ni *pro.*; niɗa ni *pro.*
these very days ódowicíkó nì kɔ̀nà *n.*
Thessalonians (biblical) Ŋítesalóníkaik^a *n.*
they ńt^a *pro.*
thick rɔ́mɔ́n *v.*; tetíŋón *v.*
thick (and round) baƙúlúmòn *v.*
thick (become) mogánétòn *v.*
thick (flat) maŋídòn *v.*
thick (mentally) miɲɔna íkèdè *v.*
thick (of brush) mogánón *v.*
thick (of undergrowth) bòmòn *v.*
thick (opaque) tìnòn *v.*
thick (optimally) lɔɓɔ́dòn *v.*
thick (sludgy) yaŋádòn *v.*
thick (undesirably) maŋádòn *v.*

thicken iɗíkétòn *v.*; iɗikitetés *v.*
thicken up (optimally) lɔɓɔ́ɗitɛtés *v.*
thickened iɗíkón *v.*
thicket tsekís *n.*; tsekísíakwᵃ *n.*
thicket (dense) môgᵃ *n.*
thicket (round) ɲalúkétᵃ *n.*
thickly lɔ́ɓɔ ideo.; màŋ ideo.
thickset kikímón *v.*
thief dzúám *n.*
thief (of grain) lokoɓél *n.*
thieve dzuesés *v.*; dzuesetés *v.*
thievery dzú *n.*; dzúnánès *n.*
thieving dzúnánès *n.*
thigh gubes *n.*
thigh meat ɲámoɗᵃ *n.*
thighbone gubesíɔ́kᵃ *n.*
thin ikárón *v.*; kɔrɔ́ɗɔ́mɔ̀n *v.*
thin (delicately) bɛɗɛ́ɗɔ̀n *v.*
thin (needle-) tiwɨ́ɗɔ̀n *v.*
thin (of a surface) kwɛxéɗɔ̀n *v.*
thin (too) ɗɛpéɗɔ̀n *v.*
thin out ilɔ́lɔ́kɛ́s *v.*
thing kɔ́rɔ́ɓâdᵃ *n.*
things kúrúɓâdᵃ *n.*; mɛnáícíkᵃ *n.*
things (newly discovered) kúrúɓàìnòìn *n.*
think tamɛ́s *v.*
think about tamɛtés *v.*
think about each other támɨnɔ́s *v.*
think back on tamɛ́súkɔtᵃ *v.*
think on ɲɛɓés *v.*; tamátámatés *v.*; tamɨ́támiés *v.*
thinker tamɛ́síàm *n.*; turúnónìàm *n.*
thinly bèdᵉ ideo.; ɗèpᵉ ideo.; kwèx ideo.
thinned out sɨlaɓánón *v.*

third (be a) kɔnɔna áɗònù *v.*
third (be the) mɨtɔna ɗɨ́ɛ áɗònì *v.*
third (one) ɗa áɗònì *pro.*
third time aɗonien *n.*; àɗònìkᵉ *n.*
thirst fetᵃ *n.*
thirsty paupáwón *v.*
thirteen toomíní ńdà kìɗi àɗᵉ *n.*
thirty toomínékwà àɗᵉ *n.*
this na *dem.*
this direction náxána na *dem.*
this kid, I tell you! ima na *interj.*
this one ɗa *pro.*; ɗa na *pro.*; naɗa na *pro.*
this way náxána na *dem.*
this year kainɔ na *n.*; nakain *n.*
thorax bakutsᵃ *n.*
thorn kàf *n.*
thornbush (dik-dik) ɲólíkàf *n.*
those (a while ago) nútsù *dem.*
those (already known) díí *dem.*
those (earlier) níkⁱ *dem.*
those (long ago) nùkᵘ *dem.*
those (over there) ki *dem.*
those (yesterday, pl.) sìn *dem.*
those areas kiyá ki *dem.*
those days ódowicíkó nùkᵘ *n.*
those ones (just there) kiɗá *pro.*
those ones (over there) kiɗa *pro.*
those places kiyá ki *dem.*
thoughts ŋátámɛta *n.*
thousand álìf *n.*
thrash ipés *v.*
thread ilɛ́kwéries *v.*; ɲéúsi *n.*; rɔ́és *v.*
threaded rɔ́ɔ́s *v.*
threaten iŋaalés *v.*; kitítésukotᵃ *v.*; zɨ́zès *v.*

threaten to displace ilɔ́lɨ́ɛtés *v.*
three àɗᵉ *num.*; àɗòn *v.*
three days from now kétsóita ke *n.*
three o'clock ɲásáatikaa tudátie ńda kiɗi ts'agús *n.*
three times àɗᵒ *num.*
three years ago kaɨnɔ nɔkᵓ *n.*; nɔkɛɨna ke *n.*
three years from now kaɨnɔ na far *n.*; nakaɨna far *n.*
thresh ipés *v.*
threshing floor ɓɔɗᵃ *n.*; ɗɨ́pɔ̀ *n.*
threshold lòkìtòŋ *n.*; lòrìòŋòn *n.*
threshold consciousness mɔɗɔ́ɗɔ́èkwᵃ *n.*
thrice àɗᵒ *num.*
thrifty toikíkón *v.*
thrive (of plants) gáruɓúɓón *v.*; karuɓúɓón *v.*
throat morókᵃ *n.*
throat infection tòmàlàɗò *n.*
throb dìkwòn *v.*
throng ɲéɓúku *n.*; ɲerípírìpᵃ *n.*
throttle iketiés *v.*
through nɛ́ɛ́ *prep.*
throw góózés *v.*; ɨmasɛs *v.*
throw a spear toɓésúƙota ɓɨsáᵋ *v.*
throw a stone zéɓès *v.*
throw a stone that way zéɓesuƙotᵃ *v.*
throw a stone this way zéɓetés *v.*
throw away góózesuƙotᵃ *v.*; ɨmásésuƙɔtᵃ *v.*
throw down gwarés *v.*
throw down carelessly futs'áts'ésuƙotᵃ *v.*
throw off iɓókésuƙotᵃ *v.*

throw stones turues *v.*; turuetés *v.*
throw this way góózetés *v.*; ɨmasɛtés *v.*
thrower (of meat) góózésíàm *n.*
thrush (rock-) nàlèmùdzòɗà *n.*
thrust ututetés *v.*; xutés *v.*; xutésúƙotᵃ *v.*
thrust (a knife) rutésúƙotᵃ *v.*
thrust repeatedly ututiés *v.*
thud ƙádiƙádès *v.*
thud! ɗùl *ideo.*
thumb kɔrɔ́ká ná zè *n.*
thumb piano lokemú *n.*
thump dìkwòn *v.*; ɨɲatɛs *v.*; ƙádiƙádès *v.*
thump a tree iwésá dakwí *v.*
thump repeatedly ɨɲatiés *v.*
thump thump kɨ́mátsᵃ *ideo.*; kùkᵘ *ideo.*
Thunbergia alata ɲápatᵃ *n.*
thunder ɗukuɗúkón *v.*; ikɨ́lɔ́n *v.*; irúrúmòòn *v.*; ƙìròn *v.*; ƙironuƙotᵃ *v.*; tɔtɔanón *v.*
thunder off itíƙíròòn *v.*; itíríƙòòn *v.*; ƙironuƙotᵃ *v.*
Thur person Ŋítéɓuríám *n.*
Thursday Ɲákásíá ts'agúsíkᵉ *n.*
thus kòtᵒ *coordconn.*
thwart kwaɲés *v.*; kwaɲésúƙotᵃ *v.*
tibia tsɛrékᵃ *n.*
tick ɲamaɗaŋ *n.*
tick (mark) totsetes *v.*
tick grass ɲamaɗaŋɨ́kú *n.*
tickbird dzàr *n.*
tickle ikwɨlɨ́kwɨ́lɛ́s *v.*
tie ɲátáyᵃ *n.*; zɨ́kés *v.*
tie around kɛkɛrɛs *v.*
tie off iliɗés *v.*; iliɗetés *v.*
tie off umbilical cord zɨ́késà ƙɔ̀ɓàᵋ *v.*
tie tightly irijɛs *v.*
tie up inénéés *v.*; inénéésuƙotᵃ *v.*; zɨ́késuƙɔtᵃ *v.*; zɨ́kɛtés *v.*

tied zíkós *v.*
tied down loosely yaŋádòn *v.*
tied down tightly tokódòn *v.*
tied off ilidʼós *v.*
tied tightly irijɔs *v.*; ŋòtsɔ̀n *v.*
tied together zíkízikánón *v.*
tight idʼɨŋón *v.*; ipɨtɔs *v.*; iridʼɔs *v.*
tighten hard ipɨtɛs *v.*
tightened hard ipɨtɔs *v.*
tightly tɨɓⁱ *ideo.*
till tɔkɔ́bɛs *v.*
till morning tsoíkᵒ *n.*; tɛrɛkɛs *ideo.*
tillable tɔkɔbam *n.*
tilled tɔkɔ́bɨtɔtɔ́s *v.*
tiller (hand) ɲɛtɛrɛkitaa na kwétɨkàᵋ *n.*
tilt ipuŋes *v.*; likés *v.*
tilt over ipuŋetés *v.*
time ɲásáatᵃ *n.*; ɲásápari *n.*
time off ɲákarám *n.*
timid xɛ̀ɓɔ̀n *v.*
timid person xɛɓásɨàm *n.*
timidity xɛɓás *n.*
Timothy Timatéwᵃ *n.*
Timothy (biblical) Timatéwᵃ *n.*
Timu Road Tímumucé *n.*
tinder gamam *n.*; lúulú *n.*
tinder (small) dʼɛ̀rɛ̀tsᵃ *n.*
tinkerbird (red-fronted) kɔkɨ́rɨkɔkᵃ *n.*
tiny dununúòn *v.*; gɔdʼɨrɨmɔ̀n *v.*; tsaúdʼɨmɔ̀n *v.*; tɔ́dʼɔ́n *v.*
tiny (opening) mɨrɨ́dʼɨmɔ̀n *v.*
tip edᵃ *n.*; edᵃ *n.*; iɲipes *v.*; kàtsᵃ *n.*; kátsêdᵃ *n.*
tip over íbodʼolés *v.*
tipped iwɨ́tsón *v.*

tipper ƙúdèsìàm *n.*; ɲétípa *n.*
tiptoe itídʼidʼésá asɨ *v.*; itsedʼítsédʼòn *v.*
tiptop (of hut) lómoloró *n.*
tire bɔrétɔ́n *v.*; dɛ *n.*
tire shoe kaetaƙáyᵃ *n.*
tire track dɛ *n.*
tired bɔ́rɔ́n *v.*; ilɔ́étɔ̀n *v.*; ilɔ́yón *v.*
tired (become) bɔrétɔ́n *v.*
tissue (osseous) ɔkᵃ *n.*
titillate ikɛdʼíkédʼés *v.*; ikwatɨkwátés *v.*
title éda na moranâdᵉ *n.*; ikedᵃ *n.*
Titus Títò *n.*
Titus (biblical) Títò *n.*
to the end dʼùdʼùŋ *ideo.*; tùtùr *ideo.*
to the rear jɨ̀rɨ̀kᵉ *n.*
toad ƙwaátᵃ *n.*; ƙwaatá na áwìkàᵉ *n.*
toast iɔ́ɓɔ́rés *v.*
tobacco lɔ́tɔ́ɓᵃ *n.*; ts'ûdᵃ *n.*
tobacco (long-leaf) loríónómor *n.*; pélédʼèkᵃ *n.*
tobacco (pounded) lɔɨtsɨ́r *n.*
tobacco cone bɔrɔkɔ́ƙᵃ *n.*; lɔ́tɔ́ɓabɔrɔkɔ́ƙᵃ *n.*
tobacco garden lɔ́tɔ́ɓàsèdᵃ *n.*
tobacco garden (grassy) mɨrɔn *n.*
tobacco grinding stone lɔ́tɔ́ɓàgwàs *n.*
tobacco horn ɲeɓuryaŋ *n.*
tobacco hunger lɔ́tɔ́ɓàɲèƙᵃ *n.*
tobacco leaves aɲawᵃ *n.*
tobacco pipe làr *n.*
tobacco user lɔ́tɔ́ɓààm *n.*
today nóódwáá *n.*
Toddalia asiatica lókódʼém *n.*
toe dɛákɔ́rɔ́ƙᵃ *n.*; kɔrɔ́ƙᵃ *n.*
toe (big) kɔrɔ́ká ná zè *n.*

455

toe bone kɔrɔ́kɔ́ɔkᵃ *n.*
toe cut lɔ́ɲɨ́zìɲɨ̀z *n.*
toenail tíbòlòkòɲ *n.*
toes (extra) ɲɛ́ɗɔ́nɨɗɔn *n.*
together ikéé kɔ̀n *n.*; kédìè kɔ̀n *n.*; kédò kɔ̀n *n.*
toilet ets'íhò *n.*; ɲótsorón *n.*
tolerate nɛɛ́s *v.*; nɛɛsúƙɔtᵃ *v.*; taɗaɲes *v.*
tomato ɲɛ́ɲaaɲá *n.*
tomb ripᵃ *n.*; tás *n.*; tásêdᵃ *n.*
tomorrow (morning) baratsᵒ *n.*; táábaratsᵃ *n.*; táábaratsᵒ *n.*
tomorrow next kétsóibarátsᵃ *n.*
tongs ɲɔkɔ́ɲɛ́tᵃ *n.*
tongue naƙaf *n.*
too jɨ̀kᵋ *adv.*
tool (handle-less) lolemukán *n.*
tool (hooked stick) pòròtᵃ *n.*
tooth kwaywᵃ *n.*
tooth gap (have a) ɲaɲálómòn *v.*
toothbrush ɲáɓʉrás *n.*; súƙútésɨ́dàkwᵃ *n.*; tsitsɨ́n *n.*
toothbrush tree ɓaláŋ *n.*
toothless ŋalólómòn *v.*
toothless gums ŋalúɓᵃ *n.*
toothpaste ɲókólíƙètᵃ *n.*
toothpick (grass) kua mɨnɛ́sɨɛ kwaɨtɨ́nɨ́ *n.*
toothy iɲɨ́sɨmòn *v.*
top gwarí *n.*; isʉkɛs *v.*; kàtsᵃ *n.*; kátsêdᵃ *n.*; súƙés *v.*
top of a gorge fòtsàiƙᵃ *n.*
top of foot dɛágwarí *n.*
top of head ikágwarí *n.*
top part gwaríêdᵃ *n.*; ikedᵃ *n.*
topi ɲémúƙetᵃ *n.*

topic mɛnééƙwᵃ *n.*; tódèèƙwᵃ *n.*
topics áƙátìkìn *n.*
Toposa Kɔrɔmɔtᵃ *n.*
Toposa dialect Kɔrɔmɔtátôdᵃ *n.*
Toposa person dzònìàm *n.*; tɔ́ɓɔ́kɨkàam *n.*
topple ɨbatés *v.*; ɨbatɛtés *v.*
topple repeatedly ɨbatiés *v.*
topsy-turvy lɔŋɔanón *v.*
torch kâʒwᵃ *n.*; ɲótótsᵃ *n.*
torment itsanɨ́tsánés *v.*
torn dzɛrɔ́sɔ́n *v.*
torpid ijíŋáánón *v.*
torrent íswᵃ *n.*
tortoise kàè *n.*
tortoise hatchling kàèìm *n.*
tortoise shell kàèƙwàz *n.*; rògìrògᵃ *n.*
torture itsanɨ́tsánés *v.*
toss góózés *v.*; ɨmasɛs *v.*; tɔrɛ́s *v.*; towates *v.*
toss (for divination) ipés *v.*
toss aside hábatsésúƙotᵃ *v.*; hábatsetés *v.*
toss away góózesuƙotᵃ *v.*; ɨmásésʉƙɔtᵃ *v.*; tɔrɛ́súƙɔtᵃ *v.*; towátésúƙotᵃ *v.*
toss in mouth iɗómóés *v.*
toss off towátésúƙotᵃ *v.*
toss out of sight isɔmɛs *v.*
toss this way góózetés *v.*; ɨmasɛtés *v.*; tɔrɛtés *v.*
totally jikɨ̂ *adv.*; kɔ́nɨ́tiákᵋ *pro.*; mùkà *adv.*; pílè *ideo.*; tsútɔ̀ *adv.*
tottering nɛrɛ́dɔ̀n *v.*
touch tábès *v.*
touch (make) tábitetés *v.*
touch all over tábodiés *v.*
touch down toɗóón *v.*
touch each other tábunós *v.*

touch lightly ikɛdíkédɛ́s *v.*; ikwatíkwátɛ́s *v.*
touch on (topic) tábès *v.*
touchable tabam *n.*
touchwood lúulú *n.*
tough diriɲíɲɔ́n *v.*; itsyátón *v.*; nikwídòn *v.*
tough (leathery) tudádòn *v.*
tough (to chew) kaŋádòn *v.*; kwaídòn *v.*
tough when cooked haúdòn *v.*
toughen ŋixítésukɔtᵃ *v.*
toughly nìkwⁱ *ideo.*; tùdᵃ *ideo.*
tousle dubɛ́s *v.*
tow béberɛ́s *v.*
towel ɲataulɔ́ *n.*
tower (celluar/radio) ɲébusitá *n.*
town ɲálaín *n.*; táùn *n.*
town-dweller ɲáláínìkààm *n.*
toxin ɲekísórìtᵃ *n.*
trace idupes *v.*; ikɛrɛs *v.*
trachea morɔ́ká ná zè *n.*
track ts'íts'ɛ́s *v.*
track footprints ts'íts'ɛ́sà dèìkàᵋ *v.*
tractor ɲɛtɛrɛkita *n.*
tractor (hand) ɲɛ́tɛrɛkitaa na kwɛ́tìkàᵋ *n.*
trade dzîgwᵃ *n.*; dzígwès *v.*; ilɔ́kɔ́tsɛ́s *v.*; ixɔtsɛs *v.*; xɔ́tsɛ́s *v.*
trade with each other xɔ́tsínɔ́s *v.*
trader ŋímutsurúsìàm *n.*
trader (being a) ŋímutsurúsìnànès *n.*
trading center ɲálaín *n.*; táùn *n.*
tradition ɲatal *n.*; ɲeker *n.*
traditional healer irésíàm *n.*
Tragia insuavis súkúsuká *n.*
trail ikɔ́kɔ́tɛ́s *v.*; muce *n.*
trail (fresh) fúfútᵃ *n.*

trailer ikɔ́rú *n.*; ɲeturɛ́ɛ́là *n.*
trailhead mucédè *n.*
train itátámɛ́s *v.*; iyoes *v.*; nɔɔsanitetɛ́s *v.*
trainer itátámɛ́síàm *n.*; ŋímaalímùàm *n.*
training ɲókós *n.*
trait (personality) ɲɛpitɛa ámáᵉ *n.*
traitor tolúónìàm *n.*
trample íbudɛ́s *v.*; iɲíkéésukotᵃ *v.*; takwitakwiɛ́s *v.*
trample termites takwiesúkota dáŋáᵉ *v.*
trample to pieces firíts'ɛ́s *v.*
transfer ijokes *v.*; ijɔ́késukotᵃ *v.*; ikɔbɛs *v.*; ilójésukotᵃ *v.*; ilɔpɛs *v.*; iméérɛ́s *v.*; iríítɛ́s *v.*; irotes *v.*
transfer here ikɔbɛtɛ́s *v.*
transfer repeatedly irotírótɛ́s *v.*
transfer there ikɔ́bɛ́sukɔtᵃ *v.*
transform beníónukotᵃ *v.*; ibéléɛ́s *v.*; ibéléìmètòn *v.*; ilotses *v.*; ilotsímétòn *v.*
transformation of land beniitesa kíjáᵉ *n.*
transgender person ɲéliwolíwo *n.*
translate ikɔbɛs *v.*; ikɔbɛtɛ́s *v.*; ilotses *v.*
translate back and forth ikɔ́bínɔ́s *v.*
transmit ijokes *v.*; ijɔ́késukotᵃ *v.*
transmit trouble ijokesa mɛnáᵋ *v.*
transparency eas *n.*
transparent bɛts'òn *v.*; tsaórómòn *v.*
transparent (of many) bɛts'aakón *v.*
transpire ikásíìmètòn *v.*; itíyáìmètòn *v.*
transplant irotes *v.*
transport iríítɛ́s *v.*; irotes *v.*; tsídzès *v.*
transport away tsídzesukotᵃ *v.*
transvestite ɲéliwolíwo *n.*
trap kotsítésukotᵃ *v.*; rúɛ́s *v.*; tɔlɔkɛ́s *v.*
trap (cage) ɲábáo *n.*
trap (large animal) ɲéritá *n.*
trap (metal) ɲétéke *n.*

trap (net) ságòsìm *n.*
trap (small-animal) lɔwídᵃ *n.*
trap (spike) ɲátatsᵃ *n.*
trap (termite) akarér *n.*
trap (termites) kokoes *v.*
trap with net ságwès *v.*
trapezius ɲálaƙamáítᵃ *n.*
trapped kòtsòn *v.*
trapped (become) kotsonuƙotᵃ *v.*
trapping tɔ̀lɔ̀kᵃ *n.*
trapping pit ɲɔ́sɔ́ɔ́ƙatᵃ *n.*
trapping with snares sâgwᵃ *n.*
trash ts'ʉts'ʉ *n.*
trash (flashflood) ɲérímama *n.*
travel ɓɛƙés *v.*; ɨlɔ́ɔ́n *v.*
travel away ɨlɔ́ɔ́nʉƙɔt ᵃ *v.*
travel here ɨlɛ́ɛ́tɔ̀n *v.*
travel preparation sùɓètᵃ *n.*
travel together ɓɛƙésɨ́nɔ́s *v.*
traveler ɓɛƙésɨ̀àm *n.*; ƙòònìàm *n.*
traveler (preparing) súɓánònìàm *n.*
traverse pídés *v.*; tɔkɛ́ɛ́rés *v.*
treacherous ɨmadɨ́mádɔ̀n *v.*
tread on takwés *v.*
treat gwadam *n.*; ɨmʉ́mwárés *v.*; irés *v.*; ɲɛmʉna *n.*
treat (medicinally) wetitésá cɛmérɨ́kàᵋ *v.*
treat a wound ɨmadɛsa ɔ́jáᵋ *v.*
treat equally ikwáánitetés *v.*
treat gently ɨɓáɓɛ́ɛ́s *v.*
treat respectfully irímɛ́és *v.*
treatment cèmèr *n.*
tree dakwᵃ *n.*
tree (sacred) lɔ́ƙɔ́ŋ *n.*; ɲɔ́ƙɔ́ŋ *n.*
tree (unknown) kɔ́rɔ́ɓàìdàkwᵃ *n.*

tree species àɗèŋèlìò *n.*; ɓàjᵃ *n.*; ɓólìs *n.*; ɓòŋ *n.*; basaúréèkwᵃ *n.*; boxoƙorétᵃ *n.*; ɗewen *n.*; dzôgᵃ *n.*; ekoɗitᵃ *n.*; èmùsìà *n.*; fàìdwᵃ *n.*; gàràjᵃ *n.*; godiywᵃ *n.*; ibétᵃ *n.*; iroroyᵃ *n.*; isókóyᵃ *n.*; ƙɔ́ɓʉƙɔ́ɓᵃ *n.*; kàrè *n.*; kɛ́láyᵃ *n.*; kómoló *n.*; kunétᵃ *n.*; kùr *n.*; lóɗíwé *n.*; lɔ́kɛ́rʉ́ *n.*; lokum *n.*; lɔ́lɔwɨ́ *n.*; lòŋìr *n.*; meleke *n.*; mókol *n.*; mozokoɗᵃ *n.*; mùs *n.*; ŋʉrʉ́sá *n.*; naarákɨlɛ *n.*; ɲáɓata *n.*; ɲákaɓurúr *n.*; ɲákátɨrɨ́ɓa *n.*; ɲamalil *n.*; ɲécaal *n.*; ɲécaal *n.*; ɲékɨsɨ́ *n.*; ɲékwaŋa *n.*; ɲéleɓuléɓu *n.*; ɲɛmaɨlɔŋ *n.*; ɲéɲéso *n.*; ɲépípa *n.*; ɲéyoroeté *n.*; ɲóɗomé *n.*; ɲókotitᵃ *n.*; ɲɔ́ƙoloƙolétᵃ *n.*; òbìjòòz *n.*; rirís *n.*; ròr *n.*; rukûdzᵃ *n.*; seger *n.*; seínení *n.*; sésèn *n.*; ts'ɔƙɔ́m *n.*; tsàl *n.*; tsereɗeɗí *n.*; tsètsèkwᵃ *n.*; tsɨkwᵃ *n.*; tɛɛté *n.*; tʉlárɔ́yᵃ *n.*; tùr *n.*; tʉ̀tʉ̀f *n.*; ʉrúsáyᵃ *n.*; wariwar *n.*; xuxûbᵃ *n.*
tree trunk dakúɓɔ́l *n.*
treeless ŋoléánètòn *v.*
tremble kìtòn *v.*; kwalɨ́kwálɔ̀n *v.*; tsábatsabánón *v.*
tremble (begin to) kitétón *v.*
tremble (make) kitítésuƙotᵃ *v.*
tremor irikíríkòn *v.*
trench ɲéƙúrumotᵃ *n.*; urúr *n.*
tri-colored ɓokóánètòn *v.*; eséánètòn *v.*
trial (legal) ɲékés *n.*
tribe dìywᵃ *n.*; ɲákaɓɨlá *n.*
Tribulus cistoides ɲesuƙuru *n.*
tribunal ɲókótᵃ *n.*
tribute meetésíicíkᵃ *n.*
tricep cwɛtéém *n.*
tricep (lower) kʉléèm *n.*
trick ɨmɔdɛs *v.*; itwáɲítésúƙotᵃ *v.*
trickle mɨrɨmɨ́rɔ́n *v.*; tɔléléɔ̀n *v.*
tricky ɨmadɨ́mádɔ̀n *v.*

trigger ɲɛɗɛ́sɛ̂dᵃ *n.*; ɲétíka *n.*
trigger (trap) iɗalɛs *v.*
trim ikwákwárɛ́s *v.*; ilimɛs *v.*
trim back ilimɛtɛ́s *v.*; isésélés *v.*
trip ilɛ́kwɛ́rɛ́s *v.*; ɲásápari *n.*; rúmánitésúkotᵃ *v.*; rúmánòn *v.*
trip (of a trap) iɗálésʉkɔta asɨ́ *v.*
trip (trap) iɗalɛs *v.*
trip repeatedly iɲatiesá kíjáᵉ *v.*
trip up ilɛ́kwɛ́rɛtɛ́s *v.*
tripod lèwèɲìdè *n.*
Triumfetta annua lɔ́mɔ́ɗaátᵃ *n.*
trochanter (greater) obólénìɔkᵃ *n.*
tromp íbuɗés *v.*
troop (of baboons) kwaár *n.*
trophy tɔ́rɔ́bɛsa na ɨ́lɔɛsɨ́ *n.*
trot isipísipòn *v.*; isɔkɨ́sɔ́kɔ̀n *v.*; isʉmʉ́sʉ́mɔ̀n *v.*
troublemaker mɛnáám *n.*
troubles mɛn *n.*; ɲɨ́tsan *n.*
trough itúɓᵃ *n.*; sɔ́kᵃ *n.*
trounce ipés *v.*; ɨrɛɛs *v.*
trousers (pair of) gwan *n.*; ɲétorós *n.*; ɲótorós *n.*
trowel ɲétʉráwèl *n.*
truck lóórì *n.*; ɲolórì *n.*
truck (small) kàè *n.*
true itsɨ́rón *v.*; tsɨ́rón *v.*; tɔɓéɔ́n *v.*
true (typically) toɓéíón *v.*
truly easíkᵉ *n.*
trumpet ikɨ́lɔ́n *v.*; ɲérʉpɛpé *n.*
trunk (elephant) gìgᵃ *n.*; komótsᵃ *n.*; òŋòrìkwètᵃ *n.*
trunk (tree) dakúɓɔ́l *n.*
trunks (pair of) ɲésiriwáli *n.*; ɲosokoloké *n.*

trust tɔnʉpɛs *v.*
truster tɔnʉpɛsíám *n.*
trustworthy tɔnʉpam *n.*
truth eas *n.*
truth (be the) mitɔna eas *v.*
truthful person easíám *n.*
try ikatɛs *v.*; kaites *v.*
try in court iniŋes *v.*
try repeatedly ikatɨ́kátɛ́s *v.*
tryst tirésíàwᵃ *n.*
tsetse fly ɲéɗɨitᵃ *n.*
tub itúɓᵃ *n.*
tubby gerúsúmòn *v.*; poŋórómòn *v.*; rexúkúmòn *v.*
tuberculosis (pulmonary) gafígáfikaɲeɗeké *n.*; ɲeɗekea bákútsìkàᵉ *n.*
tuck ipuŋes *v.*
tuck away ikɨ́ɗɨ́tsés *v.*
tuck into ɨ́bʉbʉɲés *v.*; ɨ́bʉbʉŋésúkɔtᵃ *v.*
tuck up rúbès *v.*; rúbɛsʉkɔtᵃ *v.*
tuckered ziálámòn *v.*; zíkímétòn *v.*; ziláámòn *v.*
Tuesday Ɲákásíá lèɓètsìkᵉ *n.*
tuft tsulátᵃ *n.*
tug ɗúrɛ́s *v.*; ɗʉtɛ́s *v.*
tug back and forth ilikɨ́lɨ́kɛ́s *v.*
tumble ɨ́batɛ́s *v.*; ɨ́batɛtɛ́s *v.*; ruɓétón *v.*; ruɓonukɔtᵃ *v.*
tumble down ɨ́batɛsa asɨ́ *v.*
tumble repeatedly ɨ́batiés *v.*
tumefy emites *v.*; èmòn *v.*
tumid bɔfɔ́dɔ̀n *v.*
tune out bálábálatés *v.*
tuner ɲérɛ́ɗi *n.*
tunnel wèl *n.*
tunnel (center) wèlèèkwᵃ *n.*
turaco fúlukurú *n.*
turbid kaɓúrútsánón *v.*

turgid bɔfɔ́dɔ̀n *v.*
Turkana language Pakóícétôdᵃ *n.*
Turkana person ŋɔrɛ́ám *n.*; Pakóám *n.*; rɔwáám *n.*
Turkanaland Burukáyᵃ *n.*
turkey ɲékulukúl *n.*
turn aɲireꜱ *v.*; ijᵾlɛꜱ *v.*; irɨ́ɲítéꜱ *v.*; irɨ́ŋɔ́n *v.*; iwoleꜱ *v.*
turn against tolúétòn *v.*; tolúónukotᵃ *v.*; tolúútésukotᵃ *v.*
turn against each other tolúúnóꜱ *v.*
turn around iɓóɓóŋòn *v.*; ijᵾlɛtéꜱ *v.*; irɨ́ɲítésᵾkɔtᵃ *v.*; irɨ́ŋɔ́nᵾkɔtᵃ *v.*
turn away irɨ́ɲítésᵾkɔtᵃ *v.*; irɨ́ŋɔ́nᵾkɔtᵃ *v.*; itɨ́ɨ́léꜱ *v.*
turn back this way iɓóɓóŋètòn *v.*
turn back to back kᵾkᵾmánítésukotᵃ *v.*; kᵾkᵾmánónukotᵃ *v.*
turn down imɛ́ɗéléꜱ *v.*; míjéꜱ *v.*
turn off kɔkɛtéꜱ *v.*
turn off (electrically) ts'eítésukotᵃ *v.*
turn off (of electricity) ts'oonukotᵃ *v.*
turn on (attack) tokíróòn *v.*
turn on (betray) tolúétòn *v.*; **turn on** tolúónukotᵃ *v.*
turn on (electrically) aeitetéꜱ *v.*
turn on (of electricity) aeétón *v.*
turn on each other tolúúnóꜱ *v.*
turn one's back to kᵾkᵾmanéꜱ *v.*
turn oneself around iɓéléésukota asɨ *v.*
turn oneself over repeatedly iɓilíɓíléꜱá asɨ *v.*
turn out pukéꜱ *v.*; puketéꜱ *v.*
turn out away pukésúkotᵃ *v.*
turn over bukures *v.*; bukúrésukotᵃ *v.*; bukusítésukotᵃ *v.*; iɓéléés *v.*; iɓéléetés *v.*; iɓéléìmètòn *v.*; iɓélúkáìmètòn *v.*; iɓélúkéés *v.*; ijᵾlɛtés *v.*; iwoletés *v.*
turn over (soil) iwúlákés *v.*
turn this way irɨ́ŋétòn *v.*
turn up takánétòn *v.*
turn upside-down tuɗúlútés *v.*
turned ijᵾlɔs *v.*
turned on (sexually) iɓurímétòn *v.*; kwídikwidós *v.*
turtle sídilé *n.*
tusk (elephant) òŋòrìkwàywᵃ *n.*
tusker òŋòr *n.*
tussock tsulátᵃ *n.*
tweak tᵾnés *v.*
tweak off tɔɲimɛtés *v.*
twelve toomíní ńda kidɨ léɓetsᵉ *n.*
twelve o'clock ɲásáatikaa tudátie ńdà kèdɨ kɔ̀n *n.*
twenty toomínékwa léɓetsᵉ *n.*
twice lèɓètsᵒ *num.*
twiddle ígujugujés *v.*
twilight xiŋatᵃ *n.*; xiŋatétón *v.*
twilit mígirigíránón *v.*
twin (be a) imúón *v.*
twine imɔ́jɨ́rés *v.*; itoŋes *v.*; natiɓᵃ *n.*
twinkle itweɲítwéɲòn *v.*
twins ɲímúí *n.*
twirl tɔpirɨ́pɨ́rés *v.*
twirl between hands tsapés *v.*
twirlable tsapetam *n.*
twist aɲireꜱ *v.*; imɔ́jɨ́rés *v.*; itoŋes *v.*; tɔpirɨ́pɨ́rés *v.*
twist round itútúrés *v.*
twist the truth itoŋetésá tódàᵉ *v.*
twist up imákóitetés *v.*; ipɔ́pɨ́rés *v.*; kakirés *v.*

twisted gólógolánón v.
twisted round itúturós v.
twisted up imákóòn v.
twisted up (become) imákwéètòn v.
twitch imɨmɨjɛ́s v.; irikírikòn v.
two lèɓètsᵉ num.; leɓétsón v.
two (make) leɓetsítésuƙotᵃ v.
two o'clock ɲásáatikaa tudátie ńdà kìdî àdᵉ n.
two times lèɓètsᵒ num.
two years ago kaino nótso n.; nɔkɛɨn n.
two years from now kaino na tso n.; nakaɨna tso n.
two-by-two leɓetsíón v.
type bònɨtᵃ n.; ɲákaɓɨlá n.
Typha species bulubuláta na sábàikàᵉ n.
udder ídoho n.
udder (cow) fiyòɨdwᵃ n.
Uganda Ugándà n.
ugly itópénòn v.; làlòn v.
uh ... ndaicé n.
uh-huh, sure! yóói interj.
ulcer ɗɔl n.
ulcer (stomach) bùbùɔ̀jᵃ n.
ululate iyíyéés v.
um ... átᵃ n.; ndaicé n.
umber ts'aráfón v.
umbilical cord ƙɔɓasim n.
umbilical hernia ƙɔɓa na zikîbᵃ n.
umbrella thorn tree sègᵃ n.
unadorned iɓámón v.; sɨlójómòn v.
unaffixed dolódòn v.; roiróón v.
unattractive itópénòn v.
unavailable bɨrɔ́ɔ́n v.
unbeliever nɛpɛ́ƙáàm n.

unbend idɨrítésuƙotᵃ v.
unbending kɛtérémòn v.
unbreakable lɛrédòn v.; mɛkɛlélón v.
unbreakably lèr ideo.
unburdened bùlòn v.
uncertain iɨƙón v.
unchewable mɛkɛlélón v.; ts'afɨdòn v.
unchewably ts'àf ideo.
uncle (his/her father's brother) babatᵃ n.
uncle (his/her father's sister's husband) tatatíéákwᵃ n.
uncle (his/her mother's brother) momotᵃ n.
uncle (his/her mother's sister's husband) tototíéákwᵃ n.
uncle (mother's brother) momó n.
uncle (mother's sister's husband) totóèàkwᵃ n.
uncle (my father's brother) abáŋ n.
uncle (my father's sister's husband) tátàèàkwᵃ n.
uncle (your father's brother) bábò n.
uncle (your father's sister's husband) tátóéákwᵃ n.
unclean ŋɔrɔ́ɲómòn v.; ɲɔŋɔ́rómòn v.
unclear (information) kìtsòn v.
unclouded kánón v.
uncomfortable ɗɛɲiɗɛɲɔs v.
uncomplicated ɓàŋòn v.
unconscious bàdòn v.; ifáfúƙós v.
unconscious (go) badonuƙotᵃ v.; rèŋòn v.
uncooked ts'ágwòòn v.
uncooperative with each other ɗúlúnós v.

461

uncoordinated hádaadánón *v.*; ɨɓaɲɨ́ɓaŋɔ̀n *v.*
uncover ɲáɲésʉkɔtᵃ *v.*
undependable iléjíánón *v.*; imádĩ́ɲánón *v.*
underarm bàbà *n.*
underbelly búbùèdᵃ *n.*
underclothes (pair of) ɲekúrúm *n.*
undercook kitsonukotᵃ *v.*
undercooked imʉránón *v.*; kìtsòn *v.*
underfoot dèɨ̀kàˀ *n.*
undergird titirés *v.*; titiretés *v.*
underground ɗis *n.*; jʉmááƙwᵃ *n.*
underminer ɲɛkɛsʉpan *n.*
underside búbùèdᵃ *n.*
understand enés *v.*; nesíbes *v.*; walámón *v.*
understand each other nesíbunós *v.*
understood nesíbos *v.*; nesíbunós *v.*
underwear (pair of) ɲekúrúm *n.*
undeveloped ikúrúfánón *v.*
undigestible ts'afʉ́dɔ̀n *v.*
undigestibly ts'àf *ideo.*
undivided (of cash) ɗukúdòn *v.*
undress hoɗésúkotᵃ *v.*; hoɗetés *v.*
unearth úgès *v.*; úgetés *v.*
uneducated ɨɓááŋɔ̀n *v.*
unemployed ɨlwárɔna terégù *v.*
uneven ƙumúƙúmánón *v.*
unfastened dolódòn *v.*; roiróón *v.*
unfathomable xakútsúmòn *v.*
unfixed ɨɓámɔ́n *v.*
unfurl tɔpɛtɛs *v.*; tɔpétésʉkotᵃ *v.*
uniform ɲéyúnìfòm *n.*
unintelligent ɨɓááŋɔ̀n *v.*
uninterested bɔ́rɔ́n *v.*

uninteresting itópénòn *v.*; jɔ̀lɔ̀n *v.*
unique benión *v.*; bɛnɔ́ɔ́n *v.*
unison (act in) ilíréètòn *v.*
unite kɔnɨ́tésʉkɔtᵃ *v.*
universe kíjᵃ *n.*
university yunivásìtì *n.*
unkempt sɔɓɔ́lɔ́mɔ̀n *v.*
unknowing ɨɓááŋɔ̀n *v.*
unlawful toɗyakos *v.*
unless ɗàmʉ̀s *subordconn.*; ɗɛ̀mʉ̀s *subordconn.*
unlidded lɛɓéɲémɔ̀n *v.*
unliftably ɓa *ideo.*
unload ɓuƙetés *v.*
unload a load ɓuƙetésá botáᵉ *v.*
unmanageable imákóón *v.*
unmanageable (become) imákwéètòn *v.*
unmoving wàsɔ̀n *v.*
unobserved kúbòn *v.*
unobstructed fotólón *v.*
unoccupied bùlòn *v.*; ɨɓámɔ́n *v.*; ipásóón *v.*
unoccupied (become) bulonukotᵃ *v.*
unpierced (ears) mʉɗáŋámɔ̀n *v.*
unproductive isʉ́wɔ́ɔn *v.*
unprotected ilététòòn *v.*
unrelated jalánón *v.*
unreliable iléjíánón *v.*; imádĩ́ɲánón *v.*
unresponsive ilɛtɨ́létɔ̀n *v.*; ilɛ́tʉ́ránón *v.*
unrest ɲárém *n.*
unrewarded kwɛtɨ́kɨ́nˀ *n.*; seátᵒ *n.*
unripe ts'ágwòòn *v.*
unroll tɔpɛtɛs *v.*; tɔpétésʉkotᵃ *v.*
unruly (of hair) gaúsúmɔ̀n *v.*
unsafe (of an area) tsakátsákánón *v.*
unsecured hajádòn *v.*; lajádòn *v.*
unseen kúbòn *v.*

unsettled gokirós *v.*
unsettled (homeless) tsɔnitsɔnɔ́s *v.*
unsighted múɗúkánón *v.*
unspoiled ɗòwòn *v.*
unstable ɗatólóɲòn *v.*; ikáɓóɓánón *v.*
unsteadily ɗɔ̀x *ideo.*; gwèlèjᵉ *ideo.*
unsteady ikáɓóɓánón *v.*
unstick ɨtakɛs *v.*; ɨtákésʉƙɔtᵃ *v.*
unsturdy ɗatólóɲòn *v.*
unsupple gɔkɔ́dɔ̀n *v.*
unsure ɨʉ́ƙón *v.*
until akánɨ *prep.*; ɗàmùs *subordconn.*; ɗɛ̀mùs *subordconn.*; gònè *prep.*; pákà *prep.*; pákà *subordconn.*
untouched ɗòwòn *v.*
untrue to one's word iméníkánón *v.*
untrustworthy iméníkánón *v.*
untruth yʉɛ *n.*
unused ɗòwòn *v.*; iɓámón *v.*; ɨlárɔ́n *v.*; ɨlwárɔ́n *v.*
unusual way kɔ́náxàn *n.*
unutilized ɨlárɔ́n *v.*; ɨlwárɔ́n *v.*
unwanted ɨtsárʉ́ánón *v.*
unwise iɓááŋɔ̀n *v.*
unyielding nɨkwɨ́dɔ̀n *v.*
up dìdìkᵉ *n.*; kɔ́ɔ́ kwarɔ *n.*; nɔ́ɔ́ kwarɔ *n.*
up to akánɨ *prep.*; gònè *prep.*; pákà *prep.*
up-up! kukú *nurs.*
upchuck ilɔ́ɓɔ́tɛtés *v.*
upper end ikedᵃ *n.*
upright iséréròn *v.*; ɨtsɨ́rɔ́n *v.*; tsɨ́rɔ́n *v.*
uproot ɗués *v.*; ɗuetés *v.*; rués *v.*; ruutésuƙɔtᵃ *v.*; ruutetés *v.*
upset bukures *v.*; bukúrésuƙɔtᵃ *v.*; buƙusítésuƙɔtᵃ *v.*; gaanítésuƙɔtᵃ *v.*; gaanón *v.*; iɓélúkéés *v.*; iŋóyáánón *v.*

upset (become) gaanónuƙɔtᵃ *v.*; ɨraɲímétòn *v.*
upset (emotionally) ɓarites *v.*; ɓarítésuƙɔtᵃ *v.*
upside-down tuɗúlón *v.*
upward dìdìkᵉ *n.*; kɔ́ɔ́ kwarɔ *n.*
urban center zɛƙɔ́áwa ná zè *n.*
urbanite ɲáláínìkààm *n.*
urethra xaramucé *n.*
urethral meatus kwanɨ́ékwᵃ *n.*
urge imʉ́káitetés *v.*
urge (nicotine) lɔ́tɔ́ɓàɲɛ̀kᵃ *n.*
urge on ɨsʉ́sʉ́és *v.*; itsótsóés *v.*
urinate kʉtsáƙón *v.*
urinating spot kʉtsáƙààwᵃ *n.*
urine kwatsᵃ *n.*
urine (cow) tsétᵃ *n.*
us (exclusive) ŋgwᵃ *pro.*
us (inclusive) ɲjín *pro.*
use eréges *v.*; isítíyeés *v.*; ɲákásièdᵃ *n.*
useable erégam *n.*
used to ɨtalɔs *v.*
used to (make) ɨtalɛs *v.*
used to each other náɨnɔ́s *v.*
used up bitsétón *v.*; tézètòn *v.*
useful erégam *n.*
useless ɨtsárʉ́ánón *v.*; pás *n.*
useless thing tsar *n.*
uselessness pásìnànès *n.*; tsarɨ́nánès *n.*
usher iɗimiesíàm *n.*
usher in (new year) itówéés *n.*
uterus epúáwᵃ *n.*; ɲapéryɛ́tᵃ *n.*
uterus (prolapsed) kìɓèɓè *n.*; kɨ̀tʉ̀lɛ̀ *n.*
utilize isítíyeés *v.*
utter kʉtɔnʉƙɔtᵃ *v.*

uvula ɲoɗokole *n.*
vacant bótsón *v.*; bùlòn *v.*
vacant (become) bulonuƙotᵃ *v.*
vacate bulútésuƙotᵃ *v.*
vacation ɲákarám *n.*
vaccinate itsɨpítsɨ́pɛ́s *v.*
vacillate iɲikiétòn *v.*; iɲikíɲíkòn *v.*
vagabond xikóám *n.*
vagabond (bush) ríjíkààm *n.*
vagabondage xikwᵃ *n.*
vagabondage (in the bush) ríjíkànànès *n.*
vagina dòɗᵃ *n.*
vagrancy xikwᵃ *n.*
vagrancy (in the bush) ríjíkànànès *n.*
vagrant xikóám *n.*
vague iɲúɲúánón *v.*; kìtsòn *v.*
vague (visibly) imítíròn *v.*
vain itúrón *v.*
vain (become) ɨkárímétòn *v.*
valley (wide) ɲéɓúruɓur *n.*
vanish ɨɨɗɔ́n *v.*; kúbonuƙotᵃ *v.*; wɨɗɨmónuƙotᵃ *v.*
vanishingly wɨɗⁱ *ideo.*
vanquish irɛɛs *v.*
vapid ɗɛƙwɔ̀n *v.*; jɔ̀lɔ̀n *v.*; mujálámòn *v.*
vapor lɔkapɨ́r *n.*
varicella ɲɛtʉnɛ *n.*; puurú *n.*
variety bònìtᵃ *n.*; ɲákaɓɨlá *n.*; ɲalɨ́ɲalɨ́ *n.*
various jalájálánón *v.*
vary in height iyópón *v.*
vault itúlúmòòn *v.*
veer iwítón *v.*; kwɛ́dɔ̀n *v.*
veer repeatedly aɲiriesón *v.*; iwitíwítòn *v.*
vegetable garden waicíkásèdᵃ *n.*

vegetables wà *n.*
vegetation (thick) tsekís *n.*; tsekísíàƙwᵃ *n.*
vehicle kàè *n.*; ɲómotoká *n.*
vehicle (small) kàèìm *n.*
vein seamucé *n.*; tsòrìtᵃ *n.*
vellicate irikíríkòn *v.*
velocity ɲésipíɗᵃ *n.*
velvety jamúdòn *v.*
vendue ókísèn *n.*
venerate mòròn *v.*
venom ɲekísórìtᵃ *n.*
vent (volcanic) ɲáɗúyᵃ *n.*
ventriculus ŋìl *n.*
Vepris glomerata kùr *n.*
veranda hodzíŋ *n.*
verdant ƙwɨxɨ́dɔ̀n *v.*; xɨ́dɔ̀n *v.*
verity eas *n.*
Vernonia cinerascens mɛ́rɛ́ɗɛɗɛ́ *n.*
verrucose tɔmɔtsɔkánón *v.*
verse àsàkᵃ *n.*
vertebrae gògòròjòɔ̀kᵃ *n.*
vertex ikágwarí *n.*
vertibrae (upper cervical) bɔkɔ́s *n.*
vertigo taítayó *n.*
very jɨkî *adv.*; zùkᵘ *adv.*
very much mbáyà *adv.*
vesicate bubuxánónuƙotᵃ *v.*; ileɓíléɓòn *v.*
vesicated bubuxánón *v.*
vespid dɛrɛ́ƙᵃ *n.*
vessel (blood) seamucé *n.*; tsòrìtᵃ *n.*
vessel (water) itúɓᵃ *n.*
vest ɲábʉlán *n.*; ɲéɓʉlán *n.*
vest (beaded) ɲáɓol *n.*
veterinarian ɗakɨtáriama ínóᵉ *n.*
veto ilotsesa mɛnáᵋ *v.*

viable ikásíetam *v.*
vicinity (in the) ɦyàtàkᵃ *n.*
vicious ɨɲɛ́ɛ́mɔ̀n *v.*; isɨ́lɨ́ánón *v.*
victual ŋƙam *n.*
video kúrúkúríka ni ɓɛƙɛ́s *n.*; ɲévíɗyo *n.*
view gonés *v.*; iléúrés *v.*; inwakes *v.*
view (here) gonetés *v.*
view (there) gonésúƙotᵃ *v.*
Vigna frutescens ànè *n.*
Vigna oblongifolia kɨtsàɗɔs *n.*
Vigna species ɗɔsɔ́ *n.*; málákʉr *n.*
village awᵃ *n.*
village (abandoned) on *n.*; oníáwᵃ *n.*
village (big) awa ná zè *n.*
vine ɲélɔ́kɨlɔkᵃ *n.*
vine species àdàbì *n.*; ànè *n.*; ɗilatᵃ *n.*; ɗɔsɔ́ *n.*; ewêdᵃ *n.*; iɛƙiɛƙᵃ *n.*; inwᵃ *n.*; joojo *n.*; kapʉratᵃ *n.*; kɨtsàɗɔs *n.*; kutsúbàè *n.*; loɗeɗᵃ *n.*; lókóɗém *n.*; lókúɗukuɗétᵃ *n.*; lótórobétᵃ *n.*; málákʉr *n.*; mɨ́ʒɨʒ *n.*; ɲakamɔ́ŋɔ *n.*; ɲákamúka *n.*; ɲalakas *n.*; ɲéɲeɗo *n.*; óbijoetsᵃ *n.*; simísímàtᵃ *n.*; tsɔ́ráɗoɗôbᵃ *n.*; tìl *n.*; tiritirikwáyᵃ *n.*; tɔtᵃ *n.*; tʉkʉtʉkán *n.*; urém *n.*; wɛ́ƙɛ́ƙᵃ *n.*; xoúxoú *n.*
vinery ɲéviinísèdᵃ *n.*
vineyard ɲéviinísèdᵃ *n.*
violate sexually itikiesúƙotᵃ *v.*
violence (domestic) gaɗᵃ *n.*
violent ifulúfúlòn *v.*; iréɲiánón *v.*
violent person gaɗéám *n.*
violin ɲakawᵃ *n.*
viper bɛf *n.*
viper (Gaboon) bɛfa na gógòròjìkàᵉ *n.*
virgin ɲarama na ɓétsᵃ *n.*; ɲarama na tɨ́liwᵃ *n.*

virginal ɗòwòn *v.*; tɨlɨ́wɔ́n *v.*; xɔ́dɔ̀n *v.*; xɔtánón *v.*
visage takár *n.*
viscous naíɗòn *v.*
viscously nàⁱ *ideo.*
visible ilééránón *v.*; kɛtélɔ́n *v.*; lélɔ́n *v.*; takánón *v.*
visible (completely) ùwòò *ideo.*
visible (make) kɛtélitɛtés *v.*
visit énímós *v.*
visitor wáánààm *n.*
vivacious person iɓʉrɛtésíàm *n.*
vocalist irùkààm *n.*; irukósíàm *n.*
vocals irùkᵃ *n.*
vocational school tékènɨkɔ̀l *n.*
voice morókᵃ *n.*
voice (loud) moróká ná zè *n.*
voice (soft) moróká na kwátsᵃ *n.*
voicebox gɔkᵃ *n.*
void bùlòn *v.*
volcano ɲáɗúyᵃ *n.*
vomit ɦyɛnétɔ́n *v.*; ɦyènɔ̀n *v.*; ilɔ́ɓɔ́tɛtés *v.*
vomit liquid ɦyɛnétɔ́na piɔ *v.*
vote for góózés *v.*
voter góózésíàm *n.*
voucher taatsakabáɗᵃ *n.*
vow to harm imanɛs *v.*
vowel sʉ̀pᵃ *n.*
vowels sʉpaicíká tódàᵒ *n.*
vowels (heavy) sʉpaicíká ni isaákᵃ *n.*
vowels (light) sʉpaicíká ni ɔlɔ́daákᵃ *n.*
vowels (voiced) sʉpaicíká ni nesíɓòs *n.*
vowels (voiceless) sʉpaicíká ni líîdᵃ *n.*
vreevreeew! tɨ́ɨ́tɨitɨ̈ *ideo.*
vroom! zɨ̈ɨ̈ *ideo.*

vulture kɔ̀pᵃ *n.*
vulture (African white-backed) kɔtɔl *n.*
vulture (lappet-faced) náúmɔ *n.*
wa-wa! kó *nurs.*
wad tsʼàf *n.*
waffle wasétɔ́n *v.*
waft ipúróòn *v.*
wag iwítsíwítsés *v.*
wag (tail) iwidiwides *v.*
waggle iwítsíwítsés *v.*
wail iƙúétòn *v.*; iƙúón *v.*; iƙúónuƙotᵃ *v.*; iwákón *v.*; ƙɔ̀dɔ̀n *v.*
wail (make) ƙɔditɛs *v.*
wail for itseniés *v.*
wailing iwááƙós *v.*
waist róróyᵃ *n.*
waist (of clothing) ikeda ƙwázàᵉ *n.*
waist-cloth ridiesíƙwàz *n.*
waistline róróyᵃ *n.*
wait (for/on) kɔés *v.*; kɔɛtés *v.*
wait (make) ilaritɛtés *v.*; ilwaritɛtés *v.*
wait in vain koisiés *v.*
wake suddenly burétɔ́n *v.*; tsídzètòn *v.*
wake up gonésétòn *v.*
wakefulness gòkᵃ *n.*
walk ɓɛƙés *v.*; iláítésuƙɔt *v.*; itátéés *v.*
walk (leisurely) ɲétɛmá *n.*
walk crunchily ƙɛƙɛanón *v.*
walk feebly isɔ́wɔ́ɔ̀n *v.*
walk hesitantly tsìkòn *v.*
walk laboriously ɓɛƙɛsá ziál *v.*
walk leisurely ɓɛƙɛsá wɛwɛɛs *v.*; itémɔ́ɔ̀n *v.*
walk on hands ɓɛƙɛsá kwètìkɔ *v.*
walk on knees ɓɛƙɛsá kútúŋìkᵒ *v.*

walk on tippytoes itsedítsédòn *v.*
walk slowly iɛ́mɔ́n *v.*
walk small-buttocked-ly pɛɲémɔ̀n *v.*
walk springily iŋɔ́pɨ́sɔ̀ɔ̀n *v.*
walk together ɓɛƙɛ́sɨnɔ́s *v.*
walk with cane itséƙóòn *v.*
walker ɓɛƙɛ́sɨàm *n.*
walkie-talkie durudura na tímoí *n.*
walking stick (insect) túwᵃ *n.*
walkway bácɨkᵃ *n.*
wall ɲarátátᵃ *n.*
wall (back interior) ɦyuƙún *n.*
wallet ɲɔ́pɔ́c *n.*
wallop inipes *v.*
wander ilɔ́lɨ́ɛ́sá asɨ *v.*; iwórón *v.*; térés *v.*
wander aimlessly ipɛɨ́pɛ́ɛ́sá kíjáᵉ *v.*
wander off imámádós *v.*
wanderer ɓɛƙɛsɔsɨ́àm *n.*; iwórónìàm *n.*
want bédés *v.*; ɲumés *v.*
war cɛma kíjíkàᵉ *n.*
warbler (willow) dèdès *n.*
ward ɲáwádᵃ *n.*
ward (hospital) mayaakóniicéhɔ̀ *n.*
warden (game) lɔgɛ́m *n.*
ware dzígwam *n.*; dzígwetam *n.*; dzíiƙotam *n.*
warm iɓúrɔ́n *v.*; imɛɛs *v.*
warm (make) iɓúrɨ́tésuƙɔtᵃ *v.*
warm (unpleasantly) laɲádòn *v.*
warm up iɓúrétòn *v.*; iɓurímétòn *v.*; iɓúrɨ́tésuƙɔtᵃ *v.*; ikues *v.*; ikuetés *v.*; imɔ́lɔ́ŋɛtés *v.*; iwáŋón *v.*
warming iwàŋ *n.*
warn zɨzès *v.*
warthog gaso *n.*
warthog boar bèkwᵃ *n.*

warthog piglet / *weak*

warthog piglet gasóím *n.*
warthog sow gasoŋwa *n.*
warty tɔmɔtsɔkánón *v.*
wary iŋolíŋólós *v.*
wash fítés *v.*; ilɔ́tésʉƙɔtª *v.*
wash away fítésuƙotª *v.*
wash hands fítésuƙota kwétɨ̀kàᵋ *v.*
wash up fítésuƙotª *v.*; fitetés *v.*
wasp dɛrɛ́ƙª *n.*
wasp (large) oŋoridɛrɛ́ƙª *n.*
wasp (small) ɲólídɛrɛ́ƙª *n.*
waste eletiésuƙotª *v.*; iɓalíɓálés *v.*; ilɛkɨ́lɛkés *v.*; iɲekes *v.*; iɲékésuƙotª *v.*; iɲekíɲékés *v.*
waste (time) dzuƙés *v.*
waste time of ɨlaritɛtés *v.*; ɨlwaritɛtés *v.*
wasted away kɔlɔlánón *v.*
watch fetª *n.*; iteles *v.*; ɲásáatª *n.*
watch (here) iteletés *v.*
watch (spy) toreɓes *v.*
watch (there) itélésuƙotª *v.*
watch each other itélínós *v.*
watch the sun itelesa fetí *v.*
watchful itsópóòn *v.*
watchman còòkààm *n.*; itelesíám *n.*; itelesíáma kíjáᵉ *n.*
water cue *n.*; wetités *v.*; wetitésuƙotª *v.*
water (borehole) ɲatsʉʉmácúé *n.*
water (pond) tábaricue *n.*
water (rock pool) sátíkócue *n.*
water (rock well) mɔkɔrɔ́cúé *n.*
water (tree hollow) kotímácùè *n.*
water pot cúédòm *n.*
water source cuáákª *n.*
water table jʉmúcúé *n.*
water-logged ilébìlèbètòn *v.*

water-resistant pʉrákámòn *v.*; pʉráŋámòn *v.*; pʉsélémòn *v.*
waterbuck (Defassa's) ɲéɓéɓutª *n.*
watercourse cúémúcè *n.*
watercraft itúɓª *n.*
waterfall látsóikª *n.*
waterhole tábàr *n.*
waterily tsàkª *ideo.*
watermelon nàdɛ̀kwɛ̀l *n.*
waters (amniotic) baúcùè *n.*
watershed (area) ɲɛrétª *n.*
watershed (ridge) murutª *n.*
watershed centerpoint murutéékwª *n.*
waterway cúémúcè *n.*
waterworm (red) bɨɲ *n.*
watery tsakádòn *v.*
wattle ɲétélitɛl *n.*
wave imáxánɛs *v.*; ipukes *v.*
wave (of migration) botª *n.*
wave around iwítsíwítsés *v.*
wave in eyes iwitsíwítsésá ekwitíní *v.*
wave wildly apétépétánón *v.*
waver isíƙóòn *v.*; itóŋóòn *v.*
wax (candle) sɔs *n.*
wax eloquent isiresa akáᵉ *v.*
way muce *n.*
way (it is) naɨtá *subordconn.*
way (method) ɲɛpɨtɛ *n.*
way (of doing) muce *n.*
wayfarer ɓɛƙésɨ̀am *n.*
waylay idaarɛs *v.*; tadapes *v.*; tadapetés *v.*
we (exclusive) ŋgwª *pro.*
we (inclusive) ɲjín *pro.*
weak bʉlájámòn *v.*; cucuéón *v.*; daƙwádòn *v.*; iɛ́ɓɔ́n *v.*; ɨpáláƙɔ̀n *v.*; juódòn *v.*

467

weakly dàƙwᵃ *ideo.*; jùº *ideo.*
wealth bàr *n.*; ɲámáli *n.*
wealthy bàrɔ̀n *v.*; ijákáánón *v.*
wealthy (get) bárétɔ̀n *v.*; barɔnuƙɔtᵃ *v.*
wealthy person bàrɔ̀am *n.*; bàrɔ̀nìam *n.*
wean topétésuƙotᵃ *v.*
weapon ɛ̂bᵃ *n.*
weapons kúrúɓáa ni cɛmáᵋ *n.*
wear iwales *v.*; ŋábès *v.*
wear (beads) otés *v.*
wear a feather iwalesa túkàᵉ *v.*
wear across ízokomés *v.*
wear down ilɔ́ítésuƙɔtᵃ *v.*
wear out ats'ímétòn *v.*
weary ilɔ́yɔ́n *v.*
weather dìdì *n.*
weather (cold) iɛ́ɓɔna kíjáᵉ *v.*
weather (hot) hábona kíjáᵉ *n.*
weave bɛrés *v.*; iƙɔdíƙɔ́dɔ̀n *v.*; iƙulúƙúlòn *v.*; tutukɛs *v.*
weave around ilɛ́ƙwéries *v.*
weave woof kámáriés *v.*
weaverbird tsario *n.*
web abûbᵃ *n.*
wedding beer ɲalakutsᵃ *n.*
wedding sacrifice ɲékílama *n.*; ɲɛkuma *n.*
wedge pokés *v.*; ridés *v.*
wedge-shaped liƙídímɔ̀n *v.*
Wednesday Ɲákásíá àdíkᵉ *n.*
weed dɔanés *v.*
weed species karimésém *n.*; ɲéurɛré *n.*
weed(s) dɔan *n.*
weeding dɔan *n.*
weedy tsèkòn *v.*

week ɲásaɓétᵃ *n.*
weeny gɔdírímɔ̀n *v.*
weep ƙɔ̀dɔ̀n *v.*
weep (make) ƙɔditɛs *v.*
weevil (maize) lɔkaudᵃ *n.*
weigh ipimɛs *v.*
weigh down isites *v.*
weigh words ízidesa tódaᵉ *v.*
weighed down iúƙɔ́n *v.*
weight (gain) tuɓútónuƙotᵃ *v.*
weight dwon inuɛs *v.*
weighty ìsòn *v.*
weird thing bàdìam *n.*
weirdo ƙuts'áám *n.*
welcome tébɛtés *v.*
welcome warmly ewanes *v.*; ewanetés *v.*
welcome! (plural) tébɛtaná bìtᵃ *v.*
welcome! (singular) tébɛtaná bì *v.*
well iɲáléòn *v.*; maráɲíkᵉ *v.*
well (get) iɲáléètòn *v.*
well (hand-dug) dzòn *n.*
well (in rocks) mɔƙɔr *n.*
well (natural) ɲɛlélyá *n.*
well up jiríjírètɔ̀n *v.*; jiríjírɔ̀n *v.*
well worn (of paths) díwòn *v.*
well-cooked (very) dùm *ideo.*
well-done dumúdɔ̀n *v.*
well-fed zízòn *v.*
well-known arútón *v.*; fiyoós *v.*
well-off bàrɔ̀n *v.*; ijákáánón *v.*
well-prepared toikíkón *v.*
well-seasoned ɛ̀fɔ̀n *v.*
west tábàyᵃ *n.*
westerly direction tábaixan *dem.*
western rain tsóèam *n.*
westerner tábàìam *n.*
wet dɔ̀ƙɔ̀n *v.*

wet (become) ɗɔkɔnʉkɔtᵃ v.
wet (make) ɗɔkɨ́tɛ́sʉkɔtᵃ v.
whack iɲipes v.; iɲatɛs v.
whack repeatedly iɲatiés v.
whack! pùkᵘ ideo.; zɨɗátᵃ ideo.
whale (of a) kébàdà n.; nábàdà n.; nébàdà n.
wham! gwàjᵃ ideo.; kùm ideo.
what about (when) ...? ndóó subordconn.
what about ...? ndóó prep.
what color? kɨtɔ́ɔ́sɔ̀n v.
what exactly ...? ín adv.
what if (it is) ndóó mɨ̀tɨ̀ɛ̀ v.
what shape? kɨtɔ́ɔ́sɔ̀n v.
what texture? kɨtɔ́ɔ́sɔ̀n v.
what? ìs pro.
whatcha-ma-callit ndaicé n.
whatever! hà interj.; ndéé interj.
whats-their-name tatanám n.
whatsoever mùɲ quant.
wheedle ɨmámɛ́ɛ́s v.
wheel dɛ n.
wheel (steering) ɲókokorᵒ n.
wheelbarrow ɲágaɗigáɗᵃ n.; ɲaƙaari n.
wheelchair ɲamɨɨlia ŋwáxɔ̀nɨ̀àmàᵉ n.
wheeze émɨ́tɔ̀n v.; xíƙwítós v.
whelp ŋókɨ̂ɨm n.
when náà subordconn.; náa táà subordconn.; nɛ́ɛ́ subordconn.
when (a while ago) nótsò subordconn.
when (earlier today) náà subordconn.
when (hypothetically) na subordconn.
when (long ago) nòò subordconn.
when (yesterday) sɨ̀nà subordconn.
when already térútsù adv.; tórútsù adv.
when ... had (a while ago) nànòò subordconn.
when ... had (earlier) nanáà subordconn.
when ... had (yesterday) nàsàmù subordconn.
when? ńtóódò n.
where (it is)? ndayúkᵒ n.
where? ndaíkᵉ pro.; ńtá pro.
whet banɛ́s v.
whether mɨ́sɨ̀ subordconn.
whetstone lósùàɲ n.
which (a while ago) nótsò rel.
which (a while ago, pl.) nútsù rel.
which (earlier) nákᵃ rel.
which (earlier, pl.) níkⁱ rel.
which (long ago) nòkᵒ rel.
which (long ago, pl.) nùkᵘ rel.
which (one)? ńtɛ́ɛ́n pro.
which (ones)? ńtíɛ́n pro.
which (plural) ni rel.
which (singular) na rel.
which (yesterday) sɨ̀n rel.
which (yesterday, pl.) sìn rel.
which way? ndayᵒ n.
whiff kɔ́ɨn n.
while názɛ̀ƙwà n.
while (earlier today) tenákᵃ adv.
while (long ago) tènòkᵒ adv.
while (not yet) káɗìò subordconn.
while (yesterday) tèsɨ̀n adv.
while hungry ɲéƙɨ́nᵓ n.
whimper ɨɲɨɨɲɨ̀ɔn v.; ɨɲɨɲɨ̀ɔn v.
whine ɨɲúɲúnɔ̀n v.
whip iɗitsɛs v.; inɔmɛs v.
whip (leather) ɲánɨnɔ́ n.
whip all over iléƙwéries v.

whip back and forth ìtsɔkɨ́tsɔ́kɛ́s *v.*; nìƙwɨ́nɨ́ƙɔ̀n *v.*
whip lightly irwatesa kíx° *v.*; ɨ́zaɓɨzaɓɛ́s *v.*; zaɓatiés *v.*
whippily lɛ̀ts'ᵋ *ideo.*
whippy lɛts'édɔ̀n *v.*
whirl around tɔpɨrɨ́pɨ́rɔ̀n *v.*
whirlwind lòtàbùsèn *n.*
whisper sɛsɛanón *v.*
whisperer sɛsɛanóniàm *n.*
whistle fójón *v.*; síƙón *v.*; sìƙwᵃ *n.*
whistle (metallic) ɲákápɨritᵃ *n.*
whistle (wooden) ɲétúle *n.*
whistle for iwéwérés *v.*; iwówórés *v.*
white ɓèts'òn *v.*
white (glittering) pír *ideo.*
white (make) ɓets'itetés *v.*
white (of many) ɓets'aakón *v.*
white (slightly) ɓèts'ɨɓèts'òn *v.*
white (very) lìà *ideo.*; pàkⁱ *ideo.*
white person ɓèts'òniàm *n.*; ɲémúsukitᵃ *n.*
white with black eye patches tulíánètòn *v.*
white-eye (yellow) baratɨ́gwà *n.*
white-faced ŋoléánètòn *v.*
whiten ɓets'itetés *v.*
whitish ɓèts'ɨɓèts'òn *v.*; ɓets'ɨɗɔ́ɗɔ́n *v.*; xóuxówòn *v.*
whiz by ídzesa asɨ́ *v.*
who knows? ndóó fiyè *n.*
who? ǹdò *pro.*
whoa! otí *interj.*
whole ɗàŋɨɗàŋ *quant.*; mùɲ *quant.*; mùɲùmùɲ *quant.*; tsɨ́ɗⁱ *quant.*; tsɨ́ɗitsɨ́ɗⁱ *quant.*

whoosh wààà *ideo.*
whoosh! wùòò *ideo.*
whoosh! fùùtᵘ *ideo.*
whorl iyérónuƙotᵃ *v.*
whorled iyérón *v.*
why ... of course! ɲákᵃ *adv.*
why? isiɛnɨ́kᵋ *n.*
whydah lɔɔrúkᵃ *n.*
wicked (of many) gaanaakón *v.*
wickedness gaánàs *n.*
wide zòòn *v.*
wide (of many) zeikaakón *v.*
wide awake gwɛɲémɔ́n *v.*
wide open folólómòn *v.*
wide-eyed gonésá kom° *v.*; ŋɔɓɔ́dɔ̀n *v.*; ŋɔɓɔ̀n *v.*
wide-eyedly ŋɔɓɔ́ *ideo.*
wide-legged ƙaƙótsómòn *v.*
wide-mouthed ɓolóɲómòn *v.*; laɓáɲámòn *v.*; lafárámòn *v.*
widen zoonuƙotᵃ *v.*
widened ɨatɔs *v.*
widow(er) lóméléwᵃ *n.*; ɲepúrósitᵃ *n.*
wife cekᵃ *n.*
wife (co-) ɛán *n.*
wife (his) ntsícékᵃ *n.*
wife (last) jɨ̀rɨ̀àm *n.*; kárátsɨ̀kààm *n.*
wife (my) ɲcìcèkᵃ *n.*
wife (of someone) ámácèkᵃ *n.*
wife (your) bicékᵃ *n.*
wiggle in ɨnɨƙwɨ́nɨ́ƙwés *v.*
wiggly lokilókón *v.*
wild (area) ɲáraƙɔ́áƙwᵃ *n.*; ɲáraƙwᵃ *n.*
wild animal ínwá na rijááƙɔ̀ᵋ *n.*
wild hunting dog tsoe *n.*

wild olive tree dèmìywᵃ *n.*
wilderness ɲárakɔ́ákwᵃ *n.*; ɲárakwᵃ *n.*; ɲékɨ́tɛla *n.*
wildfire kómétsʼàɗᵃ *n.*
wildlife authorities cookaika ɨnóᵉ *n.*; lɔgɛ́m *n.*
will not ńtá *adv.*
willing tsolólómòn *v.*
wilt ɨtɔ́ɗɔ́n *v.*; lajámétòn *v.*
wimpy kalɛ́ɛ́tsɛránón *v.*; sikwárámòn *v.*
win ɨlámɔ́n *v.*; ɨsʉkɛs *v.*; súkɛ́s *v.*
win the support of súbɛ̀s *n.*
wind ilúkúretés *v.*; ɨnɔɛs *v.*; lúkúɗukuɗánón *v.*; sugur *n.*
wind around ikulúkúlòn *v.*; ɨlɔkɨ́lɔ́kɛ́s *v.*; ɨlɔkɨ́lɔ́ketés *v.*; imanímánés *v.*; ɨnɔɛtés *v.*; kɛkɛrɛs *v.*; tamánétòn *v.*
wind up imakɨ́mákés *v.*
winding tukúɗukuɗánón *v.*
window (of a house) hòwèl *n.*
windpipe moróká ná zè *n.*
wine ɲéviiní *n.*
wine (Rhus natalensis) mɨsáɨcùè *n.*
wing taban *n.*
wink ɨ̀bɛ̀ɗɨ̀bɛ̀ɗɔ̀n *v.*; imɨ́jɨ́lés *v.*; irwapírwápòn *v.*
winnow ilélébés *v.*
winnow (by pouring) sɨ́kɔ́ɔ́rɛs *v.*
winnow (by tossing) fɔ́tés *v.*
wipe ŋɨ̋ɗɛ́s *v.*
wipe (rear end) ɨtɔ́tɔ́rɔ̀n *v.*
wipe clean ɨkúúlés *v.*; ɨtsɨɗɛs *v.*
wipe off kánɛs *v.*; ŋɨ̋ɗɛ́súkɔtᵃ *v.*; ɲimirés *v.*
wipe out bulútésukɔtᵃ *v.*; ɨkɔmɛs *v.*; imúɲɛsʉkɔtᵃ *v.*; imʉɲɛtés *v.*; ɨtsʉtɛs *v.*; ɨtsútésʉkɔtᵃ *v.*; kánɛ́s *v.*

wipe up kánɛ́s *v.*; ŋɨ̋ɗɛtɛ́s *v.*
wiped out ikarímétòn *v.*; kanímétòn *v.*; ziálámòn *v.*; zíkímétòn *v.*; ziláámòn *v.*
wire ɲáwáya *n.*
wiry simánón *v.*
wisdom nɔɔ́s *n.*
wise nɔɔsánón *v.*
wise person nɔɔsáàm *n.*
wiser (grow) nɔɔsánétòn *v.*
wish for kanetɛ́s *v.*; ɲʉmɛ́s *v.*; wíránɛ́s *v.*
witchdoctor ŋkwa *n.*
with ńdà *prep.*
with hunger ɲékɨ́nᵓ *n.*
Withania somnifera ikitínícɛmɛ́r *n.*; ɲónomokére *n.*
withdraw ipɛ́ɛ́rɔ̀n *v.*; ɨsúrʉ́mòn *v.*
wither ɨtɔ́ɗɔ́n *v.*; lajámétòn *v.*
wither up mɔsɔnʉkɔtᵃ *v.*
withered kɔ́rɔmɔmɔ́n *v.*; mɨtɨ́rɨ́mòn *v.*; mɔ̀sɔ̀n *v.*
withheld from rébìmètòn *v.*
withhold from rébɛs *v.*
without eating kùkᵘ *ideo.*
witness enésúkotíám *n.*; itelesíám *n.*; ŋɨtsaɗéníàm *n.*
witness (false) kérɨ́nɔ́sɨ̀àm *n.*; lóliitᵃ *n.*
wives cɨkám *n.*
wizard bàdìàm *n.*
wizard (hyena-riding) otsésíama haúùⁱ *n.*
wizardry badirɛ́tᵃ *n.*; badirétínànès *n.*; kʉtsʼánánès *n.*
wobbly ɗɔxɔ́ɗɔ̀n *v.*; gwèlèjᵉ *ideo.*
wocked gaanón *v.*
wolf down (food) ifáfúkɛ́s *v.*; ŋɔfɛ́s *v.*
woman cekᵃ *n.*
woman (foreign) fiyɔcèkᵃ *n.*
woman (old) dúnéìm *n.*; fɔ́ɗɨ́tɨ́nɨ̀àm *n.*

woman (unmarried) dekitíníàm *n.*; ɲàràm *n.*
womanhood cekínánès *n.*
womanliness cekínánès *n.*
womb epúáwᵃ *n.*; ɲapéryɛ́tᵃ *n.*
women cɨkám *n.*
women (young unmarried) ɲèr *n.*
wonders itíónàs *n.*
wonders (perform) itíónòn *v.*
woo sits'és *v.*
wood dakwᵃ *n.*
wood (piece of) dakwᵃ *n.*
woodland dakúáƙwᵃ *n.*; ríjíkaajíkᵃ *n.*
woodpecker cɛŋ *n.*
woods ríjᵃ *n.*
woodworker ɲáɓáòìkààm *n.*
woof ígòmòn *v.*
wool ɗóɗòsìts'ᵃ *n.*
woolly saúkúmòn *v.*
woozy imáúròn *v.*; itikítíkòn *v.*
word mɛnéékwᵃ *n.*; tódèèkwᵃ *n.*
work ikásíés *v.*; ikásíitetés *v.*; ɲákási *n.*; ɲetitsᵃ *n.*; terêgᵃ *n.*; tereganés *v.*; teréganitetés *v.*
work (knead) dɨbés *v.*
work (temporary) ɲéléjɨlɛjᵃ *n.*
work (the soil) tɔkóbɛs *v.*
work contract terégikabáɗᵃ *n.*
work for pay teréga na kaúdzòᵉ *n.*
work in (insert) inɨkwɨnɨƙwɛ́s *v.*
work into iwoɗíwóɗés *v.*
work of art iyomam *n.*
work on (beat) iɗiles *v.*
work over (beat) iɗiles *v.*
work project ɲéprójèkɨtᵃ *n.*
work temporarily ɨlɛjɨléjés *v.*

work with long tool iƙoríƙórés *v.*
workable ikásíetam *v.*
worked up (sexually) iɓurímétòn *v.*
worker ɲákásìàm *n.*; terégìàm *n.*
worker termite nateɓú *n.*
working for government ɲeryaŋínánès *n.*
workshop ɲókós *n.*
world kíjᵃ *n.*
World Vision Loúnoyᵃ *n.*
world's end tasálétona kíjáᵉ *n.*
worm ƙɨts'ᵃ *n.*
worm (bee-eating) gɔɗɔ́ɛ̀ *n.*
worm (biting) hoƙɨtsʼᵃ *n.*
worm (intestinal) ídèm *n.*
worn out ɨlɔ́étòn *v.*; rɛsédòn *v.*; ziálámòn *v.*; zíkímétòn *v.*; ziláámòn *v.*
worn out (become) ziláámètòn *v.*
worn smooth pikódòn *v.*
worried ísánòn *v.*; tsɨkɨɗɨ́ɗɔ́n *v.*
worried (become) ísánonuƙotᵃ *v.*
worry alólóŋòn *v.*
worse (become) gaanónuƙotᵃ *v.*
worsen gaanítésuƙotᵃ *v.*; gaanónuƙotᵃ *v.*; rúbès *v.*
worship itúrútés *v.*; wáán *n.*; wáán *v.*
worship leader wáánɨtɛtésɨ̀àm *n.*
worshipper itúrútésìàm *n.*
wort (fermenting) ɲéwɨ́ɲiwiɲ *n.*
worthless thing tsar *n.*
worthlessness tsarínánès *n.*
would have ... (earlier today) ƙánàkᵃ *adv.*
would have ... (long ago) ƙánòkᵒ *adv.*
would have ... (yesterday) ƙásàm *adv.*
wound ɔ́jᵃ *n.*
wound (bullet) bɨbɨnɔ́ɔ́jᵃ *n.*

wow! ín *adv.*; wúlù *interj.*; yáŋ *interj.*
wow! ábaŋ *interj.*
wraith kúrúkúr *n.*; lopéren *n.*; tás *n.*
wrap ipúpúŋés *v.*
wrap (with clothing) ikáburés *v.*
wrap around ilɔkɨ́lɔ́kés *v.*; ilɔkɨ́lɔ́kɛtés *v.*
wrap up gubésúƙotᵃ *v.*; ipúpúŋɛtés *v.*
wreath of reeds nàtsìkwᵃ *n.*
wreck ináƙúés *v.*; ináƙúetés *v.*; ipáríés *v.*
wrecked ináƙúós *v.*; ináƙúotós *v.*
wrest ŋusés *v.*
wrestle kóríètòn *v.*; kɔrɔanón *v.*
wrestle out ikwérɛ́ɗɔn *v.*
wretched tsúkuɗúɗón *v.*
wretched as a dog iŋókíánón *v.*
wriggle ŋuɗuŋúɗón *v.*
wriggle around akwétɛkwétánón *v.*
wriggle free ikwérɛ́ɗɔn *v.*
wriggle in inikwɨ́nɨ́kwés *v.*
wriggle into iɓitsɨ́ɓɨ́tsés *v.*
wriggle out gwɨ̀rɔ̀n *v.*
wriggly wulúkúmòn *v.*
wring jútés *v.*; tutsuɛs *v.*
wring out jútésuƙɔtᵃ *v.*; tutsúésuƙɔtᵃ *v.*
wrinkled rujanón *v.*; rujurújánón *v.*; turújón *v.*; zamujánón *v.*
wrinkly turujúrújánón *v.*
wrist kwɛtámórókᵃ *n.*
wrist knife iɓotᵃ *n.*; ɲáɓaarátᵃ *n.*
wristwatch ɲásáatᵃ *n.*
write iƙirɛs *v.*
writhe around akwétɛkwétánón *v.*
writing desk ɲéméza na íƙɨ̀ràᵋ *n.*
written iƙirɔs *v.*
wrong thing róŋ *n.*

wrongdoer ɲómɔkɔsáàm *n.*
wussy kalɛ́ɛ́tsɛránón *v.*; sikwárámòn *v.*
Ximenia americana kunétᵃ *n.*
xiphoid process toroɓóókᵃ *n.*
yank ɗúrés *v.*; ɗutés *v.*; iɓwates *v.*; ipoles *v.*
yank out ɗurɛtés *v.*; ɗutɛtés *v.*; ipolɛtés *v.*
yank over iɓwatɛtés *v.*
yank this way itsɔrɛtés *v.*
yank up ipolɛtés *v.*
yard awááƙwᵃ *n.*; ɔkɔ́tsᵃ *n.*
yawn áƙáfòn *v.*
yawning hádòlòmòn *v.*; laɓáɲámòn *v.*; lafárámòn *v.*
yeah ee *interj.*
yeah right! héé' *interj.*
yeah! ńtí *interj.*
year kain *n.*
year after next kainɔ na tso *n.*
year before last kainɔ nótso *n.*; nɔkɛin *n.*
Year of Lopíar Lopíar *n.*
Year of Lotíira Lotíira *n.*
Year of Lɔkulit Lɔkulitᵃ *n.*
Year of Nawólójam Nawólójam *n.*
yearn ítánòn *v.*
yearn for ítánésuƙotᵃ *v.*
years ago kaɨ́nɨ́kò nùkᵒ *n.*
yeast sɨ̂bᵃ *n.*
yell bofétón *v.*; bófón *v.*; iƙɨ́lón *v.*; iƙúètòn *v.*; iƙúón *v.*; iƙúónuƙotᵃ *v.*; nɔsátón *v.*
yell at iyáyɛ́ɛ́s *v.*
yeller nɔ̀sààm *n.*
yellow ɲaŋáánètòn *v.*
yellow color ɗukes *n.*
yellowish color (gazelle) kodowᵃ *n.*

yelp iƙwéón v.
yes ee interj.
yester- bàtsᵉ adv.
yesterday sáásò sɨ̀n n.
yesteryear kaɨnɔ sɨn n.
yikes! wúlù interj.
yip iƙwéón v.
yogurt ŋakiɓʉkᵃ n.
yolk (egg) ɗukes n.
you (plural) bìtᵃ pro.
you (singular) bì pro.
you dog! ŋókᵃ n.
young kwátsón v.
young (of many) kwátsíkaakón v.
young children kómósikaa ɓets'aakátìkᵉ n.
young female wâz n.
young man karatsʉ́náám n.
young monkeys lɔ́tɔ́ɓàgwàs n.
young people yús n.
young tortoise kàèìm n.
youngster im n.
your (plural) bìtᵃ pro.
your (singular) bì pro.
yours (plural) bitiɛn pro.
yours (singular) biɛ́n pro.
yourself (singular) binêbᵃ n.
yourselves (plural) bitinebitín n.
youth yús n.
youth (be a) ɨsɔ́rɔ́kánón v.
youth (male) karatsʉ́na n.; ŋɨ́mɔ́kɔka n.; ŋɨ́mɔ́kɔkáám n.
youthful (of middle-age) toipánón v.
youthful adult toipánóniàm n.
yum-yum! ɓá nurs.; mamá nurs.

yum-yum! (for milk) nʉʉnʉ́ nurs.
yummily ɗɔ̀kɔ ideo.
yummy ɗɔkɔ́ɗɔ̀n v.; gwéts'ón v.
Zanthoxylum chalybeum rukûdzᵃ n.
zebra zɨn n.
Zehneria scabra lótórobétᵃ n.
zigzag ɨkɔɗɨ́kɔ́ɗɔ̀n v.; lúkúɗukuɗánón v.
zigzagging tukúɗúkuɗánón v.
zing! fiuu ideo.; líùù ideo.; pìùù ideo.
zip over toɓésá asɨ́ v.
zipper ɲéjɨ́pᵃ n.
Ziziphus mauritiana ɨláŋ n.
Ziziphus mucronata tɨ́làŋ n.
zlop! pùkᵘ ideo.
zone ɲétɛɛr n.
zoom! wír ideo.; yír ideo.
zorilla ɲewuruŋorokᵃ n.
zucchini lomuƙe n.
zygomatic area matáŋ n.

Part IV

Grammar sketch

1 Introduction

Although the bulk of this book is devoted to the dictionary and reversal index, the following section offers an overview sketch of Ik grammar that covers most important features of the total grammatical system. Those who wish to dig deeper are encouraged to consult the fuller treatment published as *A grammar of Ik (Icétód): Northeast Uganda's last thriving Kuliak language* (Schrock 2014), which is available for free downloading from several websites on the internet.

Linguistic concepts are most easily defined with linguistic terminology. Thus, due to limitations of time and space, this sketch of Ik grammar is geared in style toward the general linguist. And yet a primary aim has been to clearly define some of the key terms used and to describe the grammatical structures in simple, straightforward language. Unfortunately, some of the discussion may still remain opaque to non-linguist readers. If such persons wish to know more, I am very willing to clarify or explain in layman's terms any point raised in this grammar sketch. Feel free to contact me any time at: betsoniik@gmail.com.

The grammar sketch begins with the language's sound system (phonology) and then proceeds to words and word-building strategies (morphology). It ends with a shallow dip into syntax. Because of its length and technical nature, the grammar sketch is probably most useful as a reference tool. However, should the reader have the opportunity, it may prove beneficial to read the sketch from front to back in order to gain a bird's-eye view of the whole system.

Learning any language from printed sources alone is rarely ideal. Rather, every learner would ideally have the chance to soak up language naturally as children do. Sadly, most adult learners do not have that luxury. Because of that, I recommend creatively mixing language-learning approaches to suit one's personality, learning style, schedule, and responsibilities. Studying grammar from a book like this one will not appeal to everyone, yet all learners will occasionally get stuck on points of grammar during the course of their learning. Just as the foregoing dictionary can help you fill in gaps where specific words need to be, this grammar sketch can help fill in holes in your understanding of how Ik works.

2 Phonology

2.1 Consonants and vowels

Ik has an array of thirty consonants and nine vowels, which are presented in Table 1. In the table's first column are shown the alphabetical letters used to represent these sounds. The second column shows the phonetic symbol for the sound used by the International Phonetic Alphabet (IPA). Then in the third column, an approximate English equivalent is given in bold typeface, or else an explanation of how the sound is made if there is no English approximation.

Those sounds in Table 1 that have a small square under the IPA symbol are pronounced with the tip of the tongue a bit farther forward than in English. Especially [d̪], [n̪], and [t̪] are affected; sometimes they are fronted so much that they touch the back of the front teeth. It is important not to pronounce [d̪] exactly like an English 'd' as this sounds more like the Ik sound [ɗ] which contrasts with [d̪]. The sounds [ɓ, ɗ, ʄ, j] are called IMPLOSIVES because they are made by 'imploding' or sucking air into the mouth rather than expelling air from the lungs. The sounds [k'] and [ts'] are called EJECTIVES because they are made by ejecting air from the throat cavity instead of from the lungs. Lastly, the sound [ɦʲ], unlike an [h], is made with the vocal chords vibrating, giving it a raspy, throaty sound. It only occurs at the beginning of words. The nine Ik vowels – [a, e, ɛ, i, ɨ, ɔ, o, ʉ, u] – operate in a vowel harmony system, which is discussed in §2.5.

2.2 Consonant devoicing

At the end of an Ik word, if silence immediately follows, voiced consonants are devoiced. In other words, they sound more like unvoiced consonants in that environment. This is similar to German, for instance, where the word *Tag* 'day' is pronounced as [tak]. Consonant devoicing most noticeably affects /d/ and /g/ in Ik, as when *êd* 'name' sounds like [êt] or when *hèg* 'marrow' sounds like [hèk].

2.3 Vowel devoicing

Ik vowels are also devoiced before a pause. This is important because every word in every grammatical context – without exception – ends in a vowel. If that final vowel is not immediately followed by another sound, then it is whispered or even left totally inaudible (for example, after the consonants /f, m, n, ɲ, ŋ, r, s, z, ʒ/). It has become a tradition in scholarly writing on Ik to write whispered vowels with the following raised (superscript) symbols: <ⁱ, ᵢ, ᵉ, ᵋ, ᵃ, ᵓ, ᵒ, ᶶ, ᵘ>.

2.4 Morphophonology

2.4.1 Deaffrication

The affricates /c/ and /j/ are occasionally deaffricated or 'hardened' into their non-affricate counterparts /k/ and /g/, respectively. This is not a general phonological

2 Phonology

Table 1: Ik sound inventory

Alphabetic	Phonetic	English equivalent
A a	[a]	as in 'father'
B b	[b]	as in 'boy'
Ɓ ɓ	[ɓ]	as an English **b** but with air sucked in
C c	[tʃ]	as in 'child'
D d	[d̪]	as in 'daughter'
Ɗ ɗ	[ɗ]	as an English **d** but with air sucked in
Dz dz	[d͡z]	as in 'adze'
E e	[e]	as in 'bait' with a shorter, crisper sound
Ɛ ɛ	[ɛ]	as in 'bet'
F f	[f]	as in 'food'
G g	[g]	as in 'good'
H h	[h]	as in 'happy'
Hy ɦy	[ɦʲ]	as an English **h** but with a raspy sound
I i	[i]	as in 'beat' with a shorter, crisper sound
Ɨ ɨ	[ɪ]	as in 'bit'
J j	[d͡ʒ]	as in 'joy'
Ɉ ɉ	[ʄ]	as a **dy** sound but with air sucked in
K k	[k]	as in 'karma'
Ƙ ƙ	[k']	1) as an English **k** with a popping release
	[ɠ]	2) as an English **g** with air sucked in
L l	[l]	as in 'love'
M m	[m]	as in 'man'
N n	[n̪]	as in 'nature'
Ñ ñ	[ɲ]	as in 'onion'
Ŋ ŋ	[ŋ]	as in 'sing'
O o	[o]	as in 'boat' with a shorter, crisper sound
Ɔ ɔ	[ɔ]	as in 'bought'
P p	[p]	as in 'play'
R r	[ɾ]	1) as a Spanish or Swahili flapped **r**
	[r]	2) as a Spanish or Swahili trilled **r**
S s	[s]	as in 'sorrow'
Ts ts	[ts]	as in 'blitz'
Ts' ts'	[ts']	as an English **ts/tz** with a hissing release
T t	[t̪]	as in 'terror'
U u	[u]	as in 'boot'
Ʉ ʉ	[ʊ]	as in 'put'
W w	[w]	as in 'wonder'
X x	[ʃ]	as in 'shoulder'
Y y	[j]	as in 'yes'
Z z	[z]	as in 'zebra'
Ʒ ʒ	[ʒ]	as in 'pleasure'

tendency in the language but is, rather, limited to a small handful of words. Moreover, the principle is applied in different ways to different words. For instance, in the word *muceé-* 'path, way', the /c/ is hardened to /k/ when the word is used in the instrumental case (see §7.7): *muko* 'on the way'. Secondly, as an instance of idiolectal variation, the plural inclusive pronoun *ɲjíní-* 'we all (including addressees)' is pronounced idiosyncratically as *ŋgíní-* by a minority of speakers. Thirdly, when the words *Icé-* 'Ik people' and *wicé-* 'children' are declined for the nominative or instrumental cases, their /c/ hardens to /k/. This type of deaffrication can be clearly seen in a case declension, like the one in Table 2. Note that, as explained later in §2.4.3, all cases have non-final and final forms:

Table 2: Case declension of *Icé-* 'Ik' and *wicé-* 'children'

	'Ik'		'children'	
	Non-final	Final	Non-final	Final
Nominative	Ika	Ik[a]	wika	wik[a]
Accusative	Icéá	Icék[a]	wicéá	wicék[a]
Dative	Icéé	Icék[e]	wicéé	wicék[e]
Genitive	Icéé	Icé	wicéé	wicé
Ablative	Icóó	Icé[o]	wicóó	wicé[o]
Instrumental	Ico/Iko	Ic[o]/Ik[o]	wico/wiko	wic[o]/wik[o]
Copulative	Icóó	Icék[o]	wicóó	wicék[o]
Oblique	Ice	Ice	wice	wice/wic[e]

2.4.2 Haplology

In Ik, when a consonant in one morpheme is made at the same place of articulation as a consonant in the next morpheme, HAPLOLOGY may occur – the deletion of the first of the two similar consonants. One example of this involves the venitive suffix {-ét-} and the andative suffix {-uƙot-}, both of which end in /t/. If another suffix containing /t/, /d/, or /s/ is attached to either of these, their final /t/ may be omitted. To illustrate this, Table 3 presents a conjugation of the verb *ŋatétón* 'to run this way'. Notice how the /t/ in {-ét-} disappears from the suffix in the forms for 2SG ('you'), 1PL.INC ('we all'), and 2PL ('you all'). The 3PL form ('they') is an exception as it does not drop its final /t/ in the same environment.

A second example of haplology occurs when a verb root ending in /g/, /k/, or /ƙ/ is followed directly by the andative suffix {-uƙot-}. When this happens, the

2 Phonology

Table 3: Haplology in ŋatétɔ́n 'to run this way'

1SG	ŋat-ɛt-ɨ́		ŋat-ɛt-ɨ́	'I run this way.'
2SG	ŋat-ɛt-ɨ́d	→	ŋat-ɛ́-ɨ̂d	'You run this way.'
3SG	ŋat-ɛt		ŋat-ɛt	'(S)he/it runs this way.'
1PL.EXC	ŋat-ɛt-ím		ŋat-ɛt-ím	'We run this way.'
1PL.INC	ŋat-ɛt-ísín	→	ŋat-ɛ-ísín	'We all run this way.'
2PL	ŋat-ɛ́t-ít	→	ŋat-ɛ́-ít	'You all run this way.'
3PL	ŋat-ɛt-át		ŋat-ɛt-át	'They run this way.'

Table 4: Haplology in verbs ending in a velar consonant

ɦyɔtɔ́g-ʉƙɔt-	→	ɦyɔtɔ́-ɔƙɔt-	'go near'
iɓók-uƙot-	→	iɓó-óƙot-	'shake off'
ipák-ʉƙɔt-	→	ipá-áƙɔt-	'swipe off'
kɔk-ʉƙɔt-	→	kɔ-ɔƙɔt-	'close up'
ŋƙáƙ-uƙot-	→	ŋƙá-áƙot-	'eat up'
oƙ-uƙot-	→	o-oƙot-	'put aside'
toríƙ-uƙot-	→	torí-íƙot-	'lead away'

final velar consonant of the verb root gets omitted in anticipation of the velar /ƙ/ in {-uƙot-}. Table 4 illustrates this by listing a few verbs ending in /g/, /k/, or /ƙ/, which disappear when the next morpheme is the andative suffix {-uƙot-}.

2.4.3 Non-final consonant deletion

Ik makes a clear distinction between NON-FINAL and FINAL forms of all morphemes and words. Presumably this is to delineate syntactic boundaries, often with stylistic overtones. Non-final forms are those that occur within a string of speech, with at least one element immediately following them. Final forms, by contrast, are those that occur at the end of a string of speech, before a pause, with nothing immediately following. This basic distinction was already shown to affect the voicing of vowels in §2.3. In the case of a small number of morphemes, it also affects consonants. Table 5 presents a few of these morphemes whose final forms contain consonants that are omitted in their non-final forms. The first column of the table shows the underlying form (UF) of the morpheme in question. This is followed in the next two columns by the non-final (NF) and

Grammar sketch

final (FF) forms that actually occur in speech. Notice how the non-final forms are missing one consonant that is fully present in the UF and the FF.

Table 5: Consonant deletion in non-final forms

UF	NF	FF	Morpheme description
-ka	-a	-k^a	accusative case suffix
-ke	-e	-k^e	dative case suffix
-ko	-o	-k^o	copulative case suffix
-´ka	-´a	-´k^a	present perfect suffix
-´de	-´e	-´d^e	dummy pronoun suffix
nákà	náá	nák^a	'earlier today'
bàtsè	bèè	bàts^e	'yesterday'
nòkò	nòò	nòk^o	'long ago'
jɨkɛ̀	jɨɨ̀	jɨk^ɛ	'also, too'
ɲákà	ɲáá	ɲák^a	'just'

2.4.4 Vowel assimilation

In addition to consonants, Ik vowels also undergo phonological changes at morpheme boundaries. For instance, when two dissimilar vowels come in contact with each other as a result of two morphemes joining together, there is a powerful urge for them to become more like each other. This VOWEL ASSIMILATION was already seen at work in Table 4, as when putting the root *torík-* 'lead' and affix *-uƙot-* 'away' together led to *torííƙot-* instead of **toríúƙot-*. It is also seen in Table 6 where the 'yester-' adverb *bàtsè* becomes *bèè* in its non-final form instead of *bàè. Ik vowel assimilation only takes place between morphemes and not inside morphemes. Inside morphemes, many combinations of dissimilar vowels are allowed, for example in *kaɨn* 'year', *mèɨ̀r* 'drongo', and *kɔɨn* 'scent'.

Ik vowel assimilation can be clearly seen throughout the lexicon, as when the transitive infinitive suffix {-és} and the intransitive infinitive suffix {-òn} are affixed to verb roots. If the verb root that these suffixes attach to ends in /a/ or /e/, the vowel of the suffix fully assimilates it. Table 6 offers a few examples of this kind of vowel assimilation in verbal infinitives.

Another environment illustrating Ik vowel assimilation is the case declension of nouns. Since all Ik nouns end in a vowel, and since seven of the eight case suffixes consist of or contain a vowel, case suffixation creates a fertile ground for

Table 6: Vowel assimilation in verbal infinitives

Transitive			
fá-és	→	féés	'to boil'
isá-ɛs	→	isɛɛs	'to miss'
itíɲá-és	→	itíɲéés	'to force'
tamá-ɛs	→	tamɛɛs	'to extol'
wa-és	→	weés	'to harvest'
Intransitive			
ƙà-òn	→	ƙòòn	'to go'
ŋká-ón	→	ŋkóón	'to stand up'
tsá-ón	→	tsóón	'to be dry'
tsè-òn	→	tsòòn	'to dawn'
zè-òn	→	zòòn	'to be big'

Table 7: Vowel assimilation in the declension of ŋókí- 'dog'

Case	NF	FF
Nominative	ŋók-á	ŋók-ᵃ
Accusative	ŋókí-à	ŋókí-kᵃ
Dative	ŋókí-è	ŋókí-kᵉ
Genitive	ŋókí-è	ŋókí-∅
Ablative	ŋókú-ò	ŋókú-∅
Instrumental	ŋók-ó	ŋók-ᵒ
Copulative	ŋókú-ò	ŋókú-kᵒ
Oblique	ŋókí	ŋókⁱ

vowel assimilation. For example, as Table 7 illustrates, in the declension of the noun root ŋókí- 'dog', the /o/ in the ablative case suffix {-o} and the copulative case suffix {-ko} partially assimilate the final /i/ of ŋókí- to /u/.

Other vowel assimilation effects are shown in the case declension of a noun like ŋʉrá- 'cane rat', as in Table 8, where the final /a/ of ŋʉrá- is assimilated by the dative, genitive, ablative, and copulative case suffixes in their non-final forms.

Grammar sketch

Table 8: Vowel assimilation in the declension of ŋᵾrá- 'cane rat'

Case	NF	FF
Nominative	ŋᵾr-a	ŋᵾr-⌀
Accusative	ŋᵾrá-á	ŋᵾrá-kª
Dative	ŋᵾré-ɛ́	ŋᵾrá-kᵋ
Genitive	ŋᵾré-ɛ́	ŋᵾrá-ᵋ
Ablative	ŋᵾrɔ́-ɔ́	ŋᵾrá-ᵓ
Instrumental	ŋᵾr-ɔ	ŋᵾr-ᵓ
Copulative	ŋᵾrɔ́-ɔ́	ŋᵾrá-kᵓ
Oblique	ŋᵾra	ŋᵾr

Ik vowel assimilation may be PARTIAL, as when the word ŋókí-kᵒ 'It is a dog' is rendered as ŋókú-kᵒ. There, the /i/ at the end of ŋókí- 'dog' only moves back in the mouth to become /u/; it does not fully assimilate to become identical to the /o/ in the suffix. But vowel assimilation can also be TOTAL, as when ŋᵾrá-é 'of the cane rat' becomes ŋᵾré-ɛ́. In that instance, the /a/ at the end of ŋᵾrá- becomes fully identical to the vowel in the suffix.

Ik vowel harmony can be REGRESSIVE as in both prior examples, where a vowel exerts pressure on a preceding one. But it can also be PROGRESSIVE, as in the example of torí-úkot- becoming torí-íkot-, where the /i/ acts ahead on the /u/.

2.4.5 Vowel desyllabification

When the back-of-the-mouth vowels /ɔ/, /o/, /ᵾ/ or /u/ wind up next to another vowel across a morpheme boundary, they may lose their status as the nucleus of a syllable and become the semi-vowel /w/ instead. When such vowel DESYLLABIFICATION occurs, the syllabic 'weight' of the vowel gets transferred to the following vowel in a process called COMPENSATORY LENGTHENING. This phonological change is evident in the transitive infinitives of verbs ending in a back vowel. Table 9 depicts how the back vowel at the end of the verb root changes to /w/ and then lengthens the vowel in the transitive suffix {-és}.

Vowel desyllabification also takes place in the case declensions of nouns. Any noun root that ends in a back vowel can have that vowel desyllabified to /w/, with the result that the following case suffix is lengthened. As Table 10 demonstrates, this happens with a noun like dakú- 'plant, tree' which ends with the back vowel /u/. In five of the eight cases – accusative, dative, genitive, ablative, copulative –

Table 9: Vowel desyllabification in verbs

tʉtsʉ-ɛs	→	tʉtswɛɛs	'to wring'
rɔ́-ɛ́s	→	rwɛ́ɛ́s	'to string'
ho-és	→	hweés	'to cut'
ó-és	→	wéés	'to call'
ru-és	→	rweés	'to uproot'

the final /u/ of *dakú-* changes to /w/ and then lengthens the case suffix. Note that in the nominative case, the /u/ of *dakú-* is desyllabified but does not lengthen the nominative suffix {-a}. This irregularity is a peculiarity of the nominative case only and is seen in many other noun declensions.

Table 10: Vowel desyllabification in nouns

Case	Non-final		
Nominative	dakw-a		
Accusative	dakú-á	→	dakw-áá
Dative	dakú-é	→	dakw-éé
Genitive	dakú-é	→	dakw-éé
Ablative	dakú-ó	→	dakw-óó
Instrumental	dak-o		
Copulative	dakú-ó	→	dakw-óó
Oblique	daku		

2.5 Vowel harmony

Ik vowels participate in a phonological system called VOWEL HARMONY. This means that the language's sound system seeks vocalic 'harmony' by ensuring that all vowels in a single word belong to the same vowel class. The vowel classes involved are the following: 1) the [+ATR] or 'heavy' vowels /i, e, o, u/ that are made with a larger cavity in the throat, giving them a 'heavier', more resonant sound, and 2) the [-ATR] or 'light' vowels /ɪ, ɛ, ɔ, ʉ/ that are made with a smaller cavity in the throat, giving them a 'lighter', less resonant sound. Where the ninth vowel /a/ fits in with these two classes is a theoretical question that has not been conclusively resolved. However, what is clear is that in Ik, /a/ sometimes behaves

Grammar sketch

as a [+ATR] vowel and other times as a [-ATR] vowel. And it certainly is found together with vowels from both classes within a single word. The Ik vowel classes anchored by the low vowel /a/ are depicted in Table 11:

Table 11: Ik vowel classes

[+ATR]		[-ATR]	
i	u	ɨ	ʉ
e	o	ɛ	ɔ
	a		

Because of vowel harmony, all the vowels in a single word will generally belong to one of the vowel classes shown in Table 11. This is clearly evident in the lexicon where verbs consisting of multiple syllables and morphemes contain either [+ATR] or [-ATR] vowels, but not both. Table 12 shows an opposing set of such verbs. Notice how all the vowels in each word belong to one vowel class.

In some situations though, /a/ blocks vowel harmony from spreading to all the morphemes in a word. For example, when the stative suffix {-án-} falls between a verb with [-ATR] vowels and the intransitive suffix {-òn-}, the /a/ in {-án-} prevents the spread of harmony to the whole word. Table 13 gives a few examples of the harmony-blocking behavior of /a/. Notice how [-ATR] vowels are found to the left of {-án-} (in bold), while the [+ATR] /o/ in {-òn-} comes after it.

Ik has three suffixes which are said to be DOMINANT in that they always spread their [+ATR] value as far as they can within a word. These include the pluractional suffix {-í-}, the middle suffix {-ím-}, and the plurative suffix {-íkó-}, all of which contain the vowel /i/. Unless an /a/ blocks the way, these three suffixes will cause all the vowels in the word they are found in to harmonize to [+ATR]. This dominant behavior is illustrated in Table 14. Notice how the [-ATR] vowels in the first column all become [+ATR] in the third column as a result of the dominance of the suffixes (in bold typeface).

Two other issues surrounding vowel harmony deserve mention. First, when two nouns are joined together to form a compound word (§4.3), vowel harmony does not occur between them. For example, the noun roots *rébè-* 'millet' and *mèsè-* 'beer' can be joined into the compound *rébèmèsè-* 'millet beer', in which, notice, the vowels belong to two different [ATR] vowel classes. An exception to this rule is when the second noun in the compound begins with the vowel /i/, in which case /i/ harmonizes the last vowel of the first noun, as when *ɲɔ́kɔkɔrɔ-ímà-* 'chick' becomes *ɲɔ́kɔkoró-ímà-* (where the first noun's /ɔ/ is harmonized to

Table 12: Vowel harmony in the lexicon

[+ATR]	
béberés	'to pull'
béberetés	'to pull this way'
béberésúƙotᵃ	'to pull that way'
[-ATR]	
bɛ́ɗɛ́s	'to want'
bɛɗɛtɛ́s	'to look for'
bɛ́ɗɛ́sʉƙɔtᵃ	'to go look for'

Table 13: Vowel harmony blocking behavior of /a/

akwétɛkwétánón	'to writhe around'
ɓɛlɛ́ɓɛlánón	'to be cracked'
gɔ́lɔ́gɔlánón	'to be crooked'
ilɔ́dɨŋánón	'to be discriminatory'
ŋúzʉmánón	'to bicker'

Table 14: Ik dominant suffixes

abʉtɛs	'to sip'	→	abutiés	'to sip continuously'
kɔ̀nɔ̀n	'to be one'	→	kóníón	'to be one-by-one'
ilɔɛs	'to defeat'	→	iloimétòn	'to be defeated'
kɔkɛ́s	'to close'	→	kokímétòn	'to close (alone)'
ɔrɔr	'stream'	→	oróríkwᵃ	'streams'
wɛ̀l	'opening'	→	wélíkwᵃ	'openings'

Grammar sketch

/o/). Second, many of Ik's clitics take on the [ATR] value of their host word, for example when the anaphoric pronoun *déé* becomes *déé* in the phrase *mɔkɔrɔ́ɛ́=déé* 'in that rock pool'. Again, the exception is when the clitic contains /i/, in which case it becomes dominant, harmonizing its host, as when *bárítínúɔ=díí* 'from those corrals' becomes *bárítínúo=díí* (where the vowels /úɔ/ become /úo/).

2.6 Tone

2.6.1 Tone inventory

Ik is a tonal language. In terms of acoustics, this means that every vowel is identified not only by where it is formed in the vocal chamber but also by the PITCH with which it is uttered. This further entails that every syllable, morpheme, word, and phrase exhibits a specific and indispensable TONE pattern. At a phonological (or psychological) level, Ik has just two tones: HIGH (H) and LOW (L). All other tones that one hears can be traced back to these two. However, for practical applications like orthography and language learning, four sub-tones must be recognized. These include: HIGH, HIGH-FALLING, MID, and LOW. High tone is pronounced with a level, relatively high pitch. High-falling tone falls quickly from relatively high to relatively low pitch, often in the presence of a depressor consonant (see §2.6.4). Mid tone is a level, relatively medium-height pitch, while low tone is either relatively low and flat or tapering off before a pause. Table 15 presents the Ik tones with their names in the first column, pitch profiles in the second, and the orthographic diacritics for writing them in the third (the same diacritics employed throughout the foregoing dictionary sections):

Table 15: Ik tones

Tone	Pitch	Symbol
HIGH	[¯]	Á á
HIGH-FALLING	[\ ]	Â â
MID	[–]	A a
LOW	[_]	À à

2.6.2 Lexical tone

As mentioned above, every word in the Ik lexicon has a tone pattern or 'melody'. That is, Ik words are not identified solely on the basis of consonants and vowels (as in non-tonal languages like English) but also on their tone pattern, which must be learned. Since every vowel and therefore every syllable bears a tone, the combination of many syllables in words produces a large inventory of tone patterns. And since the tone pattern of a word is totally unpredictable, language learners must resort to memorizing the pattern with the word. Table 16 gives a sample of the lexical tone patterns found on some short words in Ik:

Table 16: Ik lexical tone patterns

Nouns		
HH	ámá-	'person'
HL	ébà-	'horn'
MH	cekí-	'woman'
LL	ɲèrà-	'girls'
Verbs		
H	ŋáɲ-	'open'
H(L)	éd`-	'carry on back'
L	àts-	'come'

2.6.3 Grammatical tone

Ik does not have grammatical tone, whereby tone alone can carry out a grammatical function. But tone often accompanies other grammatical signals, thereby reinforcing them. Thus, in that regard, it could be said that Ik has 'semi-grammatical' tone. For example, when the suffix {-íkó-} is used to pluralize a singular noun, the tone over the singular root usually changes, as when kɔl 'ram' becomes kólíkwᵃ. Similarly, when the venitive suffix {-ét-} is added to a verb stem, it often changes the overall tone pattern, as when bédés 'to want' becomes bɛdɛtés 'to look for', whereby the tone of the root béd- goes from HIGH to MID. Indeed, many of the suffixes of the language are associated with significant tone changes to the stem. So even if one learns the tonal melodies of nouns and verbs on their own, these melodies may change in particular grammatical contexts. This type of tone changeability is one of the system's more difficult aspects.

The Ik tone system is challenging for foreigners and is not yet fully understood from an analytical point of view. Still, the good news is that with lots of practice, language learners can reasonably expect to develop a certain degree of communicative competency. For the most complete description of the tone system to

Grammar sketch

date, the reader is invited to consult §3.2 in *A grammar of Ik (Icé-tód)* (Schrock 2014). That section expands on what has been presented here and includes more detailed discussions of other features of the Ik tone system.

2.6.4 Depressor consonants

In Ik, the voiced consonants /b, d, dz, g, ɦy, j, z, ʒ/ plus /h/ act as DEPRESSOR CONSONANTS. Depressor consonants are so-called because they 'depress' or pull down the pitch of neighboring vowels. In doing so, they act almost as if they had a very low tone of their own. The effect of Ik depressors is so strong that, over time, it led to the creation of a whole new set of lexical tone patterns. For instance, all Ik verbs with a HL pattern in their roots have a depressor as the first consonant after the initial high tone: *dégèm-* 'crouch', *gúgùr-* 'hunched', *íbòt-* 'jump', *kídzìm-* 'descend', and *ts'ágwà-* 'be raw'. This is because, in anticipation of the extra-low pitch of the depressor, the language compensated by putting a high tone before it where there used to be none. As another example, all nouns with the root tone pattern HL have a depressor as the only consonant between two vowels, as in: *dóbà-* 'mud', *ébà-* 'horn', *édì-* 'name', *nébù-* 'body', and *wídzò-* 'evening'. And when these types of nouns lose their final vowel due to vowel devoicing, that is when the HIGH-FALLING contour tone comes into play, as in *dôbᵃ* 'mud', *êbᵃ* 'horn', *êdᵃ* 'name', *nêbᵃ* 'body', and *wîdzᵃ* 'evening'.

3 Morphology

3.1 Overview

MORPHOLOGY is the system by which a language grammar makes words. While the preceding chapter introduced meaningful sound units (phonemes), the present chapter describes larger meaningful units called MORPHEMES. Ik exhibits three types of morpheme: word, affix, and clitic. A WORD is defined as a free morpheme that can meaningfully stand alone. An AFFIX is a bound morpheme that must attach to a word to maintain its integrity. Affixes are indicated in this grammar by a hyphen before (and sometimes after) them, as in {-án-}, the stative adjectival suffix. A CLITIC is a hybrid: in some constructions it acts like a word standing alone, while in other constructions, it attaches to a word like an affix. Clitics may be marked in this grammar by an equals sign, as in {=kì} 'those'.

Traditionally, languages are described as having WORD CLASSES, that is, categories of morphemes that have certain characteristics. These classes include the familiar major ones like 'nouns' and 'verbs' but often several others as well. For

3 Morphology

the purposes of this grammar sketch, free-standing words and clitics are considered 'words', while affixes are not. In Ik, thirteen word classes are recognized and include the following: nouns, pronouns, demonstratives, quantifiers, numerals, prepositions, verbs, adverbs, ideophones, interjections, nursery words, complementizers, and connectives (or conjunctions). Each of these word classes is briefly introduced in the following subsections, while a full list of Ik affixes can be found later in Appendix A.

3.2 Nouns

NOUNS and verbs make up the language's only two OPEN word classes, meaning that they may have new members added to them. Nouns make up roughly 47% of the total Ik lexicon. Noun roots can be short, like *eí-* 'stomach contents', or long like *ɲákaɓɔɓwáátá-* 'finger ring', but they all have at least two syllables in their root form. This structural condition is necessary because some case suffixes delete the last vowel of the noun root when they affix to it. All Ik nouns, without a single exception, end in a vowel in their root forms. Noun roots are represented throughout this book with hyphenated forms, indicating that in actual Ik speech, any noun must have at least a case suffix. In addition to case, nouns may take singulative or plurative suffixes and may be joined with other nouns to make compound nouns. §4 is devoted to expounding on Ik nouns.

3.3 Pronouns

PRONOUNS form a CLOSED word class, incapable of admitting new members. They 'stand in' for nouns whose specific names need not always be mentioned or repeated. Pronouns make up less than 1% of the Ik lexicon and yet have great grammatical importance. Most Ik pronouns are FREE, capable of standing on their own, while others are inextricably BOUND to verbs. They may be PERSONAL, capable of specifying grammatical person, or IMPERSONAL. Other categories of pronoun include: indefinite, interrogative, demonstrative, relative, and reflexive. §5 is devoted to describing the various kinds of pronouns in Ik.

3.4 Demonstratives

DEMONSTRATIVES form another closed word class, admitting no new members. They 'demonstrate' nouns by 'pointing them out', referring to them spatially, temporally, or discursively. They too make up less than 1% of the lexicon. Many Ik demonstratives have been analyzed as clitics: They seem sometimes to act

Grammar sketch

like separate words, and yet in terms of vowel harmony, they act like suffixes. As clitics, they may be written connected to words in linguistic writing (with =), whereas in non-linguistic writing, they are written separately. For example, the phrase 'these trees' would be written as *dakwítína=ni* in linguistic publications and as *dakwítína ni* elsewhere. Ik has four kinds of demonstrative: spatial, temporal, anaphoric, and locative adverbial – all of which are discussed in §6.

3.5 Quantifiers

As their name implies, QUANTIFIERS 'quantify' the nouns that precede them. That is, they are separate words that follow nouns and convey the general quantity of the noun in terms of allness, bothness, fewness, or manyness. Specific, numeric quantity is expressed by the numerals, which are the topic of the next subsection. Ik quantifiers sometimes act more like numerals by directly following the noun they modify without an intervening relative pronoun, as in *wika kwadᵉ* 'few children'. But other times they act more like adjectival verbs by taking a relative pronoun between them and the noun they modify, for example, *wika ni kwadᵉ* 'children that (are) few'. In the former function as numerals, they have a distinct, perhaps more ancient root, as in *kwàdè*, whereas in their function as adjectival verbs, they have a truncated root in a verbal infinitive, in this case *kwàd-òn* 'to be few'. The eight known Ik quantifiers are given in Table 17:

Table 17: Ik quantifiers

Non-final	Final	
dànɨdànɨ	dànɨdàŋ	'all, entire, whole'
mùɲù	mùɲ	'all, entire, whole'
mùɲùmùɲù	mùɲùmùɲ	'all, entire, whole'
tsɨdɨ	tsɨdⁱ	'all, entire, whole'
tsɨdɨtsɨdɨ	tsɨdɨtsɨdⁱ	'all, entire, whole'
gáí	gáí	'both'
kwàdè	kwàdᵉ	'few'
kòmà	kòm	'many'

3.6 Numerals

NUMERALS convey the specific number of the noun they modify. Ik has a quinary or 'base-5' counting system, meaning that it has individual words for the numbers 1-5 and then builds numbers 6-9 by adding the appropriate number to 5, as in *tude ńda kidi ts'agús* 'five and those four', which is 9. The number 10 is technically not a numeral, but rather, a noun: *toomíní-*. Ik numerals directly follow the noun they modify, without an intervening relative pronoun. Just as the quantifiers *kwàdè* 'few' and *kòmà* 'many' can function as verbs, the numerals 1-5 can also function as verbs. Table 18 presents Ik numerals 1-9:

Table 18: Ik numerals

#	Non-final	Final	
1	kònà	kòn	'one'
2	lèɓètsè	lèɓets^e	'two'
3	àɗè	àɗ^e	'three'
4	ts'agúsé	ts'agús	'four'
5	tùdè	tùd^e	'five'
6	tude ńdà kèɗɨ kon	... ńdà kèɗɨ kɔn	'five and one'
7	tude ńda kiɗi léɓètsè	... ńdà kiɗi léɓets^e	'five and two'
8	tude ńdà kìɗì àɗè	... ńdà kìɗì àɗ^e	'five and three'
9	tude ńda kiɗi ts'agúsé	... ńda kiɗi ts'agús	'five and four'

To form numbers 11-19, Ik builds off the noun *toomíní-* 'ten' and then repeats the quinary system shown in Table 18. For example, the number 17 is expressed as *toomín ńda kiɗi túde ńda kiɗi léɓets^e* 'ten and those five and those two'. Then, after 19, the numbers 20, 30, 40, etc. are based on the compound *toomín-ékù-* 'ten-eye', as in *toomínékwa léɓets^e* 'ten-eye two', which is 20. The numbers for 100 (*ŋamíáɨ-*) and 1,000 (*álìfù-*) have both been borrowed from Swahili.

3.7 Prepositions

PREPOSITIONS are usually small particles 'pre-posed', that is, put in front of a noun to indicate what its relationship is to another noun or to the wider sentence in which it occurs. Many of the functions that prepositions fulfill in other languages are handled by cases in Ik (see §7). However, Ik still has a very small, closed group of prepositions that somehow have survived the hegemony of case.

Grammar sketch

Nonetheless, they interact closely with case as each preposition selects the case that its noun head (or host) must take. Table 19 presents all the known Ik prepositions with their meanings and the cases they require on nouns:

Table 19: Ik prepositions

Preposition	Meaning	Case required
nàpèì	'from, since'	ABLATIVE
ɗítá	'as, like'	GENITIVE
nɛ́ɛ́	'from, through'	GENITIVE
akánɨ́	'until, up to'	OBLIQUE
àkɨ̀lɔ̀	'instead of'	OBLIQUE
gònè	'until, up to'	OBLIQUE
ikóteré	'because of'	OBLIQUE
ńdà	'and, with'	OBLIQUE
pákà	'until, up to'	OBLIQUE
tònì	'even'	OBLIQUE

The following example sentences (1)-(8) offer an opportunity to see the prepositions from Table 19 in a variety of natural language contexts:

(1) napei Kaaɓɔ́ŋʉɔ **páka** awᵃ
    from Kaabong:ABL up.to home:OBL
    'from Kaabong up to home'

(2) Gógese tufúlá **ɗítá** rié.
    peg:PASS field.rat:NOM like goat:GEN
    'And the field rat is pegged up like a goat.'

(3) Atsía **nɛ́ɛ́** Tímuaƙwɛɛ nɛ.
    come:1SG from Timu:inside:GEN that
    'I'm coming from within Timu there.'

(4) Hoɗuƙoteᵉ, **akɨlɔ** cɛɛ́súƙɔtⁱ.
    set.free:IMP instead.of killing:OBL
    'Set (him) free instead of killing (him).'

(5) Duƙotuo **gone** hoo déé.
 take:SEQ up.to hut:OBL that
 'And she took (it) up to that hut.'

(6) Káátaa Tábayɛɛ **ikóteré** ɲèƙɛ.
 go:3PL:PRF West:DAT because.of hunger:OBL
 'They've gone west because of hunger.'

(7) tɛwɛɛsa kɔlilíɛ́ **ńda** lomuƙeⁱ
 sow:INF:NOM cucumber:GEN and squash:OBL
 'the sowing of cucumber and squash'

(8) **toni** Pakóíce jɨk, góƙánɨkêdᵉ
 even Turkanas:OBL also seated:IPS:SIM:DP
 'even the Turkanas as well, (were) staying there'

3.8 Verbs

VERBS comprise the second of Ik's two large open word classes. Like nouns, Ik verbs make up approximately 48% of the lexicon. Verb roots can be short like *ó-* 'call', long like *gwɛrɛjéj-* 'be coarse', or reduplicated like *diridír-* 'be sugary' and *ɨpɨrɨpír-* 'drill'. Verb roots are represented throughout this book with hyphenated forms, indicating that in actual Ik speech, any verb must have at least one suffix. That minimal suffix may be a subject-agreement suffix or a tense-aspect-mood (TAM) suffix like an imperative or optative. Ik verb stems can stand alone as an independent, self-contained clause and can have many suffixes strung together, as in *sokórítiísínàk*ᵃ 'we all have clawed' and *zeikáákotinîd*ᵉ 'and they all grew large there'. Among the many suffixes that can derive nouns from verbs or inflect verbs for different meanings, there are: deverbatives, subject-agreement markers, directionals, the dummy pronominal, modals, aspectuals, voice and valency changers, and adjectivals. All these verb-related topics (and others) are treated more fully later on in §8.

3.9 Adverbs

ADVERBS make up a catch-all category of words that modify verbs or whole clauses. The sixty-or-so Ik adverbs make up less than 1% of the total lexicon. They include 'manner' adverbs like *hɨ́ɨ́jó* 'slowly' and *zùkù* 'very', epistemic adverbs like *tsábò* 'apparently' and *tsamʉ* 'of course', and general adverbs like *ɛdá* 'only'

Grammar sketch

and *nabó* 'again'. Other important categories of adverbs are the tense-marking adverbs, certainty and contingency markers, and the conditional-hypothetical adverbs. All these types of Ik adverbs are discussed later in §9.

3.10 Ideophones

IDEOPHONES form a word class that is characterized by highly expressive words that denote physical phenomena like color, motion, sound, shape, volume, etc. They are often 'sound-symbolic' or onomatopoeic. That means that their very sound as they are pronounced evokes the physical perception they signify. For example, the ideophone *bùlùkᵘ* means 'the sound something makes when dropping into water', like 'splash!' or 'kersplunk!' in English. At present, one hundred forty Ik ideophones (1.6% of total) have been recorded, but there are certainly many more in the language. And they are probably continually created. Table 20 offers a sample of the colorful variety of Ik ideophones on record:

Table 20: Ik ideophones

Animal sounds	
bèrrr	'baaa!'
buúù	'mooo!'
ƙútú	'cluck!'
Other sounds	
ɓɛkɛ	'snap!'
gùlùjù	'gulp!'
pùsù	'plop!'
Colors	
pàkì	'pure white'
tíkí	'pitch black'
tsònì	'blood red'
Attributes	
ɓa	'unliftably heavy'
dùù	'very deep'
tsɛ̀kɛ̀	'completely full'

3 Morphology

3.11 Interjections

Like adverbs, INTERJECTIONS form a bit of a catch-all word class. Interjections include any word that expresses emotions or mental states of any kind, usually outside the grammar of a sentence. The roughly thirty Ik interjections that have been recorded make up less than 1% of the total lexicon. Ik interjections may consist of a single word like *aaii* 'ouch!' or *wúlù* 'yikes!' or a short phrase like *wika ni* 'these kids (I tell you)!' or *tíɔ jɔ́ɔ̀* 'there, there (it's okay)!'. Several of the other interjections on record are provided in Table 21:

Table 21: Ik interjections

ee Ɲakujᵃ	'oh my God!'
ee/éé	'yeah, yes'
hà	'whatever!'
maráŋ	'fine, okay!'
ɲɔto ni	'these guys (I tell you)!'
ne	'here you go!'
ńtóo(n)dó	'nah, no'
otí	'whoa!'
wóí	'aahh!'
yóói	'uh-huh … sure!'

3.12 Nursery words

NURSERY WORDS make up a small class of one-word expressions that act as commands or encouragements to babies or toddlers to do something. The ten Ik nursery words on record are lain out in Table 22 with English glosses.

3.13 Complementizers

COMPLEMENTIZERS are words that introduce reported speech or thought. For example, in the English sentence 'She said that she agrees', the word *that* is the complementizer that introduces that reported statement *she agrees*. Ik has only two complementizers. One of them, *tòìmènà-* 'that', is technically a noun and thus belongs in the noun word class. But because of its function, it is dealt with here. The word *tòìmènà-*, a compound of the verb *tód-* 'speak' and *mɛná-* 'words',

497

Grammar sketch

Table 22: Ik nursery words

bubú	'nighty-night'	for going to sleep
bá	'yummy'	for eating
dɨ	'poo'	for defecating
duudú	'sitty-sit'	for sitting down
kó	'wa-wa'	for drinking water
kɔkɔ́	'no-no'	for not touching
kukú	'up-up'	for riding on mother's back
kwàà	'pee'	for urinating
mamá	'yum-yum'	for eating
nuunú	'yum-yum'	for breastfeeding

is used with a variety of speaking and thinking verbs. The second Ik complementizer, *tàà*, is a probably a derivative of the verb *kuta* '(s)he says' that has been reduced over time. Even now it is usually used after the verb *kùt-* 'say'. Example (9) shows how *tòimènà-* is used in a sentence to introduce the clause *mitɨ́da bɔnán* 'you are an orphan'. And example (10) shows the complementizer *tàà* introducing the clause *iya ɲínikija kɔ́ɔ́kɛ* 'our land is over there':

(9) Hyeíá   **toimɛna** mitɨda bɔnán.
     know:1SG that:NOM be:2SG orphan:OBL
     'I know that you are an orphan.'

(10) Kuta   ńcie   **taa** ia   ɲíníkija   kɔ́ɔ́kɛ.
     say:3SG I:DAT that   be:3SG we:land:NOM there
     'He says to me that our land is over there.'

3.14 Connectives

CONNECTIVES or 'conjunctions' are words whose function is to join together other words, phrases, or clauses. If they are COORDINATING connectives like *ńdà* 'and', then they join grammatical units of equal status, like a word to a word, or an independent clause to another independent clause. Whereas if they are SUBORDINATING connectives like *na* 'if', then they join grammatical units of unequal status, usually a dependent clause to an independent one. Even though their role is to link grammatical units, not all of them come between the units they link. Many come before both, often as the first word in the sentence. Ik has roughly eight coordinating connectives and thirty subordinating ones – making up less than 1% of the lexicon. The coordinating connectives are presented in Table 23, while Table 24 offers a sampling of the subordinating connectives:

Table 23: Ik coordinating connectives

kèɗè	'or'
kíná	'and then, so then, then'
kòrì	'or'
kòtò	'and, but, so, then, therefore'
mísí ... mísí ...	'either ... or ...'
náàtì	'and then'
naɓó	'furthermore, moreover'
ńdà	'and'

The following natural-language examples illustrate three of the more commonly used coordinating connectives: *kèɗè*, *kòtò*, and *ńdà*. In example (11), the connective *kèɗè* 'or' joins two equal constituents, the nouns *Tábayɔɔ* and *Fetíékù*. In (12), the connective *kòtò* 'and, but, then,' links two independent but semantically related clauses, and in (13), the connective *ńdà* 'and' connects two passive clauses:

(11) Tábayɔɔ **keɗe** Fetíékù?
West:ABL or East:ABL
'From the West or from the East?'

(12) Ɨ́múkɔtiakôdᵉ, moo **koto** sáɓánɨ ínwᵃ
marry.forcibly:1SG:SEQ:DP not:SEQ but kill:IPS animal:NOM
'And from there I took (her) away as my wife, but no animal was killed.'

(13) Sáɓese basaúr **ńda** kotsana cue.
kill:SPS eland:NOM and fetch:IPS water:NOM
'Elands were killed, and water was fetched.'

In contrast to the coordinating connectives shown in Table 23 and examples (11)-(13), *sub*ordinating connectives join units of unequal status, usually a subordinate (dependent) clause to a main one. Table 24 provides a sample of the thirty Ik subordinating connectives, while examples (14)-(16) below illustrate the function of some of these connectives in a few natural-language environments:

Grammar sketch

Table 24: Ik subordinating connectives

átà	'even (if)'
dèmùsù	'before, unless, until'
ikóteré	'because'
kánɨ	'in order that, so that'
mísɨ	'if, whether'
na=	'if, when'
náà	'when (earlier today)'
nàpèì	'since'
nééɛ	'if, when'
nòò	'when (long ago)'
nótsò	'when (a while ago)'
pákà	'until'
sɨnà	'when (yester-)'
tònì	'even'

In example (14) below, the subordinating connective *dèmùsù* 'before, unless, until' introduces a dependent clause that connects semantically to the following independent one. The same grammatical structure is also evident in (15) and (16), where the connectives *mísɨ* 'if, whether' and *na* 'if, when' set off short dependent clauses that logically lead into main clauses that follow them:

(14) a. **Dɛmʉsʉ** Pakóíce   deti   riék^a,
        before   Turkanas:OBL bring goats:ACC
        'Before the Turkanas brought goats,

   b. isio   noo ŋábìàn?
      what:COP PST3 wear:PLUR:IPS
      what was typically worn?'

(15) **Mísɨ** itáána   basaúrék^e, sáɓes.
     if   reach:IPS eland:DAT kill:SPS
     'If they reach the eland, it is killed.'

(16) **Na** átsik^e,   zɛƙwɛ́tɔɔ   nayéé na.
     when come:3SG:SIM sit:3SG:SEQ here this
     'When she came, she sat down here.'

4 Nouns

4.1 Overview

Single Ik NOUNS in a speaker's mental lexicon consist minimally of a ROOT. Roots are words that cannot be analyzed into smaller parts from the perspective of modern Ik. (Historical research may reveal how roots were put together over time, but that is the domain of etymology.) When plucked from the lexicon and put into actual Ik speech, every noun root must receive at least one suffix, which must be a CASE suffix. Every noun root ends in a vowel, and case suffixes either delete or attach to this final vowel. In addition to case suffixes, an Ik noun may take on a NUMBER suffix or may be joined with one or two other nouns to form a COMPOUND. Case suffixes are fully explained later in §7, while number suffixes and compounds are covered in the rest of this chapter.

Ik number suffixes include PLURATIVES and SINGULATIVES. Many noun roots can be pluralized if they are inherently singular in number. A few others can be singularized because they are inherently plural. In addition to these standard number-markers, Ik also has special POSSESSIVE number suffixes that combine the notions of number and possession into one suffix. And yet other nouns are MASS NOUNS, naming entities in the world perceived as inherently plural unities (like dust or water). These take no suffixes but are treated grammatically as plurals. Finally, some nouns are TRANSNUMERAL, construed as singular or plural and given the appropriate singular or plural modifiers, if needed.

Compounding is the primary way Ik acquires or makes new nouns – besides borrowing them from other languages. Compounds in Ik are made by putting two or three nouns together into a new composite word with special emergent characteristics. The first noun describes or specifies the second noun to make an aggregate meaning that is often different than that of the two separate nouns. Compounding and types of compounds are discussed below in §4.3.

Ik nominal suffixes differ individually in how they affix to noun roots. With the exception of five case suffixes, all nominal suffixes first delete the final vowel of the noun to which they attach. This is known as SUBTRACTIVE morphology. The case suffixes that preserve the final vowel are the accusative, dative, genitive, ablative, and oblique. For more on how case suffixes attach to nouns, see §7.

Grammar sketch

4.2 Number

4.2.1 Pluratives (PLUR)

Ik has four ways to show that a noun is plural: three PLURATIVE suffixes and SUPPLETIVE plurals. The three plurative suffixes are: 1) {-íkó-}, 2) {-ítíní-}, and 3) {-ìkà-}. The first plurative suffix, {-íkó-}, is dominant in terms of vowel harmony, meaning it changes the vowels of a [-ATR] noun to [+ATR] unless /a/ intervenes and blocks it. For example, in some instances, the vowel /a/ spontaneously appears between the singular root and the suffix {-íkó-}. (This /a/ is a relic of an ancient singulative suffix *-at- that is no longer in use in current Ik.)

The use of {-íkó-} is limited to a small number of nouns (roughly 100); it is not applied to newly borrowed nouns. Table 25 presents several examples of nouns pluralized with this suffix. Note how the suffix harmonizes the vowels of the singular root except where the vowel /a/ blocks the leftward spread of harmony. Notice also that in some cases the suffix alters the tone of the singular root.

The second plurative, {-ítíní-}, is used to pluralize nouns that have only two syllables in their root. Table 26 gives a sample of disyllabic nouns pluralized with {-ítíní-}. Notice that if the singular noun has [-ATR] vowels, then the plurative suffix harmonizes to {-ɪ́tɪ́nɪ́-}. Unlike the suffix {-íkó-}, {-ítíní-} never alters the tone of the root, though its own tone may conform to the tone of the root.

The third plurative, {-ìkà-}, is used primarily to pluralize nouns with three or more syllables in their lexical root. Table 27 provides a sample of polysyllabic nouns pluralized with {-ìkà-}. Notice that if the singular noun has [-ATR] vowels, then the plurative suffix harmonizes to {-ɪ̀kà-}. Like {-íkó-}, {-ìkà-} sometimes alters the tone of the singular noun as well as having its own tone altered.

Secondarily, the plurative {-ìkà-} is used to pluralize a few nouns that have only two syllables in their lexical root. Why these few nouns do not take {-ítíní-} as a plurative instead is not known. A bit of speculation on this point might invoke the notion of MORA or the unit of syllable weight. Among the seven examples shown in Table 28, three of them contain the semi-vowel /w/ which may be thought to contain its own mora, as a vowel would. Likewise, two of the examples (*hòò-* and *sédà-*) contain depressor consonants which may also count for one mora. Perhaps in the remaining two (*kíjá-* and *ríjá-*), the voiced stop /j/ used to be a depressor consonant. Regardless of the historical explanation, Table 28 presents a few examples of {-ìkà-} being used to pluralize disyllabic nouns.

Table 25: The plurative suffix {-íkó-}

Singular		Plural	
abérí-	→	áberaikó-	'active termite colonies'
baratsó-	→	barátsíkó-	'mornings'
cúrúkù-	→	cúrúkaikó-	'bulls'
kɔrɔ́bè-	→	kɔrɔ́baikó-	'calves'
ƙwɛsɛ́ɛ̀-	→	ƙwéséikó-	'broken gourds'
mɔƙɔrɔ́-	→	mɔƙóríkó-	'rock wells'
taɓá-	→	taɓíkó-	'boulders'

Table 26: The plurative suffix {-ítíní-}

Singular		Plural	
aká-	→	akɨtíní-	'mouths'
bòsì-	→	bositíní-	'ears'
ɔ́já-	→	ɔ́jɨtíní-	'sores'
ɗòlì	→	ɗólítíní-	'carcasses'
ekú-	→	ekwitíní-	'eyes'
ídò-	→	ídítíní-	'breasts'
ts'úbà-	→	ts'úbɨtíní-	'stoppers'

Table 27: The plurative suffix {-ìkà-} with polysyllabic nouns

Singular		Plural	
àgɨ̀tà-	→	ágɨ̀tɨ̀kà-	'metal ringlets'
arírá-	→	aríríkà-	'flames'
bàbàà-	→	bábàìkà-	'armpits'
ɔfɔrɔƙɔ́-	→	ɔfɔ́rɔ́ƙɨ̀kà-	'dry honeycombs'
kútúŋù-	→	kútúŋìkà-	'knees'
ɲánɨnɔ́ɔ̀-	→	ɲánɨnɔ́ìkà-	'leather whips'
ɲéƙúrumotí-	→	ɲéƙúrùmòtìkà-	'gullies'

Grammar sketch

Table 28: The plurative suffix {-ìkà-} with disyllabic nouns

Singular		Plural	
awá-	→	àwìkà-	'homes'
gwasá-	→	gwàsìkà-	'stones'
hòò-	→	hòìkà-	'huts'
kíjá-	→	kíjíkà-	'lands'
kwɛtá-	→	kwɛ̀tɨ̀kà-	'arms'
ríjá-	→	ríjíkà-	'forests'
sédà-	→	sédìkà-	'gardens'

4.2.2 Suppletive plurals

Ik also has a handful of singular nouns that cannot be pluralized in a productive way with any of the three suffixes discussed above. Three of these nouns on record are truly SUPPLETIVE in that their singular and plural forms bear absolutely no resemblance to each other. These are the first three in Table 29. The last three examples in Table 29 represent nouns that are semi-suppletive; even though one can discern a similarity between the singular and plural forms, the way the two forms are derived from each other is not productive in the language:

Table 29: Ik suppletive plurals

Singular		Plural	
ámá-	↔	ròɓà-	'people'
eakwá-	↔	ɲɔtɔ́-	'men'
imá-	↔	wicé-	'children'
cekí-	↔	cɨkámá-	'women'
ɖɨ-	↔	ɖi-	'ones'
kɔ́rɔ́ɓádì-	↔	kúrúɓádì-	'things'

4.2.3 Singulatives (SING)

In contrast to pluratives, SINGULATIVES convert an inherently plural noun root to a derived singular. Ik has one such suffix that may be considered a true singulative in the contemporary grammar of the modern language, and that is {-àmà-}

or {-ɔ̀mà-}. Since this singulative is only used with personal entities, it seems likely that it is related etymologically to the word *ámá-* 'person'. Table 30 gives the only four unambiguous examples of when this singulative is used. Note that its tone pattern may be altered by the tone of the plural root:

Table 30: The Ik singulative {-àmà-}

Plural		Singular	
jáká-	→	jákámà-	'elder'
kéà-	→	kéàmà-	'soldier'
lɔŋɔ́tá-	→	lɔŋɔ́tɔ́mà-	'enemy'
ŋímɔ́kɔkaá-	→	ŋímɔ́kɔká-ámà-	'young man'

4.2.4 Possessive number suffixes (POSS)

In addition to standard pluratives and a singulative, Ik has what may be called POSSESSIVE number suffixes. These possessive suffixes – {-èdè-} in the singular and {-ìnì-} in the plural – each fuse the notions of number and possession into one morpheme. When they are affixed to a noun, they specify a) the grammatical number of the noun and b) its association with another entity (hence the 'possession'). They do not specify the number of the possessor(s). For example, the word *akedᵃ*, a stem consisting of *aká-* 'den' and {-èdè-} (nominative case) can mean both 'its den' or 'their den'. And the word *akɨn*, consisting of *aká-* 'den' and {-ìnì-} (nominative case), can mean either 'its dens' or 'their dens'.

Within the broad notion of 'possession', the possessive number suffixes {-èdè-} and {-ìnì-} can signify more specific semantic relationships like part-whole, kinship, and association. Table 31 gives some examples of {-èdè-} expressing a part-whole relationship with the unnamed entity. Note how the meanings of the noun roots are extended metaphorically to denote structural parts of things. Note also that the tone of the root may be altered in the presence of {-èdè-}.

The plural possessive suffix {-ìnì-} has two special applications with human possessors. In the first, it is used to pluralize kinship terms, where a kinship association is explicit. In the second, it refers to people associated with a certain person in general terms. Table 32 illustrates both of these nuances, showing the singular root in the first column, and in the second, the root plus {-ìnì-}.

Grammar sketch

Table 31: The Ik singular possessive {-èdè-}

Root			Part-whole	
bakutsí-	'chest'	→	bakútsédè-	'its middle part'
bùbùì-	'belly'	→	búbùèdè-	'its underside'
ekú-	'eye'	→	ekwede-	'its essence'
kwayó-	'tooth'	→	kweede-	'its edge'
ŋabérí-	'rib'	→	ŋábèrèdè-	'its side'

Table 32: The Ik plural possessive {-inì-}

Kinship				
abáŋì-	→		abáŋíní-	'my fathers (uncles)'
dádòò-	→		dádoíní-	'your grandmothers'
ŋɔ́ɔ̀-	→		ŋɔíní-	'your mothers'
tátàà-	→		tátaíní-	'my aunts'
wicé-	→		wikini-	'his/her/their/its children'
Association				
Àɗùpàà-	→		Aɗupaíní-	'the people of Aɗupa'
Dakáì-	→		Dakáiní-	'the people of Dakai'
Lójérèè-	→		Lójéreíní-	'the people of Lojere'
Ŋirikoó-	→		Ŋirikoíní-	'the people of Ŋiriko'
Tsɨláà-	→		Tsɨláíní-	'the people of Tsila'

4.2.5 Mass nouns

A small group of Ik noun roots are classified as non-count MASS NOUNS. These nouns are inherently, lexically plural. As such, they require plural demonstratives and relative pronouns. This group includes words for powders, liquids, and gases various particulate substances. Table 33 presents seven examples of mass nouns. The roots are in the table's first column, followed in the third column by the noun in a phrase with the plural demonstrative *ni* 'those'. Note that in the English gloss, the equivalent is provided but with a singular interpretation:

Table 33: Ik non-countable mass nouns

búré-	'dust'	búrá ni	'this dust'
cué-	'water'	cua ni	'this water'
kabasá-	'flour'	kabasa ni	'this flour'
sèà-	'blood'	sea ni	'this blood'
ts'údè-	'smoke'	ts'úda ni	'this smoke'

4.2.6 Transnumeral nouns

Another small group of Ik noun roots are inherently TRANSNUMERAL, meaning that they can be singular or plural depending on the speaker's intention. Whatever number is imputed to them must be reflected in the grammar of the rest of the sentence, for example in subject-agreement on the verb or in any demonstratives or relative pronouns used to modify them. Ik transnumeral nouns cannot be pluralized in any of the ways discussed up to this point. But with the bound nominal morpheme -icíká- (see §4.3.4), they can be given a sense of distributiveness or variation. Table 34 presents three examples of Ik transnumeral nouns with their singular, plural, and distributive interpretations:

Table 34: Ik transnumeral nouns

Root	ɓìɓà-	'egg(s)'
Singular	ɓiɓa na	'this egg'
Plural	ɓiɓa ni	'these eggs'
Distributive	ɓiɓaicíká-	'various kinds of eggs'
Root	gwaá-	'bird(s)'
Singular	gwaa na	'this bird'
Plural	gwaa ni	'these birds'
Distributive	gwaicíká-	'various kinds of birds'
Root	ínó-	'animal(s)'
Singular	ínwá na	'this animal'
Plural	ínwá ni	'these animals'
Distributive	ínóicíká-	'various kinds of animals'

Grammar sketch

4.3 Compounds

For word-building purposes, Ik relies heavily on COMPOUNDING, joining two or more nouns together into a new composite word. The first noun (or pronoun) in a compound retains its lexical root form (that is hyphenated throughout this book), including its lexical tone. The last noun in a compound takes whichever case ending the syntactic context calls for. For example, in the compound *riéwík*ᵃ 'goat kids', the first root *rié-* 'goat' keeps its lexical form, while the second, *wicé-* 'children', has been modified by the nominative case suffix {-ᵃ}. If compounding changes the tone of its constituent parts, it will be the first noun that affects the others. In the rare compound with three constituent nouns, the first two stay in their lexical form (not counting tone), while the third is inflected for case, for example in *Icémórídókàkà-* 'cowpea leaves', a compound of *Icé-* 'Ik', *mòrìdò-* 'beans', and *kaká-* 'leaves'. In *Icé-mórídó-kàkà-*, note that while the last two elements retain their lexical segments, their tone patterns have changed dramatically due to the influence of *Icé-* in spreading H tone throughout the word.

Ik compounds create two kinds of new meaning: 1) a narrower, more specific meaning in which the first noun specifies the second, or 2) a completely novel, unpredictable meaning. An example of the first type would be *bʉbʉnɔ́ɔ́jà-* 'ember-wound' or 'bullet wound' where the first noun *bʉbʉná-* 'ember' narrows down the possible references of *ɔ́já-* 'wound' to a wound caused by a bullet. And an example of the second type of compounded meaning would be *óbijoetsʼí-*, a compound that literally means 'rhino urine' but is actually the name of a species of vine (that nonetheless was apparently the favorite urination spot of rhinos). Through both types of meaning-making, Ik compounds add a considerable amount of expressiveness and color to the language's vocabulary.

In addition to the two broader semantic categories of compounds discussed above, five other categories of Ik compounds are recognized. These include the agentive, diminutive, internal, variative, and relational, all discussed in the sections to follow.

4.3.1 Agentive (AGT)

1 Ik forms AGENTIVE compounds by using the root *ámá-* 'person' (for singular) or *icé-* (for plural) as the last element in a compound. Although the root *Icé-* simply means 'Ik people' when standing on its own, in the agentive construction it denotes plural agents. Here 'agent' is understood broadly as any person or thing that does or is whatever is characterized by the first element in the com-

pound. The first element may be a noun, as in *dɛá-ámà-* 'messenger', literally 'foot-person', or a verb as in *ŋwàxɔ̀nɨ̀-àmà-* 'lame person', literally 'to be lame-person'. Note, however, that even though *ŋwàxɔ̀n* is a verb semantically, it has been deverbalized into a noun by the infinitive suffix {-òn}. Ik agentive compounds can be translated into English in various ways, depending on what is appropriate. Table 35 presents several examples of agentive compounds:

Table 35: Ik agentive compounds

Singlar	Plural		
aká-ámà-	aká-ícé-	mouth-person	'talker'
ɓɛkɛ́sɨ́-àmà-	ɓɛkɛ́sɨ́-ícé-	walking-person	'traveler'
itelesí-ámà-	itelesí-ícé-	watching-person	'watchman'
kɔŋɛ́sí-àmà-	kɔŋɛ́sí-ícé-	cooking-person	'cook'
ɲósomá-ámà-	ɲósomá-ícé-	studies-person	'student'
sɨsɨká-ámà-	sɨsɨká-ícé-	middle-person	'middle child'
yʉé-ámà-	yʉé-ícé-	lie-person	'liar'

4.3.2 Diminutive (DIM)

Ik forms DIMINUTIVE compounds by using the root *imá-* 'child' (for singular) and *wicé-* 'children' (for plural) as the second element in a compound. In the more literal interpretation, the first element is the animate being (animal or human) of which the second element is the 'child' or 'children', as in *dódò-ìmà-* 'lamb' or *dódo-wicé-* 'lambs'. But when the first element is inanimate, the diminutive construction conveys a sense of 'a small X' or 'small Xs', for example *kɔfó-ìmà-* 'a small gourd bowl' and *kɔfó-wicé-* 'small gourd bowls'. Lastly, the two interpretations can also get blurred, as when an animate being is perceived as smaller than normal but not as the child of anything. This can be seen, for instance, in the compound *ídèmè-ìmà-* 'earthworm', literally 'snake-child'. Table 36 offers several more examples of the diminutive compound. Notice that when the whole construction is pluralized, both elements may get pluralized, as when *ámá-ìmà-* 'someone's child' becomes *roɓa-wicé-* 'someone's (pl.) children':

Grammar sketch

Table 36: Ik diminutive compounds

Singular	Plural		
ámá-ìmà-	roɓa-wicé-	person-child	'someone's child'
bàrò-ìmà-	bárítíní-wicé-	herd-child	'small herd'
ɓisá-ímà-	ɓísítíní-wicé-	spear-child	'dart'
dómá-ìmà-	dómítíní-wicé-	pot-child	'small pot'
gwá-ímà-	gwá-wícé-	bird-child	'chick'
ŋókí-ìmà-	ŋókítíní-wicé-	dog-child	'puppy'
ɔ́já-ìmà-	ɔ́jɨ́tɨ́nɨ́-wicé-	sore-child	'small sore'

4.3.3 Internal (INT)

So-called INTERNAL compounds are made with the bound nominal root *ajɨ́ká-* 'among/inside'. When appended to plural noun, this nominal conveys a sense of interiority or internality to the noun. The internal compound, which occurs relatively rarely, is exemplified in Table 37:

Table 37: Ik internal compounds

Plural			Internal	
àwìkà-	'homes'	→	awika-ajɨ́ká-	'in/among homes'
ríjíkà-	'forests'	→	ríjíka-ajɨ́ká-	'in/among forests'
sédìkà-	'gardens'	→	sédika-ajɨ́ká-	'in/among gardens'

4.3.4 Variative (VAR)

So-called VARIATIVE compounds are made with the bound nominal root *icíká-* 'various (kinds of)'. When appended to a noun – singular or plural – this nominal morpheme communicates a sense of variety or the multiplicity of a type. As a kind of pluralizer itself, *icíká-* is may be called upon to pluralize five kinds of nouns: 1) transnumeral nouns, 2) nouns not usually pluralizeable in the usual sense, 3) inherently plural nouns, 4) already pluralized nouns, and 5) verb infinitives. Table 38 presents one example for each of these five kinds of nouns that the variative bound nominal *icíká-* can be used to pluralize:

Table 38: Ik variative compounds

Singular/Plural			Variative	
gwaá-	'bird(s)'	→	gwa-icíká-	'kinds of birds'
cɛmá-	'fights'	→	cɛmá-ícíká-	'war'
mɛná-	'issues'	→	mɛná-ícíká-	'various issues'
dakwítíní-	'trees'	→	dakwítíní-icíká-	'kinds of trees'
wetésí-	'to drink'	→	wetésí-icíká-	'drinks'

4.3.5 Relational

Ik compounding is also used to create RELATIONAL NOUNS that express the spatial or structural relationship one thing has to another. In this way, Ik metaphorically extends body-part terms to other non-bodily relationships. Table 39 presents some of the Ik body-part terms used metaphorically:

Table 39: Ik body-part terms with extended meanings

Root	Lexical meaning	Relational meaning
aká-	'mouth'	'entrance, opening'
aƙatí-	'nose'	'handle, stem'
bakutsí-	'chest'	'front part'
bùbùì-	'belly'	'underside'
dɛá-	'foot'	'base, foot'
ekú-	'eye'	'center, point'
gúró-	'heart'	'core, essence'
iká-	'head'	'head, top'
kwayó-	'tooth'	'edge'
ŋabérí-	'rib'	'side'

So then, in an Ik relational compound, terms like those in Table 39 form the second element in the compound, a position in which they denote the 'part' in a 'whole-part' semantic relationship. Accordingly, the first element in the relational compound represents the 'whole' in the structural relationship. Table 40 displays a handful of such 'whole-part' compounds:

Grammar sketch

Table 40: Ik relational compounds

Roots	Lexical meaning	Relational meaning
aká-kwáyó-	mouth-tooth	'lip'
dáŋá-àkà-	termite-mouth	'termite mound hole'
dòdî-èkù-	vagina-eye	'cervix'
fátára-bakutsí-	ridge-chest	'front of vertical ridge'
fetí-ékù-	sun-eye	'east'
kaiɗeí-áƙátí-	pumpkin-nose	'pumpkin stem'
kwará-dèà-	mountain-foot	'base of mountain'
kwaré-ékù-	mountain-eye	'saddle between peaks'
taɓá-dèà-	boulder-foot	'base of boulder'
ts'adí-ákà-	fire-mouth	'flame'

5 Pronouns

5.1 Overview

PRONOUNS 'stand in' for nouns that are not explicitly mentioned. Most Ik pronouns are free-standing words, but the subject-agreement pronominals and the dummy pronominal are suffixes that are bound to verbs (and so are treated in §8 on verbs). In a sentence, free pronouns are handled just like nouns in that they take case and modifiers. The free pronouns discussed in this section fall into the following nine categories: personal, impersonal possessum, indefinite, interrogative, demonstrative, relative, reflexive, distributive, and cohortative.

5.2 Personal pronouns

Ik PERSONAL PRONOUNS represent the various grammatical persons that can be referred to in a sentence. The name is slightly misleading in that the pronouns can also denote nonpersonal, inanimate entities expressed by 'it' and 'they' (when referring to things). The Ik personal pronoun system operates along three axes: person (1, 2, 3), number (SG, PL), and clusivity (EXC, INC). The 'first person' refers to 'I' and 'we', the second to 'you', and the third to 'she', 'he', 'it', and 'they'. 'Number' (singular or plural) obviously has to do with whether the entity is one or more than one. And 'clusivity' (EXCLUSIVE or INCLUSIVE) indicates whether the addressee of the speech is *ex*cluded from or *in*cluded in the reference of 'we'. Table 41 presents the seven Ik personal pronouns in their lexical root forms, while Table 42 presents the same but in their full case declension:

5 Pronouns

Table 41: Ik personal pronouns

1SG	ɲcì-	'I'
2SG	bì-	'you'
3SG	ntsí-	'(s)he/it'
1PL.EXC	ŋgó-	'we'
1PL.INC	ɲjíní-	'we all'
2PL	bìtì-	'you all'
3PL	ńtí-	'they'

Table 42: Case declension of Ik personal pronouns

	'I'		'you'		'(s)he/it'	
	NF	FF	NF	FF	NF	FF
NOM	ŋ́kà	ŋ́kᵃ	bìà	bì	ntsa	ntsᵃ
ACC	ɲcìà	ɲcìkᵃ	bìà	bìkᵃ	ntsíá	ntsíkᵃ
DAT	ɲcìè	ɲcìkᵉ	bìè	bìkᵉ	ntsíé	ntsíkᵉ
GEN	ɲcìè	ɲcì	bìè	bì	ntsíé	ntsí
ABL	ɲcùò	ɲcù	bùò	bù	ntsúó	ntsú
INS	ŋ́kò	ŋ́kᵒ	bùò	bù	ntso	ntsᵒ
COP	ɲcùò	ɲcùkᵒ	bùò	bùkᵒ	ntsúó	ntsúkᵒ
OBL	ɲcì	ɲcⁱ	bì	bì	ntsi	ntsⁱ

	'we'		'we all'		'you all'		'they'	
	NF	FF	NF	FF	NF	FF	NF	FF
NOM	ŋgwa	ŋgwᵃ	ɲjíná	ɲjín	bìtà	bìtᵃ	ńtá	ńtᵃ
ACC	ŋgóá	ŋgókᵃ	ɲjíníà	ɲjíníkᵃ	bìtìà	bìtìkᵃ	ńtíà	ńtíkᵃ
DAT	ŋgóé	ŋgókᵉ	ɲjíníè	ɲjíníkᵉ	bìtìè	bìtìkᵉ	ńtíè	ńtíkᵉ
GEN	ŋgóé	ŋgóᵉ	ɲjíníè	ɲjíní	bìtìè	bìtì	ńtíè	ńtí
ABL	ŋgóó	ŋgó	ɲjínúò	ɲjínú	bìtùò	bìtù	ńtúò	ńtú
INS	ŋgo	ŋgᵒ	ɲjínó	ɲjínᵒ	bìtò	bìtᵒ	ńtó	ńtᵒ
COP	ŋgóó	ŋgókᵒ	ɲjínúò	ɲjínúkᵒ	bìtùò	bìtùkᵒ	ńtúò	ńtúkᵒ
OBL	ŋgo	ŋgᵒ	ɲjíní	ɲjín	bìtì	bìtⁱ	ńtí	ńtⁱ

5.3 Impersonal possessum pronoun (PSSM)

Ik also has a special pronoun whose only function is to represent a POSSESSUM, that is, generally, an entity associated with another entity (a POSSESSOR). This pronoun has the form ɛnɨ́- and must be bound to another noun or pronoun as the last element in a compound construction. It is IMPERSONAL in that it communicates nothing about the possessor or the possessum except for the relationship of possession itself. The impersonal possessum pronoun can be used in a compound construction with personal pronouns or other nouns. Table 43 shows ɛnɨ́- in conjunction with all seven personal pronouns. It can also be used with full nouns (including deverbalized verbal infinitives) as the compound's first element. This type of possessive construction is illustrated in Table 44:

Table 43: Ik impersonal possessum with pronouns

ɲj-ɛnɨ́-	I-POSSESSUM	'mine'
bi-ɛnɨ́-	you-POSSESSUM	'yours'
nts-ɛnɨ́-	(s)he/it-POSSESSUM	'hers/his/its'
ŋgó-ɛnɨ́-	we-POSSESSUM	'ours'
ɲjíní-ɛnɨ̀-	we all-POSSESSUM	'all of ours'
biti-ɛnɨ́-	you all-POSSESSUM	'all of yours'
ńtí-ɛnɨ̀-	they-POSSESSUM	'theirs'

Table 44: Ik impersonal possessum with nouns

aɗoni-ɛnɨ́-	to be three-PSSM	'the third time'
cikámɛ́-ɛnɨ́-	women-PSSM	'the women's'
ɦyɔ-ɛnɨ́-	cattle-PSSM	'the cattle's'
Icé-ɛnɨ́-	Ik-PSSM	'the Ik's'
ɲɔtɔ́-ɛnɨ́-	men-PSSM	'the men's'
roɓe-ɛnɨ́-	people-PSSM	'the people's'
wicé-ɛnɨ́-	children-PSSM	'the children's'

5.4 Indefinite pronouns

Pronouns that are INDEFINITE stand for other entities but with a certain degree of indefiniteness or vagueness. All but one of the Ik indefinite pronouns are based on the root *kɔní-* 'one' or its plural counterpart *kíní-* 'more than one'. The other one that is not based on these roots is *saí-* 'some more/other', a root that may not actually belong with this set but is included on the basis of its English translation. Table 45 provides a rundown of these Ik indefinite pronouns:

Table 45: Ik indefinite pronouns

kɔní-	one	'another, some (SG)'
kɔ́n-áí-	one-place	'somewhere (else)'
kɔ́ní-ɛ́ní-	one-POSSESSUM	'a(n), some (SG)'
kɔní-ámà-	one-person	'somebody, someone'
kɔ́n-ɔ́mà-	one-SINGULATIVE	'some unknown person'
kíní-ámá-	many-person	'some unknown people'
kíní-ɛ́ní-	many-POSSESSUM	'some (PL)'
saí-	some	'some more, some other'

5.5 Interrogative pronouns

The role of INTERROGATIVE pronouns is to query the identity of the entity they represent. As a result, they are used to form questions. All but one of the Ik interrogative pronouns incorporate the ancient northeastern African interrogative particle *nd-/nt-*, and the one that does not has the form *isì-* 'what'. The seven Ik interrogative pronouns are presented in Table 46. Note that in the table's first column, forms are hyphenated when there is a hypothesis as to their internal morphological composition, which is reflected in the second column:

Table 46: Ik interrogative pronouns

isì-	what	'what?'
nd-aí-	?-place	'where?'
ǹdò-	who	'who?'
ńt-	?	'where?'
ńtɛ́-ɛ́ní-	?-POSSESSUM	'which (SG)'
ńtí-ɛ́ní-	?-POSSESSUM	'which (PL)'
ńtí	?	'how?'

Grammar sketch

In the formation of a question, Ik interrogative pronouns fill the same slot as the nouns they are representing. It is common for the interrogative pronoun to be 'fronted': moved for emphasis to the first place in the sentence. When this happens, the interrogative pronoun takes the copulative case (see §7.8), as exemplified in sentences (17)-(18). Both demonstrated word orders are perfectly acceptable. For more on how questions are formed in Ik, please see §10.4.3.

(17) a. Bédɨ́dà ìs?
        want:2SG what:NOM
        'You want what?'

  b. **Isio** bédɨ̂dᵃ?
     what:COP want:2SG
     'What do you want?'

(18) a. Ia ndaíkᵉ?
        be:3SG where:DAT
        'It is where?'

  b. **Ndaíó** iâdᵉ?
     where:COP be:3SG:DP
     'Where is it?'

5.6 Demonstrative pronouns

Ik also has a set of DEMONSTRATIVE pronouns that referentially 'demonstrate' or point to an entity. They are all based on either the singular form *dɨ-* 'this (one)' or the plural form *di-* 'these (ones)' that differ formally only in regard to their vowel (/ɨ/ versus /i/). The Ik demonstrative pronoun system is divided in three categories based on spatial distance from the speaker: 1) PROXIMAL, meaning near the speaker, 2) MEDIAL, meaning a relatively medium distance from the speaker, and 3) DISTAL, meaning relatively far from the speaker. The medial and distal forms, for both singular and plural, consist of the root *dɨ-/di-* preceded by the cliticized distal demonstratives *kɨ* 'that' (derived from *ke*) for singular and *ki* 'those' for plural. The only difference between the medial and distal pronouns is the tone pattern whereby the medial form has a high tone on the last syllable, while the distal form does not. Table 47 presents these pronouns in their six lexical forms, while Table 48 gives their full case declensions. Note that the medial and distal forms are indistinguishable except in the NOM, INS, and OBL cases:

Table 47: Ik demonstrative pronouns

	Singular		Plural	
Proximal	ɗí-	'this'	ɗí-	'these'
Medial	kɨɗí-	'that'	kɨɗí-	'those'
Distal	kɨɗí´-	'that'	kɨɗí´-	'those'

Table 48: Case declensions of the demonstrative pronouns

	Proximal		Medial		Distal	
	SG	PL	SG	PL	SG	PL
NOM	ɗa	ɗa	kɨɗá	kɨɗá	kɨɗa	kɨɗa
ACC	ɗíá	ɗíá	kɨɗíá	kɨɗíá	kɨɗíá	kɨɗíá
DAT	ɗéɛ́	ɗíé	kɨɗéɛ́	kɨɗíé	kɨɗéɛ́	kɨɗíé
GEN	ɗéɛ́	ɗíé	kɨɗéɛ́	kɨɗíé	kɨɗéɛ́	kɨɗíé
ABL	ɗɔ́ɔ́	ɗúó	kɨɗɔ́ɔ́	kɨɗúó	kɨɗɔ́ɔ́	kɨɗúó
INS	ɗɔ	ɗo	kɨɗɔ	kɨɗo	kɨɗɔ	kɨɗo
COP	ɗɔ́ɔ́	ɗúó	kɨɗɔ́ɔ́	kɨɗúó	kɨɗɔ́ɔ́	kɨɗúó
OBL	ɗɨ	ɗi	kɨɗɨ	kɨɗi	kɨɗɨ	kɨɗi

5.7 Relative pronouns (REL)

The role of RELATIVE pronouns is to introduce a relative clause: a clause embedded in a main clause to specify the reference of an entity in the main clause. One of the most fascinating features of the Ik relative pronoun system is that it is tensed. That is, it is able to encode the time period at which the statement contained in the relative clause holds or held true. The five time periods covered by these pronouns are 1) NON-PAST, 2) RECENT PAST (earlier today), 3) REMOVED PAST (yester-, last), 4) REMOTE PAST (a while ago), and 5) REMOTEST PAST (long ago).

The Ik relative pronouns are all enclitics based on the proto-demonstratives *na* 'this' and *ni* 'these' (see §6.2 below). Those proto-forms are identical to the non-past relative pronouns *na* 'that/which' and *ni* 'that/which (PL)' shown in Table 49. The remaining tensed relative pronouns are built from the proto-forms with a variety of ancient prefixes and suffixes such as *sɨ-/si-* and *-tso/-tsu*.

As shown in examples (19)-(20), no matter where an Ik relative clause (RC) appears in a sentence, the relative pronoun will introduce it as the first element in

Grammar sketch

Table 49: Ik relative pronouns

	Singular	Plural	
Non-past	=na	=ni	'that/which ...'
Recent past	=náa	=níi	'that/which ...'
Removed past	=sɨna	=sini	'that/which ...'
Remote past	=nótso	=nútsu	'that/which ...'
Remotest past	=noo	=nuu	'that/which ...'

the clause. The entity in the main clause that the relative clause is modifying – called the COMMON ARGUMENT – must be the last word before the relative clause. As a clitic, the relative pronoun attaches to the common argument. To learn more about the syntax of relative clauses, please see §10.3.2.

(19) Atsáá   ceka=[**náa**   ƙwaatet^a]$_{RC}$.
      come:3SG:PRF woman:NOM=REL:SG give.birth:3SG

      'The woman [who gave birth today] has come.'

(20) Tɔŋɔ́lano   rie=[**sini**   detí]$_{RC}$.
      slaughter:HORT goats:OBL=REL:PL bring:1SG

      'Let's slaughter the goats [that I brought yesterday].'

5.8 Reflexive pronoun

Ik has a REFLEXIVE pronoun that 'reflects' the impact of a verb back onto the subject of the verb. In other words, with the reflexive, the subject and object of an action are the same entity. The Ik reflexive pronoun has the form *asɨ-* in the singular and *ásɨ̀kà-* in the plural, translated as '-self' and '-selves', respectively.

These reflexive pronouns are used extensively to make SEMI-TRANSITIVE verbs: verbs falling between transitive and intransitive. For example, while the verb *ídzòn* 'to discharge, emit' is intransitive and the verb *ídzès* 'to discharge, emit, shoot' is transitive, the verb *ídzesa asɨ* 'to shoot across (literally 'to shoot -self')' is 'semi-transitive' because the subject and object of the shooting are the same entity. The full case declensions of the singular and plural reflexive pronouns are given below in Table 50, and example sentences (21)-(22) illustrate both the reflexive and the semi-transitive usages of these special pronouns:

(21) Kwatsítúƙoe   as.
      small:CAUS:COMP:IMP self:OBL
      'Humble yourself (lit: make yourself small).'

(22) Kaio   dzúíka   itídídátie   ásɨkàkᵃ.
      go:SEQ   thieves:NOM   sneak:3PL:SIM   selves:ACC
      'And the thieves went slinking away (lit: sneaking themselves).'

Table 50: Case declensions of the reflexive pronouns

	Singular		Plural	
	NF	FF	NF	FF
NOM	asa	as	ásɨkà	ásɨkᵃ
ACC	asɨá	asɨkᵃ	ásɨkàà	ásɨkàkᵃ
DAT	asɨé	asɨkᵋ	ásɨkèè	ásɨkàkᵋ
GEN	asɨé	asɨ	ásɨkèè	ásɨkàᵋ
ABL	asúó	asú	ásɨkɔ̀ɔ̀	ásɨkàᵓ
INS	asɔ	asᵓ	ásɨkɔ̀	ásɨkᵓ
COP	asúó	asúkᵓ	ásɨkɔ̀ɔ̀	ásɨkàkᵓ
OBL	asɨ	as	ásɨkà	ásɨkᵃ

6 Demonstratives

6.1 Overview

Ik's DEMONSTRATIVES grammatically point to a referent. In the case of NOMINAL demonstratives, the referent is an entity named by a noun, whereas ADVERBIAL demonstratives point to a scene or situation of some sort, encoded by a whole clause. The Ik nominal demonstratives are all ENCLITICS that come just after their host (the referent), as in *ámá=nà* 'this person'. Because the locative adverbial demonstratives function as adverbs, they tend to come at the end of the clause they are modifying. Unlike demonstrative pronouns (see §5.6), spatial and temporal demonstratives are not nouns and never take case endings.

Grammar sketch

6.2 Spatial demonstratives (DEM)

Ik's SPATIAL demonstratives locate their referent in physical space in degrees of distance from the speaker. For singular referents, there are three degrees of distance: PROXIMAL (near), MEDIAL (relatively near/far), and DISTAL (more distant). For plural referents, the language inexplicably only distinguishes between proximal and distal. The singular demonstratives are usually translated into English as 'this' and 'that' and the plural ones as 'these' or 'those'. Table 51 below presents the whole set of spatial nominal demonstratives. Notice that in their final forms (FF), their final vowels may be whispered or omitted altogether:

Table 51: Ik spatial demonstratives

	Singular		Plural	
	NF	FF	NF	FF
Proximal	=na	=na (=n)	=ni	=ni (=n)
Medial	=ne	=ne (=n)		
Distal	=ke	=ke (=kᵉ)	=ki	=ki (=kⁱ)

Spatial demonstratives usually directly follow their referent, as in (23)-(24):

(23) Eakwóó ɗa=**n**.
 man:COP this.one:NOM=DEM.SG.PROX
 'This one is a man.'

(24) Káwese koto ríjá=**ke**.
 cut:SPS then forest=DEM.SG.DIST
 'And then that forest over there was cut down.'

6.3 Temporal demonstratives (DEM.PST)

The TEMPORAL demonstratives, by contrast, locate their referent in five periods of time: NON-PAST (present and future), RECENT past (earlier today), REMOVED past (yester-, last), REMOTE past (a while ago before yesterday), and REMOTEST past (long ago). Ik has both singular and plural temporal nominal demonstratives, and these are listed below in Table 52. These temporal demonstratives are usually translated into English as 'this' and 'that' in the singular, and 'these' and 'those' in the plural, but with a sense of time rather than physical location. Recall from Table 49 that Ik's relative pronouns are identical in form to the temporal demonstratives in Table 52, except that because relative pronouns never occur before a pause, they lack the final forms (FF) of those in Table 52:

Table 52: Ik temporal demonstratives

	Singular		Plural	
	NF	FF	NF	FF
Non-past	=na	=n	=ni	=n
Recent past	=náa	=nákᵃ	=níi	=níkⁱ
Removed past	=sɨna	=sɨn	=sini	=sin
Remote past	=nótso	=nótso	=nútsu	=nútsu
Remotest past	=noo	=nokᵒ	=nuu	=nukᵘ

Just like spatial demonstratives, temporal demonstratives directly follow the noun they refer to, as example sentences (25)-(26) illustrate:

(25) Rájéte ɗɨ=nák**ᵃ**.
    return:VEN:IMP one:OBL=DEM.SG.REC
    'Give back the earlier one.'

(26) Gaana kaɨna=**nótso** Lopíaríɛ́ zùkᵘ.
    bad:3SG year:NOM=DEM.SG.REM Lopiar.GEN very
    'That year (a while back) of Lopiar was very bad.'

6.4 Anaphoric demonstratives (ANAPH)

The ANAPHORIC demonstratives locate their referent not in space or time *per se* but rather in *shared communicative context*. In other words, they point back to a referent that has either been mentioned already in the same discourse or is already known by both speaker and hearer by some other means. Ik has a singular and a plural anaphoric demonstrative which are enclitics that have the same form in both non-final and final environments (i.e., their final vowels are not omitted). These invariant anaphoric demonstratives, translated into English as 'that' in the singular and 'those' in the plural, are presented in Table 53:

Table 53: Ik anaphoric demonstratives

Singular	Plural
=déé	=díí

Grammar sketch

Ik anaphoric demonstratives also directly follow their referents, as in (27)-(28):

(27) Itíóna ɲatala=**déé**.
 be.important:3SG tradition:NOM=ANAPH.SG
 'That tradition (already discussed) is important.'

(28) Atsa=noo roɓa=**díí** Sópìà°.
 come:3SG=PST people:NOM=ANAPH.PL Ethiopia:ABL
 'Those people (already mentioned) came from Ethiopia.'

6.5 Adverbial demonstratives

6.5.1 Overview

Besides the three types of nominal demonstratives described above, Ik also has a set of ADVERBIAL demonstratives that involve both locative and anaphoric locative reference. Unlike the nominal demonstratives, the adverbial demonstratives are technically nouns themselves in that they are marked for case and can take their own nominal demonstratives. Their function, however, is adverbial.

6.5.2 Locative adverbial demonstratives

The first type of adverbial demonstrative, the LOCATIVE ADVERBIAL demonstrative, locates the state or event expressed in a clause in physical space. Ik has three sets of such demonstratives. As shown in Table 54, Sets 1 and 2 are built on degree of distance, while Set 3, in addition to degree of distance, is also split into singular and plural. These demonstratives are usually translated into English as 'here', 'there', and 'over there', depending on relative distance:

Examples (29)-(30) illustrate the locative adverbial demonstratives:

(29) Ȋtáɨa=bee kíxánee=k^e.
 reach:1SG=PST there=DEM.SG.DIST
 'I reached there yesterday.'

(30) Kaini dzígwaa naíé=ne.
 go:SEQ trade:ACC there=DEM.SG.MED
 'And they went to do trade just right there.'

Table 54: Ik locative adverbial demonstratives

	Set 1	Set 2
Proximal		náxánà- (=na)
Medial	nédì- (=ne)	
Distal	kédì- (ke)	kɨ́xánà- (=ke)
Set 3	Singular	Plural
Proximal	naí- (=na)	nií- (=ni)
Medial	naí- (=ne)	
Distal	kɔ́ɔ́ (=ke)	kií- (=ke)

6.5.3 Anaphoric locative demonstratives

The second type of Ik adverbial demonstrative are called the ANAPHORIC LOCATIVES, which are nouns with a demonstrative function. Like the locative nominal demonstratives, these demonstratives point to a specific place – or metaphorically, a specific time – while also signifying anaphorically that that place or time is already known, either from earlier in the discourse or for some other reason. Ik has two such demonstratives with roughly the same meaning: *ts'ɛ́dɛ́-* and *tɨmɛdɛ́-*, both of which are typically translated as 'there' or more rarely 'then'. Because these words are technically nouns, Table 55 presents them in a full case declension, while examples (31)-(32) illustrate them in sentences.

Table 55: Case declension of anaphoric locative demonstratives

	'there'	'there'
NOM	ts'ɛ́da	tɨmɛda
ACC	ts'ɛ́dɛ́á	tɨmɛdɛ́á
DAT	ts'ɛ́dɛ́ɛ́	tɨmɛdɛ́ɛ́
GEN	ts'ɛ́dɛ́ɛ́	tɨmɛdɛ́ɛ́
ABL	ts'ɛ́dɔ́ɔ́	tɨmɛdɔ́ɔ́
INS	ts'ɛ́dɔ	tɨmɛdɔ
COP	ts'ɛ́dɔ́ɔ́	tɨmɛdɔ́ɔ́
OBL	ts'ɛ́dɛ́	tɨmɛdɛ́

(31) Kaa=noo óŋora=jɨ̈ ts'ɛ́dɛ́ɛ́.
    go:3SG=PST elephant(s):NOM=also there:DAT
    'Even the elephants went there (place already mentioned).'

(32) Pɛlɛ́mʉɔ saa tʉmɛdɔ́ɔ́.
    appear:SEQ others:NOM there:ABL
    'And others appeared from there (place already known).'

7 Case

7.1 Overview

Ik has a CASE system. This means that every noun has a special marking to show what role it has in the sentence. The language marks this role by means of a set of case SUFFIXES (endings). Four of the cases are marked with suffixes consisting of a single vowel, while for three others, the suffix consists of /k/ plus a vowel. An eighth case, the oblique, is marked by the absence of any suffix. In the following examples, (33)-(40), notice how the word *ŋókí-* 'dog' at the end of each sentence has a different ending depending on the case for which it is marked:

(33) Atsa ŋók^a.
    come:3SG dog:NOM
    'The dog comes.'

(34) Cɛa boroka ŋókík^a.
    kill:3SG bushpig:NOM dog:ACC
    'The bushpig kills the dog.'

(35) Maa eméá ŋókík^e.
    give:3SG meat:ACC dog:DAT
    'He gives meat to the dog.'

(36) Mɨta ima ŋókí.
    be:3SG child:NOM dog:GEN
    'It is the child of the dog.'

(37) Xɛɓa ŋókú.
    fear:3SG dog:ABL
    'He fears the dog.'

(38) Kaa ŋókᵒ.
go:3SG dog:INS
'He goes with the dog.'

(39) Bɛna ŋókúkᵒ.
not.be:3SG dog:COP
'It is not a dog.'

(40) Mɨta ŋókⁱ.
be:3SG dog:OBL
'It is a dog.'

Eight examples are given above because Ik has eight cases: nominative, accusative, dative, genitive, ablative, instrumental, copulative, and oblique. Table 56 presents the non-final and final forms of the suffixes that mark all eight of these cases. Keep in mind that the null symbol <Ø> signifies either 1) that the case suffix is inaudible or, for the oblique case, 2) that there is no case suffix:

Table 56: Ik case suffixes

Case	Abbreviation	Non-final	Final
Nominative	NOM	-a	-ᵃ/-Ø
Accusative	ACC	-a	-kᵃ
Dative	DAT	-e	-kᵉ
Genitive	GEN	-e	-e/-Ø
Ablative	ABL	-o	-ᵒ/-Ø
Instrumental	INS	-o	-ᵒ/-Ø
Copulative	COP	-o	-kᵒ
Oblique	OBL	-Ø	-Ø

From Table 56, there may appear to be significant ambiguity in the Ik case system. For instance, the non-final forms of the nominative and accusative suffixes, the dative and genitive suffixes, and the ablative, instrumental, and copulative suffixes all look the same, respectively. In most cases, the key to disambiguating the suffixes is called 'subtractive' morphology. Two of the Ik case suffixes (namely nominative and instrumental) are subtractive in that they subtract or delete the final vowel of the noun to which they attach. So, for example, while the non-final forms of the nominative and accusative are identical, their morphological behavior is not: the nominative {-a} subtracts the noun's final vowel,

Grammar sketch

as when *ŋókí-* 'dog' becomes *ŋók-á* 'dog:NOM'; by contrast, the accusative suffix is non-subtractive, as in *ŋókí-à* 'dog:ACC'. Other case ambiguities like genitive versus dative and ablative versus copulative, in their non-final forms, can be resolved in the context of the sentence. Different verbs require different cases.

Since every Ik noun ends in a vowel, and since that vowel can be any of the nine (/i, ɨ, e, ɛ, a, ɔ, o, ʉ, u/), the collision of nouns and case suffixes gives rise to all kinds of vowel assimilation (see §2.4.4). The next two tables present declensions of two nouns illustrating vowel assimilation. Table 57 shows the noun *fetí-* 'sun' declined for all eight cases. In particular, notice how the vowel /o/ in the ablative and copulative suffixes partially assimilate the /i/ in *fetí-* to become /u/:

Table 57: Case declension of *fetí-* 'sun'

Case	Non-final	Final
NOM	feta	fet[a]
ACC	fetíá	fetík[a]
DAT	fetíé	fetík[e]
GEN	fetíé	fetí
ABL	fetúó	fetú
INS	feto	fet[o]
COP	fetúó	fetúk[o]
OBL	feti	fet[i]

While Table 57 shows partial vowel assimilation caused by case suffixation, Table 58 reveals an instance of total assimilation. In this table, the noun *kíjá-* 'land' is declined for all eight cases. Note how the final /a/ of *kíjá-* becomes totally assimilated by the non-final dative, genitive, ablative, and copulative suffixes.

7.2 Nominative (NOM)

The NOMINATIVE case, marked by the suffix {-a}, is the 'naming' case, whose role is to: 1) mark the subject of main clauses, 2) mark the subject of sequential clauses (see §8.10.7), and 3) mark the direct object of clauses with 1st and 2nd person subjects ('I', 'we', 'you'). Three examples ((41)-(43)) are provided below, each one illustrating one of the three grammatical roles of the nominative case. The third example contains seven sentences that show how Ik object marking is SPLIT: objects after 3-person subjects ((s)he/it, they) take the accusative case, while 1- or 2-person subjects (you, we) take objects in the nominative case:

Table 58: Case declension of *kíjá-* 'land'

Case	Non-final	Final
NOM	kíjá	kíj^a
ACC	kíjáà	kíják^a
DAT	kíjéè	kíják^e
GEN	kíjéè	kíjá^e
ABL	kíjóò	kíjá^o
INS	kíjó	kíj^o
COP	kíjóò	kíják^o
OBL	kíjá	kíj^a

Subject of a main clause

(41) Atsáá lɔŋɔ́t-a!
come:PRF enemies-NOM
'The enemies have come!'

Subject of a sequential clause

(42) Toɓuo ƙaƙaam-a kʉláɓák^a.
spear:SEQ hunter-NOM bushbuck:ACC
'And the hunter speared the bushbuck.'

Object of a clause with a 1/2-person subject

(43) a. Ŋƙíá tɔbɔŋ-a=na.
eat:1SG mush-NOM=this
'I eat this meal mush.'

b. Ŋƙɨ́da tɔbɔŋ-a=na.
eat:2SG mush-NOM=this
'You eat this meal mush.'

c. Ŋƙa tɔbɔŋɔ́-á=na.
eat:3SG mush-ACC=this
'She eats this meal mush.'

d. Ŋƙɨmá tɔbɔŋ-a=na
eat:1PL.EXC mush-NOM=this
'We eat this meal mush.'

e. Ŋkɨ́sɨ́na tɔbɔŋ-a=na.
eat:1PL.INC mush-NOM=this
'We all eat this meal mush.'

f. Ŋkɨ́tá tɔbɔŋ-a=na.
eat:2PL mush-NOM=this
'You all eat this meal mush.'

g. Ŋkáta tɔbɔŋɔ́-á=na.
eat:3PL mush-ACC=this
'They eat this meal mush.'

7.3 Accusative case (ACC)

The ACCUSATIVE case, marked by the suffix {-ka}, is also split with regard to its basic function. One of its basic functions, that for which it is named, is to mark the direct object of any clause with a 3-person subject ((s)he/it, they). Its other common function is to mark the subject *and* any object of several kinds of subordinate clauses (including relative and temporal clauses). Each of these functions is exemplified by one of the sentences in examples (44)-(47). In the first example, a sentence with a 1-person subject is also given to show the contrast:

Direct object of a clause with a 3-person subject

(44) Wetésátà mèsɛ̀-à mùɲ.
drink:FUT:3PL beer-ACC all
'They will drink all the beer.'

(45) Wetésímà mès-à mùɲ.
drink:FUT:1PL.EXC beer-NOM all
'We will drink all the beer.'

Subject and object of a subordinate clause

(46) Mee kɔ́rɔ́bádi=[náa ɲci-a detí.]
give:IMP thing:OBL=that I-ACC bring:1SG
'Give me the thing that I brought earlier.'

(47) [Noo ŋgó-á bɛ́dɨ́mɛɛ bi-a], ...
when we-ACC want:1PL.EXC you-ACC
'When we were looking for you, ...'

7.4 Dative (DAT)

The DATIVE case, marked by the suffix {-ke}, is the 'to' or 'in' case, whose role is to mark indirect objects (also called 'extended' or 'secondary' objects). These indirect objects may encode semantic notions like destination, location, recipient, experiencer, possession, and purpose. These are illustrated in examples (48)-(53):

Destination

(48) Keesíá awá-k^e.
go:FUT:1SG home-DAT
'I'm going home.'

Location

(49) Ia sédà-k^e.
be:3SG garden-DAT
'She's in the garden.'

Recipient

(50) Tɔkɔráta kabasáá ròɓà-k^e.
divide:3PL flour:ACC people-DAT
'They are dividing out flour to people.'

Experiencer

(51) Iɓálá ɲcì-è zùk^u.
appall:3SG I-DAT very
'It really appalls me.' (Lit: 'It is very appalling to me.')

Possession

(52) Ia ɦyɔa ntsí-k^e.
be:3SG cattle:NOM he-DAT
'He has cattle.' (Lit: 'There are cattle to him.')

Purpose

(53) Kaa ɲera dakúáƙɔ̀-kᵉ.
go:3SG girls:NOM wood:inside-DAT
'The girls go for firewood.'

7.5 Genitive (GEN)

The GENITIVE case, marked by the suffix {-e}, is the 'of' case, whose role is to encode a possessive or associative relationship a noun has with another noun (or, in rare cases, with a verb). Within the broad notions of possession and association are finer nuances such as: ownership, part-whole relationship, kinship, and attribution. These nuances are illustrated in examples (54)-(57):

Ownership

(54) Hɔ́nɨnɨ ɦyɔa ńtí-e ɓórékᵉ.
drive:SEQ cattle:ACC they-GEN corral:DAT
'And they drove their cattle to the corral.'

Part-whole relationship

(55) Wasá dɛɛdɛɛ kwará-ᵉ.
stand:3SG foot:DAT mountain-GEN
'He's standing at the foot of the mountain.'

Kinship

(56) Mɨ́ná cekíá ntsí-é zùkᵘ.
love:3SG wife:ACC he-GEN very
'He loves his wife very much.'

Attribution

(57) Maráŋá muceá bì-∅.
good:3SG way:NOM you-GEN
'Your luck is good.' (lit: Your way is good.)

The genitive case has two further roles. One is the NOMINALIZATION of clauses, that is, the process by which a whole clause is changed into a noun phrase that can be used as a subject or object in another clause. For example, the clause Cɛìkɔta náa eakwa ídèmèkᵃ 'The man killed the snake' can be compressed into the nominalized *cɛɛ́súƙɔta eakwéé ídèmè* 'the killing of the man of the snake' or 'the man's killing of the snake'. The other secondary role of the genitive has to do with verb *ƙámón* 'to be like'. For unknown historical reasons, this particular verb requires genitive case marking on its complement, as in *Ƙámá ròɓèè mùɲ* 'He's like all people', where *ròɓè-è* is analyzed as 'people-GEN' or 'of people'.

7.6 Ablative (ABL)

The ABLATIVE case, marked by the suffix {-o}, is the 'from' case (or in some situations 'at' or 'in'), whose function is to mark objects with the following semantic roles: origin/source, cause, stimulus, source of judgment, location of activity (versus static location, which is covered by the dative case). Each of these semantic roles of the ablative are illustrated among example sentences (58)-(62):

Origin/source

(58) Atsía   awá-ᵒ.
     come:1SG home-ABL
     'I come from home.'

Cause

(59) Baduƙota=noo ɲɛ́ƙɛ̀-ᵒ.
     die:3SG=PST   hunger-ABL
     'He died from hunger.'

Stimulus

(60) Xɛɓa ɲérà-ᵒ.
     fear:3SG girls-ABL
     'He's shy of girls.'

Source of judgment

(61) Daa   ɲcù-ᴼ.
     nice:3SG I-ABL
     'It's nice to me.'

Location of activity

(62) Cɛmáta sédìkà-ᵒ.
     fight:3PL gardens-ABL
     'They are fighting in the gardens.'

Grammar sketch

7.7 Instrumental (INS)

The INSTRUMENTAL case, marked by the suffix {-o}, is the 'by' or 'with' case. Unlike the ablative suffix {-o}, the instrumental suffix is subtractive, meaning that it first deletes the noun's final vowel. The function of the instrumental case is to mark secondary objects with such semantic roles as instrument/means, pathway, accompaniment, manner, time, and occupation. Each of these nuances are illustrated by one sentence each in example sentences (63)-(68):

Instrument/means

(63) Toɓíá=noo   gasoa   ɓɨs-ɔ.
     spear:1SG=PST warthog:NOM spear-INS
     'I speared a warthog with a spear.'

Pathway

(64) Kaini fots-o   gígìròkᵉ.
     go:3PL ravine-INS downside:DAT
     'And they went down by way of the ravine.'

Accompaniment

(65) Atsímá=naa   kúrúɓád-o ŋgóᵉ.
     come:1PL=PST things-INS we:GEN
     'We came with our things.'

Manner

(66) Rájétuo   ɲcie gáánàs-ɔ.
     answer:3SG I:DAT badness-INS
     'And he answered me with hostility.'

Time

(67) Bɨraa   ɲɛka   ódoicik-ó=ni.
     lack:3SG hunger:NOM days-INS=these
     'There is no hunger these days.'

Occupation

(68) Cɛma   fités-o   ƙwázìkàᵉ.
     fight:3SG washing-INS clothes:GEN
     'She's washing clothes.' (lit: 'She is fighting with the washing of clothes.')

7.8 Copulative (COP)

The COPULATIVE case, marked by the suffix {-ko}, is the 'is' or 'coupling' case, whose function is to link one noun to another in a relationship of exact identity. In this function, the copulative marks three kinds of nouns: 1) a focused (fronted) noun, 2) the complement of a verbless COPULA (linking verb) clause, and 3) the complement of a negative copula of identity clause. These different uses of the copulative are illustrated in examples sentences (69)-(73):

Fronted subject

(69) Ŋgó-ó=naa wetím.
 we-COP=PST drink:1PL.EXC
 'It was we (who) drank (it).'

Fronted object

(70) Emó-ó bɛ́dɨ̵.
 meat-COP want:1SG
 'It is meat (that) I want.'

Fronted secondary object

(71) Nɛkɔ-ɔ ƙaiátèè ƙàƙààƙɔ̀kɛ.
 hunger-COP go:PLUR:3PL hunt:inside:DAT
 'It is (due to) hunger (that) they keep going hunting.'

Verbless copula complement

(72) a. Ìsù-kº? Ámó-o keɗe ...?
  what-COP person-COP or
  'What is it? A person or ...?'
 b. Ámá-kº.
  person-COP
  'It's a person.'

Negative copula complement

(73) Bɛna=náá ńcù-kº.
 not.be:3SG=PST I-COP
 'It was not me!'

7.9 Oblique (OBL)

The OBLIQUE case, marked by the absence of any suffix, is the 'leftover' case. As such, it is employed to mark nouns in a variety of disparate grammatical roles and functions. Among these are the following: 1) The subject and/or object of an imperative clause, 2) the subject and/or object of an optative clause, 3) the object of a preposition, and 4) a vocative noun (used when calling someone). Each of these uses of the oblique case are demonstrated in examples (74)-(78):

Subject and/or object of an imperative clause

(74) Deté   bi   cue=díí!
     bring:IMP you:OBL water:OBL=those
     'You bring that water!'

Subject and/or object of an optative clause

(75) Ńci   nesíbine   emuti   ntsí.
     I:OBL listen:1SG:OPT story:OBL he:GEN
     'Let me listen to her story.'

Object of a preposition

(76) Túbia   ima   ńcia páka aw^a.
     follow:3SG child:NOM I:ACC until home:OBL
     'The child follows me up to home.'

(77) Kirotánía kóteré fiyekesí bì.
     sweat:1SG for   life:OBL you:GEN
     'I sweat for your survival.'

Vocative

(78) Éé wice,   atsú!
     hey children:OBL come:IMP
     'Hey children, come!'

8 Verbs

8.1 Overview

Ik verbs consist of a verbal root (written in this book with a hyphen, as in *wèt-* 'drink') and at least one of a variety of available derivational and inflectional suffixes. The language has no prefixes except those borrowed centuries ago that no longer have any active function, for example the /a/ in *ábùbùk-* 'bubble' or the /i/ in *ibóbór-* 'hollow out'. Reduplicating a verb root, partially or totally, has long been a strategy for creating a sense of continuousness or repetitiveness, as when *itsán-* 'disturb' becomes *itsanítsán-* 'torment relentlessly'.

Ik employs a large number of suffixes to create longer verb stems. Among these are the INFINITIVE and other deverbalizing suffixes that change a verb into a noun that can take case endings, demonstratives, relative clauses, etc. One very key verb-building strategy of Ik is the DIRECTIONAL suffixes that signify the direction of the verb's movement to or away from the speaker. These two directionals have also been extended metaphorically to express the beginning or completion of actions or processes. Another set of verbal suffixes deal with VOICE and VALENCY, that is, the number of objects the verb requires. Among these are the PASSIVE, IMPERSONAL passive, MIDDLE, CAUSATIVE, and RECIPROCAL.

Once a verb is taken from the mental lexicon and used in speech, it often requires SUBJECT-AGREEMENT marking, which Ik accomplishes through pronominal suffixes. Ik also has a special verbal suffix, the DUMMY PRONOUN, that goes on the verb whenever a peripheral argument, like a place or time designation, has been moved to the front of the clause or removed entirely.

The Ik verbal system has a variety of verbal paradigms based on MOOD and ASPECT. The basic distinction in mood is between REALIS and IRREALIS, or things that have happened and things that have not. Other modal distinctions include the OPTATIVE, SUBJUNCTIVE, IMPERATIVE, and NEGATIVE. As for aspect, the specification of the internal structure of a verb – complete or incomplete – Ik has suffixes that mark PRESENT PERFECT, INTENTIONAL-IMPERFECTIVE, PLURACTIONAL, SEQUENTIAL, and SIMULTANEOUS. Lastly, Ik exhibits a special set of ADJECTIVAL suffixes to cover the language's need to express adjectival concepts.

8.2 Infinitives (INF)

8.2.1 Intransitive

INTRANSITIVE verbs allow only a subject and possibly an indirect object – a direct object does not figure into their semantic schema. The Ik intransitive INFINITIVE suffix is {-ònì-}. It converts an intransitive verb to a morphological noun that can be used as a noun in a noun phrase. The infinitive is the CITATION FORM of a verb, the form one cites in a dictionary or in isolation from other words. Table 59 gives a few examples of intransitive infinitives from the lexicon:

Grammar sketch

Table 59: Ik intransitive infinitives

Root	Intransitive infinitive	
áƙáf-	áƙáfòn	'to yawn'
bòt-	bòtòn	'to migrate'
cɨ̀-	cɨ̀ɔ̀n	'to be satiated'
dód-	dódòn	'to hurt'
èf-	èfɔn	'to be tasty'
gwɨ̀r-	gwɨ̀rɔn	'to squirm'
iƙú-	iƙúón	'to howl'

Because the infinitive is a noun morphologically, it can be fully declined for case as all nouns can. Table 60 gives the case declension of the verb *wàtònì-* 'to rain', which shows some vowel assimilation effects on [+ATR] vowels, as when /io/ becomes /uo/ in the ablative and copulative cases. Table 61 does the same for the [-ATR] verb *wédɔ̀nɨ̀-* 'to detour'. Note /ɨɔ/ becoming /ʉɔ/ there as well:

Table 60: Case declension of *wàtònì-* 'to rain'

	Non-final	Final
NOM	wàtònà	wàtòn
ACC	wàtònìà	wàtònìk[a]
DAT	wàtònìè	wàtònìk[e]
GEN	wàtònìè	wàtònì
ABL	wàtònùò	wàtònù
INS	wàtònò	wàtòn[o]
COP	wàtònùò	wàtònùk[o]
OBL	wàtònì	wàtòn

8.2.2 Transitive

TRANSITIVE verbs are those that admit a subject *and* a direct object into their schematic of an active event. The Ik transitive infinitive suffix is {-ésí-}. It converts a transitive verb to a morphological noun that can be used as a noun in a noun phrase. Table 62 presents a few examples of transitive infinitives:

Table 61: Case declension of wédɔnɨ- 'to detour'

	Non-final	Final
NOM	wédɔnà	wédɔn
ACC	wédɔnɨà	wédɔnɨkᵃ
DAT	wédɔnɨè	wédɔnɨkᵋ
GEN	wédɔnɨè	wédɔnɨ
ABL	wédɔnʉɔ́	wédɔnʉ̀
INS	wédɔnɔ́	wédɔnᵓ
COP	wédɔnʉɔ́	wédɔnʉ̀kᵓ
OBL	wédɔnɨ	wédɔn

Table 62: Ik transitive infinitives

Root	Transitive infinitive	
ágʉ̀j-	ágʉjɛ́s	'to gulp'
ban-	banɛ́s	'to sharpen'
cɛ́b-	cɛ́bɛ̀s	'to roughen'
ɗóɗ-	ɗóɗɛ́s	'to point at'
erég-	erégès	'to employ'
gɨj-	gɨjɛ́s	'to shave'
ilɔ́ƙ-	ilɔƙɛs	'to dissolve'

Table 63 gives the case declension of the deverbalized noun *wetésí-* 'to drink', which shows vowel assimilation effects on [+ATR] vowels. Table 64 does the same for the [-ATR] verb for the [-ATR] verb *wɛts'ɛ́sɨ-* 'to knap'.

8.2.3 Semi-transitive

SEMI-TRANSITIVE verbs fall between transitive and intransitive in that they take an object, but the object is the reflexive pronoun *asɨ-* '-self', referring to the subject. This means that semi-transitive verbs are morphologically transitive but almost intransitive semantically. Another name for this is 'middle' (although see another Ik middle verb in §8.6.3). Table 65 provides a sample of semi-transitive verbs. No case declension is given for these because they decline the same way as the transitive infinitives shown in Table 63 and Table 64:

Grammar sketch

Table 63: Case declension of *wetésí-* 'to drink'

	Non-final	Final
NOM	wetésá	wetés
ACC	wetésíà	wetésík[a]
DAT	wetésíè	wetésík[e]
GEN	wetésíè	wetésí
ABL	wetésúò	wetésú
INS	wetésó	wetés°
COP	wetésúò	wetésúk°
OBL	wetésí	wetés

Table 64: Case declension of *wɛts'ɛ́sɨ́-* 'to knap'

	Non-final	Final
NOM	wɛts'ɛ́sá	wɛts'ɛ́s
ACC	wɛts'ɛ́sɨ̀à	wɛts'ɛ́sɨ́k[a]
DAT	wɛts'ɛ́sɨ̀è	wɛts'ɛ́sɨ́k[ɛ]
GEN	wɛts'ɛ́sɨ̀è	wɛts'ɛ́sɨ́
ABL	wɛts'ɛ́sʉ́ɔ̀	wɛts'ɛ́sʉ́
INS	wɛts'ɛ́sɔ́	wɛts'ɛ́sᵓ
COP	wɛts'ɛ́sʉ́ɔ̀	wɛts'ɛ́sʉ́kᵓ
OBL	wɛts'ɛ́sɨ́	wɛts'ɛ́s

Table 65: Ik semi-transitive infinitives

Root		Semi-transitive	
bal-	'ignore'	balésá asɨ́	'to neglect -self'
hoɗ-	'free'	hoɗésá asɨ́	'to get freed'
irɨ́ts-	'keep'	irɨtsɛsa asɨ́	'to control -self'
irʉ́ts-	'fling'	irʉtsɛsa asɨ́	'to race across'
itɨ́ŋ-	'force'	itɨŋɛsa asɨ́	'to force -self'
kɔk-	'close'	kɔkésá asɨ́	'to cover -self'
toɓ-	'spear'	toɓésá asɨ́	'to shoot across'

8.3 Deverbalizers

8.3.1 Abstractive (ABST)

The ABSTRACTIVE suffix {-ásɨ-} can be used to replace the intransitive suffix {-òni-} for converting an intransitive verb to an abstract noun, for example, when *hábòn* 'to be hot' becomes *hábàs* 'heat'. Table 66 gives several examples of abstract nouns derived from intransitive verbs:

Table 66: Ik abstract nouns derived from verbs

Intransitive infinitive		Abstract noun	
ɓàŋɔ̀n	'to be loose'	ɓaŋás	'looseness'
èfɔn	'to be tasty'	ɛfás	'(tasty) fat'
gaanón	'to be bad'	gaánàs	'badness'
ɦyètɔ̀n	'to be fierce'	ɦyɛtás	'fierceness'
kòmòn	'to be many'	komás	'manyness'
ŋwàxɔ̀n	'to be disabled'	ŋwaxás	'disability'
xèɓɔ̀n	'to be shy'	xɛɓás	'shyness'

Because verbs deverbalized by the abstractive suffix are morphological nouns, they are fully declined for case. Table 67 gives one such case declension of the abstract noun *kuɗásɨ-* 'shortness':

Table 67: Case declension of *kuɗásɨ-* 'shortness'

	Non-final	Final
NOM	kuɗásá	kuɗás
ACC	kuɗásɨ̀à	kuɗásɨ́kᵃ
DAT	kuɗásɨ̀ɛ̀	kuɗásɨ́kᵋ
GEN	kuɗásɨ̀ɛ̀	kuɗásɨ́
ABL	kuɗásɨ́ɔ́	kuɗásɨ́
INS	kuɗásɔ́	kuɗásᵓ
COP	kuɗásɨ́ɔ́	kuɗásɨ́kᵓ
OBL	kuɗásɨ	kuɗás

539

Grammar sketch

8.3.2 Behaviorative (BHVR)

The BEHAVIORATIVE suffix {-nànèsì-} is a complex suffix possibly consisting of the stative suffix {-án-} from §8.11.4 and the transitive suffix (§8.2.2) or the abstractive suffix (§8.3.1). Regardless of its composition, the suffix as a whole creates abstract concepts based on simple nouns, like *ámánànès* 'personhood' or 'personality' from *ámá-* 'person'. Table 68 provides a few more examples:

Table 68: Ik behaviorative abstract nouns

Noun root		Behaviorative	
babatí-	'his/her father'	babatínánès	'fatherhood'
cekí-	'woman'	cekínánès	'womanhood'
dzɔɗátí-	'rectum'	dzɔɗátínànès	'grabbiness'
dzúú-	'theft'	dzúnánès	'thievery'
imá-	'child'	imánánès	'childhood'
lɔŋɔ́tá-	'enemy'	lɔŋɔ́tánànès	'enmity'
ŋókí-	'dog'	ŋókínànès	'poverty'

Because behavioratives are nouns morphologically, they are declined for case. Table 69 gives the case declension for the word *eakwánánèsì-* 'manhood':

Table 69: Case declension of *eakwánánèsì-* 'manhood'

	Non-final	Final
NOM	eakwánánèsà	eakwánánès
ACC	eakwánánèsià	eakwánánèsìk[a]
DAT	eakwánánèsiè	eakwánánèsìk[e]
GEN	eakwánánèsiè	eakwánánèsì
ABL	eakwánánèsùò	eakwánánèsù
INS	eakwánánèsò	eakwánánès[o]
COP	eakwánánèsùò	eakwánánèsùk[o]
OBL	eakwánánèsì	eakwánánès

8.3.3 Patientive (PAT)

The PATIENTIVE suffix {-amá-} converts a verb to a noun that is characterized by the meaning of the verb. It is called 'patientive' because the derived noun usually has the meaning of 'patient' or object of the original verb, as when *meetés* 'to give' produces *meetam* 'gift'. Table 70 gives some examples of patientive nouns:

Table 70: Ik patientive nouns

Verb root		Patientive noun	
áts-	'chew'	ats'amá-	'chewy food'
ɓɛk-	'provoke'	ɓɛkamá-	'provocation'
dʉb-	'knead'	dʉbamá-	'dough'
dzígw-	'buy/sell'	dzígwamá-	'merchandise'
gam-	'kindle'	gamamá-	'kindling'
isúɗ-	'distort'	isuɗamá-	'falsehood'
ŋƙ-	'eat'	ŋƙamá-	'eatable'

Because patientives are nouns morphologically, they are fully declined for case. Table 71 gives the full declension of the noun *wetamá-* 'drink(able)':

Table 71: Case declension of *wetamá-* 'drink(able)'

	Non-final	Final
NOM	wetama	wetam
ACC	wetamáá	wetamák^a
DAT	wetaméé	wetamák^e
GEN	wetaméé	wetamá^e
ABL	wetamóó	wetamá^o
INS	wetamo	wetam^o
COP	wetamóó	wetamák^o
OBL	wetama	wetam

Grammar sketch

8.4 Directionals

8.4.1 Venitive (VEN)

The VENITIVE suffix {-ét-} denotes a direction *toward* a deictic center, usually (but not always) the speaker. It can be translated variously as 'here', 'this way', 'out', or 'up', but it is the Middle English word 'hither' that captures its essence nicely. The venitive suffix comes between the verb root and the infinitive suffix, whether intransitive or transitive. It can be used to augment any verb whose meaning includes motion or movement of any kind. Table 72 gives a few examples:

Table 72: Ik venitive verbs

Intransitive		Transitive	
arétón	'to cross this way'	béberetés	'to pull this way'
ɦyɔtɔ́gètòn	'to approach here'	dᵾretés	'to pull out'
ilɛ́ɛtɔn	'to come visit'	futetés	'to blow this way'
irímétòn	'to rotate this way'	hɔnetés	'to drive out'
ŋkéétòn	'to get up'	iriŋetés	'to turn this way'
tɛ́ɛ̀tòn	'to fall down'	iteletés	'to watch here'
tᵾwétɔ́n	'to sprout up'	seɓetés	'to sweep up'

Venitive infinitives are morphological nouns and thus are declined for case. See §8.2.1 and §8.2.2 for case declensions that show the relevant endings.

8.4.2 Andative (AND)

The ANDATIVE suffix {-uƙot(í)-} denotes direction *away from* a deictic center, usually the speaker (but not always). It can be translated variously as 'away', 'off', 'out', 'that way', or 'there', but it is the Middle English word 'thither' that captures its essence nicely. Unlike the venitive suffix, the andative comes after both the verbal root and the infinitive suffix (in an infinitival construction). It can be used to augment any verb whose meaning includes motion or movement of any kind. Table 73 provides a few examples of andative verbs.

Because the andative suffix comes after infinitive suffixes, whenever an andative infinitive is declined for case, it is the andative suffix that takes case endings. Table 74 gives a declension of the [+ATR] andative verb *séɓésukotí-* 'to sweep off', while Table 75 does the same for the [-ATR] verb *sɛkɛ́sᵾkɔtí-* 'to scrub off':

Table 73: Ik andative verbs

Intransitive		Transitive	
aronuƙotᵃ	'to cross that way'	hɔnésúƙɔtᵃ	'to drive off/away'
botonuƙotᵃ	'to move away'	idɛ́ɛ́sʉƙɔtᵃ	'to hide way'
bʉrɔnʉƙɔtᵃ	'to fly off/away'	ídzesuƙotᵃ	'to shoot (away)'
iɓákɔ́nʉƙɔtᵃ	'to go next to'	ígorésúƙotᵃ	'to cross over'
isépónuƙotᵃ	'to flow away'	ƙanésúƙotᵃ	'to take away'
kúbonuƙotᵃ	'to go out of sight'	maƙésúƙotᵃ	'to give away'
tʉlúɲɔ́nʉƙɔtᵃ	'to storm off'	tɔrésúƙɔtᵃ	'to toss away'

Table 74: Case declension of séɓésuƙotí- 'to sweep off'

	Non-final	Final
NOM	séɓésuƙota	séɓésuƙotᵃ
ACC	séɓésuƙotiá	séɓésuƙotíƙᵃ
DAT	séɓésuƙotié	séɓésuƙotíƙᵉ
GEN	séɓésuƙotié	séɓésuƙotí
ABL	séɓésuƙotúó	séɓésuƙotú
INS	séɓésuƙoto	séɓésuƙotᵒ
COP	séɓésuƙotúó	séɓésuƙotúƙᵒ
OBL	séɓésuƙoti	séɓésuƙotⁱ

Table 75: Case declension of sɛkésúƙɔtí- 'to scrub off'

	Non-final	Final
NOM	sɛkésúƙɔta	sɛkésúƙɔtᵃ
ACC	sɛkésúƙɔtɨá	sɛkésúƙɔtɨ́ƙᵃ
DAT	sɛkésúƙɔtɨ́ɛ́	sɛkésúƙɔtɨ́ƙᵋ
GEN	sɛkésúƙɔtɨ́ɛ́	sɛkésúƙɔtɨ́
ABL	sɛkésúƙɔtʉ́ɔ́	sɛkésúƙɔtʉ́
INS	sɛkésúƙɔtɔ	sɛkésúƙɔtᵓ
COP	sɛkésúƙɔtʉ́ɔ́	sɛkésúƙɔtʉ́ƙᵓ
OBL	sɛkésúƙɔtɨ	sɛkésúƙɔtⁱ

Grammar sketch

8.5 Aspectuals

8.5.1 Inchoative (INCH)

The INCHOATIVE suffix {-ét-} is identical to the venitive suffix described in §8.4.1, and this is because its meaning is a metaphorical extension of the meaning of the venitive. That is, the venitive meaning of 'hither' was extended to mean the beginning of a state or activity (for intransitives) or the starting up of some action or process (for transitives). The inchoative behaves morphologically (including case declensions) exactly the same as the venitive. Table 76 gives a few examples of intransitive and transitive verbs in the inchoative aspect:

Table 76: Ik inchoative verbs

Intransitive		Transitive	
aeétón	'to start ripening'	balɛtés	'to ignore'
dikwétón	'to start dancing'	ewanetés	'to take note of'
ɛkwétón	'to start early'	hoɗetés	'to liberate'
iɛɓétɔn	'to grow cold'	inákúetés	'to destroy'
lɛjétɔn	'to catch fire'	rɛɛtés	'to coerce'
tsekétón	'to grow bushy'	tajaletés	'to relinquish'
wasétɔn	'to refuse'	tamɛtés	'to ponder'

8.5.2 Completive (COMP)

The COMPLETIVE suffix {-uƙot(í)-} is identical to the andative suffix described in §8.4.2, and this is because its meaning is a metaphorical extension of the meaning of the andative. That is, the andative meaning of 'thither' was extended to mean the completion of a change of state or activity (for intransitives) or the fulfillment of some action or process (for transitives). The completive behaves morphologically (including case declensions) exactly the same as the andative. Table 77 gives a few examples of lexical verbs in the completive aspect:

8.5.3 Pluractional (PLUR)

The PLURACTIONAL suffix {-í-} denotes an action or state that is construed as inherently *plural* in its realization. This notion of plurality can mean any of the following: 1) an intransitive action done more than once or done by more than

8 Verbs

Table 77: Ik completive verbs

Intransitive		Transitive	
aeonuƙotᵃ	'to become ripe'	anɛ́súƙotᵃ	'to remember'
barɔnʉƙɔtᵃ	'to become rich'	dɔxɛ́súƙotᵃ	'to reprimand'
hábonuƙotᵃ	'to become hot'	ɦiyeésúƙotᵃ	'to learn'
hɛ́ɗɔ́nʉƙɔtᵃ	'to shrivel up'	kurésúƙotᵃ	'to defeat'
mitɔnʉƙɔtᵃ	'to become'	ŋábɛsʉƙɔtᵃ	'to finish up'
sɛkɔnʉƙɔtᵃ	'to fade away'	ŋƙáƙésuƙotᵃ	'to devour'
zoonuƙotᵃ	'to become big'	toɓésúƙotᵃ	'to plunder'

one subject, 2) a state attributed more than once or of more than one subject, 3) a transitive action done more than once, done by more than one subject, or done to more than one object. In short, the pluractional suffix conveys the idea that the application of the verb is multiple. The pluractional suffix comes just before the infinitive suffix and is a dominant [+ATR] suffix that harmonizes [-ATR] vowels. Table 78 gives a few examples of intransitive and transitive pluractional verbs:

Table 78: Ik pluractional verbs

Intransitive		Transitive	
kóníón	'to be one-by-one'	abutiés	'to sip continually'
ŋatíón	'to run (of many)'	esetiés	'to interrogate'
ŋƙáíón	'to get up (of many)'	gafariés	'to stab repeatedly'
toɓéíón	'to be usually right'	nesíbiés	'to obey habitually'
tatíón	'to drip constantly'	tirifiés	'to investigate'

8.6 Voice and valence

8.6.1 Passive (PASS)

The Ik PASSIVE suffix {-ósí-} has the unusual distinction of being able to modify both intransitive and transitive verbs. With intransitive verbs, it adds the nuance of characteristicness to the meaning of the verb, often with the help of root reduplication. With transitive verbs, it has the usual function of a passive, which is to convert the object of a transitive verb into the subject of an intransitive verb. Table 79 gives examples of both intransitive and transitive passives:

Table 79: Ik passives

Intransitive		Transitive	
botibotos	'to be migratory'	búdòs	'to be hidden'
ɓɛkɛsɔs	'to be mobile'	cookós	'to be guarded'
deƙwideƙos	'to be quarrelsome'	ɗɔtsɔ́s	'to be joined'
ɗɛɲiɗɛɲɔs	'to be restless'	júós	'to be roasted'
gúránós	'to be hot-tempered'	ɲáɲós	'to be open'
mɔɲimɔɲɔs	'to be gossipy'	ógoós	'to be left'
tsuwoós	'to be active'	tsáŋós	'to be anointed'

Another quirky feature of the Ik passive {-ósí-} is that it can function both as a passive infinitive suffix (taking case) and as a regular inflectional suffix followed by subject-agreement pronouns. When it is declined for case, it declines just like the transitive suffix {-ésí-} in §8.2.2. Example (79) below illustrates this in a sentence where the passive infinitive búdòsì- 'to be hidden' gets the accusative case. Then, example (80) shows the same passive acting as a verb proper, taking the 3PL subject-agreement pronominal suffix {-át-}:

(79) Bɛ́ɗáta   búdòsì-kᵃ.
 want:3PL hidden:PASS-ACC
 'They want to be hidden.'

(80) Búdos-átᵃ.
 hidden:PASS-3PL:REAL
 'They are hidden.'

8.6.2 Impersonal passive (IPS)

The IMPERSONAL PASSIVE suffix {-àn-} behaves like a typical passive in that it eliminates the agent of a transitive verb and promotes the object to subject. However, unlike the passive {-ósí-} described above, the impersonal passive cannot be specified for the person or number of its subject. Instead, it remains marked for 3SG regardless of who or what the subject may be. Another strange property of {-àn-} is that it can be used with intransitive verbs as well (just like the passive). When used with intransitive verbs, it has the function of downplaying the identity of the subject. For this reason, it can often be translated as 'People ...' or 'One ...', as in *Tódian* 'People say (it)'. The impersonal passive is a grammatical morpheme not listed in the lexicon, and so it must be illustrated in examples like (81)-(82):

(81) Ɨnɔ́mɛ́sànà bì.
 beat:FUT:IPS you[SG]:NOM
 'You will be beaten.'

(82) Kaíánà ƙàƙààƙɔkɛ.
 go:PLUR:IPS hunt:inside:DAT
 'People go hunting.' (Lit. 'It is gone for hunting.')

8.6.3 Middle (MID)

Ik has two MIDDLE suffixes: {-m-} and {-ím-}. Like the semi-transitive construction discussed in §8.2.3, the middle suffixes convert simple transitive verbs into something in the 'middle' of transitive and intransitive. That is, the Ik middle verbs convey that idea that if an action is done to an entity, it is the entity itself – if anything – doing it to itself alone, apart from any other explicit agent. The middles eliminate the agent and promote the patient to subject.

The middle suffix {-m-} always has a vowel between it and the preceding verb root. This vowel is usually a copy of the root vowel, as when *ɖusés* 'cut' becomes *ɖusúmón* 'to cut (alone/on its own)', but it can also have a non-copy vowel as in *bokímón* 'to get caught'. For its part, the middle suffix {-ím-} – a dominant [+ATR] suffix – is always paired with the inchoative suffix {-ét-}, thereby forming the complex morpheme {-ímét-}. Table 80 below gives some examples of these two suffixes converting transitive verbs to middle verbs.

8.6.4 Reciprocal (RECIP)

The RECIPROCAL suffix {-ínósí-} denotes a reciprocal relationship that a verb's subject has with itself. That is, the reciprocal collapses the subject and direct object of a transitive verb, or the subject and a secondary object of an intransitive verb, into just the subject of a reciprocal verb. In this regard, it is similar to the semi-transitive verbs from §8.2.3 that use the reflexive pronoun *asɨ-* '-self'. Table 81 provides a few examples of reciprocals derived from other verbs:

Grammar sketch

Table 80: Ik middle verbs

Transitive		Middle {-m-}	
ŋáɲɛ́s	'to open'	ŋáɲámòn	'to open (alone)'
pakɛ́s	'to split'	pakámón	'to split (alone)'
pulɛ́s	'to pierce'	pulúmón	'to go out'
raɟɛ́s	'to return'	raɟámón	'to return (alone)'
tɛrɛ́s	'to divide'	tɛrɛ́món	'to divide (alone)'
Transitive		Middle {-ímét-}	
áts'ɛ́s	'to chew'	ats'ímétòn	'to wear out (alone)'
iɓéléɛ́s	'to overturn'	iɓéléìmètòn	'to overturn (alone)'
kɔkɛ́s	'to close'	kokíméton	'to close (alone)'
rébès	'to deprive'	rébìmètòn	'to be deprived (alone)'
tɔrɛɛs	'to coerce'	toreimétòn	'to be coerced (alone)'

Table 81: Ik reciprocal verbs

Intransitive		Reciprocal	
ɓɛkɛ́s	'to walk'	ɓɛkɛ́sɨnɔ́s	'to walk together'
iɓákɔ́n	'to be next to'	iɓákɨnɔ́s	'to be next to each other'
tódòn	'to speak'	tódinós	'to speak to each other'
Transitive		Reciprocal	
ɦyeɛ́s	'to know'	ɦyeinós	'to be related'
iŋaarɛ́s	'to help'	iŋáárɨnɔ́s	'to help each other'
mɨnɛ́s	'to love'	mɨnɨnɔ́s	'to love each other'

Like the passive {-ósí-} discussed in §8.6.1, the reciprocal suffix can take either case endings (as a morphological noun) or subject-agreement endings (as a morphological verb). A case declension of *inínósí-* 'to cohabitate' is shown in Table 82, and in example (83) below, the reciprocal verb *iɓákɨnɔ́sɨ-* 'to be next to each other' gets the accusative case. Then, example (84) shows the same verb acting as a verb proper, with the 3PL subject-agreement marker {-át-}:

Table 82: Case declension of *ínínósí-* 'to cohabitate'

	Non-final	Final
NOM	ínínósá	ínínós
ACC	ínínósíà	ínínósíkᵃ
DAT	ínínósíè	ínínósíkᵉ
GEN	ínínósíè	ínínósí
ABL	ínínósúò	ínínósú
INS	ínínósó	ínínós°
COP	ínínósúò	ínínósúk°
OBL	ínínósí	ínínós

(83) Bédáta ɨɓákɨnɔ́sɨ-kᵃ.
want:3PL:REAL next.to:RECIP-ACC
'They want to be next to each other.'

(84) Ɨɓákɨnɔ́s-átᵃ.
next.to:RECIP-3PL:REAL
'They are next to each other.'

8.6.5 Causative (CAUS)

Ik expresses causativity with a morphological causative, the CAUSATIVE suffix {-ɨt-}. When this suffix is added to a verb with meaning X, it changes the meaning of the verb to 'cause/make (to) X'. This suffix can be used to causativize intransitive and transitive verbs and comes right after the verb root, before the infinitive marker (if present) and any other suffixes like an inchoative or pluractional. If the last vowel of the verb root is /u/, the causative may be assimilated to the form {-ùt-}. Table 83 gives several examples of causativized verbs.

8.7 Subject-agreement

Whenever Ik grammar requires verbs to agree with their subjects, one of the seven pronominal suffixes in Table 84 are used. Note that if the verb contains [-ATR] vowels, these suffixes will also be harmonized to [-ATR]. Just like the free pronouns described back in §5.2, these bound pronominal suffixes are organized along three axes: 1) person (1/2/3), 2) number (singular/plural), and 3) clusivity

Grammar sketch

Table 83: Ik causative verbs

Intransitive		Causative	
bùkòn	'to be prostrate'	bukites	'to lay prostrate'
itúrón	'to be proud'	itúrútés	'to praise'
xɛ̀ɓɔ̀n	'to be timid'	xɛɓitɛs	'to intimidate'
Transitive			
dimés	'to refuse'	dimités	'to prohibit'
naƙwés	'to suckle'	naƙwités	'to give suckle'
zízòn	'to be fat'	zízités	'to fatten'

(exclusive/inclusive). The form these pronominals ultimately take depends on the grammatical mood of the verb to which they attach. If the verb is in the irrealis mood (see §8.9.1), the suffixes appear with their underlying forms. Whereas if they are in the realis mood (see §8.9.2), the realis suffix {-a} first subtracts or deletes their final vowel. The difference in the two mood-based paradigms is depicted in Table 84. To see instances of the Ik subject-agreement suffixes in actual language use, you may refer back to example (43) in §7.2.

Table 84: Ik subject-agreement suffixes

	Irrealis		Realis	
	NF	FF	NF	FF
1SG	-íí	-í	-íá	-í
2SG	-ídì	-îd[i]	-ídà	-îd[a]
3SG	-ì	-[i]	-a	-[a]
1PL.EXC	-ímí	-ím	-ímá	-ím
1PL.INC	-ísínì	-ísín	-ísínà	-ísín
2PL	-ítí	-ít[i]	-ítá	-ít[a]
3PL	-átì	-át[i]	-átà	-át[a]

8.8 Dummy pronoun (DP)

Ik has a special verbal affix called the DUMMY PRONOUN because it represents a secondary (indirect) object that has been (re)moved. That is, the dummy pronoun is a form of object-marking on the verb, but not of direct object marking. For example, if an indirect object expressing location or time or means is moved to the front of a clause for emphasis, it leaves a trace on the verb in the form of the dummy pronoun. Seen from another perspective, the dummy pronoun is always a clue that there is a missing syntactic constituent in the clause.

The dummy pronoun has the form {-ˊdè} and is very volatile in terms of allomorphy, dramatically changing its form in different morpho-phonological environments. Once the /d/ is lost in non-final forms, vowel assimilation and vowel harmony so distort the dummy pronoun as to make it almost unrecognizable at times. Table 85 below is given to illustrate its diverse allomorphy:

Table 85: Allomorphs of the dummy pronoun {-ˊdè}

	Non-final	Final
{-ˊdè}	-ˊè	-ˊdᵉ
	-ˊɛ̀	-ˊdᵋ
	-ˊì	
	-ˊɨ̀	
	-ˊò	
	-ˊɔ̀	

Examples (85)-(86) illustrate the dummy pronoun in two different morphological forms: final and non-final. Note that the tones associated with the pronoun in these examples do not match what is shown in Table 85; this is because of local tonal interference. In terms of function, the dummy pronoun in (85) indicates that an indirect object – the destination of the verb *káátà* 'they go (went)' – has been displaced from its usual spot after the verb to a place of focus at the beginning of the sentence (*Ntsúó*). Then in (86), the dummy pronoun marks an indirect object – the location of staying – that is missing from the clause entirely. Since this sentence was taken out of context from a story, most likely the missing object had been already mentioned earlier in the discourse:

Grammar sketch

(85) Ntsúó=noo Icéá ƙáátà-**dᵉ**.
 it:COP=PAST Ik:ACC go:3PL:REAL-DP
 'It's where the Ik went (to).'

(86) J'ɛjɨkɔ́-ɔ́ sàà ròɓàᵉ.
 stay:3SG:SEQ-DP other:NOM people:GEN
 'And other people stayed (there).'

8.9 Mood

8.9.1 Irrealis (IRR)

A basic distinction in grammatical MOOD cleaves Ik verbal aspects and modalities right down the center, and this distinction is between IRREALIS and REALIS. As it applies specifically to Ik, the irrealis mood includes states and events whose *actuality* or *reality* are not expressly encoded in the grammar. Another way of saying this is that irrealis verbs in Ik can convey anything *but* whether a state or event has happened, is happening, or will happen. The morphological manifestation of the irrealis is that the final suffix of an irrealis verb – a subject-agreement pronoun – surfaces with its underlying form (see Table 84).

The verbal aspects and modalities that fall under the irrealis mood include the OPTATIVE, SUBJUNCTIVE, IMPERATIVE, NEGATIVE, SEQUENTIAL, and SIMULTANEOUS.

8.9.2 Realis (REAL)

In contrast to irrealis, the REALIS mood includes states and events whose actuality or reality *are* encoded in the grammar. That is to say, realis verbs in Ik include in their meaning the fact that something has taken place, is taking place, or will take place in the real world. The morphological manifestation of the realis mood is seen in the realis suffix {-a} that subtracts or deletes the final vowel of the subject-agreement suffix to which it attaches (again, see Table 84). In terms of verb types, the realis mood includes declarative statements in the past or non-past, questions about the past or non-past, and, rather paradoxically, negative imperatives (which one might expect to fall under irrealis).

8.10 Verb paradigms

8.10.1 Intentional-imperfective (INT/IPFV)

The INTENTIONAL-IMPERFECTIVE aspect suffix {-és-} has two functions, hence its hyphenated title. One is to denote either an intention on the part of animate subjects or an imminence on the part of inanimate subjects. It is in this role that it finds use as the usual translation for the English future tense. It is also the answer to the question, "How do you express future tense in Ik?" A second function is to denote grammatical imperfectivity: a sense that a state or event is ongoing or incomplete. The two concepts collapse into one when intention/imminence is viewed as the incomplete coming-to-be of a future state or event. And even though intention or imperfectivity may seem to fall under an irrealis mood, {-és-} can actually be used with verbs in either the realis or irrealis mood. In Table 86, {-és-} is illustrated with the verb *àts-* 'come' in its imperfective sense with a recent past tense marker (*nák*[a]) and then in its intentional (English 'future') sense:

Table 86: Ik intentional-imperfective aspect

Imperfective		
1SG	Atsésíà nàk[a].	'I was coming.'
2SG	Atsésídà nàk[a].	'You were coming.'
3SG	Atsesa nák[a].	'(S)he/it was coming.'
1PL.EXC	Atsésímà nàk[a]	'We were coming.'
1PL.INC	Atsésísìnà nàk[a].	'We all were coming.'
2PL	Atsésítà nàk[a].	'You all were coming.'
3PL	Atsésátà nàk[a].	'They were coming.'
Intentional		
1SG	Atsésí.	'I will come.'
2SG	Atsésîd[a].	'You will come.'
3SG	Atsés.	'(S)he/it will come.'
1PL.EXC	Atsésím.	'We will come.'
1PL.INC	Atsésísìn.	'We all will come.'
2PL	Atsésít[a].	'You all will come.'
3PL	Atsésát[a].	'They will come.'

8.10.2 Present perfect (PRF)

The Ik PRESENT PERFECT suffix {-´ka} denotes a state or event recently completed ('perfected') but still relevant in the present. The suffix has a 'floating' high tone that shows up on the preceding syllable of 3SG verbs, for example in *Nabʉkɔták*ᵃ 'It is finished'. The /k/ in {-´ka} disappears in non-final environments, making {-´a} an allomorph. Table 87 presents the paradigm of the present perfect with the verb *àts-* 'come' in both non-final and final environments:

Table 87: Ik present perfect aspect

	Non-final	Final	
1SG	Atsíàà ...	Atsíàkᵃ.	'I have come'
2SG	Atsídàà ...	Atsídàkᵃ.	'You have come'
3SG	Atsáá ...	Atsákᵃ.	'She has come'
1PL.EXC	Atsímáà ...	Atsímákᵃ.	'We have come'
1PL.INC	Atsísínàà ...	Atsísínàkᵃ.	'We all have come'
2PL	Atsítàà ...	Atsítákᵃ.	'You all have come'
3PL	Atsátàà ...	Atsátàkᵃ.	'They have come'

8.10.3 Optative (OPT)

The Ik OPTATIVE mood is used to express wishes, even ironic ones like 'Let the enemies come!'. Optative verbs are often introduced with imperative verbs like *Ógoe* or *Taláké*, both of which mean 'Let ...'. And all Ik optative verbs are translated into English with a sentence beginning with 'Let ...' or 'May ...'.

Morphologically, the optative is marked by a combination of tone and special irregular suffixes. All optative verbs except 3PL show a kind of high-tone 'leveling' in the subject-agreement suffixes. The leveled high tone is pushed out to the end, creating a floating high tone. This high tone is not seen except in the fact that the last syllable of the subject-agreement suffixes remains at mid-tone level. Besides tone, special irregular suffixes mark the optative in 1SG, 1PL.EXC, and 1PL.INC verbs, while standard irrealis suffixes are used for the other paradigm members. Note that the 1PL.INC may also be called the 'hortative'. Another peculiarity of the Ik optative is that there is no difference between its non-final and final forms. Table 88 presents the optative on the verb *àts-* 'come':

Table 88: Ik optative mood

1SG	Atsine.	'Let me come.'
2SG	Atsidi.	'May you come.'
3SG	Atsi.	'Let her come.'
1PL.EXC	Atsima.	'Let us come.'
1PL.INC	Atsano.	'Let us all come.'
2PL	Atsiti.	'May you all come.'
3PL	Atsáti.	'Let them come.'

8.10.4 Subjunctive (SUBJ)

The Ik SUBJUNCTIVE mood is used to encode statements that are somehow contingent or temporally unrealized. In that regard, it is an essentially irrealis verb form because it captures states or events that have not yet happened. It is also essentially irrealis in that it is marked simply by the absence of any marking. In other words, the subject-agreement suffixes surface with their underlying forms in the subjunctive mood, just as they appear in Table 84. The subjunctive is usually introduced either by *dɛmʉsʉ* 'unless, until' or *damu (kója)* 'may'. Table 89 gives the full subjunctive paradigm with the verb *àts-* 'come':

Table 89: Ik subjunctive mood

	Non-final	Final	
1SG	dɛmʉsʉ atsíí ...	dɛmʉsʉ atsí.	'unless I come'
2SG	dɛmʉsʉ atsídì ...	dɛmʉsʉ atsîdⁱ.	'unless you come'
3SG	dɛmʉsʉ atsi ...	dɛmʉsʉ atsⁱ.	'unless she comes'
1PL.EXC	dɛmʉsʉ atsímí ...	dɛmʉsʉ atsím.	'unless we come'
1PL.INC	dɛmʉsʉ atsísíní ...	dɛmʉsʉ atsísín.	'unless we all come'
2PL	dɛmʉsʉ atsítí ...	dɛmʉsʉ atsítⁱ.	'unless you all come'
3PL	dɛmʉsʉ atsátì ...	dɛmʉsʉ atsátⁱ.	'unless they come'

8.10.5 Imperative (IMP)

The IMPERATIVE mood is used to issue commands or instructions. If the recipient of the command is singular, then the suffix used is {-é}, and if the recipient is plural, the suffix is {-úó}. The singular {-e´} has a floating high tone that raises any preceding low tones to mid. Both imperative suffixes are appended to the end of the verb stem, and no subject-agreement markers are needed. Both imperative suffixes are subject to vowel devoicing before a pause, as shown in Table 90:

Table 90: Ik imperative mood

Singular			Plural		
NF	FF		NF	FF	
Atse..!	Ats^e!	'Come!'	Atsúó..!	Atsú!	'Come!'
Kae..!	Ka^e!	'Go!'	Koyúó..!	Koyú!	'Go!'
Ŋƙɛ..!	Ŋƙ^ɛ!	'Eat!'	Ŋƙúó..!	Ŋƙú!	'Eat!'
Zɛƙwɛ..!	Zɛƙw^ɛ!	'Sit!'	Zɛƙúó..!	Zɛƙú!	'Sit!'

8.10.6 Negative

Ik negates clauses by means of verblike particles that come first in the negative clause. If the negated clause has a realis verb, then the negator particle used is *ńtá* 'not'. If the negated clause has an irrealis verb, then the negator particle is *mòò* or *nòò*. Lastly, if the negated clause is past tense realis or present perfect realis, then the negator particle used is *máá* or *náá*. In the negated clause, the negator particle comes first, followed by the subject, and then the verb. Any negated verb takes the irrealis mood with the appropriate form of subject-agreement suffixes (see Table 84). To make all this more concrete, Table 91 gives example of the different negator particles used with different types of clauses.

8.10.7 Sequential (SEQ)

The Ik SEQUENTIAL aspect expresses states or events that happen in sequence. Usually a sequence of verbs starts with an anchoring non-sequential verb and/or time expression, and then a CLAUSE CHAIN begins in the sequential aspect. For example, when someone tells a story, they may start with one or two past tense realis verbs to set the stage and then continue the narrative with sequential verbs. Or if someone is giving a set of instructions, they may start with one or two imperative verbs followed by a chain of sequential verbs. Because of its versatility, the Ik sequential aspect is the language's most frequently used verb form.

Table 91: Ik negative mood

Realis		
1SG	Ńtá fiyeí.	'I don't know.'
2SG	Ńtá fiyeîdⁱ.	'You don't know.'
3SG	Ńtá fiyèⁱ.	'She doesn't know.'
Sequential		
1SG	... moo fiyeí.	'... and I don't know.'
2SG	... moo fiyeîdⁱ.	'... and you don't know.'
3SG	... mòò fiyèⁱ.	'... and she doesn't know.'
Past realis		
1SG	Máa naa fiyeí.	'I didn't know.'
2SG	Máa naa fiyeîdⁱ.	'You didn't know.'
3SG	Máà nàà fiyèⁱ.	'She didn't know.'

Morphologically, Ik sequential verbs are recognized by a combination of tone, irregular subject-agreement suffixes, and the sequential aspect suffix {-ko}. Specifically, all 1 and 2-person sequential verbs exhibit high-tone leveling in their subject-agreement suffixes, which pushes a high tone out to the right of the verb. This floating high raises the preceding low tones to mid. These tone effects, plus the irregular suffixes, and the sequential marker {-ko} are shown in Table 92. Note that the sequential paradigm also has an impersonal passive marked with the suffix {-ese}. Its function is identical to that of the impersonal passive described back in §8.6.2. For more on how the sequential aspect works in actual language contexts, skip ahead to the discussion of clause-chaining in §10.8.2.

8.10.8 Simultaneous (SIM)

The Ik SIMULTANEOUS aspect is used to express states or events that are happening simultaneously to another state or event. In contrast to the sequential, the simultaneous aspect can only be used in subordinate clauses. That is to say, simultaneous clauses usually cannot stand alone without a main clause (with some exceptions). Because of its role of supporting sequential clauses, the simultaneous aspect is also commonly found in narratives and other longer discourses. It can be given a perfective interpretation as in 'when I came' or an imperfective one as in 'while I was coming'. Morphologically, the simultaneous aspect is

Grammar sketch

Table 92: Ik sequential aspect

	Non-final	Final	
1SG	... atsiaa ...	... atsiakº.	'and I come'
2SG	... atsiduo ...	... atsidukº.	'and you come'
3SG	... àtsùò ...	... àtsùkº.	'and she comes'
1PL.EXC	... atsimaa ...	... atsimakº.	'and we come'
1PL.INC	... atsisinuo ...	... atsisinukº.	'and we all come'
2PL	... atsituo ...	... atsitukº.	'and you all come'
3PL	... àtsìnì ...	... àtsìn.	'and they come'
IPS	... atsese ...	... atses.	'and people come'

marked by the suffix {-ke}, which is affixed to the subject-agreement suffixes in their irrealis forms. Table 93 presents the simultaneous paradigm of *àts-* 'come':

Table 93: Ik simultaneous aspect

	Non-final	Final	
1SG	... atsííkè ...	... atsíík^e.	'while I was coming'
2SG	... atsídìè ...	... atsídìk^e.	'while you were coming'
3SG	... àtsìè ...	... àtsìk^e.	'while she was coming'
1PL.EXC	... atsímíè ...	... atsímík^e.	'while we were coming'
1PL.INC	... atsísínìè ...	... atsísínìk^e.	'while we all were coming'
2PL	... atsítìè ...	... atsítík^e.	'while you all were coming'
3PL	... atsátìè ...	... atsátìk^e.	'while they were coming'

8.11 Adjectival verbs

8.11.1 Overview

Since Ik does not have a separate word class of adjectives, it conveys adjectival concepts with ADJECTIVAL VERBS. These verbs have adjectival meanings but otherwise mostly behave like intransitive verbs. One way they do differ from normal intransitive verbs, though, is in the specific adjectival suffixes they can take. The next four subsections briefly describe these special adjectival suffixes.

8.11.2 Physical property I (PHYS1)

The PHYSICAL PROPERTY I adjectival suffix {-ʹd-} is found on adjectival verbs that express physical properties like appearance, size, shape, consistency, texture, and other tangible attributes. As a result, physical property I verbs are some of the language's most colorful adjectivals. Physical property I verbs all contain two syllables with LH tone pattern, and in the infinitive, they take the intransitive suffix {-ònì-}. Table 94 gives a sample of these colorful descriptive terms:

Table 94: Ik physical property I adjectival verbs

bufúdòn	'to be spongy'
ɗomɔ́dɔ̀n	'to be gluey'
dirídòn	'to be compacted'
jamúdòn	'to be velvety'
lɛts'ɛ́dɔ̀n	'to be bendy'
piɗídɔ̀n	'to be sleek'
tsakádòn	'to be watery'

8.11.3 Physical property II (PHYS2)

The PHYSICAL PROPERTY II adjectival suffix {-m-} is found in adjectival verbs that also express physical properties like appearance, color, consistency, posture, shape, and texture. It can also express less tangible attributes like strength, weakness, quality, or personality traits. Physical property II verbs usually contain two syllables with a LH tone pattern or three syllables with a LHH tone pattern (without the infinitive suffix), and in the infinitive, they take the intransitive suffix {-ònì}. Table 95 gives a sample of these descriptive adjectival verbs in two groupings.

8.11.4 Stative (STAT)

The STATIVE adjectival suffix {-án-} forms adjectival verbs that express an ongoing state characterized by the meaning of a noun or a transitive verb. Because {-án-} contains the vowel /a/, it prevents vowel harmony from spreading between the verbal root and any suffixes that follow the stative suffix (for example, infinitive or subject-agreement suffixes). Table 96 and Table 97 present a few examples of stative adjectival verbs derived from nouns and verbs, respectively:

Grammar sketch

Table 95: Ik physical property II adjectival verbs

Bisyllabic	
buɗámón	'to be black'
dúgùmɔ̀n	'to be hunched'
firímón	'to be clogged'
kikímón	'to be stocky'
kwɛts'ɛ́mɔ́n	'to be damaged'
Trisyllabic	
bulúƙúmòn	'to be bulbous'
jᵾrútᵾ́mɔ̀n	'to be slippery'
pelérémòn	'to be squinty'
ságwàràmòn	'to be shadeless'
tɛ́ƙɛ́zɛ̀mɔ̀n	'to be shallow'

Table 96: Ik stative verbs derived from nouns

Noun		Stative verb	
cué-	'water'	cuanón	'to be liquid'
ɛ́sá-	'drunkenness'	ɛsánón	'to be drunk'
kirotí-	'sweat'	kirotánón	'to be sweaty'
ɲɛ̀ƙɛ̀-	'hunger'	ɲɛƙánón	'to be hungry'
ɲèrà-	'girls'	iɲéráánón	'to be girl-crazy'

Table 97: Ik stative verbs derived from transitive verbs

Transitive		Stative	
ɓɛkɛ́s	'to provoke'	ɓɛkánón	'to be provocative'
dzɛrɛ́s	'to tear'	dzɛrɛdzɛránón	'to be torn in shreds'
itáléés	'to forbid'	itáléánón	'to be forbidden'
itukes	'to heap'	itukánón	'to be congregated'
iraŋɛs	'to spoil'	ɨráɲᵾ́nánón	'to be spoiled'

8.11.5 Distributive (DISTR)

Ik has two DISTRIBUTIVE adjectival suffixes: {-aák-} and {-ìk-}. These suffixes have the function of distributing the meaning of an adjectival verb to more than one subject. The suffix {-aák-} can be used with all kinds of adjectival verbs, including the physical property and stative varieties, while the suffix {-ìk-} has been found only with the two verbs of size, *kwáts-* 'small' and *zè-* 'large'. Moreover, it commonly occurs together with {-aák-}, as in *kwátsíkaakón* 'to be small (of many)' and *zeikaakón* 'to be large (of many)'. Table 98 gives a sampling of adjectival verbs with the distributive suffix:

Table 98: Ik distributive adjectival verbs

budúdaakón	'to be soft (of many)'
ɓets'aakón	'to be white (of many)'
gaanaakón	'to be bad (of many)'
kúɗaakón	'to be short (of many)'
maráŋaakón	'to be good (of many)'
nɔtsɔ́daakón	'to be adhesive (of many)'
semélémaakón	'to be elliptical (of many)'

9 Adverbs

9.1 Overview

The word class called ADVERBS is a catch-all category that includes words and clitics of various sorts that say something descriptive about a whole clause, for example, 'how' or 'when' it takes place, or how the speaker feels about the certainty or contingency of the clause. Accordingly, Ik adverbs can be divide up into MANNER adverbs, TEMPORAL adverbs, and EPISTEMIC adverbs. The following subsections take up each of these adverbial categories in a brief discussion.

9.2 Manner adverbs

MANNER adverbs modify whole clauses by commenting on, for example, the manner in which a state comes across or in which an action is done. Manner adverbs usually come near or at the end of the clause they modify, as shown in example sentences (87)-(88) below. Table 99 presents a sampling of these adverbs:

Table 99: Ik manner adverbs

ɗèmùsù	'fast, quickly'
hɨɨjɔ́	'carefully, slowly'
jííkì	'always'
jɨ́kɨ	'really, totally'
kɔntiákᵉ	'straightaway'
mùkà	'completely, forever'
pákà	'indefinitely'
zùkù	'very'

(87) Gaana mɛna=díí **zuku jɨ́kⁱ**.
bad:3SG issues:NOM=those very completely
'Those issues are really very bad!'

(88) Zízaaƙótùò ròɓà **mùkà**.
fat:DIST:COMP:3SG:SEQ people:NOM completely
'And the people fattened up completely!'

9.3 Temporal adverbs

9.3.1 Overview

The Ik TEMPORAL adverbs situate their clause somewhere in the course of time. Ik has sets of temporal adverbs that deal with past tense, past perfect tense, and non-past (including future) tense. The past and past perfect tense adverbs are enclitics that come directly after the verb they modify. The future tense adverbs are free adverbs that come near the end or at the end of the clause.

9.3.2 Past tense adverbs (PST)

Ik divides PAST TENSE into four time periods and marks them with adverbial enclitics. They are: 1) RECENT PAST that covers the current day and is marked with =nákà, 2) REMOVED PAST that covers yesterday (or any last or 'yester-' time period like 'yesterday' or 'yesteryear') and is marked with =bàtsè, 3) REMOTE PAST that covers a few days or weeks before yesterday and is marked with =nótsò, and finally, 4) REMOTEST PAST that covers everything before the remote past and is marked with =nòkò. Each of these tense enclitics comes directly after ther verb and has a non-final and final form. Table 100 illustrates the Ik tense markers in all their forms, and examples (89)-(90) illustrate their typical post-verbal position in a sentence:

Table 100: Ik past tense markers

	NF	FF	
Recent	=náà	=nák^a	'earlier today'
Removed	=bèè	=bàts^e	'last/yester-'
Remote	=nótsò	=nótsò	'a while ago'
Remotest	=nòò	=nòk^o	'long ago'

(89) Káá=**bee** abáŋa sáásɔ̀sɨ̀n.
go:3SG=PST2 my.father:NOM yesterday
'My father went yesterday.'

(90) Maráŋa=**noo** ɦyekesa Icé.
good:3SG=PST4 life:NOM Ik:GEN
'The life of the Ik was good (back then).'

9.3.3 Past perfect tense adverbs (PST.PRF)

The past tense can be combined with a perfect aspect to yield the PAST PERFECT tense. Unlike the simple past tense adverbs, Ik past perfect tense adverbs operate along only three periods of time: RECENT (earlier today), REMOVED (yester-), and REMOTE (before yester-). Table 101 presents the Ik past perfect tense adverbs, and example sentences (91)-(92) illustrate their use in natural contexts:

Table 101: Ik past perfect tense markers

	NF	FF	
Recent	=nanáà	=nanák^a	'had ... earlier today'
Removed	=nàtsàmù	=nàtsàm	'had ... yester-'
Remote	=nànòò	=nànòk^o	'had ... a while ago'

563

Grammar sketch

(91) Náa atsíâdᵉ, ƙaa=nanákᵃ.
when come:1SG:DP go:3SG=PST.PRF
'When I came earlier, she had (already) gone.'

(92) Ts'édɔ́ɔ́=nɛ, ts'éíƙotátà=nànòkᵒ.
then:INS=DEM die.3PL:COMP=PST.PRF
'By that (time), they had died out a while ago.'

9.3.4 Non-past tense adverbs

Ik divides the NON-PAST tense into three rather vaguely defined time periods suggested by three adverbs. They are: 1) the DISTENDED PRESENT that includes just before and just after the present and is expressed by the adverb *ts'ɔ̀ɔ̀*, 2) the REMOVED FUTURE that includes the *next* future time period (next hour, next day, next year) and is expressed by the adverb *táá*, and 3) the REMOTE FUTURE expressed by the adverb *fàrà* (occasionally *fàrò*). Table 102 arranges these adverbs in a paradigm, while (93)-(94) below illustrates them in natural sentences:

Table 102: Ik non-past tense markers

	NF	FF	
Distended present	ts'ɔ̀ɔ̀	ts'ɔ̀ɔ̀	'just/recently/soon'
Removed	táá	táá	'next___'
Remote	fàrà	fàr	'in the future'

(93) a. Atsíá=nàà **ts'ɔ̀ɔ̀**.
come:1SG=PST just
'I just came.'

b. Atsésìà **ts'ɔ̀ɔ̀**.
come:INT:1SG soon
'I will come soon.'

(94) Atsésíma **táá** baratsᵒ.
come:1PL.EXC next morning:INS
'We will come tomorrow (i.e., next morning).'

9.4 Epistemic adverbs

9.4.1 Overview

The Ik EPISTEMIC adverbs express how the speaker feels or thinks about the certainty or contingency of the clause. Accordingly, this set of adverbs can be divided into the categories of INFERENTIAL, CONFIRMATIONAL, and CONDITIONAL-HYPOTHETICAL. All of the epistemic adverbs are enclitics that follow the verb in normal main clauses, but some of them can also be moved in front of the verb.

9.4.2 Inferential adverbs (INFR)

Ik can communicate a degree of uncertainty about a situation by means of a set of INFERENTIAL tense-based adverbs. This sense of making a tentative inference based on an observation can be translated into English with such turns of phrase as 'Apparently …', 'Maybe …', 'It seems that …', 'must have', etc. Two of these inferential particles consist of the proclitic *ná* plus a past-tense particle, while the third combines *ná* with the adverb *tsamʉ*. Table 103 presents the three inferential adverbial particles in their final and non-final forms. Note that compared to the past-tense markers above in Table 100, the inferential time-scale is moved up one notch more recent. Examples (95)-(96) show the Ik inferential adverbs in context. Note that they can be placed before or after the main verb.

Table 103: Ik inferential adverbs

	NF	FF	
Recent	=nábèè	=nábàtsᵉ	'apparently earlier today'
Removed	=nátsàmʉ̀	=nátsàm	'apparently yester-'
Remote	=nánòò	=nánòkº	'apparently long ago'

(95) a. Baduƙota=**nábàtsᵉ**.
   die:COMP:3SG=INFR
   'It died, apparently.'

   b. **Nábee** baduƙotᵃ.
   INFR die:COMP:3SG
   'Apparently, it died.'

Grammar sketch

(96) **Nánoo** teremátᵃ.
    INFR   separate:3PL
    'It looks like they separated.'

9.4.3 Confirmational adverbs (CONF)

Ik can also issue a confirmation of a state or event by means of a set of CONFIRMATIONAL adverbs that are derived from the tensed relative pronouns described back in §5.7. When used, these adverbs are placed before the verb, and the verb surfaces in its non-final form, almost like a question rendered in English 'Why yes, did X *not* happen?' – meaning that, of course, it *did* happen. These suffixes are first presented in Table 104 and then demonstrated in (97)-(98):

Table 104: Ik confirmational markers

Recent	náa	'Of course____earlier today.'
Removed	sɨna	'Of course____yester-.'
Remote	noo	'Of course____long ago.'

(97) a. Ŋkákóídà=bèè?
      eat:COMP:2SG=PST2
      'Did you eat (it) up?'

    b. **Sɨna** ŋkákótíà.
      CONF eat:COMP:1SG
      'Yes, of course I did.'

(98) a. Dètà=nòò?
      bring:3SG=PST4
      'Did she bring (it)?'

    b. **Nòò** dètà.
      CONF bring:3SG
      'Yes, of course she did.'

9.4.4 Conditional-hypothetical adverbs (COND/HYPO)

If a state or event has not taken place but *could* or *would* take place, Ik can express that contingency with its CONDITIONAL-HYPOTHETICAL adverbs. There are three of these adverbs, but they are used to cover four periods of time. The first adverb covers non-past and recent past, the second removed past, and third remote past. These conditional-hypothetical adverbs are presented in Table 105:

Table 105: Ik conditional-hypothetical adverbs

	NF	FF	
Non-past	=ƙánàà	=ƙánàkᵃ	'would'
Recent	=ƙánàà	=ƙánàkᵃ	'would have ... earlier today'
Removed	=ƙásàmù̀	=ƙásàm	'would have ... yester-'
Remote	=ƙánòò	=ƙánòkᵒ	'would have ... a while ago'

The conditional-hypothetical adverbs come after the main verb:

(99) Tóída=ƙánaa ɲcìè?
tell:2SG=HYPO I:DAT
'You would tell me?'

(100) Cɛmísína=ƙánòkᵒ.
fight:1PL.INC=COND
'We all would have fought.'

10 Basic syntax

10.1 Noun phrases

The Ik NOUN PHRASE consists first and foremost of a noun 'head', either a lexical noun or a nominalized lexical verb. As a head-initial language, Ik places its noun phrase head first in the phrase. Any subordinate, supporting elements follow the head. These optional elements may include anaphoric demonstratives, possessive markers, relative pronouns/temporal demonstratives, number markers, and spatial demonstratives. The Ik noun phrase structure can be formalized as follows, where elements in parentheses are optional:

Grammar sketch

(101) Ik NP structure:
HEAD (ANAPH)(POSS)(NUM)(REL/TEMP) (DEM)

The syntactical structure of noun phrases formalized in (101) is fleshed out among the real Ik noun phrases presented below in examples (102)-(110):

(102) HEAD
wikᵃ
'children'

(103) HEAD ANAPH
wika díí
'those (specific) children'

(104) HEAD POSS
wika ɲcì
'my children'

(105) HEAD ANAPH POSS
wika díí   ɲcì
'those (specific) children of mine'

(106) HEAD ANAPH POSS NUM
wika díí   ɲcìè lèɓètsè
'those two (specific) children of mine'

(107) HEAD ANAPH POSS REL
wika díí   ɲcie [ni leɓetse]ᴿᴱᴸ
'those (specific) children of mine, two in number'

(108) HEAD ANAPH POSS NUM   REL
wika díí   ɲcie leɓetse [ní dà] ᴿᴱᴸ
'those two nice (specific) children of mine'

(109) HEAD ANAPH POSS NUM   REL   DEM
wika díí   ɲcie leɓetse [ní daa]ᴿᴱᴸ ni
'those two nice (specific) children of mine, these'

(110) HEAD ANAPH POSS NUM   TEMP DEM
wika díí   ɲcie leɓetse níi   ni
'those two (specific) children of mine from earlier, these'

10.2 Clause structure

10.2.1 Intransitive

Ik INTRANSITIVE clauses consist minimally of a verb (v) and a subject (s) in a vs constituent order. The subject may be explicit, in which case it follows the verb, or it may be implicit, in which case it is merely marked on the verb. Basic intransitive clause structure is illustrated in example (111):

(111) Epa$_V$ ŋók$^a{}_S$.
sleep:3SG dog:NOM

'The dog sleeps.'

When a tense adverb is needed, it comes directly after the verb and before any explicit subject. And any other adverbial elements like extended objects (E) or adverbs, in that order, come after the subject. This word order is shown in (112):

(112) Epá$_V$=bee$_{TENSE}$ ŋóká$_S$ kurú$_E$.
sleep:3SG=yester- dog:NOM shade:ABL

'The dog slept in the shade yesterday.'

10.2.2 Transitive

Ik TRANSITIVE clauses consist minimally of a transitive verb (v), an agent (A), and an object (o) in a VAO constituent order. The subject may be explicit, in which case it comes between the verb and object, or it may merely be marked on the verb with a suffix. The object may also be dropped, in which case it is inferred from the context. Example (113) illustrates basic transitive clause structure:

(113) Áts'á$_V$ ŋóká$_A$ ɔkák$^a{}_O$.
gnaw:3SG dog:NOM bone:ACC

'The dog gnaws the bone.'

When a tense adverb is needed, it comes directly after the verb and before any explicit subject. And any other adverbial elements like extended objects (E) or adverbs, in that order, come after the subject. This syntax is shown in (114):

(114) Áts'á$_V$=bee$_{TENSE}$ ŋóká$_A$ ɔkáá$_O$ ódàtù$_E$.
gnaw:3SG=yester- dog:NOM bone:ACC day:INS

'The dog gnawed the bone all day yesterday.'

Grammar sketch

10.2.3 Ditransitive

Ik DITRANSITIVE clauses consist minimally of a ditransitive verb (v), an agent (A), an object (O), and an extended object (E) in a VAOE constituent order. If the agent is not mentioned explicitly, then it will still be marked with a suffix on the verb. The object and extended object may be left implicit but will be understood from context. The basic ditransitive clause structure is illustrated in (115):

(115)   Maa_V   ƙaƙaama_A   ɔkáá_O   ŋókík^e_E.
        give:3SG hunter:NOM bone:ACC dog:DAT
        'The hunter gives a bone to the dog.'

10.2.4 Causative

By adding an extra element in the form of a causing agent, Ik CAUSATIVE verbs change the structure of a clause. If the original clause was a VS intransitive one, then the causative changes it to a transitive VAO. If the original clause was a transitive VAO, then the causative changes it to a ditransitive VAOE. The following two examples, (116)-(119), show causative verbs making these structural changes:

Intransitive VS → Causative VAO

(116)   Fekía_V   ŋk^a_V.
        laugh:1SG I:NOM
        'I laugh'.

(117)   Fekitéídà_VA   ŋk^a_O.
        laugh:CAUS:2SG I:NOM
        'You make me laugh.'

Transitive VAO → Causative VAOE

(118)   Wetía_V   ŋka_A   cue_O.
        drink:1SG I:NOM water:NOM
        'I drink water.'

(119)   Wetitéída_VA   ŋka_O   cuék^e_E.
        drink:CAUS:2SG I:NOM water:DAT
        'You make me drink water.'

10.2.5 Auxiliary

Ik has both true AUXILIARY verbs and PSEUDO-AUXILIARY verbs. Both types modify sentence syntax. The true auxiliaries, shown in Table 106, function as the syntactic main verb in a clause, while the *semantic* main verb follows the subject (s/A) in a morphologically defective form that consists of the bare verb stem plus a suffix {-a} (which may be the realis marker from §8.9.2). This means the constituent order of clauses with true auxiliary verbs is AUXSV for intransitives, AUXAVO for transitives, and AUXAVOE with extended objects. Again, in all these constructions, the AUX acts as the main verb from a syntactic perspective, while the defective verb carries the main meaning of the verbal schema. Another way to analyze this construction would be to say that the auxiliary verb and the defective verb *together* fill the single verb slot of the clausal syntax.

The true auxiliaries have both lexical and aspectual meanings, which are nevertheless practically identical in their semantics. However, in their lexical function, the verbs in Table 106 do not require a second, morphologically defective verb to augment them; in their strictly lexical usage, they stand alone:

Table 106: Ik true auxiliary verbs

Root	Lexical	Aspectual
erúts-	'be fresh, new'	RECENTIVE
ŋɔ́r-	'do already/early'	ANTICIPATIVE
sár-	'be still/not yet'	DURATIVE

Example (120) illustrates the use of the recentive aspectual auxiliary verb *erúts-* in an intransitive clause with the structure AUXSVE:

(120) Erútsíma$_{AuxS}$ atsa$_V$ sédà°$_E$.
RECENT:1PL.EXC come garden:ABL
'We just came from the garden.'

Example (121), on the other hand, shows the use of the anticipative verb *ŋɔ́r-* in a transitive clause with the structure AUXAVOE:

(121) Ŋɔ́rá$_{AuxA}$=naa cɛa$_V$ riááₒ baratso$_E$=nákª.
ANTICIP:3SG=PST1 kill goat:ACC morn:INS=DEM.PST1
'He already killed the goat earlier this morning.'

Lastly, sentence (122) exemplifies the durative aspectual verb *sár-* in a simple transitive clause working with the defective verb *ts'ágwa-*:

(122) Sárá_{AUX} séda_S   ts'ágwà_V.
DUR:3SG garden:NOM unripe
'The garden is still unripe.'

In contrast to the above examples, the pseudo-auxiliary verbs only mimic true auxiliaries in that they are fully lexical verbs yet ones with potentially aspectual meanings, including the completive, inchoative, and occupative. However, because they are not *syntactically* auxiliary, they take complements as any lexical verb would (direct objects for the transitive ones and extended objects for the intransitive one). The pseudo-auxiliaries are presented in Table 107 with their lexical and aspectual meanings and the cases required in their complements:

Table 107: Ik pseudo-auxiliary verbs

Stem	Lexical	Aspectual	Case required
náb-ʉkɔt-	'end, finish'	COMPLETIVE	NOM/ACC
itsyák-ét-	'begin, start'	INCHOATIVE	NOM/ACC
toɗó-	'alight, land'	INCHOATIVE	NOM/ACC
isé-ét-	'begin, start'	INCHOATIVE	NOM/ACC
cèm-	'fight, struggle'	OCCUPATIVE	INS

Each of the aspectual meanings listed in Table 107 are given one example in the following sentences. The brackets in example (123) signify that the bracketed noun phrase as a whole is the object of the verb:

Completive

(123) Nábʉkɔtíáa_{VA} [isóméésá ɲáɓúkwi]_O.
finish:1SG:PRF to.read:NOM book:GEN
'I have finished reading the book.'

Inchoative

(124) Itsyaketátaa_{VA} wáánàkᵃ_O.
begin:3PL:PRF praying:ACC
'They have begun praying.'

Occupative

(125) Cɛma_V wika_S   wáák°_E.
fight:3 children:NOM playing:INS
'The children are busy playing.'

10.2.6 Copular

Ik COPULAR clauses have relational rather than referential meanings. They link a COPULAR SUBJECT (CS) to a COPULAR COMPLEMENT (CC) which represents an entity or attribute, depending on the specific copular verb involved. The constituent order of copular clauses is therefore V-CS-CC. Ik has three distinct copular or 'be' verbs that can express five copular relationships between them. These copular verbs are presented in Table 108 below, along with the case markings their subjects and complements are obligated to have:

Table 108: Ik copular verbs

Verb	Meaning	CS case	CC case
ì-	Existence	NOM	–
	Location	NOM	DAT
ìr-	Attribution	NOM	(adverb only)
mɨt-	Identity	NOM	OBL
	Possession	NOM	GEN

The three copular verbs in Table 108 and their five potential meaning are each exemplified briefly in the example sentences (126)-(130):

Existence

(126) Ia_V   didigwarí_{CS}.
be:3SG rain.top:NOM
'Heaven [i.e. God] is (there).'

Location

(127) Ia_V   lɔŋɔ́tá_{CS}   muceék^e_{CC}.
be:3 enemies:NOM way:DAT
'Enemies are on the way.'

Grammar sketch

Attribution

(128) Ira_VCS tíyé_ADV.
       be:3SG like.this
       'It is like this.'

Identity

(129) Mɨtɨ́á_V ŋka_CS bábò_CC.
       be:1SG I:NOM father.your:OBL
       'I am your father.'

Possession

(130) Mɨta_V [awa=na]_CS   ŋgóᵉ_CC.
       be:3SG home:NOM=this we:GEN
       'This house is ours.'

10.2.7 Fronted

Ik can put special emphasis on any core nominal element by moving it to the front of the clause, before the verb, subject, and other constituents. Doing so obviously disrupts the usual syntactic structure of main clauses. Two kinds of fronting are observed in the language: 1) a CLEFT construction and 2) LEFT-DISLOCATION. In a cleft construction, the emphasized noun is moved to the front and given the copulative case. This puts it in an identifying relationship with the original clause out of which it just came. As a result, the newly arranged clause can be viewed as a kind of copular clause where the fronted element is the copular subject and the original clause the copular complement. This can in turn be formulized as: [NP:COP]_CS [CLAUSE]_CC. To make this more concrete, the next examples show the cleft construction with a simple transitive clause in (131) whose object (*mès*) gets fronted and marked with the copulative case in (132):

Cleft construction

(131) Bédɨ́mà_V   ṅgwà_A mès_O.
       want:1PL.EXC we:NOM beer:NOM
       'We want beer.'

(132) Mɛsɔɔ_CC [ŋgóá bédɨ́m.]_CS
       beer:COP we:ACC want:1PL.EXC
       'It is beer (that) we want.'

Whereas the cleft construction involves removing a clausal element from a clause and building a new clause, left-dislocation simply relocates the element to the front of the clause, but still within the same clause. In this fronted position it is given the nominative case. This type of fronting can be formulized as: [NP:NOM ‖ CLAUSE]$_{CLAUSE}$, where the double vertical line symbolize a short pause. This type of left-dislocation is illustrated between example sentences (133)-(134):

Left-dislocation

(133) Mée   eníí   kaúdza=díí.
 not:PRF see:1SG money:NOM=ANAPH
 'I haven't seen that money.'

(134) Kaúdza=díí,   mée   ení.
 money:NOM=ANAPH not:PRF see:1SG
 'That money, I haven't seen (it).'

10.3 Subordinate clauses

10.3.1 Overview

The constituent order of Ik SUBORDINATE clauses differs from that of MAIN clauses. Ik subordinate clauses exhibit an sv order with intransitive verbs, an AV order with transitives, and an AVE order with ditransitives – in short 'sv' instead of the usual 'vs'. Case marking in subordinate clauses is also different: The fronted subject/agent and *every* direct object take the accusative case.

The next two subsections deal with two key kinds of Ik subordinate clause, the relative clause (§10.3.2) and the adverbial clause (§10.3.3).

10.3.2 Relative clauses

RELATIVE CLAUSES are subordinate clauses that modify a noun within a main clause. Ik relative clauses are restrictive, meaning they can only narrow the reference of their head noun rather than merely adding extra details about it. Relative clauses are introduced by the tensed relative pronouns discussed back in (§5.7), which, within the relative clause, stand in for a noun in the main clause called the COMMON ARGUMENT (CA). As such, the common argument is a full verbal argument in the main clause, while in the relative clause, the relative pronoun fills its syntactic slot.

Grammar sketch

As a subordinate clause, an Ik relative clause exhibits a different constituent order than typical main clauses. Specifically, an intransitive relative clause has the order sv (instead of vs), and a transitive relative clause has the order oav (instead of vao). In the former (intransitive), the subject slot (s) is filled by the relative pronoun, and in the latter (transitive), it is the object (o) that is represented by the relative pronoun. Furthermore, apart for the relative pronouns themselves, all subjects and direct objects in relative clauses are marked with the accusative case – another sign of grammatical subordination in Ik.

These attributes of Ik relative clauses are illustrated in examples (135)-(136). In (135), the common argument in the main clause is *emuta* 'story', which is modified by the relative clause *nɛ éf* 'that is funny'. Note how the subject slot of the relative clause is filled by the relative pronoun *nɛ* (*na* with its vowel assimilated). Then, in (136), the common argument of the main clause is *ima* 'child', modified by the relative clause *náa ɲcia tákí* 'that I mentioned'. Since the verb of the relative clause is transitive (*tákés* 'to mean, mention'), it requires an object, which in this case is fulfilled by the relative pronoun *náa* representing the noun *ima*:

Intransitive (sv)

(135) Nesíbimaa   emuta$_{CA}$=[nɛ$_S$ éf$_V$]$_{REL}$.
       hear:1PL.EXC:PRF story:NOM=REL sweet:3SG
       'We've heard a story that is funny.'

Transitive (oav)

(136) Atsáá   ima$_{CA}$=[náa$_O$ ɲcia$_A$ tákí$_V$]$_{REL}$.
       come:3SG:PRF child=REL   I:ACC mention:1SG
       'The child I mentioned earlier has come.'

10.3.3 Adverbial clauses

The category of ADVERBIAL CLAUSES is rather broad as it includes any subordinate clause that modifies a main clause adverbially. Adverbial clause are subordinate or 'dependent' precisely because they cannot stand alone but must be linked to an independent main clause. As subordinate clauses, adverbial clauses exhibit a constituent order that differs from both main clauses and relative clauses. Specifically, intransitive adverbial clauses have the order sv, while transitive adverbial clauses have the order avo. Another correlate of subordination seen in most adverbial clauses – except for the conditional and hypothetical ones – is accusative case-marking on all core constituents (s/a/o) if they are explicitly mentioned.

Among the main kinds of adverbial clause in Ik are the following: TEMPORAL, SIMULTANEOUS, CONDITIONAL, HYPOTHETICAL, MANNER, REASON/CAUSE, and CONCESSIVE. Most types of adverbial clause – except for MANNER – have their own dedicated connective (or 'conjunction') or set of connectives, many of which are listed back in Table 24 under §3.14. Without exception, the subordinating connectives come first in the adverbial clause. Lastly, in terms of position, Ik adverbial clauses may come before or after the main clause they modify. Each of these types of adverbial clause is given one example apiece in (137)-(143):

Temporal

(137) [Noo ntsíá baduƙotâd^e]_{TEMP}, ƙɔ́ɗiak°.
 when he:3SG die:3SG:DP cry:1SG:SEQ
 'When he died, I cried.'

Simultaneous

(138) [Náa ntsíá badúƙótìk^e]_{SIMUL}, ƙɔ́ɗɛ́siak°.
 as he:3SG die:3SG:SIM cry:IPFV:1SG:SEQ
 'As he was dying, I was crying.'

Conditional

(139) [Na ntsa badúƙótùk°]_{COND}, ƙɔ́ɗiak°.
 if he:NOM die:3SG:SEQ cry:1SG:SEQ
 'If he dies, I'll cry.'

Hypothetical

(140) a. [Na ƙánoo ntsa badúƙótùk°]_{HYPO},
 if would've he:3SG die:3SG:SEQ
 'If he would've died,

 b. ƙɔ́ɗiaa ƙánòk°.
 cry:1SG:SEQ would've
 I would've cried.'

Manner

(141) Badúƙótuo [(ntsíá) tisílík^e]_{MANNER}.
 die:3SG:SEQ (he:ACC) peaceful:3SG:SIM
 'And he died peacefully (lit. 'he being peaceful').'

Grammar sketch

Reason/cause

(142) Baduƙotáá [ɗúó ídzanâdᵉ]ᵣₑₐₛₒₙ.
die:3SG:PRF because shoot:IPS:3SG:DP

'He has died because he was shot.'

Concessive

(143) [Áta ntsíá badúƙótìkᵉ]_CONCESS, ńtá ƙɔ́dɨ́.
even he:ACC die:3SG:SIM not cry:1SG

'Even if he dies, I will not cry.'

10.4 Questions

10.4.1 Overview

Questions in Ik can be formed in two mutually exclusive ways: 1) by leaving the final word in the question in its non-final form (along with a questioning intonation) or 2) by using interrogative pronouns and often rearranging the syntax of the sentence. The first method is employed with what is called POLAR or yes/no questions: those whose answer is either 'yes' or 'no'. The second method is used for CONTENT or wh-questions: those whose answer is a substantive response to such interrogative pronouns as *who?*, *what?*, *when?*, *where?*, etc. These two types of question are briefly described in the following two subsections.

10.4.2 Polar questions

Polar questions are those that elicit a 'yes' or 'no' in response. In Ik, they are formed by leaving the last word or particle of the question in its non-final form (revisit §2.3 and §2.4.3 for a review). This open-endedness of form is a fascinating way the grammar reflects the open-endedness of a question – open to a response. Besides the non-final form of the last word, polar questions are identified by a change in intonation. This interrogative intonation is enacted by what is called a BOUNDARY low tone: a low tone that attaches to the final syllable. If the final syllable already has a low tone, then the boundary tone is not audible. But if the final syllable has a high tone, the boundary tone manifests as a high-low glide.

Examples (144)-(145) illustrate these features of polar questions. Note in the first part of (144) how the present perfect suffix {-´ka} shows up in its non-final form (-´à), while in the second part, the final form is used (-´kᵃ). Then, (145) shows the interrogative boundary low tone attaching to the high tone on the final syllable of *cekúó* 'is a woman', creating a high-low down-glide (*cekúô*):

(144) a. Nábʉkɔtáà?
          finish:COMP:3SG:PRF[NF]
          'Is it finished?'

      b. Ee, nábʉkɔtákᵃ.
          yes finish:COMP:3SG:PRF[FF]
          'Yes, it is finished.'

(145) a. Cekúô?
          woman:COP[NF]
          'Is it a woman?'

      b. Ee, cekúó   ntsaᵃ.
          yes woman:COP she:NOM
          'Yes, it's a woman.'

10.4.3 Content questions

In contrast to polar questions, content questions cannot logically take 'yes' or 'no' for an answer. Rather, answers to content questions – as their name implies – must contain content relevant to the specific interrogative pronoun used to make the inquiry (Ik interrogative pronouns are listed in Table 46). So if the question contains the pronoun *ǹdò-* 'who?', the answer must include a person. Or if the question contains the pronoun *ndaí-* 'where?', the response must refer to a specific location, and so on. Ik forms content questions by placing an interrogative pronoun in the syntactic slot of the unknown entity being queried (i.e. a person, place, time, manner, etc.). For example, in (146), the interrogative pronoun *ndaí-* 'where?' is filling the normal place where an object encoding the destination of *kà-* 'go' would go. A similar thing occurs in (147), where the pronoun *isì-* 'what?' fills the direct object slot required by the verb *bɛ́d-* 'want':

(146) Keesída   ndaíkᵉ?
       go:INT:2SG:REAL where:DAT
       'You are going where?'

(147) Bɛ́dá   isìkᵃ?
       want:3SG:REAL what:NOM
       'He wants what?'

However, what is more common is for the interrogative pronoun to be fronted for emphasis. As in other instances of fronting in Ik (see §10.2.7), the fronted element takes the copulative case marker {-ko}. In (148)-(149), examples (146)-(147) are repeated in their fronted (focused) forms, and two other interrogative pronouns are used in (150)-(151) to illustrate content questions:

(148) Ndaíó ƙeesídàdᵉ?
where:COP go:2SG:REAL:DP
'Where are you going?'

(149) Isio bɛ́ɗᵃ?
what:COP want:3SG:REAL
'What does he want?'

(150) Ndoo óá ɲcìkᵃ?
who:COP call:3SG:REAL I:ACC
'Who calls me?'

(151) Ńtɛ́ɛ́nɔ́ɔ́ tákîɗᵃ?
which:COP mean:2SG:REAL
'Which (one) do you mean?'

10.5 Quotations

Quotations involve reporting someone's speech (or thought) – the speaker's own or someone else's – directly or indirectly. Ik fulfills this communicative need through the use of the verb *kʉ̀t-* 'say' followed by the actual quotation treated as an add-on clause. That is, unlike complements described below in §10.6, a quoted sentence in Ik is technically *not* an object of the verb *kʉ̀t-*. Instead, it is tacked on 'extra-syntactically' and given the oblique case (the 'leftover' case). This is proven by the fact that when the pronoun *isì-* 'what?' appears to be the object of *kʉ̀t-* with a 3SG or 3PL subject, *isì-* takes the oblique case instead of the accusative case as one would expect otherwise from case grammar (§7.3).

Many languages, English included, distinguish between direct and indirect quotative formulas, for example the direct "I said, 'I will come'" versus the indirect "I said I will come". By contrast, Ik does not distinguish the two grammatically. Instead, the proper sense has to be discerned from the context (and possibly from intonation). So the statement *Kʉtíá naa atsésí* could mean either "I said, 'I will come'" or "I said I will come", depending on factors other than syntax.

In Ik quotative sentences, if there is an addressee of the quotation, they will appear in the dative case. And the quotative particle *tàà* 'that' is often inserted

10 Basic syntax

just before the quotation, though by all appearances it is optional. The example sentences (152)-(153) provide a demonstration of the quotative construction:

(152)   Kɨtɨ́á   bie   [Pakóicéo=noo   dzígwì]_QUOTATION
        say:1SG you:DAT Turkana:COP=PST4 buy:PLUR
        'I'm telling you it was the Turkana who used to buy.'

(153)   Kɨtana   ŋgóé   taa   [atsúó   dɛ̀mɨ̀s]_QUOTATION
        say:IPS we.EXC:DAT that come:IMP quickly
        'They are saying to us, "Come quickly!".'

10.6 Complements

COMPLEMENTS are individual clauses that function as an 'argument' of the verb – as either subject or object. In other words, they are clauses within clauses. Unlike subordinate clauses which are added *onto* main clauses, complement clauses are added *into* other clauses. The main type of Ik complement clause is introduced by the COMPLEMENTIZER *tòìmɛ̀nà-* 'that', which is combination of a form of the verb *tód-* 'speak' and the noun *mɛná-* 'issues, words'. This compound word gives some evidence that Ik complement clauses (of this particular type) evolved from quotative clauses like those described above in §10.5.

Because a complement clause fits within the clausal grammar, it must somehow be declined for case (because all arguments of a verb in Ik take case, without exception). To meet this requirement, the complementizer *tòìmɛ̀nà-* bears the burden of case on behalf of the whole complement clause it is introducing. So technically, it is the complementizer – not the complement clause alone – that is the verbal argument. But because *tòìmɛ̀nà-* plus the complement is a frozen quotative formula, the whole construction can be analyzed as an argument.

To illustrate this, (154) presents a simple complement clause governed by the cognitive verb *èn-* 'see'. The {curly brackets} indicate the boundaries of the main clause from the point of view of the syntax, in which the verb *èn-* 'see' selects its object *tòìmɛ̀nà-* 'that' for the accusative case. The [square brackets] mark the boundary of the complement clause seen from the point of view of semantics, for the actual content of 'seeing' is the clause *that we have become very rich*:

(154)   {Enáta   [toimɛnaa]_OBJ   barɨkɔtɨ́máà   zùk^u]_COMPL
        see:3PL that:ACC   rich:COMP:1PL.EXC:PRF very
        'They see that we have become very rich.'

Grammar sketch

In addition to a direct object, an Ik complement clause can also function as an indirect object or even the 'complement' of a copular clause. For instance, in (155) below, *tòìmènà-* and by extension the whole complement clause is acting as the indirect object of the verb *xèɓ-* 'be afraid of, fear', which requires the ablative case. Then, in (156), the verb is the copular verb *mɨt-* 'be', which requires its nominal compliment to be in the oblique case, as is seen with *tòìmènà-*:

(155) Xɛɓíá [toimɛnɔɔ maíá sílím]ᴄᴏᴍᴘʟ
fear:1sg that:ABL ill:1sg AIDS:NOM
'I am afraid that I'm ill with AIDS.'

(156) Mɨta ja [toimɛna ńtá nesíbi mɛnákᵃ]ᴄᴏᴍᴘʟ
be:3sg just that[OBL] not hear:3sg words:ACC
'It is just that she doesn't understand instructions.'

10.7 Comparatives

Cᴏᴍᴘᴀʀᴀᴛɪᴠᴇs are grammatical constructions that allow the comparison of two entities on the basis of some shared characteristic. Ik has two strategies for doing this: 1) the mono-clausal, which involves one simple clause, and 2) the bi-clausal, which involves a complex clause. Mono-clausal comparatives place the ᴄᴏᴍᴘᴀ-ʀᴇᴇ (entity being compared) in the nominative case and the sᴛᴀɴᴅᴀʀᴅ (entity the comparee is being compared to) in the ablative case. Since most comparable attributes are expressed as intransitive verbs in Ik, the ᴘᴀʀᴀᴍᴇᴛᴇʀ (attribute) of the comparison is also an adjectival verb in such constructions. For example, in (157)-(158) below, the intransitive verbs *zè-* 'big' and *dà-* 'nice' are acting as the parameters, while their subjects are the comparees in the nominative case and their extended objects the standards in the ablative case:

(157) Zeíá ŋkà bù.
big:1sg I:NOM you:ABL
'I am bigger than you.'

(158) Daa ɗa=na kɨɗɔ́ɔ́
nice:3sg this.one:NOM=this that.one:ABL
'This one is nicer than that one.'

Bi-clausal comparatives, on the other hand, combine a main clause with a subordinate or 'co-subordinate' clause (§10.8.2). Both types are introduced by the verb *ilɔ́-* 'exceed, surpass', which acts as the INDEX of the comparison (the gauge of the degree of difference between compared entities). If the indexical verb introduces a subordinate clause, it takes the simultaneous aspect, while if it introduces a co-subordinate clause, it takes the sequential aspect. In such bi-clausal comparatives, the comparee is still the subject of the main clause, while the standard is the object of the dependent clause. The parameter remains with the main clause verb (as in mono-clausal comparatives). But unlike mono-clausals, bi-clausal comparatives can have intransitive or transitive parametric verbs. In other words, actions as well as attributes can be compared in this type of construction.

In (159), the parameter lies with the verb *tɔkɔ́b-* 'cultivate', and 'he' (marked as 3SG on the verb) is being compared with 'us' (*ŋgó-*). The index of the comparison is the verb *ilɔ́ɛ* 'he surpassing', which reveals the inequality of the compared actions of the two entities. Example (160) follows the exact same logic, only that the indexical verb *ilɔ́ɨnɨ* is in the sequential aspect instead of the simultaneous:

(159) Tokóbia edíá [ɪlɔ́ɛ ŋgók^a]_{SIM}
cultivate:PLUR:3SG grain:ACC surpass:3SG:SIM we:ACC
'He cultivates grain more than us.'

(160) Sáɓúmósáta [ilɔ́ɨnɨ toni ɲeryaŋ]_{SEQ}
kill:RECIP:3PL exceed:3PL:SEQ even government[OBL]
'They're killing each other even more than the government.'

10.8 Clause combining

10.8.1 Clause coordination

Two or more clauses can be linked in Ik through clause COORDINATION. This can result in clause ADDITION ('and'), which joins two independent clauses of equal status. It can result in CONTRAST ('but'), which joins clauses of equal syntactic status, the second of which is a counterexpectation to the first. And thirdly, clause coordination can result in DISJUNCTION ('or'), in which two clauses of equal status are presented as different possible options.

Clause addition is achieved in two ways: 1) simply adjoining the clauses with a pause in between (represented by a period or comma in writing) or 2) linking the clauses with a coordinating connective like *kòtò* 'and, but, then' or *ńdà* 'and'. These first two methods are illustrated in (161)-(162). A third way to add one clause to another is to nominalize it – change all its main parts to nouns, put them in a noun phrase, and link it up to the other clause with *ńdà*. Note from

(163) that with this third method, because the word ńdà 'and' is acting as a sort preposition, it requires its head noun(s) to be in the oblique case. Its head nouns in (163) are the subject (ŋgo) and infinitive (ŋkɛ́sɨ) – both in the oblique case:

(161) Mɨ́nɨ́a ɲécáyᵃ. Mɨ́ná   ntsa   mésɛ̀kᵃ.
      love:1SG tea:NOM love:3SG she:NOM beer:ACC

      'I love tea. She loves beer.'

(162) a. Kakiésána=noo   ńtí,
        hunt:PLUR:IPFV:IPS:REAL=PST how

        'How did people used to go hunting,

   b. ńda kaiána=noo   waa   waicíkée   ńtí?
        and go:PLUR:IPS:REAL=PST pick:NOM greens:GEN how

        and how did they used to go picking greens?'

(163) a. Itétimaa   awákᵉ,
        return:1SG:SEQ home:DAT

        'We returned home,

   b. ńda ŋgo   ŋkɛ́sɨ   tɔbɔŋɔ́ᵉ.
        and we:OBL to.eat:OBL mush:GEN

        and we ate mealmush.'

Contrast between two clauses in Ik can be expressed in two primary ways: 1) by simply adjoining the two clauses with a brief pause in between (marked with by a comma or period in writing) or 2) by linking the two clauses with the contrastive connective kòtò, which can mean 'but' as well as 'and, then, therefore, etc.'. These two types are demonstrated in examples (164)-(165), respectively:

(164) Bɛna   ɲcùkᵒ. Bùkᵒ.
      not:3SG I:COP you:COP

      'It's not me. It's you.

(165) a. Bɛɗɨkɔtɨ́a=naa   ɲémɛlɛkʉ́,
        search:COMP:1SG=PST1 hoe:NOM

        'I went and looked for the hoe,

   b. koto máa=naa ŋunetí.
        but not=PST1 find:1SG

        but I did not find (it).'

Lastly, the idea of disjunction is expressed in Ik through the use of the connectives *kèɗè* 'or' or *kòrì* 'or', as illustrated in example sentences (166)-(167):

(166) a. Tɔkɔ́bɛsɨ́da   eɗa,
       farm:IPFV:2SG grain:NOM
       'Are you farming grain,

   b. keɗe ńtá tɔkɔ́bɛsɨ̂dⁱ?
      or not farm:IPFV:2SG
      or are you not farming (it)?'

(167) a. Enída   mɛna   gaanaakátìkᵉ,
       see:2SG things:NOM bad:DISTR:3PL:SIM
       'Do you see things being bad all around,

   b. kori maráŋaakátìkᵉ?
      or good:DISTR:3PL:SIM
      or as being good all around?

10.8.2 Clause chaining

But in fact, the most common way Ik links independent clauses is through clause 'co-subordination' or CLAUSE CHAINING. To create a chain of clauses, the grammar starts with an anchoring phrase or clause to set the stage modally or temporally, and then it puts all the following mainline verbs in the sequential aspect (see §8.10.7), creating a chain of two or more clauses. When clause chaining is used in a story, the temporal 'anchor' can be a simple time expression like *kaíníkò nùkᵘ* 'in those years' or a tensed statement like *Atsa noo ámá ntanée taa Apáálɔrɛ́ŋ* 'There came a man named Apaaloreng'. In (168), the clause chain is anchored by the initial adverbial phrase *Na kónító ódoue baratsoó* 'One day, in the morning', which puts the whole sentence in a temporal frame. Thenceforth, the clause chain proceeds clause by clause, each marked as SEQ1, SEQ2, etc:

(168) a. [Na   kónító ódoue   baratsoó]_ADV
       when one day:GEN morning:INS
       'One day, in the morning,

   b. [ipuo   takáíkakᵃ]_SEQ1
      cast:3SG:SEQ shoes:ACC
      he cast (his) shoes (in divination),

c. [eguo taƙáɨ́ka ɛ́bakᵃ]_SEQ2
   put:3SG:SEQ shoes:NOM gun:ACC
   and the shoes made (the shape of) a gun,

d. [ipuo naɓó]_SEQ3
   cast:3SG:SEQ again
   and he cast (them) again,

e. [egini ɛ́bakᵃ]_SEQ4
   put:3PL:SEQ gun:ACC
   and they made a gun.'

Although the sequential aspect and clause chains are common in narratives, they are also used extensively for other types of discourse, for example, exposition and instruction. The following expository clause chain in (169) details some of the steps taken in the process of grinding tobacco leaves. Note that there are two anchoring adverbial clauses, one at the beginning and one in the third line. After each one, there is a string of one or more verbs set in the sequential aspect:

(169) a. [Náa iryámétaníɛ́ gwasákᵉ]_ADV1
          when get:IPS:SIM stone:DAT
          'When a stone is acquired,

       b. [ɲɔ́ɛ́ɛsɛ ɲaɓálaɲitᵃ]_SEQ1
          grind:INCH:SPS soda.ash:NOM
          soda ash is ground up.

       c. [náa ɲaɓálaɲitɨ́á iwídímètìkᵉ]_ADV2
          when soda.ash:ACC pulverize:MID:SIM
          When the soda ash is ground to powder,

       d. [páka ɲapúɗúmùƙòtùkᵒ]_SEQ4
          until powdery:COMP:SEQ
          until it becomes fine powder.'

Finally, the sequential aspect and clause chaining is often found operating in a set of commands or instructions. Such a clause chain may begin with one or more imperative verbs, followed by the sequential verbs in a chain of further commands or instructions. This type of clause chain is shown in (170):

(170) a. [Na bédidɔɔ berésá hoe]_ADV
          if want:2SG:SEQ to.build:NOM house:GEN
      'If you want to build a house,

    b. [kawete titírík^a, kɛɗitɨn, ńda sim]_IMP2
          cut:IMP pole:PL reed:PL and fiber
      Cut poles, reeds, and fiber,

    c. [iréɲuƙoiduo bácɨk^a]_SEQ1
          clear:COMP:2SG:SEQ area:NOM
      clear away the area,

    d. [úgiduo ripitín]_SEQ2
          dig:2SG:SEQ hole:PL:NOM
      dig holes,

    e. [otídukóé titírík^a]_SEQ3
          pour:2SG:SEQ:DP pole:PL:NOM
      and put the poles into them.'

Appendix A: Ik affixes

All of the affixes discussed in the preceding grammar sketch are listed in the table below for easy reference. When looking for an affix in the list, keep in mind that if it has two forms (for example the {-e} and {-ɛ} of the genitive case), both forms are given their own separate entry. Affixes that cannot be the terminal morpheme in a word have no final form, while those that can, have non-final and final forms.

Table 1: Full list of Ik affixes

Non-final	Final	Name	Section
-Ø	-Ø	Irrealis modality	§8.9.1
-Ø	-Ø	Oblique case	§7.9
-a	-ᵃ	Nominative case	§7.2
-a	-ᵃ	Realis modality	§8.9.2
-a	-kᵃ	Accusative case	§7.3
-a	-kᵃ	Present perfect aspect	§8.10.2
-aák-	–	Distributive adjectival	§8.11.5
-am(a)-	-am	Singulative	§4.2.3
-am(á)-	-am	Patientive	§8.3.3
-án-	–	Stative adjectival	§8.11.4
-an(ɨ)-	–	Impersonal passive mood	§8.6.2
-anoˊ	-anoˊ	First plural incl. optative	§8.10.3
-ás(ɨ)-	-ás	Abstractive	§8.3.1
-át(i)-	-át(i)	Third person plural	§8.7
ˊ-d-	–	Physical property I	§8.11.2
-e	-ᵉ	Genitive case	§7.5
-e	-kᵉ	Dative case	§7.4
-e	-kᵉ	Simultaneous aspect	§8.10.8
ˊ-è	ˊ-dᵉ	Dummy pronoun	§8.8
-eˊ	-ᵉˊ	Imperative singular	§8.10.5
-ed(e)-	-edᵉ	Possessive singular	§4.2.4

Appendix A: Ik affixes

Non-final	Final	Name	Section
-és-	–	Imperfective aspect	§8.10.1
-és-	–	Intentional modality	§8.10.1
-és(í)-	-és	Transitive infinitive	§8.2.2
-eseˊ	-eseˊ	Sequential imp. passive	§8.10.7
-èt-	–	Venitive directional	§8.4.1
-èt-	–	Inchoative aspect	§8.5.1
-ɛ	-ɛ	Genitive case	§7.5
-ɛ	-kɛ	Dative case	§7.3
-ɛ	-kɛ	Simultaneous aspect	§8.10.8
ˊɛ̀	ˊdᵉ	Dummy pronoun	§8.8
-ɛˊ	-ɛˊ	Imperative singular	§8.10.5
-ɛd(ɛ)-	-ɛdɛ	Possessive singular	§4.2.4
-ɨ́s-	–	Imperfective aspect	§8.10.1
-ɨ́s-	–	Intentional modality	§8.10.1
-ɨ́s(ɨ)-	-ɨ́s	Transitive infinitive	§8.2.2
-ɛsɛˊ	-ɛsɛˊ	Sequential imp. passive	§8.10.7
-ɛ̀t-	–	Venitive directional	§8.4.1
-ɛ̀t-	–	Inchoative aspect	§8.5.1
-ì	-ⁱ	Third person singular	§8.7
ˊì	ˊdᵉ	Dummy pronoun	§8.8
-í-	–	Pluractional aspect	§8.5.3
-í(í)-	-í(í)	First person singular	§8.8
-iaˊ -	–	First singular sequential	§8.10.7
-íd(i)-	-íd(i)	Second person singular	§8.8
-ìk-	–	Distributive adjectival	§8.11.5
-ìk(à)-	-ìkᵃ	Plurative	§4.2.1
-íkó/-íkw-	-íkᵒ	Plurative	§4.2.1
-ím(í)-	-ím(í)	First plural exclusive	§8.7
-imaˊ -	-imaˊ	First pl. exc. optative	§8.10.3
-imaˊ -	–	First pl. exc. sequential	§8.10.7
-ímét-	–	Middle II mood	§8.6.3
-ìn(ì)-	-ìn	Possessive plural	§4.2.4
-ineˊ	-ineˊ	First singular optative	§8.10.3
-ìnì	-ìn	Third plural sequential	§8.10.7
-ínós(í)-	-ínós	Reciprocal	§8.6.4

Non-final	Final	Name	Section
-ísín(ì)-	-ísín(ì)	First plural inclusive	§8.7
-ìt-	–	Causative mood	§8.6.5
-ít(í)-	-ít(í)	Second person plural	§8.7
-ítín(í)-	-ítín	Plurative	§4.2.1
-ɨ́	-ɨ́	Third person singular	§8.7
´ɨ̀	´dᵉ	Dummy pronoun	§8.8
-ɨ́(ɨ)-	-ɨ́(ɨ)	First person singular	§8.7
-ɨa´-	–	First singular sequential	§8.10.7
-ɨ́d(ɨ)-	-ɨ́d(ɨ)	Second person singular	§8.7
-ɨ̀k-	–	Distributive adjectival	§8.11.5
-ɨ̀k(à)-	-ɨ̀kᵃ	Plurative	§4.2.1
-ɨ́m(ɨ́)-	-ɨ́m(ɨ́)	First plural exclusive	§8.7
-ɨma´-	-ɨma´	First pl. exc. optative	§8.10.3
-ɨma´-	–	First pl. exc. sequential	§8.10.7
-ɨ̀n(ɨ̀)-	-ɨ̀n	Possessive plural	§4.2.4
-ɨ́nós(ɨ́)-	-ɨ́nós	Reciprocal	§8.6.4
-inɛ´	-inɛ´	First singular optative	§8.10.3
-ɨ̀nɨ̀-	-ɨ̀n	Third plural sequential	§8.10.7
-ɨ́sɨ́n(ɨ́)-	-ɨ́sɨ́n(ɨ́)	First plural inclusive	§8.7
-ɨ̀t-	–	Causative	§8.6.5
-ɨ́t(ɨ́)-	-ɨ́t(ɨ́)	Second person plural	§8.7
-ɨ́tɨ́n(ɨ́)-	-ɨ́tɨ́n	Plurative	§4.2.1
´m-	–	Middle I mood	§8.6.3
´m-	–	Physical property II	§8.11.3
-nànès(ì)-	-nànès	Behaviorative	§8.3.2
-o	-ᵒ	Ablative case	§7.6
-o	-ᵒ	Instrumental case	§7.7
-o	-kᵒ	Copulative case	§7.8
-o	-kᵒ	Sequential aspect	§8.10.7
´ò	´dᵉ	Dummy pronoun	§8.8
-òn(ì)-	-òn	Intransitive infinitive	§8.2.1
-ós(í)-	-ós	Passive mood	§8.6.1
-ɔ	-ɔ	Ablative case	§7.6
-ɔ	-ɔ	Instrumental case	§7.7
-ɔ	-kɔ	Copulative case	§7.8

Appendix A: Ik affixes

Non-final	Final	Name	Section
-ɔ	-kɔ	Sequential aspect	§8.10.7
-́ɔ	-́dᵉ	Dummy pronoun	§8.8
-ɔm(a)-	-ɔm	Singulative	§4.2.3
-ɔ̀n(ɨ)-	-ɔ̀n	Intransitive infinitive	§8.2.1
-ɔ́s(ɨ)-	-ɔ́s	Passive mood	§8.6.1
-ukot(í)-	-ukotⁱ	Andative directional	§8.4.2
-ukot(í)-	-ukotⁱ	Completive aspect	§8.5.2
-úó	-ú	Imperative plural	§8.10.5
-ʉkɔt(ɨ)-	-ʉkɔtⁱ	Andative directional	§8.4.2
-ʉkɔt(ɨ)-	-ʉkɔtⁱ	Completive aspect	§8.5.2
-ʉ́ɔ́	-ʉ́	Imperative plural	§8.10.5

References

Heine, Bernd. 1999. *Ik dictionary*. Köln: Rüdiger Köppe Verlag.
Schrock, Terrill. 2014. *A grammar of Ik (Icé-tód): Northeast Uganda's last thriving Kuliak language*. Utrecht: LOT.
Schrock, Terrill. 2015. *A guide to the developing orthography of Icetod*. Lokinene: SIL Uganda & the Ik Agenda Development Initiative.

Subject index

ablative case, 483, 582
accusative case, 482, 526, 546, 548, 575, 576, 580, 581
adjectival, 492, 535, 558–561, 582, 589–591
adverb, 482, 564, 565, 567, 569, 573
adverbial clause, 575, 577
agentive, 508, 509
allomorphy, 551
anaphoric, 488, 492, 521–523, 567
andative, 542–544
aspect, 535, 544, 553, 556, 557, 563, 589–592
ATR, 7, 485–488, 502, 536, 537, 542, 545, 547, 549
auxiliary verb, 571

boundary tone, 578

causative, 549, 550, 570
certainty, 496, 561, 565
clause chaining, 585, 586
clause structure, 569, 570
cleft construction, 574, 575
clitic, 488, 490, 518
clusivity, 512, 549
common argument, 518, 575, 576
complement, 531, 533, 574, 581, 582
complementizer, 497, 498, 581
completive aspect, 544
constituent order, 569–571, 573, 575, 576

copula, 533
copular, 573, 574, 582
copulative case, 482, 483, 516, 574, 580

dative, 480–484, 501, 525, 526, 531, 542, 580, 592
definiteness, 514
depressor consonant, 488, 502
devoiced, 478
devoicing, 478, 490, 556
dialect, 3
diminutive, 508–510
directional, 590, 592
disjunction, 585
distributive adjectival, 561
dummy pronoun, 482, 551

genitive case, 530, 531, 589

haplology, 480

ideophone, 496
imperative, 495, 534, 554, 556, 586
imperfective, 553, 557
inchoative, 544, 547, 549, 572
infinitive, 8, 9, 482, 492, 509, 535, 536, 542, 545, 546, 549, 559, 584, 590–592
instrumental case, 480, 532
intentional, 553
interrogative, 491, 512, 515, 516, 578–580

Subject index

intonation, 578, 580
intransitive, 482, 486, 518, 535–537, 539, 542, 544–547, 549, 558, 559, 569–572, 575, 576, 582, 583

left-dislocation, 575

main clause, 517, 518, 527, 557, 575–577, 581–583
modality, 589, 590
mora, 502

negative copula, 533
nominative case, 8, 485, 505, 508, 526, 575, 582
noun phrase, 530, 535, 536, 567, 572, 583

oblique case, 525, 534, 580, 582, 584
orthography, xi, xii, 488

particle, 515, 556, 565, 578, 580
passive, 499, 535, 545–548, 557, 589, 590
patient, xii, 541, 547
plurative, 486, 491, 502–504
possession, 501, 505, 514, 529, 530
possessor, 505, 514
preposition, 494, 534, 584
proclitic, 565

quotative, 580, 581

recipient, 529, 555
reciprocal, 547, 548
reduplication, 545
reflexive, 491, 512, 518, 519, 537, 547
relative clause, 517, 518, 575, 576
relative pronoun, 492, 493, 517, 518, 575, 576

reported speech, 497

semi-vowel, 484, 502
sequential aspect, 556, 557, 583, 585, 586
simultaneous aspect, 557, 583
singulative, 491, 502, 504, 505
stative adjectival, 490, 559
subjunctive mood, 555
subordinate clause, 528, 575, 576, 583
syllable, 484, 488, 489, 502, 516, 554, 578

tense, 553, 556, 562–565, 569
time expression, 556, 585

vowel assimilation, 482–484, 526, 536, 537, 551
vowel harmony, 7, 478, 484, 486, 492, 502, 551, 559

www.ingramcontent.com/pod-product-compliance
Lightning Source LLC
Chambersburg PA
CBHW060302010526
44108CB00042B/2600